2010
Gun Digest

EDITED BY
Dan Shideler

©2009 Krause Publications, Inc.,
a subsidiary of F+W Media, Inc.

Published by

Gun Digest® Books
An imprint of F+W Media, Inc.
700 East State Street • Iola, WI 54990-0001
715-445-2214 • 888-457-2873
www.gundigestbooks.com

Our toll-free number to place an order or obtain
a free catalog is (800) 258-0929.

Manuscripts, contributions and inquiries, including first class return postage, should be sent to the GUN DIGEST Editorial Offices, Gun Digest Books, 700 East State Street, Iola, WI 54990-0001. All materials received will receive reasonable care, but we will not be responsible for their safe return. Materials accepted is subject to our requirements for editing and revisions. Author payment covers all rights and title to the accepted material, including photos, drawings and other illustrations. Payment is at our current rates.

CAUTION: Technical data presented here, particularly technical data on handloading and on firearms adjustment and alteration, inevitably reflects individual experience with particular equipment and components under specific circumstances the reader cannot duplicate exactly. Such data presentations therefore should be used for guidance only and with caution. Gun Digest Books accepts no responsibility for results obtained using these data.

ISSN 0072-9043

ISBN 13: 978-1-4402-0233-9
ISBN 10: 1-4402-0233-8

Designed by Dave Hauser and Patsy Howell

Edited by Dan Shideler

Printed in the United States of America

John T. Amber
LITERARY AWARD

Wayne Van Zwoll

We are proud to note that the winner of this year's John T. Amber Literary Award is Wayne Van Zwoll, for his piece ".30-30: Short Magnum for the Frontier," which appeared in the 2009 *Gun Digest*.

Many changes have taken place in *Gun Digest* over the years, but every edition still bears the stamp of the late John T. Amber, *editor emeritus*, a man of exquisite good taste in the old-school style. Mr. Amber approached his task as an editor should: with a keen eye for detail and a genuine appreciation for a well-turned phrase.

We think that JTA – as he always signed his commentaries – would heartily approve of Wayne van Zwoll's article ".30-30: Short Magnum for the Frontier." The *Gun Digest* jury certainly does.

As its name implies, the John T. Amber Award recognizes not only the writer's knowledge but his ability to express it. We note with some dismay that, as a craft, gunwriting is a vanishing art. In this day of the blog and the unedited opinion mill, it's easy to forget that the greatest gunwriters, the truly enduring ones, not only know their subject but also know how to entertain, inform and inspire the reader. Wayne van Zwoll does.

A full-time journalist for the outdoors press, Wayne van Zwoll has published more than 2,000 articles and twice that many photos for more than two dozen magazine titles, including *Sports Afield*, *Outdoor Life* and *Field & Stream*. Once the editor of *Kansas Wildlife*, he has also edited *Mule Deer* for the Mule Deer Foundation as well as Stoeger's *Shooter's Bible*. His "Rifles and Cartridges" column in *Bugle*, flagship magazine of the Rocky Mountain Elk Foundation, has run for 21 years – longer than any other. Wayne has also authored 13 books on hunting, shooting and history.

In 1996 Wayne was named Shooting Sports Writer of the Year by the Outdoor Writers Association of America. In 2006 he received the Jack Slack Outdoor Writer of the Year award from Leupold. Now Special Projects Editor for Intermedia Outdoors, Wayne also contributes to *Petersen's Hunting* and Guns & Ammo television. He is a professional member of the Boone and Crockett Club and has served on the board of OWAA.

In addition to other enviable achievements, Wayne has taught English and Forestry classes at Utah State University, where in 2000 he earned a doctorate studying the effects of post-war hunting motive on wildlife policy. He keeps an active public speaking schedule within the outdoors industry and conservation community. When not at the desk or on the range, he reads history and jogs to keep in shape. A late starter, he completed his first marathon at age 49. He's run 16 since, including four at Boston. Wayne lives in north-central Washington State with Alice, his wife of 35 years.

The recipient of the annual John T. Amber Literary Award, which consists of a handsome plaque and a $1000 honorarium, is selected by a group of professional shooting sports editors at Krause Publications' book and magazine divisions. Every feature author appearing in *Gun Digest* is eligible for the award, and the overall excellence of this year's candidates made for a truly challenging selection process.

Congratulations, Wayne. We hope you continue to grace our pages for many years to come.

Dan Shideler
Editor
Gun Digest

Welcome to the 2010 edition of *Gun Digest*! First things first: you would not be reading this book were it not for the prior efforts of four remarkable individuals:

CHARLES R. JACOBS, who started with nothing but a blank sheet of paper and gave us the first *Gun Digest*, way back in 1944;

JOHN T. AMBER, the patron saint of *Gun Digest* who built it into the world's best-selling firearms annual;

KEN WARNER, who so ably took the helm from his predecessor and reinvigorated this truly remarkable title; and

KEN RAMAGE, who piloted *Gun Digest* into the twenty-first century in the face of an unprecedented revolution in technology and all the challenges it presented.

I was raised on *Gun Digest*. Once a year, in the long-gone Indiana of the 1960s and 1970s, my father brought home the new edition, which my brother Dave and I eagerly devoured. I mean we read it literally from cover to cover, absorbing whatever wisdom and insight that could be found in its pages. I still have some of those 40-year-old volumes, nearly all of them showing pencil marks in their catalog sections where we, with boyish enthusiasm, checked guns that we would surely buy someday. Eventually I assembled a complete collection of *Gun Digests* (which will soon be available to all at Research.GunDigest.com), from the rare 1944 First Edition, with slip-sheeted price list, to the 2008 edition.

And now, forty-some years later, I am editor of that same book. Karma? The inscrutable workings of Fate? Call it what you will, I will say simply that it is an honor – for me, it's the stuff that dreams are made of.

The front cover of this book features two new Ithaca Model 37 shotguns: a Deerslayer III slug gun and the new 28-gauge Deluxe Featherlight. A Deluxe Featherlight appeared on the cover of the first two editions of Gun Digest (1944 and 1946), and our inclusion of these two new Ithacas on our cover signifies our ongoing effort to keep Gun Digest true to its original intent: to be the firearms enthusiast's first, best source of information, entertainment and scholarship.

The Editor

It would not be unfair of you to ask who I am. I'm a shooter and firearms enthusiast, and by "firearms" I mean everything from Quackenbush air rifles to Greener Harpoon Guns to Gatlings to Smith & Wesson Model 29s and AR-15s and everything in between. Expensive guns, inexpensive guns, American guns, foreign guns, commercial guns, military guns, whatever: they're all part of my daily diet. I am not a champion marksman (as so many of my friends will be only too happy to tell you), not a certified gunsmith, but what I lack in some areas I make up for with unbridled enthusiasm for all aspects of guns and the shooting sports. Simply put, I'm an old-fashioned gun guy.

We live in the Age of Opinion. Everywhere we turn on the web, on television, on the radio – we're bombarded with opinions, opinions, opinions. It's a game we can all play. For example, I can tell you that my favorite semi-auto pistol is the Mauser C96, followed closely by the Colt 1911; my favorite revolver, the S&W New Century, the Ruger Super Blackhawk or the Colt Police Positive (tough choice there); my favorite rifle, the Remington Model 81 Woodsmaster or the 1896 Swedish Mauser; and my favorite shotgun, the Browning Auto-5 or the Remington 870. All of these selections, of course, are purely the result of my personal opinions. I hope you don't agree with me, for, as Mark Twain said, "It is difference of opinion that makes horse races."

In selecting the articles that appear in this book, I chose pieces that appealed to my tastes, trusting that a great many of you share some of them. If one of the stories herein doesn't trip your trigger, simply turn a few pages forward – the next one probably will. I do not agree with all of the opinions of the authors represented in these pages, but I certainly respect them.

In the older firearms literature, you occasionally find references to "the Hot Stove League" – those informal clusters of enthusiasts who used to gather around hot stoves in hunting shacks and gun stores to argue, gripe, theorize and pontificate about guns. No matter how heated their discussions, members of the Hot Stove League always had opinions, and they always parted friends. I hope you'll consider *Gun Digest* to be your personal Hot Stove League.

What's New – and What Isn't

You will notice that the number of articles in this edition of *Gun Digest* has increased. We did this purely because, in our opinion, there's no such thing as too much *Gun Digest*.

We have lengthened some sections; shortened others. We have added Contributing Editors in the areas of airguns, tactical arms, gunsmithing and women's perspectives. Our objective has been to pitch the largest tent possible, one large enough for all the members of the *Gun Digest* family.

We have also included a DVD with this edition, a first for *Gun Digest*. Most if not all of the contents of this DVD were collected at the 2009 SHOT Show, and we hope it gives you a behind-the-scenes look at what has to be the Greatest Show on Earth.

A Call for Papers

Gun Digest remains what it has always been: the world's leading firearms annual. Many of the pieces contained in these pages were not written by professional gunwriters but by just plain folks. We have never met a gun owner who didn't have something interesting to say, so if you would like to write something for consideration for future editions of *Gun Digest*, be our guest! All materials must be submitted in electronic format (e.g., MS-Word or .rtf files) and must be accompanied by a suitable number of high-resolution digital images (.tif or .jpg).

If you have such a manuscript, or an idea for one, contact us at:

Editor, *Gun Digest*
700 East State Street, Iola, Wisconsin 54990

Please include your street address, telephone number and email address with your submission.

Dedication

This edition is dedicated to you, the loyal reader, who has made *Gun Digest* the world's leading firearms annual.

Acknowledgments

This edition could not have been completed without the support of Jim Schlender and Brad Rucks of F+W/Krause's gun, knife and outdoors division, and without the assistance of Tom Nelsen and Dave Hauser, whose creativity, dedication and professionalism make so many of our gun books possible.

In closing, I would like to thank my gracious wife Karen for putting up with a 24/7 gun guy; and I would be remiss indeed did I not extend my affection and respect to the memories of sportsmen and raconteurs Howard H. and Joseph F. Shideler, who instilled in their children and grandchildren a love for the shooting sports that endures to this day.

Welcome to the Hot Stove League!

Cordially,
Dan Shideler, Editor
GUN DIGEST

About the covers

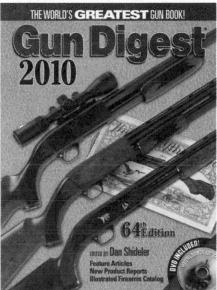

FRONT COVER If you're a shotgunner, chances are that you or someone you know has carried an Ithaca Model 37 pump at one time or another. After a turbulent period beginning in the late 1960s, Ithaca has reinvigorated itself and is once again producing shotguns commensurate with the name of Ithaca. The mainstay of the new Ithaca Gun Company of Upper Sandusky, Ohio, continues to be the bottom-ejecting Model 37 Featherlight pump gun (middle) – but the old trooper, based on a John Browning design, is now available with magnum-length chambers and interchangeable choke tubes, among other refinements. At top is the Ithaca Deerslayer III purpose-built rifled-bore slug gun, which offers excellent long-range accuracy with a variety of modern saboted loads. At bottom is the all-new, special-order Model 37 Featherlight 28-Gauge, built on a scaled receiver and available in three grades ranging from A to AAA (shown). Other models available from Ithaca include the M37 Featherlight and Ultralight in 12 and 20 gauge, the Deerslayer II slug gun, and the M37 Defense Gun. All of the company's shotguns are proudly made right here in the USA, and you can see them at www. Ithacagun.com.

BACK COVER North American Arms (NAA) of Provo, Utah, is one of the leading manufacturers of .22 mini-revolvers and self-defense semi-auto pocket pistols. In 2009, NAA introduced The Earl (top), an intriguing twist on their line of .22 rimfire revolvers. Reminiscent of Civil War-era cap and ball revolvers, The Earl features a faux loading lever that serves as a cylinder pin lock, a fixed pinched-barleycorn front sight, a 4≤ octagonal barrel and oversized rosewood grips. A limited-production item, The Earl is expected to be offered in .22 Magnum and as a .22 LR/.22 Magnum convertible model (shown). At bottom is the NAA .380 Guardian, an extremely high-quality double-action-only pocket automatic that's among the very finest of its type. For more information about NAA's distinctive product line, visit them at www.naaminis.com.

Gun Digest Staff

EDITOR Dan Shideler

CONTRIBUTING EDITORS

Holt Bodinson – Ammunition, Ballistics & Components; Web Directory
Raymond Caranta – The Guns of Europe
Wm. Hovey Smith – Blackpowder Review
John Haviland – Shotgun Review
John Malloy – Handguns Today: Autoloaders
Jacob Edson – Rifle Review

Jeff Quinn – Handguns Today: Six-guns & Others
Tom Turpin – Engraved & Custom Guns
Wayne Van Zwoll – Scopes & Mounts
Gila Hayes – Women's Perspective
Kevin Muramatsu – Gunsmithing
Michael Schoby – Airguns
Kevin Michalowski – Tactical
Larry Sterett – Handloading

John T. Amber Literary Award 3
Introduction 4

FEATURES

The Incredible 2-Bore Rifle
by John Dickson 8

Gas-Delayed Blowbacks: Junk or Cutting Edge?
by Warren Ferguson 14

Hornet Hotrod: The .19 Calhoon Badger
Don Lewis 22

The Beretta Survival Kit: The Model 84 .380 ACP
by Chris Libby 26

The Magnificent Seven
by Scott Stoppelman 32

An Introduction to the Military Handguns of Imperial Japan
by Teri Jane Bryant 38

Blowup!
by Neil Bradford 44

Custom and Engraved Guns
by Tom Turpin 46

When Bulldogs Ruled
by George J. Layman 58

The Marlin Model 90: A Case Study in Ingenuity
by Bernard H. DiGiacobbe, M.D. 66

Make Mine a .32!
by Robert H. Campbell 70

The Elusive Gerfen Rifle
by J. B. Wood 76

The Colt Official Police and S&W Military & Police
by Paul Scarlata 80

From Factory to Meat on the Table:
Gunmaking in the Val du Trompia
by Wm. Hovey Smith 88

Power and Grace: The Ruger Super Blackhawk Turns 50
by Don Findley 96

Classic .22s: There Are But Two
by John J. Quick 102

Fit to Shoot!
by Richard S. Grozick 108

The Age of Mobilubricant
by Jim Foral 118

Fun with the .45 Colt
by John W. Rockefeller 126

Oddalls: Why We Love 'Em
by Andy Ewert 132

The Xman
by Clarence Anderson 138

Updated Classics: The NEW Ithaca Model 37s 146

The .44 Special Begins Its Second Century
by John Taffin 150

REPORTS FROM THE FIELD

Editor's Picks
by Dan Shideler 161

Handguns Today: Semi-Autos
by John Malloy 164

Handguns Today: Revolvers
by Jeff Quinn 176

Rifles Today
by Jacob Edson 184

Shotguns Today
by John Haviland 192

Tactical Gear Today
by Kevin Michalowski 198

Muzzleloaders Today
by Wm. Hovey Smith 202

Airguns Today
by Michael Schoby 208

Gunsmithing Today
by Kevin Muramatsu 212

Optics Today
by Wayne Van Zwoll 216

Women's Perspective
by Gila Hayes 226

The Guns of Europe
by Raymond Caranta 232

Handloading Today
by Larry Sterett 240

Ammunition Today
by Holt Bodinson 248

ONE GOOD GUN

The Unique Kleinguenther K14 Insta-fire in 7x57 Mauser
by Mike Thomas 270

The Remington Model 760 in .300 Savage
by Steve Gash 272

A Classic Springfield Sporter
by Jim Lavin 274

The Valmet 412 Shooting System
by Steve Gash 276

TESTFIRE

Czechmate! CZ's Vz-58
by Patrick Sweeney 278

Not Your Father's BB Gun: The .50 Dragon Slayer
by Michael Schoby 280

Century International Arms M-70 AB2T Yugo Underfolder
by Pete Philippe 282

Ruger Gets Small: The LCP
by Patrick Sweeney 284

Remington's R-25
by Jacob Edson 286

Civil War Naval Artillery
by Orpheu C. Kerr 288

The Encyclopedia of Bullet Casting
by Ken Walters 289

CATALOG OF ARMS AND ACCESSORIES

GUNDEX® 306

HANDGUNS
Autoloading 317
Competition 343
Double-Action Revolvers 346
Single-Action Revolvers 353
Miscellaneous 360

RIFLES
Centerfire – Autoloaders 362
Centerfire – Lever & Slide 376
Centerfire – Bolt-Action 382
Centerfire – Single Shot 403
Drillings, Combination Guns, Double Rifles 412
Rimfire – Autoloaders 414
Rimfire – Lever & Slide Action 417
Rimfire – Bolt-Actions & Single Shots 419
Competition – Centerfire & Rimfire 425

SHOTGUNS
Autoloaders 431

Slide & Lever Actions 440
Over/Unders 446
Side-by-Side 457
Bolt Actions & Single Shot 462
Military & Police 465

BLACKPOWDER
Single Shot Pistols – Flint & Percussion 467
Revolvers 468
Muskets & Rifles 470
Shotguns 480

AIRGUNS
Handguns 481
Long Guns 483

REFERENCES
Web Directory 488
Arms Library 500

DIRECTORY OF THE ARMS TRADE
Manufacturer's Directory 529

There are big guns, and then there are BIG guns...

The incredible 2-Bore Rifle

The sheer massiveness of the enormous 2-bore is evident here along with the beautifully figured walnut stock. The barrel length is 28 inches, the overall length is 46 inches, and the length of pull is 14-1/2 inches. The action is two inches wide, as is the butt at the recoil pad.

BY JIM DICKSON

The biggest and the most powerful of anything always captures man's imagination – and the most powerful sporting rifle of all time does this in spectacular fashion. A weapon suitable for blue whales that makes traditional elephant rifles seem like smallbores, the colossal 2-bore is the all-time champion big-bore shoulder-fired sporting rifle. Firing bullets of 3500 grains with a frontal area of 1.05" diameter, having stopping power greater than five .600 Nitro Express cartridges hitting at once, the 2-bore is the ultimate charge stopper.

It is quite accurate to call the 2-bore an artillery piece, for the smaller 4-bore was once standardized as the largest practical swivel cannon – a smallish cannon that was mounted on a ship's gunwale – because anything larger kept breaking out of the mountings on the ships' rails. The 2-bore is twice the size of the standard swivel cannon of muzzleloading cannon days. In fact, the effect of a load of buckshot through the 2-bore would be exactly the same as from a large swivel cannon. It would sweep the decks of a ship of uninvited company in grand style. With piracy at an all-time high today and governments banning armed merchantmen from their ports, this opens up another possibility for this brute. Its solid shot can certainly let in enough water into a ship's hull as well as having the power to disable engines. Despite being a true cannon, however, this 26-lb. beast is a shoulder-

fired weapon and eminently practical for those tight spots that emerge in the course of hunting dangerous game. Of course it takes a real man to handle it. Aside from its weight, its recoil is like presiding over your own personal earthquake. Still, it can be fired without pain or injury as long as you roll with the punch.

There has been one other 2-bore in hunting history. About 150 years ago, the famous Victorian hunter and explorer Sir Samuel Baker had an 18-lb. muzzleloading 4-bore that fired a half-pound explosive shell, thus making it a 2-bore by the weight of its projectile. At a mere 18 lbs., it kicked viciously and Sir Samuel reported that it spun him around like a weathercock when he fired it. Not surprisingly, it never failed to kill whatever it hit. Baker named it "Baby" but the Arabs called it "Child of the Cannon." It was built in London in 1869 by Holland and Holland and was serial number 1526. Powder charges were either 10 or 12 drams of powder. With it Sam Baker once blew up a buffalo at 600 yards, as well as killing numerous elephants.

The use of explosive bullets was a development of Lieutenant Forsyth of the Bengal Army in India. It turned the

A fired and perfectly mushroomed 2500-grain 2-bore slug next to a dime.

A 6' 5" Giles Whittome and his 26-lb. 2-bore. Two giants of the firearms world.

heavy 8- and 4-gauge rifles (the terms "bore" and "gauge" are interchangeable) into proper artillery pieces for the ultimate in close-range stopping power in the close confines of the Indian jungle, where ranges were often measured in feet instead of yards. Explosive bullets contained a high explosive (not low explosive) compound that had to be mixed in a wooden bowl with a wooden spoon with nothing metallic allowed to come in contact with it at any stage.

When compounded, the mixture was put inside a two-part bullet. Molds for these bullets came in two parts, one for the bottom part and another for the top part. A screw swage forced the two molded halves together with the explosion compound in the center core and sized it to the correct barrel groove diameter. The swaged joint usually didn't break at the explosion; the bullet usually fragmented. It was made with such thick sides that it needed bone to set it off so it didn't explode on the surface. The explosive mixture detonates through

compression and percussion together (i.e., it must be confined and hit). It did not require fire to ignite it. Because of its precisely-tuned exploding properties, Forsyth's was the only successful exploding hunting bullet.

The size of the massive 2-bore discouraged other hunters and the 4-bore remained the biggest stopping rifle in use. There were a few 2-bore punt guns made for waterfowling but most of these were not shoulder-fired weapons. One should not forget that the average Victorian hunter tended to be smaller than men today and the sport and science of weightlifting and bodybuilding were late twentieth-century developments.

A BIG GUN FOR A NEW CENTURY

When the millennium arrived, the Royal Armouries in England decided to commemorate the year 2000 by an exhibition piece for their own collection that featured the number "2" in it.

Hence the 2-bore rifle. Their budget is always limited and between that and the development delays, the gun is only now being fired. In another year or two its engraving will be complete and it will be put on permanent exhibit.

The order for the 2-bore was placed with Giles Whittome, noted British maker of extra fancy exhibition-grade, best quality guns and universally recognized as the number one authority on heavy 8- and 4-gauge rifles in the world. Giles is also a very experienced African white hunter who hunted solo years ago without guides or trackers, just a couple of local natives to carry back what he shot. Lovers of best quality British guns will remember him for "The Paragon," a Nitro-proofed Damascus barrel masterpiece with every best quality feature you could put on a sidelock 12 gauge that ranks as the finest example of a British best quality shotgun in the twentieth century.

Since the 2-bore was uncharted territory, both the gun and the cartridge had to be developed. The gun is based on an

Giles Whittome in full recoil from the 2-bore. His 6' 5" frame started out leaning well into the gun but has now been pushed up straight. Note that the gun is under complete control and the barrel has not even flipped up.

Alexander Henry harpoon gun that Giles had previously found in the Royal Armouries collection. In rather bad shape, Giles offered to repair it if they would let him borrow it and record its dimensions. It is more than strong enough for the 2-bore cartridge. The lock is a typical 4-bore shotgun lock. The result is a falling block hammer rifle that looks proper for a late Victorian hunter to use. It is singularly massive because of the immense size of its cartridge. Its stock blank was originally 2-1/2" thick before shaping.

The Alexander Henry action has a non-rebounding hammer that serves to further lock the falling block in place at the moment of firing as the nose of the hammer goes into the block to strike the recessed firing pin. The recessing of the firing pin also offers protection should the gun be dropped. There is a half-cock notch on the hammer for loading the gun. The falling block release lever has a push button to release it from the trigger

guard before it can swing down, drawing the falling block with it. You don't have to worry about the immense recoil flipping it open, as the loading levers on the old M1847 Colt Walker revolvers sometimes did.

Should anyone want the gun to fire harpoons like its ancestor, Giles will gladly make a smoothbore 2-bore for harpoons, bullets, and shot. He will also furnish whatever type of harpoons and bomb lances the customer requires. *[Editor's note: Better check your local game regulations before you run out and buy any harpoons or bomb lances. – DMS]* The effectiveness of the gun on dangerous game will not suffer because dangerous game is always dealt with at close ranges where the smoothbore's accuracy is quite sufficient. A harpoon gun must be a smoothbore because the spinning that a rifled bore would impart to the harpoon would twist its rope. Anyone wanting to go whaling or simply shoot great white sharks will find this

more than adequate armament. Those who saw the movie *Jaws* will remember the attempt to kill the shark with the little Greener harpoon gun intended for pilot whales. Should anyone ever try this in real life with the 2-bore and a bomb lance on a shark of similar size, the effect would be the same as the climactic explosion at the end of the movie, with the shark's head blown off and little pieces of shark raining down everywhere. Any ocean-going sailboat owner would be very glad to have this brute and its bomb lances in his corner should he encounter a whale intent on playing that popular whale game "sink the sailboat."

A 3500-GR. BULLET

The 2-bore cartridge had to be developed from scratch. Since there had never been a 2-bore cartridge rifle, the dimensions had to be created and standardized before the gun could be

2-Bore 3500-grain bullets and loaded round next to a .455 Webley self-loading cartridge (comparable in size to a .45 ACP).

proof-fired. Once you went beyond 8-gauge, the sheer size of the barrel necessary to hold a round ball of the proper weight led early makers to go with a smaller bore diameter and make up the difference in weight with a longer conical bullet of the proper weight. Hence most 4-bores have an actual bore diameter of .935" instead of the 1.052" necessary to fire a 4-oz. round ball. They are actually proofed as 6-gauge, which would be .919". Since the cartridge shoots a 4-oz. conical, it is stamped 4-gauge. Confusing, isn't it? Actual size for a 2-bore firing a round ball is 1.325", which translates into a huge, heavy barrel, so the 2-bore's actual bore size is 1.052", which is true 4-bore for round ball but is considered 2-bore by virtue of its 8-oz. conical bullet.

There had been a few 2-bore cartridge guns made in the 1870s. Holland and Holland and Eley had gotten together and produced 2-gauge cartridges. These were 4-1/2" long and loaded with 15 drams of powder and 5 oz. of shot. No chokes were found on existing guns. Who needs it with 5 ounces of shot! There was a light load of 10 drams of powder and 3-1/2 oz. of shot for finishing off cripples in the water after the first shot into the flock by the punt gun. The last British 2-gauge shotgun was a muzzleloader proofed in 1917. The proof house had to have a new 2-bore stamp made for the proof marks.

The Eley 2-gauge paper-cased shotgun shells formed the basis of the design of the modern 2-bore case. Made of thick brass instead of a paper case, the cartridge is a monster. Its dimensions

are as follows:

Length:	4.5"
Width at mouth:	1.135"
Width at head:	1.180"
Width at rim:	1.280"
Depth at rim:	.155"
Depth of brass case:	.800"

Standard 60/40 alloy brass is used with walls of the same thickness as paper cases. This means that case life is almost unlimited when reloading, an important point considering the price of the ammunition.

Bullet diameter is 1.052" and the standard alloy is 90 percent lead and 10 percent tin. This is perfectly satisfactory for both thin-skinned and thick-skinned animals due to the immense size and power of the cartridge. This was proven true on 8-bore and 4-bore guns killing game in Victorian times. It does not lead the barrel, but should one want to shoot paper-patched bullets the bullet must be made .010" smaller diameter to accommodate the paper patch. For those wanting the ultimate in penetration, bullets are available case from 88 percent lead, 10 percent tin, and 2 percent antimony with a steel nose cap. The new 2-bore cartridge is now included in the C.I.P. Rules of Proof, which is the British equivalent of the United States' S.A.A.M.I.

The 2-bore cartridge is loaded with 24 drams of blackpowder (as befitting a Victorian gun) and a 3500-grain bullet. There is a light load of a 2500-grain bullet with 20 drams of powder as well.

Note that the weight difference alone is equal to the weight of two .470 Nitro Express elephant rifle bullets! A nitro-for-blackpowder load can easily be made for those who hate the mess and extra recoil of blackpowder.

It is worth noting that the standard load for the 4-bore, the previous big bore champion, is 14 drams of Curtis and Harvey Number 6 powder with an 1880-grain bullet. The standard 12-gauge Brenneke slug is a great favorite as a grizzly bear stopper, and it only has a 3 dram powder charge and a 1-oz. slug. The 2-bore is eight times the powder charge and eight times the bullet weight of the old reliable 12-bore Brenneke!

So how much power does the 2-bore generate? That's a question best answered by John "Pondoro" Taylor's famous knockdown formula: bullet weight in grains multiplied by velocity in feet per second multiplied by bullet diameter in inches, divided by 7000 (because there are 7000 grains in one pound). This yields some impressive ballistics for the 2-bore:

Cartridge	Taylor Value
375 H&H	40
.600 Nitro	155
2-bore, 2500 grain	544
2-bore, 3000 grain	700
2-bore, 3500 grain	825

Note that the total knockdown factor for five of the .600 Nitro cartridges is only 775, compared to the 825 of a single 3500-gr. 2-bore.

The traditional bullet energy formula for ft.-lbs. of muzzle energy (fpe) is bullet weight in grains multiplied by muzzle velocity squared divided by 450240. Velocity, however, plays too big a part in this energy formula to give accurate results on game. Bullet weight and frontal area are much more important. For example, if you double the diameter of a bullet you increase its frontal area by much more than two times, as we all learned back in our "pies are square" days (πr^2).

Take a look at the formula results below and note that because of its velocity, the little .375 H&H has over half the energy of the mighty .600 Nitro, yet the .375 has been banned for use on dangerous game in multiple African countries because of its history of failures resulting in hunters being killed, while the .600 is considered a super heavyweight stopping rifle.

Cartridge/Load	Energy (fpe)
.375 H&H Magnum, 300 grain at 2530 fps	4165
.600 Jeffrey, 900 grain at 1950 fps	7600
2-bore, 2500 grain at 1450 fps	11,675 foot pounds
2-bore, 3000 grain at 1250 fps	11,278 foot pounds
2-bore, 3500 grain	approaching 15,000 foot pounds

If one were to believe this formula we would all be using the .220 Swift on elephants, Still, no matter how you calculate it, the 2-bore always comes out on top.

Before leaving this subject, it is worth remembering that when the .280 Halger was developed in the 1920s many people saw that, according to this formula at any rate, the .280 Halger had the muzzle energy of the might .577 3" Nitro Express. There is a row of tombstones in Nairobi of hunters who thought that they could use it on lions. Among them is a brother of then British Foreign Minister, Lord Grey.

SHOOTING THE 2-BORE

To fire the 2-bore without pain or bruising, you must lean into the gun as far as possible so that y ou have room to move back without being knocked down. Grip the gun tightly so that it doesn't fly out of your hands with the kick and snug the butt against your shoulder – but not so tightly that you fully compress your body tissue before firing. You want to be able to have some cushioning give there.

Now RELAX the rest of the body and let the gun shove you upright. If you have to take a step backward that's all right too, but if you lean into the gun enough you should be able to soak up the recoil sufficiently as you are being pushed upright to prevent taking a step back. That's important, because taking a step back when dealing with a charging animal could trip you up on a tree root or something. Falling down when something big and hairy with long tusks is charging you should be avoided. Life insurance underwriters regard it as a deplorable habit.

The 2-bore kicks just as you would expect but it is entirely controllable, thanks to its huge barrel weight, careful stock design, 26-lb. overall weight, and sorbothane (not rubber) recoil pad. The shooter's use of an optional PAST recoil shoulder pad is also recommended but

not mandatory. All this makes the 2-bore far more pleasant to shoot than Sir Samuel Baker's "Baby," despite the fact that Giles Whittome's 2-bore has twice the powder charge of Baker's "little gun."

Like the 8-gauge and the 4-gauge rifles, shooting the 2-gauge can best be described as a thrill. Like the carnival roller coaster ride, it thrills you but the fun is holding onto that much power without being hurt. You know that you have controlled more power in your hands than you ever dreamed possible. You have also done something only a handful of men in the world have done.

Kings and dictators may have power but it is never as tangible as controlling a giant heavy gauge rifle as you fire it.

The effect at the other end is that of a light artillery piece instead of an elephant gun. When charged at a range of a few feet by something big with murder in its heart, you won't think is underpowered or too much gun. Those days the white hunters refer to as a "brown pants day" are best survived with the largest of weapons. While your gun bearer may hate carrying it, the 2-bore provides a neat solution to the problem of the gun bearer taking it on himself

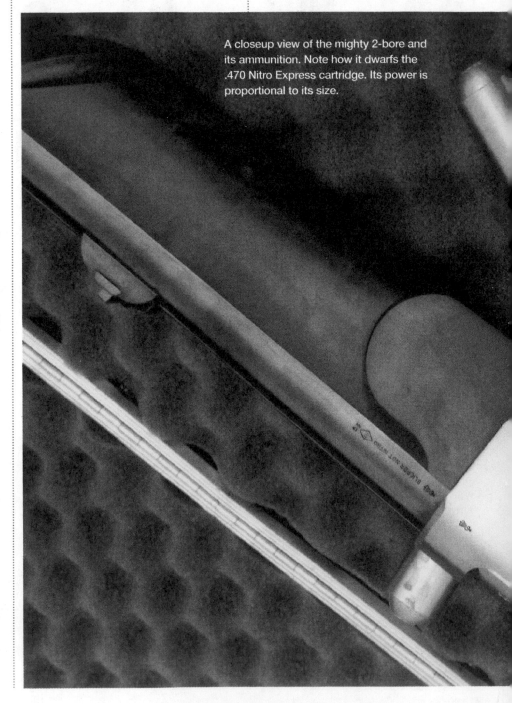

A closeup view of the mighty 2-bore and its ammunition. Note how it dwarfs the .470 Nitro Express cartridge. Its power is proportional to its size.

to fire the gun he is carrying. Just let him fire it once (being careful to catch the gun as it flies through the air) and I seriously doubt if any charging beast will be able to persuade him to fire it again. Remember that an 8-bore rifle has 200 fpe of recoil while a 4-bore rifle has 300. (I will leave the recoil of the 2-gauge to your imagination.) Reloading is as fast as any single shot and the cartridges fall out of the chamber so easily that the extractor almost seem superfulous, but it's a nice touch should more than one beast be bearing down on you.

The 21-lb. weight of the 2 gauge rifle is a serious consideration to someone considering taking it afield after game. Obviously it is not something for small men to play with and I would not recommend buying one for your wife. But is should be pointed out that the WWI German MG08-15 machinegunner carried a 50-pound weapon when the water jacket was full and the 100-round drum magazine attached. Many of these men could and did fire it offhand like a rifle when the situation demanded it. Men almost 100 years later tend to be bigger and stronger so there, should be plenty of men today who are man enough to handle this brute.

It is worth remembering that the great white hunter Frederick Selous always claimed his 4-bore single barrel muzzle loaders killed elephants better than anything else he ever saw. Finaughty and many other hunters of the day agreed with him. Today's hunters are ignorant of the power of these bygone dinosaurs of the firearms world and it is their loss, for there is nothing that will save your life faster when the chips are down than one of these shoulder cannons, over which the 2-bore reigns as king. When you read stories of how a Cape buffalo has gotten his adrenaline up and run amok taking 15 or more .375, .458 or .505 bullets before dropping, just remember that historically a single 8-bore shot in the vitals has always put a stop to that sort of thing. Now imagine what a 2-bore can do. When a previously wounded Cape buffalo or elephant that you knew nothing about lays an ambush and erupts from the bushes a few feet away, so close that you have to fire from the hip, which gun do you want? While rare, such things do happen in Africa. A poacher wounds something and then later you're confronted with the full wrath and fury of a great wounded beast you didn't even know was there. Hope you weren't on a photographic safari then.

If you want a duplicate of the Royal Armouries 2-bore rifle Giles Whittome will gladly make you one. If, like me, you prefer double barrel guns, he will make you the first 2-bore double rifle in history with whatever action type you specify. Cartridges can be either blackpowder or nitro-for-black. Whatever you please. Smokeless powder kicks less than blackpowder and also allows heavier loads if one is so inclined. It also is noncorrosive and much easier to clean up after, and I recommend it for all dangerous game hunting. I don't like charging animals disappearing behind a cloud of smoke at critical times. Giles' address is:

Giles Whittome, Gunmaker
Bassingbourn Mill
Mill Lane
Bassingbourn
Cambridge, SG8 5PP
England
Telephone 01763 248708
Fax 01763 243271
Email gileswhittome@hotmail.co.uk
Mobile 07860 445805
Prices on request, of course!

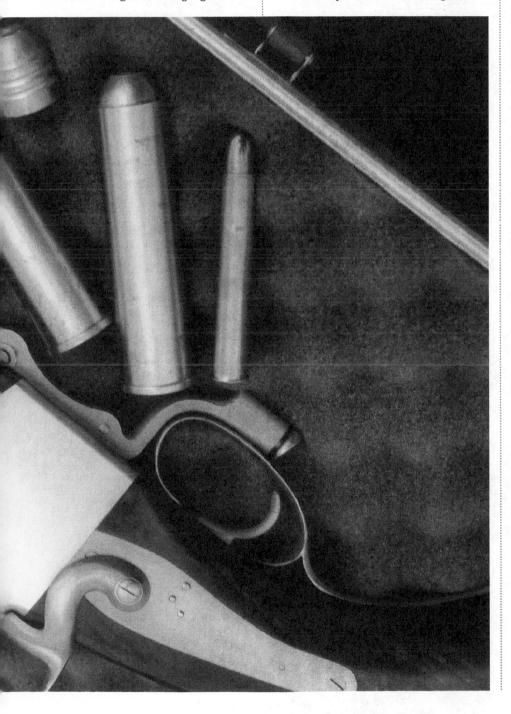

Improved firearm designs usually arise out of necessity. They are created when nations are confronted with the threat of foreign invasion and formal weapons manufacturing proves impossible - such as was the case at the end of the Second World War. It was during that era, and with a will to fight, that the Germans created new designs to resist their onward pressing foe. These firearms were crude and unreliable, yet that preliminary work on improvised firearms has lead to modern variants that usually rival the best designs coming out of long-established firms.

Pressed into a corner, a novel idea hit several German gun makers. What if you could make cheap firearms that use a portion of the expanding gas upon firing to momentarily delay opening of the action? You would not need a complicated locking system. They got to work and came up with remarkable designs. It was their initial work on gas-delayed blowback firearms initiated over 60 years ago that continues to influence respectable modern variants.

Part of the reason the Germans wanted to manufacture cheap firearms was so that scarce materials could go to the building of heavy weapons: artillery, armour and aviation. History has shown that it is these weapons, and not so much the small arms, that win battles and wars. One could even find savings in how they made firearms in general. Do away with extensive machining and the results are always less costly and may be just as effective. For example, many modern sheet metal-based assault rifles can be produced for less than their cast and machined metal rivals, but all work equally as well.

At the last stages of the war, German weapons plants could no longer cope with the demand for quality weaponry, so it became imperative that various firms begin to design firearms from the ground up which could be made quickly, simply and cost effectively. Participating weapons firms included Appel, Berliner-Spandau; Bergmann KG, Velten; Gustloff Werke, Suhlo; Walther, Zella-Mehlis; Deutsche Industrie-Werke AG,

Berlin; Rochling, Wetzlar (Coenders); Berliner-Lubecker Maschinenfabriken; ERMA, Haenel, Hessiche Industrie-Werke, Mauser, Rheinmetall-Borsig, Ruhrstahl, Spreewerk and Steyr.

Critical to the design of any full-powered autoloading firearm is how to delay the opening of the breech until residual chamber pressure upon firing decreases to safe limits. This is not a problem in locked-breech firearms in which recoil or gas unlocks the breech block from the barrel. However, locked-breech designs usually necessitate close tolerance machining and are thus expensive to produce. To solve this issue, various engineers began to consider something entirely new. They tapped a minute portion of the expanding gases of discharged ammunition to momentarily defer opening. On that account, the first gas-delayed blowback firearms came from the arms factories of Nazi Germany.

The theory behind "gas-bleed delay" is that a portion of the gas propelling the bullet flows through ports in the barrel to impinge on the inner surfaces of the slide or operating cylinder. The breech remains closed until the bullet has passed from the muzzle, by which time the pressure has dropped adequately to allow the breechblock to move rearward in standard blowback fashion. The breechblock is not wholly locked during the entire duration of the bullet's progress up the bore. It is in essence a blowback system in which the rearward movement is momentarily delayed.

VOLKSPISTOLE

Two firms stood out in developing crude by workable *Primitiv-Waffen-Programm* pistols: Walther and the more prolific Mauser. Mauser's prototype had been on the design board for years, but the first production model was ready on February 1944 and the second in June. The prototype, referred to as the M.7057, was a simple sheet metal pistol with a tipping barrel locked by camming a transverse shoulder in the slide. The pistol featured a double-action trigger, an exposed hammer spur and a thumb safety on the slide. In many respects, the M7057 was a conventional pistol made of stampings instead of milling and the project was officially abandoned in January of 1945.

The Mauser *Volkspistole* (i.e., "People's Pistol") V.7082 was originally a double-action striker-fired blowback,

JUNK OR THE CUTTING EDGE?

BY WARREN FERGUSON

Gas-Delayed Blowbacks

Author firing the Norinco M77B.

made of thick pressed steel. It was completed by October of 1944. (As a side note, many SIG-Sauer pistols of the past few decades have stamped metal slides, at least in part.) Here we see the genesis of the gas-delay concept. The arm was tested against the emerging Walther blowback design and the trials led to the rejection of double-action triggers and a petition that a breech opening delay be employed in the designs.

By using a form of delayed blowback, expensive and time-consuming manufacturing steps could be eliminated and the pistol would still be able to fire full-powered service ammunition. Remember that at the time, pistols such as the Luger and the P-38 were machined and well-engineered pieces of equipment. It was radical to think of making firearms in any other manner.

The approach in which the Mauser worked was to be expected: part of the gas propelling the bullet seeped through ports in the barrel to impinge on the inner surfaces of the slide. It featured a fixed barrel and a lift-off slide like those of many Walthers and the magazine was from the standard P-38 pistol. A long non-rifled bore extension was fitted to the end of the barrel, presumably to increase the breech opening delay.

Had the *Volkspistole* project not insisted on the use of full-powered 9mm Parabellum service ammunition rather than the low-impulse 7.65mm, 9mm Kurz or sub-loaded 9mm Parabellum, it is likely the order for additional pistols could have been filled much sooner. While this would have quickened the pace, it was not, however, a viable logistical choice. Yet as time went on, it became doubtful that these pistols could be made at all.

In a January 4, 1945, letter to *Reichs-führer-SS* Himmler, the Commanding Officer of the Replacement Army, the Staff Leader of the German Home Guard (*Volkssturm*) and the Commissioner for Armament and Equipment, Carl Walther Waffenfabrik acknowledged War Order Number 1005, Waffen SS for *Volkspistole* handguns. A few roughly-tranlated excerpts from that letter show how difficult manufacturing even People's Pistols was becoming:

"Manufacture of the pistol can begin only after completion of another ongoing project and when a workroom becomes available. The prescribed dates of delivery of February 1945, March 1945, etc., cannot be met. As soon as the plant completes the first project, Walther will communicate the shortest possible dates of delivery of the People's Pistol. The raw material request of the main committee weapons Berlin is today published. Walther asks the Hauptamt-Waffen (Head Office for Weapons) that the requested iron subscription rights and sheet metal order rights are assigned as soon as possible. Job Order SS-4924 (the present project) is priority Level I. Even so, the remaining production lines thereby already have a great deal of difficulty with the procurement of materials. Walther has therefore assigned the material procurement (for the pistols) to a lower priority since sustaining the Level I project

Dlask 294 with slide removed.

Heckler & Koch P7 M8. Courtesy of H&K USA.

has become substantially difficult."

Aside from procuring raw materials for the pistols, several drawbacks of the design were recognized early: first, the slide/barrel contact point necessitated rather close tolerances or the gas would escape, making it a blowback, something it was not designed to be. Second, gas residue soon fouled the inner wall and plugged the gas port and required constant cleaning. Third, there was a risk of case warping, splits and rim separations since the bolt was moving backward while the case was still expanding against the chamber wall by gas pressure.

From an engineering viewpoint, overcoming the last problem was achieved by fluting the chamber: thin grooves were cut longitudinally from in front of the case mouth to about one third of the case length from its base. Fluting allowed high-pressure gas to flow outside the case and thus "float" it on a layer of gas, thus reducing friction during the initial motion of the bolt. The fluting procedure prevented the cartridge case from sticking to the walls of the chamber on extraction but as a result, the mechanism became fouled black after firing.

The evolved gas-delayed blowback worked well in pistol form and even work with the stalwart 7.92mm *Pist. Patr.* 43 "intermediate" rifle round flying at over 2100 fps!

VG 1-5 SEMI-AUTOMATIC CARBINE

The German gas-delayed blowback VG 1-5 semi-automatic rifle was included within the *Primitiv-Waffen-Programm* and was intended for the *Volkssturm* troops. The chronicle of the VG 1-5, a carbine made at Gustloff Werke (Suhl), is rather elusive because few actual weapon specimens survived the war and many documents concerning it were destroyed. Few exist in private or public collections and they are both rare and expensive. A DEWAT non-functioning war trophy was at one time put on auction with a minimum bid of $10,000.

Uncovering information about the VG 1-5 is not easy. Inquiries sent to Suhl, the factory that originally built the VG 1-5, regarding the carbine passed through many hands before Elke Weiß, representative of the Suhler Jagd- und Sportwaffen GmbH weapons firm wrote me: "All materials about military guns and materials that were produced during the war in the Gustloff Werke

Selbstlader mit Kurzpatrone 44, as well as the *Versuchgerät 1-5*. Note that *Volkssturm* weapons were never adopted or given official nomenclature. The customary term *Volksgewehr* was applied by the Germans as a general reference and the various other names were conceived after the war.

Originally, the *Volkssturm* drew the greater part of its weapons from materiel captured by the *Wehrmacht*, but soon that supply was exhausted. In response, German industry exhibited remarkable resourcefulness by manufacturing serviceable weapons from basic materials and eminently uncomplicated production techniques. Machining and heat treating were kept to a bare minimum and steel tubing and sheet metal with welding, pins and rivets were used for component assembly.

The alternate weapons program was

halves like a clam shell and then welded together. Enclosing the barrel and extending behind it over the receiver was a thick-walled, machine-operating cylinder (.175"-thick, 15.5"-long steel tube, approximately 1.420" in diameter). At its front, the cylinder was sealed by a long cylindrical collar. To the rear, a half-cylindrical bolt was pinned directly to the long cylinder and a recoil spring is placed around the barrel.

The operating cylinder reciprocated and impelled the bolt with it. Following firing, normal blowback action began until the combustion gas escaped through four radial gas ports in the barrel 2.5 inches behind the muzzle to act upon the forward cylinder collar. This gas was trapped in the space created by the operating cylinder collar and the barrel. The gas pushed forward against the collar and rearward against the shoulder of the barrel. After one inch of rearward travel, the ports were exposed and normal blowback action continued. Loading was accomplished by the returning recoil spring.

After inspecting each expedient firearm, Hitler forsook all single shot models and then inspected the VG 1-5. He indicated that the VGs should have had a magazine of about 10 rounds to promote prone position shooting. The longer 30-round MP44 magazine was not to be used in the rifles. Hitler eventually discounted the Gustloff self-loading model altogether due to its expense, excessive ammunition consumption and because the MP44 assault rifle was already in production with about the same use of material and cost.

Assuredly, while serviceable, the VG 1-5 was never highly regarded compared to the MP44. Only about 10,000 of these semi-automatic carbines were manufactured for civilian resistance use during the war. Today, the VG 1-5 is exceedingly rare and is principally found only in noted arms museums. This writer was fortunately enough to examine the specimen held by the National Infantry Museum at Fort Benning, Georgia.

There is very little information relative to the field performance of the VG 1-5, but it is taken for granted that it suffered from the most typical problem of all gas-delayed blowbacks – jamming due to fouling. There is one performance report, however, worth noting. Out of Headquarters, Communications Zone, ETOUSA (European Theater of Operations, USA), Office of the Chief Ordnance Officer, came a report from a Col. H. N. Toftoy. In "ETO ORDNANCE TECHNICAL

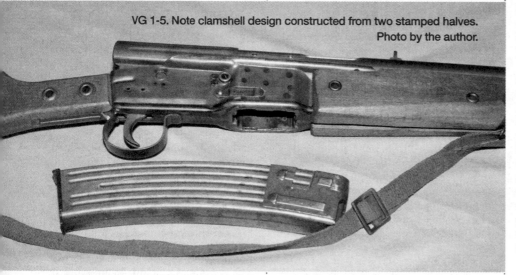

VG 1-5. Note clamshell design constructed from two stamped halves. Photo by the author.

were destroyed after the war. Since 1948 hunting guns and rifles have been produced in the former Gustloff Werke – now Suhler Jagd – und Sportwaffen GmbH so that we do not have a close connection with (the) military."

On that same note, details about the Volkspistolen are equally hard to find. Mauser-Werke Oberndorf Waffensysteme GmbH wrote: "As far as prewar products are concerned, we have to inform you that all documentation has been destroyed or dismantled...after WWII."

There ends the conventional trail. How could one find out more? What is known is that the VG 1-5 can be termed in various ways: *Selbstladegewehr, Volkssturmgewehr 1-5, Selbstladekarabiner, Volkssturm-Maschinenpistole 45, Gustloffvolkssturmgewehr, Volkssturm-Selbstladegewehr, Gustloff-Werke,*

inaugurated to field basic should arms chambered for both 7.92x57mm long cartridge and the 7.92x33mm Kurz (short) cartridges. The designs covered single shot and magazine-fed bolt action rifles and semi-automatic carbines.

Early development efforts peaked during the autumn of 1944 and the weapons were demonstrated to Adolf Hitler during November 1944, according to Germany's Minister of Production Albert Speer. Among the models demonstrated to the dictator was a delayed blowback semi-automatic firing the Kurz cartridge, with a 30-round magazine, from the Gustloff Werke, Suhl.

Karl Barnitzke, the chief draftsman at Gustloff Werke, designed the VG 1-5 to feature a barrel permanently assembled, or mated, to the receiver. A sheet metal design, the receiver was formed in two

INTELLIGENCE REPORT NO. 292" of May 24 of 1945, Col. Toftoy says:

"The design of the weapons indicates its purpose. Though crudely made it could be turned out in great numbers quickly and cheaply to arm the Volksturm [sic]. Its performance is rather poor both in functioning and easy of firing. In the three clips fired (90 rounds), seven jams were cleared. The weapon should not be fired from the hip for powder residue blows upward from the ports in the slide."

The VG 1-5 was machined to somewhat close tolerances in order to seal in the gas. However, unless the surfaces were habitually cleaned and carefully lubricated, the combined effect of accumulating gas residue and barrel expansion would sporadically cause the weapon to jam. Yet the VG 1-5 did work. Needless to say, the trigger pull, sighting system and consequent accuracy were less than could be desired.

POST WAR DEVELOPMENTS

Much has changed since some of the first German designs were field tested, and today the wartime method of breech locking, i.e., using expanding cartridge gas to delay a blowback action, has become generally accepted, appreciated and even sought out by sportsmen, police and military forces alike.

Following the war, gas-delayed blowback rifles were generally abandoned but other forms of delayed blowback firearms were attempted, all of which used WWII German technology and experience in one form or another. Early post-war delayed blowback systems from Spain, Switzerland and France have used roller-locking systems housed in stampings. The wartime innovation of chamber fluting is more recently evident in the modern French 5.56mm bullpup rifle and within the German G3/HK33/MP5 family.

The gas-delayed blowback pistol design has continued with several modern entries. When applied to sidearms, these gas designs have proven effective. More modern gas pistols include the Rogak P-18, the related but better Austrian Steyr Model GB, the German Heckler & Koch P7 variants, the Dlask 294, Network Custom Guns' M1911 drop-in gas gun conversion kit and assembled pistols, the Heritage Manufacturing Stealth pistols and their Wilson Combat cousins, the South African Du Plessis ADP and Vektor pistols, and the Chinese Norinco M20/M77B series. These designs, for the most part, will safely fire 9x19mm submachinegun ammunition, 9mm+P, and the hotter .40 S&W rounds.

What is common in each of these designs is how the design engineers overcame problems with reliability. The aforementioned drawbacks of gas-delayed designs were mastered in various ways, including fluted chambers, an insistence on jacketed ammunition (never lead bullets), and precise, quality manufacturing – something impossible during the later years of WWII.

Steyr-Daimler-Puch, widely known for its heavy machinery and firearms, first began its own studies into gas-delayed blowback pistols in the late sixties as a possible replacement for the Austrian military's aging P-38 and FN Hi Power pistols. Yet Steyr was not a newcomer in this field of research, having participating in the *Volkssturm* weapons development initiative during the final months of World War II.

The result of the firm's research and testing was the GB – *Gas Bremse*, or "Gas Brake," which featured a double-stacked magazine with an amazing 18-round capacity. Following manufacturing lessons from WWII, the GB possesses a frame that is made by welding two halves together. The resulting product is somewhat large compared to other 9mm pistols but, owing to its fixed barrel, is highly accurate.

In many respects, the GB is akin to the VG 1-5 rifle and it follows closely the construction and concept of the Mauser *Volkspistole*: it traps a small amount of gas from the barrel to channel it against the interior of the slide. Unlike most other gas guns, the GB has a conventional double-action trigger system.

The gas-delayed blowback design, depending on who made it, could be deemed as either the cutting edge or mere junk. You see, America was the initial testing ground for the GB. But before Steyr began building and marketing the GB, America's Les Rogak, a Steyr importer, put the design into production during the 1970s. In a manufacturing firm called L.E.S. or Rogak, Inc., out of Morton Grove, Illinois, Rogak brought the blueprints alive. The stainless steel Rogak P-18 featured an 18-shot capacity, as its name suggests, and a gas-delayed blowback action that appeared at first to workable and easy to manufacture.

American tastes at the time, however, did not favor 9mm pistols. Compound this with what some would suggest was less than ideal workmanship, and the P-18 was doomed to failure.

What really killed the P-18 was that its gas-delayed action was not well-suited to the 9mm Parabellum. Remember that a tight seal is required within the slide to keep the gas in and the blowback action delayed. If this cannot be achieved, all you have is a blowback pistol. The 9mm is not well suited for this arrangement.

There were attempts to salvage the P-18. These included adding fibre buffers around the barrel and relying on the strong return spring. As a result, the pistol became ammunition-sensitive and was known to jam.

In all fairness, most firearms go through a period of testing and modification, and sometimes new designs are not perfect from the outset. The P-18 was not perfect, but harsh reviews did not promote consumer confidence. Steyr, a company built on its good reputation, took legal action to stop the production of P-18s. Still, about 2,300 guns were built. Steyr, meanwhile, continued its work on the development of its GB back in Austria. Learning from the P-18 experience, the Steyr design reworked almost of the parts but, more importantly, focused on the male gas sealing bushing to ensure the pistol would be gas-delayed.

By 1980, Steyr's carbon steel GB-80 was introduced. The frame was made of two steel haves welded together, a technique first used by Nazi builders. The pistol had a chrome-lined, polygonally-rifled barrel. It was quicker to build than the Rogak by far, but workmanship did not suffer. The end product was beginning to win domestic military support, and in 1983 it looked like the GB would win a 25,000-pistol Austrian government contract – at least until a wild card was thrown in: Gaston Glock had his own plans for that contract.

Undaunted, Steyr turned to the United States XM9 military handgun trials. In the fall of 1983, the U.S. Army took possession of 30 model GB pistols for its tests. The Steyr GB went up against all the big names with the Beretta Model 92SB-F winning, as is well-known. There were some police sales in Asia and the Middle East, but the new focus was the civilian market. The GB was built in relatively small numbers and saw limited importation into the United States. From 1983 on the GBs were marketed in the US and Europe where they sold well until they were discontinued in 1986. Gun South, the US distributor, kept importing GBs until late 1988.

At one point, Austrian designers considered including a full-auto option on the GB, thus displaying their

GAS-DELAYED BLOWBACKS—JUNK OR THE CUTTING EDGE?

confidence in the safety and reliability of their gas-delayed blowback system. Some considered the GB as the ideal starting point for a competition pistol, given its fixed barrel and the ease with which a compensator could be added. Despite all it had going for it, the GB was unfortunately put on the market at the same time as countless other 9mm pistols, and competition forced its inappropriate and undeserved end.

THE GERMANS MAKE A COMEBACK

Germany's Heckler & Koch underwent its own research into gas-delay blowbacks and emerged with its P7 series of pistols. When the West German police required a new pistol, the result was a new 9x19mm semi-automatic pistol called the PSP (police self-loading pistol) by H&K. It was adopted by the West German police as the P7, and now H&K also officially titles its design the P7. Surplus PSPs have recently made it into the civilian market.

The P7 is a tough design – it was required to pass a 10,000-round service test with hot ammunition. European ammunition is usually loaded to 40,000 c.u.p. (copper units of pressure) while most American ammo makers stay around 36,000 c.u.p. Thus, the steel P7 is at its best with powerful loads. In fact, if a slightly lower velocity round is fired the pistol may not cycle correctly.

Unique to the P7's design is the employment of a squeeze cocker located at the front surfaces of the pistol grip. The squeeze cocker cocks the firing pin to provide a nice, single-action trigger pull and it also acts as a slide release. The P7 pistols use a fixed, polygonal barrel made by cold hammer forging. With its fluted chamber, the P7 will smoothly extract and eject an empty casing even if the extractor is missing.

The H&K design differs from the Steyr both in its construction and the manner in which the breech opening is delayed. After firing, a small vent in the barrel directs cartridge gas underneath the barrel into a small cylinder where the gas acts on a piston rod connected directly to the slide. As the bullet leaves the muzzle, gas pressure drops and the piston rod travels within the gas cylinder much like an automobile shock absorber. Recoil is said to be lessened this way, and this writer's range time with a P7 confirms this.

The P7's is a simple system that would be copied by others in the

years to come. Indeed, the P7 has been so successful that it has become standard issue to several military and police units including the armed forces of Germany and the New Jersey State Police with a few modifications. Further, the P7 M13 (high-capacity version) was initially a candidate for the Joint Services Small Arms Program in the early 1980s as a replacement for the older .45 ACP service pistol.

The next evolution of the P7 design was the variant feeding the .40 S&W round, the P7M10. Engineers strengthened and heightened the slide to accommodate the larger round and the result seems to attest to the fact that a gas locking system will work with powerful cartridges. The P7 is a superb piece of equipment by all possible measures.

The gas gun saga then shifted to Canada. In 1994, Canadian gunsmith Josef Dlask created a machined frame single-stack compact gas gun known as the DAC-294. Very well made, this pistol was another P7-inspired creation and used a gas piston-in-cylinder arrangement. The slim Dlask would have been a perfect compact carry gun, but the project remained in the prototype stage when Dlask moved on to producing SIG-Sauer P228 clones and the 1911s for which he is famous.

A year later, the world would see if the gas-delayed blowback system could be applied to larger and more powerful cartridges. In mid-1995 an

American firm, Network Custom Guns Inc., of Marietta, Ohio, fielded its own variant of a gas pistol, this time firing the stout .45 ACP round, in 1995. NCG's product was a drop-in conversion kit that readily changed the normally recoil-operated Model 199A1 pistol to gas-delayed action. Styled very much after the P7 system, the kit was reputed to reduce felt recoil to 50 percent less than with a standard 1911. It has proven highly accurate because there is no camming action for reloading or a removable bushing; the company boasts its pistol ejects and reloads faster than any 1911 on the market.

The conversion kit's accuracy out to 25 yards yielded groups around 1.5 inches in diameter. Company tests were done with the NCG gas gun firing .45-calibre 185-gr. jacketed truncated-cone flatpoints by Rainer Ballistics. A 16-1/2-lb. Wolfe spring was employed, and the bullet went out at 880 fps. By 1998, this 1911-type gas gun concept, now in .38 Super, began to find its way into competitive shooting where its fixed barrel proved invaluable. Currently, NCG assembles complete pistols in other race calibers such as 9x23.

As a point of interest, the firm also offers a longer threaded barrel for a suppressor, and it is in this role that the kit is best suited. Typically, a bulky, heavy suppressor prevents barrel camming after firing and the firearm must be reloaded manually – but

Schematic of Heckler & Koch P7.
Courtesy of H&K USA.

not so with the NCG kit. With kit and suppressor in place, the manufacturer claims a .45 ACP will shoot like a .22 rimfire. In any case, this set up should prove popular with shadowy forces.

In 1996 the next gas gun clan began to emerge. A series of polymer-framed 10- to 15-shot double-action-only pistols were unveiled. These were all based on the design by Alex Du Plessis, who lived originally in then-Rhodesia. From his base in South Africa, Du Plessis began his gas gun project in the 1980s and his so-called ADP pistol was shown to the world.

The prototype pistol, which used a gas-retarded blowback system like that of the Heckler & Koch P7, was produced in South Africa, and manufacturing was also taken up by Heritage Manufacturing, Inc. of Opa Locka, Florida, with a different name. In many respects, the ADP is like a smaller P7, only much less expensive. This striker-fired design has a trigger system somewhat related to the Glock's – squeezing the trigger will move the striker to its rear-most position, disengaging from the transfer bar, and allowing the striker to move forward on its own.

The American ADP became known as the Stealth C-1000 after a reported two and half years of development. With its 17-4 stainless steel and chrome molybdenum parts and polymer frame, the Stealth is light, durable and very compact. A 4-lb. double-action-only trigger activates the striker. In 1997 the Stealth Shadow 2000 variant was made available. The Shadow still has a stainless steel slide, but it is black chrome-plated to match the black frame.

The Stealths are available in both 9mm Parabellum and .40 S&W, the latter coined the C-4000 (C-4200 Shadow). Heritage's owner's manual states that the Stealth will handle +P ammunition, once again proving the suitability of the gas delay system to full-powered pistol rounds.

Back in South Africa, Truvelo Armory and Aserma had an interest in marketing the ADP line in 1998. According to Aserma, their latest ADP Mk2 represents a complete redesign and re-engineering of the original Mk1 pistol, based on market feedback. At 6.3" long by 4.6" high, it is a bit larger, and its 3.74" barrel is 0.14 inches longer than the Mk1's. Magazine capacity is the same at 10 rounds, with 15-shot versions still an option where legal. An extended barrel is available for attaching a sound suppressor.

Aserma has had a .40 S&W version

of the ADP in development. It seems that in 1995 Aserma initiated a licensing deal with Italy's Tanfoglio. This seems likely since Tanfoglio marketed the P25, a "lightweight pocket size self-defense pistol with a composite frame and a gas delayed blowback system, firing pin with drop safety mechanism, reversible magazine catch, double action only, ambidextrous safety and three dots sights."

This Italian-produced pistol has more than a passing resemblance to an ADP. It has been suggested that the P25 parts are made in South Africa and

The Norinco M77B, field-stripped.

the gun only assembled in Europe, but company officials are tight-lipped. In any case, fairly limited numbers have been circulated across Europe to date although some ADP-types were seen in the United Kingdom (ban notwithstanding). It now looks like the P25 was supplanted by the Force 99, Tanfoglio's polymer framed CZ-75-type pistol.

The ADP pistol was originally not sold in the USA due to an arrangement with Heritage Manufacturing, but is offered elsewhere in the world in .380, 9mm and .40 S&W. Designer Du Plessis recently added a fourth calibre to the line, the .45 ADP. The case for this newly invented cartridge is 3mm shorter than the .45 ACP case, and the bullets are

seated to give an overall length no more than that of the 9mm. In a sense, the .45 ADP was the parent of the .45 GAP.

Many of us have seen the ultra-futuristic Vektor CP1 9mm from Pretoria, South Africa. Vektor specializes in commercial and military products for both the local and export markets. Its products also include R4 Galils, the Vektor 40mm Automatic Grenade Launcher, and for civilized society their H5, a curious pump-action AK-type with sport stocks and scope.

The Vektor CP1's 1999 debut showed that gas-delayed blowback pistols were here to stay. Its method of operation is by now unremarkable, again the P7-type design, but its styling is unconventional to say the least. It has been called "Art Deco applied to firearms design" and has no sharp corners. Its safety is on the trigger guard in front of the trigger, a la the M1 Garand, and is tactically ambidextrous. This pistol is also available with modified sights, extended magazine releaser and a compensator as the Vektor SP1 Sport. To be expected, the Vektor SP2 is of the same design as the SP1, but it's offered in .40 S&W. This model can also be fitted with a 9mm Parabellum conversion kit, which is available as an option.

In its many forms, the Vektors should have proven suitable and very comfortable for concealed carry, but the line was recalled in 2000 by the manufacturer when it was discovered the pistol could fire when dropped or bumped. The recall notice stated that the pistol should not be loaded under any circumstance – very ominous wording indeed. The recall essentially killed the Vektors; production ceased a year later, and today they are usually only encountered in science fiction movies and television series, like the new *Battlestar Galactica*. This is a shame, as the Vektor had great potential.

So what happened to the ADP line?

50 rounds. Owners of this pistol either love it or vehemently detest it. The verdict is out on this one. Time will tell.

The most recent entry to emerge comes out of the People's Republic of China. It would seem that their engineers took a long, hard look at the German P7 and decided that they would find a way to get the same performance at a fraction of the cost. They would machine the frame and slide, but the guts of their NP-20 would be a virtual copy of the P7 gas piston layout. It too would be striker-fired and be easy to disassemble and maintain. It field strips somewhat like an oversized Walther PPK.

The Chinese then took their NP-20

and maybe some users voiced their concerns. The safety is quite positive, however, so it could be that the change to the trigger guard cocking was done for the same reason so many engineers make things – because they can.

Range shooting of the M77B by this writer showed that the pistol has good sights and is highly accurate when one figures out the feel of the trigger. It is somewhat spongy and is probably the worst feature of the design. When pulling the trigger, a lever is lifted to prevent the cocking bar from moving. Since the cocking bar does not reciprocate with the slide, it is unknown why the lever is needed at all. The ejection of the casings is very forceful and leaves the slide surfaces around the port dirty. The pistol does require a good cleaning after use.

It should be noted that this pistol is needlessly larger than the P7, ADP or Vektor. Its dimensions are approximately 1" thick, by 7-1/2" long by 5-1/2" in height. Additionally, one needs to be a behemoth to rack the slide with one's trigger finger. Nevertheless, the M77B is marketed inexpensively for about the same price as their Tokarev pistol and is very well made and finished. Were it available in the USA, it would probably sell well.

GAS RIFLES MAKE A COMEBACK

Handguns seem to be the modern focus of gas delay technology, but not exclusively. It would seem that the *Volkssturmgewehr* type of rifle might have been the inspiration for two American firearm designs that use the principles of gas delay. First, Robert M. Irwin, out of Las Vegas, Nevada, received a US patent in 1975 for a gas-locked firearm using expanding gases to delay blowback in a firearm.

In the Irwin design, and according to the patent, a portion of gas is diverted through a gas port communicating with a gas-locking chamber adjacent to the barrel. An extension arm of the breech block extends forward a distance along the rear portion of the barrel to form an elongated gas chamber between a shoulder on the rear of the barrel and a plate extending from the breech block extension. In this manner, expanding gases are trapped between the barrel shoulder and this plate to lock the breech block in a forward position while gas pressure exists in the barrel.

Paul A. Petrovich of Fowlerville, Michigan, had his own idea on this familiar theme. In 1995, he received a

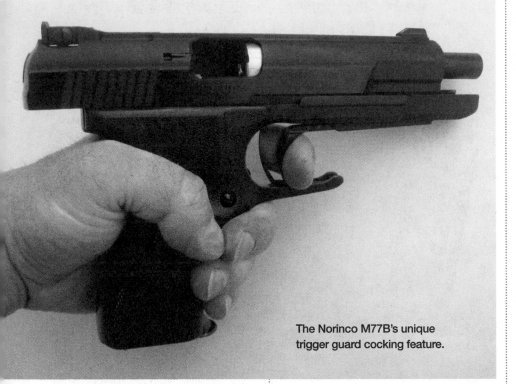

The Norinco M77B's unique trigger guard cocking feature.

It was discontinued for a while when Truvelo went off in another direction and created its distinctively shaped AK inspired rifle with integral carrying handle and rails, the Raptor. This would have been the end of the ADP were it not for Wilson Combat getting involved in 2006. The company put its name on the ADP and continues to sell it today – albeit at a higher ticket price than its cousin the Stealth.

User reports on this pistol vary widely. Some have had no problems with the new ADP and carry it as their CCW choice. Others have criticized individual parts and certain aspects of its construction. Some suggest the gas system needs a good cleaning every

one step further. They thought that the concept had great potential as a police service pistol with some changes. What they did was interesting. They modified the trigger guard in such a way that the user could rack the slide with his or her trigger finger. Pulling the front surface of the trigger guard retracts the slide and allows a cartridge to be chambered. *[Editor's note: Perhaps this idea was borrowed from the long-gone Lignose Einhandpistole of the 1920s and 1930s. –DMS]* This variant is called the Norinco M77B and the user can draw, load and fire in one go.

One could surmise that the reason for this change was perhaps safety. The NP-20 is single-action striker fired

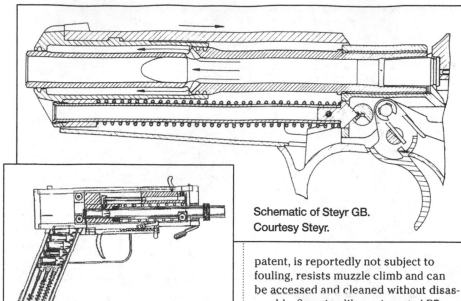

Schematic of Steyr GB.
Courtesy Steyr.

The Stephens design. From patent drawing.

US patent for a device that "improves rapidly firing guns." When such a gun fires, Petrovich's device delays departure of the gun bolt from the chamber holding a spend round's casing until barrel pressure drops to a safe level.

The device, as described in the patent, features a hollow piston which lies fore and aft along the barrel and which has an orifice linked to a barrel vent. The vent or "duct" slants forward toward the gun muzzle in a radially outward direction so as to direct expanding propellant gas from the barrel against a forward internal surface of the piston. Gas pressure keeps the piston in its most forward position and with it the bolt stays put.

Petrovich also envisioned that the piston could optionally have an escape opening at its aft end so that some of the propellant gas entering the piston would be forced rearward, thereby creating an additional forward force on the piston during and immediately after firing. Also optionally, the cylindrical wall of the piston could be made to flex outward under pressure so as to delay piston motion via friction.

OTHER ASSORTED DESIGNS

Machine pistols have also been subject to gas-delayed mechanisms. In 1990, Mark L. Stephens of Alta Loma, California, was issued a patent for his "Self cleaning automatic machine pistol and silencer for the same." This machine pistol, as described in the

patent, is reportedly not subject to fouling, resists muzzle climb and can be accessed and cleaned without disassembly. Seeming like an inverted P7, a portion of high-pressure gas from the barrel is bled through a barrel vent into a gas port tube that is telescopically inserted into the bolt. This gas acts in a forward direction in opposition to the motion of recoil. An upwardly directed nozzle within the bolt provides downward thrust on the muzzle end of the piston to avoid muzzle climb.

This design must have been well conceived indeed. A "self-cleaning" gas-delayed blowback would be useful in its own right. The design's ability to provide both a gas delay and at the same time use that same gas to dampen recoil shows incredible ingenuity. One would assume that any communication between the gas chamber and the atmosphere would negate any delay effect, but anything is possible.

Naturally, there have been any number of collet-chamber retarding systems that use the resultant high gas pressure upon firing to cause momentary dilation of the chamber or a set of fingers adjacent thereto. There have been gas-delayed blow-forward designs, too, but that is another story.

What can be mentioned, however, is the existence of two hybrid recoil-gas delay systems patented in 1996. Out of Churchill, Australia, Bernard C. Besselink has proposed two interesting self-loading firearm designs that operate on the short-recoil principle assisted by gas. In the first of these Browning HP35-derived designs, a variable volume chamber is affixed to the underside of the barrel. A vent in the barrel allows passage of pressurized gases upon firing. This retards the motion of the barrel and slide assembly allowing a

lighter slide to be used for a specific cartridge type. On the latter, a cylinder is located concentrically around the barrel and communicates with the barrel via passages. The action of propellant gases in the cylinder retards the motion of the barrel and slide assembly.

CONCLUSION

By reviewing each of the modern gas delayed blowback autoloaders, the general design gives all indication of being adequately strong to handle powerful cartridges. Gas guns started out as cheap improvised designs, but they should not be deemed as worthless junk. Today, the manufacturing practices and standards for gas guns are the same as those with conventional patterns. They are, indeed, the cutting edge of firearms technology.

With the P7, the principle has reached its highest and most costly form, while other designs were only marginally passable. Yet with the introduction of polymer frames, a full circle has been achieved. The newest gas guns are both reliable and inexpensive, something the original German engineers sought after with less than complete success. Today, countless police officers and civilians continue to stake their lives on various gas-delayed blowbacks. Thus, what started out as emergency pistol designs from WWII have been brought into wide usage and may very well continue far into the future.

AUTHOR'S NOTE: I would like to thank the following for permitting the reproduction of prints, drawings and photographs in their collections, for providing useful data, and for critique of this article: Z. Frank Hanner, E. Derntl, Steve Galloway, Bleecker Williams, John Adkins, Elke Weiss, Jay A. Bernkrant, Christine Danforth, Josef Dlask, Rodger Kotanko and Andrew Phillpotts.

Bibliography

Handrich, H. D. *Sturmgewehr! From Firepower to Striking Power.* Cobourg: Collector Grade Publications, 2004.

Hogg, Ian V. & Weeks, John S. *Military Small Arms of the 20th Century.* Iola: Krause Publications, 2000.

Hogg, Ian V.. *German Handguns: The Complete Book of the Pistols and Revolvers of Germany, 1869 to the Present.* Iola, Krause Publications, 2001.

Senich, Peter R. *German Assault Rifles: 1935-1945.* Boulder: Paladin Press, 1983.

Walter, John. *Guns of the Third Reich.* London: Greenhill Books., 2003.

The .19 Calhoon Badger topped with a 6.5x20 Leupold EFR scope and resting on a Peightal Shooting Stool incorporating an adjustable seat.

HORNET HOTROD:
The .19 Calhoon Badger

BY DON LEWIS
PHOTOS BY HELEN LEWIS

It's with regret that we note that this article, dealing with an interesting variation on the .22 Hornet, was one of the last written by the late Don Lewis.

There's no question that gunpowder made a significant impact on mankind. The black dust discovered by Friar Roger Bacon eventually became known as gunpowder when it was used by the military in large pots or vases to hurl stone balls to batter down the walls of forts and castles. As military weapons became more sophisticated, the black mixture was used in crude shoulder weapons that allowed the shooter to reach far beyond the limits of his sword, lance or longbow. Gunpowder changed the face of war; even the lowly mud soldier could dispose of the much-feared mounted knight, who was the backbone of medieval warfare, long before he could get close enough to use his axe or sword. Thomas Carlyle wrote that "gunpowder makes all men alike tall." Miguel de Cervantes, author of *Don Quixote,* lamented that the gun allowed "a base coward to take the life of the bravest gentlemen."

Friar Bacon did not live to see his black-dust mixture of charcoal, sulphur and saltpeter used as a propellant, and it's unlikely he realized completely what he had invented. Yet his puzzling, coded formula didn't stop the world from learning about the power of his mixture, and the brilliant flash and ear-splitting roar that chilled men's hearts was eventually tamed into what we now call gunpowder.

The story of the first gun is long and fascinating. Other than in a few cases, there are no exact dates or inventor's names attached to it. Still, the gun improved from the pots and vases to hand-held devices that could be used against a single enemy. Down through the years the gun was perfected from a crude barrel tied to a tiller (pole) into a shoulder weapon that performed flawlessly and produced deadly accuracy even at long ranges. It's been a fascinating journey, and the surprising part is that the road for a better cartridge is still be traveled. The .19

The family tree of the .19 Calhoon Badger, left to right: .30 M1 Carbine case, fired .301 M1 Carbine case, formed .19 Calhoon Badger case and reloaded .19 Calhoon Badger cartridge.

Calhoon Badger is solid proof of that.

It's worth noting that developing a dependable rifle stretched over several hundred years. During that time, it was learned that the cartridge was a major factor in not only killing power but in accuracy, too. As gun-making procedures became more sophisticated, which led to better performing rifles, more emphasis was being placed on the design of the cartridge. At first, big bores held the spotlight, but heavy bullets traveling at a slow pace were useless for long range accuracy. Cartridge designers became obsessed with high velocity. To obtain high velocity required reducing a bullet's weight and its caliber. After the turn of the twentieth century, hundreds of experimenters engaged in what we now call "wildcatting." This refers to simply taking a conventional case and, for the most part, swaging it down to another caliber. This sounds rather simple, but the truth is that wildcatting is far more complicated than that. With the proper swaging dies, the wildcatter can remove the case taper (thus producing a straight wall), sharpen the shoulder angle, reduce the overall length of the case and enlarge or reduce the neck to another caliber. Wildcatting gained a lot of followers and was literally a way of life for cartridge buffs from 1920 through 1940 and still has a significant group of fans today.

It's a fact that of the hundreds of wildcat cartridges cranked out back then that only a handful gained factory recognition. The .22-250 Remington is a shining example. It began life in the mid-1930s. Perhaps a dozen or more experimenters worked in developing a .22 centerfire varmint cartridge based on the .250-3000 Savage case. Although there were certainly slight differences among the various wildcatted .22-250 cartridges, their performances were pretty much the same. It was an accurate cartridge right from the start, and proved its worth on the benchrest line. However, with all it had to offer, it was fully 30 years after its birth that Remington added it to their cartridge line under the name .22-250 Remington. It's still the epitome of an accurate varmint cartridge and sets the standard that other varmint cartridges are measured by.

By the late 1980s, the varmint hunter had at his disposal a half-dozen top varmint cartridges with 300-yard range accuracy. Remington's .223, Winchester's 220 Swift, Remington's .22-250 in the factory mode and the .22 Cheetah wildcat are just some that come to mind. It's reasonable to think with so many high-quality varmint rounds available, the door would be closed to wildcatting, but that is not the case. James Calhoon, 4343 U. S. Highway 87, Havre, Montana 59501 (406-395-4079) tells me that developing a new cartridge with a caliber less than .224 had been on his mind for years. He also said that .22 caliber bullets from the bore of a .22-250, while impressive, are really overkill for many uses. Downsizing to a .22 Hornet, however, sacrifices ballistic coefficient and, consequently, range. He goes on to say that the .17 caliber, while fun to shoot, with its minimum recoil and low powder consumption, has major drawbacks including rapid fouling, difficult loading, short barrel life and the energy shortage associated with underweight bullets. These drawbacks make .17 somewhat less than a perfect varmint caliber.

From a fired .30 M1 Carbine case, the .19 Calhoon Badger is formed and reloaded with a moderate hunting powder charge and fire-formed to a straight-wall case with a 30° shoulder angle. Calhoon offers formed cases that can be reloaded and fire-formed. He also furnishes live ammo.

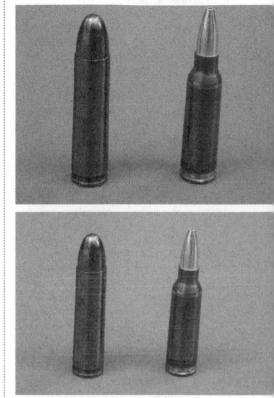

Parent cartridge .30 M1 Carbine (left); reloaded .19 Calhoon Badger cartridge (right).

In 1992, Calhoon was searching for a caliber with the best of both the .22 and .17 calibers. It was then he "stumbled" upon a cartridge called the 4.85 Experimental in a collection at a gun show. It was based on the .223 case necked down to .19 caliber. The 4.85 Experimental has a history worth noting. In the early 1970s, when the NATO countries were holding field trials for a superior infantry round, of all the calibers that were tested to the 400-meter range (.14, .17, .19, .20, .22, .27 and

A .19 Calhoon Badger re-barrel kit furnished the stainless steel barrel that is threaded into a CZ-USA Model 527 BRNO action. The barreled action is threaded into a Lone Wolf "Howler" fiberglass thumbhole stock. Peightal mounted a 6.5x20X Leupold EFR scope; the shooting table is a BR-Pivot bench. Rifle is resting on Bald Eagle front and rear rests.

.30) the entry that won was the 4.85mm Experimental. This particular version of the round featured a .222 Remington Magnum case using a .19-caliber bullet, according to data sent by Calhoon. Muzzle velocity was 3117 fps. At 550 meters, the 4.85mm bullet penetrated a steel helmet, whereas the 5.56mm (.223) only cracked the helmet at 475 meters. But during the same trials, a 62-grain bullet in the 5.56mm produced results almost identical to the 4.85mm, and the military stuck with the 5.56mm. Calhoon also says that the military opted for the .22 caliber since the likely impracticality of a smaller-diameter cleaning rod on the battlefield could cause problems.

Calhoon was certain that in the .19 he had found the right caliber, but what case would be the most efficient? At first, he used the .223 case and by 1997, Calhoon offered rebarrel kits for his .19-223 that generated velocities in the 4,000 fps range with 32-grain bullets (comparable to the 220 Swift). However, as an avid varmint hunter he could foresee the advantages of a smaller and quieter varmint cartridge. Shooting 2-lb. ground squirrels, prairie dogs, badgers and woodchucks doesn't require the man-stopping power of the military-based .223. He says, "Our tests kept leading us back to the old .22 Hornet case, and we realized that there are plenty of Hornet actions out there that could be converted to the .19 caliber."

THE .19 CALHOON HORNET

The .22 Hornet has a long and rich past. It came to life around 1930 as an improved, smokeless version of the 1885 blackpowder .22 Winchester Center Fire (WCF) case. It took the varmint clan by storm, and is still alive and well today. With all the hoopla showered on the .22 Hornet, however, it was far from a tack driver. Calhoon points out that chamber-to-case dimensions were frequently sloppy, but good enough for the accuracy achievable from the non-scoped rifles so popular back then. With factory loads, the .22 Hornet had a muzzle velocity of 2,650 fps. Compared to other black powder cartridges that offered muzzle velocities of 1200 to 1600 fps, the .22 Hornet delivered "scorching" velocities to the varmint hunters of that era. It had sufficient speed for 250-yard shooting, but its lack of accuracy made precision shooting impossible much beyond 150 yards.

A New York gunsmith by the name of Lylse Kilbourn, in an attempt to increase the Hornet's velocity, cut a reamer that straight-walled the case, pushed out the shoulder angle to 40°, and shortened the neck. With more powder room, Kilbourn's K-Hornet added several hundred feet per second to the conventional .22 Hornet. Unfortunately, accuracy was not improved to any great extent. Over the years during which I worked with the .22 Hornet, I developed a suspicion that the .224" bullet was simply too large in diameter for the tiny case, especially a case that had as long a shoulder as the Hornet's. The slow 1:16 rifling twist didn't help in the accuracy department, either. (Most modern Hornets have a 1:14 twist. This helps, but I often wonder what a 1:12 would

have done with 50 or 55-gr. bullets.)

Calhoon recognized the potential of the .22 Hornet case, and with a new caliber in mind he proceeded to design the .19 Calhoon Hornet. To eliminate chamber slop, he built the .19 Calhoon Hornet's chamber to match the Hornet brass, using .0015" for body clearance and .003" for neck clearance. He shortened the neck as much as possible and straightened the walls to gain powder capacity. He accomplished his goal without exceeding 60,000 psi, which is generally considered the top limit of chamber pressure. He said he never exceeds safe pressures to gain velocity. The .19 Hornet's 250-yard effective accuracy range is a far cry from the .22 Hornet's questionable 150-yard accurate range.

I might point out that Calhoon basically followed the footsteps of Kilbourn. He straight-walled the case and reduced the shoulder angle from 40° to 30°. However, Calhoon took an extra step by reducing the caliber from .224" to .198", and the smaller diameter bullet turned out to be a perfect mate for the tiny .22 Hornet case. The new .19-caliber wildcat brought new life to the .22 Hornet case. Not only did Calhoon's modifications increase velocities significantly (more than 3300 fps with a 36-gr. bullet) but they turned the old case into what could be called a tack driver. Our range tests produced many three-shot 100-yard groups that stayed under half an inch.

ENTER THE .19 CALHOON BADGER

The .22 Hornet uses a rimmed case, and rimmed cartridges do not feed as smoothly as cases without rims. Even though the .19 Hornet (Calhoon) was a success, Calhoon began the quest for a rimless cartridge that would feed properly through all types of actions and offer velocities in the 3,500 fps range. Being a dyed-in-the-wool wildcatter, Calhoon continued his search for a cartridge that would offer maximum reliable performance.

His search for the right case was long and complex. After going through a half dozen cases including the .221 Remington Fireball, which seemed a natural (he built three versions on that case), it was discovered that excessive powder capacity caused overheating similar to that experienced with the .222 Remington case. With Remington as the only source of brass, the .221 case was not considered suitable for the new .19 cartridge.

Meanwhile, an experimenter by the

Author's son Rev. Tim Lewis firing the .19 Calhoon Badger at a distant target. Although the rifle is topped with a 6.5x20X Leupold, the 12x40x60mm Leupold spotting scope gives a more detailed view of the target. A spotting scope is a must for the long-range varmint hunter.

Custom rifle builder Jim Peightal (left) and author Don Lewis (right). Peightal fine-tuned the bedding in this rifle. It offers superb accuracy: half an inch at 100 yards.

name of Jimmy Harrison from North Dakota, who shot both the .19 Calhoon and the .19-223 Calhoon, was also looking for something in between. In response, and after experimenting with the .357 Magnum case, Calhoon switched to the .30 M1 Army Carbine case since it had basically the same head diameter as the Hornet and was rimless. It would be compatible with the CZ 527 (BRNO) rifle action that he used to develop the .19 Calhoon Hornet. Compared to the .19 Calhoon Hornet, the .19/30 M1 Carbine wildcat held 20 percent more powder, which increased velocity from 3300 fps to 3550 fps, which translated into at least 50 yards of extra range compared to the .19 Calhoon Hornet.

Harrison tested the .19/30 on badgers and found the new cartridge in the short CZ 527 action to be a perfect marriage. On the range, its accuracy was similar to the famed 6mm PPC benchrest cartridge, and the way it disposed of badgers at ranges up to 300 yards earned it the distinction of being named the .19 Calhoon Badger.

THE PERFECT SMALL-VARMINT OUTFIT?

When you come right down to brass tacks, compromise is not what varmint rifles are about. The more a rifle and cartridge combination is focused on its purpose, the more effective it is. There's a lot of satisfaction in that. The combination of the .19 Calhoon Badger cartridge and the compact CZ 527 action forms a "varminting system" that will kill more varmints in a given time than any other rifle/cartridge combination. Optimum velocity rather than excessive velocity allows more hits due to a cooler barrel. Optimum velocities create less fouling and down time for cleaning.

Low recoil is essential for accuracy, and the .19 Calhoon Badger's light recoil improves field accuracy significantly. It offers superior ballistics, a flat trajectory and incredible accuracy. These are the requisites for a superior varmint outfit, and the .19 Badger is just that.

My .19 Calhoon Badger was originally a .19 Calhoon Hornet built by rifle builder Jim Peightal. He threaded the the .19 (Hornet) barrel and screwed it into a 521 CZ BRNO action. Since Lone Wolf did not have a drop-in stock for the BRNO action, they inletted the barreled action into their Howler thumbhole fiberglass stock. Peightal did the cleanup work and range testing. It proved to be a tack driver.

Since the .19 Calhoon can be built on some .22 rimfire actions, Dennis Olson (Box 334, 500 First Street, Plains, Montana 59859; 406-826-3790) converted a bolt from my Remington 591 (5mm Remington) rimfire to centerfire with some very nice machining. (Note that not all rimfires lock up tight enough to make the conversion, and it's imperative to discuss this with Olson.) Jim Peightal inletted the barreled action into the 591's factory stock. Range tests results by Peightal were similar to those fired with the BRNO model. The .19 Calhoon Badger was a lifesaver for the discontinued 591 Remington action since 5mm ammo was not available at that time. Since I had two .19 Calhoon Hornets, I had Peightal install the .19 Badger barrel in the BRNO action and Lone Wolf stock. Jim said he could print half-inch 100 yard five-shot groups with several different load combinations.

Calhoon himself sells both complete rifles and re-barrel kits. The kit includes a stainless steel chambered barrel (all .19-caliber barrels have a 1:13 twist) that must be threaded by a local gunsmith. A set of reloading dies is also included along with instructions for the gunsmith and a ballistic table. Calhoon also offers reloaded ammo, empty brass and components. Due to some complexities in swaging the M1 .30 Carbine case, Calhoon offers pre-formed cases for the .19 Badger that are fire-formed to exact chamber dimensions. No components are wasted in fire-forming the Badger case. The last price list currently shows a cost of $22.00 per hundred pre-formed cases plus shipping, but check with Calhoon for current pricing.

The .19 Calhoon Badger makes for a cool-shooting, low-noise varmint rig. Using Calhoon's Double HP bullets, which are electrochemically silver-coated on the outside to cut down fouling and barrel wear, there's no need for constant bore cleaning. I use Slick 2000, but most chemical bore cleaners wash out the fouling about as well.

The .19 Badger Badger is a unique varmint cartridge. It can't compare with the 220 Swift, .19-223 Calhoon or .204 Ruger in velocity, nor does it have the killing range of these more powerful cartridges. Still, it offers precision bullet placement up to 300 yards, which is a long distance to be sure. In fact, I suspect that too much emphasis is being put on super-range field shooting today. Varmint shooting is a precise sport. It is far from just shooting and hoping to hit the target.

With today's sophisticated shooting gear and top optics, the responsible hunter can be precise, but only up to a point. My wife, Helen, who is a super off-hand shot, is capable of excellent bullet placement at shots up to 100 yards from the offhand position and much, much farther when using a rest. However, not everyone (myself included) can shoot that well. Unless a varmint hunter specializes is long-range shooting, most field shots will be under 350 yards. Making a precise bullet placement shot at 275 yards takes more skill than shooting a half dozen times before connecting at 600 yards. Quality shooting beats quantity hunting.

I may be going out on the proverbial limb, but I believe the .19 Calhoon Badger will satisfy the most demanding varmint hunter. Top it with a high-quality variable-power scope, and it offers a lifetime of satisfaction both on the range and in the field.

BY **CHRIS LIBBY**
PHOTOS BY **KAYLA NASAN, BETH LIBBY & CHRIS LIBBY**

Different strokes for different folks, as we used to say back in our disco days. Here's one author's thoughts on the perfect survival gun.

1980-vintage Beretta Model 84 advertisements and current Model 84FS.

THE BERETTA SURVIVAL KIT:
The Model 84 .380 ACP

One of the most written-about topics in gun magazines and outdoor sporting literature in the 1970s and 1980s was "survival weapons." Noted authorities gave their opinions on which firearms to carry into the hills in an emergency situation, in case of a natural disaster or a nuclear or similar attack. Readers were advised to prepare to defend themselves and family in possible situations where civil authority would be unavailable or non-existent, as society as we knew it would most likely disintegrate rapidly.

The virtues and flaws of various rifles, handguns and shotguns were discussed, along with caliber and ammunition selection choices. Many readers, primarily civilian shooters and hunters, were suddenly faced with the prospect of selecting a firearm not only on the basis of personal defense, target shooting and hunting, but also for self-defense and survival in a post apocalyptic world.

As a teenager growing up in the early 1980's I read every gun book and magazine I could lay my hands on, cover to cover and several times over. Even as a youth I could understand the wisdom of having a survival weapon, particularly a handgun, "just in case." A good rifle or shotgun is essential in an emergency sit-

The author taking aim with the model 84FS Beretta. The .380 ACP round is effective for self-defense purposes, provided proper shot placement is utilized in vital areas.

(below right) The Beretta is a potent handful of deadly firepower in a very compact package.

uation, but I realized that a personal defense weapon such as a handgun is more likely to be closer at hand should the need for a weapon unexpectedly arise.

Back then one could take firearms-related literature to school to read in study hall and only be subjected to a frown – unlike today, when a similar "offense" would likely provoke disciplinary action. Anyway, one fine day in school during the Reagan era I was reading a popular gun magazine when I spotted an advertisement from Beretta. The boldface headline read "The Beretta Survival Kit." It featured the small but deadly model 84 in .380 ACP. The pistol held 13 shots in the magazine plus one in the tube, giving the gun a 14-shot total capacity. The ad stated that "Beretta sportsmen and sportswomen are born survivors" and "Police and military specify them for protection," as well as "Our model 84 is exceptionally reliable, safe, and delivers tremendous firepower. But only if you need it." The ability to fire 14 rounds without reloading had a great deal of appeal to consumers in an era when many police departments were still armed with six-shot revolvers.

I was hooked! This was the gun I needed, just in case "it" ever hit the fan. Although I knew that my chances of needing a survival gun for an actual survival purpose were slim to none, there was always the remote chance. I already had an airgun and a .22 rifle, but I yearned for a centerfire handgun. The Beretta would make an excellent all-purpose handgun in my eyes. The .380 cartridge was more powerful than a .22 rimfire, yet the gun was much smaller and lighter (22.5 oz.) and more controllable than a .357 or .44 Magnum, allowing for accurate rapid fire. I could wear it when I was hunting as a backup gun. I could take it on canoe and camping trips with my father. It would be perfect for concealed carry when I obtained my gun permit in the future. Berettas have always had a reputation for exceptional accuracy, and I knew this would be a tackdriver. The .380 ACP Beretta would be the perfect trail gun, powerful enough to ward off or dispatch predators and superb for close-range shots at small game such as rabbits, partridge and squirrels. This Beretta would indeed fit the bill as a survival gun, as well as an all-around sidearm.

Months passed by, and I somehow had convinced my mother to sign for a handgun (this was in 1984 and most of the males in my family and rural community owned guns). I had a little money saved up, so a trip to the local gun shop to check out the merchandise was in order. There on the table was the Beretta .380 ACP I had drooled over in the magazines! I picked up the Beretta 84 – it was a beautiful deep rich blue with walnut grips and fit my hand like a glove, but the price tag took my breath away. I wanted that gun more than anything in the world (well, almost anything; swim suit model Christie Brinkley trumped the Beretta!). But the cost of the Be-

From top to bottom: Colt 1991A1 .45 ACP, Beretta 84FS .380 ACP, Beretta 92FS 9mm. The 84FS .380 in the middle is far easier to conceal as well as to carry around all day, whether on the street or in the outdoors.

retta was far too much for my meager high school job earnings. The cash was burning a hole in my pocket and I had to walk out the door with something. I ended up settling for a five-shot Rossi Model 88 .38 Special, which cost less than half of the price of the handsome high- capacity Beretta. The Rossi was a nice little sporting weapon, but it was NOT the 14-shot .380 Beretta advertised as a "Survival Kit" for sportsmen. As the paperwork was being filled out for the Rossi, I kept glancing over at the Beretta .380. Later that evening as I examined the Rossi .38, I knew I had made a mistake as I still truly wanted the Beretta. I have regretted not waiting for, saving for and buying the Beretta ever since.

College, family obligations, and other "firearms deals," as well as price gouging at gun shows, had all one way or another kept me from getting a Beretta 84 over the last two decades or so. Every time a Model 84 caught my eye, either the price was over-inflated or I lacked the cash. I continued to search for one, not so much for use as a "survival" weapon, but for use as a Trail Gun.

I'm happy to report that I finally had the opportunity to obtain a slightly used model 84FS Beretta for a decent price at the Kittery Trading Post in southern Maine. I couldn't wait to get the formalities done and to get out the door with my "new" pistol. I would soon discover that my dream gun for over the past two and a half decades had been well worth the wait!

THE BERETTA 84FS

The 84FS differs from the original Model 84 as it comes in a matte black

At 22.5 oz. unloaded, the Beretta 84 can be carried all day without causing undue burden (unlike heavier and larger weapons) and be drawn at a moment's notice. The Beretta 84FS offers 14 rounds of potent .380 ammunition, enough to defend against almost any threat encountered on the trail.

This young lady finds the Beretta a comforting companion in the wild, tucked high and tight on her hip in a holster.

"The model 84FS (13/1 shot) in the shooters right hand, is virtually identical to the model 85FS (8/1 shot) in the shooters left hand, aside from the magazine capacity and grip width."

This shooter finds the .380 ACP Beretta accurate and enjoyable to shoot. This is a FUN plinking gun!

smaller and therefore far easier to shoot and conceal. In the past I worked as a correctional officer and as a member of the Correctional Emergency Response Team (CERT). In these roles I received extensive training with the .40-caliber Beretta Model 96, the department-issued weapon at that time. The 96 is a BIG weapon and would prove cumbersome to carry as a concealed weapon, in my opinion, due to its size and weight. The 92/96 guns really need to be carried in a belt holster, as they are full-sized handguns. The 84FS is almost identical in operation to its .40-caliber big brothers but far easier to handle and carry, as it is much smaller. Comparing the Beretta 80 Series Cheetah .380 to the larger 92/96 pistols is like comparing a Ford Mustang to a Lincoln Town car.

BUT WHAT ABOUT THE .380 CARTRIDGE?

For a sidearm that is going to be carried for miles on the trail or street with

The Model 84's blowback recoil system, although sturdy and dependable, requires a firm grip to rack the slide in order to chamber a round.

military finish and its trigger guard is squared off. The gun has an ambidextrous safety; when "off" a bright red dot is showing. My gun came with two 10-shot magazines, a Clinton-era product. I wasted no time in ordering a couple of 13-shot magazines online from Mec-Gar, a top-of-the-line magazine manufacturer, as the decade-long ban had long since expired.

The grip on the 84FS is thicker than on the almost identical model 85FS, which holds eight rounds in its .380 magazine. I don't find that the thicker grip on the 84 hinders its ability to be effectively concealed or carried unobtrusively, and I do prefer the 13-shot magazines as opposed to the 10. If I am going to carry a gun that was originally designed to hold a 13-shot magazine, and not under any legal restrictions, then the thought of stuffing a 10-shot magazine home in its place just doesn't set right. The Beretta is a modern design with a magazine safety; the gun will not fire without a magazine in place, just like the majority of the pistols made by Smith & Wesson.

This feature is beneficial for most, and there are quite a few in law enforcement who are alive today as they were able to render their S&W service weapons inoperable by disengaging the magazine during a life or death struggle. If a bad guy attempts to get your weapon away from you, and you are able to disengage the magazine during the scuffle as many others have in the past, the weapon will not fire, giving you a few precious moments to either launch a vicious counterattack or run like hell.

The Beretta 80 Series pistols – the Model 81 in .32 ACP; the Models 84, 85 and 86 in .380 ACP; and the Model 87 in .22 LR, all collectively known as members of the Cheetah family – are blowback operated, and are almost identical to the larger 92FS and Military M-9 models in 9mm Parabellum. The open-slide design vitually eliminates jamming. Current as well as former law enforcement and military personnel who have been trained in the use of these Beretta handguns will find the 80 series to be quite familiar, as well as much little probability of being drawn from its holster, the moderately powerful but deadly .380 cartridge is enough for most situations, aside from traveling in grizzly bear country. The .380 ammo has improved since the 1980s. While the ballistics of the 95-gr. ball loading are more or less the same as they were when the cartridge was introduced in 1908, Winchester, Remington, CorBon and Federal – as well as other manufacturers – currently produce excellent self-defense hollowpoint ammo that also doubles as potent small game loads. Full patch or full metal jacket offers the best penetration if you are concerned about predators, but the current hollowpoint ammo gives excellent expansion, with penetration very close to that of FMJ.

My favorite cartridge for the trail is the CorBon 90-gr.JHP, which has a listed velocity of 1050 fps and energy of 220 fpe. This cartridge provides me with an aggressive combination of expansion, penetration, and accuracy, good for any small game and varmints one might encounter on the trail, as well as a very capable self-defense load should an unfortunate situation ever present itself. If restricted to hardball by law, as some states do, I would not feel improperly armed with a .380 ACP hardball. Full metal jacketed .380s will penetrate deeper than expanding jacketed hollow point bullets, and with proper shot placement in a vital zone can be devastating for small game or self defense. In fact, this gun and caliber are issued (or on the "approved list") by many law enforcement agencies in the United States as backup and or undercover weapons.

The Author, along with a varmint that was humanely harvested with the Beretta .380 and a single 95-gr. American Eagle FMJ cartridge.

Most of the high-velocity self-defense .380 ACP ammunition produced by the major ammunition manufacturers matches and or exceeds most over-the-counter standard-velocity .38 Special cartridges and greatly exceeds the majority of .22 fimfire ammunition when fired from average handgun-length barrels. Average 90-gr. loads in the .380 ACP (aka 9mm Browning Short, 9mm Kurz and 9mm Corto) obtain approximately 1000 fps at the muzzle according to manufacturer's specifications: that's 200 fpe, folks! Not a magnum by any stretch of the imagination, but still a powerful cartridge. The cross sectional density of the .355" .380 projectile creates a larger entrance wound in its target than a .22-, .25- or .32-caliber bullet. If the hollowpoint bullet exits its target, the exit wound will be larger on departure, assuming full or at least partial expansion has occurred, allowing increased blood loss and trauma. If the bullet doesn't exit the target, all the energy is thus exhausted in the animal, creating a greater shock effect (at least in theory). In a vital zone such as the heart, brain or central nervous system, both solid and hollowpoint bullets will most likely be lethal.

Shot placement is vital, regardless of the caliber used. A well-aimed .380 hollow-point or FMJ bullet will dispatch any small and medium game I may encounter while on the trail, as well as offering protection against larger predators. Shot placement is the key to effective and humane dispatching of game animals, regardless of size. This holds true in self-defense situations as well. The fact is, at close range, with careful marksmanship and an accurate weapon, big game such as deer can be taken with the .380 or lesser cartridges if the animal is hit in a vital area such as the brain, spine, or heart. I am NOT recommending the .380 ACP as a big game hunting cartridge, but in a survival situation, under the right conditions, it could be highly effective. The mild recoil of the Beretta also allows quick recovery back on target, which allows the shooter to fire several shots off very quickly. This ability to deliver numerous fast, accurate shots is important in a defensive type of situation, regardless if one is being confronted on the trail by a large predator or being attacked in a dimly-lighted parking garage by several assailants.

SO HOW'S IT SHOOT?

Soon after acquiring my Beretta 84FS I had a chance to test it out as a pest

de-animation tool. Living in a rural area has its mixed blessings, and varmints are part of the deal. A large raccoon had been destroying property and crops in the area, and the financial loss was growing larger every day. There was also the safety issue to consider: with children in my home and elsewhere in the neighborhood, a large varmint that was spotted frequently during daylight hours and that displayed little fear of humans constituted a recipe for disaster. There has been an epidemic of rabies that has spread throughout New England during the past decade, which made the risk even greater. Unfortunately, the animal was wise to live traps and avoided them. With no other viable alternative, the decision was made to euthanize the pest at the first opportunity.

I took a stand out near the vegetable garden one evening and awaited the masked bandit. The Beretta 84FS was loaded with American Eagle 95-gr. FMJ bullets. I had not yet had the opportunity to sight the gun in with CorBon hollowpoints so I passed on using them. I was, however, quite comfortable with the knowledge that the American Eagle hardball was shooting to point of aim.

As dusk approached the raccoon arrived, intent on destroying more food crops. Using a two-handed stance I thumbed back the hammer and carefully lined up the sights at a distance of approximately 16 yards. The single action trigger pull was slick – so slick, in fact, that I could almost swear that the trigger pulled my finger! The Beretta barked, and the crop destruction and property damage ended with a single shot between the eyes. The powerful little 9mm bullet mercifully dropped the big varmint in its tracks. Just as the ad slogan stated back in the 1980s, the gun delivered "tremendous firepower. But only if you need it." The Beretta still had 13 shots in it, but one precisely-placed shot was all that was needed. I then lowered the hammer using the safety-decocking lever.

The Beretta shot where I aimed it, as I knew it would. I had sighted the gun in previously with the American Eagle ammunition, and knew it was potentially more accurate than the sub-2.5" groups I had managed at 20 yards. I'm positive that a better shot than I could shoot a tighter group, and most likely at a greater distance. This gun, however, is not designed for long range target shooting, but it is certainly more than adequate for small game hunting at 20-25 yards or less and for plinking sessions. The double action trigger pull is smooth with no drag or creep whatsoever; in single action it is clean and crisp. Overall quality of my Model 84FS is second to none, and the gun lives up to Beretta's reputation for excellence and stellar performance.

The Beretta 84FS is too large to be classified as a pocket pistol (at least in the grip area); however it is still much smaller and easier to conceal than the majority of pistols and revolvers of larger caliber. The Walther PP/PPK series (which I am partial to) and its clones are noticeably smaller, but they're limited to only about half of the Beretta's 14-round capacity.

The Beretta .380 is just as useful today for self defense and survival as when it was first offered in the late 1970s. This gun makes for an excellent off duty/concealed carry weapon for law enforcement officers and civilians alike. Moreover, it not only makes for a potent personal- or home-defense weapon, it also doubles as a superb trail gun. The combination of firepower, accuracy and dependability makes the Beretta 84 Series in .380 a sound choice as a durable hunting sidearm, a camp gun or as a fishing/tackle box gun. Where legal, the pistol can be easily stashed in a backpack or pack basket, vehicle glove box, slipped in a purse, carried in a holster either concealed or open, or even tucked into a belt under a loose shirt.

When you hold this precision made piece of fine Italian steel in the hand, you get the sense that you are holding something that will last for several generations to come. To be sure, when Beretta advertised the Model 84 .380 as a "Survival Kit" in the early 1980s, they were right on the mark.

The Model 84FS is both rugged and dependable, perfect for extend-ed outings in the wilderness, be it hiking, camping, canoeing, hunting or running a trap line.

The Magnificent Seven

BY SCOTT STOPPELMAN

As quietly as possible my dad lowered the drop window in the pilot house of the old 65' wooden tugboat we were on. The heavy-duty diesel engine was at idle, slowly chuffing toward shore. As soon as the deep forefoot of the tug grounded in near silence on the sandy beach – a rarity in Southeast Alaska – I leaned out of the window with my Model 64 Winchester .30-30 and took aim at one of the two little island deer on the beach some 100 or so yards away.

"Wait," Dad whispered to me. "Let's not take any chances. Use my rifle with the scope." We quickly swapped rifles and I was now armed with pop's pre-'64 Model 70 Winchester that had been re-barreled to .284 Winchester from its original .308 Win. This rifle had always been an accurate one and had taken its share of game in Dad's hands including deer and elk. It had been very professionally barreled and bedded by the late Seattle gunsmith Stan Baker.

At the shot, the first deer dropped feet-in-the-air stone dead, the fast stepping 140-gr. Sierra bullet having nearly disintegrated inside the chest cavity of the little blacktail (they don't often go much more than 125 lbs.). My next shot missed due in part to my excitement at having just taken my first deer at age 15. Dad called the shot high so I settled down and dropped this deer just like the first in instantaneous fashion. By the time we rowed the skiff ashore, both deer were still.

Rarely have I seen animals drop so quickly from a body shot. By today's standard, some would consider the bullets performance sub-par owing to the breaking up and lack of total penetration, but both bullets made it inside the chest cavity, which is what they are supposed to do, and did expand – somewhat of an understatement – to cause the trauma necessary for quick humane kills.

Thus began a long and happy association with the 7mm (or .284" as measured). While this caliber has never been a lucky one for me for hunting, it

(left) Ruger 77 Old Model rebarreled from .270 to .284 Winchester.

(below) Best of the 7mms, left to right: 7mm Remington Magnum, 7mm Weatherby Magnum, 7X64 Brenneke, .280 Remington, .284 Winchester, 7X57 Mauser, 7mm-08 Remington.

nonetheless remains my favorite because of its sterling qualities. Let's take a look at some of the classic 7mm cartridges still available to today's shooter.

7X57 MAUSER

Perhaps the most efficient of all the 7mms, the 7X57 is also the oldest smokeless 7mm still in common use today, some 117 years after its birth. Developed in 1892 for the Mauser military rifle, it quickly became a world standard and was chambered in military Mausers and sporting rifles for use on all continents. When the British came up against the 7mm-armed Boers in South Africa they took quite a beating. Likewise at San Juan Hill, future president Theodore Roosevelt's Rough Riders faced the 1893 Spanish Mauser rifle so chambered, much to their dismay, and

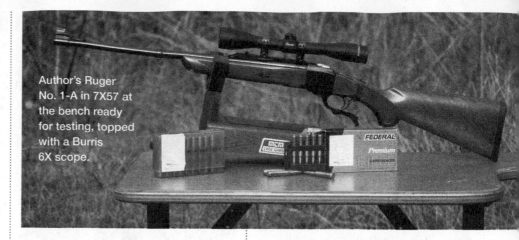

Author's Ruger No. 1-A in 7X57 at the bench ready for testing, topped with a Burris 6X scope.

while the Riders won the day, they took serious casualties and left with a great respect for the little 7X57 round as well as the enemy marksmen's skill.

I currently own two rifles chambered in 7X57. One is a late-production Ruger No. 1-A Light Sporter single-shot and the other is a custom job built around a BRNO-made Brazilian service rifle Mauser action. This rifle was given the full treatment to make it a classic sporter such as those made famous by Mauser and the best British "Bond Street" gunmakers of England such as Rigby and Westley Richards. This was a collaboration between me and a local gunsmith who did all of the metal work, while I did all of the woodwork except the checkering, which was performed by Fajen. The

Four excellent 7mm sporting rifles, (l to r): Ruger M77 MKII in 7X64 Brenneke; Ruger No. 1 in 7X57; custom BRNO Mauser in 7X57; and pre-'64 Winchester M70 in .284 Winchester.

barrel is 24" long, of Shilen manufacture and adorned with express rear sights and barrel band front sight as well as the classic barrel band front sling swivel. The action was left untapped for scope mounts in order to make it a true "iron sight gun" in keeping with the desired look. While not a target rifle with such sighting equipment, it sure can't be faulted for its appeal. Still, it'll shoot 2" groups with good loads.

The Ruger is altogether different as, in addition to its classic looks, it came from the factory designed to take a scope and is meant to shoot. The 1-A is equipped with open sights and the supplied scope rings attach directly to a quarter rib on the barrel via a dovetail system that is one of the best. Ring spacing, however, can be a challenge at times, depending on scope configuration.

A Burris 6X sits atop this Ruger and has proved totally satisfactory in all respects. With good handloads this rifle shoots under an inch with a great number of loads and bullet weights, contrary to the #1's reputation for being fussy. The barrel's twist of 1:8.6 allows a wide range of bullets to perform well. My favorite loads consist of full charges of Reloder 19 and 22 behind the 140-gr. Nosler Ballistic-Tip or Partition for around 2800 fps at the muzzle.

In preparation for a Montana antelope hunt a couple of years ago, the rifle was fired at ranges from 100 to 300 yards for bullet placement confirmation. Two shots at 100 yards were touching about 3 inches high. At 200 yards, two shots were about an inch apart, and at 300 yards two holes appeared in the target less than three inches from each other and about 6 inches low. The rifle was taken hunting, with high expectations.

Anyone who says shooting an antelope in Montana is a sure thing has never hunted the public lands where I prefer to hunt. We got skunked and not for the first time either. Sure can't blame the rifle though – just my typical hunting luck.

The 7X57 round has probably been used to take every game animal on earth including elephant and while there are a number of more appropriate cartridges available for large game, it has done it with aplomb in skilled hands. It's still a popular round in Africa.

.280 REMINGTON

Introduced in 1957, this excellent round is nothing more than a necked-down .30-06 with its shoulder moved forward a bit to keep it from being chambered in the .270 Winchester, where pressures created by the oversize bullet could be dangerous, or in a .30-06.

In 1983, as a present to myself for being gone on a tugboat in Alaska for a couple of months, I indulged myself in a new rifle. I looked hard for and finally found a Ruger M77 in Jack O'Connor's favorite, the .270 Winchester. Not long afterward, I became particularly enamored of the .280 Remington, which was enjoying a resurgence in popularity at the time. As O'Connor himself once said in another context, "I could scarcely relish my vittles 'til I had one." As the .270 Ruger's accuracy was less than earth-shattering anyway, I decided to use it

The author and his son Nathaniel, who inherited the .284 M70 from his grandfather. This is the same rifle the author used to take his first deer 40 years earlier.

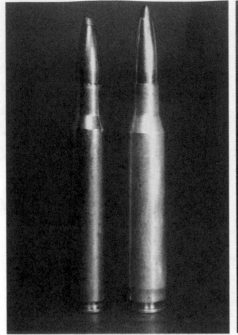

Two nearly identical rounds, in terms of performance: the 7X64 Brenneke (left) and the .280 Remington. The Remington is slightly longer but the Brenneke has similar case capacity.

as the platform for a custom project so it was off to the gunsmith to re-barrel to .280 with a 24" Douglas barrel with a twist of 1:9.

While this rifle didn't change my overall hunting luck, it did end a long dry spell on elk when I used it to put down a decent bull at over 200 yards with two 160-gr. Nosler bullets that left the muzzle at over 2900 fps. That load consisted of a near caseful of H4831 in Remington cases lit by the CCI 200 primer. I suspect that this barrel, besides being a very accurate one, is also a "fast" barrel. A shooting friend who owns an improved version of the .280 has not yet been able to match my velocities. In fact my handloads are nearly the equal of some factory 7mm Remington Magnum loads. Best loads with this rifle have achieved the following velocities: 140 gr. @ 3190 fps; 150 gr. @ 3050 fps; 160 gr. @ 2910 fps; and 175 gr. @ 2840 fps. All of these are accurate and develop at or over 3000 ft/lbs of muzzle energy. *[Editor's note: While these loads have proven safe in the author's rifle, they might not be in yours. Never exceed load data published by the powder manufacturers, and work up to maximum loads. –DMS]*

Some of the most enjoyable time spent with this rifle has been in the shooting of NRA Sporting Rifle matches.

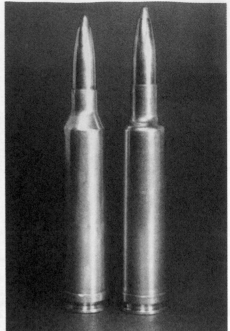

Two other nearly identical rounds, performance-wise: the 7mm Remington Magnum (left) and the 7mm Weatherby Magnum. Note the radiused shoulder on the Weatherby.

In this game, most any rifle is allowed and some use their service rifles and others use hunting type rifles. As I was already competing with M1s and M1As in NRA High Power matches, I opted to use my .280 and did very well with it. My best score netted on this course was a 314-12X of a possible 320. My "match" load is a fairly run-of-the-mill load using the Speer 145-gr. hunting bullet ahead of 57.5 grs. of IMR 4350. Not an exotic load but it shoots very well. This rifle and caliber remain one of my very favorites.

REMINGTON'S LITTLE 7MM-08

While I have no personal experience with this round I have a nephew who owns one in the form of a Remington 700 BDL and speaks very highly of it. He reports shooting sub-MOA (minute of angle) groups with boring regularity. This should come as no big surprise as this cartridge is one of several based on the very accurate and useful .308 Winchester of 1952. It is simply necked down to .284-caliber with no other changes. All of the .30- based rounds seem to be very accurate whether necked up or down, the latest being the 338 Federal.

Case capacity is nearly the equal of the old 7X57 and expected handloaded velocities would be essentially equal.

(top) Express rear sight, barrel band front swivel and ebony forend tip are classic touches of elegance on the 7x57 BRNO Mauser. (middle) Burris 6X scope is attached to the Ruger via Ruger rings mounted directly on the barrel rib, an excellent mounting system. (bottom) The Ruger owes much of its styling to the Farquharson rifle of the nineteenth century.

Factory 7mm-08 fodder is loaded to higher pressures than the older round owing to the existence of many very old 7X57 Mauser rifles whose condition is questionable.

As is always the case with similar rounds individual rifles may perform better as regards velocity than another, and this can be attributed to all of the many variables present in individual rifles, things like chamber dimension, barrel length, barrel twist and even individual chronographs. But as Frank Barnes states in *Cartridges of the World*, "If you can say a cartridge is as good as the 7mm Mauser, you're saying it is a very good cartridge indeed. And that's what we're saying."

While I have toyed with the idea of a 7mm-08, it hasn't happened yet. I am so pleased with my Ruger 1-A in 7X57 that it's hard to imagine what the point would be as the one real (or imagined) advantage the 7mm-08 has over the 7X57 is its shorter length (2.8"), which allows it to be chambered in short-action bolt action rifles, which the longer (3.06") 7X57 cannot. However, in a single-shot rifle like the Ruger #1 this becomes a moot point.

Since its introduction in 1980, the 7mm-08 has gained a good reputation for accuracy and is used by more than a few target shooters because of it. It is also a good game-getter for animals up to and including elk and has done well on similar-sized African antelope species. It should be around well into the future.

7MM REMINGTON AND WEATHERBY MAGNUMS

These two are lumped together because there is essentially no real difference in their potential in any department. Simply put, what one will do the other will do. Again, this will depend on those pesky variables that can drive rifle cranks around the bend. The Weatherby predated the Remington by quite a few years, 1944 compared to 1962 for Big Green.s 7mm. If you place one round

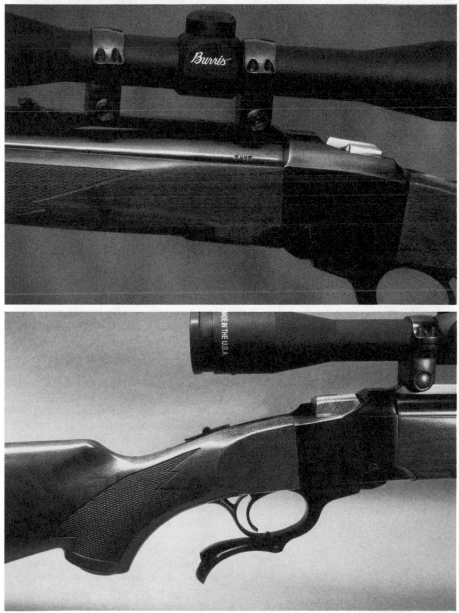

(left) The Douglas barrel used in the .270-to-.284 conversion. The original rear sight from the Ruger was used. (bottom) Brazilian crest on the receiver ring of the BRNO.

alongside the other, it's obvious there cannot be much difference in velocity potential. The Weatherby round, like all cartridges designed by the high-velocity guru Roy Weatherby, has the distinctive rounded or radiused shoulder. The Remington version is based on a wildcat 7mm magnum developed by elk outfitter Les Bowman of Wyoming.

Recently I played with the Weatherby version for a while to see if I could safely achieve 3000 foot seconds with the 175-gr. bullet, which was one of the original goals in developing the 7mm mags in the first place. It's not easy to accomplish, either, at least using the platform I had, which was a Remington Model 700 Classic with 24" barrel. Weatherby rifles often have 26" barrels with long throats or "freebore" ahead of the chamber. This is supposed to allow increased velocity without excessive pressure. The Remington rifle had no such freebore, nor the longer barrel. Thus while the goal of 3000 fps was met, it took lots of careful experimentation with lots of different powders, bullets and primers. Hodgdon H870, a very slow ball powder, was what finally gave the hoped-for speed using the Hornady spire point. I felt, however, in the end that pressure signs were getting a little too close to the "hold on to your hat" level for comfort. Two more inches of barrel as would be provided by the Weatherby rifle would no doubt have yielded the desired speed with less pressure, all else being equal.

In the midst of the loading project, I took the time to make comparisons between cases, not only between different brands in the same chambering but also between the Remington and Weatherby 7mms. A given charge filled the one case to about the same point,

indicating capacities so similar that, once again, velocity potential apparently would have more to do with individual rifles than anything else. A number of faster-stepping 7mm mags have been developed in recent years, some belted some not, and while they may offer some velocity advantage over the two older rounds it will be at the expense of more recoil and reduced barrel life. Rounds like the Remington 7mm UltraMag appear to be of grossly overbore capacity, and the above statement would certainly apply to it. It seems doubtful that there is really a need for much more of a 7mm mag than the Remington or Weatherby rounds, both already well established proven game-getters.

7X64 BRENNEKE

This cartridge could rightly be called the grandfather of the .280 Remington, coming as it did some 40 years previously. In 1917 German designer Wilhelm Brenneke gave us this fine cartridge, of which there is also a rimmed version, the 7X65R, for use in single-shots, drillings and double rifles.

Case design and powder capacity are nearly identical to the later .280 but they are not interchangeable. Just as the .280 is a little longer in headspace than the .270 and '06, so the 7X64 is a tad longer than the .280 in that dimension. Its rim and body diameters are also slightly smaller as well.

I had been looking for a suitable 7X64 rifle for some time and it was becoming an exercise in frustration, as most guns so chambered are of European manufacture and somewhat more costly than most domestic products. I was aware that Ruger had made a small run of their

fine Model 77 Mk II bolt action rifle in this caliber some years ago, but being a rarity they were priced accordingly. So it was with some surprise that while I made my way around a local gun show, one such rifle caught my eye. It was topped with a Leupold scope for a reasonable price in pre-owned, unfired condition. The deal was quickly struck and the 7X64 had a new owner.

The bubble of my excitement soon burst, however, when upon swabbing the cobwebs out of the bore I noticed that either the rifle was possessed of a very long throat or was eroded. Closer examination revealed merely the long throat – so long in fact that shorter bullets could be just barely started into the case mouth and chambered without coming close to the lands. Longer bullets could be seated to 3.8" OAL and still clear. This would be okay in a single-shot rifle where magazine length is not an issue, but not so with the bolt rifle.

In this case the magazine was actually a little longer than many such rifles, allowing an overall loaded length of 3.4". Still, the disparity between allowable mag length and loaded round maximum length was great. As the rifle was unfired, I was in a bit of a quandary: should I shoot it or sell it unfired? I decided to touch bases with Ruger's service department. I won't bore you with the several ensuing conversations, some of which grew a little heated, but it was finally agreed by both sides to send the rifle back for examination of its throat. I was informed, however, that in all likelihood it was "within spec." And so it

proved when the rifle was returned with no work performed. Apparently Ruger chose for some reason to use European specs rather than SAAMI specs when they chambered for the 7X64. Perhaps they had intended for the bulk of these rifles to be sold overseas. The Germans in particular seem to love long throats in their rifles.

Okay, fine, so I'd just shoot it. Initial shooting with three different factory loads turned out surprisingly well, so handload development began. Drawing on my experience with the .280 Remington, I managed to work up loads for this round with no trouble. What works well in one should work well in the other, I thought, and initial results bore this out. The 1:8.6 twist in the 7X64, being close to the .280's 1:9 twist, would seem to indicate similar potential in bullet weights as regards accuracy; but with two inches less barrel length it was also expected that velocity would suffer to some degree. It did, but not enough to send me screaming for antidepressants.

Top speed with the 160-gr. Nosler Partition was 2850 fps, which was achieved with Sellier and Bellot cases, which are thinner and have more capacity than Remington or Federal cases. The S&B cases do, however, seem prone to neck spits at random times for some reason, perhaps because of the thinness. To gain this velocity, IMR 4831 was used as opposed to Hodgdon's version of the same. I could not burn enough H4831 to reach 2800 fps in the 22"-barreled Ruger.

Accuracy in this rifle was mostly very good – right up until it went to hell! This stymied me at first; I thought something had happened in the load chain. It turned out that the problem was a crack in the stock in the web area ahead of the trigger well. This was repaired with Brownells epoxy and pins and the rifle went back to shooting well until it gave up again. This time it was a vertical crack in the recoil lug area that was repaired in similar fashion and the barrel free-floated for extra measure. The next trip to the range confirmed that all was OK when factory loads again went into around an inch and subsequent trips with handloads yielded some very nice groups, all of which makes me a happy camper.

The business of long throats has been discussed before by many but I recall the words of the late Finn Aagard. He states with authority, and I paraphrase, that "a long throat is supposed to be bad for accuracy but it is hard to prove." Having now dealt with this issue several times myself in various rifles in several calibers, I completely concur with Aagaard's opinion.

.284 WINCHESTER

The .284 mentioned at the outset of this piece is still in the family. When Dad quit hunting due primarily to age and loss of interest, he offered the rifle to me since he remembered that I had taken my first two deer with it in Alaska all those years ago. As I already had the .280, which I like to think is a tad better though it really isn't, I suggested he give it to my son Nathaniel for the day he may chose to try hunting himself.

Introduced in 1963 for use in the Winchester Models 88 lever-action and 100 autoloader, the .284 was meant to give .270-like performance in a shorter action cartridge. The case itself is an interesting design in that it is nearly as big around at the head as the magnums, measuring as it does a full .500". The .30-06-based rounds measure a nominal .473" in the same place. Its case has less body taper and a steep shoulder, which when all added up gives it essentially the same capacity as the '06 though somewhat shorter. It also has a rebated rim, i.e., its rim is smaller in diameter than the body or head of the case. This was not at all normal for American case design at that time, though is not all that unusual today. At any rate it is a cartridge fully capable of the same potential for accuracy and game-getting as any other .30-06 based cartridge. The barrel on this rifle is 22", so even with some of pop's steamier loads it cannot quite equal the 24" barrel on my .280 for bullet speed but comes quite close. No animal hit with a top load from either would know the difference.

Perhaps Jack O'Connor said it best in an *Outdoor Life* article I have dated from 1964 in which he compares the .270, .280 and the then-new .284 Winchester: "If one of these cartridges is noticeably better than the other when loaded to the same pressure and fired with the same type of action, I am not astute enough to see it." Having worked with all three I would only say, if you add the 7X64 to

Targets like this one fired with the Ruger 7X64 Brenneke are one of the reasons why the author likes the .284" bullet diameter.

the mix you have a winning hand of four of a kind.

FINAL THOUGHTS

More than a little ink has been drawn from the well over the years, extolling the virtues of one bullet diameter over another. It's often stated that because of superior sectional density, bullets of smaller diameter of the same weight as a larger caliber fly better or penetrate better. Such stuff makes for interesting conversation and ballistic tables, but in reality trying to make a big case – so to speak – for say a 175-gr. 7mm bullet over a 180-gr. .308 diameter bullet seems like hair-splitting. Much is dependent on the quality of the bullet because when that is equal and two such similar caliber bullets are properly placed, the result will be the same. Actual differences in trajectory or bullet path, wind-bucking ability (if there is such a thing), brush-bucking ability (there really isn't any such thing) and penetration are so slight as to be properly relegated to grist-for-the-mill status, at least as regards cartridges and rifles to be used primarily for hunting.

What it all boils down to really is what a shooter likes or what has the most appeal or charisma, if such a word can properly be applied to inanimate objects. For me, the 7mm caliber has all that, but I readily admit that it has little if any advantage other similar calibers. I just like it – and that's enough for me.

AN INTRODUCTION TO THE
Military Handguns of Imperial Japan

Early Tokyo Arsenal Showa 4.2 (February, 1929) Type 14 and late Nagoya Arsenal-Toriimatsu Showa 20.5 (May, 1945) Type 14 show differences in cocking knobs and grips, as well as addition of magazine retention spring on front of grip. Shown with service medals from the Manchurian (left) and Chinese (right) campaigns.

BY **TERI JANE BRYANT**

It seems as though WWII-era Japanese handguns have never received the attention that their German counterparts have. Maybe the author can change that!

I hear it all the time at gun shows: "They're just copies of Lugers, aren't they?" Well, no, they're actually nothing like Lugers, but in a way the question is not surprising. Japanese handguns are very little known, especially in Canada, where I live, and several do have the same general shape as the famous German pistol. Many people have never even seen one Japanese handgun, let alone a collection. However, I have found them to be a fascinating and challenging field of study, and the attention my display gets at gun shows suggests others agree.

THE TYPE 26

When Japan began to modernize its military in the late 1800s, it first chose a foreign handgun, the Smith & Wesson

Model 3 in .44 Russian, for its army and navy. Between the late 1870s and mid-1890s it imported an estimated 16,000 of these revolvers in several variations. Japanese industry progressed rapidly, though, and soon it had an indigenous

design, the Type 26 revolver, so named because its design was completed in the twenty-sixth year of the reign of the Meiji Emperor, i.e. in 1893.

The Type 26, a break-top, double-action only revolver, combined features

Japanese cartridges. From left to right: 9mm revolver; early 8mm Nambu with cupro-nickel jacketed bullet; 8mm Nambu with copper-jacketed bullet adopted in 1942; 7mm Nambu for the Baby; .44 Russian for the early imported Smith & Wessons; .32 ACP for officer's private purchase sidearms and a few small-volume domestic pistols.

of many of its contemporaries, most noticeably a Smith & Wesson-style latch and a left side plate that swings open like that of the French M1892 revolver. Like its contemporaries, it is chambered for a rather underpowered cartridge, which is similar to the .38 S&W but with a much thinner rim. However, its main flaw is that the cylinder locks up only at the moment of firing. As a result, if the cylinder brushes against something, an empty chamber can easily rotate into the firing position. Modern buyers unfamiliar with this peculiarity often mistake the free rotation of the cylinder as a sign of breakage, but that is just how these guns were made.

More than 59,000 Type 26 revolvers were produced. Although they were obsolete by the 1920s, Japan's chronic shortage of small arms meant they were still in widespread use in 1945, and hence almost all are either very battered or were arsenal refurbished during the 1930s. Specimens with the original finish have much deeper bluing than arsenal reworks and are most easily distinguished by the heat tempered bluing on the hammer, which has a purplish, iridescent appearance.

THE NAMBUS

Shortly after the introduction of the Type 26, Captain (later Lt. General) Kijiro Nambu joined the Tokyo Artillery Arsenal and began work on small arms. Nambu had the same broad influence on small arms development in Japan that John Browning had in the USA. His work touched everything from handguns to rifles and machine guns.

Nambu's first production handgun design was an eight-shot, semi-automatic with a shoulder-stock/holster. Now called the Grandpa Nambu, only about 2,400 were produced between 1902 and 1906, for private purchase by officers. However, this early model included two features that were extremely influential. First, it introduced the 8mm bottle-necked cartridge that became the standard Japanese pistol and submachine gun round. The 8mm Nambu is similar in size to the 7.65mm Luger round, but with a lower velocity that makes it ballistically more similar to the .380 ACP. Second, it had a mechanism based on a downward-swinging locking block, variants of which were used in several subsequent models. When the pistol is fired, the barrel and bolt recoil together about 3mm. Then the locking block swings down into an aperture in the rear of the frame, freeing the bolt to continue its rearward movement. Luger afficionados will recognize this as totally different from the upward-breaking toggle action on the much more common Parabellum pistol. In fact, if the mechanism had any German inspiration, it was more likely the Mauser Broomhandle, which also had a downward-swinging locking block, and with which Nambu would have been familiar.

A direct follow-on from the Grandpa was the Papa Nambu, which dropped the shoulder-stock and incorporated some minor improvements such as a slightly larger trigger guard and an aluminum (rather than wooden) magazine base. Tokyo Arsenal and the private firm Tokyo Gas and Electric (TGE) produced

Papa Nambu and Baby Nambu. The latter was designed to compete with European pocket semi-automatics in the market for private purchases by officers.

more than 10,000 of these pistols between 1906 and the mid-1920s. The Japanese referred to it as the "Riku-shiki" (Army-Type), which was ironic, since the Army never adopted it officially, while the Navy did, in 1909. Once again, a chronic shortage of weapons resulted in the Papa continuing in service until 1945, by which time decades of use in the Navy's salt-spray environment had left most of them in very rough condition. Like the Type 26 revolver, only a handful of mint specimens are known.

Many Japanese officers found the full-size Nambu pistols too bulky and purchased smaller European and American semi-automatics, such as the 1910 and 1914 Mausers, 1903 Colt and 1910 Browning, for their personal use. To provide a domestic alternative for this market, Nambu developed a three-quarter-size version of his pistol. Known as the Baby Nambu, this pocket-sized pistol was mechanically identical to its full-size counterparts but fired a unique bottle-necked 7mm cartridge with muzzle energy similar to that of the .32 ACP. Since they were almost twice the price of a European pistol, they were mostly purchased by senior officers and therefore led pampered lives. Only 6,500 were produced, 90

percent by Tokyo Arsenal and the rest by Tokyo Gas & Electric. Their rarity and extremely high level of craftsmanship have made them among the most sought-after of Japanese pistols.

THE TYPE 14

The 1920s saw the development of Japan's most common sidearm, the Type 14. Adopted by the Army in 1925 (the fourteenth year of the reign of the Taisho Emperor, Hirohito's father) and by the Navy in 1927, approximately 280,000 were produced between late 1926 and August, 1945. While broadly similar in design to its predecessors, it was much easier to produce and incorporated several improvements, such as dual recoil springs. The first 102,000 or so produced up until September of 1939 had a small, rounded trigger guard. Those produced thereafter had an extended trigger guard to allow the use of a gloved finger in cold weather. The large trigger guard version is sometimes referred to as the "Manchurian Model," "Kiska Model," or "Winter Trigger Guard Model." However, these terms have fallen into disfavour since all pistols produced after September of 1939 had the large guard regardless of where

or in what season they were issued.

Type 14 pistols are easily dated since the year and month of production were recorded just below the serial number on the right rear of the frame. They are recorded using the Japanese emperor-based system of dating, with the year of the Emperor's reign first, followed by a period or comma and then the month. For example, a marking of "18.6" indicates the sixth month (June) of the eighteenth year of Emperor Hirohito's reign. To convert these imperial dates to Western style, simply add 1925 (e.g., "Year 18" was 1925+18=1943). The only exception was the first 100-150 or so pistols produced, which were made during the last months of the reign of Hirohito's father, i.e. in 1926. These do not have a reign name character in front of the date, which could range from 15.8 to 15.12, and bear low serial numbers of up to around 100 (note

(left top) Here the Type 14 bolt is shown fully forward, with the locking block in the "up" (locked) position. (bottom) After firing the bolt and barrel move rearward 3mm, then the locking block drops down and allows the bolt to continue rearward. Note the notch in the bottom of the bolt, into which the locking block fits when the bolt is forward and the action is locked.

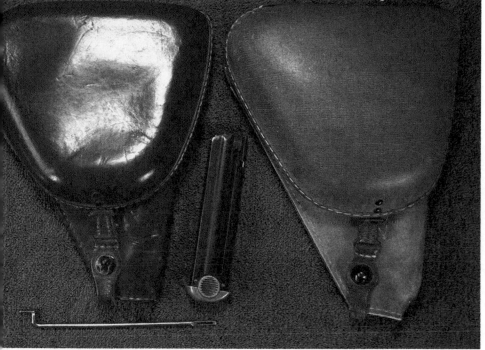

Early models of Type 14 holster had a solid leather closure strap (right). In 1939 a spring –loaded strap was adopted (middle). In late 1942, rubberized canvas was adopted as a leather substitute. It proved much more resistant to rot in tropical climates (right). Also shown are an early magazine (left, with nickel plating), a late magazine (blued, with a notch in the lower front for the magazine retention spring), and a cleaning rod.

that guns with the dates 1.8 to 15.1, a character in front of the date, and serial numbers in the 72000 to 87000 range were made much later, during Hirohito's reign, and are relatively common). If you find one of these ultra-rare pistols, known as "Taisho" Type 14s after the name of Hirohito's father's reign, you have really hit the jackpot!

The Type 14 was Japan's primary sidearm for 20 years. It had several strong points, such as ease of disassembly, great "pointability," a very light trigger that breaks at around 2.5 lbs., good inherent accuracy and mild recoil, all of which made it easy to shoot well. On the other hand, it had three major defects. First, it was prone to misfires due to striker tip breakage and inadequate power of the striker spring. To combat this problem a spare striker was issued with each pistol, and the striker length was reduced from 87mm to 73mm and then 65mm to lighten it.

Rubberized canvas holster shows typical Type 14 features: pouch for two, 15-round boxes of cartridges, slot for spare striker to right of ammo pouch, and use of lanyard to draw pistol. Like many Japanese holsters, this one has a tag identifying the soldier to whom it was issued, in this case Superior Private Toru Sayama.

Second, the safety required two hands to operate, since it was located too far forward on the left side and had to be rotated 180 degrees. Third, the bolt locked back on the magazine follower after the last shot, making reloading slow and awkward unless one is fortunate enough to have been blessed with three hands. Since the Japanese had a rather limited idea of the military use of handguns, neither of the latter two design shortcomings was considered worthy of corrective action. Indeed, in December of 1939 another highly visible change was introduced that made reloading even slower: a magazine retention spring was added. This spring protrudes through the lower part of the front grip strap and prevents magazine loss by catching a released magazine after about 3mm of downward travel

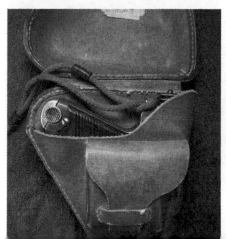

so that it can be manually extracted. Despite these shortcomings, the Type 14 continued in service with the Japanese coast guard until the 1960s!

There were five producers of Type 14s, and numerous variations in cocking knobs, grips, etc. One could make a very interesting collection of just Type 14 variations and their holsters, which themselves come in at least eleven major varieties. Late war Type 14s, particularly those from 1944, the peak year of production, are often available in excellent condition at reasonable prices and therefore make an excellent representative Japanese pistol for the World War II collector, or a starting point for a more ambitious Japanese collection. Their often rough finish should not be confused with actual wear and tear, a common mistake. While early Japanese pistols such as the Baby Nambu had fit and finish equal to the best anywhere, as World War II progressed, less and less attention was paid to cosmetic issues such as polishing and bluing. Eventually poorly trained schoolgirls made up a large part of the labour force in arms factories, resulting in poor quality and an appalling rate of workplace injuries. Oddly, very rough Type 14 pistols made in the last month or two of production (July and August, 1945) are prized by many collectors specifically because of their crudity. These pistols, known as "last ditch," combine poorly made new parts with those scavenged from earlier rejects or damaged pistols sent in for repair. They usually lack final inspection stamps in the area near the date and should definitely not be fired. (Of course, like any antique firearm, even earlier, higher-quality Japanese pistols should be inspected by a competent gunsmith for safety before firing.)

Just before the Type 14 went into production, Lt. General Nambu retired and established the Nambu Rifle Manufacturing Company. Initially it produced only training rifles, but by the late 1930s, after merging with two other companies and assuming the name Chuo Kogyo (Central Industries), it became the largest private producer of military small arms in Japan. Besides pistols, it made the famous "knee mortar" and Type 100 submachine guns, among others. A successor company operated in post-war Japan until the 1970s, when it was absorbed by Minebea, the Japanese bearing maker. The company's pistol-making heritage was preserved when it was granted a contract to produce SIG pistols under license for today's Japanese Self-Defence Forces.

THE NOTORIOUS TYPE 94

The last major design used by the Imperial Japanese military was the Type 94. Its designation results from its adoption by the Army in 1934, which was 2694 by the Japanese calendar (it was never adopted by the Navy). Contrary to reports in some early sources, this pistol was never intended for civilian sale; it was designed at the specific request of the military.

This unusual pistol broke with previous Nambu designs in two important respects. It had a hammer and firing pin rather than a spring-driven striker, and the locking block was a downward-floating wedge. Considered by many to be a good candidate for the title "world's ugliest pistol" or even "world's worst military handgun," the Type 94 perhaps deserves reappraisal. Its small grip and compact overall size actually were ideal for the smaller stature of Japanese soldiers, who averaged only 5'3" and 123 lbs. Its compactness was especially appreciated by those working in confined spaces, such as pilots and tankers. The holster magnified the advantage, as its tailored design contrasted sharply with the bulky clamshell designs issued with most prior Japanese sidearms. The safety was also better positioned and can be operated with one hand.

On the down side, the design of the Type 94's locking mechanism was weak and prone to premature wear, the

Type 94 with holster, cleaning rod and spare magazine. The Showa 18.7 date translates to July, 1943.

The Type 94 had an exposed sear bar. When the safety is off, pressing on the forward portion (indicated by the pencil tip) will fire the pistol.

sights are poor and the trigger is long and creepy. However, by far its most notorious feature was undoubtedly its exposed sear bar on the left side. Pressing on its forward tip when the safety is disengaged allows the pistol to be fired without depressing the trigger. Although inherently an undesirable, unsafe feature, in practice such discharges require sufficiently focused pressure on a small area that they were never a serious operational issue. About 71,000 Type 94s were made by Chuo Kogyo, the only producer. Frequent changes in machining and the placement of markings and the late-war use of slab wooden grips instead of the earlier checkered bakelite mean there are also numerous variations for the serious collector to pursue. "Last ditch" Type 94 pistols often show even worse quality than the late Type 14s and, although of great historical interest, they should certainly not be fired.

TIPS FOR THE BEGINNING COLLECTOR

If you've been keeping score, you have

Papa, Grandpa and Baby. There are now excellent sources of reference information available to guide the beginning collector or help the established one reach new depths of understanding. Two outstanding reference books have been published recently. The most comprehensive is *Japanese Military Cartridge Handguns 1893-1945* by Harry Derby and James Brown. Mr. Brown's *Collector's Guide to Imperial Japanese Handguns 1893-1945* is also available at a very modest price for those on a strict budget (it even has some new information that has turned up since the larger volume came out, as well as advice on valuation). Online resources are also available, such as my website, www. nambuworld.com. I strongly recommend doing some research before you plunge into a purchase, as few sellers know what they really have due to the specialized nature of Japanese weapon collecting. Joining a group like Banzai, the Japanese militaria collectors' association, is also a good idea: I have found the advanced collectors very forthcoming with help and advice as they warmly welcome newcomers to the field.

Very few Japanese handguns made their way to Canada, so many people ask me why I chose such an obscure field to collect. My long-term interest in Japan was one factor, but I also thought it would be interesting to do something no one else in my area was doing. In addition, although they can be hard to find, especially in Canada, when they do turn up, prices are still quite reasonable compared to some of the more popular collectible handguns like Colts and Lugers. You probably won't find one at your local gun shop even in the USA, but if your curiosity has been piqued, you can often find them on the major gun auction websites, Banzai's newsletter or one of the bulletin boards devoted to Japanese weapons and militaria (see my website for a list of them). Be careful, though: once you get started you may end up a "Nambu nut" like me!

NOTE: Teri Jane Bryant's interest in guns and militaria was sparked by visiting gun shows with her father as a child. Japan began to fascinate her when she visited the country on an exchange during her university years. Her two interests came together when she saw a battered Type 14 for sale cheap at a gun show. She has since developed an extensive Japanese collection and published numerous articles on Japanese weapons and militaria. She can be reached at tallteri@shaw.ca.

probably figured out by now that total production of handguns by Imperial Japan during the entire period 1893-1945 was less than 450,000, even including a small number of rare weapons produced late in the war, such as the Hamada. (By comparison, Germany made several million Lugers during the same period, not to mention the many other sidearms it adopted.) Most Japanese handguns were destroyed at the end of WWII; most of those that survived were brought home as war trophies by US troops. Many of these pistols are still being dug out of attics, garages and closets and put on the market by the heirs of the servicemen who brought them back. A good start to a collection would be a Type 26 revolver, two Type 14s (small and large trigger guard versions) and a Type 94. These examples would represent over 90% of all the Japanese handguns made. From there one can easily branch out into collecting the many variations of either the Type 14 or Type 94, or (if one's budget allows) attempt to complete the "Nambu Family" with the rarer types such as the

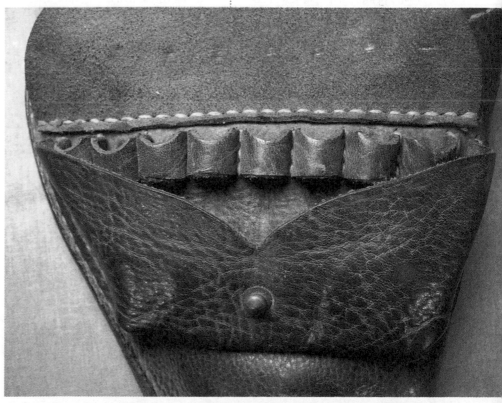

Baby Nambu holsters, like those for the Type 26, Grandpa and Papa, had individual loops for spare cartridges in their ammo pouches.

*It takes an honest man to tell a story like this.
Many of us have done, or have come close to
doing, the very thing the author describes. Is
there a moral here? You better believe it!*

BLOW UP!

BY NEAL BRADFORD

Short and simple: I should be dead, because there is no logical reason why anyone should be alive after blowing up a gun as I did. My wish is that by writing this story I can keep you alive by not making the same or a similar error.

It happened almost two years ago, buit I remember it all too well. In addition to my .357 Magnum revolver, I had four rifles for which I decided to reload ammunition: an old .32-40 Winchester for which shells are not commonly available; a .38-55 for which I have to special-order the ammunition; a pre-'64 M70 Winchester .30-06, which I had completely restored; and a new .300 WSM in a M700 Remington. So, after much studying, I came home with a new RCBS kit, .300 WSM dies, primers, and only one kind of powder, H-4350.

After loading and shooting over 80 rounds of .300 WSM, I was enjoying the reduced cost per shell, but it was already mid-March and I had hundreds of hours of work to do on my farm in Washington state.

It was sometime in June of 2007 when my friend Patrick stopped to see me and brought some gifts to go with my reloading stuff. There was a case tumbler, a set of .30-06 loading dies, three or four smaller items, and a can of HS-6 pistol powder, even though I still did not yet have the dies to load for my .357 revolver. I put it all on the shelf and went back to work on the farm.

By August 1, with my normal work up to date, I decided to reload some more and improve my shooting accuracy before hunting season. This time I was loading for my restored M70 in .30-'06. Since the book called for a low of 53 gr. and a high of 57 gr. of H-4350, I loaded some shells at 54 gr. That, I was sure.would keep me well within the safe range.

On August 10 I drove 28 miles up into the mountains of Gifford Pinchot National Forest to a lonely spot where we had set up a safe firing range.

Now that my M70 had a new sissy pad, newly finished stock, new barrel, new bluing and new scope, I was ready to prove that the hours I had spent in refinishing it had not been in vain and that I could shoot a good tight group with that new barrel. I set up the shooting bench with sandbags and everything I needed. I wanted to know what the gun could do before I did any off-hand shooting.

When I touched off that first shell, all hell broke loose. My prized 'pre-64 M70 Winchester, which my dad handed down to me, blew into hundreds of pieces. Small chips of the stock were raining down on my head. The bar-

rel landed 34 feet from where I pulled the trigger. There was blood dripping from my right thumbnail. My face felt partially numb from the blast, so I touched it with my left hand and my palm came away covered with blood. I discovered later that only my safety glasses, which I wear all the time, saved my eyes. The lenses were covered with little chip marks from flying metal.

What went wrong? I had to know. So as quickly as possible I gathered up all the pieces that were close by and easy to find, threw them in the car and asked myself, "What next?"

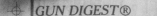

This is what a bad reload can do. After I searched a 100-ft. radius, this is all I could find. I never found the bolt.

BELOW LEFT: This was my pride and joy, a pre-'64 Winchester Model 70 in .30-06. I had refinished the stock, adding a sissy pad, and I had the metal reblued.

I was alone and 28 miles from home with only one way to get there. I had to drive . . . at least until I found a Forest Service truck or a sheriff's patrol car. I wiped the blood off my glasses so I could see and started down the mountains. As it turned out, I was only twelve miles from home when I met the first car of any kind, but by then I knew that I could make it to the house.

After three days of doctor visits, I loaded the gun and my metal detector into the car and drove back to the mountains. With the metal detector I searched a 100-foot radius from my firing position and never found the bolt or any other pieces of the gun.

On the way home, I stopped at the home of another friend, Keith, in nearby Amboy. I knew that he was a marksman in the Marines and now he both repaired guns and built custom rifles that are sold at auction at NRA banquets. I wanted to know if he and his expert friends could determine what went wrong. The poor guy took one look at what was left of my gun and went white with the fear

that one of his reloads caused the explosion. I had to assure him that it was not his reloads that I was shooting. It took a while, but after he calmed down, he took one of the remaining shells I had loaded with 54 gr. and gently removed the bullet from the case. Then he poured out the powder on a white paper, and with a bad-news expression said, "That's pistol powder." Pistol powder!

Keith then went to his supply room and returned with three canisters of powder. Upon comparison and talking to me he concluded that I had loaded 54 gr. of HS-6 into those .30-06 cases instead of 54 gr. of H-4350.

It was only then that I realized what I had done: in early April my wife had asked me to put my reloading powder in the safe because the grandkids were coming to visit. Then the gifts that Patrick had brought me, including the HS-6 for my .357 revolver, had gone onto the same shelf from which I removed my H-4350 – or what I thought was my H4350.

And finally, having played it safe and purchased only one type of rifle

powder, I had reloaded for my M70 without checking my powder container and without a thought of that HS-6.

By the way: it takes only 9 gr. of HS-6 to load a .44 Magnum shell. Keith later informed me that although my '06 was designed to withstand a chamber pressure of 50,000 psi, he and his mathematical friends figured that my 54 gr. of HS-6 pushed that pressure up somewhere between 235,000 and 285,000 psi.

The bottom line? Slow down. Never assume you know what you have. When reloading, check each powder container and each measurement to prove that you are right.

No, I still don't know why I'm alive after such an explosion only nine inches from my face. Maybe that Old Man Upstairs still has a job for me that I do not yet know about. As my friend Keith suggests, "Maybe that job was to write this story and keep someone else alive by not making a similar error."

Believe it: yes you can. You can mix them up. I've seen it done.

CUSTOM AND ENGRAVED GUNS

BY TOM TURPIN

A magnificent .416 Rigby rifle from the shop of Ryan Breeding. Starting with a Granite Mountain Arms double square-bridge magnum Mauser action, Pac Nor barrel, and lovely stick of Turkish walnut, Breeding does the rest in his shop. On this rifle, he fitted a Swarovski Z6 1-6 extended eye-relief scope mounted in Talley rings with bases milled into the double square bridges. Sights and accessories are all shop-made in the Breeding shop. Photo courtesy of Ryan Breeding.

This takedown .275 Rigby was built on a Granite Mountain Arms Kurz action fitted with Joe Smithson scope mounts. The barrel is octagonal with integral front sight ramp, sling swivel studs and quarter-rib by Ralf Martini. Steve Nelson then machined square threads on the barrel to mate up with the special-order square threads in the receiver. Square threads were used to withstand repeated assembly/disassembly. By depressing a button in the forend escutcheon, the barrel unscrews from the action. Nelson then made a pattern stock to precisely fit the client and then machined a lovely stick of exhibition grade walnut using the pattern. After finishing with many coats of hand-rubbed oil, he checkered the stock with a fleur-de-lis ribbon pattern designed just for this client.

Bob Evans then executed the engraving duties. Since the client is of Norse ancestry, the designs were all taken from Norse mythology and the gold runes on the quarter rib are the client's initials. After Evans finished the engraving, George Komadina rust blued the metalwork. Evans then selectively French grayed the engraving.

When the rifle was finished but before engraving, the client just had to take his rifle on a moose hunt in Sweden where he dropped a nice bull on the first morning with a single well-placed shot. A good omen! Photos by Tom Alexander

These two images are of the first Jack O'Connor Commemorative Rifle. Roger Biesen crafted the rifle in the same style as his father Al had done in 1959 to Jack's favorite rife of all time. I believe Al, who just turned 91 years old, did quite a bit of "supervising" building this rifle. A third generation Biesen, Roger's daughter Paula Biesen-Malicki, engraved Jack's best ram, the Pilot Mountain ram, on the buttplate. Photos courtesy of the Biesen family

A personal job for engraver Brian Powley. Powley purchased this Series 70 National Match Colt Gold Cup new in 1978. The gun is all original except for the engraving, custom ivory grips, and the grip screws. Powley even has the original box that the pistol was in when he purchased it.

The pistol is multi-caliber in that, in addition to the original .45 ACP N.M. barrel, it has been fitted with a Bar-Sto custom barrel chambered in a J.D. Jones wildcat cartridge, the .41 Avenger. (The Avenger is simply a .45 ACP necked down to accept .41 caliber.)

The numerous colors in the engraving come from using 24K gold, rose gold, green gold, platinum, silver, brass, and copper inlays. Photos by Brian Powley

I haven't spoken with Mike Dubber about this commission, but I'd wager a king's ransom that it was done for a native Kentuckian. Dubber embellished this Colt Bisley Flat-Top model exquisitely with scroll, gold inlay, and carved ivory grips. As the TV commercial once said, it just doesn't get any better than this. Photos by Sam Welch.

This rifle was crafted, at the instructions of the client, for a specific task. It was designed to be a tree stand gun! The client wanted a technically perfect rifle of the highest quality, but he wanted no glitz and no glamour. Custom maker Dave Norin set about accomplishing the instructions by selecting a 1908 Brazilian Mauser action. He blue printed the action, installed a Model 70 type three-position safety, and installed a .30-caliber barrel, and chambered it for the .30-06 cartridge. He fitted Ted Blackburn bottom metal, with the Oberndorf style trigger guard bow, to the action. He then stocked it with a piece of excellent, but very plain, walnut. The client, and this writer believes he succeeded admirably. Photo by Tom Alexander Photography

Starting with a VZ-24 Mauser action and a Krieger barrel, custom maker Dave Norin crafted this wonderful lightweight deer rifle. He used Fisher rounded bottom metal, Biesen buttplate, and a Fisher grip cap and crafted the stock with a very nice stick of English walnut. He checkered the stock with a point pattern featuring a mullered border at 22 lpi. Ken Hurst did the engraving. Photo by Tom Alexander Photography

This lovely custom Dakota Model 10 belongs to my colleague and friend, Terry Wieland. In addition to being a fantastically talented writer, Terry is also a connoisseur of fine firearms, particularly rifles. This Dakota is no exception. Starting with a Model 10 action and .25 caliber barrel from Dakota, a magnificent stock blank from Bill Dowtin of Old World Walnut, and a grip cap and sling swivels from Brownells, and a set of Talley scope bases and rings from Gary Turner of Talley Manufacturing, Terry delivered the goods to Master custom maker James Flynn. Flynn did all the stock and metal work on this rifle with the exception of the superb case coloring and bluing. That specialized talent was entrusted to Doug Turnbull. Chambered for the .250/3000 Savage cartridge, it is Terry's idea of what a fine single shot rifle should look like.

As an interesting aside, the blank from which James Flynn crafted the stock (using chisels, rasps, and other hand tools with no machine-shaping involved) came from the Caucasus Mountains, the source of true Circassian walnut. Bill Dowtin related that on a trip to the area, he came across a little man in Georgia that had cut up a tree using a chainsaw. Dowtin bought three blanks from him, all from the root section below ground level. The tree was estimated to be a minimum of 300 years old. Photos by Terry Wieland

This fine rifle began life as a factory Remington Model 700 chambered for the .30-06 cartridge. Custom Maker Gary Stiles then cleaned up the metalwork and added a Model 70 type safety, a set of Dakota bottom metal, and checkered the bolt knob. Using a nice stick of Turkish walnut from Luxus Walnut, he fashioned the excellent custom stock, adding Talley sling swivel bases, a Dakota skeleton grip cap, an ebony forend tip with widow's peak, a bearskin covered recoil pad, and checkered the stock in a 24 lpi wraparound pattern with ribbons. He then mounted a Leupold VX-III 2.5-8 variable scope in Talley mounts. Engraver Ron Nott completed the job with his tasteful scroll engraving. Photos courtesy of Gary Stiles

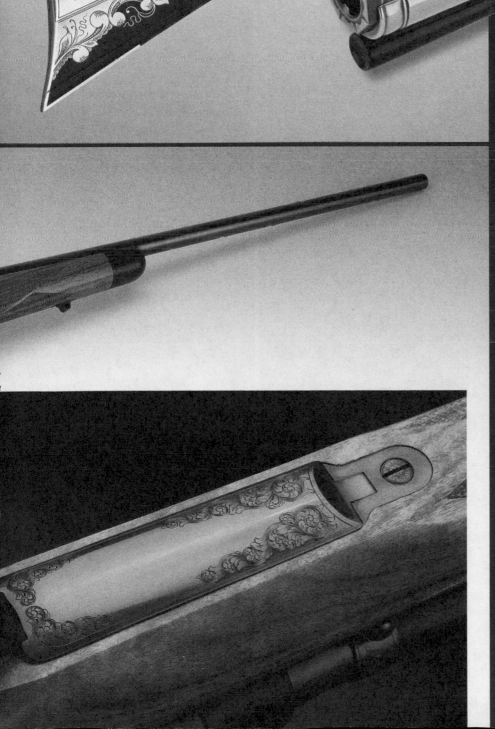

This superb "Kentucky" flintlock rifle was made entirely by hand by Hugh Toenjes. He started the stock with a square blank of curly maple and fashioned the stock fully by hand. No stock duplicator or other "high tech" machinery was used. He finished the stock by hand rubbing a combination of various stains, boiled linseed oil, tung oil and Japan dryers. This finishing alone took three weeks to complete.

All the brass furniture was crafted from solid stock using primarily a file and hacksaw. The two exceptions are the trigger guard and butt plate, which were fashioned from rough sand castings.

Using a rough octagon barrel blank that had only been deep drilled, Toenjes rifled it by hand using his own style of rifling. He honed it to his specifications and filed a breech plug from solid stock and fitted it to the barrel. After proof firing the barrel for accuracy, which produced several five shot groups measuring 1-1/4 inches at 100 yards, he draw filed the flats to the final dimensions, ready for inletting.

Toenjes made the lock from a combination of rough castings and springs filed out by hand. Toenjes also did all the stock decoration, as well as all the metal engraving.

This exquisite rifle is a wonderful example of Old World craftsmanship and talent. All photos by Robert Fogt Photography.

This very nice "southpaw" rifle is from the shop of Robert Mercer. Mercer built the gun for a very special purpose, not for a client, but as a gift for his son. He started the project with a Montana 1999 action and a Krieger barrel. He fitted the 7mm barrel to the action and chambered it for the .280 Ackley Improved cartridge.

He then stocked the rifle in a very nice stick of English walnut and checkered it in a 26 lpi fleur-de-lis pattern. Finally, he mounted a Leupold scope in Talley rings and bases. Jerome Glimm did the lovely engraving. Mercer told me that since he finished the rifle and gave it to his son, their target bill has gone down considerably. The rifle seems to consistently deliver nothing bigger than .5 MOA groups. Photo by Tom Alexander Photography

Starting with a post-war FN large ring action, Al Lofgren set about crafting a fine .30-06 hunting rifle. Dave Norin did all the metalwork on the rifle, including fitting a McFarland checkered bolt knob and Talley scope mounts. Lofgren crafted the stock from a nice stick of English walnut. He fitted a skeleton grip cap and butt plate to the stock but filled the openings with ebony inlay, which he checkered. A superb and unusual job. Photo by Tom Alexander Photography

If this rifle reminds you of an early Rigby magazine rifle, then gunmaker Reto Buehler has accomplished the job he set out to do. He started with a Steyr M98 Mauser action. At the time, he had in the shop a 1910 Oberndorf Mauser built for Rigby, so he copied the barrel contour in a new Pad Nor 9.3mm barrel, and Reto fitted the new barrel to the action and chambered it for the 9.3x62 cartridge. He added the square bridges to the action, as well as Recknagel side swing scope mounts. To the barrel, he shop-made and added an express and ladder rear sight, just like the original Rigby. He retained the original military magazine box, but added a straddle type floorplate to which he built in a hinged lever floorplate release. While it is a new rifle, it is very reminiscent of the early 1900 products. A very masterful job. Photos courtesy of Reto Buehler.

Engraver Lee Griffiths, responding to general guidelines from a client, came up with this design for engraving the client's Perazzi shotgun. According to Lee, the client suggested bugs, stinging nasty bugs on each side, and butterflies on the bottom. Lee admitted that the spider on the break lever was his idea.

IMPORTER-Perazzi-USA
MONROVIA - CALIFORNIA

When I asked him how he came up with the design, he told me "eat enough spicy foods and have enough bad nightmares, and you can come up with stuff like this!" Perhaps not everyone's taste in design, the execution is marvelously done. This job won the Engravers Choice Merit award at the 2009 FEGA/ACGG combined Exhibition in Reno. Photos by Sam Welch

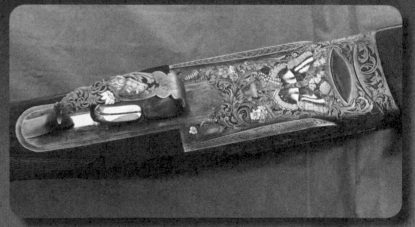

CUSTOM AND ENGRAVED GUNS

One of the premiere gunmakers in the world is D'Arcy Echols. His work with bolt-action rifles is among the finest on this planet. Not the most extravagant, not the flashiest, and not the most attention getting, mind you, but he is among a handful of the very best artisans building rifles.

Echols began work on this rifle with a Winchester Model 70 Classic action, which was completely reworked in the Echols shop. A 7mm barrel was then fitted to the action and chambered for the 7mm Remington Magnum cartridge. All the accessories – bottom metal, scope mounts, sling swivels and studs, etc., are all custom made in the Echols shop. Echols then crafted a superb stock from a stick of excellent, but not ornate, English walnut. The final task was fitting a Schmidt & Bender 3-12 Zenith scope to the rifle in Echols mounts. This rifle will hold its own with any. Photo courtesy of D'Arcy Echols

This wonderful double rifle is a No. 11 Jeffery's Express Rifle, chambered for the .475 #2 Cordite cartridge. It features Krupp steel barrels, 24 inches in length. It is a non-ejector rifle and weighs 11-1/2 lbs. From all indications, it was manufactured between 1907 and 1909. The rifle has been completely reconditioned and restocked to "As New" condition.

The metalwork was completely restored by Pete Mazur. All metal parts were reconditioned and refinished using proper period finishes. The engraving was recut as required.

Darwin Hensley, one of our very best stockers, restocked the rifle. The blank that Hensley selected is a stick of exhibition grade Turkish walnut of exceptional quality, and the styling of the stock is distinctively Hensley's.

Of special note, Mazur custom-fitted an original Purdey folding peep sight to the barrels. The owner of the rifle now shoots 1-1/2-inch groups at 25 yards instead of the previous 8-inch groups using the "normal" leaf sights. Photo by Tom Alexander Photography

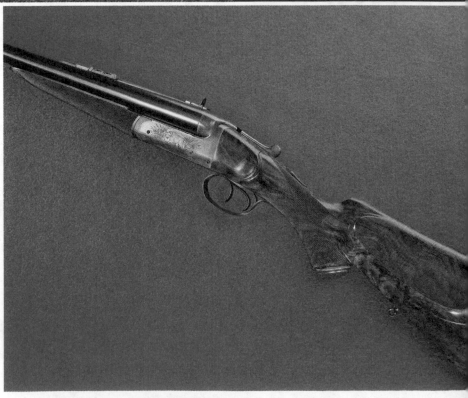

This fine pair of rifles was crafted to support the American Custom Gunmakers Guild Foundation. Larry Potterfield of Midway started the process by donating two consecutively serial numbered Remington Model 700 short actions. Douglas then donated two air-gauged chrome moly barrels, one in .222 and the other in .257. Fred Wenig donated two Bastogne walnut stock blanks, and Leupold followed with two 4-12 variable scopes, also with consecutive serial numbers. John Maxson did the stocks including checkering each in a 20 lpi borderless checkering pattern. Brian Powley did the modest engraving on the rifles. All work and parts of these rifles were donated. A silent auction is underway from March 1 to November 1. On November 1 the winner of the auction will be announced, with proceeds going to the ACGG Scholarship Fund. Anyone wanting to bid should check the ACGG website (www.acgg.org) for details. Photo by Tom Alexander Photography

This wonderful Sabatti shotgun is the work of one superb craftsman, Mr. Joe Rundell. Starting with the barreled action, Rundell devoted over 3000 highly talented hours to turning the rough metalwork into a masterpiece. Not only did Rundell do all the engraving, inlay work, and finishing, he also stocked the gun in a stick of fabulous walnut and did all the stock carving as well. At the annual combined Firearms Engravers Guild of America/American Custom Gunmakers Guild Exhibition, Joe and his Sabatti won the Engravers Choice Award, the Best Engraved Shotgun Award, and the Metal on Metal Inlay award. Photos by Tom Alexander Photography

This very unusual rifle is the combination of several highly talented artisans. Bob Snapp did the metalwork on this Martini barreled action. Though Bob can do metalwork on any firearm, he is most at home working on single shot rifles like this Martini. Kent Bowerly fashioned the stock from a magnificent stick of crotch grain walnut and carried out the unique checkering pattern. Bob Evans then designed and executed the one-of-a-kind engraving pattern. All of the symbols are from the Kwakiutl Indian tribe of coastal SW British Columbia. Photos by Tom Alexander Photography

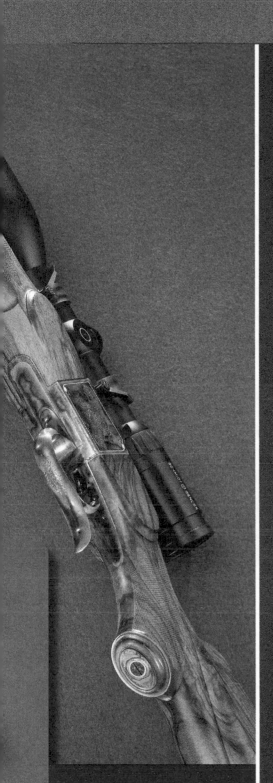

This single shot 7mm STW features the metalwork of Steve Heilmann, the engraving of Denis Reece, the bluing and finishing of Pete Mazur, the color case hardening of Doug Turnbull, and the stockwork of Keith Heppler. The action used is a Hagn. The rifle exhibits marvelous work from a group of superb artisans. Photos by Tom Alexander Photography

Think the Colt 1873 Single Action Army won the West? Think again!

When Bulldogs Ruled

BY GEORGE J. LAYMAN

Colt, Remington, Smith & Wesson and Merwin & Hulbert didn't manufacture them, but during the late nineteenth century they were among the Old West's most well-known pocket revolvers. Though the second definition of "bulldog" in Webster's is "…a small, short-barrel pistol of large caliber…" the genuine British Bulldog may further be defined as "any of the nineteenth century-produced, double-action, stubby short-barreled revolvers chambered for medium to large calibers."

At the end of the Civil War, many ex-soldiers, civilians, and city folk took their chances on a new life in the yet unsettled and lawless areas of the American West. Those who dared the long trek prepared themselves with everything from general supplies to reliable firearms for hunting and self-defense. These future Westerners were a sophisticated lot when it came to choosing their rifles, pistols and shotguns, and did so according to their financial means. By the 1870s, many Western townships forbade carrying firearms openly, thus many had to conceal their arms to circumvent the restriction. By 1875, both the Midwest and the California coast

This close-up of a Belgian-made British Bulldog (maker unknown) shows the quality of the simple engraving pattern common to these imported revolvers.

were beehives of activity, chock-full of gold-seekers, gamblers, homesteaders, and other opportunists. The market was ripe for a small size, large-caliber revolver that was concealable but powerful enough for a serious gunfight or other armed dispute. Most of all, the revolver had to be affordable in price.

Though Remington brought out a number of pocket revolvers to include a double action by 1870, as well as Smith & Wesson's Baby Russian, a competitor from abroad surprised U.S. manufacturers with the introduction of what was to be a very well-received wheelgun. Just before 1874, a small double-action, big-bore revolver with a short 2-1/2" barrel made its abrupt debut in the

With the loading gate down, the cylinder is readied for loading. Most cylinders on British Bulldogs were of an unlocked type: unless the trigger was pulled back or the hammer cocked, the cylinder would spin freely.

West. It was a unique big-bore revolver of excellent quality and was made by the English gun manufacturer P. Webley & Son. It was called the British Bulldog.

THE WEBLEY INFLUENCE

Upon its introduction in the early 1870s, Webley's new British Bulldog had become an immediate sensation in Victorian England since the carrying of firearms in Great Britain was accomplished quite discreetly. Thus the pocketsize, highly concealable Bulldog fit right into the period of Sherlock Holmes and Jack the Ripper. Webley firearms were well known in the United States for their high degree of workmanship. Even George Armstrong Custer owned a pair of Webleys (the Royal Irish Constabulary Model) prior to his death in June of 1876 at the Little Big Horn. Soon after its invasion of the United States arms market, the self-cocking Webley British Bulldog was being sold through American gun dealers such as Nathaniel Curry of San Francisco and E.C. Meacham of St. Louis. With population surges in areas west of the Mississippi growing by the day, many were glad to see a compact, inexpensive, double-action revolver with plenty of wallop to boot. The new Webley catchphrase "British Bulldog" would evolve into one of the most famous revolver trademarks from the 1870s up to the turn of the century. The term

Bulldog became a legend in its own time. By 1876, several European and American imitators jumped on the Bulldog bandwagon, marketing copies of self-cockers marked "British Bulldog" over the topstrap. Many of the European Webley copies came from Belgium and their overall finish and quality was noticeably inferior to the genuine British-made variations. Quite a number of these – both domestic and foreign – were stamped with such markings as "Western Bull Dog," "British Lion," "Boston Bulldog," etc., and, not surprisingly, many were indeed well made. The 1880 Homer Fisher catalog listed several of these for sale in .44 Webley (.44 Bulldog) at $7.50, each which was far below the $18.00 price tag of a Colt or Smith & Wesson. Both the Webley British Bull Dog and its imitations were also being offered in .32 rimfire or centerfire as well as .41 rimfire and .38 and .44 centerfire. Webley even listed a "Holster Size Frontier Model" Bulldog in .38 and. 44 centerfire with a 4" barrel and a lanyard on the grip.

The quality of Belgian-made British Bulldogs was often quite good, but a lower grade of metallurgy often caused their internal parts to wear out much more quickly than those of the Webley- or U.S.- made British Bulldog.

design compared to the British type since it had a saw handle-style grip, plus a larger frame somewhere between a medium- and full-size revolver. It also had a 2-1/2" full round barrel as opposed to the oblong type most common to the British-style versions. Not easy to find nowadays, these revolvers were manufactured by Iver Johnson Co. of Worcester, Massachusetts, for the Meacham company, to be sold under the American Bulldog trade name. It should be mentioned that the Iver Johnson Co. independently marketed their own series of Bulldog revolvers, some of which were marked Boston Bulldog, British Bulldog, and oddly enough, American Bulldog as well.

Though the Meacham American Bulldog is not marked Iver Johnson, the giveaway is one of the company's trademarks – an American eagle – on the stocks. Removing the grips however, does show a serial number on the frame in two places. With its reddish gutta percha grips, these 44-caliber five-shooters are extremely well-made; much better than most other Bulldogs. It is here where a degree of confusion exists between the British and American Bulldog revolvers. It appears the basic cosmetic difference is that the British-style Bulldog retains the classic parrot's beak or bird's-head grip, and the American Bulldogs were supplied with a "saw handle" flat-base grip. Some early ads made reference that their American

This Belgian British Bulldog has most of its nickel worn away, but the proofmark "R" and the Bulldog logo are partially visible on the frame behind the barrel.

would soon become a household word among pistoleros of the day, and gain almost equal footing with the Colt Peacemaker, the Smith & Wesson Russian models and other famous handguns.

It is quite obvious that the British

AMERICAN BULLDOGS

The E.C. Meacham company had at least four different Bulldogs in their 1884 catalog, among which were an "American Bulldog" somewhat unique in

Bulldogs were made exclusively in .38 caliber, with the British Bulldog with bird's-head grips being made only in .44 caliber. Additionally, the Meacham catalog also listed an "American" British Bulldog complete with bird's-head grips and in both calibers, too.

Another very interesting British Bulldog is the illustration on the same page beneath the aforementioned "American" Bulldog in the 1884 catalog. This particular revolver is advertised as a "new design" English British Bulldog and has a remarkable resemblance to the later Webley series of military break-open revolvers. Together with its flat-base saw handle grips (listed as a "Smith & Wesson handle"), the text states that when chambered for the .38 S&W, they are marked "American Bulldog." A footnote goes on to say that the revolver ". . .is made to compete with Colt's and resembles them in model and fine workmanship. . . ." Equipped with an octagonal 2-1/2" barrel, the arm is something of a hybrid between a Webley of the future and a Colt double-action Lightning with a flat butt! At least a dozen or more Belgian-made Bulldog copies with bird's-head grips have been seen by the author in .38 caliber only, with

American or British Bulldog markings.

Unquestionably, the U.S.-made copies are generally better from a quality standpoint than their Belgian counterparts. The Meacham Arms American Bulldog sold for $3.31 in 1881 and was quite the bargain when compared to a full-size Colt. It could also be had with extras such as pearl or ivory stocks, and engraved frames. It is curiously amusing to note that in the Meacham advertisement, for 31 cents less, one could have the same revolver marked "British Bulldog"!

The design of the American Bulldog from Meacham Arms differed from the majority of British Bulldogs in that it uses a spring-charged vertical flat latch to retain the cylinder pin. The typical British Bulldog used a pull-out, rotating extractor pin which, when pulled upward and turned right, allowed removal of the hollow cylinder pin as well. A short, oblong-shaped 2-1/2" barrel was standard on most Bulldogs regardless of origin. However, some are listed with 2-1/4" and 2-3/4" tubes in certain advertisements. Depending on caliber, they could be five-, six-, or seven-shooters! Noteworthy is that the Webley Bulldogs had unfluted cylinders,

whereas most U.S. and European copies had the fluted type. Unfluted cylinders, however, have been observed on several Liege-made Belgian copies.

Colt didn't introduce a self-cocker until 1877 (the Model 1877 "Lightning" and "Thunderer" models), and it seemed the Bulldog owned the market for the double-action class of big-bore pocket revolvers. In truth, the Bulldogs' fast-firing characteristics had a hand in spreading the popularity of the double-action revolver as a whole. Mechanically, the British and American Bulldogs were quite sturdy and simple; however, the finish and smooth mechanics of these Bulldogs were still not up to par with those of a Smith & Wesson or a Colt. A light strain on the wallet was their obvious strongpoint. Though the later Colt Lightning/Thunderer series of double actions would be the stiffest competition, the Colt's lockwork proved complicated and prone to breakage under hard use. They nevertheless became immensely popular.

The British Bulldog, however, was not without its own mechanical problems. Too-vigorous operation of the double-action trigger would eventually cause the lockwork to begin mis-indexing, as

The British Bulldog's design was simplicity at its best. Withdrawing the steel extractor rod from the cylinder pin hollow and turning it right, allows the cylinder pin to be removed from the frame, leaving three pieces after disassembly.

the hand would skip a cylinder notch. Many of the British Bulldogs encountered today seem to display this malfunction, and finding one that functions correctly in double action is not easy. Most seem to work better as single actions!

One of the minuses of some Bulldogs was their "freewheeling" cylinder that would spin if the hammer wasn't cocked or the trigger pulled back. Costwise, the most expensive Bulldog was the Webley Frontier Model, which sold (in 1880) for $17.50 when the cheapest Webley was $9.50. In 1884, the E.C. Meacham catalog still had the lowest price of $3.00 for a Bulldog, "an unbeatable price," as they noted. With the Colt double action at $13 to $17.50 each, it was without doubt the Bulldog which could easily fit the leanest budget of the average individual.

Some ads for the Bulldog boasted it could fire seven shots in five seconds. Promoters of the well-made Forehand & Wadsworth British Bulldog stated this quite confidently. Sold in .32, .38 and .44 caliber, the .32 S&W version had a seven-round cylinder. The Forehand & Wadsworth Bulldog, introduced in 1880, began cutting into sales of the Webley product. Nathaniel Curry noted the Forehand & Wadsworth Bulldog was "...decidedly the best and cheapest of the low-grade American self-cocking revolvers...."

In the beginning, few consumers were aware that the Bulldog had a competitive edge on the products of the large U.S. gunmakers. The British Bulldog soon took a back seat, however, because these bigger companies had been in existence for many years and enjoyed well-established reputations. Bulldogs were in far more widespread use than most will realize, but many may ask, if so many were in circulation, why are there so

A comparison of the hammer styles of both the author's American Bulldog and the Forehand & Wadsworth British type (right). The two U.S.-manufactured revolvers were America's best "Bulldog" and produced in the same city. Note the flatter, larger contours of the American version compared to the rounded lines of the British style, which has a shorter spur. Mechanically, the American version has a smoother action; the Forehand & Wadsworth has a rebounding hammer feature.

few pictures of them in the holsters of Westerners? The answer is quite likely that Bulldogs were out of sight, hidden in the pockets of their users.

In due time, people began wondering why no Bulldog-style revolvers were being made by any of the major American manufacturers. A testimony to this was a letter in 1876 written by a Californian to Smith & Wesson, in which he asked,

"Why don't you put something on the market to compete with Webley's Bulldog? The pistols have an immense popularity on this coast and people don't hesitate to pay $25 to $30.00 for them either...."

Sales techniques of the day kept the Bulldog market steadily popular with some advertisements stating, "the pistols are the most substantial of their class, the price we quote them makes them substantial bargains." In late 1895, Montgomery Ward Company advertised; "big bargains, American Bulldog [author's note: possibly unsold, smaller-caliber versions of the earlier Meacham product sold back to Iver Johnson, who re-sold them to Montgomery Ward] revolver, sold in .32 and .38 caliber...." The ad further stated "these guns are not toys, but good, big guns." Top prices now were $1.89 each. Montgomery Ward also advertised a "Frontier Bulldog 6-shot, in 44 WCF for $3.85" but judging from the illustration of this revolver, it appears to be an inferior-quality Belgian-made mass-produced copy of a Webley Frontier Model.

THE BULLDOG OUT WEST

Other notable gun dealers who regularly offered Bulldogs of all types included Liddle & Kaeding and Shreve & Wolfman, both located in San Francisco. One of Liddle & Kaeding's advertisements in the publication *Pacific Life* in

The Forehand & Wadsworth British Bulldogs are serial-numbered on the grip of the frame and on the rear of the cylinder. It is estimated no more 90,000 F & W Bulldogs were manufactured; however, the serial numbers drastically overlap with other F&W revolvers, as seen on this specimen in the 85,000 range.

These Pistols are the most substantial of their class. The price at which we now quote them makes them a genuine bargain.

Rubber Stock, Nickel Plated.
SAW HANDLE.
Cut represents exactly the 38-cal.
AMERICAN
"BRITISH BULL-DOG"

Central Fire, Double-Action, Five-Shot.
Length of Barrel, 38 Cal., 2 1-2 in.;
44 Cal., 2 3-4 in. Weight, 38 Cal.,
16 ounces; 44 Cal., 19 ounces.

No. 101, Cent. Fire, 38 Cal., Round Barrel. S. & W. Cartridge........... $3 00
No. 102, Cent. Fire, 44 Cal., Round Barrel, with Gate, Webley Cartridge... 3 00

These Pistols were made to compete with Colt's and resemble them in model and fine workmanship. The price at which we now quote them makes them a genuine bargain.

Rubber Stock, Nickel Plated
SAW HANDLE.
Cut represents exactly the 38 cal.
NEW DESIGN
(ENGLISH)
BRITISH BULL-DOG.

Central Fire, Double Action, Five-Shot.
Length of Barrel, 2 1-2 inches.
Weight, 20 ounces.
THE 38 CAL. ARE STAMPED "AMERICAN BULL-DOG."

No. 380, Cent. Fire, 38 Cal., Octagon Barrel, S. & W. Cartridge................. $6 87
No. 440, Cent. Fire, 44 Cal., Round Barrel, Webley Cartridge...................... 7 50

A pair of unique British Bulldogs (manufacturers unknown) is this duo seen in the 1884 Meacham catalog. The upper "American" British Bulldog has some interesting features as it is equipped with an almost identical cylinder pin and takedown latch as found on the Iver Johnson American Bulldog. Sold as an "American"-style British Bulldog, it is nevertheless supplied with a parrot beak grip. Compounding the confusion is that it mentions it has a "Smith & Wesson" handle! The lower catalog cut displays a very scarce and unusual type of British Bulldog that resembles both a pre-WWI Webley and a Colt double-action Lightning. The mention of it also having a "Smith & Wesson" handle seems suited to the illustration, and overall it is a very advanced-looking British Bulldog apparently introduced to compete with Colt's double-action.

1876 listed numerous Colt, Smith & Wesson and Wesson & Harrington revolvers, but most emphatically stressed the Bulldog's merits, noting: ". . .available also is the much celebrated double-action self-cocking Bulldog pistol." The heyday of the Bulldog continued.

In the historical arena, many notables of the old West had their own affinities for the Bulldog. One known user of the Bulldog during its halcyon days was John Henry Tunstall. Tunstall employed William Bonney, aka Billy the Kid, when he first came to New Mexico. Billy was close to Tunstall, who took the teenager

under his wing. Tunstall's diary noted, "I never went anywhere without my Bulldog." After Tunstall's murder by the Murphy-Dolan faction, Billy became hostile to those elements and played a violent role in the Lincoln County War. At the time of his death, it is rumored that Billy was in possession of a .41 Colt Thunderer with the backstrap engraved "Billy." This has never been authenticated, but it was known he had a self-cocker on his person when he was shot at the Maxwell ranch. There is a distinct possibility that Billy could have had a double-action Bulldog on his person – perhaps even Tunstall's own revolver, obtained after his mentor had been killed. Nothing substantiates this, however.

A place where the British Bulldog was always reported in detail was in Bodie, California. It seems the newspapers of this town had an affinity for reporting incidents involving Bulldog revolvers. The paper carried various accounts in the late 1870s and early 1880s, some of which included that a mining employee on October 2, 1879, put a Bulldog to his head and took his own life. Another article mentioned that a miner staying at "Spanish Dora's brothel" was robbed of $15.00 and his British Bull Dog. One very interesting Bodie news story was the January, 1881 vigilante lynching of an adulterous man who used a Forehand & Wadsworth 38-caliber Bulldog to kill the husband of a woman he was seeing!

One notable fan of the British Bulldog was outlaw Bob Dalton. In 1892 when the Dalton gang raided Coffeyville, Kansas, during the botched bank jobs in that town, nearly the entire band was killed or seriously wounded. The Condon Bank bookkeeper, Tom Babb, found a 38-caliber British Bulldog in the vest pocket

Identifying the actual manufacturer of the Meacham Arms Co. American Bull Dog was easy if one knew that the American eagle logo was a trademark of the Iver Johnson Company! The grips on this specimen are perfect, without cracks or developing hairlines.

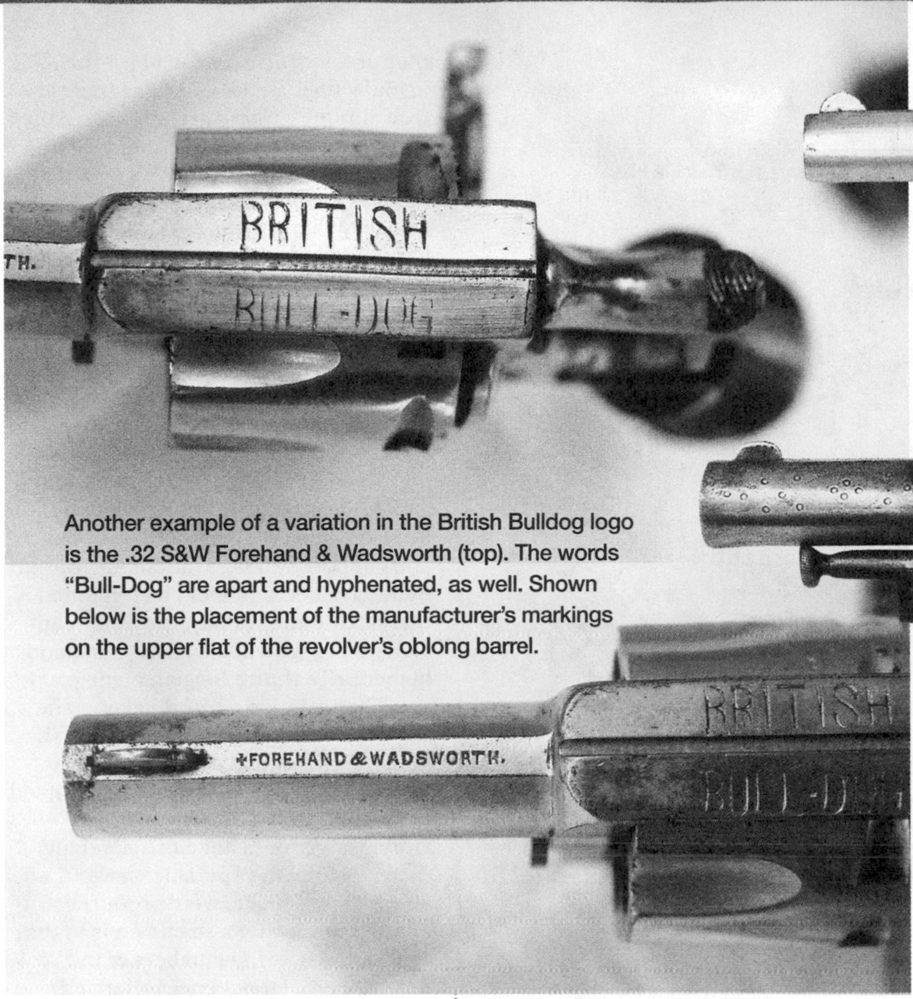

Another example of a variation in the British Bulldog logo is the .32 S&W Forehand & Wadsworth (top). The words "Bull-Dog" are apart and hyphenated, as well. Shown below is the placement of the manufacturer's markings on the upper flat of the revolver's oblong barrel.

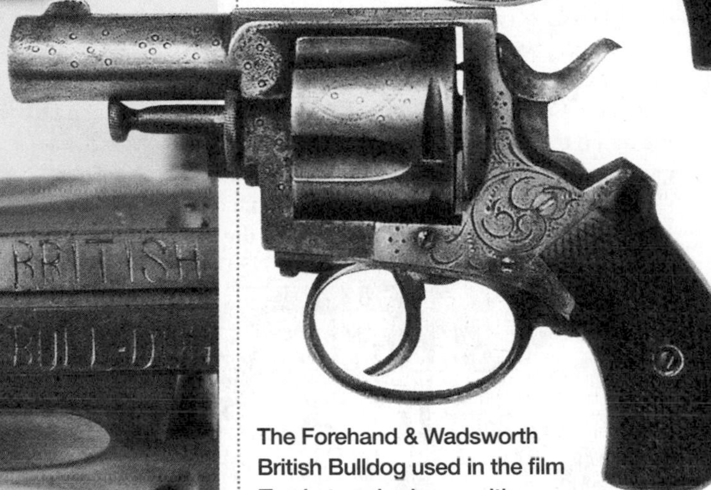

The Forehand & Wadsworth British Bulldog used in the film *Tombstone* is shown with a unique 44-caliber engraved Belgian British Bulldog with a worn gold-brushed finish that is disappearing with time.

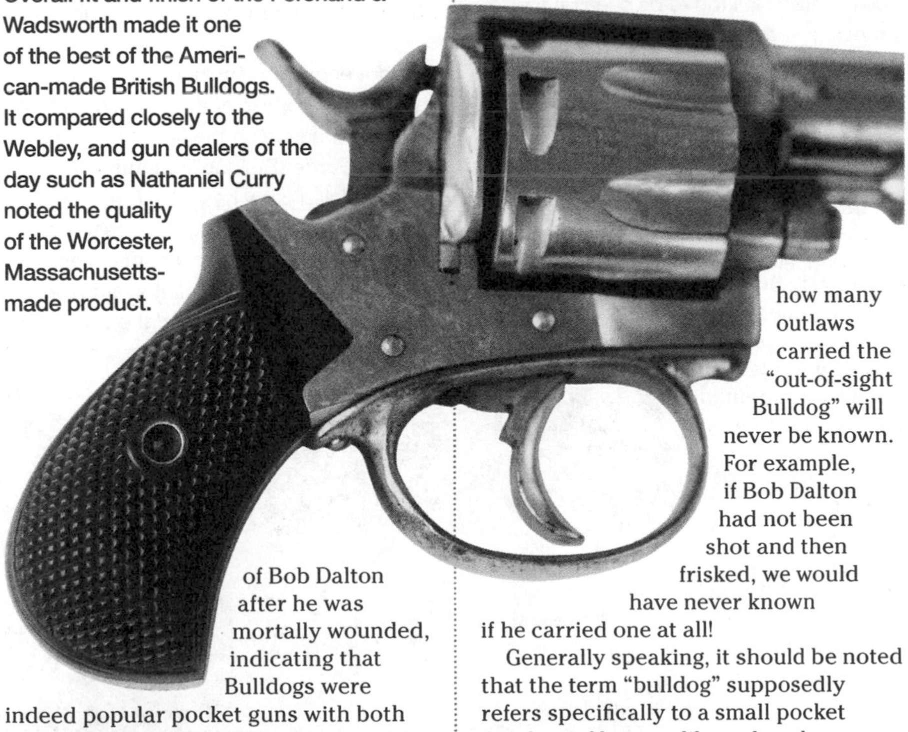

Overall fit and finish of the Forehand & Wadsworth made it one of the best of the American-made British Bulldogs. It compared closely to the Webley, and gun dealers of the day such as Nathaniel Curry noted the quality of the Worcester, Massachusetts-made product.

how many outlaws carried the "out-of-sight Bulldog" will never be known. For example, if Bob Dalton had not been shot and then frisked, we would have never known if he carried one at all!

of Bob Dalton after he was mortally wounded, indicating that Bulldogs were indeed popular pocket guns with both outlaw and law-abiding citizen alike. The revolver he carried on that day is now in the Dalton Museum in Coffeyville. Just

Generally speaking, it should be noted that the term "bulldog" supposedly refers specifically to a small pocket revolver of large caliber – but the general design was so popular that smaller calibers of 32 and 38 were also marketed

as Bulldogs. *[Editor's note: During this same period, Connecticut Arms & Manufacturing Co. of Naubuc, Connecticut, also manufactured a single-shot .44 derringer called the Hammond Bulldog. –DMS]* The British and American Bulldogs were as popular in the East as in the West, but received more attention in the Wild West. Even Charles Strauss, the mayor of Tucson, Arizona, carried a beautifully engraved British Bulldog with fancy stocks in the early 1880s. This particular specimen is on display at the Arizona Historical Society.

THE BULLDOG AS A COLLECTIBLE

Modern-day Old West fans have taken a liking to the Bulldog. Some of today's shooters have resurrected them and a number of obsolete brass manufacturers have recently informed the author that there has been a noticeable demand for .44 Webley/Bulldog cases in the last five years. At the present time, double

This full left hand view of the Iver Johnson/ Meacham Arms American Bulldog shows its design held several improvements over the Webley British Bull- dog. The barrel on the Amer- ican Bulldog could be removed from the frame as a separate piece, where the British models had the barrel permanently attached to the frame by sweating, brazing or some other method, and then ground smooth at several points. Though sold in three calibers (.32, .38, and .44), the last must have been the most popular as few examples of the American Bulldog in the smaller calibers are encountered.

This Forehand & Wadsworth British Bulldog is owned by Peter Sherayko of Caravan West Productions and is perhaps the best- known British Bulldog to be seen on the movie screen. This particular revolver was used by actress Joanna Pacula's character "Big Nose Kate" in the epic 1993 Western *Tombstone*. Though used only in the card table dispute in one scene in the beginning, it shows that informed attention to detail ensures that historically correct firearms, such as the British Bulldog, get their due.

they are, for the most, all of pre-1898 manufacture, which classifies them as true antiques. There are, however, some that may have been built after 1898, but these would probably be made as double-actions in the "suicide special" category that are easy to spot as many have dated patent markings. Production of the classical British Bulldogs began to wane in the mid-1890s, but by that time there were plenty in circulation.

It is the Webley-made British Bulldog most collectors see as the genuine forerunner of all Bulldogs. Costwise, Webley variations have lately risen as high as $400, depending on condition and grade. At gun shows or auctions, Bulldogs of all different varieties, makes, and calibers still seem abundant, but the Bulldog collector should be reminded that next to the Webley, the American- made Bulldogs will normally command a higher price than a Belgian-made prod- uct. The varieties of the Belgian-made Bulldogs are, however, endless and the guns vary radically in overall quality.

For a comparison of value, a Forehand & Wadsworth Bulldog is noticeably more expensive (aside from a Webley) than any foreign copy, since fewer than an estimated 90,000 were produced. Though the author's specimen is in the 85,000 range, serial numbers of the F&W revolver serial numbers overlapped so radically that one cannot reliably date them. The F&W British Bulldog is

The dot engraving flanking the logo on this Belgian copy is of a very plain pattern. Note the marking on the upper example has the words "Bulldog" together. The lower Belgian copy has "Bull Dog" as separate words stamped to be read from the right whereas the upper specimen must be read from the left. It seems foreign manufacturers have marked the trademark logo in varying methods and styles.

actions are not allowed in Single Action Shooting Society competition, but may make for an interesting novelty – or "side" –match. It would be nice to see the "self-cockers" allowed to have their own category in the future. It is important to mention here that the Bull- dog revolver made a comeback in the 1970s when Charter Arms Company in Connecticut added a "Bulldog" revolver to its line. Keeping with tradition, they chambered it for a 44-caliber cartridge, namely the powerful .44 Special. The five-shot wheelgun had a 3-1/2" barrel, rounded butt, and was an improvement on an old design. The Charter Arms Bulldog, however, got bad press when it was used in several murders by David Berkowitz, later convicted in the Son of Sam cases in New York City.

The British Bulldog is quickly becoming the new generation of classical ordnance of the Old West to find acceptance in collector circles. One of the niceties of Bulldog collecting is that

Side by side, the rear frames of the American Bulldog (left) and the British Bulldog (right) clearly show the smooth, fluid lines of the former contrasted to the squarish look of the latter.

A comparison of the Iver Johnson/Meacham Arms Co. 44-caliber American Bulldog vs. a 44-caliber Belgian British Bulldog. Note the size of the former–built with a larger frame than the Belgian copy, comfortable in large hands.

Note the petite, well-contoured lines of the Forehand & Wadsworth British Bulldog (top), contrasted to a typical Belgian Bulldog. The F&W is far less "boxy" than its European counterpart.

yet not listed in *Flayderman's Guide to Antique American Firearms and their Values* since so few exist. It should be mentioned that Forehand & Wadsworth also produced another double action with bird's-head grips that was marked on the frame "American Bulldog." Its production numbers are unknown and the author has seen no early advertisements for it. Some of the Belgian copies have medium- to lower-grade engraving, which can enhance value, and there are other lower-quality specimens being found with oblong bores!

Until the last 10 years, it appears that Bulldogs in all categories were often lumped into the "scrap iron" category of antique firearms. Times have indeed changed! In general, an upsurge in value is starting to occur to the Bulldog, much like that which transpired in the 1950s and '60s when Smith & Wessons and Merwin & Hulberts were inexpensive on the gun show circuit–but have now become premium antique firearms.

Currently, the Bulldog is still quite affordable, and there should be enough for everybody, at least for the present. Prices have been on the rise over the last decade, indicating growing interest in the once-neglected area of Bulldog collecting. Having been a student of these little fistfuls of power for well over 30 years, I've found that out of the 300-plus Bulldogs I have owned or examined, there are more than 30 variations from my own examinations alone. With the huge numbers of manufacturers, designs, calibers, special features, etc., one can create his own collecting theme on a single specimen within this family of firearms. Even the various styles of the legendary logo, "British Bulldog" on these ultra-compact belly guns, is an area of study itself!

As a final tribute, it should be remembered that the basic design of the Webley British Bulldog influenced the future of the large-frame, break-top Webley military revolver that served admirably in three major wars. The nostalgia of the Bulldog is not far from my mind each time I travel to Worcester, Massachusetts and pass by the city's old mills and factories. It's bittersweet to recall that this area of New England was once the capital of domestic Bulldog revolver manufacture in the United States.

BY BERNARD H. DiGIACOBBE, M.D.
PHOTOS BY GEORGE E. DVORCHAK JR., M.D.

A CASE STUDY IN INGENUITY: The Marlin Model 90

Those who are familiar with Marlin's imported line of L. C. Smith double shotguns may be surprised to learn that Marlin once offered a sturdy over/under shotgun made entirely in America. We're delighted that Drs. DiGiacobbe and Dvorchak have reintroduced it to us.

"**I**f you have a difficult job, give it to a lazy man and he will find an easy way to do it." And that's just what Ole Horsurd and the good old boys at Marlin did for Sears, Roebuck and Company.

Following the technical and market success of the expensive Browning Superposed and Remington 32 shotguns, Sears, Roebuck and Company petitioned Marlin in 1936 to produce a moderately priced over/under shotgun, one that would be competitively priced with the then-popular repeating shotguns. Because double guns require meticulous attention to the dimensioning and fitting of the many individual components, more than a simple compromise in the standards of external finish would be required to achieve this goal. Marlin used a design by Ole Horsurd (patent no. 2,376,350) that not only met this goal but also provided a lightweight, well-balanced gun with a surprising array of advanced technical features as well. This feat was achieved in part by utilizing internal components of simple shapes that were easy to manufacture with the available technology of the day. More importantly, these parts would function reliably without the critical attention to dimensioning and fitting usually associated with double guns. They were thus able to use ingenuity of design as a substitute for the labor intensive and expensive fitting of the individual components.

The most technically advanced feature of the Marlin Model 90 was its firing system with in-line strikers with in-line restraining sear sur-faces located behind the concentric coil springs.

As this is almost exactly like the earlier 1880s-vintage British Woodward "Acme" side-by-side, it leads one to wonder if Horsurd's simple solution was not to simply copy and adapt a previously-proven concept. Either way, the direct approach of the in-line strikers is more efficient and resulted in a significantly shorter lock time than the acutely angled firing pins required by other conventional over/under designs. The Model 90, however, did not include the intercepting safeties that were a feature of the Woodward side-by-side!

This pattern of vertically arranged strikers did however preclude the use of a conventional top lever and spindle to activate the bottom locking bolt. So, the Model 90 utilized a vertical lever pivoted in its mid-portion and located to the right of the strikers to connect the top lever to the bottom locking bolt. As on some original Parkers, avoiding the large passageway for the spindle resulted in a stronger frame.

Ole Horsurd's patent drawings demonstrate a horizontal cocking lever with a perpendicular upright projection, similar to the cocking lever on a Browning Superposed. However, as anyone familiar with Marlin lever action rifles knows, the Marlin engineers are not averse to placing the pivot point of a lever below the receiver to gain a significant mechanical advantage. On the Model 90, they utilized a vertical cocking lever pivoted within the hollow (and thus thickened) anterior bow of the trigger guard. Placing the cocking lever below the cocking slide thus allows the cocking lever to multiply the linear motion of the cocking rod located in the bottom of the receiver. Because of the extended range of motion of this and other components, their functioning is unaffected by subtle dimensional inaccuracies. The design did however require a

Overall view of the gun. Despite its utilitarian external finish, the Marlin Model 90 demonstrates surprising good handling characteristics thanks to the overall light weight and favorable balance. The depth of the fore-end is offset by the use of a pistol grip stock maintaining favorable barrel-hand relationship.

While some will find the thickness of the anterior bow of the trigger guard objectionable, it does allow for ideal geometry of the cocking lever and thus should be appreciated for its functional significance.

split front hook and split rear locking lug to accommodate the cocking rod. Like the bulkier top slide of the Remington 32, this system is to be appreciated for its functional beauty rather than mere aesthetics.

The design of the conventional sliding top safety is an excellent example of how ingenuity was substituted for the precise fitting of individual components. The especially long trigger blades are pivoted at their extreme forward positions. This maximizes the distance to the restraining surface of the safety at the very back of the trigger blades. Thus, even with loose fitting, these components will function satisfactorily by preventing contact of the mid-portion of the trigger blades with the sears.

Otherwise, the internal components have a surprisingly modern appearance. Stampings are utilized wherever feasible and wire or coiled wire springs are used throughout. These wire springs are not only cheaper than conventional leaf springs, but they are also significantly less prone to breakage. Whether fitted with conventional double triggers or the non-selective inertia type trigger introduced in 1954, these trigger components are mounted on a separate sub-frame assembly.

Costs restraints mandated the use of a conventional full-length hinge pin under the bolt rather than stub hinge pins as used on the contemporary Remington 32. Not only is a full-length hinge pin inherently stronger, it also allows for a worn, loose gun to be readily re-tightened by simply fitting a larger pin. Of greater significance, the increased depth of this system allowed for greater freedom of design of the internal components of the firing system. In addition, it allowed the use of larger components, which are not only easier to manufacture than smaller components but are also better suited to restrain the forces of the powerful main springs of the firing mechanism.

All of these ingenious mechanisms were housed within an equally advanced frame. The tangs and their vertical cross supports were forged integral with the frame and, together with the use of a through-bolt for the butstock resulted in a rigid system that without resorting to expensive fittings of any of the components. The thickened anterior portion (but not bottom and posterior portion) of the trigger guard was also forged integral with the frame. As on the current Ruger over and under, the vertical seam between the monobloc and frame extends to the very top of the receiver without an expensive-to-fit horizontal shroud covering the top of the seam. The inner surfaces of the receiver were subtly relieved to reduce friction upon the opening and closing of the barrels.

However, as every silver lining has a cloud, there is unfortunately a large rectangular window at the bottom of the receiver that accommodates the bolting lug. The anterior bearing surface of this lug is supported by the receiver as on a Browning Superposed. However, unlike the Browning Superposed with its neatly fitted cocking lever, the loose fitting of the cocking slide and, worse yet, the large gap beneath the cocking slide is more than a little unsightly. A plate to cover this area, perhaps an easy-to-fit round plate, would have been a valuable addition to the design. While Marlin did experiment with aluminum frames, none was offered for sale.

Because of the metal alloy used in the Model 90's frames, they could not be blued with conventional blueing techniques. This accounted for the frames' unusual blue-black finish. Perhaps the most important feature of the frames, however – and one that contributed to the ideal handling characteristics of the gun – was the use of a smaller and lighter frame for the 16- and 20-gauge versions that were introduced in 1937,

as well as an even smaller frame for the .410 version that was introduced in 1939.

Similarly, the Marlin Model 90s were fitted with thin-walled lightweight barrels that also contributed to their good handling characteristics. Side ribs were fitted (with soft solder) until about 1950. After this, the barrels were separate except for small stub ribs affixing the muzzles. Surprisingly, a top rib was never fitted. Instead, an approximately 1/8"- wide matted surface was embossed along the top surface of the upper barrel. To those of us accustomed to top ribs, even on repeaters, it is surprising how well Marlin's system works. It is worth noting at this point that many of the top British quality over and unders of the first half of the century were devoid of top ribs and/or full-length ribs as a weight-saving contrivance that saved approximately 1/8 of a pound! Whether Marlin omitted the top rib as a cost saving or weight saving maneuver is insignificant; what is significant is how well their system works. And, if you agree with me, we're not alone. In 1936, Browning cataloged a model of their Superposed with a stripped matted barrel surface replacing the top rib. Sim-

No apologies needed! The large size of these components not only makes them easier to manufacture, but less prone to malfunction from acquire congealed lubricants and rust. Also note the use of coil springs and music wire springs as well as fabricated components and sub-frame for the trigger mechanism and Sears. Surprisingly modern features for a gun designed in 1936! Less obvious is the arch of the bottom of tang in an effort to lower the axis of the barrels in the shooter's grip to promote favorable handling characteristics.

ilarly, the minimal sculpting of the top of the monobloc was an appropriate choice given the cost constraints imposed.

On the earlier versions of the Marlin Model 90, the forend was secured to the lower barrel by a U-shaped flat spring within the forend. This not only considerably simplified production but also resulted in an especially neat appearance. Unfortunately, removing or reattaching the forend required considerable effort. On the earliest versions, the forend iron extended above the hinge but not all of the way to the top of the frame, similar to the system used by Browning on their Superposed. The last series of forends utilized a more conventional latch mechanism to secure it to the barrels. On most Model 90s, however, the forend iron did extend all the way to the top of the surface of the frame as in the model shown in the accompanying photographs. While the choke designation was not indicated on the barrels, the models fitted with 28" barrels were choked full and modified and the 26" barrel versions were choked improved cylinder and modified. The 30" barrels were offered in 12-gauge only and were choked full and modified.

All of these design advantages resulted in a gun that was surprisingly well balanced (at the hinge joint) and light in weight. The 12-gauge versions weighed approximately 7-1/2 lbs. The 16- and 20-gauge guns weighed only 6-1/4 lbs., while the .410 versions weighed a scant 5-3/4 pounds. The favorable handling characteristics were no doubt enhanced by the narrowness of the forend used in conjunction with a pistol grip configuration of the butstock. In addition, the concave shape of the bottom tang allowed the gun to be appropriately grasped closer to the axis of the lower barrel despite the increased depth the receiver required by the under-bolting.

Between its introduction in 1937, and before production was halted in 1942, for World War II, approximately 15,000 Model 90s were produced. Those sold through Sears, Roebuck and Company after World War II were sold under the Ranger trade name. When production was resumed after World War II, approximately 11,000 double-trigger versions were produced between 1952 and 1957. Those sold through Sears Roebuck were sold under the J.C. Higgins name, although the Marlin name was included on post-World War II Sears models. While production ceased in 1959, sales from inventory continued until 1963, and between 1953 and 1963 approximately 8,200 single, non-selective trigger versions were sold. A word of caution at this point: those interested in buying a Marlin Model 90 on the used gun circuit should be aware that parts and repairs are no longer offered by the factory; however, as of this writing parts can be obtained through the Gun Parts Corporation (formerly known as Numrich).

At this point, two Model 90 variations are worth noting. One was the combination gun variant offered in .22 Long Rifle/.410 with an estimated fewer than 500 produced. On special order, .22 Hornet/.410 or .218 Bee/.410 versions were available. Another rare version was the Skeeting version produced in 1939 and 1940. These were special ordered guns intended for skeet shooting or upland game hunting and were proof tested with special heavy loads and had specially adjusted chokes. They were also fitted with special figure American black walnut and featured hand engraving.

So, why the demise of the Marlin Model 90? Well, in sales as in wing shooting, timing is everything, and timing could not have been worse for the Marlin Model 90. It was introduced at a time when Americans were enamored with repeaters rather than doubles. In fact, the resurgent interest in doubles did not occur until the late 1970s, long after production of Marlin Model 90 ceased. The gun was also introduced during the

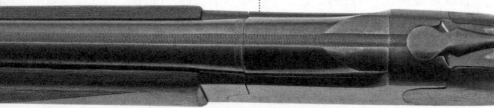

Although the stippled stripe along the top surface of the barrel may at first seem pretentious, it does function surprisingly well as a top rib. It also totally eliminates the extra weight associated with a conventional top rib.

The least flattering view of the Marlin Model 90 shows the protruding bottom lugs and cocking rod. Realize however that they do contribute to the forward restraint of the barrel assembly and provide for a full length sliding bolt at the rear of these lugs.

View of the monobloc. While the simple shapes and minimal contouring of the top surface greatly simplified production, they in no way impede the handling characteristics nor functionality of the gun.

Eliminating the Model 90's side ribs saved both money and weight.

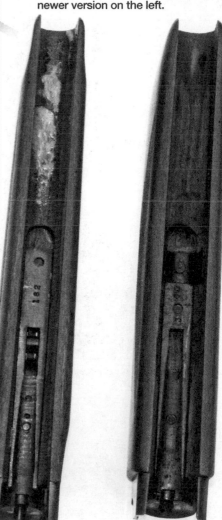

fate if it had been manufactured to better standards of external finish and, perhaps manufactured overseas where this increased quality of finish could have been achieved at a lower cost. As for the legacy of the

As a cost-saving measure, ejectors were not fitted, a shortcut that in no way impeded the function of the shotgun. Notice the thin walls of the chambers, accounting in part for the light weight and overall handling characteristics of the Model 90.

hard times of the 1930s, a time when few people could afford a new gun – and those who could, could generally afford the more expensive Browning Superposed or Remington 32. Worse yet were the good times of the American economy following World War II. Not only had American labor become too expensive to permit production of a double gun in this country, but because of the increased cost of American labor, these same workers wanted and were able to afford a double gun of finer external finish. It is interesting to speculate what would have been the Model 90's

Marlin Model 90, it offered an inexpensive, well-balanced over/under with an array of technical advancements to several generations of shooters who would not buy or could not afford a double of finer finish. Now, decades later, their children and grandchildren can purchase many of these same technical advancements in a more expensive double.

Inside view of the forends with the newer version on the left.

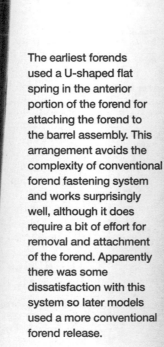

The earliest forends used a U-shaped flat spring in the anterior portion of the forend for attaching the forend to the barrel assembly. This arrangement avoids the complexity of conventional forend fastening system and works surprisingly well, although it does require a bit of effort for removal and attachment of the forend. Apparently there was some dissatisfaction with this system so later models used a more conventional forend release.

Make mine a .32!

BY ROBERT H. CAMPBELL

The Charter Arms .32 proved to be surprisingly true at moderate range. This is a neat field gun. At 19 ounces you do not know it is there.

Seasoned handgunners will probably flip to the pages in this book showing .44 and .45 ballistics. But some will realize that small calibers are great for just plain ol' shooting. I am a hunter and consider personal defense important, but I own quite a few "unnecessary" handguns that give me great pleasure. We all should own a good .22 or two and I haven't met a man so big and burly he cannot appreciate the rimfire. But mention that you enjoy shooting a .32 and your testosterone level becomes suspect.

Nevertheless, the .32 has its place in my shooting life and it is often a better fit between the .22 and .45 than the .38. The .32 is an ideal fit for small game and for breaking new shooters into the centerfire shooting game. While I own and use as many handguns as finance and matrimonial harmony will allow, a good .32 won't break the bank. Plus, often as not, in a midsize handgun the .32 is very accurate.

I hadn't owned a .32 revolver in some time until quite recently. However, my youngest child is just becoming interested in handguns and she is able to handle them as long as they're on the light side. Little sister often fires a .22 /.410 over/under with her name on it. She sometimes helps her Dad load ammunition. Her interest wanes at times but she is a good range buddy and helper. I think a .32 is a good starting point for her in centerfire shooting.

My youngest son, in contrast, is a military intelligence officer who is proficient with any number of tools from the Ek Commando knife to the SAW. But on his own time and his own dime he loves cowboy shooting. A Ruger Single Six .22 and a USFA Rodeo .45 Colt are among his favorites. He practices with his Smith & Wesson Chiefs Special .38 and Novak Custom .45 automatic because they are "obligatory." But his .32 is a Ruger Single-Six "Baby Vaquero" chambered in .32 H&R Maghnum.

THE RUGER BIRDSHEAD .32 H&R MAGNUM

First, big brother's .32. The birdshead grip Ruger illustrated has been called a Baby Vaquero because it features fixed sights and a color case hardened frame as well as fixed sights. This

The bird's-head grip of the Ruger .32 Magnum is comfortable and eye-catching, a good choice for all-around service in such a light handgun.

is a very friendly, fast-handling and ac-curate cowboy gun. (The Baby Vaquero, alas, has been discontinued by Ruger.)

You may argue that a serious hand-gunner should have a pistol with ad-justable sights. I have been involved in shooting as serious as it gets and that is why I never underestimate rug-ged fixed sights. I appreciate fixed sights and, truth be told, the wide notch and prominent post found on modern revolvers is a big improve-ment over what was once the norm.

The Ruger is a handy revolver with good performance, and it proved accu-rate in initial testing with Black Hills 85-gr. JHP. A two-inch group at 25 yards gave me an incentive to keep firing and experimenting with the .32 H & R Mag-

These two .32s are neat, good shooting revolvers just perfect for recreation.

num. Frankly, I have not had much truck with the .32 Magnum because I felt it was a mistake to tout it as a defense car-tridge. I still believe it is not enough for that application. But as a field car-tridge for raccoon and the like it is a sure shot. When the bullet strikes a steel target at the range with sufficient ve-locity, the timbre is much the same as a .38. The Ruger is a good recreation-al shooter for my son and something that could bring home meat if need be.

THE SMITH & WESSON .32 REGULATION POLICE

The second revolver was a good find, obtained more with little sister in mind. This is a Smith & Wesson double action .32 Regulation Police (pre-Model 31) of

The old .32 Regulation Police proved accurate with factory ammunition. The average factory load clocked a little over 600 fps.

If you have fat fingers you may have a difficult time of it with the .32. We used a single stage in loading just a few rounds with Starline Brass as there was no need to resize the brass.

LOADING .32-CALIBER SHOTSHELLS

There are no .32-caliber factory shotshell cartridges available. Don't let that bother you!

Loading .32 caliber shotshells is relatively simple. Take a spent case and punch two wads out of a cardboard box (shoebox material works well). Load 2.0 grains of Titegroup into the case; in general, lighter powder charges give better patterns than heavy ones. Put one wad over the powder charge and seat it firmly, making sure it's centered in the case. Now pour in a weighed 65 grains of small birdshot. Then place the overfill wad over the shot charge and give the case a good crimp.

The results are pretty good, beating the .22 LR shotshell by a wide margin and coming close to the .38 Special shotshell's effectiveness at close range.

sembling a miniature Military and Police .38, this is a friendly and well-made revolver. I did not approach the .32 Smith & Wesson Long completely in the dark. As a teenager I had taken squirrels and rabbits with my grandfather's Colt Detective Special .32 (chambered for the Colt New Police .32, a .32 Smith & Wesson Long with a flat-point bullet). I did not realize at the time that the factory ammunition I fired was breaking perhaps 650 fps. But it did the business. I did some of my first handloading with a Lee Loader and swaged wadcutters from the now defunct Taurus bullet company. I never remember having more than a dozen or so loaded cartridges on hand at a time for hunting, but I learned how to bring home the meat on a limited budget. The Colt .32 of my grandfather's taught me a great deal about marksmanship. This was a smooth revolver with good sights and a clean trigger break. I hadn't a nickel to spare, and the .32 was cheap to feed. But the Colt went by the wayside when I obtained my first S&W Model 10 .38 Special and the rest is history.

THE ADVANTAGES OF HANDLOADING

The .32 Smith & Wesson Long is often regarded as a pipsqueak but it is feisty for its size. It's about 35 percent more powerful than the shorter .32 Smith & Wesson (sometimes referred to as the .32 S&W Short), but that is damning with faint praise. The .32 S&W Long is easy to fire well and often quite accurate. Realistically, a well-placed .22 is probably as effective and the .22 Magnum a better field gun. A 98-gr. RNL bullet at 650 fps simply is not a powerhouse. But as is the case with many other calibers, a handloader can completely transform this cartridge. A 100-gr. SWC at 800 fps is just one example.

The .32 H & R Magnum is a cartridge I once dismissed out of hand, but the cartridge has grown on me, largely due to the excellent handguns that chamber it. Factory loads are limited as they must be safe in any number of revolvers of dubious strength. It is interesting that the .32 Magnum is ballistically similar to the old .32 French Long automatic pistol cartridge. This long .32 Automatic is hotter than many realize and quite accurate to boot. I have tested the factory loads for the .32 Magnum and while they are okay as far as they go, the cartridge comes alive with handloading. The factories must ensure that their

Top to bottom: a factory 98-gr. RNL, a 100-gr. Magnus SWC in the .32 Smith & Wesson Long case, and the .32 H & R Magnum with the 85-gr Hornady XTP. The handloads are by far the more useful.

loads are safe in the old top-break revolvers by H&R, Iver Johnson and other makers as well as the many light-frame hideouts chambered for the .32 Magnum. An 85-gr. JHP at 1100 fps may not qualify as a Magnum in your book, but

(below) Sierra, Hornady, Magnus. If we could use only one bullet it would have to be the cast SWC. The flat nose and sharp shoulder should do just fine for small game. We have whacked pretty big bunnies with less. (bottom) The Magnus 100-gr. SWC performed well. When fired into ballistic simulant, the nose often smeared.

THE NEW KID ON THE BLOCK: THE .327 FEDERAL

Now we have a new .32-caliber star on the horizon! The .327 Federal is a cartridge with the energy to match comparable .357 Magnum defense loadings. The .327 obviously has been given the ".327" designation in order to give the impression of equivalence with the popular .357 cartridge. After all, ".357 SIG" sounds better than "9mm Bottlenecked Long" and ".32 Magnum Magnum" doesn't roll off the tongue smoothly. Nevertheless, a .32 Magnum Magnum is pretty much what the .327 Federal is.

The .327 Federal breaks about 1350 fps with the 115-gr. Gold Dot bullet. This is comparable to the 110-gr. .357 Magnum loading from three- and four-inch revolvers. Horse sense would tell us recoil energy would be the same but that is not the whole story. The .327 Federal works its pressure over a smaller area and the revolvers chambered for the .327 are generally heavier than comparable .357s because of their necessarily thicker cylinders with smaller chambers. Whatever the physics, the .327 kicks less than the .357 while giving the same energy. The thick cylinder may allow even greater velocity than factory loads given careful handloading, but the .327 is pretty hot as issued so hot-rodding it is not recommended. The Gold Dot bullet as in this caliber has been a strong performer in every other caliber, offering a good balance of expansion and penetration.

As of this writing, the revolvers that chamber the .327 Federal are six-shooters built on five-shot .357 frames. Even six 32-caliber chambers still leave plenty of steel as an insurance policy. As an added benefit to .32 revolver aficionados, any revolver chambered in the .327 Federal, such as the Ruger SP101 and the Charter Arms Patriot, will also chamber the .32 S&W, the .32 S&W Long, the .32 Colt New Police, and the .32 H&R Magnum.

Time will tell, but the .327 looks like a winner.

---

compared to the .32 Smith & Wesson Long it certainly is a vast improvement.

I have several favorite bullets for the .32s, and have used most in both the Short and Long .32 revolvers. A hardcast 100-gr. SWC as offered by Magnus Bullets is accurate and tough enough for small thin skinned game including turkey and bobcat. Certain pests and varmints are well advised to get out of the way of a 100-gr. bullet at over 1200 fps. However, I have also enjoyed excellent results with the jacketed bullets.

Sure enough, the Charter Arms Undercoverette is a five-shot .32. For those who are recoil shy or simply don't need a .38, this is a nifty little revolver.

The Hornady 85- and 100-gr. JHP bullets seem to be the most popular. The Sierra 90-gr. JHP is wonderfully accurate and seems to give a degree of expansion. The Hornady 85-gr. XTP is accurate and offers more penetration. The velocity champ is the Hornady 60-gr. XTP. This one is an eye-opener at about 1,400 fps with proper loads.

I have tried quite a few combinations in the Ruger .32 Magnum with good results. While I am impressed with the Hornady 60-gr. bullet in terms of velocity, it strikes considerably below the point of aim with fixed sights. While I could easily remedy this situation by filing the front sight, the end results would be a revolver not usable with heavier bullets including my favorite cast bullet loads. My all-around, go-anywhere/do-anything loads remain those using the 100-gr. SWC. When I wish to use a jacketed bullet in the 85- to 90-gr. range, the point of impact is close enough for field work at 25 yards or so. I have found the .32 Magnum responds well to careful loading. But there are cautions!

I have done quite a bit of work with the .32 Smith & Wesson Long cartridge. I soon realized that a relatively large portion of the case is taken up with powder and we are working with small variations in powder charge. Minor differences in weight result in pressure being driven up substantially. We are often working with loads with ranges of 1.9 to 2.1 grains of powder. While this is certainly economical, you really have to monitor your powder weight and use caution. With the .32 Magnum you use larger powder charges but the basic relationship remains the same. We also use slower-burning powders in the Magnum with some loads and powder charges over ten grains.

OTHER CONSIDERATIONS

There have been reports of short cartridge case life with the .32 H&R Magnum. I cannot comment as I have endured no such instances, but I hedged my bests by obtaining a new supply of Starline brass for both the .32 S&W Long and the .32 S&W Short. I have never regretted this investment. I've enjoyed good results with the same bullets in either caliber, including the inexpensive 78-gr. RNL bullet from Oregon Trail and the 100-gr. SWC from Magnus. I have even used jacketed bullets experimentally in the .32 Smith & Wesson Long. There is insufficient velocity to instigate good bullet upset but there was some expansion with the Sierra bullet at 800 fps. I have chosen to limit velocity in my girl's Smith & Wesson .32 to 800 fps with the 100-gr. bullet. There is no point is stressing this fine old revolver when I have a Magnum available.

Interestingly, my first experiments with the .32 S&W Long were impressive. I fired a single round of the 98-grain factory load into a 273-page hardback book. The bullet stopped at about 50 pages, slightly deformed. This is average performance for the 650 fps load. Among the first loads tested in the Smith & Wesson Regulation Police was a number using enough HP38 to reach 780 fps. The additional130 fps advantage was obvious as the bullet completely penetrated the book and exited! Sometimes a little goes a long way.

When loading the .32 Smith & Wesson Long, all went smoothly although my fingers are a little fat to handle the cartridge cases! I adhere to a strict rule in loading the Starline cases with moderate loads for general use. I do not hot-rod my Starline .32 Smith & Wesson brass for use in the .32 Magnum. Any .32 Smith & Wesson Long round in my loading room is a load safe in the Smith & Wesson Regulation Police. In the .32 Magnum, I have experimented with hot loads and always use the Magnum case.

How well do my .32 S&W Long loads shoot? After a bit of experimentation in discovering a load that strikes the point of impact with the fixed-sight Smith & Wesson, I was able to find several loads that will group into two to three inches at fifteen yards. That is more than adequate for the intended use. The Ruger

The Hornady XTP, Sierra JHP and Magnus SWC all gave excellent results in both .32 calibers and all three handguns.

.32 Smith & Wesson Long Reloading Data in 4" Smith & Wesson Regulation Police

Starline brass, Winchester primer. Data shown for comparison purposes only.

Bullet	Charge (Gr.)/Powder	Muzzle Velocity	15 yard group (")
98-gr. Speer WC	1.7/Bullseye	707 fps	3.0
	1.8/231	713 fps	2.5
100-gr. Magnus	5.0/2400	660 fps	4.0
	5.5/2400	773 fps	3.5
	1.9/231	735 fps	2.8
	2.4/231	790 fps	2.5
	2.4/HP38	780 fps	1.9
	1.8/Titegroup	780 fps	2.0
	2.0/Titegroup	860 fps	2.5
85-gr. Hornady JHP	2.4/HP38	750 fps	2.3
	2.7/HP38	800 fps	2.5
	2.5/Unique	650 fps	3.0
90-gr. Sierra JHP	2.3/HP38	760 fps	2.8
	2.6/HP38	811 fps	3.0

.32 H&R Magnum Reloading Data

Starline brass, Winchester primer. Data shown for comparison purposes only.

Bullet	Charge (Gr.)/Powder	Muzzle Velocity	25-Yd. Group (")
77-gr. RNL	2.4/HP38	790 fps	3.0
	3.0/Titegroup	945 fps	2.0
100-gr. Magnus	2.5/Red Dot	755 fps	2.5
	3.1/Unique	850 fps 1	.9
	4.2/Unique	1134 fps	2.0
	4.0/AA #5	826 fps	2.5
	10.5/H110	1130 fps	2.0
	8.3/2400	1130 fps	2.25
	3.3/231	860 fps	1.8
	11.1/Lil' Gun	1201 fps	1.9
	11.0/Lil' Gun	1050 fps	2.5 (15 yards/ Charter Arms snubbie)
60-gr. Hornady XTP	4.0 Clays	1410 fps	3.0
	7.0/True Blue	1500 fps	2.6
85-gr. Hornady JHP	8.3/2400	1044 fps	2.0
	5.0/Long Shot	1167 fps	2.25
	3.3/HP38	1003 fps	2.0
	11.5/H110	1109 fps	1.9
	12.0/IMR 4227	1200 fps	2.6
	12.0/Lil' Gun	1255 fps	2.0
	5.0/231	1300 fps	2.0
90-gr. Sierra JHP	8.3/2400	1100 fps	3.0
	10.0/Lil' Gun	1156 fps	2.25
	11.5/Lil' Gun	1227 fps	2.0
	11.0/Lil' Gun	1010 fps	3.0 (15 yards/ Charter Arms snubbie)
	10.5/IMR 4227	1200 fps	2.5
	9.0/H110	990 fps	2.25
	3.0/Bullseye	870 fps	2.0
100-gr. XTP	2.6/Red Dot	764 fps	3.0
	3.0/Unique	829 fps	3.2
	4.2/Unique	1122 fps	2.5
	10.5/H110	1119 fps	2.0

We used Starline brass for the heavy loads with complete satisfaction.

The Smith & Wesson .32 proved accurate and reliable with a box of MagTech picked up at the shop – it was the least expensive and worked just fine.

revolver will do two and one half inches for five shots at 25 yards, with an occasional brilliant group a bit smaller. This is a revolver that is very friendly to lead bullets and when my son returns home for Christmas he will have a number of boxes at his command!

As for the .32 H&R Magnum, I was thoroughly impressed with the improvements I was able to achieve, all with no high pressure signs and excellent accuracy. I was able to improve factory load performance by one hundred to one hundred fifty feet per second on average, while retaining excellent accuracy. This is with the strong Ruger single action. As for the maximum loads listed, these loads are intended only for conversational and educational value. *For actual use, the shooter is well advised to begin fifteen per cent below my maximum and use caution.* This is a caliber that truly demands an experienced handloader to achieve its potential. All loading data is given for informational purposes only. What is safe in my revolvers is not necessarily safe in yours.

I also compared these loads in a lightweight Charter Arms .32 Magnum. Most .32 Magnum revolvers are six-shot versions of the five-shot .38. Not the Undercoverette, a purpose-designed lady's gun. This revolver features a five-shot .32 Magnum cylinder. This certainly gives an extra degree of strength for the few of us who will handload for this revolver. But the oft-touted advantage of an additional shot in the six-shot .32s versus the five-shot .38 is shot to pieces with this revolver. Just the same, it is very easy to shoot well and proved out a good performer with full-power Magnum loads. There were a couple that showed sticky extraction but they were at the very top end. After all, a load program with only one handgun doesn't tell us much and the Char-

ter was a valuable addition to it. When using the Smith & Wesson and Taurus light-frame revolvers they will perform in a similar fashion. So cut the charges fifteen percent or so for light revolvers.

I have never experienced any case life problems with the .32 Smith & Wesson Long and expect my Starline and commercial brass to last quite a while. But we have been warned of poor results with competing brass. In fact, I suffered loose primer pockets with some brass after a handful of loads. Common sense tells us to use Starline brass and use the heaviest loads sparingly.

Heavy .32 revolvers may be able to handle loads somewhat stiffer than those shown here. However, given the variety and age of all the .32 revolvers out there, my editor and I have decided not to tempt overzealous hand-

loaders by showing any real firecrackers. Being the strongest of the .32s, the Ruger certainly has the most flexibility in regard to diet. The Charter Arms Undercoverette also has some potential but with its two-inch barrel and the need to load considerably lighter, you must put the results in perspective. On the other hand, the Charter is small enough to disappear into the pocket. With a 100-gr. bullet at 1,000 fps it would be enough to deliver the *coupe de grace* to downed game or protect your recoil-shy spouse if she cannot handle a .38 loaded with wadcutters.

Overall, I am satisfied with the results from my .32s. Well, from my kid's .32s. Me, I'm too mean and knurly to fool with a .32 – but come to think of it, I sure seem to be using them a lot lately!

A close view of the Gerfen rifle and the best cartridges.

WINCHESTER
Supreme

20 Supreme
Centerfire Rifle
Cartridges

THE ELUSIVE
Gerfen Rifle
BY J. B. WOOD

In the single-shot falling-block rifle, over the past hundred years, there have been no really new designs. Any gun of this type would usually have some elements that could be traced back to Aydt, or Fraser, or Browning. Even the excellent Ruger of modern times has some Fraser and Farquharson echoes, though it is an improvement on both designs.

In the last decade of the previous century, though, there was a falling-block rifle that was unlike any of these. It was the work of Raymond Gerfen of San Antonio, Texas. There were numerous fine little features hidden in the Gerfen rifle's mechanism, but the most immediately noticeable was the shape of the breechblock – it was cylindrical, except, of course, for the flat cartridge contact face at the front.

The rear top of the receiver extended over the breechblock, and when locked in place the top of the block entered a recess in the extension. Below, the round rear of the block was solidly supported by the rear of the receiver, offering a full 180 degrees of contact.

From this description, you can see that it's an extremely strong system.

The massive finger lever locked securely over a cross-pin at the rear. As the breechblock reached full-down position on opening, the ejector was lever-connected to a tip-over plunger with a helical-coil spring, and its function was the same regardless of the speed of the breech opening. Inside the breechblock, the head of the firing pin bears on a rocker lever, the lower tip of the lever being hit by a cylindrical coil-spring-powdered striker. A prop-type sear with good length and leverage directly contacts the top projection of the trigger. When the striker is cocked, an indicator pin protrudes, just to the rear of the safety.

At the rear of the trigger, a lever

The Gerfen rifle with cartridge box.

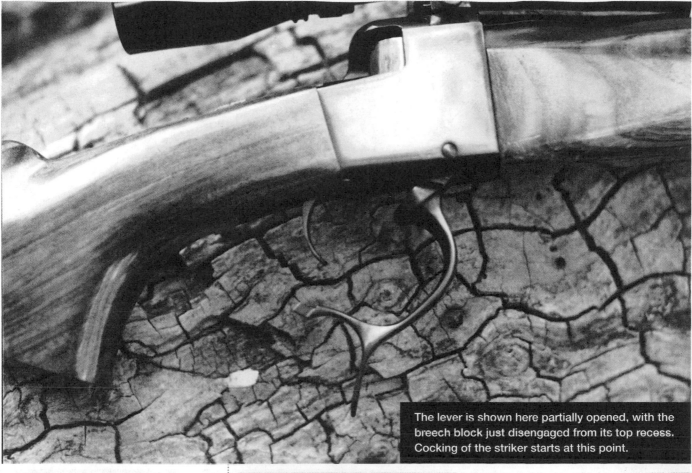

The lever is shown here partially opened, with the breech block just disengaged from its top recess. Cocking of the striker starts at this point.

extends upward to engage the tang-mounted manual safety. When the safety is moved rearward to on-safe position (this is automatic, when the breech is opened), a shelf on the lever bears directly on the inside of the receiver. At the same time, a lug on the lever blocks the striker. It is a very secure system.

At the front of the trigger, another arm bears on the trigger plunger and spring, and at that point there is also an over-travel or stop screw. The tension of the trigger spring is also screw-adjust-

J. B. Wood at the range with the Gerfen rifle. The casual rest is an MTM "Shooting Stick."

able. On the rifle that I tested around 20 years ago, there was no need for any adjustment. The trigger pull was a crisp four lbs.

In addition to the mechanical excellence of the design, the Gerfen rifle also had nice lines and fine balance. I examined and fired two of the guns, in

.243 and .30-06 chambering, and both rifles showed extremely beautiful workmanship. The operation of the action was easy and smooth, evidence of good fitting and good mechanical leverage in the design. At the range, I fired the .30-06 rifle from a casual rest at 50 and 150 yards. The test gun came with a variable

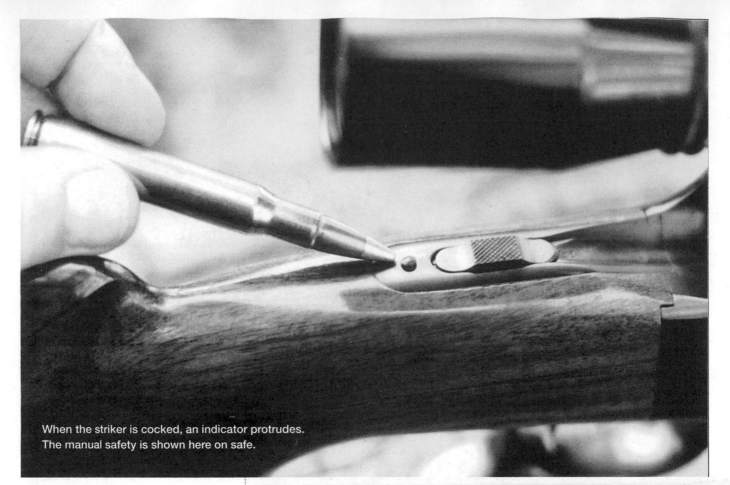

When the striker is cocked, an indicator protrudes. The manual safety is shown here on safe.

6X-18X Burris scope in a Burris mount. I used Winchester Supreme 180-grain Silvertip cartridges. At 50 yards, the result was a single ragged hole that measured one-half inch. At 100 yards, one three-shot group measured just seven-eighths of an inch.

As some readers will know, I am primarily a handgun shooter. If the Gerfen rifle performed this well for me, imagine what it could do in the hands of a real "rifle person"! At the time, Ray Gerfen told me that the barrel used in this particular gun was of unknown European origin, obtained from a surplus dealer. He did note that it was of hammer-forged construction.

With any falling-block single-shot gun, the cleaning of the chamber and bore can be done from the rear by simply opening the action. For more thorough cleaning, removal of the lever and breechblock assembly may be necessary. There is an interdependence of parts that could make this an interesting endeavor. However, instructions for this were supplied with the rifle.

The fore-end is attached by a screw in the front tip that enters a long post attached to the receiver. This leaves

Receiver marking on the Gerfen rifle.

the underside of the fore-end smooth and unbroken, and also offers no barrel contact that might affect accuracy. The barrel is screwed directly into the receiver and is further secured by a large Allen screw. There is a gas vent aligned with the breech face.

With the lever partially opened, just to the point where cocking tension begins, it is possible to move the safety

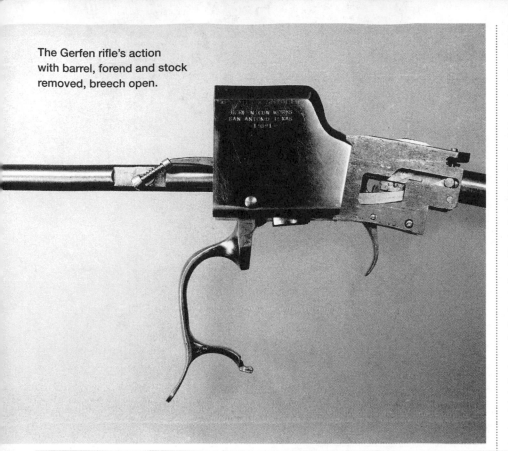

The Gerfen rifle's action with barrel, forend and stock removed, breech open.

to off-safe, pull the trigger, and ease the lever to the closed position. This lowers the striker to the "fired" position without snapping the gun on an empty chamber. This is a good thing to know when putting it away after use.

Back in the early 1990s, Ray Gerfen made exactly 18 of these rifles, and all but one are currently owned by members of the Gerfen family. Since all of the Gerfen rifles were custom-made, a list of specifications would be of little use. However, for those who might be interested, the .30-06 test rifle, with scope, weighed 8-3/4 lbs. The overall length was 39-7/8". When the Gerfen riffles were made, the price quoted for the Model "G90" rifle was $600. Today, for a gun of this quality, multiply that figure by three. I wish, now, that I had purchased one. Because of the designer/maker's age and state of health, no more will ever be made.

Unless some wise entrepreneur acquires the right to make it, that is. In case one of those is reading this, the address is R. Gerfen, 4422 Black Hickory Woods, San Antonio, TX 78249. Here's hoping!

The underside, with the breech opened. Note the stop screw and the spring tension screw, just forward of the trigger.

What were the most popular law enforcement handguns of the twentieth century? The answer might surprise you.

THE COLT OFFICIAL POLICE AND S&W Military & Police

BY PAUL SCARLATA
PHOTOS BY JAMES WALTER

Two Boston PD officers wearing early bulletproof vests. They are armed with Colt O.P. revolvers. (Courtesy Boston PD Records Center & Archives)

I want all of you readers under the age of 30 to sit down before we go any further. I want you seated because I don't want anyone getting dizzy and falling down when I tell you that:

There was a time when American

1944. Canadian infantry officers in the Netherlands. They are wearing holstered No. 2 S&W revolvers. (Courtesy of Clive Law)

police officers DID NOT carry semi-auto pistols!

Yes, children, it's true. From the 1870s until the last decade and a half of the twentieth century, the weapon in the holster of the vast majority of American cops was a revolver. I know some of you are having trouble visualizing this concept, but that's not the end of the story. Not only did the guardians of law and order carry revolvers, but the weapon in question was usually a "plain Jane" blue steel revolver with a barrel of four to six inches, fitted with wooden grips and fixed sights.

I can hear the gasps of disbelief emanating from the readership. "No stainless steel? No adjustable sights? No recoil absorbing, synthetic grips? How could they possibly function with such primitive equipment?" Well, the answer to that question consists of two words: Damn well!

Those of us who are "experienced" shooters remember when the choice of centerfire handguns available to the public was limited. In fact, until 1954 there was only one (!) American-made, centerfire pistol capable of firing a serious cartridge: the .45-caliber Colt M1911. But even this well-respected icon received little notice from the average civilian shooter or police officer. To us Americans, when the word "handgun" was mentioned, the image that immediately came to mind was the revolver.

During the latter half of the nineteenth century, most American police forces did not issue handguns. Officers were usually supplied with a truncheon and a set of handcuffs, and those desiring to carry firearms were required to buy their own. Standards, when they existed at all, were usually limited to what were acceptable calibers and size. Period photos show these nineteenth-century constables wearing long coats and tall hats but nary a holster in sight. This was because most urban agencies required that the handgun be carried out of sight, which was why small, .32-caliber, top-break designs predominated.

The situation began to change in the 1890s as urban police departments became better trained, organized and armed. One of the first was the NYPD, whose new commissioner, Theodore Roosevelt, equipped all officers with a

The equipment of a member of the Boston Police Department, circa 1960. (Courtesy Boston PD Records Center & Archives)

Colt Official Police Revolver. Note the exposed ejector rod, characteristic Colt style grips with medallion and round blade front sight. Except for the latter, the O.P. remained basically unchanged during its long production life.

Smith & Wesson's .38 Hand Ejector Military & Police revolver underwent a number of styling changes. This is a 1940 production gun, one of the last commercial grade revolvers to leave the factory before they switched over to wartime production. It is a "five screw" frame gun with the "skinny" barrel and a lanyard ring.

Colt Official Police Revolver

SIX SHOTS, DOUBLE ACTION

Jointless Solid Frame
Simultaneous Ejection
Swing-out Cylinder

CALIBERS:
.22 Long Rifle (See page 7).
.32-20 (.32 Winchester).
.38 Special. (Using in the same arm .38 Short Colt; .38 Long Colt; .38 Colt Special; .38 Colt Special Hi-Speed; .38 S. & W. Special (full and mid-range loads); .38 S. & W. Special High Velocity; .38-44 S. & W. Special Hi-Speed).

The Famous Colt Matted Frame Top

The "Official Police" Revolver as well as all Colt Service Revolvers, is furnished with the patented Colt matted frame top, eliminating all possibility of light reflection and glare and aiding in sighting. Both of the raised ribs running lengthwise along the top of the frame are deeply cut in a crosswise direction, giving a matted effect which has become unusually popular among shooters. This feature is found only in Colt Revolvers.

General Specifications

LENGTHS OF BARREL: 2, 4, 5 or 6 inches (.22 Cal. 6 in. only). (.32-.20 Cal. 4, 5, 6 in. only.)
LENGTH OVER ALL: With 6 inch barrel, 11¼ inches.
STOCKS: Checked Walnut.
TRIGGER: Checked.

SIGHTS: Fixed, Non-reflecting, giving "Patridge" effect in sighting.
FINISH: Full Blued (or Full Nickel Plated), top of frame matted to eliminate reflection and glare. (.22 cal. Blued only).
WEIGHT: With 6-inch barrel, (.38 caliber) 34 ounces.

Simplicity of design and care in manufacture, resulting in extreme durability, reliability and accuracy make the Official Police Revolver a most acceptable model for all around service. The ample grip with its checked wood stocks is so designed as to snugly fit the hand, regardless of size, while the action is surprisingly smooth and easy for so powerful an arm. The extreme safety in handling provided by its COLT POSITIVE LOCK especially adapts it for service wherever a safe, dependable Arm of medium size and weight to handle the powerful caliber .38 Colt Special cartridge is desirable.

Special Features

Adopted by such Police Departments as New York City, Chicago, San Francisco, Portland, Ore., St. Louis, Los Angeles and many smaller cities, as well as the State Police of Maryland, Delaware, Pennsylvania, Connecticut, New Jersey, etc., etc. Much of the unequalled durability of the Official Police Revolver is due to its sturdy one-piece frame, as well as the exacting care employed in finishing and fitting every part.

5

A page from a 1940 Colt catalog extolling the virtues of their Official Police Revolver. Note that they refer to its cartridge as the ".38 Colt Special."

standard handgun, the Colt .32 New Police revolver – and insisted they receive marksmanship training. This also signified an important technological change as the New Police was a swing-out cylinder revolver. Even then the NYPD was a trendsetting agency and many departments followed suit and adopted the new Colt.

That same year S&W introduced their first swing-out cylinder revolver, the .32 Hand Ejector Model of 1896, which was taken into service by the Philadelphia PD, among others. The race was now on, as these two titans of the American handgun industry began a non-stop, no holds barred competition to see who could capture the lion's share of the U.S. police market.

The year 1899 saw S&W's introduction of the .38 Hand Ejector Military & Police revolver. This medium frame (K-frame), swing-out cylinder revolver was their attempt to garner a military contract. And while the government purchased several thousand, Colt's .38-caliber New Model Army & Navy revolvers remained the standard military sidearm.

The next big step occurred during the first decade of the new century. As is the case today, American police tended to ape the army when it came to sidearms, and the military's acceptance of the .38 Colt revolver convinced many that an upgrading of equipment was called for. While the .32 revolver's popularity with police would continue for a few more decades, the writing was on the wall for all to see: the .38 revolver would be THE next American police handgun of choice. The timing was opportune as the army was getting ready to ditch the .38 wheelgun in favor of one of the new fangled semi-auto pistols. With military sales drying up, Colt began to court police departments and their rivals from Springfield were not far behind!

Cutaway view of a 1960s vintage M&P revolver. (Courtesy of Michael Jon Littman)

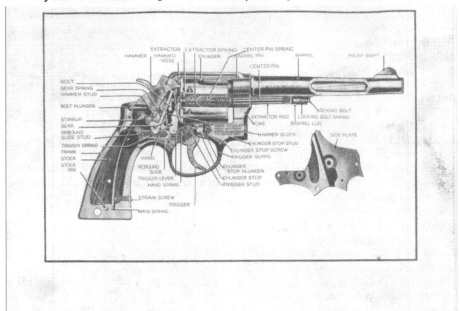

SMITH & WESSON, INC.

SPRINGFIELD, MASS., U.S.A.

THE S&W M&P

The S&W .38 Hand Ejector – let's just call it the M&P – utilized a swing-out cylinder that was locked into the frame by means of a spring loaded center pin passing through the ejector rod and projecting out of the rear of the cylinder. When the cylinder is closed, the end of the center pin snaps into a recess in the recoil plate, locking the cylinder in place. To open, a thumb latch on the left side of the frame is pushed forward, forcing the center pin out of the locking recess and allowing the cylinder to be swung out to the left. Pushing back on the ejector rod forces out a star-shaped extractor, ejecting all the spent cartridge cases simultaneously.

In 1902 the locking system was strengthened by the addition of a underlug on the barrel with a spring-loaded pin that locked into the front end of ejector rod. This system has proven so practical that it has been used on all subsequent S&W revolvers down to the present day.

But perhaps more historically significant was the new cartridge introduced with the M&P. Known as the .38 S&W Special it consisted of a straight-walled, rimmed case 1.14" in length loaded with a 158-gr. lead round-nosed bullet with a rated velocity of approximately 850 fps. This was an definite improvement over the army's .38 Long Colt and within a five years would completely dominate the medium-caliber revolver market to the point where even Colt was chambering revolvers for it.

1908 saw Colt attempt to interest police agencies with a modified New Model Army & Navy revolver: the New Army. They also introduced the smaller .38 Police Positive, which weighed a convenient 22 oz. The Police Positive would prove very popular and it, along with a short-barreled version, the Detective Special, would remain in production until the 1980s. But many agencies wanted a more robust sidearm and to answer this demand, in 1927 the Colt Official Police (O.P.) was released on the market.

THE COLT OFFICIAL POLICE

The O.P. used the same size of frame (I-frame) as the New Army but the frame and trigger guard were reshaped to make it more comfortable and attractive. Unlike some of the earlier Colts, cylinder rotation direction was clockwise and cylinder locking was strenghtened by a single peripheral recess for each chamber engaged by a bolt at the rear of the cylinder. Lastly, a pivoting firing pin replaced the fixed protuberance used on its predecessors.

Lockup was via a pin contained in the recoil plate that entered a recess in the center of a rotating ratchet at the rear of the cylinder, locking it securely in place. To unload the O.P., a latch on the left of

To load or unload both the M&P and O.P., the cylinders were swung out to the left side. Both were traditional "six shooters."

the frame was pulled to the rear (exactly the opposite of the M&P), allowing the cylinder to be be swung out on a crane to the left. As with the S&W, pushing on the ejector rod activated a star-shaped extractor, extracting the spent cartridge cases simultaneously. Both the O.P. and M&P swing out cylinders permitted fast, fumble-free reloading, although it would be many more decades before the perfection of the revolver speedloader really speeded things up.

The O.P. weighed approximately 11 oz. more then the Police Positive and so, depending on what size revolver the customer wanted, Colt had the waterfront covered. In regard to weight, the M&P split the difference between the two Colts.

Toth revolvers function identically – except to unlatch the S&W's cylinder, the thumb latch on the left side of the frame is pushed forward....

...while that of the Colt is pulled to the rear.

Then their cylinders were swung out to the left and their ejector rods pushed to the rear to extract the spent cases from the cylinder.

This entrepreneurial battle royale began with Colt – who traditionally received "better press" – having a distinct advantage. Within a few years, the O.P. was the standard issue sidearm of (among others) the NYPD, LAPD, Chicago, San Francisco, Kansas City, St. Louis, and Portland police departments. The highway patrols of Pennsylvania, New Jersey, Delaware, Maryland and Connecticut (to say nothing of the FBI) soon followed, and sales of the O.P. on the police and civilian markets boomed.

While the O.P. usually outsold the M&P, the S&W was without a doubt the #2 product on the North American police market. Among the more notable agencies adopting it were the police departments of San Antonio, New Orleans, Atlanta, Omaha, Dallas, Philadelphia, and Charleston. Larger agencies included the Michigan and Virginia State Police and the Provincial Police of British Columbia, Quebec and Ontario. Over the years, many agencies approved the use of both revolvers and it was possible to find Colts and Smiths in service concurrently.

Unlike the O.P., the M&P underwent a number of changes and improvements during its production life, the most notable being:

1902: the addition of a underlug on the barrel with a spring loaded pin that locked into the front of the ejector rod.
1904: an optional square butt grip frame and larger grips.
1907: the trigger mechanism was modified to provide a lighter DA trigger pull.
1915: the hammer rebound safety was replaced with a spring activated hammer block which was further improved in 1926.
1944: a mechanically activated, positive hammer block safety.

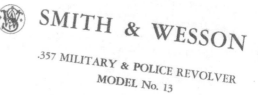

In 1940 Great Britain placed large orders for S&W revolvers to supplement their standard Enfield and Webley revolvers. S&W chambered the M&P for the standard British .380" Mark I cartridge, which was nothing more then the old .38 S&W loaded with a 200-gr. lead bullet (later a 178-gr. FMJ bullet). Deliveries continued until late 1945,

SMITH & WESSON
.357 MILITARY & POLICE REVOLVER MODEL No. 13

PARTS LIST • INSTRUCTIONS FOR USE • MAINTENANCE
SPECIFICATIONS • GUARANTEE

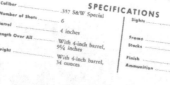

SPECIFICATIONS

Caliber	.357 S&W Special	Sights	Fixed, ⅛-inch serrated ramp front, square notch rear.
Number of Shots	6		
Barrel	4 inches	Frame	Square butt
Length Over All	With 4-inch barrel, 9¼ inches	Stocks	Checked walnut Service with S&W monograms
Weight	With 4-inch barrel, 34 ounces	Finish	S&W Blue
		Ammunition	.357 S&W Magnum, .38 S&W Special Hi-Speed, .38 S&W Special, .38 S&W Special Midrange

SMITH & WESSON
@ A BANGOR PUNTA COMPANY
Springfield, Massachusetts, U.S.A.

Instruction manual for a S&W .357 Magnum Model 13 revolver. This model, with a 3" barrel, was adopted by the FBI. (Courtesy of Michael Jon Littman)

This M&P revolver, made in 1975, has the late style ramp front sight, larger grips, and improved lockwork. It sports the less common (for that era) 6" barrel.

with about 600,000 being delivered to British and Commonwealth forces.

In January 1942, to cut costs and speed up production, British production of the M&P was standardized with a Parkerized finish, smooth wooden grips and 5" barrel. S&W referred to this variation as the "Victory Model," and a "V" prefix was added to the serial number.

With the United States' entry into the war, the U.S. Government placed orders for Victory Model revolvers, which differed from the British pattern in that they were chambered for the .38 Special cartridge and were fitted with 2" and 4" barrels. Over 300,000 U.S. Victory Models were issued to the U.S. Navy, Coast Guard, Merchant Marine and security guards at government installations. Numbers of them eventually saw combat, mainly in the Pacific theater.

While Colt concentrated on producing other weapons for the war effort, beginning in 1942 a version of the O.P., known as the Colt Commando, was produced with a Parkerized finish, smooth trigger and hammer, plastic grips and 2" or 4" barrel. The government bought approximately 48,000 Commando re- volvers, most of which were used by defense plant guards and government security agencies.

S&W TAKES THE LEAD

After the war, both companies resumed production of commercial-grade guns for the police and civilian market. As it had been before 1941, the O.P. proved a bigger seller – but the situation was about to change. During the war years, Colt had concentrated on building 1911 pistols and other weaponry, letting their revolver line languish. S&W, on the other hand, had upgraded their manufacturing processes and had a large pool of trained workers. With the war's end, Colt was stuck with outdated equipment and a shortage of skilled labor.

Additionally, Colt revolvers required more hand-fitting and detail work, which significantly increased their price compared to the competition. Lastly, while

The Colt Commando was a wartime version of the O.P. with a Parkerized finish and plastic grips. (Photo courtesy of Charles Pate)

S&W embarked on a long-term R&D program to improve their revolvers, Colt's management seemed content to live off their reputation and did little to improve equipment, efficiency, their labor force and, most significantly, the product. This recipe for disaster led to S&W's capturing an ever-increasing share of the police and military market.

1948 saw the venerable M&P's designation changed to the Model 10. Seven years later, S&W introduced a K-frame revolver chambered for the .357 Magnum cartridge: the Model 19 Combat Magnum. Police agencies seeking more powerful weapons bought them as fast as they could be produced. Colt attempted to play catchup by re-chambering the O.P. for the .357 cartridge and adding a heavy barrel, adjustable sights and larger grips. Known as the Colt 357 Magnum, sales were disappointing. The popularity of S&W K-frame revolvers, however, continued to grow as such prestigious agencies as the New York State Police, FBI and Royal Canadian Mounted Police adopted them. S&W also sold large numbers of them to police and military forces in Europe, Latin America and Asia.

The handwriting was now on the wall. Colt went through a series of new owners, none of whom seemed interested in innovation; the product line remained stagnant; and quality control took a hit while a series of labor disputes adversely affected production and the company's reputation.

As is evident from a 1976 survey taken by the New York State Criminal Justice Services, by that time, the police market was S&W's private preserve The sidearms used by the 45 state police agencies responding to the survey broke down as follows:

S&W revolvers: 30
Colt revolvers: 4
Both: 4
Other: 1 (S&W 9mm pistol)
Revolver brand not indicated: 6

In an attempt to stay solvent, Colt began dropping models and 1969 found the O.P. missing from the catalog. The name was briefly revived with the Mark III Official Police revolver, but sales were so disappointing that production ceased after only three years. Many shooters and collectors found it disturbing that Colt's product line, reputation and popularity had sunk to such low levels.

The S&W Model 10 continued to be

the firm's bread and butter product, although with the advent of the troublesome – and more violent – 1970s, .357 K-frame revolvers soon became their most popular law enforcement product. Beginning in the late 1980s, the 9mm (and later .40-caliber) semi-auto pistol became the police sidearm of choice, and today it is rare to see an American police officer with a holstered revolver at his side.

Here is the target Vince produced with the M&P. No complaints there! (below) While the Colt's grouping was not quite as good as the Smith's, the difference was minimal.

Specifications

Colt Official Police

Caliber	.38 "Colt Special" (Colt's proprietary .38 Special)
Overall length	9.25"
Barrel length	4"
Weight	33.5 oz.
Capacity	6
Sights	Front, rounded blade; rear, square groove in topstrap
Grips	Checkered walnut

S&W .38 Hand Ejector Military & Police

Caliber	.38 S&W Special
Overall length	9.2"
Barrel length	4"
Weight	29 oz.
Capacity	6
Sights	Front, rounded blade; rear, U-shaped groove in topstrap
Grips	Checkered walnut or hard rubber

Opinions regarding this change of equipment are varied, with both sides making many good points in favor of their preferred weapon but such discussions – which always threaten to become heated – is beyond the scope of this article.

WHICH IS THE BETTER-SHOOTING REVOLVER?

You knew we were going to get around to burning gunpowder sooner or later, didn't you? Accordingly I obtained samples of each revolver: my brother

Offhand shooting was performed at a "regulation" seven yards. Note the fumes from the lubricated, lead bullets.

All test firing was performed with Blacks Hills ammunition.

mance of this pair only serves to buttress my long-held belief that they are one of the most practical type of handguns ever invented. I contend that for over a century they were proved capable of performing any law enforcement task they were called upon to perform and – despite the present popularity of the semi-auto pistol – still are!"

I then pressed him to choose a "winner." After a few moments of hesitation he said, "The M&P. But then I'm prejudiced."

NOTE: I would like to thank Vincent Scarlata, John Rasalov, Charles Pate, Michael Jon Littman, Donna Wells, Jeff Hoffman and Clive Law for supplying materials used to prepare this report. And I'm indebted to Black Hills Ammunition (PO Box 3090, Rapid City, SD 57709. Tel. 800-568-6625) for their kind cooperation in furnishing ammunition.

Bibliography

Boothroyd, Geoffrey. *The Handgun*. New York: Bonanza Books, Inc., 1967.

Canfield, Bruce N. *America's Military Revolvers*. Fairfax, VA: *American Rifleman*, Volume 145, No. 5. The National Rifle Association. May 1997.

Canfield, Bruce N. *U.S. Infantry Weapons Of World War Ii*. Lincoln, RI: Andrew Mowbray Publishers. 1996.

Ezell, Edward Clinton. *Handguns of the World*. New York: Barnes & Noble Books, 1981.

Haven, Charles T. and Frank A. Belden. *A History of the Colt Revolver*. New York: Bonanza Books, 1940.

Henwood, John. *America's Right Arm - The Smith & Wesson Military and Police Revolver*. Pacifica, CA: John Henwood. 1997.

Hogg, Ian V. & Weeks, John. *Pistols of the World*. Northfield, IL: DBI Books, Inc., 1982.

Jinks, Roy G. *History of Smith & Wesson*, 10th edition. North Hollywood, CA: Beinfeld Publishing, Inc. 1996.

Johnson, George B. and Hans Bert Lockhoven. *International Armament*, Volume 2. Cologne: International Small Arms Publishers. 1965.

Neal, Robert J. & Roy G. Jinks. *Smith & Wesson 1857-1945*. Livonia, NY: R&R Books. 1996.

Pate, Charles W. *U.S. Handguns of World War II*. Lincoln, RI: Andrew Mowbray Publishers.1998.

Wells, Donna. *Boston Police Department*. Portsmouth, NH: Arcadia Publishing, 2003.

Vincent provided a very nice M&P made around 1940 while my fellow collector of oddities, John Rasalov, was able to supply an O.P. Despite its being of 1930 vintage, the latter was in very good condition and as mechanically sound as the day it left the factory.

First, several observations as to each revolver's strong and weak points: I found the S&W to be the better balanced of the two, making it a more naturally pointing revolver. Double-action trigger pulls are a subjective matter and while some prefer the way the Colt's stroke has a noticeable stage just before it breaks, I prefer the lighter, stage-free pull of the M&P.

The O.P. was graced with a superior set of sights: a wide, square notch at the rear and the blade of ample proportions up front. While having the same style of sights, the Smith's were smaller and harder to align quickly. In addition, the tip of M&P's hammer spur actually obscured the rear notch until the hammer was slightly cocked. For the life of me I cannot fathom this, and wish someone could explain the reason for it.

When it comes to grips it was a tie. Both were horrible! I do not understand why it took the firearms industry several centuries to figure out that the odds of hitting the target would be greatly improved by a set of hand-filling, ergonomically-correct grips?

In keeping with the proper historical spirit I decided to limit me test firing to the type of ammunition that was most widely used during the era during in which this pair or revolvers had seen service. Black Hills Ammunition kindly supplied a quantity of .38 Special cartridges loaded with the traditional 158-gr. LRN bullets.

While I served as cameraman, my brother Vincent fired a series of six-shot groups with each revolver from a rest at a distance of 15 yards. As can be seen in the photos, both shot to point of aim and produced some very nice six-shot groups. I then set up a pair of USPSA targets at seven yards, and Vince ran two dozen rounds through each revolver, firing them both one-handed and supported.

What can we deduce from this expenditure of ammunition? Inasmuch as my brother Vince did all the shooting, I will quote him:

"I can make several observations," he says. First of all, both revolvers proved capable of excellent accuracy, whether fired from a rest or offhand. And while the Colt's sights were of a more practical design, I shot slightly better with the S&W. Whether or not this was due to the fact that I have much more experience with S&W revolvers, I can't really say. The grips on both revolvers were poorly designed and I believe something as simple as the addition of a grip adapter would improve handling to a significant degree. The Tyler-T Grip Adapter was first marketed in the 1930s and I can understand why! As regards recoil control, with its greater weight, I found I could shoot the O.P. faster but, considering the rather sedate ammunition we used, the difference was not all that great."

Vince summed it all up by saying, "I have long been a fan of the fixed-sight, double-action revolver and the perfor-

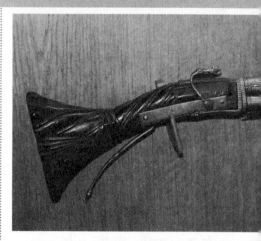

FROM FACTORY TO MEAT ON THE TABLE:
Gunmaking
in the Val du Trompia

BY WM. HOVEY SMITH

A FAIR double shotgun engraved on false sideplates for FAIR Presiden's Luco Rizzini's father. Each side plate features a portrait of one of Rizzini's daughters.

A s the line of hunters slowly proceeded up the forested slopes of Mount Prati Alti that towered over Lake Montedoglio, I did not have time to consider the historic, cultural and scenic attributes of my surroundings. I was hunting the European wild boar, and fresh rootings told me that the hog was not far away.

This part of the hunt was being done the old-fashioned way as recent rains

Davide Pedersoli in his Western U.S. hunting clothes. He likes this style and often purchases them when he is in the U.S.

provided ideal stalking conditions. The rocks and trees were overgrown with moss and grasses, reminding me of mountain creeks that I have hunted in Alaska and the Rocky Mountain states, but in Italy they did not have nasties like devil's club and stinging nettles.

Spread apart at about 40-yard intervals, our host Pierangelo Pedersoli anchored the left part of the line. Aurelio Boninsegni, the owner of the 200-hectare La Conca agricultural preserve, was beside me and ballistician Alberto Riccadonna and editor Emanele Tabasso were to my right.

I had hunted hogs many times in the U.S. and sometimes on my own property, but this was the first time I had hunted the European wild boar in its native habitat. The footing on the moss-covered boulders was treacherous. I was looking for a safe place to make my next step when a noise from ahead and a glimpse of something big and black informed me that the boar was on the move and very close.

As I wanted a European hunting experience, the gun I carried was particularly appropriate. It was a Davide Pedersoli .54-caliber early American Jaeger rifle whose Germanic antecedents had been designed for this type of work. Pierange-

lo was carrying a 12-gauge double slug-shotgun, Alberto a Pedersoli double Kodiak rifle and Emanele, Pedersoli's new Hawken rifle.

True to the Jaeger style, my rifle was a relatively short-barreled large-caliber gun intended to deliver a heavy ball into large game animals, particularly wild boars. Often these were .75-caliber, but the Pedersoli version was .54-caliber and its 27-1/2" barrel was rifled to stabilize a Thompson/Center Arms 430-gr. MaxiBall. This gun was introduced into the United States by Dixie Gun Works and was one of the late Butch Winter's favorite muzzleloaders. He liked it because of its quick handling and easy shooting characteristics. Jaegers were historically produced in both flintlock and percussion versions. Although I would have happily shot either, my gun

(left) The author shooting the 8X57 JRS combination gun. Although the author shot this gun twice, he actually hunted with another gun. (below) Danilo Liboi (L) and Marco Ramanzini (R) shown in different, but typical, central European hunting garb. The Italians who big game hunt do not wear as formal a dress as the English do when hunting. Camouflage is sometimes worn, but often their clothes are dark greens and muted browns. I found the German ex-military fleck camo that I wore with its dark colors to be particularly effective in the dark forest with its muted colors.

was fired by a #11 percussion cap and stoked with 106 grains of Swiss FFg black powder.

I had fired the gun only twice before the hunt. The first shot was off-hand and the bullet hit an inch or so above the bull at about 40 yards. When the shot broke I was aiming three inches to the left. The second shot, with a closer hold, confirmed that that the gun was shooting to the right. I also fired two shots with a Fair over-under rifle-shotgun combination gun that I might use the next day.

My favorite style of rifle for off-hand shooting has always been the set-triggered Hawken design. The forward-weighted barrel aids in steady off-hand holding that is nearly impossible with broom-straw weight tubes. Smaller-diameter barrels make guns lighter to carry, but I must shoot from a rest to make consistent shots beyond 30 yards with feather-weight barrels. I have made off-hand killing shots at a walking boar at 85 yards with one of my Hawken rifles and used another to hit 1"x2" kill zone on an alligator's brain at 30 yards. The Jaeger I was using and the Hawken rifle that Emanele carried exhibited the excellent off-hand shooting characteristics of their designs.

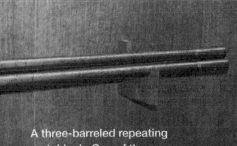

A three-barreled repeating matchlock. One of the many fine firearms in the Luigi Marzoli Museo delle Armi in the Castello in downtown Bresca.

The FAIR 20-ga. by 9.3X74 JR combination gun and the Davide Pedersoli .54-caliber Jaeger rifle that the author used to take a mouflon and European wild boar.

"Enough shooting," our host had said. "It is time to hunt."

HUNTING, ITALIAN STYLE

I was in distinguished company. Marco Ramanzini, Danilo Liboi and Tabasso have editorial responsibilities for the magazines *Diana*, *Sentieri di Cacca* and *Caccia a palla* while Pierangelo Pedersoli and Luca Rizzini are presidents of the gun-making companies Davide Pedersoli and FAIR (Fabbrica Armi Isidoro Rizzini), respectively. My responsibility as an outdoor writer was to take the Pedersoli Jaeger and a FAIR rifle-shotgun combination gun and cleanly kill a game animal with each of them. I had only seen these guns a few hours before and fired only a shot or two with each of them.

The author with his European wild boar at the kill site. As boars, go this is an average boar that weighed about 175 lbs. On preserves where the game is regularly hunted, the hogs are often harvested before they reach their maximum weights of some 600 lbs.

Another task was that Pierangelo Pedersoli was attempting to convince the Italian government that muzzleloading guns were effective on game and that it would be advantageous to have special seasons for these guns. He had invited me and the other writers to help publicize muzzleloading hunting. For me this hunt was more about shooting well than taking trophy animals.

This was very much a two-way interchange. Just as these Italian editors and writers were interested to learn about my American exploits with muzzleloaders, I wanted to hear about European hunting. The basic difference was that in Europe, hunting is more of a group experience whereas in the U.S. it is commonly a solitary undertaking, even though game drives with hunters and standers are practiced in some parts of the U.S.

"Often," Ramanzini explained, "these will be quite large affairs. There may be 40 dogs used to move the game and perhaps 50 people participating in the hunt. Large tracts of land are driven at one time. It is not unusual for a hunting club to take 200 to 400 boars a year, as well as much other game. This is a cooperative effort. The hunter who kills gets the trophy, but all share in the meat.

"At each kill honor is paid to the animal by placing a broken branch into its mouth as a 'last meal,' and very often a ceremony with horn playing, banqueting and toasting is done at the conclusion of the hunt."

It came as something of a shock when I told them that the only aspect of European hunting traditions that was practiced in the United States was blooding the face of a young hunter when he took his first big-game animal. Some more pensive hunters might spend a few seconds over the animal reflecting on the hunt, but mostly it was gut and drag to get the animal back to camp as soon as possible.

When asked why this was so, I replied, "Remember that America was settled by those who were escaping wars, famine and religious persecutions. Things were so terrible at home that they risked their lives to cross the Atlantic and settle in what was often a hostile environment. These were not the titled nobility of Europe, but people who needed to feed their families. Many European traditions

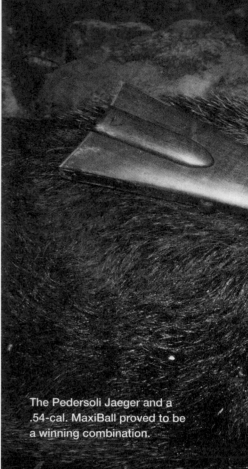

The Pedersoli Jaeger and a .54-cal. MaxiBall proved to be a winning combination.

FAIR Presiden's Luco Rizzini discusses on of the combination guns that he brought to the hunt. FAIR has seriously investigated almost every potential option of the over-under design. They produce the gun in all common shotgun gauges and in 12 and 20 gauge also offer a variety of European and American rimmed and rimless rifle cartridges. There is even a single-shot rifle built on a 28-gauge gun that is a particularly handsome stalking rifle.

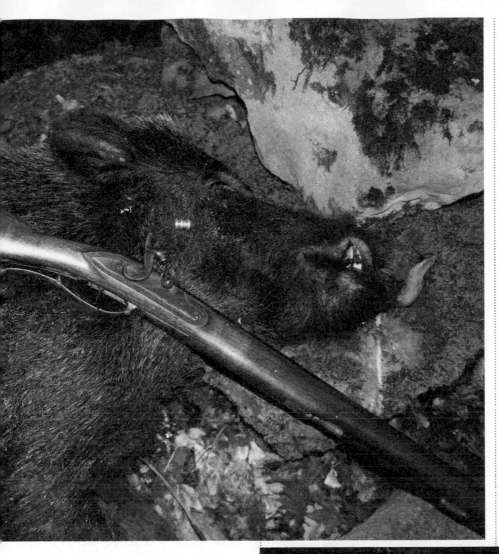

preserves, they must relinquish their hunting licenses in their home provinces to obtain one in another. They may also only buy and possess ammunition for guns they have on license.

Non-Italian hunters may not hunt on public hunting areas but are restricted to hunting on shooting preserves. La Conca specializes in agriturismo (agricultural tourism) and maintains four former home sites where tourists can experience something of rural life while living in modern comfort, including swimming pools. These farms had been abandoned, and Boninseqni rebuilt the old farmhouses using wood that he cut and milled on the property. Vallorsaia, where we stayed, once kept cows on the ground floor; the second floor was used for living quarters and the third for drying vegetables and fruits. The address was Paradiso 15, and for me the game animals and settings lived up to the billing as a hunter's paradise.

THE HUNT CONTINUES

But I had a boar to contend with. Getting ready for a possible shot, I cocked the hammer and set the trigger – carefully holding my trigger finger outside of the trigger guard. Although only 25 yards away, the boar was moving away at a trot and twisting this way and that on its path. This was a going-away shot that was partly obscured by intervening rocks and trees. Perhaps smelling one

were left behind in favor of what a man could accomplish with his own hands as fast as possible. For most Americans, even though they might belong to clubs, big game hunting is still a solitary undertaking with one man taking one animal per trip.

"Native Americans, with cultures tens of thousands of years, did have complex hunting traditions; but Europeans in the New World largely left their hunting traditions behind."

On the trip from Gardon in the Val du Trompia through Bresca, Verona, Florence and down the Apennine Mountains to the la Conca reserve near the historic city of Sansepoicro, Pierangelo Pedersoli talked non-stop for over an hour about Italy's complex hunting and gun laws. Both are very closely controlled by a series of restrictive licenses that govern gun ownership for target shooters, collectors and hunters and for self-defense. Hunters are licensed, for example, to hunt only within their provinces. With the exception of hunting on shooting

Aurelio Boninsegni shown in his homemade buckskins with the author's mouflon. He became interested in muzzleloading and purchased his first rifle from Dixie Gun Works. He later found that the guns were actually made in Italy and soon after formed a relationship with Pierangelo Pedersoli that has endured for decades. He made his buckskins from the leather derived from the animals he took. He is truly an Italian buckskinner.

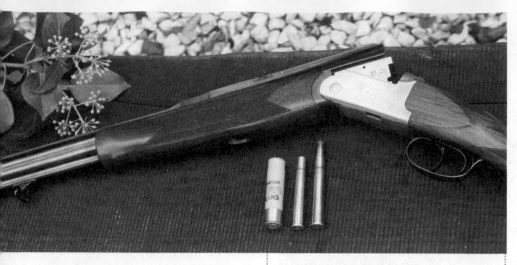

The FAIR combination 20x9.3X74R combination gun shown with fired 20-gauge and 9.3 cases and a loaded 9.3 cartridge. This cartridge is on a par with the 35 Whelen, but uses a heavier bullet to produce more muzzle energy.

of the other hunters, he hesitated in a clearing across the creek, briefly offering a shot at 40 yards. I quickly put the sights on the animal and touched the set trigger.

Smoke from the gun obscured the result. I heard crashing noises, and Boninseqni said, "Bravo. Multo bravo." The 175-lb. boar was down and dead. When the bullet was recovered, it had expanded to .75-caliber and exhibited a perfect mushroom. It had passed through both lungs and the heart. I was very grateful that my quick, off-hand shot had struck the animal well. Pierangelo had a shot at a running hog and missed, but others of our group took a fallow deer stag, a doe and two mouflon. It had been a good day, and we returned for supper.

We were served in typical Italian style at a long table that now sat where the cow stalls were located. Amid ancient beams, rocks and boards; we were had several courses starting with a pasta dish, then salad, meats, dissert and coffee accompanied by local wines. Particularly memorable were wild boar backstraps and homemade Italian lasagna. Some of the cooking was done in a wood-fired *furno* (outside stone oven) by Luca, one of Boninsegni's two sons. The main part of the meal had been prepared by Boninseqni's wife and daughters. Another son, Davide, assisted in the hunting operations and cleaned the game. The entire operation was a family business with everyone working

very hard to make it succeed.

The next hunt was to be from a shooting stand using FAIR's rifle-shotgun combination gun. I selected one with a 20-ga. rifled barrel and the classic 9.3X74R rifle barrel. This cartridge was designed for heavy animals like large boar, European moose and African plains game. On the American side of the Atlantic, it would also be appropriate for elk and caribou. The prominent rim makes this cartridge easy to extract in break-open guns. I had always wanted to shoot something with the 9.3, and this hunt offered that opportunity.

In the early morning light with wisps of fog still hanging from yesterday's rains, Boninsegni made motions for me to bend over and be quiet as we entered the box blind overlooking a feeding station. There were three fallow-deer does eating corn about 30 yards away and a stag feeding on acorns in the valley bottom 80 yards away. Fallow deer are handsome animals but often fight and break their horns. Rut had not started, and this stag had intact horns. It was a fine trophy, and one that I wanted.

Supposing that the stag would join the does at the corn, I hesitated to shoot. When the deer passed behind a tree I slowly raised the gun to the shooting window, poked the barrel out of the blind and took the safety off. I had to watch the does carefully to make sure that they did not spook and warn the stag.

Unfortunately, the stag had apparently learned that bad things happen to heavily-horned deer that go to the corn. He continued feeding on acorns and passed out of sight. Drat! He had offered a good-enough shot opportunity, and if I had been using the Jaeger instead of a gun that I had never shot, I would have taken it. Since I thought that there was a good possibility of the stag coming closer, my

plan had been to let it approach.

Boninsegni pointed to the side of the blind. My vision was obstructed by the wooden sides of the shooting box, and I had not seen a mouflon. Half-standing and swinging around, I aimed at the sheep and pulled the front trigger. I was impressed by the gun's mild recoil. Then it dawned on me that I had shot it with the rifled-slug barrel. That was fine as the range was close, and the slug would likely cause more internal damage than the bullet from the 9.3X74R, which was meant for much heavier game.

The sheep showed no indication of being hit. It bounded off the trail and went down the hill. Boninseqni indicated that he heard it fall. I reloaded and put the gun on safe and we exited the blind. The animal had gone 25 yards before collapsing.

"Perfecto," Boninsegni remarked as he examined the sheep. The 20-gauge slug had diagonally raked the animal and exited through the off-side shoulder. Although I had not fired at the trophy stag that I wanted, I was satisfied with the result: two shots – two dead animals. I had fulfilled my obligations, aided in no small measure by my previous experiences using these types of guns and a double dose of good luck.

Pierangelo Pedersoli took a gold-metal class mouflon at 80 yards using his 12-gauge slug-shotgun. I was not surprised that his smoothbore gun did so well. I also own one and have used it to take deer in the U.S. as well as a blue wildebeest, guinea fowl and other birds in Africa. At home I often load one barrel with a round ball for deer and another with shot for small game.

These hunts are expensive. To a base fee for housing and meals, trophy fees are added for each animal. The mouflon goes for 200 to 2,000 Euros, fallow deer from 250 to 1,500 Euros and boars for 10 Euros a kilogram. My boar, for example, would have cost about $1,200. Seasons vary, but everything is open during the last half of October.

GUNMAKING IN THE VAL DU TROMPIA

During my Italian expedition, I was fortunate to be able to learn more about the Italian gunmaking industry and its truly exceptional products.

The historic gunmaking city of Gordone is located in the steep mountain valley of the Mella River about a 30-minute drive north of Brescia in the Tuscan province of Brescia. The presence of

The Guns

Type	Maker	Barrel	Caliber	Length	Weight	Features
Jaeger	Davide Pedersoli	Single	.54	43.5 in.	8.25 lbs.	Set triggers
Hawken	Davide Pedersoli	Single	.54	48.5 in.	10 lbs.	Set triggers
Kodiak	Davide Pedersoli	Double	.54	45.25 in.	9.3lbs.	Double triggers
Slug-Shotgun	Davide Pedersoli	Double	12 gauge	45 in.	6.25 lbs.	Double triggers
Combination	FAIR	Over-Under	12 gauge X 8.57 JRS	45 in.	6.4 lbs.	Double triggers, Aluminum alloy frame
Combination	FAIR	Over-Under	20 gauge X 9.3X74R	45.0 in.	7 lbs.	Double triggers, steel frame

iron ore, wood for gunstocks and water-power resulted in the establishment of iron foundries and gun-making activities in the 1400s. Fine examples of these early efforts can be seen in the Luigi Marzoli Musco delle Armi in the Castello in Brescia. This fortress also houses the Museo del Risorgimento where arms are exhibited from the revolution that led to the establishment of the modern Italian state in the 1840s.

Arms making in the narrow confines of the valley has its advantages and disadvantages. Perhaps nowhere else on earth are located so many arms-making companies and related activities. These include a proof house, engraving shops, a 100-year-old gunmaking school and suppliers of related goods and services. The valley is so small that there is no railroad service, and the access road through the historic town is sometimes choked with traffic. There is no room for factory expansions except by adding more stories to existing structures.

All gun designs began with a pattern and model. Here a First Model Brown Bess musket is being designed for future production.

The valley is also subjected to periodic flooding, making it prudent to put multi-million-dollar machinery on upper floors with resultant increases in building and gun-construction costs.

Despite, and perhaps because of, these constraints, companies like Beretta and smaller firms like Davide

The engraved action of the FAIR 20-gauge by 9.3X74 R showing a wild boar on the action. The 20-gauge barrel is rifled for slug shooting, and it was this barrel that the author used to take a mouflon at close range. The "R" designation indicates that this is a rimmed cartridge particularly designed for break-open guns. Another of the FAIR combination guns was chambered for the 8X57 JRS, which is a rimmed version of the 8 mm German service cartridge of World War II. This cartridge uses a different bullet from the 8X57 JR that was chambered in many drillings and combo guns brought home by servicemen after World War II. Both cartridge are made by Norma and are available in the U.S. It is dangerous to use the wrong ammo in these guns because of changes in pressure loadings and bullet diameters. This is well understood in Europe, but not in the U.S.A.

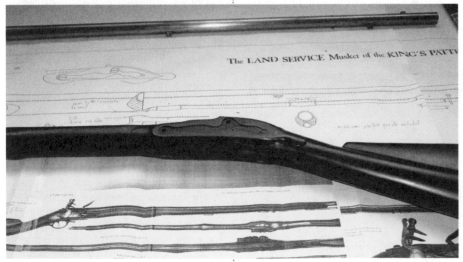

The LAND SERVICE Musket of the KING'S PATT

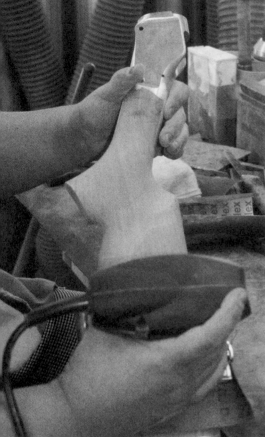

Sanding the action and stock together ensures that the lines will blend perfectly between the wood and steel. The action is that of a Pedersoli Winchester high wall.

Pedersoli and FAIR have modernized to produce very-high-quality arms from the best materials using modern techniques. Computer-controlled CNC (computer numerical control) equipment enables a variety of guns to be made on the same machines, requiring only changes of computer programs to switch from one model to another. This saves considerable space over the former practice of having separate

production lines for each gun. Because of the lack of space, Italian gunmakers in Gordone were among the first to adopt this new technology. Some 700,000 guns a year are made in this small valley.

The firms of Davide Pedersoli and FAIR are typical of companies that passed from fathers to progressive generations of sons and daughters. The present generation of Pedersolis includes Pierangelo Pedersoli and his sons Stefano and Paula. Stefano takes an active part in the business while Paula is still in school, and he shares his father's hunting interests. I have shot Pedersoli's replica guns for decades and have met the family at numerous SHOT Shows. This connection led to my being invited for the hunt and factory visit.

Making high-quality replicas of historic firearms for shooters, re-enactors and hunters has given Davide Pedersoli a world-wide market. Although the firm's largest volume of sales are in the U.S., there is also keen interest in his guns in Europe, Russia and South Africa. Unlike in the U.S. where hunting muzzleloaders may be of advanced designs, muzzleloaders used in other countries are usually restricted to traditional patterns or are regulated as cartridge arms. Pedersoli guns regularly sweep both U.S.

and international muzzleloading shooting events and are increasingly winning black-powder cartridge competitions.

Changes in market demand requires the ability to make rapid responses, and Pedersoli and other Italian gunmakers have the capabilities to adapt to different product lines as needed. FAIR, for example, formerly produced more side-by-side shotguns. Facing decreasing sales of these traditional shotguns and rising interest in over-unders, they now emphasize over-under shotguns, combination guns and double rifles while still offering luxury-grade side-by-sides.

FAIR's investigation of the ramifications of the over-under design includes offering models with either aluminum or steel frames. These guns may have one smoothbore shotgun barrel and one rifled shotgun barrel, rifle-shotgun combinations on both 20- and 12-ga. frames chambered for a variety of rimed and rimless rifle cartridges including the .22 Hornet, .270 Winchester, .308 and .30-06. Other options include a single-barreled rifle on a 28-ga. frame with a lower chamber holding a spare cartridge. Sixteen and 36-gauge (.410) shotguns are also offered with appropriately-sized frames.

FAIR hasn't neglected the over-under

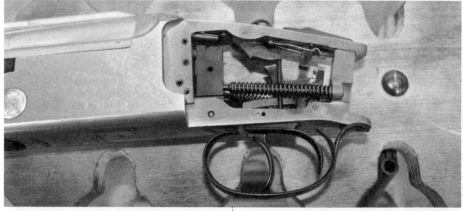

The assembled, but unblued, action of a FAIR combination gun.

shotgun, with competition, hunting, sporting clays and waterfowl versions being offered in 12 and 20 gauges. There is also the LX600 Battue slug gun with rifled bores regulated for the 3-inch Battue slug.

Decorative possibilities offered by both Pedersoli and FAIR include engraving on false side plates by FAIR and gold inlays and engraved models offered by both companies. Once the base guns have been produced, the possibilities of using local craftsmen to make unique

The Game

Hunter	Boar	Mouflon	Fallow Deer	Metal Grade
Smith	X	X		
Pedersoli		X		Gold
Riccadonna			X – Doe	
Fair		X		Platinum
Libio			X – Stag	
Ramanzini			X – Doe	

Note: It is perhaps interesting that two of the most experienced hunters, Riccadonna and Ramanzini, apparently chose does for the table, having already collected a sufficient number of horns from common European game.

Racks of guns being readied for packing and shipment. For most gun companies in Gardone 90 percent of the production is exported.

Barrel straightening at the Davide Pedersoli factory. This important step is still done by eye and hand. No machine has yet been developed to do this as well.

examples of the gunmaker's art are limited only by the client's desires. Both firms plan to offer high-grade production and custom guns which may be paired with identical plainer-finished models for field use.

WOOD, METAL AND A GREAT DEAL OF SKILL

Wood, steel, brass and nowadays high-strength aluminum alloys are components of modern Italian firearms. At Pedersoli these are produced in-house, as are the barrels. A combination of contract and in-house production is employed at FAIR because of lack of space to make all of their guns' components.

Good gunstock wood is becoming increasingly scarce, and Pedersoli gets most of his from North America. Planks are sawn and made into blanks that are later milled into finished stocks. During assembly the final inletting is done with hand tools.

Machining operations inside the computer controlled machines consist of the machine selecting a particular tool, verifying that it is not broken, performing a particular operation, replacing the tool, choosing another, performing another operation, replacing the tool, choosing another and so on until the machining operations are completed. In this manner frames, action parts and other components are milled to a very

high degree of precision and sorted into individual boxes for assembly.

Pedersoli rifles all of his barrels in-house. Each barrel is rifled, broached and straightened to insure maximum smoothness and accuracy. As is reasonably common, but not universally practiced, FAIR shoots each of its rifles for accuracy. If they do not pass the shooting test, their barrels are adjusted until they shoot within very narrow limits. These tests are particularly important for the company's double rifles.

Both companies guns undergo a rigorous final inspection prior to shipment to ensure that they are up to quality standards. Quality – in respect to the materials used, machining of the parts and final fit and finish – of the guns is very important to both firms.

Luca Rizzini perhaps expresses it best when he speaks of Italian-made guns compared to less expensive products from Russia, Turkey and the Far East: "We make quality guns that are branded and sold by companies all over the word. Our guns have the highest qualities in regard to design, the materials used and workmanship. In the case of some of our less costly competitors from abroad, they are frequently deficient in that the designs they copied are good, but often the parts are not properly heat treated to provide long-lasting performance. Or, in the case of Russian production, the materials are of good quality; but the designs are poor.

"It is true that we cannot compete on price with those who only think of guns as commercial products and do not use them. Our guns are made by people who not only make beautiful objects, but also shoot and hunt with them. We know what it takes to make a good gun, have hundreds of years of experience to draw upon, have the materials and tools to produce them and, as importantly, we use the guns we make. Buyers can pay less, but their hunting and shooting experiences will be considerably degraded with lesser-quality guns."

All told I had a good hunt, a fine visit and shot some excellent guns. Brescia and Gardone are off the popular tourist routes, but for gun enthusiasts these are places that are well worth visiting. Most gun makers have in-house showrooms, and it is often possible to special-order guns to fit individual requirements. If you must convince a spouse to include Brescia on your Italian trip, Venice is only a two-hour train ride away.

Every half-century or so, a new revolver comes along that changes everything. Ruger's Super Blackhawk is one of them.

POWER & GRACE:
The Ruger Super Blackhawk turns 50

BY **DON FINDLEY**
PHOTOS BY **CHRIS DUNCAN PHOTOGRAPHY**

RUGER PRODUCES THE FIRST SINGLE ACTION IN .44 MAGNUM

Remington Arms designed and perfected the .44 Magnum cartridge in the early to mid-1950s. Smith and Wesson produced the double action revolver to deliver it. S&W introduced their .44 Magnum double action revolver, later known as the Model 29, in 1956. That same year Sturm, Ruger & Co. produced the first single action in .44 Magnum, the Ruger Blackhawk.

The Ruger .44 Blackhawk was built around a cast chrome-moly steel cylinder frame and a one-piece aluminum grip frame. Unbreakable, high-quality music wire coil springs were incorporated throughout. An adjustable Micro rear sight was set flush in the heavy flattop frame. The front sight was a ramp style with an 1/8"-wide blade.

The .44 Blackhawk was offered only with a 6-1/2" barrel. The grip frame was anodized black; steel parts were polished and blued. Grip panels were varnished American walnut. The fluted cylinder had a six-round capacity. Empty weight was 40 oz. and the retail price was $96.00. The .44 "Flattop," as it was referred to, was a phenomenal success. Production could not keep up with demand.

Some arms "experts" complained that the .44 Blackhawk's grip frame was too small for the .44 Magnum's heavy recoil and that more room was needed for the trigger finger. Some said the gun was too light in weight; maybe a steel grip frame and a longer barrel for a better balance? By the summer of 1958, Sturm, Ruger an-

Ruger's original revolver chambered for the powerful .44 Magnum, the Ruger Blackhawk ("Flattop") with a box of Remington 1956 production ammunition.

swered some of their critics by offering the .44 Blackhawk in two additional barrel lengths, a 7-1/2" (catalog code BKH47) and 10" (BKH40), along with the standard 6-1/2" (BKH46).

ENTER THE SUPER BLACKHAWK

Sturm, Ruger & Company moved their manufacturing operation from the small, wood-frame shop at 29 Station Street, Southport, Connecticut, in 1959 to an all-new modern facility at Number 1 Lacey Place (still in Southport). Ruger's first new product produced at the new

First year production (1959) Super Blackhawk, the essence of power and grace.

factory was an improved .44 Magnum single action revolver, designed for "maximum shooter comfort": the Super Blackhawk.

Like the original Flattop, the new Super Magnum was constructed of chrome molybdenum steel. New features included integral ribs designed to protect the adjustable rear sight as well as to strengthen the cylinder frame; a wide serrated target style trigger; and a wide-spur, low-profile, serrated hammer. The square-back, steel trigger guard, contoured to help control recoil, was a dragoon style with a little added room for the trigger finger. The six round cylinder was non-fluted.

The Super Blackhawk's front sight was a ramp style with an eighth inch-matted blade. The rear sight was a Micro with an adjustable click screw for windage and elevation. Grip panels were varnished walnut with the Ruger logo medallion set in each panel. The Super Blackhawk (factory ctaalog code

Official announcement of the Ruger Super Blackhawk. Original Factory letter dated August 19, 1959.

S47) was available in 7-1/2" barrel length only. The revolver's finish was polished blue and its overall weight was a heft 48 oz. polished and blued. Retail price was $120.00. The Super Blackhawk came packaged in a cloth-lined, fitted mahogany case with brass hardware; serial numbers began at number 1. In the Super Blackhawk, Ruger had created a magnificent revolver engineered

STURM, RUGER & CO., INC.

SOUTHPORT, CONNECTICUT

August 19, 1959

To: RUGER Distributors

Subject: New RUGER Revolver: "Super Blackhawk"

Gentlemen:

It is with genuine great pride that we announce the introduction of the "Super Blackhawk" revolver, the largest and most luxurious single-action revolver ever made.

Chambered for the very powerful .44 Magnum cartridge, the "Super Blackhawk" has a 7 1/2" barrel, a rakish cylinder frame with integral ribs to protect the adjustable rear sight, a large steel grip frame, a wide serrated trigger, and a lower, wider, knurled hammer. The non-fluted cylinder and square-back trigger guard add immeasurably to the handsome design of this magnificent firearm.

Each "Super Blackhawk" will be packed in a mahogany, cloth-lined case. The suggested retail price will be $120.00. Dealer price: $91.88. The net Distributor price is $68.56 and with the 10% Federal Tax your cost is $75.42.

The "Super Blackhawk" is the first new RUGER to come from our new factory. We are constantly working on new models, and you can rely on us to continue our policy of producing quality products, designed and produced to meet the demands of world-wide gun enthusiasts.

Now in production, shipments of the "Super Blackhawk" are scheduled for early October. We look forward to receiving your stock order to cover your initial requirements for this outstanding gun, a masterpiece of power and precision.

Yours very truly,

STURM, RUGER & CO., INC.

E. P. Nolan
Sales Manager

EPN/jn

to better handle the powerful .44 Magnum, a gun whose graceful lines and perfect balance made the it a single action that set the standard for future arms makers to follow. The Ruger Super Blackhawk was truly a combination of power and grace.

The introduction of the new single action came in a factory letter dated August 19, 1959, to all Ruger distributors: "It is with genuine great pride that we announce the introduction of the Super Blackhawk revolver, the largest and most luxurious single action revolver ever made. Projected availability date; early October, 1959."

Gun writers had nothing but praise for the new Super Blackhawk. Captain Leo Milligan of *Shooting Times and Country Magazine* wrote, "The .44 Magnum Super Blackhawk incorporates the best features of every sixgun made since 1836." (Samuel Colt patented his first revolver in 1836.) Elmer Keith, the undisputed dean of single action shooters, wrote, "This is just about what I have wanted and worked for 40 years now in a single action and is by far the finest single action sixgun ever produced."

Though Ruger did not set out to manufacture their new revolver in varying configurations, a different variation was produced the first year, much to the delight of collectors. An estimated 300 guns were assembled with a longer grip frame, 3/16" longer than the frame

Front cover of the 28th Anniversary Edition, 1974 *Gun Digest* with artwork by James M. Triggs. Ruger's New Model Super Blackhawk with a cut-away drawing to illustrate safety features of Ruger's new line of single action revolvers.

standard for the Super Blackhawk. In collectors circles these guns are known as "Long Frame Supers." These longer frame guns range from the very first guns produced to the highest serial number recorded at serial number 3111. The longer frames were randomly installed and are mixed with Super Blackhawks with standard frames. For example, serial number 9 has a long frame, while number 10 was shipped with the standard frame. The grip panels on these long frame guns were stamped, on the back, with the letter "C." The longer frames were hand-fitted to the gun. Grip panels were also hand-fitted to individual frames (these grips will interchange

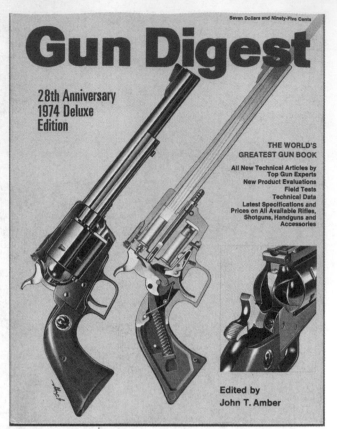

Seven Dollars and Ninety-Five Cents

Gun Digest

28th Anniversary 1974 Deluxe Edition

THE WORLD'S GREATEST GUN BOOK

All New Technical Articles by Top Gun Experts
New Product Evaluations
Field Tests
Technical Data
Latest Specifications and Prices on All Available Rifles, Shotguns, Handguns and Accessories

Edited by John T. Amber

from one long frame to another but in some cases the fit is less than perfect from one gun to another). The production of these few Super Blackhawks with longer frames was no doubt purely unintentional and as of today no one has come up with an official explanation for their existence. One can only speculate.

In a factory letter dated December 8, 1960, sales manager E.P. Nolan sent this notice: "The factory that constructed the mahogany cases was destroyed by fire. Super Blackhawks will now be packaged in a very

Super Blackhawk as shipped with original two-piece, red and black box, 1970.

STURM, RUGER & CO.
SOUTHPORT, CONN. U.S.A.

RUGER SUPER BLACKHAWK
.44 MAGNUM CAL.

RUGER.

SUPER "BLACKHAWK"
.44 MAGNUM CAL. REVOLVER
Catalog No. S47   7½" Bbl.
STURM, RUGER & CO., INC.
SOUTHPORT, CONN. U.S.A.

fine paperboard case. To offset the difference between boxes, the new suggested retail price is now $116.00." The paperboard case was replaced by a red and black, two-piece box before the end of 1961. At about this time the finish was changed from the standard blued finish to a high polish "deep" blue. Earlier Supers had a more "dull" blue similar to the Ruger Flattops.

By the end of 1962 the .44 Ruger single action was offered only in the Super Blackhawk. Ruger had discontinued the Flattop in both .357 and .44 Magnum. The walnut grip panels were now oil finished. and an unmarked aluminum sight replaced the Micro sight. The ejector rod housing was also changed from steel to black anodized aluminum.

Approximately 600 Super Blackhawks were shipped with 6-1/2" barrels (instead of the standard 7-1/2") in 1966. What happened was this: a number of .44-caliber barrel blanks were cut to 6-1/2 inches by mistake by a machinist who mistook them for blanks for the Blackhawk in .41 Magnum caliber. Instead of scrapping the barrels, Ruger installed them in Super Blackhawks and marketed them through Ruger distributors. These guns were never listed in Ruger's advertisements or catalogs.

THE BRASS FRAME SUPER BLACKHAWK

The Super Blackhawk was listed in distributor price sheets, beginning in January of 1965, with your choice of a steel or solid brass grip frame. Catalog code for the brass frame Super was S47B. The retail price at that time was still $116.00 in either brass or steel. If you wanted to install a brass grip frame on your Ruger single action, the brass grip frame (catalog code BRG) was offered as an accessory under "component parts" for $20.00. Some fitting was required.

Although the S47B was listed in 1965, none was shipped until 1968, and only a small number was produced. They were dropped from factory price sheets by January of 1968. In a factory letter dated May 22, 1968, E.P. Nolan answered a customer's inquiry related to the availability of the Super Blackhawk with a brass grip frame in this manner: "Because of the demand for regular production items we were obligated, for simplicity reasons, to drop the S47B from our line." Because these guns were produced in such a small number (estimated at fewer than 100) they are extremely rare. Before you pay serious

One of the features of Ruger's new Super Blackhawk was a Micro sight with integral ribs, 1959.

Ruger's new .44 Magnum came with a wide spur, a serrated hammer . . .

. . . and a wide serrated target style trigger, 1959.

money for a S47B, check with Sturm, Ruger's record department to verify that the brass frame was installed by the Factory and is not after-market.

The brass frame Super was produced again in 1972. Various other Ruger Blackhawks, along with the Old Army, were also produced in 1972 with factory-installed brass frames at an additional cost of $20.00 per gun (the cost of a Super Blackhawk was the same as one with a steel frame). Only the Old Army was listed in Ruger's advertising as offered with the factory-installed brass frame. Production numbers, as in 1968, were low in all models.

THE NEW MODEL SUPER BLACKHAWK

At Sturm, Ruger & Company, as a design is advanced from the drawing board to the "tool room" and eventually to the field for testing, efforts

Long Frame Super Blackhawk serial number 588, one of approximately 300, 1959.

to improve the product never cease, often times even after the product goes into production. Starting in 1965 and continuing into 1966, in an effort to create a safer handgun, designers at Ruger worked to incorporate a "hammer drop proof safety" into their single actions. They were not able to come up with a practical design. In the late 1960s they renewed their efforts. These renewed efforts evolved into a totally new concept that eventually became the basis for Ruger's "New Model" single action.

In 1973 Ruger made firearm design history. Sturm, Ruger & Company introduced a line of single action revolvers that could safely be carried with all six

Super Blackhawk with factory-installed brass grip frame, 1972.

Super Blackhawk with a high polish, deep blue finish, 1962.

One of 600 Super Blackhawks shipped with a 6-1/2" inch barrel, 1966.

chambers loaded, the Ruger New Model. For over 100 years, standard practice had been to carry your single action six-shooter safely with only five chambers loaded and the hammer resting over the sixth empty chamber. The New Model eliminated this requirement. As the

hammer is cocked on the Ruger New Model single action, a transfer bar comes into position between the firing pin and the hammer. The transfer bar system eliminates the possibility of an accidental discharge, even if the gun is dropped. To rotate the cylinder, simply open the loading gate. When the gate is open the hammer cannot be cocked. When the hammer is cocked the gate cannot be opened, making an accidental discharge, while loading or unloading, virtually impossible.

Serial numbers for the New Model Super Blackhawk, factory code S47N, began at number 81-00000. The feel and balance were the same as on the older Super Blackhawks. The finish and

quality remained the same. Gone, from the left side of the cylinder frame, were the familiar three-screw heads; replaced by two hardened pivot pins. The New Model Ruger single action is the result of a brilliant concept and advanced engineering. In a 1973 new products review, *American Rifleman* magazine declared, "It is the best-designed and safest single action revolver to date."

2009 celebrates 50 years of continuous production for the Super Blackhawk. The New Model Super Blackhawk is now available in barrel lengths from 4 5/8" to 10 1/2" in both blued and stainless steel. The Super Blackhawk, in either the old or New Model, remains the essence of power and grace.

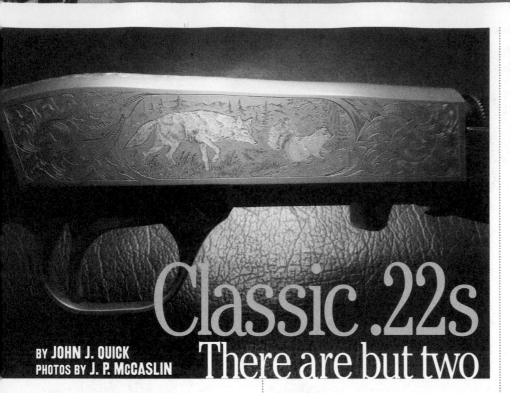

Classic .22s
There are but two

BY JOHN J. QUICK
PHOTOS BY J. P. McCASLIN

Want a strong opinion? Read on. . . .

It is indeed a rather bold statement to assert that only two .22 caliber rifles are worthy of the esteemed designation "classic." But in today's world, the term "classic" seems to be used with very little discretion. All too often we hear of something regarded as an "instant classic," which more aptly means it will probably be forgotten in a few years. But what if we demand that the term honors only those things that are universally praised by several generations and that hold a value and influence that only increase over time? Regarding all of the .22 rifles made during the twentieth century, how many really deserve to be recognized as a genuine classic, establishing a new standard for all that follow?

If you were opening a new firearms museum to honor the rifles of the past century and only had enough space to display two .22s, which would you select? I've had a never-ending interest in .22 rifles for over 30 years, and I believe I have finally arrived at an appropriate answer to the above question. My museum would display a high grade Browning .22 automatic and a Winchester Model 52 sporter.

When I researched the long history of both of these guns, several similarities come to light. Both the Browning and the Winchester have histories that begin during the second decade of the twentieth century. Each came to represent a major development in the history of .22 rifles that continues to this day. Both guns have been produced in at least four major grades or variations, which is one sure sign of a collectible. Today the most sought-after models of each of these rifles are commonly valued at $3,000 or more. And as further proof of continuing interest in both rifles, during the 1990s, thoroughly researched volumes were published that were devoted to the Browning .22 automatic and the Winchester Model 52: Homer C. Tyler's *Browning .22 Caliber Rifles, 1914 - 1991* and Herbert G. Houze's *The Winchester Model 52*. Most importantly, both rifles are still readily available, as the Browning autoloader remains in production, and the Winchester 52 sporter, as a reissue, was produced again from 1993 to 2000.

Let's take a closer look at our two truly classic .22s.

BROWNING .22 AUTOMATIC

The John M. Browning-designed .22 automatic rifle will always be regarded as a significant development in the history of twentieth century firearms, becoming the first production autoloading rifle to be chambered for the ever-popular .22 LR rimfire cartridge. And in many regards, it has never been equalled or surpassed.

One of Browning's principal aims in developing his new semi-automatic rifle was to design a receiver that is solid on the top and both sides, whereby the shooter's face is, in Browning's own words, "protected from gases and flying particles while firing." Empty shells are ejected downward out the bottom of the receiver when the breechblock cycles backward. Though initially regarded as a design to enhance safety, a receiver with completely smooth sides and top surface would allow its manufacturers to eventually adorn this gracefully shaped rifle with engravings the like of which no other .22 rifle could claim. More than any other feature, the beautifully engraved receivers would transform Browning's reliable little rifle into a work of art.

Another feature unique to the Browning .22 autoloader allows it to be taken down or put together in a matter of seconds, no tools required. After you push forward the small barrel lock on the end of the forearm, a quarter-turn of the barrel disengages it from the threaded receiver. The barrel can then be properly cleaned from the breech end or the rifle easily transported or stored in a much smaller space. (The breech end of the barrel also includes a barrel adjusting ring, which according to John Browning's patent application, provides "a simple and effective means for taking up play that may occur between the barrel and the frame.") To the credit of its designer,

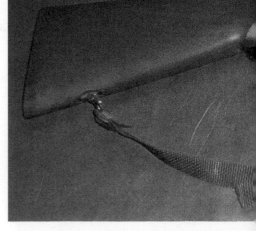

Winchester's re-issue 52B Sporter – a full-sized rifle designed for the serious sportsman.
RIGHT: Beautifully executed checkering enhances the walnut stock of 52B Sporter.

no other .22 rifle of the past century has such a simple takedown feature.

Browning's new rimfire rifle was first manufactured by Fabrique Nationale (FN) in Belgium during 1914. Under license by Browning, his .22 semi-automatic rifle was also produced and sold in the U.S. by Remington as the Model 24, from 1919 to 1935. With slight variations from the rifle simultaneously made by FN in Belgium, the Model 24 was eventually offered in a premier grade comparable to that of the FN Grade III. Although hundreds of thousands of the FN rifles were sold around the world, the rifle was unavailable in the U.S., except for the rare exception, until 1956, when it was finally imported and marketed as the "Browning .22 automatic." Manufacture of the rifle continued in Belgium through 1973, and it has always been these rifles (1956-73) that have aroused so much interest among collectors, especially the remarkably crafted Grade III models.

The Grade III rifles featured highly polished French walnut stocks with superb metal-to-wood fit and finely executed skip-line checkering. And, of course, the receivers were graced by extraordinary engravings. The hand-engraved receivers featured highly detailed game scenes with three pheasants on the left side, and a hound with a rabbit or duck in its mouth on the top of the receiver. Photographs cannot do justice to the consummate work of these European master engravers, many of whom initialled or signed their name on the lower side of the receiver. It is these

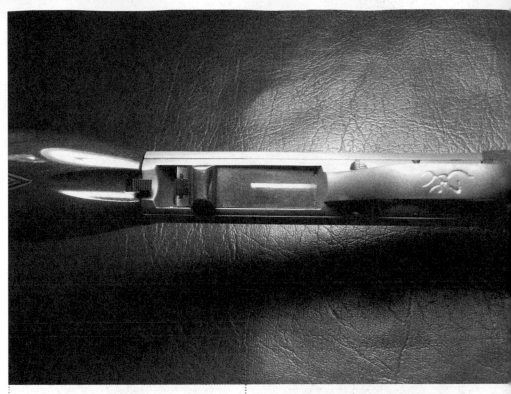

FN Grade III Browning rifles, with their elaborately engraved gray chromed receivers, that command a price of $2500-$3500 among today's collectors.

The Grade II rifles, no longer made today, had a traditional pattern of checkering and an engraved chrome receiver featuring game scenes with much less detail than those of the Grade III. The Grade I rifles, then as now, were hand-checkered in a pattern similar to that

Browning's autoloader ejects spent rounds from the bottom of the receiver.

of the Grade II models but featured a blued receiver with very simple but tasteful scroll engraving. When production ceased by FN in Belgium in 1974, over a half-million Browning/FN .22 autoloaders had been sold in the U.S., Europe, Canada, South America and Australia. The little Browning became the most universally well liked and

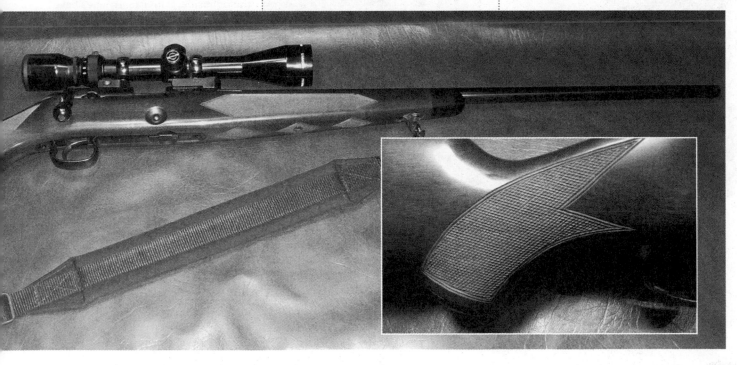

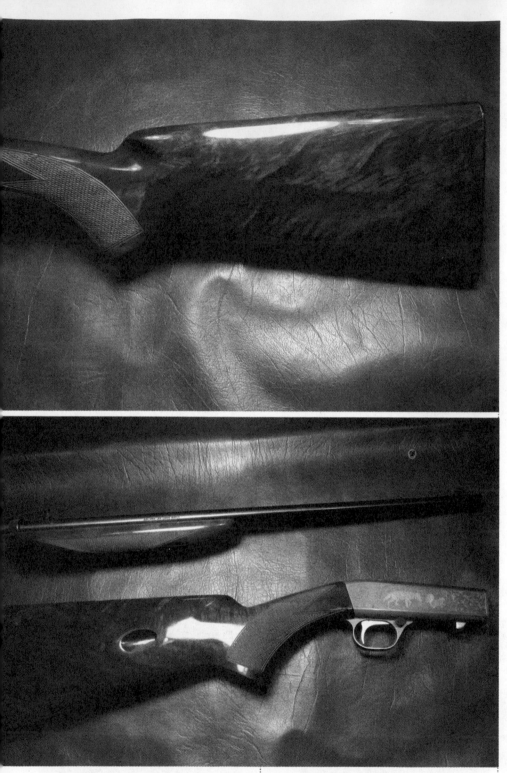

TOP: Highly figured walnut is characteristic of the present day Browning Grade VI autoloader. ABOVE: John Browning's revolutionary design with easy takedown to facilitate cleaning and transport.

mains a handsome and delightful gun to shoot. Always reliable, it possesses the required accuracy for use as a squirrel rifle out to about 50 yards.

Unfortunately, mounting a scope detracts from the slim, graceful lines which have always made the Browning so appealing. Even loading the Browning reveals its old-fashioned charm, with a loading slot on the right side of the buttstock and a magazine tube that is withdrawn from an opening in the buttplate. And there is absolutely no other rifle as perfectly balanced as the Browning .22. It remains a distinct pleasure just to shoulder the Browning. The specifications list its weight at 4-3/4 lbs. but the rifle actually feels a couple of pounds lighter because of its excellent balance. During my mid-teens, I hunted squirrels with a friend who owned a Grade I model and always felt neither of us really deserved or appreciated this elegant little .22 autoloader. Simply put, it was a gentleman's rifle. It still is.

A few years ago, I finally purchased a new Browning .22. I selected a Grade VI with the gray and gold receiver, as the gold plating seemed to contrast a little too much against a dark blued receiver. Unlike the FN Grade III rifles, which had completely hand engraved receivers, the Miroku Grade VI uses laser etching with only the final touching up by hand. Tastefully executed game scenes adorn the top and both sides of the receiver, with a beagle chasing a rabbit on the left side, the head of a beagle on the top, and a fox in pursuit of a squirrel on the right side. Both game scenes have detailed backgrounds and floral accents.

The trigger is gold plated and the bottom of the trigger guard has an engraved "buck mark." This familiar Browning insignia, along with all the animals engraved on the receiver, is beautifully highlighted with 24k gold inlay. The checkering on the forearm and semi-pistol grip has a double line border and is sharply cut at 22 lpi. But more than anything else, it is this rifle's extraordinary wood that always commands my attention. The extra-select claro walnut possesses a highly figured grain which can only be appreciated in hand. Its fascinating pattern produces an almost shimmering effect – the wood could be suitable for a custom rifle costing five times as much.

With its superbly hand engraved receiver and skip-line checkering, the Belgian-made FN Grade III will always be the most collectible and valued Browning .22 autoloader. But

recognized .22 rifle around the world.

In 1974, FN production in Belgium was replaced by manufacture in Japan by Miroku. The Grade II and III models remained in production, along with the standard Grade I, through 1984. The new Grade VI debuted in 1987 with an engraved receiver finished in blue and gold or gray and gold. It is still sold by Browning today, along with the Grade I. Though easily overlooked compared to the more collectible grades, the standard or Grade I Browning .22 re-

WINCHESTER 52B
SPORTER / POWER-AINTS
AMMO

.43" – 5 SHOTS / 50 YARDS

Even with high-speed hollowpoint ammo, the Winchester 52B re-issue is capable of superb accuracy.

today's Grade VI made in Japan continues the tradition of producing a perfectly reliable, unique and elegant .22 rifle. Everyone who handles this flawless .22 wants to take it home.

I remain hopeful that someday a FN Grade III in mint condition will be a part of my collection. And I'm not the only one who feels this way, for sure. For the Browning semi-auto .22 remains the premier .22 autoloader of all time – truly classic.

WINCHESTER MODEL 52

Perhaps the high grade Browning .22 rifle can be fully appreciated without firing a single round but not the Winchester Model 52 sporter. Above all else, this was a rifle designed for the serious shooter. From the very beginning, its remarkable accuracy endeared to any and all target shooters. Their widespread acclaim would soon lead to the title of "The King of .22 Caliber Rifles."

Although production of the Win-

chester Model 52 sporting rifle didn't begin until 1934, its direct ancestor, the Model 52 target rifle, was introduced 15 years earlier. Winchester's post-war Production Planning Committee had decided to discontinue the Model 1885 Single Shot and replace it with a military-style bolt action target rifle. With the end of World War I in 1918, company officials anticipated that returning soldiers would lead to an increase in target shooting, and also possible future contracts with the U.S. government for an appropriate .22 target rifle for training purposes. Pre-production samples of the Model 52 target were introduced to the public at the National Match rifle competition at Caldwell, New Jersey, in August of 1919. Members of the American Small Bore Team used the sample Model 52s during the matches with great success, winning several awards. In an article published in *Arms and the Man*, only two weeks after the Model 52's spectacular debut, David North stated, "they are the pioneers of a line of rifles which should

delight the experienced and meticulous marksman" – certainly a very early acknowledgment that still rings true today.

Actual production of the Model 52 began in the spring of 1920. Winchester's initial advertisements for the rifle stated that weighing 8-1/2 lbs. with a 28" barrel, the Model 52 had the same feel as the Springfield army rifle, and they already claimed it to be the "greatest small bore rifle every placed on the market." A noteworthy feature of the Model 52's bolt was the use of double extractors that gripped both sides of the rimmed cartridge. This helped assure proper feeding into the chamber, resulting in precise accuracy.

Bullet shaving at the mouth of the chamber was a common problem in other rifles of this era, and Winchester's engineers boasted proudly of their flawless design. And the Model 52 was soon used to shatter a host of records, including the first 10-shot perfect score at 100 yards ever accomplished in a national competition (by Virgil Richards in July of 1920). It would be almost 40 years before Anschutz would finally dethrone the Winchester Model 52 as the world's premier target rifle.

The first major improvements to the Model 52 came in 1930 with a redesigned target stock and the introduction of the "Speed Lock," a new trigger and firing pin design that reduced cartridge ignition time after the trigger was pulled. The company's president, John M. Olin, had been an enthusiastic supporter of the Model 52 and eventually endorsed the development and production of a sporting version in the summer of 1934. Known as the Model 52 Sporting Rifle, or Model 52 Sporter, it was given an elegant shaped walnut stock with cheekpiece and finely cut checkering. Weighing 7 lbs., it featured a lighter-weight 24" barrel, with a Lyman receiver sight as standard equipment. It also incorporated the Model 52 target rifle's bolt and speed lock mechanism.

From the beginning, the Model 52 Sporter was envisioned as a deluxe grade firearm that could serve equally for small game hunting and as a target rifle. An important early supporter in the development of the Sporter model was Lt. Col. Townsend Whelen, who wrote a review of it in 1935 for *Outdoor Life* titled "The First Efficient .22 Hunting Rifle." This article indicates the proper place for the Model 52 Sporting Rifle in the development of .22 firearms during the twentieth century. As the

Browning .22 automatic can be considered the grandfather of many of the .22 autoloaders that followed, the Model 52 Sporter became the first .22 sporting rifle to possess target grade accuracy. As such, it influenced the development of an entirely new type of rifle – a .22 sporter designed for the serious shooter who demands extraordinary accuracy. Many years later, competitive rifles began to appear – the Anschutz Model 52 Sporter, the Remington 541S, the Kimber Model 82 Classic – but the Winchester Model 52 Sporter secured its place in history in July of 1934.

The Model 52A Sporting and Target rifles appeared in 1935. Throughout its production, mechanical improvements were shared by both the target and sporting versions. The 52A featured a new receiver with an improved safety and redesigned Speed Lock components. The third version of the sporter, the 52B, debuted in 1938, again with a newly redesigned lock and safety mechanism. Shortly before, Remington introduced their Model 37 Rangemaster which many shooters believed had a superior trigger action. But with their overwhelming war contracts, Winchester had to wait until the end of World War II before offering any further improvements. During 1951, the company announced its "revolutionary," newly-designed "Micro-Motion" trigger, fully adjustable and vibration-free. The forward section of the trigger guard housed two adjustment screws,

one to limit overtravel and the other, the amount of trigger pull. This new Model 52C also featured a redesigned receiver, firing pin and bolt. Tapped screw holes for a scope mount also became a standard feature on the new receiver. The 52C Sporter was given a new reshaped stock which included a much more prominent cheekpiece. Though production of the 52C target rifle began in1951, the 52C Sporter didn't debut until 1953.

The Model 52C would be the ultimate and final version of Winchester's Model 52 Sporting Rifle. Production continued through 1959, with records showing a final shipment date of January of 1960. From 1953 to 1959, average production of the 52C sporter was only about 200 rifles per year. This rarity helps to account for the over $3,000 price tag for a mint condition 52- 52C sporting rifle. This value is three to five times higher than that of the equivalent Model 52 target rifle, which continued in production as the Model 52D, then 52E, through 1980.

In 1993, Winchester surprised collectors of high-quality .22 rifles by reissuing their classic 52B Sporting Rifle as part of their limited edition Historic Rifles series. Prior to its introduction, it was announced that only 6,000 Sporters would be made, but it was publicized during 1996 that an additional 3,000 would be produced. This new reissue was a chance of a lifetime to own a legendary rifle about which I had read so much during my boyhood in the 1960s.

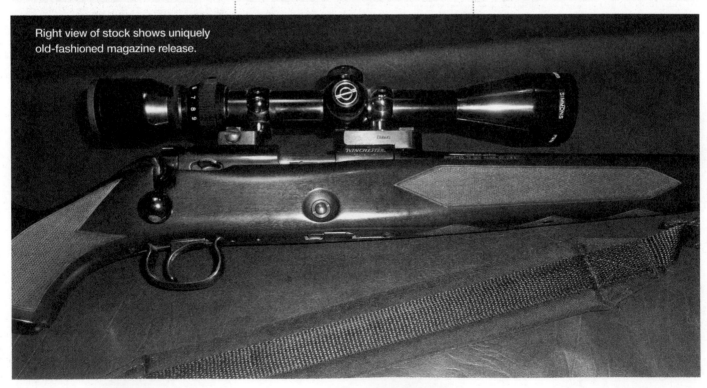

Right view of stock shows uniquely old-fashioned magazine release.

The new 52 sporter could be more accurately named the 52B/C Sporter, for although the rifle has the preferred stock of the former 52B Sporter, it incorporates the mechanical improvements of the original 52C Sporter, most notably, the Micro-Motion trigger mechanism. The new 52B is superbly made, and if not quite as stunningly beautiful as the high grade Browning .22 autoloader, it is nonetheless a very handsome rifle and a faithful reproduction of the revered original. The walnut stock features a sculpted cheekpiece and is finely checkered in the original pattern, including the three distinctive diamond shaped patterns on the bottom of the forend. In the center of the middle checkering diamond is located the forend adjustment screw that allows the shooter to apply pressure against the bottom of the barrel.

The reissue comes with a free-floating barrel, and Winchester claims the rifle will usually shoot more accurately if the adjustment screw does not touch the barrel. The original forend cap was black plastic but has now been upgraded and made of ebony. The stock's pistol grip features a metal cap, and a touch of class is continued with inclusion of the original checkered metal buttplate. Swivel bases allow for easy attachment of a sling, a necessary addition for hunting with a rifle which weighs 8 lbs., including scope. Fortunately, the stock also retains the push-button magazine release, located three inches forward of the bolt handle. I have always felt this feature retains some of the old fashion charm so lacking in an era of composite and laminate stocks. The new sporter is equipped with a medium-heavy, 24" barrel, without sights, but drilled and tapped for either scope bases or a receiver sight. The breech end features a match chamber which has a pronounced effect on accuracy. Most .22 rifles have a slightly larger size "sporting" chamber. But independent tests have verified that barrels equipped with a tighter fitting "match" chamber typically produce 50-yard groups only half as large as those shot from standard barrels.

Shooting the new 52B Sporter gives the same impression as given by the rifle's appearance, that of high quality and absolute precision. It is, above all else, a .22 bolt action magazine rifle for the demanding shooter. And it will reward one's diligent practice with outstanding results. The bolt, trigger and safety lever are all stoutly built and when handled, they impart a feeling of assurance that leaves a lasting impression.

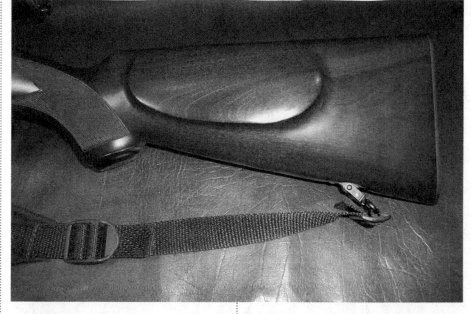

The renowned Micro-Motion trigger mechanism includes two adjustable screws located forward of the trigger guard: one marked PULL, the other OT (for over-travel). There is barely any perceptible movement of the trigger before it releases the firing pin – the "micro-motion" designation is quite fitting. Because of the very limited amount of trigger movement required for firing, Winchester's design prevents accidental shots by restricting how much the pull can be decreased by the adjustment screw. And though I have sometimes wished for about a pound less of trigger pull, the trigger action overall is so close to perfect that I gladly accept it as-is. Shooting the new 52B reveals its close heritage to the record-setting Model 52 Target rifles of yesteryear.

After attaching Burris bases, I equipped my second generation sporter with a Simmons 3-9x40 Prohunter scope. Capable of target grade accuracy, this classic rifle deserves a scope with high magnification. By 1937, Winchester claimed their Model 52 Target rifle was capable of shooting 1.25" ten-shot groups at 200 yards. I've never attempted to replicate this claim with my 52 Sporter, but I have spent a few hours shooting at 50 yards and have not been disappointed.

Using Winchester .22 Power-Points, my Weatherby MK XXII will shoot five-shot groups of 7/16" at 25 yards. Using the same ammo, the 52B sporter will get the same results but at 50 yards. Winchester's high velocity Power-Points have become my favorite choice for squirrel hunting in the oak and hickory

Stock cheekpiece is featured on both original and re-issue 52B Sporters.

groves during late autumn, in pursuit of the almost mythical 100-yard head shot. Kimber claims that every .22 rifle they now produce will shoot a 50-yard group measuring less than .40" before it leaves the factory. The best my 52B will shoot with premium target ammo is 3/8" (.375"). Achieving less than half-inch groups at 50 yards with any sporter requires diligent practice and intense concentration. Both the original and reissue Model 52 sporters reward such dedication and effort with results never realized by the casual plinker. The new line of Kimber .22s are undeniably very fine rifles, but the 52-52C Sporting Rifles have a historical significance all their own – the first high quality .22 rimfire sporters – a man-sized .22s built for the serious sportsman.

Fortunately the reissued Winchester is often available for sale in the bi-weekly publications, for a price considerably discounted from the final list price of $662. Having talked with a gun dealer who owns both the original and second generation 52 Sporters, he has been equally impressed with the new rifle's appearance and shooting precision – so impressed, in fact, that he actually bought two of the reissued models.

I remain very impressed as well. Along with the high grade Browning .22 automatic, the Winchester 52 sporter is one of the two true classic .22s.

Fit to Shoot!

To paraphrase "Red" Sanders, "Shotgun fit isn't everything — it's the only thing." Here author Grozik shows us what's involved in custom-fitting a shotgun.

BY RICHARD S. GROZIK

The looming heat and humidity of a mid-summer Missouri morning hung heavy in the air as we stepped into the bustling workshop of Fred Wenig's Custom Gunstocks. Fans were already humming in a futile attempt to hold back the oppressive weather. For my friend and hunting partner of 30 years, it was a long-avoided event, and, no doubt, a cold day in hell. He was finally going to have three of his favorite Western shotguns custom-stocked to fit him.

This trip really began in a duck blind decades before when I suggested to him that the Winchester Model 12 he was mounting to his 6'3" needed, at the very least, more length of pull to keep him locked into the gun. A stubborn traditionalist, he resisted my modest proposal to modify his pet Model 12 buttstock. But under my constant seasonal barrage he finally surrendered and had a local gunsmith install a solid red Winchester pad on his "perfect repeater." Immediately, he began to make shots on ducks that surprised us both, and he made them consistently. With the simple addition of a recoil pad, he

increased his gun's length of pull to 14-3/4 inches. This, coupled with the Model 12's agreeable drop at comb and heel, helped to make the gun more a part of him. Without worrying about adjusting his physique to the gun for each shot, he could now focus beyond the barrel

Master stockmaker Elbert Smith (right) evaluates customer's pad-enhanced Winchester Model 12 field grade to make sure the gun is a correct fit. The gun's stock dimensions will be used to restock a Winchester Model 12 Duck and 12- and 20-ga. Winchester Model 50 autoloaders.

and concentrate on taking his birds.

We had journeyed to Fred Wenig's that hot summer day to have his Model 12 stock dimensions, and some new fancy-figured American black walnut, affixed to his Model 12 3" Duck and his Winchester Model 50 12- and 20-ga.

Restocked Model 50 12-ga., a thing of beauty and a joy forever.

shotguns. I also brought along a 12-ga. Fox AE grade (circa 1910) side-by-side for Fred to refit with some attractive English walnut to accommodate my 6'4" anatomy. We had come to the right place, because "walnut" is Fred Wenig's middle name. For more than 40 years he has been securing the world's finest American, English, Bastogne, and Claro walnut to satisfy his customers. In addition to the random samples strewn about his front office, and the floor-to-ceiling stacks in his woodshop, Fred has several caches of stock blanks stored and drying all around his home town of Lincoln, Missouri. His extensive walnut inventory will please even the most discriminating sportsman.

After spending a considerable part of my life adjusting my shooting form to fit a variety of factory-dimensioned shotgun stocks, I finally decided to spend a little time and money to be property measured for a custom-fitted gunstock. That decision to visit Fred Wenig 25 years ago had a profound effect on my shooting performance and satisfaction. I learned that factory shotgun stocks are built for the "average" individual. Most of these guns have a 14" or 14-1/4" length-of-pull, a 1-1/2" or 1-5/8" drop

(top) Promising stock blanks are sponged with water to reveal wood figure and grain structure. (middle) Pre-cut Model 12 forearms are bathed with water to find the right color and figure to match the buttstock blank. (bottom left) Fred Wenig wets down a handsome piece of English walnut (*Juglans regia*) that will be used to restock author's 90-year-old AE Fox double. (bottom right) Partial view of Wenig's large inventory of rough-inletted factory stocks that is used to profile customer's personal stock dimensions.

0at comb, a 2-1/2" drop at heel, thickish combs, and offer little or no cast-off (lateral bend to the right) or, for southpaws, cast-on (lateral bend to the left). Shotgunners are anything but average and require a fit gun to shoot well under all conditions. A custom stockmaker considers several anatomical factors when fitting a customer. The length of pull and circumference of the grip will be determined by the length of your arm and the size of your hand. Broad shoulders may require some cast-off, a bony cheek a thicker comb, etc. A correctly fitted buttstock will make you one with your gun, will help eliminate the common nemesis of lifting your head off the stock, and will make your gun's muzzle an extension of your vision.

Good shooting is no mystery. It is a combination of good gun fit, proper gun mounting technique, consistent follow-through, and a lot of practice. But you must first begin with a gun that fits. A shotgun is not aimed, it is pointed. A tailored gunstock enables you to instinctively and consistently align the gun barrel with your line of sight. On crossing shots, it also helps you stay with the gun to continue swinging through the target. It is no secret that two of the main reasons for missing with a shotgun (custom-stocked or not) are improper gun mounting and shooting behind the target because of poor follow-through. Either or both will leave you hitless afield. To overcome them, practice bringing the shotgun up securely to your cheek with a minimum of head movement. Create a good shoulder pocket in which to solidly anchor the butt of the stock. Train your leading hand and shoulders to move as a unit to keep the shotgun swinging through the target as you pull the trigger. Of course, good posture and balanced footwork are also factors that contribute to good shooting form. Like any other sport, the more muscle memory and hand/eye coordination you can develop, the better you will perform.

Shotgunning is not an exact science, but if you want to score consistently on clay target fields and game fields, you will need a stock that fits you like a well-tailored suit. For the casual shooter, the fuss and expense may not be worth it. But if you are a serious shotgunner, you will eventually arrive at a set of stock dimensions that will enable you to perform your best. And while trial and error is one method of determining the best fit for you, a visit to a custom stockmaker like Fred Wenig will save you considerable time and aggravation.

After introductions, my partner and I joined Fred and Company for breakfast at a down-home restaurant on Lincoln's main street, just a short walk from the workshop. We discussed the current state and fate of the shooting sports and the importance of introducing the younger generation to the joys of hunting and clay target shooting. Between bits of buttermilk pancakes, my partner explained in great detail what he wanted done to his guns. Fred listened intently, offering advice and suggestions on wood selection and gunfitting.

With my friend's "modified" Model 12 Field Grade in hand, Elbert Smith recorded the exact length of pull, drop and cast dimensions of the gun. If the measurements were indeed correct, all of my partner's guns would be re-stocked to 14" length of pull, 1-5/8" drop at comb, 2-7/16" drop at heel, with a 1/2-inch cast-off. To make sure the measurements were allowing my partner to sight down the center of the barrel with his master eye, he was instructed to mount the empty and open-breached Model 12 and point it at Elbert's nose. Standing a yard or so off the end of the muzzle, Elbert told my friend to mount and point the Model 12 several times. Elbert wanted to make sure the gun's dimensions would truly allow my partner to correctly and con-sistently mount and point all the guns he was having restocked. As it turned out, the padded Model 12 was indeed a perfect fit for him and no additional stock adjustments would be required.

For customers who are uncertain of their correct stock measurements, Wenig will trundle out his over/under try gun that can be adjusted for length-

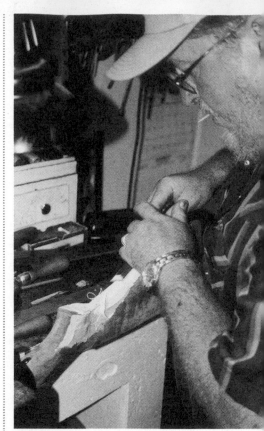

(above) Plastic putty is chiseled and rasped to achieve proper stock dimensions and contours. (left) With profiled factory stock attached to customer's gun, a laser is inserted into the muzzle to make sure the stock dimensions are centering light beam on target grid on the workshop wall 20 feet away.

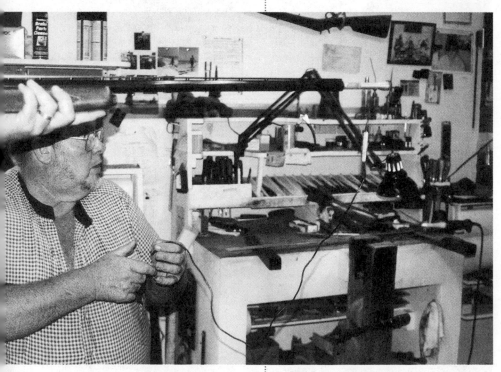

When we returned to the shop, Fred and his vice-president, Elbert Smith, immediately began to choreograph the team of craftsmen who would restock my friend's battery of Winchesters. By noon, his three guns would be sporting new buttstocks, complete with pads, ready for field-testing.

of-pull, drop, and cast dimensions to determine the proper fit. However, be-cause they have fitted so many shoot-ers over the years, and have such a large selection of buttstock patterns in both repeating and double shotguns to choose from, the try-gun is seldom used in the shop. They do take it to

the Grand American Trap Shoot and similar venues to fit new customers.

In addition to translating length-of-pull and drop dimensions, the try-gun can also be adjusted for down pitch. Down pitch is the distance the barrel(s) drops down from a straight line con-necting the top heel of the buttstock with the top rear of the receiver. The angle at which the butt of the stock is cut determines the down pitch. Chest, shoulder, and cheek anatomy all figure into the down pitch equation that allows the barrel(s) to be served level with the line of sight. The less down pitch, the more upward influence on the barrel(s) and vice versa. Zero to two inches is the normal range of down pitch. Field and trap shooters often prefer little to no down pitch to help them compen-sate for rising targets, offering some-what of a built-in lead. Many American shotguns from the late nineteenth and early twentieth century were built con-

Before the customer's blank is augured into the duplicating machine, it is band-sawed to approximate the shape of the finished stock.

ture content in walnut is a key factor in the stockmaking process. Freshly harvested walnut trees are usually quarter-sawn into the planks before they are cut into 3"-thick stock blanks. Most of the highly figured wood comes from the root, lower trunk and crotch sections of the tree. These "green" blanks are full of water, and the drying process must be carefully monitored to control the rate of moisture reduction. If the water is removed from the wood too quickly, the walnut can warp, crack and even crust over and collapse. The first few weeks of during are critical. Kiln drying is still the most practical and preferred method. Once the moisture content in the wood reaches 18 to 20 percent, the blank is considered stable enough for air curing in a humidity-controlled environment. Often the porous end grains at the head and butt of the blank are sealed with pitch or paraffin to ensure that the wood continues to dry uniformly. Depending on the care given the wood and the conditions of the drying process, some blanks may be ready for stocking within six months. But because of the density of the higher grades of American and English walnut, the longer and more lovingly it is air-dried, the better it tolerates inletting, checkering, and finishing. Some of Fred's private stock has been air-drying for decades.

As profiled stock (top) is traced with stylus, a wood bit cuts identical dimensions into the customer's blank (bottom).

siderable down pitch and drop to help accommodate the "head erect" style of shooting that was popular at that time. As such, most of these vintage guns are excellent candidates for restocking to longer and straighter dimensions.

Much anticipated, the next order of business was wood selection. My hunting partner decided that since the restocking of his guns was going to be a lifetime investment, he wanted the best American black walnut Wenig offered – the Special Selection grade. We followed Fred and Elbert into a large back room of the workshop and began browsing through mountainous stacks of walnut that were sorted by type and grade. It was mind-boggling. As we wandered among the aromatic walnut, Fred and Elbert sponged down likely looking blanks with water to highlight the grain and figure in the wood. Eventually, my mesmerized partner selected three stunning pieces of black walnut that were remarkably similar in figure and color. Fred quickly produced forearm blanks to match.

As we walked toward the front of the shop Fred explained that because so much black walnut is being exported to the Orient for furniture and other uses, even the plainer grades of the wood are becoming difficult to keep in inventory. The black walnut my partner chose was indeed Special Selection. Some would even refer to it as Exhibition Grade quality. The feather crotch

figure ran completely through the butt-stock of each blank, with straighter grain flowing, as it should, into the grip areas. Such densely grained walnut is stronger, inlets more precisely, and accepts checkering well. Some of the erratic-figured, burl walnut blanks may have knots, voids or other minor imperfections that are revealed after duplicating and must be expertly repaired and blended before final finishing.

Along with grain structure, the mois-

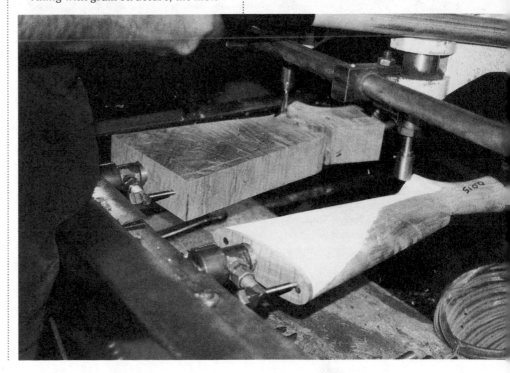

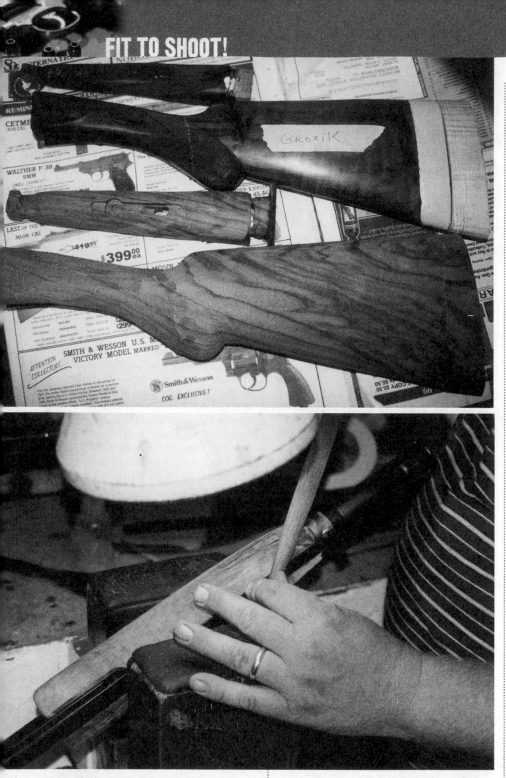

(top) With one-inch wood extension temporarily affixed for added length-of-pull, author's original Fox buttstock is used as duplicating template for his English walnut blank. (above) New forearm wood on Model 12 Duck is contoured with hand file.

When the moisture content of a blank stabilizes around 12 percent, it is ready for the craftsman. After the walnut has been mated to metal, care must still be taken in overly dry or wet climates to prevent the wood from shrinking, swell-

ing, warping, cracking, etc. All wood, raw or finished, continually reacts to its environment. Climate control is a perennial concern. A little common sense in the field and some gun-room vigilance will help prevent any unpleasant surprises from season to season. As an additional precaution against unwanted moisture, some stockmakers prefer to band-saw the blank in an outline of the desired stock design (pistol grip, straight grip, Monte Carlo, etc.) then allow it to dry a while longer before plying their craft. A completely stabilized

stock blank is their ultimate goal.

Before the selected blank is augured into the duplicating machine, a stock with the customer's required dimensions must be profiled. As in the case of my Fox, which only needed an inch of length added to it, the original stock can also be used as the duplicating template. But to preserve the finish of the original stock, a roughed-out stock of plain grade from Wenig's extensive inventory of factory duplicates is often used for the profiling procedure. Usually, the drop dimensions of these factory stocks must be raised to reflect modern standards before the proper fit can be achieved. This build-up is accomplished with a well-known staple of the automotive trade, plastic body putty. After mixing, the putty is applied liberally to the areas of the buttstock where the build-up is needed. It is allowed to dry, then is rasped and sanded to blend smoothly with the contours of the stock. This profiled duplicating stock is then quickly and carefully inletted to the customer's gun. The length-of-pull, drop and cast dimensions are painstakingly measured again and, if needed, adjusted with a wood rasp to duplicate the required specifications. Once again, the gun is given to the customer to check the fit and feel.

When the stocker and customer are satisfied with the dimensions, a laser pointer is inserted into the muzzle of the gun and the customer is asked to mount and point the gun at a patterning grid on the workshop wall some 20 feet distant. After several shots with the laser, the stock dimensions can be adjusted to make sure the gun in pointing precisely where the customer is looking. In my partner's case, the stock profiled for his Model 12 Duck required a few strokes of the wood rasp on the comb to give him the drop he needed to center the laser on the grid. The profiled stocks for his Model 50s were dead on target. However, because of their through-bolts, the Model 50 stocks required a little more time to be mated to metal. Once all three of the stocks were properly profiled and laser tested, they were removed from the guns and readied to take center stage on the stock duplicating machinery. Each profiled stock is precisely positioned and mounted on the duplicating machine so that when the operator traces over it with the hand-guided stylus, its exact dimensions, inletting, and contours are cut into the customer's blank that in mounted alongside it.

Today's gunstock duplicating machinery is really an offshoot of America's turn-of-the-nineteenth century gun trade. Unlike British bespoke guns, whose stocks are hewn entirely with drawknives, spokeshaves, gouges, chisels and other hand tools, American gunmakers devised ingenious machinery to render stock blanks within a whisker of final fit, significantly reducing costly hand labor. Modern stock duplicating equipment continues in that tradition. However, the final fit and finish of any properly stocked gun is still dependent on the experienced hand and educated eye of the master craftsman.

Showered in a steady stream of pungent walnut chips, the duplicating machine operator employs a series of gradually smaller tracing stylists and carving bits to reduce the blank to within .606" to .015" of the profiled stock's exact dimensions and inletting. This extra margin of wood left on the customer's blank allows the stockmaker to compensate for any flaws in the walnut he may encounter during the restocking process.

When the stock blank is removed from the duplicating machine, it is delivered to the stockmaker's bench where it is meticulously hand-grafted to gunmetal. Every custom stockmaker's goal is to make the walnut appear as if it grew around the metal. With the help of simple hand chisels and gouges, the craftsman carefully snugs the receiver against the head of the stock. This work is critical, especially when stocking sidelocks and other shotguns that require extensive and precise inletting

Restocked Model 12 Duck is checked to make sure the barrel is properly aligned with customer's master eye. (below) Customer shoulders fully restocked Model 12 Duck. Sanding, checkering, and finishing of buttstock and forearm will soon follow.

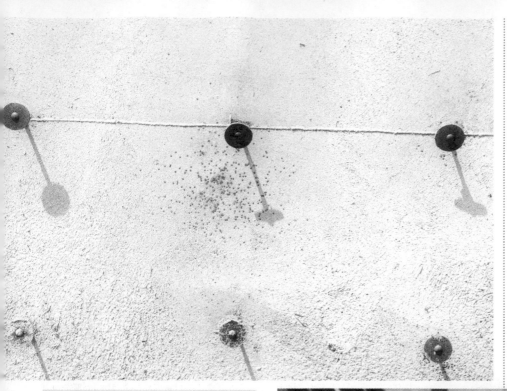

inletting black and is carefully shaved away by the stockmaker a sliver at a time. This time-consuming procedure is performed repeatedly until a perfect fit between wood and metal is achieved. In anticipation of future refinishing, most custom stockmakers leave a thin margin of wood (called "proud wood") above the inletted metal surfaces.

Once the new buttstock has been inletted to the gun, the customer goes through another session of gun mounting, "nose" pointing, and laser testing the make sure the stock dimensions are correct. Of the three guns restocked for my partner that morning, only his Model 50 12-ga. required a minor comb reduction to put it back on target. As we handled and admired the guns, the workshop became strangely quiet. It was lunchtime. The entire restocking process for all the guns had taken less than four hours.

After a quick lunch, my friend and I jumped into Fred's air-conditioned Suburban and were driven out west of town

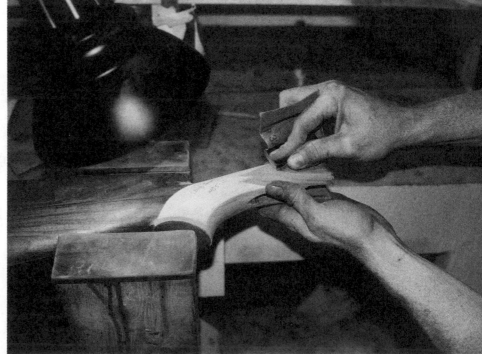

around the head and jaws of the stock. If this area of the stock has any gaps or high points, recoil and the elements can exploit them to crack or split even the most densely grained walnut. To make sure the wood is properly inletted against the metal, the bearing surfaces of the receiver are brushed with a thin film of inletting black. When the head of the stock is pressed against the receiver metal, the wood is marked with the

(top left) Modified choke pattern of 1-1/8 oz. of No. 7-1/2 lead shot at 25 yards. (above) Careful hand sanding brings walnut to a marble-like smoothness. (left) Author looks on as Elbert Smith applies a fresh coat of paint on metal backstop prior to pattern testing.

to field-test the guns at his shooting grounds. A metal storage shed, a large

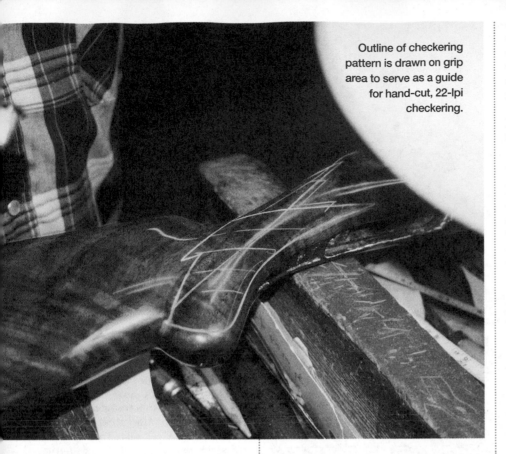

Outline of checkering pattern is drawn on grip area to serve as a guide for hand-cut, 22-lpi checkering.

vince us that all the guns were shooting where they should, and after sweating through our clothes in the noon-day sun, we headed back to the workshop to discuss what type of checkering and finish my friend wanted on his Winchesters.

Always partial to the mellow, dark-honey sheen of the original stock finish found on high grade Model 12s from the 1940s and 1950s, my partner brought along a pristine, half-a-century-old Super Field Model 12 to show Fred the type of finish he wanted on his guns. He also wanted the Super Field checking pattern duplicated on his Model 12 Duck. The new wood on his Model 50 would wear the same checkering pattern as the original stock and forearm from his Premier Skeet grade Model 50 20-ga.

At this point, the guns were handed over to the finishing department where Fred said the buttstock and forearm of each gun would be hand-sanded to marble smoothness with progressively finer grits of sandpaper. Wood whiskers would be raised and sanded repeatedly in preparation for the filler that is applied to close the pores of the wood. When the sanding process is complete, the wood is stained the desired color and turned over the master checkerer Darrel Smith. He pencils an outline of the checkering pattern on to the grip areas, clamps the wood into his checkering cradle, and, with knowing eyes and steady hands, begins to work his 22-lines-per-inch magic on the black

metal target board, and a portable clay-target trap were positioned on a long, narrow strip of fescue between towering cornfields. We uncased the guns and began the patterning process. Two of my partner's shotguns rang the metal backstop with perfectly thrown patterns. The Model 50 12-ga., however, was centering its patterns of 1-1/8 oz. of #7-3/4 shot a little low of the mark, even though its stock dimensions were identical to the other two guns. All things being equal, the only conclusion we could draw was that when my partner had the choke of the 30" barrel gun opened up from full to modified, it caused the pattern to print low. For patterning purposes, all of the guns were deliberately mounted and aimed, rifle-like, at the target boards. Perhaps the way my friend was sighting down the Model 50's ventilated rib also had something to do with its low-shooting tendencies. The real proof of their performance would be demonstrated in how well the gun powdered clay targets, where instinctive mounting and quick shooting demands a fit gun.

Proving to all assembled that proper gun fit dramatically improves shooting consistency, my old duck hunting partner left clay target powder wafting in the air after each shot. As we fed the portable trap, he seamlessly switched off

between all three guns, hitting clay targets at every angle. Even his enigmatic Model 50 12-ga. auto gave no indication of shooting low as he crushed target after target with the restocked gun. After expending several boxes of shells to con-

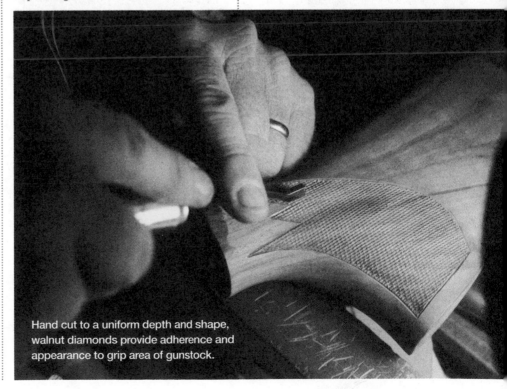

Hand cut to a uniform depth and shape, walnut diamonds provide adherence and appearance to grip area of gunstock.

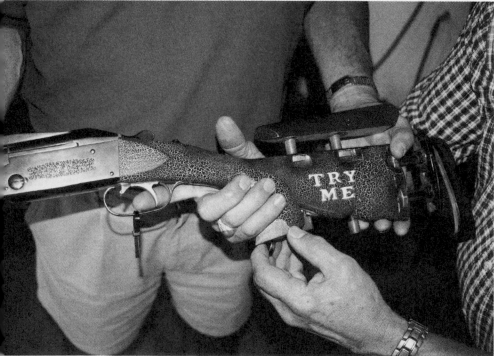

the wood to the finishing department.

It was decided that the satin glow of Wenig's regular lacquer stock finish would give my partner's Special Selection wood the vintage Winchester look he wanted on all his guns. To achieve it, each stock and forearm receives two sealer coats of catalyzed lacquer. After drying, the sealer is scuffed down with 320-grit sandpaper and seven to 12 more coats of lacquer are sprayed on the wood in the dust-free finishing booth. Before the final three topcoats of satin (or gloss) sheen are applied, the finish is scuffed again with 600-grit sandpaper and polished with fine steel wool. To remove any possible surface contamination, the finish is also whipped down with lacquer thinner then towel and air-dried. After the final topcoat has cured, the tape is removed from the checkering and a liberal coat of linseed oil is brushed over the diamonds. The lacquer finishing process usually requires two full days to complete. The lustrous finish is not only handsome, it is also extremely durable for field use.

Wenig also offers a traditional, hand-rubbed oil finish. After applying numerous coats of linseed oil to the walnut, the stock finisher uses 400- to 600-grit wet/dry sandpaper to sand the wood dust in with the oil until all surface pores on the stock are filled and smooth. Additional coats of oil are rubbed into the wood, allowed to dry, then buffed with fine steel wool and a soft cloth. This treatment produces a warm glow that only an oil finish can give walnut. After the final buffing, a few more coats of oil are slowly hand-rubbed into the wood. Oil finishing is a time-consuming process and, depending on the porosity of the wood, may require from five days to two weeks to complete. Because of its tighter grain, English walnut accepts an oil finish more readily than does the more porous black walnut. Gunstocks receiving an oil finish are checkered after the finish has been applied.

When Fred called later that summer to say the guns were ready to be shipped, my partner and I decided to once again make the eight-hour trek to Lincoln. In addition to our monetary investments, we both had a lot of sentiment in the guns and were unwilling to risk any delivery mishaps. We drove up to Fred's shop a week before the opening day of dove season. He knew we were anxious to give the guns a workout in the dove fields as a prelude for the upcoming upland bird and waterfowl seasons. In anticipation of our arrival, he had the

(top) With checkering and inletted surfaces covered with masking tape, finisher applies catalyzed lacquer to buttstock. (above) Try-Gun can be adjusted to determine correct length-of-pull, drop and cast dimensions for customers who are unsure of their ideal measurements. Here, Wenig adjusts pistol grip length for customer.

walnut. Darrel believes 22-lpi checkering is a good compromise between beauty and utility, especially on the more porous black walnut. Usually, only English

walnut can accept the fine checkering (32-lpi and up) that is seen in the more ornate patterns on high-grade guns. If the checkering wraps around the grip or forearm, Darrell measures his work in half-inch intervals to ensure his line is maintained over the contours. Using a hand-held MMC machine for rough outlining, and razor-sharp hand checkering tools, he cuts mirror-image, sharp-pointed diamonds that are flawless and functional. After he completes his work, if the stock is to receive a lacquer finish, he carefully covers the checkering and inletting with masking tape, then sends

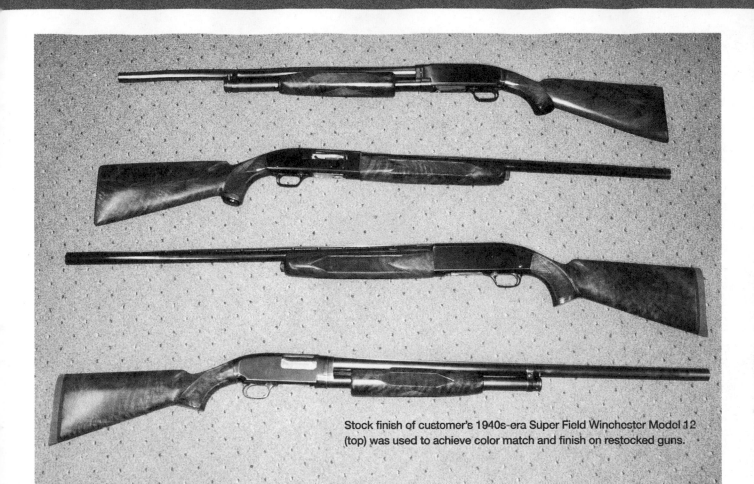

Stock finish of customer's 1940s-era Super Field Winchester Model 12 (top) was used to achieve color match and finish on restocked guns.

Fred Wenig poses with author's restocked, oil-finished AE Fox 12-ga.

guns waiting for us in his front office.

The transformation from amorphous wood blanks to custom gunstocks was complete, and it was breathtaking. We spent a long time admiring and shouldering the beautifully restocked shotguns before casing them for the return trip home. As we zipped up the canvas cases, my partner glanced over at me with a satisfied gleam in his eyes that also told me he was going to be tough to beat on the clay target range and in the duck blind for many seasons to come.

As with most labor-intensive endeavors, custom stock work can be costly. Depending on the quality of wood selected, inletting complexity, checkering pattern, wood finish, stock accessories, etc., you can easily invest more that the original cost of your gun. But if you want a lifetime of shooting pleasure, custom stockwork is an investment that will pay both tangible and intangible dividends down through the years. Good work – properly inletted, checkered, and finished – is a joy to behold and to shoot. Forced to choose between

upgrading my guns with fine walnut or embellishing them with hand engraving, I would opt for the good wood every time. As spectacular as custom engraving can be, only God can grow a tree.

With the well-respected Missouri stockmaking firms of Bishop and Fajen a fading memory, Wenig Custom Gunstocks, Inc., carries on in their tradition and continue to refine the American system of manufacturing begun by Parker Brothers, L.C. Smith, A.H. Fox, Winchester and others. This small Midwestern company is using modern American machinery and time-honored hand craftsmanship to produce a standard of gunstocking excellence that can compare with the best the world has to offer, at a fraction of the time and cost.

If you strive to perform your best afield, or if you just enjoy the compelling beauty of well-figured walnut, spend the time and money on a gunstock that fits you to perfection. In the grand scheme of a lifetime of shooting, it is a very small price to pay.

Less being better than more, the easiest way to get in trouble was to dunk a the whole clip into the can of Mobilubricant.

We're delighted to offer another fascinating piece of scholarship by one of Gun Digest's *favorite authors, this one dealing with a nearly-forgotten chapter in the story of the 1903 Springfield.*

The age of Mobilubricant

BY JIM FORAL

In the natural world, the adage "You have to learn to walk before you can run" has never been proven wrong. After all, mammals don't drop from the womb and immediately take off on a trot, nor does the hatchling free itself from the shell and instantly take flight.

The same is true for mechanical systems, as design and engineering bugs are isolated and eliminated. As first issued, the 1903 Springfield rifle and ammunition combination required almost immediate modernization. Every nation's ordnance department was leaning toward the ballistic advantages of high speed pointed bullets, and

there was a crying need to bring the new U.S. service arm into conformity. The nineteenth century-styled 220-gr. round-nosed bullet was replaced in 1906 with an up-to-date, svelte 150-gr. spire point. An astonishing 2,700 feet per second, an improvement by 500 fps, was achieved at safe pressures.

The Springfield rifle toddled into the next year without a match load having been developed for it, and the 1907 Palma marked the last time this important contest was shot with the Krag. In 1908, the new service rifle was fired in its inaugural international competition, the Olympic Games, held that year in

Bisley, England. The Springfield came out of the gate at an all-feet-off-the-ground gallop. The Americans carried off the rifle championships of the world, winning all but one team event, and that by but a single point. Those with but a cursory understanding of the wheels within wheels involved might have felt that the Springfield had finally struck its gait.

The victorious Americans, however, were mindful that they were nursing a limp that threatened to rob them of their victory and their medals. They had squinted through their bores and had seen the micro-stalactites dangling near the muzzle, and they had felt them with

Frankford Arsenal 1921 Match cartridge with "Tin Can" bullet (Gary Muckell collection)

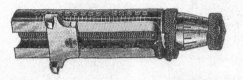

O'HARE MICROMETER

Made for the Springfield Rifle Model 1903

This Micrometer has all others beaten a dozen ways. First—It's Made in America. The Army Navy Marine Cavalry Engineers Naval Academy and all the Rifle Teams in the Service uses this Micrometer. All of our State Teams at The Great National Match use the O'Hare Micrometer. The great records made in the last Two National Matches at Camp Perry is largely due to the use of The O'Hare Micrometer. **Price $5.00.**

A close look at the P.J. O'Hare sight micrometer. The smart shooters selected this sight adjuster almost without exception.

a tight patch on their wiping rods. As the Springfield system was put through its paces, a lameness manifested itself as lumpy, metallic bore fouling that attached itself so tenaciously it had to be dissolved to be removed.

DOPING IT OUT

The Olympic ammunition contract had been awarded to the United States Cartridge Company. Shortly after the Games, U. S. C. Co. issued a statement on the subject of cleaning that, when condensed, amounted to a publicly conducted head scratching. The noticeable overuse of the word "seems" was indicative of the collective uncertainty of the time. There was no current strategy to check or retard the fouling, but a strong ammonia-based solution was developed as an efficient means of eliminating it.

Dissolved into the solution of four ounces of water and six ounces of stronger ammonia water (28 percent) were 200 grains of ammonium carbonate and an ounce of ammonium persulfate. The ingredients were readily obtainable at most city drug stores. This "ammonia dope" was made up fresh for each cleaning. Both fresh and stale solution were especially corrosive to steel exposed to the air. Rusting started within a few minutes and slackness could ruin a bore overnight. The dope's use was onerous and required a commitment to doing it right. The chamber was corked with a rubber stopper and the fluid poured into the muzzle through a rubber tube. For a half hour – and no longer – the

rifle was set aside to percolate while the dissolved jacket material turned the solution a blue color. The bore was then wiped thoroughly dry and oiled. The practice of some was to then dust the bore with graphite and burnish with a slightly oversized cotton patch.

U. S. C. Co. offered hope that a better way was around the corner: "It seems probable that we shall be able in time to evolve other satisfactory methods of cleaning a barrel, and riflemen should not be disappointed when they find original results are not entirely satisfactory."

Army Ordnance specifications for bullet jackets in the early smokeless days called for an alloy known as cupro-nickel, a metallic compound comprised of 60 percent copper and 40 percent elemental nickel. Strong enough to hold the lead core against deformation, cupro-nickel took the rifling readily but was not so hard as to excessively wear the lands. In the Krag and Model 1903-gr. cartridges, loping along at 2,000 to 2,300 feet per second, cupro-nickel fouling took the form of an innocuous wash and

caused no problems. When the cupro-nickel patched 150-gr. flat-based spitzer came to be known officially as the Model 1906 Ball, and its velocity at the muzzle had been accelerated to a dizzying 2,700 fps, serious trouble became evident.

A chemical affinity existed between the nickel in the jacket and the steel in the barrel. This attraction, at the 1906 velocity, caused a scraping of the jacket metal to stick in the bore, creating a rough spot. Each succeeding bullet deposited its quota until the ironed-over accumulation of alloy formed lumpy clusters along the last few inches of bullet travel. These deposits built up quickly and were absolutely fatal to accuracy and all but impossible to dislodge with the ordinary wiping rod and scratch brush. Twenty-five shots through a clean barrel, it was said, was all it too to foul it so severely that groups past the mid-ranges were thoroughly ravaged.

As soon as the 1908 Olympic Games were completed, Dr. Walter Hudson, that generation's great problem solver, wrote that the German silver was "the most resistant metal that has so far been found suitable." Not as an afterthought certainly, he also intimated everyone's fond desire: "The discovery of some better material by one of America's shooters would be most welcome." In 1909, writer E.C. Crossman broadcasted that either a change in rifling pitch or jacket composition was the route to eliminate the fouling. Further he advocated patience; the government and military target shooting experts would squash this fouling bugbear. Credentialed and experienced civilians would lead the way, as they'd done in the past. An occasionally vocal rabble earnestly held that the metal-jacketed bullet, for any purpose, was a "temporary makeshift" soon to be superseded by some yet-to-be-

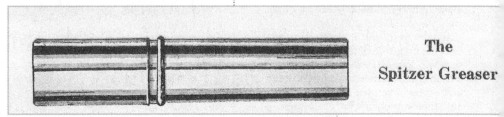

The Spitzer Greaser

There were all sorts of ways to carry Mobilubricant to the firing line. The company clerk could provide typewriter ribbon tins for free, but for those flush enough to spring for store-bought, the P.J.O'Hare spitzer greaser only set them back a quarter.

MOBILE LUBRICANT

3-ounce Cans, Price, 25 cents

O'Hare's proprietary equivalent to the name brand Mobilubricant, in a handy compact package.

discovered homogenous material. Until this marvel presented itself, humanity would have to content itself with cupronickel. That bullets were jacketed with this infernal alloy was tantamount to a confession by the cartridge makers either of incompetence or a desire "to ruin rifle barrels and so increase gun sales."

For the singular virtue of this contrary metal, its ability to grip rifling, an extreme price was being exacted. Across the country, the troops stared at the clock while their vertical gun barrels steeped in that wretched ammoniac pickle, and collectively lamented that this was the best resolution that could be hoped for. On the ranges, inside the cantonments and drill halls, and wherever America's military men assembled themselves in late 1908, there was much wailing and gnashing of teeth because of it.

History had proven that a metal jacket for a bullet driven faster than 1,800 feet per second was absolutely essential. Capt. Townsend Whelen himself had been a vocal champion of steel as the ideal bullet jacket material. With plenty of old-school support, he had continually gone on record touting its superiority. All of the armies of Europe, apart from England, were using them in the continental bloodletting of 1914. But steel jacketing wasn't perfect. Even the mildest steel jacket would wear the bore faster than would cupro-nickel, but even when shooting steel-sheathed bullets the Springfield's barrel life was calculated to be in the neighborhood of 4,000-5,000 shots. Their use required a premium, hard, and costly grade of barrel steel, and the U.S. War Department wasn't willing to lavish the expense on an expendable battle rifle. Even when plated, steel mantles were prone to rust, which would have compromised the military consideration of indefinite storage, thus precluding the adoption of steel jackets.

Isolated from military guidance, some

civilians dreamed up novel but ineffective ways to mechanically rid their bores of cupro-nickel fouling. Pushing and pulling a wiper with a tight patch dusted with emery flour was one citizen's inspiration that resulted in a ruined bore and the fouling virtually unmolested. Capt. Whelen warned his readers that this method removed steel five times as fast as it did the nickel fouling.

Another devised a guide to follow the rifling lands and fashioned a jig to hold a tiny steel scraper that cold-chiseled out the fouling. His success was incomplete. A brass screw repeatedly driven through the bore head first was another exercise. By and by, much of the fouling was stripped out this way, and the bore was good for another 25 shots. The original formula Hoppe's #9, advertised to remove metallic fouling, stubbornly refused to do so. A boreful of acidic vinegar, the resort of another misguided soul, was equally ineffective.

Once the weight of the troublesome cure had exceeded a pound, the search for a hoped-for ounce of prevention began in earnest. The collective mental wheels were set in motion. The military "sharps" reminded themselves that the familiar lead alloy slug, without protective lubrication or insulating paper patch, left a severe metallic fouling. It was also remembered that the 1900-era Krag metal-cased 220-grainer had been anointed beneficially by two lube-laden grooves hidden inside the case neck. Unlike the Japan-waxed Krag roundnose,

the new 150-gr. M1905 Ball lacked the traditional cannelured grip to clench a greasy or waxy substance.

AN UNLIKELY SOLUTION

We still owe a debt to the individual struck with the inspiration that grease applied directly to the smooth government spitzer might serve as a lubricating

New World's Records!

Remington Metallic Ammunition has proven its supreme accuracy and reliability. All World's Records for Long Runs of consecutive Bulls-Eyes from 300 to 1200 yards are now held by shooters who used Remington .30 Springfield 180-Grain Palma-Olympic Match Ammunition.

REMINGTON UMC

1921

At Camp Perry, Ohio—
1st Sgt. T. B. Crawley, U.S.M.C., shooting in the Winchester Match made 176 Consecutive Bulls-Eyes at 800 yards.
(World's Record)
1st Sgt. J. W. Adkins, U.S.M.C., shooting in the Western Match made 80 Consecutive Bulls-Eyes at 900 yards.
(World's Record)
1st Sgt. J. W. Adkins, U.S.M.C., shooting in the Wimbledon Match made 75 Consecutive Bulls-Eyes at 1000 yards.
(World's Record)

At Sea Girt, N. J.—
Marine Gunner C. A. Lloyd, U.S.M.C., shooting in the Rogers Match made 101 Consecutive Bulls-Eyes at 600 yards.
(World's Record)
Sgt. Thos. J. Jones, U.S.M.C., shooting in the Libbey Match made 66 Consecutive Bulls-Eyes at 1100 yards.
(World's Record)
Sgt. Edwin F. Holzhauer, U.S.M.C., shooting in the Spencer Match made 41 Consecutive Bulls-Eyes at 1200 yards.
(World's Record)

At Wakefield, Mass.—
Sgt. Thos. J. Jones, U.S.M.C., shooting on the new 10-inch Bulls-Eyes made 132 Consecutive Bulls-Eyes at 300 yards.
(World's Record)

Americans Win With Remington

The team representing the United States at the International Matches held at Lyons, France, August, 1921, won the big event — the Free Rifle Team Match—and W. R. Stokes of the American Team won the Free Rifle Individual Match, all shooting Remington .30 Springfield 180-Grain Palma-Olympic Match Ammunition.

On The Small Bore Ranges

The new Remington .22 Long Rifle N. R. A. Target Cartridges were used by Mr. P. E. Lahm in making a new record for the Small Bore Palma course of 224 out of 225. The course consists of 15 shots each at 150, 175, and 200 yards. Capt. F. G. Bonham won the Small Bore Wimbledon using the same ammunition with a score of 99 out of 100. The match was 20 shots at 200 yards.

Remington for Shooting **Right**

Copper-jacketed bullets finally spelled the end for Mobilubricant in the early 1920s.

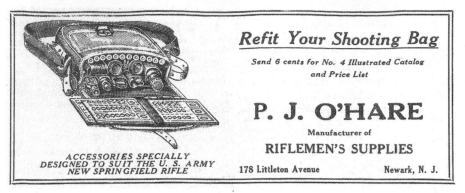
P.J. O'Hare even provided the range pack to carry the gear he sold.

element. The brainstorm might have come upon this unrecorded someone during a barracks session of meticulously stripping away the thick layers of the packing grease Cosmoline from every pore of a freshly-issued 1903 Springfield. Accomplished with gasoline and plenty of rags, this drudgery was the bane of each Army recruit. When done, there was plenty of the amber-colored Cosmoline to be discarded. At some point it was smeared onto the exposed points of the bullets of the New Springfield cartridges, and this contrived system underwent an unofficial and haphazard trial. The Cosmoline melted readily and decomposed, leaving behind a charred residue of abrasive carbon. Otherwise, it worked after a fashion but its inability to tolerate friction-generated heat became evident. Some tried common Vaseline, with a predictably similar result. Ordinary graphite was tried and set aside as another failure. It soiled everything and didn't reduce the fouling. What was needed was a grease that took heat without liquefying.

The realization that such a substance already existed – as an automotive lubricant, no less – was a natural deduction that occured to any number of wide-awake amateur diagnosticians. Thankfully, their quest wasn't a year-long exercise in trial and error. Mobilubricant appears to have been one of the first products tried. And it worked. When a coating was applied to each exposed bullet surface by dipping, lumpy bore deposits reportedly vanished and didn't return. Word was spread throughout military circles and as the initially small band of Mobilubricant believers increased, its use was soon service-wide.

Physically, Mobilubricant was simply a heavy grease used largely for automotive lubrication. It was made by the Vacuum Oil Company of Buffalo, New York, an industry pioneer dating back to 1866. It was very similar to Cosmoline in appearance and identical to the various automotive cup greases in characteristics. A significant advantage was that considerably greater heat was needed to render it fluid than was the case with Cosmoline or any ordinary gun grease.

Nearly all of the top-flight military shooters endorsed the greasing practice. When he became totally convinced of Mobilubricant's ability to prevent the nagging cupro-nickel fouling, Capt. Townsend Whelen, this country's eminent authority on all things marksmanship- and ordnance-related, ultimately gave his prelatic blessing.

The logical presumption among the masses was that since the Mobilubricant was a grease, its function was that of a lubricant. Capt. Whelen expressed his disagreement when he wrote: "In fact it would seem that it does not lubricate at all, but rather coats the bore with a substance of about the consistency of celluloid, which acts to a certain extent to prevent metal fouling and wear." A pair of chemists – one a professor – whom I consulted validated my own interpretation of Whelen's statement. We agreed with Whelen's apparent assertion that Mobilelubricant formed a micro-thin barrier that prevented the bullet's direct contact with the bore. It was for this reason, and not because of the grease's lubricating properties, that Mobilubricant was so effective in eliminating metallic fouling.

Mobilubricant was not a snake oil-type curative hawked by a traveling huckster. Its value was unquestionable and well known, and several supplemental benefits were attributed to it. There was no dissention that the slick micro-plating of grease made bore cleaning much less of a chore. Lower temperatures from less friction added

On the thousand-yard range at Bisley with the American Olympic rifle team, among the first to contend with the effects of cupro-nickel fouling in July of 1908. The man looking into the camera is C.B. Winder of Winder Musket fame. The long-faced individual, second in line, is K.K.V. (Kellogg Kennon Venable) Casey, the most outstanding long distance rifleman of the era and the man Chauncey Thomas called "the best shot ever to face a target." Photo from the September,1908 issue of *Recreation* magazine.

The Victorious American Rifle Team at Bisley.
On the 1,000 yards range.

Greasing the spitzer by the dip-and-twirl method.

somewhat to the useful life of the barrel. In addition, a noticeably higher average accuracy was maintained, translating to higher scores. This was not wishful thinking, but documented beyond contention. It may have been just the sales talk of a mail order merchant, but P.J. O'Hare insisted that the decreased friction resulted in reduced recoil. Secondary advantages considered, the worth of Mobilubricant as a sure-fire remedy to the annoying Springfield fouling could almost be considered a bonus.

IT'S ALL IN THE WRIST

For the benefit of civilians continually sampling the military .30 caliber discipline, Capt. Whelen periodically republished concise instructions for proper, trouble-free greasing. "The bullet should be pushed down into the grease to where it enters the shell, and given a twirl with the fingers, then withdrawn, and the grease adhering to it in only a thin coating is all that is necessary."

Mobilubricant was not regarded as a potion with supposed lucky or magical properties. Once its benefits had been established, its use developed into a fixed and optionless habit. A shooter showing up at a match between 1909 and 1920 who failed to plunge the points of his issued .30-1906 cartridges into the indispensable Mobilubricant was

a notable exception. Among U.S. military and civilian marksmen, at a match held for the sole purpose of winning, the application of Mobilubricant or some offshoot variant wasn't just common, it was, according to Whelen, "almost universal." Another period authority chose the words "almost to a man." Novice competitors learned the drill by mimicking the mechanical yet careful dip and twirl of an NCO at an adjacent firing point. Greasing the bullet thereafter was a ritual done by rote.

Prior to becoming a familiar name in the post-War shooting press, C. (Charles) S. Landis was a budding columnist and an ardent Springfield competitor. In a 1919 treatise, the seasoned veteran advised the hopeful novice on the matter of essential equipment. "Any rifleman aspiring to success in military rifle shooting needs a good outfit," he wrote. All the essentials fit into a modest-sized satchel. To move the rear sight, a very few got by with sensitive fingers, but most depended on the requisite micrometer sight adjuster. The well-informed knew that sight black was not a luxury. Equally vital was a small can of Mobilubricant. "I am a firm believer in the efficiency and benefit of using grease on metal cased bullets as a means of reducing the amount of metal fouling," Landis reported. Whelen rehashed the same basic guidance periodically. On going to the firing point, he cautioned: "See that you have rifle, ammunition properly greased, micrometer, score book, pencil, telescope rest, Mobilubricant, and sight black."

Generally, competitors unceremoniously dunked their bullets into an open container of the Mobilubricant,

a practice not conducive to uniformly filming the projectile only. Some thought was devoted to shielding the case neck, thus foolproofing the application process. A lot of shooter's kits held a simple typewriter ribbon tin. These held enough lube for the entire firing line but were compact and totally dirtproof when closed. P.J. O'Hare cataloged his own grease; "Mobile Lubricant" was put out in the same style of container. A .30-caliber hole punched into the lid of either can blocked entry at the case neck and was a low-tech makeshift that worked. Whelen recommended a steel washer with a .310" hole be floated on the grease. The "spitzer greaser" put out by O'Hare was a telescoping metal tube with an airtight cover. By an "ingenious arrangement" it lubed only the bullet.

Sooner or later the lubed cartridge would get dropped in the sand or fall into the dirt on the shooting mat. If fired, the bullet became a file that gnawed the precious rifling. The one sure safe way to grease bullets was one at a time, just before loading them into the rifle. Getting the Mobilubricant where it was not wanted or needed was the unavoidable consequence of using it. Inescapably, properly and sparingly lubricated projectiles of magazine-fed cartridges contacted internal action parts and left behind at least a grimy trace. Each successively chambered round distributed the grease over a larger area and added its share to the ever-accumulating aggregate. As firing warmed the chamber, the grease flowed to pervade all the metal not already covered. Sloppily-greased bullets compounded the trouble and sped the process. The common practice of haphazardly dunking all the bullets of a five shot stripper clip at once besmeared everything in their path from magazine well to throat.

Summarized from the authoritative viewpoint, Whelen once recorded this observation: "It is almost impossible to use it without getting the chamber heavily coated with grease."

When the rifle chamber was violated with Mobilubricant, the incompressible grease prevented normal case obturation. This gas-sealing expansion was necessary during the high pressure phase of discharge to hold the shell in place and reduce the already considerable rearward thrust on the locking system. Practically, the skim of grease decreased the size of the chamber and gave a greater density of loading. Chamber pressure increases of 5,000 psi, according to Whelen, could realistically be expected. Compounding the trouble was the tapered cartridge case being virtually unrestrained by the chamber walls. With far more force than ever intended, the case head slammed straight back against the bolt face, excessively stressing the locking lugs.

The 1903 Springfield receivers were heat treated with the same underdeveloped methods used to case harden the frame of its predecessor, the Krag-Jorgensen. The heat gauging process was accomplished, not by instrument, but by the trained eye of old-school master hands, scrutinizing color in the furnaces. Unavoidably, some steel got "burnt" and escaped detection. These brittle receivers were produced during the infamous period of the "Low Numbered Springfields" that we have all been warned about for the past 90 years. Heat-treated overly-hard bolts sometimes shed their lugs, particularly if the lugs' bearing surfaces were uneven.

In 1913, E.C. Crossman provided figures contrasting theoretical bolt thrust for dry and greased contaminated chambers. In a normally dry chamber, the bolthead received a thrust of 5,000-6,000 lbs. With a greased case it took a hammer blow of 8,700 pounds. A rash of sheared bolt lug reports appeared in the 1913 rifleman's journals and the inference was that the use of the Mobilubricant contributed to the failures. Capt. Whelen, however, was convinced that the real culprit was the "defective temper" of the lugs and was totally uncompromising with this stance. The safety margin built into the Springfield would contain pressures in excess of proof loads, he maintained. Even if the bolt held, a frangible receiver couldn't be counted on to stay in one piece.

The odds were long that detonation would occur, but it happened often enough that after a while such incidents failed to make the front page. Blown-up Springfields, in the 'teens, were not unheard of. Some burst from firing an 8mm Mauser cartridge and for other assorted reasons. The ones wrecked from the cause of greased chambers were anything but rare, and we'll probably never know the full extent of it.

Surplus Mobilubricant often resulted in another handicap. With an over-greased bore swabbed with Hoppe's #9 and stowed muzzle up at a July shoot, the resultant grease/solvent slurry seeped into the bolt body

and collected along the mainspring. Upon firing, inertia flung the fluid rearward into the shooter's eye. An instinctive and long-lasting flinch was the usual consequence.

ALTERNATIVES TO MOBILUBRICANT?

In 1914, Chas. Newton brought out his proprietary Wire Point bullets, jacketed with pure unalloyed copper. Western Tool and Copper Works in Oakland, California, introduced a modest line of expanding bullets, jacketed with the same element, in that same year. Whelen used a lot of the Newton 172-gr. spitzers and was openly fond of them. By 1918, he'd gathered enough experience to form an opinion: "Copper seems to be proving superior to cupro-nickel as a bullet jack-

et material, as it does not metal foul so badly and is superior to steel as it does not wear the barrel of the rifle so badly." In the course of tests, one finding was as indisputable as it was unexpected: copper-jacketed projectiles wore a rifle's bore no more than a lead alloy bullet. Its fouling amounted to little more than a wash, easily removable with a swabbing of stronger ammonia. By early 1919, many of the modern factory loaded commercial bullets were sheathed with copper and tin plated to prevent the formation of verdigris. The swing to copper seemed certain. The War Dept. was beginning to see the light but was cautiously slow to abandon its proven cupro-nickel. Change within Army Ordnance didn't happen overnight.

Whelen regarded the banner years of 1918-19 as an unparalleled period of

REMINGTON UMC

Civilian America on the Rifle Range

No. 5
American Marksmen Series
Painted for Remington UMC
by F. X. Leyendecker

Our dapper demonstrator is outfitted by P.J. O'Hare with all the essential gear. The spitzer greaser containing Mobilubricant is at his left hand. This painting, one of a series commissioned by Remington Arms in 1916-17, was executed by Frank X. Leyendecker, a popular illustrator of the day.

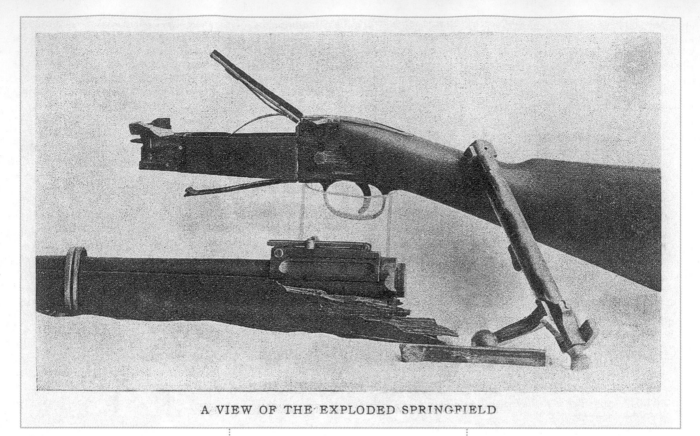

A VIEW OF THE EXPLODED SPRINGFIELD

discovery and enlightenment in the field of rifle refinement and in interior and exterior ballistic science. More had been accomplished, Whelen wrote in the summer of 1919, in those two years than "in all the centuries since the grooved barrel was invented." The days of untested "expert" opinion, guesswork, and clinging to unfounded archaic beliefs were replaced with a new era of proving or disproving old-time theory beyond doubt. This great step toward ballistic modernization was the work of a few – and yet unsung – men coupled with the full resources of the DuPont ballistic laboratories being placed at their disposal.

For a time in early 1920, the shift was to a safer wax-based alternative to grease, and Whelen kept his readers posted on the experimental trials of waxy, graphite-incorporating compounds. Fundamentally, fine graphite was added to molten Japan wax or Ceresine, and the mixture was constantly stirred to keep the black lead in suspension. The bullets were then dipped into this blend, taking pains to avoid getting any on the case neck, and allowed to quickly harden. Carnaba and beeswax, softened with Vaseline, were tried by some. Machine rest tests at Frankford Arsenal proved that the wax/graphite treated bullets grouped with National Match ammunition tested

at the same time. Cold-weather shooting, however, produced erratic results at the target. It was theorized that the wax didn't melt completely during the bullet's excursion through the bore, and the remaining solids unbalanced the projectile, spoiling groups. Contemporary speculation – based on the bullet's vapor trail and the inordinately slick passage of a white flannel patch and its gray emergence from the muzzle – was that lubrication was totally provided by the graphite. The wax acted simply as a carrier for the soft carbon. Despite the prominence of those who touted the system, these waxy preparations, after fair trial, fell by the wayside.

The lead article in the August 15, 1921, number of *Arms and the Man*, under the byline of Steven Trask, carried the dumbfounding title "FRANKFORD CONDEMNS GREASE." Had this been a newspaper headline, the big scoop would have rated an EXTRA! in red 72-point type heading the page. After 13 years with cupro-nickel and Mobilubricant, experts at Army ordnance had finally gotten around to officially and definitively testing the combination to determine the actual effects, risks, and wisdom of its use.

In the Spring of 1921, Frankford Arsenal technicians conducted a series of experiments in order to conclu-

The smithereens of a Springfield dismantled by "unknown causes" in June, 1916. By the firer's admission, the bullets were lubricated.

sively ascertain facts and establish figures. The rifleman was provided an amassment of data fresh from the arsenal's pressure gun in a report over the signature of Major Townsend Whelen, then newly promoted and commanding the Ordnance Dept. at Frankford Arsenal, Pennsylvania.

Two other preparations tested alongside the Mobilubricant were ordinary drug store grade Vaseline and the trendy Cavalry bullet grease, a substance that incorporated cocoa butter and blue ointment to stiffen the principal ingredient, which was petroleum jelly. A number of rifles were fired with and without grease to learn if an accuracy edge was apparent either way. There was no advantage with judiciously applied lube, but accuracy suffered markedly with excessive lubrication. An analysis in Frankford's well-equipped ballistic labs revealed what really went on inside a Mobilubricated bore. The cupro-nickel jacket left behind a harmless, non-accumulating, almost transparently thin coating of metal. Shot dry, the same plating was evident, as was the alloy's predisposition to gather into lumpy bunches near the muzzle. To simulate how the average soldier was known to have done it, Mobilubricant was smeared onto the bullets of 1920 Match cartridges and the case necks also received their dab. Just ahead of the chamber, the greased ammunition's pressure spiked to a maximum of 65,000 psi, contrasted to 51,000 psi for normal dry cartridges. Substituting Vaseline for Mobilubricant, the rear end pressure registered in excess of 71,000 psi and wrecked the pressure gauge, which was considerably stronger than the Springfield rifle. In summary, the Frankford Arsenal staff concluded what every veteran marksman had known for a decade. Mobilubricant entirely prevented patchy and lumpy metallic fouling. They determined also that its misuse presented a danger not to be regarded lightly. Unless it was applied with the greatest of care, pressures could be dangerously increased, as could the backthrust on the bolthead of the rifle. Major Whelen's closing was hardly a revelation: "It is believed that it is not safe to use it because experience with troops has shown that extreme care can not be insured in its use."

SLIPPERY WHEN WET

That the technical description of the 1921 National Match ammunition was published in the same *Arms and the Man* issue was hardly a coincidence. It was intended to be seen while the Major's counsel was fresh and most timely. The noteworthy feature of these cartridges was the 170-gr. bullet, jacketed with the standard cupro-nickel, electrically plated with a thin wash of tin. The frosted silvery metal was to vaporize instantly on firing and coat the bore. Arsenal experiments had indicated that the tin functioned as a lubricant and prevented the build-up of cupro-nickel fouling.

Competitors were particularly and firmly cautioned that the use of grease in any form with the 1921 Match ammo was "positively dangerous." The chamber pressure had been increased to achieve the desired 2,700 fps and there was a lessened margin of safety. Conceivably, grease could run pressures 50 percent higher, and every effort was made to make this well-known. The likelihood of damage to the rifle, and its operator's precious person, was clear and forcefully stated in black and white. Repetition for emphasis was preached at orientation classes at Camp Perry and by its watchful range officers.

People could have not been more

sternly warned. Still, the compulsion to grease the service ammunition had been ingrained for nearly a generation. Mobilubricating the "Tin Can" ammunition was the equivalent of running with scissors: someone could lose an eye. Someone almost did. Against all advice, a Major on the Texas team snuck a tin of Mobilubricant to the line, did the dip and twirl, and his rifle fragmented in front of his face. He suffered an ulcerated eye and was in considerable pain for some time. Major Julian Hatcher, an Ordnance officer detailed to the National Matches that year, eyewitnessed a rifle wrecked by a slippery bullet. Several other similar instances were reported, all blamed on the outlawed grease.

For a time, Whelen was sold on tin as the marksmen's liberator from the shackles of cupro-nickel. Tin's fouling reduction properties were first discovered during World War One by French artillerists. Their projectiles' copper rotating bands smeared a thick cupric deposit onto the deep grooves of the 6" guns. Accuracy slumped and the predicament was a desperate one. The French

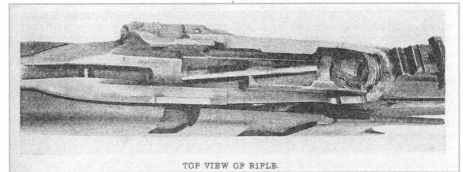

TOP VIEW OF RIFLE.

learned that tin sheets placed within the powder charge plated the bore and reduced the problem significantly.

With this same end in mind, Du Pont introduced two canister powders incorporating flaked tin about 1921. Serious over-plating and public acceptance issues cropped up right from the start, and these were not popular propellants. Plating the bullet to coat the bore, however, was Townsend Whelen's own private brainstorm. After the 1921 Matches, he lamented finally that after so much was expected of the favored tin plating, in the end it was "just another metallic fouling."

THE END OF THE MOBILUBRICANT ERA

The concluding scenes of the days of Mobilubricant on the range played out during the shooting season of 1921.

At one time indispensable, spitzer greasers and typewriter tins filled to the brim with lube were reduced to relics of a bygone era almost overnight.

The need for Frankford Arsenal to perfect and adopt a copper alloy jacket material continued in earnest. The program was spurred and progress was double-timed to completion. In charge of Frankford's Small Arms Department, now Col. Townsend Whelen co-ordinated the effort. Gilding metal, a compound consisting of nine parts copper to one part zinc, was once considered too soft to envelop the high speed 150-gr. service bullet, but renewed testing proved that it was in many ways superior to cupronickel. Most importantly, gilding metal didn't smite the bore with a plague of lumpy deposits of itself. In the course of a few months, gilding metal supplanted cupro-nickel altogether, and the world was suddenly a better place. Commercially, Western Cartridge Company patented a variation comprising 90 percent copper, 8 percent zinc, and 2 percent of the wonder-working tin. Lubaloy was its trade name and Western had it ready for

Another Springfield that let go. This didn't happen every day, and grease wasn't always the cause, but it was usually high on the list of suspects.

the sportsman in 1922. That same year, Western, with its 180-gr. Lubaloy-clad match bullet, beat all its rivals for a contract to provide the long range cartridges for the Palma competition.

Cupro-nickel was not just a transitory state of the art bullet jacket metal and a stepping stone to something better; it was the aggravation of a generation. More than an imperfect solution to a vexing dilemma, Mobilubricant was very much the "necessary evil" that Whelen once considered it. Freed from the fetters of cupro-nickel and unhobbled by Mobilubricant, the Springfield rifle strutted into the 1920s, having stylishly and faultlessly hit its stride.

For years during the Magnum Era, the .45 Colt languished as a dinosaur, a holdover from a long-dead age. But it's a great old cartridge nevertheless, as the author will only be too happy to tell you.

Author's Bounty Hunter with six JHP handloads.

Fun with the .45 Colt

BY JOHN W. ROCKEFELLER

Sixguns for the .45 Colt have been around since 1873, when Colt first chambered the round in their Single Action Army revolver. The Colt revolver became the official service sidearm of the United States Army…and the handgun of choice for every westerner who could get his hands on one!

The .45 Colt was originally loaded with 40 grains of blackpowder behind a lead round-nose bullet of 250 grains. When I first started shooting .45 Colt sixguns, nearly 50 years ago, the blackpowder had been replaced with smokeless and the primers were non-corrosive, but the bullet remained essentially the same.

Colt had discontinued production of their Single Action Army revolver in 1941, dropping their fine New Service double-action in 1946 but, by 1955, they were once again offering their Single Action Army revolver in .45 Colt for $125.00

Manufacturer	Bullet Weight & Type	Muzzle Velocity (fps)	Muzzle Energy (fpe)
CCI Blazer	200-gr. JHP	1000	444
Federal	225-gr. SWC-HP	830	345
Hornady	255-gr. Cowboy	725	298
Remington	225-gr. SWC	960	460
Remington	250-gr. LRN	860	410
Speer	250-gr. Gold Dot HP	900	450
Winchester	225-gr. Silvertip HP	920	423
Winchester	250-gr. LRN	860	420
USA Cowboy (Win.)	250-gr. Lead	750	312

JHP=Jacketed Hollowpoint; SWC-HP=Semi-Wadcutter Hollowpoint; LRN=Lead Round-Nose

– a rather high price at the time. I could not afford a Single Action Army then, but I was able to pick up a New Service in .45 Colt at a local pawn shop and, a bit later, a Smith & Wesson .455 Hand Ejector, which I shipped off to a gunsmith in Walterville, Oregon, to be rechambered to .45 Colt. My mismatched pair of sixguns were good shooters, though, thanks to their hump-backed frames and skinny grips, they tended to kick a bit.

My current .45 Colt revolver, a Christmas present from my wife Marlene, is a German-made single-action sixgun from H. Weihrauch, a.k.a. Arminius. Stamped "BOUNTY HUNTER" on its color case-hardened frame, it has fixed sights and a 4-3/4" barrel. Thanks to its "plow handle" grip, it's a lot more pleasant to shoot than were my old double-actions!

Factory ammunition for the .45 Colt is loaded to a SAAMI maximum average pressure of 14,000 C.U.P. or, in other words, to the same pressure as the original blackpowder loads of the late nineteenth century. Since factory ammunition is loaded with bullets weighing anywhere from 200 to 255 grains, it follows that not all loads will shoot to the the same point on the target. My old Colt and Smith & Wesson sixguns had sights properly "regulated" for the heavier 250-gr. slugs but would shoot low with lighter bullets. My Arminius revolver, on the other hand, shoots high with the 250-gr. bullets, yet prints dead on with

SPEER swaged-lead bullets for 45 Colt including 200-gr. SWC, 230-gr. RN, 250-gr. SWC, and .457" Round Ball for author's "double-ball" loads.

loads using a 225-gr. slug.

Factory ammo is fine, but I am primarily a handloader, and most of my shooting over the years has been done with my own handloads – mostly with bullets I cast myself. The .45 Colt is an easy cartridge to handload, but it does have a few faults.

First of all, the .45 Colt has a rather narrow rim and, aside from the fact that it is easy for the extractor to slip past the rims when ejecting empties, it also doesn't give the shellholder of your press much to hold onto. Back in the old days, when I was loading on a Herters press using an old Lyman All-American die set with a steel sizing die, and even though I was lubricating my cases, it was not uncommon for a case rim to pull through the shellholder, often ruining both the case AND the shellholder. Today, I put up my handloads on my RCBS Partner press using a Lyman Multi Deluxe die set with a tungsten carbide sizer and, since I got away from the old-fashioned steel sizer dies, I don't recall ever having a case rim pull through the shellholder.

Also, the .45 Colt was designed for blackpowder, and the cavernous case can easily hold two or three charges of fast-burning smokeless powder...which can easily wreck the gun! I prefer to use my RCBS Little Dandy pistol powder

Home-cast bullets from Lyman molds were sized to .454" in author's Lyman # 4500 lubricator-sizer. Shown on the RCBS Accessory Base Plate, right to left, are Lyman #454190 250-gr., #452424 255-gr., and 452664 250-gr.

Lyman formerly offered the Silver Star bullets commercially, as cast in Lyman mould #454664, a flat-point bullet designed to feed safely in lever-action rifles with tubular magazine.

Laser-Cast bullets from Oregon Trail Bullet Company include, left to right, 200-gr. RNFP, 225-gr. TC, 250-gr. RNFP, 255-gr. SWC, and 300-gr. FP. These bullets are not all that expensive.

measure when loading handgun rounds, racking up my primed cases in a Lyman or MTM loading tray and moving the hand-held measure from case to case to drop powder charges. I then check each case under a strong light to insure that each case got a powder charge, and that no case got two charges.

You can obtain brass for the .45 Colt by shooting up factory ammo and reloading the empties but, since factory ammunition is fairly expensive, I would just as soon start out with virgin brass. Hornady offers brass in boxes of 100; Remington; Winchester brass comes in bag of 100; and you can buy Starline brass in bags of 500 or 1000.

I have cast most of my bullets for the .45 Colt over the years and, if you don't mind a bit of hot, hard work, it is a simple matter to turn scrap wheelweights into good cast bullets for your sixgun. Since I had a pretty good stockpile of cast bullets on hand, I decided to dig out

Oregon Trail Bullet Company offers the *Laser-Cast Reloading Manual*, First Edition. Handloads with bullets, left to right, include 200-gr. RNFP, 225-gr. TC, 250-gr. RNFP, 255-gr. SWC, and 300-gr. FP.

Author likes to use the RCBS Little Dandy pistol powder measure for metering handgun charges. Shown here are the Little Dandy measure, 24 rotors in an MTM 12 gauge shotshell box, and RCBS 5-0-5 powder scales used to check charge weights. Note the oversized knob on the rotor in the Little Dandy powder measure.

an assortment of bullets for my .45 Colt, including the Lee 452-252-SWC and 452-255-RF bullet molds, Lyman #454190 and #4542424 molds, and RCBS 45-250-FN and 45-255-SWC moulds.

In slugging my Bounty Hunter, I found it had a groove diameter of .451", while chamber throats slugged .457". I felt that

MY FAVORITE .45 COLT LOADS

When the .45 Colt came out in 1873, it was the most powerful revolver cartridge to be had. Designed as a service round for the U.S. Army and, particularly for the Cavalry, it was capable of shooting through a horse broadside. Cowboys preferred it because it was capable of stopping a charging bull with a head shot or, if a man was hung up in his stirrup and being dragged, capable of killing the horse.

At the onset of the twentieth century, the .45 Colt was still the best of the big-bore sixguns, outslugging the .44-40 Winchester and .38-40 Winchester rounds that held second and third place. The .44 Smith & Wesson Special, introduced in Smith & Wesson's New Century swing-out cylinder gun, also known as the "Triple Lock," fell far behind the .45 Colt in stopping power.

Sometime after 1900, the ammo makers started loading smokeless powder in factory ammunition but, really, their smokeless powder loads were no more effective than the old blackpowder loads. They simply loaded to blackpowder pressure levels using fast-burning powders when, actually, they could have achieved higher velocities with slower-burning powders without exceeding the modest pressures of the blackpowder rounds. Also, they stuck with the old, inefficient round-nose lead bullets with those tiny flat points that produce minimal shock effect in flesh, punched ragged holes in paper targets, and ricochet badly.

Fortunately, improvements were made by private individuals such as the late, great Elmer Keith, who not only experimented with more efficient smokeless powder handloads operating at higher pressures, but also developed superior cast bullet designs for use in .38-, .44-, and .45-caliber sixguns.

Keith's handloads, initially using a DuPont powder called SR-80 (now discontinued) and later with Hercules 2400 Rifle powder, produced much higher velocities than the factory loads but at somewhat higher pressures. Keith's loads for the 45 Colt, using his 260-gr. bullet from Ideal mould #454424, cranked

out 1000 f.p.s using a powder charge I'm not comfortable in repeating here. Used in the old Colt Single Action, Colt New Service, or the Smith & Wesson New Century, such loads were definitely "pushing the envelope," and I would recommend not experimenting with them in these old guns today.

When I started shooting the .45 Colt in my double-actions, the Colt New Service and the rechambered Smith & Wesson .455 Hand Ejector, about 1960 or 1961, I went by the data found in my 42nd edition *Lyman Reloading Handbook*, which recommended Hercules Unique behind the 260-gr. Keith Cast Plain Base, with a suggested load of 8.0 grains for 790 feet per second, and a maximum load of 10.3 grains Unique for 980 fps.

My "pet load" for the .45 Colt was put up with the 260-gr. Keith semi-wadcutter bullet, dropped from a single-cavity mould stamped "IDEAL" and "454424" and backed with 8.0 grains Hercules Unique. I didn't exceed 8.0 grains in my Colt New Service or in my rechambered Smith & Wesson .455 Hand Ejector, since this load gave me all the "kick" I really wanted – which is probably why I never wrecked either gun!

While this old handloading manual is a treasured memento, the data found in it is no longer to be relied on. Nowadays I get my handloading data from much more recent sources: manuals from Accurate, Hodgdon, Hornady, Laser-Cast, Lyman, Nosler, Sierra, and Speer, all with copyright dates of 2000 or later.

When it comes to mild loads for ordinary shooting chores, I rather like the 7th Edition *Hornady Handbook of Cartridge Reloading* because it covers a wide range of powders and also offers several velocity levels to choose from. The *Hornady Handbook* lists loads for their 200-gr. SWC bullets at velocities ranging from 800 to 1100 fps, while loads listed for their 255-gr. flat point Cowboy bullet offer velocities ranging from 650 to 900 feet per second, as fired from a Ruger Bisley Blackhawk with 7-1/2" barrel. Powders listed include offerings by Accurate, Alliant, Hodgdon, IMR, and Winchester.

One powder that is not listed in the Hornady Handbook is Ramshot's True Blue so, since True Blue IS listed in Lyman's *Pistol & Revolver Handbook*, Third Edition, let's take a look:

	Powder	Sugg. Starting Grains	Velocity f.p.s.	Pressure C.U.P.	Max Load Grains	Velocity f.p.s.	Pressure C.U.P.
200 grain Cast #4542460	True Blue	8.5	925	9,800	9.5	1021	13,100
250 grain Cast #452664	True Blue	7.4	834	11,800	8.3	917	13,700
255 grain Cast #452424	True Blue	7.2	854	11,400	8.0	926	13,600

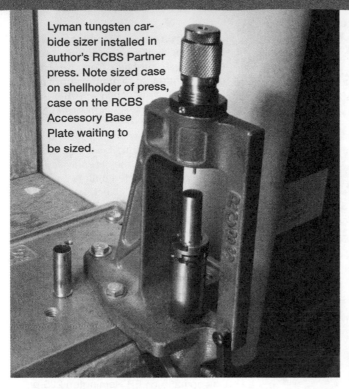

Lyman tungsten carbide sizer installed in author's RCBS Partner press. Note sized case on shellholder of press, case on the RCBS Accessory Base Plate waiting to be sized.

Cast bullets from RCBS moulds, left to right, 45-185-0SWC, 45-200-SWC, 45-230-RN, 45-250-FN, and 45-255-SWC.

Soft, swaged-lead bullets, left to right, Speer 200-gr. SWC, Speer 230-gr. LRN, Speer 250-gr. SWC, and Hornady 255-gr. FP Cowboy.

Handloads with author's home-cast bullets from molds, left to right, Lee 452-252-SWC and 452-255-RF, Lyman #454190 250-gr. and Lyman #452424 255 gr, and RCBS 45-200-FN and 45-255-SWC.

.454" was the best compromise, so I sized all cast bullets to .454" in my Lyman #4500 lubricator-sizer.

However, it is not strictly necessary to cast your own bullets and you may, if you wish, buy commercial cast bullets available from companies such as the Oregon Trail Bullet Company. These bullets are quite reasonably priced. Finally, there are the soft, swaged-lead bullets from Hornady and Speer, and jacketed bullets from Hornady, Nosler, Sierra, and Speer. The swaged lead bullets are essentially the same as those used in factory loads with lead bullets, while the jacketed pills are primarily useful for hot handloads for hunting game.

Handloading data for the .45 Colt appears in all manuals, including loads that are safe in all guns, and more powerful loads that are only safe in strong guns such as the Ruger Blackhawk or the Thompson/Center Contender. Loads for "weak" guns (such as the old Colt SAA) must be held to pressures not over 1,400 C.U.P. Loads for "strong" guns can be loaded to pressures as high as 20,000 C.U.P. However, when it comes to plebian pursuits such as plinking, paper punching, or potting small game, there is little point in using hot handloads or in wasting expensive jacketed bullets. Such shooting can be conducted quite effectively with mild loads using lead bullets.

I prefer to limit the use of swaged-lead bullets to what are known as "cowboy action" loads, i.e., loads with a muzzle velocity somewhere around 750 feet per second. It is noteworthy

Author's Arminius sixgun is stamped "BOUNTY HUNTER" on right side of the frame.

that both Hornady and Winchester load their "cowboy" loads to this velocity – and I suspect they know what they are doing! Loading data for "cowboy action" loads can be found in several reloading guides such as the *Alliant Powder Reloaders Guide*, the *Hodgdon Basic Reloading Manual*, the *IMR Smokeless Powder Reloaders' Guide*, the *Ramshot Load Guide*, and the *VihtaVuori Reloading Guide*. These booklets can be had on a complimentary basis by writing to the respective powder manufacturers and requesting them.

Some good powders for "cowboy action" loads include Alliant American Select, Hodgdon Titegroup, IMR Trail Boss, Ramshot True Blue, and VihtaVuori N-320. IMR's Trail Boss powder was, by the way, especially designed for use in "cowboy action" loads.

All loads for the .45 Colt should have the bullets tightly crimped, as the initial resistance provided by the crimp boosts pressures sufficiently so that the powder can burn more

FUN WITH THE .45 COLT

Hornady offers these swaged lead "Cowboy" bullets in boxes of 200, virgin brass cases in boxes of 100, and "Cowboy" factory loads in boxes of 20 rounds.

uniformly. Also, recoil tends to pull bullets forward, causing them, in some instances, to protrude from the face of the cylinder to tie up the gun. The heavier the bullet, and the stiffer the recoil of your loads, the more likely this is to occur.

Jacketed hollow point bullets are fairly expensive but, if you need greater stopping powder, they are the way to go. However, jacketed bullets must be driven to at least 750 feet per second to prevent getting one stuck in the bore, and to at least 850 feet per second in order for the bullet to expand properly. Also, unless you are loading for one of the "strong" guns, such as the Ruger Blackhawk, loads must be held to 14,000 C.U.P or less.

A good bullet for a "stopper" load to

Factory loads for the 45 Colt, left to right, include CCI Blazer 200-gr. JHP, Federal Champion 225-gr. SWC-HP, Hornady Cowboy 255-gr. FP, Remington 225-gr. SWC, Remington 250-gr. LRN, Speer 255-gr. GDHP, Winchester 225-gr. STHP and Winchester Cowboy with 250-gr lead bullet.

HEAVY HANDLOADS FOR THE .45 COLT

While most of us are aware that the heavy handloads should be used ONLY in "strong" guns that can handle the higher pressures, it should also be noticed that such loads should only be used in good, strong, solid-head brass cases, also known as "web head" cases.

Unfortunately, ammo makers continued to offer balloon-head brass well into the 20th century, both for rifle and revolver rounds. Some Remington brass that I bought for my .45 Colt six-guns and my .45-70 rifle, 40-odd years ago, was of balloon-head or, perhaps I should say, semi-balloonhead construction. These were headstamped REM-UMC, though I also found some stamped R-P. On the other hand, brass headstamped WESTERN

and W.R.A.CO was of solid-head construction.

While I don't mind using old, solid-head brass for mild loads, I prefer to use more recent brass for heavy handloads, e.g., Federal cases stamped F-C or FEDERAL, Remington brass stamped R-P, Starline brass stamped *-*, or Winchester brass stamped W-W or WINCHESTER. Old brass, even solid head cases, should be relegated to mild loads or to your cartridge collection.

Note: While the following loads are okay for the Ruger Blackhawk and Bisley and the older, heavy-frame Vaquero, they should NOT be used in Ruger's recently introduced New Vaquero, which has a smaller-diameter cylinder and was intended to handle the light loads used in "Cowboy Action" shooting! Elmer Keith used heavy loads like these in "weak guns" such as the Colt Single Action Army, the Colt New Service, and the Smith & Wesson "Triple Lock" or Hand Ejector. My advice is: DON'T!

Data from: Laser-Cast Reloading Manual: .45 Colt (Ruger Blackhawk/Bisley/Old Vaquero Only)

	Powder Type	Starting Grains	Velocity (fps)	Maximum Grains	Velocity (fps)	Overall Length(")
255 Lead SWC						
	2400	16.0	907	17.5	1009	1.595
	Unique	7.6	825	10.1	1039	1.595

Data from: Accurate Smokeless Powder Loading Guide, Number Two: .45 Colt; Ruger Blackhawk/Bisley/Old Vaquero & T/C Only)

	Powder Type	Starting Grains	Velocity (fps)	Maximum Grains	Velocity (fps)	Pressure (C.U.P.)
255 Lead SWC						
	No.7	13.6	1010	15.1	1148	19,700
300 Lead FN						
	No. 9	13.5	798	15.0	907	17.600

DISCLAIMER: Inasmuch as neither I nor the publisher have any control over how the data listed above might be used, neither I nor the publisher will be responsible for any results obtained. If you choose to handload your own ammunition, you, and you alone, are responsible for your own safety, and the safety of others.

be used in one of the weaker sixguns is Speer's 225-gr. jacketed hollowpoint which, according to the *Speer Reloading Manual*, can be loaded atop a MAXIMUM load of 13.0 grains of Alliant Blue Dot, which will drive this bullet to 1036 fps when fired from a Smith & Wesson Model 25-5 with 67" barrel. Heavier loads are listed in various manuals, with the notation that these are to be used only in Ruger Blackhawk revolvers or in Thompson/Center Contender pistols.

Ruger Blackhawk revolvers in .45 Colt are built on the same heavy frame as their Super Blackhawk in .44 Magnum, with cylinders of 1.730" diameter, as compared to a cylinder diameter of 1.680" for the old Colt Single Action Army. The Bounty Hunter is also made in .44 Magnum, however, and their .45 Colt is built on the same frame. The cylinder of my Bounty Hunter measures 1.732" in diameter, according to my RCBS dial caliper, so I have no reservations about shooting the heavier loads in my German-made sixgun.

While I don't hunt deer with my Bounty Hunter and certainly would not take it after heavier game, my wife Marlene and I were once taking a walk along the Paul Stock Nature Trail north of Cody, Wyoming, when we encountered a sign on the fence:

"WARNING! BLACK BEAR IN AREA!"

The sign made my wife a little nervous so, the next time we went out, I packed my Bounty Hunter, stoked with some heavy handloads. We never did see the black bear, but that big sixgun was a comfort to have along!

Jacketed bullets of 240 to 260 grains can be driven to velocities of 1200 feet per second or more from strong guns, while the lighter 225-gr. Speer JHP can be driven to more than 1300 feet per second. Heavier 300-gr. bullets are also

available for the .45 Colt or, at least, they CAN be used, though I suspect they are better suited to the .454 Casull or the .460 Smith & Wesson Magnum. Jacketed bullets of this weight are offered by Hornady, Nosler, Sierra, and Speer, while the Oregon Trail Bullet Company offers a Laser-Cast 300-gr. flat point, if you prefer a cast bullet.

Naturally, you cannot drive a 300-gr. slug as fast as a lighter bullet. A velocity of 1100 feet per second is about all you can hope for, even in a "strong" gun, and then only from a 7-1/2" barrel. Expect brutal recoil when shooting such heavy loads and, also, expect the bullet to shoot extremely high.

On a lighter note, the .45 Colt can be a lot of fun with less serious handloads. Have you ever shot a "double ball" load? Using a moderate powder charge, 7.0 grains of Hodgdon Universal, I load a single .454" lead down into the case. I then seat another ball atop that and crimp it. On firing, the two balls will separate in flight, yet stay close enough together to make two holes in a large sighting-in target at 25 yards.

How about a .45 Colt shotshell? You can put up shotshells for the .45 Colt using the empty plastic shot capsules from Speer. These come in boxes of 25, with blue plastic capsules and white base wads.

Data for "Reloading Handgun Shotshells" is found in the *Speer Reloading Manual* and, while there is no data for the .45 Colt, data for the .44 Magnum can be used for the .45 Colt. Listings for the .44 Magnum include 7.3 grains of 231 Ball so, using my RCBS Little Dandy powder measure, I loaded up twelve with 7.0 grains 231 (rotor #11) and a dozen with 7.4 grains 231 (rotor #12).

While the old .45 Colt is not the only big-bore revolver cartridge worth considering, it's still a grand old cartridge, and it remains one of my favorites after all these years.

What more can I say? Good luck, good shooting – and happy handloading!

They're not as common today as they once were, but unusual vintage handguns can still be a lot of fun. The author shares four of his favorites with us.

ODDBALLS–
Why we love 'em

BY ANDY EWERT

Generally speaking, the reasons for owning a handgun fall under two categories: need and desire. Protection, law enforcement, and recreation are functions of need. But when one owns numerous handguns, possession may be more a function of desire than need.

A good number of veteran handgunners who have all they need, myself included, find themselves in this predicament. Today's new-product-driven marketplace is awash in brand name revolvers, semi-autos, and other action types for every conceivable purpose. Specialization has replaced utility as marketers cajole us at every opportunity to discard the old in favor of the new and improved.

There is a subset of handguns on the market today that time has passed by. They're usually old and long out of production; made of steel; of obscure, sometimes foreign origin; and usually a bit "dated" looking, compared with their modern counterparts. They go by the names Astra, Webley, Ballaster Molina, and Makarov, to name a few. I refer to this subset affectionately as "oddballs" and I love 'em. So do other like-minded independents who snap them up for no other reason than pure desire to own, shoot, and admire. Not that they're incapable of meeting the needs they were designed for. They do, usually very well, but not with the pizzazz of high-capacity firepower, exotic materials, or block-busting ballistics.

Oddballs are usually encountered unexpectedly and off the beaten path: in small town gun shops, at rummage and garage sales, in the shadowy corners of gun shows, or on the back pages of pulpy firearms-peddler publications. You can even find them on the Internet if you are willing to drill. At first glance, they appear to be second-rate, second-class clunkers. Ah, but as we know, appearances can be deceiving.

Oddballs are an eclectic bunch.

Some date to before the turn of the twentiethth century, but most originate from the 1900s to the 1960s. Many are of military origin and from Old World

One of few successful 9mm Parabellum blowback designs, the Astra 600 is impressively accurate and reliable.

countries. They're often referred to by the unenlightened as obsolete, surplus, or, most cruelly, as old iron.

THE WEBLEY NO.1 MARK VI

My favorite oddball is the Webley No.1 Mark VI, the last in a distinguished line of break-top, self-extracting, double-action revolvers. Manufactured in England from 1915 to 1928, the Mark VI served with distinction across the British Empire, from the trenches of France during World War I and the African deserts in World War II to across former possessions for decades after production ceased. Webleys still appear in active duty from time to time, usu-

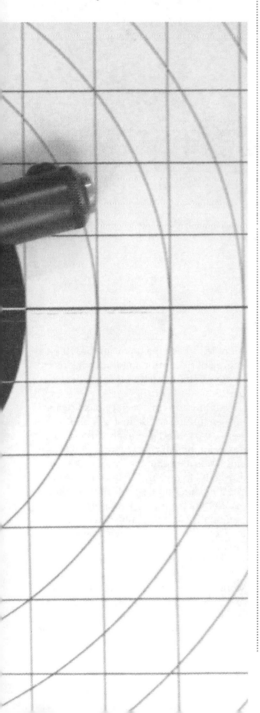

ally in the hands of irregular mountain warriors prowling the border regions of middle-eastern civilization.

Chambered for the .455 Webley Revolver, Mk 2 cartridge, the Mark VI's 265-grain round-nose lead slug, traveling at a leisurely 600 fps, delivers a lethal blow up close. The sixgun itself exudes a rich heritage of exotic places, hard combat with determined foes, and empiring. Its 6" barrel and 2 lb. 6.5-oz. heft balances well and steadies without muscle fatigue. The Mark VI is rugged, fast to reload, and is capable of delivering its payload fast and true. It earned the reputation as arguably the best combat revolver ever produced.

The Webley No.1 Mark VI was available in the U.S. at least since the 1960s at move-'em-out prices. To heighten their appeal, importers converted many to the more available and affordable .45 ACP cartridge. And a good thing they did. Today, as back then, .455 ammo costs more than twice its ACP peer. You can still find Mark VIs about, but not at rock bottom prices. I acquired mine without dickering at a Milwaukee, Wisconsin, gun show after a protracted search.

Its markings indicate that my Mark VI dates to 1916 and is of Royal Navy issue. Like many of its brothers, this Brit was converted to .45 ACP, which is fine by my wallet and .45 reloading dies. In excellent condition, it accommodates ACP cartridges in half- or full-moon clips for speedy loading, or .45 Auto Rims for slightly improved accuracy.

Fired offhand at 25 yards, it will place six 250-gr. lead flatpoint slugs, powered by 3.5 grains of Bullseye, at approximately 700 fps, into a group you can cover with your hand. Not bad for an octogenarian! Recoil is mild. To be on the safe side, I keep reloads near factory .455 levels and forego stouter ACP ballistics.

The Webley's V-notch rear and squared front sights are conducive to good shot placement. Its single action trigger pull is accommodating, less so double action. The issue hard rubber grips are non-slip and the right size. My Webley's boxy, high-center-of-gravity look draws stares on the firing line, but so what?

THE ASTRA 600

My second favorite oddball is the curious Astra 600. This single-action, enclosed hammer, blowback 9mm Parabellum originates from an extended family of military- and civilian-issue semi-automatic handguns produced by Unceta y Compania in Spain's historic firearms manufacturing region. It should be noted that the 600 is one of very few successful (read durable) blowback 9mm Parabellum designs. The Astra's long, narrow, tubular look sets it decisively apart from other handguns.

Introduced in 1943, the 600 carries a history as interesting as the Webley's. During World War II, the German military required more sidearms than its indigenous manufacturers could supply. Impressed with the Astra 400 9mm Largo semi-auto used by both sides during the Spanish Civil War and by the *Wehrmacht* in limited quantities during early World War II, Germany ordered 38,000 Astra 600 pistols, specifying they chamber the German military-issue 9mm Parabellum cartridge and feature a 5-1/4" barrel, compared with the 400's 6" tube. The magazine release was also modified to a button located on the lower side of the left grip frame. The Germans designated their supplemental sidearm the Pistole Astra 600/43.

Some 10,000-plus 600s made it to Germany before the shifting tides of war ended deliveries. A number of the 28,000 undelivered pistols were sold for issue to the Portuguese Navy, and later exported as surplus. Others ironically were delivered to West Germany after the war, this time for police use. Astra 600 production terminated in 1946 with a total run of approximately 60,000 pistols.

I came across my 600 through a classified ad several years ago. The pistol is marked "MRP" (Marina Republica Portugal) on the frame, indicating naval issuance. It appears never to have been used and, other than a few storage dings, is as it was when it arrived in Portugal 60-plus years ago. Fit and finish are as fine as any semi-auto I've encountered. Evidently, the Spanish aimed to please their German customers.

By today's double-action, high-capacity, locked-breech 9mm semi-auto standard, the 600's design is past its prime. Single-action, nine-shot 9mms with a grip safety and fixed sights are passe. However, at the range it's another matter.

The Astra's rigidly secured barrel is promotes unusally good accuracy. Despite a stiff trigger and rudimentary (though user-friendly) sights, on a good day I can place a magazine full of economical, Russian steel-cased 115-gr. 9mm ball into a bit over 2 inches at 25

A small sampling of "oddballs" includes (top to bottom) England's Webley No.1 Mark VI, converted to .45 ACP; Argentina's Ballester-Molina in .45 ACP; Spain's Astra 600 in 9mm Parabellum; and the 9X18mm Makarov, this example manufactured in the former East Germany. Exotic history, old-world, quality manufacture, and uniqueness set them apart from today's handguns. Despite their age and foreign pedigree, all are more than capable in defense or informal target shooting. They're still available at reasonable prices, though not as reasonable as in times past, if one takes the time to search.

yards. I challenge any wondernine to do noticeably better. Perhaps with tailored handloads one might cut this to under 2 inches, but why bother? I have no use for costly hollowpoints and other high-performance rounds for punching holes in paper.

Recoil from blowbacks tends to be more pronounced than that of comparable locked-breeched pistols. The 600's heavy slide and impressive recoil spring mitigate the sensation satisfactorily.

THE BALLESTER-MOLINA

Oddball number three is Argentina's home-grown Ballester-Molina .45 semi-auto. This Colt 1911 variant represents a successful attempt to upgrade the proven John Browning design – a quarter of a century or more before doing so became popular.

Produced by Hispano Argentina de Automovites, S.A. around 1935, the Ballaster's developers did away with the 1911's grip safety, switched to a pivoting-type trigger from Colt's bar-type design, and added a larger grip tang than the Colt. In my experience, all three changes are for the better. The 1911's laterally mounted safety makes its grip counterpart redundant. The Ballaster's pivoting trigger is noticeably smoother its Colt counterpart, and its extended tang provides needed protection to the web of the shooting hand. Others may take a different view, but I know what works for me.

The Ballester-Molina had its moment in history, albeit brief and murky. A number of the pistols were supplied to the British Special Operations Executives for use on convert missions during World War ll. Why it was chosen

is unclear. Perhaps its origin provided a degree of deception in identifying users. History is mum on its performance in battle.

Judging from the variety of slide markings encountered, Ballester-Molinas were distributed profusely among various branches of the Argentine military and law enforcement communities during its five-year, 100,000-pistol production run. Mine, acquired through a print advertisement, is marked "Armada Nacional," indicating naval issue. (Judging from the condition of surplus naval pistols I've come across, sailors didn't spend much time with sidearms.)

Like its oddball peers, the Ballester-Molina reflects quality manufacturing. All parts fit tightly and function as they should. The pistol's smooth, evenly applied parkerized finish is as attractive as it is practical, particularly in a marine environment. Available on the U.S. surplus firearms market periodically for almost four decades, this sidearm never was popular, but it always seems to sell. It remains an economical alternative to the Colt 1911.

Though certainly nowhere near as prestigious as its legendary American stepfather, the Ballester-Molina more than holds its own at the range with stock military 1911s. With a smooth pull, courtesy of the aforementioned pivoted trigger, and adequately proportioned fixed sights, my Ballaster groups 230-gr. ball comparably with other unaltered military 1911s and is totally reliable. Lead SWC handloads improve accuracy and function good enough for perforating paper, but not for lifesaving. I'm perfectly content to stick with factory ball or equivalent handloads and avoid the cost and uncertainty of modification.

THE MAKAROV

My last oddball dates back to the Cold War. The Russian Markarov semi-automatic is an interesting product of German and later Russian desire to produce a compact, lightweight, 9mm blowback for their armed forces. Interestingly, firearms producers in Italy, France, Germany, England, Israel, and the U.S. have attempted to do this on and off since before the First World War through the 1980s. Perhaps someone somewhere is at it today.

German efforts, led by small arms manufacturer Carl Walther and ammunition maker Gustave Genschow, at the request of the *Luftwaffe*, culminated in a shortened, lower-operating-pressure, 9mm cartridge and some prototype pistols – but no production sidearm – by the war's end. Russia, suitably impressed by the German weapons technology that bloodied it so, discovered documentation detailing Germany's 9mm blowback project. The Russians adopted the cartridge and pistol concepts, added their own touches, and introduced the *Pistolet Makarova* in 1951. This double-action sidearm, chambered for a special 9X18mm cartridge referred to as the 9mm Markarov, was adopted by some East Bloc countries and later China, along with parts of Soviet-influenced Africa, Asia, and South America. To meet these geographically dispersed needs, Markarovs were produced in Russia and, with Soviet assistance, in Bulgaria, China, and the former East Germany.

After the fall of the Iron Curtain, all sorts of East Bloc hardware ranging from firearms to greatcoats and jet aircraft became available in the U.S. When Markarovs made it to our shores, favorable reviews begin popping up and the pistols began to disappear. Those that didn't suddenly were more expensive. New batches arrived, including Markarovs manufactured with adjustable sights for the U.S. civilian market.

Some firearms authorities refer to the Markarov as obsolete. True, it's a product of the 1950s and has been supplanted in parts of the former Soviet Union by a high-capacity, double-action, full-power Wondernine. But when grasping this compact eight shooter, you realize there is an ideal size for a belt pistol and this is it. For someone lugging a sidearm around in battle, the Makarov strikes a workable balance between full-size and pocket pistol in power, bulk, and weight. I carry mine in a briefcase during the day and park it on the bedroom nightstand when the sun goes down. I don't feel undergunned.

My Makarov is of German 1960s vintage, apparently unissued, and without a scratch. It came to my door in a box along with a spartan shoulder holster and extra magazine. Fit and finish are the traditional German standard – excellent, not surprising since it came from the captured Walther plant in Zella-Mehlis, in what was then Russian-occupied East Germany.

With Russian 9X18mm ball, featuring a 94-gr. FMJ bullet at around 1,050 fps,

The Author believes this Cold War-era EastGerman 9X18-mm Makarov strikes a reasonable balance between power and size. Surplus holster and economical Russian ball ammunition suit range needs, while translated operating manual provides a wealth of useful and interesting data, including shooting from horseback! Like its fellow oddballs, this Mak is reliable and suitably accurate for a combat pistol.

I can place my shots offhand within the span of my fingers at 25 yards. This is quite good for an almost-but-not-quite pocket pistol with a 5" sighting radius. The basic square-rear-notch and square-front sights suit my 50-year-old+ bifocaled eyes well. The single action trigger pull is adequate for defense or informal paper punching. Its double action pull, however, is atrocious. Recoil is surprisingly sharp and a bit painful in extended shooting sessions, but not unbearable.

ODDBALLS: WHERE TO FIND 'EM

As you can see, oddballs are all about history, high quality manufacture, and innate uniqueness. I've only scratched the surface of this fascinating group. All four of the handguns profiled here are capable of protecting one's hide and hearth, besides piercing X-rings, potting small game, or making tin cans dance.

Taking the oddball plunge requires forethought. I favored the pulp route in locating most of mine, perusing *Shotgun News* and *Gun Digest Magazine* until my fingers are black with ink. I also keep an eye on importers' websites. *(Editor's note: We've also found a fair number of oddballs at AuctionArms.com, Gunbroker. com and GunsAmerica.com.–DMS)*

If you don't have a Federal Firearms License, you'll have to find someone who does and, for a modest fee, will conduct your transaction in accordance with federal, state, and any local laws. Surplus arms dealers periodically receive new shipments, some large, some small. Once an oddball catches on, they're gone in a hurry, so it pays to move fast. I'm completely satisfied with my three sight-unseen purchases. Most surplus arms dealers have reasonable return policies.

Another route is to canvas gun shows. Some dealers specialize in ordering quantities of surplus firearms, marking them up for profit, and selling them one by one at shows. Although more costly than placing orders with an accommodating FFL owner, this approach permits buyers to examine the merchandise, sometimes still coated in cosmoline and wrapped in waxed paper, along with mysteriously marked crates of imported ammunition, holsters, magazines, and all sorts of miscellaneous paraphernalia. Getting to know these dealers and maintaining dialog gives you an edge in getting in on the ground floor of new offerings.

The final option is akin to panning for gold. Visiting small town gun shops, hardware stores, garage and yard sales, and pawn shops is an adventure in search and discovery. It's truly amazing what a diversity of firearms and miscellaneous second-hand Americana awaits you.

During one foray to a southern Ohio sporting goods store, for example, I came across a *Waffenamt* acceptance-marked Astra 600, complete with original holster bearing its German owner's name – and priced to sell. I let that one get away and I've regretted it ever since. This way of procuring oddballs is admittedly time- and fuel-consuming, but it's fun. As a city slicker, I find exploring small towns a pleasurable exploit in itself.

A bit of advice for beginners: When buying an oddball, always spend the extra money required for prime specimens. Worn out, battered, malfunc-

Webley No.1 Mark VI converted to .45 ACP along with homemade period holster, full- and half-moon clips, and detailed literature that add luster to this historic, battle-tested old timer. Despite its reputation for ruggedness, author keeps reloads to .455 levels, though surplus .45 ACP ball has been fired through converted Webleys for decades without reports of mishaps.

tioning wrecks are frustrating at best, a danger to human health at worst. There is no guarantee that you'll be able to find replacement parts or gunsmiths capable of performing proper repairs. Be forewarned: Buying long-out-of-production oddballs is not without risks.

YOU'VE FOUND AN ODDBALL – NOW WHAT?

So you've found your prize, lightening your bankroll in the process, and are admiring it in your easy chair. If you have any doubts about your handgun's caliber, operation, condition, or disassembly, you have more work to do.

Operating manuals or literature detailing your prize's specifications, disassembly, functioning, and idiosyncrasies are usually available. I unexpectedly came across a translated Soviet Markarov operating manual and a wonderful booklet detailing the Webley at local gunshows. Using the Internet can speed up literature location. Gun magazines, books, specialty firearms publications, and *Gun Digests* from the past are treasure troves of information on oddballs.

With oddballs, there are a few "best practices" to observe.

#1: Examine your newly acquired handgun thoroughly for signs of wear or damage. Do this by field stripping it (or further disassembling it if you're capable) using *The Gun Digest Book of Firearms Assembly/Disassembly* (separate volumes for semi-automatic pistols and revolvers) by J.B. Wood and the *NRA Guide to Firearms Assembly* (separate volumes for handguns and rifles and shotguns). Many valuable out-of-print books dealing at least in part with oddball handguns can be found at Amazon.com.

Some oddballs are tricky to take apart and/or reassemble. The Astra 600 leads my menagerie in this characteristic. With its powerful recoil spring, you have to be careful: a slip of the fingers sends a piece of steel flying at eye-threatening velocity.

If you have any doubts about your handgun's operating condition or safety, take it to a reputable gunsmith before your first trip to the range.

#2: Do not use ammunition exceeding the operating pressures your sidearm was designed for. *Cartridges of the World* by Frank Barnes and reloading manuals list factory load specs. Exceeding these jeopardizes your hide and your prize. Remember, most oddballs were built before the advent of high-pressure +P loads and their ilk. To be safe, stick to standard factory ball or equivalent handloads.

#3: Select your ammunition with care. If you're lucky, your oddball is chambered for a common caliber. If not, be prepared to dig deeper into your wallet. Be sure to keep track of your empties at the range. The reliability of most semi-automatic oddballs begins to suffer with hollow point and lead bullets. Military surplus ammunition is a cost-effective option, but proceed with care. Some of it is great while others are less so. Thanks to entrepreneurial importers, ammunition is today a global commodity. You can purchase ammunition from Asia to Eastern Europe and Australia and many locales in between. Try to stay away from corrosive or "semi-corrosive" ammunition if possible, unless you enjoy mandatory, extended strip-down cleaning sessions.

If you have a real oddball that you can't find ammo for, or don't know the proper caliber, consult The Old Western Scrounger at (304) 262-9870. If Dangerous Dave Cumberland can't help you out, you're in trouble. After firing your oddball for the first time, examine the fired cases for any signs of cracks or blown primers. Either indicates something amiss with either with the gun or ammunition. It may be time to contact a gunsmith.

RELOADING FOR ODDBALLS

Reloading saves money and solves problems. Varying tolerances in firearms and ammunition are normal. You want to keep variances within a range where safety, performance, and case life are maximized. The first way is by measuring your bore diameter. Do this by driving an oversize, soft lead slug through the bore and measuring it with calipers. When buying or casting bullets, keep them close to bore diameter or a little over for optimum accuracy.

The second way to maintain tolerances is to periodically measure your fired cases. When they exceed your manual's recommended maximum length, trim with a case trimmer and chamfer the rough edges with a chamfering tool.

Slight case bottom bulges in blowback empties are not unusual, as are blackened case mouths. If you notice signs of excess pressure, such as unusually heavy recoil or flattened or pierced primers, consult your reloading manual and back off the powder charge.

If oversize chamber variance is a problem (split cases are the warning sign), you may want to purchase a custom resizing die manufactured to your handgun chamber's dimensions. I followed this route with a World War II vintage Japanese Arisksa rifle and saved mucho dinero in prolonging the life of pricey Norma brass.

Now you see the big picture of owning and using oddballs. They're not for everyone, but for those eccentric, nostalgic pistoleros who treasure quality manufacturing and are willing to forgo the trendy for the uncommon, the desire for oddballs burns hot and bright. For us, desire is what it's all about.

Bibliography

Barnes, Frank C. *Cartridges of the World.* Iola, Wisconsin: Krause Publications, 2006.

Ezell, Edward C. *Handguns of the World.* New York: Barnes and Noble Books, 1993.

Gangarosa, Gene Jr. "Germany's ULTRA Pistols," *Gun Digest*, 53rd Annual Edition, Iola, Wisconsin: Krause Publications, 1998.

Gebhardt, James F. (translator). *The Official Makarov Pistol Manual.* El Dorado, Arizona: Desert Publications, 1995.

Hogg, Ian V. *The New Illustrated Encyclopedia of Firearms.* Secaucus, New Jersey: Wellfleet Press, 1993.

James, Garry. *Guns & Ammo The Big Book of Surplus Firearms: The Best of Volumes I, II, and III.* Los Angeles: Petersen Publishing Company, 1998. (Webley Mk VI.)

Malloy, John. "Blowback Nines." *Gun Digest 1993, 47th Annual Edition.* Northbrook, Illinois: DBI Books, 1992.

Metcalf, Dick. "East Meets West – The 9 mm Makarov Arrives!" *Shooting Times* Nov. 1993.

Shimek, Robert T. *Guns & Ammo The Big Book of Surplus Firearms, The Best of Voumes I, II, and III.* Los Angeles: Petersen Publishing, 1998. (Astra Models 400, 600, and 300.)

Shimek, Robert T. *Guns & Ammo The Big Book of Surplus Firearms, The Best of Voumes I, II, and III.* Los Angeles: Petersen Publishing, 1998. (Makaro.v)

Skennerton, Ian. *Small Arms Identification Series: .455 Pistol, Revolver No. I MK VI.* Labrador, Australia: Ian D. Skennerton, 1997.

Thompson, Jim "Surplus Handguns For Home Defense." *Guns & Ammo Surplus Firearms, Vol. VI.* Los Angeles: Petersen Publishing, 1998.

THE Xman

BY CLARENCE ANDERSON

So, who *was* the greatest gun writer? "Whelen, 'Mister Rifleman,' of course," the proletariat roars, and although partisans of Elmer Keith and Jack O'Conner cannot be entirely suppressed, there might appear to be no other serious contenders. But when *American Rifleman* Editor C. B. Lister described in 1939 "the outstanding writer of his time in the field of guns and ammunition," the first "to write technical articles for magazines of general circulation" (at which he was "plainly most successful"), who "filled a unique place and has left an indelible mark on American military and sporting shooting ideas," he was not referring to Col. Whelen, much-admired and highly-respected as he then was. Lister was talking about one whose fame has been eclipsed not only by the longevity of contemporaries such as Whelen and Keith, but also by the circumstances of his own tragic death. That man was Edward C. Crossman, "Ned" to his friends, or "Xman," as he sometimes called himself.

If Crossman harbored any fond memories of his birthplace in Iowa, he elected to withhold them from his readers; in fact, it is only because it is recorded on U. S. census returns (of questionable reliability) that we know the state of his birth. An offhand remark in *Outers'* magazine reveals that he had made his way to California by 1906, because he was in that year assigned as a member of the National Guard to duty at a "refugee camp" set up in Oakland for survivors of the great San Francisco earthquake and fire of 1906. The Guard remained armed with the Krag, but in the hands of the Regulars who relieved them, Crossman obtained his first look at the rifle that would many years later inspire his most memorable work, *The Book of the Springfield*.

His path from Iowa to California was evidently not direct, because he once briefly mentioned spending a year on a gold-dredge working the Colorado Riv-

The XMan also found time to pen a brief testimonial for Winchester's top-of-the-line Model 21 shotgun. Courtesy Mike Manges

Praise by Critical Captain Crossman for the

WINCHESTER
TRADE MARK
Model 21 Shotgun

Captain Edward C. Crossman . . . one of the world's best known authorities on sporting firearms. Contributing Editor of Outdoor Life. Author of standard books on shooting.

After THREE years . . .

"As to my observation of the ability of the Model 21 . . . to 'take it' . . . my own gun, one of the first . . . to reach the Pacific Coast several years ago . . . has been used ever since . . . in Skeet, and for many months . . . was a sort of 'public' gun, grabbed by most anybody . . . to try . . . There is no question as to (its) ability to take punishment and deliver unbroken and reliable service . . . The number of shots through this gun are far more than the average man fires in all his life at game . . . and I was told lately of one of these guns in use in a Washington, D. C., club which had gone over the 100,000 mark! . . . The layman . . . certainly needs no factory 'dope' to tell him that the gun works more easily and smoothly than any other double gun, American or foreign. I own two fine English guns, neither of which, by scale measurement, opens as easily, hammers down, as this Model 21."
—EDWARD C. CROSSMAN

After FIVE years . . .

"Some five years of observation of this Winchester Model 21 in the Skeet game forces me sadly to the conclusion that it has the most reliable single trigger on the market, and that the gun will take more grief than any American or foreign gun offered to the shooter."—EDWARD C. CROSSMAN

Both quotations reprinted, by permission, from the Sporting Goods Journal, Captain Crossman's department "Richochets."

A youthful Crossman in a formal studio portrait. Courtesy Jim Foral

tion of one's own "first gun." If any such reminiscence appears among the writings of Crossman, it has eluded the due diligence of this researcher. However, references to his early encounters with various U. S. service rifles abound. On the basis of this inadequate evidence, it thus appears possible that Crossman's interest in shooting was, if not acquired, then greatly stimulated through service in the National Guard.

In his first book, *Small Bore Rifle Shooting*, published in 1927, Crossman declares, "I started to shoot a rifle in 1892, a military rifle at the time of the Spanish War." He expands upon that statement in his third volume, *Military and Sporting Rifle Shooting* (1932), by explaining that "my own first qualification score was fired with the Remington-Lee .45-70 Navy rifle," a rather peculiar choice for an infantryman, fired from the back-position popular in the black-powder era. This chronology, however, conflicts with the age of 28 set down for him in the Census of 1910 (or 48 in the Census of 1930), which if correct places his birth in 1882. By that reckoning, his age in 1892 would have been a trifle young – 10 years old – for service in the National Guard, even though cases were not unknown of boys only a little older who enlisted by lying about their ages. It would thus appear he misreported his age for the Census; so much for official government statistics!

WRITING FOR A LIVING

This apparent chronological discrepancy, however, is far less interesting than another disclosure from the Census of 1910: that Crossman was already, at this early date, describing his profession as "correspondent, magazines." The occupation of his wife Blanche, two years his junior, was given as "singer," and their only child Edward B. (or Jim) Crossman – to whom Col. Brophy dedicated his epic treatise, *The 1903 Springfield Rifles* – was recorded as being nine months of age. If writing was indeed Crossman's primary source of income (remembering that Whelen and his other colleagues had "day jobs"), this circumstance almost certainly qualifies him to be called our first "professional" gun writer.

Bear in mind that the earliest sporting periodicals, most of them weeklies such as *Forest and Stream,* paid their contributors *nothing,* and only with the launching of "modern" monthly sporting magazines in the 1890s did it become possible for writers to earn something more tangible than the satisfaction of seeing their own words in print. How well these publications paid their contributors cannot easily be estimated, except to assume their rates were several rungs down the wage ladder from the major magazines of the time, such as *Harper's* and *Scribner's.*

The earliest Crossman article to come into my possession, "The Telescopic Sight," appeared in the June of 1910 issue of *Outers'-Recreation,* one of the oldest sporting periodicals of the day and arguably the most prestigious. Whelen, Julian Hatcher, and C. S. Landis were other *Outers'* regulars. The November issue began an exhaustive three-part examination of the development of the first group of commercially-produced M1903 sporters: "The Metamorphosis of the New Springfield." One of the most historically important pieces Crossman ever wrote, it detailed his collaboration with his own "discovery," Los Angeles gunsmith Ludwig Wundhammer, and popular novelist and hunter Stuart Edward White in designing this now legendary quintette of sporting Springfields. Prior to his safari of 1910, White had been no friend of bolt-actions, but the Springfield that Crossman designed for that occasion performed so superbly that it immediately became his all-around favorite rifle.

Whelen was, during these same months of 1909 and 1910, developing his own Springfield sporter, sharing ideas by mail with Crossman. Regrettably, neither of these two lifelong comrades quite got around to explaining how they met, but Lieutenant Whelen's first posting after receiving his commission in 1902 was Monterrey, California, and he later wrote

er between Arizona and Colorado. Even briefer and less specific was his mention of "an old college chum," the only evidence he ever provided about his education. Did he graduate? Crossman's mathematical adroitness and meticulous attention to detail suggest he possessed the requisites of an engineer, but to the "advanced education" question on the 1930 census form, his response was "no."

Somewhere in the work of almost every other important gun writer there will be found warmly remembered recollections of boyhood hunting or shooting outings, and to that pivotal event in the lives of most riflemen, the acquisi-

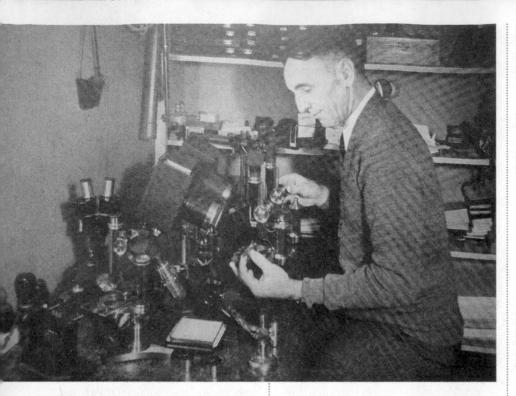

Crossman at home in his ballistics laboratory. The custom-built microscope reportedly cost Crossman $1000. Courtesy Jim Foral

in the *Rifleman* that he had known Crossman "since the beginning of the century when we collaborated in writing on sporting rifles." By 1910, they had become *such* fast friends that Crossman – a partisan for the West who could scarcely mention the East without sneering – crossed the continent to visit Whelen at his new quarters near New York City.

Crossman's residence by 1908 – "the little shack with the gingerbread trimmings," as he called it – was within the city limits of Los Angeles. In later years, his name would become well known to readers of the *Los Angeles Times,* but that would not have been true in 1908 when, in the issue of May 11, he was reported as having tied for first place in a competition among members of the California National Guard. Thereafter, his name would appear, usually as winner or runner-up, in a multitude of matches covered by the *Times.* Ned, however, was *not* the first Crossman to be make the *Times* for his marksmanship: in the January 21 issue of the same year, "Woman Takes Medal" told the story of Blanche winning third place in a revolver match hosted by the Los Angeles Rifle and Revolver Club. There is much more to tell about this remarkable woman, but for the present suffice it to say that "colleague and shooting partner," as much as "wife," describes her role in Ned's life.

Crossman's demonstrated shooting talent, with smooth bores as well as grooved, was critical in the develop-

ment of his career, because it was the synergistic combination of his shooting with his writing that so quickly catapulted him into the front rank of American arms authorities – a trajectory parallel, in fact, to that of Whelen. Both men won many matches, but neither could fairly be ranked at the level of Pope, Farrow, and the other true "greats" in target competition. Both, however, were close enough to such masters in skill to speak with unimpeachable authority on the subject of rifle accuracy.

By 1909, when Crossman was only 27 (according to the Census, at any rate), his standing in the world of arms and riflemen was already such that the "grand old man of the American rifle game," Dr. Walter Hudson, considered it worth his while to visit this young man at his little shack in Los Angeles. No doubt the Doctor had additional reasons to travel to the West Coast, but the implications of such a congenial relationship between the two speaks for itself.

So what kind of living was Crossman eking out as "correspondent, magazines"? Not a grand one, we can be sure, because he affirmed that lack of the necessary funds compelled him to decline an invitation in 1912 from his prosperous friend White to accompany the latter on his second African safari. (On the other hand, Crossman's lavishly engraved Bob Owen sporter, shown in *Book of the Springfield,* does not suggest destitution.) Fate provided Crossman with com-

pensation for this lost African opportunity in the form of a less-costly invitation to join the American team traveling to Buenos Aires that same year to compete in the Pan-American Rifle Matches. How he was selected for the team, he never explained, but the opportunity to observe and critically analyze foreign rifles and shooting styles made a lasting impression, to judge by his later references to this event.

The *Norte-Americanos* narrowly defeated the Mauser-equipped Argentinians, but were bested the following year of 1913 when the same match was conducted at Camp Perry, Ohio. Once again, the foreign riflemen and their unfamiliar equipment provided grist for Crossman's analytical mill. Much could be learned, he believed, by comparing the foreign with the domestic. Crossman always showed the most scrupulous impartiality, which sometimes stirred resentment ("made the eagle scream," in Crossman's words) when he occasionally pronounced some foreign idea or design superior to its American counterpart.

THE TIME OF HIS LIFE

Great wars change everything, an axiom made manifest in the career of Ned Crossman. Before *the* Great War, World War I, he would have been seen as a thinker of obvious intelligence and originality, a writer as popular as he was prolific, and a shooter of international reputation. However, his experimental work for the U. S. Army during the war, and immediately afterwards, provided him with the experience to stand alone as an authority in almost every facet of firearms use and design. If in respect to breadth and depth of technical expertise he had any contemporary rival, the brilliant Julian Hatcher of the Ordnance Dept. seems the most likely candidate, although the latter, compared to Crossman, did not write nearly so much for popular consumption.

To train officers as rifle instructors for the hundreds of thousands of raw recruits required for the war, the Army authorized the organization of a Small Arms Firing School at Camp Perry in early 1918, "the most important and most famous in U. S. history," in the opinion of long-time NRA officer C. B. Lister. And in an exhibition of good sense extraordinary for the Army bureaucracy, Lt. Col. Smith Brookhart, then President of the NRA, was allowed to hand-pick "outstanding civilian riflemen for his staff" at the School.

In this providential way, Sgt. Crossman of the California National Guard came to be commissioned a Captain in the regular Army, along with his old friend from the L. A. gun club, Grosvenor Wotkyns. "I learned the rifle thoroughly during the war, as we had 2000 of them [mostly the U. S. Model 1917] at the firing school at Camp Perry, where I was first an Instructor, later an Experimental Officer," he wrote in the May, 1921, issue of *Outers'*. (Crossman's evaluation of the M1917 – a better battle rifle than the M1903, he thought – in the February and March *Outers'* was the first to appear in print, and quite possibly remains the most thorough.) And in the issue of April, 1922, discussing his testing of ammunition purchased by the government, he adds, "we fired more than a million rounds per month." He renewed his target-shooting friendship with famed sniper Capt. Herbert McBride (author-to-be of the classic

A Rifleman Went to War), who had resigned from the Canadian service when America entered the war, and been assigned after gaining his U. S. commission to the School at Perry. (He later contributed a chapter to Crossman's *Military and Sporting Rifle Shooting*.) Often in later years Crossman referred to this exciting period as the time he "lived for seven months under canvas."

All this shooting at Perry, incredibly, was but a prelude to his experimental work for the Army after the war ended. But before commencing the amazing series of ballistic tests in Florida that were to figure so prominently in his later career – when he was still assigned, following Perry, to the Infantry School of Arms, at Ft. Benning, Georgia – Crossman was sent in 1919 "by the War Dept. on a trip through every arms plant, arsenal, cartridge factory, and powder plant in this country to observe manufacturing and experimental methods," he related in the *Rifleman* of Jan. 15, 1924. The idea was to apply his findings to the work he would soon be undertaking for the Experimental Dept. of the Infantry School. He remained on the road two months for this purpose.

1919 proved to be one of the most eventful years in his life, because he was appointed Chief Range Officer, and Assistant Executive Officer, for the National Matches scheduled for July and August. That year, the U. S. Navy had obtained permission for the first time to host the Nationals at its newly constructed range in Caldwell, N. J., only 20 miles from New York. To stimulate greater public interest in the event, the Navy had planned many spectacular events and live-fire demonstrations, and rules which formerly restricted civilians from competing in certain matches had been abolished. But by far the most revolutionary innovation at Caldwell was the introduction of .22 RF competition in a variety of different classes, the organization of which events fell in large part to Crossman as Range Officer. Small-bore shooting in a quasi-military style was part of the overall effort, inspired by the war, to "teach our civilians how to shoot straight" and "make good the claim that Americans are a nation of riflemen – not a nation of pool-hounds, bleacherites, and lounge-lizards." Crossman later referred to Caldwell many times, but most fully in his July, 1919, *Outers'* critique, "The Flat-Feet Hold the National Rifle Matches."

In Crossman's *Small Bore Rifle Shooting*, published in 1927 as the first textbook for the new sport and a work so thorough and comprehensive that it remained definitive for decades, the Xman said relatively little about his role in establishing the immediately and immensely popular game of small-bore shooting, i.e., outdoor competition at 50 to 200 yards, to distinguish it from the indoor, or gallery, offhand small-bore matches that flourished in the late nineteenth century. So great was enthusiasm for the outdoor event and the modern rifles soon developed for it, such as the Model 1922 Springfield, that interest in the latter swiftly waned. It was at Caldwell that Winchester unveiled prototypes of possibly the greatest target rifle of all time, the Model 52, which had been "in the works" because it was originally envisaged as a military training rifle. Crossman never claimed credit for discovering the long-range accuracy potential of the .22 LR cartridge, popularly believed to be unstable beyond about 50 yards, but rather took pains to acknowledge T. K. Lee and others for the experiments that paved the way to Caldwell.

By 1936, however, he seems to have felt the time was finally ripe to unburden himself, in the December issue of *National Sportsman*, of the whole sto-

Crossman's beloved wife Blanche takes careful aim with a Colt Model 1911. Courtesy Jim Foral

ry of the introduction of small-bore competition to the National Matches of 1919 "in spite of the NRA officials then against the move." He had "sold the idea to Col. Harlee, the Executive Officer" of the matches, but it was also necessary to hold "the threat of a separate small-bore association over the head of the NRA if it did not forget its old-fogey ideas that the small-bore was fit only for kids!" This kind of bureaucratic resistance to reasonable innovation, whether in the Army or old-boy organizations like the NRA, usually provoked Crossman to outbursts of invective – except when the immediate circumstances (such as wearing a uniform) obliged him to exercise restraint!

Caldwell, in 1919, was especially significant to Crossman for reasons purely personal. Blanche competed in both rifle and pistol events, none of which she won, although she out-shot a great number of male contestants, and was "the only woman ever to fire through a National Match and qualify as Sharpshooter over the Army course." With no encouragement from Ned, she also entered tryouts for the 20-place Dewar Match team, and to the astonishment of everyone present, most especially her husband, earned the dedication that appears in *Small Bore Rifle Shooting*: "To the only girl who has made a place on an international rifle team." The match was shot later that year, with Blanche achieving scores, Crossman reported, that bettered the average of the British team. The following year she again won a place on the U. S. team, and not even a "face full of powder and gas" from a punctured primer at Perry in 1920 daunted her enthusiasm. Her pluck and performance inspired Crossman to write a chapter in *Small Bore Rifle Shooting* that otherwise might not have been included: "The Riflewoman." (Conspiracy theorists may point out that Crossman was also Captain of the Dewar teams from 1919 through 1921, but one can be *absolutely* sure that aspirants to the team would have tolerated no favoritism on his part. Moreover, he devoted a paragraph in "The Riflewoman" to explaining why well-meant favoritism toward "the girls" was condescending and counterproductive.)

A NEW DIRECTION

Late in 1919, Crossman was reassigned from Ft. Benning to the newly created Small Arms Ballistic Station near Miami, Florida, and thus began the most event-

ful period of his career. In "Shooting at the Sky," from the May, 1923, *Outers'*, he described, among other experiments, the fantastic exercise of firing a .30 Browning machine gun mounted in a vertical position, to analyze the dispersion and retained energy of the spent bullets. The following issue of *Outers'* continued the story with this addition: "In January of 1920, Maj. Wilhelm [Crossman's C.O.] moved his station with its heavy and elaborate equipment ($200,000 worth), its 70 enlisted men and half-score of officers and civilian experts, to Daytona to make use of its twice-washed slate of white sands," which would facilitate the recovery of spent bullets fired in maximum-range testing. A battery of three .30 Brownings could be fired simultaneously in testing different powders and bullets on barrel erosion. And weather balloons, geophones, and "more anemometers than I supposed were in possession of the entire Army" taught Crossman virtually everything there was to know about the effects of wind on moving projectiles. Crossman seems to have been second in command at the station, with the position of Fire Control Officer.

Crossman was "having the time of my life," and being paid for it, but in addition the Army permitted him the use of all this equipment, which included a Mann machine-rest, to conduct his own private experiments when off-duty. This prerogative, needless to say, he exploited to the full. "We made more elaborate experiments with the .22 LR cartridge during our work in Florida than has been done by anybody before or since," he asserted in *Small Bore Rifle Shooting*. ("We" included Capt. Wotkyns, father of the .22 Hornet a decade later.) His tour of commercial arms factories in 1919 had acquainted him with everyone of influence in the industry, and therefore Remington Arms, aspiring to convert the M1917 manufactured under contract during the war into a commercially viable sporting rifle, turned to Crossman for assistance. He made arrangements with his old friend Wundhammer to design a stock for Remington (and later did the same for the Ross and

A uniformed
Captain E. C. "Ned" Crossman (left)
circa 1920. Courtesy Jim Foral

Newton arms companies), suggested other modifications, and in due time was sent a prototype Model 30 Remington for testing and evaluation at Daytona, all of which was reported in "Looking Over a War Baby," in the May, 1921, *Outers'*.

The good times were interrupted in March of 1921, when Crossman was hospitalized in Walter Reed Hospital in Washington. In later articles, he referred several times to this incident, which was serious enough to prevent him from shooting for an entire year – for Crossman, an eternity – yet never troubled to explain what his problem had been. C. B. Lister's *Rifleman* obituary for Crossman reported that stomach ulcers, "the bane of many an officer," had forced his retirement from the Army while still working at Daytona, although it seems odd that such an infirmity would preclude recreational shooting. Could his illness have been mis-diagnosed?

Crossman was clearly proud of his brief military service, because afterwards, his bylines never failed to include his rank of Captain. Yet it would be hard to imagine one more temperamentally ill-suited to function cheerfully within so generally inflexible and closed-minded a bureaucracy as the regular Army. Never was there a man less able to practice blind obedience, or suffer fools gladly; such fools, for example, as the "feeble-minded military morons" who "used to insist that the soldier must shoot in his blouse with the collar buttoned up." This complaint is found in *Small Bore Rifle Shooting,* but similar sentiments were expressed throughout his work.

Fortunately for Crossman, the unique circumstances under which he was "invited" into the service by old friends within the Army, and the extraordinary nature of his assignment after the war ended, permitted him to escape most of the usual Army discipline and regimentation. The experimental station in Florida, staffed by such kindred spirits as Wotkyns, bore more resemblance to a gun club than any typical Army post, and Crossman was spared the kind of bureaucratic senselessness that in the next war engendered the immortal acronyms "snafu" and "fubar." Or, at any rate, largely spared, because after he was out of uniform, he occasionally revealed hints of friction with Army policies, as in his comments from the *Rifleman* of January 15, 1924: "such iconoclastic attitudes sometimes results in the Chief of Ordnance not loving you" but "an iconoclastic attitude is sometimes needed for Ordnance pigheadedness."

BACK TO CALIFORNIA

Ordnance pigheadedness notwithstanding, the most productive period of Crossman's life, unquestionably, was his service with the Army from early 1918 to some time in 1921; the wealth of knowledge and experience acquired during that time became a savings account from which he made withdrawals for the remainder of his life. After leaving the Army and returning to his "dear Southern California," the course of his career becomes more difficult to follow. He continued of course to write regularly for *Outers',* occasionally for *Field and Stream,* and probably others, and also for *Arms and the Man,* and its

successor, the *Rifleman* (charity work, as the NRA paid contributors little).

He continued as well to serve the arms industry as a consultant, which he never spoke of as an activity involving filthy lucre, although it is only reasonable to assume he was being compensated for his time and expertise, and probably on a scale higher than that for magazine writing. The work for Remington previously described was by no means the first of its kind: in 1908, he was the first American, at the behest of *Outers',* "to import and shoot the .280 Ross on game and report in print"; in 1910, he "tried out and baptized the .22 Hi-Power 'Imp'" for Savage Arms; and in 1914, with a Savage Model 99 test gun he "killed the first game killed with the .250/3000 anywhere, by anybody." His stature in the trade was such that "few new guns, cartridges, or accessories have appeared on the American market during the past 20 years which have not borne the mark of Ned Crossman's experience passed along to the manufacturer after examining preliminary samples," Lister asserted in 1939.

The archives of the *Los Angeles Times* provide sporadic traces of Crossman's activities during the Roaring Twenties and Hard-Time Thirties: in 1922, he was mentioned as winning his class in a trap shoot (and he later took up

skeet with a vengeance, organizing the first L. A. skeet club); in 1924, he was "victorious in rifle contest"; again in 1924 (and now residing in Santa Monica) it was announced that he had been elected a Life Director of the NRA (not that this honor suppressed his criticisms of the "more or less dumb" organization); in 1925, he won the Price Trophy; in 1926, he was "victor in rifle shoot"; in 1927, he had "best shooting card in rifle tilts at Schuetzen Park," presumably an off-hand contest.

During the 1930s, he was often mentioned in the *Times* as a firearms and ballistics expert witness testifying in criminal cases; "I entered into this work in 1924 at the request of the L. A. County Sherif – reluctantly because I did not like police work, courts, lawyers...and the spectacle of some poor devil on trial," he recounted in *The Book of the Springfield*. He wrote elsewhere that he ordered built to his specifications in 1926 (at a cost, he said, of $1000) the first bullet-comparison microscope used on the West Coast. "I have had occasion a number of times in the past dozen years to glance at the waxen face of somebody

Crossman (top row, left) seems proud of his team: the Los Angeles Rifle and Revolver Club.

LOS ANGELES RIFLE AND REVOLVER CLUB.
Winners of the Championship of the United States in the National Inter-club Military Match.
Top row, left to right: E. C. Crossman (team coach), H. C. March, Dr. L. Felsenthal, I. O. Gardiner, D. R. Dickey, W. R. Jackson, E. D. Neff, Colonel Cook (executive officer of the N.R.A.)
Bottom row: A. F. Goldsborough, R. J. Fraser, W. G. Hansen, G. L. Wotkyns, A. L. Thomson, Sergeant-Major Decius (range officer).

Blanche Crossman was no wallflower. Here she assists shooter Alvan Fischer in setting up a paper shotgun pattern target. Courtesy Jim Foral

hit squarely with a .22 bullet, and then to investigate the conditions of the killing," he noted in a discussion of rimfires for *Outdoor Life* in December, 1937.

The L. A. Rifle and Revolver Club, which in *Small Bore Rifle Shooting* he said "I organized" in 1908, and for which served as Secretary for over two decades, absorbed much of his time, as it was one of the most – if not *the* most – active clubs in the country, regularly sending teams (coached by Crossman, if he did not shoot with them) to the National Matches and other competitions. Wotkyns was club Treasurer for many years and White another long-standing member. Crossman knew what it takes to organize and, more importantly, *sustain,* a shooting club: "the organizer...must fix firmly in his mind that 95% of his members will not lift a hand to help." His methodical study of the art and psychology of coaching other shooters was the fruit of decades of experience at the firing line. When the L. A. Police Dept. required an expanded practice range, Crossman, well known to the department for his forensic work, was the obvious choice to design it.

MAGAZINE JOBS

Crossman authored the firearms department ("Arms, Ammunition, and the Game Trail") of the most venerable sporting periodical of them all, *Forest and Stream*, beginning at least as early as January of 1929 and continuing until the last months of its survival in mid-1930. Founded as a weekly in 1873, and modernized into a monthly magazine in the 'teens, *Forest and Stream* failed, however, to compete successfully with its newer rivals, and finally succumbed to the financial crisis that began in 1929. Regrettably, issues including his work have thus far eluded this collector.

Following this truncated affiliation with *Forest and Stream*, Crossman presumably occupied himself with writing the two books published in 1932 (*Military & Sporting Rifle Shooting* and *The Book of the Springfield*). But in April of 1932, there appeared his initial columns as firearms editor of two unusual magazines less well-remembered now than their merits deserved: *National Sportsman,* in print before the turn of the century, and, coming along after Wilson's "war to make the world safe for democracy," its sibling *Hunting and Fishing*. Edited by William H. Foster, the inventor of skeet, this pair, zealous in their promotion of conservation issues and with possibly the most imaginative cover art in the business, claimed for decades the highest combined circulation of any sporting periodicals – as high as a phenomenal 700,000 readers by the mid-1930s. Circulation figures should always be regarded with suspicion, but no other sporting magazine between the 'teens and the '40s seems to have disputed this braggadocio. To be frank, they lacked the prestige as well as the bulk of *Outers',* but the latter, like so many other distinguished old marques, did not survive the first years of the Great Depression.

Also in 1932, he was "dragged out of my peaceful shack on my 160 acres of timber in the Oregon woods...at the request of the NRA," as he related in the October issue of *Hunting and Fishing*, "to be manager, captain, and coach, of the U.S. team, and also run the [entire] rifle shoot," for the Los Angeles Olympics of that year. (Far too large a job for one man, he recruited friends to assist.) This Oregon property, apparently acquired well before the war, he described elsewhere as a "timber claim," meaning perhaps that it was granted by the federal government on condition of being developed in some way, such as logging, because he also mentioned a local man hired to fell timber. In *Military and Sporting Rifle Shooting*, Crossman referred to "living most of two years in the Oregon backwoods...45 miles from the railroad...with deer coming into my clearing often...I staged quite a few extemporaneous shooting matches with my neighbors." For hunting experience under differing conditions of climate and terrain, the contrast between the rainforest of Oregon and the desert mountains of southern California and Mexico could not easily be exceeded.

HIS LAST POST

"Well, gun bugs, here's your man. If you don't already know him, you ought to hang your head. If you do, you know he writes the liveliest, soundest gun stuff that's published, and has been doing it for 30 years at least." With these erudite lines in the June issue of 1937, the editor of *Outdoor Life* announced that Crossman would thereafter "air his forceful views" as the magazine's new firearms editor, replacing for reasons unknown none other than "Mr. Rifleman," Townsend Whelen. Although Crossman had written many pieces for *Outdoor Life* before the war, his best work afterwards had appeared in *Outers'*. "Just Offhand," he called his new column, and it immediately demonstrated that his views had lost none of their force, but seemed, rather, to be more pungent than ever.

Crossman's three books have been reprinted in two recently published editions (Wolfe and Paladin presses), although the Samworth first editions may be purchased at a cost no greater than these reprints. Readers of these books *only*, however, miss much of the singular spirit of Crossman, because in those more carefully considered works, the "forceful views," wisecracks, and snappy patter that more truthfully portray his ebullient personality were held under tighter rein. That personality is fully revealed in his magazine articles and especially in the columns dashed off for *National Sportsman, Hunting and Fishing*, and *Outdoor Life*. Crossman's light-hearted banter – or, depending upon circumstances, ferocious invective – contrasts so dramatically with the staid and sober, warm but humorless style of Whelen, that it might be imagined the two would probably prove incompatible. Of course, that mistaken assessment does not allow for a comradeship tempered in the summer heat of Perry and Sea Girt and other shooting grounds famous to riflemen.

A PARTNER FOR LIFE

For the Census of 1930, Blanche listed her occupation as "musician, radio broadcast," an intriguing facet of her life never mentioned by Crossman, who mentioned her often. Almost the only personal information regarding his wife that Crossman vouchsafed to his readers was that she had never touched a gun before their marriage in 1905. He actively discouraged her first tentative expressions of an interest in shooting, as he tells the tale in *Small Bore Rifle Shooting*, although perhaps this narrative exaggerates his reluctance for dramatic effect. But to such a meticulous and analytical observer as Crossman, it must have been immediately obvious, when he finally acceded to her entreaties, that this lady possessed a true natural talent in all the elements essential to good shooting. And although many women prove themselves to be "naturals" when introduced to a .22RF or other firearm of light recoil, the remarkable skill Blanche quickly developed with the famously hard-kicking straight-gripped Springfield was a wonder. (Whelen re-

marked that even many Regulars complained about the recoil of the "new" Springfield when it supplanted the Krag.)

In addition to her interest (and success) in competitive shooting, Blanche is frequently identified by Crossman as assisting in the firearms and accessories testing that, especially after he left the Army, played so large a part in their lives. (A wonderful photograph of her firing a Springfield equipped with an experimental scope mount appears on page 507 of Brophy's great paean to the M1903.) Blanche is probably portrayed in some of the numerous photos of unidentified women in shooting positions, their faces hidden by buttstocks, that appear in Crossman's own works, but page 291 of *Military and Sporting Rifle Shooting* is, owing to the rifle depicted, almost certainly a portrait of her. And when Crossman tested for his "Just Offhand" column a Model 70 newly chambered by Winchester for the powerful .375 H&H cartridge, he included a photo of Blanche bravely touching it off.

THE END

Even today when women are vastly more active in the shooting sports than was the case in Crossman's day, any serious rifleman or hunter would surely think himself blessed to share a home with such a partner. Consider, however, the feelings of a man whose *life*, not merely his recreational enthusiasms, was wrapped-up in shooting, and perhaps you will appreciate the

blow that fell on Crossman October 21, 1938: Blanche was killed in an auto accident. No significant details of the accident were reported by the *Los Angeles Times*, but Crossman, for reasons unknown, and under the influence, of course, of grief and despondency, blamed himself. The *Times* of January 18, 1939 reported that "Police Expert Tries Suicide – Capt. Crossman, Arms Expert, Saved From Death by Car Fumes," going on to explain that he had been found behind the wheel of his car by a servant in his garage. The hospital to which he had been taken predicted "he has an even chance to recover."

It was not to be; the *Times* of January 20, 1939 included this obituary: "Grieving Officer Dies as Desired." Crossman's suicide note to Coroner Nance, "who many times called Capt. Crossman as an expert witness during inquests," was reproduced in full: "Dear Frank, This is of course a suicide. No inquest is necessary, and for the sake of my family, will you keep the matter as quiet as possible. Reason for suicide – the death of my beloved wife – from motor car accident, which was my own fault."

The matter could *not* be kept as quiet as possible in a city in which he had been a well-known personality for four decades, but in his *Rifleman* obituary, in *Outdoor Life*, and in all the other sporting periodicals which noted his untimely demise, no hint of the actual circumstances was disclosed. The last "Just Offhand," appearing in the issue of March, 1939, included this incontrovertible statement by *Outdoor Life*: "His passing will leave a wide gap...that gap, perhaps, will never be filled. Capt. Crossman was unique."

To Lister's obituary in the *Rifleman*, Whelen added "A Tribute": "I know of no other shooter who was so well-versed in the technique of the grooved barrel, or so familiar with the allied sciences. Sometimes scathing in his criticisms, he never failed to give justice where it was due. He was a delightful companion to those who knew him well, generous to a fault, his greatest weakness that he would spend his last penny on his friends if permitted. We rifleman have lost a very great friend, a wise counselor and coach, and a helpful scientist. I, one of his oldest friends, mourn his loss, and the help and comradeship I have sensed the many times we lay side by side on the firing range."

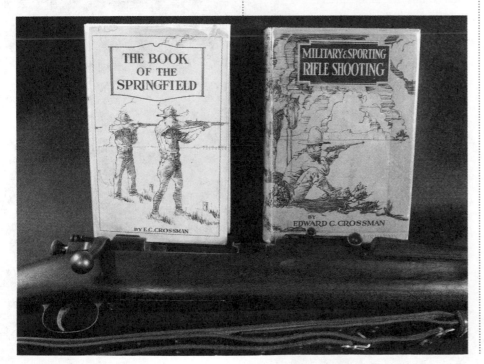

Two of Crossman's classics, shown with the rifle he knew so well: the 1903 Springfield.

UPDATED CLASSICS:
The NEW Ithaca Model 37s

One major highlight of the 2009 SHOT Show in Orlando came from an unlikely source, the Ithaca Gun Company, when they unveiled their new 28-gauge Model 37 Featherlight pump. In a show that was dominated by semi-auto pistols and ARs, one of the most talked-about guns turned out to be a sweet little honey of a shotgun that practically begged you to throw it up to your shoulder.

Younger shooters might have only a passing familiarity with the Ithaca name, and that's a pity, for the Ithaca name is respected by shotgunners all over the world. The company began way back in 1883 by a consortium of New York businessmen, chief among whom were William Henry Baker and L. C. Smith. These two giants of the shotgun world and their partners located their new enterprise in Ithaca, New York, and named it, appropriately enough, the Ithaca Gun Company. Over the years, the Ithaca Gun Company's double- and single-barrel trap guns, as well as its enormously popular New Ithaca Double (NID), attracted an impressive collection of high-profile endorsers, including John Philip Sousa, Annie Oakley, E. C. "Ned" Crossman, Capt. Charles Askins, and the editors of *Fur-Fish-Game*, *Outdoor Life* and *Field and Stream*.

As popular as the Ithaca's double guns were, however, the shotgun that most shooters associate with the company, the Model 37 pump gun, didn't start out as an Ithaca at, all but as the Remington Model 17. Designed by a pair of true masters, John M. Browning and John Pederson, the hammerless, 20-gauge Model 17 featured a unique bottom-ejecting design that was said to be stronger and more impervious to foul weather than competing side-ejecting pump guns. Introduced in 1921, the Remington Model 17 was a modest seller, with only around 73,000 units being produced before it was dropped in 1933. In 1930, Remington introduced a 12-gauge version designated the Model 29. It, too, was dropped in 1933, after 38,000 units had been shipped, to make room for Remington's new side-ejecting Model 31.

We can only speculate why the Remington Models 17 and 29 failed to catch on, but a clue lies in the overwhelming success of Winchester's Model 12 pump gun. With its streamlined good looks, enormous strength and beefy action, the Model 12 pretty much set the standard for slide-action shotguns, and the Remington's just couldn't compete effectively with it.

And the Model 12 wasn't just goring Remington's ox; it caused Ithaca a good deal of trouble, too, as more and more shooters traded in their doubles for the "modern" Winchester pump.

Ithaca wasn't content to sit back and watch Winchester steal its lunch, so the company made plans to introduce their own pump gun based on the Remington Model 17 as soon as Remington's patents expired in 1933. When the new Ithaca pump was being tooled up, however, it was discovered that Remington's patents didn't actually expire until 1937. When they did, Ithaca was positioned to introduce what was – and is – to many shooters the most graceful pump shotgun ever produced: the Model 37.

There's a lot to like about the Model 37. It's a natural pointer, due in no small part to its trim dimensions and light weight. (The steel-framed 12-ga. Featherlight generally runs less than 7.5 lbs., while the aluminum-framed Ultralight weighs 16 ounces less.) Unlike other pump guns, the Model 37 featured a single action bar on the left side of the action, and it was beefy enough that it didn't flex and bind up the action. And, of course, the Model 37 was a take-down gun, which was a definite plus in those pre-choke tube days: just unscrew the maga-

The Deerslayer III produced respectable 100-yard groups out of a fresh barrel. These are the first three shots.

zine tube, give the barrel a counterclockwise quarter-turn, and off it came. You could then install any other M37 barrel of the same gauge, even one of the ultra-accurate smoothbore Deerslayer barrels that the company began offering around 1958.

Aesthetically, the Model 37 was quite an improvement over the Remington Model 17. The folks at Ithaca trimmed away some of the M17's awkward angularity, with the result being a uniquely stylish, almost voluptuous grace. And here we must confess that there's something so naturally feminine about the way that the top of the M37's receiver curves down into the comb that we find it a pleasure to put our hand there.

Ithaca Gun Company stayed in the hands of the Smith family until 1967, when they sold it to a group of Colorado inves-

**12" x 18" (30 cm x 45 cm)
Splattering Target**

tors. Ithaca continued its product development, introducing the world's first 10-gauge magnum autoloader, the mighty Mag 10, as well as marketing a number of rimfire and centerfire rifles, some of which were imported from overseas. Unfortunately, Ithaca Gun Company fell victim to the economic malaise of the late 1970s and filed for Chapter 11 bankruptcy in 1979.

In 1985, the company was relocated to Kings Ferry, New York, by its new owners, Ithaca Acquisition, Inc.

In 1987, Ithaca did two things that respectively delighted and horrified M37 fanciers: they gave the Model 37 a three-inch chamber but changed the Model 37's name to the Model 87 – sacrilege!

By this time, however, Remington's Model 870 had well established itself as the most popular pump gun in the world, and the new Model 87 couldn't compete with it. In 1996, the company – now known as Ithaca Gun Company, LLC – changed the shotgun's name back to the Model 37, but by then it was too late. Production became irregular, service became questionable, and it seemed that the clock had finally run out on the good old Model 37.

But not quite. In 2005 the assets of the company were purchased by Dave Dlubak, an Ohio-based businessman. Dlubak – doing business as Ithaca Gun Company USA, LLC – relocated the company to Upper Sandusky, Ohio, midway between Toledo and Columbus. In 2007, Dlubak's company, once again known simply as Ithaca Gun Company, resumed production of the Model 37.

Dlubak assembled a crack team of engineers and machinists who have ushered the Model 37 into the twenty-first century. Ithaca shotguns are now built using state-of-the-art computer modeling and manufacturing techniques, and it's no exaggeration to say that the finest Ithaca pump guns of all time are being built right now, as you read this, in Upper Sandusky, Ohio. Moreover, they're being built by workers who know exactly what the Ithaca name means to pump gun fans.

Ithaca Gun Company now specializes in Model 37s only, of which there are four main flavors: the traditional Featherlight and Ultralight; the Deerslayer II; the Deerslayer III; and the short-barreled Defense Gun. All the new Model 37s have a one-piece receiver, and all 12- and 20-gauge guns have 3-inch chambers and Briley choke tubes (with the exception of the Defense Gun); but only the Featherlight and Ultralight have retained the removable-barrel feature. To the dismay of the few of us who like the old "'tweener," the 16-gauge guns offered by the earlier Ithaca companies have been discontinued, at least as of this writing.

Thanks to Mike Farrell and the other fine folks at Ithaca Gun Company, *Gun Digest* staffers recently had an opportunity to testfire a trio of new Ithaca M37s at our range in central Wisconsin: a field grade 12-gauge; a 12-gauge Deerslayer III and a new Grade AAA 28-gauge M37. We weren't disappointed. First up was the Deerslayer III. Its

24-inch fluted heavy barrel made it look like a serious purpose-built slug gun, and that's exactly what it turned out to be. Our sample gun carried a Nikon 3x9 variable scope, and with some new premium Winchester Supreme Elite Sabots, we found that, after the barrel was broken in, we could shoot sub-two-inch groups at 100 yards as long as our ammunition

The TRUGLO font sight on the new M37s replaces the old Raybar sight, but it lights up just as brightly.

held out. But it wasn't only its accuracy that really impressed us about the Deerslayer III; it was its remarkably crisp, light trigger pull and slick slide that put the smiles on our faces. Several shooters commented that they had never racked a smoother pump gun.

The Deerslayer III's Monte Carlo stock was a big help in lining up the scope without a lot of fidgeting, and a laminated thumbhole stock is available for those who appreciate the extra measure of control that such a stock offers. We wished that we had more time to spend with the Deerslayer III, because at around 10 lbs. with scope, it was a pleasure to shoot.

There's bound to be some debate about what is truly the Rolls-Royce of pump-action slug guns. Some will say it's the Remington 870-based Tar-Hunt DSG; others will choose the Deerslayer III. Since both guns perform so well, it's likely to come down to a matter of personal preference; but the Ithaca's extremely slick slide and snappy trigger pull will undoubtedly appeal to connoisseurs. At a suggested retail of around $1200, it's not exactly inexpensive, but you get what you pay for.

We then moved on to the 12-ga. Field Grade Featherlight. This is as close as you can get to the classic M37s of years gone by but it has a 3-inch chamber and interchangeable choke tubes. The classic corncob forend is long gone, having been replaced by a nice geometric checker-

ing pattern. Anyone who's ever shot a well-built M37 knows how shooter-friendly they are, and the Field Grade was no exception. Clays just didn't stand a chance with it. Everyone shot it well, from tiny Corrina Peterson up to linebacker-size Tom Nelsen.

The Field Grade Featherlight 12 gauge retails for around $850. That's on the high side for pump guns, true, but few who shot the gun would maintain that it's not worth it. When a 5-foot-nothing lady such as Corrina can pick up an M37 for the first time in her life and outshoot the rest of our staff with it, well, that gun's got some serious mojo going on.

Next came our chance with the new 28-gauge Grade AAA. We believe that this was the very same gun that we saw at the SHOT Show back in January. It was almost as much fun just to hold this gun, with its slender scaled frame and 28" barrel, as it was to shoot it (well, almost). Contributing Editor Jake Edson dusted every bird we threw up with the tiny, pointy little gun. Like all the other M37s we tested, it had a light, quick slide, and Mr. Edson – no slouch with a shotgun, he – cranked out several doubles so fast that if you closed your eyes you'd think he was shooting an over-under or a Browning Auto-5. If we had any suggestions for the Grade AAA 28-gauge, it would be to replace the dull black recoil pad with a plain horn or hard rubber buttplate. Who needs a recoil pad on a 28, anyway? And perhaps one other point deserves mention: the serial number on our sample 28, stamped on the lower border of the right side of the receiver, looked ENORMOUS.

The new 28-gauge Featherlight starts at around $1000 in its Grade A dress; for that you get nice but not super-deluxe wood and a plain roll-engraved receiver. Naturally, there's a cost associated with gold inlays and ultra-fancy wood, and we suspect that Ithaca will build you a 28-gauge as fancy as your checkbook will allow. Those who favor the 28 gauge for upland hunting may decide that the Remington 870 Express is all they really need, while others will prefer the very elegant Browning BPS Hunter. We have shot all three and have done rather well with them. Still – and perhaps for no other reason than plain old sentimentality – we

Ithaca's new 28-gauge Featherlight is a graceful, perfectly proportioned field gun.

The M37 Featherlight takes down into a compact package that fits most short-sized hard cases.

rather like the new 28-gauge Ithaca.

Some shooters may have issues with the red-orange TRUGLO front sights that graced both the 12- and 28-gauge Feather-lights, but to us, Ithaca fans of long stand-ing, they just wouldn't be M37s without a luminescent front sight, whether it be a TRUGLO or the old-fashioned Raybar. Like them or not, you will certainly know they're there, even on overcast days. On bright, sunshiny days, they glow like the neon sign at Duffy's Tavern.

Our very first shotgun, purchased back in 1974, was an Ithaca Deluxe Feath-erlight 20-ga. As fond as we are of that old 20-gauge, the

(above) The gold inlaid engraving on the Grade AAA 28-gauge M37 belies the fact that it's a serious, pointy little upland gun. (below) The M37's single action bar is a brawny affair that gives the M37 its legendarily smooth stroke.

quality of the new Ithaca M37s is even better. In terms of fit, finish and function, we found nothing to complain about and plenty to praise. With annual production at around 3,500 M37s of all types, you won't see as many of them in the fields or on the lines as you would, say,

Gun Digest Group Publisher Jim Schlender puts the Ithaca Deerslayer III through its paces at the bench.

Rem-ington 870s. But if you get a chance to shoot a new Ithaca M37, we recommend you take it. In our opinion, it may well be the smoothest, slick-est, sweetest pump gun on the market. You might agree.

For more information on the new Ithaca 37s, the company probably wouldn't mind it one bit if you visited their website at www.IthacaGun.com.

The .44 Special

BEGINS ITS SECOND CENTURY

BY JOHN TAFFIN

Taffin shooting the USFA .44 Special Single Action.

THE ROAD TO THE .44 SPECIAL

In 1857, two entrepreneurs, Horace Smith and Daniel Wesson, produced the first successful cartridge-firing revolver, the Smith & Wesson #1. This little seven-shot, tip-up revolver was chambered for what would become the most popular cartridge of all time, the .22 rimfire. They would go on to build both .22 and .32 rimfires in the Models 1, 1-1/2, and 2, and they had plans to bring out a big-bore version, but those plans were pushed to the back burner with the coming of the Civil War in 1861.

Meanwhile, over at the Colt factory, Sam Colt had decided cartridge cases would never catch on and shooters would always want to load their own using powder, ball, and cap. When Colt received a very lucrative contract to build 1860 Army Model .44s for the Northern Army not, only was the company's immediate future assured but there definitely was no further thought of building cartridge-firing revolvers. Smith & Wesson kept producing their

In the early 1980s S&W resurrected the .44 Special Model 24 for a limited run. This matched pair of 4" sixguns wear carved ivory stocks by Bob Leskovec and are carried in floral carved Tom Threepersons holsters from El Paso Saddlery.

little pocket guns, which were quite popular as hideout weapons during the 1860s, but they did not forget their plans to build a .44-caliber version.

Sam Colt died in 1862, but his ideas persisted and percussion revolvers remained as the number one focus of the Colt Company. Then it happened! I can let my imagination run loose and see the executives of Colt sitting around the boardroom in late 1869 when the messenger arrives. He talks to the president, Richard Jarvis, who immediately scowls. He shares the information with the rest of the group. That other gun company, that Smith & Wesson group, had just announced a large-frame, break-top, six-shot, cartridge-firing .44 sixgun!

The new Smith & Wesson was known as the American and was chambered in both .44 Centerfire and .44 Henry Rimfire. Then when the U.S. Army ordered 1,000 .44 S&W Americans, Colt really knew they had some catching up to do.

Meanwhile, someone else was taking a serious look at the first .44 from Smith & Wesson: the Russians. They eventually negotiated a large contract for 150,000 guns with the Springfield firm to supply single-action sixguns for the Czar's army. However, they insisted on a change in the ammunition that would affect all future cartridge-cased ammu-

Smith & Wesson 4" .44 Specials: 1950 Target with shortened barrel, Model 624, Model 24-3, and original 4" 1950 Target.

was changed with a hump at the top to prevent the grip's shifting in the hand when the gun was fired, and a spur was placed on the bottom of the trigger guard. (The argument still remains as to just what that spur was for: to parry a sword thrust? To keep the sixgun from falling when carried in a sash? To serve as a steadying rest for the middle finger when firing the revolver? All these theories have been advanced.) This sixgun became known as the Model #3 Russian. With the removal of the spur and a slightly redesigned grip frame, the Model #3 Russian evolved into the New Model #3 in 1878 chambered in, of course, .44 Russian. The New Model #3 is without a doubt the epitome of Smith & Wesson single action production, and could easily be argued as the finest single-action sixgun to come from the nineteenth century. It was beautifully

nition. The original .44 S&W American was made just like the .22 Rimfire and used an outside lubricated heel bullet; that is, the diameter of the main body of the bullet was the same as the diameter of the outside of the brass case, but the lower part of the bullet was slightly smaller in diameter to fit inside the cartridge case. The Russians made a great improvement in ammunition when they asked for a bullet of uniform diameter with lube grooves inside the case itself. The result was the .44 Russian and the beginning of modern ammunition.

Those first Russian contract guns were nothing more than American models chambered in .44 Russian. Eventually the rounded back strap

John Gallagher converted this Ruger New Model 50th Anniversary .357 Magnum Blackhawk to an easy-packin' 4" .44 Special.

built with tight tolerances that actually worked against it in a black powder age with the fouling resulting from shooting.

In 1881, Smith & Wesson looked at that beautiful New Model #3 and redesigned it with a double-action mechanism, and so the first Double Action Model arrived in .44 Russian. These are not the finest-looking double-action sixguns ever made, far from it, but they were dependable and would represent the best big-bore double-action sixguns from Smith & Wesson for more than 25 years. In fact, the Double Action .44 would stay in production right up to the eve of World War I.

By the late 1890s, Colt was producing swing-out cylindered double-action revolvers, and Smith & Wesson soon followed suit. In 1899, Smith & Wesson produced their first K-frame, the Military & Police, which would go on to be one

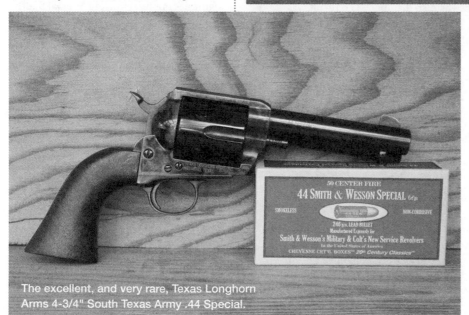

The excellent, and very rare, Texas Longhorn Arms 4-3/4" South Texas Army .44 Special.

of the most popular revolvers of the twentieth century. It was chambered in .38 Special, but the engineers at Smith & Wesson were looking at something a bit bigger. In 1907, the Military & Police was enlarged to what we now know as the N-frame, fitted with an enclosed ejector rod housing, and had a third locking mechanism added. By this time, the M&P locked at the back of the cylinder and the front of the ejector rod; this new sixgun received a third lock with the crane locking into the back of the ejector rod housing.

The new sixgun had many names, including the .44 Hand Ejector 1st Model, New Century, Model of 1908, .44 Military, but it is best known among collectors and shooters alike as the Triple Lock. Such a beautifully built sixgun deserved a new cartridge, and that cartridge was the .44 Special. To arrive at the .44 Special, the .44 Russian was simply lengthened from .97" to 1.16". But having gone to the edge of perfection, Smith &

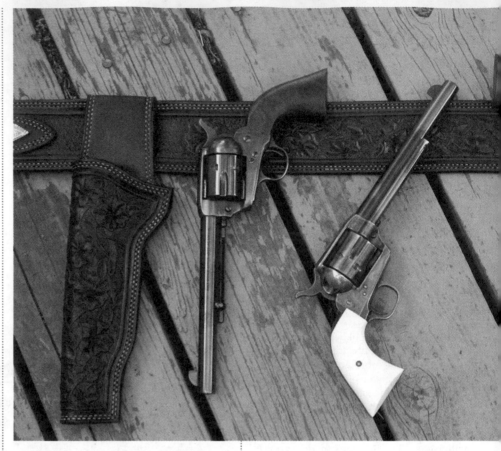

1st, 2nd, and 3rd Generation 7-1/2" .44 Special Colt SAAs with leather by Circle Bar T.

The most popular bullet for the .44 Special is the Keith design; this version is from RCBS.

Wesson then drew back. The longer cartridge in a stronger sixgun was loaded to duplicate the .44 Russian! The Russian carried a bullet of approximately 250 grains at a muzzle velocity of about 750 fps. They should have at least duplicated the .45 Colt round and bumped the .44 Special up to 850-900 fps – and 1,000 fps would have been even better. It would remain the task of experimenters in the 1920s through the 1940s to discover the real potential of the .44 Special.

SMITH & WESSON .44 SPECIALS

The Triple Lock, perhaps the finest double-action revolver ever produced, had a very short life span, lasting only until 1915 with just over 15,000 being manufactured. They sold for $21 at

a time when one dollar was a lot of money, but because of an attempt to save $2 on its price, the Triple Lock died. True! It was replaced by the .44 Hand Ejector 2nd Model, which lacked the third lock, a shortcut that allowed it to retail for $2 less than the Triple Lock. To add insult to injury, the Triple Lock's shrouded ejector rod housing was also dropped. The result was simply a larger Military & Police.

More 2nd Models were built than 1st Models, about 2,000 more, but it would take 35 years to accomplish. Both the Triple Lock and the 2nd Model are rarely, very rarely, found in other chamberings such as .45 Colt, .44-40, and .38-40; however they were first and foremost .44 Specials. As soon as the Triple Lock was replaced by the 2nd Model, sixgun connoisseurs began calling for a return to the Triple Lock. As so often happens with gun companies, the pleas for the return to what a double-action sixgun should be fell on deaf ears, at least until 1926.

What individual shooters could not do, Wolf and Klar, a gun dealer in Fort Worth, Texas, could do. An order was placed with Smith & Wesson for several thousand revolvers chambered in .44 Special with the enclosed ejector rod

housing. Except for the missing third lock, these revolvers were every bit as good as the 1st Models and were eagerly accepted by shooters and especially by Southwestern lawmen. The 4", fixed sighted, double-action .44 Special Smith & Wesson was just about the perfect defensive sixgun in the 1920s, and there is some doubt that it has ever been

An excellent choice for a hunting bullet in the .44 Special is the Speer original jacketed bullet with a lead core in a full copper cup.

became the Model 21 and the Target version was dubbed the Model 24.

The Model 21 demands prices in four figures today. In the early 1970s I purchased a 5" Model 21 for $65 and since it was not considered rare or a collector's item at that time, I converted it to a Target Model with a 1950 Target barrel cut back to 5" and a S&W adjustable rear sight installed. One of the top gunsmiths in the country did the work and it is a beautiful sixgun, but imagine what it would be worth today if I had left in its original condition!

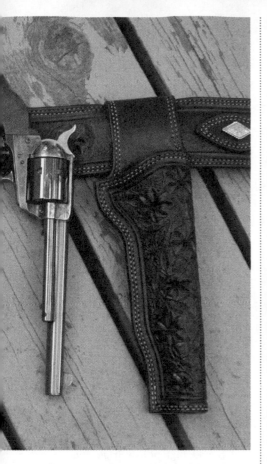

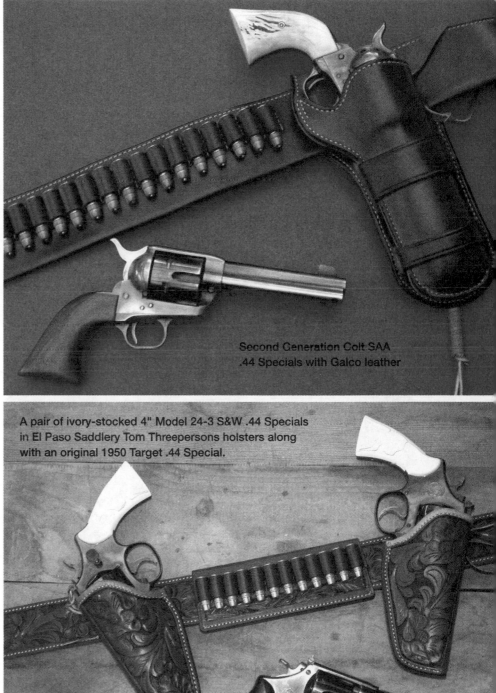

Second Generation Colt SAA .44 Specials with Galco leather

A pair of ivory-stocked 4" Model 24-3 S&W .44 Specials in El Paso Saddlery Tom Threepersons holsters along with an original 1950 Target .44 Special.

pushed to second place. This 3rd Model, also known as the Model 1926, would be produced until the start of World War II, when all production of civilian arms ceased, and then resurrected in 1946 for only a short time until the next model appeared. As great as the Model 1926 was, it did not replace the 2nd Model as both were produced simultaneously until the eve of World War II.

The Model 1926 is even more rare than the Triple Lock, with only about 6,500 being produced in the two runs from 1926 to 1941 and 1946 to 1949. Just as with the 1st and 2nd Models, this 3rd Model was offered in both fixed-sight and target-sight versions. By 1949, the Model 1926 was about to be changed to become the 4th Model Hand Ejector of 1950. The Model 1950 was offered in two versions: the rare fixed-sight Military Model with only about 1,200 being produced, and the magnificent 1950 Target Model. Both were offered in barrel lengths of 4", 5", and 6-1/2" with the 4" 1950 Target being rare and the 5" Target extremely so. Just under 5,100 4th Model Target .44 Specials were made from 1950 to 1966. In 1957, when all Smith & Wessons lost their personality and became mere model numbers, the 4th Model Military

(top) This pair of .44 Specials built on S&W and Ruger .357 Magnums were finished in matte blue by Hamilton Bowen for heavy-duty field use. (middle) In the mid-1980s Smith & Wesson offered a limited number of stainless steel .44 Special Model 624s. (above) The Freedom Arms Model 97 is the finest production .44 Special single-action ever produced.

Eight years later I actually came upon a 6-1/2" Model 1950 Target. I had placed a Winchester 1886 on layaway at the Gunhaus and when George called me to tell me about the Smith & Wesson, I backed off the Winchester and took the 1950 Target instead.

Then I did it again! I wanted the 6-1/2" 1950 Target, but I also wanted a 4" version even more and had the barrel shortened to four inches. Strike Two! Fortunately, thanks to regular readers of *Guns* and *American Handgunner*, I have been contacted about .44 Special Smith & Wesson sixguns for sale and in recent years have purchased three 4" .44 Specials, a 1926 Model made the same year I was, a 1950 Military, and a 1950 Target, as well as a 6-1/2" Model 1950 Target. There will be no Strike Three and the sixguns will be enjoyed exactly as the beautiful works of art they really are.

Not only was the 1950 Target a magnificent sixgun in its own right, it became the basic platform for the .44 Magnum. In 1954 Smith & Wesson began experimenting with a new Magnum in a 4" 1950 Target with special heat-treating and the cylinder re-chambered to the longer .44. When the .44 Magnum became reality, it was a 1950 Target with a longer cylinder, bull barrel, high polish Bright Blue finish, and adjustable sights consisting of a white outline rear sight and a front ramp sight with a red insert. The 1950 Target with its special heat-treating could handle the .44 Magnum, but shooters could not, and an extra half-pound was added to the weight by going to the longer cylinder and bull barrel.

The coming of the .44 Magnum pushed the .44 Special aside very quickly. Some shooters, such as sheriff of Deaf Smith County Texas, Skeeter Skelton, sold his 4" 1950 Target .44 Special and replaced it with a 4" .44 Magnum, only to find it was a lot harder to pack all day and the ammunition was much too powerful for law enforcement use. Of course, a handloader could tailor-make .44 Magnum ammunition at the .44 Special level, but if one is going to shoot .44 Special ammunition, why carry the heavier sixgun? Skeeter admitted he was sorry he ever sold his .44 Special.

In 1966 Smith & Wesson dropped the 1950 Target/Model 24 from production. Of course, as always happens, when something disappears a demand appears. It would be Skeeter Skelton who would help keep the fire burning for .44 Specials by publishing an article in the early 1970s about converting the Smith & Wesson .357 Magnum Highway

This first-year production .44 Special Triple Lock is carried in a George Lawrence #34 Elmer Keith holster.

Patrolman to .44 Special. In those days Smith & Wesson .44 Special barrels were still available so it was simply a matter of re-chambering the .357 cylinder to .44 Special and fitting a new barrel.

It would take a while, but finally in 1983 Smith & Wesson brought back the .44 Special as the Model 24-3. To ensure selling all of these guns they promised to make only so many. They were offered in both 4" and 6-1/2" versions with a production run of one year and 7,500 being produced. They

Two S&W .44 Specials that command high collector prices now are the five-shot 696 and the Mountain Lite.

sold quickly; in fact the demand for these resurrected .44 Specials was greater than the number produced. Now what? Smith & Wesson had backed themselves into a corner by promising only to produce a certain number, and yet the market was out there for more .44 Specials. This dilemma was solved by offering the stainless-steel version, the Model 624, with the same barrel lengths from 1985 to 1987. Both the blued 24-3 and stainless-steel 624 .44 Specials were also specially ordered and offered as 3" round-butted versions by Smith and Wesson distributors.

The Smith & Wesson .44 Special died in 1966, was resurrected in 1983, and died again in 1987. However, the .44 Special is too good to stay buried for very long. In 1996, the Smith & Wesson .44 Special returned as the Model 696, a stainless steel, five-shot L-frame with a 3" barrel and round butt grip frame. It was followed by the Model 396Ti, the same basic revolver with an alloy frame and titanium cylinder. And then after nearly 20 years we got back to basics with a full-sized, six-shot, N-frame .44 Special: the Model 21-3, a 4" round-butted, fixed-sight, blue steel revolver with an enclosed ejector rod. It first appeared as the Thunder Ranch Special and now is a standard catalog item.

Smith & Wesson also produces two 4" .44 Magnums, the Model 29 Mountain Gun with the tapered barrel of the 1950 Model and the 26-oz. scandium/titanium 329PD. If the truth

RUGER'S FIRST FACTORY .44 SPECIAL!

The .44 Special sixgun many of us have been waiting for since 1955 is finally here!

It was in that wonderful year that Ruger introduced their first centerfire revolver, the .357 Magnum Blackhawk (known to sixgunners today as the Flat-Top). It was the same size as the Colt Single Action Army but in addition to its virtually unbreakable coil spring action, it also had a flat-topped frame fitted with a Micro adjustable rear sight. Elmer Keith reported the next step would be a .44 Special. However, before that happened the .44 Magnum arrived. Ruger tried to chamber the .357 Blackhawk in .44 Magnum, but with further proof-testing the cylinder and frame proved to be too small and one of their prototypes blew. The frame and cylinder of the Blackhawk were subsequently enlarged to properly house the .44 Magnum and the .44 Special became a dead issue.

Thanks to Lipsey's ordering 2,000 .44 Specials built on the original sized frame, Ruger is now doing what they intended to do more than 50 years ago. The .44 Special Flat-Top New Model Blackhawk is available in an all-blued steel sixgun with the choice of 4-5/8" or 5-1/2" barrel length. I have been shooting one of each and they have proven to be superb sixguns. Suggested retail price is $579 from your local dealer. Don't miss this one!

be known, both of these Magnums are better suited to .44 Special use. Just this past year S&W introduced, or I should say re-introduced, the Model 1950 Target as the Model 24-6 Classic with the same 6-1/2" barrel length as the original. The .44 Special is definitely alive and well at Smith & Wesson.

COLT .44 SPECIALS

In 1913 Colt began chambering the Single Action Army in .44 Special. From then until 1941, only 506 Single Action Army Models would be so chambered, and only one Flat-Top Target, which belonged to Elmer Keith. In the beginning these sixguns were marked on the left side, "RUSSIAN AND S&W SPECIAL 44". One of the most beautiful examples of an engraved .44 Special so inscribed was the 7-1/2" personal sixgun of Ed McGivern shipped to him by Colt in 1919; it is pictured in *A Study Of The Colt Single Action Army Revolver* by Graham, Kopec, and Moore. In 1929, barrel markings were changed to "COLT SINGLE ACTION ARMY .44 SPECIAL".

I had one of these 7-1/2" .44 Special Colts marked the same as the McGivern Colt as related in my book *Big Bore Sixguns* (Krause Publications 1997).

As I relate in that book:

My new wife solidly entrenched herself in my heart forever our first Christmas together as she presented me with a brand new 6-1/2" .44 Special Smith & Wesson Model 1950 Target. I had begun a lifelong love affair with the .44 Special. Not only did my wife present me with

Two very easy-carrying .44 Specials by Andy Horvath and Bob Baer.

Andy Horvath built this .44 Special "Fitz Special" on a Colt New Service.

my first .44 Special, she also combined with a very special .44 Special to make it possible for me to meet another vocal proponent of the .44 Special. It has always been my regular habit to read section 640 GUNS every day in the morning paper's want ads expecting to find maybe one special sixgun per year. In the early 1970's the ad read Colt Single Action .44 and old belt and holster.

The address was a trailer park just outside of town and I hustled over to find a 1st Generation 7-1/2" Colt Single Action with cartridge belt and holster. The owner explained the .44 had belonged to his uncle and he wore it regularly as a sheriff in Colorado, and the pitting on the top strap were from his blood when he was shot and was more concerned about having himself patched up than cleaning the Colt. As I handled the Colt I could scarcely contain myself. Except for the minor pitting on the top strap, the old Colt .44 Single Action was in excellent shape mechanically and the case coloring had turned a beautifully aged gray. The left side of the barrel was marked "RUSSIAN AND S&W SPECIAL 44". A very rare single action!

How much? I asked as I contemplated my budget. $450. I was sorely tempted but with paying for three kids to attend private school, I felt it was out of the question. I reluctantly thanked the man for his time and left. My excitement stayed high all the way home and it was impossible to contain my disappointment as I told my wife all about the Colt .44 Special. She was more than a little surprised I was able to resist buying that beautiful sixgun.

Later that day she headed out to do some shopping and I asked her to stop at the local boot repair shop. I had been so stirred up by the .44 Colt I had forgotten

to pick up my finished boots. When she returned home she handed me the boots with a slight smile on her face. As I took the boots I realized they felt a few pounds heavier than normal. In the left boot was the Colt! She had gone out on her own and purchased the .44 Special! You hold on tightly to a wife such as this one!

After doing a little research on the Colt and finding out how really rare it was, we decided it belonged to a collector not a shooter as I was. So we traded it for the $450 we paid for it plus two shooting Colt sixguns, a 2nd Generation Colt Single Action Army 5-1/2".44 Special and a 7-1/2" New Frontier chambered in .45 Colt. But that isn't the end of the story as this Colt .44 Special and Russian was my ticket to meeting someone very special.

Later that year I attended the NRA Show in Salt Lake City and carried pictures of the old Colt, especially a close-up of the barrel inscription, all for a purpose. I was looking for one particular individual. When I found him dressed in a dark suit, wearing colored shooting glasses and a white Stetson, I simply handed him the picture of the barrel close up. He grabbed me by the arm and said: "Son, let's go find a place to talk." The man was Skeeter Skelton and I had found the way to his heart. Skeeter was second only to Elmer Keith in praising the virtues of the .44 Special during his writing career. Keith retired his .44 Specials after the .44 Magnum arrived; Skelton tried the .44 Magnum, found the Special better for most purposes, and went back to his first love.

The 1st Generation Colt Single Action Army was dropped from production in 1941, never to be seen again. After the war, Colt made it very clear they had no intention of ever resuming production. Television changed all that! A whole new generation of shooters and would be shooters discovered the Colt Single Action Army through all the B Western movies that filled the screens in the early days of television and then were followed by the made-for-TV westerns. Shooters wanted Colt Single Actions and in 1956 the 2nd Generation Single Actions appeared.

The .44 Special arrived in the Single Action Army one year later in 1957 with both 5-1/2" and 7-1/2" barrel lengths. For some unknown reason the 2nd Generation .44 Specials were never offered with 4-3/4" barrels. While not as rare as the 1st Generation .44 Specials, just over 2,300 were offered before they were removed from production in 1966. A companion sixgun to the Single Action Army was the New Frontier, a modernized version of the old Flat-Top Target Model of the 1890s. These are very rare with only 255 total being made with 5-1/2" and 7-1/2" barrels from 1963 to 1967. They are also some the finest single actions ever produced by Colt.

By 1974, the Colt machinery was wearing out and the decision was made to drop the Colt Single Action Army once again. This time instead of 15 years it only took two years to resurrect the Single Action, as the 3rd Generation began

USFA offers the barrel marking as found on the original Colt Single Action .44 Special.

production in 1976. This time around the .44 Special would be produced from 1978 to 1984 in all three barrel lengths: 4-3/4", 5-1/2", and 7-1/2" and a total production of about 15,000 with about 375 Buntline Specials with 12" barrels. Colt just recently announced the return of the .44 Special Single Action Army to their catalog. The .44 Special was also offered as the New Frontier from 1980 through 1984 when all New Frontier production ceased. Something over 3,500 3rd Generation .44 Special New

Frontiers were produced and only with 5-1/2" and 7-1/2" barrels. Most shooters hold 2nd Generation .44 Specials in much higher esteem than their counterparts among 3rd Generation examples and the prices demanded reflect this.

Colt not only produced the first big-bore double-action revolvers a few years before Smith & Wesson – the Model 1878 in .45 Colt – but they would also be the first to produce what we consider a modern double-action revolver., i.e., one with a swing-out cylinder. These Army and Navy Models on the .41 frame would evolve into the larger New Service in 1898. Immensely popular, the New Service overtook the Single Action Army in total production numbers due to the fact that more than 150,000 New Services chambered in .45ACP with 5-1/2" barrels and known as the Model 1917 were ordered for the use of the troops in World War I.

The .44 Special, as with the Single Action Army, first appeared in the Colt New Service in 1913. Before it was dropped, the .44 Special New Service was offered as a standard model with barrel lengths of 4-1/2", 5 1/2", and 7-1/2" with either blue or nickel finish, or the beautifully shooting New Service Target Revolver with a choice of either a 6" or 7-1/2" barrel. Stocks were checkered walnut and the trigger was checkered, as were the front and back straps; the finish was a deep blue; sights were adjustable, with a choice of a Patridge or bead front sight.

Colt's ultimate .44 Special New Service was the deluxe target revolver, the Shooting Master. This 6"-barreled revolver featured a hand-finished action, sights and a top strap that were finished to eliminate glare. It represented the highest-quality revolver that Colt could build until the Python arrived in 1955. Along with the Colt Single Action Army, the New Service was dropped in 1941.

New Services chambered in .44 Special are very hard to find, at least at my price level. A few years ago a reader came to the rescue with a late-model New Service in .44 Special, which he offered to send to me for inspection. It had several problems: it was out of time, its lanyard ring was missing, and someone had installed a Smith & Wesson adjustable rear sight while leaving the front sight intact. This, of course, resulted in a sixgun that shot way high. But it had possibilities and it came for very reasonable price. The 4-1/2" New Service .44 Special was sent off to Milt Morrison of QPR (Qualite Pistol & Revolver), one of the few gunsmiths

Excellent powders for reloading for the .44 Special are Unique, #2400, and H4227.

qualified to work on the old New Service. He totally tuned and tightened it, fitted a ramp front sight and re-blued it. A lanyard ring was found and installed, and stag grips were located and fitted to the frame. The final result is one of the finest New Service .44 Specials around.

In the time between the two World Wars, John Henry FitzGerald ("Fitz") was Colt's representative, traveling to all the shooting matches, working on shooters' Colts and generally sharing shooting information. He is best known for his Fitz Special built on the Colt New Service: "Perhaps some would like to ask why I cut up a good revolver and here is the answer: The trigger guard is cut away to allow more finger room and for use when gloves are worn…. The hammer spur is cut away to allow drawing from the pocket or from under the coat without catching or snagging in the cloth and eliminates the use of thumb over hammer when drawing….The butt is rounded to allow the revolver to easily slide into firing position in the hand…. The top of the cut-away hammer may be lightly checked to assist in cocking for a long-range shot." It was common knowledge among his contemporaries that Fitz always carried a pair of .45 Colt Fitz Specials in his two front pockets. He definitely knew how to use them.

I've wanted to have a Fitz Special ever since I was the kid learning to shoot big-bore sixguns in the 1950s, and just recently decided to have one made up on a Colt New Service. I found what I thought would be the perfect candidate for a Fitz Special, a 5-1/2" Late Model New Service in .45 Colt. Although having considerable pitting on the right side

From top left counterclockwise: First came the .44 Special Triple Lock of 1908, then the Model 1926, which was used as the platform for the .38-44 Heavy Duty of 1930 which in turn became the building block for the .357 Magnum of 1935.

of the barrel and part of the cylinder, it was mechanically perfect and the interiors of both barrel and cylinder were like new. Instead of sending it off to be converted, I shot it first and found it shot much too well to touch as it placed five shots, fired double-action standing at 50 feet, in less than 1-1/2". By now I have learned not to fix what ain't broke, so it remains untouched.

Thanks to a reader I came up with a Late Model New Service chambered in .44 Special. It needed some help and made a perfect candidate for a Fitz Special, so off it went to one of the premier gunsmiths in the country, Andy Horvath. Horvath said of this New Service: "It's got a few miles on it and somebody got a little carried away with the buffing wheel. I bushed the cylinder to get out most of the endplay, and installed a ball lock on the crane to help with the lock-up. Instead of cutting the old barrel I just made a new one using up a piece of Douglas barrel blank too short for anything else. The grip frame has been shortened and rounded and fitted with fancy walnut grip panels, and the top of the hammer serrated for shooting single action by starting the hammer back with the trigger and then grabbing the hammer with your thumb." The end result is a .44 Special Fitz Special that is one of the finest in existence, built by one of

the finest gunsmiths ever. My everyday working load for .44 Special sixguns, the 250-gr. Keith bullet over 7.5 gr of Unique in the short barrel of the "Fitz" registers 830 fps, or just about the perfect equivalent of Fitz's .45 Colt loads.

OTHER .44 SPECIAL SINGLE ACTIONS

The .44 Special has never been the everyman's cartridge but rather the favorite of true connoisseurs of big-bore single-action and double-action sixguns. As a result, production numbers are usually very low for any company

producing single-action sixguns exclusively. In 1954, Great Western began producing a single action, the Frontier Six-Shooter, in Los Angeles. Bill Wilson, president and one of three founders, had contacted Colt in 1953 and was assured they had no plans to resurrect the Colt Single Action Army. The Great Western looked so much like a Colt Single Action Army they actually used real Colts in the early advertising. In fact, some of the Great Western parts came from Colt. When Colt resumed production of the Single Action Army in 1956, Great Western's demise was only a matter of time. They lasted until 1964.

No one really knows how many Great Westerns were produced in eight years, or if they do they aren't telling. The standard caliber was .45 Colt, but the GW was also offered in .22, .38 Special, .357 Magnum, .357 Atomic, .44 Magnum, and .44 Special. The last two are especially rare and, until recently, I had only seen one of each in my lifetime and purchased both of them. In the past few years, again thanks to readers, I have come up with two 5-1/2" Great Western .44 Specials, one unfired and nickel-plated with factory pearls, and the other standard blue and case colored with plastic stag grips. The nickel plated version required considerable 'smithing to put it into shooting condition but all have now proven to be excellent sixguns.

Bill Grover started Texas Longhorn Arms in 1981 building a single-action sixgun different than anything ever previously offered. It was his belief Sam

Southwest lawmen who were true pistoleros often chose the 4" 3rd or 4th Model Hand Ejectors from Smith & Western chambered in .44 Special.

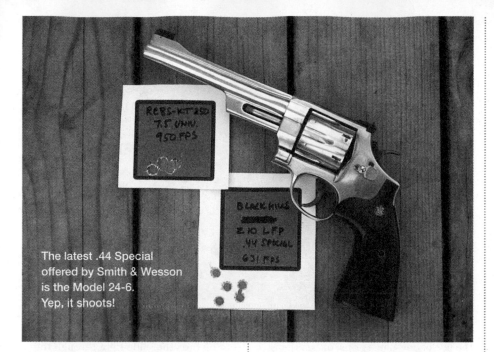

The latest .44 Special offered by Smith & Wesson is the Model 24-6. Yep, it shoots!

Colt was left-handed and his designs show this. I am right-handed and I load and unload a Single Action Army by switching the sixgun to my left hand, working the ejector rod with my right hand and also using my right hand to reload and then switching the sixgun back to my right hand for either holstering or shooting. Grover's idea was to reverse everything. That is, both the ejector rod housing and the loading gate are on the left side of the sixgun and the cylinder rotates counterclockwise. This allows the right-handed shooter to hold the gun in his right-hand while both loading and unloading operations are performed with the left hand. The sixgun never leaves the shooting hand.

Grover's first right-handed single actions included the West Texas Flat-Top Target with a 7-1/2" barrel, the South Texas Army with fixed sights and a 4-3/4" barrel, and the Improved Number Five with a 5-1/2" barrel. Texas Longhorn Arms' version of Keith's Famous #5SAA managed to maintain the flavor of the original while being stronger and replacing Keith's favorite cartridge of the 1920s-1950s with his choice from 1955 on, the .44 Magnum. Even with its larger frame and cylinder, the TLA Improved Number Five still maintains Colt-style balance rather than seeming overly large. Both the West Texas Flat-Top Target and the South Texas Army were offered in .44 Special, and like the Great Westerns, are very rarely seen. Texas Longhorn Arms, unfortunately, closed their doors in the mid-1990s and their beautiful

.44 Special sixguns are no more.

I first ran into USFA (United States Firearms Co.) at a SHOT Show in the early 1990s. Arrangements were made to do a test and evaluation of their single actions, and one of those sixguns ordered was a blued and case colored 7-1/2" version with the barrel marked "RUSSIAN AND S&W SPECIAL 44". At the time USFA was importing Uberti parts and assembling and finishing them in this country. That .44 was beautifully finished and fitted up tightly with very little cylinder movement either fore, aft, or side-to-side. The goal of USFA was to eventually provide an All-American made sixgun and they have now arrived at that point. Their Single Action Army is a beautifully made, totally American .44 Special.

USFA offers the Single Action Army and the Flat-Top Target both made the old way as Single Actions were before World War II. Since my original Colt Single Action Army with its 7-1/2" barrel marked with both .44 Special and .44 Russian was sold, I decided to replace it with the USFA version. In fact, at the 2004 SHOT Show I ordered two USFA .44 Specials, one to replace the old Colt, with identical markings, and a full blue Flat-Top Target also with a 7-1/2" barrel. These are beautiful (I know I'm overusing the word but they really are!) .44 Special sixguns and are made as well or better as any the old revolvers we now call classic. They are finely finished, tight with no cylinder play either front to back or side to side, and they shoot as good as they look.

THE FREEDOM ARMS MODEL 97

One exception to the rule of a full-sized, six-shot .44 Special is the Freedom Arms Model 97. This little sixgun, smaller than the Colt SAA, has a cylinder that is 1.575" in diameter; however it is an extremely strong five-shot little sixgun built to very tight tolerances and with the bolt cut on the cylinder in between chambers so there is no weak point there. My most-used standard load for the .44 Special for more than 40 years has been the 250 gr. Keith hard cast bullet over 7.5 grains of Unique. With this load, a 250-grain Keith bullet clocks out at just over 1,000 fps from the 5-1/2" barrel of the Model 97 .44 Special; and the same RCBS Keith bullet over 17.0 grains of H4227 gives 1,002 fps. These are easy shootin' and very accurate loads from this .44 Special.

For heavy-duty use in the Freedom Arms .44 Special, Speer's 225-gr. jacketed hollow point over 16.0 grains of #2400 gives 1,240 fps and the exceptional accuracy of four shots into 5/8". This bullet is not the normally-encountered jacketed hollowpoint but rather the copper cup with a lead core. The standard Keith load using RCBS's version clocks out at 1,270 fps from the short-barreled Model 97. Switching over to Ray Thompson's design, Lyman's #431244GC, 17.5 grains of #2400 also travels well over 1,200 fps and shoots equally well. The Model 97 has a relatively short cylinder; however, all these loads with the Keith bullet chamber with room to spare. *[Editor's note: These loads have proven safe in the author's Freedom Arms Model 97. Other, older .44 Specials may not tolerate them; thus we do not recommend their use.]*

Most double action connoisseurs hold the original .44 Special in the highest esteem even to the point of labeling the old Triple Lock as the finest revolver ever built. It has had no equal let alone been surpassed by any other factory produced .44 Special; until now. The .44 Special Model 97 from Freedom Arms is the number one challenger to the title.

RUGER .44 SPECIAL BLACKHAWKS

In 1953 Bill Ruger modernized the single action and introduced the Single-Six .22 with the first major change (coil springs instead of flat springs) since the Paterson arrived in 1836. Two years later the Single-Six was increased to the same size as the Colt Single Action Army; its frame was flat-topped, adjustable sights were added, and we had the

.357 Magnum Blackhawk. Ruger had the full intention of bringing this same sixgun out in .44 Special, and if we lived in a perfect world that is exactly what would have happened; however we don't, and it didn't. The coming of the .44 Magnum in 1956 changed all that and instead the Blackhawk frame and cylinder were enlarged to become the .44 Magnum Blackhawk. Ruger never did produce a .44 Special Blackhawk.

What Ruger did not do, custom sixgunsmiths can do. Earlier mention was made of Skeeter Skelton's article converting the .357 Magnum Highway Patrolman from Smith & Wesson into a .44 Special. In that same article he also covered the conversion of the Three Screw .357 Magnum Ruger Blackhawk to .44 Special. The Three Screw .357 Blackhawks are divided into two categories: the Flat-Top, which was produced from 1955 to 1962, and the Old Model, from 1963 to 1972. Both of these .357 Blackhawks were built on the same size of frame as the Colt Single Action Army. When the New Model arrived in 1973, the .357 Magnum-size frame was dropped and instead the .357 Magnum Blackhawk was built on the same size frame as the .44 Super Blackhawk. Converting a New Model to .44 Special results in a .44 Magnum-size sixgun.

To convert a .357 Magnum Blackhawk to .44 Special, it is only necessary to re-chamber the cylinder and fit a different barrel. That's the basic idea, but different sixgunsmiths take over from here and exercise their artistic side. Gunsmiths I know of who can convert the Three Screw .357s to very special .44 Specials include Bob Baer, Hamilton Bowen, David Clements, Ben Forkin, John Gallagher, Alan Harton, Andy Horvath, Gary Reeder, and Jim Stroh, and I have considerable hands-on experience with examples built by these different gunsmiths/metal artists. Some of these men re-bored the existing barrel to .44 Special; others fitted custom barrels; and others used .44 Magnum barrels from other Ruger Blackhawks. Barrel lengths offered include but are not limited to the standard 4-5/8", 5-1/2", and 7-1/2", as well as 3-1/2" and 4" Sheriffs Model styles. Colt 3rd Generation .44 Special or .44-40 New Frontier barrels can even be fitted to Three Screw Blackhawk frames.

Grip frames can be polished bright or re-anodized; Flat-Top grip frames can be installed on Old Model frames to give more of a Colt feel, or stainless steel Old Army grip frames can be fitted to either

Great .44 Special sixguns from the middle part of the twentieth century: Great Western SA, 2nd Generation Colt SAA, and a pair of 3rd Generation Colts.

Three Screw Model. Even Colt two-piece grip frames can be attached to allow the use of one-piece grips, or 'smiths can use the new Colt-style, two-piece grip frame offered by Power Custom and sold through Brownells. Some Ruger .357s came with an extra 9mm cylinder which allows two .44 cylinders to be used, one Special and the other in .44-40. No matter what route is chosen, nor which of these gentlemen does the work, the result is an easy-handlin', easy-packin', easy-shootin' .44 Special.

With the coming of the Ruger 50th Anniversary .357 Magnum Flat-Top in 2005, we suddenly had a new platform for building Colt SAA-size .44 Specials on a Ruger. Both Ben Forkin and John Gallagher have converted 50th Anniversary .357 New Model Blackhawks to .44 Special for me with the former using a 7-1/2" New Frontier barrel and the latter opting for a custom 4" barrel. I have to say it again: they are beautiful sixguns!

HUNTING WITH THE .44 SPECIAL

In these days of heavy-loaded .44 Magnums and .45 Colts – let alone the .454 Casull, .475 Linebaugh, and .500 S&W – is the .44 Special still viable for hunting? I had taken deer-sized game in the 125- to 250-lb. pound class, but what about bigger game? The most popular big game animal, second only to deer, is the poor man's grizzly: wild hogs, feral pigs, Russian boars. For a feral hog hunt I chose the .44 Special loaded with a hollowpoint cast bullet (Lyman's #429421 Keith) at 1,200 fps muzzle velocity from the 7-1/2" .44 Special Texas Longhorn Arms West Texas Flat-Top Target.

On the first pig, the bullet went in

right behind the upper part of the front leg and, as we found out later, came out on the other side right through the center of the upper part of the leg on the off-side. The bullet gave total penetration in a 500-lb. animal! That was to be the end of it, as far as I was concerned.

I intended to take one pig and be on my way. But there were two pigs there, and the dead pig's big buddy would have none of that. By now he was up on his feet and using his snout to move that 500-pounder. He was not about to leave. So! At the shot he turned around, started to run, and I put a second shot in him and down he went. The smaller, 500-lb. pig had 4" tusks, while this 650-pounder had tusks curling around for a full 6". We would later find out the .44 Special hollowpoint had gone through the heart of the second boar, the second shot was only two inches away from the first shot, and the bullet was perfectly mushroomed and lodged under the hide on the far side. In both cases the .44 Special bullets did everything a sixgun, load, and bullet combination are supposed to do.

In 1966, the .44 Special was pronounced old, antiquated, out of date, ready for the bonepile. Skeeter Skelton started the resurrection of sixguns firing this first big-bore cartridge of the twentieth century and I have tried to carry the torch since his passing in 1988. I'm sure Skeeter is smiling as he sees all the .357 Three Screw Blackhawks being turned into .44 Specials, as well as the new .44 Special sixguns from USFA and Freedom Arms and the revival of S&W's N-frame .44 Special. The .44 Special is ready for its second century of service.

Editor's PICKS

T he able Contributing Editors of *Gun Digest* will perhaps forgive me if I take a moment and comment on just a few guns and gadgets that tripped my personal trigger during the past year. Some of these are doubtless discussed elsewhere in this volume, but what can I say? I was here first.

Lord Tennyson wrote, "*In the spring a young man's fancy lightly turns to thoughts of love.*" Well, it's spring, and although I can't rightly be termed a young man anymore, I'm in love – with **Ithaca's new 28-gauge Model 37 pump shotgun**. My first shotgun, nearly 35 years ago, was a new Ithaca 20-ga. Deluxe Featherweight, and it pained me when Ithaca fell on tough times a few years ago. Now, however, Ithaca is back is competent hands in their new headquarters in Upper Sandusky, Ohio, and although the company's production is limited to around 3500 guns per year, the guns it does produce are gems. The new 28-ga. M37 is available in three grades, A to AAA, with prices starting around a cool grand. I handled an AAA Grade at the 2009 SHOT Show and, brother, that was it for me. Ithaca's new 28-ga. is available on special order only, and I fully intend to order one as soon as I've bailed out the banks, the Big Three, Moe's Pizza, and apparently everybody else.

It's a shame that many younger shooters are unaware of the Ithaca Model 37. Based on the sainted John Browning's patents for a bottom-ejecting shotgun, the M37 always struck me as the quintessential upland pump. It is so refined, so exquisitely styled, so just plain pretty, that even today I have a hard time passing one up on the used-gun rack. What really

Ithaca's 28-ga. M37.
This one's a Grade AA.

hurt the M37, in my opinion, was the fact that it wasn't offered with a 3" chamber until it was rechristened the Model 87 some 20 years ago, and by that time the brand's prestige had already dimmed. In 2005, however, Dave Dlubak acquired the company, and he's really turned it around. I've spoken to Dave and to Ithaca's management team, and I'm glad to report that they are True Believers in the grand old name of Ithaca.

But even bigger news may be in the offing for Ithaca. They've got an all-new, *100% American-made* 12-ga. over/under prototyped, and I hope like hell it makes it all the way to production. Until then, the 28-ga. M37 will do quite nicely for me.

Ithaca's back, folks. (See www.ithacagun.com.)

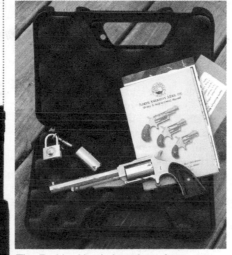

The Earl by North American Arms.

Then there's **The Earl by North American Arms**. For those of you who came in late, NAA is the pre-eminent manufacturer of .22 mini-revolvers (and they field a pretty good team of centerfire pocket pistols, too). The Earl is the latest of NAA's mini-guns, and it's a pip: a five-shot .22 Magnum that looks for all the world like an 1858-pattern Remington percussion revolver. It's made entirely of stainless steel (except the grips, of course) and even includes a faux "loading lever" that serves as a cylinder pin release. It even has a 4" octagonal barrel with a barleycorn front sight.

Initially available in only .22 Magnum rimfire, a .22 Mag/.22LR conversion cylinder is expected to be offered soon, perhaps by the time you read this. At a suggested retail of $289 for the .22 Mag version, I'd have an awfully tough time passing up The Earl.

Some shooters condemn all .22 mini-guns as "mouse guns" or worse, but I beg to differ. A .22 in my shirt pocket sure beats a .45 left at home. Besides, The Earl really isn't meant as a self defense gun; NAA's affable president Sandy Chisholm says "it might become your favorite plinker." I can see that. (See naaminis.com.)

This Charter Arms .357 Target Bulldog did pretty well at 25 yards offhand.

I'm happy to report that it seems that **Charter Arms** has really gotten its act together. A few months ago I had the chance to spend some time with their **.357 Target Bulldog Stainless** and was impressed. While its double-action trigger pull was a bit stagy until a few hours of shooting smoothed it out, its single-action pull was one of the nicest I've ever seen. Its 4" barrel and neoprene grips made it quite comfortable to shoot even with fast-steppin' 125-grainers, and it shot right on the money. With a suggested retail of $449 and a street price substantially less, the five-shot .357 Target Bulldog strikes me as a good buy for the woods bum who wants something small but substantial on his belt. It should serve well as a home defense revolver, too. Those who remember the quality of Charter Arms' first Bulldogs back in the mid-'70s will find a lot to like in the .357 Target Bulldog. Welcome home, Charter Arms! (See www.charterfirearms.com.)

I have to admit, with all due embarrassment, that until recently I had never owned an AR. I've had plenty of M1 Carbines and AKs and SKSs in addition to the usual complement of Krags and Trapdoors and '03s and Mausers, but somehow the planets never lined up sufficiently for me to buy an AR. That oversight has been corrected in the form of a **Remington R-15 VTR** in .223. As a life-long fan of Remington autoloaders (from the Model 8 of 1906 on up to today's Model 750 Woodsmaster), I'm kind of glad that my first AR had the

With a street price of around $1200 as of this writing, Remington's R-15 VTR is a superbly accurate AR.

Remington name on it. A camo-dipped version of a Bushmaster Predator, my R-15 shoots consistent .75" groups at 100 yards if I hold my mouth right. Frankly, I remain amazed by its performance. To anyone who ever questioned whether an AR is a legitimate sporting arm, the R-15 definitely answers in the affirmative. I can't wait to introduce it to some Indiana woodchucks. (See www.remington.com.)

Speaking of Remington, I like the looks of Remington's new **.30 Remington AR** cartridge. I have a soft spot for the old .30 Remington Autoloading cartridge (sort of a rimless .30-30 Winchester), and the new Remington .30 is a worthy successor. Based on a cut-down, necked .450 Bushmaster case, the stubby new .30 provides low-end .308 Winchester ballistics with a 125-gr. spitzer. Make no mistake: the short .30 Remington AR case can't accommodate the longer 150- to 165-gr. bullets like a .308 bolt rifle can, but for someone who wants a real deer-level cartridge in an AR platform, it should prove decisive. I'm not going out on too much of a limb when I predict that this is one

case that will be extensively wildcatted.

By now you've read all the compliments for **Mossberg's 464 .30-30 lever-action**, and I'll throw a few more on the pile. We wrung one out pretty thoroughly last year

Tne new .30 Remington AR.

and it performed just as advertised: short lever throw, positive ejection, easy loading, etc. Externally it resembles a hybrid between a Marlin 336 and a late-model Winchester 94, but there's an impressive amount of steel in its upper receiver. With a street price hovering around $400, the 464 should find friends among those who believe that a .30-30 is all you really need for woods-range deer hunting. For beginning hunters, it should be an absolute peach. Now: where's that 464 in .22LR? (See www.mossberg.com.)

Younger hunters – and some not-so-young – will find plenty of value in the Mossberg 464 .30-30.

It seems like I spend at least 25% of my life tying things to the back of trucks: boats, canoes, coolers, unruly children, etc. Since my half-hitches usually come out looking like granny knots, I'm happy to have found the **No-Knot Ropelok by Grabber Outdoors**. The Ropelok is heavy-duty

The Ropelok is as simple as it looks and makes life a lot easier.

8' or 15' poly rope combined with a lever-activated cinching device that's superior to plain knots and ratcheting straps, at least for my needs. Just slip the rope through the Ropelok, draw up the slack, and press the lever. That's it. It's like an automatic knot. Since the Ropelok is made out of polymer, it can't scratch or mar automotive or boat surfaces. (See www.warmers.com.)

I belong to the school that holds that you can't have too many gadgets. And a couple of the more enticing gadgets I've seen lately are the **Superior Concepts 10/22 Laser Stock** and **Accessory Band**. The Laser Stock first: This is a nifty aftermarket stock for the Ruger .22 autoloader that incorporates an easily-adjustable laser sight. The switch for the sight is inset into the left side of the stock's forend, where it falls naturally under the thumb. A little pressure on the switch and *zing!* a brilliant laser dot is projected as far out as you're likely to use one. It's available in a wide variety of stockl styles, from tactical to plain-jane.

The Accessory Band is one of those slap-my-forehead-why-didn't-I-think-of-that things: an accessory mount that replaces the barrel band of the 10/22. For those such as I who possess only limited gunsmithing skills (okay, very limited), it's a no-brainer. (See www.laserstock.com.)

The BreakOut Safety Tool. A good idea in a handy package.

Rounding out this brief review is the **BreakOut Safety Tool** by **World Class Safety Products**. The BreakOut is a combination window-breaker, seatbelt-cutter and LED signal light that should be standard equipment in your car. Available in a variety of configurations, the BreakOut is a well-thought-out auto accessory that seems superior (to me, anyway) to many hammer-style emergency tools. For one thing, it clips onto your car's sun visor, where it's always within easy reach. I've never forgotten what my Driver's Ed instructor told me: "The next poor SOB upside-down in that water-filled ditch could be you!" If so, I'd rather be there with a BreakOut on my sunvisor than without one. (See www.breakoutsafetytools.com.)

Superior Concepts Laser Stock (laser visible at end of forend) and barrel-band Accessory Mount.

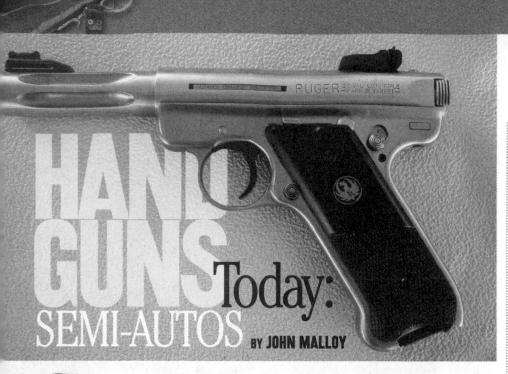

HAND GUNS Today: SEMI-AUTOS

BY JOHN MALLOY

At the time of this writing in 2009, our country is experiencing an economic downturn. Among the things that are still selling well are firearms and ammunition. Some makers of autoloading handguns report that they are making all they can and selling all they make. Not only autoloading handguns, but AR- and AK-type rifles, and revolvers, and some types of shotguns, appear to be selling in record quantities.

Ordinarily, this would be a happy state of affairs for the firearms industry. However, the conditions are special.

In the previous edition of this publication, I noted that two important things pertinent to the future of autoloading handguns had not occurred by that earlier press time. The US Supreme Court had not yet rendered a decision related to the right to keep and bear arms. The November 2008 elections, which included the presidential election, had not yet taken place.

Now, those events are well in the past, and our questions relating to our autoloading handguns (and firearms in general) have been answered — or have they? Time will tell, as the saying goes.

Apart from — or at least only peripherally related to — the political situation, new things are happening in the world of autoloading handguns.

Perhaps the most interesting is the recent rise in popularity of the down-sized .380-caliber autoloading pistol. A decade or so ago, the little ".25-sized .32" pistols chambered for the .32 ACP cartridge appeared on the scene. They filled a niche for the growing number

of people who held concealed firearms licenses, which are now offered in most of our states. For those unable to conceal a larger handgun, the new little .32s provided something potentially more effective than most .22- and .25-caliber "vest-pocket-size" pistols.

Now, the new small .380s, only a little bit larger in gun size, but with a cartridge offering more bullet weight and frontal area, seem to provide more effectiveness with just a bit more size and weight. They might be considered "hip-pocket-size" pistols. At least six companies have brought out new scaled-down .380 pistols.

The Colt/Browning 1911 design — fast approaching its 100th birthday also — is still king of the hill in the world of autoloading handguns. By my informal count, at least 28 companies offer pistols of 1911 type. This year, several companies are introducing new 1911s. At least a few more new 1911s that were previously introduced are now in production.

Striker-fired full-size polymer-frame service-type pistols have carved out a niche in the past few years, and you will see new offerings this year.

Other countries have a stake in the firearms industry, and we have, introduced here, self-loading handguns from Turkey, Germany, Israel, Italy, Brazil, Argentina, and other sources. The Philippines firearms industry continues to grow. Here in the United States, the "traditional" gun-making areas of the country have been joined by unlikely locations in Ohio and Tennessee. New handguns are even being designed and produced in California, a state that seems

Ruger's new stainless-steel Mark III Hunter has a fluted 4-½" barrel and special grips.

to do everything possible to discourage the firearms industry.

Frame-mounted rails have taken the place of hooked trigger guards as the current fad of choice. Hardly anyone uses the rails, but anyone who has a pistol with a rail might use the rail, so they are gaining in popularity.

What handgun caliber actually fires the most shots each year? I can't point to any definite research, but my suspicion is that the .22 Long Rifle would be the winner. .22-caliber pistols are popular for target shooting, plinking, small-game hunting, training and recreational shooting. A number of new .22-caliber pistols are being announced, and .22 conversion kits for centerfire autoloaders remain popular.

There are a number of new ideas that have been developed into new pistols, and I think you will be interested in reading about them. Also, I'll continue to include pistol-caliber autoloading carbines and unconventional pistols, because they use pistol-caliber ammunition. Also related are "short barrel rifles" that use autoloading handgun cartridges, and long-range semi-automatic pistols that use rifle cartridges. It all makes for a fascinating group of guns showing amazing creativity.

With all this information in mind, let's take a look at the new guns themselves:

Akdal

The Akdal Ghost pistols were introduced at the January 2009 SHOT Show, are of a "Glock-type" design, and are chambered for the 9 x 19mm cartridge.

With a barrel length of 4-¼" inches, the length is 7-3/8". The grip has a flared shape unlike that of the Glock, and there are other differences. The Ghost TR01 has fixed sights, and the Ghost TR02 has adjustable sights on a different slide.

Akdal pistols are made in Turkey. A representative expected sales to begin in the United States during 2009, perhaps under a different brand name.

American Classic

Recall that, with the demise of the Spanish Llama pistols a few years ago, we lost a source of affordable 1911-type .45-caliber handguns. Last year, S&B Distributors introduced the American Classic line, new 1911-style pistols made by a new source in the Philippines. The company believes the new American Classic pistols will fill the niche vacated by Llama.

The pistols are now in production, and S&B is shipping two different models (let's consider them "mil-spec" and "enhanced") at a rate of about 200 a month.

Armalite

For the second year in a row, the Armalite AR-26, a new .45-caliber pistol, was a no-show at the annual SHOT Show. Armalite representatives report that the prototype works fine. However, the AR-26 project has been put on the back burner, as the volume of production of their AR-15 and AR-10 rifle lines is taking most of the company's attention.

ATI

American Tactical Imports has a number of pistols of interest to us here, imported from Turkey and Germany.

The American Tactical C-45 and CS-9 are ported pistols in, respectively, .45 ACP and 9mm calibers. They are conventional double-action (DA) pistols made by the Tisas firm in Turkey. The .45 has a 4.7" barrel, while the 9 has a 4" barrel. Both variants are available in black, two-tone, or chrome. The ATI catalog also introduced some other Tisas-made pistols.

From Germany comes the GSG-5PK. (The GSG stands for "German Sport Guns.") It is a .22-caliber semi-automatic of unconventional appearance for a pistol. Well, not too unconventional if you expect it to look like a .22-caliber pistol version of an MP5 submachinegun. With its 4.7" barrel, it is no lightweight, cataloged at about 5 lbs. with its 10-round magazine.

Beretta

A few recently-introduced variants have sneaked quietly into Beretta's pistol line.

The PX4 Storm SD is one. This "Special Duty" pistol was designed to meet U.S. SOCOM military specifications. With its standard Picatinny rail and 4.6" barrel, it runs about 29 oz. and measures 8.2" x 5.7". The SD's polymer frame is a dark earth color and features modular backstraps to fit different hands.

The PX4 Storm Sub-Compact, previously offered as a 9mm, is also available now in .40 S&W chambering. Same 3" barrel and same 26-oz. weight. However, the staggered-column magazine holds 10 rounds compared to the 13-round capacity of the 9mm.

Beretta is proud of winning a U.S. military contract for up to 450,000 pistols, calling it the largest U.S. handgun contract since World War II. The Beretta Model 92 FS has been used by the U.S. military since 1985, so Beretta thinks it has stood the test of time.

Bersa

The Argentine-made Bersa line has some new variants. The Thunder 9 and Thunder 40 Pro Series pistols now have frame rails, loaded chamber indicators, polygonal-rifling barrels and special sights. Each pistol comes with two magazines — 17 rounds in 9mm and 13 in .40 S&W.

In progress are special variants, the BP 9 and BP 40, which will be Bersa's first polymer-frame pistols. Tentative plans were to introduce the new pistols late in 2009.

In this recent period of interest in the .380 cartridge, Bersa continues its longtime line of double-action .380 pistols. New is the Thunder 380 Concealed Carry, a "slimline" eight-shot pistol with bobbed

The Akdal Ghost TR01 is a new 9mm "Glock-type" pistol from Turkey.

The prototype of the Chiappa 1911-22, a new .22-caliber pistol styled after the 1911 design. The new .22 will be made in America and marketed by MKS Supply.

CZ's new 2075 RAMI BD is a new variant with a decocking lever and a lighter recessed slide.

Here is a sneak preview of the prototype of the new Detonics DTX pistol. The DAO handgun is a departure for Detonics, with polymer frame and striker-fire mechanism.

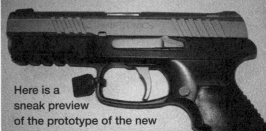
Guncrafter Industries' two calibers — the .45 ACP and their special .50 GI. The big .50 has a rim rebated to the same diameter as the .45.

Colt now offers a 1911 with an integral accessory rail. What to call it? How about "Colt Rail Gun?" Malloy tries one out and finds it to be a good shooter.

FNH's exotic-looking PS 90 carbine is now available in a version with a C-More Red Dot sight.

This specimen is in Olive Drab green color.

Teresa Starnes, president of Double Star, is the only woman in charge of a company that makes 1911-type pistols. Here, she proudly displays the new Double Star .45.

hammer and short tang.

Bersa handguns are imported by Eagle Imports.

Browning

Is there space in Browning's .22-caliber Buck Mark line to squeeze in another variant? Apparently so, for displayed at the 2009 SHOT Show was the Buck Mark Practical URX. The pistol has a 5-½" tapered bull barrel, and has the ambidextrous "ultragrip." The front sight is from Truglo/Marbles. The new .22 was too new to appear in the 2009 Browning catalog.

Another uncataloged offering was the Hi Power Mark III with a new digital green camo finish. Other visual features, such as black grips, remain the same.

Century

The Arcus 9mm pistols announced by Century International Arms last year are in good supply now. The Arcus is based generally on the Browning Hi Power design, with the addition of a conventional double-action trigger mechanism and other modifications. Century points out that the Arcus pistols are manufactured in Eastern Europe, "in a picturesque town near the Black Sea." They are being used by Iraqi police and military forces now.

The Arcus Model 98 DA is a full-size pistol with a 4.7" barrel and a 15-round magazine. It weighs about 34 oz. The compact version, Model 98 DAC, had a

4" barrel and weighs a couple of ounces less. Magazine capacity is 13 rounds, the same capacity as the original Hi Power. Two magazines come with each Arcus pistol.

Charles Daly

Several new introductions in the Charles Daly line this year.

A prototype of a new steel-frame 1911-style pistol was displayed at the 2009 SHOT Show. Dubbed the Charles Daly G4 1911, the gun will be made by Bul, Ltd. in Israel. Several versions—Standard, Target, Tactical—will be offered, all with 5" barrels and 7-round magazines. A .22-caliber conversion kit will also be offered.

Striker-fired polymer-frame service pistols are popular now, and Charles Daly is also entering that niche. The new pistol, named the CD 9, is made in Turkey. It comes with a 4-½" barrel and 15-round magazine. A 10-round magazine will be available for areas in which the local government doesn't trust its citizens. Looking into the future, a tactical model is planned for later availability. Also, CD 40 and CD 45 variants are in the plans for later introduction.

Longtime readers of this publication may remember the excellent Jericho Model 941 pistol, originally made in Israeli, in 9mm and .41 Action Express. The .41 AE faded away, but the Jericho pistol became the Baby Eagle, the Uzi Eagle, and then the Baby Eagle again. Now it is the Jericho once more, and Charles Daly is offering it in 9, .40 and .45 chamberings in full-size, mid-size and compact versions. Barrel lengths run from 3.5" to 4.4", and magazine capacities are between 10 and 15 rounds, depending on model.

Chiappa

Those with an interest in firearms might be familiar with the Chiappa name in the context of nice Italian-made replicas of historical firearms, and of blank pistols styled after firearms.

A departure was introduced at the 2009 SHOT Show, at which the prototype of a new .22-caliber 1911-style pistol was displayed. The new Chiappa Model

1911 – 22 will be made of U.S. and Italian parts, and will be built right here in the USA, in Dayton, Ohio. The introduction, scheduled for Spring 2009, will consist of a Standard variant with fixed sights, and a Target version with adjustable sights and adjustable trigger. The Target model is envisioned as suitable for entry-level bullseye shooting—a complete pistol at a price competitive with 1911 .22-caliber conversion kits.

The frame and slide are made of Chiapp-palloy, an alloy that will take conventional cold blue. The pistol's takedown is like that of a 1911, and 1911 grips and sights will interchange.

The new Chiappa pistols will be distributed by MKS Supply, the distributors of Hi-Point autoloaders and Charter Arms revolvers.

Colt

Frame rails for autoloading pistols have been gaining popularity for some years. For 2009, Colt has offered a new Colt with an accessory rail, suitable for attaching a tactical light or a laser. What to call it? Simple. The new "Colt Rail Gun" has a forged stainless-steel frame and slide. The rail is machined into the forward reach of the frame. The Colt Rail Gun is loaded with niceties such as a palm-swell upswept beavertail tang, extended safety lever, Novak rear sight, ventilated burr hammer and eight-round magazine. .45 ACP, of course. I have had a chance to shoot one, and it shot very well indeed. It is just possible that the extra

The Glock 29 is the "sub-compact" 10mm pistol that is now offered with "short frame" treatment.

weight of the rail on the forward portion of the frame may provide a little bit of extra steadiness.

Colt's Combat Elite has many of the same features as the Rail Gun. The major visual differences are that it has no frame rail, and it is a two-tone pistol. The frame is stainless steel, and the slide is forged blued carbon steel. Grips are special half-checkered, half-smooth rosewood, with the word "Colt" at the midpoint. .45 ACP, of course.

The return of the 10mm Delta Elite was announced last year, and it is back in production now. The all stainless-steel pistol is enhanced with features similar to those of the previous two pistols.

The World War I replica was introduced last year. This year, the Colt Custom Shop is offering a Presentation Grade of the original pistol with engraving, smooth ivory grips and royal-blue finish. It comes in a walnut presentation case.

With the new interest in pistols for the .380 cartridge, it would seem an opportune time for the reintroduction of Colt's nice little Mustang and Pony .380 pistols. The Colt representatives with whom I spoke were mum on that possibility.

CZ

Regular readers of this publication may recall that last year, the semi-automatic pistol version of the little European "Skorpion" submachinegun was introduced by TG International.

Well, who better to handle the Czech-designed gun than the modern Czech company of CZ? CZ-USA has taken over, and now offers the intriguing Skorpion pistol as the CZ VZ 61, commemorating the 1961 adoption of the original submachinegun by special Czech forces. Caliber is the original .32 ACP. Frames are new, and allow semi-automatic fire only. Barrel is 4-½" and overall length is 10-½". Weight with a 20-round magazine is only 2-½ lbs. (Remember that 2-½ lbs. is 40 oz., about the weight of a Colt 1917 revolver.) The Skorpion is perhaps not for everyone, but it is an interesting little pistol.

Also new for 2009 from CZ is the SP-01 Phantom. The full-size 9mm pistol, built on the CZ 75 design, has a polymer frame—with integral rail—and has a relieved slide that also reduced weight. At 28 oz., the Phantom is 33 percent lighter.

The P-07 Duty pistol has the simplified Omega trigger system, reportedly an improvement on the original CZ 75's trigger design. The decocker mechanism can be changed to a manual safety by simply changing parts, which are included. The new P-07 Duty has a slide with a new pro-file, covering a 3.8" barrel. Overall length is 7.2", and the pistol weighs 27 oz.

A new variant of the compact CZ Rami pistol, the CZ 2075 Rami BD, has been introduced. It has a decocking lever, lighter recessed slide and 3-dot sights. Caliber is 9mm, barrel length is 3 inches, and weight is 23.5 oz.

CZ markets the Dan Wesson 1911 pistol line. Several new variants of Dan Wesson pistols (*q.v.*) were also introduced.

Dan Wesson

Several new models from Dan Wesson.

A new variant of the Dan Wesson line, the CCO (Concealed Carry Officer) is offered. It has a steel "Commander" slide with an aluminum "Officer" frame, which has a slightly-bobbed heel of the grip frame. The new .45 has a 4-¼" barrel and weighs 27 oz.

The PM 9 is the only 9mm pistol carried in the Dan Wesson line. Some people just have to have a 9mm 1911, and Dan Wesson wants to accommodate them. The PM 9 has a Clark rib-style slide and a fiber-optic front sight.

The new Marksman pistol is essentially their flagship full-size Pointman Seven with a more classic appearance. Slide retraction grooves are only at the traditional rear position, and the trigger is flat and solid.

The Sportsman, Model RZ-10, is similar to the Marksman, but is chambered for the zippy 10mm Auto cartridge. Full-size, with 5" barrel and 8.75" in overall length.

Detonics

Detonics, recently relocated to Millstadt, IL, offers a growing line of 1911-type pistols of different sizes and styles.

The big eye-catcher at the 2009 SHOT Show, however, was a prototype of their new DTX pistol. This pistol is a real departure for Detonics. It has a polymer frame, and is striker fired, with no manual safety. It is true double-action-only (DAO), with restrike capability. The trigger requires only .55" of travel, and has a 5-½-lb. pull.

At first glance, the most noticeable feature of the Detonics DTX is the increased angle of the grip frame. Various studies, dating back from the WWII techniques of Col. Rex Applegate, to those of the present leadership team of Detonics, were used to design a pistol that could be used for stressful situations in which point shooting is the best response. The slantier grip, lack of manual controls and short, relatively light double-action trigger give a pistol very suitable for such fast shooting. Good square sights and the controllable trigger also allow precise shots.

When will it be available? Because of the early stage of development, company officials could not give an estimate of an actual production date.

Double Star

The Double Star .45 pistol exists! Introduced as a prototype last year, the new Double Star 45 was in inventory in early 2009, and was ready for shipping. Recall that Double Star began making forged 1911 frames with an integral rail about five years ago. Eventually, the company decided to offer a complete pistol.

The firm's primary business is AR-15 type rifles. The recent surge of demand for such arms made company officers reconsider the idea of going ahead with pistol production. A new manufacturing facility was recently constructed, and the decision was made to expand rifle production and also begin pistol production.

The new 1911 has a number of niceties today's shooters seem to like. Beside the rail, the pistol has a ventilated trigger and burr hammer, and a beavertail tang. A stainless-steel 5" match barrel resides in a slide topped by Novak sights.

I had a chance to fire one of the new .45s. Although a two-handed hold is the most practical hold for most pistol shooting, I think the one-handed "Bullseye" hold allows better evaluation of a trigger. The Double Star 45 had an excellent trigger, and I enjoyed making pivoted steel targets swing side to side at 25 yards.

EAA

European American Armory is aware that rails are "in." Both the Tanfoglio-designed Witness full- and compact-size steel pistols are available now with accessory rails. The polymer-frame Witness pistols also have rails, moulded into the forward part of the frame. Full-size,

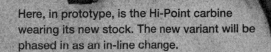

Here, in prototype, is the Hi-Point carbine wearing its new stock. The new variant will be phased in as an in-line change.

compact and "carry" polymer Witness pistols have this treatment.

Some have wondered about the status of the unique "tube chamber" Witness that was beautifully introduced in prototype on these pages two years ago. Apparently, development has stopped on that project.

Ed Brown

Ed Brown offers its Special Forces 1911 in desert tan color this year. These 5" single-column pistols come with an eight-round "8-Pack" magazine.

A limited run of engraved Classic Custom pistols will be made. This variant, a high-quality 5" full-size pistol is Ed Brown's top-of-the-line handgun.

EMF

Over many years, EMF has created a tradition of replicas of single-action revolvers and other historical firearms. A company slogan, "The Best in Cowboy Guns Since 1956" reinforces this idea of early-American firearms.

Kimber's Celia Crane is happy to display the company's new Crimson Carry II, a .45 that is factory-equipped with Crimson Trace Lasergrips.

Few remember that EMF originally stood for "Early and Modern Firearms." Now, EMF has revitalized the "modern" portion of the name. Two new series of autoloading handguns have been introduced.

The EMF Model 1911 line is made 100% in the United States (in Tennessee, of all places). The basic variant is the 1911-A1, an essentially "mil-spec" 5" .45 with parkerized finish. The gun can come with either a flat or arched mainspring housing, and choice of grips. Commemorative military models with some tasteful engraving will be offered. They will have "ultra ivory" grips with insignia of either the Army, Navy, Air Force or Marines, and come with the appropriate service medallion and a presentation case. The 1911 Combat Model is an enhanced variant with lightened burr hammer and upswept beavertail tang, and choices of sights, grips and finishes. Scheduled for availability during 2009 was the 1911 CCC (Concealed Carry Compact) Model. These 4-¼" variants will have eight-round magazines and choices of sights and finishes.

Interesting as the EMF 1911 line is, the other pistol offering was the center of attention at the EMF booth at the 2009 SHOT Show.

The new pistol is called the FMK Model 9C1. Chambered for the 9mm cartridge, the polymer-frame pistol has a 4" barrel, is under 7" long and weighs about 23 oz. The sights are "fixed," but, interestingly, each pistol comes with interchangeable front and rear sights to adjust for elevation and windage. So, a shooter can adjust for load and range, and still have the ruggedness of fixed sights. Capacity of the 9C1 is 10 + 1. Trigger action is true DAO, with second-strike capability. Surprisingly, the pistol is made in California, the only gun to be recently approved.

Perhaps the most striking feature of the FMK 9C1 is its lettering. Patriotic Americans may enjoy reading the pistol when not shooting it. In small letters, abbreviated wording of the U.S. Constitution's Bill of Rights appears on the slide. Other patriotic (and possibly politically-incorrect) phrases such as "In God We Trust," "Thank You, U.S. Soldiers" and "Proudly American" also appear in different places on the pistol. I think it is safe to say that there is nothing similar in this niche.

FNH

Selected models of FNH USA pistols are now available with a new FNP Shooters Pack. In a lockable hard case with the

pistol are a polymer belt holster, adjustable paddle assembly and a double magazine pouch. Both holster and magazine pouches are tension-adjustable for retention. Also included is a yellow polymer dummy barrel that can be installed in the pistol — simply replacing the original barrel — for training purposes. Special models of the FNP-45, FNP-40 and FNP-9 are offered in this Shooters Pack.

The interesting-looking PS 90 carbine is now available with a special C-More "red dot" sight installed. The little 5.7x28mm rifle is offered in black or olive drab color stocks, and with 10- or 30-round magazines.

Girsan

The Turkish Girsan company has been in business since 1994, making 9mm Yavuz pistols, based on the Beretta 92 action design. At the January 2009 SHOT Show, Girsan displayed a number of new offerings. A Beretta-styled Yavuz pistol, the T40 is now available in .40 S&W chambering. Magazine capacity for the new .40 is 10 rounds.

Also introduced is a new .45-caliber pistol. Using a similar DA trigger mechanism, the pistol has been expanded to .45 ACP caliber, and has been given a tilting-barrel locking system. With a 4" barrel, the pistol measures 7-¾" long, and weighs about 32 oz. (without magazine). The magazine, incidentally, holds 9 rounds, giving the pistol 9 + 1 capacity.

If you are keeping count, chalk up another new .380 for 2009. The Girsan MC 14 is a new introduction in that caliber. However, it is not one of the "downsized" .380s, but is built in the style of pocket pistols of the last century. With a barrel length of just under 4 inches, it is 6-¾" long and weighs about 22 oz. It is conventional double action. A similar pistol, the MC 13, is also available in .32 ACP caliber.

Glock

Glock has introduced three different variants for 2009.

Two years ago, Glock brought out an "SF" (Short Frame) version of the .45-caliber Model 21. Subtle changes in the frame reduced the distance from backstrap to trigger, and many shooters liked the new feel. Now, Glock has given the "SF" treatment to its powerful 10mm Auto lineup.

The full-size 15 +1 Glock Model 20 10mm is now available with the SF frame. With its 4.6" barrel, it is eight inches long and weighs only about 28 oz.

The "sub-compact" Glock 29 in the 10mm chambering is also available as an SF variant. With a 3.8" barrel, it is 6.8

inches long and weighs 25 oz.

The Glock 22, a .40 S&W pistol, changes the feel of the grip in a different way. The shape and surface of Glock grip frames has changed over the years. The original "pebble" finish gave way to checkering on the front and back straps, and finger grooves on the front. Now, the Glock 22 RTF2 gives us a new variant. The grip frame has a pattern of tiny pyramids to provide better purchase for the shooting hand. Thus it is termed a "rough textured frame" or RTF. If this were not enough to set it apart, the 22 RTF2 also has distinctive arcuate grasping grooves on the slide.

GSG

GSG (German Sport Guns) makes a nifty autoloading carbine styled a bit like the German HK MP-5 submachinegun. The GSG carbine was cleverly named the GSG-5.

Now, a pistol version has been introduced, which is of interest to us here. With no stock and a 4.7" barrel, the big new 22 pistol is about 15 inches long, and weighs about 5 lbs. It has the letter-filled name of GSG-5PK. It is available with 10, 15 or 22-round magazines.

The GSG-5PK is being imported and distributed by American Tactical Imports. (See ATI)

Guncrafter

Regular readers of this report will remember that in the 2004 edition of this publication, a new company, Guncrafter Industries, introduced a new 1911 pistol. The unique aspect of this pistol was that it was redesigned and enlarged to handle a powerful new cartridge with a half-inch bullet diameter—the .50 GI.

The original pistol is now called the Model 1, and there is now a second version. The Model 2 is distinguished by its full-profile (no scallops) slide, and an accessory rail on the frame. Caliber is .50 GI, of course.

However, the Guncrafter firm will make either model of the big pistol in .45 ACP caliber if a shooter wants one. Then, a conversion kit can be acquired to later make it into a .50 GI.

In addition, the company offers "The American," an enhanced regular-size .45-caliber 1911, under the Guncrafter Industries name. Chalk up one more 1911, if you are keeping score.

A new product introduced at the 2009 SHOT Show was a .50-caliber conversion kit for the Glock 21. The kit consists of a magazine and a complete top end (slide, barrel and all associated parts). This is a "drop-in" installation for those who feel they don't have enough caliber options with Glock's standard offerings, or just want a bigger caliber. The .50-caliber Glock conversion kit can be acquired from Guncrafter or from American Tactical Imports.

HK

Heckler & Koch's P 30 pistol was recently designed as a modern 9mm police and security arm. It is conventional double action, but can use other trigger modes such as DAO or HK's Law Enforcement Modification (LEM). A Picatinny rail is moulded into the front of the polymer frame. Capacity is 15 + 1, and it has ambidextrous controls.

The original 3.85" barrel was felt by some to be a bit short, so now there is the P 30 L. The "L" stands for "Long Slide." We must remember that in terminology, things can be relative. The P 30 L has about a half-inch longer barrel, slide and sight radius. With its lengthened 4.45" barrel, the slightly larger pistol's weight goes up from 26 to 27.5 oz.

High Standard

High Standard had added a new .45 to its 1911 pistol line. The

The new Kahr P380 is Kahr's smallest handgun. Weighing in at about 11 oz. (with magazine), the little pistol has 6+1 capacity.

The Kriss .45 was introduced last year in carbine form, and is offered this year as a "short barrel rifle." Requiring extra federal paperwork and money, the new variant can be said to have an exotic appearance.

One of the new pistols offered by Legacy Sports International is the BUL Cherokee, a 9mm polymer-frame pistol made in Israel. This version is the Cherokee Compact.

The exotic-looking .380-caliber Magnum Research Micro Desert Eagle uses a unique blowback system. The Micro Eagle's trigger is double-action-only, and the barrel length is 2.2 inches.

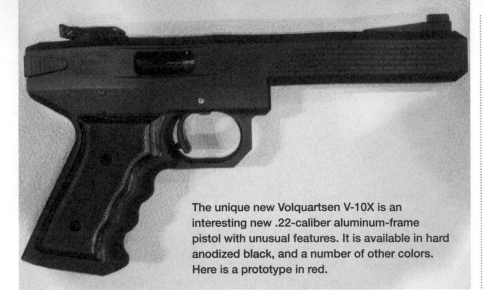

The unique new Volquartsen V-10X is an interesting new .22-caliber aluminum-frame pistol with unusual features. It is available in hard anodized black, and a number of other colors. Here is a prototype in red.

new Compact Elite has a 3-5/8" barrel. The parkerized small .45 has niceties such as a beavertail tang, skeletonized hammer and trigger and checkered wood grips. Capacity is 6 + 1.

High Standard also offers the Sentinel Model. (Like S&W and Colt, High Standard apparently felt they might as well recycle some early company names.) Small .45s with no sights have been recently offered by Colt and Kimber, and the new Sentinel also comes without sights. Some pocket pistols of the early 20th century were made without sights, and it is interesting to see this trend come back now.

High Standard's line of .223-caliber AR-type rifles has a new addition, of interest to us here as a pistol-caliber carbine. The new 9mm carbine uses Colt 9mm magazines and can come with the carry handle upper, or as a flat-top. The lower receiver uses a removable magazine block. This gives the owner the option of later converting the 9mm carbine to a .223, if that change is desired.

Since this seems to be the year of the .380, it is worth noting that the DAO stainless-steel AMT .380 BackUp pistol, an early compact .380, is offered by High Standard.

Hi-Point

Green- and tan-colored service auto-loaders are offered by other companies, so Hi-Point has gone so far as to offer its first green-colored .40 and .45-caliber pistols. Mechanically identical to current Hi-Point pistols, the new 40G and 45G models were scheduled for availability in early 2009.

The economical Hi-Point carbine, available in 9mm and .40 S&W chamber-

ings, will be wearing a new stock before too long. The new stock, displayed in prototype at the 2009 SHOT Show, is a ventilated unit with a cushioned butt pad. It incorporates rails for mounting lights or lasers or other accessories. Like most of Hi-Point's changes, it will probably sneak in, with little fanfare, as an in-line change.

For those who like the little carbine, good news! The long-awaited .45-caliber variant of the Hi-Point carbine was scheduled to enter production in the last half of 2009.

Hogue

The Hogue Avenger is now a reality for American shooters. Initial production was scheduled to go to Europe, but now the new gun is available in the United States, at least in conversion-kit form.

Recall that the Avenger system will work on a standard 1911 frame. It replaces the 1911 slide but makes it a very different gun. The barrel is fixed, and the sights are always in alignment with the barrel. The unique mechanism unlocks after the bullet has left the barrel, and movement is in a straight line. Putting an Avenger upper unit on a 1911 frame can convert the pistol into a match-ready race gun, says Peter Spielberger, the designer of the Hogue Avenger.

At the present, the Avenger is supplied as a kit with all the instructions and tools included. Someone with a sense of humor named the tools the APT (Avenger Pin Tool) and VST (Very Special Tool).

The Avenger conversion kit is not a firearm by itself, so can be shipped and sold freely. The conversion units are being produced at the rate of 700 per year, of which 300 will go to Europe. Eventu-

ally, complete pistols will be marketed, but no time frame has been planned.

ISSC

A .22-caliber Glock? The ISSC M22 pistol certainly looks like one. The Austrian pistol is shaped like a Glock, and until the eye catches the external hammer peeking out at the rear of the slide, it is easy to mistake it for one. The familiar Glock-style trigger safety is part of the design, but because it is hammer-fired, a manual safety on the slide is included.

Designed as a training pistol for those armed with a Glock, the new .22 can, of course, be used for plinking, target shooting, and other recreational shooting. The blowback pistol has a 4-lb. trigger. With its 4" match barrel, the M22 has an overall length of 7". Weight with a magazine is about 24 oz. A version with a longer barrel and slide is also in the works.

The new .22 Long Rifle pistol is imported by Austrian Sporting Arms.

Iver Johnson

The Iver Johnson 1911-style pistols are finally a production reality. Planned in .45 and .22 LR variants, the .45 was in stock by early 2009, and plans were to begin shipping during the spring. The .22 version will come later.

Many companies are offering non-traditional finishes now, and Iver Johson plans to offer a Dura-Coat "Snakeskin" pattern finish as an option with their .45-caliber 1911. The prototype of the new finish was displayed at the 2009 SHOT Show.

Malloy learns about the inner workings of the Hogue's Avenger conversion kit from Peter Spielberger, the inventor of the design. The Avenger is now available as a conversion kit for 1911 pistols.

Even though the IJ 22 was not yet ready for shipping at the time of this writing, the company offers .22-caliber conversion kits which work on any .45-caliber 1911.

Kahr

Kahr started out years ago with a small DAO 9mm pistol. Over the years they have enlarged the basic design to include .40- and .45-caliber handguns. Now, things are going the other way, and Kahr offers the new, much smaller model P380, chambered for the .380 ACP cartridge.

Like the latest larger Kahr variants, the P380 has a polymer frame, a DAO trigger mechanism, a tilting-barrel locking system and a matte stainless-steel slide. The pistol is scaled down to match the .380 cartridge. The barrel length is 2.5 inches. Overall size is 4.9" long by 3.9" high; the little .380 can easily hide beneath a 4x6 index card. It thus falls into what I consider the "subcompact" class. (Kahr, however, calls it a "micro-compact").

Advertised weight is just under 10 oz. — 9.97 oz., to be exact. They are cheating a little, though, as this figure is without a magazine. With the magazine, the weight goes up to a bit over 11 oz. (As this is two ounces lighter than the 13-oz. weight of the old Colt .25 Auto of 1908, I still am impressed with how light the P380 is.) Capacity of the Kahr P380 is 6 + 1.

Kahr is proud of the fact that the little .380 has "real" sights, with both front and rear sights dovetailed into the slide. Night sights are available.

Kahr also produces Thompson long guns and pistols (q.v.).

Kimber

Kimber's 1911 line has some new models. All the new guns are in .45 ACP.

Last year the stainless-steel Raptor II was introduced with a 5" barrel as a "Custom" pistol. New this year are the Pro Raptor II with a 4" bull barrel and full-length frame, and the Ultra Raptor II with a 3" barrel and short aluminum frame. Raptor pistols have special scaled gripping surfaces on the metal, and logo grip panels carry out the "Raptor" theme. To refresh your memory, here are Kimber's model codes: Custom guns have 5" barrels, Pro series guns are 4-inchers and Ultra pistols have 3" barrels.

Crimson Carry II pistols are equipped with Crimson Trace Lasergrips. Grip-mounted lasers are becoming ever more popular, and these are nicely done. The grips have a rosewood finish and double-diamond checkering. The pistols are two-tone, with bright aluminum frames

and blued slides. They are available in Custom, Pro and Ultra variants, and are very attractive pistols.

Two new items have been added to the Tactical pistol line. The Tactical Custom HD II has a new stainless-steel frame. The Tactical Entry II has an elongated forward frame with an integral rail that allows attaching a light or laser or other accessory. The Tactical series guns have ambidextrous safeties, beavertail tangs, night sights, extensive checkering, and other embellishments.

Kriss

Produced by TDI (Transformational Defense Industries), the Kriss .45 ACP carbine was introduced last year. Of unconventional appearance, the Kriss design was originally developed as a submachinegun, with a polymer frame and a unique recoil-reducing mechanism. The action was redesigned for semi-automatic fire, and a longer 16" barrel was used to produce the carbine.

Some people just have to have a gun that looks like a submachinegun, even if it isn't one. So, for 2009, the Kriss is also offered with the short submachinegun barrel. Yes, it is considered a "short barrel rifle" so it takes BATF paperwork and extra money to own one, but if someone wants one, it is available.

Also announced was another caliber option. A 16" carbine in .40 S&W chambering will be offered. The new .40 carbine will use a 30-round .40-caliber Glock-type magazine. Scheduled availability was set for the second half of 2009.

Legacy

Legacy Sports International is known as a provider of rifles and shotguns. Now, the company offers two new autoloading pistols.

The ever-popular 1911 design is offered by Legacy as the "Citadel." Made in the Philippines, the Citadel is an enhanced 1911 offered in two sizes. The Full Size variant has a 5" barrel, beavertail tang, lightened hammer and trigger, Novak-style sights, and ambidextrous manual safety. Each pistol comes with two eight-round magazines.

The Compact (Concealed Carry) version is a smaller pistol with a 3.5" barrel and shorter grip frame. It does not have the ambidextrous safety, but has a bushingless barrel and full-length guide rod. The Compact pistol comes with two six-round magazines.

Citadel 1911 pistols were first displayed at the January 2009 SHOT Show. Pistols were in stock, ready for shipping, at that time.

For those wanting a 9mm pistol of a different design, Legacy offers polymer BUL 9mm pistols. Israeli BUL pistols have a good reputation, and have been offered by other companies under other names. Legacy is offering the polymer-frame, conventional double-action 9mm pistols under the BUL name.

The BUL Cherokee (full size) is based on the CZ 75 trigger mechanism in a polymer frame, locked by a tilting-barrel

The S&W Model SW1911ES ("extended slide") .45 has a short grip frame and longer 4-½" barrel and slide.

system. Barrel length is about 4-3/8", with an overall length of close to 8-½". A Cherokee Compact is also offered, with a shorter 3-9/16" barrel. Frames for both variants are the same, with barrel and slide length differentiating the guns. Each BUL pistol comes in a lockable hard case with two 17-round magazines and a nifty little cleaning kit.

Les Baer

The Les Baer H.C. 40, introduced last year, is in the catalog now as a production item. We'll assume that H.C. stands for "high capacity," as the double-column magazine holds 18 rounds. With one in the chamber, that means 19 rounds of .40 S&W ammunition. The pistol is built on a double-stack Caspian frame and has an accuracy guarantee of 2-½" at 50 yards.

Magnum Research

Using a different operating concept from any of the other new .380-caliber pistols, Magnum Research has introduced its new small-size DAO 380. The "Micro Desert Eagle" has a 2.2" barrel. It measures 4.5" x 3.7"; it could hide under a 3x5 index card if the butt didn't stick out. Weight is a hair under 14 oz.

The pistol is described as "gas assisted blowback system." What on earth does that mean? A Magnum Research representative was kind enough to give me an examination of the inner workings of the pistol, which shows some interesting ideas. The frame is light aluminum (a new 6066 alloy), but to counter recoil, the slide is steel, with dual recoil springs. The fixed barrel is very subtly ported, and the porting assists in recoil control. The 2.2" barrel is very subtly octagon-shaped to allow slide clearance for free operation.

The little Micro Desert Eagle was the star of Magnum Research's new offerings. However, the big Desert Eagle pistol reached its 25th anniversary in 2009. The first version, in .357 Magnum, was introduced in 1984. Later chamberings were .44 Magnum and then .50 Action Express (.50 AE), the big boomer of conventional autoloading handguns. The pistol today is offered in these three calibers. From 2009 on, all Desert Eagle pistols will be manufactured in a new facility in Minnesota.

To celebrate the 25th year of the Desert Eagle, Magnum Research panned to offer 250 commemorative pistols. The pistols will have silver titanium finish with gold-plated triggers, hammers and levers. Each one will come with a walnut display case and a medallion. Caliber? .50 AE, of course.

Nighthawk

Nighthawk Custom's new 1911 9mm Lady Hawk was sized with slim frame and grips to fit women's smaller hands. Introduced last year too late to make the catalog, the pistol sold well — to men! A company representative told me that 80 percent of sales were to men. Now, they will not put "Lady Hawk" on the slide unless requested by the customer.

The T3 pistol, originally designed as a compact 1911-style .45, uses a "Commander" 4-½" slide on a short "Officer" frame. This size proved to be popular, and new Nighthawk T3 variants are now available in 9mm and .40 S&W.

Para

Para's big news is that the company has changed location. The new headquarters is in Charlotte, NC. The first product made at and shipped from the Charlotte plant was their new GI Expert pistol, in early 2009. After that, the schedule called for production of the company's rifle line. By mid-2009, all manufacture, assembly and distribution was scheduled to be from North Carolina.

That said, the big news in Para's firearms line is indeed their GI Expert pistol, the first item to come from North Carolina. There has been a tendency in the past few decades to enhance the basic 1911 design. Components have been added or modified to suit the gun to special purposes. Lately, though, it seems that a lot of people just want a basic 1911 without a lot of bells and whistles. Para has given substantial thought to a basic .45, and the GI Expert at first glance looks very much like a WWII-era 1911A1. However, some subtle additions have been made. The crisp trigger mechanism uses a trigger of medium length, which should be satisfactory to those who can't decide between a short trigger and a long one. The tang has been slightly lengthened and reshaped to prevent hammer bite by the skeletonized burr hammer. The sights are higher, and both rear and front sights are dovetailed into the slide. The magazine holds eight rounds instead of seven, and the barrel is stainless steel. All in all, the GI Expert seems a basic .45 that even a purist could love.

Robar

After the polymer-frame Glock pistol became popular, some shooters were impressed by the design but didn't really like the polymer frame. Eventually, replacement frames made of aluminum became available. Now Robar of Phoenix, AZ, has introduced a line of complete pistols using the basic Glock mechanism in either aluminum or stainless-steel frames.

Robar believes the metal frame offers positive advantages. The "Alloy Xtreme" frames do not flex, and features such as a "beavertail" tang and better access to the magazine release are possible. Also, interchangeable grip inserts can be added to the lower rear portion of the grip. Stainless-steel frames have the same features, and add additional weight

The experimental STI-QS 7mm pistol looks a bit like a 1911, but uses a special delayed blowback action and fixed barrel.

which helps to control recoil.

Robar also has a "Robar Revive!" program to upgrade existing Glock pistols with metal frames and other features.

Rock River

Rock River Arms makes a number of items of interest to us here, including 1911-style pistols, .223-caliber long-range pistols and 9mm AR-style carbines.

For 2009, a .40 S&W caliber carbine was added to the line, but was not available for display at the January SHOT Show because the .40-caliber magazines were not ready.

Rohrbaugh

Last year, I reported that the new Rohrbaugh .380 pistol was "almost in production," but it turned out the introduction was held up by the magazines not being ready. Now, the .380 is in full production, just in time to catch the wave of renewed interest in that caliber.

The Rohrbaugh .380 has basically the same specifications as the original all-metal 9mm, weighing 12.8 oz. With its 2.9" barrel, it measures 5.2" x 3.7". The magazine holds six rounds, giving 6 + 1 capacity. Variants with and without sights are available.

The new Rohrbaugh .380 is about the same size as the company's 9mm pistols. The .380 weighs 12.8 oz. and has 6+1 capacity.

Ruger

New variants of the products of Sturm, Ruger & Co. tend to slip in and out of the Ruger lineup with little fanfare. So, let's take a look at the new pistol variants.

The original .22-caliber Mark III Hunter pistol was introduced a few years ago in a long-barrel version. In 2009, a new Mark III Hunter was introduced. The stainless-steel pistol is very distinctive with its 4-½" fluted barrel. For those of us whose first .22 autoloader was the old Ruger Standard model, the new Ruger Mark III pistols are loaded with features. The takedown is still the same, and the manual safety button is still the same. Slowly introduced over the intervening years are a last-shot holdopen (I used an extended plastic follower in my old Mark I to trap the bolt), a loaded chamber indicator and a magazine disconnect. The basic Ruger design has lasted from 1949 into 2009: 60 years and still going strong.

The .22-caliber Charger pistol, a 10"-barrel silhouette and hunting pistol based on the 10/22 rifle action, was introduced last year. New for 2009, the original model with the laminated wood stock is joined by a variant with a black "Axiom" synthetic stock.

Also introduced last year were two new polymer-frame pistols: the SR 9 9mm service-style pistol and the little LCP .380 carry pistol. Since their introduction, some potential problems developed, and Ruger has resolved the situation. For people who purchased SR 9 or LCP pistols in the early days of 2008, Ruger has issued a recall notice. SR 9 pistols with serial number prefix "330" and LCP pistols with serial number prefix "370" are involved. If you have such a pistol, contact Ruger at 1-800-784-3701 or e-mail SR9recall@ruger.com or LCPrecall@ruger.com. They will send a shipping box so you can return the pistol free of charge for a no-cost upgrade. A free extra magazine will be included when the refitted pistol is returned to you. Ruger reports that turnaround is about one week.

Sarsilmaz

Last year, the Turkish Sarsilmaz K2 was introduced. It is a 15 + 1 9mm based on the CZ 75 mechanism. Announced at that time, but not present for display, was the K2C, a compact with a shorter barrel, but using the full-size frame. The 9mm K2C is now in production, and is a catalog item.

The K2 has also been expanded into a .45 ACP version. The new K2-45 has 14 + 1 capacity. With a barrel about 4-½" long, the overall length is 8 inches. The big staggered-column .45 weighs about 40 oz. Finishes are black or white chrome.

Sarsilmaz makes pistols for other companies under other names also.

SIG Sauer

SIG Sauer introduced a new .380 pistol for 2009. The new SIG is different than most of other companies' new .380 introductions, though. It is a single-action, aluminum-frame pistol with the appearance of a 1911 that has been reduced in every dimension. Its black aluminum frame carries a stainless-steel slide which can be left natural or covered with black Nitron. Grips are available in black or natural aluminum. The grooved aluminum grips give the little pistol a distinctive look. With its 2.7" barrel, the pistol measures 5.5" x 3.9", thus falling into my subcompact class (able to hide under a 4x6 index card). The new .380 weighs 15 oz. and has 6 + 1 capacity.

The larger double-action .380 P232 is now available with a new slide design and new sights. Finishes are natural stainless or black Nitron.

A new concept in SIG Sauer products is a long-range pistol. It is a modification of the company's P556 (5.56mm NATO/.223 Remington) semi-automatic rifle. The new P556 pistol has no provision for a stock, and has a 10" barrel. It is available with a polymer forearms or an "alloy quad rail" SWAT version. Weight is about 6.5 lbs. Overall length is 20.5 inches. Such

pistols are catching on for recreational shooting as well as for law-enforcement applications. I had a chance to shoot the new P556 pistol, and it is fun to shoot. Interestingly, the guns are marked "PISTOL USE ONLY." You can't put a stock on one.

Smith & Wesson

S&W's two most recent pistol lines—the SW1911 and the polymer-frame M&P series—now dominate the firm's autoloading pistol offerings. A number of new variants appeared for 2009.

In the 1911 line, new is a full-size 9mm, a departure from the traditional .45 ACP chambering. Added to the full-size 5" version (which appeared first), and the "Commander" sized 4-¼" variant, a new 3" compact version has been added.

S&W has also come to the conclusion that the butt of an autoloading handgun is the hardest part to conceal. Using the shortened six-round frame, they have mated the 4-¼" barrel and slide to it, rather than the shorter 3" components. The compact "extended slide" pistol is cataloged as the SW1911ES.

Smith & Wesson is proud of specialty metals in some of the company's guns. In the 1911 line, a new full-size variant in black melonite finish has a titanium firing pin. The model designation? SW1911TFP.

In the M&P polymer-frame pistol line, the full- and compact-size M&Ps have a new optional feature. An ambidextrous thumb safety is now offered for the M&P line. Although the catalog shows it only on the M&P9, it will be available also on the .40 S&W and .357 SIG variants.

Although the catalog shows availability only on the full-size frame, the M&P Compact guns will be available with Crimson Trace Lasergrips.

Springfield

Springfield continues its extensive line of 1911-type handguns, but its new introductions are in the polymer frame XD line.

The new XD(M) has a number of new

SIG Sauer's new .380, the P238, is a little pistol based in general design on the 1911. Grip panels on this two-tone specimen are of aluminum.

The new Vltor Standard Model Fortis will be available in the Bren Ten's original 10mm Auto chambering, and in .45 ACP. (right view).

features. Either by coincidence (unlikely) or by design (probably), all the new features start with the letter "M." They include a Multi-use carry case, Main-focus sights (low and holster-friendly), Mould-tru backstraps (interchangeable), Multi-adjust rail system (longer rail), Maximum reach magazine release (works from either side), Minimal error disassembly (easier), Mega-capacity magazine (16 in .40, 19 in 9mm), Melonite (black oxide), Minimal reset trigger (short travel reset), Model contour frame (better grip), Mega-lock texture (better purchase on grip), Major grasp slide serrations (deeper) and Match-grade barrel.

Just in case these items don't give you the picture of the new XD(M), it also has a different contour slide, with beveled sides. Barrel length is 4-½", and the gun is available in black, olive-drab green, or two-tone finishes. It comes in a case with two magazines, a holster, a double magazine pouch, cable lock and cleaning brush. Cataloged now in .40 and 9mm, a .45 ACP version is in the works.

STI

STI International, maker of 1911-type autoloading pistols, introduced a revolver (of all things) last year. This year, the firm offers another departure. The 9mm STI GP6 pistol has a polymer grip over a steel frame, and a polymer accessory rail is included. It is conventional double action, but has ambidextrous thumb safeties. Other ambidextrous controls are the magazine release and the slide stop. The barrel is 4-¼" long, and the overall length is 8". Weight is 26 oz.

STI also displayed a very interesting experimental pistol, a joint venture between STI in America and the QS firm in Italy. The pistol is roughly of 1911 shape, but has a fixed barrel and is described as

a delayed blowback. (I do not know the exact mechanical aspects). The pistol has the SFS (Safe Fast Shooting) system described on these pages in past years. The cocked hammer can be pushed forward, which motion automatically applies the thumb safety to its upward position. When the safety is depressed, the hammer automatically recocks.

Still, perhaps the most interesting aspect is the ammunition. The cartridge is named the 7mm Penna, or 7x23mm. The case is the same length as the Super .38 or .45 ACP (.898"), but is only .311" in diameter (about the diameter of a .32 Auto bullet, not cartridge). The nominal 7mm bullet measures .277". The cartridge comes in two loadings.

A very light (aluminum) bullet weighs 15 grains and reaches the zippy speed of 2800 feet per second (fps) from the muzzle. Needless to say, it loses velocity very rapidly and probably loses stability in short order. The concept is that it could be a useful close-range defense load – it could be very effective at close range, yet quickly slow down without endangering other people. A more conventional load is also in progress. A 70-gr. bullet still comes out at 1400 fps. Components are being made in Italy by Fiocchi. This is an interesting development.

Taurus

Lots of new pistols from Taurus, a company that calls itself the "World's Foremost Pistol Maker." Let's start with the PT 738, Taurus' entry into the small .380 market.

Taurus, in their catalog, calls the model 738 the "TCP" pistol. I neglected to ask what the significance of "TCP"

The STI-QS experimental pistol uses the 7mm Penna cartridge. Here, from left, are a Fiocchi 70-gr. bullet, empty cartridge case, 15-gr. aluminum bullet load, 70-gr. jacketed bullet load, and a .45 ACP for comparison.

was, and can only guess. Tiny Compact Pistol? At any rate, the DAO model PT 738 has a polymer frame and holds 6 + 1 rounds of .380 ammunition. The barrel is a relatively long 3.3", for an overall length of 5". Three variants are offered: the 738B has a blued slide and weighs 10.2 oz; the 738SS has a stainless-steel slide and weighs 10.2 oz; the 738 TI has a titanium slide and weighs just 9 oz. An extension magazine is available that increases capacity to 8 + 1.

The slim look is in for small carry pistols, and Taurus' PT709SLIM pistol has trimmed down. A 9mm, the 709 is a conventional double action. It has a "trigger safety" and a manual thumb safety. Barrel length is 3.2 inches, and overall length is 6.2 inches. Several variants of the SLIM pistol are offered in black, stainless, and titanium. All weigh 19 oz. except the titanium version, which goes 17 oz. Capacity is 7 + 1 or 9 + 1.

Taurus' little .22 and .25 conventional double action pistols are now available with polymer frames. The 22PLY and 25 PLY (I can break this code) have 8 + 1 and 9 + 1 capacity, respectively. Barrels are 2.3", and they each weigh 10.8 oz.

The PT 2045 is a new polymer-frame .45. The pistol is conventional double action, with "Strike Two" capability. The staggered-column magazine gives 12 + 1 capacity. With a 4.2" barrel, it weighs 31.5 oz. The 2045 is available with either a blue or stainless slide.

The 1911 line has several new variants. The PT 1911 has, logically, been a .45, but now both 9mm and .38 Super choices are available, either in blue or stainless. Both calibers are 5" pistols with 9 + 1 capacity. Another new Taurus .45 is the 1911 HC, a wide-frame full-size pistol with 12 + 1 capacity. (I feel certain that HC stands for "high capacity").

The Polymer-frame 24/7, Taurus' original entry into the polymer-frame service pistol niche, is now available in a high-capacity variant, the 24/7 PLS. This variant of the pistol has grown — the barrel is a full five inches, and the grip is longer. Weight, however, is a moderate

Walther's new .380-caliber pistol, the PK380, has a polymer frame and is hammer-fired. This is the "bicolor" version.

31.5 oz. The new 24/7 is available in 9mm and .38 Super with 18 + 1 capacity, and in .40 S&W with 16 + 1 capacity.

Thompson

The line of Thompson "Tommy Gun" long guns and pistols is produced by Kahr Arms. Introduced last year were a "Short Barrel Rifle" variant of the 1927A1 semi-automatic carbine, and a 1927A1 semi-automatic pistol. These variants are in production and are now catalog items.

The 45-caliber 1927A1 Thompson pistol (aka TA5) is available in three configurations: the pistol with a 50-round drum, the pistol with a 100-round drum (Wow!), and the pistol with a special 10-round drum, for those states that do not trust their citizens with more than 10 rounds at a time.

Tisas

A new double-action full-size pistol was introduced by the Turkish Tisas firm two years ago, and was given the name Zigana last year. For 2009, a whole family of Zigana pistols is now offered. Calibers are 9mm and .45 ACP, with differences in grips and finishes. Rails and porting are available on some models.

Some variants of Tisas pistols are now being imported by American Tactical imports. (See ATI)

Vltor

In the last edition of this publication, Vltor's Fortis pistol was a concept. Vltor Weapon Systems planned to reincarnate the Bren Ten of the early 1980s, a design approved by the late Jeff Cooper. The Bren Ten failed through no fault of the design — the company producing it ran into financial problems.

The Fortis project moved very quickly, and the design became reality. A year later, Vltor displayed a number of working models of the Fortis at the January 2009 SHOT Show. Plans were to be at full production before the end of 2009.

The Fortis can be thought of as an "improved" Bren Ten. Although the Fortis looks, feels and operates like the original design, there is no parts interchangeability. This extends to the magazines, which were a problem with the original Bren Ten. The magazine problem was solved by using magazines designed for EAA's Witness pistols, which have the advantage of proven reliability. A different floorplate is used, however.

The Fortis guns were planned to be offered in a standard 5" two-tone model, and a 4" Special Forces variant. Calibers will be the original 10mm Auto (14 + 1), and .45 ACP (10 + 1).

A lot of people have been hoping for the revival of the Bren Ten design. Want more information? Try www.fortispistol.com.

Volquartsen

Is there room for a new design of precision .22 pistol? Volquartsen thinks so. Their recently-introduced V-10X pistol is CNC-machined from aluminum billet material. The finished pistol can be hard anodized to almost any color the shooter desires. Displayed at the 2009 SHOT Show were prototypes in red and blue.

The grip frame has front finger grooves, matching the contours of the grips. The pistol comes with adjustable sights, and is drilled and tapped for top and bottom rails. A compensator and balance weights will also be available. The pistol uses a 6" barrel internal in the frame, a cylindrical bolt and an adjustable trigger mechanism. It is designed to use Ruger .22 pistol magazines.

The new V-10X was scheduled for Spring 2009 availability.

Walther

Walther already had their splendid PPK pistols in .380 caliber. With all the current interest in that caliber, how would they go about adding a new .380? Why not take the polymer-frame P22 and turn it into a .380?

The Robar metal-frame Glock-style pistol uses interchangeable backstraps to fit the shooter's hand.

A new offering from Wilson Combat is the Sentinel pistol, a compact 9mm variant in the company's 1911 line.

It wasn't that simple, of course, but the new Walther PK380 is about the same size, and looks much like the earlier .22 pistol. The new .380, like the .22, is hammer-fired. The trigger mechanism is conventional double-action. The pistol has ambidextrous manual safeties on the slide, and ambidextrous magazine releases. Several different variants were offered, with black or nickel slides, and with lasers to fit the integral frame rails.

The new Walther PK380 has a 3.7" barrel, measures 6.2"x5.2", and weighs 19.4 oz. Capacity is 8 + 1.

Wilson

New from Wilson Combat is the Bill Wilson Carry Pistol. The compact 1911-style .45 is patterned after the pistol Wilson himself actually carries. It has a 4" barrel and weighs 35 oz. A noticeable feature is the gently-rounded butt, which gives it a graceful look reminiscent of the nice old Colt pocket automatics of a century ago.

The Sentinel pistol is a 1911 in 9mm chambering, with a 3.6" barrel and short grip. With a lightweight frame, it weighs 27 oz.

Wilson Combat has been fitting some models with their special grooved "G10" grips. The grips have a "sticky" feel that allows the shooter better purchase on the pistol.

Postscript

The year 2010 gives the firearms community a unique opportunity. The Boy Scouts of America (BSA), founded in February 1910, reaches its 100th birthday this year. Shooting has been part of the Boy Scout program ever since BSA's formation. The 2010 National Jamboree will feature 21 different shooting ranges. During 2010, the BSA Centennial, consider supporting their shooting programs. The Jamboree could use Instructors and donations. Local area programs throughout the year can use similar assistance, too. Contact your nearest Boy Scout council office for information.

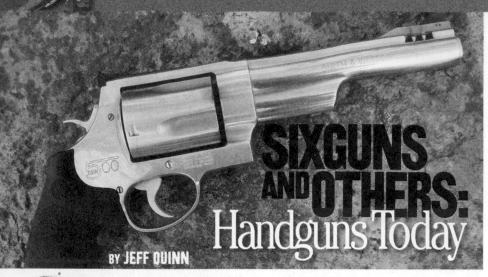

SIXGUNS AND OTHERS: Handguns Today

BY JEFF QUINN

Those of you who are long-time readers of the *Gun Digest* will recognize this section as having been written by my good friend John Taffin in years past. Mr. Taffin is alive, well, and still writing, but with his books, magazines, and other commitments, he has passed the writing of this section of *Gun Digest* on to me, and I am honored that both he and the editor of this legendary gun annual have bestowed upon me the privilege to try to adequately fill those big boots. I, as much as any of you, will miss Mr. Taffin's writing of this section of the *Digest*, as many, including myself, consider him to be the best gunwriter of our time. Anyway, here we are, and it is at an historic time in our nation. Civilian gun sales in the U.S. are at an all-time high since anyone started keeping records on such things.

As I type this, there are five different bills submitted in Congress aimed at curtailing the ownership of firearms, and totally eliminating some types of firearms from production. It is indeed interesting times for gun owners. Still, 2009 has some exciting firearms reaching production, and in this brief review, I will try to touch on some of the most interesting sixguns on the market today, along with a couple of other interesting handguns, including one newly-designed single shot and a lever action handgun that has historical roots and nostalgic memories for fans of old Western TV shows. Let's get started!

AWA (American Western Arms)

AWA, as always, has some high quality 1873 Colt replicas, from their basic Classic series (which is a fine example of what a single action sixgun should be) to their Ultimate, which has a coil mainspring and can be upgraded with better

stocks and finishes in addition to engraving. AWA also offers an octagon-barrel model, which is something that really sets it apart from the other Single Action Army replicas on the market, with a distinctive, classic look. Of particular interest is the Lightningbolt, a short, pump-action *handgun* version of the old medium-frame Colt Lightning Magazine Rifle. Offered in three different models (blued, case-hardened, and the White Lightning hard chrome finish) the Lightningbolt pistol is in production right now and should prove to be popular with shooters who want something a bit different but with an Old West flavor. It holds five rounds in a tubular magazine under its 12" barrel and is chambered for the .45 Colt cartridge. AWA also has a neat holster rig custom built to carry this one-of-a-kind handgun.

Beretta

Beretta entered the world of revolvers, and particularly Single Action Army Colt replicas, a couple of years ago with their purchase of Uberti. Uberti has been a well-known maker of fine quality

replica firearms for decades, and with that acquisition, Beretta introduced their Stampede line of high quality, well-finished replica sixguns. Beretta offers the Stampede with blued, nickel, or deluxe blued finishes.

The blued models have case-colored frames and a standard blue-black finish, while the deluxe has a bright charcoal blue finish to the grip frame, trigger guard, and barrel. The stocks are either walnut or black plastic, while the Bisley models have black plastic stocks only. In addition to the standard barrel lengths, the Stampede Marshall has a shorter 3.5" barrel, a birds-head grip frame and walnut stocks. Also, the Stampede and Stampede Marshall are offered with an Old West finish that resembles an original aged and worn Colt. The Stampede series is offered in a choice of .357 Magnum or .45 Colt chamberings.

Bond Arms

Bond Arms is a Texas outfit that manufactures what is probably the finest example of the Remington pattern derringers ever built. It is certainly the strongest. The Bond is a stack-barrel derringer that swings open at the hinge pin for loading and unloading, just as the original Remington Double Derringer .41 rimfire did. The barrels are fired one at a time, and interchangeable barrels are available to allow for changing the caliber quickly and easily. The most popular seems to be their .45 Colt/.410 shotshell version, but other caliber choices include the .22 Long Rifle, .32 H&R, 9x19mm, .38 Special/.357 Magnum, .357 Maximum, .40 S&W, 10mm, .44 Special, .44 WCF, .45 GAP, .45 ACP, and .45 Colt. There should be enough

Editor Quinn shooting the Freedom Arms .500 Wyoming Express.

choices there for everyone, but being a fan of the .22 Magnum cartridge, I would like to see that versatile little chambering offered as well.

The Bond Arms derringer is not in the same class as the cheap zinc-frame derringers that we have seen offered during the last half of the past century. The Bond is made from quality materials, and built to last. While offering only two shots before reloading is required, these handguns are very compact and very flat, making it easy and comfortable to carry in a back pocket or in a lightweight hip holster while working around the homestead, or out for a walk in snake country. The .410 shotshell does a real number on poisonous snakes and can also serve very well as gun to repel carjackers. At arms-length, a faceful of .410 shot will change the mind of any carjacker, and the payload is easy to deliver from the barrels of the Bond derringer.

Charter Arms

Charter Arms has been producing reliable, affordable revolvers for decades now. I have owned Charters chambered for the .22 Magnum, .32 H&R, .38 Special, .357 Magnum, .44 Special, and that most-useful of cartridges, the .22 Long Rifle. Charters have always seemed to me no-frills, solid little handguns, and they have never let me down.

Back in my younger days while working undercover for a State Attorney General's Office, I was associating with some of the coarser types of our society. They are by nature a suspicious lot, and the slightest hint that something was out of place could result in a distasteful outcome, to me at least. In those days, I relied upon a Charter .38 tucked into the top of my boot. I had slicked the action, removed the front sight, and bobbed the hammer spur. It was there to resolve up-close and personal social conflicts, and was very comforting to have along. I still have that little five-shot revolver, and it is as useful and reliable as ever. It has never let me down.

Charter Arms makes a variety of small and medium-sized revolvers. One of their latest is chambered for the relatively new .327 Federal cartridge. The .327 Federal is what the .32 H&R Magnum should have been. The .327 Federal launches a .312" diameter bullet at true magnum velocities, and Charter was one of the first to chamber for the cartridge after its initial introduction. Of course, Charter still makes their .44 Bulldog, which is the flagship of the Charter line, having developed a cult-like following over the past few decades. As I type this, Charter is also working on a new revolver that will handle rimless cartridges such as the 9mm Luger and .40 S&W cartridges. I have not yet handled one, but it looks to be promising, and should be in production by the time that you read this.

Cimarron

Cimarron Firearms of Fredericksburg, Texas, has long been a supplier of quality replicas of classic firearms, and they continue that tradition today. Cimarron offers several varieties of 1873 Colt Single Action Army replicas, but they also supply shooters with replicas of some of the lesser-known sixguns of the Old West. Cimarron offers some unique and interesting replicas of the old conversion revolvers that bridged the gap from percussion cap-and-ball guns to modern cartridge revolvers.

I especially like the Smith & Wesson replicas offered by Cimarron, such as the Schofield and Russian models. Many shooters today are not aware of the fact that had it not been for the Russian purchase of a large quantity of S&W sixguns, the company might have folded in the nineteenth century, and the modern double-action revolver that we know today might have

Freedom Arms 25th Anniversary Revolver.

Ruger .44 Special Blackhawk Flattop with Simply Rugged Western Rig.

Freedom Arms Model 83 .500 Wyoming Express is the Perfect Packin' Pistol for use against teeth and claws.

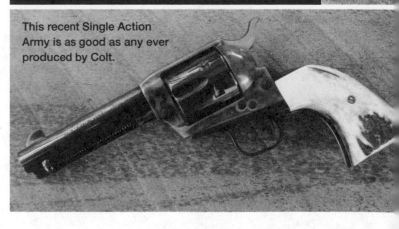

This recent Single Action Army is as good as any ever produced by Colt.

never been. Anyway, Cimarron markets replicas of the S&W Number 3 Russian, which is both historical and fun to shoot. These Cimarron Smith & Wesson replicas are offered in .38 Special, .44 WCF, .44 Russian, and .45 Colt chamberings. Of course, Cimarron still has many varieties of their Model P SAA replicas, offered in a wide choice of calibers, barrel lengths, and finishes. Their Thunderer revolvers are not really a copy of any old gun, but are a dandy example of what a Single Action Army can be with a modified bird's head grip. Very handy and easy to shoot, the Thunderer – and its little brother, the Lightning – offer the grip frame of the double action Colt Thunderer with the reliability of the Single Action Army.

The latest sixgun on the market from Cimarron is their .22 Long Rifle Plinkerton. *["Plinkerton"? Yes, Plinkerton. – DMS]* This is a no-frills revolver patterned after the Colt SAA, but it's made of a non-ferrous alloy with steel chamber liners and a steel inner barrel. The two that I have fired performed pretty well. There is also a version with an extra cylinder for the .22 Magnum cartridge. Best of all, this revolver is selling for under 200 bucks in most places. It is a really good buy, and a dandy sixgun to start a youngster out shooting.

Colt

Colt is one of the most recognized names in the world of firearms, steeped in tradition and history. There has probably never been a Western movie made that did not have a Colt or copy thereof on the set somewhere. Colt is what we picture when we think Western sixgun. Most of the shapes, the feel, and the lines of today's single action revolvers can be traced back to the Colt Single Action Army and to the Colt revolvers which preceded it. Today, Colt is still producing the Single Action Army revolver. While quality has varied over the past few decades, the examples of the

SAA that I have examined and fired over the past three years show that the Colts now leaving the factory are as good as any that have been produced. The Single Action Army is offered in either blue/casehardened or nickel finishes, in several caliber choices.

EAA (European American Armory)

EAA Corp in Rockledge, Florida, has a couple of revolver lines. Their Bounty Hunter is a Colt SAA replica, which is offered in .22 LR/Magnum, .38/.357 Magnum, .44 Magnum, and .45 Colt in a choice of blued, nickel, or blued/case-hardened finishes. The Bounty Hunter uses a transfer bar safety system, but retains the traditional feel to the action and loads/unloads in the half-cock hammer position. The .22 LR/Magnum version has an alloy frame, but the centerfire guns are made of steel. The .22 is also offered in a choice of six or eight-shot models.

EAA's double-action revolver is called the Windicator. This small-framed revolver is offered as a steel-framed .357 Magnum or as an alloy-framed .38 Special. It has synthetic rubber grips, a matte blued finish, and a choice of either a 2" or 4" barrel. They are good, basic, reliable revolvers at an affordable price.

Freedom Arms

Freedom Arms is an All-American success story. Mr. Wayne Baker started the company back about 25 years ago, having already been successful in the construction and mining businesses. Starting with a philosophy dedicated to building the finest revolvers every made, they achieved that goal and continue to hold to that standard today.

I am often asked why I like firearms so much, and the answer is a complex one. However, a large part of my love of guns is my appreciation for well-crafted machines. Firearms are still some of the

best-built machines in the world. Many still exhibit a great deal of craftsmanship in their design and execution. While many things that we use everyday are made to be disposable, from appliances to electronics, guns are still built to last, and many are built to a higher standard than most everything else that we use.

That having been said, there is no finer example of skilled craftsmanship in the world than a Freedom Arms revolver. Built at first to harness the power of the .454 Casull cartridge, FA revolvers now are offered chambered for the .17 HMR, .22 LR/Magnum, .32 H&R, .327 Federal, .32 WCF, .357 Magnum, .41 Magnum, .44 Magnum, 45 Colt, .454 Casull, and .500 Wyoming Express cartridges. They are also introducing their own .224-32 FA cartridge, firing a .22-caliber bullet from a necked-down .327 Federal case. Two different frame sizes are currently offered: the original Model 83 and the more compact Model 97.

I have fired many different Freedom Arms revolvers, and have found each one to be an amazing piece of workmanship. Holding a Freedom Arms revolver is like holding a work of art, but a working work of art! I have never fired one that wasn't accurate. Freedom takes care in the way that they align the chambers with the barrel, and it pays off in accuracy. Capable of taking the largest game on earth – and they have done so many times – Freedom Arms revolvers are built for those who appreciate fine workmanship and want to buy the very best.

News flash: Freedom Arms has been working for a couple of years on a new single-shot pistol. I have had the pleasure of shooting the prototype gun at ranges out to 600 yards, and find it to be worthy of the Freedom Arms name. It has interchangeable barrels and extractors to easily switch calibers, and the one that I spent the most trigger-time with was chambered for the 6.5mm JDJ cartridge. I found it to be very accurate, and easy to shoot well.

Ruger 4" Redhawk .45 Colt makes for a powerful, compact outdoorsman's gun.

Smith & Wesson 632 Pro Comp chambered for the .327 Federal Magnum.

Legacy Sports

Legacy Sports has been the distributor for the Puma rifles for several years now, and for 2009, the manufacture of these has been moved from Brazil to Italy. Along with this move, Legacy has a new Puma handgun called the Bounty Hunter, modeled after the "Mare's Laig," a cut-down '92 Winchester carried by Steve McQueen in the old *Wanted, Dead or Alive* TV series. McQueen's character, Josh Randall, a bounty hunter by trade, carried .45-70 cartridges in his belt for effect, but the '92 Winchester was of course built to handle much shorter cartridges. The Bounty Hunter from Legacy is chambered for either the .44 Magnum, .44 WCF, or .45 Colt cartridges, has a 12" barrel and a six-shot magazine. It wears a large loop lever and an abbreviated buttstock, and it just drips with nostalgia.

Legacy Sports also has a new line of 1873 Colt replicas, made in Italy and called the Puma Westerner. They are traditionally styled and offered with a blued/case-hardened finish, nickel plated, or in stainless steel. Grips are one-piece walnut or imitation ivory, with a smooth or checkered option with the walnut.

Magnum Research

Magnum Research is still making the BFR ("Biggest, Finest Revolver," or so it's said) revolver. Made almost entirely of stainless steel, the BFR is a large single action revolver made in two different frame lengths. The shorter frame size still handles some very powerful revolver cartridges such as the .50 Action Express, .454 Casull, and the .475 Linebaugh/.480 Ruger, in addition to the little .22 Hornet. The long frame handles some truly powerful revolver cartridges like the .460 and .500 S&W Magnums, and also rifle cartridges like the .30-30 Winchester, .450 Marlin, and .45/70 Government. The BFRs are well made, built in the USA, and in my limited experience with them, they shoot very well.

North American Arms

NAA has been producing fine little miniature revolvers for many years now, and most shooters are familiar with them. Built mainly with short barrels and chambered for either the .22 Short, .22 Long Rifle or .22 Magnum cartridges, these are handy little five-shot pocket guns that serve as snake repellant in areas where poisonous snakes are a problem, but are mainly carried for protection when nothing larger can be easily or comfortably concealed. While it is hard to hit a target at long range with these short-barreled revolvers, up close and personal, they can be very effective.

The newest offering from NAA is a .22 Magnum five-shot revolver dubbed "The Earl." This one has a 4" barrel, and the retainer for the cylinder pin gives it the look of an old percussion Remington style sixgun. It can be had with just the magnum cylinder, or with a .22 Long Rifle conversion cylinder as well. Weighing in at just over 8.5 oz., this looks like a dandy little trail gun, and I am anxious to get my hands on one for a full review. They should be available by the time you are read this.

Rossi

Rossi is better known for their handy and affordable rifles and shotguns, but they still produce a limited line of double action revolvers as well. Chambered in either .38 Special or .357 Magnum, you have a choice of blued steel or stainless, and either a 2", 4" or 6" barrel. The two-inch guns have fixed sights, but the longer barreled guns have adjustable sights. They are well-built and affordable revolvers, with a nice exterior finish. Rossi revolvers are a lot of gun for the money.

Ruger

Sturm, Ruger, & Company has been in the revolver business since 1953 and was largely responsible for the comeback of the single-action sixgun.

When Western TV shows and movies were creating a demand for the old-style sixguns, Ruger filled the need by creating the Single-Six, a rimfire revolver that is still in production today. The ones built 56 years ago are still in use today, and will shoot right along side the newer versions. The little sixguns just do not wear out. I own several Single-Sixes myself, and would not choose to be without at least one.

Ruger sixguns have proven themselves in the field for many years, whether chambered for the rimfires or the larger, more powerful centerfire magnums. This year, Ruger celebrates the fiftieth anniversary of their flagship single-action sixgun, the Super Blackhawk. The Super was introduced to the world the same year that I was: 1959. While my design is showing its age, the Super Blackhawk is as relevant and useful today as it was way back then. The Anniversary Super Blackhawk is certainly worthy to wear the name, with a rich, deep blue finish that is reminiscent of the early Supers. The Anniversary Super comes in a special white cardboard box, with a pistol rug to protect the beautiful finish and gold trim.

Also new this year from Ruger is a gun that is dear to the hearts of single-action sixgunners, and Ruger fans in particular. Back in 1956, Ruger had the very successful .357 Blackhawk in production, and had a .44 Special version of that gun in the works. As fate would have it, Bill Ruger found out about the .44 Magnum cartridge that was in development by Remington and Smith & Wesson. Bill Ruger immediately scrapped the .44 Special project and began working on the .44 Magnum Blackhawk instead, actually beating Smith & Wesson in getting the .44 Magnum into production by a few weeks. Anyway, while .44 Special fans could always shoot the shorter cartridge in their .44 Magnum Blackhawks, the .44 Magnums were built on a slightly larger frame than the pre-1973 .357 Magnum

Taurus Model 941 .22 Magnum.

Cimarron's New Plinkerton .22 Long Rifle sixgun.

Ruger celebrates the 50th anniversary of their Super Blackhawk .44 Magnum with this limited edition sixgun.

Blackhawks, and shooters still longed for the production of a Ruger Blackhawk .44 Special built upon the old .357-sized frame.

Custom gunsmiths have made out pretty well over the past few decades converting small-frame .357 Flattops and Three-Screws into .44 Special Blackhawks. Skeeter Skelton lobbied Ruger for many years to build a .44 Special on the early small Blackhawk frame, to no avail. After his passing, John Taffin has been carrying the flag for those of us who still wanted a .44 Special Blackhawk that was built on the older, handier original-sized Blackhawk frame. Finally, Ruger is producing such a sixgun, and it was worth the wait. The New Model .44 Special Blackhawk is built on a frame the size of the original Blackhawk, and it even has a Flattop frame with Micro rear sight. Mine is very, very accurate, has tight tolerances, and shoots well. It wears the XR-3 grip frame, which is a very close copy of the profile of the the grip of the old Colt Single Action Army and 1851 Navy revolvers. The grips are well-textured black plastic, and the sixgun itself is a delight to handle. The .44 Flattop balances well, handles quickly, and points like the finger of God. It is only available from dealers who buy through Lipsey's, a wholesaler in Baton Rouge, Louisiana. Ruger is also bringing back their Bisley Vaquero sixgun, now built upon the slightly smaller New Vaquero frame, as the Bisley New Vaquero.

Of course, Ruger has also built a name for itself producing rugged, reliable, and accurate double-action revolvers, and they are still in production. The Redhawk and Super Redhawk sixguns are well-suited to outdoorsmen and hunters, with many of them available with scope rings included to mount optics. For many years, Ruger produced the Redhawk with a choice of 7.5" or 5.5" barrel, but they now offer the Redhawk with a 4" barrel, which makes it much better suited as an everyday packing gun. It still wears good adjustable sights, and serves well as a primary hunting arm, but the shorter barrel makes it much easier to carry around while doing other chores or just bumming around the woods.

Another very handy but powerful Ruger double action is their Super Redhawk Alaskan, which is a version of their Super Redhawk with an abbreviated barrel, cut off right at the front of the cylinder frame extension. These sixguns are very handy to carry on the belt, and are available chambered for the .44 Magnum or .454 Casull/.45 Colt. In the past, the Alaskan was also offered chambered for the .480 Ruger cartridge, and hopefully, it will be again despite the fact that it appears to have been discontinued. A very few were produced last year chambered in .480 Ruger with a five-shot cylinder. I have one of these, and it is a very handy and powerful revolver.

The talk of the SHOT show this past January at the 2009 SHOT Show in Orlando, Florida, was Ruger's entry into the pocket revolver market with their new LCR. The LCR is like nothing else, with a unique polymer grip frame/trigger guard unit that houses all of the fire control parts, such as the trigger and hammer. It is a double-action only design with a concealed hammer, five shot steel cylinder, and an aluminum cylinder frame. I had the pleasure of firing the LCR at the New Hampshire Ruger factory back in December of 2008, and the little revolver is a lightweight, easy-to-shoot firearm. The trigger pull is wonderful, at least on that test gun, and was plenty accurate for social work as well. Chambered for the .38 Special, and Plus P rated, I believe that it will be very popular, and anxiously await the arrival of a production gun for a full review. As you read this, they should already be available on gun dealer's shelves.

Smith & Wesson

The name Smith & Wesson to me has always meant revolvers. That is just the first thing that pops into my mind: revolvers. Smith & Wesson makes some excellent auto pistols, and has done so for decades. They also makes rifles and shotguns, but to me, and many others, S&W means revolvers. That is quite understandable, for Smith & Wesson has been making revolvers for almost 160 years. Some of my all-time favorite sixguns, like the Models 34, 43, 51, 63, and 651 rimfire kit guns bear the S&W logo. Same with the K-frame twenty-twos. I love .22-caliber sixguns, and Smith & Wesson always has a few in the lineup.

As the older models fade from production, new ones are added, like the reintroduction for 2009 of the Model 18. The Model 18 is a K-frame .22 Long Rifle sixgun that is well-balanced and easy to carry, but still has enough heft in its blued-steel frame to make it easy to shoot well. As a kid, I often read the words of one of my favorite gun writers, Bob Milek, and his adventures with his Model 18 Smith. After being dropped from the catalog a few years ago, I am glad to see that it is back in production.

On the other end of the power scale, Smith & Wesson has an ever-expanding lineup of variations of their huge X-Frame chambered for the .460 XVR and the .500 S&W Magnums. The big X-Frame guns are widely popular. The .460 XVR is a very versatile handgun cartridge, and the revolvers that are chambered for it can also fire the .454 Casull, .45

Taurus makes dozens of compact revolvers, including this Model 85.

Colt, and .45 S&W cartridges. The .500 S&W Magnum has been on the market for a few years now, and is a popular choice for not only big game hunters, but for those who just want to own and shoot the most powerful double-action production revolver that they can find. The Big 500 throws a heavy chunk of lead at magnum velocities, and some of the shorter-barreled 500s carry on the hip pretty well.

Between these two extremes, S&W offers a wide variety of chamberings and frame sizes. One of the newest is the Model 632 Carry Comp Pro that is chambered for the hot little .327 Federal cartridge. With a 3" ported barrel and adjustable sights, the 632 is both a good little defensive revolver, as well as a handy little six-shot trail gun. It can shoot the .32 S&W, .32 S&W Long, .32 H&R Magnum, and .327 Federal cartridges, making it a versatile little package. The .327 Federal throws bullets as light as 60 grains and as heavy as at least 135 grains, all at magnum velocities. My favorite factory load is the 100-gr. American Eagle, which throws that jacketed softpoint bullet out at almost 1400 fps from the Smith's 3" barrel.

There is still a huge selection of S&W .357 and .44 Magnum revolvers from which to choose, along with the .41 Magnum and .45 Colt in a couple of models. In the extremely popular J-frame size, S&W rules the market with the top sellers in the five-shot pocket revolver class of .38 Special and .357 Magnum firearms. There is a huge variety of both lightweight and all-steel revolvers in that section of their catalog, and they also offer one snub-nosed .22 Magnum as well. While Smith & Wesson is now a full-line manufacturer of many classes of firearms, they are still very much involved in supplying fine quality revolvers to the world.

Taurus

Taurus has so many revolvers on the market that I cannot keep up with them. In the world of revolvers, there is nothing hotter on the market now than the Taurus Judge. This .45 Colt/.410 shotshell revolver has proved to be very popular, and production still has not caught up with demand after about two years on the market already.

The Judge is, to me, primarily a .410 shotshell revolver with the .45 Colt being secondary. Properly loaded with .410 birdshot or buckshot, it would be ideal to repel attackers at close range, and it is a natural for those who walk

Charter Arms
Target Bulldog .44 Special.

Thompson-Center
G2 Contender single shot pistol.

USFA 12-22 "Twelve Shot Sixgun" holds
a handful of .22 Long Rifle cartridges.

USFA Omni Target
Flattop Target sixgun.

Freedom Arms
New single-shot pistol.

AWA Lightningbolt slide action handgun.

Ruger is now making a Bisley version of their New Model Vaquero.

in the woods or desert where poisonous snakes are a problem. Right now, Taurus has about a dozen different variations of the Judge, in a variety of finishes, all-steel or lightweight, two barrel lengths, and with either a 2.5" or 3" chamber. Just introduced is an even more compact version of the Judge, based upon the small Model 85 frame size, called the Public Defender. It should prove to be wildly popular as well.

While still on the Taurus website, their Colt SAA replica called the Gaucho seems to be out of production. That is a shame. Mine is a very accurate, good-looking and easy-handling sixgun. Hopefully, it is just not in the production cycle for now, and will come back soon.

Of course, Taurus still makes many double-action revolvers, from compact pocket models to those capable of taking large game, and their Models 94 and 941 are some great little rimfire trail guns. In the defensive gun market, small pocket revolvers are very popular, and Taurus is well represented in that field. They offer both lightweight and all-steel versions of their basic Model 85. Right now, Taurus USA catalogs almost four dozen different small-frame revolvers built for concealed carry. They also manufacture a large variety of double-action revolvers that are suitable for hunting small and large game, as well as for target competition and casual plinking.

Thompson-Center

Thompson-Center has been the leader in single shot handguns for decades now. In the past few years, T-C has entered the muzzleloading and centerfire rifle markets in a big way, but they certainly have not neglected their single-shot handgun line. Introducing their Encore pistol several years ago as a big brother to their popular Contender pistol, the Encore line has expanded with many caliber offerings, making the Encore a very powerful and versatile pistol. Offered in 17 different calibers, with a choice of walnut or synthetic rubber stock material and blued steel or stainless, the Encore is a simple yet thoroughly modern hunting pistol capable of cleanly harvesting small game and vermin, then switching barrels and taking the largest game on earth.

While building the Encore line of single shot pistols, T-C did not ignore their original Contender pistol. Upgrading the design to the new G2 Contender, they offer this pistol in 13 different chamberings. While smaller than the Encore, the G2 can still handle the big .45-70 Government cartridge. The Contender is, and always has been, a handy, versatile break-open single shot, and is still the leader in this type of hunting handguns.

Uberti

Aldo Uberti began in 1959 the company that would become a leader in the world of replica firearms, starting with cap-and-ball replicas, then moving on to other replica firearms from the history of the American West. Today, Uberti is a premier producer of replica firearms, many of which we would not be able to enjoy and shoot, were it not for replicas. Original examples of some of our beloved sixguns are either too rare or expensive for most of us to enjoy.

Uberti recreates these fine sixguns using modern steel and technology, producing firearms that are in many ways superior to the originals. While almost everyone in the replica business replicates the Colt Single Action Army, Uberti doesn't stop there. One of my favorite sixguns is the 1875 Remington. Uberti makes very good replicas of both the 1875 and 1890 Remington revolvers.

Other makers have attempted in recent years to build quality replicas of the Remingtons, but I have yet to see a production gun. Uberti seems to have no problem in producing these in quantity, and they are well-made and accurate sixguns.

The 1875 Remington Outlaw and Frontier are available in blued/color case-hardened or nickel finishes, and the 1890 Police is available in blued/color case-hardened only. The 1875 is chambered for the .45 Colt cartridge, and the 1890 Police also adds the option of the .357 Magnum chambering. The Cattleman is the bread and butter of the Uberti sixgun line, and it is a 1873 Colt Single Action Army replica of very good quality. Offered in a variety of finishes from matte blue to nickel to the highly polished and charcoal blued Frisco with imitation mother of pearl grips. The Cattleman is available withf 4-3/4", 5.5", and 7.5" barrels, in addition to the shorter-barreled Cattleman Bird's Head, which can be had with a 3.5", 4" or 4-3/4" barrel. Chamberings include the .357 Magnum, .44 WCF, and .45 Colt.

Uberti's Stallion is a slightly smaller SAA replica chambered in .22 Long Rifle or .38 Special. It's offered with either fixed or adjustable sights, with the .22 Long Rifle version having the option of a brass grip frame and trigger guard. The Bisley replica is offered in blued/ case-hardened only, in either .357 Magnum or .45 Colt. The top of the line Cattleman is called the "El Patron." It is a special revolver in a choice of stainless steel or blued/case-colored finish, complete with Wolff springs and tuned for a better, smoother action. The El Patron wears one-piece checkered walnut grips and is available in .357 Magnum or .45 Colt chamberings.

Uberti offers an impressive line of quality cap-and-ball replica sixguns, but I still prefer their cartridge guns, and one of my favorite Uberti sixguns is their top-break Smith & Wesson replica. Offered in blued or nickeled steel, these are excellent quality replicas of the Number 3 Schofield and Russian sixguns. The Schofield wears your choice of a 5" or 7" barrel and is chambered in .45 Colt, .38 Special, or .44 WCF. The Russian is offered in .44 Russian or .45 Colt, and there is even a hand-engraved version of the 7" Schofield offered as well.

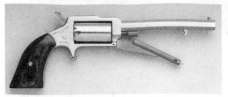

North American Arms "The Earl," shown here with "loading lever" opened.

USFA (United States Fire Arms)

USFA is celebrating 15 years of producing some of the best-built Colt SAA replicas ever produced. Their quality is comparable to any Colt ever built, and in addition to the SAA replica, they also offer some unique firearms of their own, such as the Omni-Potent Six-Shooter, which is kind of a single-action version of the old double-action Colt Model 1878. This fine sixgun is like no other, and is offered as either a fixed-sight or a Flattop Target version. The Omni-Potent Six-Shooter has a unique grip that is reminiscent of the old double-action Colt Thunderer, but in a single-action sixgun. They are beautifully finished and wear checkered walnut stocks. Like most of the USFA lineup, the caliber choices are .32 WCF, .38 Special, .38 WCF, .44 Special, .44 WCF, and .45 Colt. They also offer a short-barreled version of the Omni-Potent, called (appropriately enough) the Snubnose. The Snubnose is available with a choice of a 2", 3" or 4" barrel. This is the definitive single-action belly gun. It has a lanyard ring on the butt and wears two-piece walnut stocks.

Another unique revolver from USFA is the new 12/22. This is a .22 Long Rifle "twelve gun" that offers a lot of firepower for a revolver. Offered in high polish blued or nickeled finishes with a choice of 4-3/4", 5.5", or 7.5" inch barrel, it wears white plastic stocks and looks like a genuine Single Action Army sixgun, but cranks out 12 shots before reloading, just like the sixguns in an old Western movie. The latest from USFA is their Shooting Master Magnum series sixguns. These look like nothing else to ever come out of Hartford. First offered in .357 magnum, with .41 and .44 Magnums slated for later, the Shooting Master has an adjustable rear sight and fiber optic front. The most unusual feature of these new sixguns is the finish of the frame. Offered in a choice of black, gray, brown, tan, or two shades of green, this ain't your traditional single action revolver! The Shooting Master is built as a hunting gun, and it should serve in

that role very well. The non-glare finish will certainly not endear itself to single-action purists, but it should prove to be very practical in the field.

This about wraps up my attempt to cover the revolver scene for 2009, and is by no means a comprehensive list of everything available to revolver fans. While it looks like the semi-auto pistols are here to stay, there is still a large selection of fine firearms available to us who love the simplicity, accuracy, and convenience of the grand old sixgun, along with the precision and rifle-like accuracy of a good single shot pistol. In this section, I have just hit the high spots, and am sure that in the months ahead, that more new firearms will be introduced that will pique the interest of sixgun shooters. The design of a firearm that holds a half dozen cartridges in a revolving cylinder has been declared

obsolete by many for about the last 100 years, but the sixgun is far from dead, and is still by far the best design found to date to easily handle the best and most powerful of the world's handgun cartridges.

The USFA Snubnose is the ultimate single-action belly gun.

The Uberti New Model Russian is a faithful replica of the Smith & Wesson Russian revolver.

Uberti Cattleman SAA replica with charcoal blue finish.

Uberti Stallion Rimfire Target sixgun.

Compact .357 Magnum double action sixgun from Rossi.

RIFLES Today

BY JACOB EDSON

Jake Edson is Managing Editor of Deer & Deer Hunting Magazine.

It's pretty clear which way the rifle market is trending these days. AR-style rifles continue to pour into gun shops, but stores big and small are unable to keep them in stock. This isn't surprising news for many shooters, and yet AR-style rifles weren't immediately accepted by the industry as a whole. For many years, the assault rifle stereotypes lingered — possibly because the gun is still used by so many branches of military, and a large portion of the general public viewed the entire AR-line as synonymous with the M16/M4.

Perhaps now, though, these perceptions are finally changing. Today, the AR is embraced in almost every corner of the shooting industry. Even big game hunters are now reaching for this platform as more and more of us are introduced to it.

If you don't understand the appeal of AR-style rifles you probably have never shot one. Simply put, these guns are a blast to shoot. Plus, the modular design allows endless modification and customization. And now, with even America's largest gunmaker, Remington, offering multiple AR models, the gun seems to have settled firmly into a respected sector of the shooting industry. In fact, the AR really has come full circle, because today's latest trend is to build derivatives of not the AR-15 — which is a .223/5.56 caliber weapon — but its predecessor, the larger-framed AR-10.

Up and down the product lines of most AR manufacturers (and there are now more than 60 manufacturers of AR-style rifles and parts) you can now find an assortment of calibers, from the miniscule 9mm Luger, up to big game hunting calibers such as .243 Win., 7mm-08 Rem., and the original AR-10, the .308 Win.

Larger calibers have even been designed specifically for the platform,

including the .450 Bushmaster, .458 SOCOM and .50 Beowulf.

That's not to say all other rifle designs are obsolete. In fact, bolt actions continue to be the favorite among the majority of shooters. In large part, our fascination in turnbolts stems from our love for long-range shooting. And that is precisely where the bolt-action market continues to advance. Tactical and varmint rifles are the fastest growing categories. And surprise, the AR-style guns have influenced this market as well — contributing to current trends toward modular stock designs in many of the newest tactical bolt actions. The other major movement is toward consumer-adjustable triggers. Almost every major bolt-action manufacturer has added a newly revamped trigger to their turnbolt lines.

With that, here's a look at the latest rifles.

ArmaLite

The AR designation got its start with Eugene Stoner and the Fairchild ArmaLite Corporation more than 50 years ago with the AR-10 .308 rifle. ArmaLite sold its rights to the "AR-10" and "AR-15" names to Colt in 1959, but the "original" AR-10 continues to flourish with its creator. The AR-10T features a free-floated, triple-lapped, stainless steel, match grade barrel. And now, the "T" is also chambered in 7mm-08 Rem., .260 Rem., .338 Federal and .243 Win. The rifle is equipped with new lightweight, freefloat handguards and a Picatinny railed upper. Plus, like all of ArmaLite's AR-10 flattop uppers, it is equipped with forward assist.

Barrett

Barrett's new M98B bolt-action rifle is chambered in .338 LM for military and law enforcement applications where a 7.62 NATO or even .300 Win. Mag. might not provide the long range punch necessary for every situation. This long-range tactical rifle features a short-throw bolt

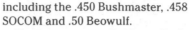

If there's a finer production bolt gun made than the Kimber 84M, we're not sure what it might be.

design and skeletonized aluminum stock with adjustable comb height and elevation. The modular design allows the user to adapt the rifle to fit their exact needs. The trigger is set at 2.5 lbs. and is shaped for a straight rearward pull. Two nuts prevent the adjustment screws from changing weight with repeated use and can be easily accessed from the top with the receiver broken down. A muzzle brake reduces rise and recoil, which Barrett says is similar to a 20-gauge shotgun. I can believe that, because the rifle weighs 13.5 lbs.!

Benelli

While Benelli's big introduction of 2009 is a shotgun, the company has added to its R1 line of semi-automatic rifles with the R1 Limited Edition. This premium grade R1 rifle is chambered in .30-06. It displays all of the style, balance and attention to detail expected in a fine European hunting rifle — including a highly figured AAA-Grade satin walnut stock and fore-end with 28 line-per-inch, fine-line checkering. The receiver features detailed engraving, gold inlay and highly polished bluing. On the inside, the gun features the R1's clean, efficient A.R.G.O. operating system. However, the

Limited is just that, and is only available through Benelli USA World Class Dealers.

Browning

Much like Benelli, Browning's big news for 2009 is an all-new semi-auto shotgun. Yet Browning has added to both its X-Bolt and A-Bolt rifle lines. For a lighter X-Bolt, try the new Micro Hunter with a satin, walnut stock sized for smaller shooters and shorter 20- and 22-inch barrels. The Micro Hunter is available in .22-50 Rem., .243 Win., 7mm-08 Rem., .308 Win., 270 WSM, 7mm WSM, 300 WSM and 325 WSM. It weighs in at 5 lbs., 6 oz., with the Super Short Action receiver and 6 lbs., 7 oz. in Short Action models. The X-Bolt Varmint Stalker goes the other way. It is features a medium-heavy barrel in four classic varmint calibers — .223 Rem., .22-250 Rem., 243 Win., and .308 Win. — with 24" or 26" barrels. The Varmint Stalker weighs about 8 lbs. All the X-Bolt models have a glass bedded and free-floating barrel. They feature the four-screw-per-base X-Lock scope mounting system, Inflex recoil pad and a bolt unlock button to allow the chamber to be opened with the safety in the on position. This year also

finds Super-Short Actions available on the standard X-Bolt models chambered in .223 Rem., and .22-250 Rem.

The already-expansive A-Bolt line gets two additions, the A-Bolt Target and Target Stainless. Both feature a new target-style stock with adjustable comb and a wide, flat fore-end. Both Target models are available in .223 Rem., .308 Win., and 300 WSM.

The BAR line gets a makeover, too, with a handsome new satin nickel finish and Grade II walnut stocks. These new BARs offer a near custom shop look with the same BAR action shooters have come to expect. In addition, 7mm-08 Rem., and .325 WSM have been added to the BAR caliber options.

Finally, the T-Bolt line of rimfire rifles gets the addition of left-hand models across the board. Improvements in materials and design have Browning promising greater accuracy and smoother operation, while the rifles still feature the popular rotary 10-round Double Helix magazine and an adjustable trigger. Lots of fun on the range.

Bushmaster

Bushmaster features a dizzying array of AR-15 rifles, each model with slightly different components. However, two new models are quite noteworthy. The first is the Bushmaster .450. This rifle is chambered for the new Bushmaster .450 round, developed in affiliation with Hornady. The big bore load is tamed by a tweaked AR-type gas impingement operating system and Izzy muzzle brake. The cartridge is adapted from a 6.5mm case with the neck cut off to accommodate a 250-grain Hornady SST FlexTip .450 caliber bullet. The five-round AR-style magazine is fitted with a single stack follower to allow for the diameter of the cartridge. Bullet velocity is reported at 2,200 fps. The chromoly steel barrels are rifled with a 1:24 twist to get the heavy bullet spinning.

The Bushmaster O.R.C. (Optics Ready Carbine) was developed because most sporting AR shooters will want to stick a scope on their pet rifles. Of course, add-on iron sights can be attached to the upper and milled gas block, but the flattop is optics-ready right out of the box. Meanwhile, the 16" barrel is chrome-lined in both the bore and chamber to provide accuracy, durability and maintenance ease. The six-position telescoping stock reduces overall length by 4 inches when compressed.

The Bushmaster BA50 rifle is designed for military, law enforcement and recre-

ational shooters who asked Bushmaster for a highly-accurate, low-recoil .50 BMG rifle. The bolt-action gun is designed to remain familiar to AR fans. It features lower and upper receivers machined from aluminum and a manganese phosphate finish. The Bushmaster barrel is free floated within a vented forend. The high-efficiency recoil-reducing brake limits felt recoil.

Finally comes Bushmaster's exclusive license deal with Magpul Industries for the production, future development and sales of Magpul's Masada weapon system. Renamed the Bushmaster ACR (Adaptive Combat Rifle), this weapon is one of the most anticipated releases of the year. At press time only a handful of ACRs were available for viewing, but the product is slowly coming online for military, law enforcement and civilian shooters. It will initially be offered in 5.56 NATO, but the key feature of this weapon system is its tool-less adaptability to a variety of calibers.

Basically, the Bushmaster ACR keeps the fundamentals of the Masada concept, such as the gas piston operating system, tool-less, quick change barrel and relocated charging handle and adds features such as a firing pin block and true ambidextrous controls. For those unfamiliar with the Masada prototypes, the weapon system is a combination of many rifle designs, incorporating a short-stroke gas system similar to the AR-18, the upper receiver charging handle location of the FN SCAR and the liberal use of polymer components popularized by Heckler & Koch. It maintains the M16 or AR15 trigger pack and barrel, while the quick-change barrel, adjustable gas regulator and charging handle, integral flip-up front sight, and storage compartments located in the stock are Magpul innovations. The first ACRs will be offered with 12.5", 16" and 18" barrels and three stock configurations. The 7.62×39mm conversion kits are promised but not yet in production.

Chapparal

Chapparal Arms Co. is already known for its high quality reproductions, including a beautiful Winchester Model 1873. But now the company is reproducing possibly the most popular rifle of all time, the venerable Winchester 1894. These high-quality '94s are available in .44 Rem. Mag, 44/40 WCF, .45 Colt, .30/30 WCF and .410 ga. The accurate reproductions feature high-grade wood and rich bluing. Each rifle is sold in a carefully designed nylon carry-case.

The Benelli RI Limited semi-auto is almost too pretty to take out in the field.

Today's classy Browning BAR LongTrac Grade II is a far cry from the original BAR.

Browning X-Bolt Varmint.

Southpaws who are interested in a straight-pull rimfire bolt rifle should take a look at Browning's T-Bolt Left Hand Varmint.

For those who think the M1892 was the sweetest, best-designed pistol-caliber lever carbine ever designed (and many do), the Charles Daly Large Loop in .45 Colt has a lot going for it.

Remington's ultra-funky, all-business Model 700 Target Tactical.

One of the most powerful lever-actions ever produced: the Marlin 1895 MXLR in .338 Marlin Express.

The short-action Marlin XS7 bolt gun.

Mossberg's wood-stocked 4x4 now has the LBA trigger. So does the synthetic version, by the way.

Mossberg's Model 817 Varmint in .17 HMR is a serious, purpose-built small game and varmint rifle.

Charles Daly

To complement its line of 1892 lever action standard and take down models, Charles Daly has added the 1892 Lever Action Large Loop carbine in .45 Colt. The rifle features a 20" barrel, walnut stock and saddle ring. Although this gun is a reproduction of the 1892 factory rifle, it features modern CNC machining and a carefully designed over-sized lever loop.

CZ USA

Brno Rifles is the newest brand in the CZ-USA family. It brings a high-end line of fixed-breech firearms from a well-known plant in Brno, Czech Republic, to the growing CZ family of firearms. The Brno Stopper is an over/under double rifle chambered in .458 Win. Mag. It features a select-grade walnut stock, elegant checkering and a semi-Schnabel fore-end. It offers a single mechanical trigger, short radius iron sights for fast shooting, and a barrel mounted sling attachment point.

The Brno Effect single-shot rifle weighs only 6 lbs. and features select walnut, a single set trigger, automatic safety, iron sights and includes scope bases. It is chambered in .30-06.

The Brno Combo gun is a great companion for predator calling or mixed bag hunts. The gun features 23-1/2" barrels: A 12-gauge, 3" magnum with Improved Modified choke sits over your choice of .243 Win., .308 Win., or .30-06. Features include an automatic safety, extractors, barrel mounted sling attachment and quarter rib iron sights. The shotgun barrel is fired with the rear trigger, while the front trigger includes a set function for precision shooting with the rifle barrel.

DPMS

DPMS Panther Arms follows the trend of offering multiple AR platforms in a variety of calibers. The Panther REPR comes with an 18" fluted, chrome-moly steel REPR contour barrel with 1:10 twist. The gun is chambered in 7.62 NATO and comes with a phosphated steel bolt and carrier that is heat-treated. The flattop receiver is thick walled and hard coated, with dust cover, shell deflector and forward assist machined as one unit. It comes with a Magpul Precision Rifle Stock in Coyote Brown and a Micro Gas Block. The rifle weighs 9.5 lbs. empty.

The popular Panther Sportical is also now offered in a 7.62 NATO configuration with 16" chrome-moly steel heavy barrel and A2 flash hider. The upper features a snag-free design and smooth-side look with no dust cover, shell deflector or forward assist. The raised Picatinny rail makes for easy optics mounting. It weighs 8.3 lbs.

FNH USA

FNH USA is now offering a full line of SPR bolt-action tactical precision rifles. The A3 G is chambered in .308 Winchester and offers controlled round feed, blade ejection, a two-lever trigger and a three-position safety. The 24" cold hammer-forged barrel is fluted, with a hard-chromed bore and is held to +/-.001" headspace to produce sub-1/2-MOA accuracy.

The FN A1 and A2 rifles are based on the Winchester Model 70 action. They offer massive external claw extractors for reliable ejection. A variety of barrel lengths and designs are available. The one-piece steel MIL-STD 1913 optical rail with an additional 20 MOA of elevation is factory-installed.

The PSR I rifle features the same rail, but also comes with a three-lever trigger that works on the simple principle of a pivoting lever. The trigger has a pull weight range from 3 to 5 lbs. and is factory set to 3-3/4 lbs.

The FNAR Standard and Heavy are based on the legendary BAR. The Standard is chambered in .308 Win., and offers an ambidextrous magazine release with a 20" cold hammer-forged fluted barrel. The gun features a one-piece, receiver-mounted MIL-STD 1913 optical rail. The pistol grip tactical stock is adjustable for comb height, cast on or cast off and length of pull.

Civilian shooters can now experience the versatility of FN's SCAR with the civilian-legal semi-auto versions of the U.S. Special Operations Command's newest service rifles. The SCAR 16S is chambered in 5.56 NATO, while the SCAR 17S fires the 7.62 NATO cartridge. Both feature the gas-operated, short stroke piston system for reduced fouling and user-interchangeable, free floating barrels. Fully–ambidextrous operating controls are intuitively placed and three accessory rails enable mounting of a wide variety of tactical lights and lasers. The side-folding polymer stock is fully adjustable for comb height and length of pull.

Harrington & Richardson

H&R Handi-Rifles offers accurate, affordable, single-shot rifles in a range of calibers all the way up to .500 S&W. The smaller-framed Compact Handi-Rifle is available in .223 Rem., .243 Win., and 7mm-08 Rem. Plus, the new Handi-Rifles in .44 and .357 Mag. are also available in versatile combo gun packages. Choose from a .44 Magnum/12-gauge slug gun combo or a .357 Mag/20-gauge slug gun combo. Each of these single-shot break-action combo rifles comes with two barrels that can be interchanged on the fly.

Heckler & Koch

The MR556 rifle is a descendent of the HK416 in a semi-automatic civilian version. It fires 5.56 NATO cartridges using the same HK gas piston system found on the HK416. The rifle is being produced at HK's brand new manufacturing facility in Newington, New Hampshire. It features a free-floating four-quadrant rail system/handguard, adjustable buttstock and 10-round magazine. The rifle weighs 8.6 pounds empty and offers a high-quality HK cold hammer forged barrel with a 1:7 twist.

Kimber

The Model 84M is known for its light weight and accuracy. Now, the 84M Classic Stainless is available in .243 Win., 7mm-08 Rem. And .308 Win. Each rifle features a stainless barreled action in a classic walnut stock. In addition, the Model 84M Montana is now available in .204 Ruger and .223 Rem.

The new Model 8400 Police Tactical is chambered in .300 Win. Mag., and Kimber is adding several new chamberings to its lines, including .280 Ackley Improved in the Model 8400 Classic Select and Montana models; 7mm Rem. Mag., in the 8400 Classic and Sonora; and .270 Win., and .30-06 Sprg., in the 8400 SuperAmerica.

Legacy Sports International

Legacy Sports is the importer of several new hunting and target rifles. First, the Howa line expands with the Ranchland Full Camo Combo. This package starts with a Howa M-1500 rifle and a Nikko Stirling 3-10x42mm riflescope and a high-quality one-piece base. All of this wears the same King's Desert Shadow camo pattern. The M-1500 features a Hogue OverMolded stock, and shooters can choose from six calibers from .223 Rem. to .308 Win.

The Puma line is new to many U.S. shooters but offers great shootability and good value. The Puma .22 LR is only 33.5" long and features a 16" barrel. It is available with wood or synthetic stock and comes with a 50-round drum magazine for extended shooting sessions. Of course, a 10-round stick magazine is available for use in areas with magazine capacity restrictions. This rimfire is a blast to shoot and is made by Pietta of Italy. *[Editor's Note: It's nice to see this PPSh-styled fun-gun back in production after several years' absence. Originals have become quite collectible in some circles. – DMS]*

The Puma line also includes a variety of lever-action centerfires made by Chiappa Firearms. The M-92 is offered with 20" or 24 1/4" octagonal barrels and 16" or 20" round barrels. Available calibers include .357 Mag., .44 Mag., .44/40 and .45 Colt. The M-86 is available in .45-70 Gov't and is available in 26" rifle and 22" carbine versions.

Marlin

The Marlin XL7 series of bolt-action rifles has received plenty of acclaim, and now Marlin announces the XS7 short action series of bolt-action rifles. The XS7 series is offered in three classic

Browning's X-Bolt Micro is a trim, snappy little rifle.

short action hunting calibers: .243 Win., 7mm-08 Rem., and .308 Win. The rifle comes in composite stock versions in standard black, compact black (with a shorter length of pull) and Realtree APG HD. The XS7 series exhibits all the proven features of the XL7, including are an accuracy enhancing Pro–Fire trigger system; Soft–Tech recoil pad; raised cheek piece; precision button rifled barrel with target-style recessed muzzle crown; fluted bolt; pillar bedded stock; and barrel nut construction to ensure proper headspace for improved accuracy.

The original XL7 also gets a bit of a makeover with more options, including attractive American walnut and brown laminated hardwood stock versions.

This year, Marlin is taking the guide rifle to the extreme with the introduction of the Model 1895SBL. The new 1895SBL is chambered for the legendary .45-70 Govt., and is built to handle the worst weather with a stainless steel barrel, receiver, trigger guard plate, loading gate and enlarged loop lever. Other distinguishing features include a weather-impervious laminated stock, heavy 18-1/2" barrel and six-shot tubular magazine. The 1895SBL features the XS Ghost Ring Sight System. It also comes standard with a XS lever rail that provides a rock-solid mounting platform for a variety of optics.

The popular Marlin Model 925 rimfire expands to include a .22 Win. Mag. It features a 22" Micro-Groove rifled barrel and a black synthetic stock with molded-in checkering and swivel studs. The T-900 Fire Control System, standard on most Marlin bolt-action rimfire rifles, enhances accuracy for target shooting or small game hunting.

Finally, Marlin announces two new lever action rifles chambered for the new .338 Marlin Express. This round is the latest offering in the Marlin Express family of cartridges and drives a 200-gr. bullet at 2,565 fps from a 24" barrel. The 338MXLR features a 24" stainless steel barrel, full pistol grip and black/grey, two-tone laminated stock. The 338MX version is designed for hunters who prefer traditional blued rifles. It features a 22" barrel and walnut stock.

Mossberg

Mossberg's big news is the new Lightning Bolt Action Trigger System for its centerfire bolt-action rifles. The LBA gives the shooter the flexibility to adjust the trigger pull without taking the rifle to a gunsmith. A simple twist of a standard screwdriver can adjust the trigger from 2 to 7 lbs. The design of the LBA trigger's sear engagement offers a crisp, creep-free trigger pull, while the trigger blade blocks the sear from releasing the striker unless the blade is fully depressed. The trigger is available on the full line of 4x4 and 100ATR bolt-action rifles.

The 4x4 line receives an additional upgrade with the availability of a "classic" stock. New 4X4 Classic models feature walnut, laminate and synthetic polymer stocks, each featuring Monte Carlo-style cheek pieces, slim-line grips, and soft, recoil absorbing buttpads. A detachable box magazine, smooth, quick-handling bolt, free-floating, 22" button-rifled barrel, and factory-installed Weaver-style scope bases round out the features.

The 100ATR line's newest member is the Night Train II. The model features the LBA trigger, a free-floating 22" button-rifled barrel, plus a factory-mounted Barska 6-24x60mm scope, muzzlebrake, Harris bipod and neoprene comb raising kit with foam cheek pad inserts. The integral top-load magazine offers a 4+1 capacity in .308 Win.

Mossberg also expands its line of 464 lever-action rifles with a 464 Pistol Grip model in .30-30 Win. The design centers on improved accuracy, performance and value. The new pistol-gripped 464 lever-action features diamond patterned cut checkering on the pistol grip and forearm for a stylish look and an easy grip in the field.

For rimfire fans, the all-new 817 Varmint combines the sleek style and handling of the standard 817 bolt-action with a bull barrel. Chambered in .17 HMR caliber, the action rests in a tough black synthetic stock and features a 21" free-floating barrel, recessed muzzle crown and factory-installed Weaver-style scope bases.

Another rimfire is aimed specifically at young shooters. The 801 Half Pint from Mossberg International is small, affordable and a perfect starter gun. This .22 LR has a 12-1/4" length of pull and 16" barrel. It weighs only 4 lbs. As the young shooter becomes more familiar with the gun, and more experienced, the removable single-shot magazine plug can be replaced with an optional 10-shot magazine.

Remington

Big Green made a huge splash last year with its entry into AR market. This year, the company continues to follow the market trend with the release of its own larger-caliber AR, the R-25. This rifle features a flattop upper, Picatinny gas block and fluted barrel with recessed hunting crown. The traditional two-stage trigger found on most AR rifles has been exchanged for a crisp, single-stage version that comes factory set at about 5 lbs. The rifle is available in .243 Win., 7mm-08 Rem., and .308 Win. It is compatible with all DPMS .308 Win.-type magazines. If this rifle doesn't legitimize the AR platform as a real big game hunting option, I don't know what will.

Of course, with the ease in adaptability of the AR platform, Remington fans also shouldn't be surprised that the company has added a few new models to the R-15 line. Most notable is the R-15 Hunter chambered for the brand new .30 Remington AR round. The rifle is similar to past R-15s but is chambered for the first .30 caliber round specifically produced to fit in an AR-15-sized upper. Remington reports big game hunting ballistics out past 200 yards, and the rifle I was able to test fire had little more kick than a standard .223 Rem.

The R-15 VTR SS Varmint features a 24" stainless barrel with the patent-pending Remington triangular barrel contour. The innovative barrel is meant to deliver repeat-shot accuracy of traditional heavy barrels without the weight. The R-15VTR Thumbhole features the maneuverability and rock-solid stability of a Bell & Carlson thumbhole stock. It has a 24" olive drab barrel that is fluted and features a recessed hunting crown.

Of course, the expansive 700 line also gets some new additions. First off, every rifle in the line gets the new X-Mark Pro adjustable trigger. This crisp, clean trigger comes factory set at 3.5 lbs. but is user adjustable with a 2-lb. range.

The Model 700 XHR brings the revolutionary triangular barrel contour from the varmint/target field to the big game realm. The barrel design shaves weight while maintaining the rigidity of a traditional heavy barrel. Plus the surface area facilitates rapid cooling for more accurate follow-up shots. The XHR is available in nine calibers from .243 Win. to 300 Rem. Ultra Mag.

The same barrel and trigger also find their way onto the new Model 700 Target Tactical. This rifle comes in .308 Win., and features a Bell & Carlson Medalist stock with adjustable comb and length of pull. The 5-R hammer-forged tactical target rifling is based on M-24 rifling for extreme accuracy.

Two new Remington varmint rifles are available. The Model 700 VTR Desert

Recon offers the same features as the 700 VTR with the addition of Digital Desert camo. Meanwhile, the 700 Varmint SF comes with a 26" heavy-contour barrel that is fluted for weight reduction and rapid cooling. The concave dish crown protects the rifling and promotes the best possible bullet flight.

Lefties get another option with the Model 700 SPS Synthetic in .270 Win., .30-06, 7mm Rem. Mag., and 300 Win. Mag.

Rock River Arms

Rock River Arms is also producing a wide range of AR-style rifles in multiple calibers. Its standard LAR 15 rifles are chambered in the .223 Wylde chamber, which was designed as a match chambering for semi-automatic rifles. It will accommodate both .223 Rem. and 5.56mm NATO ammunition. It is relieved in the case body to aid in extraction and features a shorter throat for improved accuracy. Other available chamberings are the LAR-458 in .458 SOCOM, the LAR-6.8 in 6.8 SPC, the LAR-8 in .308/7.62 and the LAR-9 in 9mm Luger. I expect the LAR-8 Varmint A4 to be a hot-seller among sportsmen. It features a 26" stainless bull barrel with 1:10 twist and weighs in at 11.6 lbs. The rifle promises 1 MOA accuracy at 100 yards.

Rossi

Rossi Firearms introduces its newest version of the Trifecta youth gun system. The system originally included easily interchangeable .243 Win. .22 LR and 20-gauge barrels. Now, Rossi offers more versatility and knock-down power with the option of choosing either a .243 Win., or .44 Magnum barrel. The Trifecta system features a removable cheek piece to gain the proper fit with each barrel option. Remove the cheek piece when using the 20-gauge shotgun barrel for proper alignment of the front-bead sight. With the cheek pad in place, the stock is perfect for using the .22 LR or either of the centerfire barrels with a scope. Both centerfire rifle barrels include a scope mount base that accepts any standard Weaver-style rings. The set also includes a hammer extension, custom carrying case and all-purpose strap. This year, the Trifecta is available in three laminate stock colors: green/brown, pink/black and gray/black.

Ruger

Sturm, Ruger has added several models to two of its most popular lines. Perhaps the most striking are three M77 Hawkeye Predator rifles in .223 Rem.,

Remington's M700 VTR Desert Recon Camo.

Remington might be on to something with this triangular barrel business. Every one we've fired has been dead-on. This one is the Model 700 XHR.

The Remington R-15 Hunter in .30 Remington AR is a lot like the .223 version – only moreso!

Remington's R-15 VTR SS is Big Green's top-of-the-line varminting AR.

The Ruger M77 Hawkeye Predator in .204, .22-250 or .223.

The Ruger M77 Hawkeye Tactical with Hogue overmolded stock.

Savage's Model 10BAST should appeal to tactical fans who like having several places to hang their stuff.

The ban-compliant SIG-Sauer 556 SCM.

Thompson/Center (now owned by Smith & Wesson) has entered the entry-level bolt gun sweepstakes with its new Venture.

Fans of the pre-'64 Winchester Model 70 will find a lot to like in the new M70 Featherweight Deluxe.

.22-250 Rem. and .204 Ruger calibers. They feature green and brown laminate stocks and matte stainless barrels and receivers. The .223 Rem. features a 26" barrel, while the .22-250 Rem. and .204 Ruger rifles come with 24" barrels. The Ruger two-stage target trigger, designed for precise shot placement, and the full-length medium weight barrels deliver long-range accuracy.

Ruger also announces the introduction of an M77 Hawkeye Tactical rifle. These bolt-action rifles, available in .223 Rem., .243 Win., and .308 Win., feature Hogue OverMolded synthetic stocks, alloy steel barrels, and receivers in the Hawkeye Matte Blue finish. They feature the Ruger two-stage target trigger and 20" heavy barrels. The rifles weigh 8.75 lbs. and are shipped with a Harris bipod.

The third addition to the line is the M77 Hawkeye Compact rifle. These 16-1/2"-barreled rifles have an overall length of 35-1/2 inches, and are ideal for heavy brush. The Hawkeye Compact rifles are available in a Hawkeye Matte Blued with an America walnut stock or the Hawkeye Matte Stainless model with a black laminate stock. The rifles are offered in eight short action calibers, including .300 RCM, 7.62x39 and 6.8SPC. The walnut and blued models weigh approximately 5.75 lbs., while their laminate and stainless counterparts average 6.25 lbs. each. They feature the smooth and crisp Ruger LC6 trigger, Mauser-type controlled feeding and a powerful claw extractor.

Ruger has also added models of the Mini-14 Ranch Rifle and Mini-14 Tactical Rifle. The blued 16-1/8"-barreled ATI Mini-14 comes equipped with a six-position collapsible/side folding buttstock. The stock features an adjustable cheekrest, a rubber buttpad, four picatinny rails, storage for batteries inside the stock tube, and six sling swivel stud mounting locations. The stock folds to the left side of receiver and the rifle can be fired from the folded position. The ATI Mini-14 weighs about 8 lbs. and has an overall length of 37-3/4" with the stock extended.

The Mini-14 Tactical Rifle features a 16-1/8" blued alloy steel barrel with flash suppressor, black synthetic stock, and is shipped with one 20-round magazine. It weighs approximately 6.75 lbs.

Sako

The new A7 from Sako boasts a bolt body machined from a solid piece of forged steel for superior strength and a smooth throw. The A7 features a lightweight composite stock with unique textured wave patterns for a sure grip in any weather. The barrel is cold-hammer forged with a hand-cut crown. The single-stage trigger system is crisp and precise, adjustable from 2 to 4 lbs. The A7 is available in 12 calibers and features a two-position safety with bolt-lock release. It comes with scope mount bases and features a detachable synthetic magazine with steel feed lips. It's a sharp-looking rifle.

Savage

Savage is rolling out several new tactical-style bolt-action rifles, headlined by the new modular sniper system in the Model 10 BAS. These rifles are based on the long-established 110 action but are built on a modular aluminum chassis that features the same three-dimensional bedding system included in the company's new Accu-Stock. But unlike the standard AccuStock, this system accepts most AR-style buttstocks and pistol grips, allowing the user to customize his bolt rifle – a tasty touch that will appeal to those accustomed to the feel of black guns. The 10 BAS will come in two configurations, the BAS with a M4-style buttstock and the BAS/T with a target-style, multi-adjustable buttstock that borrows from Savage's Model 12 Palma target rifle. Other features include the Savage Accu-Trigger, a 10-round detachable magazine, a 24" free-floating, fluted heavy barrel, a proprietary Savage muzzle brake, and an oversized bolt handle.

Savage also announces two new Model 10 precision law enforcement rifles with the standard AccuStock. This stock uses an aluminum spine and 3D bedding cradle molded into polymer composite, giving it many of the same properties of high-end aftermarket stocks. The Model 10 FCP features a 24" heavy, fluted barrel, matte finish and is available in .308 Win. and .223 Rem. Calibers. The Model 10 Precision Carbine comes in Digital Green camo and features a 20-inch medium-contour barrel.

Savage is also expanding its successful line of camouflage package guns with the addition of snow camo. The rifles will include full-coverage Realtree Hardwoods Snow camo on the stock, barrel, action, bases, rings and scope. The new additions include the Model 93 R17 XP Camo in .17 HMR and Model XP Predator Package in all current calibers, plus the addition of .243 Win.

SIG Sauer

SIG Sauer introduces the new SIG556 Classic semi-automatic rifle (chambered in – you guessed it! – 5.56) with an adjustable stock

Ruger ATI Mini-14

that snaps into a folded position and features an adjustable length of pull. The redesigned trigger housing improves access to the controls. The Classic is also available with a new diopter sighting system. The rear rotary diopter sight utilizes aperture calibrations from close-quarter ranges out to 100, 200 and 300 meters. Another new option is the SIG SCM. It features a fixed A2-style stock, 16" barrel with crowned muzzle, and it ships with a "pre-1994 ban" 10-round magazine.

Smith & Wesson

Smith & Wesson jumped into the long-gun market with both feet with its I-bolt. The gun features a T/C Precision barrel, three-position linear safety and X-bed stock and comes with a Weaver-style scope mount Posi-Lug system that locks the mount to the receiver for a stable optics platform. The I-bolt also features the Tru-Set trigger, which is adjustable from 3 to 6 lbs. I-bolts are available in .25-06 Rem., .270 Win., and .30-06 in black synthetic or Realtree AP HD. They also feature the advanced Weather Shield corrosion protection system.

New this year, Smith & Wesson also adapted its M&P15 to the Soviet 5.45x39 cartridge. The rifle looks the same as a standard M&P15, but internally, it's a new rifle with a new bolt to accept the differing rim diameter of the 5.45 cartridge.

The barrel is also customized to .221" with a 1:8-1/2 turn. It is clearly marked "5.45x39mm" to avoid any confusion with standard 5.56 NATO barrels. The magazine is also 5.45 specific. So what's the point of all this, considering the 5.45 isn't all that much different, ballistically speaking, from the 5.56 NATO round? In one word: economy. Surplus 5.45 ammunition can be had at almost half the price of 5.56 NATO rounds and even the high-end stuff is substantially less expensive, if you know where to shop.

Stag Arms

Stag Arms' follows the trend of offering a larger bore AR style rifle with its Stag 7 in 6.8 SPC. This rifle features a 20.77" stainless steel barrel, A3-style flattop upper, two-stage trigger and Hogue grip. Designed for sporting use, it comes with a five-round magazine. Like the rest of the Stag Arms line, it is available in a true left-hand model.

Steyr Arms

The STEYR SSG 08 is designed for sport shooting and tactical defense. It features an aluminum folding, adjustable cheek piece and butt plate with height marking, and an ergonomical, exchangeable pistol grip. Additional features include a Versa-Pod, muzzle brake, a

Picatinny rail, UIT rail on the stock and various picatinny rails on the forend.

Thompson/Center

Thompson/Center has introduced a new bolt gun called the Venture. Whereas the company's Icon is what we might call a top-shelf gun, the Venture is designed to deliver top-end accuracy at an entry-level price. It offers a 5R rifled match-grade barrel and match grade crown, adjustable precision trigger and a classic style composite stock. The rifle is guaranteed to deliver minute of angle accuracy at a reasonable price point. The venture is available in .270 Win., 7mm Rem. Mag., .30-06, and 300 Win. Mag.

Weatherby

The biggest news from Weatherby is in the rimfire market. The Mark XXII is now available in .22LR and .17 HMR. It features an eight-groove, target grade, button-rifled barrel, built to exact Olympic competition specifications. The fully adjustable single stage trigger allows for precise adjustment from 2 to 4.4 lbs. A raised comb Monte Carlo walnut stock is precision cut checkered, and the gun features a quick release magazine.

Meanwhile, the new Mark XXII SA was created in cooperation with Magnum Research to offer a semi-automatic rimfire that can boast the accuracy of a bolt-action. This rifle is also available in both .22 LR and .17 HMR. It features a newly designed bolt for more accurate firing pin placement, a quick-release rotary magazine, a hand-tuned trigger and a 20" contoured button-rifled barrel. The chamber is tighter and has a shorter tapered throat to perfectly center the bullet in the rifling prior to firing for enhanced accuracy. Another innovation is the rear cleaning port, which allows easy cleaning of the chamber and barrel.

The Vanguard line gets two new

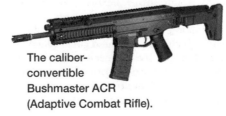

The caliber-convertible Bushmaster ACR (Adaptive Combat Rifle).

models with the Vanguard Predator and Vanguard Carbine. The Predator features a factory-tuned, fully adjustable trigger, injection molded composite stock, low density recoil pad and a complete Natural Gear camo finish. It is available in .223 Rem., .22-250 Rem., and .308 Win. The Vanguard Carbine weighs just 6.75 lbs. and features a 20" barrel. It is available in .223 Rem., .22-250 Rem., .243 Win., 7mm-08 Rem., and .308 Win.

Winchester

The Model 70 is back — and in a big way. Winchester Repeating Arms is offering the famous M70 in six new configurations. Each Model 70 features the M.O.A. Trigger System, operating on a simple pivoting lever principle. This trigger mechanism has been completely redesigned to exhibit zero take up, zero creep and zero overtravel. The pull weight ranges from 3 to 5 lbs. and is factory-set at 3-34. Of course the Model 70 still features an improved three-position safety, hammer-forged barrels and the classic blade-type ejector.

The Super Grade is available in five calibers and features a fancy grade walnut stock, one-piece bottom trigger guard and flush-mount hinged floorplate. The Extreme Weather SS features a Bell and Carlson composite stock, free-floating fluted stainless barrel and is available in 11 calibers. The Coyote Light features a medium-heavy fluted stainless barrel that is mounted in a skeletonized aluminum bedding block set in a lightweight carbon fiber composite stock. It is available in six short action and WSM calibers. The Model 70 Featherweight and Sporter models both feature satin finished walnut stocks, controlled round feeding, bedded actions and free-floating barrels along with Pachmayer Decelerator recoil pads. The Featherweight has a schnabel fore-end, and is available in 14 calibers from .22-250 Win. to .338 Win. Mag. The Sporter offers a sculpted cheeckpiece and comes in 10 calibers. Finally, the Ultimate Shadow comes with a lightweight rubberized composite stock. It features WinSorb recoil pad and weighs just 6.5 lbs. It's available in nine popular calibers.

Hunters and collectors will also be interested in Winchester Theodore Roosevelt Safari Centennial Model 1895 lever rifles. Both a Custom Grade and High Grade model feature intricate engraving and are chambered in .405 Win. This is a limited run with only 1,000 Custom Grade rifles and 1,500 High Grades available.

SHOT GUNS Today

BY **JOHN HAVILAND**

The nearly incalculable number of shotgun brands and models makes a person wonder who shoots all these guns and where. But it comes into focus when you consider all the target games and bird and big game hunting done with shotguns. During the last year I used shotguns to shoot sporting clays and trap and hunt southern bobwhite quail, grouse on mountain ridges, pheasants on the plains and waterfowl in the muck and mud. Let's see what new guns are out there for all that shooting and more.

Benelli

Benelli is making a 12- and 20-gauge set of limited edition guns based on its Legacy autoloader. The World Class Curator 12- and 20-gauges are limited to 250 specially numbered sets. The guns have AAA-grade walnut stocks and forearms with a satin finish and checkering of 28 lines per inch. A sterling silver medallion that can be custom engraved is set into the grip cap. Matched walnut butt plates are standard and rubber recoil pads are included.

The left side of the Curator's lower receiver is engraved with scrollwork and a medallion portraying a pair of chukar partridges set against a gold-overlaid mountain landscape. Below, floral engraving and cinquefoils frame an engraving of a bounding hare. On the right hand face, the gold details a rising ring-necked pheasant and a landing mallard duck.

The 12- and 20-gauge guns have 26" barrels and identical stock dimensions, but the 12 weighs 7.3 lbs. and the 20 six lbs.

Benelli is celebrating the sale of its two millionth shotgun with 200 World Class BiMIllionaire shotguns each in 12 and 20 gauge. Each gun in this limited release is specially numbered on the bottom of the receiver. The BiMillionaire is stocked in AAA-Grade walnut with a satin finish and the grip and forearm checkered 28 lines per inch. The BiMillionaire comes with a sterling silver medallion that can be custom engraved and set into the grip cap.

The gun's two-tone receiver is covered with floral scrollwork engraving that surrounds gold-accented game scenes. The left face of the receiver features a duck in flight and the right side displays the Spinone Italiano, northern Italy's classic gun dog. A half rosette with entwined gold overlay and shaded background accents both sides of the BiMillionaire's receiver base. The 12- and 20-gauge guns have 26" barrels and identical stock dimensions, but the 12 weighs 7.3 lbs. and the 20 six lbs.

Browning

The Maxus has replaced Browning's Gold autoloading shotgun. The Maxus has several new features and a gas system that fouls less to keep the gun shooting longer before cleaning.

The Power Drive Gas System on the Maxus features a gas piston with large exhaust ports to quickly bleed powder gases from heavy loads to soften recoil. The piston has a 20 percent longer stroke than other systems to reliably cycle light loads down to 1-1/8 oz. target shells. A rubber seal inside the gas piston keeps powder residue out of the action for cleaner operation. Recoil is further dampened with an Inflex Technology recoil pad. The pad is designed with materials with "directional deflection" to pull the comb down and away from the shooter's face.

The Lightning Trigger System on the Maxus produces a trigger with a light pull and a minimum of travel. Locktime averages .0052 seconds. The trigger assembly is also easily removed for cleaning. The safety button is set for right-handed shooters, but it is simple to reverse for left-hand use.

The Speed Lock Forearm uses a lever to lock and remove the forearm, eliminating the traditional screw-on cap. With the forearm removed, the plug in the tube magazine can be removed in a few seconds by using the Turnkey Magazine Plug that works with any vehicle or house key. The Speed Load Plus system takes the first shell fed into the magazine and runs it into the chamber. The Maxus also has a magazine cut-off that allows you to remove the duck shell in the chamber and replace it with a goose load when a goose is flying into range. *[Editor's note: It's nice to see that these features, once standard on the old Browning Auto-5, have found a home in the new Maxus. – DMS]* The magazine cutoff's best benefit is that the chamber can

Gail Haviland is posing with her Remington 11-87 Sportsman Turkey with the ShurShot stock she used to take her spring gobbler.

Browning Maxus Stalker

quickly be unloaded to safely cross the untold numbers of fences and ditches a hunter meets during a day afield. Pushing a latch quickly unloads all the shells in the magazine.

For now, Browning offers its Maxus in 12-gauge in 3" and 3-1/2" inch models. The receiver is aluminum and the barrel has a lightweight profile with flat ventilated rib. The composite stock has a close radius pistol grip with molded textured gripping and Browning's Dura-Touch Armor Coating for a sure grip in all weather conditions. All that adds up to a weight of 6-7/8 lbs.

Surely we will soon see walnut stocked upland, target and deer models.

The Browning Citori 625 over/under line has been expanded to include the 20- and 28-gauge and .410 in Field and Sporting models. The Citori 625 Feather Field has an aluminum receiver that reduces the weight of the 12-gauge Field by ¾ of a pound, to just under seven lbs. The Feather Field in 20-gauge weighs 5-1/2 lbs. All Feather Fields feature an engraved receiver. Forearms wear a Schnabel tip and stocks have a tight radius grip.

The Silver Sporting autoloading has a stock that can easily be adjusted up to 3/4" longer with three 1/4" spacers that fit between the stock and the Decelerator recoil pad.

I hunted with a similar Silver Hunter 20-gauge last fall to shoot mountain grouse and ducks. At 6 lbs., 5 oz., the Hunter was a light carry after blue grouse on the high ridges of grass and sparse stands of Douglas firs. The gun traced the steep downward pitch of the grouse when they flushed and an ounce of 6s tumbled them. In December's sleet and snow, the Hunter and I lay in a mud swamp beneath the whistling wings of greenhead mallards. When the ducks started to set in, tipping side to side to spill air from their wings, I wiped the muck from the gun and sat up. The ducks backpedaled, but it was too late.

Ithaca

David Dlubak and crew and crew in Upper Sandusky, Ohio, have been working for several years to resurrect the Ithaca Model 37 pump shotgun. All that work has paid off and Ithaca is up and running with five Model 37s and a special order 28-gauge pump.

The Ithaca Featherlight 12- and 20-gauge upland gun is made with a steel receiver while the Ultralight has an aluminum receiver and weighs about a pound less. Both models feature a ventilated rib, lengthened forcing cone, engraving on the receiver flats, three Briley choke tubes in 26, 28 or 30 inch barrels and a TRUGLO fiber optic red bead. The black walnut stocks and forearms have point pattern laser cut checkering. The ventilated rib on the barrels is held in place with a single screw.

The Deerslayer III is built on the Model 37 action with a fluted heavy walled rifled barrel with a 1:28 inch twist in 12 gauge and 1:24 inch twist for 20-gauge. Ithaca claims it shoots 4" groups at 200 yards because of the heavy barrel and because the barrel mates in the receiver with threads for a tight lockup. A Weaver optic base on the top of the receiver is included. A Pachmayr 750 Decelerator pad helps soak up recoil from slug loads. The gun is shipped with a hard case.

The Model 37 Defense 12-gauge has an 18-1/2" inch barrel with a cylinder bore and parkerized finish on the metal. The walnut stock wears a Pachmayr Decelerator pad and the "corncob" forearm has ring tail grooves like Model 37s of

Amy Brown is hammering away at sporting clays. Amy, and millions of other shooters, keep dozens of shotgun companies in business.

yesteryear. The gun holds four rounds in the magazine.

The Featherlight 28-gauge is a special order gun with a three inch chamber and a ventilated rib 26 or 28 inch barrel and black walnut stock and forearm. The "A Grade" has some engraving, the "AA" full cover engraving on the receiver. The "AAA" Grade has engraving and gold inlays of three flushing game birds and a pointing dog.

John Browning would be pleased the Model 37 he designed is back in production.

Legacy Sports

After a brief hiatus, Verona shotguns are back. Legacy Sports is importing the Verona line of side-by-side, over/under and autoloading guns.

The over/unders are made with nickel-plated steel receivers scaled to the 12-, 20- and 28-gauges and the .410-bore on a 28-gauge receiver. The chrome-lined 28 inch barrels come with full, improved modified, modified, improved cylinder and skeet choke tubes. The Hunting Combo is a two barrel set for the 20- and 28-gauge.

The Verona box lock side-by-side is made by Fausti in Italy. The receiver is color case hardened with laser engraved long sideplates. The straight grip stock has extended panels of point pattern checkering and the forearm is semi-beavertail. The 12- and 20-gauge models are on the same size receiver while the 28-gauge is made on a reduced size frame. All the guns have automatic ejectors and safeties and full, improved modified, modified, improved cylinder and skeet choke tubes.

The Verona autoloading guns feature an inertia driven pivoting bolt head that

Erik Smith used a Browning Silver 20-gauge shooting steel shot to take this wood duck.

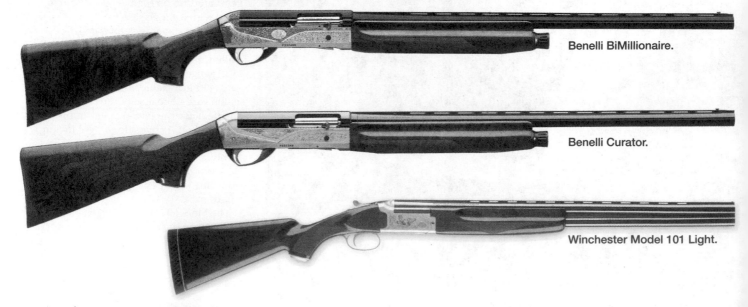

Benelli BiMillionaire.

Benelli Curator.

Winchester Model 101 Light.

locks into an extension of the barrel that reached back into the receiver. This is the same type of operating system used on Benelli and Franchi shotguns, and in fact the Verona guns look suspiciously similar to Franchi guns.

The Verona 12- and 20-gauge guns with 3" chambers have an aluminum receiver that is blued, nickel or grey and with a walnut or black synthetic stock and forearm. Twelve-gauge guns with 3-1/2" chamber have a black synthetic stock and forearm.

Slug guns have been added to the Escort line of 12- and 20-gauge pumps and autoloaders. Badger Barrels makes the 22" barrels with cut rifling and a 1:26 twist to shoot sabot slugs. A cantilever optic sight base is attached to the barrels and extends back over the receiver.

Merkel

The German Merkel company is so immersed in tradition that it has never offered screw in choke tubes on its over/under or side-by-side shotguns. That has kept companies such as Briley busy installing choke tubes on Merkel guns. But Merkel will break with convention this year by offering Briley screw-in chokes on a couple of its over/under guns. Merkel will find great acceptance of these guns because choke tubes make shotguns useful over a wider range of shooting and hunting.

I had the chance to shoot a Merkel Model 1620 EL side-by-side 20 gauge on a pleasant afternoon hunting Alabama bobwhite quail last January. We walked the edges of green grass fields behind a pointing dog. The quail flew in an arc across the open or in a beeline through the timber. The 20 came up in the cups of my hands and the little birds tumbled. After several months of northern winter, the sun felt warm and good on my shoulders.

New England Firearms

New England Firearms has introduced the Pardner Pump Cantilever Slug Gun 12-gauge with a fully rifled 22" barrel. The gun uses Ultragon rifling. The six oval-shaped lands and grooves impart bullet spin without leaving cuts on sabot jackets or lead slugs. The result is a better gas seal and less loss of pressure, which equals higher velocity and better accuracy. To round out this serious slug hunting combination, the Pardner Pump Slug Gun features a strong steel receiver, double action bars and a Monte Carlo-style stock in American Walnut or Black Synthetic, all at an attractive price.

Remington

The 887 Nitro Mag pump is Remington's new shotgun. The 887's barrel and receiver are sealed with a polymer ArmorLokt coating that protects all external metal from rust. The overmolding on the barrel also forms the sighting rib and front sight base. The trigger plate is also formed from polymer and holds a trigger assembly and shell carrier similar to the 870's. The carrier incorporates a "Flexi-Tab" that allows easy removal of shotshells from the magazine. The 887's bolt has dual locking lugs that fasten into the barrel tang. Right and

These bobwhite quail were taken with a Merkel 2000 over/under.

left extractors made of steel ensure that fired shells fly out of the chamber.

The 887's 28" barrel is chambered in 3-1/2" 12-gauge. The Synthetic model weighs 7-3/8 lbs. and has a black synthetic forearm and a SuperCell recoil pad on its stock, modified screw in choke tube and a Hi-Viz fiber optic front bead with interchangeable light pipes. The Waterfowl weighs 7-1/2 lbs. and is covered with Realtree Advantage Max-4 camouflage and has an Extended Over Decoys Rem Choke for nontoxic waterfowl loads.

The 12-ga. Model 870 SPS Super Slug's ShurShot synthetic stock has a large opening that allows a quick grasp of a near vertical grip that right- and left-handed hunters can use and an ex-tended forend for a secure grip. A Super-Cell recoil pad soaks up the cruel recoil from slug loads. The ShurShot stock also has molded-in swivel studs. A cantilever

Weaver-style optical sight base is mounted on its rifled barrel. The 870 Express Compact and Compact ShurShot are a bit shorter in the barrel and stock for smaller stature shooters. The Compact has a black synthetic stock with rough texture grip panels. A pink stock and forearm with an overlay camo pattern is also available to match feminine fashion wear.

The 870 Express Tactical line has been expanded to include the Express

Merkel's Einar Hoff is shooting a Merkel Model 1620 EL side-by-side 20 gauge at Alabama quail on a pleasant afternoon.

Tactical with a gray powder coat finish and an 870 Tactical with XS Ghost Ring Sights. The XS Ghost Ring Sights have a front XS blade and an XS Ghost Ring rear sight mounted on the receiver, adjustable for windage and elevation. The guns handle both 2-3/4" and 3" loads. A two-round magazine extension holds seven rounds under an 18-1/2" bar-rel with an Extended Tactical RemChoke tube.

Anymore, with hard hitting 20-ga. slugs and shotshell loads like Federal's new 1-1/2 oz. of HEAVYWEIGHT, the only thing a 20-gauge gun gives up to the 12 is a couple of pounds of weight. Remington has a couple of new 20-gauge guns:

The Model 870 Express ShurShot Fully Rifled – Canti-

A 4" barrel extension is an innovative feature on TriStar's new Viper Turkey/Waterfowl 12- and 20-ga. pumps.

The Browning Silver Sporting autoloader has a stock that can easily be adjusted up to 3/4" longer with three 1/4" spacers that fit between the stock and the Decelerator recoil pad.

Remington's new Model 887 Nitro Mag, here shown in Maxx4 camo.

Weatherby has extended its line of SA-08 autoloading shotguns with synthetic stocked 12- and 20-ga. models.

lever (FR-CL) has a .8" diameter 18-1/2" barrel with a 1:24 twist for 20-ga. sabot slugs. The barrel and receiver are finished in a black-oxide coating to match the synthetic fore-end and ShurShot stock. The gun's Weaver-style optic base is fixed to the barrel and extends back over the receiver. It weighs 6-3/8 lbs.

Four Model 870 Express Compact 20-ga. pump shotguns feature synthetic forearms and stocks with a shorter length of pull than standard 870s and an Adjustable Length of Pull System that adjusts LOP incrementally up to 1" with two 1/4" and one .5" spacers on the butt. A SuperCell recoil pad caps it off. The Express Compact weighs 6 lbs. with a 21" barrel and is offered with Black Synthetic, Realtree Hardwoods, Mossy Oak and pink camo stocks. The Express Compact Jr. has an 18-1/4" barrel and weighs 5-3/4 lbs.

The Model 11-87 Compact Sportsman also has the Adjustable Length of Pull System, a 21" barrel with a modified screw-in choke tube and synthetic stock and forearm. It weighs 6-1/2 lbs.

TriStar

A 4" barrel extension is an innovative feature on TriStar's new Viper Turkey/ Waterfowl 12- and 20-ga. pumps. The Viper's barrel is 24 inches long and is threaded to accept screw-in choke tubes for turkey hunting. With the choke tube removed, a 4" barrel extension screws in to lengthen the barrel to 28 inches for a smooth swing on waterfowl or upland birds. The seam is nearly unnoticeable between the barrel and extension. The muzzle of the barrel extension is threaded to accept choke tubes.

Weatherby

Weatherby has extended its line of SA-08 autoloading shotguns with synthetic stocked 12- and 20-ga. models. The Black Synthetic reduces weight a few ounces and sells for about $50 less than walnut stocked models.

All SA-08 models now have a dual valve system to help the guns cycle all 2-3/4" and 3" loads. The dual valve system has two valves that adjust gas bleed-off to compensate for different loads. The Light Load valve cycles 12-ga. loads from 7/8 oz. through 1-1/8 oz. and 20-ga. from 3/4 oz. to 7/8 oz. loads. The Heavy Load valve cycles everything from 2-3/4" to 3" magnum 2-oz. loads in the 12 gauge and 7/8 oz. loads to Federal's new turkey load of 1-1/2 oz. of HEAVYWEIGHT shot.

Winchester

The Winchester Speed Pump has been given some style refinements and renamed the Super X Pump. The Super X Shadow Field comes in 12 gauge with 3" chambers and 26" or 28" barrels. The synthetic stock and forearm have grip panels and some stylish triangles and lines. The Shadow Field comes with full, modified and improved cylinder choke tubes.

The Super X Defender has an 18 " barrel with a cylinder bore. It has a ringtail forearm for a sure grip and control while firing its five-round magazine dry.

The external metal and synthetic stock and forearm of the autoloading Super X3 Gray Shadow are covered with a gunmetal gray Perma-Cote Ultra Tough finish. The Gray Shadow has an Active Valve gas system and Inflex recoil pad to soak up the recoil of 12-gauge 3-1/2" shells.

The Winchester Model 101 Light over/under 12-gauge weighs a pound less than other Model 101s. The Light weighs 6 lbs. with a 26" barrel and 6 lbs., 5 oz. with a 28" barrel. The Light's aluminum receiver is decorated with a quail on the right side and flushing pheasants on the left. The bottom is engraved with a springer spaniel holding a bird. The walnut stock wears a ventilated Pachmayr Decelerator pad. Full, modified and improved cylinder choke tubes are included.

TACTICAL GEAR Today

BY KEVIN MICHALOWSKI

Mossberg's new Night Train II .308 looks good in digital camo.

Can anyone remember a time when there wasn't a Law Enforcement section at the SHOT Show? For a fairly new addition to the program, the LE section has really taken off. I can't remember the exact year, but it must have been two or three years after the creation of the section, when it became clear that such an area would be amazingly popular. As the shuttle bus I was riding pulled up to the convention center, an older gentleman turned to his partner in the seat next to him and said, "Well there certainly seems to be plenty of black pants and brown shirts again this year."

For once in my life I decided to bite my tongue and allow these two members of the braided leather suspender crowd to waddle on to whatever booth they would be manning. I was off in search of black nylon and Velcro and didn't need anyone getting in my way.

Cut to 2009 and the opening bell of the SHOT Show at Orlando's Orange County Convention Center. Once again I was thinking about people getting in my way. Only this time it was people wearing "black pants and brown shirts" blocking the aisles in the Law Enforcement section. Regardless of what people say about overall attendance of the 2009 SHOT show, things in the Law Enforcement section were hopping right from the start. Special thanks for the level of activity in the section can largely be attributed to the Obama Gun Sales Team, which was, at the time of the SHOT show, preparing for an historic Presidential inauguration ceremony. Call it *Fear and Loathing in Orlando.*

Tactical Guns

The big news was, of course the torrid pace of black gun sales. To spend too much time talking about wholesale and retail sales of the AR-15s and their clones would be to overstate the obvious. Suffice to say that everything with detachable magazine, pistol grip and bayonet lug was in high demand. But it wasn't just the black guns flying off the shelves. It was accessories as well. Everything from picatinny rails to collapsible stocks became hot commodities following the 2008 presidential election and the pace did not slow down as the inauguration approached. Demand was so strong that many manufacturers complained of an inability to get part parts.

Early in 2009 some makers were telling tales of woe about receiver shortages. Apparently manufacturers with the ability to machine AR components were not keeping pace with demand and backorders measured in months were common. All this led to some spillover sales for other models. Buyers were placing orders on everything from Springfield Armory's M-1A to the PTR-91 (a G-3 clone) to AK variants. It seemed that dealers just wanted to have some type of black rifle in stock for the coming spring.

But the truth is a black rifle is a black rifle. One AR clone works pretty much like another and the proliferation of black gun makers didn't really have anything new. A couple different variations on the gas-piston AR upper are now on the market, but they really didn't offer anything new and radical. All the hoopla and buying frenzy was based more on fear upcoming legislation than on anything new in the design arena. Still, as far as I'm concerned, any guns sales are good gun sales. And more buyers of black rifles mean more voters when the issue finally comes to the fore.

Well, there was one AR variant that really caught my eye. The AT-14 marketed by **American Tactical Imports** brings a whole new dimension to the AR platform. Now you can have an AR that fires .410 shotgun shells. Imagine the possibilities. If you thought the lever-action .410 shotguns that hit the market a few years back were fun, the AT-14 should put those to shame. This, of course, is not the first military style rifle to be chambered for the .410. There are still some of the old SMLE conversions floating around out there and the Saiga AK-styled shotguns. But the AT-14 looks to be infinitely more enjoyable.

The AT-14 is currently offered in two styles: the Classic and the Compact, both with five-round magazines, but a 15-round magazine will be available soon. The gun is a smooth bore, open-choke .410 shotgun. Both models have barrels at just over 20", and an overall length of 37.8". The Compact version of the AT-14 differs from the Classic version in its weight, with the Compact weighing in at just 5.73 lbs., while the Classic version tips the scales at 6.28 lbs.

Other big news in area of long guns is the release of the SCAR 16C, the civilian version of **FN**'s popular Special Combat Automatic Rifle, the MK 16. Chosen by the U.S. Special Operations Command as its next generation modular assault rifle, the MK 16 is a selective-fire 5.56x45mm NATO rifle with both full and semi-automatic capability using a short-stroke gas-piston system. The system offers three interchangeable barrels that can, if required, be switched by the individual operator in just minutes. The weapon is completely ambidextrous with a fully

free-floating barrel, multiple integral MIL-STD 1913 mounting rails and a telescoping, folding stock with adjustable cheekpiece. Having gotten my hands on the SCAR MK-16 I can tell you from personal experience it to completely controllable in both semi- and full-auto fire and just about perfect in the area of ergonomics. Like all FN products I've carried and tested, the MK-16 was totally reliable under a variety of conditions, but don't take my word for it. I think the USSOCOM trials were a bit tougher than my tests.

As is true with most military firearms, the public started clamoring for a civilian-legal version of the SCAR almost before USSOCOM got their first deliveries. Well, the folks in Belgium followed through with a semi-auto version that should keep shooters happy for years to come.

Another well know name in the firearms industry: **Mossberg** unveiled a couple very nice additions to their product line at the 2009 SHOT show. One is an old favorite that is now available to the general public; the other is a nice addition to the precision rifle community that gives shooters and even smaller agencies a suitable price point to get started.

The first is the venerable Mossberg Model 590A1 combat shotgun. This is the military version of the well-known Model 500. But for those who don't know the subtle differences, the Model 590A1 is beefed up for the rigors of military and police use. This is the only 12-gauge pump shotgun ever to pass the stringent U.S. Military Mil-Spec 3443 standard.

All models will come standard with heavy-walled barrels, metal trigger guards and safety buttons in a durable Parkerized finish. A full range of sighting options are also available in front bead, ghost ring rear or 3-dot configurations. Several variations of stocks will also be available with wood, synthetic, speed feed and adjustable aluminum. All 590A1 models come drilled and tapped from the factory making it easy to mount a picatinny rail, scope base or other optic options. Other accessories available for the 590A1 include heat shields, picatinny rails as well as orange buttstocks and

forearms for training purposes.

And there's even an optional bayonet. I haven't yet come up with a practical application for the bayonet, but it sure looks good. And that's good enough for me.

Mossberg has also moved up a notch in the tactical rifle market with its new 100ATR Night Train II bolt-action rifle. The Night Train II is a .308 Winchester bolt-gun equipped with the new adjustable LBA™ (Lightning Bolt Action) Trigger System and free-floating 22" button-rifled barrel. While I haven't fired the Night Train II, my initial observations and my first hands-on experience tell me this is nicely balanced and mobile tactical rifle. What I really like about the unit is that the Night Train II comes complete with a factory-mounted Barska 6-24 x 60mm variable scope; muzzlebrake; Harris Bipod; and neoprene comb raising kit with foam cheek pad inserts — all factory installed and ready to roll and all for one money as the auctioneers like to say. MSRP is just under $1,000, meaning you might be able to find it for about $800 some places. Now this is not a high-dollar package and it is not meant

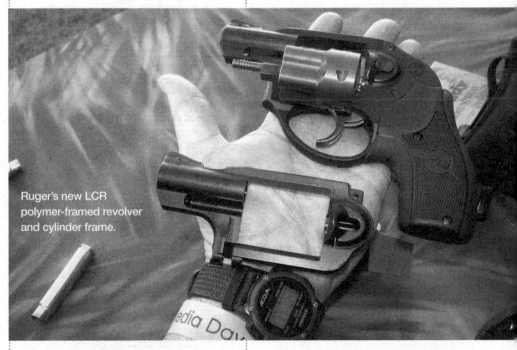

Ruger's new LCR polymer-framed revolver and cylinder frame.

to be. Instead, it should prove to be a good, serviceable rifle with a few nice bells and whistles. It should be a solid improvement over the original Night Train, which got a bad rap in some internet forums largely because people were comparing that gun to rifles costing six times more.

Personally, I want to shoot it. Look over that new trigger system and take

a good hard look through the Barska glass. Right now, I see no reason it will not live up to its billing and do what it is reasonably expected to do.

On the handgun side, the big news for 2009 revolved around small guns, with **Ruger**'s new LCR (light compact revolver) being the talk of the show floor. This polymer-framed revolver might not qualify as a true tactical arm, but you can be sure the little 12-oz. powerhouse will certainly end up as a back-up gun with some police officers on the street.

I say powerhouse because the LCR is designed to digest a steady diet of +P loads. Ruger, in creating the little five-shot revolver, uses a radical mix of design elements and the latest, greatest materials to ensure that the gun remains tough as nails while shaving every ounce. The coating used on the aluminum frame is not new, but it is the first time anyone ever thought to put it on a firearm offered to the commercial market. Another trademark look of the LCR is the radically fluted (almost reverse rebated) cylinder. There certainly is no extra metal left on that thing. Early reports are that the little gun has a bit of

bark, as one would expect with a 12-oz. revolver and +P loads, but is certainly controllable and well up to its task as a close-range defense gun.

This is the second year in a row that Ruger has kept the lid on a "secret" project in order to make a big splash at the SHOT show. The 2008 introduction of the LCP, Ruger's first entry into the pocket pistol market, came with equal

Les Baer's AR-based Police Special, possibly the finest civvie M4 available.

folks who don't make guns.

There is one notable exception. **Colt** had something really cool. The folks in Hartford, who spent lots of time making M-4s for the soldiers in the sandbox have developed the slickest folding stock for that rifle I have ever seen. Now I don't know about you, but I always thought the original collapsible stock on the AR-15/M-16, making it the CAR-15, was a bit of an afterthought. It appears to me it was whipped up without any real engineering and designed simply to fit over the buffer tube there in the stock.

After 30-some years of that traditional system, Colt put some thinking into a new folding stock and came up with a dual-fold mechanism that actually gets the butt out of the way and still allows shooter to fire the gun while the stock is folded. I'm told it was designed with motorcycle officers in mind, but a quick look says it will be a huge asset for paratroopers and vehicle operators. Now the folded version can be fired without any part of the stock banging into or hanging up on your forearm. Very nice.

Emergency Stuff

Here's a smooth segue. Let's go from guns to getting shot. We want one, but not the other. But the truth of the matter is that if bad guys are trying to get the upper hand, you might just end up with someone getting shot or cut. Then what do you do?

Well, SHOT 2009 brought us two great answers. The first is QuikClot, offered exclusively in the U.S. by **Adventure Medical Kits**. Their Field Trauma Kit retails for about $40 and has everything you need to deal with something like a gunshot wound or other severe injury. QuikClot, when applied to a GSW or severe cut works chemically fill to stop the bleeding in just minutes. You can apply your bandage over the top and alert the doctors at the emergency room that you have used the product. They will know what to do.

It is my opinion that every shooting range (public and private) and every police vehicle and ambulance in the country should have at least one of these kits readily available at all times. There's no telling when you'll need it and you likely won't need it often, but when you need it the QuikClot should be handy.

But, just for the sake of argument, let's say you don't have space in your kit for the Field Trauma bag from Adventure Medical Kits. Well, if that's the case, you should have the SWAT tourniquet from Remote Medical International. In this case SWAT stands for Stretch, Wrap and Tuck. It is just that easy to apply this flexible tourniquet. And, cooler still, the directions are printed right on the tourniquet in such a manner that you will get the proper tension and pressure on the wound when you stretch the material until the visual indicators are correct. I know that was a long sentence, but it just sounds better than, "Pull on the rubber band until the pattern looks like a checkerboard." On second thought, that last sentence is a pretty fair indication on how to use the SWAT tourniquet. At about $10 each, buy one and slip it in the pocket of your cargo pants. Just take it out and transfer it to your other pants before you do the laundry.

A Good Belt

Speaking of an easy way to move things around your duty belt, a new attachment system by **Uncle Mike's Law Enforcement** takes all the headaches out of trying to rearrange your duty belt. No longer do you need to take everything thing off and reweave the whole belt if you want to change flashlight holsters or swap out a handcuff case. The new system lets you

fanfare and market interest. When these little revolvers get into gun shops they likely will not stay on the shelves long.

Saying that someone has come out with another 1911 typically gets only a raised eyebrow and perhaps a monosyllabic "hmm" as a response. After 98 years, what more can you do with that classic design? The answer to that rhetorical question came from a rather unlikely source. The folks at **Doublestar** down in Tennessee are well known for making fine AR-15 rifles and carbines. Well, soon they will be well known for making a top-notch 1911 pistol. It seems what you can do with the 1911 is invest in high quality machinery and parts and make sure they're assembled with the utmost diligence and care. That's what they are doing over at Doublestar and their 1911 should give anyone who loves that grand old sidearm the chance to say, "Now that's a nice pistol."

The same is true for **Les Baer**. The company that carries his name has been making top-grade guns for a long time now by doing just what I described above: Taking top-quality parts and putting them together better than anyone else. But this year Les has a new twist as he's building up a double-stack .40 S&W on the 1911 platform. You might say, "It's been done before."

To which I would say, "Not the way Les does it."

And the same would hold true for his Police Special AR-variant. People are calling this thing the best-shooting M-4 clone they have ever seen. In one package you are getting patrol carbine size and precision accuracy, with 100-yard groups coming in at about a half an inch. Which means that rifle can shoot better than most of us can. That's just the way Les makes his stuff.

That about does it for the gun portion of my SHOT show Tactical Gear round-up. But I should let it be known that I only put the gun stuff on top of this article because this is *GUN Digest*. From my perspective most of the coolest innovations and biggest changes announced at the 2009 SHOT show came on the gear side of the equation. And they came mostly from flip tabs, open snaps and go. I know what you're thinking. "How tough can it be?" Well, my driver's license says I weigh 225 pounds and I was having a tug-o-war using a duty belt and a double magazine pouch with a guy who went at least 180. The attachment points didn't budge and the newly designed seams take up less space on the belt. It's as if every item is a quarter inch narrower thanks to the way Uncle Mikes is sewing its pouches and other belt accessories. If you don't believe me, get to a retailer and check it out. This is a cool belt.

Light 'Em Up

And if you get a belt you need to get a flashlight to hang on it. I like flashlights because, well, I'm afraid of the dark. Don't ask. There was an incident. This may be hard to believe, but flashlight technology is advancing like Rosie O'Donnell at a buffet line. I still remember when a flashlight was simply a metal tube designed to hold dead batteries.

Today, flashlights are amazing tools that provide illumination and, in some cases, an alternative to force. And the coolest one in the new Light for Life, by **5.11 Tactical**. Thanks to the perfection of new technology the Light For Life offers 90 minutes of run time at 90 lumens with a 90-second recharge time…all without using batteries. On the high setting, you can blast 270 lumen, but that shortens the run time.

My first look at the Light for Life gave me mixed feelings. The technology of the quick-recharge capacitors is awesome, but the light was larger than I expected. Probably because I'm used to a Streamlight or Blackhawk Gladius. While the Light for Life was large, it was incredibly light. In my opinion, I'd like to see the same technology in a light that's smaller and tough enough to break a car window. I think those days are coming.

Bushnell introduced another ultra-cool light. The HD™ Torch takes flashlight technology in a new direction. While conventional flashlight produce circular patterns of light that are uneven and irregular, the new HD Torch projects a perfectly square and uniform beam of light. The benefit is that the light beam is consistent from center to edge without dim areas or doughnuts of light.

Without the shadows that are typical with traditional flashlights, the HD

Torch makes objects stand out from their background for better definition and clarity. It is a great tool when searching for lost objects because the square beam lets the user search by quadrant or zone for more precision and efficiency. The HD torch can easily light up an entire wall without moving from side to side.

In the toughness department, the HD Torch is constructed of aircraft-grade aluminum and produces 165 Lumens of light with its powerful LED. Run time is 1.5 hours. It is powered by two 3-volt lithium batteries. There are two operating modes: high and safety-strobe for emergency use.

Another thing on the cool scale is the "Find Me" feature, a glowing "B" rear button that allows serves as a battery life indicator. The flashlight comes with two batteries and a lanyard all for just $80.

Night Vision

The **ATN** PS22-3 Day/Night Tactical Kit with Trijicon 4x32 ACOG 1 QRM is the ultimate operators sighting system by combining the ATN PS22-3 front sight with one of the best names in the daytime optical area – **Trijicon**. The PS22-3 uses ATN's standard third-generation image intensifier tubes (IIT). They have a micro channel plate, GAAs photocathode, and a completely self-contained integral high-voltage power supply. These tubes provide a combined increase in resolution, signal to noise and photosensitivity over tubes with a multi-alkali photocathode. Generation 3 is the standard for the USA military. Highlights of the Gen 3 specifications are the typical SNR of 22 and resolution of 64 lp/mm.

This thermal imaging unit is so good, you won't believe the things you can see.

The PS22-3 is packaged with a Trijicon 4x32 ACOG 1 QRM riflescope. Trijicon 4x32 ACOG scope TA01NSN with Amber Center Illumination for M4A1 fits the AR15/M16 flat-top rifles and includes the TA51 mount. Modifications to this Trijicon Special Forces TA01 NSN model include an integral rear ghost ring aperture and a tritium glow-in the-dark front sight (yellow center illumination) for close-quarter-combat/back-up sighting, and includes a flat-top adapter, back-up iron sights and dust cover.

Yes. It is about $5500, but if you need to see in

Colt Industries' new folding stock for the AR-15/M-16.

the dark and stop bad guys before they stop you, spend the money.

And Finally, The Big News

It seems everyone had a press conference of some sort at the SHOT show – which, of course, means a reporter can get kind of jaded. One announcement, however, really made an impression. BAE Systems is now under the one banner that is easily recognizable to cops around the world: **Safariland**. I guess if you are going to capitalize on brand identity in the LE community, Safariland is the one to go with. BAE Systems is a multi-billion-dollar company with their fingers in all sorts of things. But when it came to LE gear they were the umbrella for everything from Hatch gloves to Monadnock batons, Hiatt handcuffs and, of course Safariland holsters and gear. In total, BAE is bringing 19 companies and product lines under one banner; everything from duty gear to forensics equipment. This will be the 800-lb. gorilla in the marketplace and I fully expect they will continue to offer the best products, but now in one easy-to-find location. This might be the wave of the future, a few big players like Safariland, Blackhawk and 5.11 Tactical. We'll keep watching.

Until next time: stay safe.

FN's SCAR 16C, the civilian version of FN's popular Special Combat Automatic Rifle/MK 16.

BY WM. HOVEY SMITH

MUZZLE LOADERS Today

*T*he once old is now new, and the new will once more become old again.

This proverbial statement typifies the present state of the muzzleloading gun industry. There are new replica version of historic firearms, guns that are truer in spirit than in form to the originals, those that are adaptive variants of cartridge guns and new designs.

In the present American market, a competitive inline muzzleloader would appear to need to incorporate all, or most, of the following features:

- Fiber optic sights with the option of mounting a scope or other optical sight.
- Chambering that accommodates elongated .50-caliber bullets.
- Easy to operation function.
- Action, or barrel, parts that move, and remove, to provide easy loading and cleaning.
- Removable breech plug allowing 209 ignition and also be adaptable for musket and #11 percussion caps.
- Stainless-steel barrel option.
- Camo-clad stocks.
- Aluminum ramrod that can take a variety of fittings.
- Availability in several price ranges to appeal to larger market segments.
- Capability of digesting a 150-grain load of pellets or loose powder.
- Overbored or chamfered muzzle for easy bullet seating.
- Recoil pad or other recoil-reduction system.

Once an innovative feature has been pioneered by one company on its inline guns, it does not take long for it to be established as "the new industry standard" and for other companies to produce guns incorporating the new development. The result is that each year brings better muzzleloaders; older patterns are retired; and we who shoot these front-loading guns are the beneficiaries.

Some companies, such as Remington, have withdrawn from the muzzleloading market; CVA and Thompson/Center have stopped, or almost stopped, making side-lock muzzleloaders while more companies are producing substitute powders and accessories.

The Traditions Continue

"Just you wait a gall-darn minute!" I can hear some crusty buckskin-clad character shouting. While sales of inline guns dominate the American muzzle-loading market, new replicas of flint and percussion guns are being produced and are enormous fun to use.

A case in point is Davide Pedersoli's Howdah Hunter double-barreled pistol. Of several options available in .50 caliber, 20-gauge and this year in .58-caliber, I used the double .50-caliber version to hunt hogs from a tower stand in Texas. It takes skill to use primitive guns effectively, but they can be mastered.

This triumph over the adverse aspects of shooting traditional matchlock, flint or percussion guns has enduring appeal as does recapturing something of the feel of holding history in your hands.

Hunting Handguns

Black powder hunters are a subset of hunters and those who prefer the short guns are a tiny fraction of that group. To be a successful handgun hunter, the first step is to learn how to shoot pistol. I did bullseye shooting with cartridge guns for years before I hunted with muzzleloading pistols. The second task is developing effective loads. Mine have ranged from 4 grains of FFFFg for a .22 revolver to 100 grains of Triple Seven pellets for a .50-caliber Encore combined with bullets weighing bullets from 30 to 370 grains.

The penultimate event in handgun hunting is to apply the same sighting and trigger

MDM's break-open .50-cal. pistol. Let's hope it makes it to production someday.

pull discipline that was learned on the target range when a 300-lb. hog is in front of you snapping its teeth.

This is not the jab-the-gun-at-the-target-and-yank-the-trigger shooting style so often shown on TV. Such shots will likely result in a missed animal at 20 yards, or, worse yet, a bad hit. My own standard is if I can shoot squirrels with the pistol and load with a degree of consistency, then I am ready to hunt big game with that gun. It is also helpful to employ a rest, one that taken with you or improvised, as often as possible.

Muzzleloading handguns for small game include any that are .36-caliber and smaller and all percussion revolvers, including the .44s. Standouts in this group include the Traditions Crockett Pistol, a .32-caliber single shot, and the .44-caliber target-sighted Remington-pattern revolvers. Squirrels, rabbits, raccoons, armadillos and the like are suitable targets. I particularly like the now-discontinued Ruger Old Army revolver's adjustable sights that allowed it to be precisely sighted for a given load. Replica Colt and Remington revolvers without adjustable sights often shoot high, making them difficult to hit with. However, some Remington replicas with adjustable sights are available in stainless steel, which partly makes up for the Old Army's regrettable demise.

Apex

Loaded with 40-grains of FFg Triple Seven and using a CCI Magnum #11 cap, the Old Army will develop 458 ft/lbs of muzzle energy. Will it kill deer? The answer is yes, but only when bullets are precisely delivered at ranges of less than 20 yards. If a hunter has the fortitude to pass on every deer beyond that range and the ability to put that ball into the heart or spine, this load will take deer. The heart-shot deer will run and there will be no exit wound to give a good blood trail. It is unwise to hunt with such a gun unless you have a dog to help recover your animals. I use the Old Army to finish off game that is down and dying and to kill alligators with brain shots delivered at ranges of a few inches.

The most common big-game-capable muzzleloading pistols that are likely to be encountered are Traditions' Buck-hunter and Buckhunter Pro. These .50-caliber single shots have adjustable rear sights, but are best used with pistol scopes. My load for an early Buckhunter with a #11 nipple and a 12-1/2" barrel was 80 grains of FFg black powder and a 275-gr. Silver Lightning .44-caliber lead boattail in a sabot.

Because of its 15" barrel and ability to burn a larger powder charge, I purchased a 209X50 Thompson/Center Arms Encore pistol. This gun has an excellent set of adjustable sights, and I use them because it makes for a convenient holster carry. This is, by far, the most capable muzzleloading handgun that was once generally available. (Barrels can still be purchased through T-C's custom shop.) With a load of two 50-gr. Pyrodex or Triple Seven pellets, an over-powder Wonder Wad and a 370-grain T/C MaxiBall, I have taken several deer, hogs weighing over 300 lbs., and warthog. I've also used it to finish off a blue wildebeest. This load can be depended on to penetrate about 27" of tough game animal and plow through bone to do it.

For those who must shoot flint, there is one traditionally-styled gun that will get the job done. This is the Davide Pedersoli Bounty, which has a 14" .50-caliber barrel. I load this gun with 85 gr. of FFg GOEX black powder and a 295-gr. PowerBelt bullet. The problem is that

A variety of pistols suitable for handgun hunting. How many can you name?

Not a muzzleloader, but a black powder cartridge rifle: the Pedersoli aluminum-framed rolling block.

The .72-cal. Gibbs rifle from Pedersoli is a light gun that will give your shoulder a nice talking-to.

I had to hang two pounds of lead shot onto the end of the barrel so that I could hold onto the gun. I slowly worked up to this load watching pressure signs along the way (i.e., by how easily the vent plug removed).

A recent addition to the Pedersoli line is the Howdah Hunter. Since it was said to be "a hunter," I was audacious enough to hunt with the double-barreled .50-caliber pistol even though it had no rear sight. Because of the gun's relatively short 10-1/4" barrels, I installed musket cap nipples and worked up a load of 65 gr. of FFg Triple Seven, Wonder Wad and 370-gr. MaxiBall for the right barrel and the same powder charge and a 270-gr.

Buffalo Bullet Maxi Ball-et for the left. Two loads were used so that the barrels would shoot to about the same point of aim. I took a 200-lb. Texas boar hog with this gun at a range of 20 yards. The first shot was a spine shot to down the animal and the second barrel was used to finish it. The Howdah Hunter will hunt, but is for the close-range work, like shooting tigers off elephants' backs from the howdah.

These pistols and loads illustrate a variety of capabilities (see accompanying table.) The North American Arms Companion as a .22-caliber muzzleloader is not well sighted and develops even less power than a high speed .22 short. It is

CVA's Apex is a nicely-styled contemporary inline.

The Author's Hunting Loads

Name	Caliber	Powder	Bullet	Velocity (fps)	Energy (fpe)
North American Arms	.22	4 gr. FFFFg	30 gr. HB	344	7.88
Traditions Crockett	.32	20 gr. FFFg	44 gr. Round ball	1250	153
Ruger Old Army	.45	45 gr. Triple Seven*	143 gr. Round ball	1201	458
CVA Hawken	.50	65 gr. FFg	245 gr. Ball-et	902	443
Traditions Buckhunter Pro	.50/.44	80 gr. FFg	300 gr.**** Sabot	930	576
T/C Scout	.50	85 gr. FFg*	370 gr. MaxiBall	867	618
Pedersoli Bounty	.50	85 gr. FFg***	295 gr. PowerBelt	1060	736
Pedersoli Howdah L. Barrel	.50	60 gr. Triple Seven*	370 gr. MaxiBall	1022	853
Pedersoli Howdah R. Barrel	.50	60 gr. Triple Seven	270 gr. Maxi Ball-et	1088	710
T/C Encore	.50	100 gr. Pyrodex*	370 gr. MaxiBall	1024	858
Pedersoli H.F. 1807	.58/.45*	85 gr. FFg.	250 gr. Sabot	704	275
T/C Encore Turkey Barrel	12-gauge	110 gr. FFg**	.690" Round Ball	731	481

Notes:
All powder measurements by volume.
*Loads used a lubricated Wonder Wad between the powder and bullet.

**Ball contained in a Winchester Red AA wad for 1-¼ oz. shot.
***Required the addition of a counterweight taped on the end of the barrel to prevent the pistol from flying from the hand with the shot.
**** Not original bullet used on hunt.

not a toy and can penetrate ½ of pine or 40 sheets of typing paper. I mostly use it for finishing off crippled squirrels. I was not impressed with the performance of the 12-gauge round ball fired from the smooth bore 24" turkey barrel fitted to the Encore pistol frame. I did kill deer with this load, but the animal indicated no signs of being hit. The .690" round ball passed through it, cutting like an arrow rather than expanding.

Of the guns that I have used, the Encore 209X50 muzzleloading pistol is my preferred gun for hunting deer-sized game, with the longer-barreled Traditions Buckhunter Pros offering good performance in a less-expensive package.

Because of the small market for big-game-capable muzzleloading handguns, they are often only offered by companies for a year or two and then discontinued. In short, if a potential user sees one that he likes, it is best to buy it. Traditions has their Buckhunter Pro in redesign and have not set a date for its reintroduction. Similarly, MDM has shown a break-barrel muzzleloading pistol at previous SHOT Shows and plans to introduce it within the next few years.

CVA

CVA's Apex is a new, good-looking, break-open muzzleloading rifle that offers advanced features such as a pull-

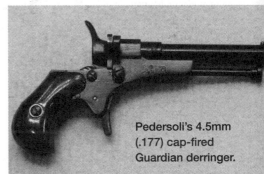

Pedersoli's 4.5mm (.177) cap-fired Guardian derringer.

out trigger group, externally adjustable trigger, redesigned stock and premium-quality interchangeable rimfire and centerfire blued or stainless barrels.

The company went through a learning curve to produce this gun. It took features like the excellent trigger and Bergara Barrels from their Accura and the concept of interchangeable barrels from their Optima Elite and combined them to make the Apex, although barrels will not interchange between the two models. The Apex is available in .45 and .50 calibers as a muzzleloader and presently with .45-70, .300 Win. Mag., .30-06, .270, 7mm-08, .243, .223, .222, .22-250 and .22 Rim-Fire barrels with more to come. As a muzzleloader, it retails for between $575-$650.

For approximately the same price, the older Optima Elite is offered in a break-action combo with both muzzleloading and centerfire barrels in .30-06, .270 and

Pedersoli's double-barreled Howdah Hunter (here broken down) is a replica of the mid-Victorian Howdah pistol. Should be just the thing if a tiger leaps up on your elephant! Note the skull-popper grip cap.

Thompson Center Bone Collector.

.243. For states that require muzzle-loaders with open ignition, the bolt-action Elkhorn Pro offer that option at prices of about $300 for the Elkhorn and $150 for the striker-fired .50-caliber Buckhorn. The Buckhorn and falling-barrel Wolf are CVA's entry priced models with the last being sold for about $200, depending on options. The weights of these guns increase from 6.3 lbs. for the Buckhorn to 8 lbs. for the muzzleloading version of the Apex. This added weight makes the heavier guns more comfortable to shoot with 150-gr. loads and increases the likelihood of making accurate off-hand shots.

In a class by itself the CVA Electra, which employs a battery, circuit boards and electric ignition, is reputed to be enjoying robust sales for those who want to move beyond impact ignition in muzzleloading guns for easier shooting and accurate shot placement.

Knight Rifles

Knight was in somewhat of a holding pattern this year with the principal change being the discontinuance of the Revolution rifle although its Rolling Block muzzleloader (about $400) uses the same frame and much resembles it. Also absent from its current catalogue is the TK-2000 muzzleloading shotgun. Its place is apparently taken by the 12-ga. cartridge barrel offered in the Wurfflein (muzzleloader with rifle or shotgun barrel combo $700-$850). *[Editor's note: It's good to see the grand old name of Wurfflein resurrected after a century or so! – DMS]* There are also new chambering for .444 Marlin and 12-ga. slug barrel in the drop-barreled Wurfflein and some new camo patterns for the Rolling Block and Shadow (about $350). One aspect of the Wurfflein's barrels that improves their accuracy is that the forends are free-floated by being attached to a hanger, rather than being screwed onto the barrel, thus removing one source of shot-to-shot variation.

Davide Pedersoli

Davide Pedersoli is noted for its extensive line of replica firearms and has added some variants to its line. The Gibbs Rifle, which has been available in .45 caliber and 12-ga. shotgun, will also be offered with a .72-caliber rifled barrel

for about $1400. This derivation was produced by the expedient of rifling the existing cylinder-bored shotgun and putting sights on it. The result is a single-barreled large-bore gun that could be used on deer, hogs and black bear if employed with patched hardened lead balls and charges of 100-150 grains of FFg black powder. Stiff charges will be uncomfortable to shoot in the 7-¾-lb. gun. The concept is good, but the gun needs a heavier, longer barrel in this caliber.

On the tiny end of the scale, Pedersoli has also introduced a small 4.5mm (.177) Guardian derringer ($236) that uses a 209 primer to fire lead BBs – just the thing for dispatching a trapped mouse in the hunt cabin. New cartridge variants include a handsome Sharps Old West (about $1900) in either maple or walnut stocks, brass name plate and stock keys, that is chambered in .45-70. This 1874-style Sharps accepts the company's extensive line of sights and accessories. Also new is an aluminum-framed model of the rolling block Mississippi Hunter in .45-70, .38-55, .45 L.C. and .357 Magnum. This rifle is drilled and tapped for users who opt for modern optical sights.

Thompson-Center Arms

I first ran into Michael Waddell nearly a decade ago at Realtree's factory in Columbus, Georgia. He was then a champion turkey caller who had started a few weeks before at Realtree. Nowadays he is a family man with young children and his own "Bone Collector" TV show. Thompson/Center credits him with designing their Bone Collector (about $650) that is based on the aluminum Triumph falling-barrel action, a recoil-absorbing stock and hand-detachable breechplug with, what else, a Realtree AP camo finish.

This gun combined with the company's extensive Encore muzzleloading and cartridge gun line, the newer Endeavor (around $800) frame, the falling-breach Omega ($350-$700) and that old standby,

the T/C Hawken ($750) rifle in percussion ignition offer a variety of capable guns for the muzzleloading hunter. My current choice would be between the Omega, which is a simple design that functions very well, and the Hawken percussion rifle in long guns. I consider the highest evolution of the Encore design to be 209X50 muzzleloading pistol.

Traditions

Unlike its competitors, Traditions has expanded its line of side-lock muzzleloading guns and even included a new flintlock Pirate Pistol. The company has also improved the PA Pellet Flintlock

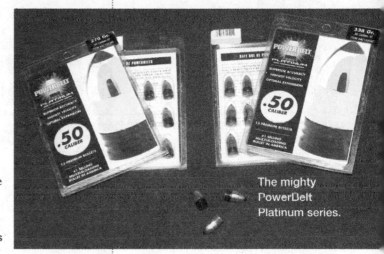

The mighty PowerBelt Platinum series.

by adding a larger specially-hardened frizzen. Also uncommon is that this flint-lock is offered in right and left-handed versions. The PA Pellet weighs in at 7 lbs. and retails for about $400, depending on options. The heavyweight in the line is the Rex Over/Under .50-caliber muzzleloading rifle. This gun weighs 12 lbs. and costs about $1,700. I used a 150-grain load of Hodgdon's new IMR Red Hot pellets and a 338-gr. PowerBelt bullet to drop a doe in its tracks this year, and I have an African trip planned for next year for Cape Buffalo. I am also undergoing weight training in preparation for carrying this gun all day and still have enough arm strength to use it when the Cape buffalo appears.

In inline persuasion, Traditions' new gun for 2009 is the Vortek, which has an aluminum action featuring the front-of-trigger-guard opening mechanism used in the company's drop-barreled muzzleloaders. This gun also has a drop-down trigger group and a new accelerator breech plug to allow for easier cleaning. The gun weighs 7-½ lbs., and not the

How PowerBelt bullets are made.

Accessories

Although I shoot a variety of bullets, I have followed the evolution of PowerBelt bullets from the start of the company, when they were called BlackBelts, to the present. Michael McMichael, who started the company, conceived of the notion of loading a plastic-skirted projectile made of soft lead that was sufficiently under-bore-size to be easily loaded and slug-up to groove diameter when it was fired. Over the years I have shot PowerBelts in .45 caliber in Africa and the USA. and in .50 caliber from a number of pistols and rifles on deer and hogs. I have been pleased with their performance.

A few years ago I did a factory visit and Idaho bear hunt with Dan Hall using prototype Platinum PowerBelts. The silver-colored bullets are still soft lead coated with copper, but with a new

12-½ as stated in the catalog.

Variants on the company's Pursuit drop barreled rifles include the Tip-up in .45-70 for Mississippi and Louisiana hunters and the Outfitter with interchangeable muzzleloading and centerfire rifle barrels in .243, 270, .308 and .30-06. These sell for about $500 with American-made Wilson barrels. Remaining in the line are the Pursuit muzzleloading rifles, the Yukon drop breech, Tracker 209 striker-fired inline and Evolution bolt action. The Northwest edition of the Pursuit has exposed ignition in the drop-barreled gun for the states that require it. Traditions' bottom-dollar inline is the Tracker, a 6-½-lb. gun that generally retails for less than $200 and will accept scope mounts. This lightweight gun is best used with loads of about 100 grains of powder and bullets not weighing over 300 grains.

For the first time Traditions is offering its miniature shooting cannon in kit form. These have .50-.69 caliber barrels in both land and naval patterns at prices of between about $200-$250.

Other Makers

Still in the muzzleloading business,

Knight's new Shadow break-open.

but with not much happening in regards to new guns, MDM is still producing its distinctive line of drop-barrel muzzleloaders, and Rossi continues to offer very attractive packages with muzzleloading, centerfire rifle, shotgun and/or rimfire barrels in various combinations. Dixie Gun Works and Navy Arms still offer their lines of imported muzzleloading firearms. No changes were made this year in Savage's model 10ML-II, which is the only muzzleloader designed to use some smokeless powders.

molecular arrangement to make the metal slicker in the bore. One shot at 30 yards fatally wounded the bear, although another was used to kill it. These bullets expand well with either hollow or protected points and only the 444-gr. version is now offered in a flat-point version. The steel-pointed Dangerous Game Bullet has now been discontinued. McMichael said that he cannot recommend the 444-gr. bullets for Cape Buffalo because he fears that the soft lead will expand prematurely

Traditions Vortek with rubber overmolded stock drop out trigger assembly and quick removal breechplug.

Silver Stag knife. These knives are also available with customer-supplied handle material.

In the powder arena, Hodgdon has purchased GOEX and will continue that firm's black powder production at the Louisiana plant. They also announced a new line of IMR White Hot pelletized black power substitute powder. This is available in 50-grain FFg-equivalent pellets. This product joins their existing line of substitute products including loose and pelletized Pyrodex and Triple Seven. Next year I will have more to say about these and other black powder substitutes, including some that are citric-acid based and another made in South Africa.

All told, muzzleloading in 2009 exhibited a vitality that is nothing short of amazing for a technology that only 50 years ago was considered to have reached its highest stage of development in the early 1870s. What's possibly left to do? How about a three-shot .50-caliber muzzleloading revolver with a 15" barrel? Revolvers in .45-70 are already being made. The muzzleloading version's frame would be about as deep and would require some new innards, but it could contain sufficient powder to make hunters out of front-stuffing revolvers. Put adjustable sights on it and the result would be a very heavy, but effective, gun. Projected sales would be very small indeed.

on the mud-caked hide and ribs and not penetrate sufficiently to take out both lungs on broadside shots. On soft-skinned animals, he says, the bullet works fine.

Modern manufacturing methods in their plant in Nampa, Idaho, ensures top-notch quality for these bullets. I have used them to make kills on deer out to about 135 yards and on kudu and zebra and they have performed very well. Besides their killing capabilities, the best thing about them is the ease with which they can be reloaded for a second shot.

Two knives attracted my attention last year. One is the Texas Buck Buster made by Rodney Parish. This is a one-stop cleaning tool that can skin, gut and quarter whitetail deer very well. Better practiced than I, Parish can skin and quarter a deer in about five minutes using his tool. This product was once licensed to Do All and produced under that brand. That arrangement was dissolved, and Parish offers his original version which he heartily endorses.

The other notable knife is produced by Silver Stag knife company in Blaine, Washington. This, and all the company's knives, are handled in deer or elk antler. The company offers the unique service of putting your antler materials on your special-order knife, which can be as small as a patch knife to as large as a sword. These handles can be installed with or without scrimshaw engraving. I cannot think of a better way to preserve the memory of a youngster's first black-powder buck than having a knife made using the animal's antlers.

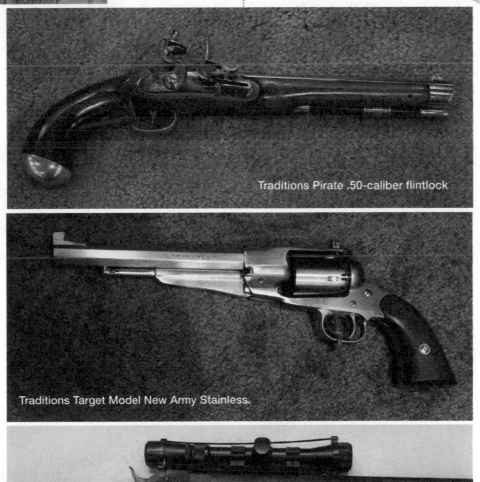

Traditions Pirate .50-caliber flintlock

Traditions Target Model New Army Stainless.

Pedersoli's aluminum-framed Mississippi Hunter rolling block.

AIRGUNS Today

BY MICHAEL SCHOBY

A majority of hunters and shooters still regard airguns with the nostalgic nod to their days as a youth, rambling around their backyard plinking cans and maybe even occasionally attempting to wing an intruding starling or ground squirrel. But the fact is today's airguns are a far cry from the prized Red Ryder of *Christmas Story* lore. In reality, modern air rifles and air pistols possess what could be considered very adult attitudes, boasting all the engineering and technology of more powerful centerfire arms (including price).

While models designed for the beginning shooter are certainly still available, take a deeper look on the store shelves and you'll spy numerous airguns that can deliver tack-driving performance and enough down-range energy to take down varmints, predators and even large game.

One of the latest trends driving both accuracy and power in the airgun world is the increased interest in PCP models or precharged pneumatics, guns that use a reservoir of compressed air to launch the projectile, be it a pellet or BB. These guns boast virtually no recoil and some models can push a pellet at more than 1,100 fps, a fact that will astound most gunpowder purists. The trend toward PCPs grew into fashion in Europe, but has made its way to our shores in the past few years as noted by many of today's top offerings by manufacturers doing business in the states.

Whether you're curious about the latest PCP model or high-performing traditional powered airguns, following are some of today's guns to consider.

Air Force Air Guns Edge

The Edge is one serious competition-grade airgun and, though it boasts many precision-class features, is approved by the Civilian Marksmanship Program (CMP) for Sporter-class competition. It features an ambidextrous cocking knob, adjustable length of pull and an adjustable forend for a perfect fit to the shooter. The Edge boasts Air Force Air Guns' TS1 precision target sight along with a hooded front site to reduce glare and enhance sighting, and you can get it in any color you want as long as it's red or blue.

The .177-caliber air rifle has a max fill pressure of 3000 psi or 200 bar of pneumatic pressure, which delivers pellets at 500 to 550 fps. It can handle up to 100 shots on a single tankful of compressed air for lots of shooting before needing to refill. The length of pull is adjustable between 10-1/2 and 15-1/2 inches, the trigger pull is set at 1-1/2 lbs. and the entire gun weighs in at a solid 6-3/4 lbs. Overall length is between 34-1/4 inches and 39-1/4 inches, depending on how a shooter adjusts it to fit. ($600; airforceairguns.com)

Beeman Falcon R

The Falcon R will garner the most high-end gun enthusiast's appreciation with its attention to detail and respect for classic firearm styling. Just some of the luxury features of this PCP tack-driver include custom designed, fine grain wood stocks in either beech or walnut. The Breech Block receiver is manufactured from aircraft-grade #7075 aluminum alloy for reduced weight without sacrificing steel-hard strength. The Lothar Walther barrels come in match grade or 12-groove versions.

The bolt-action Falcon R has an eight-pellet magazine and the two-stage, multi-adjustable trigger is factory set at

The top-quality Beeman Falcon R has a free-floating barrel for extreme accuracy.

2 lbs. A single attachment point between the stock and barrel creates a free-floating action for optimal accuracy; this is a feature you don't often find on an airgun. The Falcon R is available in .177, .22, and .25 calibers and delivers a velocity of 970, 860 and 710 fps respectively. Regardless of caliber, each variation has a total length of 43-1/2 inches and tips the scales at just over 7-1/3 lbs. This is one sweet shooter, but it comes at a sweet-shooter's price. Expect to pay more than a grand for this high-end

The AirForce Edge has plenty of serious target features, and it's available in red or blue finish to boot!

Gamo's Hunter Extreme is a .177- or .22-cal. scorcher that shoots pellets at an advertised 1,300 and 1600 fps, respectively.

air rifle. ($1,185 for .177 and .22 models, $1,200 for the .25; beeman.com)

Crosman Benjamin Marauder PCP

Through its Benjamin brand Marauder PCP, Crosman has found a way to get 3,000-psi performance (the industry norm) out of a 2,000-psi delivery system. Available in both .177- and .22-caliber multi-shot, bolt-action versions, each caliber delivers pellets at 1,100 fps and 1,000 fps respectively.

The Marauder features a dark, finished hardwood stock with an ambidextrous raised comb and custom checkering. The choked and internal shrouded barrel works to both limit the audible report and enhance accuracy. Other features include a two-stage, adjustable match-grade trigger, machined aluminum breech with a groove designed to accept 11 mm scope mounts, an auto-indexing 10-round clip and a built-in pressure gauge to display the gun's current air charge. The Marauder can operate off compressed air, supplied by Benjamin's patented hand pump, or the gun can be powered from CO_2. A single tank will deliver a minimum of 35 to 45 shots. (crosman.com)

Crosman Recruit

Throughout its history, Crosman has been responsible to introducing the joy of shooting to young participants and it continues this effort with the Recruit, a .177-caliber BB/pellet combo rifle powered by a multi-pump pneumatic charging system. The butt stock is fully adjustable to accommodate shooters of various sizes and is built on Crosman's pneumatic frame. It is finished in an all-black synthetic stock, and the receiver is grooved to accept optics.

The reservoir holds up to 200 BBs and the manual clip holds 5 pellets. The multi-pump pneumatic can deliver velocities of up to 680 fps with BBs and 645 fps with pellets. (crosman.com)

Gamo Hunter Extreme

Designed for serious airgun hunters, Gamo's Hunter Extreme sends PBA Raptor .177-caliber pellets downrange at a blistering 1,600 fps and .22-caliber pellets at an equally impressive 1,300 fps. It is a spring-piston, break-barrel air rifle with a rifled, bull barrel for superior accuracy. The hardwood stock is checkered and boasts a raised cheekpiece for right-handed shooters. The stock is also fitted with a rubber recoil pad. It also features an automatic cocking safety along with a two-stage adjustable trigger.

Trigger pull is set at 3-3/4 lbs., while the unscoped gun stretches 48-1/2 inches and weighs a hefty 9 lbs. It is set for 58 lbs. cocking effort, so the Hunter Extreme certainly doesn't fall under the "Toy" category. The receiver is topped with a grooved rail for the company's

3x9-50 illuminated center glass-etched reticle. The Hunter Extreme is a great option for small- and medium-sized game. ($530; gamousa.com)

Ruger Airhawk

If you're looking for a gun that truly combines quality with value, the Ruger Airhawk delivers. At a price point below $200, the Airhawk is as stylish as it is functional. The break-barrel rifle is powered by a spring piston and boasts a beautifully shaped ambidextrous thumbhole stock with raised cheek pieces on both sides and a checkered forearm for a sure grip. A fine-looking rifle that bears a passing resemblance to the RWS Diana Model 34, the Airhawk isn't actually

The Airhawk is licensed by Ruger and is a serviceable entry-level air rifle with enough power to get most jobs done.

The Winchester/Daisy 850XS22 .22.

The Winchester/Daisy 1100XSU .177.

The Crosman Benjamin Marauder is a PCP gun that can be charged through the use of the patented Benjamin hand pump; it also functions as a CO_2 gun.

manufactured by Ruger and has offshore roots. As of this writing, the Airhawk isn't being promoted on Ruger's website, but it is well-represented on several retailers' webpages including Cabela's and Pyramyd Air.

The blued, rifled barrel features a muzzlebrake for reduced recoil (though there is little anyway), which is also softened by the ventilated rubber recoil pad. The brake also serves as a convenient handhold when cocking the rifle. The gun weighs in at a hefty 9 lbs. and has an overall length of just over 44-3/4 inches. The mainspring tube offers 11 mm dovetails for easy mounting of the 3x9-40 mm scope that comes with the gun, but some airgun purists balk at the effectiveness of how well the scope will remain in place given the extreme vibration from a spring-powered gun that delivers pellets at a solid 1,000 fps. ($180)

AIR POWER PLANTS

A quick look at today's airguns reveals countless configurations that run the gamut from traditional hunting rifle designs to target models that look like something out of a science-fiction movie. Despite the variety, all airguns are powered in three basic ways.

Spring Piston

When most people think airguns, they're probably thinking of a spring-piston powered gun, thanks to the classic Daisy Red Ryder BB Gun. Spring-piston airguns are probably the easiest and most affordable to shoot and maintain. And while the Red Ryder works off a cocking lever, most models actually are powered through a break barrel design whereby the gun is cocked by holding the stock in one hand and the barrel in the other and then breaking the airgun in half at the breech.

The classic spring piston air rifle: the Daisy Red Ryder.

By breaking the airgun in half, a piston inside the receiver compresses a strong spring, which is locked into place by a trigger sear. Pull the trigger and the spring expands rapidly forward, pushing and compressing a column of air that launches the pellet or BB through the barrel. Besides the under-lever of the Red Ryder and the simple break barrel design, other designs include a side-lever and even an over-lever.

The strength of springs and size of the pistons allow for a wide variance of power delivered by various spring-piston models, and it is this power plant that typically delivers the most recoil because of the action of the spring's release with each shot.

CO_2

These guns are powered by carbon dioxide, either in a small cartridge inserted in the gun or loaded from a bulk tank in the airgun's reservoir. It's a fairly common power plant design and can deliver blistering power, particularly when a cartridge is new or the gun is newly charged.

One challenge that faces shooters of CO_2, however, is the effect temperature can play on the pressure of the gas. At room temperature, a typical CO_2 cylinder produces about 1,000 psi of pressure. But change the temperature up or down just a few degrees and the pressure changes with it. This can really affect the point of impact of a CO_2 gun. Serious shooters, whether on

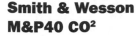

The Crosman Recruit has a buttstock that's widely adjustable for length of pull.

Smith & Wesson M&P40 CO²

Because you love to shoot airguns doesn't mean you're limited to long arms. There are a number of air pistol offerings as well for the avid target shooter and a fun model under the Smith & Wesson brand (as licensed to Soft Air USA) is a replica model of S&W's M&P 40 semi-auto. The air version is powered by CO² for a maximum shooting distance of 131 feet, delivered at 380 fps.

It is a semi-auto, non-blowback model, which means the slide doesn't come back when fired. It holds 15 BBs

Licensed by S&W, the M&P40 CO² pistol looks just like the real thing.

in the magazine. It will fire 250 BBs on a single CO² cartridge. The gun features the BAXS Accuracy System to maximize the power delivered by the pressurized carbon dioxide gas. The plastic-bodied gun has a textured grip, a variety of realistic finishes and, as mandated by federal law, an orange tip so it can't be confused for a real 40 cal. semi-auto. The M&P 40 is 7-1/2 inches long and weighs 1-1/2 lbs. ($60, smith-wesson.com)

Winchester 1100XSU and 850XS22

Winchester air rifles, made by Daisy, are attracting attention with a couple of top-performing models in 2009. The Winchester 1100XSU is a .177-caliber pellet rifle that shoots a maximum velocity of 1,100 fps. The 1100XSU features a single pump under-lever action that is more simple than it may sound, but you merely open the bolt, release the cocking lever lock, extend a cocking lever, release the lever latch and return the cocking lever under the forearm. Load a pellet into the action and the gun is ready to shoot.

The 1100SXU features a rifled steel barrel, rear button safety and a solid walnut stock with a checkered forearm and grip. It is topped with Tru-Glo fiber-optic front and rear sights for fast and clear target acquisition even in low light. The rifle also comes with a 4x32 Winchester Air Rifle scope if you prefer optics to open sights. The gun has a maximum shooting distance of 335 yards, is 46-1/2 inches long and weighs 8-3/4 lbs. This is another super small game option. The Winchester Air Rifle 1100SXU Under-Barrel Lever Cocking pellet rifle has an MSRP of $439.99.

For those who prefer the extra smackdown of a .22-caliber pellet, there's the Winchester 850XS22. It launches ammo at 850 fps for a reported shooting distance of 305 yards. Like the 1100SXU, the single-pump, break-barrel action rifle boasts a solid walnut stock, Tru-Glo fiber-optic front and rear sights (with the rear sight fully adjustable) and comes with the 4x32 scope.

The 850XS22 utilizes a rear button safety and weighs in at just over 7-1/2 lbs. It is 45 inches long. This is a shooter for a hunter with confidence in his abilities to take game with a single shot. The 850XS22 (850 FPS velocity/.22 cal.) has an MSRP of $319.99. (daisy.com)

---

the range or heading into the woods, will want to allow their gun to sit awhile in the ambient temperature and then sight it in before shooting targets or game. These guns are good for allowing quick second shots and recoil is less than in a spring-piston model.

A frequently-heard complaint about CO² guns is that once pressure begins to fall off, it does so noticeably and rapidly. Offsetting this disadvantge, however, is the relatively high rate of fire (for an airgun, anyway) of which most CO² guns are capable.

Pneumatic

Pneumatic airguns use compressed air stored in a reservoir to power their shots. The way the air is compressed in the gun varies. The most common type is the multi-stroke or pump-up type of pneumatic airgun. To compress the air, the gun is pumped usually between two and 10 times, typically using a forend pump lever.

Multi-stroke pneumatics are moderate in power, but usually compact, lightweight and delivers relatively little, if any, recoil. Because of the time and effort needed to pump them, however, quick second shots are virtually impossible at game or birds. They typically get harder to pump as the air compresses, making them difficult options for young or physically weaker shooters.

Single-stroke pneumatics are available and for close range shooting, these guns remain tack drivers. However, because they are powered by a single stroke or pump, these guns lack in power and aren't great choices for the hunter or longer distance shooter.

PCP (Pre-Charged Pneumatic)

First finding popularity among European hunters where strict gun laws often meant it was the only type of gun allowed for the field, pre-charged pneumatics (PCPs) are growing in popularity among

American shooters. Compressed air can either be obtained from a larger bottle (such as a scuba bottle) or it can be manually pumped into the reservoir of the gun with a high-pressure hand pump. Since the reservoir holds multiple shots often one charge will last a single outing, making this a great design for hunters and serious shooters. The guns are super accurate, powerful and generate little recoil. The downside is a higher starting cost as new PCP owners not only need to buy a gun, but also the accessories needed to load the gun with the compressed air.

PCP airguns have been used to take varmints, feral hogs and – believe it or not – small deer. Doing so requires close range and ideal conditions. It's ironic that while PCP airguns represent the cutting edge of modern airgun technology, Meriwether Lewis took an early PCP air rifle on his famous expedition with William Clark – way back in 1803!

GUNSMITHING Today

BY KEVIN MURAMATSU

As a gunsmith it's always fun to discover what the multitude of intellects called the American public will come up with. I've found that the tools of the trade that are the most helpful to the gunsmith or home hobbyist are often those that substitute for a third arm. In a similar fashion, those add-ons to our guns, the accessories for men, usually fill a similar role, like a more ergonomically shaped stock or sights that are easier for aging or faulty eyes to see. So it is kind of fun, in a geeky way, to flip through a Brownells catalog. I think every time I've done so, I've noticed something new. Whoever came up with that screw-driven sight pusher concept should be raised to sainthood. And whenever someone comes up with a new gun or somesuch, all sorts of minor tools – and occasionally major ones – for fixing, stripping, or doing whatever to it inevitably appear. Examples would be things like the hex-shaped Glock front sight installation tool or the rebound spring installation tool for Smith & Wesson revolvers, the clamshell vice block for AR receivers, and the aforementioned sight pushers.

In light of this, it's rather sad when a political climate discourages innovation and excellence. As I write, the fear of multiple firearm prohibitions and bans looms over the firearm industry like the sword of Damocles. Some companies continue to produce new products; after all, if you don't go forward, you fall behind. One axiom (a rather important one) in business is if a venture is unlikely to make a profit, then it is probably wise not to explore that venture. Some of the most well-known companies in the firearms industry are currently expanding to meet the demand for new guns and gear. Others, fearing harmful legislation, resist that otherwise profitable expansion, since to invest in new tooling, production space or employees could sink the company should some ludicrous anti-gun law be passed. The result is long, long, backlogs for production, with the supply, in my opinion, unlikely to catch up to the demand for some time, if ever.

Likewise, it's my belief that the pace of newly-introduced products for the care, maintenance, and enhancement of firearms has slowed perceptibly. Even at the most recent SHOT show, I expected a glut of new and neat gadgets or parts to slap onto the average Joe's gun – but a glut was not what I found. Sure, there was some pretty cool stuff, but not in the amounts I expected. I mean, who wants to develop a new widget, or the gun that the widget goes onto, if that widget may well be banned in the foreseeable future?

Fortunately, there are still some innovators out there who are flipping the proverbial bird to the haters in the ether. As will be detailed below, even now, there are still new tools and chemicals, accessories, parts, sights, and workable gimmicks this year designed to make your shooting and gunsmithing more exciting, easier, or both. (I'm still waiting for the all-in-one super tool, though.)

Keep It Clean, Guys

Much of the new items for gunsmithing use come in the arena of cleaning and maintenance. An oft-neglected component of firearms ownership, this field is a great one for experimentation in the industry. See, lots of guys who own guns never clean them until they don't work anymore. This means baked-on, caked-on crud, rust and such that needs to be removed. So new cleaners, cleaning tools, and whatzits are discovered in a fairly regular fashion

For example, **G96 Products**, maker of lubricants, solvents and such, has a new formula which was submitted to Big Brother to meet a new Mil-Spec, 63460E, whatever that stands for. *[Editor's Note: It's the U.S. DoD military procurement specification for "Lubricant, Cleaner and Preservative for Weapons and Weapons Systems." – DMS]* According to Alan Goldman, the owner of the company, one of the criteria in the specifications was dropped after testing in order for more of the competition to pass the bar in a subsequent retesting. Having used the G96 Gun Treatment aerosol extensively and having found it to be an excellent product, I may not need to take that claim with a grain of salt. Living in Minnesota, I'm always interested in a lube that claims works to well below and well above 0° F!

G96 Gun Treatment by G96 Products

Birchwood Casey, maker of many fine finishing products, has come up with a new way to rust-proof your gun. It's called called Perma-Fin. This material is a liquid spray-on protectant that is applied with an airbrush. They supply a kit with two bottles of fluid and the airbrush to hose the gun down with, and when you run out of the stuff, you can buy the bottles separately. It is not a binary compound and it does not require baking. You will need an air compressor for the airbrush. If all you have is the 1200 psi squeezer in your garage, go to the wife's craft store, or Walmart, and get a small one. You don't need a manly compressor to Perma-Fin your rifle.

Perma-Fin spray-on protectant by Birchwood Casey

OTIS has expanded their lineup of compact flexible cable cleaning systems. I'm a big fan of these kits, having had to use an AR-15 pistol grip kit to do a quick cleanout of my bore once, after falling into the creek. A combination bore brush and mop in all the fun calibers is now available for quickie cleans. Of course, the familiar soft packs are there for more detailed cleaning.

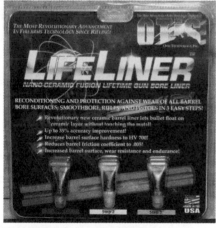

Combination bore brush and mop from OTIS

What really caught my eye, however, is that OTIS is now marketing a three-part kit that is designed to refurbish your worn bore. They claim an accuracy enhancement of up to 35% in used barrels, a little less in new barrels. This system serves to first clean, lap, and then deposit an ultrathin ceramic coating in the bore that also fills the pores in the metal and thus reduces the friction coefficient of the bore. This makes the gun more accurate, allows higher velocity, increases the wear resistance and endurance of the barrel, and makes the firearm much easier to clean. Just the thing to try on your old shooter-grade carbine's worn barrel.

and I am crazy paranoid about keeping lead contamination away from my kids, so this is going to be one of the first things I buy this year. As my kids grow older and I start taking them shooting, sanitation will be a priority, so this is a welcome addition to the shop and the home.

Pacific Tool & Gauge adjustable throating reamer

bullet in a chamber that may not have a long enough freebore to chamber that bullet, he can now use this reamer

A fun addition to your range bag is a CO_2-powered cleaner called SACS, from **Lanigan Performance Products**. Using a cartridge, it shoots bore-specific wads from bore to muzzle, picking up crud and fouling on the way. A universal device, it only requires adaptors to fit any caliber of rifle or pistol, and it is small enough to fit in a small pouch in a pocket of your bag. Such a bag is included with the kit, along with several wads, a bottle of CLP, and some other run-of-the-mill, yet handy, cleaning stuff.

Otis Lifeliner bore treatment

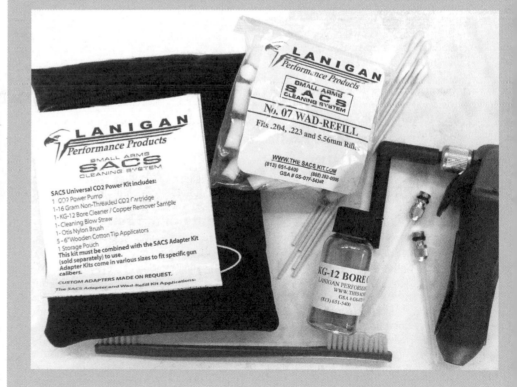

Tetra Gun is selling a new wipey thingy called a Lead Removal Cloth. Similar to the lubricated gun cloths and silicone impregnated cloths already on the market, this product combines the cleaning and protective properties of the latter while also removing lead residue. I've got three small children at home

Tetra GunLead Removal Cloth

Cool Tools

In the tools category are a couple of new things and a couple of things we should have thought of before.

Pacific Tool & Gauge has developed an adjustable throating reamer for chambering match-grade target guns. If a fellow wants to use a super-heavy

to easily determine how much longer the freebore needs to be, and then cut it custom, whip-bam-whoop. This will make doing such a task much easier and quicker and should be a welcome addition to the custom gunsmith's tool box. They will be available in multiple calibers and are piloted to the particular bore sizes. I want one. One of each.

Reamer and gauge set by Clymer
Precision Tools

Clymer Precision Tools has begun
marketing their reamers and gauges
together in one package with a slight
discount on the set. I can't recall anyone
else using this simple concept before,
but I may be mistaken. Since we need a
reamer and the accompanying go and
no-go gauges anyway, why not get them
all together at the same time, from the
same source? Duh.

Brownells' torque wrench line has
expanded. Already available is their
Magna-Tip adjustable torque handle.
Coming soon are a series of fixed break
handles available in several different
settings. This way you can get dedicated
wrenches for action screws and
scope mount and ring installation.
I can't tell you how many times I've
snapped the heads off of screws
in the shop using my incredible
physical prow-
ess. Using a
torque wrench
should help to prevent that by
enabling the gunsmith or hobbyist
to consistently tighten any screw to
its ideal tightness, exactly.

Brownells fixed torque tool

While **Wheeler Engineering** has for
some time marketed their F.A.T. Wrench
torqueing tools, and they are now
providing them in a handy Professional
Scope Mounting Kit with all the tools a
fellow may need to professionally mount
a riflescope, such as the wrench, driver
bits, levels, and ring lapping tool. Available for 30mm tubes and 1" tubes, the
kit can also be purchased as a combo
set with tooling for both sizes of scope
tubes.

One of the neatest little instruments
I've seen in this field is the borescope.
Gradient Lens Corporation, the makers of the Hawkeye Borescope, have
introduced a new version that gives a
45˚ view of the bore. This can give you a
more three-dimensional perspective as
you view the rifling; and that perspec-

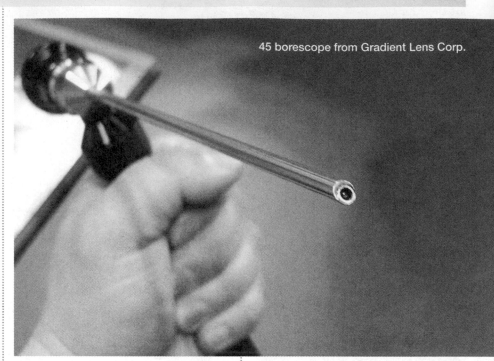

45 borescope from Gradient Lens Corp.

tive, I think, will come in very handy for
those who do a lot of barrel inspections.
Of course the traditional 90˚ viewers are
still available, and newly appearing is a
unit using an LED light source, a setup
demanded by the company's customers.

Sights and Such

Limbsaver has expanded with a new
concept in the fiber optic realm. Fiber
optic sights have been very helpful for
the aged or colorblind eyes among the
many shooters and hunters in America,
as well as making the sights much more
visible and easy to use in low lighting.
Last year they combined, in yet another
simple yet brilliant concept, fiber optic
light tubes of two different colors, one
inside the other (red inside of green, for
example) to enhance the contrast per-
ceived by the shooter. This year this line
of sights has expanded to include the
Dual Color Micro Sight for installation
on shotgun ribs. Not only does
it have those two contrasting
colors, it is also very low
profile and will fit the ribs of
most of the shotguns out in
the market.

Another company on the cutting edge
of fiber optic innovation is the **Williams
Gun Sight Company**. They already
have a vast assortment of sights for our
projectile projectors, and now more
are available for handguns such as the
H&K USP, Kimber fixed-sight models,
assorted Kahr pistols, Taurus 1911, and
the new Ruger SR9. The beautiful thing
about these sights is that if you don't
like the color, you can change it. I can't
see the red light tubes on anyone's FO
sights. So I replace them with yellow or
green. Much better.

**Rib-mounted Dual Color
Micro Sight by
Limbsaver**

AR-15 Goodies

In the black rifle arena, the sky's the limit. Everyone and their brother seems to be coming out with something new in this very large niche. One of the most interesting is the Omega X handguard from **Daniel Defense**. It is a rifle-length sight

Omega X handguard
by Daniel Defense

pocket handguard for use on carbines. "Uh...what's that?" you say. This handguard is designed to give more forend space for accessories to hang onto, and to give more room for guys who like to hold the handguard as far out toward the muzzle as possible – and it fits on guns with the short carbine gas system. It clamshells on in two pieces, the top fitting around the fixed front sight assembly. These pieces clamp to a proprietary barrel nut, so the gun will have to be partially disassembled for installation. It is rock solid, and best of all, is less than two inches wide and lightweight. Even with full size rail covers, it feels slimmer than standard plastic handguard pieces. Much nicer for those of us with small hands but who like to hold the handguard with our weak arm extended.

The flavor of the moment in the AR realm is the retrofit piston operating system. Several companies are now offering some incarnation of this ultimate update, some of which are end user-installable, while others require a trip to the factory or a visit to a certified installer. Look for more entries in this niche to add to those available from **Patriot Ordnance Factory**, **Adams Arms**, **Primary Weapons Systems**, **Bushmaster**, **CMMG**, **Colt**, **HK**, and probably a couple others.

Target Stuff

More and more shooters are exploring the long range target disciplines and so need a very accurate rifle. In addition tow good optics and mounts, a quality barrel, top-notch ammunition and and good technique, an accuracy-enhancing stock is a necessity. A new entry into this market is the **JP Enterprises** MOR-07 chassis system. It is built in three sections (action block, stock, and handguard) with the handguard and action block made of big chunks of hard coat anodized aluminum. The company plans on additional models of action block and handguard beyond the original Remington 700 style short action set. Simply switching out the short action for a long action receiver block, or for a block made to any particular spec, allows the MOR to potentially fit onto any bolt action rifle in existence while using the same stock and handguard. The stock is adjustable for length and cheek weld and folds to the left side for more compact storage in a smaller case. According to the company, it should also fit most factory and aftermarket triggers available for the Remington 700. It will be available alone or with JP's proprietary barreled action as a complete rifle.

Whether you are a professional gunsmith or shooter, or just a home hobbyist there are plenty of ways to improve and enhance our everyday firearms. Just exploring a **MidwayUSA** or **Brownells** catalog will overload your mind with potential projects. From building a 1000-meter gun to swapping sights on your XD, whatever you need is available.

And if something just isn't available, then design and market it yourself. The gunsmithing field, like any other, is driven greatly by innovation. While new stuff appears on a regular basis, truly new ideas are rare. Even the relatively simple task that requires the third hand can benefit from an intelligently designed assistant in the form of a fixture, jig, or manipulator extraordinaire. Man, if I had come up with the idea a few years back for those sight installation fixtures, I could buy my own island. That may be a little bit of dreamweaving, but I still want the ultimate gunsmithing tool in my toolbox.

The question is: who's gonna build it?

MOR07 chassis system for
Remington M700 by
JP Enterprises

OPTICS Today

BY WAYNE VAN ZWOLL

Wayne fires a McMillan rifle with a 2-1/2x Sightron. Small, lightweight scopes are often best!

You know, of course, that if you hunted with a Remington 721 shipped in the 1950s and equipped with a Weaver K4 scope, you'd kill as many deer as with a modern rifle and the most sophisticated optics – that if you entered long-range competition with a Lyman Super Targetspot sold then, you'd score as high as with the latest high-power glass.

OK. These days some deer are killed at extremely long range. Some would

probably still be afoot if every hunter held his shots to 400 yards – a reasonable limit for the K4. But by and large, modern scopes pose no greater threat to game than did those of my youth. Shooters skilled enough to clean targets with a vintage Lyman would gain few if any Xs with a modern Leupold.

Still, riflemen dote on perfection. And they're much more apt demand it of their hardware than of themselves. With brighter, sharper sight pictures, they want bigger tubes and wider power ranges. They also crave options: rangefinding and illuminated reticles, re-settable windage and elevation dials, turret-mounted parallax dials, quick-focus eyepieces, water-repellent lens coatings. Throw in long eye relief that doesn't change as you crank up the magnification, plus cap-less, waterproof, low-profile knobs that spin with the crisp clickety-snick of target dials. And, now, built-in laser rangefinders.

The basic components and properties that defined worthy rifle-scopes a half-century ago remain. Strip the gingerbread, and a good sight still comprises high-quality lenses and precisely machined, carefully fitted parts – all secured against the recoil of cartridges that release bullets with bomb-blast violence.

Here's a rundown of rifle-scopes new for 2009, with notes on the most intriguing binoculars and spotting scopes. You'll find traditional glass here too – optics so good they don't need changing. Perhaps if they appear often enough in print, makers will keep them around. Not all that's new is better than all that's old.

A final note: Lately I've chosen to hunt without a rifle-scope – not every time, but often. I like it. The most memorable part of any hunt is the approach. Irons force you to get close. The approach is commonly long and difficult; but the last yards are more exciting, the shot more intimate than if you fired from afar. While iron sights no longer come as standard equipment on many rifles, you can get excellent irons from Lyman

(lymanproducts.com), Williams (williamsgunsight.com) and XS (XSsights.com). They give lever rifles and short bolt guns an agility you won't sense with a scope. And there's something just plain right about clenching that receiver in your fist as you head for the horizon, the way hunters did long before glass sights blocked their grip and made the hunt an exercise in long shooting.

Aimpoint

In 1975 Swedish inventor Gunnar Sandberg came up with what he called a single-point sight. You couldn't look through this sight; you looked into the tube with one eye while your other registered a dot superimposed on the target. Sandberg refined the device and founded a company. Aimpoint came to define a new type of optical sight, with an illuminated dot suspended in a field you can see from almost anyplace behind the sight. And you needn't worry about parallax. The front lens of an Aimpoint is a compound glass that corrects for parallax – unlike red dot sights whose reflective paths shift with eye position.

Aimpoint's doublet lens brings the dot to your eye in a line parallel with the sight's optical axis, so you'll hit where you see the dot, even when your eye is off-axis. A 1x Aimpoint gives you unlimited eye relief, and it's easy to use with both eyes open. Current Aimpoints

Not everyone on your block will have Alpen's pink binocular; but this is, optically, a real bargain, and a portion of sales go to breast cancer research.

The new Burris SpeedBead mounts easily on a shotgun without screws or pins.

(some with magnification) boast what the firm calls Advanced Circuit Efficiency Technology. It reduces power demand; batteries last up to 50,000 hours with a brightness setting of 7 (on a scale of 1 to 11). These sights are lightweight and compact, too. The lightest of the 9000 series weighs just 6.5 oz. Positive windage and elevation clicks each move point of impact 13mm at 100 meters. Sturdy enough for military use, Aimpoint sights have been adopted by armed forces in the U.S. and France, and they serve sportsmen in 40 countries. One of every 10 moose hunters using optical sights in Sweden carries an Aimpoint.

A few years ago, on the receiving end of a game drive in a Swedish forest dark under a dripping fog, I spied a pair of moose hoofing through the trees at a brisk pace. The red dot in my Aimpoint cut through the gloom and glued itself to a shoulder. Bang! The moose stumbled, recovered. I found it dead a short distance farther into the woods. Two other moose, both shot on the go in heavy cover, have convinced me that nothing beats an Aimpoint for fast shots in dim conditions. At the range, I've fired minute-of-angle groups with the same sight. 'Nuf said! (Aimpoint.com)

Alpen

Building a new optics company takes patience and tenacity. The Alpen people have shown a lot of both over the last decade. And their recipe for success is paying off. "Value. We focus on value." Vickie Gardner insists on it from the manufacturers. Rifle-scopes, spotting scopes and binoculars with Alpen's label have been winning industry "best buy" awards like Michael Phelps collected Olympic gold. The list of new items this year is short, but the catalog is still chock-full of bargains.

Top-end Rainier binoculars now come in 8x32 and 10x32 versions that are 20 percent lighter than the 42mm originals but still wear BAK4 lenses, phase-corrected coatings, a locking diopter dial and twist-out eyecups. The AlpenPro Porro series includes an 8x30 that's ideal for the woods. For 2009 the company has announced an 8-16x42 zoom binocular. You may prefer the more traditional roof-prism Wings, of open-frame design. Choose 8x42 or 10x42, ED or standard lenses. You'll get the features of Alpen's best glasses. The new 8.5x50 delivers a very bright image at modest cost. While pink binoculars might not top your shopping list, Alpen carries a pair (8x25 and 10x42) to draw attention to breast cancer research – where the firm has pledged a portion of pink sales. The Rainier 20-60x80 spotting scope accommodates a camera adapter, for photography at long range. Straight and angled eyepieces index easily.

AR rifle-scopes for air guns were developed to endure double-shuffle recoil. Alpen has a new pocket monocular that really does fit in a shirt pocket. The 8x25 (or 10x25) glass is great for a peek into timber when you're traveling light. (Alpenoutdoors.com)

ATK

Last year the Nitrex label, once put on Speer ammunition, was adopted by ATK for a new line of rifle-scopes. ATK (which, incidentally, also owns Speer) just added several scopes to this series. The 1.5-5x32, 3-9x42, 3-10x50 and 6-20x50 AO now wear the "TR-one" label, while five new sights make up the "TR-two" group. All these 1" scopes feature five times magnification – top-end power is five times the lowest setting. All deliver 4" eye relief and a choice of TrexPlex or EBX reticle. There's a 2-10x42, a 2-10x50, a 3-15x42, a 3-15x50, and a 4-20x50. You can specify an illuminated reticle in the 3-15x50, a fine crosswire in the 4-20. Choose matte or silver finish. While the TR-one 6-20x50 AO has a front-end parallax ring, the 3-15x and 4-20x TR-two scopes have turret-mounted focus/parallax dials. These scopes weigh from 23 to 28 ounces. The 4-20x50 has 1/8-minute windage and elevation clicks; the others change in 1/4-minute increments. All Nitrex scopes have fast-focus eyepieces.

The Leica Ultravid, now with ED glass, ranks among the very best binoculars in the world.

As is customary in the American market, ATK kept reticles in the second focal plane. They don't change dimensions as you turn the power dial. I like the generous tube sections on these scopes, for easy mounting on a variety of rifles and the almost-constant eye relief across the power range. Checking windage and elevation movements on a 3-9x42 TR-one (with the rifle snug in a Caldwell Steady Rest), I found the dials gave a reliable return to zero. Bright, sharp images, a flat field and minimal color fringing belie the modest price of the TR-one scopes. While the new TR-two models cost a bit more, they're still bargains in my view. The 42mm front lens carries as much glass as can be clamped in low rings. So my choice would be the 3-15x42. ATK has also slapped the Nitrex brand on 25-ounce roof-prism binoculars, 8x42 and 10x42. Phase-corrected lens coatings enhance images; the click-detent diopter dial won't creep off your preferred setting. Eleven-ounce compact versions, 8x25 and 10x25, are available too. (Nitrexoptics.com)

Barrett

The Barrett Optical Ranging System – BORS – is not a sight. It's a sight attachment, a 13-oz. device you pair with a scope. It includes a small ranging computer powered by a CR-123 lithium

Leupold's 4.5-14x50 Tactical scope helps this Surgeon rifle in .338 Lapua shoot into one hole.

battery and featuring a 12x2-character liquid crystal display with a four-button keypad. Factory-installed cartridge tables tailored to your loads enable the computer to give you precise holds for long-distance shooting. The BORS also comprises an elevation knob, a knob adapter and a set of rings that affix the computer to your sight. The rings mount to any M1913 rail and are secured with hex nuts that endure the beating of Barrett rifles in .50 BMG. After you press the 6-o'clock power button on the BORS unit, you're ready to engineer a shot. The screen shows zero range and indicates any cant (tipping of the rifle off vertical), which at long range can cause you to miss. The BORS unit automatically compensates for vertical shot angles. You can adjust the scope for up to 90 degrees of inclination and declination, in increments of 2 degrees! At extreme range, temperature and barometric pressure matter, too. Both come on-screen when you press the 9-o'clock button. To determine range, you specify target size, then move the horizontal wire of your reticle from top to bottom of the target, or vice versa. The range appears in yards or meters. Now you can use the elevation knob to dial the range. The BORS unit must know your load, of course. You provided that data earlier; the unit stores it as a ballis-

tics table. It can hold up to 100 tables for instant access. At the end of this process – which takes longer to explain than to do – you can hold dead-on even at extended range. If the battery dies, you can use the scope as if the electronics were not there. I've attached a BORS unit to a Barrett rifle with Leupold Mark 4 LR/Tactical 4.5-14x50 scope. Recoil and blast from this .50 haven't fazed the instrument. (Barrettrifles.com)

Brunton

Since its start in the 1890s, Brunton has served people who live in the outdoors. Field geologists were the first customers. The product line has grown to include all manner of camping gear, from transits and compasses and GPS units to cookwear and stoves. Binoculars have lately brought Brunton to hunters. Topping that line is the Epoch, a full-size roof-prism glass with 43mm objectives. Choose from 7.5x, 8.5x and 10.5x magnification. At $1,639, the 8-15x35 zoom costs about $340 more. Like its fixed-power stable-mates, it has lockable, twist-out eyecups and accepts a doubler to increase magnification. Less expensive Eterna and Echo binoculars still boast fully multi-coated lenses. Eterna 8x45 and 11x45 versions earned a "Best Buy" rating from *Consumer's Digest*. The 8x32 and 10x32 are more portable; the 15x51 with tripod adapter can serve as a spotting scope. But Brunton also makes traditional spotting scopes, from the compact 12-36x50 Echo and 18-38x50 Eterna to full-size 20-60x80 spotting scopes with ED (extra-low dispersion) fluorite glass. Brunton imports rifle-scopes to sell under the NRA banner. At $109 and $119, fixed-power 4x32 and 6x42 scopes offer good value. A 6-24x50 AO target scope lists for just $149 with mil-dot reticle. Variables, from 1.5-6x40 to 6-24x50, start around $100. Word on the street is that Brunton will focus more and more on camping and orienteering hardware. (Brunton. com and nrasportsoptics.com)

Burris

Two new rifle-scopes join the extensive Burris line in 2009. The Six Series comprises a 2-12x40 and a 2-12x50, both with 30mm tubes and up to 4-1/2" of eye relief. The "Six", of course, refers to a six-times power range. Decades ago, when variables started to gain traction with hunters, the 3-9x led the pack. For years, three-times power range seemed sufficient. Then, as shooters demanded more power, came a four-times option. It appeared most notably in 3-12x and 4-16x scopes. Last season I hunted with a scope featuring six-times magnification – more range, I must say, than I needed. But there's no question a 2-12x scope is versatile! I'm pleased Burris has kept the 40mm objective for hunters like me who favor low scope mounting and a relatively compact sight.

On another front, Burris has improved its 1.6-oz. reflex-style red dot sight. FastFire II is now waterproof (fully submersible!). Made to fit Picatinny rails, it's ideal not only for rifles but for handguns and shotguns. A battery-saver mode extends the life of the lithium CR2032 battery to five years. Burris has also announced FastFire mounts for popular lever rifles, and a mounting plate you can sandwich between receiver and buttstock on repeating shotguns. Called SpeedBead, the red dot sight on the shotgun mount should excel on slug guns. I tried this sight recently, on an 1100 Remington at a clay-target range. The first bird escaped, but after that, the red dot found the target as quickly as would a front bead, and there was no barrel to obscure rising birds. Hitting became easy quickly!

Burris hasn't forgotten the long-range shooter. Its Ballisic Plex and Ballistic Mil-Dot reticles are available in 30mm Euro Diamond and Black Diamond series, and the 1-inch Signature Select and Fullfield II lines. Illuminated reticles define the Fullfield II LRS scopes, which employ flat battery housings on the turret. Fullfield 30s (3-9x40 and 3.5-10x50) feature 30mm tubes at affordable prices. A 1" Timberline series, from 4x20 to 4.5-14x32 AO, fills the "compact" slot. The company also lists a red dot sight: the 1x, 5-oz. tube-style 135. Like many optics firms, Burris is expanding its tactical line. Fullfield II Tactical scopes and Fullfield TAC30 variables (3-9x40, 3.5-10x50 and 4.5-14x42, new last year) have been joined by a 3x AR-332 prism sight, and an AR-Tripler, which you position on a pivot mount behind a 1x red dot sight for extra magnification. Burris catalogs an XTS-135 SpeedDot tube sight, and 1-4x24 and 1.5-6x40 XTRs (Xtreme Tactical Riflescopes). FastFire II complements AR-style battle rifles. The Burris catalog also lists spotting scopes, binoculars and the 4-12x42 Laserscope, a laser-ranging sight. (Burrisoptics.com)

Bushnell

Still new on the Bushnell website is the company's Elite 6500-series rifle-scopes: 2.5-16x42, 2.5-16x50 and 4.5-30x50. The nearly-seven-times magnification range is the broadest in the industry. Bushnell 4200 2.5-10x50 and 6-24x40 scopes are new, and there's now a 3200-series 3-9x40 with Ballistic Reticle. The affordable Trophy series has grown by two: 1x28 red dot and 1x32 red/green dot sights. New 36mm and 42mm Excursion EX binoculars (8x and 10x) sell for $230 to $320 – reasonable prices, given their fully multi-coated optics with PC-3 phase correction. An Excursion spotting scope, with folded light path, comes in 15-45x60 and 20-60x80 versions. Bushnell's most field-worthy laser range-finders may well be the Scout 1000 with ARC, technology that takes shot angle into account so you get a corrected range for accurate shooting at steep vertical angles. The 6.6-oz. instrument fits in a pocket; single-button control makes it easy to use with one hand. In bow mode, it delivers accurate reads between 5 and 100 yards. Rifle mode sets it for reads from 100 to 800 yards. The 5x24 Scout 1000 can range reflective objects to 1,000 yards. If you're GPS-literate, you no doubt have a GPS unit. If not, you may want to dip a toe in the water with Bushnell's Backtrack, a straightforward instrument that stores up to three locations and can bring you back to them. Promoted as an aid to finding your car in a parking lot, it can also help you locate downed game in the hills. (Bushnell.com)

Cabela's

Obviously, Cabela's does not manufacture rifle-scopes. It markets them. The Cabela's brand goes on optics made by and imported from established optics firms that also build rifle-scopes, binoculars and spotting scopes for companies many people think make their own products. These manufacturers have the advantage of what you'll remember from Econ 101 as economies of scale. They own the best of machines and technology and enjoy modest labor costs. So it should come as no surprise if you find Cabela's optics good bargains. The Alaska Guide series of rifle-scopes includes fixed-powers as well as 11 variables. Most useful for big game and varmint hunters: 3-9x, 4-12x AO and 6.5-20x AO scopes, with 40mm objectives and 1" tubes. All list for less than $400. I've relied on a $200 4x Cabela's scope on remote hunts and found it both bright and durable. If the times are really pinching you, consider the Pine Ridge line – it's less expensive still. There's also a series of Cabela's tactical scopes with interchangeable turrets and left-side parallax knobs. The 2-7x32, 3-9x40, 3-12x40 and 6-18x40 start at less than $100, with fully multi-coated lenses and fast-focus eyepieces and adjustable objectives. The company also imports spotting scopes, laser range-finders and roof-prism binoculars. Its catalog includes optics from Nikon, Leupold, Swarovski, Zeiss and other well-known optics makers. (Cabelas.com)

Docter

The Carl Zeiss Jena factory in Thuringia, Germany, began producing Docter optics in 1991. Late in 2006 Merkel USA became the U.S. importer. While it has yet to launch a major marketing campaign here, Docter Optic has wooed hunters Stateside with a series of rifle-scopes featuring 1" tubes and rear-plane reticles. The 3-9x40, 3-10x40, 4.5-14x40 AO and 8-25x50 AO Docter Sport scopes boast qualities of more costly scopes . Docter's line also includes 1" 6x42 and 8x56 fixed-power Classic models, plas 30mm variables: 1-4x24, 1.5-6x42, 2.5-8x48 and 3-12x5 with fast-focus eyepieces, resettable windage/elevation dials and lighted reticles. The electronically controlled Unipoint dot is of constant size, while the first-plane main reticle varies with magnification (and stays in constant relationship with the target). Doctor catalogs three binoculars: 8x42, 10x42 and a bright 8x58. They're of roof-prism design with center focus and four-layer achromatic front lenses. A central diopter dial with vernier scale ensures precise focus down to just 3 feet! All Docter binoculars have aluminum/magnesium bodies and twist-up eyecups. (Merkel-usa.com and docter-germany.com)

Elcan

A subsidiary of Raytheon, Elcan is an optics firm and an acronym: Ernst Leitz, Canada – the Leitz optical company dating to 1849 in Germany. Elcan has been building infrared-sensitive scopes for military units since the 1980s, but it's now pursuing civilian sales with DigitalHunter, a truly innovative rifle-scope. DH1 has an alloy tube and multi-coated optics. It mounts on a Picatinny rail or Weaver bases – but not in scope rings because the body is not round. There's no turret either. A flat panel serves as a control center. You make every adjustment by pressing buttons. Turn the sight on with a button. Pick magnification, from 2.5x to 13.5x, with buttons. Choose one of four downloaded reticles – or design your own – with buttons. As this scope lacks a power ring and windage/elevation dials, it lacks a clear optical path. You cannot see through this scope. The image comes from a digital display triggered by light hitting a sensor. Because target image and reticle share a common plane, you can forget about parallax. DigitalHunter also has long, non-critical eye relief, though in bright light you must press your brow against the flexible eye-shade to get an acceptable image.

Alas, image is the scope's singular weakness. It cannot match what you're used to seeing through high-quality optics. It is, to date, dim and grainy. To be fair, so was early television. Surely technology will come to the rescue. Already it has given DH1 superior windage and elevation adjustments. Each push of a button moves point of impact exactly .2". There's no backlash, and you won't lose track of where you are on the adjustment range because each move stays in an electronic memory bank. No need to hold high at long range. The scope self-adjusts after you install ballistic data specific to your load. For each shot after zeroing, you need only enter the range on the control panel and aim in the middle!

I tested this feature with a .30-06 to ranges beyond 400 yards. Groups were perfectly centered with dead-on holds! Of course there's a battery, and the DH1 will run out of juice after 5 hours of use (sooner in cold weather). You can get more field time by switching the scope to sleep mode; it comes to life almost instantly at your command. Turn it off, and you'll wait about 3 seconds to reboot. At 28 oz., the scope is not light. Neither is it cheap. But the price has dropped substantially in the last two years. Figure about $1200 for the DH1. A new model has a removable tinted cap instead of a tinted front lens, so it can read infrared (you'll need an infrared flashlight) and give you a bright target at night! DH1s can be converted to IR. (Elcansportingoptics.com)

A quick-focus eyepiece and generous eye relief complement excellent optics in this Meostar R1.

Kahles

A subsidiary of Swarovski, Kahles operates independently. This year, there's not much new from the Austrian firm. But there's plenty of high-quality glass already in the line. Helia C sights include 1" fixed-power and 30mm variable and fixed scopes, with front-plane reticles. Helia CT scopes were designed for the U.S. market. The 2-7x36, 3-9x42 and 3-10x50 have compact 1" tubes and second-plane reticles that do not appear to change size during magnification changes. Kahles catalogs four 30mm CBX models, 1.1-4x24 to 12x56, with lighted rear-plane reticles. CS (30mm) and CL (1") variables, also designed for American tastes, have a Multizero turret (optional) that allows you to preset zeros for as many as five loads or distances. Color-coded dials give you instant access to each zero in the field, and accurate returns. The company's newest rifle-scope series, the KX, is also the most affordable. It comprises 3-9x42, 3.5-10x50 and 4-12x50 models with 1" tubes. Kahles has pushed many new products to market recently, including several fine binoculars. But its history is one of more conservative growth. In 1898 in Vienna, Karl Robert Kahles combined the Opto-Mechanical Workshop of Karl Fritsch with the Simon Plossl Company to form the Kahles Company. Two years later it was selling Telorar rifle-scopes. The Helia scope series came along in 1926. Bombing during World War II all but ruined the Kahles factory; however, Freidrich Kahles III had it rebuilt and introduced some of the first variable-power rifle-scopes. Later Kahles pioneered multi-coating of lenses, now standard on most scopes. (Kahlesoptik.com)

Leica

Geovid laser-ranging binoculars now boast the HD fluorite glass of Leica's Ultravid HD binocular series. Fluorite lenses enhance brightness and resolution, and can reduce overall weight slightly. All four Geovids (8x42, 10x42, 8x56 and 12x56) have alloy frames and deliver accurate range reads as far as 1,200 yards. The Ultravid line, which has replaced the time-honored Trinovid, includes 8x20 and 10x25 compact models, and full-size roof-prism glasses from 8x32 to 12x50. HD models feature fluorite in every lens, plus proprietary Aqua-Dura lens coating on exposed glass. This hydrophobic compound beads water and makes lens cleaning easier. Duovid 8 + 12x42 and 10 + 15x50 binoculars offer an instant choice of magnification. Leica Televid 62 and 77 spotting scopes have been joined this year by an 82mm Televid HD. The German company's biggest news, though, is a pair of new rifle-scopes, a 2.5-10x42 and a 3.5-14x42. Specs aren't available at this writing, but you should see these scopes by mid-summer.

A few years ago Leica marketed a series of scopes manufactured by Leupold. The relationship wasn't publicized and soon dissolved. These new Leicas are the first rifle-sights produced in-house in the firm's 100-year history! (Leica-camera.com)

Leupold

Two years ago, Leupold introduced its VX-7 scopes, with a range of features and refinements that defined the best the company could bring to market. The low-profile VX-7L, with a concave belly up front, came along last spring (3.5-14x56 and 4.5-18x56, complementing the VX-7 in 1.5-6x24, 2.5-10x45 and 3.5-14x50). These sights have European-style eyepieces and "lift and lock" SpeedDial W&E dials. Xtended Twilight glass features scratch-resistant DiamondCoat 2 lens coating. The power selector ring is matched to a "Ballistic Aiming System" so you can tailor magnification and reticle to the target and distance. Nitrogen was replaced by Argon/Krypton gas to better prevent fogging. The VX-7 is still top-of-the-line. But in 2009 a new VX-3 series replaces the flagship Vari-X III. Nearly 40 models are listed, all with VX-7's Xtended Twilight lenses and DiamondCoat 2. Cryogenically treated stainless adjustments move 1/4, 1/8 and 1/10 m.o.a. per click in standard, competition and target/varmint versions. An improved spring system ensures precise, positive erector movement. The fast-focus eyepiece has a removable rubber ring. These features appear as well on the new FX-3 6x42, 6x42 AO, 12x40 AO and two scopes designed for metallic silhouette shooting: 25x40 AO and 30x40 AO. You'll find 18 reticle options for the VX-3 and FX-3 series, and five finishes for the 1-inch and 30mm 6061-T6 aircraft alloy tubes.

For black powder rifles and shotguns firing slugs, Leupold now markets two UltimateSlam scopes. The 2-7x33 and 3-9x40 incorporate what the firm calls a Load Selector Ring. After zeroing, you choose a load designation that matches your ammo, then dial that number on the ring every time you shoot The SA.B.R. (for Sabot Ballistics Reticle) reticle comprises two dots and a tight center circle, stacked vertically on a heavy Duplex wire. It all means faster aim at normal hunting ranges (to 300 yards). In the Mark 4 tactical line, there's a new ER/T M1 4.5-14x50 sight with a front-plane reticle. As in European scopes, this reticle stays in constant relationship to the target throughout the magnification span, so you can range a target at any power.

As for oldies, Leupold's FX II 2.5x20 Ultralight scope remains one of my favorites for lever-action carbines. It sits tight to the receiver in extra-low rings, slides easily into scabbards, adds just 7-1/2 oz. to the rifle's weight and has all the magnification you need for big game to 200 yards. For bolt rifles with longer reach, I still prefer the lightweight 4x33 and 6x36 scopes in Leupold's FX II line. My friend Pat Mundy hints of a return of the 3x. "But no promises." The M8 3x ranks among my first picks for hunting elk. I've used that magnification on bulls from 30 to 300 yards. (Leupold.com)

Meopta

European optics are renowned for quality. Meopta's Czech-made R1 4-16x44 Long Range Target Scope boasts low-profile target knobs and an adjustable objective up front, with a 30mm tube and a rear-plane plex or mil dot reticle. Meostar hunting scopes – eight variables and two fixed-powers – also have the second-plane reticle Americans prefer (except the 3-12x56). I've used the 30mm Artemis 3000 3-9x42, a superb sight! The 2000 and illuminated 2100 series are similar, but with steel 30mm tubes. Choose one of four variables: 1.5-6x42, 2-8x42, 3-9x42, 3-12x50. Or a 4x32, 6x42 or 7x50 fixed-power. A pair of range-finding reticles completes Meopta's list of eight. The illuminated versions offer seven levels of brightness, with an "off" detent between each for one stop control. Mcopta W/E adjustments move independently no matter how how close to their limits. The company offers a Meostar S1 spotting scope (75mm objective) with standard or APO glass, straight or angled heel and 30x wide-angle or 20-60 zoom eyepiece. There's a collapsible 75mm scope too. A 12x50 binocular accepts a 2x doubler. Roof-prism binoculars include 7x, 8x and 10x models with 42mm objectives, plus a 7x50, a 10x50 and an 8x56. (Meopta.com)

Millet

Starting out as a supplier of scope mounts, iron sights and related items, Millet soon joined myriad other firms importing rifle-scopes from the Orient. In 2006 Millet introduced target and varmint scopes – a 4-16x and a 6-25x with turret parallax/focus dials, target knobs and the option of illuminated reticles. Buck Gold hunting scopes, 1.5-6x44 to 6-25x56, cover a range of applications. Windage and elevation dials have coil-spring returns and finger-friendly rims. Lighted reticles are available on the high-power models; so too turret-mounted focus. Fast-focus eyepieces come on all. The Buck Silver series comprises 3-9x, 4-12x and 6-18x variables, plus a 2x LEE scope, all with 1" tubes. The 30mm Tactical series, including a 10x and 1-4x and 4-16x variables, catalogs a lighted Donut-Dot reticle option. Millet's Zoom Dot red dot sight fits rails on handguns and tactical carbines. You'll find Millet rails for popular sporting rifles too. The firm still sells a variety of handgun sights, plus an extensive selection of mount bases and rings. (Millettsights.com)

Nightforce

Made in Idaho. *Idaho?* Yep. Nightforce proudly puts its scopes up against all comers. Four-times magnification gives you great versatility from this 30mm line, from the 3.5-15x50 and 3.5-15x56 NSX to the 5.5-22x50 and 5.5-22x56, the 8-32x56 and 12-42x56. Compact scopes for hunting (a 1-4x24 and a 2.5-10x24) have been joined this year by a 2.5-10x32. Like all but two benchrest models, the new 2.5-10x has a turret-mounted focus/parallax dial. (The 8-32x56 and 12-42x56 bench scopes wear front-sleeve parallax rings, plus resettable 1/8-minute windage and elevation dials.) Also new: the 3.5-15x50 F1, with first-plane reticle. The reticle stays in constant relationship to the target throughout the power range. All Nightforce scopes feature main tubes of lightweight bronze alloy. Dissimilar alloys in the erector assembly guarantee repeatable movement. The illuminated reticles (up to 10 choices per scope model) are distinctive in form and appealing because they cover so little of the field.

Nightforce also markets accessories for competitive and tactical shooters. Mil radian knobs click in mils (.1 per click). Or choose quarter-minute graduations – or a turret with 1-minute elevation and half-minute windage clicks (for big changes in yardage with short dial movement). A "zero-stop" turret has an elevation dial that can be set to return to any of 400 detents in its adjustment range. One-piece steel scope bases have a recoil lug to better secure the mount. Choose from five heights of steel rings. Unimount, machined from 7075-T6 alloy, features titanium crossbolts and a 20-minute taper for long shooting. It stays with the scope, for fast sight changes on Picatinny rails. Nightforce NXS riflescopes may well endure the toughest tests in the industry. Each sight must remain leak- and fog-proof after submersion in 100 feet of water for 24 hours, freezing in a box cooled to a minus 80 degrees F, then heating within an hour to 250 degrees F. Every scope gets hammered in a device that delivers 1,250 Gs – backward and forward! Lens coatings must pass mil-spec abrasion tests. Starting at over $1,200, NXS scopes aren't cheap. But then, they're not cheap. To help with those long shots, get the Nightforce Ballistic Program for Windows, or the abbreviated version for Pocket PCs. (Nightforceoptics.com)

Nikon

A new Monarch "African" rifle-scope series tops Nikon's list of new products. The 1-4x20 has a 1" tube; the 1.1-4x24, available also with an illuminated reticle, is a 30mm sight. Both scopes provide 4 inches of eye relief for fast aim and plenty of recoil space. They feature German #4 reticles and 1/2-minute click adjustments. The African rifle-scopes round out a line tilted to high-power

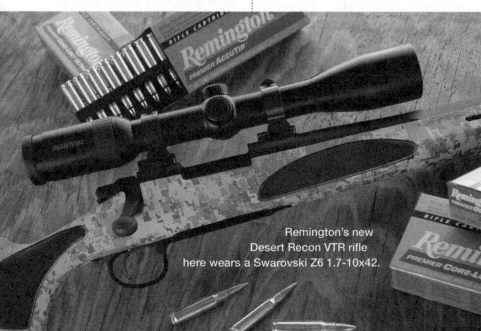

Remington's new
Desert Recon VTR rifle
here wears a Swarovski Z6 1.7-10x42.

optics by the 2008 debut of a 8-32x50ED SF with 1/8-minute adjustments and a turret dial to refine focus and zero-out parallax. The 4-16x50SF and 2-8x32, recent additions, are more versatile. For 2009 Nikon has trotted out a pair of "Coyote Special" rifle-scopes – a 3-9x40 and a 4.5-14x40. Both feature BDC (Bullet Drop Compensating) reticles and camouflage finish. A reflection-fighting screen is included for the front lens. A new Omega 1.65-5x36 scope for muzzle-loaders has a practical power range and

Sightron has an extensive optics line. This 10x42 binocular is new, excellent, reasonably priced.

trim front end. So does the suspiciously similar 1.65-5x36 SlugHunter. Both have BDC reticles, though these are slightly different, to fit trajectories of the most common bullets. Omega's parallax setting is 100 yards, that of the SlugHunter 75. Their best feature: 5 inches of eye relief! Both scopes (and a 3-9x40 SlugHunter) have 1" tubes and quarter-minute clicks.

Nikon's EDG binocular series (7x4, 8x42, 10x42, 8x32 and 10x32) appeared a year ago. ED glass, open-bridge design and a locking diopter have boosted sales. Now the company lists an EDG Fieldscope, also with ED glass. Pick the 85mm or 65mm version. Zoom eyepieces (16-48x and 20-60x) interchange with Nikon fixed-power eyepieces. On the binocular front, Nikon has once again bolstered its mid-priced lines. The All Terrain group now includes 8.5x45 and 10.5x45 Monarch X binoculars. You might recognize that moniker – the same as on a Nikon rifle-scope series with 30mm tubes and turret-mounted focus dials. The 2.5-10x and 4-16x feature Nikoplex and mil dot reticles, both

etched. The 2.5-10x is available with an illuminated mil dot. Still new at market: Nikon's IRT 4-12x42 laser rangefinding scope that reads reflective objects to 800 yards and delivers 1-yard accuracy out to 400. A BDC reticle helps with holdover. The sight can also give you continuous reads on moving game. (Nikonsportoptics.com)

Pentax

The 2009 binocular line-up at Pentax includes a new 7x50 Marine binocular with built-in compass on a liquid bearing (for quick dampening). It has an LED illuminator. Waterproof, with twist-up eye-cups and a click-stop diopter ring, the rubber-armored 7x50 has all the best features of its roof-prism kindred from the Denver-based firm. DCF roof prism binoculars come in 8x, 10x and 12.5x, with 32mm to 50mm objectives. DCFs feature phase-corrected prisms in aluminum and polycarbonate shells. A Porro prism PCF line includes 8x40, 10x50, 12x50 and 20x60 glasses. Less costly XCF Porros in 8x40, 10x50, 12x50 and 16x50 are great values. Last year I tried a new 9x28 BCF LV roof-prism binocular and found it one of the best lightweights (13 oz.!) I'd ever used. The 3mm exit pupil is adequate for all but the dimmest light. I like the twist-out eyecups and click-stop diopter. The surface is easy to grip. This spring 8x36 and 10x36 DCF NV roof-prism glasses join the 9x28. Their bigger exit pupils but compact size promise good hunting!

Pentax has added a 3-15x50 Game-seeker to its premier rifle-scope line. Five-times magnification offers more versatility than you'll likely need. Like the SL 3-9x32 I carried on a moose hunt last year, it is optically excellent. (That 12-ounce 3-9x32, incidentally, was perfect for my Ruger carbine in .300 RCM. It had the resolution to pick out a sliver of moose antler 107 yards away in timber! Neither my guide nor my hunting partner saw that moose until it fell.) The Gameseeker stable

includes eight 1" variable models and 4x32 and 6x42 fixed-powers. The 30mm Lightseeker 30 series comprises 3-10x40, 4-16x50, 6-24x50 and 8.5-32x50 scopes. A new pair of Pioneer II scopes has just appeared, in 3-9x40 and 4.5-14x42 versions that feature 1-inch tubes with fully multi-coated glass. The Whitetails Unlimited rifle-scope series has been dropped; reflex-style red dot sights remain. Among Pentax spotting scopes, the compact PF-63 Zoom with fixed 20-50x eyepiece is a bargain. It and the top-quality PF-65ED "make weight" for mountain hunting, while PF-80ED and PF-100ED scopes excel when weight isn't an issue. Interchangeable eyepieces include 32x, 46x and 20-60x for the 37-oz. PF-65ED, which also accepts a Pentax PF-CA35 camera adapter for 35mm SLRs. (Pentaxsportoptics.com)

Schmidt & Bender

Recent changes in the administration of this venerable German firm have not shifted its primary focus. Neither did the celebration, last year, of its first half-century in business. A small company by most standards, S&B caters to people who want the very best in optical sights. Its roots lie in the hunting field, but lately it has brought innovation to the tactical table. Two years ago a S&B 3-12x was adopted by the U.S. Marine Corps for its .30- and .50-caliber sniper rifles. The 34mm Police/Marks-man scopes have boldly raised the bar as regards not only tube diameter but sophistication. Lighted mil dot reticles, as on S&B's 4-16x42 P/M II, come with an 11-setting turret-mounted rheostat. An automatic shutoff saves battery – but the previous setting is automatically engaged when you hit the illumina-tion switch again. A side-mounted focus/parallax adjustment shares the left-side turret spot, and cleverly covers the illumination battery cage. Visible "gauges" on the windage and elevation knobs show you where the reticle is in its adjustment range. Flash-dot reticles incorporate a beam-splitter to illuminate a dead-center dot – which vanishes at a touch if you want to use a standard black reticle. For 2009, S&B has announced its first 1" variable rifle-scope, a 2.5-10x40 with second-plane reticle to satisfy U.S. hunters. Called the Summit, this 16-oz. scope has a pleasing profile and, praise be, a relatively short eyepiece. There's tube enough for easy mounting on most rifles. (Schmidt-bender.de or email scopes@cyberportal.net)

Shepherd

The problem with any front-plane reticle is that it grows in apparent size as you dial up the power. So at long range, where targets appear small and you want precise aim, the reticle can obscure the aiming point. Up close, when you power down for quick shots in thickets, the reticle shrinks, becoming hard to see quickly. A second-plane reticle stays the same apparent size throughout the power range. The advantage of a front-plane reticle is that it remains the same size relative to the target throughout the power range. It can be used quickly as a range-finding device at any magnification because the reticle subtends the same area regardless of power.

Shepherd scopes offer both reticles. You get an aiming reticle that doesn't change size and a range-finding reticle that varies in dimension with power changes. Superimposed, they appear as one. The range-finding reticle comprises a series of circles of decreasing diameter, top to bottom. To determine yardage, match a deer-size (18") target with one of the circles, located in the front focal plane. Correct holdover is factored in because the circles are placed to compensate for bullet drop. A trio of range-finding reticles suit the trajectories of popular cartridges. Vertical and horizontal scales are marked in minutes of angle so you can compensate for wind. The newest Shepherd scope, a 6-18x M556 is specially designed for AR-style rifles. (Shepherdscopes.com)

Sightron

It was a start-up company just a few years ago, a new player in the already-competitive arena of sports optics. But Sightron delivered an imported rifle-scope line of impressive quality at modest prices. It grew. The 2009 catalog lists more than 50 scopes in SI, SII and SIII series. New SIII Long Range models feature 30mm tubes, turret-mounted focus/parallax dials and reticles that include mil dot and an illuminated German #4A. Target knobs are tall enough for easy access but not ungainly. From the 3.5-10x44 to the 8-32x56, these scopes feature fully multi-coated optics in one-piece tubes, with resettable ExacTrack windage and elevation adjustments and a fast-focus eyepiece. External lenses wear "Zact-7," a seven-layer coating to transmit the most light possible. A hydrophobic wash disperses raindrops. Eye relief: 3.8 inches.

The SII series comprises a broad range of scopes with 1" tubes and most of the features of the SIIIs. A 1.25-5x20 Dangerous Game sight with over 6 inches of clear tube for mounting has replaced the 2.5x20 that has served me very well on hard-kicking rifles. Big field! Bright images! The SII series now has 4.5-14x40 and 6.5-20x50 scopes with side-focus dials. Sightron has also brought back its 12x42 fixed-power – Hooray! It and the 6x42 hunting scope make long shots easy. High-power variables and the 36x benchrest sights have front-ring parallax adjustments. I like the dot reticle. It's also available in the 5-20x42. Silver finish remains an option on selected models, so too Sightron's Hunter Holdover reticle with a couple of simple hash marks on the lower wire. Specify it on 3-9x42, 3-12x42 and 45.5-14x42 SIIs, and on the 3-9x40 SI.

The SI series for 2009 includes five scopes "back by popular demand." Sightron catalogs two ESDs (Electronic Sighting Devices) masquerading as red dot sights. They feature 33mm tubes, 11-stop rheostats and four reticles you can change with the twist of a dial. New on the binocular front are SIII 8x42 and 10x42 binoculars. I have a 10x42 at hand now. It's optically excellent, a solid value! Also listed: new SIIs and SI roof-prism 8x32 and 10x32 binoculars. (Sightron.com)

Steiner

Had you kept track over the last decade, you'd have noticed Steiner making a purposeful departure from the military profiles that for years defined the brand. Sleek roof-prims binoculars have dominated the news at this European firm. But for 2009 the Predator Pro line has two new Porro prism IF binoculars, and there's a 21-oz. Wildlife Pro 8x30 Porro glass with center focus, the first of its type in Steiner's stable in 20 years! Still the flagship of Steiner's line is the Peregrine XP. This center-focus, open-bridge binocular focuses down to 6-1/2 feet. Large (30mm) eyepieces have twist-up eyecups and flexible wings that can be folded back to ensure against fogging from face moisture. Exterior lens surfaces have hydrophobic "NANO Protection." It beads rainwater so you can see clearly even in a storm. Peregrine XP (8x44 and 10x44) is waterproof and lightweight, with a rugged magnesium frame. It comes with a neoprene hood and a clever Click-Loc strap. The NRA has awarded Peregrine XP its coveted Golden Bullseye Award for excellence, a feather in Steiner's cap! (Steiner-binoculars.com)

Swarovski

There's little new at Swarovski this year – which is hardly an indictment. The Austrian optics (and crystal) maker has introduced a steady stream of new products over the last decade, each an improvement on products many shooters thought were beyond improvement. The SLC binoculars I'd used for years were eclipsed by the EL series. The PH rifle-scopes gave way to the Z6, with

Trijicon's ACOG (Advanced Combat Optical Gunsight) has a big following among AR shooters.

six-times magnification. Swarovski borrowed from subsidiary Kahles to produce a Ballistic Turret capable of storing several zero settings. You determine those zeroes with ballistics tables or by live firing, then set a color-coded elevation dial. Change the load and zero; then return to your original in a wink. Ballistic Turret is an option on 1" 4-12x50 and 6-18x50 AV scopes. An even simpler way to engage long-range targets is the BR reticle. Its ladder-type bottom wire has 10 hash-marks. BR is available in three AV scopes, plus 1.7-10x42 and 2-12x50 Z6 sights. By the way, there is a new Z6: a 2.5-15x56. Like the other three 30mm Z6s, you can specify an illuminated reticle. The switch, atop the eyepiece, has an automatic shutoff and a blinking battery warning. It has two memory locations, one for daytime and one for night use. Turn the switch, and the reticle gets the default illumination for prevailing conditions. These Z6s are very fine scopes; they deliver brilliant, razor-edged images. The 1-6x24 boasts the broadest power range of any "dangerous game" sight. At a generous 4-3/4", its eye relief is longer than even that of its stable-mates. (Swarovskioptik.com)

Trijicon

"We just sold our 500,000th ACOG," said Tom Munson. The ACOG (Advanced Combat Optical Gunsight) vaulted Trijicon into the limelight as an optics maker. Tough and ideally suited for fast shooting with AR-type rifles, the ACOG has endeared itself to military units. But Trijicon didn't stop there. It now offers

hunters traditional scopes, and early this spring announced a new reflex-style red dot sight. Labeled RMR (for Ruggedized Miniature Reflex), it can be ordered with an LED (light-emitting diode) that adjusts automatically for changing light conditions; or you can specify a dual-illuminated, battery-free RMR with Trijicon fiber optics and tritium. Both versions have windage and elevation screws – as does the company's RedDot sight. Like the LED RMR, it is powerd by a 17,000-hour lithium battery. The RMR has an alloy housing, the RedDot sight a nylon-polymer frame. Either can be paired with the ACOG.

The newest Trijicon AccuPoint scope is a 5-20x50. It features target knobs and a turret-mounted focus/parallax dial. Like the 1-4x24, 1.25-4x24, 3-9x40 and 2.5-10x56, the 5-20x50 employs both tritium and fiber optics to illuminate the reticle without a battery. An adjustable cover lets you trim light from the fiber optic coil. Last year AccuPoint came with plex and crosswire-and-dot reticles, as alternatives to its original super-fast delta. To acquaint hunters with the famous ACOG, Trijicon now markets a 4x32 version to civilians. It includes an adjustable rail mount and a bullet drop compensator useful to 800 meters. The Michigan-based company continues to produce iron sights with tritium inserts (green, orange and yellow) for handguns and carbines. "We're busy," smiles Tom. (Trijicon.com)

TruGlo

Its luminescent shotgun beads and

rifle-sight inserts, with tritium and fiber-optic elements, served shooters well. Now TruGlo offers red dot sights and rifle-scopes too. Waterproof and compatible with any Weaver-style mount, the red dot sights come in tube or reflex (open) styles. Choose 1x or 2x, 1-inch, 30mm or 40mm tubes. An 11-stop rheostat controls reticle brightness. Dual-Color (red and green) Multi-Reticles (pick instantly from four, including the special turkey circle) come standard in some models. All versions of the tube sight have unlimited eye relief, multi-coated lenses, click-stop windage/elevation adjustments. Reflex red dot sights weigh as little as 2 oz. This light-weight model boasts a 4-minute dot with manual and light-sensitive automatic brightness modes. Multi-Reticle, Dual-Color reflex sights offer four reticles in red or green. They're parallax-free beyond 30 yards. Like many optics firms now, TruGlo markets several series of rifle-scopes, topped by the Maxus XLE in 1.5-6x44, 3-9x44 and 3.5-10x50 (also with BDC). The Infinity label goes on 4-16x44 and 6-24x44 scopes with adjustable objectives. To make long-distance hits easier across a variety of loads, each comes with three replaceable BDC elevation knobs. Tru-Brite Xtreme Illuminated rifle-scopes feature dual-color plex and range-finding reticles. Choose a 3-9x44, 3-12x44 or 4-16x50. Muzzleloader versions are available. The 4x32 Compact scope for rimfires and shotguns, a 4x32 for crossbows and a 1.5-5x32 illuminated crossbow model round out the TruGlo line of 1" scopes. New for 2009: a fiber optic AR-15 gas block front sight with protected green bead (it will also mount on Picatinny and Weaver rails). TruGlo offers an expanded line of illuminated iron sights and beads. (Truglo.com)

Vortex

Two lines of rifle-scopes from Vortex differ primarily in front-lens glass and W&E dials. Viper sights comprise six models, from the 1" 2-7x32 to the 30mm 6.5-20x50 AO. Front lenses are of what the company calls XD or extra-low dispersion glass. Dials reset to zero. There's a fast-focus eyepiece. Eye relief ranges from 3.1 to 4.0 inches. Diamondback rifle-scopes share the aircraft-alloy tubes, argon-gas fog-proofing and fully multi-coated optics of the Viper series; but they lack the resettable dials and XD glass, so they don't cost as much. Choose a 1.75-5x32 or one of six other models in versatile power ranges (2-7x to 4-12x) with BDC (bullet drop

The Zeiss Victory Varipoint 1.1-4x24 now features front-plane reticle with rear-plane lighted dot.

compensating) reticles – but not BDC mechanisms.

The widest selection in the Vortex family comes under the Crossfire banner, a line of affordable rifle-scopes from 1.5-4x32 to 8-32x50. It includes 2-7x32 and 4x32 sights for rimfires, a 2x20 handgun scope and a 3x32 for crossbows. As with the Vipers, you get tall target knobs (and 30mm tubes) on the most powerful scopes, low-profile dials on others. Nitrogen gas prevents fogging. Specify a mil dot or illuminated mil dot reticle on the 6-24x50 AO. Vortex also offers a red dot sight, the Strikefire, with fully multi-coated lenses. Choose red or green dots at any time. The sight has a 30mm tube 6 inches long and weighs 7.2 oz. The 2x optical doubler is a useful feature. There's unlimited eye relief, and the Strikefire is parallax-free beyond 50 yards.

Vortex spotting scopes include two new models. The 20-60x80 Nomad complements the budget-priced 20-60x60 Nomad (specify straight or angled eyepiece for both). Adapters allow you to mount most pocket-size digital cameras so you can photograph through your Nomad. At the top end, there's the new Razor HD, with apochromatic lenses and an 85mm objective. The 15" scope weighs 66 ounces with an angled 20-60x eyepiece and rotating body. It has coarse and fine focusing wheels in front of the eyepiece. The die-cast magnesium alloy body is argon-gas purged. (800-426-0048)

Weaver

It was inevitable, I suppose, that after the Grand Slam would come the Super Slam. Weaver's most recent scope line includes 2-10x42, 2-10x50, 3-15x42, 3-15x50 and 4-20x50 models. The scopes are quite similar to the ATK line (Weaver is owned by ATK), from the five-times magnification range to the 1" tubes to the turret-mounted focus/parallax dials. They're not identical, though. Weaver has endowed these sights with pull-up windage and elevation knobs (no caps to lose). A three-point erector design, argon gas purging and scratch-resistant lens coating make them field worthy. Euro-style versions with 30mm tubes and front-plane reticles are available.

Weaver's Classic Extreme scopes, new last year, remain in the stable with the Grand Slam and Classic V-Series – both of which offer Ballistic-X reticles this year. Fixed 4x38 and 6x38 K-Series scopes survive. I'm delighted. They're among the best buys in the industry! No

With an 85mm objective and a 20-60x eyepiece, the Vortex Razor weighs 66 oz.

frills, just fine optics in a lightweight, foolproof package that looks good on any rifle. New in 2009 is a 4-20x50 Tactical scope with 30mm tube, front-plane mil dot reticle and side-focus parallax dial. For long shooting at small targets, Weaver T-series sights excel. I like the T-24s announced a couple of years ago. Choose a 1/2-minute or 1/8-minute dot reticle. Target adjustments on dual-spring supports ensure quick, repeatable changes. (Weaveroptics.com)

Zeiss

No question, Zeiss is out for more U.S. market share. The highly rated Conquest rifle-scope series was followed last year by 8x45 and 10x45 T* RF binoculars, which feature a laser range-finding unit that requires no "third eye" emitter but delivers 1,300-yard range on reflective targets. This unit is fast – you get a read in about a second – and the LED self-compensates for brightness. The binocular itself is top-drawer, and wears rain-repellent LotuTec coating. You can program the RF with computer data to get holdover for six standard bullet trajectories. This year, the Zeiss news is mostly about scopes. The Victory Varipoint 1.1-4x24 T* and 1.5-6x42 T* are getting a #60 reticle, with a crosswire in the front focal plane and a lighted dot in the rear. So the main reticle stays in constant relationship to the target (for easy ranging), while the dot subtends a tiny area even at high power. A left-side turret knob controls dot brightness on the 1.1-4x24; three other Varipoints (2.5-

10x42T*, 2.5-10x50T*, 3-12x56T*) have automatic brightness control. Another headline for 2009: second-plane reticles in 2.5-10x50T* and 3-12x56T* Diavari scopes. Hewing to tastes of U.S. hunters, these reticles stay the same apparent size throughout the power range, so do not block out targets at high magnification. Reticle choices include the #60, Z-Plex and Rapid-Z 800.

Big news for pistol shooters is the first Zeiss handgun scope. This 2-7x has more power than most of us need. But it's a trim, well-shaped sight, with non-critical eye relief and plenty of tube for rings. It is optically superb. So is the Victory PhotoScope, 85T* FL, also new this spring. This 85mm spotting scope with fluorite lens and 45-degree 15-45x eyepiece has at its midpoint a square compartment – not too bulky or obtrusive – housing a 7-megapixel camera, so you can shoot photos through that powerful lens (35mm equivalent: 600mm f2.4 to 1800mm f3.3). The camera uses a 7.4-volt lithium ion battery and SD card to deliver images in standard file formats. PhotoScope 85T* FL weighs 6-1/2 lbs.

Not to be outdone in the range-finder market, Zeiss has introduced the Victory 8x26T* PRF, a "one-touch" device that gives you an LED read to 1,300 yards. In scan mode, it updates distance every 1.5 seconds. Its most distinctive feature may be a Ballistic Information System (BIS) that can be programmed to give you proper holdover for your rifle's load – instantly. (Zeiss.com)

We are happy to include in this edition a notable first: a column written from a woman's perspective. That woman, Gila Hayes, is 10-year veteran of Washington State police departments, where she served as Department Firearms Instructor. In addition, Ms. Hayes has a long career writing for publications including *Woman's Outlook, American Guardian, SWAT Magazine, Women & Guns,* and *GUNS Magazine.* With her husband Marty, she operates The Firearms Academy of Seattle, Inc., a practical firearms training school. In addition, Gila has recently started a second business, the Armed Citizens Legal Defense Network (http://www.armedcitizensnetwork.org/).

Women's PERSPECTIVE

BY GILA HAYES

s women's participation in the world of guns becomes increasingly ordinary, the variety of firearms that work really well for women is greater than ever before. Remember when an anemic .25 ACP with pearly pink grips was the pistol most gun store clerks

Short hands just fit well around a 1911, as the author shows here with Para Ordnance's new 9mm LTC.

Ruger's reinvention of the snub-nosed revolver has cutting-edge good looks.

trotted out for women? Fortunately, that doesn't happen too often anymore, due in part to the increasing variety of very serviceable handguns, shotguns and rifles that fit women's needs. Still, I marvel at the shooting industry's proclivity for coloring a product pink and dubbing it a "ladies' gun."

That kind of marketing is straight out of the mid to late 1950s. If in doubt, consider the amusing history of the ill-fated Dodge La Femme and similarly patronizing General Motors attempts at "women's cars"! When the color concept petered out with merciful rapidity, Detroit's marketing geniuses came to their senses and began promoting creature comforts like heated seats, adjustable pedals and steering wheels,

and child-friendly seating.

In the gun industry of 2009, countless variations on ergonomic firearms offer women guns that fit and function properly with quite a reasonable selection from which to choose — no matter the color!

Handgun Choices

On handguns, proper fit is largely determined by the measurement between the backstrap and the face of the trigger. On revolvers, shooters have traditionally custom fit the gun to their hand size with replacement grips. The latest trend in semi-auto pistols is the small-to-large interchangeable back strap insert, as found on Smith & Wesson's M&P, Walther's PPS, several models of Heckler

Mossberg's Super Bantam Model 500's stock is adjustable between 12" and 13" LOP, plus one of the color options is the distinctive Pink Marble.

& Koch handguns, the Beretta Storm, FNH's FNP handguns, Springfield's XD(M), and the Ruger SR9, to list only what comes quickly to mind. SIG Sauer achieves a similar end result with the modular SIG Sauer 250.

The classic 1911 design has long been an ergonomic favorite among female .45 shooters, with the thin grips around the single column magazine and the short trigger reach accommodating a strong grip. Think about this: how powerfully can you hold an object around which your fingers only reach halfway, compared to gripping something your

With their latest innovation, the LaserGuard, Crimson Trace returns to its roots – a laser sight positioned on the front of the trigger guard.

fingers nearly encircle? Thus the thin-gripped 1911 is a natural choice for the smaller-handed shooter.

Does recoil matter? Of course it does, but in shooters of either gender, tolerance to recoil is an individual matter. It is not unusual to see a woman operating a .45 ACP pistol with the same skill as her male counterpart. With good training and well-practiced trigger control, the larger handgun calibers are certainly controllable. Only when tactical engagements require intensely brief shot-to-shot times, do we begin to see the generally smaller and more lightly

muscled female shooter better served by lighter recoil.

Because there are plenty of highly ranked men shooting 9mm 1911s in competition, I hesitate to identify models like Kimber's Aegis as "women's guns." Not everyone wants to put up with the hard bump of .45 caliber recoil and its muzzle rise. Para Ordnance, Springfield Armory and Kimber, as well as exclusive shops like STI, Wilson Combat and Cylinder and Slide, all stock a variety of excellent 1911 choices in alternative calibers.

Several years ago, Springfield Armory and Para Ordnance both brought out 9mm 1911 pattern pistols on what was essentially shrunken frames. Para's Carry 9 is a slim, 9mm micro version of Para's popular light double-action pistol. Eight round magazines, plus one in the chamber, make it a nine-shooter.

An exciting new development is chambering the originally 9mm Springfield Enhanced Micro Pistol (EMP) to fire the effective .40 caliber ammunition. The ingenious EMP design remains a favorite with women who love the 1911 single-action operation, but want a smaller grip than the traditional officers model. Now we even have a caliber choice!

The original 9mm EMP is built around a nine-round magazine so it's about a 1/4" longer through the grip than the Para Carry 9. The new .40 caliber EMP has an eight-round magazine.

I would be remiss if mention of the Glock 19 was lost in all the "new-and-improved" chatter! If there is one semi-automatic pistol which shooters, new

and old, male and female, find adaptable to their training, practice, and defense needs, it is the Glock 19. The Glock Safe Action eliminates the need to accustom the shooter to a thumb safety or decocker, and that mid-sized frame sure soaks up recoil. Though less suitable for beginners, the smaller Glock 26 may well have eclipsed J-frame revolvers as women's single most popular personal protection choice.

Both the Glock 19 and 26 cannot be beat for reliable operation; the array of holsters and carry options made for Glocks cannot be surpassed; and there are hundreds of aftermarket products such as grip reductions, laser sights, night sights, and other replacement parts of all kinds made for Glocks.

How Small Is Too Small?

Too often, people erroneously recommend extremely small, light guns to first-time women gun buyers. At the Firearms Academy of Seattle, which my husband and I operate, we see with heartbreaking regularity novice female shooters who come to class with ultra-light snubby revolvers, or tiny, 8-oz. .380s. Not only are the abbreviated frames often too small for these new shooters to attain a serviceable shooting grip, the recoil in such a light gun is jarring.

Having acknowledged the extreme disadvantage of training with miniaturized pistols, it is hard to ignore the attraction they pose for the well-trained

Possibly the hottest semi-auto at the 2009 SHOT Show: Kahr Arms' P380.

Angela Harrell w/HK P30
Heckler & Koch's Angela Harrell shows off features of their P30, which also includes grip backstrap inserts in varied sizes.

concealed carry practitioner. Women licensed to carry a concealed handgun face additional concealment challenges, owing to the skimpiness of women's fashions coupled with ladies' generally smaller physiques. Today, our concealed carry gun choices are many and varied.

Kel-Tec and North American Arms enjoy continued loyalty to their respective P-3AT and Guardian semi-autos in .380 ACP, though in 2008, Ruger enchanted many with their LCP. In 2009, SIG Sauer and Kahr Arms entered the mini-380 market with models that also deserve serious consideration.

Kahr Arms' P380 is a miniaturized version of their already miniscule PM9 pistol. Thus, like the – dare we say larger? – PM9, the P380 is an elegantly simple double-action-only pistol with a stainless steel slide atop a polymer frame. With no external safety, the striker-fired design uses a double action only trigger with a light, but long, pull. Kahr pistols position the barrel very low in the gripping hand, which tames the .380 muzzle rise in this small, 10-oz. frame.

Beyond the smaller dimensions, the new Kahr .380 features rounded edges appropriate to a deep concealment pistol, and honest-to-goodness sights, something sorely lacking on most miniaturized .380s. Dimensionally, the P380 is slightly shorter from slide to mag base plate than a Kel-Tec, though both use six-round magazines. The Kahr is heavier, and its price about double. Like other Kahr pistols, its locked breech design operates on the short recoil principle, unlike the blowback operation of NAA's Guardian.

Though Colt's Manufacturing hasn't made the Colt Government Pocketlite for over a decade, SIG Sauer's new single-action semi-auto P238 is so reminiscent of that early pocket pistol that I thought I was suffering a flashback when first I saw it. Closer inspection showed that the little single action was identical in height and length to the old Colt .380, though its blocky slide profile is pure SIG.

Both the SIG P238 and Kahr P380 herald good things for the concealed carry practitioner. The Kahr is a little smaller and considerably thinner, while the SIG P238 has the single action operation to which some experienced shooters are so partial.

Revolver Innovations

But not all the innovation focuses on semi-automatic pistols! It is entirely possible that the new product generating the greatest interest at the 2009 Shooting, Hunting and

Outdoor Trade Show (SHOT Show) was Ruger's completely redesigned, ultra-lightweight five-shot .38 Special revolver. Recently, Ruger has made a concerted play for the hearts of serious self-defense shooters, in 2008 with their pocket-sized .380 and now with their all-new Lightweight Compact Revolver (LCR).

The LCR is an intriguing re-invention of the double-action revolver: an all-new wheel gun comprising an aluminum frame, polymer housing around the firing mechanism, and a fluted steel cylinder. Sized like all five-shot snubbies, the LCR weighs between 13 and 13.5 oz., depending on grip option selected.

The innovative LCR has a large, curving trigger guard that should accommodate chubby or gloved trigger fingers, a black pinned front sight blade, and the modular design that accept a variety of replacement grips, including an OEM LaserGrip option.

Ruger's new revolver promises to address one challenge that wheel guns pose for some women: their stiff trigger pull. According to Ruger, "The LCR's trigger pull force builds more gradually, and peaks later in the trigger stroke, resulting in a trigger pull that feels much lighter than it actually is…This results in more controllable shooting, even among those with smaller, weaker hands who find traditional DAO triggers difficult to operate."

A ridiculously over-booked SHOT Show schedule cost me the chance to test fire the all-new revolver, but no less an authority than Massad Ayoob enthusiastically told me that the recoil was quite manageable.

Another innovation making ever-widening ripples in the revolver market is the .327 Federal cartridge. I couldn't help but notice that Smith &

Springfield Armory's beautiful new .40 caliber EMP.

Wesson now joins Ruger in producing a revolver chambered for the smaller .327. Now both the Ruger SP101 and S&W's J-framed Model 632 fire six rounds of high pressure, magnumized .32-caliber ammo. The jury is still out on cartridge effectiveness as it has only been with us since November of 2007, but Smith & Wesson's presence brings additional prestige to the new cartridge, giving it "legs," so to speak. I am told that other manufacturers, including Charter Arms and Taurus, have also embraced the new caliber.

Sighting Improvements

Small, hard-to-use sights are the single most troubling characteristic shared by most ultra-small handguns, and they pose problems not only for men but for women, too. The solution? Crimson Trace's LaserGrip and now the new LaserGuard. The LaserGuard is a sleek half-sleeve attaching to Glock, Kahr Arms, Kel-Tec, and Ruger LCP trigger guards to position an aiming laser to the front of the trigger guard.

The design is reminiscent of Crimson Trace's first laser sight, introduced some 15 years ago. It was a complex aftermarket assembly that they painstakingly installed on Glock pistols. Since then, the Crimson Trace laser aiming products have grown increasingly innovative, while continuing to augment traditional sights without compromising conventional sighting and without replacing any of the handgun's operating parts.

Crimson Trace even has several laser sighting options for AR-15 rifles. Not being a big fan of vertical foregrips, I am partial to the slightly more complex LG-525, which I have installed on my AR. I am comforted by the increased low light functionality it adds to the .223 rifle.

Beyond Handguns

If there is one gun that exemplifies this decade's gun industry growth, it must surely be the AR-15 rifle. It seems that companies manufacturing "black rifles" have doubled, if not tripled. Even mainline Smith & Wesson has their famous logo on an AR-15! The good news for women is the light recoil of the .223 cartridge, as well as a plethora of aftermarket accessories to custom fit the rifle to their needs. An AR-15 promises hours of shooting fun, plus a serious tactical rifle for defense emergencies.

With long guns, police raid vests and bulky body armor interfere with stock fit. While most women shooters won't be kitted out that way, the short stocks manufactured to accommodate SWAT and military operators also fit short-statured shooters! While some do fine with collapsible stocks, I prefer the cheek weld of a fixed A-1 stock, which is 5/8" shorter than the common A2 version.

Cavalry Arms injection-molds AR furniture in a variety of colors and has

1911 and .45 ACP are no longer synonymous. Major manufacturers like Kimber have 9mms on the 1911 pattern.

Peggy Tartaro, editor of *Women & Guns*, deserves recognition for putting out a magazine exclusively for women who shoot.

KNOWLEDGE IS POWER

Women shooters are also serious about knowing how to shoot their guns well. Twenty years ago, *Women & Guns* magazine started a gun publication solely for women. Editor Peggy Tartaro recently told me that she is inspired by Virginia Woolfe's famous title, "A Room of One's Own," and her goal has been to provide female shooters with a magazine of their own, and thus their own voice. She is proud to note that, "unlike virtually any other women's magazine, *Women & Guns* has, with rare exceptions, used actual women gun owners on our covers and pages throughout its history."

Tartaro believes that the gun industry has "failed itself by not working harder with minorities, women and the urban population in general." Her magazine is not heavily focused on gun rights issues, though its publisher, the Second Amendment Foundation, is a leader in that effort.

Live-fire educational initiatives that women truly appreciate include programs like Women on Target or the Ladies Action Shooting Camp, a competition training program taught by top female shooters, including Kay Clark-Miculek, Lisa Munson, Sheila Bray, and Julie Goloski, just to name a few. Sponsorship by Smith & Wesson and USPSA keeps tuition reasonable.

For more information, visit www.women shooters.com.

A pink backstrap insert identifies the Smith & Wesson M&P Breast Cancer Awareness model.

Mossberg has what is in my opinion the most tastefully done pink gun ever! They've dressed up a Model 500 Super Bantam 20-gauge shotgun in a stock pattern dubbed "Pink Marble." Veins of a dark, contrasting hue run through the pink of the stock and forend. The darker colors tie in the pink to the blued steel of the shotgun's action and barrel. Of course, Super Bantams also come in several camo patterns, black synthetic or the more traditional wooden stock.

The 20-gauge Super Bantam has the added benefit of 12" to 13" LOP adjustability that can be a make-or-break feature for short shooters. If a 13" stock fits, the shooter can choose between 12- and 20-gauge in the Bantam line. The Mossberg tang-mounted safety makes it almost ambidextrous, and it is certainly the most ergonomic place to put a shotgun's safety.

The pink marble Mossberg stock is genuinely attractive. In other instances, I've seen pink accessories that looked as if they were simply slapped onto a black gun with little aesthetic consideration. These make me think of wearing boots with a chiffon ball gown. Bold design contrast can look great, but some mind must be paid to design principles to carry it off!

What Women Want

The prevalence of pink at the 2009 SHOT Show convinced me that the gun industry continues to court the female market, but I wonder if color-coding is intelligent marketing. I looked to women

the A1-length butt stock in their product line up. Although not every woman shooter will go all googly-eyed over colored AR furniture, this manufacturer stocks green and brown butt stocks and handgrips, and in the past has run pink, red, yellow and purple choices.

Hunting rifles to fit women seem fewer and farther between, owing to long 14" length of pull (LOP) stocks on most of the bolt-action rifles. Youth models, with a 13" LOP, generally find their way into women's hands, and for my money, Remington's compact Model Seven Youth rifle combines quality construction with caliber choices, ranging from .223 to 7mm-08 Rem., suitable for a variety of hunts. The Model Sevens are slightly more compact and half a pound lighter than Remington's ubiquitous Model 700.

The Remington Model 700, however, has a left-handed youth model. That's important to women, because ladies exhibit eye cross dominance at a higher rate than men. Right-handers with left eye dominance usually simply shoot a rifle or shotgun from the left shoulder, so that left-handed action could make a big difference, even though caliber choices are limited to .243 and 7mm-08.

The ever-popular shotgun is the other long gun on which certain models and modifications make considerable difference for female shooters. Length of pull is again the critical factor, and once more, youth models reduce stock length by about an inch. Often these shorter shotguns are 20-gauges. As with

handguns, ability with a 12- or 20-gauge shotgun is an extremely individual attribute. Plenty of women can keep up with or even outshoot the gents at the gun club with a 12-gauge shotgun – if it fits her properly.

Hogue's famous soft rubbery overmolded short butt stocks are a great help when adjusting a 12-gauge for shorter shooters. A really short woman, or one who simply likes a short stock, will be delighted, as was I, with the fit of Hogue's 12" LOP stock for Remington 870s and Mossberg 500s.

Smith & Wesson's Model 632 puts six of the new .327 Magnum cartridges in the cylinder.

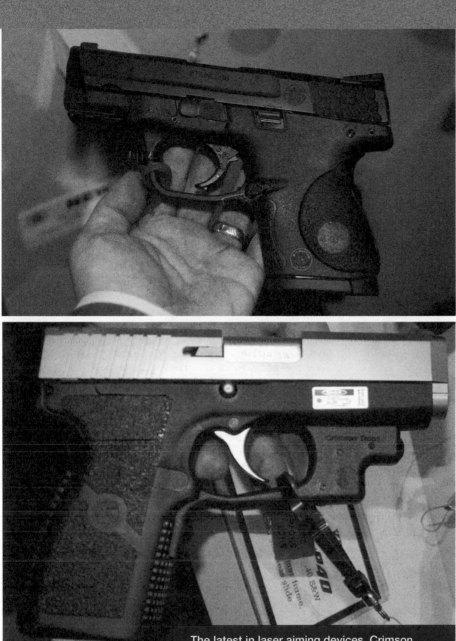

Crimson Trace teams with Smith & Wesson to offer an OEM LaserGrip option that puts a laser in the M&P backstrap insert.

The latest in laser aiming devices, Crimson Trace's LaserGuard, shown on Kahr Arms' CW9.

Walther's 9mm PPS is ultra-slim, but the back-strap insert gives some grip size adjustment.

from various walks of life for perspective.

Suzi Huntington, retired San Diego police officer, now managing editor of *American Cop* magazine, dislikes pink guns, feeling they trivialize women. "A gun should not be viewed as a fashion accessory, but as a deadly weapon. It's got one job to do and it's pretty damn hard to get anybody to believe you mean business when the darn thing is pink," she commented, adding, "I think the pink goodies marketed for breast cancer awareness are wonderful. That's a legitimate and noble cause and that's about where this pink thing should end!"

On the other hand, *Concealed Carry Magazine* editor Kathy Jackson, also the woman behind www.corneredcat.com, is annoyed by implications that shooting and self defense are masculine activities. She sees no reason for women to want to be treated like one of the guys. "We can be as absolutely feminine as we want to be, as long as we're competent and capable. People will take the competence and visible capability seriously, whether it's pink and frilly or not," she told me.

Theresa Dec is an avid competition shooter who opines, "I am not a man. I will not do things like a man. I will, however, shoot quickly, accurately and safely. It's great to tease the guys I shoot with, that not only are they being beat by a girl, they are being beat by a girl with a pink gun."

Most women queried found the idea of pink accents on a wholly sporting firearm acceptable and often appealing, while attempting to feminize purely defensive guns raised some hackles. Not once in my inquiries did a woman complain that she couldn't find firearms that fit her needs.

Viewed that way, it seems that women shooters have a reasonable variety of equipment choices, both colored and plain. The ergonomic challenges of all smaller shooters are fewer than in earlier years, though shooters always welcome innovations that fit guns and equipment to individual needs, especially with shotguns and rifles.

Pink doesn't necessarily make a gun "perfect for women," but the ability to fit a firearm to "her" size, conceal it if appropriate, and trust it to function reliably, may well make a gun a woman's favorite!

EUROPEAN GUNS TODAY:
Highlights of IWA 2009

BY M. RAYMOND CARANTA
Aix-en-Provence, France

The 36th IWA and outdoor classic gun show was held in Nurnberg this year – as it is every year – from March 13 to 16th, 2009.

The IWA (the German acronym for the International Trade Fair for Hunting and Sporting Arms and Accessories – Europe's counterpart to our own SHOT Show) gathered 1132 exhibitors from 53 nations, including the United States, as compared to 1046 last year, for an 8 percent increase and acknowledged 32,000 professional visitors, a slight increase over last year's attendance.

As all the great international companies are present both at the American SHOT Show held in February and at the European IWA, this report will mainly cover the new or most original products displayed by the more typical exhibitors and those of particular interest for our national shooters and hunters. Therefore, the new products of major companies such as

Beretta, Browning FN, BSA, Franchi, Glock, Heckler und Koch, Merkel, Pedersoli, Perazzi, Sako, Steyr, Tanfoglio, Tikka, Umarex and Walther, for instance, are not mentioned hereunder.

Concerning our selection, the American reader should understand that, in regard to handguns, for instance, in Europe, target shooting is performed according to the ISU (International Shooting Union) rules, with the exception of IPSC. Therefore, our most popular calibers are the .22 Long Rifle, 9mm Luger and .38 Special.

The .22 W. Magnum RF, .32 ACP, .357 Magnum, .44 Magnum and .45 ACP are also available in large shops, but much less common. Other calibers such as the .380 ACP (stupidly classified as "war material" since 1939), .38 Super Auto, .40 SW and .41 Magnum, are quite rare and expensive when available, restricting their use mostly to handloaders.

Here is our selection:

ANICS
(ANICS GROUP, 7 Vorontsovo Pole St. MOSCOU 105062, Russie. www.anics.com)

ANICS is a Russian company specializing in the manufacture of CO_2 pellets guns of .177 caliber.

The ANICS "Berkut" A-2002 pistol features a revolutionary conveyer type 22-shot magazine for .177 pellets; CO_2 cartridge capacity is 75 shots.

Anschutz
(Anschutz J.G. GmbH, Daimlerstrasse 12, D-89079 ULM – Donautal. www.anschutz-sport.com)

Anschutz is a name well-respected throughout the world for accuracy and fine workmanship.

In the "hunting rifles line," the Anschutz Model 1770 bolt action rifle chambered in .223 Remington with a three-shot magazine capacity is 42" long and weighs 7.5 lbs. Barrel length is 22", and trigger pull is factory-adjusted to 2.5 lbs.

Baïkal
**(Izhevsky Mekhanichesky Zavod,
8, Promyshlennaya Str.
Izhevsk 426063, Russie
www.baïkalinc.ru)**

The most famous Russian gunmaker, Baïkal has introduced a full line of sporting guns in all the international calibers and systems. This year, we have noted for you a nice self-loading .22 LR rifle, a Biathlon repeating air rifle and a fancy CO_2 machine pistol for .177 BBs.

The Baïkal "MP-661 K Drozd" CO_2 fancy machine pistol in .177 BB caliber, has a 400-round magazine capacity with an adjustable firing rate of 300 rpm, 450 rpm and 600 rpm (muzzle velocity = 393 fps). It operates with 6 AA-type batteries. Overall length is 27.6"; weight is 4.9 bbs.

The Baïkal "MP-161 K" self-loading .22 LR rifle, featuring a nine-round magazine capacity and a highly modern ergonomic polymer stock, is 39" long with a 20" barrel. It weighs 6.4 lbs.

The Baïkal "M-571 K PCP" compressed air five-shot international competition ISU rifle is 43.3" long with a 15.75" barrel and weighs 9-7 lbs. Operating pressure is the standard 200 bar value.

Blaser
**(Blaser Jagdwaffen GmbH, Ziegelstadel, 1,
D-88316Isny im Allgau. www.blaser.de)**

This year, the general trend, as far as bolt rifles were concerned, was toward "modular systems." In this connection, we have noticed at the German Blaser booth, the "R93" modular system, enabling the fast and easy conversion of any "R93" center fire rifle into a convenient .22 LR five-shot bolt action.

Several right or left hand versions are available with semi-weight, stützen and varmint or match barrels, and special forearms matching Safari or match barrels.

For 2009, Benelli displayed at IWA its 2009 "Concept gun" – a veritable celebration of energy, relentlessly flowing fluidity, and undeniable grace.

Benelli
(Benelli Armi SPA, Via della Stazione, 50. I-61029 URBINO www.benelli.it)

For 2009, Benelli has introduced a new .223 hunting rifle and a striking new "concept gun" shotgun.

The Benelli "MR1" self loading .223 Rem hunting five-shot rifle featuring a delayed blowback action is available with 12.5", 16" or 20" barrels. With the short barrel and flash-hider, it weighs 7 lbs. Features include a rotating bolt head with three lugs and techno-polymer stock.

Being the discoverer of the original pre-production CZ 75 pistol at the Madrid 1975 Gun Show, this writer could not resist mentioning the new CZ 75 P-07 with its so attractive look, regardless of whether it will be imported in the United States.

Ceska Zbrojovk
(Ceska Zbrojowka, Svatopluka Cecha, 1283, 68827 Uhersky Brod, République Tchèque. www.czub.cz)

Among the new items shown at IWA, we have noted the CZ 550 "Exclusive" bolt action rifle chambered in .30-06, the Brno "Stopper" over-under chambered in .458 Win Mag, and the beautiful CZ 75 P-07 16-shot 9 mm Luger pistol with polymer receiver. Empty weight is 27.5 oz.; loaded, it weighs 34 oz. Of course, all of them will be imported in the United States.

The Brno "Stopper" over-under rifle, chambered in .458 Win. Mag, features independent 23.6" barrels and weighs 9 lbs.

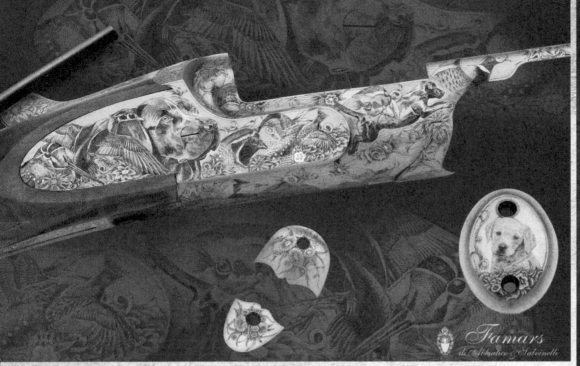

Academia "Il Bulino"
**(Il Bulino srl, Via Repubblica 197,
I-25068 Sarezzo (Brescia). www.ilbulinosrl.com)**

Il Bulino, Italian for "The Chisel," is is a fascinating
Italian school of engraving, teaching young people this
perrenial art which took its early origin in the prehis-
toric times. These young masters have already being
able to create absolutely outstanding masterpieces of
classic art and remarkable modern designs. Some of
their best work is shown.

EUROPEAN GUNS TODAY

An advance view of what the Italian FABARM "Iris" bolt action rifle will be.

FABARM (FABARM, Via Averolda, 31, Zona Industriale, I-25039 Travagliato (BS). www.fabarm.com)
This year, this well-known Italian shotgun maker has displayed at IWA eight new versions of its Axis, Elos and Waterfowl over-under shotguns, a Classic Grade IV side-by-side, a Martial Ultrashort 18" pump shotgun and, in preview, the Iris bolt action rifle.

Renato Gamba's Daytona K2 over-under featuring his patented interchangeable and detachable trigger group.

Renato Gamba
(SAB [SOCIETA ARMI BRESCIANE] Renato Gamba, Via Artigiani, 93, I-25063 Gardone Val Trompia (BS) www.renatogamba.it)

Renato Gamba was, when John T. Amber was the Gun Digest's chief editor in the 1970s, the flamboyant gunmaker of the "Italian Miracle" years... and a jolly good fellow! Since then, he is still at work, making on request outstanding Daytona, Prince, London Gold, Ambassador and Mustang double over-under and side-by-side shotguns. Gamba's "Daytona K2" has won, in 2008, at Beijing, a bronze Olympic medal at the Skeet Event, in the capable hands of Antony Terras.

Peter Hambrusch
Peter Hambrusch is an Austrian ferlacher who has designed a top precision side–by-side double outside hammer rifle chambered in .450/.400 caliber, featuring quite a sophisticated action. As a matter of fact, it consists of a self-cocking mechanism, the two hammers of which can also be individually cocked when breaking the barrel. Moreover, this gun is also fitted with a conventional safety at the rear of the tang, and a patented Hambrusch Safety Sidelock System.

The outstanding new Hambrusch side-by-side .450/400 caliber rifle (copyright DWJ Special Edition and Roland Zeitler).

Historical Weaponry
(www.piecesof history.co.uk)

This is a British company publishing a nice 114-page fullsize catalog of historical Japanese, Chinese and European swords and fractional-scale models of suits of armour.

The Black Knight is a suit of armour 2/3 size model 26-3/4" high.

The Peter Hofer gold inlaid small caliber side-by-side.

Peter Hofer
(Peter Hofer, Kirchgasse 24, A-9170 Ferlach, Autriche www.hoferwaffen.com)

Peter Hofer is a famous Ferlach gunmaker displaying a wonderful small gold inlaid side-by-side with two braces of barrels, one rifled in .22 caliber, and the other one, smoothbore in .410 Magnum.

The colorful Feinwerkbau 700 Evolution match air rifle as per ISU regulations. Overall length is 39 to 41 inches; weight is approximately 8 lbs. Muzzle velocity is 560 fps.

Feinwerkbau
(Feinwerkbau, Westiger & Altenburger, Neckarstrasse, 43, D-78727 Oberndorf/Neckar. www.feinwerkbau.de)

At Feinwerkbau, we have been able to see a new version of their famous Model 700 .177-caliber competition air rifle, the 700 Evolution, with an universal stock designed both for right-hand and left-hand shooters.

Grunig and Elmiger
(Grunig & Elmiger AG, Industriestrasse 22, CH-6102 Malters (LU). www.gruenel.ch)

This is a famous Swiss company making top-class ISU long range competition custom rifles, mostly for the 300-meter programs.

Grunig and Elmiger's FT 300 free rifle is currently available in 10 international competition calibers, from the 6 mm PPC to the .308 Win. Single shot; available in right hand only. Trigger pull adjustable from 4 to 9 oz. Weight is approximately 13 lbs.

The Russian KBP MTs-255 revolving shotgun.

KBP
(KBP, 17 Krasnoarmeysky Prospekt 300041 Tula Russie. www.tulatskib.ru)

This is a new and impressive Russian company, holder of four gold medals in its country, who first offers six hunting rifles including the bolt action MTs-19 in .308 Win and 9X64 calibers and five different self-loading models available in .22 LR, .308 Win, 9X64 and 7.62 mm Mossin-Nagant. In addition, KBP lists also four over-unders, two custom grade richly engraved, side-by-side, a conventional automatic gas-operated 12-gauge MTs-22 shotgun and an original pump repeater Rys (Lynx) chambered in the same caliber, but weighing only 6 Ibs., with a seven-shot capacity. However, their most interesting achievement is the MTs-255 revolving shotgun available in 12, 20, 32 and .410 Magnum chamberings, with a five-shot cylinder capacity!

Match Guns
(Matchguns Srl, Via Cartiera 6/d, I-43010 Vigatto (Parma) www.matchguns.com)

This year, this leading Italian specialist of top grade ISU competition handguns has released the new .22 LR MG free pistol for 50-meter slow fire shooting.

The Match Gun MG5 pistol is a dropping-bolt single-shot design fitted with four adjustable stabilizers. Barrel length is 11.4 inches; weight is 39.8 oz. plain.

Pardini K10 air pistol.

Pardini (Pardini Armi, Via Italica, 154-A, I-55043 Lido di Camaiore (Lucca). www.pardini.it)

Giampiero Pardini has been a noted Italian pistol champion who created, in the eighties, his own target pistol manufacturing company specialized in ISU competition models. Since then, his guns have won several major international events, namely at the Olympic Games of Atlanta, Sidney, Athens and, last year, Beijing (silver and bronze, in "Rapid fire"). For 2009, Pardini has designed a new "K10" target air pistol in .177 caliber.

Voere
(Voere, Untere Sparchen 56, A-6330 Kufstein/Tirol www.voere.de)

This reputable Austrian company has introduced this year at IWA the new modular LBW Luxus 20-03' bolt action hunting rifle available in four caliber groups and 22 basic calibers, plus custom options. Thanks to Voere's "Variosystem," the bolt travel is short for small calibers and long for others. The bolt features three solid locking lugs with a small opening angle, and the magazine is single row with three- (standard) or five-round (magnum) capacity. Average weight is around 6.6 lbs., depending on caliber.

The LBW Luxus 20-03 rifle is fitted with modular barrels and stocks, enabling its owner to easily change caliber at will.

Krieghoff
Krieghoff GmbH, Boschstr. 22, Postfach 2610, D-89016 Ulm/Donau www.krieghoff.de)

This famous German company displayed at IWA a beautiful "Trumpf Drilling" available in 12 or 20-gauge for the two side-by-side smooth-bore upper barrels and in 11 different calibers, from 6X70R to 9,3X74R, for the lower rifled barrel. Available barrel lengths are 22" and 24". Weight varies from 6.8 to 8 lbs.

The new Krieghoff "Trumpf Drilling."

SIG Sauer
(JP Sauer & Sohn GmbH, Sauerstrasse 2-6, D-24340 Eckernforde. www.sauer-waffen.de)

The latest Sig-Sauer handgun creation on the European IPSC market is their P220 X-Six .45 ACP eight-shot pistol. It has a six-inch barrel and weighs 44 oz. unloaded.

Sig-Sauer P220 X-Six pistol.

HANDLOADING Today

Today's factory ammunition is probably the best it has ever been in the history of factory ammunition. However, handloading permits the use of bullet weights not available in factory loads, and it is often the only way to obtain ammunition for obsolete cartridges and wildcats. Plus, it's fun and the best – and sometimes only – way to tailor loads to improve accuracy. Also, given the impending legislative climate, this might be a good time to consider "rolling your own."

To produce quality handloads you need equipment and components. What follows is a look at the newest available to handloaders.

Bullet pullers are necessary to remove a bullet from a cartridge when it's the wrong bullet for the powder charge, or to salvage the powder and primed case. Sometimes a handloader will decide to replace the bullet with a different bullet design of the same weight. It's a simple process with the correct equipment,

Excellent loading data is available in the complimentary loading guide published by the various powder companies, such as these for Accurate, VihtaVuori, and Ramshot powders.

Some of the .50 caliber cartridges which handloaders can reload. Left to right: .502 Sabre, .50 ACP, .50 Spotter, .510 DTC Europa, .50 BMG, .500 Phantom, .500 Cyrus, .500 Jeffery, .500 Smith & Wesson.

but a time-consuming task.

Forster Products has a new Universal Bullet Puller designed for use with the Forster Co-Ax Press, as well as any standard loading press using 7/8" x 14 thread dies. The die is capable of pulling bullets from .17 caliber to .458 caliber using one of the 21 hardened steel collets available separately. In addition to the die, and a proper size collet, a 9/16" wrench is needed to tighten and loosen the collet screw.

RCBS (www.rcbs.com) has a new Bullet Puller designed to pull .416 or .50 BMG bullets using the correct collet. (The collets are sold separately.) Designed for use on the AmmoMaster .50 BMG or AmmoMaster 2 RCBS presses, this puller has 1-1/2" x 12 threads and can be used with any press capable of accepting dies of this size.

RCBS had one of the first presses available to load the .50 BMG cartridge, and for 2009 the firm expanded the line of accessories for "Big Fifty" reloading. In addition to the Bullet Puller,

The Redding G-Rx Push Thru Base Resizing Die does an excellent job of returning the base section of the .40 S&W cases to original specs.

there's a new Military Crimp Remover, Carbide Primer Pocket Uniformer, Priming System, and Case Trimer Kit. The Case Trimmer will handle, with the correct collet and pilot, all the big cases from the .338 Lapua to the .50 BMG, including most of the Sharps and English Nitro cases, such as the .500 Nitro Express.

The Crimp Remover is designed to be used with the RCBS Trim Prep Center or the RCBS Accessory Handle. It cuts away the primer pocket crimp found on most military .50 BMG brass, permitting easier repriming. The Uniformer utilizes a carbide cutter to square the bottom of the primer pocket and uniform the

240 ⊕ **GUN DIGEST**®

depth to permit easier primer seating to a consistent depth.

The new .50 BMG Priming System consists of a bench-mounted, lever-operated device with Safety Shield 20-primer capacity tube. A primer pick-up tube and flat and oval primer seating plugs are a part of the system.

Handloaders who have an RCBS Progressive Press set to load handgun cartridges will appreciate the new Bullet Feeder for such presses. Designed for use with jacketed bullets only—no cast lead bullets—the Feeder is 110-115 VAC operated. It mounts next to the Press, and has a hopper capacity of approximately 200 bullets. The collator unit orients the bullets to drop into the feed mechanism and is said to increase the loading rate by as much as 50 percent. Adapters allow the loading of 9mm/.38 Spl/.357 Magnum, 10mm/.40 S&W, and .45 ACP FMJ or jacketed bullets.

New RCBS reloading dies include those for the .300 and .338 RCM and .50-95 Winchester Express cartridges, plus seven of the big English calibers from the .404 Jeffery to the .505 Gibbs. (The other five are the .450/.400 (.400 Jeffery), .450 Rigby Rimless, .470 Nitro Express, .500 Jeffery, and the .500 Nitro Express. The .500 Jeffery and .505 Gibbs dies have 1" die bodies and require a press adapter bushing to fit loading presses designed for use with 1-1/2" x 123 thread dies.)

RCBS now has loading dies for the .460 Steyr cartridge, but again these dies have 1-1/2" x 12 threads, and can only be used with loading presses such as the AmmoMaster Single Stage with the .50 BMG Conversion Kit installed, or the AmmoMaster 2.

RCBS has reloading dies for untold different cartridges, not counting wildcats, from the .17 Remington Fireball to the .505 Gibbs. In addition, the firm can produce "special order" die sets. based on the dimensioned drawings, or three cases fired in the chamber of the rifle or handgun for which the loading dies are desired. Such dies are expensive, and orders must be prepaid, and are not subject to cancellation or return for credit.

Loading data from RCBS is among the best, and currently the firm has a handbook titled *Shotshell Reloading*, plus the new *Speer Reloading Manual No. 14* covering the metallics. The new shotshell book is one of the most up-to-date on the market today, and features over 2,000 loads for the various gauges. The *Speer* manual continues the tradition started years ago. It has hundred of loads, plus technical data to assist handloaders in the production of accurate reloads. (RCBS also has a software program(RCBS.LOAD) and a 30-minute DVD on handloading that can even benefit "old pros."

If you handload for any cartridge not currently being produced by one of the major ammunition manufacturers you may have difficulty locating a supply of suitable brass. If you have a rifle, or handgun, for which you already have loading dies, great. If you do not have the dies, **Huntington Die Specialities** (www.huntingtons.com) may already have the proper dies in stock, or they can make them for you from a chamber cast, or three empty cases fired in that chamber. Huntington may also have the brass you need for a foreign, wildcat, or obsolete cartridge.

Two other sources for suitable brass include **Quality Cartridge** (www.qual-cart.com) and **Jamison International V LLC** (jamisoninstl@rushmore.com). Both companies can also provide components and custom-loaded ammunition. (These companies do not sell less-than-full box quantities of the bras or loaded ammunition, and the smallest quantity available is usually 20 rounds.)

Quality Cartridge currently lists over 300 different calibers, and has the capability to supply custom cases for nearly any wildcat cartridge you can think of, from 5mm to over .550" in size. This firm can also convert your 5mm Remington M591 or M592 bolt action rifle to fire a 5mm centerfire cartridge, without permanently altering the rimfire capability. *[Editor's Note: Aguila is now making loaded 5mm Remington ammunition if you'd prefer not to alter your Remington. It's unknown how long this production will continue, however. – DMS]*

Jamison currently has brass for at least a dozen of the big-bore English cartridges, from the .416 Rigby to the .577 Snider, plus cases for several of the old Sharps. Need cases for the Snider or the .577/.450 Martini-Henry? Jamison produces them.

This handloader firmly believes you can never have too much information on a subject, especially handloading. **Blue Book Publications** has a new 792-page *Ammo Encyclopedia* by Michael Bussard that every handloader needs on their reference shelf. It contains 60 chapters, and while it does not actually contain loading data, it has about everything

The new Hornady L-N-L Case Preparation Center features a powder trimmer, chamfer/dedurring tool, primer pocket cleaner, and five neck brushes.

Accessory tools to fit are also available.

The RCBS .50 BMG Priming System is lever operated, has a 20-primer capacity tube with Safety Shield, and comes with flat and oval primer seating plugs.

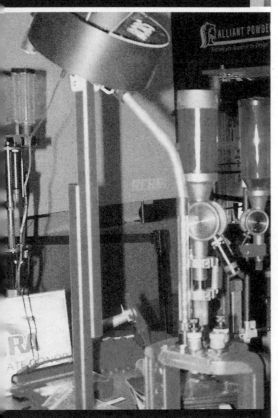

Owners of a RCBS Progressive Press set up for handgun loads will appreciate this new Bullet Feeder. The Feeder mounts next to the press, and is 110-115 VAC operated, with a hopper capacity of approximately 200 bullets. It's said to increase the loading rate by up to 50 percent, and adapters are available to load most handgun cartridges from 9mm to .45 ACP.

and more. Beginning with Chapter 38 it covers many of the centerfire — current, obsolete, sporting, military, proprietary and wildcat — cartridges. Dimensional drawings are provided for most of the cartridges, and while the quality of the drawings is not equal, nor drawn to the same scale for all, the information is still valuable. Not every wildcat cartridge ever designed or developed is featured, but that would be an impossibility. What is presented covers a wide field, and there are no SAAMI specs or standardized drawings for most wildcats. (The .257 Roberts Improved exists in a dozen or more versions, differing in neck length, shoulder angle, overall case length, case taper, etc., for example. Shortening the case, necking it down, expanding the neck, and other modifications add more wildcats to the same basic case, and the .257 Roberts was itself a wildcat in the beginning.)

Chapters 53 and 54 are devoted to formulas and useful reference data, including chamber pressures, barrel lengths, sectional densities, ballistic coefficients, loading densities, burning propellants emissions, etc. It's handy to have it all in one volume, and there's even a glossary and a pair of indices.

Dealers handling **Western Powders** (www.accuratepowder.com and www.ramshot.com) should have available copies of the latest load guides for the **Accurate** and **Ramshot** powders, respectively. The Accurate guide has new loads for eight additional cartridges, from the 5.7x28mm FN to the .338 Federal, plus a good number of 12 gauge shotshell loads. The handgun loads range from the 5.7x288mm FN to the .500 Smith & Wesson, while the rifle loads cover cartridges from the .17 Remington to the .458 Lott. Ramshot has data for the same eight new metallics as Accurate, but since it's a different powder the loads are different, as they are for the centerfire handgun cartridges. Rifle cartridges for which Ramshot loads are provided are not exactly the same as those for the Accurate powder data, plus Ramshot loads data is provided for five of the most popular handgun cartridges used in Cowboy Action Shooting. Load data for 12 gauge shotshells is also listed in the Ramshot Guide.

Redding Reloading Equipment (www.redding-reloading.com) has new dies for the .30 Remington AR, .338 Marlin Express, .416 Ruger, and a Comp Seater die for the .357 SIG cartridge. Another great die from Redding is the G-Rx Push Thru Base Sizing Die for .40

S&W brass. When the .40 S&W cartridge is fired in most autoloading pistols, it develops a slight bulge near the base. Using the new die irons out or swages this bulge, returning the case to original dimensions in this location. (Conventional full length resizing dies often do not size this area of the fired cases due to the shell holder and die junction.) An optional bottle adapter and HDPE collection bottle are also available to save having to pick up each sized case as it exits the die.

Other new items from Redding include a Case Neck Gauge, Flash Hole Deburring Tools, Primer Pocket Uniformers, and a dip-in dry Imperial Application Media consisting of high density ceramic spheres pre-charged with Imperial Dry Neck Lube. This new Media will handle all case necks from .17 caliber upward.

Redding hasn't added any new bullet moulds to the SAECO line, but current sizes range from .22 to .45. The available moulds include bullet designs suitable for smokeless or black powder use. Depending on the caliber and bullet weight, the moulds can be had in a choice of 1, 2, 3, or 4-cavity sizes.

Shiloh Sharps (www.shilohrifle.com) is known for their excellent line of single shot percussion and cartridge rifles based on the original M1863 and M1874 Sharps designs. Today's Sharps rifles may not have the history of an original, but the new Sharps will be of better materials and have a better finish in most instances. The firm also has some reloading equipment designed for use

Left to right: .223 Remington, .30-06 Springfield, .50 BMG case, .338 Xtreme, and .308 Winchester. The .338 Xtreme is another cartridge which can be handloaded to achieve different results.

The new RCBS Case Trimmer Kit, with the correct collets and pilots, will handle all the big cases, from the .338 Lapua to the .50 BMG shown here.

with the rimmed Sharps cases or similar cartridges. A hand-operated depriming tool can deprime those big cases in a hurry. Slip the case over the de-priming rod, slip the case rim into the notch and squeeze the lever. Quick and easy! The end of the lever features a primer pocket cleaning tool, and the handle is threaded to hold a case neck cleaning brush.

Shiloh carries reloading equipment of RCBS and Redding, plus a few others not always easy to locate, such as the MVA Visible Power Measure with non-sparking brass hopper and micrometer adjustable scale. A Case Annealer for those work-hardened case necks, a drop tube for those large capacity cases, and a good 50-hole loading block are other handy Shiloh items. Constructed of solid wood with brass tube and funnel, the drop tube can be used for single cases, or with a loading block, and the 50-hole Shiloh Loading Block is thick enough the tall "fifties" will not tip over. Another handy item is the "paper cartridge kit" for those shooters of muzzleloading black powder rifles. It's complete with cartridge paper, two dowels, glue stick, funnel for filling, and complete directions for use.

Not handloading equipment, but a handy reference is the Sharps Company Cartridge Poster designed by artist Robert Auth. It features a buffalo hunter scene with Sharps rifle and shooting sticks, and thirty Sharps cartridges,

from the .36 caliber paper to the .50-140-700 3-1/4".

Brooks' Moulds (www.brooksmoulds.com) will produce custom bullet moulds to a customer's specifications for any design up to 1.55" in length. Precision machined using case iron blocks to fit SAECO handles, and lathe bored, the moulds may be built with nearly any nose shape, groove diameter and number, desired.

Barnes Bullets (www.barnesbullets.com) has a host of new products for handloaders, from new bullets to the copper Club, which (for a nominal fee) permits immediate access to load data for new Barnes bullets as such becomes available from the Barnes ballistics lab. The new bullets range from a 30-gr. .22 Hornet Varmit Grenade design to the 480-gr. .450/400 Banded Solid, plus there's a new line of Barnes Buster heavy-for-caliber handgun/rifle bullets slated for availability about the time you read this. The *Barnes Reloading Manual No. 4* lists data for all Barnes bullets up to the time of publication, but you may not find the mid-2009 designs featured.

Handloaders for the British big-bore cartridges will find Barnes has suitable designs available for most of them, .416, .404, .470, .500, .505, .577, and .600 Nitro Express. (Yes, if you handload for the .600 Nitro, Barnes has a 900-gr. Banded Solid bullet available.)

Barnes Reloading Manual No. 4 features loading data, using Barnes bullets,

for many of the newer cartridges, including Winchester's Short and Super Shot Magnums, 6.8mm SPC, .338 Federal, and .375 Ruger. (Owners of a rifle chambered for the .375 Whelen cartridge might want to check out the loading data for the .375 Scovill in the Barnes manual.) In addition, those handloaders set up for the big bores will appreciate the data for the .470 and .577 Nitro Express, .505 Gibbs, and the .50 BMG cartridges.

Handgun cartridges for which loading data is provided range from the .221 Remington Fireball to the .500 Smith & Wesson, include in the .45 GAP. No data for cartridges such as the .25 ACP or .256 Magnum are featured, nor does the rifle section feature any .17 caliber loads. Other features of this 696-page manual include five interesting articles, trajectory tables — short, medium, and long range — energy tables, an excellent glossary, a history of the company, and much more. There's even a section of muzzleloading data for smokepole users, plus dozens of color photographs throughout of successful hunters, all users of Barnes bullets.

VihtaVuori's *Reloading Guide, Edition 7*, has data for more than 50 centerfire rifle cartridges, and two dozen handgun cartridges. This includes revised data for 15 cartridges, from the .204 Ruger to the .45-70 Gov't., including the 6.5x47 Lapua, .260 Remington, and .338 Lapua, using N100 and N500 Series powders. Cowboy Action Shooting loads are provided for five of the most popular cartridges. (This guide has a great "Powder Burning Rate Chart" just inside the front cover that lists the burning rates from fast to slow for 11 brands of smokeless powders that most U. S. handloaders will encounter. It also has a chart inside the back cover for listing favorite personal loads.)

Reliable ballistic data is now available for most **Lapua** bullets through the Lapua website (www.lapua.com) and Quick Target Unlimited ballistic software. Check it out. The data was assembled using continuous Doppler radar measurements, and is stated to be more accurate than using the single number ballistic coefficient method.

Speer's new *Reloading Manual No. 14* is the largest the firm has ever produced. Naturally, it's geared to the use of Speer-manufactured bullets, such as the 115-gr. Gold Dot Hollow Point in the .327 Federal cartridge, but not exclusively.

A couple of sources for reloading data for wildcat and older cartridges are *Wildcat Cartridges, Combo Edition*, and *Pet Loads, Complete Volume*, both published by the **Wolfe Publishing Company** (www.riflemagazine.com). The wildcat tome contains all the articles, with loading data, featured in volumes I and II, covering cartridges from the .14/221 to the .460 Van Horn. The articles are interesting and the loading data may be the only source available, since wildcat loading data is relatively scarce. The *Pet Loads* volume, by Ken Waters, features loads for all the cartridges originally featured in supplements 1 through 24, and again the articles are not only interesting but informative.

Hodgdon has a new Reloading Data

The RCBS Bullet Puller is massive, but it pulls .50 BMG or .416 Barrett bullets with ease.

Center that handloaders with access to the web can use. Just click on any of the three available web sites – www.hodgdon.com, www. imrpowder.com, or www.wwpowder. com. The first page you see on one of these sites will allow you access. Click on the designated area marked Reloading Data Center, read the warnings and click on I agree. One the next page, pick your reloading preference, and click on either "cartridge" or "shotshell."

The Hodgdon Reloading Data Center shows 52 different powders, including IMR 4007 SSC, and Winchester AA Lite and Super Handicap powders. Loading data is available for 84 handgun cartridges from the .17 Bumble Bee to the .500 Smith & Wesson, and 144 rifle cartridges from the .17 Ackley Hornet to the .50 BMG. (Starting and maximum loads, pressures, and velocities are provided for each cartridge.)

Shotshell handloaders can select from literally thousands of 10, 12, 16, 20 and 28 gauge, plus .410-bore loads. Bismuth, steel, Hevi-Shot, and lead shot, including buckshot, plus slug loads are presented. The RDC data is continually updated with the latest car-

tridges and components. It provides handloaders using Hodgdon, IMR, and Winchester powders with over 20,000 recipes for handgun, rifle, and shotshell cartridge loads. It's easy to navigate and sort by cartridge, bullet weight, shell size, shotgun loads, powder type, and manufacturer brand, and it's available 24 hours a day, seven days a week.

In addition to lots of new cartridges, unprimed cases, bullets, and loading data for the cartridges, the Really Big News at **Hornady Manufacturing** (www.hornady.com) are the Lock-N-Load Case Preparation Center, the L-N-L Ammo Concentricity Gauge, and the 1500 GS Electronic Scale. The L-N-L Power Case Prep Center literally provides in one location everything necessary to prepare an empty cartridge case for reloading. It features a power trimmer, chamfer/deburring tool, primer pocket cleaner, and five neck brushes. Primer pocket reamers, uniformer, and flash hole deburring tools can be purchased separately. The Center can be mounted on the bench with four lag screws or bolts. The vertically mounted L-N-L case trimmer is crank adjustable, with the other features mounted on the face of the base portion of the Center.

The new L-N-L Ammo Concentricity Tool allows a shooter to measure bullet run-out and to true-up his handloads, or even factory ammunition. Place the cartridge on the included 60° universal centers in the tool, roll it, and read the dial indicator, accurate to 0.001". If the reading is unsatisfactory, use the threaded pressure-point adjuster to adjust the run-out to zero. Simple, and quick.

The new Hornady Lock'N Load AP EZ-Ject Press will be a big hit with handloaders tired of manually removing each loaded cartridge from the final station. The loaded cartridge, from .25 ACP to .45-70 Gov't., is automatically ejected into a trap suspended on the left of the press. The system is standard on all new L-N-L AP presses, and older models can be upgraded.

Hornady has also introduced loaded

Hornady's new L-N-L Ammo Concentricity Tool allows a shooter to measure bullet run-out to 0.001" and adjust it. Center the cartridge, roll it, read, and adjust. Simple and quick!

ammunition for two new cartridges, .338 Marlin Express and .416 Ruger, in addition to a load for the .300 H & H Magnum, and loads for four of the English big bores, .404 Jeffery, .450, .470 and .500 Nitro Express. There's also a new load for the .50 BMG cartridge, featuring the 750-grain A-MAX bullet. Naturally, the firm now has loading dies for these cartridges, plus shell holds, and unprimed brass. (Hornady introduced unprimed cases for a number of other cartridges also, including the 6.8mm SPC, .30 TC, .32 Winchester Special, and .450 Bushmaster.)

Hornady has more than 20 new bullets available for handloaders, including GMX and FTX designs, plus DGX (Dangerous Game) models for the .404 Jeffery, .470 and .500 Nitro Express cartridges. By the time you read this there may be others.

Anyone handloading for one of the service rifle cartridges of the World War II era knows the surplus ammunition was usually Berdan primed, provided you could find such ammunition in the correct caliber. A source of Boxer-primed new case for nine such cartridges is **Graf & Sons** (www.grafs.com). Graf has loaded ammunition, primed and unprimed cases for cartridges from the 6.5x50mm Japanese to the 8x56R Hungarian Mannlicher, including the 7.5x54mm French, 7.5x55mm Swiss, and the 7.92x33mm Kurz. The firm also handles a wide assortment of reloading equipment and components.

Lyman's 49th *Reloading Handbook* covers about everything a handloader needs to know, with plenty of data on both metallics and shotshells.

Handloaders who cast their own bullets may have a bit of trouble find a source of lead, etc. They should check out the **Bulletman** (www.bulletmetals.net). Pure lead and several alloys, including linotype metal, are available.

Battenfeld Technologies (www.battenfeldtechnologies.com), known for their Caldwell Lead Sled, now has a Lead Sled Plus, allowing the handloader to test out new loads with comfort. Designed to handle two 25-lb. barbell weights, or up to 100 lbs. of lead shot or sand bags, the LSP is similar to the original Lead Sled in size, and smaller than the Lead Sled PFT. The LSP can reduce recoil up to approximately 95 percent. (There's also a new "large" weight bag available which will hold approximately 20 pounds of sand for use on the Lead Sleds.)

Handloaders needing a shooting rest, but not the recoil reduction feature, should check out the new Caldwell 7 Rest Shooting Rest. Designed high enough, and offset to accommodate the extended magazine of AR-15 rifles and clones, the 7 Rest folds to accommodate left or right-handed shooters. (The 7 Rest folds nearly flat for storage or transportation.) The forearm and buttstock supports are overmolded and screw-adjustable for height.

From the **Frankford Arsenal** division of Battenfeld there's a new DS-750 Digital Electronic Scale with a 750-grain capacity. Powered by two AAA batteries, and complete with integrated protective cover, the DS-750 resembles one of the TI-83 Graphing Calculators, but smaller; it's ideal for use in the field at the shooting bench. Accurate to 0.1-grain, the DS-750 has overload protection, and auto shutoff after 60 seconds to conserve the batteries. Auto calibrated, with tare and counting functions, the DS-750 measures in grains, grams, carats, and ounces, with a blue backlit LCD display. Complete with carry pouch, pan, and calibration weights, the scale is only slightly larger than the Micro Reloading Scale and is suitable for use on the regular reloading bench or at the range for load development.

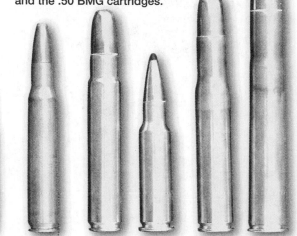

Left to right: .223 Remington, .30-06 Springfield, .416 Ruger, .338 Marlin Express, .404 Jeffery, and .470 Nitro Express Cartridges. The last four are new Hornady loads, and loading dies are available. New Hornady loads not shown include the .450 Nitro Express, .500 Nitro Express, and the .50 BMG cartridges.

Not new, but always needed at the reloading bench are the Frankford Arsenal Powder Funnel Kit and the Perfect-Fit Reoading Tray. The Funnel Kit features a large funnel, extension tube, and 16 quick-change specific nozzles to accommodate case necks from .17 to .45 caliber. The Kit is packed in a plastic case with marked cavities. The Trays are available in a dozen sizes to accommodate cases from the .25 ACP to the .500 Nitro Express. Except for tray No. 9, which holds only 45 cases, the other 11 trays have a 50-case capacity. Each tray will accommodate cases whose base or rim diameter is approximately the same. Tray No. 1, for example, will host .22 Hornet, .25 ACP, 5.7x28mm FN, and similar cases, while No. 9 will accommodate .470 N.E., .50-70 Gov't., .500 N.E., etc. cases.

Handloaders loading for only a couple of calibers, or using their own fired brass may not have the problem, but sorting range brass can be a headache. **Lamb Labs** (www.lamblabs.com) can help, at least for pistol range brass, with their Shell Sorter. Consisting of an arrangement of screened trays, the Shell Sorter can separate .45 ACP, .40 S& W, and 9mm/.380 fired cases by caliber in seconds. Just dump in the mixed cases and shake. Simple and quick.

Most handloaders who load many cartridges have a tumbler or vibratory-type case cleaner/polisher. You fill it with fired cases and media, close it, turn it on and let it run. But how long, or when is it time to check it?

The new Dillon press for reloading the .50 BMG cartridge is massive, with three 1" diameter steel posts supporting the die head. The leverage available for resizing the .50 BMG case is tremendous, and the access space to the shell holder area is ample.

UniqueTek Inc. (www.uniquetek. com) has a Time-Out Case Cleaner Timer that will ease the situation a bit. It operates on a regular 115 VAC circuit, features an easy-to-read LCD display with a NiNH battery for memory backup, and has dual outlets. It permits operation of the cleaner, thumbler or vibratory, (15 amp/1 hp/1875 watt), from one minute to 10 hours.

Sinclair International (www. sinclairintl.com) always hs some new products for handloaders. There are a couple of new Powder Drop Tubes to fit most Sinclair, Redding and RCBS powder measures, and the Neil Jones measures without an adapter. Four lengths (4", 6", 8", and 10") are available in two sizes,

.22 caliber and up, and 6.5mm and up. Bushings may be required. A special 4" drop tube is available for the .27 and .20 caliber cartridges, and custom lengths are possible for the others, if required. (Sinclair drop tubes are now available with bushings to fit Lyman, Dodd, Bruno, and older Sinclair/Culver powder measures, and have the same features as those for the Redding, RCBS measures.)

Other new Sinclair handloading products include a Case Neck Brush Power Screwdriver Adapter, a 17/20 Caliber Piloted Flash Hole Tool, a Case Neck Sorting Tool, and the R.F.D. Culver Style Powder Measure. The Screwdriver Adapter permits case neck brushes to be used in any power screwdriver,

hand-held drill, etc., and speeds up the cleaning process. The new .17 and .20 caliber Piloted Flash Hole Tool utilizes stainless steel pilots which index from the case mouth to ensure case-to-case chamfer depth. (Sinclair has a .50 BMG Flash Hole Deburring Tool and Primer Pocket Uniformer that handloaders of the Big Fifty should find handy.)

The new R.F.D. Culver Style Powder Measure is produced on CNC machinery and features an aluminum body with brass metering insert that throws from 0 to 85 grains with four "clicks" between each number on the insert. It will fit onto the Sinclair 11-1100 Measure Stand and comes with a 16-oz. powder hopper and two drop tubes.

Case neck wall thickness is important to accurate handloads and the new Case Neck Sorting Tool works for cartridges from .22 through .45 caliber with the Sinclair Stainless Steel Neck Pilots. (It works with .17 and .20 caliber cases with the use of an optional carbide alignment rod and matching pilots.) The new tool can be used by both left and right-handed reloaders, and its low profile and low center of gravity provide the user with a more stable working platform. Currently Sinclair neck pilots are available in 17 popular sizes, including 10mm/.40 and .41/.416 caliber. (A dial or electronic indicator is necessary for use with this tool, and Sinclair currently has five different models from which to choose, if needed, including those produced in the U. S. by the **L. S. Starrett** firm.)

The balance-type powder scale used to be standard, and many handloaders still use them to produce thousands of accurate handloaded cartridges. Today, electronic scales are becoming popular and **Denver Instrument** (www.Denver-InstrumentUSA.com) has such a scale with a capability of 1,851 grains and a 0.02-grain readability. It weighs less than 2.5 lbs., stabilizes in three seconds, and has a pan nearly four inches in diameter.

Ammunition testing and adjustment is possible with the German-manufactured **Bersin device**. Distributed in the U. S. by **Century International Arms, Inc.** (www.centuryarms.com) the Bersin is available in four sizes, S (small) M (medium), L (large), and Ultra L, with the last for cases such as the Remington Ultra Magnum and Winchester Short Magnum, etc. It measures and adjusts concentricity to 0.0001" and helps to sort out cartridges with irregular case surfaces and lengths. Said to be capable of improving group sizes by as much as 50 percent, the Bersin can be used on

One of the best reference volume for handloaders needing case dimensions is the *Ammo Encyclopedia* by Michael Bussard. Published by Blue Book Publications, it does not feature loading data, but it contains considerable other information pertinent to handloading.

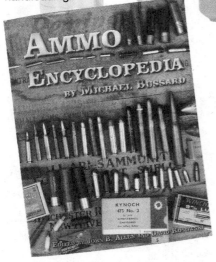

The lastest Norma Precision AB reloading manual provides handloading data for all but the latest cartridges. Naturally, Norma components, cases, powders, and bullets, are emphasized. (Norma produces cases and loaded ammunition for a dozen big bore cartridges from the .375 H & H to the .505 Gibbs, plus more than two dozen hunting and target cartridges. Additional new scheduled cartridges include three new Norma Magnums, the .300, .338, and .375 to join the .308 and .358 Norma Magnums.

Barnes Reloading Manual No. 4 not only has loading data for rifle and handgun cartridges, but plenty of other useful information. Trajectory tables—short, medium, and long range—energy tables, and interesting articles are all contained between the covers of this 696-page volume.

commercial ammunition, or handloads. **MTM Molded Products Co.** (www.mtmcase-gard.com) has new 10-round Case-Gard Ammo Boxes to house .50 BMG and .416 Barrett cartridges. The cartons or boxes in which commercial .50 BMG cartridges are packaged are flimsy and if you handload the .50 BMG using surplus brass, you probably purchased the fired brass loose or in bulk. The new MTM boxes cradle the rounds at the shoulder, not the tip, and are built to last. Each box will hold ten .50 BMG, .50 DTC, .460 Steyr, HS .460, .416 Barrett, or .338 Xtreme cartridges.

MTM has many other cartridge cases, loading trays, die storage boxes, self-adhesive loading labels, and while not new, there is a great three-ring binder for recording handloading data. This Handloaders Log provides an excellent way to store personal loads and information in a loose-leaf fashion.

More and more serious handloaders are paying attention to the small details, checking individual bullets for weight variations and diameters, case neck thickness, etc. **Rampro Corporation** (www.ramproco.com) has a new Universal Reloaders Gauge capable of measuring more than seven different variation of bullets and/or cartridges from .22 to .470 Nitro Express. User friendly and

precision machined, the Gauge includes a digital LCD indicator with 0.0005" resolution. The complete kit includes the stand, LCD indicator, indicator tips, cartridge measuring fixture, .22 caliber holder, .220 and .300 caliber pilots (other calibers optional), cartridge centering locators, mounting hardware and instructions. Thus case trimmed length, seated bullet concentricity, cartridge ovality and distortion, bullet diameter and length, bullet seated overall length, and more can be checked all on the same tool. Now, all that's needed is such a tool for use with the .50 BMG cartridge to shrink those 1,000-yard groups.

Shooters who handload dangerous game cartridges are, or should be, cognizant of **Woodleigh** bullets manufactured in Australia (www.woodleighbullets.com.au). The firm produces more than 130 different bullet types in calibers from 6.5mm to .700 Nitro. The majority of the bullets are roundnose softpoints, with a few flat nose and protected point. Three dozen of the bullets are full metal jacket designs intended for maximum penetration. The lightest weight bullets are the 130 grain .277" for the .270 Winchester, and the heaviest are the 1,000-gr. .700" projectiles. (Woodleigh bullets are used by several U. S. ammunition manufacturers in their

"big bore" loads. **Huntington Die Specialties** stocks the Woodleigh bullets as components for handloaders.)

Woodleigh may soon be distributing the new "Hydrostatic Stabilization" bullets on which patents are pending. Constructed of a specially formulated copper alloy, the new HS bullets produce breech pressures similar to gilding metal jacketed softpoint bullets of the same weight. Featuring a depressed nose, shallow driving bands and full bore body, the HS is designed to cut a clean hole to promote profuse bleeding, and to travel in a straight line following impact. Following the principle used in the brass extrusion industry to produce hollow bars, the HS bullet produces a pressure ring following impact, and travels onward in a low pressure cavitation bubble. The result is massive hydraulic shock transfer, increased penetration and stabilization. (HS bullets striking bone are said to have a better orientation to the original line of travel than conventional round, flat, or pointed nose bullets.) As components, the new HS bullet will not be inexpensive, but none of the big bore bullets is cheap, and what's the price of a bullet compared to the cost of the hunt, anyway?

Ballistic Products' new "ITX" shot sports a sharp cutting band around the circumference.

AMMUNITION TODAY: Ammunition, ballistics and components BY HOLT BODINSON

In terms of the quality of our ammunition and the selection of handloading components, these are the best days of our lives. Just consider for a moment that this year has brought us three new rifle cartridges – the .30 Remington AR, .338 Marlin Express and the .416 Ruger – five new reloading powders and counting – a variety of new bullets – lead-free, rimfire ammunition – and even a steel shot load for the tiny .410.

Recession? Nothing is slowing down or holding back the constant innovation and flow of new products from the ammunition industry.

A-Square

After relocating its ammunition manufacturing plant to Chamberlain, South Dakota, A-Square is fully up to production this year with calibers ranging from the 6.5-06 A-Square to the .700 Nitro Express. For big game hunting, especially in Africa, no ammunition approaches the versatility of A-Square's unique Triad loads. For each major caliber, A-Square loads three bullets with the same weight, same profile and same trajectory. One is a monolithic solid; one is a bonded core, controlled expansion soft point; and the third is a thin jacketed soft point designed for rapid, maximum expansion. In short, Triad ammunition provides the hunter with the opportunity to match the bullet to the game at a moment's notice with the assurance that all three loads will shoot to the same point of impact. The Triad is a revolutionary development in the design of big game ammunition. See the Triad and the whole A-Square line at www.asquarecompany.com.

Alliant Powder

Alliant is introducing five spherical powders under the "Power Pro" label.

A member of the ATK group, Alliant is introducing five new spherical handloading powders this year under the "Power Pro" label. They're designed specifically for magnum pistol, varmint rifle, medium rifle, large rifle and magnum rifle. Handloading data is available at www.alliantpowder.com. The big surprise though is a new powder under the "Reloader" series, Reloader 17.

Reloader 17 snuck into the line without a lot of fanfare. It's a very special powder with a unique chemistry. Made in Switzerland by Nitro Chemie, Reloader 17 is formulated for the short magnum cases and has a burn speed similar to IMR-4350.

Its advantage is that the chemicals that determine the burn rate are saturated into the powder grains rather than being applied to the exterior surface of the grain. The result is a smoother, longer release of energy, producing sensational velocities in the short magnums at normal working pressures. For example, loaded with Reloader 17, the 7mm WSM produces 3,356 fps with a 130-gr. BTSP; the 300 WSM, 3,343 fps with a 150-gr. BTSP. If you shoot a short magnum, you must try Alliant's RE-17. (www.alliant-powder.com.)

Ballistic Products

Ballistic Products offers the most diverse and innovative selection of shotshell reloading components and manuals available. They've just introduced a new, soft, non-toxic shot composed of iron, tungsten and a polymer binder. Going under the "ITX" label, the pellets are perfectly spherical with a broad cutting band around the circumference. Ballistic Products emphasizes that ITX is much softer than other tungsten blends and is similar in density to Bismuth. See their store at www.ballisticproducts.com.

Baschieri & Pellagri (B&P)

Long known for their premium quality shotshells, B&P builds their ammunition using hulls made under the Gordon System patent that features an active, cushioning base wad that reduces felt recoil. This year B&P has used the Gordon hull to develop 12-gauge steel, target loads featuring 7/8 - 1 oz. of #7 and #8.5 shot driven at lead shot velocities for ideal target performance out to 35 meters. Look for them under the F2 Mach and F2 Legend Professional Steel labels. (www.baschieri-pellagri.com and www.kaltronoutdoors.com)

Barnes Bullets

Building on the success of their "Tipped Triple-Shock X Bullet" that combines the accuracy and controlled expansion of the conventional Triple-Shock X Bullet with a higher ballistic coefficient offered by the addition of a pointed polymer tip, Barnes is introducing five new Tipped TSX boattail bullets ranging from a .243 (80-gr.) to a 7mm (150-gr.). The conventional Triple-Shock lineup continues to expand as well with a new 6.8 mm (85-gr.) and a .308 (110-gr.).

One of the nightmares of the muzzleloading crowd is a potential ban on lead hunting bullets. Barnes has an answer: the .50-caliber, solid copper, sabot Spit-

Barnes' new manual is highly focused on the modern "Triple Shock" lines.

Fire line. Now offered with a streamlined polymer tip, the Spit-Fire has also been wrapped in a new, easy-loading sabot that's just the answer to tight or fouled bores. For the handgun hunting enthusiast, there is the new "Barnes Buster." Designed for the .44, .45 and .500 magnums and the .45-70 rifle, the Buster is a non-expanding, deep penetrating bullet intended for wild boar, bear, and even dangerous game like Cape buffalo. Buster bullet weights have yet to be announced. New, too, is an expanded line of lead-free, rifle and handgun bullets for

Barnes "Buster" bullet for handguns and .45-70s is a non-expanding, deep penetrating big game bullet.

The tungsten core of Barnes' new MRX bullet ensures deep penetration and high retained energy at long range.

the military and law enforcement communities, offering every quality from precision long range accuracy (TAC-LR) to barrier defeating designs (TAC-XP and TAC-X). For updated bullet specifications go to www.barnesbullets.com and www.barnesbullets.com/mle.

Berger Bullets

With the increasing popularity of the .204 Ruger cartridge for varmint hunting, Berger will offer a long, 55-gr. bullet for the .20-calibers. It should prove ideal for the windy plains of the prairie dog towns. New, too, later in the year, are a number of VLD and conventional bullet designs being developed for the .338 calibers in bullet weights of 200-300 grains. (www.bergerbullets.com)

Berry's Manufacturing

Berry's offers an extensive line of copper plated lead handgun bullets at very attractive prices. A new design that is proving to be exceptionally accurate is their hollow base handgun bullet that is offered in 9mm (124-gr.), .40 (155-gr.) and .45 (185-gr.). The .40 and .45 caliber hollow base bullets are premium target bullets that are "double struck," or

sized, after being plated to insure they are 100% symmetrical. See Berry's full line of plated, non-plated and "cowboy" bullets at www.berrysmfg.com.

Black Hills Ammunition

Consistently providing some of the most accurate ammunition on the market, Black Hills is offering a variety of new loadings based on Barnes bullet designs that include the TAC-XP bullet in 9mm, .40 S&W and .45 ACP; the 55-gr. TSX and 55-gr. highly frangible MPG bullet in the .223, and a 85-gr. TSX bullet in the .243 Win. (www.black-hills.com.)

Brenneke USA

Long known for their advanced shotgun slug designs, Brenneke is marketing a unique lead-free, .30-caliber (155-gr.) bullet named the Brenneke "Quik-Shok Copper." Similar in concept to Polywad's Quik-Shok rimfire ammunition and shotgun slugs, the Brenneke bullet features a deep, hollow cavity capped with a polymer tip. Upon impact, the front portion of the new bullet fragments into four copper petals, creating four additional wound channels, while the solid rear section assures deep penetration. The new bullet will be offered in loaded ammunition for the .308 and .30-06 with velocities of 2,953 fps and 2,789 fps respectively. See the complete Brenneke line at www.brennekeusa.com.

Barnes' older Triple Shock design has been upgraded with a polymer tip.

Black Hills Ammunition is famous for their rigorous quality control and accuracy standards.

CCI

Something old and something new. CCI is introducing a new and improved, four wing musket cap for traditional muzzleloaders this year and a 30-gr., lead-free .22 WMR cartridge under CCI's "TNT Green" label. See the details at www.cci-ammunition.com.

Century International Arms

As the major USA importer and manufacturer of surplus military firearm models, Century is in unique position to ferret out great ammunition deals from across the globe.

Under their "Hotshot" brand of commercial sporting ammunition, Century offers Boxer primed, non-corrosive, soft point loads in a variety of popular calibers ranging from the 7.62 Nagant to the .30-06. Selling for $12.87/box, Hotshot rifle ammo is the buy of the century. (www.centuryarms.com)

Extreme Shock

With its successful line of frangible rifle and handgun ammunition based on bullets featuring powdered tungsten cores, Extreme Shock is bringing its proprietary technology to bear on the shotgun shell market. Their new .50-caliber, BD-50J slug weighing 325 grains is a copper-jacketed, compressed tungsten core, 12 ga. sabot round with a muzzle velocity of 1,800 fps. It's designed for rifled shotgun bores and offers maximum expansion on soft tissue. A bit

more on the radical side is Shock Shot, compressed cylinders of tungsten powder, equating roughly to #4 and #6 round shot and #00 buckshot. The tactical cylindrical shot delivers extremely wide and open patterns at close range and more ragged and lethal wound channels. Extreme Shock ammunition is wild stuff. See it all at www.extremeshockusa.net.

Federal Premium

Introduced several years ago, Federal's proprietary 12-gauge "FLITECONTROL" wad has a proven track record of delivering exceptionally uniform and dense shot patterns. This year the FLITECONTROL wad technology is being introduced in both the 10-gauge and

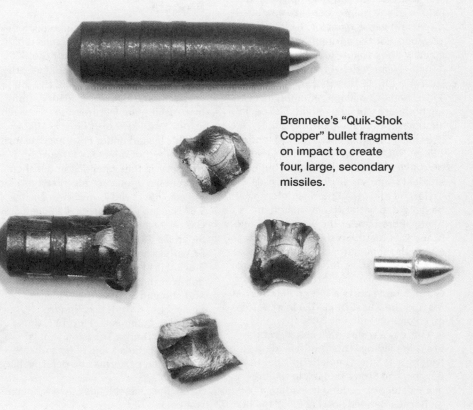

Brenneke's "Quik-Shok Copper" bullet fragments on impact to create four, large, secondary missiles.

CCI has upgraded the quality and performance of the classic musket cap.

20-gauge turkey and waterfowl lines. The new 10- and 20-gauge waterfowl lines now include the loading of Federal's devastating Black Cloud shot.

Even the diminutive .410 is getting some attention due to the popularity of the .410/45LC "Judge" revolver by Taurus. Federal has developed two specialized loadings for the Judge based on 000 buckshot and #4 lead shot. Interesting!

If steel shot is your only option in the field or at the range, there are new steel target and game loads for the 20- and 12-gauge. For the varmint hunter, there's a new V-Shok coyote loading for the 3-inch 12-gauge delivering 1-1/2 oz. of HEAVYWEIGHT BB's in a FLITECONTROL wad at 1,350 fps. With the increasing popularity of lightweight .38 Special snubbies for personal protection, Federal is bringing back the non-fouling 125-gr. NyClad, hollowpoint load featuring a nylon-coated soft lead HP bullet at an ideal snubby velocity of 830 fps.

Garand and M1A target shooters will be delighted with two new match loads being offered under the American Eagle brand that feature pressure curves to match the semi-automatic gas systems and a harder, staked-in primer to reduce the possibility of slamfires. The .30-06 Garand load sports a 150-gr. FMJ at 2,740 fps and the 7.62x51mm M1A load, a 168-gr. HP match bullet at 2,650 fps.

There is a wide range of new centerfire rifle loadings this year based on Federal's Trophy Bonded Tip, Speer, Barnes, and Sierra bullets. In the big game category, Federal is loading a 286-gr. Barnes Banded Solid at 2,550 fps in the .370 Sako and 500-gr. Barnes Triple-Shock X-Bullet at 2,280 in the .458 Lott. The .338 Federal round will be chambered in an AR-10 platform this year, and Federal is making sure it will be economical to shoot by introducing a 200-gr. soft point load in the popular Power-Shok line. Finally, in the rimfire category, Federal is reintroducing its Olympic winning Ultramatch load consisting of a 40-gr. solid at 1,080 fps. See it all at www.federalpremium.com.

Fiocchi

One of the most common questions raised by our handgun ballistics tables is the inclusion of a listing for the .450 Short Colt cartridge, also known as the .450 Adams. Believe it or not, the 150-year-old cartridge is still loaded – and by a major manufacturer, too.

Yes, the .450 Short Colt is available, and it's loaded under Fiocchi's "Historic Cartridge for Collector's Firearms" category. In that category, under their current handgun cartridge listings, Fiocchi also offers the 7.5 Swiss Ordnance, 7.62 Nagant, 7.63 Mauser, .30 Luger, 8mm Gasser, 8mm Lebel, 8mm Steyr, 9mm Steyr, .38 S&W Short, .380 Long, .44 S&W Russian and. 455 Webley. This year Fiocchi is highly focused on their new non-toxic lines that include rifle, pistol and shotgun ammunition. Fiocchi's answer is a proprietary Tundra Tungsten Composite. Fiocchi claims that their Tundra Tungsten shot is safe for all chokes and older pre-steel barrels and performs and deforms like lead shot.

See their latest loads at www.fiocchi usa.com.

Hodgdon

After buying the IMR Powder Company in 2003 and licensing the Winchester branded powders in 2006, Hodgdon has emerged as the largest handloading powder company in the world. Not standing on their laurels for one moment, this year Hodgdon acquired the only black powder manufacturer in the United States, GOEX Powder, Inc., with a history going back to 1802 when it was founded originally as a DuPont company. The only easy way to keep track of Hodgdon and its three powder subsidiaries is through the web at www. hodgdon.com, www.goexpowder. com, www.imrpowder.com,and www.wwpowder.com.

Hodgdon has just released its new 5000+ loads reloading manual that does a good job of covering the latest cartridges like the .300 and .338 Ruger Compact Magnums,. 30 T/C and .327 Federal. Hodgdon also offers an annual muzzleloading manual and basic reloading manual. (www.hodgdon.com)

Hornday

Hornady has developed a new non-toxic, monolithic game bullet made from gilding metal rather than a softer copper alloy. Called the "GMX," it sports a hollow nose cavity capped with a polymer tip, a 10-degree boattail base and has a ballistic coefficient that equals its streamlined SST and InterBond counterparts. Performance specifications call for the GMX to expand 1.5 times its original diameter, retain 95 percent of

Federal has designed two specialty loads for the popular Taurus .410 "Judge" revolver.

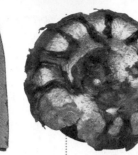

Federal is bringing back the popular 125-gr. .38 Special NyClad round for snubnose revolvers.

Hornady's new DGX bullet is a steel jacketed soft point designed for game like the Cape buffalo.

its original weight and perform across a wide range of velocities from 2,000 fps to 3,400 fps. Initially, it will be available in .270-, 7mm-, .30-, and .338-calibers.

There are two brand new cartridges this year: the .416 Ruger Compact Magnum and the .338 Marlin Express. Loaded with either Hornady's 400-gr. steel jacketed soft point (DGX) or their steel jacketed solid (DGS) at 2,400 fps, the .416 Ruger should be a fantastic complement to Ruger's short, handy Hawkeye Alaskan rifle. The .338 Marlin Express puts some power and range in Marlin's lever action line with a 200-gr. FTX Flextip bullet at 2,565 fps. With a ballistic coefficient of .430, the .338 FTX bullet matches the ballistics of the 180-gr. .30-06 bullet out to 400 yards.

Speaking of big game cartridges, Hornady will be offering classic loads for the .404 Jeffery, .470 Nitro Express and the .500 Nitro Express this year, so stock up.

Finally, there's a new "Critical Defense" line of handgun ammunition for the .380 Auto, 9mm Luger, .38 Special and .38 Special +P. The Critical Defense bullet incorporates a soft polymer insert in its hollow point that insures 100% percent reliable expansion when fired through the toughest of clothing. (www.hornady.com)

Hornady now offers classic ammunition for the .404 Jeffery, .416 Rigby, .470 Nitro Express and .500 Nitro Express.

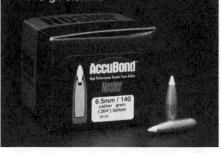

Lapua

Is the .222 Remington due for a comeback? Maybe so; it's still a popular light game cartridge in Europe. This year Lapua is producing a true match grade .222 case with extremely tight tolerances in wall thickness and neck concentricity. The .222 has always been an inherently accurate cartridge. Lapua's new brass might make it even better.

Promoting their .338 Lapua Magnum for long range target shooting, Lapua is introducing a heavy 300-gr., extra low drag, Scenar hollowpoint match bullet for the .338. Other precision brass case offerings of interest include the .220 Russian, 6.5x47 Lapua, 6.5 Grendel and the 6.5-284. The full Lapua story is at www.lapua.com.

Norma

Although it receives little press, Norma's extensive line of match ammunition has been at the forefront of international competition for years. Recently, USA's David Tubb, 11-time NRA High Power Champion and five-time NRA Long Range Champion, developed a new match cartridge in cooperation with Norma. Named the 6XC, the short, compact cartridge features a moly-coated 105-gr. 6mm open point match bullet at 3,018 fps. Zeroed at 300 yards, it is 3.5 inches high at 100 and only 9.8 inches low at 400. It's short enough to fit in an AR platform, giving us the ultimate across-the-board rifle. Norma reports that the accuracy of the 6XC exceeds that of their legendary 6mm Norma Benchrest cartridge, and that's saying a lot. See Norma's extensive lines of hunting and match ammunition at www.norma.cc.

Nosler

Introducing the largest Partition bullet ever offered, Nosler

is fielding a .458-caliber, 500-gr. Partition that is ideally matched to large and dangerous game in the .458 Win., .458 Lott and .460 Weatherby. Nosler's AccuBond line has developed a well-deserved reputation for outstanding accuracy and structural integrity. The line is being expanded this year with the introduction of a highly desirable and long awaited 6.5mm 140-gr. AccuBond. The .30-caliber 168-gr. bullet has been an outstanding match bullet for decades, so Nosler is introducing a 168-gr. Ballistic Tip hunting bullet

Nosler is introducing the largest Partition bullet they've ever made: the 500-gr. .458.

A long awaited addition to the Nosler Partition line is the new 140-gr. 6.5mm.

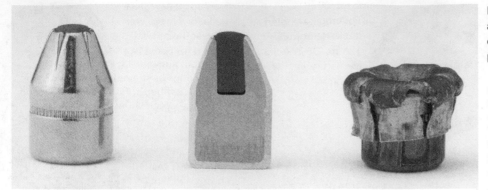

that combines accuracy with excellent terminal performance on soft skinned game. See their complete catalog and the company store at www.nosler.com.

Pinnacle Ammunition

Bismuth is back on the market under the auspices of a new company, Pinnacle Ammunition. The shell is still being loaded by Eley but is now being imported and sold under the Bis-Maxx brand. It's still a bit pricey, but it is a safe waterfowling load for all those classic shotguns with pre-steel era barrels. Pinnacle is also introducing a new steel pellet designed by Polywad. Polywad called it a "Squound" because it was neither square nor round. Pinnacle calls it "Aerosteel." The pellet looks ever so much like a miniature Foster slug. It flies nose first and is far less wind sensitive than normal shot. It's an exciting development. Read all about it at www.pinnacleammo.com.

Polywad

Polywad's highly creative R&D program is continually spinning off new product designs for a number of commercial ammunition companies as well as offering a substantial line of shotshells themselves. Recently their focus has been on the development of a totally green shotshell payload. They've got it. Going under their "GreenLite" shotshell label, the new shell is designed for small upland bird shooting out to 35 yards and clay targets out to 40 yards+. The 20- and 28-gauge shells feature a soft steel payload of roughly #7.5 shot enclosed in a heavy Kraft paper shot cup. Between the shot cup and the powder is a column of polymer powder. There is no over-powder wad.

When a GreenLite shell is fired, the only residues left in the field are steel shot, a bit of Kraft paper and a puff of polymer powder – all of which are bio- and photo-degradable.

The company's full line of innovative products is at www.polywad.com.

Precision Ammunition

One of the leaders in the non-toxic industry, Precision Ammunition offers an extensive line of handgun, rifle and

Hornady's Critical Defense handgun ammunition utilizes a polymer tip to ensure the hollow point expands after passing through clothing layers.

shotgun ammunition using projectiles formed from a matrix of copper. Precision calls it their Copper-Matrix NTF Non-Toxic Frangible Ammunition line, and it is torched off using RUAG's GreenFire lead-free primers! It doesn't get much greener! (www.precisionammo.com)

Prvi Partisan

This notable Serbian ammunition company not only offers an extensive selection of affordable rifle and handgun ammunition and components but has earned a reputation for loading many of the harder-to-get military cartridges. Among its latest catalogued offerings of loaded ammunition and components are the 6.5x52 Carcano, 7.5x54 French, 7.5x55 Swiss, 7.65x53 Argentine, 7.62x33 Kurz, 8x56 RS Mannlicher and possibly my favorite, the 8x50R Lebel. See their complete catalog at www.prvipartisan.com.

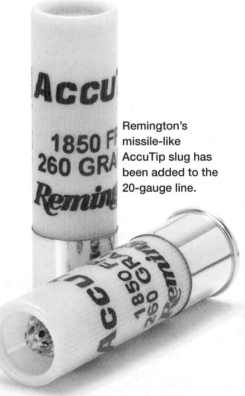

Remington's missile-like AccuTip slug has been added to the 20-gauge line.

Polywad's "GreenLite" shotshells leave nothing in the field but steel shot, Kraft paper and fine polymer dust.

Remington

Big Green has a new short proprietary cartridge that revs up the power factor of their lightweight R-15 AR platform rifle. Wouldn't you know it, it's called the .30 Remington AR, and it should prove to

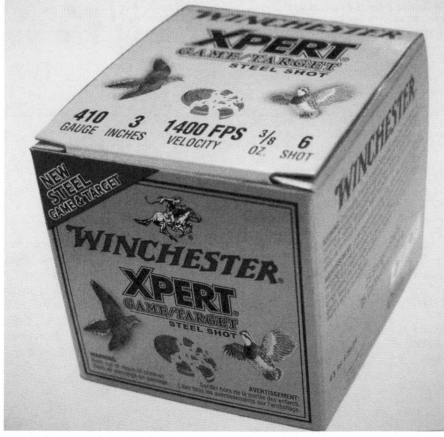

Remington's compact .30 AR cartridge is designed to bring deer hunting capability to the AR rifle.

be a great deer load. Remington sums it up by stating "It hits like a .308 and carries like a .223." Initially, there are three loadings for the new AR cartridge: a 125-gr. Core-Lokt, a 125-gr. AccuTip and a 123-gr. FMJ, all at 2,800 fps. Given the popularity of the AR today, I expect we will see a number of other makers chambering the new round.

In the varmint field, Remington is introducing two frangible, iron-tin core, lead-free loads for the .223 (45 grains at 3,550 fps) and the .22-250 (45 grains at 4,000 fps). They should prove to be destructive and ricochet free. Sharing a berth now with Bushmaster, Remington is offering a load for the .450 Bushmaster featuring a 250-gr. soft point at 2,200 fps. Their excellent and high-tech AccuTip Bonded Sabot Slug line has been expanded to include a 260-gr. 20-gauge loadings in the 2-3/4" and 3" shells at 1,850 fps and 1,900 fps respectively. Finally, like most ammunition companies, Remington is fielding 12- and 20-gauge steel game and target loads this year. See this great company at www.remington.com.

Sierra

Sierra reports they've had a hard time just keeping up with demand this year, much less introducing a number of new products. It's been a common observation in the ammunition and components industry. Nevertheless, Sierra does have a new bullet – the 155-gr. .30 caliber HPBT Palma MatchKing – which should keep your .308 match rifle super-sonic out to 1,000 yards. See the bullet smiths at www.sierrabullets.com.

Speer

Responding to the increasing popularity of the 327 Federal, Speer is making its 115-gr. Gold Dot bullet loaded last year in Federal Premium ammunition available as a handloading component. Similarly, their TNT Green bullets, formerly available only in Federal Premium and CCI loaded ammunition, will be available as components for the first time. Much to Speer's credit, the company continues to offer some of the most

Winchester's .410 steel load features 3/8 oz. of #6 shot at 1,400 fps.

Winchester has led the pack with the release of its lead-free, tin bullet in the .22 LR.

Winchester's Bonded PDX1 provides FBI protocol assurance for self-defense.

Winchester's new .45- and .50-caliber Dual Bond handgun bullets are designed for the largest game.

difficult-to-find bullets to the handloading clan, including a 75-gr. SPFN for the .25-20 Win. and a 130-gr. SPFN for the 7-30 Waters. See their whole component list at www.speer-bullets.com.

Winchester Ammunition

At the 2009 Shot Show, I watched a Winchester engineer conduct the complete FBI handgun ammunition protocol with Winchester's new Bonded PDX1 ammunition. The results were impressive. The new bullet, which is a bonded core hollowpoint, consistently expanded to 1.5X its diameter and punched through glass, clothing and other media without deviating from its track. Available in the 38 Special (130 grains), 9mm Luger (124 and 147 grains), 40 S&W (165 and 180 grains) and 45 Auto (230 grains), the PDX1 bullet may be the ultimate self-defense pill.

Winchester is carrying their bonded technology over to rifle ammunition with the introduction of the Super-X Power Max Bonded line featuring a bonded core, protected hollowpoint bullet designed specifically for deer hunting. It's available in .270 Win. (130 grains), .270 WSM (130 grains), .30-30 (150 grains), .30-06 (150 grains), .300 WSM (150 grain), .300 Win. Mag. (150 grains) and .308 Win. (150 grains).

What about handgun hunting ammunition and shotgun slugs? Winchester is introducing a third new projectile design called the Supreme Elite Dual Bond. The Dual Bond handgun bullet and shotgun slug feature both a bonded core and two bonded jackets, one inside the other. Winchester calls it "the bullet within a bullet," and it's designed for big game up to and including brown bears. Upon impact, a massive hollowpoint initiates expansion up to 2X original bullet diameter, the jackets roll back into a classic talon profile, and due to complete bonding of the jackets and core, the bullet retains nearly 100 percent of its original weight. This year, Dual Bonds will be loaded in the .454 Casull (260 grains), .460 S&W (260 grains), and .500 S&W (375 grains) and as 2-3/4" and 3" shotgun sabot rounds in the 20- and 12-gauges.

Winchester's rimfire line receives quite a facelift with the addition of a 32-gr. Expediter LRHP delivering a muzzle velocity of 1,640 fps and tin base, lead-free bullets in both the .22 LR and .22 Win. Mag. Expanding their lead-free offerings, Winchester is also loading a 55-gr., tin core bullet in the .223 Super-X line and steel shot loads for the .410 and 28 gauge under the Xpert Game and Target line. Our ammunition has never been better! (www.winchester)

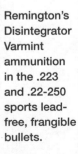

Remington's Disintegrator Varmint ammunition in the .223 and .22-250 sports lead-free, frangible bullets.

Many manufacturers do not supply suggested retail prices. Others did not get their pricing to us before press time. All pricing can vary dependent on the exact brand and style of ammo selected and/or the retail outlet from which you make your purchase. Pricing has been rounded to the nearest dollar and represents our best estimate of average pricing. An * after the cartridge means these loads are available with Nosler Partition or Swift A-Frame bullets. Listed pricing may or may not reflect this bullet type. ** = these are packed 50 to box, all others are 20 to box. Wea. Mag.= Weatherby Magnum. Spfd. = Springfield. A-Sq. = A-Square. N.E.=Nitro Express.

Cartridge	Bullet Wgt. Grs.	VELOCITY (fps)					ENERGY (ft. lbs.)					TRAJ. (in.)				Est. Price/ box
		Muzzle	100 yds.	200 yds.	300 yds.	400 yds.	Muzzle	100 yds.	200 yds.	300 yds.	400 yds.	100 yds.	200 yds.	300 yds.	400 yds.	
17, 22																
17 Remington Fireball	20	4000	3380	2840	2360	1930	710	507	358	247	165	1.6	1.5	-2.8	-13.5	NA
17 Remington Fireball	25	3850	3280	2780	2330	1925	823	597	429	301	206	0.9	0.0	-5.4	NA	NA
17 Remington	25	4040	3284	2644	2086	1606	906	599	388	242	143	+2.0	+1.7	-4.0	-17.0	$17
204 Ruger	32	4225	3632	3114	2652	2234	1268	937	689	500	355	.6	0.0	-4.2	-13.4	NA
204 Ruger	40	3900	3451	3046	2677	2336	1351	1058	824	636	485	.7	0.0	-4.5	-13.9	NA
204 Ruger	45	3625	3188	2792	2428	2093	1313	1015	778	589	438	1.00	0.0	-5.5	-16.9	NA
221 Fireball	50	2800	2137	1580	1180	988	870	507	277	155	109	+0.0	-7.0	-28.0	0.0	$14
22 Hornet	34	3050	2132	1415	1017	852	700	343	151	78	55	+0.0	-6.6	-15.5	-29.9	NA
22 Hornet	35	3100	2278	1601	1135	929	747	403	199	100	67	+2.75	0.0	-16.9	-60.4	NA
22 Hornet	45	2690	2042	1502	1128	948	723	417	225	127	90	+0.0	-7.7	-31.0	0.0	$27**
218 Bee	46	2760	2102	1550	1155	961	. 788	451	245	136	94	+0.0	-7.2	-29.0	0.0	$46**
222 Remington	40	3600	3117	2673	2269	1911	1151	863	634	457	324	+1.07	0.0	-6.13	-18.9	NA
222 Remington	50	3140	2602	2123	1700	1350	1094	752	500	321	202	+2.0	-0.4	-11.0	-33.0	$11
222 Remington	55	3020	2562	2147	1773	1451	1114	801	563	384	257	+2.0	-0.4	-11.0	-33.0	$12
22 PPC	52	3400	2930	2510	2130	NA	1335	990	730	525	NA	+2.0	1.4	-5.0	0.0	NA
223 Remington	40	3650	3010	2450	1950	1530	1185	805	535	340	265	+2.0	+1.0	-6.0	-22.0	$14
223 Remington	40	3800	3305	2845	2424	2044	1282	970	719	522	371	0.84	0.0	-5.34	-16.6	NA
223 Remington	50	3300	2874	2484	2130	1809	1209	917	685	504	363	1.37	0.0	-7.05	-21.8	NA
223 Remington	52/53	3330	2882	2477	2106	1770	1305	978	722	522	369	+2.0	+0.6	-6.5	-21.5	$14
223 Remington	55	3240	2748	2305	1906	1556	1282	922	649	444	296	+2.0	-0.2	-9.0	-27.0	$12
223 Remington	60	3100	2712	2355	2026	1726	1280	979	739	547	397	+2.0	+0.2	-8.0	-24.7	$16
223 Remington	64	3020	2621	2256	1920	1619	1296	977	723	524	373	+2.0	-0.2	-9.3	-23.0	$14
223 Remington	69	3000	2720	2460	2210	1980	1380	1135	925	750	600	+2.0	+0.8	-5.8	-17.5	$15
223 Remington	75	2790	2554	2330	2119	1926	1296	1086	904	747	617	2.37	0.0	-8.75	-25.1	NA
223 Remington	77	2750	2584	2354	2169	1992	1293	1110	948	804	679	1.93	0.0	-8.2	-23.8	NA
223 WSSM	55	3850	3438	3064	2721	2402	1810	1444	1147	904	704	0.7	0.0	-4.4	-13.6	NA
223 WSSM	64	3600	3144	2732	2356	2011	1841	1404	1061	789	574	1.0	0.0	-5.7	-17.7	NA
222 Rem. Mag.	55	3240	2748	2305	1906	1556	1282	922	649	444	296	+2.0	-0.2	-9.0	-27.0	$14
225 Winchester	55	3570	3066	2616	2208	1838	1556	1148	836	595	412	+2.0	+1.0	-5.0	-20.0	$19
224 Wea. Mag.	55	3650	3192	2780	2403	2057	1627	1244	943	705	516	+2.0	+1.2	-4.0	-17.0	$32
22-250 Rem.	40	4000	3320	2720	2200	1740	1420	980	660	430	265	+2.0	+1.8	-3.0	-16.0	$14
22-250 Rem.	50	3725	3264	2641	2455	2103	1540	1183	896	669	491	0.89	0.0	-5.23	-16.3	NA
22-250 Rem.	52/55	3680	3137	2656	2222	1832	1654	1201	861	603	410	+2.0	+1.3	-4.0	-17.0	$13
22-250 Rem.	60	3600	3195	2826	2485	2169	1727	1360	1064	823	627	+2.0	+2.0	-2.4	-12.3	$19
220 Swift	40	4200	3678	3190	2739	2329	1566	1201	904	666	482	+0.51	0.0	-4.0	-12.9	NA
220 Swift	50	3780	3158	2617	2135	1710	1586	1107	760	506	325	+2.0	+1.4	-4.4	-17.9	$20
220 Swift	50	3850	3396	2970	2576	2215	1645	1280	979	736	545	0.74	0.0	-4.84	-15.1	NA
220 Swift	55	3800	3370	2990	2630	2310	1766	1300	1000	850	650	0.0	0.0	-4.7	-14.4	NA
220 Swift	55	3650	3194	2772	2384	2035	1627	1246	939	694	506	+2.0	+2.0	-2.6	-13.4	$19
220 Swift	60	3600	3199	2824	2475	2156	1727	1364	1063	816	619	+2.0	+1.6	-4.1	-13.1	$19
22 Savage H.P.	71	2790	2340	1930	1570	1280	1225	860	585	390	190	+2.0	-1.0	-10.4	-35.7	NA
6mm (24)																
6mm BR Rem.	100	2550	2310	2083	1870	1671	1444	1185	963	776	620	+2.5	-0.6	-11.8	0.0	$22
6mm Norma BR	107	2822	2667	2517	2372	2229	1893	1690	1506	1337	1181	+1.73	0.0	-7.24	-20.6	NA
6mm PPC	70	3140	2750	2400	2070	NA	1535	1175	895	665	NA	+2.0	+1.4	-5.0	0.0	NA
243 Winchester	55	4025	3597	3209	2853	2525	1978	1579	1257	994	779	+0.6	0.0	-4.0	-12.2	NA
243 Winchester	60	3600	3110	2660	2260	1890	1725	1285	945	680	475	+2.0	+1.8	-3.3	-15.5	$17
243 Winchester	70	3400	3040	2700	2390	2100	1795	1435	1135	890	685	1.1	0.0	-5.9	-18.0	NA
243 Winchester	75/80	3350	2955	2593	2259	1951	1993	1551	1194	906	676	+2.0	+0.9	-5.0	-19.0	$16
243 Winchester	85	3320	3070	2830	2600	2380	2080	1770	1510	1280	1070	+2.0	+1.2	-4.0	-14.0	$18
243 Winchester	90	3120	2871	2635	2411	2199	1946	1647	1388	1162	966	1.4	0.0	-6.4	-18.8	NA
243 Winchester*	100	2960	2697	2449	2215	1993	1945	1615	1332	1089	882	+2.5	+1.2	-6.0	-20.0	$16
243 Winchester	105	2920	2689	2470	2261	2062	1988	1686	1422	1192	992	+2.5	+1.6	-5.0	-18.4	$21
243 Light Mag.	100	3100	2839	2592	2358	2138	2133	1790	1491	1235	1014	+1.5	0.0	-6.8	-19.8	NA
243 WSSM	55	4060	3628	3237	2880	2550	2013	1607	1280	1013	794	0.6	0.0	-3.9	-12.0	NA
243 WSSM	95	3250	3000	2763	2538	2325	2258	1898	1610	1359	1140	1.2	0.0	-5.7	-16.9	NA
243 WSSM	100	3110	2838	2583	2341	2112	2147	1789	1481	1217	991	1.4	0.0	-6.6	-19.7	NA
6mm Remington	80	3470	3064	2694	2352	2036	2139	1667	1289	982	736	+2.0	+1.1	-5.0	-17.0	$16
6mm Remington	100	3100	2829	2573	2332	2104	2133	1777	1470	1207	983	+2.5	+1.6	-5.0	-17.0	$16
6mm Remington	105	3060	2822	2596	2381	2177	2105	1788	1512	1270	1059	+2.5	+1.1	-3.3	-15.0	$21
6mm Rem. Light Mag.	100	3250	2997	2756	2528	2311	2345	1995	1687	1418	1186	1.59	0.0	-6.33	-18.3	NA
6.17(.243) Spitfire	100	3350	3122	2905	2698	2501	2493	2164	1874	1617	1389	2.4	3.20	0.0	-8.0	NA
240 Wea. Mag.	87	3500	3202	2924	2663	2416	2366	1980	1651	1370	1127	+2.0	+2.0	-2.0	-12.0	$32

Many manufacturers do not supply suggested retail prices. Others did not get their pricing to us before press time. All pricing can vary dependent on the exact brand and style of ammo selected and/or the retail outlet from which you make your purchase. Pricing has been rounded to the nearest dollar and represents our best estimate of average pricing. An * after the cartridge means these loads are available with Nosler Partition or Swift A-Frame bullets. Listed pricing may or may not reflect this bullet type. ** = these are packed 50 to box, all others are 20 to box. Wea. Mag.= Weatherby Magnum. Spfd. = Springfield. A-Sq. = A-Square. N.E.=Nitro Express.

Cartridge	Bullet Wgt. Grs.	VELOCITY (fps)					ENERGY (ft. lbs.)					TRAJ. (in.)				Est. Price/ box
		Muzzle	100 yds.	200 yds.	300 yds.	400 yds.	Muzzle	100 yds.	200 yds.	300 yds.	400 yds.	100 yds.	200 yds.	300 yds.	400 yds.	
240 Wea. Mag.	100	3395	3106	2835	2581	2339	2559	2142	1785	1478	1215	+2.5	+2.8	-2.0	-11.0	$43
25																
25-20 Win.	86	1460	1194	1030	931	858	407	272	203	165	141	0.0	-23.5	0.0	0.0	$32**
25-35 Win.	117	2230	1866	1545	1282	1097	1292	904	620	427	313	+2.5	-4.2	-26.0	0.0	$24
250 Savage	100	2820	2504	2210	1936	1684	1765	1392	1084	832	630	+2.5	+0.4	-9.0	-28.0	$17
257 Roberts	100	2980	2661	2363	2085	1827	1972	1572	1240	965	741	+2.5	-0.8	-5.2	-21.6	$20
257 Roberts+P	117	2780	2411	2071	1761	1488	2009	1511	1115	806	576	+2.5	-0.2	-10.2	-32.6	$18
257 Roberts+P	120	2780	2560	2360	2160	1970	2060	1750	1480	1240	1030	+2.5	+1.2	-6.4	-23.6	$22
257 Roberts	122	2600	2331	2078	1842	1625	1831	1472	1169	919	715	+2.5	0.0	-10.6	-31.4	$21
257 Light Mag.	117	2940	2694	2460	2240	2031	2245	1885	1572	1303	1071	+1.7	0.0	-7.6	-21.8	NA
25-06 Rem.	87	3440	2995	2591	2222	1884	2286	1733	1297	954	686	+2.0	+1.1	-2.5	-14.4	$17
25-06 Rem.	90	3440	3043	2680	2344	2034	2364	1850	1435	1098	827	+2.0	+1.8	-3.3	-15.6	$17
25-06 Rem.	100	3230	2893	2580	2287	2014	2316	1858	1478	1161	901	+2.0	+0.8	-5.7	-18.9	$17
25-06 Rem.	117	2990	2770	2570	2370	2190	2320	2000	1715	1465	1246	+2.5	+1.0	-7.9	-26.6	$19
25-06 Rem.*	120	2990	2730	2484	2252	2032	2382	1985	1644	1351	1100	+2.5	+1.2	-5.3	-19.6	$17
25-06 Rem.	122	2930	2706	2492	2289	2095	2325	1983	1683	1419	1189	+2.5	+1.8	-4.5	-17.5	$23
25 WSSM	85	3470	3156	2863	2589	2331	2273	1880	1548	1266	1026	1.0	0.0	-5.2	-15.7	NA
25 WSSM	115	3060	284	2639	2442	2254	2392	2066	1778	1523	1398	1.4	0.0	-6.4	-18.6	NA
25 WSSM	120	2990	2717	2459	2216	1987	2383	1967	1612	1309	1053	1.6	0.0	-7.4	-21.8	NA
257 Wea. Mag.	87	3825	3456	3118	2805	2513	2826	2308	1870	1520	1220	+2.0	+2.7	-0.3	-7.6	$32
257 Wea. Mag.	100	3555	3237	2941	2665	2404	2806	2326	1920	1576	1283	+2.5	+3.2	0.0	-8.0	$32
257 Scramjet	100	3745	3450	3173	2912	2666	3114	2643	2235	1883	1578	+2.1	+2.77	0.0	-6.93	NA
6.5																
6.5x47 Lapua	123	2887	NA	2554	NA	2244	2285	NA	1788	NA	1380	NA	4.53	0.00	-10.7	NA
6.5x50mm Jap.	139	2360	2160	1970	1790	1620	1720	1440	1195	985	810	+2.5	-1.0	-13.5	0.0	NA
6.5x50mm Jap.	156	2070	1830	1610	1430	1260	1475	1155	900	695	550	+2.5	-4.0	-23.8	0.0	NA
6.5x52mm Car.	139	2580	2360	2160	1970	1790	2045	1725	1440	1195	985	+2.5	0.0	-9.9	-29.0	NA
6.5x52mm Car.	156	2430	2170	1930	1700	1500	2045	1630	1285	1005	780	+2.5	-1.0	-13.9	0.0	NA
6.5x52mm Carcano	160	2250	1963	1700	1467	1271	1798	1369	1027	764	574	+3.8	0.0	-15.9	-48.1	NA
6.5x55mm Light Mag.	129	2750	2549	2355	2171	1994	2166	1860	1589	1350	1139	+2.0	0.0	-8.2	-23.9	NA
6.5x55mm Swe.	140	2550	NA	NA	NA	NA	2020	NA	NA	NA	NA	0.0	0.0	0.0	0.0	$18
6.5x55mm Swe.*	139/140	2850	2640	2440	2250	2070	2525	2170	1855	1575	1330	+2.5	+1.6	-5.4	-18.9	$18
6.5x55mm Swe.	156	2650	2370	2110	1870	1650	2425	1950	1550	1215	945	+2.5	0.0	-10.3	-30.6	NA
260 Remington	125	2875	2669	2473	2285	2105	2294	1977	1697	1449	1230	1.71	0.0	-7.4	-21.4	NA
260 Remington	140	2750	2544	2347	2158	1979	2351	2011	1712	1448	1217	+2.2	0.0	-8.6	-24.6	NA
6.5 Creedmoor	120	3020	2815	2619	2430	2251	2430	2111	1827	1574	1350	1.4	0.0	-6.5	-18.9	NA
6.5 Creedmoor	140	2820	2654	2494	2339	2190	2472	2179	1915	1679	1467	1.7	0.0	-7.2	-20.6	NA
6.5-284 Norma	142	3025	2890	2758	2631	2507	2886	2634	2400	2183	1982	1.13	0.0	-5.7	-16.4	NA
6.71 (264) Phantom	120	3150	2929	2718	2517	2325	2645	2286	1969	1698	1440	+1.3	0.0	-6.0	-17.5	NA
6.5 Rem. Mag.	120	3210	2905	2621	2353	2102	2745	2248	1830	1475	1177	+2.5	+1.7	-4.1	-16.3	Disc.
264 Win. Mag.	140	3030	2782	2548	2326	2114	2854	2406	2018	1682	1389	+2.5	+1.4	-5.1	-18.0	$24
6.71 (264) Blackbird	140	3480	3261	3053	2855	2665	3766	3307	2899	2534	2208	+2.4	+3.1	0.0	-7.4	NA
6.8mm Rem.	115	2775	2472	2190	1926	1683	1966	1561	1224	947	723	+2.1	0.0	-3.7	-9.4	NA
27																
270 Winchester	100	3430	3021	2649	2305	1988	2612	2027	1557	1179	877	+2.0	+1.0	-4.9	-17.5	$17
270 Win. (Rem.)	115	2710	2482	2265	2059	NA	1875	1485	1161	896	NA	0.0	4.8	-17.3	0.0	NA
270 Winchester	130	3060	2776	2510	2259	2022	2702	2225	1818	1472	1180	+2.5	+1.4	-5.3	-18.2	$17
270 Win. Supreme	130	3150	2881	2628	2388	2161	2865	2396	1993	1646	1348	1.3	0.0	-6.4	-18.9	NA
270 Winchester	135	3000	2780	2570	2369	2178	2697	2315	1979	1682	1421	+2.5	+1.4	-6.0	-17.6	$23
270 Winchester*	140	2940	2700	2480	2260	2060	2685	2270	1905	1590	1315	+2.5	+1.8	-4.6	-17.9	$20
270 Win. Light Magnum	130	3215	2998	2790	2590	2400	2983	2594	2246	1936	1662	1.21	0.0	-5.83	-17.0	NA
270 Winchester*	150	2850	2585	2336	2100	1879	2705	2226	1817	1468	1175	+2.5	+1.2	-6.5	-22.0	$17
270 Win. Supreme	150	2930	2693	2468	2254	2051	2860	2416	2030	1693	1402	1.7	0.0	-7.4	-21.6	NA
270 WSM	130	3275	3041	2820	2609	2408	3096	2669	2295	1564	1673	1.1	0.0	-5.5	-16.1	NA
270 WSM	140	3125	2865	2619	2386	2165	3035	2559	2132	1769	1457	1.4	0.0	-6.5	-19.0	NA
270 WSM	150	3120	2923	2734	2554	2380	3242	2845	2490	2172	1886	1.3	0.0	-5.9	-17.2	NA
270 Wea. Mag.	100	3760	3380	3033	2712	2412	3139	2537	2042	1633	1292	+2.0	+2.4	-1.2	-10.1	$32
270 Wea. Mag.	130	3375	3119	2878	2649	2432	3287	2808	2390	2026	1707	+2.5	-2.9	-0.9	-9.9	$32
270 Wea. Mag.*	150	3245	3036	2837	2647	2465	3507	3070	2681	2334	2023	+2.5	+2.6	-1.8	-11.4	$47
7mm																
7mm BR	140	2216	2012	1821	1643	1481	1525	1259	1031	839	681	+2.0	-3.7	-20.0	0.0	$23
7mm Mauser*	139/140	2660	2435	2221	2018	1827	2199	1843	1533	1266	1037	+2.5	0.0	-9.6	-27.7	$17
7mm Mauser	145	2690	2442	2206	1985	1777	2334	1920	1568	1268	1017	+2.5	+0.1	-9.6	-28.3	$18
7mm Mauser	154	2690	2490	2300	2120	1940	2475	2120	1810	1530	1285	+2.5	+0.8	-7.5	-23.5	$17

Many manufacturers do not supply suggested retail prices. Others did not get their pricing to us before press time. All pricing can vary dependent on the exact brand and style of ammo selected and/or the retail outlet from which you make your purchase. Pricing has been rounded to the nearest dollar and represents our best estimate of average pricing. An * after the cartridge means these loads are available with Nosler Partition or Swift A-Frame bullets. Listed pricing may or may not reflect this bullet type. ** = these are packed 50 to box, all others are 20 to box. Wea. Mag.= Weatherby Magnum. Spfd. = Springfield. A-Sq. = A-Square. N.E.=Nitro Express.

Cartridge	Bullet Wgt. Grs.	VELOCITY (fps)					ENERGY (ft. lbs.)					TRAJ. (in.)				Est. Price/ box
		Muzzle	100 yds.	200 yds.	300 yds.	400 yds.	Muzzle	100 yds.	200 yds.	300 yds.	400 yds.	100 yds.	200 yds.	300 yds.	400 yds.	
7mm Mauser	175	2440	2137	1857	1603	1382	2313	1774	1340	998	742	+2.5	-1.7	-16.1	0.0	$17
7x57 Light Mag.	139	2970	2730	2503	2287	2082	2722	2301	1933	1614	1337	+1.6	0.0	-7.2	-21.0	NA
7x30 Waters	120	2700	2300	1930	1600	1330	1940	1405	990	685	470	+2.5	-0.2	-12.3	0.0	$18
7mm-08 Rem.	120	3000	2725	2467	2223	1992	2398	1979	1621	1316	1058	+2.0	0.0	-7.6	-22.3	$18
7mm-08 Rem.*	140	2860	2625	2402	2189	1988	2542	2142	1793	1490	1228	+2.5	+0.8	-6.9	-21.9	$18
7mm-08 Rem.	154	2715	2510	2315	2128	1950	2520	2155	1832	1548	1300	+2.5	+1.0	-7.0	-22.7	$23
7mm-08 Light Mag.	139	3000	2790	2590	2399	2216	2777	2403	2071	1776	1515	+1.5	0.0	-6.7	-19.4	NA
7x64mm Bren.	140					Not Yet Announced										$17
7x64mm Bren.	154	2820	2610	2420	2230	2050	2720	2335	1995	1695	1430	+2.5	+1.4	-5.7	-19.9	NA
7x64mm Bren.*	160	2850	2669	2495	2327	2166	2885	2530	2211	1924	1667	+2.5	+1.6	-4.8	-17.8	$24
7x64mm Bren.	175					Not Yet Announced										$17
284 Winchester	150	2860	2595	2344	2108	1886	2724	2243	1830	1480	1185	+2.5	+0.8	-7.3	-23.2	$24
280 Remington	120	3150	2866	2599	2348	2110	2643	2188	1800	1468	1186	+2.0	+0.6	-6.0	-17.9	$17
280 Remington	140	3000	2758	2528	2309	2102	2797	2363	1986	1657	1373	+2.5	+1.4	-5.2	-18.3	$17
280 Remington*	150	2890	2624	2373	2135	1912	2781	2293	1875	1518	1217	+2.5	+0.8	-7.1	-22.6	$17
280 Remington	160	2840	2637	2442	2556	2078	2866	2471	2120	1809	1535	+2.5	+0.8	-6.7	-21.0	$20
280 Remington	165	2820	2510	2220	1950	1701	2913	2308	1805	1393	1000	+2.5	+0.4	-8.8	-26.5	$17
7x61mm S&H Sup.	154	3060	2720	2400	2100	1820	3200	2520	1965	1505	1135	+2.5	+1.8	-5.0	-19.8	NA
7mm Dakota	160	3200	3001	2811	2630	2455	3637	3200	2808	2456	2140	+2.1	+1.9	-2.8	-12.5	NA
7mm Rem. Mag. (Rem.)	140	2710	2482	2265	2059	NA	2283	1915	1595	1318	NA	0.0	-4.5	-1.57	0.0	NA
7mm Rem. Mag.*	139/140	3150	2930	2710	2510	2320	3085	2660	2290	1960	1670	+2.5	+2.4	-2.4	-12.7	$21
7mm Rem. Hvy Mag	139	3250	3044	2847	2657	2475	3259	2860	2501	2178	1890	1.1	0.0	-5.5	-16.2	NA
7mm Rem. Mag.	150/154	3110	2830	2568	2320	2085	3221	2667	2196	1792	1448	+2.5	+1.6	-4.6	-16.5	$21
7mm Rem. Mag.*	160/162	2950	2730	2520	2320	2120	3090	2650	2250	1910	1600	+2.5	+1.8	-4.4	-17.8	$34
7mm Rem. Mag.	165	2900	2699	2507	2324	2147	3081	2669	2303	1978	1689	+2.5	+1.2	-5.9	-19.0	$28
7mm Rem Mag.	175	2860	2645	2440	2244	2057	3178	2718	2313	1956	1644	+2.5	+1.0	-6.5	-20.7	$21
7mm Rem. SA ULTRA MAG	140	3175	2934	2707	2490	2283	3033	2676	2277	1927	1620	1.3	0.0	-6	-17.7	NA
7mm Rem. SA ULTRA MAG	150	3110	2828	2563	2313	2077	3221	2663	2188	1782	1437	2.5	2.1	-3.6	-15.8	NA
7mm Rem. SA ULTRA MAG	160	2960	2762	2572	2390	2215	3112	2709	2350	2029	1743	2.6	2.2	-3.6	-15.4	NA
7mm Rem. WSM	140	3225	3008	2801	2603	2414	3233	2812	2438	2106	1812	1.2	0.0	-5.6	-16.4	NA
7mm Rem. WSM	160	2990	2744	2512	2081	1883	3176	2675	2241	1864	1538	1.6	0.0	-7.1	-20.8	NA
7mm Wea. Mag.	140	3225	2970	2729	2501	2283	3233	2741	2315	1943	1621	+2.5	+2.0	-3.2	-14.0	$35
7mm Wea. Mag.	154	3260	3023	2799	2586	2382	3539	3044	2609	2227	1890	+2.5	+2.8	-1.5	-10.8	$32
7mm Wea. Mag.*	160	3200	3004	2816	2637	2464	3637	3205	2817	2469	2156	+2.5	+2.7	-1.5	-10.6	$47
7mm Wea. Mag.	165	2950	2747	2553	2367	2189	3188	2765	2388	2053	1756	+2.5	+1.8	-4.2	-16.4	$43
7mm Wea. Mag.	175	2910	2693	2486	2288	2098	3293	2818	2401	2033	1711	+2.5	+1.2	-5.9	-19.4	$35
7.21(.284) Tomahawk	140	3300	3118	2943	2774	2612	3386	3022	2693	2393	2122	2.3	3.20	0.0	-7.7	NA
7mm STW	140	3325	3064	2818	2585	2364	3436	2918	2468	2077	1737	+2.3	+1.8	-3.0	-13.1	NA
7mm STW Supreme	160	3150	2894	2652	2422	2204	3526	2976	2499	2085	1727	1.3	0.0	-6.3	-18.5	NA
7mm Rem. Ultra Mag.	140	3425	3184	2956	2740	2534	3646	3161	2715	2333	1995	1.7	1.60	-2.6	-11.4	NA
7mm Firehawk	140	3625	3373	3135	2909	2695	4084	3536	3054	2631	2258	+2.2	+2.9	0.0	-7.03	NA

30

Cartridge	Bullet Wgt. Grs.	Muzzle	100 yds.	200 yds.	300 yds.	400 yds.	Muzzle	100 yds.	200 yds.	300 yds.	400 yds.	100 yds.	200 yds.	300 yds.	400 yds.	Est. Price/ box
7.21 (.284) Firebird	140	3750	3522	3306	3101	2905	4372	3857	3399	2990	2625	1.6	2.4	0.0	-6.0	NA
30 Carbine	110	1990	1567	1236	1035	923	977	600	373	262	208	0.0	-13.5	0.0	0.0	$28**
303 Savage	190	1890	1612	1327	1183	1055	1507	1096	794	591	469	+2.5	-7.6	0.0	0.0	$24
30 Remington	170	2120	1822	1555	1328	1153	1696	1253	913	666	502	+2.5	-4.7	-26.3	0.0	$20
7.62x39mm Rus.	123/125	2300	2030	1780	1550	1350	1445	1125	860	655	500	+2.5	-2.0	-17.5	0.0	$13
30-30 Win.	55	3400	2693	2085	1570	1187	1412	886	521	301	172	+2.0	0.0	-10.2	-35.0	$18
30-30 Win.	125	2570	2090	1660	1320	1080	1830	1210	770	480	320	-2.0	-2.6	-19.9	0.0	$13
30-30 Win.	150	2390	2040	1723	1447	1225	1902	1386	989	697	499	0.0	-7.5	-27.0	-63.0	NA
30-30 Win. Supreme	150	2480	2095	1747	1446	1209	2049	1462	1017	697	487	0.0	-6.5	-24.5	0.0	NA
30-30 Win.	160	2300	1997	1719	1473	1268	1879	1416	1050	771	571	+2.5	-2.9	-20.2	0.0	$18
30-30 Win. Lever Evolution	160	2400	2150	1916	1699	NA	2046	1643	1304	1025	NA	3.00	0.20	-12.1	NA	NA
30-30 PMC Cowboy	170	1300	1198	1121			638	474				0.0	-27.0	0.0	0.0	NA
30-30 Win.*	170	2200	1895	1619	1381	1191	1827	1355	989	720	535	+2.5	-5.8	-23.6	0.0	$13
300 Savage	150	2630	2354	2094	1853	1631	2303	1845	1462	1143	886	+2.5	-0.4	-10.1	-30.7	$17
300 Savage	180	2350	2137	1935	1754	1570	2207	1825	1496	1217	985	+2.5	-1.6	-15.2	0.0	$17
30-40 Krag	180	2430	2213	2007	1813	1632	2360	1957	1610	1314	1064	+2.5	-1.4	-13.8	0.0	$18
7.65x53mm Arg.	180	2590	2390	2200	2010	1830	2685	2280	1925	1615	1345	+2.5	0.0	-27.6	0.0	NA
7.5x53mm Argentine	150	2785	2519	2269	2032	1814	2583	2113	1714	1376	1096	+2.0	0.0	-8.8	-25.5	NA
308 Marlin Express	160	2660	2430	2226	2026	1836	2513	2111	1761	1457	1197	3.0	1.7	-6.7	-23.5	NA
307 Winchester	150	2760	2321	1924	1575	1289	2530	1795	1233	826	554	+2.5	-1.5	-13.6	0.0	Disc.
307 Winchester	180	2510	2179	1874	1599	1362	2519	1898	1404	1022	742	+2.5	-1.6	-15.6	0.0	$20
7.5x55 Swiss	180	2650	2450	2250	2060	1880	2805	2390	2020	1700	1415	+2.5	+0.6	-8.1	-24.9	NA
7.5x55mm Swiss	165	2720	2515	2319	2132	1954	2710	2317	1970	1665	1398	+2.0	0.0	-8.5	-24.6	NA
30 Remington AR	123/125	2800	2465	2154	1867	1606	2176	1686	1288	967	716	2.10	0.00	-9.7	-29.4	NA

Many manufacturers do not supply suggested retail prices. Others did not get their pricing to us before press time. All pricing can vary dependent on the exact brand and style of ammo selected and/or the retail outlet from which you make your purchase. Pricing has been rounded to the nearest dollar and represents our best estimate of average pricing. An * after the cartridge means these loads are available with Nosler Partition or Swift A-Frame bullets. Listed pricing may or may not reflect this bullet type.
** = these are packed 50 to box, all others are 20 to box. Wea. Mag.= Weatherby Magnum. Spfd. = Springfield. A-Sq. = A-Square. N.E.=Nitro Express.

Cartridge	Bullet Wgt. Grs.	VELOCITY (fps)					ENERGY (ft. lbs.)					TRAJ. (in.)				Est. Price/ box
		Muzzle	100 yds.	200 yds.	300 yds.	400 yds.	Muzzle	100 yds.	200 yds.	300 yds.	400 yds.	100 yds.	200 yds.	300 yds.	400 yds.	
308 Winchester	55	3770	3215	2726	2286	1888	1735	1262	907	638	435	-2.0	+1.4	-3.8	-15.8	$22
308 Winchester	150	2820	2533	2263	2009	1774	2648	2137	1705	1344	1048	+2.5	+0.4	-8.5	-26.1	$17
308 Winchester	165	2700	2440	2194	1963	1748	2670	2180	1763	1411	1199	+2.5	0.0	-9.7	-28.5	$20
308 Winchester	168	2680	2493	2314	2143	1979	2678	2318	1998	1713	1460	+2.5	0.0	-8.9	-25.3	$18
308 Win. (Fed.)	170	2000	1740	1510	NA	NA	1510	1145	860	NA	NA	0.0	0.0	0.0	0.0	NA
308 Winchester	178	2620	2415	2220	2034	1857	2713	2306	1948	1635	1363	+2.5	0.0	-9.6	-27.6	$23
308 Winchester*	180	2620	2393	2178	1974	1782	2743	2288	1896	1557	1269	+2.5	-0.2	-10.2	-28.5	$17
308 Light Mag.*	150	2980	2703	2442	2195	1964	2959	2433	1986	1606	1285	+1.6	0.0	-7.5	-22.2	NA
308 Light Mag.	165	2870	2658	2456	2263	2078	3019	2589	2211	1877	1583	+1.7	0.0	-7.5	-21.8	NA
308 High Energy	165	2870	2600	2350	2120	1890	3020	2485	2030	1640	1310	+1.8	0.0	-8.2	-24.0	NA
308 Light Mag.	168	2870	2658	2456	2263	2078	3019	2589	2211	1877	1583	+1.7	0.0	-7.5	-21.8	NA
308 High Energy	180	2740	2550	2370	2200	2030	3000	2600	2245	1925	1645	+1.9	0.0	-8.2	-23.5	NA
30-06 Spfd.	55	4080	3485	2965	2502	2083	2033	1483	1074	764	530	+2.0	+1.9	-2.1	-11.7	$22
30-06 Spfd. (Rem.)	125	2660	2335	2034	1757	NA	1964	1513	1148	856	NA	0.0	-5.2	-18.9	0.0	NA
30-06 Spfd.	125	3140	2780	2447	2138	1853	2736	2145	1662	1279	953	+2.0	+1.0	-6.2	-21.0	$17
30-06 Spfd.	150	2910	2617	2342	2083	1853	2820	2281	1827	1445	1135	+2.5	+0.8	-7.2	-23.4	$17
30-06 Spfd.	152	2910	2654	2413	2184	1968	2858	2378	1965	1610	1307	+2.5	+1.0	-6.6	-21.3	$23
30-06 Spfd.*	165	2800	2534	2283	2047	1825	2872	2352	1909	1534	1220	+2.5	+0.4	-8.4	-25.5	$17
30-06 Spfd.	168	2710	2522	2346	2169	2003	2739	2372	2045	1754	1497	+2.5	+0.4	-8.0	-23.5	$18
30-06 Spfd. (Fed.)	170	2000	1740	1510	NA	NA	1510	1145	860	NA	NA	0.0	0.0	0.0	0.0	NA
30-06 Spfd.	178	2720	2511	2311	2121	1939	2924	2491	2111	1777	1486	+2.5	+0.4	-8.2	-24.6	$23
30-06 Spfd.*	180	2700	2469	2250	2042	1846	2913	2436	2023	1666	1362	-2.5	0.0	-9.3	-27.0	$17
30-06 Spfd.	220	2410	2130	1870	1632	1422	2837	2216	1708	1301	988	+2.5	-1.7	-18.0	0.0	$17

30 Mag.

Cartridge	Bullet Wgt. Grs.	Muzzle	100 yds.	200 yds.	300 yds.	400 yds.	Muzzle	100 yds.	200 yds.	300 yds.	400 yds.	100 yds.	200 yds.	300 yds.	400 yds.	Est. Price/ box
30-06 Light Mag.	150	3100	2815	2548	2295	2058	3200	2639	2161	1755	1410	+1.4	0.0	-6.8	-20.3	NA
30-06 Light Mag.	180	2880	2676	2480	2293	2114	3316	2862	2459	2102	1786	+1.7	0.0	-7.3	-21.3	NA
30-06 High Energy	180	2880	2690	2500	2320	2150	3315	2880	2495	2150	1845	+1.7	0.0	-7.2	-21.0	NA
30 T/C	150	3000	2772	2555	2348	2151	2997	2558	2173	1836	1540	1.5	0.0	-6.9	-20.0	NA
30 T/C	165	2850	2644	2447	2258	2078	2975	2560	2193	1868	1582	1.7	0.0	-7.6	-22.0	NA
300 REM SA ULTRA MAG	150	3200	2901	2622	2359	2112	3410	2803	2290	1854	1485	1.3	0.0	-6.4	-19.1	NA
300 REM SA ULTRA MAG	165	3075	2792	2527	2276	2040	3464	2856	2339	1898	1525	1.5	0.0	-7	-20.7	NA
300 REM SA ULTRA MAG	180	2960	2761	2571	2389	2214	3501	3047	2642	2280	1959	2.6	2.2	-3.6	-15.4	NA
7.82 (308) Patriot	150	3250	2999	2762	2537	2323	3519	2997	2542	2145	1798	+1.2	0.0	-5.8	-16.9	NA
300 RCM	150	3300	3056	2825	2606	2397	3627	3110	2658	2262	1914	1.1	0.0	-5.4	-16.0	NA
300 RCM	165	3140	2921	2713	2514	2324	3612	3126	2697	2316	1979	1.3	0.0	-6.0	-17.5	NA
300 RDM	180	3000	2802	2613	2432	2258	3597	3139	2729	2363	2037	1.5	0.0	-6.5	-18.9	NA
300 WSM	150	3300	3061	2834	2619	2414	3628	3121	2676	2285	1941	1.1	0.0	-5.4	-15.9	NA
300 WSM	180	2970	2741	2524	2317	2120	3526	3005	2547	2147	1797	1.6	0.0	-7.0	-20.5	NA
300 WSM	180	3010	2923	2734	2554	2380	3242	2845	2490	2172	1886	1.3	0	-5.9	-17.2	NA
308 Norma Mag.	180	3020	2820	2630	2440	2270	3645	3175	2755	2385	2050	+2.5	+2.0	-3.5	-14.8	NA
300 Dakota	200	3000	2824	2656	2493	2336	3996	3542	3131	2760	2423	+2.2	+1.5	-4.0	-15.2	NA
300 H&H Magnum*	180	2880	2640	2412	2196	1990	3315	2785	2325	1927	1583	+2.5	+0.8	-6.8	-21.7	$24
300 H&H Magnum	220	2550	2267	2002	1757	NA	3167	2510	1958	1508	NA	-2.5	-0.4	-12.0	0.0	NA
300 Win. Mag.	150	3290	2951	2636	2342	2068	3605	2900	2314	1827	1424	+2.5	+1.9	-3.8	-15.8	$22
300 Win. Mag.	165	3100	2877	2665	2462	2269	3522	3033	2603	2221	1897	+2.5	+2.4	-3.0	-16.9	$24
300 Win. Mag.	178	2900	2760	2568	2375	2191	3509	3030	2606	2230	1897	+2.5	+1.4	-5.0	-17.6	$29
300 Win. Mag.*	180	2960	2745	2540	2344	2157	3501	3011	2578	2196	1859	+2.5	+1.2	-5.5	-18.5	$22
300 W.M. High Energy	180	3100	2830	2580	2340	2110	3840	3205	2660	2190	1790	+1.4	0.0	-6.6	-19.7	NA
300 W.M. Light Mag.	180	3100	2879	2668	2467	2275	3840	3313	2845	2431	2068	+1.39	0.0	-6.45	-18.7	NA
300 Win. Mag.	190	2885	1691	2506	2327	2156	3511	3055	2648	2285	1961	+2.5	+1.2	-5.7	-19.0	$26
300 W.M. High Energy	200	2930	2740	2550	2370	2200	3810	3325	2885	2495	2145	+1.6	0.0	-6.9	-20.1	NA
300 Win. Mag.*	200	2825	2595	2376	2167	1970	3545	2991	2508	2086	1742	-2.5	+1.6	-4.7	-17.2	$36
300 Win. Mag.	220	2680	2448	2228	2020	1823	3508	2927	2424	1993	1623	+2.5	0.0	-9.5	-27.5	$23
300 Rem. Ultra Mag.	150	3450	3208	2980	2762	2556	3964	3427	2956	2541	2175	1.7	1.5	-2.6	-11.2	NA
300 Rem. Ultra Mag.	150	2910	2686	2473	2279	2077	2820	2403	2037	1716	1436	1.7	0.0	-7.4	-21.5	NA
300 Rem. Ultra Mag.	180	3250	3037	2834	2640	2454	4221	3686	3201	2786	2407	2.4	0.0	-3.0	-12.7	NA
300 Rem. Ultra Mag.	180	2960	2774	2505	2294	2093	3501	2971	2508	2103	1751	2.7	2.2	-3.8	-16.4	NA
300 Rem. Ultra Mag.	200	3032	2791	2562	2345	2138	4083	3459	2916	2442	2030	1.5	0.0	-6.8	-19.9	NA
300 Wea. Mag.	100	3900	3441	3038	2652	2305	3714	2891	2239	1717	1297	+2.0	+2.6	-0.6	-8.7	$32
300 Wea. Mag.	150	3600	3307	3033	2776	2533	4316	3642	3064	2566	2137	+2.5	+3.2	0.0	-8.1	$32
300 Wea. Mag.	165	3450	3210	3000	2792	2593	4360	3796	3297	2855	2464	+2.5	+3.2	0.0	-7.8	NA
300 Wea. Mag.	178	3120	2902	2695	2497	2308	3847	3329	2870	2464	2104	+2.5	-1.7	-3.6	-14.7	$43
300 Wea. Mag.	180	3330	3110	2910	2710	2520	4430	3875	3375	2935	2540	+1.0	0.0	-5.2	-15.1	NA
300 Wea. Mag.	190	3030	2830	2638	2455	2279	3873	3378	2936	2542	2190	+2.5	+1.6	-4.3	-16.0	$38
300 Wea. Mag.	220	2850	2541	2283	1964	1736	3967	3155	2480	1922	1471	+2.5	+0.4	-8.5	-26.4	$35
300 Warbird	180	3400	3180	2971	2772	2582	4620	4042	3528	3071	2664	+2.59	+3.25	0.0	-7.95	NA

Many manufacturers do not supply suggested retail prices. Others did not get their pricing to us before press time. All pricing can vary dependent on the exact brand and style of ammo selected and/or the retail outlet from which you make your purchase. Pricing has been rounded to the nearest dollar and represents our best estimate of average pricing.
An * after the cartridge means these loads are available with Nosler Partition or Swift A-Frame bullets. Listed pricing may or may not reflect this bullet type.
** = these are packed 50 to box, all others are 20 to box. Wea. Mag.= Weatherby Magnum. Spfd. = Springfield. A-Sq. = A-Square. N.E.=Nitro Express.

Cartridge	Bullet Wgt. Grs.	VELOCITY (fps)					ENERGY (ft. lbs.)					TRAJ. (in.)				Est. Price/ box
		Muzzle	100 yds.	200 yds.	300 yds.	400 yds.	Muzzle	100 yds.	200 yds.	300 yds.	400 yds.	100 yds.	200 yds.	300 yds.	400 yds.	
300 Pegasus	180	3500	3319	3145	2978	2817	4896	4401	3953	3544	3172	+2.28	+2.89	0.0	-6.79	NA
31																
32-20 Win.	100	1210	1021	913	834	769	325	231	185	154	131	0.0	-32.3	0.0	0.0	$23**
303 British	150	2685	2441	2210	1992	1787	2401	1984	1627	1321	1064	+2.5	+0.6	-8.4	-26.2	$18
303 British	180	2460	2124	1817	1542	1311	2418	1803	1319	950	687	+2.5	-1.8	-16.8	0.0	$18
303 Light Mag.	150	2830	2570	2325	2094	1884	2667	2199	1800	1461	1185	+2.0	0.0	-8.4	-24.6	NA
7.62x54mm Rus.	146	2950	2730	2520	2320	NA	2820	2415	2055	1740	NA	+2.5	+2.0	-4.4	-17.7	NA
7.62x54mm Rus.	180	2580	2370	2180	2000	1820	2650	2250	1900	1590	1100	+2.5	0.0	-9.8	-28.5	NA
7.7x58mm Jap.	150	2640	2399	2170	1954	1752	2321	1916	1568	1271	1022	+2.3	0.0	-9.7	-28.5	NA
7.7x58mm Jap.	180	2500	2300	2100	1920	1750	2490	2105	1770	1475	1225	+2.5	0.0	-10.4	-30.2	NA
8x56 R	205	2400	2188	1987	1797	1621	2621	2178	1796	1470	1196	+2.9	0.0	-11.7	-34.3	NA
8mm																
8x57mm JS Mau.	165	2850	2520	2210	1930	1670	2965	2330	1795	1360	1015	+2.5	+1.0	-7.7	0.0	NA
32 Win. Special	165	2410	2145	1897	1669	NA	2128	1685	1318	1020	NA	2.0	0.0	-13.0	-19.9	NA
32 Win. Special	170	2250	1921	1626	1372	1175	1911	1393	998	710	521	+2.5	-3.5	-22.9	0.0	$14
8mm Mauser	170	2360	1969	1622	1333	1123	2102	1464	993	671	476	+2.5	-3.1	-22.2	0.0	$18
325 WSM	180	3000	2841	2632	2432	2242	3743	3226	2769	2365	2009	+1.4	0.0	-6.4	-18.7	NA
325 WSM	200	2950	2753	2565	2384	2210	3866	3367	2922	2524	2170	+1.5	0.0	-6.8	-19.8	NA
325 WSM	220	2840	2605	2382	2169	1968	3941	3316	2772	2300	1893	+1.8	0.0	-8.0	-23.3	NA
8mm Rem. Mag.	185	3080	2761	2464	2186	1927	3896	3131	2494	1963	1525	+2.5	+1.4	-5.5	-19.7	$30
8mm Rem. Mag.	220	2830	2581	2346	2123	1913	3912	3254	2688	2201	1787	+2.5	+0.6	-7.6	-23.5	Disc.
33																
338 Federal	180	2830	2590	2350	2130	1930	3200	2670	2215	1820	1480	1.80	0.00	-8.2	-23.9	NA
338 Marlin Express	200	2565	2365	2174	1992	1820	2922	2484	2099	1762	1471	3.00	1.20	-7.9	-25.9	NA
338 Federal	185	2750	2550	2350	2160	1980	3105	2660	2265	1920	1615	1.90	0.00	-8.3	-24.1	NA
338 Federal	210	2630	2410	2200	2010	1820	3225	2710	2265	1880	1545	2.30	0.00	-9.4	-27.3	NA
338-06	200	2750	2553	2364	2184	2011	3358	2894	2482	2118	1796	+1.9	0.0	-8.22	-23.6	NA
330 Dakota	250	2900	2719	2545	2378	2217	4668	4103	3595	3138	2727	+2.3	+1.3	-5.0	-17.5	NA
338 Lapua	250	2963	2795	2640	2493	NA	4842	4341	3881	3458	NA	+1.9	0.0	-7.9	0.0	NA
338 RCM	200	2950	2744	2547	2359	2179	3865	3344	2881	2471	2108	1.6	0.0	-6.9	-20.0	NA
338 RCM	225	2775	2598	2427	2264	2106	3847	3372	2944	2560	2216	1.8	0.0	-7.7	-22.2	NA
338 Win. Mag.	200	2960	2658	2375	2110	1862	3890	3137	2505	1977	1539	+2.5	+1.0	-6.7	-22.3	$27
338 Win. Mag.*	210	2830	2590	2370	2150	1940	3735	3130	2610	2155	1760	+2.5	+1.4	-6.0	-20.9	$33
338 Win. Mag.*	225	2785	2517	2266	2029	1808	3871	3165	2565	2057	1633	+2.5	+0.4	-8.5	-25.9	$27
338 W.M. Heavy Mag.	225	2920	2678	2449	2232	2027	4259	3583	2996	2489	2053	+1.75	0.0	-7.65	-22.0	NA
338 W.M. High Energy	225	2940	2690	2450	2230	2010	4320	3610	3000	2475	2025	+1.7	0.0	-7.5	-22.0	NA
338 Win. Mag.	230	2780	2573	2375	2186	2005	3948	3382	2881	2441	2054	+2.5	+1.2	-6.3	-21.0	$40
338 Win. Mag.*	250	2660	2456	2261	2075	1898	3927	3348	2837	2389	1999	+2.5	+0.2	-9.0	-26.2	$27
338 W.M. High Energy	250	2800	2610	2420	2250	2080	4350	3775	3260	2805	2395	+1.8	0.0	-7.8	-22.5	NA
338 Ultra Mag.	250	2860	2645	2440	2244	2057	4540	3882	3303	2794	2347	1.7	0.0	-7.6	-22.1	NA
8.59(.338) Galaxy	200	3100	2899	2707	2524	2347	4269	3734	3256	2829	2446	3	3.80	0.0	-9.3	NA
340 Wea. Mag.*	210	3250	2991	2746	2515	2295	4924	4170	3516	2948	2455	+2.5	+1.9	-1.8	-11.8	$56
340 Wea. Mag.*	250	3000	2806	2621	2443	2272	4995	4371	3812	3311	2864	+2.5	+2.0	-3.5	-14.8	$56
338 A-Square	250	3120	2799	2500	2220	1958	5403	4348	3469	2736	2128	+2.5	+2.7	-1.5	-10.5	NA
338-378 Wea. Mag.	225	3180	2974	2778	2591	2410	5052	4420	3856	3353	2902	3.1	3.80	0.0	-8.9	NA
338 Titan	225	3230	3010	2800	2600	2409	5211	4524	3916	3377	2898	+3.07	+3.80	0.0	-8.95	NA
338 Excalibur	200	3600	3361	3134	2920	2715	5755	5015	4363	3785	3274	+2.23	+2.87	0.0	-6.99	NA
338 Excalibur	250	3250	2922	2618	2333	2066	5863	4740	3804	3021	2370	+1.3	0.0	-6.35	-19.2	NA
34, 35																
348 Winchester	200	2520	2215	1931	1672	1443	2820	2178	1656	1241	925	+2.5	-1.4	-14.7	0.0	$42
357 Magnum	158	1830	1427	1138	980	883	1175	715	454	337	274	0.0	-16.2	-33.1	0.0	$25**
35 Remington	150	2300	1874	1506	1218	1039	1762	1169	755	494	359	+2.5	-4.1	-26.3	0.0	$16
35 Remington	200	2080	1698	1376	1140	1001	1921	1280	841	577	445	+2.5	-6.3	-17.1	-33.6	$16
35 Rem. Lever Evolution	200	2225	1963	1721	1503	NA	2198	1711	1315	1003	NA	3.00	-1.30	-17.5	NA	NA
356 Winchester	200	2460	2114	1797	1517	1284	2688	1985	1434	1022	732	+2.5	-1.8	-15.1	0.0	$31
356 Winchester	250	2160	1911	1682	1476	1299	2591	2028	1571	1210	937	+2.5	-3.7	-22.2	0.0	$31
358 Winchester	200	2490	2171	1876	1619	1379	2753	2093	1563	1151	844	+2.5	-1.6	-15.6	0.0	$31
358 STA	275	2850	2562	2292	2039	NA	4958	4009	3208	2539	NA	+1.9	0.0	-8.6	0.0	NA
350 Rem. Mag.	200	2710	2410	2130	1870	1631	3261	2579	2014	1553	1181	+2.5	-0.2	-10.0	-30.1	$33
35 Whelen	200	2675	2378	2100	1842	1606	3177	2510	1958	1506	1145	+2.5	-0.2	-10.3	-31.1	$20
35 Whelen	225	2500	2300	2110	1930	1770	3120	2650	2235	1870	1560	+2.6	0.0	-10.2	-29.9	NA
35 Whelen	250	2400	2197	2005	1823	1652	3197	2680	2230	1844	1515	+2.5	-1.2	-13.7	0.0	$20
358 Norma Mag.	250	2800	2510	2230	1970	1730	4350	3480	2750	2145	1655	+2.5	+1.0	-7.6	-25.2	NA
358 STA	275	2850	2562	2292	2039	1764	4959	4009	3208	2539	1899	+1.9	0.0	-8.58	-26.1	NA

Many manufacturers do not supply suggested retail prices. Others did not get their pricing to us before press time. All pricing can vary dependent on the exact brand and style of ammo selected and/or the retail outlet from which you make your purchase. Pricing has been rounded to the nearest dollar and represents our best estimate of average pricing. An * after the cartridge means these loads are available with Nosler Partition or Swift A-Frame bullets. Listed pricing may or may not reflect this bullet type. ** = these are packed 50 to box, all others are 20 to box. Wea. Mag.= Weatherby Magnum. Spfd. = Springfield. A-Sq. = A-Square. N.E.=Nitro Express.

Cartridge	Bullet Wgt. Grs.	VELOCITY (fps)					ENERGY (ft. lbs.)					TRAJ. (in.)				Est. Price/ box
		Muzzle	100 yds.	200 yds.	300 yds.	400 yds.	Muzzle	100 yds.	200 yds.	300 yds.	400 yds.	100 yds.	200 yds.	300 yds.	400 yds.	
9.3mm																
9.3x57mm Mau.	286	2070	1810	1590	1390	1110	2710	2090	1600	1220	955	+2.5	-2.6	-22.5	0.0	NA
9.3x62mm Mau.	286	2360	2089	1844	1623	NA	3538	2771	2157	1670	1260	+2.5	-1.6	-21.0	0.0	NA
370 Sako Mag.	286	3550	2370	2200	2040	2880	4130	3570	3075	2630	2240	2.4	0.0	-9.5	-27.2	NA
9.3x64mm	286	2700	2505	2318	2139	1968	4629	3984	3411	2906	2460	+2.5	+2.7	-4.5	-19.2	NA
9.3x74Rmm	286	2360	2136	1924	1727	1545	3536	2896	2351	1893	1516	0.0	-6.1	-21.7	-49.0	NA
375																
38-55 Win.	255	1320	1190	1091	1018	963	987	802	674	587	525	0.0	-23.4	0.0	0.0	$25
375 Winchester	200	2200	1841	1526	1268	1089	2150	1506	1034	714	527	+2.5	-4.0	-26.2	0.0	$27
375 Winchester	250	1900	1647	1424	1239	1103	2005	1506	1126	852	676	+2.5	-6.9	-33.3	0.0	$27
376 Steyr	225	2600	2331	2078	1842	1625	3377	2714	2157	1694	1319	2.5	0.0	-10.6	-31.4	NA
376 Steyr	270	2600	2372	2156	1951	1759	4052	3373	2787	2283	1855	2.3	0.0	-9.9	-28.9	NA
375 Dakota	300	2600	2316	2051	1804	1579	4502	3573	2800	2167	1661	+2.4	0.0	-11.0	-32.7	NA
375 N.E. 2-1/2"	270	2000	1740	1507	1310	NA	2398	1815	1362	1026	NA	+2.5	-6.0	-30.0	0.0	NA
375 Flanged	300	2450	2150	1886	1640	NA	3998	3102	2369	1790	NA	+2.5	-2.4	-17.0	0.0	NA
375 Ruger	270	2840	2600	2372	2156	1951	4835	4052	3373	2786	2283	1.8	0.0	-8.0	-23.6	NA
375 Ruger	300	2660	2344	2050	1780	1536	4713	3660	2800	2110	1572	2.4	0.0	-10.8	-32.6	NA
375 H&H Magnum	250	2670	2450	2240	2040	1850	3955	3335	2790	2315	1905	+2.5	-0.4	-10.2	-28.4	NA
375 H&H Magnum	270	2690	2420	2166	1928	1707	4337	3510	2812	2228	1747	+2.5	0.0	-10.0	-29.4	$28
375 H&H Magnum*	300	2530	2245	1979	1733	1512	4263	3357	2608	2001	1523	+2.5	-1.0	-10.5	-33.6	$28
375 H&H Hvy. Mag.	270	2870	2628	2399	2182	1976	4937	4141	3451	2150	1845	+1.7	0.0	-7.2	-21.0	NA
375 H&H Hvy. Mag.	300	2705	2386	2090	1816	1568	4873	3793	2908	2195	1637	+2.3	0.0	-10.4	-31.4	NA
375 Rem. Ultra Mag.	270	2900	2558	2241	1947	1678	5041	3922	3010	2272	1689	1.9	2.7	-8.9	-27.0	NA
375 Rem. Ultra Mag.	300	2760	2505	2263	2035	1822	5073	4178	3412	2759	2210	2.0	0.0	-8.8	-26.1	NA
375 Wea. Mag.	300	2700	2420	2157	1911	1685	4856	3901	3100	2432	1891	+2.5	-.04	-10.7	0.0	NA
378 Wea. Mag.	270	3180	2976	2781	2594	2415	6062	5308	4635	4034	3495	+2.5	+2.6	-1.8	-11.3	$71
378 Wea. Mag.	300	2929	2576	2252	1952	1680	5698	4419	3379	2538	1881	+2.5	+1.2	-7.0	-24.5	$77
375 A-Square	300	2920	2626	2351	2093	1850	5679	4594	3681	2917	2281	+2.5	+1.4	-6.0	-21.0	NA
38-40 Win.	180	1160	999	901	827	764	538	399	324	273	233	0.0	-33.9	0.0	0.0	$42**
40, 41																
400 A-Square DPM	400	2400	2146	1909	1689	NA	5116	2092	3236	2533	NA	2.98	0.00	-10.0	NA	NA
400 A-Square DPM	170	2980	2463	2001	1598	NA	3352	2289	1512	964	NA	2.16	0.00	-11.1	NA	NA
408 CheyTac	419	2850	2752	2657	2562	2470	7551	7048	6565	6108	5675	-1.02	0.00	1.9	4.2	NA
405 Win.	300	2200	1851	1545	1296		3224	2282	1589	1119		4.6	0.0	-19.5	0.0	NA
450/400-3"	400	2050	1815	1595	1402	NA	3732	2924	2259	1746	NA	0.0	NA	-33.4	NA	NA
416 Ruger	400	2400	2151	1917	1700	NA	5116	4109	3264	2568	NA	0.00	-6.00	-21.6	0.00	NA
416 Dakota	400	2450	2294	2143	1998	1859	5330	4671	4077	3544	3068	+2.5	-0.2	-10.5	-29.4	NA
416 Taylor	400	2350	2117	1896	1693	NA	4905	3980	3194	2547	NA	+2.5	-1.2	15.0	0.0	NA
416 Hoffman	400	2380	2145	1923	1718	1529	5031	4087	3285	2620	2077	+2.5	-1.0	-14.1	0.0	NA
416 Rigby	350	2600	2449	2303	2162	2026	5253	4661	4122	3632	3189	+2.5	-1.8	-10.2	-26.0	NA
416 Rigby	400	2370	2210	2050	1900	NA	4990	4315	3720	3185	NA	+2.5	-0.7	-12.1	0.0	NA
416 Rigby	410	2370	2110	1870	1640	NA	5115	4050	3165	2455	NA	+2.5	-2.4	-17.3	0.0	$110
416 Rem. Mag.*	350	2520	2270	2034	1814	1611	4935	4004	3216	2557	2017	+2.5	-0.8	-12.6	-35.0	$82
416 Rem. Mag.*	400	2400	2175	1962	1763	1579	5115	4201	3419	2760	2214	+2.5	-1.5	-14.6	0.0	$80
416 Wea. Mag.*	400	2700	2397	2115	1852	1613	6474	5104	3971	3047	2310	+2.5	0.0	-10.1	-30.4	$96
10.57 (416) Meteor	400	2730	2532	2342	2161	1987	6621	5695	4874	4147	3508	+1.9	0.0	-8.3	-24.0	NA
404 Jeffrey	400	2150	1924	1716	1525	NA	4105	3289	2614	2064	NA	+2.5	-4.0	-22.1	0.0	NA
425, 44																
425 Express	400	2400	2160	1934	1725	NA	5115	4145	3322	2641	NA	+2.5	-1.0	-14.0	0.0	NA
44-40 Win.	200	1190	1006	900	822	756	629	449	360	300	254	0.0	-33.3	0.0	0.0	$36**
44 Rem. Mag.	210	1920	1477	1155	982	880	1719	1017	622	450	361	0.0	-17.6	0.0	0.0	$14
44 Rem. Mag.	240	1760	1380	1114	970	878	1650	1015	661	501	411	0.0	-17.6	0.0	0.0	$13
444 Marlin	240	2350	1815	1377	1087	941	2942	1753	1001	630	472	+2.5	-15.1	-31.0	0.0	$22
444 Marlin	265	2120	1733	1405	1160	1012	2644	1768	1162	791	603	+2.5	-6.0	-32.2	0.0	Disc.
444 Marlin Light Mag	265	2335	1913	1551	1266		3208	2153	1415	943		2.0	-4.90	-26.5	0.0	NA
444 Mar. Lever Evolution	265	2325	1971	1652	1380	NA	3180	2285	1606	1120	NA	3.00	-1.40	-18.6	NA	NA
45																
45-70 Govt.	300	1810	1497	1244	1073	969	2182	1492	1031	767	625	0.0	-14.8	0.0	0.0	$21
45-70 Govt. Supreme	300	1880	1558	1292	1103	988	2355	1616	1112	811	651	0.0	-12.9	-46.0	-105.0	NA
45-70 Lever Evolution	325	2050	1729	1450	1225	NA	3032	2158	1516	1083	NA	3.00	-4.10	-27.8	NA	NA
45-70 Govt. CorBon	350	1800	1526	1296			2519	1810	1307			0.0	-14.6	0.0	0.0	NA
45-70 Govt.	405	1330	1168	1055	977	918	1590	1227	1001	858	758	0.0	-24.6	0.0	0.0	$21
45-70 Govt. PMC Cowboy	405	1550	1193				1639	1280				0.0	-23.9	0.0	0.0	NA
45-70 Govt. Garrett	415	1850					3150					3.0	-7.0	0.0	0.0	NA

Many manufacturers do not supply suggested retail prices. Others did not get their pricing to us before press time. All pricing can vary dependent on the exact brand and style of ammo selected and/or the retail outlet from which you make your purchase. Pricing has been rounded to the nearest dollar and represents our best estimate of average pricing. An * after the cartridge means these loads are available with Nosler Partition or Swift A-Frame bullets. Listed pricing may or may not reflect this bullet type.
** = these are packed 50 to box, all others are 20 to box. Wea. Mag.= Weatherby Magnum. Spfd. = Springfield. A-Sq. = A-Square. N.E.=Nitro Express.

Cartridge	Bullet Wgt. Grs.	VELOCITY (fps)					ENERGY (ft. lbs.)					TRAJ. (in.)				Est. Price/ box
		Muzzle	100 yds.	200 yds.	300 yds.	400 yds.	Muzzle	100 yds.	200 yds.	300 yds.	400 yds.	100 yds.	200 yds.	300 yds.	400 yds.	
45-70 Govt. Garrett	530	1550	1343	1178	1062	982	2828	2123	1633	1327	1135	0.0	-17.8	0.0	0.0	NA
450 Bushmaster	250	2200	1831	1508	1480	1073	2686	1860	1262	864	639	0.00	-9.00	-33.5	0.00	NA
450 Marlin	350	2100	1774	1488	1254	1089	3427	2446	1720	1222	922	0.0	-9.7	-35.2	0.0	NA
450 Mar. Lever Evolution	325	2225	1887	1585	1331	NA	3572	2569	1813	1278	NA	3.00	-2.20	-21.3	NA	NA
458 Win. Magnum	350	2470	1990	1570	1250	1060	4740	3065	1915	1205	870	+2.5	-2.5	-21.6	0.0	$43
458 Win. Magnum	400	2380	2170	1960	1770	NA	5030	4165	3415	2785	NA	+2.5	-0.4	-13.4	0.0	$73
458 Win. Magnum	465	2220	1999	1791	1601	NA	5088	4127	3312	2646	NA	+2.5	-2.0	-17.7	0.0	NA
458 Win. Magnum	500	2040	1823	1623	1442	1237	4620	3689	2924	2308	1839	+2.5	-3.5	-22.0	0.0	$61
458 Win. Magnum	510	2040	1770	1527	1319	1157	4712	3547	2640	1970	1516	+2.5	-4.1	-25.0	0.0	$41
450 Dakota	500	2450	2235	2030	1838	1658	6663	5544	4576	3748	3051	+2.5	-0.6	-12.0	-33.8	NA
450 N.E. 3-1/4"	465	2190	1970	1765	1577	NA	4952	4009	3216	2567	NA	+2.5	-3.0	-20.0	0.0	NA
450 N.E. 3-1/4"	500	2150	1920	1708	1514	NA	5132	4093	3238	2544	NA	+2.5	-4.0	-22.9	0.0	NA
450 No. 2	465	2190	1970	1765	1577	NA	4952	4009	3216	2567	NA	+2.5	-3.0	-20.0	0.0	NA
450 No. 2	500	2150	1920	1708	1514	NA	5132	4093	3238	2544	NA	+2.5	-4.0	-22.9	0.0	NA
458 Lott	465	2380	2150	1932	1730	NA	5848	4773	3855	3091	NA	+2.5	-1.0	-14.0	0.0	NA
458 Lott	500	2300	2062	1838	1633	NA	5873	4719	3748	2960	NA	+2.5	-1.6	-16.4	0.0	NA
450 Ackley Mag.	465	2400	2169	1950	1747	NA	5947	4857	3927	3150	NA	+2.5	-1.0	-13.7	0.0	NA
450 Ackley Mag.	500	2320	2081	1855	1649	NA	5975	4085	3820	3018	NA	+2.5	-1.2	-15.0	0.0	NA
460 Short A-Sq.	500	2420	2175	1943	1729	NA	6501	5250	4193	3319	NA	+2.5	-0.8	-12.8	0.0	NA
460 Wea. Mag.	500	2700	2404	2128	1869	1635	8092	6416	5026	3878	2969	+2.5	+0.6	-8.9	-28.0	$72
475																
500/465 N.E.	480	2150	1917	1703	1507	NA	4926	3917	3089	2419	NA	+2.5	-4.0	-22.2	0.0	NA
470 Rigby	500	2150	1940	1740	1560	NA	5130	4170	3360	2695	NA	+2.5	-2.8	-19.4	0.0	NA
470 Nitro Ex.	480	2190	1954	1735	1536	NA	5111	4070	3210	2515	NA	+2.5	-3.5	-20.8	0.0	NA
470 Nitro Ex.	500	2150	1890	1650	1440	1270	5130	3965	3040	2310	1790	+2.5	-4.3	-24.0	0.0	$177
475 No. 2	500	2200	1955	1728	1522	NA	5375	4243	3316	2573	NA	+2.5	-3.2	-20.9	0.0	NA
50, 58																
505 Gibbs	525	2300	2063	1840	1637	NA	6166	4922	3948	3122	NA	+2.5	-3.0	-18.0	0.0	NA
500 N.E.-3"	570	2150	1928	1722	1533	NA	5850	4703	3752	2975	NA	+2.5	-3.7	-22.0	0.0	NA
500 N.E.-3"	600	2150	1927	1721	1531	NA	6158	4947	3944	3124	NA	+2.5	-4.0	-22.0	0.0	NA
495 A Square	570	2350	2117	1896	1693	NA	5850	4703	3752	2975	NA	+2.5	-1.0	-14.5	0.0	NA
495 A Square	600	2280	2050	1833	1635	NA	6925	5598	4478	3562	NA	+2.5	-2.0	-17.0	0.0	NA
500 A-Square	600	2380	2144	1922	1766	NA	7546	6126	4920	3922	NA	+2.5	-3.0	-17.0	0.0	NA
500 A-Square	707	2250	2040	1841	1567	NA	7947	6530	5318	4311	NA	+2.5	-2.0	-17.0	0.0	NA
500 BMG PMC	660	3080	2854	2639	2444	2248	13688		500 yd. zero			+3.1	+3.9	+4.7	+2.8	NA
577 Nitro Ex.	750	2050	1793	1562	1360	NA	6990	5356	4065	3079	NA	+2.5	5.0	-26.0	0.0	NA
577 Tyrannosaur	750	2400	2141	1898	1675	NA	9591	7633	5996	4671	NA	+3.0	0.0	-12.9	0.0	NA
600, 700																
600 N.E.	900	1950	1680	1452	NA	NA	7596	5634	4212	NA	NA	+5.6	0.0	0.0	0.0	NA
700 N.E.	1200	1900	1676	1472	NA	NA	9618	7480	5774	NA	NA	+5.7	0.0	0.0	0.0	NA

Notes: Blanks are available in 32 S&W, 38 S&W and 38 Special. "V" after barrel length indicates test barrel was vented to produce ballistics similar to a revolver with a normal barrel-to-cylinder gap. Ammo prices are per 50 rounds except when marked with an ** which signifies a 20 round box; *** signifies a 25-round box. Not all loads are available from all ammo manufacturers. Listed loads are those made by Remington, Winchester, Federal, and others. DISC. is a discontinued load. Prices are rounded to the nearest whole dollar and will vary with brand and retail outlet. † = new bullet weight this year; "c" indicates a change in data.

Cartridge	Bullet Wgt. Grs.	VELOCITY (fps)			ENERGY (ft. lbs.)			Mid-Range Traj. (in.)		Bbl. Lgth. (in).	Est. Price/ box
		Muzzle	50 yds.	100 yds.	Muzzle	50 yds.	100 yds.	50 yds.	100 yds.		
22, 25											
221 Rem. Fireball	50	2650	2380	2130	780	630	505	0.2	0.8	10.5"	$15
25 Automatic	35	900	813	742	63	51	43	NA	NA	2"	$18
25 Automatic	45	815	730	655	65	55	40	1.8	7.7	2"	$21
25 Automatic	50	760	705	660	65	55	50	2.0	8.7	2"	$17
30											
7.5mm Swiss	107	1010	NA	NA	240	NA	NA	NA	NA	NA	NEW
7.62mm Tokarev	87	1390	NA	NA	365	NA	NA	0.6	NA	4.5"	NA
7.62 Nagant	97	790	NA	NA	134	NA	NA	NA	NA	NA	NEW
7.63 Mauser	88	1440	NA	NA	405	NA	NA	NA	NA	NA	NEW
30 Luger	93†	1220	1110	1040	305	255	225	0.9	3.5	4.5"	$34
30 Carbine	110	1790	1600	1430	785	625	500	0.4	1.7	10"	$28
30-357 AeT	123	1992	NA	NA	1084	NA	NA	NA	NA	10"	NA
32											
32 S&W	88	680	645	610	90	80	75	2.5	10.5	3"	$17
32 S&W Long	98	705	670	635	115	100	90	2.3	10.5	4"	$17
32 Short Colt	80	745	665	590	100	80	60	2.2	9.9	4"	$19
32 H&R Magnum	85	1100	1020	930	230	195	165	1.0	4.3	4.5"	$21
32 H&R Magnum	95	1030	940	900	225	190	170	1.1	4.7	4.5"	$19
327 Federal Magnum	100	1500	1320	1180	500	390	310	-0.2	-4.50	4-V	NA
32 Automatic	60	970	895	835	125	105	95	1.3	5.4	4"	$22
32 Automatic	60	1000	917	849	133	112	96			4"	NA
32 Automatic	65	950	890	830	130	115	100	1.3	5.6	NA	NA
32 Automatic	71	905	855	810	130	115	95	1.4	5.8	4"	$19
8mm Lebel Pistol	111	850	NA	NA	180	NA	NA	NA	NA	NA	NEW
8mm Steyr	112	1080	NA	NA	290	NA	NA	NA	NA	NA	NEW
8mm Gasser	126	850	NA	NA	200	NA	NA	NA	NA	NA	NEW
9mm, 38											
380 Automatic	60	1130	960	NA	170	120	NA	1.0	NA	NA	NA
380 Automatic	85/88	990	920	870	190	165	145	1.2	5.1	4"	$20
380 Automatic	90	1000	890	800	200	160	130	1.2	5.5	3.75"	$10
380 Automatic	95/100	955	865	785	190	160	130	1.4	5.9	4"	$20
38 Super Auto +P	115	1300	1145	1040	430	335	275	0.7	3.3	5"	$26
38 Super Auto +P	125/130	1215	1100	1015	425	350	300	0.8	3.6	5"	$26
38 Super Auto +P	147	1100	1050	1000	395	355	325	0.9	4.0	5"	NA
9x18mm Makarov	95	1000	NA	NA	NA	NA	NA	NA	NA	NA	NEW
9x18mm Ultra	100	1050	NA	NA	240	NA	NA	NA	NA	NA	NEW
9x23mm Largo	124	1190	1055	966	390	306	257	0.7	3.7	4"	NA
9x23mm Win.	125	1450	1249	1103	583	433	338	0.6	2.8	NA	NA
9mm Steyr	115	1180	NA	NA	350	NA	NA	NA	NA	NA	NEW
9mm Luger	88	1500	1190	1010	440	275	200	0.6	3.1	4"	$24
9mm Luger	90	1360	1112	978	370	247	191	NA	NA	4"	$26
9mm Luger	95	1300	1140	1010	350	275	215	0.8	3.4	4"	NA
9mm Luger	100	1180	1080	NA	305	255	NA	0.9	NA	4"	NA
9mm Luger	115	1155	1045	970	340	280	240	0.9	3.9	4"	$21
9mm Luger	123/125	1110	1030	970	340	290	260	1.0	4.0	4"	$23
9mm Luger	140	935	890	850	270	245	225	1.3	5.5	4"	$23
9mm Luger	147	990	940	900	320	290	265	1.1	4.9	4"	$26
9mm Luger +P	90	1475	NA	NA	437	NA	NA	NA	NA	NA	NA
9mm Luger +P	115	1250	1113	1019	399	316	265	0.8	3.5	4"	$27
9mm Federal	115	1280	1130	1040	420	330	280	0.7	3.3	4"V	$24
9mm Luger Vector	115	1155	1047	971	341	280	241	NA	NA	4"	NA
9mm Luger +P	124	1180	1089	1021	384	327	287	0.8	3.8	4"	NA
38											
38 S&W	146	685	650	620	150	135	125	2.4	10.0	4"	$19
38 Short Colt	125	730	685	645	150	130	115	2.2	9.4	6"	$19
39 Special	100	950	900	NA	200	180	NA	1.3	NA	4"V	NA
38 Special	110	945	895	850	220	195	175	1.3	5.4	4"V	$23
38 Special	110	945	895	850	220	195	175	1.3	5.4	4"V	$23
38 Special	130	775	745	710	175	160	120	1.9	7.9	4"V	$22
38 Special Cowboy	140	800	767	735	199	183	168			7.5" V	NA
38 (Multi-Ball)	140	830	730	505	215	130	80	2.0	10.6	4"V	$10**

Notes: Blanks are available in 32 S&W, 38 S&W and 38 Special. "V" after barrel length indicates test barrel was vented to produce ballistics similar to a revolver with a normal barrel-to-cylinder gap. Ammo prices are per 50 rounds except when marked with an ** which signifies a 20 round box; *** signifies a 25-round box. Not all loads are available from all ammo manufacturers. Listed loads are those made by Remington, Winchester, Federal, and others. DISC. is a discontinued load. Prices are rounded to the nearest whole dollar and will vary with brand and retail outlet. † = new bullet weight this year; "c" indicates a change in data.

Cartridge	Bullet Wgt. Grs.	VELOCITY (fps)			ENERGY (ft. lbs.)			Mid-Range Traj. (in.)		Bbl. Lgth. (in).	Est. Price/ box
		Muzzle	50 yds.	100 yds.	Muzzle	50 yds.	100 yds.	50 yds.	100 yds.		
38 Special	148	710	635	565	165	130	105	2.4	10.6	4"V	$17
38 Special	158	755	725	690	200	185	170	2.0	8.3	4"V	$18
38 Special +P	95	1175	1045	960	290	230	195	0.9	3.9	4"V	$23
38 Special +P	110	995	925	870	240	210	185	1.2	5.1	4"V	$23
38 Special +P	125	975	929	885	264	238	218	1	5.2	4"	NA
38 Special +P	125	945	900	860	250	225	205	1.3	5.4	4"V	#23
38 Special +P	129	945	910	870	255	235	215	1.3	5.3	4"V	$11
38 Special +P	130	925	887	852	247	227	210	1.3	5.50	4"V	NA
38 Special +P	147/150(c)	884	NA	NA	264	NA	NA	NA	NA	4"V	$27
38 Special +P	158	890	855	825	280	255	240	1.4	6.0	4"V	$20
357											
357 SIG	115	1520	NA	NA	593	NA	NA	NA	NA	NA	NA
357 SIG	124	1450	NA	NA	578	NA	NA	NA	NA	NA	NA
357 SIG	125	1350	1190	1080	510	395	325	0.7	3.1	4"	NA
357 SIG	150	1130	1030	970	420	355	310	0.9	4.0	NA	NA
356 TSW	115	1520	NA	NA	593	NA	NA	NA	NA	NA	NA
356 TSW	124	1450	NA	NA	578	NA	NA	NA	NA	NA	NA
356 TSW	135	1280	1120	1010	490	375	310	0.8	3.5	NA	NA
356 TSW	147	1220	1120	1040	485	410	355	0.8	3.5	5"	NA
357 Mag., Super Clean	105	1650									NA
357 Magnum	110	1295	1095	975	410	290	230	0.8	3.5	4"V	$25
357 (Med.Vel.)	125	1220	1075	985	415	315	270	0.8	3.7	4"V	$25
357 Magnum	125	1450	1240	1090	585	425	330	0.6	2.8	4"V	$25
357 (Multi-Ball)	140	1155	830	665	420	215	135	1.2	6.4	4"V	$11**
357 Magnum	140	1360	1195	1075	575	445	360	0.7	3.0	4"V	$25
357 Magnum FlexTip	140	1440	1274	1143	644	504	406	NA	NA	NA	NA
357 Magnum	145	1290	1155	1060	535	430	360	0.8	3.5	4"V	$26
357 Magnum	150/158	1235	1105	1015	535	430	360	0.8	3.5	4"V	$25
357 Mag. Cowboy	158	800	761	725	225	203	185				NA
357 Magnum	165	1290	1189	1108	610	518	460	0.7	3.1	8-3/8"	NA
357 Magnum	180	1145	1055	985	525	445	390	0.9	3.9	4"V	$25
357 Magnum	180	1180	1088	1020	557	473	416	0.8	3.6	8"V	NA
357 Mag. CorBon F.A.	180	1650	1512	1386	1088	913	767	1.66	0.0		NA
357 Mag. CorBon	200	1200	1123	1061	640	560	500	3.19	0.0		NA
357 Rem. Maximum	158	1825	1590	1380	1170	885	670	0.4	1.7	10.5"	$14**
40, 10mm											
40 S&W	135	1140	1070	NA	390	345	NA	0.9	NA	4"	NA
40 S&W	155	1140	1026	958	447	362	309	0.9	4.1	4"	$14***
40 S&W	165	1150	NA	NA	485	NA	NA	NA	NA	4"	$18***
40 S&W	180	985	936	893	388	350	319	1.4	5.0	4"	$14***
40 S&W	180	1015	960	914	412	368	334	1.3	4.5	4"	NA
400 Cor-Bon	135	1450	NA	NA	630	NA	NA	NA	NA	5"	NA
10mm Automatic	155	1125	1046	986	436	377	335	0.9	3.9	5"	$26
10mm Automatic	170	1340	1165	1145	680	510	415	0.7	3.2	5"	$31
10mm Automatic	175	1290	1140	1035	650	505	420	0.7	3.3	5.5"	$11**
10mm Auto. (FBI)	180	950	905	865	361	327	299	1.5	5.4	4"	$16**
10mm Automatic	180	1030	970	920	425	375	340	1.1	4.7	5"	$16**
10mm Auto H.V.	180†	1240	1124	1037	618	504	430	0.8	3.4	5"	$27
10mm Automatic	200	1160	1070	1010	495	510	430	0.9	3.8	5"	$14**
10.4mm Italian	177	950	NA	NA	360	NA	NA	NA	NA	NA	NEW
41 Action Exp.	180	1000	947	903	400	359	326	0.5	4.2	5"	$13**
41 Rem. Magnum	170	1420	1165	1015	760	515	390	0.7	3.2	4"V	$33
41 Rem. Magnum	175	1250	1120	1030	605	490	410	0.8	3.4	4"V	$14**
41 (Med. Vel.)	210	965	900	840	435	375	330	1.3	5.4	4"V	$30
41 Rem. Magnum	210	1300	1160	1060	790	630	535	0.7	3.2	4"V	$33
41 Rem. Magnum	240	1250	1151	1075	833	706	616	0.8	3.3	6.5V	NA
44											
44 S&W Russian	247	780	NA	NA	335	NA	NA	NA	NA	NA	NA
44 S&W Special	180	980	NA	NA	383	NA	NA	NA	NA	6.5"	NA
44 S&W Special	180	1000	935	882	400	350	311	NA	NA	7.5"V	NA
44 S&W Special	200†	875	825	780	340	302	270	1.2	6.0	6"	$13**
44 S&W Special	200	1035	940	865	475	390	335	1.1	4.9	6.5"	$13**
44 S&W Special	240/246	755	725	695	310	285	265	2.0	8.3	6.5"	$26
44-40 Win. Cowboy	225	750	723	695	281	261	242				NA

Notes: Blanks are available in 32 S&W, 38 S&W and 38 Special. "V" after barrel length indicates test barrel was vented to produce ballistics similar to a revolver with a normal barrel-to-cylinder gap. Ammo prices are per 50 rounds except when marked with an ** which signifies a 20 round box; *** signifies a 25-round box. Not all loads are available from all ammo manufacturers. Listed loads are those made by Remington, Winchester, Federal, and others. DISC. is a discontinued load. Prices are rounded to the nearest whole dollar and will vary with brand and retail outlet. † = new bullet weight this year; "c" indicates a change in data.

Cartridge	Bullet Wgt. Grs.	VELOCITY (fps)			ENERGY (ft. lbs.)			Mid-Range Traj. (in.)		Bbl. Lgth. (in.)	Est. Price/box
		Muzzle	50 yds.	100 yds.	Muzzle	50 yds.	100 yds.	50 yds.	100 yds.		
44 Rem. Magnum	180	1610	1365	1175	1035	745	550	0.5	2.3	4"V	$18**
44 Rem. Magnum	200	1400	1192	1053	870	630	492	0.6	NA	6.5"	$20
44 Rem. Magnum	210	1495	1310	1165	1040	805	635	0.6	2.5	6.5"	$18**
44 Rem. Mag. FlexTip	225	1410	1240	1111	993	768	617	NA	NA	NA	NA
44 (Med. Vel.)	240	1000	945	900	535	475	435	1.1	4.8	6.5"	$17
44 R.M. (Jacketed)	240	1180	1080	1010	740	625	545	0.9	3.7	4"V	$18**
44 R.M. (Lead)	240	1350	1185	1070	970	750	610	0.7	3.1	4"V	$29
44 Rem. Magnum	250	1180	1100	1040	775	670	600	0.8	3.6	6.5"V	$21
44 Rem. Magnum	250	1250	1148	1070	867	732	635	0.8	3.3	6.5"V	NA
44 Rem. Magnum	275	1235	1142	1070	931	797	699	0.8	3.3	6.5"	NA
44 Rem. Magnum	300	1200	1100	1026	959	806	702	NA	NA	7.5"	$17
44 Rem. Magnum	330	1385	1297	1220	1406	1234	1090	1.83	0.00	NA	NA
440 CorBon	260	1700	1544	1403	1669	1377	1136	1.58	NA	10"	NA

45, 50

Cartridge	Bullet Wgt. Grs.	VELOCITY (fps)			ENERGY (ft. lbs.)			Mid-Range Traj. (in.)		Bbl. Lgth. (in.)	Est. Price/box
		Muzzle	50 yds.	100 yds.	Muzzle	50 yds.	100 yds.	50 yds.	100 yds.		
450 Short Colt/450 Revolver	226	830	NA	NA	350	NA	NA	NA	NA	NA	NEW
45 S&W Schofield	180	730	NA	NA	213	NA	NA	NA	NA	NA	NA
45 S&W Schofield	230	730	NA	NA	272	NA	NA	NA	NA	NA	NA
45 G.A.P.	185	1090	970	890	490	385	320	1.0	4.7	5"	NA
45 G.A.P.	230	880	842	NA	396	363	NA	NA	NA	5"	NA
45 Automatic	165	1030	930	NA	385	315	NA	1.2	NA	5"	NA
45 Automatic	185	1000	940	890	410	360	325	1.1	4.9	5"	$28
45 Auto. (Match)	185	770	705	650	245	204	175	2.0	8.7	5"	$28
45 Auto. (Match)	200	940	890	840	392	352	312	2.0	8.6	5"	$20
45 Automatic	200	975	917	860	421	372	328	1.4	5.0	5"	$18
45 Automatic	230	830	800	675	355	325	300	1.6	6.8	5"	$27
45 Automatic	230	880	846	816	396	366	340	1.5	6.1	5"	NA
45 Automatic +P	165	1250	NA	NA	573	NA	NA	NA	NA	NA	NA
45 Automatic +P	185	1140	1040	970	535	445	385	0.9	4.0	5"	$31
45 Automatic +P	200	1055	982	925	494	428	380	NA	NA	5"	NA
45 Super	185	1300	1190	1108	694	582	504	NA	NA	5"	NA
45 Win. Magnum	230	1400	1230	1105	1000	775	635	0.6	2.8	5"	$14**
45 Win. Magnum	260	1250	1137	1053	902	746	640	0.8	3.3	5"	$16**
45 Win. Mag. CorBon	320	1150	1080	1025	940	830	747	3.47			NA
455 Webley MKII	262	850	NA	NA	420	NA	NA	NA	NA	NA	NA
45 Colt	200	1000	938	889	444	391	351	1.3	4.8	5.5"	$21
45 Colt	225	960	890	830	460	395	345	1.3	5.5	5.5"	$22
45 Colt + P CorBon	265	1350	1225	1126	1073	884	746	2.65	0.0		NA
45 Colt + P CorBon	300	1300	1197	1114	1126	956	827	2.78	0.0		NA
45 Colt	250/255	860	820	780	410	375	340	1.6	6.6	5.5"	$27
454 Casull	250	1300	1151	1047	938	735	608	0.7	3.2	7.5"V	NA
454 Casull	260	1800	1577	1381	1871	1436	1101	0.4	1.8	7.5"V	NA
454 Casull	300	1625	1451	1308	1759	1413	1141	0.5	2.0	7.5"V	NA
454 Casull CorBon	360	1500	1387	1286	1800	1640	1323	2.01	0.0		NA
460 S&W	200	2300	2042	1801	2350	1851	1441	0	-1.60	NA	NA
460 S&W	260	2000	1788	1592	2309	1845	1464	NA	NA	7.5"V	NA
460 S&W	250	1450	1267	1127	1167	891	705	NA	NA	8.375-V	NA
460 S&W	250	1900	1640	1412	2004	1494	1106	0	-2.75	NA	NA
460 S&W	395	1550	1389	1249	2108	1691	1369	0	-4.00	NA	NA
475 Linebaugh	400	1350	1217	1119	1618	1315	1112	NA	NA	NA	NA
480 Ruger	325	1350	1191	1076	1315	1023	835	2.6	0.0	7.5"	NA
50 Action Exp.	325	1400	1209	1075	1414	1055	835	0.2	2.3	6"	$24**
500 S&W	275	1665	1392	1183	1693	1184	854	1.5	NA	8.375	NA
500 S&W	350	1400	1231	1106	1523	1178	951	NA	NA	10"	NA
500 S&W	400	1675	1472	1299	2493	1926	1499	1.3	NA	8.375	NA
500 S&W	440	1625	1367	1169	2581	1825	1337	1.6	NA	8.375	NA
500 S&W	500	1425	1281	1164	2254	1823	1505	NA	NA	10"	NA

Note: The actual ballistics obtained with your firearm can vary considerably from the advertised ballistics. Also, ballistics can vary from lot to lot with the same brand and type load.

Cartridge	Bullet Wt. Grs.	Velocity (fps) 22-1/2" Bbl.		Energy (ft. lbs.) 22-1/2" Bbl.		Mid-Range Traj. (in.)	Muzzle Velocity
		Muzzle	100 yds.	Muzzle	100 yds.	100 yds.	6" Bbl.
17 Aguila	20	1850	1267	NA	NA	NA	NA
17 Hornady Mach 2	17	2100	1530	166	88	0.7	NA
17 HMR	17	2550	1902	245	136	NA	NA
17 HMR	20	2375	1776	250	140	NA	NA
5mm Rem. Rimfire Mag.	30	2300	1669	352	188	NA	24
22 Short Blank	—	—	—	—	—	—	—
22 Short CB	29	727	610	33	24	NA	706
22 Short Target	29	830	695	44	31	6.8	786
22 Short HP	27	1164	920	81	50	4.3	1077
22 Colibri	20	375	183	6	1	NA	NA
22 Super Colibri	20	500	441	11	9	NA	NA
22 Long CB	29	727	610	33	24	NA	706
22 Long HV	29	1180	946	90	57	4.1	1031
22 LR Pistol Match	40	1070	890	100	70	4.6	940
22 LR Sub Sonic HP	38	1050	901	93	69	4.7	NA
22 LR Standard Velocity	40	1070	890	100	70	4.6	940
22 LR AutoMatch	40	1200	990	130	85	NA	NA
22 LR HV	40	1255	1016	140	92	3.6	1060
22 LR Silhoutte	42	1220	1003	139	94	3.6	1025
22 SSS	60	950	802	120	86	NA	NA
22 LR HV HP	40	1280	1001	146	89	3.5	1085
22 Velocitor GDHP	40	1435	0	0	0	NA	NA
22 LR Hyper HP	32/33/34	1500	1075	165	85	2.8	NA
22 LR Expediter	32	1640	NA	191	NA	NA	NA
22 LR Stinger HP	32	1640	1132	191	91	2.6	1395
22 LR Lead Free	30	1650	NA	181	NA	NA	NA
22 LR Hyper Vel	30	1750	1191	204	93	NA	NA
22 LR Shot #12	31	950	NA	NA	NA	NA	NA
22 WRF LFN	45	1300	1015	169	103	3	NA
22 Win. Mag. Lead Free	28	2200	NA	301	NA	NA	NA
22 Win. Mag.	30	2200	1373	322	127	1.4	1610
22 Win. Mag. V-Max BT	33	2000	1495	293	164	0.60	NA
22 Win. Mag. JHP	34	2120	1435	338	155	1.4	NA
22 Win. Mag. JHP	40	1910	1326	324	156	1.7	1480
22 Win. Mag. FMJ	40	1910	1326	324	156	1.7	1480
22 Win. Mag. Dyna Point	45	1550	1147	240	131	2.60	NA
22 Win. Mag. JHP	50	1650	1280	300	180	1.3	NA
22 Win. Mag. Shot #11	52	1000	—	NA	—	—	NA

NOTES: * = 10 rounds per box. ** = 5 rounds per box. Pricing variations and number of rounds per box can occur with type and brand of ammunition. Listed pricing is the average nominal cost for load style and box quantity shown. Not every brand is available in all shot size variations. Some manufacturers do not provide suggested list prices. All prices rounded to nearest whole dollar. The price you pay will vary dependent upon outlet of purchase. # = new load spec this year; "C" indicates a change in data.

10 Gauge 3-1/2" Magnum

4-1/2	2-1/4	premium	BB, 2, 4, 5, 6	Win., Fed., Rem.	$33	1205
Max	2	premium	4, 5, 6	Fed., Win.	NA	1300
4-1/4	2	high velocity	BB, 2, 4	Rem.	$22	1210
Max	18 pellets	premium	00 buck	Fed., Win.	$7**	1100
Max	1-7/8	Bismuth	BB, 2, 4	Bis.	NA	1225
Max	1-3/4	high density	BB, 2	Rem.	NA	1300
4-1/4	1-3/4	steel	TT, T, BBB, BB, 1, 2, 3	Win., Rem.	$27	1260
Mag	1-5/8	steel	T, BBB, BB, 2	Win.	$27	1285
Max	1-5/8	Bismuth	BB, 2, 4	Bismuth	NA	1375
Max	1-1/2	steel	T, BBB, BB, 1, 2, 3	Fed.	NA	1450
Max	1-3/8	steel	T, BBB, BB, 1, 2, 3	Fed., Rem.	NA	1500
Max	1-3/8	steel	T, BBB, BB, 2	Fed., Win.	NA	1450
Max	1-3/4	slug, rifled	slug	Fed.	NA	1280
Max	24 pellets	Buckshot	1 Buck	Fed.	NA	1100
Max	54 pellets	Super-X	4 Buck	Win.	NA	1150

12 Gauge 3-1/2" Magnum

Max	2-1/4	premium	4, 5, 6	Fed., Rem., Win.	$13*	1150
Max	2	Lead	4, 5, 6	Fed.	NA	1300
Max	2	Copper plated turkey	4, 5	Rem.	NA	1300
Max	18 pellets	premium	00 buck	Fed., Win., Rem.	$7**	1100
Max	1-7/8	Wingmaster HD	4, 6	Rem.	NA	1225
Max	1-7/8	heavyweight	5, 6	Fed.	NA	1300
Max	1-3/4	high density	BB, 2, 4, 6	Rem.		1300
Max	1-7/8	Bismuth	BB, 2, 4	Bis.	NA	1225
Max	1-5/8	Hevi-shot	T	Hevi-shot	NA	1350
Max	1-5/8	Wingmaster HD	T	Rem.	NA	1350
Max	1-5/8	high density	BB, 2	Fed.	NA	1450
Max	1-3/8	Heavyweight	2, 4, 6	Fed.	NA	1450
Max	1-3/8	steel	T, BBB, BB, 2, 4	Fed., Win., Rem.	NA	1450
Max	1-1/2	FS steel	BBB, BB, 2	Fed.	NA	1500
Max	1-1/2	Supreme H-V	BBB, BB, 2, 3	Win.	NA	1475
Max	1-3/8	H-speed steel	BB, 2	Rem.	NA	1550
Max	1-1/4	Steel	BB, 2	Win.	NA	1625
Max	24 pellets	Premium	1 Buck	Fed.	NA	1100
Max	54 pellets	Super-X	4 Buck	Win.	NA	1050

12 Gauge 3" Magnum

4	2	premium	BB, 2, 4, 5, 6	Win., Fed., Rem.	$9*	1175
4	1-7/8	premium	BB, 2, 4, 6	Win., Fed., Rem.	$19	1210
4	1-7/8	duplex	4x6	Rem.	$9*	1210
Max	1-3/4	turkey	4, 5, 6	Fed., Fio., Win., Rem.	NA	1300
Max	1-3/4	high density	BB, 2, 4	Rem.	NA	1450
Max	1-5/8	high density	BB, 2	Fed.	NA	1450
Max	1-5/8	Wingmaster HD	4, 6	Rem.	NA	1227
Max	1-5/8	high velocity	4, 5, 6	Fed.	NA	1350
4	1-5/8	premium	2, 4, 5, 6	Win., Fed., Rem.	$18	1290
Max	1-1/2	Wingmaster HD	T	Rem.	NA	1300
Max	1-1/2	Hevi-shot	T	Hevi-shot	NA	1300
Max	1-1/2	high density	BB, 2, 4	Rem.	NA	1300
Max	1-5/8	Bismuth	BB, 2, 4, 5, 6	Bis.	NA	1250
4	24 pellets	buffered	1 buck	Win., Fed., Rem.	$5**	1040
4	15 pellets	buffered	00 buck	Win., Fed., Rem.	$6**	1210
4	10 pellets	buffered	000 buck	Win., Fed., Rem.	$6**	1225
4	41 pellets	buffered	4 buck	Win., Fed., Rem.	$6**	1210
Max	1-3/8	heavyweight	5, 6	Fed.	NA	1300
Max	1-3/8	high density	B, 2, 4, 6	Rem. Win.	NA	1450

12 Gauge 3" Magnum (cont.)

Max	1-3/8	slug	slug	Bren.	NA	1476
Max	1-1/4	slug, rifled	slug	Fed.	NA	1600
Max	1-3/16	saboted slug	copper slug	Rem.	NA	1500
Max	7/8	slug, rifled	slug	Rem.	NA	1875
Max	1-1/8	low recoil	BB	Fed.	NA	850
Max	1-1/8	steel	BB, 2, 3, 4	Fed., Win., Rem.	NA	1550
Max	1-1/16	high density	2, 4	Win.	NA	1400
Max	1	steel	4, 6	Fed.	NA	1330
Max	1-3/8	buckhammer	slug	Rem.	NA	1500
Max	1	slug, rifled	slug, magnum	Win., Rem.	$5**	1760
Max	1	saboted slug	slug	Rem., Win., Fed.	$10**	1550
Max	385 grs.	partition gold	slug	Win.	NA	2000
Max	1-1/8	Rackmaster	slug	Win.	NA	1700
Max	300 grs.	XP3	slug	Win.	NA	2100
3-5/8	1-3/8	steel	BBB, BB, 1, 2, 3, 4	Win., Fed., Rem.	$19	1275
Max	1-1/8	steel	BB, 2, 4	Rem.	NA	1500
Max	1-1/8	steel	T, BBB, BB, 2, 4, 5, 6	Fed., Win.	NA	1450
Max	1-1/8	steel	BB, 2	Fed.	NA	1400
4	1-1/4	steel	T, BBB, BB, 1, 2, 3, 4, 6	Win., Fed., Rem.	$18	1400
Max	1-1/4	FS steel	BBB, BB, 2	Fed.	NA	1450

12 Gauge 2-3/4"

Max	1-5/8	magnum	4, 5, 6	Win., Fed.	$8*	1250
Max	1-3/8	lead	4, 5, 6	Fiocchi	NA	1485
Max	1-3/8	turkey	4, 5, 6	Fio.	NA	1250
Max	1-3/8	steel	4, 5, 6	Fed.	NA	1400
Max	1-3/8	Bismuth	BB, 2, 4, 5, 6	Bis.	NA	1300
3-3/4	1-1/2	magnum	BB, 2, 4, 5, 6	Win., Fed., Rem.	$16	1260
Max	1-1/4	Supreme H-V	4, 5, 6, 7-1/2	Win. Rem.	NA	1400
3-3/4	1-1/4	high velocity	BB, 2, 4, 5, 6, 7-1/2, 8, 9	Win., Fed., Rem., Fio.	$13	1330
Max	1-1/4	high density	B, 2, 4	Win.	NA	1450
Max	1-1/4	high density	4, 6	Rem.	NA	1325
3-1/4	1-1/4	standard velocity	6, 7-1/2, 8, 9	Win., Fed., Rem., Fio.	$11	1220
Max	1-1/8	Hevi-shot	5	Hevi-shot	NA	1350
3-1/4	1-1/8	standard velocity	4, 6, 7-1/2, 8, 9	Win., Fed., Rem., Fio.	$9	1255
Max	1-1/8	steel	2, 4	Rem.	NA	1390
Max	1	steel	BB, 2	Fed.	NA	1450
3-1/4	1	standard velocity	6, 7-1/2, 8	Rem., Fed., Fio., Win.	$6	1290
3-1/4	1-1/4	target	7-1/2, 8, 9	Win., Fed., Rem.	$10	1220
3	1-1/8	spreader	7-1/2, 8, 8-1/2, 9	Fio.	NA	1200
3	1-1/8	target	7-1/2, 8, 9, 7-1/2x8	Win., Fed., Rem., Fio.	$7	1200
2-3/4	1-1/8	target	7-1/2, 8, 8-1/2, 9, 7-1/2x8	Win., Fed., Rem., Fio.	$7	1145
2-3/4	1-1/8	low recoil	7-1/2, 8	Rem.	NA	1145
2-1/2	26 grams	low recoil	8	Win.	NA	980
2-1/4	1-1/8	target	7-1/2, 8, 8-1/2, 9	Rem., Fed.	$7	1080
Max	1	spreader	7-1/2, 8, 8-1/2, 9	Fio.	NA	1300
3-1/4	28 grams (1 oz)	target	7-1/2, 8, 9	Win., Fed., Rem., Fio.	$8	1290
3	1	target	7-1/2, 8, 8-1/2, 9	Win., Fio.	NA	1235
2-3/4	1	target	7-1/2, 8, 8-1/2, 9	Fed., Rem., Fio.	NA	1180
3-1/4	24 grams	target	7-1/2, 8, 9	Fed., Win., Fio.	NA	1325
3	7/8	light	8	Fio.	NA	1200
3-3/4	8 pellets	buffered	000 buck	Win., Fed., Rem.	$4**	1325

NOTES: * = 10 rounds per box. ** = 5 rounds per box. Pricing variations and number of rounds per box can occur with type and brand of ammunition. Listed pricing is the average nominal cost for load style and box quantity shown. Not every brand is available in all shot size variations. Some manufacturers do not provide suggested list prices. All prices rounded to nearest whole dollar. The price you pay will vary dependent upon outlet of purchase. # = new load spec this year; "C" indicates a change in data.

12 Gauge 2-3/4" (cont.)

4	12 pellets	premium	00 buck	Win., Fed., Rem.	$5**	1290
3-3/4	9 pellets	buffered	00 buck	Win., Fed., Rem., Fio.	$19	1325
3-3/4	12 pellets	buffered	0 buck	Win., Fed., Rem.	$4**	1275
4	20 pellets	buffered	1 buck	Win., Fed., Rem.	$4**	1075
3-3/4	16 pellets	buffered	1 buck	Win., Fed., Rem.	$4**	1250
4	34 pellets	premium	4 buck	Fed., Rem.	$5**	1250
3-3/4	27 pellets	buffered	4 buck	Win., Fed., Rem., Fio.	$4**	1325
Max	1	saboted slug	slug	Win., Fed., Rem.	$10**	1450
Max	1-1/4	slug, rifled	slug	Fed.	NA	1520
Max	1-1/4	slug	slug	Lightfield		1440
Max	1-1/4	saboted slug	attached sabot	Rem.	NA	1550
Max	1	slug, rifled	slug, magnum	Rem., Fio.	$5**	1680
Max	1	slug, rifled	slug	Win., Fed., Rem.	$4**	1610
Max	1	sabot slug	slug	Sauvestre		1640
Max	7/8	slug, rifled	slug	Rem.	NA	1800
Max	400	plat. tip	sabot slug	Win.	NA	1700
Max	385 grains	Partition Gold Slug	slug	Win.	NA	1900
Max	385 grains	Core-Lokt bonded	sabot slug	Rem.	NA	1900
Max	325 grains	Barnes Sabot	slug	Fed.	NA	1900
Max	300 grains	SST Slug	sabot slug	Hornady	NA	2050
3	1-1/8	steel target	6-1/2, 7	Rem.	NA	1200
2-3/4	1-1/8	steel target	7	Rem.	NA	1145
3	1#	steel	7	Win.	$11	1235
3-1/2	1-1/4	steel	T, BBB, BB, 1, 2, 3, 4, 5, 6	Win., Fed., Rem.	$18	1275
3-3/4	1-1/8	steel	BB, 1, 2, 3, 4, 5, 6	Win., Fed., Rem., Fio.	$16	1365
3-3/4	1	steel	2, 3, 4, 5, 6, 7	Win., Fed., Rem., Fio.	$13	1390
Max	7/8	steel	7	Fio.	NA	1440

16 Gauge 2-3/4"

3-1/4	1-1/4	magnum	2, 4, 6	Fed., Rem.	$16	1260
3-1/4	1-1/8	high velocity	4, 6, 7-1/2	Win., Fed., Rem., Fio.	$12	1295
Max	1-1/8	Bismuth	4, 5	Bis.	NA	1200
2-3/4	1-1/8	standard velocity	6, 7-1/2, 8	Fed., Rem., Fio.	$9	1185
2-1/2	1	dove	6, 7-1/2, 8, 9	Fio., Win.	NA	1165
2-3/4	1		6, 7-1/2, 8	Fio.	NA	1200
Max	15/16	steel	2, 4	Fed., Rem.	NA	1300
Max	7/8	steel	2, 4	Win.	$16	1300
3	12 pellets	buffered	1 buck	Win., Fed., Rem.	$4**	1225
Max	4/5	slug, rifled	slug	Win., Fed., Rem.	$4**	1570
Max	.92	sabot slug	slug	Sauvestre	NA	1560

20 Gauge 3" Magnum

3	1-1/4	premium	2, 4, 5, 6, 7-1/2	Win., Fed., Rem.	$15	1185
Max	1-1/4	Wingmaster HD	4, 6	Rem.	NA	1185
3	1-1/4	turkey	4, 6	Fio.	NA	1200
Max	1-1/4	Hevi-shot	2, 4, 6	Hevi-shot	NA	1250
Max	1-1/8	high density	4, 6	Rem.	NA	1300
Max	18 pellets	buck shot	2 buck	Fed.	NA	1200
Max	24 pellets	buffered	3 buck	Win.	$5**	1150
2-3/4	20 pellets	buck	3 buck	Rem.	$4**	1200
3-1/4	1	steel	1, 2, 3, 4, 5, 6	Win., Fed., Rem.	$15	1330

20 Gauge 3" Magnum (cont.)

Max	7/8	steel	2, 4	Win.	NA	1300
Max	1-1/16	high density	2, 4	Win.	NA	1400
Max	1-1/16	Bismuth	2, 4, 5, 6	Bismuth	NA	1250
Mag	5/8	saboted slug	275 gr.	Fed.	NA	1900

20 Gauge 2-3/4"

2-3/4	1-1/8	magnum	4, 6, 7-1/2	Win., Fed., Rem.	$14	1175
2-3/4	1	high velocity	4, 5, 6, 7-1/2, 8, 9	Win., Fed., Rem., Fio.	$12	1220
Max	1	Bismuth	4, 6	Bis.	NA	1200
Max	1	Hevi-shot	5	Hevi-shot	NA	1250
Max	1	Supreme H-V	4, 6, 7-1/2	Win. Rem.	NA	1300
Max	7/8	Steel	2, 3, 4	Fio.	NA	1500
2-1/2	1	standard velocity	6, 7-1/2, 8	Win., Rem., Fed., Flo.	$6	1165
2-1/2	7/8	clays	8	Rem.	NA	1200
2-1/2	7/8	promotional	6, 7-1/2, 8	Win., Rem., Fio.	$6	1210
2-1/2	1	target	8, 9	Win., Rem.	$8	1165
Max	7/8	clays	7-1/2, 8	Win.	NA	1275
2-1/2	7/8	target	8, 9	Win., Fed., Rem.	$8	1200
Max	3/4	steel	2, 4	Rem.	NA	1425
2-1/2	7/8	steel - target	7	Rem.	NA	1200
Max	1	buckhammer	slug		NA	1500
Max	5/8	Saboted Slug	Copper Slug	Rem.	NA	1500
Max	20 pellets	buffered	3 buck	Win., Fed.	$4	1200
Max	5/8	slug, saboted	slug	Win.,	$9**	1400
2-3/4	5/8	slug, rifled	slug	Rem.	$4**	1500
Max	3/4	saboted slug	copper slug	Fed., Rem.	NA	1450
Max	3/4	slug, rifled	slug	Win., Fed., Rem., Fio.	$4**	1570
Max	.9	sabot slug	slug	Sauvestre		1480
Max	260 grains	Partition Gold Slug	slug	Win.	NA	1900
Max	260 grains	Core-Lokt Ultra	slug	Rem.	NA	1900
Max	260 grains	saboted slug	platinum tip	Win.	NA	1700
Max	3/4	steel	2, 3, 4, 6	Win., Fed., Rem.	$14	1425
Max	250 grains	SST slug	slug	Hornady	NA	1800
Max	1/2	rifled, slug	slug	Rem.	NA	1800

28 Gauge 2-3/4"

2	1	high velocity	6, 7-1/2, 8	Win.	$12	1125
2-1/4	3/4	high velocity	6, 7-1/2, 8, 9	Win., Fed., Rem., Fio.	$11	1295
2	3/4	target	8, 9	Win., Fed., Rem.	$9	1200
Max	3/4	sporting clays	7-1/2, 8-1/2	Win.	NA	1300
Max	5/8	Bismuth	4, 6	Bis.	NA	1250
Max	5/8	steel	6, 7	NA	NA	1300

410 Bore 3"

Max	11/16	high velocity	4, 5, 6, 7-1/2, 8, 9	Win., Fed., Rem., Fio.	$10	1135
Max	9/16	Bismuth	4	Bis.	NA	1175
Max	3/8	steel	6	NA	NA	1400

410 Bore 2-1/2"

Max	1/2	high velocity	4, 6, 7-1/2	Win., Fed., Rem.	$9	1245
Max	1/5	slug, rifled	slug	Win., Fed., Rem.	$4**	1815
1-1/2	1/2	target	8, 8-1/2, 9	Win., Fed., Rem., Fio.	$8	1200
Max	1/2	sporting clays	7-1/2, 8, 8-1/2	Win.	NA	1300
Max		Buckshot	5-000 Buck	Win.	NA	1135

ONE GOOD GUN:
The Unique Kleinguenther K14 Insta-fire in 7 X 57 Mauser BY MIKE THOMAS

I had been thinning my modest accumulation of rifles and was not looking for another when I happened upon the Kleinguenther. However, my admitted weakness for the 7x57mm (7mm Mauser) chambering would not permit me to pass on it. I won't attempt to resurrect the hypothetical "all around cartridge" debate, but it is difficult to imagine any game animal in most of our country that could not be successfully hunted with a 7x57 rifle.

Like many of us, my knowledge of Kleinguenther rifles was quite sketchy but I knew they had a reputation for accuracy and high quality. I had seen a few published photographs of the rifles and had read a bit about them over the past twenty or so years.

Robert Kleinguenther of Kleingunether Distinctive Firearms in Seguin, Texas began importing the German-made Voere bolt-action rifle in the early 'seventies. According to the catalog section of *Gun Digest's* 26th Edition (1972), the rifle is referred to as the M-V-2130, listing Kleinguether as the importer. In the 1973 *Gun Digest*, what appears to be the same rifle is called the Kleinguenther K14. It was listed as such through the 1978 edition of the annual publication. The rifle was also called the K14 Insta-Fire, in reference to its fast lock time, made possible by a striker travel that was about one-third that of a conventional Mauser action.

Mr. Kleinguenther worked for Weatherby for many years before relocating to Texas and starting his own business in 1970. He had direct involvement with Voere in the development of what was to become the Model K14 Insta-Fire. One readily notes the Weatherby styling similarity, which is likely no coincidence. The rifle I have is a standard model complete

While the Kleinguenther K14 bears a strong outer resemblance to a Mark V Weatherby, it has a number of unique features that set it apart from the Weatherby and other bolt-action rifles.

with glossy-finished walnut stock, white line spacers, and rosewood fore end tip and grip cap. Centered in the grip cap is a diamond-shaped white plastic or acrylic inlay. The grip and both sides of the forearm have a well-executed skip-line checkering pattern.

As expected, wood-to-metal-fit is excellent. The receiver and barrel were well polished prior to bluing; the result is a mirror-like final finish. The retail price of a standard K14 was higher than that of a Ruger or Remington bolt-action, but less than that of a Weatherby Mark V. The K14 appeared to have been a very good buy for the times. Since several thousand K14s were imported into the United States, they are far from rarities. However, these rifles do not often surface on the used gun market. Perhaps the owners recognize good rifles and hang onto them.

The K14 is a comparatively big rifle. Some would consider it quite heavy by today's standards, but rifle weight is a subjective factor, despite some armchair conjecture indicating otherwise. While one hunter may be bothered by an extra pound or so of rifle weight, another may have no objection. Unloaded and without a sling, my rifle weighs 8 lbs., 12 oz. with a 2.5X-8X Leupold Vari-X III installed. The 24" barrel (26" in magnum chamberings) tapers to a fairly thin .585" at the muzzle. Action length is 9" and the massive three-lug bolt weighs about 17 oz., almost 20 percent more than a comparable Ruger 77 bolt.

The fluted bolt body of the K14 is .845"

in diameter. To handle the possibility of escaping gas, three ports are drilled in the bolt body. Bolt lift is 60 degrees. For some reason (easier to quickly grasp, perhaps?) the bolt handle is not bent downward nearly as far as most other bolts, causing it to extend from the stock farther than necessary. However, the bolt operates very smoothly, more so than any bolt-action I am familiar with other than a Krag action. Bolt "wobble" is comparatively minimal.

The single trigger is adjustable and breaks in a clean manner. As purchased, mine was set and remains at around 2.5 lbs., probably close to the minimum adjustment. This may be a little light for a hunting rifle, but like rifle weight, we all have preferences. A double-set trigger was also available for the K14.

The trigger also is used to operate the bolt stop. With the bolt pulled back and the trigger depressed, the bolt can be removed. The K14's safety, which consists of a horizontal checkered knob on the right side of the rear of the bolt's shroud, moves up and down; down to engage the safety, up to fire. I am aware of no other rifle safety quite like this one. Initially, there was a significant degree of awkwardness in using the mechanism, but that diminished with familiarity.

Before opening, the magazine/floorplate assembly of the K14 appears to be similar to that of many other bolt-action rifles. Inside the front of the trigger guard is a release button that can be pushed forward. Doing so allows the entire, 7-1/4"-long, one-piece hinged trigger guard and floorplate to swing open. The magazine box remains in the well until a spring-loaded button on the top edge of the receiver (in the middle of the ejection port) is pushed. The five-cartridge box is similar to most other box magazines. This all may seem needlessly complicated. Perhaps it is, but the magazine can loaded from topside like other bolt-action rifles.

Another unusual feature of the Kleinguenther is that the recoil lug is not an integral component of the receiver. Instead, it is neatly welded to the bottom of the receiver. While this probably makes no comparative difference from the standpoint of strength, it is unlike other bolt-action rifles.

As to the K14's stock: in the early 1970s enties there were few, if any, production rifles that had any sort of bedding compound applied to their stocks' inletting. As with other unique characteristics of the K14, the application of stock bedding material was handled a bit differently than one might imagine in that the work was not performed at the Voere plant. After the completed rifles were delivered to Robert Kleinguenther's KDF facility, the barreled actions were pulled from their stocks. Bedding material was applied just under the receiver tang, in the web behind the trigger, and in the recoil lug area. It was also applied in forend in the form of a thin band 7/8" wide, the middle of which was about 2-3/4" behind the forend tip. No doubt this was step was performed in the interest of accuracy by providing consistent upward pressure to the otherwise free-floated barrel.

All K14 rifles came with a 1-1/2" accuracy guarantee for 100-yard three-shot groups. Each rifle was test fired at the KDF facility for verification. Presumably, Robert Kleinguenther fired most, if not all, of the groups.

In the 13th Edition of *Guns Illustrated* (1981), Hal Swiggett wrote a piece titled "The Kleinguenther K15 Really Does Shoot Half-Inch Groups!" Swiggett evaluated the K14's successor, sometimes referred to as the Improved K15 Insta-Fire. The major difference between the two models is a side-mounted safety and a more conventional floorplate/magazine box assembly on the newer rifle. Regarding the accuracy guarantee, Swiggett mentioned the fact that Mr. Kleinguenther continually fine-tuned and improved his bedding technique. In so doing, the accuracy guarantee correspondingly "shrunk from the 1-1/2" groups of the early K14s to 1" three-shot groups and finally to the 1/2" three-shot groups of later production K15s. The last year the K15 was listed in the catalog section of *Gun Digest* was in 1988.

Depending on one's perspective, a 1-1/2" group may not sound very impressive today, but it remains quite acceptable for a hunting rifle. In fact, if a rifle will hold its zero and the barreled action never shifts in the stock, consistent 1-1/2" groups are far better than the occasional

half-inch group from a rifle that won't hold a zero overnight. I've worked with more than a few such troublesome rifles.

A long-time, prolific gun writer, the late Bob Hagel, wrote an article for *Rifle* magazine (#34, July-August, 1974) titled "Kleinguenther's K14" in which he evaluated one of these rifles in great detail. Hagel knew what he was talking about when it came to rifles, having had many decades of experience handloading, hunting, guiding, and using firearms on a far more regular basis than the majority of us. The K14 Hagel evaluated was chambered for the .308 Norma Magnum. In a summation toward the end of his article, the author remarked that the K14 was the most consistently accurate sporter he had encountered up to that time. Using a variety of different bullets and weights ranging from 110 to 220 grains, Hagel obtained an average accuracy of 1-1/8" for three-shot 100 yard groups.

Thus far, I have fired fewer than 250 rounds from my K14. Almost all of those have been handloads that were developed for use in another 7x57 rifle. None of the loads were worked up specifically for the Kleinguenther other than increasing the overall cartridge length to accommodate the long throat. I have found no information on the barrel twist rate for the K14 and I have not measured it. The standard twist rate for the 7x57 cartridge was originally 1:8-3/4 for the old military rifles in order to effectively stabilize the long 175-gr. roundnosed bullets. Twist rates have varied somewhat over the last century and some rifles (particularly newer ones) may have rates of 1:9, 1:9-1/2, or 1:10. How much difference these rates will make from an accuracy standpoint with a variety of bullet weights, I cannot say. The basic rule that suggests lighter, shorter bullets shoot more accurately in barrels with slower twist rates is sometimes suspect, so experimentation is required for best results.

The Kleinguenther shot well with the only factory ammunition I fired in it, some very old Western 175-gr. roundnosed soft points. The most accurate load so far has used the 150-gr. Nosler Partition bullet at around 2,500 fps muzzle velocity. I found I could

beat the factory accuracy guarantee by a small margin with this bullet and Accurate Arms 4350 powder. Best groups have been around 1-1/4". Another bullet that showed promise of decent accuracy was Hornady's 154-gr. Interlock spirepoint. I have much work to do and many bullets to try, however, before I make a final assessment of the K14's accuracy capability.

Surprisingly, my K14 has a "slow" barrel. Despite its 24" length, chronographed muzzle velocities run about 100-150 fps slower than the same loads from a Ruger M77 with a 22" "fast" (?) barrel. However, a review of trajectory tables affirmed that such a velocity decrease is insufficient to make much difference in the field. With a 200-yard zero, an increased bullet drop of 1-1/2" at 300 yards is indeed a trivial amount. If you go much beyond that range, however, trajectory shortcomings actually do limit the usefulness of the cartridge. Nevertheless, the 7x57 is

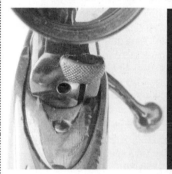

The unusual safety is an up/down button on the right side of the rear of the bolt shroud; down for safe, up to fire.

certainly a very capable 300-yard hunting cartridge in the hands of an experienced rifleman.

So what's the big deal about the Kleinguenther K14? Its uncanny resemblance to a Mark V Weatherby may be a bit much for those who don't care for such styling. Some might call it a large and hefty rifle. The barrel is too long to suit some tastes, not to mention odd features like the unconventional safety, magazine release, and the floorplate/trigger guard assembly. To top it off, Kleinguenther's 1970s accuracy guarantee of 1-1/2" three-shot groups at 100 yards is rather ho-hum when judged by contemporary standards.

However, the fact that the K14 is a very finely-built rifle rather than just a tool is plenty of justification for some folks to own one. Features such as overall excellent craftsmanship, exceptional wood-to-metal-fit, and deep, lustrous blue retain desirability and are always in style regardless of the year or even the decade of production.

The hinged floorplate and trigger guard assembly is a one-piece unit. The detachable magazine box is similar to that found on other bolt-action rifles.

ONE GOOD GUN:
Remington Model 760
.300 Savage

BY STEVE GASH

Remington's Model 760 slide-action made a fine woods rifle for a variety of big game in 1952 – and still does.

new. The bluing was good, and the only rust was on the right side of the front-sight ramp.

I studied the white fingerprints. I figured that I could (probably) not make it look any worse, so I moistened a small piece of 0000 steel wool with Hoppe's No. 9, and gingerly rubbed the white spots. To my delight and amazement, the paint, epoxy, or whatever came right off, and the underlying finish was in fairly decent shape; it was at least 60%, maybe better. The original aluminum buttplate still had stock finish on its sides. It was a big step forward in the rehabilitation.

As I delved into the M-760's history, I became caught up in its mystique. The

A firearm can become "One Good Gun" by several means. It can be a family heirloom, one you've owned since your youth, or one you've just wanted to own since your youth. The Remington M-760 .300 Savage is of the latter category, and sometimes good fortune befalls us without warning. This happened to me recently as I perused the wares at a local emporium of fine firearms. I spied a well-worn Remington Model 760 "Gamemaster" that gazed longingly back at me from the rack. "Probably another .30-06, .308, or some other pedestrian caliber," I ruefully mused as I glanced at its hangtag. Gasp! It read ".300 Savage," a caliber for which I'd been searching a long time. I promptly checked it out. The slide shuttled back and forth like it was on greased glass, and the trigger pull wasn't too bad. After a (very) short haggle period, the M-760 followed me home.

The old rifle had been used and abused in a couple of spots. Some cretin mistakenly thought that the large slots in the forend cap were just like those on the Model 870 shotgun, and had tried to "unscrew" it. Of course, it wouldn't budge,

The M-760 offered convenient scope mounting and powerful calibers not previously offered in a pump. It was very popular with the growing legion of shooters of Remington's M-870 shotgun.

and the implement used (I suspect a large tire iron) had left ghastly gouges in both slots. Further insult was inflicted by some previous handler, who had apparently poked his paws into a vat of white-colored epoxy before picking up the rifle, and subsequently left his fingerprints on the buttstock and forend.

As I cleaned several decades of gunk from the metal parts, I found that it was in excellent mechanical shape. Everything worked. The bore was bright and the six-groove rifling looked as good as

Model 760 was introduced in 1952 in just three calibers: the .30-06, .35 Remington, and .300 Savage. While the M-760 in various guises would be produced until 1980, the .300 Savage was discontinued in 1958, with a total of 41,751 of this chambering produced, while a total of 971,712 M-760 rifles (and 67,726 carbines) were made. Remington uses a letter code for the month and year a rifle was assembled and sent to the warehouse. This rifle has "D" and "YY" on the left side of the barrel, indicating September of 1952

.300 Savage Factory Load Data
Test Rifle: Remington Model 760, 22-inch barrel, 1:12 twist

	Listed Velocity (fps)	Actual	Standard Deviation	Group (")
Federal 150-grain SP, no. 300A	2,630	2,566	8	1.18
Federal 180-grain SP, no. 300B	2,350	2,352	10	2.16
Remington 150-grain Core-Lokt PSP, #R30SV2	2,630	2,515	14	1.39
Remington 180-grain Core-Lokt, #R30SV3	2,350	2,231	31	1.50
Winchester 150-grain PP, no. X3001	2,630	2,583	9	1.62

Testing done at 100 yards from a bench rest with a Burris 3-9x40 Fullfield II scope set at 9x. Accuracy is the average of three, 5-shot groups.

The old M-760 still offers hunters a slick action, minute-of-deer accuracy, plenty of power, and classic lines, as it has for over a half century.

– the year of the M-760's introduction. Of the 63,735 M-760s sold that year, only 14,431 were in .300 Savage.

According to the Remington website (www.remington.com), the Model 141 was Remington's pump-action big game rifle until it was discontinued in 1950. In 1952, the new and spiffy M-760 debuted. It was designed by L. R. Crittendon and William Gail, Jr., and during its production run the M-760 was offered in a total of 12 calibers.

The M-760's design features were quite modern for its day. A rotating bolt with 14 lugs mated into corresponding cuts in the barrel extension. This made the M-760 much stronger than its predecessor, the M-141. The availability of the powerful .30-06, heretofore chambered only in bolt-action rifles, helped make the M-760 a hit, and this caliber was the most popular.

The M-760's forearm has twin action bars similar to the M-870 shotgun that was introduced just two years earlier. These bars actuate a carrier that holds the bolt, so that pumping the forend back rotates and unlocks the bolt and cocks the hammer. A horseshoe-shaped extractor riveted onto the bolt face pulls a cartridge from the chamber, and a plunger ejector flips the round to the side. A forward shove on the forend strips a cartridge off the box magazine, and as the bolt goes into the barrel extension, it rotates into battery. All in all, it was a pretty slick system – then and now. The factory instruction sheet is still available from Remington, as is the parts diagram.

The solid receiver allowed the mounting of a scope directly over the bore, and all but the very earliest M-760s came factory drilled and tapped. Those that weren't could be sent back to Remington, which would perform this alteration for the meager sum of $6.50.

The rifle came with a one-piece Weaver base installed, so I checked the screws and mounted a Burris 3-9x40 Fullfield II scope. Someday I'll replace it with a period-correct Weaver K4, but first I had to test my new treasure.

Fortunately, a fair variety of factory ammo for the .300 Savage is available today. Federal and Remington both make 150- and 180-gr. softpoint loads, and Winchester produces a 150-grain Power Point. I tested them all, and the results are shown in the accompanying chart. All exhibited minute-of-deer accuracy, averaging 1.57 inches, which I thought it was pretty good for a 56-year-old rifle. The only hiccup was that the magazine sometimes failed to feed; I suspect a weak spring.

Winchester still lists new .300 Savage cases, but they're seasonal merchandise. Fortunately a friend had given me a good supply of once-fired cases. Reloaders should be aware that the M-760 has a 1:12 twist, which may not stabilize some of the long and/or heavy bonded and lead-free bullets available today. As would be expected, medium burning-rate powders like IMR-3031, IMR-4064, N-140, H4895, and Varget perform best in the .300 Savage. All the loading manuals have data.

To some, the M-760 might appear as just another old clunker, but I see only history, not only in its clever and efficient design, and its classic old cartridge, but also its time in the woods, as evidenced by the scratches and dings

The .300 Savage was offered in the M-760 from its introduction through 1958. A total of 41,751 .300 Savages was produced, about 4% of the total M-760 production.

Early M-760s magazines for shorter cartridges like the .300 Savage featured filler blocks fore and aft, and were marked by caliber.

here and there. Surely it has taken deer; has it tangled with a bear?

Personally, I plan to make my own history with the M-760 during this fall's Missouri deer season. Handloads have to be developed, and their accuracy checked. This expedition is surely not the M-760's first, and I fervently hope it will not be our last.

THE REMINGTON MODEL 760: FURTHER READING

Eugene Myszkowski, *Remington Auto-loading & Pump-Action Rifles*. Excalibur Publications, 2002.

Myszkowski, "Models 76 & 7600 Pump-Action Rifles," *The American Rifleman*, October 2005.

Warren Page, "Slide, .30-06, Slide," by Warren Page. *Gun Digest* 7th Edition (1953), DBI, Inc.

Paul Scarlata, "Remington's Model 760 GameMaster," *Shooting Times*, March 2009.

Dean Boorman and Roy Marcot, "Remington Model 760 Gamemaster Slide-Action Rifles," in *The History of Remington Firearms*. Lyons Press, 2005.

Harold Murtz, "Remington Model 760 Slide Action Rifle, Carbine," in *The Gun Digest Book of Exploded Firearms Drawings*. Gun Digest Books, 2005.

ONE GOOD GUN:
A Classic Springfield Sporter BY JIM LAVIN

Sometimes a shooter's favorite rifle remains in its original factory stock for years, awaiting the day when its owner has the inclination and the means to have a custom stock built for it. On a rare occasion, it's the other way around, with the gun stock blank awaiting the arrival of the hardware.

In the early 1960's I owned a U.S. Model 1903-A3 Springfield military rifle of WWII vintage. Shortly after I got it, my uncle Lou, a woodworking hobbyist, restocked the barreled action in an old sporter stock that was lying around, as he wanted to experiment with glass bedding. When he was finished with it, the re-stocked Springfield was a thing

The author's reincarnated Springfield Sporter in its new stock.

of no special beauty, adorned as it was with a botched-up checkering job that came with the stock. Yet this was the classic custom sporter of the early twentieth century – or very close to it. The original 1903 Springfield action was finely made, with its sculpted com-

ponents having been milled from bar stock steel, a very costly and labor-intensive process.

The metal work on the '03 Springfield had an aura of quality about it. Thus, in its heyday, it was a natural choice for custom rifle-builders and their clients. A great favorite of the rich and famous, it went along on many an African safari as the "light rifle." Teddy Roosevelt owned one, as did novelists Ernest Hemingway and Stewart Edward White, among others. But this particular rifle was not a keeper. Still, the experiment

was instructive in that I saw a certain mystique about the rifle. It had charisma. In short, I was sufficiently impressed with the aesthetic potential of a sporterized Springfield that I resolved to have a really nice one made up someday.

To digress for a moment, around that point, I got Uncle Lou to re-stock a model 1956 Mannlicher-Shoenauer carbine for me. He purchased a fancy-grade European walnut stock blank directly from a supplier in Christchurch, New Zealand. It was kiln-dried to a moisture content of 8 percent and had a Janka hardness rating of 1500 lbs. (American black walnut has a rating of 1,000 lbs.) Although the amount of figure in the stock did not measure up to my expectations, I was more than pleased with the overall result. I didn't know anyone else who owned a Mannlicher-Shoenauer, much less a custom-stocked one. To a gun nut – well, it just doesn't get any better. I immediately had uncle Lou order me another stock blank of New Zealand walnut from the same supplier, this time an "exhibition grade" blank at somewhat greater cost (about $35 or so). I squirreled that stock blank away, as I was already set for life with my custom Mannlicher-Shoenauer. To show up anywhere with equipment like that, I would be "properly turned out," as the folks at Abercrombie & Fitch used to say.

Several years went by and sad to say, uncle Lou passed away. In addition to the loss of a good friend, my chance of owning an inexpensive yet very classy custom "ought-six" had slipped away. Then one day in 1999, disaster struck. An accidental fire destroyed my house and its entire contents, including my beautiful Mannlicher-Shoenauer carbine. I received a check for $1000 from the NRA Insurance Plan, which covered the cost of my new deer rifle, a Winchester Model 70 Classic Featherweight in 6.5 x 55mm Swedish Mauser.

Amazingly, one of the few things that survived the fire undamaged was the stock blank of New Zealand walnut. A few years later, I moved to central Florida, and I now hunt deer and wild boar on the Georgia border, where the cover is so thick that an animal that is not anchored with the first shot is likely to escape. "Those hogs will run off with

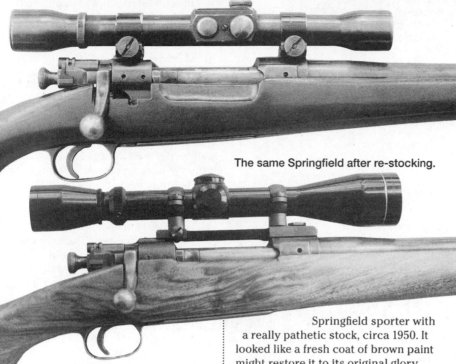

Author's c. 1950 sporterized Springfield before re-stocking.

The same Springfield after re-stocking.

your bullet," I was warned by locals. I also heard it said in these parts that the wild boar is "the poor man's grizzly bear." I then decided that I might need a cartridge with more authority than my little 6.5 x 55 mm Swede, perhaps something on the order of a 30-06. A friend offered to lend me a spare Savage rifle in that chambering and I soon shot a 140-lb. boar with one well-placed bullet straight through the boiler room. The hog traveled about 50 feet and piled up, its head submerged in a puddle of water. It was quite dead. Suddenly, I decided that there was definitely going to be another "ought-six" in my future.

I began to cruise the local gun shows and shops in search of a nice clean Springfield Model 1903. I did find a few but they were selling in the $700-$800 range, and I was not about to pay that much for what was to become a second rifle. Then I hit upon the idea that I could get around the high cost of a decent Springfield rifle if I were lucky enough to find one that somebody else had already sporterized many years ago, a common practice in the 1950s. The ideal specimen, in my mind, would be a nice, clean barreled action bedded in a truly wretched stock, one so awful that the whole rifle would be a complete turn-off. This now became my Holy Grail.

Many months later, at a local gun shop I spotted a 1918-vintage high-numbered

Springfield sporter with a really pathetic stock, circa 1950. It looked like a fresh coat of brown paint might restore it to its original glory. Perhaps someone had applied too much stain at some point, as there was no evidence of anything resembling wood beneath the surface. There were cracks in the tang area as well as chips missing in several places. The stock was not checkered and the plain steel buttplate was badly rusted. It was as sorry a gunstock as I had ever laid eyes on, but the barreled action had not been botched and the barrel was in its original 24" configuration. This was the Holy Grail indeed! Priced at $150 plus tax, this was a fantastic bargain for the barreled action alone. It was in very good condition except for some heavy wear in the trigger guard and magazine floorplate area, where the blueing had been completely worn off. However, the metal showed no pitting anywhere and the bore was bright. The action was as slick as glass.

I bought it.

Inwardly, I wished the gun had retained more of its original blueing, but nonetheless I began to relish the anticipation of once again owning a custom sporter. I still had that New Zealand walnut stock blank, but a major obstacle loomed just ahead: getting the stock blank transformed into a custom

stock. Doubt set in. Then, on a hunch, I sat down at the computer. In a stroke of fortune, I found there were several mass-production stockmaking companies advertising on the Internet. One of them offered the option of "customer-supplied wood." This was exactly what I was hoping for!

After considering the various style options available, I decided on the "Modern Classic," which could be shaped and inletted for $75. A Pachmayr Decelerator recoil pad would be $40 extra. I promptly shipped the stock blank off. While I was waiting to get the stock back, I took the old Springfield to a local gunsmith to remedy a problem I had not noticed before. The rifle had, of course, been designed for use with open sights. However, with a scope in place, it interfered with the swing of the safety lever over and across the cocking piece of the bolt. The previous owner of the rifle had left it permanently set in the "off" position and mounted the scope on top of it. This would not do. Therefore, I had the gunsmith install a Dayton Traister safety, designed to replace the original safety.

When the shaped and inletted stock was returned to me, the style was exactly as ordered, and the shaping was excellent despite the rough toolmarks all over the exterior surface. Miraculously, it seemed a striking new stock had emerged after all those years hidden away inside the old blank. I packed it up with the old rifle and took it to a gun shop to be glass bedded at a cost of $85.

When the work was completed, I gazed upon the barreled action bedded in the new stock for the very first time. Even with its coarse surface, it had the look of an expensive sporter and although its component parts were quite old, a modern sporting rifle had just come into being. In my mind, it was brand new.

At this writing, I have just completed the stock-finishing job and, as the photos will attest, I shall be properly turned out for those hogs on Opening Day. As for that New Zealand walnut stock blank, in a strange way I feel happy for the thing. After 40-odd years' gestation in a closet and against great odds, it had finally become part of a real hunting rifle.

The New Zealand walnut stock, roughly shaped but not yet finished.

The Valmet Model 412 S shooting System offered a wide array of barrel sets that could be selected to meet almost any shooting challenge, and the barrels fit a common receiver with little or no fitting.

ONE GOOD GUN (OR TWO):
The Valmet 412 Shooting System
BY STEVE GASH

Combination guns and double rifles have always held a fascination for a small but devoted cadre of shooters, and while such arms have been around for decades, few have captured the hearts (or wallets) of American shooters. One model that made a brief but significant excursion into our collective gun consciousness was the Valmet Model 412 Shooting System.

Valmet literature of the day touted that "No longer do you need several guns in the rack. The Valmet Shooting System is all the gun you need to own." Although most shooters cringe at the thought of a philosophy that limits gun accumulation, the justifications for such a system are sound. There is a certain seduction of the "one gun for everything" argument, the reduced weight and bulk for your battery while traveling, and the sheer satisfaction of owning something truly unique.

Valmet's Combo Gun

The Valmet M-412 is such an arm. Its receivers accept multi-caliber barrel sets that offer true flexibility, and cost considerably less than other types (i.e., a drilling). The Valmet 412 also exhibits more pizzazz than the utilitarian Savage Model 24.

The story of the 412 begins in 1980, when the firm of Valmet Industrial Ma-

chinery and Products, Inc., established Valmet USA in Elmsford, New York, and began offering the Model 412 Shooting System with comprehensive line of over/unders with multi-barrel sets that worked on one receiver, usually with little or no fitting.

There were three basic configurations that lasted until Valmet discontinued the line in 1989 and importation was taken over by Tikka: the double rifle, the combination gun, and shotguns.

Extractors were standard on the 412K series, although ejectors could be had on some models (designated 412KE). A single selective trigger was also standard, but double triggers were a special order option. A two-piece firing pin was said to reduce breakage. All guns had automatic safeties, except the trap and skeet shotguns, which had non-automatic safeties. Various high-grade models were produced, including the "engraved model" in (at least) 1984 and 1985. Some of these were described as having "full scroll" and "game scene" coverage. Non-detachable sling swivels were provided on rifle as well as shotgun models. A top sighting rib and side ribs were provided on the shotguns, but not on models with rifle barrels.

The over/under shotguns were offered in both hunting and target versions. Barrel lengths on the 12-gauge guns were 26,

28, and 30 inches, with fixed chokes in the then-usual pairings of Improved Cylinder/Modified, and Modified/Full. The 26" and 28" 12 gauges had 2-¾" chambers; the 30" 12s were 3" magnums. The 412KE series added the 20 gauge with 26" or 28" barrels, both with 3" chambers. The Trap model had Improved, Modified and Full chokes, while the skeet gun was bored Skeet & Skeet.

Guns of either gauge with 26" barrels had a "standard" buttstock and no recoil pad, as did the 28" 12 gauges. The 30" 12 gauge was equipped with a Monte Carlo stock with recoil pad, as was the 28" 20 gauge. Stocks were made of nicely figured European walnut, and checkered at a functional 18 lines-per-inch.

The double rifle and the combination gun had 24" barrels throughout their production run. Double-rifle calibers in 1980 were the .308 Winchester and .30-06 Springfield. The combination gun was a 12-gauge shotgun with a fixed Improved-Modified choke over the popular .222 Remington, .308, or .30-06. In 1981, the .243 and .375 Winchesters – not the .375 H&H Magnum, as has been reported – were added to both models.

In 1982, the .223 Remington was added to the combination gun. This rounded out the line until 1984, when the 9.3x74R was offered in the double rifle. In Europe, combination guns were also offered with the rifle barrel chambered in 5.6x52R (.22 Savage High Power to us), and the 6.5x57R. Rifle and shotgun-rifle barrels had flip-up rear sights and blade front

Regulation of the rifle barrels for windage was accomplished by moving the bottom barrel right or left, relative to the top barrel. Note the opposing screws for the adjustment. While relatively imprecise, it worked.

sights. All barrels accepted a base with 1" rings for easy scope mounting.

An integral part of the "Model 412 Shooting system" was the availability of extra barrel sets, which were offered in basically the same configurations as complete guns. The utility of this concept was not lost on many shooters, and at gun shows and on the internet one stills sees multi-barrel Valmet sets.

In 1980, the Valmet double rifle listed for $679; by 1989, the price had risen to $999 and $1099 for the ejector model. Even so, this was still well below the cost of a more traditional British side-by-side double rifle.

Ingenious Features

A couple of new design features distinguished the new M-412 from previous Savage M-300 and M-330 offerings. The barrels rotate on trunnions rather than a full-length hinge pin. A single-selective trigger was operated mechanically, not by inertia, so the second barrel could be fired if the first barrel didn't. A barrel selector button was located on the single trigger. Cocking indicators on the tang pop up ever so slightly when the barrel(s) is cocked, and recede into the receiver upon firing.

One of the M-412's more ingenious elements is the sliding top latch (called the "locking bolt" in the Valmet parts list). This metal cover engages an angled flat on either side of the barrel, a la the Remington M-3200 and Krieghoff. This part, along with the trunnions, eliminates the need for any underlugs, and makes for a slimer, trimmer receiver. All barrels were joined in a monoblock.

The M-412 System included a comprehensive array of 12- and 20-gauge shotgun barrels, and combination sets of a 12-gauge shotgun barrel over several different rifle chamberings, and there were double-rifle barrels in various calibers to tempt the more seriously afflicted.

Barrel regulation is a major cost factor in traditional double rifles, but two unique devices in the M-412 neatly handle this problem. There is a sliding adjustment on the shotgun/rifle and double-rifle sets at about their mid-point. Loosening a set screw allows the slider to be moved fore or aft. This either pushes the barrels further apart or draws them closer together. This action moves the point of impact of the lower barrel, relative to the top barrel. Lateral adjustment for windage is accomplished by loosening opposing lock screws at the muzzle, and moving the lower barrel right or left, again, relative to the top barrel.

"Regulating" the rifle barrels is actually pretty easy. Here's the drill. For best results, attach the scope mount and suitable glass. Then zero the top barrel; ignore the bottom barrel for the moment. For the best accuracy, hold the forend in your hand, and rest your hand on the bench rest. After you get the top barrel hitting to point-of-aim, fire a 3-round group with the bottom barrel. Use a large backer, as this group can be anywhere. To raise the point of impact of the bottom barrel, mover the slider to push the barrels further apart. It's best to get elevation regulated first, so fire another group. Repeat above.

When you're satisfied with the up-and-down, adjust the muzzles for windage. Caution: a little of either adjustment goes a long way, so make small movements, and re-test. Eventually, the points of impact will converge. Honest.

My introduction to the Valmet Shooting System came at the 1980 NRA Annual Meetings when I was struck by a display of guns with extra barrel sets. A fine gentleman named Robert T. Sheridan introduced himself as the Valmet Sporting Goods Division's Vice President, and began to extol the virtues of the M-412 over/under series. Soon I was enthralled.

Most interesting to me at the time were the double rifles. The Valmet M-412 double rifles were then available in only .30-06 Springfield and .308 Winchester, but more calibers were added later. Here was a double rifle that a) looked like a fine, European firearm (which, of course, it was); b) didn't cost an arm and a leg; and c) the barrels of which easily could be made to shoot together. I was also taken by the combination of a 12-gauge over one of my all-time favorite rifle calibers, the .222 Remington.

I am a firm believer in the utility, simplicity, and the instant barrel selection of double triggers, and was delighted when Mr. Sheridan said that he would see to it that the receiver was so equipped. Interestingly, on the double-trigger model, the front trigger fires the top barrel, just opposite of what you'd think, so this takes a little getting used to. But it makes for instant barrel selection, and it works.

After some discussion with Mr. Sheridan as to calibers and such, I placed an order for a representative system. The primary gun was to be a double-trigger double rifle in .308, along with two additional barrel sets, one a 20-ga. with automatic ejectors, and combo barrels in 12-ga. over .222. I also ordered a scope mount and a hard case that held it all.

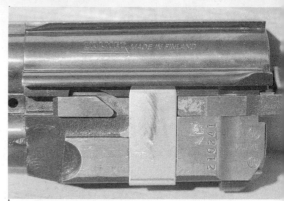

Each barrel set was uniquely marked with caliber or gauge. These 20-gauge barrels are marked with the chamber length of 76 mm (3") and chokes (IC and M). Note the automatic ejectors.

It's a Hunter

In November of 1984, I added a set of 30" 12-gauge barrels (also with auto ejectors) with which to hunt waterfowl and turkeys, so I dare say that the set was and is truly complete.

In the 1980s, I lived in Denver, and the great wilderness of Wyoming was but a few interstate miles away. A coworker named John and I hunted turkeys along Crazy Woman Creek in the Powder River Basin. Wyoming allowed the use of centerfire rifles as well as shotguns on Merriam's turkeys, so I used the 12-gauge/.222 Valmet.

One fine morning, we spotted a flock of turkeys walking complacently up a draw. We sprinted up a hill one gully over in an attempt to head them off. As I topped the ridge, the flock stopped in a sea of waist-high sagebrush at about 100 yards to reconnoiter the situation. I sat down and carefully fired a 55-gr. FMJ bullet from the .222 at a fat gobbler. The entire assemblage took off running, but the one I had fired at soon lagged behind. As I approached, the gobbler's red and white head poked up from the sage at about 15 yards. I quickly fed him 1-½ ounces of copper-plated BBs, and that was that.

The Valmet 412 Shooting System offered the American shooter a comprehensive array of over/under guns that could be crafted to meet virtually any shooting challenge. While it's no longer imported stateside, those of us who are intrigued by totally unique yet fully functional firearms can still find Valmet 412 guns with a little searching. It's well worth the effort.

> Superficially it looks like an AK. Inside, it isn't, and that scores you lots of cool points.

CZECHMATE!
CZ's Vz-58

BY PATRICK SWEENEY

In these uncertain times, you have to have the essentials. A good rifle, a stack of ammo cans, lots of magazines – they're all not just good to have, but nearly requirements or proof of US citizenship. But even while we're taking care of the essentials, we can't lose sight of coolness. Being prepared is good; being cool while doing it is even better.

Your gun club buddies will parse every detail of your guns. Brand, caliber, accessories, all will be viewed, judged and rated. Your "man points" total will be duly noted, and ranked with the rest of the pack. Do you want to score higher? Then get cool iron.

Back in 1958, when the Berlin Wall was still a gleam in Nikita Krushchev's eye, the vZ-58 (technically the *7.62 mm samopal vzor 58* or "7.62 mm submachine gun model 1958") was Czechoslovakia's attempt at solidarity with the Evil Empire. They actually believed the Soviet's promises and jumped whole-hog into design and manufacture of small arms, something they'd been good at for quite a while. What they didn't realize was that the promises of friendship and brotherhood actually meant "you build what we need." So the original plans they had of a new family of small arms, chambered in a new cartridge, were dashed. They

had to make everything in the existing Soviet chambering of 7.62X39.

With a change of chambering and magazine dimensions, the vZ-58 on the drawing boards in 7.62X45 became the vZ-58 in 7.62X39. It looks like an AK, but it isn't. The only things from an AK you can use in your vZ-58 are the ammunition, the magazine pouches and the cleaning kit. First off, the vZ-58 is a pound lighter than an AK. The action is not a rotating bolt, but one more like the Beretta M-92's locking system. It also uses a striker and not a hammer. The piston that drives the bolt and carrier is not attached, but is a simple

rod located above the handguard.

The magazines are different: they're made from aluminum, lighter, with a built-in bolt hold-open. The safety is above and behind the trigger and does not cover the ejection port. It is a bit more ergonomic than the AK, but its chief virtue is that it does not make a resounding "clack" when you move it one way or the other. And the ejection port? There isn't one. When the bolt cycles, the whole top of the vZ-58 slides back, exposing the action and feed lips, and thus there is no way for an empty to get hung up and non-ejected. (I've seen that happen on the supposedly "fail-safe" AK.) Of course, the drawback to the wide-open action is that if you get your fingers in there while the bolt closes, you're going to get one heck of an owie out of it. Garand thumb may be embarrassing, but vZ-58 fingertips can be very painful.

Being a bit lighter, the vZ-58 has a bit more recoil than an AK, but not so much that you'd notice unless you shot them side-by-side. The vZ-58 as imported comes one of three ways: folding, traditional synthetic and modern synthetic. The folding stock is a marvel of minimalist design, being an extension rod with a buttplate attached to it. If you want the smallest package possible when folded, then your vZ-58 will have to come this way. Me, I'm not so enamored of folding stocks that I'd go for this one, but I do have to admire its spartan design. The traditional synthetic is right out of the 1950s: chipped wood mixed into a slurry with an epoxy, and squirted into moulds. That was the height of commie fashion in the 1950s, learned from the late-WWII German attempts at mak-

Not bad, for iron sights, frozen benches and stiff fingers from the cold.

The vZ-58 magazine has a bolt hold-open tab on it, so you know when you're empty.

When the bolt goes back, the whole cover opens up.

The wide-open action means no hung-up brass (or steel) cases. It also means keep your fingers out of there.

ing stocks. It is durable, comfortable, well-proportioned and distinctive. The modern synthetic is your basic "Dragunov" style stock, with the upper and lower arms of the stock growing out of the back of the receiver and the bottom of the pistol grip, respectively.

For my test gun I went with the traditional stock, and found it comfortable to shoot. The trigger is your basic long-travel type, not too heavy, but certainly not what someone who has 1,000-yard sniper rifle expectations will find suitable. Then again, this isn't a thousand-yard rifle. The trigger is plenty good enough to get hits as far as the accuracy is good for, including a high percentage of hammered 300-meter targets on the military qual course. The safety takes a bit of practice, but after a while it isn't a problem.

As for reliability, all I can say is the rifle never gave me a problem. Now, testing a military self-loading rifle with only a couple of thousand rounds is not a big test, but it is indicative. The rifle never stumbled, not even when I was shooting it in single-digit winter temperatures. The open sights make accuracy work almost as much of a test of the shooter as it is of the rifle, and I'm not sure you can really say one batch or brand of ammo is more accurate than another, but the rifle definitely wanted to shoot well. If I took my time, I could shoot 3 MOA groups, this from the bench in the dead of winter. It's a shame the Czechs and Slovaks never took the next step and fitted the vZ-58 with a scope mount of some kind for use as a DMR. The milled-steel receiver would have been a solid place to bolt on a base or rail of some kind, and with a low-power scope on it the vZ-58 could probably turn in some really good groups.

When the Czechs and Slovaks went their separate ways after the Iron Curtain fell, they split the inventory of vZ-58 rifles. That left them each with about half a million rifles, for an army of perhaps 50,000. That means a lot of spare rifles to be taken apart, imported, and reassembled as US-compliant, uber-cool rifles. Even a short while ago an AK was uncommon. Now they're everywhere, and if you want to stand out from the crowd you have to extend yourself. So extend yourself to the nearest gun shop that deals in cool gear, and get yourself a vZ-58 with some spare magazines. Your AK mags don't fit, won't work, and are too heavy anyway. Or give CZ-USA, the importer, a buzz at (913) 321-1811 or visit them at cz-usa.com.

TEST FIRE

NOT YOUR FATHER'S BB GUN:
The .50 Dragon Slayer
BY MICHAEL SCHOBY

Ever since reading the *Journals of Lewis and Clark* I have been fascinated with big-bore air rifles (for readers who are unfamiliar with this work, Captain Lewis took a very unique air rifle on his "Voyage of Discovery"). While the actual model and caliber are debated, the most recent consensus is that the rifle was a Girandoni 22-shot repeating .46-caliber air rifle that was used for hunting as well as impressing the natives.

Big-bore air rifles were nothing new in 1804 when Lewis and Clark sallied forth to the western frontier. In fact far from it; Europeans had been using air-powered rifles for hunting as well as military service for years. While they have been around since the mid-1600's, they were pretty widely unknown as they were so prohibitively expensive that the average man couldn't begin to afford one.

Jump forward to today – and not much has changed. Big-bore air rifles are still being made, but the number of known custom makers can be counted without removing your shoes, and those who make affordable big-bore air rifles are so backed up with work that actually obtaining a rifle is akin to getting a handgun permit in New York City. It just doesn't happen.

Enter the Koreans, namely ShinSung. ShinSung has quietly been mass producing quality big-bore air rifles for quite some time now, but their latest offering, the .50 caliber Dragon Slayer, is sure to launch them from relative anonymity into the limelight. While there are lots of reasons this rifle should turn heads, the caliber selection doesn't

hurt. There are lots of cool things that start with the number fifty. Take for example the .50 BMG, the .50 Action Express, the .50-110 Sharps, and the rapper, .50 Cent…okay, so not all things that start with .50 are to my liking, but the new Dragon Slayer sure is.

These rifles are being made exclusively for Pyramyd Air. Pyramyd is offering two versions, the first being just the basic rifle; the second, a full-blown, ready-to-whack kit complete with a massive Leapers 4-16 x 50mm scope with illuminated reticle, a side-mounted laser, an adjustable bipod and a hard case. Since I was already getting strange looks from my significant other on why I was ordering a .50 caliber "pellet gun," I decided to go ahead and get one with all the bells and whistles.

When the Dragon Slayer arrived, I was impressed with its overall craftsmanship. At first the rifle looks massive, (and it ain't small by any stretch of the imagination) but it balances well and feels good in the hand, and the stock, even thought it looks radical, fits extremely well to my 6'1" frame. The barrel

The complete Dragon Slayer package comes with a bipod, Leaper's scope and a laser.

is deeply blued and looks substantial, even with a half-inch hole bored into it. In short, I was excited to get some air into it and get it to the range.

How It Works

Big-bore air guns operate on a totally different principle than most people associate with air rifles. Most airguns found in an average household today either operate with a spring/piston design (the common break-barrel) or are pneumatic (the old reliable pump-up) or run on compressed CO_2 canisters. In order to generate enough pressure and air volume to be effective at pushing a big slug, big-bore airguns typically are of the Pre-Charged Pneumatic variety (PCP for short). They have a high-pressure air tank mounted somewhere on the rifle (generally under the barrel but sometimes in the buttstock or replacing it entirely). This air tank is capable of holding extremely highly pressurized air, in the case of the Dragon Slayer around 3,000 psi.

Now 3,000 psi is a figure worth putting in perspective. An average truck tire has between 35 to 55 psi, while a garage air compressor generally generates around 100 psi and a Sheridan Blue Streak pump-up pellet rifle gets to about 1,000 psi. So how does one get 3,000 psi? There are really only three ways: scuba tanks, high-pressure hand pumps and an electric high-pressure air generator. Of the three, the scuba tank is probably the most effective and easiest to use. However, if you don't live

Author Mike Schoby testing the Dragon Slayer at the range. For testing, three shots were fired before the pressure tank was topped off to ensure maximum consistency.

by a scuba shop, a hand pump is pretty convenient, as well as easy to take afield. The generator, while effective, is way too costly for the average shooter.

Loading the Dragon Slayer

Loading the Dragon Slayer is pretty straightforward. I chose to use a Swedish-made FX hand pump I already had. Pumping up the tank initially took a couple hundred of pumps, but once some pressure built up, it went rather quickly.

After the rifle was fully charged, the mechanism was simple. The charging handle (bolt) is located on the right side of the action. Pulling the charging handle rearward opens the breech and cocks the trigger, allowing you to insert a standard .50-caliber lead round ball into the action port on the left side and return the charging handle to the full forward position – much like

A close up of the built-in pressure gauge on the air tank. It accurately shows available pressure to 3,000 psi.

working a bolt on a bolt action rifle. The safety lever is located inside the trigger guard and is designed to move either left or right for safe or fire.

Once the safety is removed, you merely aim, fire and repeat. It is that simple. I found that a fully-charged air tank provided about five shots of reasonable velocity and reduced the pressure by only around 10 percent. By always working within the top 10 percent of the pressure range, standard deviation remained fairly consistent, and it was easy to top it off with a couple dozen pumps. Upon further testing I found the best groups, most power and least deviation to occur in the first three shots.

Accuracy Test

While most shooters are excited about the bore diameter and power level of the Dragon Slayer, the real excitement comes from downrange. In the accuracy department, the Dragon Slayer is excellent. To be honest, I had my doubts about the accuracy potential of a .50-caliber round ball, but I shouldn't

have. At 25 yards, I fired three shots that looked like the proverbial cloverleaf. They were so close it appeared to be one ragged hole. Moving out to 50 yards, the group opened up somewhat but stayed tight enough to hit a golf ball every time. Of course the longer the shot string sequence, the more deviation occurred, but when testing with the first three shots on a newly charged tank the accuracy was astounding.

The loading port of the Dragon Slayer is intentionally short and is designed to accommodate commonly available lead round balls (intended for .50 muzzleloaders) or swaged pellets. The two varieties that Pyramyd sells are either a 225-gr. roundnose or a 200-gr. hollowpoint. While some added energy could possibly be obtained from the pellets due to their greater mass, I liked the accuracy and velocity increase offered by the 180-gr. round balls. Also, they're extremely economical to boot.

So How Powerful Is the 'Slayer?

When it comes to production air rifles, the Dragon Slayer is a powerhouse, producing around 200 fpe (ft. lbs. of energy) at the muzzle. To put this in perspective, most .177 and .22 spring-action pellet rifles generate between 15 and 35 fpe, with some magnum models putting out around 60 fpe, so the .50 Dragon Slayer opens new worlds for air charged hunters. But if a shooter thinks that just because the Dragon Slayer fires the same projectile as a .50 muzzleloader it will have similar energy, he is sadly mistaken. When propelled by a 100-gr. charge of black powder, that same .50 lead ball produces over 1,500 fpe at the muzzle.

All that being said, I did some field penetration tests using wet newspaper and hard 3/4" boards to simulate bone, and the penetration was pretty spectacular. While velocity is good for shocking game, when too much velocity is applied to a pure lead slug, penetration can often suffer as the round projectile will tend to flatten out, "pancaking" on the surface. However, when pushed at the modest velocities of the Dragon Slayer, the ball only slightly deforms and penetrates very well. Penetration of six to eight inches in wet newspaper was pretty consistently achieved, as was shooting through as much as 1.5 inches of hard board.

So how does this translate on game? To begin with, the Dragon Slayer is more than adequate for any small game and is very viable on predators such as fox,

The charging handle (or bolt) works very similiar to that of a bolt action rifle. Pull it back to open the breech, which also cocks the trigger.

raccoon and coyote. On large game, say up to deer-sized animals, I have no doubt if ranges were kept short (under 40 yards) and only broadside shots were taken, the Dragon Slayer would be more than adequate where legal. (Note: Most states do not allow the use of air rifles for anything larger than small game and predators but, where the practice is legal, hunters have been successfully using the Dragon Slayer on a whole host of deer sized game as well as various African antelopes).

On this particular afternoon, the basic Dragon Slayer .50 is available from Pyramyd Air (PyramydAir.com) at just over $600, with the entire kit (minus compressor or pump) going for close to $800. True, that's more expensive than most higher-end air rifles, but if you want to shoot a big-bore air rifle, it's about as economical as it gets.

ShinSung Dragon Slayer Specifications

Weight:	8.80 lbs
Barrel Length:	20.5 inches
Overall Length:	41.30 inches
Capacity:	1 round
Barrel:	Steel, fully rifled
Front Sight:	None
Rear Sight:	None
Scope Mount:	11mm dovetail
Trigger:	Two-stage adjustable
Buttpad:	Rubber
Action:	Sidelever
Powerplant:	Pre-charged pneumatic 3,000 PSI
Price:	$619.00 rifle only, $799 for the kit
Available at:	www.Pyramidair.com

The Yugo Underfolder field-strips simply.

TEST FIRE

Century International Arms M-70 AB2T Yugo Underfolder

BY PETE PHILIPPE
of www.GunWebsites.com and www.AK47review.com, with assistance from Scott Loomis

The Century M-70 AB2T Yugo Underfolder is a well-made, accurate and historically interesting version of the AK47 (Kalashnikov) rifle. Shooters and collectors looking for an affordable AK47 would do well with this rifle from Century International Arms (CIA).

The M-70 AB2T is a modern version of the Yugoslavian Kalashnikov with an underfolder shoulder stock. The Yugoslavians started building their version of the Kalashnikov in the 1960s with the M64. The M-70 AB1 & M-70 AB2 are later Yugoslavian versions of the Soviet Kalashnikov rifles.

The Yugoslavians added some distinctive features to the standard Kalashnikov including a thicker RPK-style receiver with "bulges" on either side of the forward receiver for strength, a folding grenade sight with a gas system shutoff on the gas block, a ventilated gas tube, three air cooling gaps between the upper and lower handguards instead of two, no "swell" in the lower handguard, a black plastic pistol grip with thumbrest, night sights and a push-button lock on the receiver cover to keep it in place while using the rifle as a grenade launcher. These features make the Yugoslavian Kalashnikov an interesting rifle for many collectors.

The CIA Yugo M-70 AB2T has an underfolding shoulder stock. The clever design allows the rifle to be folded even with 30-round magazine inserted. It can also be fired with the stock extended or when it is folded. There is a cutout on the inside of the right stock strut

so that the safety clears and has room to operate when the stock is folded.

The M-70 AB2T's black synthetic hanguards and pistol grip retain some features of the original Yugoslavian Kalashnikov but give this rifle a modern look and make it comfortable to shoot.

The CIA reproduction is built in the United States with many quality Yugoslavian and US-made parts including a receiver made by DC Industries, Inc.; a barrel made by Green Mountain; a trigger group made by Tapco; and black plastic handguards and pistol grip. The parts are assembled into the rifle and given a blemish-free grey parkerized finish. The US-made receiver is marked only on the rifle's underside so it does not clutter the clean lines along the sides of the rifle. The receiver is stamped with:

> Century International Arms, Inc.,
> MOD: M70AB2
> Cal 7.62 x 39
> DC Industries, Inc.
> St. Paul, Minnesota, USA

The CIA M-70 AB2T is 34-1/4" long overall with 16-1/2" barrel. Weight is 7.5 lbs. empty. The M-70 is unique in the respect that its receiver is heavier and made with thicker gauge steel than other Kalashnikov rifles. The rugged, time-tested design of the Kalashnikov allows it to work under extreme conditions, and the CIA M-70 AB2T lives up to the reputation of its illustrious Soviet predecessor.

A simple disassembly of the receiver cover, recoil spring, bolt carrier and bolt allow the shooter access to all the areas of the rifle that need periodic cleaning and maintenance. The included manual explains safety rules and use of the rifle along with instructions on how to disassemble the rifle for cleaning and maintenance.

Unique Yugoslavian Kalashnikov Parts

Using the Kalashnikov operating system on the DC Industries receiver offers the same thicker "RPK-style" receiver as the original Yugoslavian rifle. The US-made barrel by Green Mountain is not chrome-lined, but neither were those of the original Yugoslavian M-70 barrels. In this way CIA has created a close reproduction that is legal and affordable in the USA.

Most of the CIA M-70 AB2T rifles still retain the factory markings on the rear sight block that they bore when they left the Zastava factory. Some are marked with: "ZASTAVA-KRAGUJEVAC, YUGOSLAVIA"; some aren't.

An obvious addition to the Yugoslavian Kalashnikov is the grenade sight and gas cut-off. When the grenade launching sight is extended (opened), it cuts off gas flow to the piston. This keeps the bolt from cycling normally. The grenade launching sight is used to align the rifle at an upward angle to lob grenades long distances. The grenade launcher itself (not included) is a muzzle attachment which simply replaces the slant brake and holds rifle-launched grenades on the muzzle. Rubber practice grenades that work with 7.62x39mm blanks are available from time to time at gun shows and on internet auction sites. They can be a lot of fun to shoot.

The CIA Yugo AK's have the Tapco G2 trigger. The DCI receiver is cut for a double-hook trigger (note the cutout on both sides of the receiver at the top of the trigger). Another feature unique to the Yugoslavian Kalashnikov is the built-in flip-up night sights Both the front and rear night sights fold down when not in use. The glow-in-the-dark radium-painted dots are no longer available on most of the CIA M-70 AB2Ts, but it's not too difficult to repaint new luminescent dots.

Shooting Tests at 25 and 50 yards

In order to test the accuracy of the M-70 AB2T, we took a random rifle off the shelf of a local gun shop (not one handpicked by CIA) out to the local shooting spot and shot a few types of 7.62x39 ammunition at 25 yards and again at 50 yards. Granted, this was hardly a scientific test, but we wanted to show how well this rifle would do out of the box in the hands of a typical shooter. We did use the same shooter shooting the same ammo out of the same magazines at both distances.

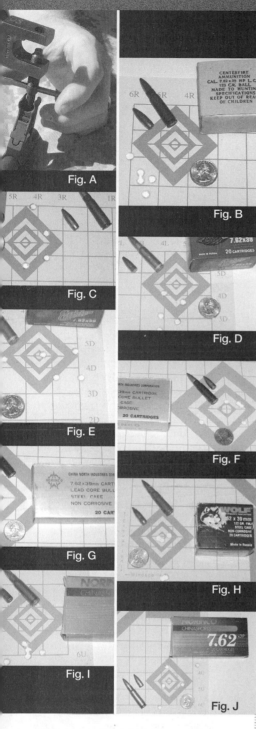

Fig. A

Fig. B

Fig. C

Fig. D

Fig. E

Fig. F

Fig. G

Fig. H

Fig. I

Fig. J

The test procedure was as follows: We loaded five magazines with five types of 7.62x39mm ammo, using a mix of currently available ammo and some popular types that are no longer imported. We loaded ten rounds of each brand of ammo into each magazine.

The shooter used the iron sights on the rifle. He shot from a prone position using the magazine as a monopod, with no sand bags, no shooting rest. We wanted to simulate typical "field conditions," so no other shooting aids were used. Our shooter shot five rounds of each brand at the 25-yard target, then again at the 50-yard target. We didn't need to adjust the sights on this rifle, but we took a Kalashnikov (AK/SKS) sight tool with us just in case we needed it. Our version from Tapco (www.tapco.com) can adjust both the windage and elevation.

Our tests showed that this rifle was very accurate out of the box, as the accompanying photos show.

(Fig. A) We didn't need to adjust the sights on this rifle, but we took a Kalashnikov (AK/SKS) sight tool with us anyway. This version from Tapco (www.tapco.com) can adjust both the windage and elevation.

(Fig. B) The Klimovsk ammo shot well at 25 yards with a tight group a little less than two inches.

(Fig. C) At 50 yards the Kilmovsk ammo did open up a bit to about two inches with a called flyer.

(Fig. D) The Golden Bear also shot well at 25 yards with a bit larger group than the others, but still under two inches.

(Fig. E) The Golden Bear actually stayed fairly consistent at 50 yards and was one of our tighter groups at three inches.

(Fig. F & G) This Chinese lead core ammo held consistent groups under three inches at both distances.

(Fig. H) The Wolf ammo shot well but inconsistently. Three of the five rounds were within an inch, but two flyers created a 2"+ group.

(Fig. I) At 50 yards the Wolf opened up to our largest group at just over four inches.

(Fig. J) The second brand of Chinese lead core ammo shot less consistently than the other. At 25 yards the group was tight and under two inches, but but it opened up to almost four inches at 50 yards.

Note on the Ammunition Tested

All Chinese firearms and ammo were banned from importation in 1994, so some of these brands of ammo are harder to find today. Most of the ammunition in this shooting comparison is non-reloadable steel case with non-corrosive Berdan primers.

Klimovsk 123-gr. H.P.
Steel case, lead core. Klimovsk Stamping Plant (Russia)
Note: The Russian Klimovsk ammo is not as easy to find as Wolf or the various flavors of Barnaul "Bear" brand ammo. But the Klimovsk was available at many gun shows and at online auctions and websites for sale for a long time and is occasionally still available in bulk.

Golden Bear 123-gr. FMJ
Bimetal brass plated steel case, lead core.Made at the JSC Barnaul Machine-Tool Plant (Russia).
Note: This is one of the easier brands to find at the time this article is being written (late 2008). It shoots consistently and is fairly inexpensive.

Norinco / China North Industries Corp.
Steel case, lead core "match" ammunition. Made in China.
Note: Norinco ammo has not been imported for many years. However it is still possible to find Chinese 7.62x39 ammo from time to time.

Wolf Performance 122-gr. FMJ
Steel case, lead core. Made at the Tula Cartridge Works (Russia).
Note: Wolf ammo is another brand that is fairly common and available at the time of this review. There are other brands from Wolf including different box designs, case styles, bullet weights and bullet types (e.g., FMJ, HP).

Norinco / Chinasports 122-gr FMJ
Copperwashed steel case, lead core. Made in China.
Note: Another Chinese brand that is more difficult to find.

Final Thoughts

According to Century Arms, the company has manufacured more than 15,000 M-70s so far and over 12,000 of them are the M-70 AB2T model. The M-70 AB2T should still be available for perhaps another year. With a street price generally between $600 and $800 at this writing and considering its trouble-free performance, the Century Arms M70AB2T Yugo Underfolder represents an extremely good buy for the budget-conscious AK fancier.

Acknowledgments
The author wishes to thank the following firms and individuals for their help in preparing this testfire:
• Tucson Gun and Western Artifacts (www.TucsonGun.net)
• Century International Arms (www.CenturyArms.com)
• Members of The AK Forum (www.theAKforum.net)
• Additional technical information provided by the KCA (Kalashnikov Collectors Association) (www.KalashnikovCollectorsAssociation.com)

RUGER GETS SMALL: The LCP

BY PATRICK SWEENEY

The buzz for weeks before the announcement was that Ruger was going to unveil something new. I had an inside track, as I had been told to assemble a bunch of .380 ammo for an upcoming article. I was prepared for a Ruger .380, but not this one. I envisioned something nearly as big as a 1911, and as indestructible as a *Koenigstiger*. What I found was a flat, compact, easily-carried .380 that would do for daily carry in the hottest of climates.

The Ruger LCP is all of 9.4 oz., with a 2.75" barrel and a six-round magazine holding .380 Auto ammunition. Unlike some very small .380s and .32s, it does not require a single type of ammo, but can fire any and all .380 you can find. The sights are fixed and cast/machined into the top of the slide. The construction is interesting, using a steel slide and barrel (a locked-breech barrel, by the way, not typical in pocket .380s) and a glass-filled polymer frame with an aluminum chassis inside of it.

The double-action trigger is easy enough to shoot well, but heavy enough to keep you out of trouble packing it. Please use a good holster, and don't just put it in your pocket to carry. That's a really good way to get the nickname "lefty" or "the dear departed."

You don't buy a pocket .380 so you can go out to the range and shoot buckets of ammo. However, you do buy it to protect yourself, and for that you need a reliable firearm. To that end I put a bunch of ammo through the LCP to see

how it would fare. In a word: marvelously. First, the pistol really is too small for my hands. I can get hold of it, but that hold is not pretty nor is it comfortable. The lack of external safeties is a good idea, for I'm not sure I could work them and still hold the pistol. Those of you with smaller hands will actually be better-suited to shooting the Ruger LCP than I was, an interesting change of situation. However, if you want ultra-concealable, you have to put up with a small handgun. The recoil is not great, although with the hotter loads it can be a bit sharp. Again, if you want the benefits of a really compact gun, you get them with the drawbacks of a small gun.

One example is the Cor-Bon 90-gr. JHP. In most cases, when Cor-Bon prints a velocity figure on a box, you can take it to the bank. If they say it is 30% of lightspeed, it usually is. However, ask-

Short barrels means lower velocities, and that means not all bullets will expand. The excellent XTP just wasn't pushed fast enough to do its typical job of expansion.

Little guns can be work to shoot, and the Ruger LCP is one of the littlest guns.

These Gold Dots expanded, but you get expansion at the cost of penetration. You'll have to decide which you prefer.

at the recoil as the Cor-Bon ammo tried its best to deliver the printed speed.

As in so many instances, Hornady ammo was superbly accurate. I get some flak from others for testing every handgun at 25 yards, pocket pistols included, but the Ruger did not let me down. The velocity/accuracy chart is not a misprint, and you should not be snide at four inches. Remember, this is with a pocket .380, a 2.75" barrel, and fixed sights, while pressing through a long double-action trigger. That kind of performance is to be admired, not rejected. The Hornady XTP ammunition shot brilliantly, and their new Critical Defense was not too shabby either.

The rest of the ammo, FMJ and Gold Dots, worked as well as the rest. You'd expect jacketed round-nose ammo to feed, and here you would not be disappointed. Some find Gold Dots to be a bit chancy in some of their guns. I have not, and in the LCP it worked flawlessly. Well, flawlessly with one exception. The ATK Frangible ammo had a peculiar problem: The second shot, first feeding after firing, would always jam, and always in the same way. The rest of the magazine would not, nor would any other type of ammo. I figure it is either me or the ammo. So I do not plan on having a 100% reliable pocket pistol if I ever have to go into a training shoot-house with frangible ammo and the LCP. I'm not worried.

Partway into my testing Ruger announced a recall of the LCP. They had reports of a very few pistols that, when dropped on their muzzles on a hard surface, would occasionally discharge. In the customary Ruger fashion

they stepped up to the bar and told everyone who owned one they'd get a free fix. And a spare magazine. I had testing to do, so I made sure I didn't drop it before I could ship it back. You can easily check to see if the one you're looking at is either fixed, or past the change. Those with a 370 prefix that have been fixed will have a small diamond engraved on the new hammer. No diamond? Contact Ruger to send it in. All LCP pistols built after that were begun with a new prefix of 371. Oh, as an interesting aside, the aluminum chassis inside the polymer is the firearm of record. That polymer thing you hold? Just an extra part, but not the firearm itself.

Ruger barrels are all cut with enfield-style rifling and thus have no problems with lead bullets. So I tried a few reloads, stuff I'd had on hand long after I'd given up reloading for the .380. Those too fed with ease and worked without problem. In all, I've put something like 1,200 rounds through this cute little blaster and had not a problem. Well, I've had the problem of hanging on to it, it being so small and all. There's also the work of wrestling 1,200 rounds into the magazine, but after a while you get used to it. Not that the magazine is troublesome, just small.

For practice and cost, you can shoot FMJ or reloaded lead bullets. But for defense, you'll probably want JHPs. Some might not, and will depend on penetration to get the job done. For those willing to give up a few inches of penetration for expansion, you can count on some, if not all, the expansion you want. I tested a few loads in ballistic gelatin, and if you are willing to depend on nine inches, you can use expanding bullets. If you need more you have to go with hardball.

Once you get over the idea of packing a big gun on your freshly-acquired concealed carry permit, you'll start looking for smaller ones. The Ruger is perhaps the smallest .380, at a very attractive price point, that you can consider.

Four inches at 25 yards is plenty good for defense. The LCP can deliver if you can.

Note the lower lugs on the barrel. The LCP is a locked-breech pocket pistol. How often do you see that?

ing a 90-gr. JHP to do 1050 fps out of a barrel so short is asking for too much. I was not surprised when the chrono read less, but I was also not surprised

Chronograph Results *in ballistic gelatin*

Ammunition	Muzzle Velocity (fps)	Group at 25 Yards (")	Penetration (")
Hornady 90-gr. XTP	772	4	9-10
Hornady 90-gr. Critical Defense	827	4.5	11
ATK Frang 75-gr.	1085	6	not tested
Blaser Brass 95-gr. FMJ	798	5	12
CCI 90-gr. GDHP	906	4.5	8
Blazer Al. 95-gr. TMJ	811	6	13
Cor-Bon 90-gr. JHP	978	5	9

TEST FIRE

Remington's R-25

BY JACOB EDSON

A thing of beauty is a joy forever: Remington's "beauty shot" for the new R-25 hunting rifle.

Maybe it was inevitable. Rifle making is a business after all, and it simply makes sense for the country's largest gunmaker to jump into the fastest growing segment of the firearm market. It really wasn't all that surprising, then, two years ago when Remington (which happens to be owned by the Cerberus Capital Management, the same company that owns Bushmaster Firearms) released its R-15 rifle. Still, it was big news.

Remington's R-15 really legitimized AR-style rifles as mainstream sporting platforms – something AR fans have been working hard at for years. Remington's marketing team helped, offering the gun only in camouflage coloration to avoid the sometimes-nasty language heaped on so-called "black rifles." But Big Green wasn't done. After Cerberus also acquired DPMS/Panther Arms, a leader in the market for larger-framed ARs chambered for big game rounds, Remington announced it would release a new R-25 rifle in .243 Win., 7mm-08 Rem., and .308 Win. The gun, the R-25, began shipping this year.

This is it, AR fans! Whether you are an admirer of the Remington, Bushmaster and DPMS models or you prefer ArmaLite, or Colt, or one of the more than 60 other manufacturers of AR rifles and parts, Remington's R-25 is exactly what we have been waiting for. Basically, the R-25 is the final exclamation point announcing the AR platform's relevance as a big game sporting rifle.

The rifle itself (more on that in a minute) isn't groundbreaking. But the fact that it is being offered by possibly the most respected maker of hunting guns in the world? That is. Now, the R-25 is available for all of us who appreciate AR-style guns. But it's also right there in the faces of hunters and shooters who undoubtedly had heard about the platform but had never really thought about it. And while the buzz in AR circles might have peaked with the R-15, the R-25 has created its own buzz in a group of gun owners who previously weren't talking about the platform.

That includes hunting writers. Not long after Remington announced the R-25, I contacted Linda Powell, Remington's press relations manager, to see if she could provide one to test fire. Powell said she would do her best, but demand for the test rifles was extremely high. It seemed every hunting writer in the country wanted to try out the new gun, many of whom had never fired an AR. My hope was to land an R-25 chambered in .308 Win. in time for Wisconsin's gun deer season. My position on the waiting

As it happened, the R-25's testfire conditions were reasonably close to what a deer hunter might encounter.

list didn't make that happen, but Powell was able to rush me her SHOT Show gun in early December as long as I promised to have it back by the end of the month. What arrived was a very respectable and well-designed hunting version of the original AR-10. Here's what I found:

My first impression when I opened the factory-supplied hard case was that this is indeed a hunting rifle. The Mossy Oak Treestand coating is sharp. It covers the forged aluminum upper and lower, as well as the turned aluminum handguard with a much more scratch- and wear-resistant film than I imagined. Still, I am glad they left the barrel, gas block and control surfaces black. For one thing, I think it looks cool. But more importantly, you can find the rifle if you set it down against a brush pile.

The four-round magazine adds to the hunter-friendly styling and is a smart choice, because some states limit the number of rounds that can be loaded in a big game hunting rifle. The camo coating also seems to contribute to a tight mesh between the upper and lower receiver, with almost no slop. The entire rifle has a tight feel, and the action was tight and crisp.

The 20" free-floated, button-rifled ChroMoly barrel is also a good choice. One knock on ARs chambered in .308 Win., (especially those with 16" or 18" barrels) has been that the barrel is not long enough to achieve maximum efficiency from the round. However, many bolt-action .308s come with a 22" barrel, and you certainly aren't giving up much performance by dropping those additional two inches. What you get is a more balanced gun that is easy to carry, even at almost 9 pounds. As expected, the interior of the barrel appeared well polished, without any blemishes.

The flattop receiver sports a full-length Picatinny rail for unlimited optics mounting options. *Gun Digest Magazine* advertising representative Ted Willems and I mounted a Burris Fullfield II LRS in 3-9x40mm for our day at the range. With standard high-mount rings, the optic was at the perfect height for a firm cheek meld to the buttstock.

I also thought the length of pull was about perfect for me, and I can sometimes be particular about the length of my stocks. Part of this pleasant fit, I'm sure, can be attributed to the in-line design of all ARs. They just always seem to sit better in a variety of shooting positions because the rifle's center runs from the muzzle to buttstock in one straight line.

Remington equips the R-25 with a single-stage "hunting" trigger. If you've never shot an AR before, you might find it slightly creepy, but the trigger on our test rifle did break cleanly at 5 lbs. The trigger isn't adjustable like the new X-Mark Pro trigger now offered on Big Green's venerable Model 700 line, but a bunch of companies are offering aftermarket models if you want to give the trigger a tune up. Really, though, this trigger isn't bad, and it will probably only bother shooters who are used to finely-tuned target guns.

The rifle performed flawlessly at the range, and conditions certainly weren't optimal on the 10° F day Willems and I chose to test the rifle. We did not experience any cycling problems; the brass and primers all appeared clean and accuracy was much better than I expected considering the conditions.

Willems and I ran through about 100 rounds of various Remington and Hornady .308 loads so quickly we didn't realize where it all went. That's probably my biggest complaint with the gun: It's so easy and fun to shoot, you can burn up several hundred dollars of ammunition before you know what happened. The recoil is certainly less than on a lightweight bolt-action .308 Win., and in all honesty (if someone else is supplying the ammo) I could shoot that gun all day long.

The rifle produced sub-1.5 MOA accuracy with all the ammo we tried at 100 yards and sub-1 MOA accuracy with most of the match-grade ammunition. Personally, I was more happy to see that the barrel retained its accuracy with the rounds this gun was created to be fed – expanding hunting bullets – than with the match ammo.

I also tried the rifle from a variety of positions. Again, the fit and balance were excellent. I shot the R-25 better offhand than any of my bolt-action hunting rifles.

A few other features are worth noting. The grip and stock-placed sling swivels are a nice standard feature for a hunting rifle, especially considering that with a scope, mounts and full magazine of ammo the R-25 can push into the 10-lb. range. And though we certainly didn't have a great need for it in December, the fluted barrel will be appreciated in warmer climates. However, the grooves aren't overly deep because the barrel is already pretty slim compared to some of the fluted heavy barrels I've seen. The deep recessed crown is nice, because hunters are notorious for finding ways to damage the crown of their barrel, which can severely limit accuracy.

Of course, one of the greatest attributes of any AR is the ability to customize it. The R-25 lower is compatible with all aftermarket AR .308 Win. type magazines and accessories. Remington

The proof is in the paper. The R-25 shot this respectable five-shot group at 100 yards with hunting ammo under just about the worst possible conditions.

currently only offers complete rifles, but a hunter could easily purchase a DPMS (or some other brand) upper to convert one rifle into two, or three different calibers. I'm thinking .308 Winchester. for deer, .338 Federal for bears and .243 Winchester for coyotes.

To sum it up, the R-25 isn't a revolutionary take on the AR platform. But it is a good, solid hunting version that is simply a blast to shoot. It has good accuracy, it has features that should sit perfectly with the gun's intended user – and, perhaps most importantly, it further breaks down the stereotypes often laid upon a great design.

Editor's Note: American humorist Robert Henry Newell (1836-1901) was a contemporary of Mark Twain. His pen name, "Orpheus C. Kerr," was a pun on the phrase "Office Seeker," which refers to a political appointee who advances on the basis of his connections rather than his talents. In this brief satire, first published in 1863 in the form of a letter to a friend, Newell pokes fun at the U. S. Ordnance Department and the military procurement process in general. Not much has changed, has it?

Civil War Naval Artillery

BY ORPHEUS C. KERR

By invitation of a well-known official, I visited the Navy Yard yesterday, and witnessed the trial of some newly-invented rifled cannon. The trial was of short duration, and the jury brought in a verdict of "innocent of any intent to kill."

The first gun tried was similar to those used in the Revolution, except that it had a larger touch-hole, and the carriage was painted green, instead of blue. This novel and ingenious weapon was pointed at a target about sixty yards distant. It didn't hit it, and as nobody saw any ball, there was much perplexity expressed. A midshipman did say that he thought the ball must have run out of the touch-hole when they loaded up, for which he was instantly expelled from the service.

After a long search without finding the ball, there was some thought of summoning the Naval Retiring Board to decide on the matter, when somebody happened to look into the mouth of the cannon, and discovered that the ball hadn't gone out at all. The inventor said this would happen some times, especially if you didn't put a brick over the touch-hole when you fired the gun.

The Government was so pleased with this explanation, that it ordered forty of the guns on the spot, at two hundred thousand dollars apiece. The guns to be furnished as soon as the war is over.

The next weapon tried was Jink's double back-action revolving cannon for ferry-boats. It consists of a heavy bronze tube, revolving on a pivot, with both ends open, and a touch-hole in the middle. While one gunner puts a load in at one end, another puts in a load at the other end, and one touch-hole serves for both. Upon applying the match, the gun is whirled swiftly round on a pivot, and both balls fly out in circles, causing great slaughter on both sides.

This terrible engine was aimed at the target with great accuracy; but as the gunner has a large family dependent on him for support, he refused to apply the match. The Government was satisfied without firing, and ordered six of the guns at a million dollars apiece. The guns to be furnished in time for our next war.

The last weapon subjected to trial was a mountain howitzer of a new pattern. The inventor explained that its great advantage was, that it required no powder. In battle it is placed on the top of a high mountain, and a ball slipped loosely into it. As the enemy passes the foot of the mountain, the gunner in charge tips over the howitzer, and the ball rolls down the side of the mountain into the midst of the doomed foe. The range of this terrible weapon depends greatly on the height of the mountain and the distance to its base.

The Government ordered forty of these mountain howitzers at a hundred thousand dollars apiece, to be planted on the first mountains discovered in the enemy's country.

These are great times for gunsmiths, my boy; and if you find any old cannon around the junk-shops, just send them along.

There is much sensation in nautical circles arising from the immoral conduct of the rebel privateers; but public feeling has been somewhat easier since the invention of a craft for capturing the pirates, by an ingenious Connecticut chap.

Yesterday he exhibited a small model of it at a cabinet meeting, and explained it thus:

"You will perceive," says he to the President*, "that the machine itself will only be four times the size of the *Great Eastern***, and need not cost over a few million dollars.

"I have only got to discover one thing before I can make it perfect. You will observe that it has a steam-engine on board. This engine works a pair of immense iron clamps, which are let down into the water from the extreme end of a very lengthy horizontal spar. Upon approaching the pirate, the captain orders the engineer to put on steam. Instantly the clamps descend from the end of the spar and clutch the privateer athwart-ships. Then the engine is reversed, the privateer is lifted bodily out of the water, the spar swings around over the deck, and the pirate ship is let down into the hold by the run. Then shut your hatches, and you have ship and pirates safe and sound."

The President's gothic features lighted up beautifully at the words of the great inventor; but in a moment they assumed an expression of doubt, and says he:

"But how are you going to manage, if the privateer fires upon you while you are doing this?"

"My dear sir," says the inventor, "I told you I had only one thing to discover before I could make the machine perfect, and that's it."

So you see, my boy, there's a prospect of our doing something on the ocean next century, and there's only one thing in the way of our taking in pirates by the cargo.

Last evening a new brigadier-general, aged ninety-four years, made a speech to Regiment Five, Mackerel Brigade, and then furnished each man with a lead pencil. He said that, as the Government was disappointed about receiving some provisions it had ordered for the troops, those pencils were intended to enable them to draw their rations as usual.

I got a very big pencil, my boy, and have lived on a sheet of paper ever since.

Yours, pensively,

ORPHEUS C. KERR

* Abraham Lincoln, who had a genuine interest in weapons design.
** Launched in 1858, the *S. S. Great Eastern* was the largest steam sail ship ever built (705' long).

With justifiable pride, we present this truly monumental work by cast-bullet master Kenneth Walters.

THE ENCYCLOPEDIA OF
Bullet Casting

BY KENNETH WALTERS

Introduction

The Encyclopedia of Bullet Casting is a really big table *[Editor's note: He ain't kiddin'!]* that contains physical dimensions and casting rate data for hundreds and hundreds of bullet moulds using many of the popular bullet casting alloys. Bullet casting rate data has never been available before. That is really odd because, as we'll see shortly, rate data can save you a lot of money. Even cast bullet physical dimensional data has been limited. Manufacturer's catalogues, for example, never tell you a bullet's length. That too is odd because you need bullet lengths in order to figure out if a particular bullet is going to be accurate in your rifle. We'll examine this in detail shortly. And the internet makes all this information even more important because most internet bullet mould ads don't tell you much about the mould being advertised. The Encyclopedia of Bullet Casting solves all these problems and more.

Before the advent of the internet I saw maybe two very old seven-cavity Ideal Armory moulds in 20+ years and I never saw an old 10-cavity Cramer mould. Moulds like these from long forgotten companies, however, are now readily available on the internet. Where can you find data about moulds from long forgotten companies? In the Encyclopedia of Bullet Casting.

Now, of course, virtually all the companies who make bullet moulds have their catalogues online. Those catalogues, however, only cover currently-made moulds. Discontinued ones are not listed. But the Encyclopedia may have them.

The Encyclopedia of Bullet Casting contains detailed information on over 600 bullet moulds, both old and new. Well over 600,000 bullets were cast to generate this information using over 10 tons of bullet alloy. It took me over 20 years to do this. Though no listing of this type could ever be complete, the Encyclopedia covers a lot. It is, in fact, the only time this sort of thing has ever been done. Most of what I'm going to discuss, however, isn't the data in the Encyclopedia but rather how to use it. I'll show you how to pick a bullet for a particular gun, how to maximize your bullet production, how to save money and a lot more. Also because I like really strange guns, you'll find bullets for a lot of weird firearms in the Encyclopedia. The regular stuff is, of course, covered in great detail, too, but bullets for unusual firearms are very well represented.

One last point before we get started. The greatest use for this information, I suspect, will be looking up physical dimensions and bullet casting rate data for bullet moulds advertised on the web. Ads on the web for bullet moulds almost always tell you virtually nothing about the moulds being offered for sale. Why that is true I don't know but it is. The Encyclopedia, however, can easily solve this problem. But even though this is probably the most practical use of this information, you can, as we'll see shortly, use it for a lot more.

Data Layout

The Encyclopedia of Bullet Casting is a huge table, each line of which is broken down into the sections indicated below. The title of each section is underlined. Next to each underlined heading there is, usually, a brief description of what that particular piece of information means. Data within the Encyclopedia is laid out by increasing bullet diameter and, for a constant diameter, by increasing bullet weight because that is the most convenient form for someone trying to figure out what bullet mould to buy for a particular gun.

Mould Block Description

Maker: The name of the firm that made the mould. As many of these moulds are quite old, some of these firms no longer exist. Old moulds, however, can be found on the internet.

Mould: The name given to the mould by its maker.

Cavities: The number of cavities in the mould. This is sometimes called block size. A mould with four or more cavities, incidentally, is called a gang mould.

Comments: See discussion in text.

Used Together: See discussion in text.

Material: The material that the mould was made from, aluminum (A), brass (B) or iron (I).

Experimental Data

Alloy: Lead, linotype, wheelweights (WW), 30 to 1 lead to tin by weight (30 to 1) and a mystery alloy (MA). A blank in this column indicates linotype.

Casting Time: How many hours a particular mould was studied. The normal casting study was exactly two hours long.

Total Bullets Cast

Visually Acceptable Bullets: the number of bullets that passed a very harsh visual inspection.

Experimental Results

Bullet Description

Average: Measurements taken on visually acceptable bullets.

Diameter

Weight

Length

Bullets Per Hour: Total Bullets Cast divided by Casting Time.

Visually Acceptable BPH (Bullets Per Hour): Visually Acceptable Bullets divided by Casting Time.

Rate Of Twist: discussed below.

There is one calculation for each of these bullets that I didn't include: the percentage that were visually acceptable. You can compute that by dividing the number in the column titled Visually Acceptable Bullets by the number in the column titled Total Bullets Cast. I didn't include this because I didn't want to suggest, however inadvertently, that one brand of mould block was better than another. Including the percent visually acceptable would, I thought, have been just too judgmental.

Most of the data is for bullets made from linotype. Linotype is 4 percent tin, 12 percent antimony and 84 percent lead by weight. Back when newspapers were printed using type, this is the alloy that that type was made from. My reason for using linotype so extensively is that its chemical composition never changes, so the linotype I bought when I started this study back in 1986 is exactly the same as the linotype I bought when this work was ending in 2008. Alloy consistency is absolutely vital in guaranteeing consistency in the dimensional and casting rate data. Guaranteeing consistency is also why all the casting studies were, except when there was an equipment failure, exactly two hours long. Alloys other than linotype show up in the Encyclopedia when they are the right alloy for the corresponding gun.

Now let's look at some of the phrases you'll see In the Encyclopedia in the Comments and Used Together columns. Here you'll occasionally see phrases such as "2 at once." When you see this in the Comments column, there will also be a number in the Used Together column. In these cases I'm using two non-identical blocks simultaneously. The number in the Used Together column helps you find the other block. There are also phrases like "1 in a 4" in the Comments column. That means that this particular bullet was made from one cavity in a four-cavity mould. Each of the three other cavities produced a different bullet. Once again the number in the Used Together column will lead you to the other bullets from such a mould. We'll look at examples like this later.

In the more complex casting studies, incidentally, time is always recorded but it is only recorded once per study. So if I was using several blocks simultaneously or if I was using a block with several different cavities cut into it, only one of the corresponding lines in the Encyclopedia will have an entry in the Casting Time column. The others will be left blank.

How To Read The Encyclopedia

Let's look at an example: the information provided in the first entry in the Encyclopedia for NEI mould number 31.224.

From the Mould Block Description section, under the heading "Maker" we see that Northeast Industrial (NEI) made this mould. Under the heading "Mould" we see that NEI's name for this mould is 31.224. According to the NEI naming convention, this mould should yield a 31 grain, 0.224" diameter bullet. The "1" in the "Cavities" column indicates that this was a single cavity mould. The "B" in the "Material" column means that this mould was made from brass.

From the section titled "Experimental Data," we see from the column titled "Alloy" that the alloy was linotype. Remember, linotype is indicated by a blank. The Casting Time was six hours. Since cast-

ing studies were almost always exactly two hours long, this mould was studied three times. During these three studies the Total Bullets Cast was 544 and the number of Visually Acceptable Bullets was 425.

From the section titled "Experimental Results," we see that the average Diameter for a visually acceptable bullet was 0.224", the average Weight was 28 grains and the average Length was 0.341". The Bullets Per Hour (BPH) is computed by dividing the Total Bullets Cast (544) by the Casting Time (6), or 90.67. The Visually Acceptable BPH (Bullets Per Hour) is computed by dividing the number of Visually Acceptable Bullets (425) by the Casting Time (6), or 70.84. Obviously these numbers have been rounded up in the Encyclopedia. Under the column titled the "Rate of Twist" is the rate of twist you'll need in your rifle to stabilize this bullet.

Rate Of Twist

On the internet you can find numerous sites that explain the rate of twist in great detail by looking up the "Greenhill Formula." Here I'm only going to cover the basics. The Greenhill formula (Rate of Twist = 125 x bullet diameter x bullet diameter ÷ bullet length), developed in the 1870's, is used to compute the rate of twist your rifle should have in order to stabilize a bullet. Those internet sites will also explain how to measure your rifle barrel's rate of twist. Greenhill values, incidentally, are only used with rifle projectiles.

Though some people go REALLY nuts over the fine print here, and there is a lot of fine print, don't. Just pick a bullet from the Encyclopedia that has a rate of twist as close to that in your rifle as you can.

Why include Greenhill calculations for all the bullets if these calculations are only used for rifle projectiles? Because that is a lot easier than trying to identify those bullets that could not possibly end up being used in a rifle.

Despite the Greenhill formula's popularity with cast bullet rifle shooters, bullet length measurements have never been available before. So if you are a fan of the Greenhill formula, the Encyclopedia is the only place where you are going to find all the data you need.

Does the Greenhill formula work? That's a really good but loaded question. Some very serious rifle shooters swear by it. Some swear at it. If I were younger and a really good rifle shot, it would be fascinating to do shooting studies to figure out just how reliable this idea is.

If you want a very interesting long-term project that would be of considerable value, be my guest.

Selecting A Rifle Bullet

When you want to select a mould for a particular gun, the best place to start is a *Lyman Reloading Handbook*. You should own at least two. You want a recent edition, #48 or later, and you want an early one, #47 or earlier. Lyman made major changes in their powder recommendations starting with their 48th edition. You want a copy of both of their sets of powder recommendations.

Start by looking your cartridge up in a Lyman Handbook. Note the recommended bullet weights and suggested sizing die. Then go to the Encyclopedia and look at all the entries for bullets whose diameters are between 0.007" inches below to 0.007" above Lyman's recommended sizing diameter. Remember that the Encyclopedia is laid out by increasing diameters, so finding this range is easy.

Why plus or minus 0.007" from Lyman's recommended sizing diameter? Because anything up to about 0.007" over Lyman's recommended diameter can be sized down using a lubricator/sizer and anything 0.007" or so below can be bumped up. I'll explain that shortly.

A sizing die in a lubricator/sizer can reduce a cast bullet's diameter by several thousands of an inch by just squeezing it. Squeezing a bullet by more than 0.007", however, is a pain. If you really have to do that, the only way I know of is to size the bullet twice using two slightly different diameter sizing dies and taking off several thousands of an inch with each sizing die. It would be a lot easier to buy a mould that cast a bullet that is closer to the desired diameter.

An undersized cast bullet can be bumped up. Just load the bullet into a cartridge and fire it. When the powder charge goes off and the bullet enters the rifling it will expand. It bumps up to the correct diameter because of the resistance to the rifling on the front end and the pressure of the expanding gas on the back.

What do you do if the cartridge of interest isn't covered in the Lyman Handbooks? Search the web. The best place to start is Accurate Arms' website (www.accuratepowder.com) because they will provide, on demand, modern smokeless loading data for virtually any cartridge firearm, even very old, long forgotten black powder guns.

One of my more accurate rifles is a

single shot Remington-style rolling block made by Lone Star and chambered in .50-70. It has a rate of twist of one turn in 26 inches. According to the *47th Lyman Reloading Handbook*, .50-70s use cast bullets sized to 0.511". Lyman's recommended bullet weights are 422 and 489 grains. To look up potential bullets for this cartridge in the Encyclopedia, look for bullet diameters between 0.504"

and 0.518", plus or minus 0.007" from Lyman's recommended sizing diameter, with weights between 400 and 520 grains that have a calculated rate of twist close to 1:26. In the Encyclopedia, such an entry for this rate of twist would have a value of 26. You'll notice, incidentally, that I've increased the weight range here. I did that because other bullet mould maker's weight ranges for

.50-70 bullets are a bit wider than what Lyman recommends.

How many entries are there in the Encyclopedia that meet these criteria? Based on the diameter range, you'll find over 90 (Table 2). Restricting it to bullets weighing between 400 and 520 grains brings it down to just under 30 (Table 3).

TABLE 2

MOULD BLOCK DESCRIPTION						EXPERIMENTAL DATA				EXPERIMENTAL RESULTS					
Maker	Mould	Cavities	Comments	Used Together	Material	Alloy	Casting Time (hrs.)	Total Bullets Cast	Visually Acceptable Bullets	BULLET DESCRIPTION AVERAGE			Bullets Per Hour (BPH)	Visually Acceptable BPH	Rate Of Twist
										Diameter	Weight	Length			
Ballisti-Cast	1454-2	4			I		2.00	380	257	0.504	368	0.792	190	129	40
Navy Arms	450 Smith	1			I		3.00	265	36	0.504	282	0.680	88	12	47
Ballisti-Cast	1454-1	4			I		2.00	428	243	0.504	369	0.794	214	122	40
Ballisti-Cast	1454 (2 of these)	4	3 @ once	10	I			4800	3389	0.504	369	0.794	277	196	40
Ballisti-Cast	1454	4	3 @ once	11	I		19.00	2616	2217	0.504	369	0.794	138	117	40
Ballisti-Cast	1454 (2 of these)	4	4 @ once	12	I		2.00	420	361	0.504	369	0.794	210	181	40
T/C	Maxi-Hunter	1			I	lead	2.00	289	153	0.505	346	0.756	145	77	42
NFI	300.510	2			I	lead	4.00	770	513	0.505	309	0.686	193	128	47
NEI	860.510	1			I	ww	7.00	744	347	0.506	935	2.231	106	50	14
NEI	500.510	1			I	30/1	2.00	282	150	0.506	535	1.107	141	75	29
Ballisti-Cast	1465	4			I	ww	2.00	708	318	0.507	541	1.102	354	159	29
CBE	512.975-1	1			B	ww	2.00	226	171	0.508	966	2.002	113	86	16
CBE	512.975	1	2 of these		B	ww	2.00	234	86	0.508	965	2.000	117	43	16
Hoch	510.425	1			I	30/1	2.00	220	112	0.508	429	0.921	110	56	35
CBE	512.975-2	1			B	ww	2.00	264	114	0.508	963	1.999	132	57	16
NEI	625.510	1			I	30/1	2.00	252	152	0.509	669	1.339	126	76	24
NEI	860.510	1			I		2.00	125	63	0.509	886	2.237	63	32	15
NEI	350.508	1			I		2.00	165	68	0.509	357	0.861	83	34	38
CBE	510.510	1			B		2.00	133	57	0.509	473	1.050	67	29	31
Hoch	513.715	1			I	ww	6.00	578	368	0.510	703	1.465	06	61	22
Hoch	513.715	1			I	30/1	2.00	195	140	0.510	721	1.466	98	70	22
NEI	300.510	2			I		0.67	56	32	0.510	281	0.690	84	18	47
NEI	420.512	1			I	30/1	4.00	495	273	0.510	448	0.927	124	68	35
Ballisti-Cast	1435-27	5			I	lead	2.00	930	756	0.510	358	0.666	465	378	40
Rapine	515.365	1			A	lead	3.00	390	224	0.510	362	0.748	130	75	44
Ballisti-Cast	1435	5	2 of these		I	lead	8.00	4035	2716	0.511	356	0.664	504	340	49
NEI	625.510	1			I		2.00	115	41	0.511	621	1.342	58	21	24
Hoch	512.760	3			I	lead	4.00	654	394	0.511	740	1.470	164	99	22
Ballisti-Cast	1435-26	5			I	lead	2.00	825	265	0.511	355	0.662	413	133	49
Hoch	510.425	1			I		2.00	122	84	0.512	398	0.923	61	42	35
Hoch	513.715	1			I		2.00	102	70	0.512	669	1.472	51	35	22
NEI	630.511	1			I	30/1	2.00	253	113	0.512	674	1.340	127	57	24
RCBS	50-515-FN-2	1			I	ww	2.00	243	174	0.512	541	1.101	122	87	30
RCBS	50-515-FN	1	2 of these		I	ww	6.00	986	827	0.512	541	1.101	164	138	30
RCBS	50-515-FN	1	3 of these		I	ww	16.00	2089	1349	0.512	541	1.101	131	84	30
SAECO	542	1			I		6.00	334	237	0.512	562	1.218	56	40	27
NEI	640.512	1			I		2.00	101	82	0.512	667	1.433	51	41	23
NEI	420.512	4			A	ww	2.00	552	405	0.512	433	0.931	276	203	35
NEI	630.511	1			I		2.00	114	74	0.512	628	1.344	57	37	24
Hoch	513.445	1			I	30/1	4.00	507	322	0.513	445	0.953	127	81	34
RCBS	50-515-FN-3	1			I	lead	2.00	207	156	0.513	558	1.098	104	78	30
SAECO	583	1			I		6.00	348	195	0.513	610	1.332	58	33	25
Hoch	512.760	3			I	ww	2.00	318	152	0.513	705	1.475	159	76	22
Hoch	512.760	3			I		2.00	153	62	0.513	677	1.473	77	31	22
NEI	640.512	1			I	30/1	1.88	241	81	0.513	714	1.430	128	43	23
NEI	420.512	1			I		6.00	405	299	0.513	420	0.933	68	50	35
Hoch	512.400	3			I		14.00	1776	1290	0.513	367	0.797	127	92	41
Hoch	512.400	3	2 @ once	16	I			700	372	0.513	367	0.797	117	62	41
Ballisti-Cast	1435-2	5			I		2.00	590	238	0.513	326	0.667	295	119	49
Hoch	513.445	1			I	ww	32.12	5153	2888	0.513	438	0.954	160	90	35
CBE	512.975-2	1			B		2.00	97	40	0.513	905	2.011	49	20	16
Ballisti-Cast	1435	5	2 of these		I		3.00	1465	886	0.513	325	0.667	488	295	49
Ballisti-Cast	1465	4			I		2.00	306	153	0.514	510	1.107	153	77	30
Ballisti-Cast	1465	4	2 @ once	5	I		2.00	268	123	0.514	510	1.107	134	62	30
Ballisti-Cast	1465 (1 of 3)	4	3 @ once	28	I			1488	1320	0.514	510	1.107	124	110	30
CBE	512.975-1	1			B		2.00	100	43	0.514	904	2.007	50	22	16
Ballisti-Cast	1435-1	5			I		2.00	580	197	0.514	324	0.668	290	99	49
Lyman	515141	1			I		6.00	399	187	0.514	416	0.969	67	31	34
Ballisti-Cast	1417	5			I		2.00	455	188	0.514	420	0.853	228	94	39
Lyman	515142	1			I		10.00	654	200	0.514	488	1.051	65	20	31

TABLE 2 (continued)

Maker	Mould	Cavities	Comments	Used Together	Material	Alloy	Casting Time (hrs.)	Total Bullets Cast	Visually Acceptable Bullets	Diameter	Weight	Length	Bullets Per Hour (BPH)	Visually Accept-able BPH	Rate Of Twist
NEI	630.512	1			A		17.00	875	595	0.514	651	1.398	52	35	24
NEI	715.511	1			A		6.00	283	136	0.514	702	1.496	47	23	22
Rapine	515.385	1			A	lead	4.00	512	254	0.514	395	0.817	128	64	41
NEI	420.512	4			A		2.00	388	199	0.514	410	0.933	194	100	35
Lyman	515141	2			I		2.00	202	82	0.514	412	0.976	101	41	34
Lyman	515141	1			I		1.00	76	32	0.515	411	0.970	76	32	34
RCBS	50-515-FN	1	2 of these		I	lead	2.00	292	215	0.515	557	1.099	146	108	30
Hoch	513.445	1			I		4.00	252	163	0.515	414	0.956	63	41	35
RCBS	50-515-FN-3	1			I		2.00	119	98	0.515	508	1.103	60	49	30
RCBS	50-515-FN	1	2 of these		I		12.00	1199	668	0.515	509	1.103	100	56	30
RCBS	50-515-FN-2	1			I		2.00	123	89	0.515	510	1.102	62	45	30
NEI	630.512	1			A		3.00	148	38	0.515	654	1.406	49	13	24
RCBS	50-450-FN	1			I		2.00	129	89	0.515	443	0.969	65	45	34
RCBS	50-515-FN-1	1			I	30/1	2.00	232	136	0.515	553	1.105	116	68	30
RCBS	50-515-FN	1	2 of these		I		12.00	1271	841	0.516	511	1.106	106	70	30
Rapine	515.365	1			A		6.00	445	266	0.516	334	0.760	74	44	44
RCBS	50-515-FN	1	3 of these		I		0.67	59	49	0.516	509	1.104	88	73	30
Rapine	540.300-1	1			A	30/1	2.00	284	144	0.516	304	0.642	142	72	52
NEI	385.515	1			I		4.00	276	167	0.516	354	0.833	69	42	40
Lee	52 Wilkinson	2	2 of these		A	lead	2.00	430	326	0.516	361	0.885	215	163	38
RCBS	50-515-FN-1	1			I		2.00	121	97	0.517	513	1.110	61	49	30
Lyman	515139	1			I		2.00	160	116	0.517	314	0.726	80	58	46
RCBS	50-515-FN-2	1			I	lead	2.00	184	126	0.517	557	1.101	92	63	30
Rapine	515.385	1			A		8.00	676	172	0.517	359	0.821	85	22	41
Rapine	540.300-2	1			A		2.00	169	161	0.518	273	0.651	85	81	51
RCBS	50-515-FN-4	1			I		2.00	144	103	0.518	510	1.106	72	52	30
NEI	490.540	2	1 in a 2	26	A	lead	4.00	269	123	0.518	494	1.071	67	31	31
NEI	500.540	2	1 in a 2	26	A	lead		269	115	0.518	502	1.073	67	29	31
Rapine	540.300-2	1			A	lead	2.00	216	164	0.518	313	0.650	108	82	52
Rapine	540.300	1	2 of these		A	lead	12.00	1827	1247	0.518	313	0.648	152	104	52
Rapine	540.300-1	1			A	lead	2.00	268	164	0.518	312	0.646	134	82	52

TABLE 3

Maker	Mould	Cavities	Comments	Used Together	Material	Alloy	Casting Time (hrs.)	Total Bullets Cast	Visually Acceptable Bullets	Diameter	Weight	Length	Bullets Per Hour (BPH)	Visually Accept-able BPH	Rate Of Twist
Hoch	510.425	1			I	30/1	2.00	220	112	0.508	429	0.921	110	56	35
CBE	510.510	1			B		2.00	133	57	0.509	473	1.050	67	29	31
NEI	420.512	1			I	30/1	4.00	495	273	0.510	448	0.927	124	68	35
NEI	420.512	4			A	ww	2.00	552	405	0.512	433	0.931	276	203	35
Hoch	513.445	1			I	30/1	4.00	507	322	0.513	445	0.953	127	81	34
NEI	420.512	1			I		6.00	405	299	0.513	420	0.933	68	50	35
Hoch	513.445	1			I	ww	32.12	5153	2888	0.513	438	0.954	160	90	35
Ballisti-Cast	1465	4			I		2.00	306	153	0.514	510	1.107	153	77	30
Ballisti-Cast	1465	4	2 @ once	5	I		2.00	268	123	0.514	510	1.107	134	62	30
Ballisti-Cast	1465 (1 of 3)	4	3 @ once	28	I			1488	1320	0.514	510	1.107	124	110	30
Lyman	515141	1			I		6.00	399	187	0.514	416	0.969	67	31	34
Ballisti-Cast	1417	5			I		2.00	455	188	0.514	420	0.853	228	94	39
Lyman	515142	1			I		10.00	654	200	0.514	488	1.051	65	20	31
NEI	420.512	4			A		2.00	388	199	0.514	410	0.933	194	100	35
Lyman	515141	2			I		2.00	202	82	0.514	412	0.976	101	41	34
Lyman	515141	1			I		1.00	76	32	0.515	411	0.970	76	32	34
Hoch	513.445	1			I		4.00	252	163	0.515	414	0.956	63	41	35
RCBS	50-515-FN-3	1			I		2.00	119	98	0.515	508	1.103	60	49	30
RCBS	50-515-FN	1	2 of these		I		12.00	1199	668	0.515	509	1.103	100	56	30
RCBS	50-515-FN-2	1			I		2.00	123	89	0.515	510	1.102	62	45	30
RCBS	50-450-FN	1			I		2.00	129	89	0.515	443	0.969	65	45	34
RCBS	50-515-FN	1	2 of these		I		12.00	1271	841	0.516	511	1.106	106	70	30
RCBS	50-515-FN	1	3 of these		I		0.67	59	49	0.516	509	1.104	88	73	30
RCBS	50-515-FN-1	1			I		2.00	121	97	0.517	513	1.110	61	49	30
RCBS	50-515-FN-2	1			I	lead	2.00	184	126	0.517	557	1.101	92	63	30
RCBS	50-515-FN-4	1			I		2.00	144	103	0.518	510	1.106	72	52	30
NEI	490.540	2	1 in a 2	26	A	lead	4.00	269	123	0.518	494	1.071	67	31	31
NEI	500.540	2	1 in a 2	26	A	lead		269	115	0.518	502	1.073	67	29	31

The lowest value in Table 3, and hence the one closest to the desired rate of twist of one turn in 26 inches, corresponds to RCBS mould 50-515-FN and Ballisti-Cast bullet 1465. Ballisti-Cast 1465, incidentally, is an exact copy of RCBS 50-515-FN. RCBS produces only single cavity moulds for this bullet and I wanted a four-cavity block. So I had Ballisti-Cast copy this RCBS mould.

The Encyclopedia tells us a lot about these two bullets. I've cast them using pure lead, 30:1 (30 parts lead to one part tin by weight), wheelweights and linotype. I've also used several identical

RCBS 50-515-FN

	MOULD BLOCK DESCRIPTION					EXPERIMENTAL DATA			EXPERIMENTAL RESULTS					
Maker	Mould	Cavities	Comments	Material	Alloy	Casting Time (hrs.)	Total Bullets Cast	Visually Acceptable Bullets	BULLET DESCRIPTION AVERAGE			Bullets Per Hour (BPH)	Visually Accept-able BPH	Rate Of Twist
									Diameter	Weight	Length			
RCBS	50-515-FN-1	1		I		2.00	121	97	0.517	513	1.110	61	49	30.0
RCBS	50-515-FN-2	1		I		2.00	123	89	0.515	510	1.102	62	45	30.1
RCBS	50-515-FN-3	1		I		2.00	119	98	0.515	508	1.103	60	49	30.0
RCBS	50-515-FN-4	1		I		2.00	144	103	0.518	510	1.106	72	52	30.3
RCBS	50-515-FN	1	2 of these	I		12.00	1199	668	0.515	509	1.103	100	56	30.0
RCBS	50-515-FN	1	2 of these	I		12.00	1271	841	0.516	511	1.106	106	70	30.1
Ballisti-Cast	1465	4		I		2.00	306	153	0.514	510	1.107	153	77	29.8
RCBS	50-515-FN-2	1		I	lead	2.00	184	126	0.517	557	1.101	92	63	30.3
RCBS	50-515-FN-3	1		I	lead	2.00	207	156	0.513	558	1.098	104	78	29.9
RCBS	50-515-FN	1	2 of these	I	lead	2.00	292	215	0.515	557	1.099	146	108	30.1
RCBS	50-515-FN-2	1		I	ww	2.00	243	174	0.512	541	1.101	122	87	29.7
RCBS	50-515-FN	1	2 of these	I	ww	6.00	986	827	0.512	541	1.101	164	138	29.7
RCBS	50-515-FN	1	3 of these	I	ww	16.00	2089	1349	0.512	541	1.101	131	84	29.7
Ballisti-Cast	1465	4		I	ww	2.00	708	318	0.507	541	1.102	354	159	29.2
RCBS	50-515-FN-1	1		I	30/1	2.00	232	136	0.515	553	1.105	116	68	30.1

RCBS single cavity iron-moulds. That is why some of the moulds in the Encyclopedia are listed with a –1, -2 or –3 added to the end of their name. I added that. I scratched it into the exterior of the blocks so that I could tell identical moulds apart. And I've used more than one of these blocks at a time. Under the "Comments" heading, such data are indicated by the phrases "2 of these" or "3 of these." As we will see shortly doing this can greatly increase hourly casting rates. Another way to increase hourly casting rates is to use a gang mould, i.e. a mould with four or more cavities. That's why I had the Ballisti-Cast mould made.

The table marked "RCBS 50-515-FN" contains all the entries from the Encyclopedia for this mould and its Ballisti-Cast copy. There is a lot we can learn here. Let's start by looking at the bullet diameters and lengths.

Overall, these moulds and alloys the average bullet diameters and lengths did not change all that much. There is some variability, of course, but it is minor. Since changing alloys does not significantly affect bullet diameters and bullet lengths, and since only bullet diameters and bullet lengths are important to the Greenhill formula, then the rate of twist needed to stabilize a bullet does not change significantly when changing alloys. Said another way, bullet alloy doesn't have a significant impact on potential bullet accuracy. That's odd. The Greenhill formula predicts this but I would have never thought of this!

Is there any way to investigate this idea experimentally? Sure. Look at the graph entitled "Lone Star 50-70." Lone Star is a company that makes really beautiful

Remington-style rolling block rifles. This plot shows a set of shooting studies done with a Lone Star rifle chambered in 50-70 using this RCBS 50-515-FN bullet and a couple different bullet alloys. Note that I did about as well when shooting this bullet cast from linotype as I did when

shooting this bullet cast from wheel-weights (ww). True I also changed the powder (from Unique to 5744) but I did get nearly identical results from both of these alloys. So just maybe the Greenhill formula is right. Maybe you can change bullet alloys without adversely changing

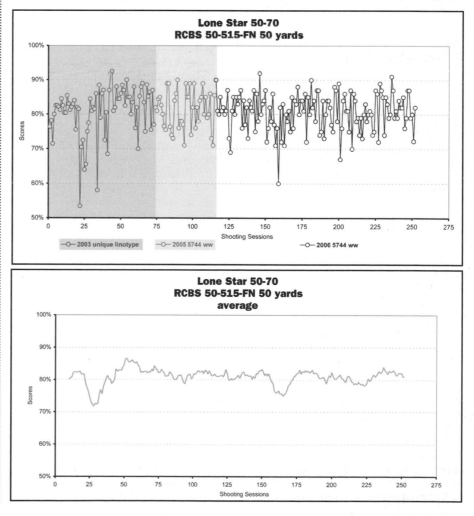

64TH EDITION, 2010

on target performance.

Changing alloys, incidentally, expanded the range of bullet weights. Remember we were originally looking for bullets that weighed between 400 and 520 grains. Now we have a weight range of 508 to 553 grains. Why did this increase in the weight range happen? This happened because more alloys are being considered here than were considered by Lyman when they made up the loading data for this round. And the new alloys, the ones Lyman didn't use, have a higher lead content and hence a higher weight. This sort of weight range expansion doesn't happen often, but it does tend to occur with really heavy bullets because the Encyclopedia has data for a wider range of bullet alloys than the Lyman Handbooks do.

This example, incidentally, illustrates another point. Remember earlier that I said that when a series of moulds were used together that the number in the Used Together column could help you find all the blocks? In Table 3 you see the number 28 in the "Used Together" column. The other two blocks that were used here will have the number 28 in their entry in the Encyclopedia as well. This is just an arbitrary number used to identify such sets of moulds.

Visual Inspections

Now let's consider visual inspection techniques. The bullet casters I've known over the decades have come in two versions. Some do extremely harsh visual inspections and reject a lot of bullets. I fall into this group. I reject, on average, 30 percent of all my cast bullets. Any visual imperfection gets a bullet tossed, no matter how minor. If it isn't perfect it is remelted. The other type of bullet caster rejects very few bullets. Most of them will shoot just about anything unless it is grossly deformed.

How do you decide if a bullet fails visual inspections? Decades ago I published an article with pictures of every visual defect I had ever seen. For each I tried to figure out the probable cause and a possible solution. Now I simply pitch anything that doesn't look perfect. The 15th *Handloader's Digest*, incidentally, has an article of mine entitled "The Art Of Bullet Casting," printed under a pen name, that goes into this in great detail.

Hourly Casting Rates

The Encyclopedia has two types of hourly production rate data. If you pitch almost nothing, then for your visual acceptable rate data use the data under the heading Bullets Per Hour. The visual

rejection rate here is zero. If you pitch a lot of bullets then use the hourly rate data under the heading Visually Acceptable BPH (Bullets Per Hour). If your visual inspections fall between these two extremes, just average these two numbers. The Encyclopedia, incidentally, is the only source for this kind of hourly rate information.

Look at the RCBS 50-515-FN table again. One of the bigger impacts on these casting rates is the alloy. For wheelweights using one single cavity mould the rate numbers are 122 Bullets Per Hour and 87 Visually Acceptable BPH, i.e. 122/87. For a single mould using linotype the rate numbers are 61/49, 62/45, 60/49 and 72/52. For pure lead they are 92/63 and also 104/78. Finally for 30 to 1 the numbers are 116/68. Obviously changing alloy has a major impact on bullet casting rates.

And changing alloy will also save you money. Remember we noted earlier that a rifle that can stabilize a linotype bullet should also stabilize that same bullet made from wheelweights? Wheelweights are significantly cheaper than linotype. These .50-70 bullets are really heavy and thus require a lot of alloy. So switching from linotype to wheelweights will greatly increase your hourly casting rates and significantly reduce your costs for no significant change in accuracy.

Alloy isn't the only thing that can have a major impact on hourly casting rates. Look at the RCBS 50-515-FN table again. Another way to increase casting rates is to use two identical moulds. Such entries correspond to the comment "2 of these" in the Comments column. For all of these alloys, using two identical moulds dramatically increases bullet-casting rates.

This makes sense. After you fill a mould, the alloy in that mould has to cool. That takes time. You can either sit there and wait or you can use a second mould. One mould is cooling while you are filling the other. Using two moulds almost always significantly increases casting rates.

Does using three identical moulds increase casting rates yet again? Not always. There is one example of this in the RCBS 50-515-FN table and there are others throughout the Encyclopedia. Later we'll examine how to tell if using three or more moulds is actually worth the cost.

How about increasing casting rates by using a gang mould, i.e. a mould with four or more cavities? Does this increase casting rates? Almost always!

Speeding up bullet casting has always been of interest to bullet casters. That's

why there are gang moulds. That's why many bullet casters use more than one block at a time. They may use two moulds casting the same bullet or two moulds casting very different bullets. But decades ago people did something else. They would have custom moulds made where each cavity cast a different bullet. In the Encyclopedia such moulds are identified by phrases like "1 in a 2" or "1 in a 4." Some firms still offer this option but this idea has lost its appeal. I bought mine back when this was a brand new, red-hot idea. I would not recommend doing this. These special order moulds are expensive and not worth the money.

If you cast more than one bullet at a time, incidentally, either by using several bullet moulds or a specialty mould that has cavities for more than one bullet, always cast bullets that are <u>very clearly different</u>. If they aren't ,you are going to spend a great deal of time separating them.

Selecting a Pistol Bullet

The most striking difference between rifle and pistol moulds is the huge selection of pistol moulds. SAECO, for example, makes only one rifle mould for many rifle calibers. But everybody who makes pistol moulds makes a lot of them. So when using the Encyclopedia to select a pistol mould you are almost always going to end up with a very long list of possible bullets.

Because of this much wider selection, I use a different set of selection criteria. I look for bullets in the Encyclopedia with a diameter range from −0.002" below Lyman's recommended sizing die to +0.005" above. The range here can be smaller because there are so many more pistol bullets to choose from. Also I change the weight range. I use whatever Lyman recommends plus or minus 10 percent. And one criterion is dropped: the rate of twist. That, remember, is only used with rifle moulds.

Speed and cost are also important. I figure out just how many bullets I'm going to need. Pistol moulds come in three speeds: slow (one and two cavity blocks), medium (three and four cavity moulds) and fast (five or more cavities). And they come in three matching price ranges, relatively inexpensive, expensive and very expensive. Slow speed moulds are inexpensive. Medium speed moulds are not cheap. And high-speed moulds are expensive. Speed costs and sometimes it costs a lot! When I pick a pistol mould I restrict my search in the Encyclopedia to one of these three speed/price ranges.

And speed shows up in another way.

Two of the most popular alloys for pistol bullets are wheelweights and linotype. Wheelweights are, or at least should be, inexpensive. They also usually yield much higher hourly casting rates. But wheelweight bullets are noticeably less accurate than linotype bullets in high-pressure cartridges. I'm positive about that because I've done extensive shooting studies using both wheelweight and linotype bullets. Using wheelweights in a .44 Special revolver, for example, works just fine but using wheelweights in a .44 Magnum can lead to accuracy problems.

Casting rates and alloy, then, are important selection criteria when picking pistol bullets from the Encyclopedia. I look for a mould that has a really high Visually Acceptable BPH (bullets per hour) rate. This will greatly reduce the casting time and vastly reduce the number of visual rejects. And I consider the alloy. If it is a high-pressure cartridge, like the .44 Magnum, I only consider data from the Encyclopedia for linotype bullets. If it is a low-pressure cartridge, like the .44 Special, then this alloy restriction does not apply.

Now let's consider an example. Let's look at the Encyclopedia to select a bullet for the .44 Magnum. We start with the diameter range. Lyman recommends a sizing die of 0.429 inches so we look in the Encyclopedia for bullets with diameters between 0.427" and 0.434". You'll find over 50. Lyman recommends a weight range between 200 and 300 grains. So we will consider bullets weighing between 180 and 330 grains. This drops the number of bullets being considered only slightly. Let's assume that you want to cast several thousand bullets but you are not going to mass-produce them. You might consider making several thousand bullets to be mass-production but I don't. I view mass-production as making more than 10,000. So, because this isn't mass production, we want a single three- or four-cavity block. This reduces the number of moulds still being considered to just over a dozen.

Because this is a high-pressure cartridge we are going to eliminate any wheelweight bullets. That causes another minor drop in the number of possibilities. Finally we look for really high numbers in the column entitled Visually Acceptable BPH (bullets per hour). Three choices remain. They are SAECO #420, SAECO #442 and H&G #23. Ballisti-Cast now makes H&G moulds but changed H&G's names by adding 600 to each one. So the Ballisti-Cast equivalent to this H&G mould would be Ballisti-Cast mould #623. These three

(SAECO #420, SAECO #442 and BC #623) are excellent bullets. I've made well over 50,000 of them and I'm in the process of making 100,000 more. They are easy to cast and they are very accurate! You couldn't possibly do better.

Another Example

The casting rate data in the Encyclopedia isn't limited to just looking for a bullet for a particular rifle or pistol. You can also use it in other ways. Consider another example. One of the guns I want to shoot next year is a blackpowder cartridge rifle. I've got six. Any of them would be fine. Casting up the several thousand bullets I'm going to need is going to take time. The question is would it take significantly less time if I picked a particular rifle?

Answering this question is easy. Go to the Encyclopedia and look up all the bullets for each gun. You'd do that exactly like we did in the rifle example but you would do it for all the guns you were considering rather than just one. I made up a Table similar to the one shown for the 50-70 bullets, the RCBS 50-515-FN table, but with entries for each of my blackpowder cartridge rifles. Once I made up this list of potential bullets the answer to my question was obvious. One of these blackpowder cartridges rifles is a .43 Beaumont. The .43 Beaumont can use a very heavy .44 Magnum cast bullet. I didn't know that. A very heavy .44 Magnum cast bullet can be made from a six cavity Ballisti-Cast mould. Most rifle moulds have only one or two cavities. Using a six-cavity mould cuts down the casting time substantially.

And there are other ways to reduce the casting time, and the cost, in this example. Remember wheelweights work well in low-powered cartridges. A blackpowder round is a low-powered cartridge. So you can use wheelweights. Wheelweights, in fact, are a much better choice here than linotype because they are so inexpensive. And casting rates with wheelweights are always higher than casting rates with linotype. Wheelweight bullets aren't good for all applications but they are excellent for this one.

Was the .43 Beaumont in the Lyman Handbooks? No. I got the loading data from the Accurate Arms website. As indicated earlier, the Accurate Arms website is a really good source for data for unusual cartridges.

Another Use for the Rate Data

Now let's look at the rate data for

SAECO #442, SAECO's classic 44 Special bullet. For a double cavity mould, the number of visually acceptable bullets per hour is 93. Buy an 8-cavity block and this number jumps to 225. So increasing the number of cavities in the mould increases the casting rate.

Suppose you want to cast up several thousand of these 44 caliber bullets. I typically shoot 3600 of these annually. If I use a double cavity mould it will take me 3600/93 or 38.7 hours to cast up this many bullets. This double cavity block is relatively inexpensive so I'm spending time but saving money. If I use an eight-cavity mould, it will take me only 3600/225 or 16 hours. This eight-cavity mould is very expensive so I'm spending money but saving time. Because of the Encyclopedia's rate data I can see exactly how much time I'm going to save if I buy the more expensive block. Doing this kind of rate/cost comparison has never been possible before.

Also note that rate numbers don't just scale up. If they did, then the rate of this SAECO eight cavity mould would be 4 x 93 or 372 visually acceptable bullets per hour. Clearly that didn't happen. The actual rate for this eight-cavity mould was only 225 visually acceptable bullets per hour. Bigger moulds certainly do have higher bullet casting rates, but those rates almost never are as high as you might expect. The Encyclopedia has a lot of data where you can clearly see how much of an hourly rate increase you'll get if you buy a bigger mould.

There is another twist to this rate data, namely using multiple moulds. The number of visually acceptable bullets per hour you get when you use two SAECO 4-cavity #442 simultaneously is 310. That, oddly enough, is a massive improvement over using one SAECO 8-cavity mould where this figure was only 225. Why did this happen? Why is it that using two SAECO four cavity moulds can substantially out produce one SAECO eight cavity mould?

Using Multiple Moulds

Using two or more moulds simultaneously is an art. There are dozens of examples of this in the Encyclopedia. The reason that there are dozens of examples is that I was trying to figure out just exactly how to use multiple moulds to maximize production rates and minimize visual rejections. I had a lot of failures. What I finally discovered was that there are three critical points when using several moulds simultaneously. First, run your casting furnace full open. Turn the thermostat all the way to the top. That will give you the best mould block fill out because you have really hot bullet metal. Second, use enough moulds so that there is a very long cooling time for each. After you fill a mould, it just sits there cooling off as you are filling the other moulds. You want to use enough mould blocks so that this cooling time for any one block is <u>long</u> because long cooling times limit visual imperfections. Finally, never ever use moulds that produce bullets that are the least bit similar in appearance. If you do, you'll spend hours separating them.

How do you know how many blocks to use? Start out with two. Note the total number of visually acceptable bullets you made per hour. Then add a third. If the total number of visually acceptable bullets per hour goes up significantly, then adding the third mould helped. If the number of visually acceptable bullets per hour didn't go up, then either drop back to using only two moulds or try a different mould for your third block. Do you have to stop at using just three moulds? No! Use the same criteria in deciding if adding a fourth block helps.

Obviously in the SAECO #442 example, using multiple gang moulds really helped. But this idea isn't just limited to gang moulds. It can be used with single cavity blocks as well as we saw earlier in the RCBS 50-515-FN Table.

Rate Data that Isn't in the Encyclopedia

What do you do if you want hourly rate data for a bullet that is not listed in the Encyclopedia? Is there any way to fill in the holes? Yes!

There are four steps to this. First, look for bullets in the Encyclopedia with approximately the same weight. If you are buying a mould on the internet, the internet ad should list the bullet's diameter and weight. If it does not, e-mail the seller and ask. Use the stated weight plus or minus ten percent when looking up entries in the Encyclopedia. Second, look for rate data in the Encyclopedia for blocks with the same number of cavities. Third, look for rate data for the alloy you are interested in. Fourth, restrict your search to moulds made from the same material (aluminum, brass or iron). Average the rate numbers for any remaining blocks.

Let's give this a whirl and see how well it does. Suppose you wanted to estimate the casting rate for a double cavity iron SAECO #442 mould. Yes, I know that this mould is in the Encyclopedia, but I want to estimate it anyway because then I can use the actual data in the Encyclo-

pedia to see just how well this estimating process works.

The first selection criteria is weight. This bullet weighs 245 grains when cast from linotype. Searching the Encyclopedia for bullets weighing between 220 and 270 grains yields just over 50. Restricting this list to double cavity moulds drops this number down to six. All six of these blocks were used with linotype, so the third of our selection criteria, alloy, doesn't have an effect here. The final selection criterion is the material from which the block is made. All SAECO moulds are made from iron. One of our remaining six blocks is an aluminum mould, so it can be eliminated. So we have five remaining moulds, all of which fit each of our four selection criteria. Averaging the rate numbers for these five gives a Bullets Per Hour value of 119 and a Visually Acceptable BPH value of 85. The actual measured rate numbers for this mould were 122 and 93. So our estimate wasn't perfect but it was pretty darn close.

Buying Bullet Moulds on the Internet

A lot of bullet moulds are offered on the internet on the online auction sites. Virtually all of these ads have pictures either of the bullets a mould produces or, more likely, of the cavities in the mould. Pay really close attention to the cavities. If they are covered in rust or have pitting, don't buy. If the picture isn't good enough to see these details, e-mail the seller and ask for a better picture.

Also pay close attention to what the ad says. You are looking for the maker, the maker's name for this mould, the bullet's diameter and the bullet's weight. Remember that the Encyclopedia is laid out by increasing bullet diameters so knowing the diameter is going to make finding your mould in the Encyclopedia a LOT easier. And knowing the weight will help if you do not find the mould in the Encyclopedia because, as we just saw, if you know the weight you can estimate the hourly casting rates. If any of this information isn't listed in the ad, e-mail the seller and ask for it.

It is also a good idea to watch the auction sites for a while before buying anything so that you can get an idea of what moulds should cost. For example, I like really old gang moulds. Ideal Armory moulds were last manufactured in the early 1950s and they appear on eBay every now and then. I've seen them sell for as little as $75 and for as much as $450. $75 is a real bargain if the block is in ex-

cellent shape but $450 is well past nuts even if the mould is virtually perfect. The problem is that you can get novice bidders who just have to have something. Get two such bidders going after the same old mould and prices can really get out of control. If you see that happening do not bid! A mould like that will be offered again eventually and will probably sell at a significantly lower price.

Also know that there are several kinds of Internet mould block sellers. Some sellers, for example, go to a mould block manufacturer and buy a large number of moulds and then turn around and auction them. I suppose if you buy a large number of blocks from a manufacturer you can get a really good price. But these moulds at auction frequently sell for more than you would have paid if you had bought them new directly from the manufacturer. So if you are bidding on a brand new mould, check the price at the manufacturer's website first.

Other sellers are clearly just selling junk. You can look at the pictures posted on the web and know that this is true. But such blocks sell and quite often for a very high price. Auction fever, I guess.

You really need to avoid getting caught up in auction fever. Whenever you are considering buying a used mould on the web find a similar block on a mould block manufacturer's web page so that you can know, approximately, what this mould would cost new. Never ever bid more for a used mould than half the new block price!

And remember that there isn't just one mould that will work for you. As we saw in the numerous examples, you can use the Encyclopedia to finds lots of blocks that will work in your gun. You do not absolutely have to have some mould that is being offered on an auction site. If you are going to buy from an on-line auction site, wait until you can get what you want and get it at a very good price!

I suspect that the major use of the data in the Encyclopedia will be looking up casting rates and physical dimensions for bullets offered for sale at on-line auction sites. But remember that the data in the Encyclopedia has other uses. You can use it to pick a bullet for your particular rifle or pistol. You can use it to see if the rate increase you'll get from using two moulds or from using a gang mould is worth the money. And the rate data in the Encyclopedia can help you not only to maximize your bullet production but also to minimize your costs by helping you select the least expensive alloy that will work well in your particular firearm.

Now, on to the Encyclopedia!

MOULD BLOCK DESCRIPTION						EXPERIMENTAL DATA			EXPERIMENTAL RESULTS					
Maker	Mould	Cavities	Comments	Used Together	Material	Alloy	Casting Time (hrs.)	Total Bullets Cast	Visually Acceptable Bullets	BULLET DESCRIPTION AVERAGE			Bullets Per Hour (BPH)	Visually Acceptable BPH	Rate Of Twist
										Diameter	Weight	Length			
NEI	31.224	1			B		6.00	544	425	0.224	28	0.341	91	71	18
RCBS	22-055-SP	2			I		6.00	1166	882	0.224	54	0.638	194	147	10
RCBS	22-055-SP	2			I		2.00	450	342	0.225	53	0.645	225	171	10
NEI	45.224	5			A		6.00	2145	1864	0.225	42	0.498	358	311	13
Lyman	225438	2			I		5.50	1148	645	0.225	43	0.509	209	117	12
Lyman	225462	2			I		6.00	1196	719	0.225	57	0.666	199	120	10
NEI	72.224	2			I		2.00	432	341	0.225	73	0.817	216	171	8
NEI	45.224	1			I		2.00	274	193	0.225	50	0.564	137	97	11
SAECO	221	4			I		6.00	1758	1161	0.226	56	0.668	293	194	10
SAECO	221	1			I		6.00	555	428	0.227	56	0.668	93	71	10
SAECO	243	2			I		6.00	1032	825	0.246	81	0.802	172	138	9
Hoch	260.113	1			I		6.00	608	353	0.249	106	0.907	101	59	9
Rapine	250.021 RB	2			A		1.00	258	74	0.252	22	0.252	258	74	32
Lyman	252435	2			I		6.00	1418	922	0.253	49	0.470	236	154	17
H&G	117	2			I		2.00	296	204	0.254	51	0.475	148	102	17
Old West	259.095	2	1 in a 2	4	B		8.00	493	184	0.254	96	0.815	62	23	10
Old West	259.106	2	1 in a 2	4	B			493	155	0.254	106	0.899	62	19	9
H&G	32	2			I		6.00	932	510	0.258	56	0.494	155	85	17
NEI	72.257	2			A		6.00	912	578	0.258	69	0.589	152	96	14
Lyman	257231	1			I		5.50	696	373	0.258	104	0.886	127	68	9
RCBS	25-100-ГN	2			I		2.00	336	280	0.260	101	0.855	168	140	10
Lyman	25720	1			I		6.00	876	498	0.260	73	0.629	146	83	13
SAECO	257	2			I		6.00	1030	720	0.261	95	0.824	172	120	10
NEI	115.257	2			A		6.00	794	414	0.262	111	0.932	132	69	9
SAECO	264	2			I		2.00	356	236	0.266	134	1.094	178	118	8
RCBS	6.5-140-SP	2			I		6.00	890	527	0.266	137	1.117	148	88	8
NEI	62.280	1			B		6.00	551	416	0.282	59	0.451	92	69	22
Lyman	287405	2			I		6.75	1040	374	0.286	141	1.065	154	55	10
SAECO	071	2			I		4.00	610	486	0.287	151	1.044	153	122	10
NEI	95.313	2			I	lead	2.00	522	308	0.295	99	0.553	261	154	20
Rapine	290.035 RB	2			A		2.00	446	284	0.298	36	0.298	223	142	37
Hoch	310.205	1			I		6.00	480	216	0.304	201	1.093	80	36	11
Lyman	311441	1			I		6.00	665	208	0.305	109	0.079	111	35	17
SAECO	315	1			I		6.00	491	255	0.305	163	1.012	82	43	12
RCBS	30-180-SP	2			I		8.00	1038	480	0.308	173	1.064	130	60	11
RCBS	30-085-RN	2			I		2.00	358	232	0.309	70	0.500	179	116	22
Lyman	311465	1			I		6.00	549	203	0.309	116	0.740	92	34	16
NEI	163.308	2			A		6.00	718	261	0.309	154	0.934	120	44	13
NEI	182.308	1			I		2.00	209	145	0.309	190	1.073	105	73	11
Lee	C309-160-R	1			A		6.00	694	279	0.310	146	0.902	116	47	13
SAECO	307	2			I		2.00	332	195	0.310	168	0.978	166	98	12
NEI	145.308	2			A		6.00	682	368	0.310	138	0.834	114	61	14
Lee	C309-170-F	1			A		6.00	691	209	0.310	159	0.936	115	35	13
SAECO	254	4			I		6.00	1384	1069	0.311	111	0.740	231	178	16
SAECO	315	4			I	lead	2.00	684	639	0.311	179	1.008	342	320	12
CBE	311.199	1			B		2.00	237	141	0.311	189	1.120	119	71	11
NEI	85.309	2			A		6.00	766	418	0.311	81	0.517	128	70	23
H&G	S216	4	1 in a 4	14	I		14.00	898	297	0.311	87	0.517	64	21	23
H&G	113	4	1 in a 4	14	I			898	530	0.311	88	0.568	64	38	21
Lyman	311359	2			I		6.00	1070	466	0.311	107	0.737	178	78	16
NEI	118.308	2			A		6.00	730	320	0.311	112	0.690	122	53	18
Lee	C309-180-R	1			A		6.00	657	181	0.311	165	0.998	110	30	12
RCBS	30-180-FN	2			I		4.00	488	251	0.311	179	1.029	122	63	12
NEI	95.313	2			I		0.33	56	22	0.311	89	0.555	168	66	22
SAECO	315	4			I		2.00	460	376	0.312	163	1.012	230	188	12
SAECO	315	4	2 @ once	18	I		10.00	1688	1559	0.312	163	1.012	169	156	12
RCBS	32-077-RN	2			I		2.00	428	272	0.312	73	0.490	214	136	25
SAECO	302	4			I		6.00	1432	1171	0.312	110	0.725	239	195	17
SAECO	315	4	2 of these		I		6.00	2419	2237	0.312	163	1.014	403	373	12
H&G	93	4	1 in a 4	14	I			898	524	0.312	88	0.546	64	37	22
NEI	108.312	2			A		6.00	756	406	0.312	99	0.620	126	68	20
Lee	C309-200-2R	1			A		6.00	582	160	0.312	185	1.111	97	27	11
SAECO	315	4			I		2.00	484	409	0.312	163	1.015	242	205	12
H&G	87	2			I		6.00	1006	846	0.313	81	0.508	168	141	24
Ideal	308-257-110	8			I		2.00	1200	916	0.313	109	0.694	600	458	18
SAECO	305	4			I		12.00	3216	2778	0.313	168	0.973	268	232	13
SAECO	327	8			I		6.00	3296	2062	0.313	72	0.471	549	344	26
Lyman	311419	2			I		7.00	1120	428	0.313	85	0.500	160	61	25
Lee	311-93-1R	6			A		6.00	2244	815	0.313	85	0.531	374	136	23
H&G	361	4			I		6.00	1212	934	0.314	106	0.623	202	156	20
Frankfort Arsenal	30RB	5			B		1.00	428	56	0.314	42	0.324	428	56	38
H&G	S26	6			I		6.00	2550	1472	0.314	85	0.536	425	245	23
CBE	311-92-R	4			B		2.00	595	433	0.314	84	0.535	298	217	23

	MOULD BLOCK DESCRIPTION					EXPERIMENTAL DATA				EXPERIMENTAL RESULTS					
Maker	Mould	Cavities	Comments	Used Together	Material	Alloy	Casting Time (hrs.)	Total Bullets Cast	Visually Acceptable Bullets	BULLET DESCRIPTION AVERAGE			Bullets Per Hour (BPH)	Visually Accept-able BPH	Rate Of Twist
										Diameter	Weight	Length			
SAECO	327	1			I		12.00	1000	680	0.314	73	0.476	83	57	26
Mountain	315BB180	1			B		2.00	170	95	0.315	172	1.035	85	48	12
Lee	311-93-1R	2			A		6.00	1048	316	0.315	86	0.537	175	53	23
H&G	65	4			I		8.00	2180	1485	0.316	93	0.623	273	186	20
Lee	TL314-85-WC	2			A		6.00	1042	368	0.317	82	0.431	174	61	29
NEI	115.316	2	1 in a 2	2	A		6.00	419	271	0.318	116	0.693	70	45	18
RCBS	32-170-FN	2			I	30/1	2.00	588	235	0.320	181	0.911	294	118	14
Hoch	322.210	1			I	30/1	2.00	305	182	0.321	214	1.099	153	91	12
Hoch	210.322	1			I	ww	2.00	321	141	0.321	211	1.102	161	71	12
NEI	175.318	1			I		2.00	212	176	0.321	168	1.089	106	88	12
Hoch	322.210	1			I		2.00	183	123	0.322	198	1.103	92	62	12
SAECO	538	1			I	ww	2.00	317	210	0.322	202	1.057	159	105	12
RCBS	32-170-FN	2			I		2.00	286	169	0.322	169	0.920	143	85	14
RCBS	08-170-FN-1	2			I	ww	2.00	624	425	0.323	177	0.903	312	213	14
RCBS	08-170-FN-1	2			I	ma	2.00	644	571	0.323	180	0.902	322	286	14
RCBS	8mm Nambu	2			I		6.00	750	441	0.323	98	0.605	125	74	22
NEI	125.324	1			I		8.00	749	497	0.323	126	0.843	94	62	16
NEI	150.322	2	1 in a 2	2	A		6.00	419	191	0.323	143	0.786	70	32	17
RCBS	08-170-FN	2	2 of these		I	ma	4.00	1232	1036	0.323	180	0.902	308	259	15
RCBS	08-170-FN	2	2 of these	25	I	ma		284	251	0.323	180	0.902	142	126	15
RCBS	08-170-FN-2	2			I	ma	2.00	484	376	0.324	180	0.903	242	188	15
RCBS	08-170-FN	2	2 of these		I		4.38	996	799	0.324	168	0.908	227	182	14
SAECO	081	3			I		8.00	1356	787	0.324	185	1.059	170	98	12
SAECO	632	4			I		2.00	420	300	0.324	158	0.895	210	150	15
SAECO	632	4	2 @ once	18	I			1672	1511	0.324	158	0.895	167	151	15
SAECO	632	4	3 @ once	9	I		6.00	892	707	0.324	158	0.895	149	118	15
RCBS	08-170-FN-2	2			I		2.00	294	236	0.324	168	0.907	147	118	15
RCBS	08-170-FN-1	2			I		2.00	262	220	0.324	168	0.909	131	110	15
SAECO	538	1			I		2.00	204	113	0.325	190	1.058	102	57	13
H&G	116	4	1 in a 4	14	I			898	656	0.325	100	0.611	64	47	22
H&G	226	2			I		8.00	1248	803	0.325	119	0.641	156	100	21
NEI	160.322	4			A		6.00	1184	794	0.325	164	0.888	197	132	15
H&G	116	2			I		6.00	914	626	0.326	100	0.614	152	104	22
Lee	C329-205-1R-1	1			A		2.00	217	172	0.330	189	1.044	109	86	13
Lee	C329-205-1R	1	2 of these		A		6.00	1016	755	0.330	189	1.044	169	126	13
Lee	C329-205-1R-2	1			A		2.00	188	141	0.330	189	1.045	94	71	13
RCBS	33-200-FN	2			I	30/1	2.00	524	232	0.337	210	0.961	262	116	15
NEI	215.338	1			I	30/1	2.00	392	160	0.339	231	1.075	196	80	13
RCBS	33-200-FN	2			I		2.00	260	168	0.339	195	0.965	130	84	15
RCBS	33-200-FN	2			I		2.00	240	76	0.340	195	0.976	120	38	15
RCBS	33-200-FN	2			I		6.00	748	379	0.341	198	0.971	125	63	15
NEI	225.348	1			A		8.00	489	180	0.349	214	1.033	61	23	15
RCBS	348-200-FN	2			I		6.00	712	371	0.350	191	0.917	119	62	17
LBT	200.349 LFN	2			A		6.00	1004	537	0.351	187	0.855	167	90	18
SAECO	402	4			I		6.00	1192	845	0.353	199	0.860	199	141	18
NEI	171.375	2			I		1.00	138	75	0.354	170	0.679	138	75	23
CBE	363.190	4			B		2.00	432	356	0.356	175	0.769	216	178	21
SAECO	910	6			I		6.00	1800	1223	0.356	142	0.699	300	204	23
Lyman	358429	4			I		6.00	1276	878	0.356	160	0.747	213	146	21
H&G	X279	2			I		2.00	372	257	0.357	81	0.423	186	129	38
H&G	251	2			I		2.00	306	260	0.357	141	0.586	153	130	27
Lyman	356637	4			I		6.00	1624	1289	0.357	146	0.689	271	215	23
RCBS	09-115-RN	2			I		2.00	316	201	0.358	110	0.613	158	101	26
SAECO	910	2			I		2.00	344	147	0.358	143	0.702	172	74	23
Lyman	358242	4			I		6.00	1604	987	0.358	87	0.462	267	165	35
H&G	307	4	1 in a 4	15	I			2753	1689	0.358	112	0.629	66	40	26
H&G	264	4	1 in a 4	15	I			2753	1698	0.358	118	0.652	66	40	25
RCBS	09-124-CN	2			I		2.00	304	164	0.358	121	0.606	152	82	27
Cramer	16H	5			I		2.00	665	632	0.358	133	0.574	333	316	28
Ballisti-Cast	921	6			I		2.00	768	596	0.358	185	0.896	384	298	18
Ballisti-Cast	921	6	2 @ once	6	I			564	480	0.358	185	0.896	282	240	18
Ballisti-Cast	921	6	3 @ once	11	I			3966	3342	0.358	185	0.896	209	176	18
Ballisti-Cast	921	6	4 @ once	12	I			300	223	0.358	185	0.896	150	112	18
SAECO	382	2			I		2.00	340	147	0.359	155	0.713	170	74	23
H&G	377	4			I		4.00	884	727	0.359	142	0.675	221	182	24
H&G	39 BB	2			I		6.00	814	586	0.359	153	0.734	136	98	22
SAECO	382	2			I		2.00	336	206	0.359	154	0.710	168	103	23
SAECO	358	4			I		6.00	1680	1253	0.359	152	0.658	280	209	25
Lee	356-125-2R	6			A		6.00	2196	568	0.359	118	0.573	366	95	28
H&G	115	4	1 in a 4	15	I			2753	1861	0.359	119	0.617	66	44	26
Lyman	356634	4			I		6.00	1520	1064	0.359	128	0.583	253	177	28
H&G	511	6			I		8.00	2850	1672	0.359	134	0.601	356	209	27
H&G	50	4			I		6.00	1592	1198	0.359	137	0.599	265	200	27

MOULD BLOCK DESCRIPTION						EXPERIMENTAL DATA				EXPERIMENTAL RESULTS					
Maker	Mould	Cavities	Comments	Used Together	Material	Alloy	Casting Time (hrs.)	Total Bullets Cast	Visually Acceptable Bullets	BULLET DESCRIPTION AVERAGE			Bullets Per Hour (BPH)	Visually Acceptable BPH	Rate Of Twist
										Diameter	Weight	Length			
NEI	165.358	1			A		55.00	4901	1812	0.359	152	0.688	89	33	23
Lyman	358315	2			I		6.00	790	350	0.359	199	0.915	132	58	18
Hensley	63-358-145	6			I		2.00	1002	791	0.359	133	0.658	501	396	25
H&G	376	2			I		2.00	282	206	0.359	174	0.734	141	103	22
SAECO	358 (1 4 & 1 8)		2 @ once		I		14.00	9216	8158	0.359	151	0.655	658	583	25
SAECO	358	4	2 of these		I		2.00	796	672	0.359	152	0.658	398	336	25
H&G	378	2			I		6.00	782	515	0.359	142	0.655	130	86	25
SAECO	358 (2 4 & 1 8)		3 @ once		I		12.00	7036	6393	0.359	151	0.656	586	533	25
Lee	358-105-SWC	2			A		6.00	1000	443	0.359	98	0.518	167	74	31
H&G	224	2			I		2.00	384	332	0.359	123	0.616	192	166	26
Cramer	16H	10			I		2.00	1050	986	0.359	139	0.576	525	493	28
SAECO	358	8			I		14.00	7384	5705	0.359	150	0.653	527	408	25
SAECO	358	8	2 @ once	19	I		6.00	2208	2005	0.359	150	0.653	368	334	25
SAECO	358	8	2 @ once	20	I		18.00	5936	5424	0.359	150	0.653	330	301	25
SAECO	358	8	2 @ once	22	I			3840	3275	0.359	150	0.653	274	234	25
SAECO	358	8	4 @ once	13	I			384	362	0.359	150	0.653	192	181	25
SAECO	358-2	4			I		2.00	520	382	0.359	152	0.659	260	191	25
H&G	333	2			I		6.00	1072	917	0.360	65	0.259	179	153	62
Cramer	358-8-148	8			I		2.00	1112	872	0.360	129	0.567	556	436	29
Cramer	29	3			I		2.00	435	359	0.360	145	0.658	218	180	25
Cramer	16H	10	2 of these		I		2.00	1060	991	0.300	138	0.585	530	496	28
RCBS	38-158-CM	2			I		4.00	578	336	0.360	148	0.667	145	84	24
Cramer	16H	10			I		2.00	1120	687	0.360	137	0.594	560	344	27
H&G	376	4			I		6.00	1132	970	0.360	173	0.732	189	162	22
Lyman	358063	4			I		6.00	1488	821	0.360	139	0.581	248	137	28
NEI	300.358	1			A		8.00	490	198	0.360	294	1.300	61	25	13
Cramer	358-158-ID	3			I		2.00	423	275	0.360	147	0.714	212	138	23
H&G	331	2			I		6.00	842	712	0.361	119	0.619	140	119	26
H&G	322-4	2			I		2.00	304	212	0.361	181	0.875	152	106	19
Hensley	358.150	6			I		6.00	2328	1421	0.361	141	0.575	388	237	28
Ideal	358.432	7			I		6.00	2072	1200	0.361	154	0.647	345	200	25
NEI	170.358	2			A		6.00	666	412	0.361	162	0.717	111	69	23
NEI	200.358	1			A		8.00	584	259	0.361	189	0.894	73	32	18
NEI	200.358	1			B		11.00	764	220	0.361	189	0.894	70	20	18
NEI	300.358	2			A		4.00	428	164	0.361	299	1.315	107	41	12
Rapine	380.100	2			A		6.00	1042	428	0.361	105	0.516	174	71	32
H&G	50	10			I		2.00	1170	713	0.362	137	0.590	585	357	28
SAECO	395	2			I		6.00	816	495	0.362	190	0.846	136	83	19
Ideal	358.432	7			I		2.00	924	459	0.362	151	0.636	462	230	26
H&G	279	4	1 in a 4	15	I		42.00	2753	1055	0.362	95	0.479	66	25	34
NEI	136.358	2			A		6.00	748	475	0.362	129	0.578	125	79	28
Cramer	25A	5			I		2.00	725	642	0.362	151	0.712	363	321	23
LBT	100.363 RN	2			A		6.00	1132	653	0.363	95	0.469	189	109	35
Lyman	356402	4			I		8.00	2116	1215	0.363	120	0.624	265	152	26
H&G	279	2			I		6.00	914	757	0.363	95	0.483	152	126	34
Ideal	358.311	7			I		2.00	805	505	0.364	153	0.738	403	253	22
NEI	100.363	1			B		8.00	547	357	0.364	107	0.489	68	45	34
RCBS	375-RB	2			I	lead	2.00	488	360	0.366	78	0.372	244	180	45
H&G	375	2			I		6.00	942	722	0.366	100	0.471	157	120	36
LBT	100.363 RN	1			A		6.00	772	218	0.366	95	0.446	129	36	38
Hoch	368.150	1			I	lead	4.25	520	247	0.367	168	0.687	122	58	24
Rapine	366.158	2			A		2.00	270	124	0.368	149	0.691	135	62	25
Hoch	368.150	1			I		4.00	366	188	0.368	154	0.687	92	47	25
NEI	290.375	1			I	lead	2.00	280	245	0.373	325	1.176	140	123	15
RCBS	375-RB	2			I		2.00	366	352	0.374	69	0.365	183	176	48
NEI	171.375	2			I	lead	2.00	402	185	0.376	189	0.685	201	93	26
NEI	277.375	1			I	30/1	2.00	371	215	0.376	297	1.241	186	108	14
NEI	380.375	1			I	30/1	2.00	274	89	0.376	393	1.447	137	45	12
NEI	290.375	1			I	30/1	2.00	355	226	0.376	320	1.177	178	113	15
SAECO	373	1			I	30/1	2.00	366	150	0.377	257	0.940	183	75	19
SAECO	373	2			I		6.00	686	365	0.377	251	0.980	114	61	18
NEI	277.375	1			I		2.00	147	108	0.378	276	1.245	74	54	14
RCBS	378-312-BPS-1	2			I	lead	2.00	364	255	0.378	320	1.282	182	128	14
RCBS	378-312-BPS	2	2 of these		I	lead	2.00	504	420	0.378	320	1.283	252	210	14
RCBS	378-312-BPS-2	2			I	lead	2.00	388	319	0.378	320	1.284	194	160	14
SAECO	373	1			I		4.00	343	183	0.378	240	0.947	86	46	19
NEI	380.375	1			I		2.00	143	65	0.378	367	1.452	72	33	12
RCBS	378-312-BPS-0	2			I		2.00	228	152	0.379	293	1.279	114	76	14
NEI	290.375	1			I		2.00	168	122	0.379	297	1.182	84	61	15
RCBS	378-312-BPS-1	2			I		2.00	214	182	0.379	292	1.290	107	91	14
LBT	304.378	2	1 in a 2	1	A		6.00	285	139	0.379	304	1.259	48	23	14
RCBS	378-312-BPS	2	3 of these		I		2.00	534	477	0.379	292	1.287	267	239	14
SAECO	738-2	4			I	ww	2.00	684	544	0.379	250	0.942	342	272	19

Maker	Mould	Cavities	Comments	Used Together	Material	Alloy	Casting Time (hrs.)	Total Bullets Cast	Visually Acceptable Bullets	Diameter	Weight	Length	Bullets Per Hour (BPH)	Visually Acceptable BPH	Rate Of Twist
										BULLET DESCRIPTION AVERAGE					
SAECO	738	4	2 of these		I	ww	4.00	1748	1311	0.379	249	0.939	437	328	19
RCBS	378-312-BPS	2	2 of these		I		2.00	570	391	0.379	292	1.291	285	196	14
SAECO	738-1	4			I	ww	2.00	684	481	0.380	249	0.936	342	241	19
RCBS	378-312-BPS-2	2			I		2.00	348	280	0.380	292	1.293	174	140	14
Disston	100.380	5			A		1.00	315	91	0.380	100	0.415	315	91	44
NEI	240.375 J	1			A		6.00	531	207	0.380	247	0.987	89	35	18
SAECO	738-2	4			I		2.00	448	435	0.382	237	0.948	224	218	19
SAECO	738	4	2 of these		I		2.00	784	702	0.382	236	0.947	392	351	19
Hoch	381.200	3			I		8.00	1254	760	0.383	192	0.750	157	95	24
SAECO	738-1	4			I		2.00	452	434	0.383	234	0.946	226	217	19
NEI	200.41	2			I	lead	2.00	534	369	0.383	173	0.555	267	185	33
H&G	121	2			I		2.00	252	179	0.384	184	0.636	126	90	29
H&G	121	4			I		6.00	1084	866	0.385	184	0.636	181	144	29
NEI	205.41 LC	1			B		6.00	446	240	0.387	199	0.719	74	40	26
Rapine	386.185 HB	1			A		6.00	531	304	0.388	172	0.706	89	51	27
CBE	401.150	4			B		2.00	524	437	0.402	145	0.538	262	219	38
SAECO	047	4			I		2.00	484	351	0.402	192	0.706	242	176	29
H&G	396	2			I		2.00	276	229	0.402	195	0.669	138	115	30
NEI	160.404	1			I		6.00	572	341	0.403	160	0.575	95	57	35
Lyman	401043	2			I		6.00	898	510	0.403	166	0.610	150	85	33
SAECO	043	4			I		8.00	1716	1195	0.403	164	0.623	215	149	33
Lyman	401638	4			I		6.00	1408	1101	0.404	168	0.607	235	184	34
NEI	250.404	1			I		12.00	807	551	0.404	242	0.842	67	46	24
Lyman	401633	2			I		6.00	782	257	0.404	199	0.724	130	43	28
NEI	right cylinder	2			A		6.00	752	371	0.405	170	0.509	125	62	40
NEI	200.41	2			I		2.00	260	183	0.406	157	0.558	130	92	37
RCBS	40-400-BPS	1			I		2.00	155	121	0.406	380	1.373	78	61	15
RCBS	40-400-BPS	1	3 of these		I		2.00	255	169	0.406	380	1.373	128	85	15
SAECO	640	3	2 of these		I	ma	6.00	1554	1099	0.407	367	1.196	259	183	17
Hoch	409.335	1			I	30/1	2.00	252	126	0.407	340	1.095	126	63	19
SAECO	640-2	3			I	ma	2.00	525	409	0.408	368	1.195	263	205	17
Lee	410-195-SWC	6			A		6.00	1872	1198	0.408	187	0.649	312	200	32
Hoch	409.335	1			I		6.00	461	306	0.409	314	1.097	77	51	19
SAECO	640-1	3			I		2.00	309	250	0.410	346	1.208	155	125	17
SAECO	640	3	2 of these		I		6.00	1539	1315	0.410	345	1.205	257	219	17
H&G	368	2			I		2.00	350	195	0.410	80	0.245	175	98	86
SAECO	640-2	3			I		2.00	321	276	0.410	344	1.202	161	138	18
SAECO	740	1			I	30/1	6.00	853	421	0.410	419	1.336	142	70	16
RCBS	41-210-SWC	2			I		2.00	298	214	0.411	200	0.684	149	107	31
RCBS	40-400-BPS-2	1			I		2.00	142	123	0.411	362	1.366	71	62	15
RCBS	40-400-BPS	1	2 of these		I		2.00	269	236	0.411	362	1.367	135	118	15
Rapine	408.336 PB	2			A		6.00	722	206	0.411	309	1.089	120	34	19
RCBS	40-400-BPS-3	1			I		2.00	140	116	0.411	361	1.368	70	58	16
Lyman	410459	4			I		6.00	1296	941	0.412	206	0.754	216	157	28
RCBS	40-300-S	2			I		6.00	686	522	0.412	301	0.988	114	87	21
H&G	258	2			I		6.00	724	530	0.412	210	0.770	121	88	28
SAECO	740	1			I		4.00	282	129	0.412	391	1.344	71	32	16
SAECO	418	4			I		24.00	4879	4415	0.412	209	0.693	203	184	31
SAECO	640	1			I	30/1	2.00	312	109	0.412	379	1.214	156	55	18
SAECO	412	8			I		16.75	7504	5373	0.413	177	0.602	448	321	35
SAECO	412	8	2 @ once	5	I			592	536	0.413	177	0.602	296	268	35
SAECO	412	8	2 @ once	19	I			2160	1750	0.413	177	0.602	360	292	35
SAECO	412	8	2 @ once	24	I		2.00	672	577	0.413	177	0.602	336	289	35
SAECO	412 (1 4 & 1 8)		2 @ once		I		12.00	7920	6866	0.413	178	0.606	660	572	35
SAECO	640	1			I		2.00	146	106	0.413	352	1.219	73	53	18
SAECO	412	4			I		2.00	400	342	0.413	180	0.610	200	171	35
NEI	260.423	1			I	30/1	2.00	360	117	0.415	273	0.866	180	59	25
RCBS	416-350-FN	1			I	30/1	2.00	292	111	0.415	361	1.075	146	56	20
NEI	260.423	1			I		2.00	198	101	0.416	253	0.872	99	51	25
RCBS	416-350-FN	1			I		2.00	148	109	0.417	335	1.080	74	55	20
NEI	260.419	1			I		2.00	197	108	0.417	254	0.834	99	54	26
NEI	225.44	2			I	lead	2.00	332	180	0.420	219	0.579	166	90	38
NEI	250.421	1			I		4.00	373	232	0.423	249	0.838	93	58	27
NEI	208.44	1			I	30/1	2.00	356	239	0.423	213	0.672	178	120	33
NEI	208.44	1			I		2.00	194	115	0.425	199	0.675	97	58	33
SAECO	420	8			I	ww	6.75	4446	3811	0.428	200	0.603	659	565	38
SAECO	433-2	4			I		2.00	388	279	0.428	276	0.832	194	140	28
Ballisti-Cast	943	5			I		4.00	1235	922	0.429	295	0.939	309	231	25
Ballisti-Cast	943	5	2 @ once	6	I		2.00	505	427	0.429	295	0.939	253	214	25
Ballisti-Cast	943	5	2 @ once	27	I		4.00	865	649	0.429	295	0.939	216	162	25
Ballisti-Cast	943	5	3 @ once	11	I			3350	2704	0.429	295	0.939	176	142	25
Ballisti-Cast	943 (1 of 3)	5	3 @ once	28	I		12.00	1890	1663	0.429	295	0.939	158	139	25
Ballisti-Cast	943	5	4 @ once	12	I			255	191	0.429	295	0.939	128	96	25

Maker	Mould	Cavities	Comments	Used Together	Material	Alloy	Casting Time (hrs.)	Total Bullets Cast	Visually Acceptable Bullets	Diameter	Weight	Length	Bullets Per Hour (BPH)	Visually Acceptable BPH	Rate Of Twist
NEI	190.427	2			A		6.00	680	421	0.429	181	0.602	113	70	38
NEI	190.427	1			B		6.00	414	113	0.429	184	0.607	69	19	38
Lee	429-214-1R	2			A		6.00	776	248	0.430	202	0.670	129	41	34
CBE	430-240-R	4			B	ww	62.00	24074	18285	0.430	240	0.745	388	295	31
RCBS	520-Hodge	1			I	30/1	2.00	223	11	0.430	246	0.518	112	6	45
H&G	443	2			I		6.00	1062	927	0.430	86	0.247	177	155	94
SAECO	444	1			I		6.00	466	234	0.430	193	0.589	78	39	39
H&G	23	4			I		6.00	1276	1019	0.430	195	0.622	213	170	37
H&G	240	2			I		2.00	310	204	0.430	188	0.624	155	102	37
Lyman	429421	4			I		6.00	1216	836	0.430	236	0.775	203	139	30
SAECO	420-2	4			I		5.25	1444	976	0.430	190	0.604	275	186	38
RCBS	44-200-CM	1			I		4.00	530	391	0.431	188	0.570	133	98	41
H&G	379-5	2			I		2.00	236	154	0.431	321	0.962	118	77	24
SAECO	442	2			I		2.00	244	185	0.431	235	0.782	122	93	30
H&G	367	2			I		2.00	232	187	0.431	261	0.760	116	94	31
H&G	X240	2			I		2.00	326	212	0.431	97	0.352	163	106	66
NEI	310.429	2			A		6.00	618	434	0.431	314	0.987	103	72	24
SAECO	420	4	2 of these		I		2.00	952	706	0.431	192	0.609	476	353	38
CBE	430.240-R	4			B		1.62	324	284	0.431	229	0.751	200	175	31
SAECO	433	4	2 @ once	17	I			320	282	0.431	279	0.841	160	141	28
SAECO	420 (2 4 & 1 8)		3 @ once		I		2.00	1227	1113	0.431	191	0.606	614	557	38
NEI	192.429	4			A		6.00	1296	736	0.431	182	0.749	216	123	31
NEI	196.429	1			B		4.00	277	108	0.431	183	0.572	69	27	41
SAECO	420	8			I		29.00	13640	9453	0.431	190	0.602	470	326	39
SAECO	420	8	2 @ once	20	I			5968	5060	0.431	190	0.602	332	281	39
SAECO	420	8	2 @ once	21	I			528	472	0.431	190	0.602	264	236	39
SAECO	420	8	2 @ once	24	I			640	464	0.431	190	0.602	320	232	39
SAECO	442-2	4			I		2.00	408	345	0.431	228	0.787	204	173	30
Lyman	429215	4			I		8.00	1628	781	0.431	232	0.783	204	98	30
RCBS	44-250-SWC	1			I		21.00	1600	907	0.431	241	0.751	76	43	31
SAECO	420 (1 4 & 1 8)		2 @ once		I		30.00	15960	13579	0.431	191	0.608	532	453	38
SAECO	442	8			I		6.00	1968	1349	0.431	236	0.783	328	225	30
SAECO	442	8	2 @ once	23	I		7.00	2120	1621	0.431	236	0.783	303	232	30
SAECO	442	8	2 @ once	27	I			1040	923	0.431	236	0.783	260	231	30
SAECO	442 (2 4 & 1 8)		3 @ once		I		20.00	10864	9311	0.431	236	0.783	543	466	30
SAECO	442 (1 of 3)	8	3 @ once	28	I			2896	2708	0.431	236	0.783	241	226	30
SAECO	420	4			I		7.00	1512	1228	0.431	193	0.614	216	175	38
SAECO	433-1	4			I		2.00	434	281	0.431	279	0.841	217	141	28
SAECO	442	4	2 of these		I		2.00	668	619	0.431	232	0.786	334	310	30
Rapine	451.210	2			A		6.00	784	273	0.432	198	0.651	131	46	36
SAECO	442 (1 4 & 1 8)		2 @ once		I		6.00	3091	2486	0.432	236	0.785	515	414	30
SAECO	442	4			I		2.00	368	282	0.432	237	0.786	184	141	30
SAECO	433	2			I		2.00	232	128	0.432	279	0.832	116	64	28
SAECO	433	4	2 of these		I		28.00	9052	7555	0.432	279	0.832	323	270	28
H&G	379-5	4			I		6.00	880	699	0.432	320	0.956	147	117	24
NEI	185.429	1			A		14.00	1089	225	0.433	125	0.347	78	16	68
Ideal	424-98-210	6			I		2.00	780	563	0.433	200	0.638	390	282	37
Lee	421-300-HB	1			A		2.00	195	169	0.433	290	0.999	98	85	24
NEI	240.429	2			A		6.00	658	314	0.434	251	0.801	110	52	29
RCBS	43-370-FN	2			I		6.00	666	517	0.440	372	1.069	111	86	23
NEI	560.458	1			I	lead	2.00	194	153	0.445	556	1.386	97	77	18
Disston	150.445	5			A		1.00	280	199	0.445	147	0.440	280	199	56
RCBS	44-370-FN-2	2			I	lead	2.00	360	280	0.446	408	1.035	180	140	24
RCBS	44-370-FN	2	2 of these		I	lead	12.00	3052	2177	0.446	409	1.036	254	181	24
RCBS	44-370-FN-1	2			I	lead	2.00	312	265	0.446	409	1.037	156	133	24
NEI	560.458	1			I		2.00	120	95	0.447	508	1.393	60	48	18
NEI	535.458	1			I	30/1	2.00	252	155	0.447	545	1.433	126	78	17
RCBS	44-370-FN-1	2			I		2.00	204	141	0.448	374	1.040	102	71	24
RCBS	44-370-FN	2	2 of these		I		2.00	366	277	0.448	373	1.040	183	139	24
RCBS	44-370-FN-2	2			I		2.00	188	160	0.449	373	1.040	94	80	24
SAECO	458-2	4			I	ww	2.00	724	593	0.449	255	0.672	362	297	37
SAECO	458-1	4			I	ww	2.00	684	621	0.449	256	0.673	342	311	37
NEI	220.450	1			I	30/1	2.00	333	174	0.449	222	0.610	167	87	41
H&G	362	2			I	lead	2.00	616	391	0.451	164	0.482	308	196	53
SAECO	458	8			I	ww	24.00	15191	11931	0.451	258	0.678	633	497	38
SAECO	458-2	4			I		2.00	504	375	0.451	240	0.676	252	188	38
NEI	225.44	2			I		2.00	232	138	0.452	200	0.583	116	69	44
SAECO	458	4	2 of these		I		4.00	1248	1085	0.452	241	0.676	312	271	38
SAECO	458-1	4			I		2.00	492	395	0.452	241	0.676	246	198	38
NEI	204.451	2			A		2.00	292	141	0.452	195	0.547	146	71	47
NEI	186.451	2			A		2.00	322	121	0.452	171	0.482	161	61	53
RCBS	451-RB	2			I		2.00	312	273	0.453	122	0.448	156	137	57
NEI	255.451	4			A		6.00	1356	763	0.453	242	0.623	226	127	41

Maker	Mould	Cavities	Comments	Used Together	Material	Alloy	Casting Time (hrs.)	Total Bullets Cast	Visually Acceptable Bullets	Diameter	Weight	Length	Bullets Per Hour (BPH)	Visually Acceptable BPH	Rate Of Twist
										BULLET DESCRIPTION AVERAGE					
Lyman	452664	4			I		2.00	416	236	0.453	237	0.648	208	118	40
H&G	339	2			I		2.00	244	193	0.453	254	0.727	122	97	35
Lee	452-255-RF	6			A		6.00	1542	828	0.453	240	0.642	257	138	40
SAECO	458	8			I		44.00	12991	8936	0.454	242	0.676	295	203	38
SAECO	458	8	2 @ once	23	I			2112	1562	0.454	242	0.676	302	223	38
SAECO	069	4			I		6.00	1284	940	0.454	184	0.606	214	157	43
NEI	275.451	1			I		2.00	180	136	0.454	255	0.727	90	68	35
Cramer	5G	10			I		2.00	840	699	0.454	181	0.593	420	350	43
H&G	265	2			I		8.00	1082	816	0.454	195	0.675	135	102	38
H&G	34	8			I		10.00	3792	2303	0.454	219	0.680	379	230	38
H&G	34	6			I		44.00	16225	10419	0.454	221	0.681	369	237	38
H&G	34	6	3 @ once	10	I		17.33	3888	3195	0.454	221	0.681	224	184	38
H&G	22	6			I		6.00	1908	1501	0.454	241	0.714	318	250	36
SAECO	069	4			I		6.00	1204	901	0.454	186	0.608	201	150	42
Modern-Bond	B-452-650	6			I		2.00	690	399	0.455	218	0.656	345	200	39
Ballisti-Cast	990-5	4				lead	6.00	1880	1506	0.455	422	1.007	313	251	26
RCBS	45-235-CM	2			I		2.00	240	175	0.455	216	0.592	120	88	44
Ideal	452.400	6			I		2.00	522	386	0.456	226	0.684	261	193	38
NEI	475.454	1			I	30/1	2.00	250	164	0.456	528	1.332	125	82	20
P&C	45-500-DWC	1			A		6.00	332	97	0.456	483	1.223	55	16	21
RCBS	45-255-SWC	2			I		6.00	714	497	0.456	250	0.722	119	83	36
NEI	225.451	4			A		6.00	1320	844	0.457	212	0.660	220	141	40
NEI	525.458 H	1			I	lead	2.00	216	187	0.457	539	1.460	108	94	18
NEI	425.458	1	2 of these		I	ma	10.00	1674	1445	0.457	440	1.259	167	145	21
NEI	475.454	1			I		4.00	208	99	0.457	487	1.334	52	25	20
H&G	390-5	2			I	lead	2.00	342	282	0.458	427	1.015	171	141	26
SAECO	020	1			I	lead	2.00	217	167	0.458	561	1.319	109	84	20
NEI	425.458-1	1			I	ww	2.00	300	266	0.458	439	1.257	150	133	21
NEI	530.458	4			A	ww	16.00	5040	2694	0.458	504	1.354	315	168	19
Hoch	458.515	1			I	ww	10.00	1035	804	0.458	509	1.346	104	80	20
NEI	250.456	4			A		6.00	1276	914	0.458	244	0.676	213	152	39
Lyman	457125	1			I		6.00	351	76	0.458	488	1.327	59	13	20
H&G	347-4	2			I		6.00	630	379	0.458	317	0.870	105	63	30
CBE	458.400	1			B		2.00	159	95	0.458	373	0.955	80	48	28
Hoch	458.515	1			I		12.00	752	593	0.458	481	1.351	63	49	19
Hoch	458.515	1			I	30/1	2.00	295	164	0.458	517	1.346	148	82	20
Ballisti-Cast	990-5	4			I		2.00	272	175	0.459	386	1.010	136	88	26
Ballisti-Cast	990-5	4	3 @ once	8	I			252	120	0.459	386	1.010	126	60	26
NEI	425.458-2	1			I	ww	2.00	305	241	0.459	437	1.251	153	121	21
NEI	425.458	1	2 of these		I	ww	6.00	1055	707	0.459	438	1.256	176	118	21
NEI	425.458-1	1			I	ma	2.00	260	231	0.459	443	1.258	130	116	21
NEI	525.458 H	1			I		2.00	148	95	0.459	491	1.467	74	48	18
NEI	575.458	1			I	30/1	2.00	265	163	0.459	588	1.361	133	82	19
RCBS	45-500-BPS-1	1			I		2.00	133	85	0.459	476	1.349	67	43	20
NEI	525.458	1			I		2.00	131	42	0.459	522	1.424	66	21	19
Lee	457-450-F	1			A		6.00	380	48	0.460	427	1.114	63	8	24
NEI	575.458	1			I		2.00	122	93	0.460	546	1.365	61	47	19
NEI	425.458	1	2 of these	25	I	ma	2.00	142	131	0.460	440	1.258	71	66	21
Hoch	459.300	3			I		20.00	3006	1905	0.460	281	0.772	150	95	34
Hoch	459.300	3	2 @ once	16	I		6.00	695	367	0.460	281	0.772	116	61	34
SAECO	021	2			I		6.00	578	282	0.460	403	1.152	96	47	23
RCBS	45-500-BPS	1	2 of these		I		5.00	782	432	0.460	476	1.350	156	86	20
RCBS	45-500-FN	1			I		6.00	392	218	0.460	492	1.316	65	36	20
RCBS	45-500-BPS	1	3 of these		I		2.00	296	174	0.460	476	1.351	148	87	20
Lee	457-340-F	1			A		6.00	538	152	0.460	323	0.855	90	25	31
SAECO	017	4			I		6.00	912	651	0.460	329	0.914	152	109	29
RCBS	45-500-BPS-3	1			I		2.00	163	109	0.460	477	1.352	82	55	20
H&G	390-5	2			I		14.00	1252	963	0.461	389	1.020	89	69	26
SAECO	015	8			I	ww	2.00	1135	823	0.461	309	0.815	568	412	33
SAECO	015	4			I		2.00	368	326	0.461	295	0.827	184	163	32
RCBS	45-500-BPS-2	1			I		2.00	131	99	0.461	477	1.351	66	50	20
SAECO	020	1			I		6.00	342	209	0.461	512	1.327	57	35	20
SAECO	015	4	2 @ once	17	I		2.00	312	240	0.461	295	0.827	156	120	32
NEI	425.458-1	1			I		2.00	152	113	0.462	414	1.263	76	57	21
NEI	530.458	4			A		2.00	260	147	0.462	478	1.357	130	74	20
NEI	425.458-2	1			I		2.00	155	131	0.462	413	1.265	78	66	21
NEI	425.458	1	2 of these		I		2.00	270	205	0.462	414	1.262	135	103	21
SAECO	015 (1 4 & 1 8)		2 @ once		I		2.00	984	736	0.462	295	0.824	492	368	33
NEI	535.458	1			I		2.00	124	79	0.463	506	1.437	62	40	19
SAECO	015	8			I		21.25	6200	3946	0.464	295	0.820	292	186	33
SAECO	015	8	2 @ once	21	I		2.00	520	268	0.464	295	0.820	260	134	33
SAECO	015	8	2 @ once	22	I		14.00	3952	2690	0.464	295	0.820	282	192	33
SAECO	015	8	3 @ once	7	I			1312	960	0.464	295	0.820	210	154	33

Maker	Mould	Cavities	Comments	Used Together	Material	Alloy	Casting Time (hrs.)	Total Bullets Cast	Visually Acceptable Bullets	Diameter	Weight	Length	Bullets Per Hour (BPH)	Visually Acceptable BPH	Rate Of Twist
SAECO	015	8	4 @ once	13	I			408	312	0.464	295	0.820	204	156	33
H&G	S357	6			I		6.00	1650	1338	0.476	293	0.722	275	223	39
H&G	357	6			I		6.00	1494	810	0.477	416	1.005	249	135	28
Hilte	ML50MAX-3	3			A		N/A	6	N/A	0.494	338	0.915	N/A	N/A	33
NEI	445.500	1			I	ww	2.00	273	166	0.499	447	0.999	137	83	31
NEI	510.500 PP	1			I		2.00	133	77	0.500	496	1.113	67	39	28
RCBS	50-400-SWC-2	1			I		2.00	177	99	0.500	384	0.885	89	50	35
RCBS	50-400-SWC-1	1			I		2.00	178	141	0.500	379	0.877	89	71	36
NEI	445.500	1			I		2.00	148	115	0.500	418	1.002	74	58	31
RCBS	50-400-SWC	1	3 of these		I		2.00	263	248	0.500	381	0.883	132	124	36
RCBS	50-400-SWC	1	2 of these		I		2.00	231	181	0.501	380	0.881	116	91	36
RCBS	50-400-SWC-3	1			I		2.00	163	95	0.501	381	0.885	82	48	36
NEI	325.500	1			I		6.00	456	265	0.502	329	0.766	76	44	41
Ballisti-Cast	1454	4	2 of these		I		8.00	2440	1392	0.502	368	0.790	305	174	40
Ballisti-Cast	1454 (2 of these)	4	3 @ once	7	I		6.25	1216	840	0.502	368	0.790	195	134	40
Ballisti-Cast	1454 (2 of these)	4	3 @ once	8	I		2.00	504	320	0.502	368	0.790	252	160	40
Ballisti-Cast	1454 (2 of these)	4	3 @ once	9	I			1656	1029	0.502	368	0.790	276	172	40
Ballisti-Cast	1454 (2 of these)	4	4 @ once	13	I		2.00	384	307	0.502	368	0.790	192	154	40
Ballisti-Cast	1454-2	4			I		2.00	380	257	0.504	368	0.792	190	129	40
Navy Arms	450 Smith	1			I		3.00	265	36	0.504	282	0.680	88	12	47
Ballisti-Cast	1454-1	4			I		2.00	428	243	0.504	369	0.794	214	122	40
Ballisti-Cast	1454 (2 of these)	4	3 @ once	10	I			4800	3389	0.504	369	0.794	277	196	40
Ballisti-Cast	1454	4	3 @ once	11	I		19.00	2616	2217	0.504	369	0.794	138	117	40
Ballisti-Cast	1454 (2 of these)	4	4 @ once	12	I		2.00	420	361	0.504	369	0.794	210	181	40
T/C	Maxi-Hunter	1			I	lead	2.00	289	153	0.505	346	0.756	145	77	42
NEI	300.510	2			I	lead	4.00	770	513	0.505	309	0.686	193	128	47
NEI	860.510	1			I	ww	7.00	744	347	0.506	935	2.231	106	50	14
NEI	500.510	1			I	30/1	2.00	282	150	0.506	535	1.107	141	75	29
Ballisti-Cast	1465	4			I	ww	2.00	708	318	0.507	541	1.102	354	159	29
CBE	512.975-1	1			B	ww	2.00	226	171	0.508	966	2.002	113	86	16
CBE	512.975	1	2 of these		B	ww	2.00	234	86	0.508	965	2.000	117	43	16
Hoch	510.425	1			I	30/1	2.00	220	112	0.508	429	0.921	110	56	35
CBE	512.975-2	1			B	ww	2.00	264	114	0.508	963	1.999	132	57	16
NEI	625.510	1			I	30/1	2.00	252	152	0.509	669	1.339	126	76	24
NEI	860.510	1			I		2.00	125	63	0.509	886	2.237	63	32	15
NEI	350.508	1			I		2.00	165	68	0.509	367	0.861	83	34	38
CBE	510.510	1			B		2.00	133	57	0.509	473	1.050	67	29	31
Hoch	513.715	1			I	ww	6.00	578	368	0.510	703	1.465	96	61	22
Hoch	513.715	1			I	30/1	2.00	195	140	0.510	721	1.466	98	70	22
NEI	300.510	2			I		0.67	56	32	0.510	281	0.690	84	48	47
NEI	420.512	1			I	30/1	4.00	495	273	0.510	448	0.927	124	68	35
Ballisti-Cast	1435-27	5			I	lead	2.00	930	756	0.510	358	0.666	465	378	49
Rapine	515.365	1			A	lead	3.00	390	224	0.510	362	0.748	130	75	44
Ballisti-Cast	1435	5	2 of these		I	lead	8.00	4035	2716	0.511	356	0.664	504	340	49
NEI	625.510	1			I		2.00	115	41	0.511	621	1.342	58	21	24
Hoch	512.760	3			I	lead	4.00	654	394	0.511	740	1.470	164	99	22
Ballisti-Cast	1435-26	5			I	lead	2.00	825	265	0.511	355	0.662	413	133	49
Hoch	510.425	1			I		2.00	122	84	0.512	398	0.923	61	42	35
Hoch	513.715	1			I		2.00	102	70	0.512	669	1.472	51	35	22
NEI	630.511	1			I	30/1	2.00	253	113	0.512	674	1.340	127	57	24
RCBS	50-515-FN-2	1			I	ww	2.00	243	174	0.512	541	1.101	122	87	30
RCBS	50-515-FN	1	2 of these		I	ww	6.00	986	827	0.512	541	1.101	164	138	30
RCBS	50-515-FN	1	3 of these		I	ww	16.00	2089	1349	0.512	541	1.101	131	84	30
SAECO	542	1			I		6.00	334	237	0.512	562	1.218	56	40	27
NEI	640.512	1			I		2.00	101	82	0.512	667	1.433	51	41	23
NEI	420.512	4			A	ww	2.00	552	405	0.512	433	0.931	276	203	35
NEI	630.511	1			I		2.00	114	74	0.512	628	1.344	57	37	24
Hoch	513.445	1			I	30/1	4.00	507	322	0.513	445	0.953	127	81	34
RCBS	50-515-FN-3	1			I	lead	2.00	207	156	0.513	558	1.098	104	78	30
SAECO	583	1			I		6.00	348	195	0.513	610	1.332	58	33	25
Hoch	512.760	3			I	ww	2.00	318	152	0.513	705	1.475	159	76	22
Hoch	512.760	3			I		2.00	153	62	0.513	677	1.473	77	31	22
NEI	640.512	1			I	30/1	1.88	241	81	0.513	714	1.430	128	43	23
NEI	420.512	1			I		6.00	405	299	0.513	420	0.933	68	50	35
Hoch	512.400	3			I		14.00	1776	1290	0.513	367	0.797	127	92	41
Hoch	512.400	3	2 @ once	16	I			700	372	0.513	367	0.797	117	62	41
Ballisti-Cast	1435-2	5			I		2.00	590	238	0.513	326	0.667	295	119	49
Hoch	513.445	1			I	ww	32.12	5153	2888	0.513	438	0.954	160	90	35
CBE	512.975-2	1			B		2.00	97	40	0.513	905	2.011	49	20	16
Ballisti-Cast	1435	5	2 of these		I		3.00	1465	886	0.513	325	0.667	488	295	49
Ballisti-Cast	1465	4			I		2.00	306	153	0.514	510	1.107	153	77	30
Ballisti-Cast	1465	4	2 @ once	5	I		2.00	268	123	0.514	510	1.107	134	62	30
Ballisti-Cast	1465 (1 of 3)	4	3 @ once	28	I			1488	1320	0.514	510	1.107	124	110	30

MOULD BLOCK DESCRIPTION						EXPERIMENTAL DATA				EXPERIMENTAL RESULTS					
Maker	Mould	Cavities	Comments	Used Together	Material	Alloy	Casting Time (hrs.)	Total Bullets Cast	Visually Acceptable Bullets	BULLET DESCRIPTION AVERAGE			Bullets Per Hour (BPH)	Visually Acceptable BPH	Rate Of Twist
										Diameter	Weight	Length			
CBE	512.975-1	1			B		2.00	100	43	0.514	904	2.007	50	22	16
Ballisti-Cast	1435-1	5			I		2.00	580	197	0.514	324	0.668	290	99	49
Lyman	515141	1			I		6.00	399	187	0.514	416	0.969	67	31	34
Ballisti-Cast	1417	5			I		2.00	455	188	0.514	420	0.853	228	94	39
Lyman	515142	1			I		10.00	654	200	0.514	488	1.051	65	20	31
NEI	630.512	1			A		17.00	875	595	0.514	651	1.398	52	35	24
NEI	715.511	1			A		6.00	283	136	0.514	702	1.496	47	23	22
Rapine	515.385	1			A	lead	4.00	512	254	0.514	395	0.817	128	64	41
NEI	420.512	4			A		2.00	388	199	0.514	410	0.933	194	100	35
Lyman	515141	2			I		2.00	202	82	0.514	412	0.976	101	41	34
Lyman	515141	1			I		1.00	76	32	0.515	411	0.970	76	32	34
RCBS	50-515-FN	1	2 of these		I	lead	2.00	292	215	0.515	557	1.099	146	108	30
Hoch	513.445	1			I		4.00	252	163	0.515	414	0.956	63	41	35
RCBS	50-515-FN-3	1			I		2.00	119	98	0.515	508	1.103	60	49	30
RCBS	50-515-FN	1	2 of these		I		12.00	1199	668	0.515	509	1.103	100	56	30
RCBS	50-515-FN-2	1			I		2.00	123	89	0.515	510	1.102	62	45	30
NEI	630.512	1			A		3.00	148	38	0.515	654	1.406	49	13	24
RCBS	50-450-FN	1			I		2.00	129	89	0.515	443	0.969	65	45	34
RCBS	50-515-FN-1	1			I	30/1	2.00	232	136	0.515	553	1.105	116	68	30
RCBS	50-515-FN	1	2 of these		I		12.00	1271	841	0.516	511	1.106	106	70	30
Rapine	515.365	1			A		6.00	445	266	0.516	334	0.760	74	44	44
RCBS	50-515-FN	1	3 of these		I		0.67	59	49	0.516	509	1.104	88	73	30
Rapine	540.300-1	1			A	30/1	2.00	284	144	0.516	304	0.642	142	72	52
NEI	385.515	1			I		4.00	276	167	0.516	354	0.833	69	42	40
Lee	52 Wilkinson	2	2 of these		A	lead	2.00	430	326	0.516	361	0.885	215	163	38
RCBS	50-515-FN-1	1			I		2.00	121	97	0.517	513	1.110	61	49	30
Lyman	515139	1			I		2.00	160	116	0.517	314	0.726	80	58	46
RCBS	50-515-FN-2	1			I	lead	2.00	184	126	0.517	557	1.101	92	63	30
Rapine	515.385	1			A		8.00	676	172	0.517	359	0.821	85	22	41
Rapine	540.300-2	1			A		2.00	169	161	0.518	273	0.651	85	81	51
RCBS	50-515-FN-4	1			I		2.00	144	103	0.518	510	1.106	72	52	30
NEI	490.540	2	1 in a 2	26	A	lead	4.00	269	123	0.518	494	1.071	67	31	31
NEI	500.540	2	1 in a 2	26	A	lead		269	115	0.518	502	1.073	67	29	31
Rapine	540.300-2	1			A	lead	2.00	216	164	0.518	313	0.650	108	82	52
Rapine	540.300	1	2 of these		A	lead	12.00	1827	1247	0.518	313	0.648	152	104	52
Rapine	540.300-1	1			A	lead	2.00	268	164	0.518	312	0.646	134	82	52
Rapine	515.370	1			A	lead	2.00	282	46	0.519	368	0.834	141	23	40
Rapine	520.375	1			A	lead	1.75	264	64	0.519	375	0.778	151	37	43
Rapine	520.300	1			A	lead	2.00	303	112	0.519	298	0.641	152	56	53
Ideal	50-Gov	6			I		2.00	462	344	0.520	431	1.022	231	172	33
Rapine	520.300	1			A		2.00	148	100	0.520	271	0.650	74	50	52
Lee	52 Wilkinson-2	2			A		2.00	262	174	0.520	330	0.890	131	87	38
Romano	50 Maynard	1			I	lead	21.00	2400	1706	0.520	397	0.866	114	81	39
Lee	52 Wilkinson	2	2 of these		A		2.00	368	286	0.520	330	0.891	184	143	38
Rapine	540.300	1	2 of these		A		2.00	245	221	0.521	279	0.653	123	111	52
Rapine	515.370	1			A		2.00	140	83	0.521	336	0.841	70	42	40
Rapine	520.357	1			A	lead	2.00	236	29	0.521	361	0.880	118	15	39
Lee	52 Wilkinson-1	2			A		2.00	272	196	0.521	330	0.893	136	98	38
NEI	490.540	2	1 in a 2	3	A		6.00	295	107	0.521	455	1.078	49	18	32
Romano	56-50	1			I		2.00	170	34	0.521	309	0.724	85	17	47
Rapine	520.375	1			A		2.00	149	100	0.521	341	0.784	75	50	43
NEI	500.540	2	1 in a 2	3	A			295	161	0.522	461	1.082	49	27	32
Rapine	515.357	1			A	lead	2.00	279	110	0.522	365	0.885	140	55	39
Rapine	540.300-1	1			A		2.00	153	105	0.523	285	0.655	77	53	52
Rapine	520.357	1			A		2.00	148	73	0.523	327	0.888	74	37	39
Rapine	515.357	1			A		2.00	146	76	0.525	333	0.893	73	38	39
NEI	365.525 HB	1			I		2.00	151	135	0.528	330	0.785	76	68	44
RCBS	530-R	1			I	lead	2.00	303	233	0.530	225	0.530	152	117	66
RCBS	530-R	1			I		2.00	168	161	0.533	205	0.533	84	81	67
NEI	525.544	1			I	lead	2.00	267	162	0.535	529	1.076	134	81	33
LBT	636.535	2	1 in a 2	1	A			285	142	0.535	637	1.349	48	24	27
Rapine	535.370	1			A	lead	2.00	280	86	0.539	385	0.731	140	43	50
Rapine	535.370	1			A		2.00	148	109	0.540	352	0.740	74	55	49
Rapine	544.475	1			A	lead	2.00	253	93	0.545	486	1.022	127	47	36
Lee	54 Gardner V2	1			A		2.00	173	36	0.547	342	1.085	87	18	34
Lee	54 Gardner V1	1			A		2.00	175	135	0.547	386	1.081	88	68	35
Rapine	544.475	1			A		2.00	118	96	0.547	443	1.029	59	48	36
Rapine	546.375	1			A		6.00	442	242	0.548	351	0.742	74	40	51
Rapine	560.500	1			A	lead	2.00	218	85	0.552	550	1.046	109	43	36
Hoch	555.350	1			I	lead	2.00	211	155	0.553	353	0.641	106	78	60
Rapine	556.360	1			A	lead	4.00	501	195	0.553	353	0.636	125	49	60
NEI	525.544	1			I		2.00	133	69	0.554	484	1.077	67	35	36
Hoch	555.350	1			I		2.00	142	112	0.556	321	0.641	71	56	60

MOULD BLOCK DESCRIPTION						EXPERIMENTAL DATA				EXPERIMENTAL RESULTS					
Maker	Mould	Cavities	Comments	Used Together	Material	Alloy	Casting Time (hrs.)	Total Bullets Cast	Visually Acceptable Bullets	BULLET DESCRIPTION AVERAGE			Bullets Per Hour (BPH)	Visually Accept-able BPH	Rate Of Twist
										Diameter	Weight	Length			
Rapine	556.360	1			A		2.00	142	99	0.557	322	0.642	71	50	60
NEI	420.556	1			I	lead	2.00	250	211	0.559	445	0.838	125	106	47
Lyman	562 RB	1			I		6.00	508	232	0.561	242	0.576	85	39	68
NEI	420.556	1			I		2.00	137	115	0.562	405	0.842	69	58	47
Rapine	560.500	1			A		2.00	107	89	0.564	500	1.050	54	45	38
Lee	58 Wilkinson	2			A	lead	2.00	362	229	0.575	436	0.895	181	115	46
RCBS	58-500-M	1			I		4.00	257	126	0.578	474	1.019	64	32	41
NEI	542.577	1			I	30/1	2.00	247	200	0.578	562	0.946	124	100	44
NEI	900.577	1			A	ww	2.00	187	74	0.579	967	1.578	94	37	27
Edington	58 Wilkinson	1			I		2.00	208	109	0.579	367	0.904	104	55	46
NEI	900.577	1			A		2.00	92	41	0.579	928	1.580	46	21	27
NEI	542.577	1			I		2.00	120	86	0.580	520	0.947	60	43	44
Lee	58 Williams	1			A		2.00	157	119	0.580	420	0.970	79	60	43
Lee	58 Wilkinson	2			A		2.00	192	168	0.581	381	0.900	96	84	47
NEI	58 Maxi	2			A		6.00	378	168	0.584	542	1.065	63	28	40
Lee	58 Wilkinson	1			A		2.00	153	101	0.585	450	0.975	77	51	44
NEI	525.586	4			A		6.00	736	316	0.590	511	0.921	123	53	47
Lee	58-350-REAL	2			A		6.00	550	183	0.592	321	0.640	92	31	69
Lee	58-440-REAL	2			A		6.00	510	106	0.592	405	0.776	85	18	57
NEI	670.586	2			A		5.00	264	82	0.593	644	1.117	53	16	39
NEI	900.622	1			A		16.00	671	170	0.623	860	1.298	42	11	37
Lyman	12 g Sabot	1			I	lead	2.00	170	33	0.665	514	0.771	85	17	72
Lyman	12 g. Sabot HB	1			I		2.00	110	63	0.667	454	0.780	55	32	71
Lyman	690 RB	1			I		6.00	347	214	0.687	447	0.690	58	36	86
Lee	69 Williams HB	1			A		2.00	122	68	0.695	492	0.968	61	34	62
Lee	69 Wilkinson	1			A		2.00	144	129	0.698	563	0.963	72	65	63
Lyman	12 g. Slug	1			I	lead	2.00	159	56	0.706	479	0.786	80	28	79
Lyman	12 g. Slug HB	1			I		2.00	114	82	0.706	427	0.791	57	41	79
NEI	1765.820	1			A		2.00	89	17	0.822	1720	1.564	45	9	54
NEI	2800.843	1			A		6.00	152	115	0.848	2288	1.900	25	19	47
NEI	3500.955	1			A		2.00	54	34	0.958	3453	2.222	27	17	52
NEI	3000.100	1			I	lead	n/a	40	11	0.999	2158	1.366	n/a	n/a	91
			totals:				2828.00	616235	427786						

2010 GUN DIGEST Complete Compact CATALOG

GUNDEX® 306

HANDGUNS

Autoloading 317
Competition 343
Double-Action Revolvers . 346
Single-Action Revolvers . . 353
Miscellaneous 360

RIFLES

Centerfire—Autoloaders . . 362
Centerfire—Lever & Slide . 376
Centerfire—Bolt-Action . . 382
Centerfire—Single Shot . . 403
Drillings, Combination
     Guns, Double Rifles . . . 412
Rimfire—Autoloaders 414
Rimfire—Lever &
     Slide Action 417
Rimfire—Bolt Actions
     & Single Shots 419
Competition—Centerfire
     & Rimfire 425

SHOTGUNS

Autoloaders 431
Slide & Lever Actions 440

SHOTGUNS (cont.)

Over/Unders 446
Side-By-Side 457
Bolt Actions &
     Single Shot 462
Military & Police 465

BLACKPOWDER

Single Shot Pistols—Flint
     & Percussion 467
Revolvers 468
Muskets & Rifles 470
Shotguns 480

AIRGUNS

Handguns 481
Long Guns 483

REFERENCES

Web Directory 488
Arms Library 500

**DIRECTORY OF THE
ARMS TRADE**

Manufacturer's
     Directory 529

Numbers

1862 Pocket Navy Percussion
     Revolver 465

A

Accu-Tek AT-380 II 380 ACP Pistol . . .313
Airforce Condor Rifle 479
Airforce Talon Air Rifle 479
Airforce Talon SS Air Rifle 479
Airrow Model A-8S1P Stealth Air Rifle .479
Airrow Model A-8SRB Stealth Air Rifle .479
Anschutz 1416D/1516D Classic Rifles .415
Anschutz 1710D Custom Rifle 415
Anschutz 1827BT Fortner Biathlon
     Rifle 421
Anschutz 1903 Match Rifle 421
Anschutz 1907 Standard Match Rifle . .421
Anschutz 1912 Sport Rifle 421
Anschutz 1913 Super Match Rifle 421
Anschutz 2007 Match Rifle 421
Anschutz 64-MP R Silhouette Rifle 421
Anschutz Super Match Special
     Model 2013 Rifle 421
Armalite AR-10(T) Rifle 422
Armalite AR-10A2 358
Armalite AR-10A4 Special Purpose
     Rifle 358
Armalite AR-10B Rifle 358
Armalite AR-24 Pistol 313
Armalite AR-50 Rifle 399
Armalite M15 A4 Carbine 6.8 &
     7.62x39 422
Armalite M15A2 Carbine 358
Armalite M15A4(T) Eagle Eye Rifle . . .422
Armoury R140 Hawken Rifle 466
Army 1860 Percussion Revolver 464
Arrieta Sidelock Double Shotguns 453
ARS Hunting Master AR6 Air Pistol 477
ARS Hunting Master AR6 Air Rifle 479
Arsenal, Inc. SLR-106CR 358
Arsenal, Inc. SLR-107CR 358
Arsenal, Inc. SLR-107F 358
Auto-Ordnance 1911A1 Automatic
     Pistol 313
Auto-Ordnance 1927 A-1 Commando . .359
Auto-Ordnance 1927A-1 Thompson . . .358
Auto-Ordnance TA5 Semi-Auto Pistol . .313
Auto-Ordnance Thompson M1/M1-C . .359
AyA Model 4/53 Shotguns 453

B

Baby Dragoon 1848, 1849 Pocket,
     Wells Fargo .464
Baer 1911 Bullseye Wadcutter Pistol . .339
Baer 1911 Custom Carry Auto Pistol . . .313
Baer 1911 National Match Hardball
     Pistol 339
Baer 1911 Premier II Auto Pistol 313
Baer 1911 Prowler III Pistol 314
Baer 1911 S.R.P. Pistol 314
Baer 1911 Stinger Pistol 314

GUNDEX

Baer 1911 Ultimate Master Combat
  Pistol 339
Baer 1911 Ultimate Recon Pistol. 313
Baer H.C. 40 Auto Pistol 313
Ballard 1875 #3 Gallery Single Shot
  Rifle. 399
Ballard 1875 #4 Perfection Rifle 399
Ballard 1875 #7 Long Range Rifle. 399
Ballard 1875 #8 Union Hill Rifle. 399
Ballard 1875 1 1/2 Hunter Rifle 399
Ballard Model 1885 High Wall Special
  Sporting Single Shot Rifle. 399
Ballard Model 1885 High Wall Standard
  Sporting Single Shot Rifle. 399
Ballard Model 1885 Low Wall
  Single Shot Rifle 399
Barrett Model 82A-1 Semi-Automatic
  Rifle. 359
Barrett Model 95 Bolt-Action Rifle 378
Barrett Model 99 Single Shot Rifle 399
Beeman HW100 479
Beeman HW70A Air Pistol. 477
Beeman P1 Magnum Air Pistol 477
Beeman P3 Pneumatic Air Pistol. 477
Beeman R1 Air Rifle 479
Beeman R1 Carbine 479
Beeman R11 MkII Air Rifle 479
Beeman R7 Air Rifle 479
Beeman R9 Air Rifle 479
Beeman RX-2 Gas-Spring Magnum
  Air Rifle 479
Beeman/Feinwerkbau 700 P
  Aluminum or Wood Stock 479
Beeman/Feinwerkbau P44 477
Beeman/Feinwerkbau P56 477
Beeman/Feinwerkbau P70 Field
  Target 479
Beeman/FWB 103 Air Pistol 477
Beeman/HW 97 Air Rifle 480
Benelli Cordoba Shotgun. 428
Benelli Legacy Shotgun. 427
Benelli M2 Field Shotguns. 427
Benelli M2 Tactical Shotgun 461
Benelli M3 Convertible Shotgun 461
Benelli M4 Tactical Shotgun 427
Benelli Montefeltro Shotguns. 427
Benelli Nova Pump Shotguns 436
Benelli R1 Rifle 359
Benelli Super Black Eagle II Shotguns .428
Benelli Supernova Pump Shotguns. . . .436
Benelli Supersport & Sport II
  Shotguns. .428
Benelli Ultra Light Shotgun 427
Benjamin & Sheridan Co2 Pistols 477
Benjamin & Sheridan Pneumatic
  (Pump-Up) Air Rifle. 480
Benjamin & Sheridan Pneumatic
  Pellet Pistols 477
Beretta 1873 Renegade Short
  Lever-Action Rifle 372
Beretta 3901 Shotguns 428

Beretta 471 Side-By-Side Shotguns . . .453
Beretta 686 Onyx O/U Shotguns. 443
Beretta A391 Xtrema2 3.5 Auto
  Shotguns. .429
Beretta AL391 Teknys Shotguns. 429
Beretta AL391 Urika and Urika 2
  Auto Shotguns 429
Beretta Competition Shotguns. 443
Beretta CX4 Storm 480
Beretta CX4/PX4 Storm Carbine 359
Beretta DT10 Trident Shotguns. 442
Beretta DT10 Trident Trap Top
  Single Shotgun 458
Beretta Express SSO O/U Double
  Rifles. 408
Beretta Gold Rush Slide-Action Rifle
  and Carbine 372
Beretta Model 21 Bobcat Pistol 314
Beretta Model 3032 Tomcat Pistol 314
Beretta Model 455 SXS Express Rifle. .408
Beretta Model 80 Cheetah Series
  DA Pistols .314
Beretta Model 92FS Pistol. 314
Beretta Model M9 315
Beretta Model M9a1 315
Beretta Model PX4 Storm 314
Beretta Model PX4 Storm
  Sub-Compact 314
Beretta Model U22 Neos. 314
Beretta Series 682 Gold E Skeet, Trap,
  Sporting O/U Shotguns. 442
Beretta Silver Pigeon O/U Shotguns . . .443
Beretta Stampede Single-Action
  Revolver 349
Beretta SV10 Perennia O/U Shotgun . .442
Beretta UGB25 XCEL Semi-Auto
  Shotgun. 428
Beretta Ultralight O/U Shotguns 443
Bersa Thunder 380 Series Pistols. 315
Bersa Thunder 45 Ultra Compact
  Pistol 315
Bersa Thunder 9 Ultra Compact/40
  Series Pistols 315
Bf Classic Pistol. 339
Bill Hanus 16-Gauge Browning Citori
  M525 Field 443
Bill Hanus Nobile III by Fabarm. 453
Blaser R93 Bolt-Action Rifle 378
Blaser R93 Long Range Sporter 2
  Rifle. 422
Bond Arms Century 2000 Defender . . .356
Bond Arms Cowboy Defender. 356
Bond Arms Ranger 356
Bond Arms Snake Slayer 356
Bond Arms Snake Slayer IV 356
Bond Arms Texas Defender Derringer .356
Bostonian Percussion Rifle 466
Breda Altair .429
Breda Echo .429
Breda Grizzly. 429
Breda Xanthos. 429

GUNDEX

HANDGUNS

RIFLES

SHOTGUNS

BLACKPOWDER

AIRGUNS

REFERENCE

DIRECTORY OF
THE ARMS TRADE

GUNDEX

Brown Model 97D Single Shot Rifle . . .399
Browning A-Bolt Composite Stalker . . .379
Browning A-Bolt Eclipse Hunter
  w/Boss, M-1000 Eclipse w/Boss,
  M-1000 Eclipse WSM, Stainless
  M-1000 Eclipse WSM 380
Browning A-Bolt Hunter. 378
Browning A-Bolt Hunter FLD 378
Browning A-Bolt Medallion 379
Browning A-Bolt Micro Hunter and
  Micro Hunter Left-Hand. 379
Browning A-Bolt Mountain Ti 379
Browning A-Bolt Rifles 378
Browning A-Bolt Stainless Stalker,
  Stainless Stalker Left-Hand 379
Browning A-Bolt Target 378
Browning A-Bolt White Gold Medallion,
  RMEF White Gold, White Gold
  Medallion w/Boss 379
Browning Bar Safari and Safari
  w/Boss Semi-Auto Rifles. 360
Browning Bar Shorttrac/Longtrac
  Auto Rifles. 360
Browning Bar Stalker Auto Rifles 360
Browning BL-22 Rifles 413
Browning BLR Lightweight w/Pistol
  Grip, Short and Long Action;
  Lightweight '81, Short and
  Long Action. 372
Browning BLR Rifles 372
Browning BPS 10 Gauge Camo Pump
  Shotgun. 437
Browning BPS Micro Pump Shotgun. . .437
Browning BPS NWTF Turkey Series
  Pump Shotgun 437
Browning BPS Pump Shotguns. 436
Browning BT-99 Trap O/U Shotguns. . .458
Browning Buck Mark Pistols 315
Browning Buck Mark Semi-Auto Rifles .410
Browning Citori High Grade Shotguns. .445
Browning Citori O/U Shotguns. 444
Browning Citori XS Sporting O/U
  Shotguns. .445
Browning Citori XT Trap O/U Shotgun .445
Browning Cynergy O/U Shotguns 443
Browning Gold Auto Shotguns 429
Browning Gold Golden Clays Auto
  Shotguns. .430
Browning Gold Light 10 Gauge Auto
  Shotgun. 430
Browning Gold Nwtf Turkey Series
  and Mossy Oak Shotguns. 429
Browning Hi Power 9mm Automatic
  Pistol. 315
Browning Maxus 430
Browning Model 1885 High Wall
  Single Shot Rifle 399
Browning Sa-22 Semi-Auto 22 Rifles . .410
Browning Silver Auto Shotguns. 430
Browning T-Bolt Rimfire Rifle 415
Browning X-Bolt Hunter. 380
Browning X-Bolt Micro Hunter 380

Browning X-Bolt RMEF Special Hunter.380
Browning X-Bolt RMEF White Gold. . . .380
Browning X-Bolt Varmint Stalker 380
BSA Magnum Supersport Air Rifle,
  Carbine 480
BSA Meteor Air Rifle 480
BSA Superten MK3 Air Rifle 480
BSA Superten MK3 Bullbarrel 480
Bushmaster 11.5" Barrel Carbine 361
Bushmaster 450 Rifle and Carbine . . .361
Bushmaster 6.8 Spc Carbine. 361
Bushmaster A2/A3 Target Rifle 422
Bushmaster BA50 Bolt-Action Rifle. . .380
Bushmaster Carbon 15 .223 Pistol . . .316
Bushmaster Carbon 15 Flat-Top
  Carbine 361
Bushmaster Carbon 15 Top Loader
  Rifle. 361
Bushmaster DCM-XR Competition
  Rifle. 415
Bushmaster DCM-XR Competition
  Rifle. 422
Bushmaster Gas Piston Rifle. 361
Bushmaster Heavy-Barreled Carbine . .361
Bushmaster M4 Post-Ban Carbine . . .361
Bushmaster M4A3 Type Carbine 361
Bushmaster Modular Carbine 361
Bushmaster Orc Carbine. 361
Bushmaster Pit Viper 3-Gun
  Competition Rifle. 415
Bushmaster Superlight Carbines. 360
Bushmaster Target Rifle 361
Bushmaster Varminter Rifle. 361
Bushmaster Varminter Rifle. 423
Bushmaster XM15 E25 AK Shorty
  Carbine 361
Bushmaster XM15 E2s Dissipator
  Carbine 361

C

C. Sharps Arms 1874 Bridgeport Sporting
  Rifle. 400
C. Sharps Arms 1875 Classic Sharps. .400
C. Sharps Arms Custom New Model
  1877 Long Range Target Rifle 400
C. Sharps Arms Model 1875 Target
  & Sporting Rifle. 399
C. Sharps Arms New Model 1885
  Highwall Rifle 400
Cabela's 1874 Sharps Sporting Rifle. . .400
Cabela's Blackpowder Shotguns. 476
Cabela's Blue Ridge Rifle 466
Cabela's Kodiak Express Double Rifle .466
Cabela's Traditional Hawken. 466
Carbon One Bolt-Action Rifle 381
Century International AES-10 Hi-Cap
  Rifle. 362
Century International Gp WASR-10
  Hi-Cap Rifle. 362
Century International M70 Sporter
  Double-Trigger Bolt Action Rifle 381

Century International M70AB2
  Sporter Rifle 362
Century International WASR-2
  Hi-Cap Rifle. 362
Charles Daly Enhanced 1911 Pistols . .316
Charles Daly Field Pump Shotguns. . . .437
Charles Daly Field Semi-Auto
  Shotguns. .431
Charles Daly M-5 Polymer-Framed
  Hi-Cap 1911 Pistol 316
Charles Daly Maxi-Mag Pump
  Shotguns. .437
Charles Daly Model 1892 Lever-Action
  Rifles. 372
Charles Daly Model 206 O/U Shotgun .445
Charles Daly Superior II Semi-Auto
  Shotguns. .431
Charter Arms Bulldog Revolver. 342
Charter Arms Dixie Derringer 349
Charter Arms Dixie Derringers 356
Charter Arms Mag Pug Revolver. 342
Charter Arms Off Duty Revolver 342
Charter Arms Pink Lady Revolver 342
Charter Arms Southpaw Revolver. . . .342
Charter Arms Undercover Revolver . . .342
Charter Arms Undercover Southpaw
  Revolver 342
Cheytac M-200 381
Cimarron 1860 Henry Rifle Civil War
  Model 372
Cimarron 1866 Winchester Replicas. . .372
Cimarron 1872 Open Top Revolver. . . .349
Cimarron 1873 Deluxe Sporting Rifle . .372
Cimarron 1873 Long Range Rifle 372
Cimarron 1873 Short Rifle. 372
Cimarron Billy Dixon 1874 Sharps
  Sporting Rifle 400
Cimarron Bisley Model Single-Action
  Revolvers .349
Cimarron Lightning SA 349
Cimarron Model "P" Jr. 349
Cimarron Model 1885 High Wall Rifle . .400
Cimarron Model P 349
Cimarron Quigley Model 1874
  Sharps Sporting Rifle 400
Cimarron Silhouette Model 1874
  Sharps Sporting Rifle 400
Cimarron Thunderer Revolver. 350
Cimarron U.S.V. Artillery Model
  Single-Action. 349
Cobra Big Bore Derringers 356
Cobra Enterprises CA32, CA380 Pistol.316
Cobra Enterprises FS32, FS380
  Auto Pistol. 316
Cobra Enterprises Patriot 45 Pistol . . .316
Cobra Long-Bore Derringers 356
Cobra Standard Series Derringers 356
Colt Rail Gun 317
Colt Special Combat Government
  Carry Model 317
Colt 1918 WWI Replica 317

Colt 38 Super. 317
Colt Accurized Rifle. 423
Colt Defender 317
Colt Gold Cup Trophy Pistol 339
Colt Match Target Competition
  HBAR II Rifle. 423
Colt Match Target Competition
  HBAR Rifle 423
Colt Match Target HBAR & M4 Rifles . .423
Colt Match Target M4 363
Colt Match Target Model Rifle. 362
Colt Model 1991 Model O Auto Pistol . .317
Colt New Agent 317
Colt Series 70 317
Colt Single-Action Army Revolver 350
Colt Special Combat Government. 339
Colt XSE Lightweight Commander
  Auto Pistol. 317
Colt XSE Series Model O Auto Pistols . .317
Comanche I, II, III DA Revolvers 342
Comanche Super Single-Shot Pistol . . .356
Competitor Single-Shot Pistol 339
Connecticut Shotgun Manufacturing
  Company RBL Side-by-Side Shotgun. 453
Cook & Brother Confederate Carbine . .466
Cooper Model 21 Bolt-Action Rifle 381
Cooper Model 22 Bolt-Action Rifle 381
Cooper Model 38 Bolt-Action Rifle 381
Cooper Model 57-M Bolt-Action Rifle . .415
Crosman 2240. 477
Crosman 3576 Revolver 477
Crosman C11 477
Crosman Model .2260 Air Rifle 480
Crosman Model 1088 Repeat Air Pistol 477
Crosman Model Classic 2100 Air Rifle .480
Crosman Model Powermaster 664SB
  Air Rifles .480
Crosman Model Pumpmaster 760
  Air Rifles .480
Crosman Model Repeatair 1077 Rifles .480
Crosman Pro77 477
Crosman T4. 477
CVA Accura. 466
CVA Apex 466
CVA Buckhorn 209 Magnum. 466
CVA Kodiak Magnum Rifle 466
CVA Optima 209 Magnum
  Break-Action Rifle. 466
CVA Optima Elite Break-Action Rifle. . .466
CVA Wolf 209 Magnum Break-Action
  Rifle. 466
CZ 2075 Rami/Rami P Auto Pistol 319
CZ 452 American Bolt-Action Rifle 416
CZ 452 Lux Bolt-Action Rifle 416
CZ 452 Varmint Rifle. 416
CZ 513 Rifle. 410
CZ 527 American Bolt-Action Rifle 381
CZ 527 Lux Bolt-Action Rifle 381
CZ 550 American Classic Bolt-Action
  Rifle. 382

CZ 550 Magnum H.E.T. Bolt-Action
  Rifle. 382
CZ 550 Safari Magnum/American
  Safari Magnum Bolt-Action Rifles. . . .382
CZ 550 Ultimate Hunting Bolt-Action
  Rifle. 382
CZ 550 Varmint Bolt-Action Rifle. 382
CZ 584 Solo Combination Gun 408
CZ 589 Stopper Over/Under Gun 408
CZ 75 B Auto Pistol. 318
CZ 75 B Compact Auto Pistol 318
CZ 75 BD Decocker. 318
CZ 75 Champion Competition Pistol . . .339
CZ 75 Champion Pistol 318
CZ 75 Kadet Auto Pistol 318
CZ 75 Sp-01 Phantom. 318
CZ 75 Sp-01 Pistol 318
CZ 75 Tactical Sport 318
CZ 750 Sniper Rifle. 382
CZ 83 Double-Action Pistol 318
CZ 85 B/85 Combat Auto Pistol. 318
CZ 97 B Auto Pistol 318
CZ 97 BD Decocker. 319
CZ Bobwhite and Ringneck Shotguns. .453
CZ Canvasback. 446
CZ Hammer Coach Shotguns 453
CZ Mallard. 446
CZ P-01 Auto Pistol. 319
CZ Redhead 446
CZ Sporting Over/Under 446
CZ Woodcock 446

D

Daisy 1938 Red Ryder Air Rifle. 480
Daisy Avanti Model 887 Gold Medalist .481
Daisy Avanti Model 888 Medalist 480
Daisy Model 105 Buck Air Rifle 480
Daisy Model 105 Buck Air Rifle 481
Daisy Model 4841 Grizzly 480
Daisy Model 717 Air Pistol. 477
Daisy Model 747 Triumph Air Pistol . . .478
Daisy Model 753 Elite 481
Daisy Model 840B Grizzly Air Rifle 480
Daisy Model 853 Legend. 481
Daisy Powerline® 1000 Break Barrel . .481
Daisy Powerline® 201 478
Daisy Powerline® 500 Break Barrel . . .481
Daisy Powerline® 5170 Co2 Pistol 478
Daisy Powerline® 5501 Co2
  Blowback Pistol. 478
Daisy Powerline® 693 Air Pistol 478
Daisy Powerline® 800 Break Barrel . . .481
Daisy Powerline® 880 Air Rifle 481
Daisy Powerline® 901 Air Rifle 481
Daisy Powerline® Model 15XT Air
  Pistol 477
Daisy Powerline® Targetpro 953 Air
  Rifle. 481
Dakota 76 Classic Bolt-Action Rifle. . . .382
Dakota 76 Traveler Takedown Rifle . . .382

Dakota Double Rifle. 408
Dakota Legend Shotgun 454
Dakota Longbow T-76 Tactical Rifle . . .382
Dakota Model 10 Single Shot Rifle 401
Dakota Model 97 Bolt-Action Rifle. 383
Dakota Predator Rifle. 383
Dakota Premier Grade Shotgun 454
Dan Wesson Commander Classic
  Bobtail Auto Pistols. 319
Dan Wesson DW RZ-10 Auto Pistol . . .319
Dan Wesson DW RZ-10 Sportsman . . .319
Dan Wesson DW RZ-45 Heritage 319
Dan Wesson Firearms Pointman
  Seven Auto Pistol 319
Davey Crickett Single Shot Rifle 416
Desert Baby Eagle Pistols. 319
Desert Baby Micro Desert Eagle Pistol .319
Desert Eagle Mark XIX Pistol 319
Dixie 1873 Deluxe Sporting Rifle. 373
Dixie Deluxe Cub Rifle. 467
Dixie Early American Jaeger Rifle 466
Dixie Engraved 1873 Sporting Rifle. . . .373
Dixie Lightning Rifle and Carbine 373
Dixie Magnum Percussion Shotgun . . .476
Dixie Pedersoli 1857 Mauser Rifle 467
Dixie Sharps New Model 1859 Military
  Rifle. 467
Dixie U.S. Model 1816 Flintlock
  Musket 467
Dixie Wyatt Earp Revolver. 464
DPMS Panther Arms AR-15 Rifles 363
DPMS Panther Arms Classic Auto
  Rifle. 363
DSA 1R Carbine 363
DSA CQB MRP, Standard MRP 363
DSA DCM Rifle. 364
DSA DS-MP1. 383
DSA S1 364
DSA SA58 Bull Barrel Rifle 365
DSA SA58 Carbine 365
DSA SA58 Congo, Para Congo. 364
DSA SA58 G1 365
DSA SA58 Gray Wolf 364
DSA SA58 Medium Contour 365
DSA SA58 Mini OSW 366
DSA SA58 Predator. 364
DSA SA58 Standard 365
DSA SA58 T48 364
DSA SA58 Tactical Carbine 365
DSA Standard 363
DSA Std Carbine 363
DSA Xm Carbine 363
DSA Z4 GTC Carbine With C.R.O.S. . . .363

E

EAA Bounty Hunter SA Revolvers. 350
EAA Windicator Revolvers 342
EAA Witness Compact Auto Pistol 320
EAA Witness Elite Gold Team Auto . . .340

GUNDEX

EAA Witness Full Size Auto Pistol.....320
EAA Witness-P Carry Auto Pistol.....320
EAA Zastava Ez Pistol.....320
EAA/Baikal IZH61 Air Rifle.........481
EAA/Baikal IZH-M46 Target Air Pistol..478
EAA/HW 660 Match Rifle.........423
EAA/Zastava M-93 Black Arrow Rifle..383
Ed Brown Classic Custom.....320
Ed Brown Executive Pistols.........320
Ed Brown Hunting Series Rifles.....383
Ed Brown Kobra and Kobra Carry.....320
Ed Brown Model 704 Bushveld.......383
Ed Brown Model 704 Express.......383
Ed Brown Model 704, M40A2
  Marine Sniper.................423
Ed Brown Special Forces Carry Pistol..320
Ed Brown Special Forces Pistol.....320
EMF 1860 Henry Rifle............373
EMF 1863 Sharps Military Carbine....467
EMF 1866 Yellowboy Lever Actions...373
EMF 1873 Great Western II.........350
EMF 1875 Outlaw Revolver.........350
EMF 1890 Police Revolver.........350
EMF Great Western II Express
  Single-Action Revolver...........350
EMF Hartford Single-Action Revolvers.350
EMF Model 1873 Frontier Marshal....350
EMF Model 1873 Lever-Action Rifle...373
EMF Model 1873 Revolver Carbine...373
EMF Old West Hammer Shotgun.....454
EMF Old West Pump (Slide Action)
  Shotgun.......................437
EMF Premier 1874 Sharps Rifle......401
Escort Over/Under Shotguns........446
Escort Pump Shotguns............437
Escort Semi-Auto Shotguns.........431
Euroarms 1861 Springfield Rifle.....467
Euroarms Harpers Ferry Rifle.......467
Euroarms Volunteer Target Rifle.....467
Euroarms Zouave Rifle............467
Excel Arms Accelerator MP-17/MP-22
  Pistols........................321
Excel Arms Accelerator Rifles........366

F

Firestorm Auto Pistols..............321
Fox, A.H., Side-by-Side Shotguns.....454
Franchi 48AL Field and Deluxe
  Shotguns.....................431
Franchi 720 Competition Shotgun.....431
Franchi Inertia I-12 Shotgun.........431
Franchi Model 720 Shotguns.........431
Franchi Renaissance and Renaissance
  Sporting O/U Shotguns...........446
Freedom Arms Model 83 22 Field
  Grade Silhouette Class...........340
Freedom Arms Model 83 Centerfire
  Silhouette Models.............340
Freedom Arms Model 83 Field
  Grade Revolver.................351

Freedom Arms Model 83 Premier
  Grade Revolver.................351
Freedom Arms Model 97 Premier
  Grade Revolver.................351
French-Style Dueling Pistol.........463

G

Gamo Hunter Air Rifles.........482
Gamo P-23, P-23 Laser Pistol.......478
Gamo PT-80, PT-80 Laser Pistol......478
Gamo Shadow Air Rifles..........481
Gamo Viper Air Rifle............481
Gamo Whisper Air Rifles..........482
Garbi Express Double Rifle.........408
Garbi Model 100 Double Shotgun....454
Garbi Model 101 Side-by-Side Shotgun 454
Garbi Model 103 A & B Side-by-Side
  Shotguns.....................454
Garbi Model 200 Side-by-Side
  Shotgun.......................454
Glock 17/17C Auto Pistol.........321
Glock 19/19C Auto Pistol.........321
Glock 20/20C 10mm Auto Pistol.....321
Glock 21/21C Auto Pistol.........321
Glock 22/22C Auto Pistol.........321
Glock 23/23C Auto Pistol.........321
Glock 26 Auto Pistol.............321
Glock 27 Auto Pistol.............322
Glock 29 Auto Pistol.............322
Glock 30 Auto Pistol.............322
Glock 31/31C Auto Pistol.........322
Glock 32/32C Auto Pistol.........322
Glock 33 Auto Pistol.............322
Glock 34 Auto Pistol.............322
Glock 35 Auto Pistol.............322
Glock 36 Auto Pistol.............322
Glock 37 Auto Pistol.............322
Glock 38 Auto Pistol.............322
Glock 39 Auto Pistol.............322
Glock Model 20 SF Short Frame Pistol.321
Glock Model 29 SF Short Frame Pistol.322
Gonic Model 93 Deluxe M/L Rifle.....467
Gonic Model 93 M/L Rifle.........467
Gonic Model 93 Mountain Thumbhole
  M/L Rifles....................467

H

Hammerli 850 Air Magnum.........482
Hammerli AP-40 Air Pistol.........478
Hammerli AR 50 Air Rifle..........482
Hammerli Model 450 Match Air Rifle...482
Hammerli Nova................482
Hammerli Quick...............482
Hammerli Razor...............482
Hammerli SP 20 Target Pistol.......340
Hammerli Storm Elite............482
Harper's Ferry 1803 Flintlock Rifle....468
Harper's Ferry 1805 Pistol.........463
Harrington & Richardson Buffalo
  Classic Rifle.................401

Harrington & Richardson CR-45LC....401
Harrington & Richardson Excell
  Auto 5 Shotguns...............432
Harrington & Richardson Pardner
  Pump Field Gun Full-Dip Camo.....438
Harrington & Richardson Topper
  Models.......................458
Harrington & Richardson Topper
  Trap Gun......................459
Harrington & Richardson Ultra Lite
  Slug Hunter...................458
Harrington & Richardson Ultra
  Slug Hunter Thumbhole Stock......458
Harrington & Richardson Ultra
  Slug Hunter/Tamer Shotguns.......458
Harrington & Richardson Ultra
  Varmint/Ultra Hunter Rifles.........401
Harrington & Richardson/New England
  Firearms Handi-Rifle/Slug Gun
  Combos.......................401
Harrington & Richardson/New England
  Firearms Stainless Ultra Hunter with
  Thumbhole Stock...............401
Hawken Rifle.................468
Heckler & Koch Mark 23 Special
  Operations Pistol..............323
Heckler & Koch P2000 Auto Pistol....323
Heckler & Koch P2000 SK Auto Pistol.323
Heckler & Koch USC Carbine........366
Heckler & Koch USP Auto Pistol.....322
Heckler & Koch USP Compact Auto
  Pistol.......................323
Heckler & Koch USP Compact
  Tactical Pistol................323
Heckler & Koch USP45 Tactical Pistol.323
Henry .30/30 Lever-Action Carbine...373
Henry "Mini" Bolt Action 22 Rifle.....416
Henry Acu-Bolt Rifle............416
Henry Big Boy Lever-Action Carbine...373
Henry Golden Boy 22 Lever-Action
  Rifle.........................413
Henry Lever Octagon Frontier Model..413
Henry Lever-Action Rifles..........413
Henry Pump-Action 22 Pump Rifle....413
Henry U.S. Survival Rifle AR-7 22.....410
Heritage Rough Rider Revolver......351
High Standard 10X Custom 22 Pistol..323
High Standard Olympic Military 22
  Pistol........................324
High Standard Sport King 22 Pistol....324
High Standard Supermatic Citation
  Series 22 Pistol................324
High Standard Supermatic
  Tournament 22 Pistol...........324
High Standard Supermatic Trophy
  22 Pistol....................323
High Standard Supermatic Trophy
  Target Pistol..................340
High Standard Victor 22 Pistol.......323
High Standard Victor Target Pistol....340
Hi-Point 9mm Carbine............366
Hi-Point Firearms 40sw/poly and
  45 Auto Pistols................323

Hi-Point Firearms Model 380 Polymer
Pistol.........................323
Hi-Point Firearms Model 9mm
Compact Pistol 323
Hoenig Rotary Round Action
Combination 408
Hoenig Rotary Round Action Double
Rifle.........................408
Howa Camo Lightning M-1500 384
Howa M-1500 Ranchland Compact....383
Howa M-1500 Thumbhole Sporter 384
Howa M-1500 Ultralight 2-n-1 Youth ...384
Howa M-1500 Varminter Supreme and
Thumbhole Varminter Supreme 384
Howa/Axiom M-1500................384
Howa/Hogue M-1500..............384
Howa/Hogue M-1500 Compact Heavy
Barrel Varminter 384
H-S Precision Pro-Series Bolt-Action
Rifles........................384

I

IAC Model 87W-1 Lever-Action
Shotgun.......................438
Ithaca Gun Company Deerslayer III
Slug Shotgun 438
Ithaca Gun Company Model 37
28 Gauge Shotgun 438

J

J.P. Henry Trade Rifle 468
J.P. Murray 1862-1864 Cavalry Carbine468

K

Kahr 380 ACP Pistol 325
Kahr CW Series Pistol.............325
Kahr K Series Auto Pistols 324
Kahr MK Series Micro Pistols 324
Kahr P Series Pistols..............324
Kahr PM Series Pistols............324
Kahr T Series Pistols.............324
Kahr TP Series Pistols............324
Kel-Tec P-11 Auto Pistol 325
Kel-Tec P-32 Auto Pistol 325
Kel-Tec P-3at Pistol..............325
Kel-Tec PF-9 Pistol 325
Kel-Tec PLR-16 Pistol............325
Kel-Tec PLR-22 Pistol............325
Kel-Tec RFB 384
Kel-Tec SU-22CA 410
Kenny Jarrett Bolt-Action Rifle.......384
Kentucky Flintlock Pistol 463
Kentucky Flintlock Rifle 468
Kentucky Percussion Pistol.........463
Kentucky Percussion Rifle..........468
Kimber CDP II Series Auto Pistol 326
Kimber Compact Stainless II Auto
Pistol........................326
Kimber Custom II Auto Pistol........325
Kimber Eclipse II Series Auto Pistol ...326

Kimber Gold Match II Auto Pistol.....326
Kimber Marias O/U Shotgun 446
Kimber Model 8400 Bolt-Action Rifle...385
Kimber Model 8400 Caprivi Bolt-Action
Rifle.........................385
Kimber Model 8400 Talkeetna Bolt-Action
Rifle.........................385
Kimber Model 84M Bolt-Action Rifle ...385
Kimber Pro Carry II Auto Pistol 325
Kimber Rimfire Target 341
Kimber SIS Auto Pistol 326
Kimber Stainless II Auto Pistols......325
Kimber Super Match II............340
Kimber Tactical Custom HD II Pistol ...326
Kimber Tactical Entry II Pistol 326
Kimber Team Match II Auto Pistol.....326
Kimber Ultra Carry II Auto Pistol 326
Kimber Valier Side-by-Side Shotgun...454
Knight 52 Models................469
Knight Bighorn..................468
Knight Extreme 468
Knight Long Range Hunter 468
Knight Rolling Block Rifle 468
Knight Shadow Rifle 468
Knight TK2000 Next G-1 Camo
Muzzleloading Shotgun...........476
Kolar AAA Competition Skeet O/U
Shotgun.......................447
Kolar AAA Competition Trap O/U
Shotgun.......................447
Kolar Sporting Clays O/U Shotguns ...447
Korth USA Pistol Semi-Auto 326
Korth USA Revolvers..............342
Krieghoff Classic Big Five Double Rifle.409
Krieghoff Classic Double Rifle.......409
Krieghoff Hubertus Single-Shot Rifle...402
Krieghoff K-20 O/U Shotgun 447
Krieghoff K-80 Single Barrel Trap Gun .459
Krieghoff K-80 Skeet O/U Shotguns ...447
Krieghoff K-80 Sporting Clays O/U
Shotgun.......................447
Krieghoff K-80 Trap O/U Shotguns 447
Krieghoff KX-5 Trap Gun...........459

L

L.A.R. Grizzly 50 Big Boar Rifle.......385
Lanber Semi-Automatic Shotguns.....432
Le Mat Revolver 464
Le Page Percussion Dueling Pistol ...463
Lebeau-Courally Boss-Verees O/U
Shotgun.......................447
Lebeau-Courally Boxlock Side-By-Side
Shotgun.......................454
Lebeau-Courally Express Rifle SxS ...409
Lebeau-Courally Sidelock
Side-by-Side Shotgun............454
Les Baer Custom Ultimate AR 223
Rifles........................366
Ljutic LM-6 Super Deluxe O/U
Shotguns......................447
Ljutic LTX Pro 3 Deluxe Mono Gun....459

Ljutic Mono Gun Single Barrel
Shotgun.......................459
London Armory 1861 Enfield
Musketoon 469
London Armory 2-Band 1858 Enfield ..469
London Armory 3-Band 1853 Enfield ..469
LR 300 Rifles...................367
Lyman Deerstalker Rifle 469
Lyman Great Plains Hunter Model 469
Lyman Great Plains Rifle...........469
Lyman Plains Pistol 463
Lyman Trade Rifle 469

M

Magnum Baby Desert 478
Magnum Research BFR Single-Action
Revolver 351
Magnum Research Desert Eagle 478
Magnum Research Magnumlite Rifles..410
Magnum Research Mountain Eagle
Magnumlite Rifles 385
Markesbery KM Black Bear M/I Rifle...470
Markesbery KM Brown Bear Rifle 470
Markesbery KM Colorado Rocky
Mountain Rifle..................470
Markesbery KM Grizzly Bear Rifle.....470
Markesbery KM Polar Bear Rifle......470
Marlin 70PSS Papoose Stainless Rifle .411
Marlin L. C. Smith O/U Shotguns 447
Marlin L. C. Smith Side-by-Side
Shotgun.......................454
Marlin Model 1894 Cowboy 374
Marlin Model 1894 Lever-Action
Carbine.......................374
Marlin Model 1894C Carbine........374
Marlin Model 1894SS 374
Marlin Model 1895 Cowboy
Lever-Action Rifle 375
Marlin Model 1895 Lever-Action Rifle ..374
Marlin Model 1895 SBL R...........375
Marlin Model 1895G Guide Gun
Lever-Action Rifle 374
Marlin Model 1895GS Guide Gun 375
Marlin Model 1895M Lever-Action Rifle.375
Marlin Model 1895MXLR Lever-Action
Rifle.........................375
Marlin Model 1895XLR Lever-Action
Rifle.........................375
Marlin Model 336C Lever-Action
Carbine.......................373
Marlin Model 336SS Lever-Action
Carbine.......................373
Marlin Model 336W Lever-Action Rifle .373
Marlin Model 338MXLR.............374
Marlin Model 39A Golden
Lever-Action Rifle 413
Marlin Model 444 Lever-Action Sporter.374
Marlin Model 444XLR Lever-Action
Rifle.........................374
Marlin Model 60 Auto Rifle 410
Marlin Model 60SS Self-loading Rifle ..411

Marlin Model 795 Auto Rifle 411
Marlin Model 915YN "Little Buckaroo". .417
Marlin Model 917 Bolt-Action Rifles. . . .416
Marlin Model 925M Bolt-Action Rifles . .417
Marlin Model 982 Bolt-Action Rifle 417
Marlin Model 983 Bolt-Action Rifle 417
Marlin Model XLR Lever-Action Rifles. .373
Marlin XL7 Bolt Action Rifle. 386
Marlin XS7 Short-Action Bolt-Action
  Rifle. 386
Maximum Single-Shot Pistol 356
MDM Buckwacka In-line Rifles 470
MDM M2K In-line Rifle. 470
Meacham Highwall Silhouette
  or Schuetzen Rifle. 402
Meacham Low-Wall Rifle. 417
Merkel Boxlock Double Rifles 409
Merkel Drillings 409
Merkel K1 Model Lightweight
  Stalking Rifle. 402
Merkel K-2 Custom Single-Shot
  "Weimar" Stalking Rifle. 402
Merkel KR1 Bolt-Action Rifle. 386
Merkel Model 1620 Side-by-Side
  Shotgun. 455
Merkel Model 2000CL O/U Shotgun . . .448
Merkel Model 2001EL O/U Shotgun . . .448
Merkel Model 280EL, 360EL Shotguns.455
Merkel Model 280SL and 360SL
  Shotguns. 455
Merkel Model 47E, 147E
  Side-by-Side Shotguns. 455
Merkel Model 47EL, 147EL
  Side-by-Side Shotguns. 455
Merkel Model SR1 Semi-Automatic
  Rifle. 367
Mississippi 1841 Percussion Rifle. 470
Morini CM 162 El Match Air Pistols 478
Mossberg 100 ATR Bolt-Action Rifle. . .386
Mossberg 464 Lever Action Rifle. 375
Mossberg 4x4 Bolt-Action Rifle 386
Mossberg 930 Autoloader 432
Mossberg Model 464 Rimfire Lever-Action
  Rifle. 414
Mossberg Model 500 Bantam Pump
  Shotgun. 438
Mossberg Model 500 Special Purpose
  Shotguns. 461
Mossberg Model 500 Sporting Pump
  Shotguns. 438
Mossberg Model 590 Special Purpose
  Shotgun. 461
Mossberg Model 702 Plinkster Auto
  Rifle. 411
Mossberg Model 801/802 Bolt Rifles. . .417
Mossberg Model 817 Varmint
  Bolt-Action Rifle 417
Mossberg Model 835 Ulti-Mag Pump
  Shotguns. 438
Mossberg Model 935 Magnum
  Autoloading Shotguns. 432

N

Navy Arms "John Bodine" Rolling
  Block Rifle. 403
Navy Arms 1861 Musketoon 471
Navy Arms 1866 Yellow Boy Rifle. 375
Navy Arms 1873 Gunfighter
  Single-Action Revolver 352
Navy Arms 1873 Springfield Cavalry
  Carbine. 402
Navy Arms 1873 Winchester-Style
  Rifle. 375
Navy Arms 1874 Sharps #2
  Creedmoor Rifle 402
Navy Arms 1874 Sharps #2
  Creedmore Rifle 375
Navy Arms 1874 Sharps "Quigley"
  Rifle. 402
Navy Arms 1874 Sharps No. 3
  Long Range Rifle 403
Navy Arms 1875 Schofield Revolver. . .352
Navy Arms 1885 High Wall Rifle 402
Navy Arms Bisley Model
  Single-Action Revolver 352
Navy Arms Brown Bess Musket 471
Navy Arms Country Hunter 471
Navy Arms Founder's Model
  Schofield Revolver 352
Navy Arms Iron Frame Henry 375
Navy Arms Military Henry Rifle 375
Navy Arms New Model Russian
  Revolver 352
Navy Arms Parker-Hale 1853
  Three-Band Enfield. 471
Navy Arms Parker-Hale 1858
  Two-Band Enfield 471
Navy Arms Parker-Hale Volunteer Rifle 471
Navy Arms Parker-Hale Whitworth
  Military Target Rifle 471
Navy Arms Pennsylvania Rifle 471
Navy Arms Scout Small Frame
  Single-Action Revolver 352
Navy Arms Sharps Sporting Rifle 402
Navy Arms Side-by-Side Shotgun. 476
Navy Model 1851 Percussion Revolver.464
New England Firearms Handi-Rifle. . . .403
New England Firearms Huntsman. 471
New England Firearms Pardner and
  Tracker II Shotguns. 459
New England Firearms Sidekick 471
New England Firearms Sportster
  Single-Shot Rifles 417
New England Firearms
  Sportster/Versa Pack Rifle 404
New England Firearms Stainless
  Huntsman 471
New England Firearms Survivor Rifle . .403
New England Pardner Pump Shotgun. . .438
New Model 1858 Army Percussion
  Revolver 464
New Ultra Light Arms 20RF Bolt-Action
  Rifle. 417

North American Arms "The Earl"
  Single-Action Revolver 353
North American Arms Black Widow
  Revolver 353
North American Arms Guardian
  DAO Pistol 327
North American Arms Mini Revolvers . .352
North American Arms Mini-Master 352
North American Companion Percussion
  Revolver 465
North American Super Companion
  Percussion Revolver. 465

O

Olympic Arms Big Deuce Pistol. 327
Olympic Arms Cohort Pistol. 327
Olympic Arms Enforcer 1911 Pistol. . . .327
Olympic Arms K23P AR Pistol. 328
Olympic Arms K23P-A3-TC AR Pistol. .328
Olympic Arms K3B Series AR15
  Carbines 367
Olympic Arms K8 Targetmatch AR15
  Rifles. 424
Olympic Arms K9, K10, K40, K45
  Pistol-Caliber AR15 Carbines 367
Olympic Arms Matchmaster 5 1911
  Pistol. 327
Olympic Arms Matchmaster 6 1911
  Pistol. 327
Olympic Arms ML-1/ML-2 Multimatch
  AR15 Carbines 424
Olympic Arms OA-93 AR Pistol. 328
Olympic Arms Plinker Plus AR15
  Models 367
Olympic Arms Schuetzen Pistol
  Works 1911 Pistols. 328
Olympic Arms SM Servicematch
  AR15 Rifles. .423
Olympic Arms UM Ultramatch AR15
  Rifles. 424
Olympic Arms Westerner Series 1911
  Pistols. 327
Olympic Arms Whitney Wolverine
  Pistol. 328

P

Pacific Rifle Big Bore African Rifles. . . .472
Pacific Rifle Model 1837 Zephyr 471
Para USA LDA Hi-Capacity Auto
  Pistols 329
Para USA LDA Single-Stack Auto
  Pistols 329
Para USA PXT 1911 Single-Action
  High-Capacity Auto Pistols 328
Para USA PXT 1911 Single-Action
  Single-Stack Auto Pistols 328
Para USA PXT Limited Pistols 329
Para USA Warthog 329
Pardini K58 Match Air Pistols 478
Pedersoli Mang Target Pistol 463
Peifer Model TS-93 Rifle 472
Perazzi MX10 O/U Shotgun 448

Perazzi MX12 Hunting O/U Shotguns . .448
Perazzi MX20 Hunting O/U Shotguns . .448
Perazzi MX28, MX410 Game O/U
   Shotgun. .448
Perazzi MX8 O/U Shotguns. 448
Perazzi MX8 Special Skeet O/U Shotgun . .
   448
Perazzi MX8/20 O/U Shotgun 448
Perazzi MX8/MX8 Special Trap,
   Skeet O/U Shotguns 448
Phoenix Arms HP22, HP25 Auto
   Pistols 329
Picuda .17 Mach-2 Graphite Pistol 329
Piotti Boss O/U Shotgun 448
Piotti King No. 1 Side-by-Side Shotgun .455
Piotti Lunik Side-by-Side Shotgun. 455
Piotti Piuma Side-by-Side Shotgun 455
Pocket Police 1862 Percussion Revolver465
Pointer Over/Under Shotgun 449
Prairie River Arms PRA Bullpup Rifle . .472
Puma Model 92 Rifles and Carbines . . .376

Q

Queen Anne Flintlock Pistol 463

R

Remington 40-XB Rangemaster Target
   Centerfire 425
Remington 40-XBBR KS 425
Remington 40-XC KS Target Rifle. 425
Remington 40-XR Custom Sporter 425
Remington 572 BDL Deluxe
   Fieldmaster Pump Rifle. 414
Remington 597 Auto Rifle 411
Remington 700 XHR Extreme
   Hunting Rifle 388
Remington Genesis Muzzleloader. 472
Remington Model 105 CTI Shotgun . . .432
Remington Model 1100 G3 Shotgun . . .433
Remington Model 1100 Tac-4 433
Remington Model 1100 Target
   Shotguns. .433
Remington Model 11-87 Sportsman
   Shotguns. .432
Remington Model 552 BDL Deluxe
   Speedmaster Rifle 411
Remington Model 700 Alaskan Ti 388
Remington Model 700 BDL Rifle 387
Remington Model 700 CDL
   Classic Deluxe Rifle 387
Remington Model 700 Mountain
   LSS Rifles .387
Remington Model 700 SPS Rifles 387
Remington Model 700 Varmint SF
   Rifle. 389
Remington Model 700 VLS/VLSS
   TH Rifles 388
Remington Model 700 VSSF-II/Sendero
   SF II Rifles .388
Remington Model 700 VTR
   Varmint/Tactical Rifle 389

Remington Model 700 XCR Camo
   RMEF 388
Remington Model 700 XCR Rifle. 388
Remington Model 700 XCR Target
   Tactical Rifle 389
Remington Model 750 Woodsmaster . .368
Remington Model 7600/7615
   Pump Action 376
Remington Model 770 Bolt-Action Rifle.389
Remington Model 798/799
   Bolt-Action Rifles. 390
Remington Model 870 and Model
   1100 Tactical Shotguns 461
Remington Model 870 Classic
   Trap Shotgun 439
Remington Model 870 Express
   Shotguns. .439
Remington Model 870 Express
   Super Magnum Shotgun. 440
Remington Model 870 Express Tactical 440
Remington Model 870 Marine Magnum
   Shotgun. 439
Remington Model 870 Special Purpose
   Shotguns (SPS) 440
Remington Model 870 SPS Shurshot
   Synthetic Super Slug 440
Remington Model 870 Wingmaster
   Shotguns. .438
Remington Model 887 Nitro Mag Pump
   Shotgun. 441
Remington Model Five Series 417
Remington Model R-15 Modular
   Repeating Rifle 368
Remington Model R-25 Modular
   Repeating Rifle 368
Remington Model Seven CDL/CDL
   Magnum 389
Remington Model SP-10 Magnum
   Shotgun. 433
Remington Model SPR18 Single Shot
   Rifles. 404
Remington Model SPR453 Shotgun . . .432
Remington No. 1 Rolling Block
   Mid-Range Sporter 404
Remington Premier Over/Under
   Shotguns. .449
Remington SPR100 Single-Shot
   Shotguns. .459
Remington SPR210 Side-by-Side
   Shotguns. .455
Remington SPR220 Side-by-Side
   Shotguns. .456
Remington SPR310 Over/Under
   Shotguns. .449
Richmond, C.S., 1863 Musket. 472
Rizzini Artemis O/U Shotgun 449
Rizzini Express 90L Double Rifle 409
Rizzini S782 Emel O/U Shotgun 449
Rizzini S790 Emel O/U Shotgun 449
Rizzini S792 Emel O/U Shotgun 449
Rizzini Sidelock Side-by-Side Shotgun .456
Rizzini Upland EL O/U Shotgun 449

Rock River Arms Basic Carry Auto
   Pistol 329
Rock River Arms LAR-15/LAR-9
   Pistols 329
Rock River Arms Standard A2 Rifle . . .368
Rocky Mountain Hawken. 472
Rogers & Spencer Percussion
   Revolver 465
Rohrbaugh R9 Semi-Auto Pistol 329
Rossi Matched Pair Single-Shot
   Rifle/Shotgun 417
Rossi Matched Pairs 404
Rossi Matched Pairs 460
Rossi Matched Set 460
Rossi Model 851 343
Rossi Model R351/R352/R851
   Revolvers .343
Rossi Model R971/R972 Revolvers. . . .343
Rossi Muzzleloaders 472
Rossi R461/R462/R971/R972 343
Rossi R92 Lever-Action Carbine 376
Rossi Single-Shot Rifles 404
Rossi Single-Shot Shotguns 459
Rossi Tuffy Shotgun 459
Ruger 10/22 Autoloading Carbine 412
Ruger 10/22 Deluxe Sporter 412
Ruger 10/22-T Target Rifle 412
Ruger 22 Charger Pistol 330
Ruger 22/45 Mark III Pistol 330
Ruger 77/17 Rimfire Bolt-Action Rifle . .418
Ruger 77/22 Bolt-Action Rifle 390
Ruger 77/22 Rimfire Bolt-Action Rifle . .418
Ruger Bisley Single-Action Revolver. . .353
Ruger Compact Magnums. 390
Ruger Engraved Red Label O/U
   Shotgun. 449
Ruger Gold Label Side-by-Side
   Shotgun. 456
Ruger Gp100 Revolvers 343
Ruger K10/22-RPF All-Weather Rifle . .412
Ruger K77/22 Varmint Rifle. 418
Ruger KP944 Autoloading Pistol 330
Ruger LCP. 330
Ruger M77 Hawkeye Rifles. 390
Ruger M77VTTarget Rifle 391
Ruger Magnum Rifle 390
Ruger Mark III Standard Autoloading
   Pistol 330
Ruger Mark III Target Model
   Autoloading Pistol 341
Ruger Mini Thirty Rifle. 369
Ruger Mini-14 Ranch Rifle
   Autoloading Rifle. 368
Ruger Model 96 Lever-Action Rifle 414
Ruger New Bearcat Single-Action 354
Ruger New Model Bisley Vaquero. 354
Ruger New Model Blackhawk/Blackhawk
   Convertible 353
Ruger New Model Single Six & New
   Model .32 H&R Single Six Revolvers .353
Ruger New Model Super Blackhawk. . .353

Ruger New Model Super Blackhawk Hunter 353
Ruger New Vaquero Single-Action Revolver 353
Ruger No. 1 RSI International 405
Ruger No. 1-A Light Sporter 405
Ruger No. 1-B Single Shot 404
Ruger No. 1-H Tropical Rifle 405
Ruger No. 1-S Medium Sporter 405
Ruger No. 1-V Varminter 405
Ruger NRA Mini-14 Rifle 369
Ruger P90 Manual Safety Model Autoloading Pistol 330
Ruger P95 Autoloading Pistol 330
Ruger Red Label O/U Shotguns 449
Ruger Redhawk 343
Ruger SP101 Double-Action-Only Revolver 343
Ruger SP101 Revolvers 343
Ruger SR9 Autoloading Pistol 329
Ruger Super Redhawk Revolver 344
RWS 34 Panther 482
RWS 460 Magnum 482
RWS 48 482
RWS 9B/9N Air Pistols 478
RWS Model 34 482

S

Sabre Defence Sabre Rifles 369
Sabre Defence Sphinx Pistols 331
Saiga Autoloading Shotgun 433
Sako 75 Deluxe Rifle 392
Sako 75 Hunter Bolt-Action Rifle 392
Sako 75 Varmint Rifle 392
Sako 85 Finnlight 392
Sako A7 American Bolt-Action Rifle . . .391
Sako Model 85 Bolt-Action Rifles 391
Sako TRG-22 Bolt-Action Rifle 425
Sako TRG-42 Bolt-Action Rifle 391
Savage Classic Series Model 14/114 Rifles 392
Savage Cub T Mini Youth 420
Savage Mark I-G Bolt-Action Rifle 418
Savage Mark II Bolt-Action Rifle 418
Savage Mark II-FSS Stainless Rifle . . .418
Savage Milano O/U Shotguns 450
Savage Model 10 BAS Law Enforcement Bolt-Action Rifle 394
Savage Model 10 Predator Series 395
Savage Model 10FP/110FP Law Enforcement Series Rifles 394
Savage Model 10GXP3, 110GXP3 Package Guns 393
Savage Model 10ML Muzzleloader Rifle Series .473
Savage Model 10XP Predator Hunting Bolt-Action Rifle Package 395
Savage Model 11/111 Hunter Series Bolt Actions .393
Savage Model 110-50th Anniversary Rifle 394

Savage Model 11FXP3, 111FXP3, 111FCXP3, 11FYXP3 (Youth) Package Guns 393
Savage Model 12 F Class Target Rifle .395
Savage Model 12 F/TR Target Rifle . . .395
Savage Model 12 Precision Target Palma Rifle .395
Savage Model 12 Precision Target Series Benchrest Rifle 395
Savage Model 12 Series Varmint Rifles 393
Savage Model 16/116 Weather Warriors 393
Savage Model 16FXP3, 116FXP3 SS Action Package Guns 393
Savage Model 25 Bolt Action Rifles . . .392
Savage Model 30G Stevens "Favorite" .420
Savage Model 64G Auto Rifle 412
Savage Model 93FSS Magnum Rifle . .419
Savage Model 93FVSS Magnum Rifle .419
Savage Model 93G Magnum Bolt-Action Rifle 419
Savage Model 93R17 Bolt-Action Rifles 419
Second Model Brown Bess Musket 473
Seecamp LWS 32/380 Stainless DA Auto 331
Sheriff Model 1851 Percussion Revolver 465
Shiloh Rifle Co. Sharps 1874 Long Range Express 405
Shiloh Rifle Co. Sharps 1874 Montana Roughrider 406
Shiloh Rifle Co. Sharps 1874 Quigley . .406
Shiloh Rifle Co. Sharps 1874 Saddle Rifle 406
Shiloh Rifle Co. Sharps Creedmoor Target 406
SIG 556 Autoloading Rifle 370
SIG SAUER 1911 Pistols 331
SIG SAUER 250 Compact Auto Pistol .331
SIG SAUER Mosquito Pistol 332
SIG SAUER P220 Auto Pistols 331
SIG SAUER P220 Carry Auto Pistols . .332
SIG SAUER P226 Pistols 332
SIG SAUER P229 DA Auto Pistol 332
SIG SAUER P232 Personal Size Pistol .332
SIG SAUER P239 Pistol 332
SIG SAUER SP2022 Pistols 332
SKB Model 585 O/U Shotguns 450
SKB Model 85TSS O/U Shotguns 450
SKB Model GC7 O/U Shotguns 450
Smith & Wesson 1000/1020/1012 Super Semi-Auto Shotguns 434
Smith & Wesson 586 478
Smith & Wesson 60LS/642LS Ladysmith Revolvers 344
Smith & Wesson Elite Gold Shotguns . .456
Smith & Wesson Elite Silver Shotguns . .450
Smith & Wesson Enhanced Sigma Series Dao Pistols .334
Smith & Wesson I-Bolt Rifles 395
Smith & Wesson J-Frame Revolvers . . .344

Smith & Wesson K-Frame/L-Frame Revolvers 345
Smith & Wesson M&P Auto Pistols 332
Smith & Wesson M&P Revolvers 344
Smith & Wesson M&P15 Rifles 370
Smith & Wesson M&P15PC Camo 371
Smith & Wesson Model 10 Revolver . . .345
Smith & Wesson Model 14 Classic 344
Smith & Wesson Model 1911 Sub-Compact Pro Series 333
Smith & Wesson Model 21 346
Smith & Wesson Model 22A Pistols . . .341
Smith & Wesson Model 29 Classic 346
Smith & Wesson Model 317 Airlite Revolvers 345
Smith & Wesson Model 329PD Airlite Revolvers 346
Smith & Wesson Model 340/340PD Airlite SC Centennial 345
Smith & Wesson Model 351PD Revolver 345
Smith & Wesson Model 360/360PD Airlite Chief's Special 345
Smith & Wesson Model 3913 Traditional Double Actions 333
Smith & Wesson Model 4013TSW Auto 333
Smith & Wesson Model 41 Target 341
Smith & Wesson Model 438 345
Smith & Wesson Model 442/637/638/642 Airweight Revolvers 344
Smith & Wesson Model 460V Revolvers 347
Smith & Wesson Model 500 Revolvers .347
Smith & Wesson Model 60 Chief's Special 344
Smith & Wesson Model 617 Revolvers .345
Smith & Wesson Model 625/625JM Revolvers 346
Smith & Wesson Model 629 Revolvers .346
Smith & Wesson Model 63 344
Smith & Wesson Model 632 Powerport Pro Series 345
Smith & Wesson Model 637 345
Smith & Wesson Model 64/67 Revolvers 345
Smith & Wesson Model 640 Centennial DA Only 345
Smith & Wesson Model 642 345
Smith & Wesson Model 649 Bodyguard Revolver 345
Smith & Wesson Model 686/686 Plus Revolvers 346
Smith & Wesson Model 908 Auto Pistol 333
Smith & Wesson Model 910 DA Auto Pistol 333
Smith & Wesson Model CS45 Chief's Special Auto .334
Smith & Wesson Model CS9 Chief's Special Auto .334
Smith & Wesson Model M&P15VTAC Viking Tactics Model 371

Smith & Wesson Model S&W500
(163565) 346
Smith & Wesson Model SW1911
Pistols 333
Smith & Wesson Models 620 Revolvers346
Smith & Wesson N-Frame Revolvers . .346
Smith & Wesson Night Guard
Revolvers 344
Smith & Wesson X-Frame Revolvers . .346
Spiller & Burr Revolver 465
Springfield Armory Custom Loaded
Champion 1911A1 Pistol 334
Springfield Armory Custom Loaded
Long Slide 1911A1 Pistol 335
Springfield Armory Custom Loaded
Micro-Compact 1911A1 Pistol 335
Springfield Armory Custom Loaded
Ultra Compact Pistol 335
Springfield Armory EMP Enhanced
Micro Pistol 334
Springfield Armory Gi 45 1911A1
Auto Pistols 334
Springfield Armory Leatham Legend
TGO Series Pistols 341
Springfield Armory M-1 Garand
American Combat Rifles 426
Springfield Armory M1A Rifle 371
Springfield Armory M1A Super Match . .425
Springfield Armory M1A/M-21 Tactical
Model Rifle 425
Springfield Armory Mil-Spec 1911A1
Auto Pistols 334
Springfield Armory Tactical Response
Loaded Pistols 335
Springfield Armory Trophy Match Pistol 341
Springfield Armory XD Polymer Auto
Pistols 334
Stevens Model 200 Bolt-Action Rifles . .395
Stevens Model 512 Gold Wing
Shotguns 450
Steyr LP10P Match Air Pistol 478
Steyr Mannlicher Classic Rifle 395
Steyr Pro Hunter Rifle 395
Steyr Scout Bolt-Action Rifle 395
Steyr SSG 69 PII Bolt-Action Rifle 396
STI Eagle 5.0, 6.0 Pistol 341
STI Executive Pistol 341
STI Texican Single-Action Revolver . . .354
STI Trojan .341
Stoeger Coach Gun Side-by-Side
Shotguns 456
Stoeger Condor O/U Shotguns 450
Stoeger Model 2000 Shotguns 434
Stoeger Model P350 Shotguns 441
Stoeger Uplander Side-by-Side
Shotguns 456
Stoner SR-15 M-5 Rifle 371
Stoner SR-15 Match Rifle 426
Stoner SR-25 Carbine 371
Stoner SR-25 Match Rifle 426
Super Six Classic Bison Bull 347

T

Tactical Response TR-870 Standard
Model Shotguns 462
Tar-Hunt RSG-12 Professional Rifled
Slug Gun .460
Tar-Hunt RSG-16 Elite Shotgun 460
Tar-Hunt RSG-20 Mountaineer
Slug Gun .460
Taurus 132 Millennium Pro Auto Pistol .336
Taurus 138 Millennium Pro Series 336
Taurus 140 Millennium Pro Auto Pistol .336
Taurus 145 Millennium Pro Auto Pistol .336
Taurus 851 & 651 Revolvers 347
Taurus Model 100/101 Auto Pistol 336
Taurus Model 111 Millennium Pro Auto
Pistol 336
Taurus Model 17 "Tracker" 347
Taurus Model 1911 335
Taurus Model 2045 Large Frame Pistol 335
Taurus Model 22PLY Small Polymer
Frame Pistols 335
Taurus Model 24/7 335
Taurus Model 416/444/454 Raging
Bull Revolvers 348
Taurus Model 425 Tracker Revolvers . .348
Taurus Model 44 Revolver 347
Taurus Model 444 Ultra-Light 348
Taurus Model 4510 Judge 347
Taurus Model 58 Pistol 335
Taurus Model 605 Revolver 348
Taurus Model 608 Revolver 348
Taurus Model 609TI-Pro 336
Taurus Model 617 Revolver 348
Taurus Model 62 Pump Rifle 414
Taurus Model 65 Revolver 347
Taurus Model 650 CIA Revolver 348
Taurus Model 651 Protector Revolver . .348
Taurus Model 66 Revolver 347
Taurus Model 709 "Slim" 337
Taurus Model 72 Pump Rifle 414
Taurus Model 731 Revolver 348
Taurus Model 738 TCP Compact Pistol 336
Taurus Model 800 Series 335
Taurus Model 817 Ultra-Lite Revolver . .348
Taurus Model 82 Heavy Barrel
Revolver .347
Taurus Model 85 Revolver 347
Taurus Model 850 CIA Revolver 348
Taurus Model 90-Two Semi-Auto Pistol 336
Taurus Model 911B Auto Pistol 336
Taurus Model 917 335
Taurus Model 92 Auto Pistol 336
Taurus Model 94 Revolver 347
Taurus Model 940B Auto Pistol 337
Taurus Model 941 Revolver 348
Taurus Model 945B/38S Series 337
Taurus Model 970/971 Tracker
Revolvers 348
Taurus Model 99 Auto Pistol 336

Taurus Model PT-22/PT-25 Auto
Pistols 335
Taurus Raging Bull Model 416 347
Taurus Single-Action Gaucho
Revolvers 354
Taurus Thunderbolt Pump Action 376
Tech Force 35 Air Pistol 478
Tech Force 6 Air Rifle 483
Tech Force 99 Air Rifle 483
Tech Force S2-1 Air Pistol 478
Tech Force Ss2 Olympic Competition
Air Pistol .478
Thompson Custom 1911A1
Automatic Pistol 337
Thompson TA5 1927A-1 Lightweight
Deluxe Pistol 337
Thompson/Center 22 LR Classic Rifle .412
Thompson/Center Bone Collector 473
Thompson/Center Encore "Katahdin"
Carbine .406
Thompson/Center Encore 209x50
Magnum .473
Thompson/Center Encore Pistol 357
Thompson/Center Encore Rifle 406
Thompson/Center Encore Rifled
Slug Gun .460
Thompson/Center Encore Turkey Gun .460
Thompson/Center Fire Storm Rifle 473
Thompson/Center G2 Contender Pistol 357
Thompson/Center G2 Contender Rifle .406
Thompson/Center Hawken Rifle 473
Thompson/Center Icon Bolt-Action
Rifle 396
Thompson/Center Icon Precision
Hunter Rifle 396
Thompson/Center Omega 473
Thompson/Center Stainless Encore
Rifle 406
Thompson/Center Triumph Magnum
Muzzleloader 473
Thompson/Center Venture Bolt-Action
Rifle 396
Tikka T3 Hunter 396
Tikka T3 Lite Bolt-Action Rifle 396
Tikka T3 Stainless Synthetic 396
Tikka T3 Varmint/Super Varmint Rifle . .396
Time Precision 22 RF Bench Rest Rifle 426
Traditions 1874 Sharps Deluxe Rifle . . .407
Traditions 1874 Sharps Sporting
Deluxe Rifle 407
Traditions 1874 Sharps Standard Rifle .407
Traditions ALS 2100 Home Security
Shotgun .434
Traditions ALS 2100 Hunter Combo . . .434
Traditions ALS 2100 Series
Semi-Automatic Shotguns 434
Traditions ALS 2100 Slug Hunter
Shotgun .434
Traditions ALS 2100 Turkey
Semi-Automatic Shotgun 434

Traditions ALS 2100 Waterfowl Semi-Automatic Shotgun 434
Traditions Buckskinner Carbine. 473
Traditions Classic Series O/U Shotguns. .451
Traditions Deerhunter Rifle Series 474
Traditions Elite Series Side-by-Side Shotguns. .456
Traditions Evolution Long Distance Bolt-Action Blackpowder Rifle. 474
Traditions Hawken Woodsman Rifle . . .474
Traditions Kentucky Pistol. 463
Traditions Kentucky Rifle. 474
Traditions Mag 350 Series O/U Shotguns. .451
Traditions PA Pellet Flintlock. 474
Traditions Pennsylvania Rifle 474
Traditions Pursuit Break-Open Muzzleloader. 474
Traditions Rolling Block Sporting Rifle .407
Traditions Shenandoah Rifle. 474
Traditions Tennessee Rifle 474
Traditions Tracker 209 In-Line Rifles. . .475
Traditions Trapper Pistol 463
Traditions Uplander Series Side-by-Side Shotguns. .457
Traditions Vest-Pocket Derringer 463
Traditions William Parker Pistol. 463
Tristar Brittany Classic Side-by-Side Shotgun. 457
Tristar Cobra Pump. 462
Tristar Hunter EX O/U Shotgun. 451
Tristar Sharps 1874 Sporting Rifle 376
Tristar Viper Semi-Automatic Shotguns 434

U

U.S. Fire Arms 1910 Commercial Model Automatic Pistol 337
U.S. Fire Arms 1911 Military Model Automatic Pistol 337
U.S. Fire Arms Ace .22 Long Rifle Automatic Pistol 337
U.S. Fire Arms Rodeo Cowboy Action Revolver 355
U.S. Fire Arms Single-Action Revolver .355
U.S. Fire Arms Standard Lightning Magazine Rifle 377
U.S. Fire Arms Super 38 Automatic Pistol. 337
U.S. Fire Arms U.S. Pre-War. 355
Uberti 1847 Walker Revolvers. 465
Uberti 1848 Dragoon and Pocket Revolvers .465
Uberti 1851-1860 Conversion Revolvers .354
Uberti 1858 New Army Revolvers 465
Uberti 1860 Henry Rifle. 377
Uberti 1861 Navy Percussion Revolver 465
Uberti 1866 Yellowboy Carbine, Short Rifle. 376

Uberti 1870 Schofield-Style Top Break Revolver 355
Uberti 1871-1872 Open Top Revolvers. 354
Uberti 1873 Bisley Single-Action Revolver 354
Uberti 1873 Buntline and Revolver Carbine Single-Action 355
Uberti 1873 Cattleman Bird's Head Single Action. 354
Uberti 1873 Cattleman Single-Action . .354
Uberti 1873 Sporting Rifle 376
Uberti 1874 Sharps Sporting Rifle. 407
Uberti 1885 High-Wall Single-Shot Rifles. 407
Uberti Lightning Rifle 377
Uberti Outlaw, Frontier, and Police Revolvers .355
Uberti Springfield Trapdoor Rifle 377
Ultra Light Arms Bolt-Action Rifles . . .396
Ultra Light Arms Model 209 Muzzleloader. 475

V

Verona 501 Series O/U Shotguns 451
Verona 702 Series O/U Shotguns 451
Verona LX680 Competition Trap O/U Shotguns. .451
Verona LX680 Skeet/Sporting/Trap O/U Shotgun. 451
Verona LX680 Sporting O/U Shotgun . .451
Verona LX692 Gold Hunting O/U Shotguns. .451
Verona LX692 Gold Sporting O/U Shotgun. 451
Verona LX702 Gold Trap Combo O/U Shotguns 452
Verona LX702 Skeet/Trap O/U Shotguns. .452
Verona Model 401 Series Semi-Auto Shotguns. .435

W

Walker 1847 Percussion Revolver 465
Walther CP99 Compact. 478
Walther Lever Action 483
Walther LP300 Match Pistol 478
Walther P22 Pistol. 338
Walther P99 Auto Pistol. 338
Walther PPK/S. 478
Walther PPK/S American Auto Pistol . .338
Walther PPS Pistol 337
Weatherby Athena Grade V and Grade III Classic Field O/U Shotguns 452
Weatherby Mark V Bolt-Action Rifles . .396
Weatherby Orion D'Italia O/U Shotguns. .452
Weatherby SBS Athena D'Italia Side-by-Side Shotguns 457
Weatherby Vanguard Bolt-Action Rifles 397
White Alpha Rifle. 475
White Lightning II Rifle. 475

White Model 2000 Blacktail Hunter Rifle. 475
White Model 97 Whitetail Hunter Rifle. .475
White Model 98 Elite Hunter Rifle 475
White Thunderbolt Rifle. 475
White Tominator Shotgun 476
Wilson Combat Elite Professional 338
Wilson Combat Tactical Rifles. 371
Winchester Apex Swing-Action Magnum Rifle 475
Winchester Model 1000B 483
Winchester Model 1000SB 483
Winchester Model 1000X 483
Winchester Model 1000XS 483
Winchester Model 1895 Safari Centennial High Grade 377
Winchester Model 70 Bolt-Action Rifles 398
Winchester Model 70 Coyote Light 398
Winchester Model 70 Featherweight. . .398
Winchester Model 70 Sporter 398
Winchester Model 70 Ultimate Shadow. 398
Winchester Model 800X 483
Winchester Model 800XS 483
Winchester Select Model 101 O/U Shotguns. .452
Winchester Super X Pump Shotguns . .441
Winchester Super X Rifle 371
Winchester Super X2 Auto Shotguns . .435
Winchester Super X2 Sporting Clays Auto Shotguns 435
Winchester Super X3 Flanigun Exhibition/Sporting 435
Winchester Super X3 Shotguns 435
Winchester Wildcat Bolt Action 22. 420
Winchester X-150 Bolt-Action Magnum Rifle 475

Z

Zouave Percussion Rifle 475

Includes models suitable for several forms of competition and other sporting purposes.

Accu-Tek AT-380 II
380 ACP

Auto-Ordnance 1911A1
Standard

Auto-Ordnance
1911PKZSEW

Auto-Ordnance Deluxe

Baer Custom
Carry

Baer Premier II

ACCU-TEK AT-380 II 380 ACP PISTOL
Caliber: 380 ACP, 6-shot magazine. **Barrel:** 2.8". **Weight:** 23.5 oz. **Length:** 6.125" overall. **Grips:** Textured black composition. **Sights:** Blade front, rear adjustable for windage. **Features:** Made from 17-4 stainless steel, has an exposed hammer, manual firing-pin safety block and trigger disconnect. Magazine release located on the bottom of the grip. American made, lifetime warranty. Comes with two 6-round stainless steel magazines and a California-approved cable lock. Introduced 2006. Made in U.S.A. by Excel Industries.
Price: Satin stainless **$262.00**

ARMALITE AR-24 PISTOL
Caliber: 9mm Para., 10- or 15-shot magazine. **Barrel:** 4.671", 6 groove, right-hand cut rifling. **Weight:** 34.9 oz. **Length:** 8.27" overall. **Grips:** Black polymer. **Sights:** Dovetail front, fixed rear, 3-dot luminous design. **Features:** Machined slide, frame and barrel. Serrations on forestrap and backstrap, external thumb safety and internal firing pin box, half cock. Two 15-round magazines, pistol case, pistol lock, manual and cleaning brushes. Manganese phosphate finish. Compact comes with two 13-round magazines, 3.89" barrel, weighs 33.4 oz. Made in U.S.A. by ArmaLite.
Price: AR-24 Full Size. **$550.00**
Price: AR-24K Compact **$550.00**

AUTO-ORDNANCE 1911A1 AUTOMATIC PISTOL
Caliber: 45 ACP, 7-shot magazine. **Barrel:** 5". **Weight:** 39 oz. **Length:** 8.5" overall. **Grips:** Brown checkered plastic with medallion. **Sights:** Blade front, rear drift-adjustable for windage. **Features:** Same specs as 1911A1 military guns-parts interchangeable. Frame and slide blued; each radius has non-glare finish. Introduced 2002. Made in U.S.A. by Kahr Arms.
Price: 1911PKZSE Parkerized, plastic grips **$627.00**
Price: 1911PKZSEW Parkerized **$662.00**
Price: 1911PKZMA Parkerized, Mass. Compliant (2008)..... **$627.00**

AUTO-ORDNANCE TA5 SEMI-AUTO PISTOL
Caliber: 45 ACP, 30-round stick magazine (standard), 50- or 100-round drum magazine optional. **Barrel:** 10.5", finned. **Weight:** 6.5 lbs. **Length:** 25" overall. **Features:** Semi-auto pistol patterned after Thompson Model 1927 semi-auto carbine. Horizontal vertical foregrip, aluminum receiver, top cocking knob, grooved walnut pistolgrip.
Price: **$1,143.00**

BAER H.C. 40 AUTO PISTOL
Caliber: 40 S&W, 18-shot magazine. **Barrel:** 5". **Weight:** 37 oz. **Length:** 8.5" overall. **Grips:** Wood. **Sights:** Low-mount adjustable rear sight with hidden rear leaf, dovetail front sight. **Features:** Double-stack Caspian frame, beavertail grip safety, ambidextrous thumb safety, 40 S&W match barrel with supported chamber, match stainless steel

barrel bushing, lowered and flared ejection port, extended ejector, match trigger fitted, integral mag well, bead blast blue finish on lower, polished sides on slide. Introduced 2008. Made in U.S.A. by Les Baer Custom, Inc.
Price: **$2,960.00**

BAER 1911 CUSTOM CARRY AUTO PISTOL
Caliber: 45 ACP, 7- or 10-shot magazine. **Barrel:** 5". **Weight:** 37 oz. **Length:** 8.5" overall. **Grips:** Checkered walnut. **Sights:** Baer improved ramp-style dovetailed front, Novak low-mount rear. **Features:** Baer forged NM frame, slide and barrel with stainless bushing. Baer speed trigger with 4-lb. pull. Partial listing shown. Made in U.S.A. by Les Baer Custom, Inc.
Price: Custom Carry 5", blued **$1,995.00**
Price: Custom Carry 5", stainless **$2,120.00**
Price: Custom Carry 4" Commanche length, blued **$1,995.00**
Price: Custom Carry 4" Commanche length, stainless **$2,120.00**

BAER 1911 ULTIMATE RECON PISTOL
Caliber: 45 ACP, 7- or 10-shot magazine. **Barrel:** 5". **Weight:** 37 oz. **Length:** 8.5" overall. **Grips:** Checkered cocobolo. **Sights:** Baer improved ramp-style dovetailed front, Novak low-mount rear. **Features:** NM Caspian frame, slide and barrel with stainless bushing. Baer speed trigger with 4-lb. pull. Includes integral Picatinny rail and Sure-Fire X-200 light. Made in U.S.A. by Les Baer Custom, Inc. Introduced 2006.
Price: Bead blast blued **$3,070.00**
Price: Bead blast chrome **$3,390.00**

BAER 1911 PREMIER II AUTO PISTOL
Caliber: 38 Super, 400 Cor-Bon, 45 ACP, 7- or 10-shot magazine. **Barrel:** 5". **Weight:** 37 oz. **Length:** 8.5" overall. **Grips:** Checkered rosewood, double diamond pattern. **Sights:** Baer dovetailed front, low-mount Bo-Mar rear with hidden leaf. **Features:** Baer NM forged steel frame and barrel with stainless bushing, deluxe Commander hammer and sear, beavertail grip safety with pad, extended ambidextrous safety; flat mainspring housing; 30 lpi checkered front strap. Made in U.S.A. by Les Baer Custom, Inc.
Price: 5" 45 ACP **$1,790.00**
Price: 5" 400 Cor-Bon **$1,890.00**
Price: 5" 38 Super **$2,070.00**
Price: 6" 45 ACP, 400 Cor-Bon, 38 Super, from........ **$1,990.00**
Price: Super-Tac, 45 ACP, 400 Cor-Bon, 38 Super, from . **$2,280.00**

Baer 1911 Stinger

Beretta 92FS

Beretta Bobcat

Beretta PX4 Storm

Beretta Tomcat

Beretta U22 Neos

Beretta PX4 Storm Sub-Compact

BAER 1911 S.R.P. PISTOL
Caliber: 45 ACP. **Barrel:** 5". **Weight:** 37 oz. **Length:** 8.5" overall. **Grips:** Checkered walnut. **Sights:** Trijicon night sights. **Features:** Similar to the F.B.I. contract gun except uses Baer forged steel frame. Has Baer match barrel with supported chamber, complete tactical action. Has Baer Ultra Coat finish. Introduced 1996. Made in U.S.A. by Les Baer Custom, Inc.
Price: Government or Commanche length **$2,590.00**

BAER 1911 STINGER PISTOL
Caliber: 45 ACP, 7-round magazine. **Barrel:** 5". **Weight:** 34 oz. **Length:** 8.5" overall. **Grips:** Checkered cocobolo. **Sights:** Baer dovetailed front, low-mount Bo-Mar rear with hidden leaf. **Features:** Baer NM frame. Baer Commanche slide, Officer's style grip frame, beveled mag well. Made in U.S.A. by Les Baer Custom, Inc.
Price: Blued **$1,890.00**
Price: Stainless **$1,970.00**

BAER 1911 PROWLER III PISTOL
Caliber: 45 ACP, 8-round magazine. **Barrel:** 5". **Weight:** 34 oz. **Length:** 8.5" overall. **Grips:** Checkered cocobolo. **Sights:** Baer dovetailed front, low-mount Bo-Mar rear with hidden leaf. **Features:** Similar to Premier II with tapered cone stub weight, rounded corners. Made in U.S.A. by Les Baer Custom, Inc.
Price: Blued **$2,580.00**

BERETTA MODEL 92FS PISTOL
Caliber: 9mm Para., 10-shot magazine. **Barrel:** 4.9". **Weight:** 34 oz. **Length:** 8.5" overall. **Grips:** Checkered black plastic. **Sights:** Blade front, rear adjustable for windage. Tritium night sights available. **Features:** Double action. Extractor acts as chamber loaded indicator, squared trigger guard, grooved front and backstraps, inertia firing pin. Matte or blued finish. Introduced 1977. Made in U.S.A.
Price: With plastic grips **$650.00**

BERETTA MODEL 80 CHEETAH SERIES DA PISTOLS
Caliber: 380 ACP, 10-shot magazine (M84); 8-shot (M85); 22 LR, 7-shot (M87). **Barrel:** 3.82". **Weight:** About 23 oz. (M84/85); 20.8 oz. (M87). **Length:** 6.8" overall. **Grips:** Glossy black plastic (wood optional at extra cost). **Sights:** Fixed front, drift-adjustable rear. **Features:** Double action, quick takedown, convenient magazine release. Introduced 1977. Made in U.S.A.
Price: Model 84 Cheetah, plastic grips **$650.00**

BERETTA MODEL 21 BOBCAT PISTOL
Caliber: 22 LR or 25 ACP. Both double action. **Barrel:** 2.4". **Weight:** 11.5 oz.; 11.8 oz. **Length:** 4.9" overall. **Grips:** Plastic. **Features:** Available in nickel, matte, engraved or blue finish. Introduced in 1985.
Price: Bobcat, 22 or 25, blue **$335.00**

Price: Bobcat, 22, Inox **$420.00**
Price: Bobcat, 22 or 25, matte **$335.00**

BERETTA MODEL 3032 TOMCAT PISTOL
Caliber: 32 ACP, 7-shot magazine. **Barrel:** 2.45". **Weight:** 14.5 oz. **Length:** 5" overall. **Grips:** Checkered black plastic. **Sights:** Blade front, drift-adjustable rear. **Features:** Double action with exposed hammer; tip-up barrel for direct loading/unloading; thumb safety; polished or matte blue finish. Made in U.S.A. Introduced 1996.
Price: Matte **$435.00**
Price: Inox **$555.00**

BERETTA MODEL U22 NEOS
Caliber: 22 LR, 10-shot magazine. **Barrel:** 4.5"; 6". **Weight:** 32 oz.; 36 oz. **Length:** 8.8"; 10.3". **Sights:** Target. **Features:** Integral rail for standard scope mounts, light, perfectly weighted, 100 percent American made by Beretta.
Price: **$250.00**
Price: Inox **$350.00**

BERETTA MODEL PX4 STORM
Caliber: 9mm Para., 40 S&W. **Capacity:** 17 (9mm Para.); 14 (40 S&W). **Barrel:** 4". **Weight:** 27.5 oz. **Grips:** Black checkered w/3 interchangeable backstraps. **Sights:** 3-dot system coated in Superluminova; removable front and rear sights. **Features:** DA/SA, manual safety/hammer decocking lever (ambi) and automatic firing pin block safety. Picatinny rail. Comes with two magazines (17/10 in 9mm Para. and 14/10 in 40 S&W). Removable hammer unit. American made by Beretta. Introduced 2005.
Price: **$600.00**
Price: 45 ACP **$650.00**

BERETTA MODEL PX4 STORM SUB-COMPACT
Caliber: 9mm, 40 S&W. **Capacity:** 13 (9mm); 10 (40 S&W). **Barrel:** 3". **Weight:** 26.1 oz. **Length:** 6.2" overall. **Grips:** NA. **Sights:** NA. **Features:** Ambidextrous manual safety lever, interchangeable backstraps included, lock breech and tilt barrel system, stainless steel barrel, Picatinny rail.
Price: **$600.00**

Beretta Model M9

Bersa Thunder 380

Beretta Model M9A1

Browning Hi-Power 9mm

Browning Buck Mark Standard

Browning Buck Mark Stainless Plus UDX

BERETTA MODEL M9
Caliber: 9mm Para. **Capacity:** 15. **Barrel:** 4.9". **Weight:** 32.2-35.3 oz. **Grips:** Plastic. **Sights:** Dot and post, low profile, windage adjustable rear. **Features:** DA/SA, forged aluminum alloy frame, delayed locking-bolt system, manual safety doubles as decocking lever, combat-style trigger guard, loaded chamber indicator. Comes with two magazines (15/10). American made by Beretta. Introduced 2005.
Price: **$650.00**

BERETTA MODEL M9A1
Caliber: 9mm Para. **Capacity:** 15. **Barrel:** 4.9". **Weight:** 32.2-35.3 oz. **Grips:** Plastic. **Sights:** Dot and post, low profile, windage adjustable rear. **Features:** Same as M9, but also includes integral Mil-Std-1913 Picatinny rail, has checkered frontstrap and backstrap. Comes with two magazines (15/10). American made by Beretta. Introduced 2005.
Price: **$750.00**

BERSA THUNDER 45 ULTRA COMPACT PISTOL
Caliber: 45 ACP. **Barrel:** 3.6". **Weight:** 27 oz. **Length:** 6.7" overall. **Grips:** Anatomically designed polymer. **Sights:** White outline rear. **Features:** Double action; firing pin safeties, integral locking system. Available in matte, satin nickel, gold, or duo-tone. Introduced 2003. Imported from Argentina by Eagle Imports, Inc.
Price: Thunder 45, matte blue **$402.00**
Price: Thunder 45, stainless **$480.00**
Price: Thunder 45, satin nickel **$445.00**

BERSA THUNDER 380 SERIES PISTOLS
Caliber: 380 ACP, 7 rounds **Barrel:** 3.5". **Weight:** 23 oz. **Length:** 6.6" overall. **Features:** Otherwise similar to Thunder 45 Ultra Compact. 380 DLX has 9-round capacity. 380 Concealed Carry has 8 round capacity. Imported from Argentina by Eagle Imports, Inc.
Price: Thunder 380 Matte **$310.00**
Price: Thunder 380 Satin Nickel **$336.00**
Price: Thunder 380 Blue DLX **$332.00**
Price: Thunder 380 Matte CC (2006) **$315.00**

BERSA THUNDER 9 ULTRA COMPACT/40 SERIES PISTOLS
Caliber: 9mm Para., 40 S&W. **Barrel:** 3.5". **Weight:** 24.5 oz. **Length:** 6.6" overall. **Features:** Otherwise similar to Thunder 45 Ultra Compact.

9mm Para. High Capacity model has 17-round capacity. 40 High Capacity model has 13-round capacity. Imported from Argentina by Eagle Imports, Inc.
Price: Thunder 9mm Para. Matte **$402.00**
Price: Thunder 40 High Capacity Satin Nickel **$419.00**

BROWNING HI POWER 9MM AUTOMATIC PISTOL
Caliber: 9mm Para., 13-round magazine; 40 S&W, 10-round magazine. **Barrel:** 4-5/8". **Weight:** 32 to 39 oz. **Length:** 7.75" overall. **Metal Finishes:** Blued (Standard); black-epoxy/silver-chrome (Practical); black-epoxy (Mark III). **Grips:** Molded (Mark III); wraparound Pachmayr (Practical); or walnut grips (Standard). **Sights:** Fixed (Practical, Mark III, Standard); low-mount adjustable rear (Standard). Cable lock supplied. **Features:** External hammer with half-cock and thumb safeties. Fixed rear sight model available. Commander-style (Practical) or spur-type hammer, single action. Includes gun lock. Imported from Belgium by Browning.
Price: Mark III **$979.00**
Price: Standard, fixed sights, from **$999.00**
Price: SMark III, Digital green (2009) **$985.00**

BROWNING BUCK MARK PISTOLS
Common Features: Caliber: 22 LR, 10-shot magazine. **Action:** Blowback semi-auto. **Trigger:** Wide grooved style. **Sights:** Ramp front, Browning Pro-Target rear adjustable for windage and elevation. **Grips:** Cocobolo, target-style (Hunter, 5.5 Target, 5.5 Field); polymer (Camper, Camper Stainless, Micro Nickel, Standard, STD Stainless); checkered walnut (Challenge); laminated (Plus and Plus Nickel); laminated rosewood (Bullseye Target, FLD Plus); rubber (Bullseye Standard). **Metal finishes:** Matte blue (Hunter, Camper, Challenge, Plus, Bullseye Target, Bullseye Standard, 5.5 Target, 5.5 Field, FLD Plus); matte stainless (Camper Stainless, STD Stainless, Micro Standard); nickel-plated (Micro Nickel, Plus Nickel, and Nickel). **Features:** Machined aluminum frame. Includes gun lock. Introduced 1985. Hunter, Camper Stainless, STD Stainless, 5.5 Target, 5.5 Field all introduced 2005. Multiple variations, as noted below. Made in U.S.A. From Browning.
Price: Hunter, 7.25" heavy barrel, 38 oz., Truglo sight **$429.00**
Price: Camper, 5.5" heavy barrel, 34 oz. **$329.00**
Price: FLD Camper Stainless URX, 5.5" tapered bull barrel, 34 oz. **$359.00**
Price: Standard URX, 5.5" flat-side bull barrel, 34 oz. **$399.00**
Price: Standard Stainless URX, 5.5" flat-side bull barrel, 34 oz. **$439.00**
Price: Micro Standard URX, 4" flat-side bull barrel, 32 oz. . . . **$399.00**

Browning FLD Plus Rosewood UDX

Charles Daly Empire EFS

Charles Daly M-5 Government

Browning Stainless Camper

Cobra Patriot 45

Cobra Patiot 380

BROWNING BUCK MARK PISTOLS (cont.)
Price: Micro Standard Stainless URX, 4" flat-side bull barrel,
32 oz. **$439.00**
Price: Challenge, 5.5" lightweight taper barrel, 25 oz. **$399.00**
Price: Contour 5.5 URX, 5.5" barrel, 36 oz. **$469.00**
Price: Contour 7.25 URX, 7.25", 39 oz. **$479.00**
Price: Contour Lite 5.5 URX, 5.5" barrel, 28 oz., adj. sights . **$519.00**
Price: Contour Lite 7.25 URX, 7.25" barrel, 30 oz., adj. sights **$529.00**
Price: Bullseye URX, 7.25" fluted bull barrel, 36 oz. **$549.00**
Price: Bullseye Target Stainless, 7.25" fluted bull barrel,
36 oz. **$719.00**
Price: 5.5 Target, 5.5" round bull barrel, target sights,
35.5 oz. **$579.00**
Price: 5.5 Field, 5.5" round bull barrel, 35 oz. **$579.00**
Price: Plus Stainless UDX (2007) **$509.00**
Price: Plus UDX (2007) **$469.00**
Price: FLD Plus Rosewood UDX (2007) **$469.00**
Price: Stainless Camper, 5.5" tapered bull barrel (2008) **$379.00**
Price: Practical URX Fiber-Optic, 5.5" barrel (2009) **$379.00**
Price: Lite Splash 5.5 URX **$489.00**
Price: Lite Splash 7.25 URX **$509.00**

BUSHMASTER CARBON 15 .223 PISTOL
Caliber: 5.56/223, 30-round. **Barrel:** 7.25" stainless steel. **Weight:** 2.88
lbs. **Length:** 20" overall. **Grips:** Pistol grip, Hogue overmolded unit
for ergonomic comfort. **Sights:** A2-type front with dual-aperture slip-
up rear. **Features:** AR-style semi-auto pistol with carbon composite
receiver, shortenend handguard, full-length optics rail.
Price: . . . . **NA**
Price: Type 97 pistol, without handguard **$1,055.00**

CHARLES DALY ENHANCED 1911 PISTOLS
Caliber: 45 ACP. **Barrel:** 5". **Weight:** 38 oz. **Length:** 8.75" overall. **Grips:**
Checkered double diamond hardwood. **Sights:** Dovetailed front and
dovetailed snag-free low profile rear sights, 3-dot system. **Features:**
Extended high-rise beavertail grip safety, combat trigger, combat
hammer, beveled magazine well, flared and lowered ejection port. Field
Grade models are satin-finished blued steel. EMS series includes an
ambidextrous safety, 4" barrel, 8-shot magazine. ECS series has a
contoured left hand safety, 3.5" barrel, 6-shot magazine. Two magazines,

lockable carrying case. Introduced 1998. Empire series are stainless
versions. Imported from the Philippines by K.B.I., Inc.
Price: EFS, blued, 39.5 oz., 5" barrel **$649.00**
Price: EMS, blued, 37 oz., 4" barrel **$649.00**
Price: ECS, blued, 34.5 oz., 3.5" barrel **$649.00**

CHARLES DALY M-5 POLYMER-FRAMED HI-CAP 1911 PISTOL
Caliber: 9mm Para., 12-round magazine; 40 S&W 17-round magazine;
45 ACP, 13-round magazine. **Barrel:** 5". **Weight:** 33.5 oz. **Length:** 8.5"
overall. **Grips:** Checkered polymer. **Sights:** Blade front, adjustable
low-profile rear. **Features:** Stainless steel beaver-tail grip safety,
rounded trigger-guard, tapered bull barrel, full-length guide rod, matte
blue finish on frame and slide. 40 S&W models in M-5 Govt. 1911, M-5
Commander, and M-5 IPSC introduced 2006; M-5 Ultra X Compact in
9mm Para. and 45 ACP introduced 2006; M-5 IPSC .45 ACP introduced
2006. Made in Israel by BUL, imported by K.B.I., Inc.
Price: M-5 Govt. 1911, 40 S&W/45 ACP, matte blue **$749.00**
Price: M-5 Commander, 40 S&W/45 ACP, matte blue **$749.00**
Price: M-5 Ultra X Compact, 9mm Para., 3.1" barrel,
7" OAL, 28 oz. **$749.00**
Price: M-5 Ultra X Compact, 45 ACP, 3.1" barrel, 7" OAL,
28 oz. **$749.00**

COBRA ENTERPRISES FS32, FS380 AUTO PISTOL
Caliber: 32 ACP, 380 ACP, 7-shot magazine. **Barrel:** 3.5". **Weight:**
2.1 lbs. **Length:** 6-3/8" overall. **Grips:** Black composition. **Sights:**
Fixed. **Features:** Choice of bright chrome, satin nickel or black finish.
Introduced 2002. Made in U.S.A. by Cobra Enterprises of Utah, Inc.
Price: **$165.00**

COBRA ENTERPRISES PATRIOT 45 PISTOL
Caliber: 45 ACP, 6, 7, or 10-shot magazine. **Barrel:** 3.3". **Weight:** 20
oz. **Length:** 6" overall. **Grips:** Black polymer. **Sights:** Rear adjustable.
Features: Stainless steel or black melonite slide with load indicator;
Semi-auto locked breech, DAO. Made in U.S.A. by Cobra Enterprises
of Utah, Inc.
Price: **$380.00**

COBRA ENTERPRISES CA32, CA380 PISTOL
Caliber: 32 ACP, 380 ACP. **Barrel:** 2.8". **Weight:** 22 oz. **Length:** 5.4".
Grips: Black molded synthetic. **Sights:** Fixed. **Features:** Choice
of black, satin nickel, or chrome finish. Made in U.S.A. by Cobra
Enterprises of Utah, Inc.
Price: **$157.00**

Prices given are believed to be accurate at time of publication however, many factors affect retail pricing so exact prices are not possible.

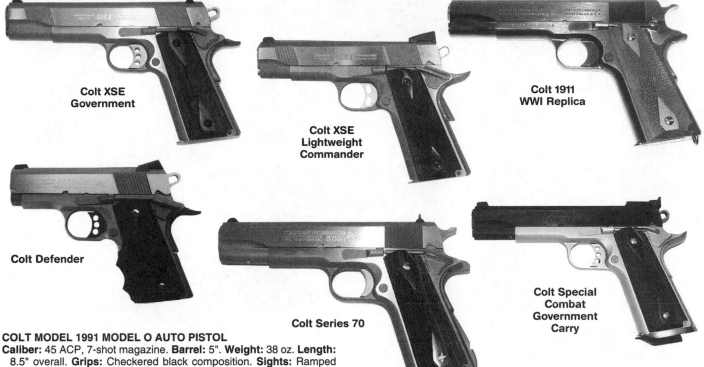

Colt XSE Government

Colt XSE Lightweight Commander

Colt 1911 WWI Replica

Colt Defender

Colt Series 70

Colt Special Combat Government Carry

COLT MODEL 1991 MODEL O AUTO PISTOL
Caliber: 45 ACP, 7-shot magazine. **Barrel:** 5". **Weight:** 38 oz. **Length:** 8.5" overall. **Grips:** Checkered black composition. **Sights:** Ramped blade front, fixed square notch rear, high profile. **Features:** Matte finish. Continuation of serial number range used on original G.I. 1911A1 guns. Comes with one magazine and molded carrying case. Introduced 1991.
Price: Blue $786.00
Price: Stainless $839.00

COLT XSE SERIES MODEL O AUTO PISTOLS
Caliber: 45 ACP, 8-shot magazine. **Barrel:** 4.25", 5". **Grips:** Checkered, double diamond rosewood. **Sights:** Drift-adjustable 3-dot combat. **Features:** Brushed stainless finish; adjustable, two-cut aluminum trigger; extended ambidextrous thumb safety; upswept beavertail with palm swell; elongated slot hammer. Introduced 1999. From Colt's Mfg. Co., Inc.
Price: XSE Government (5" bbl.) $944.00
Price: XSE Government (4.25" bbl.) $944.00

COLT XSE LIGHTWEIGHT COMMANDER AUTO PISTOL
Caliber: 45 ACP, 8-shot. **Barrel:** 4.25". **Weight:** 26 oz. **Length:** 7.75" overall. **Grips:** Double diamond checkered rosewood. **Sights:** Fixed, glare-proofed blade front, square notch rear; 3-dot system. **Features:** Brushed stainless slide, nickeled aluminum frame; McCormick elongated slot enhanced hammer, McCormick two-cut adjustable aluminum hammer. Made in U.S.A. by Colt's Mfg. Co., Inc.
Price: Stainless $944.00

COLT DEFENDER
Caliber: 45 ACP, 7-shot magazine. **Barrel:** 3". **Weight:** 22-1/2 oz. **Length:** 6.75" overall. **Grips:** Pebble-finish rubber wraparound with finger grooves. **Sights:** White dot front, snag-free Colt competition rear. **Features:** Stainless finish; aluminum frame; combat-style hammer; Hi Ride grip safety, extended manual safety, disconnect safety. Introduced 1998. Made in U.S.A. by Colt's Mfg. Co., Inc.
Price: 07000D, stainless............................$885.00

COLT SERIES 70
Caliber: 45 ACP. **Barrel:** 5". **Weight:** NA. **Length:** NA. **Grips:** Rosewood with double diamond checkering pattern. **Sights:** Fixed. **Features:** Custom replica of the Original Series 70 pistol with a Series 70 firing system, original rollmarks. Introduced 2002. Made in U.S.A. by Colt's Mfg. Co., Inc.
Price: Blued $919.00
Price: Stainless $950.00

COLT 38 SUPER
Caliber: 38 Super. **Barrel:** 5". **Weight:** NA. **Length:** 8.5" **Grips:** Checkered rubber (stainless and blue models); wood with double diamond checkering pattern (bright stainless model). **Sights:** 3-dot. **Features:** Beveled magazine well, standard thumb safety and service-style grip safety. Introduced 2003. Made in U.S.A. by Colt's Mfg. Co., Inc.
Price: Blued $837.00
Price: Stainless $866.00
Price: Bright Stainless $1,090.00

COLT 1918 WWI REPLICA
Caliber: 45 ACP, 2 7-round magazines. **Barrel:** 5". **Weight:** 38 oz. **Length:** 8.5". **Grips:** Checkered walnut with double diamond checkering pattern. **Sights:** Tapered blade front sight, U-shaped rear notch. **Features:** Reproduction based on original 1911 blueprints. Original rollmarks and inspector marks. Smooth mainspring housing with lanyard loop, WWI-style manual thumb and grip safety, black oxide finish. Introduced 2007. Made in U.S.A. by Colt's Mfg. Co., Inc.
Price: Blued $990.00

COLT RAIL GUN
Caliber: 45 ACP (8+1). **Barrel:** NA. **Weight:** NA. **Length:** NA. **Grips:** Rosewood double diamond. **Sights:** White dot front and Novak rear. **Features:** 1911-style semi-auto. Stainless steel frame and slide, front and rear slide serrations, skeletonized trigger, integral; accessory rail, Smith & Alexander upswept beavertail grip palm swell safety, tactical thumb safety, National Match barrel.
Price: .... **TO BE ANNOUNCED**

COLT NEW AGENT
Caliber: 45 ACP (7+1). **Barrel:** 3". **Weight:** 25 oz. **Length:** 6.75" overall. **Grips:** Double diamond slim fit. **Sights:** Snag free trench style. **Features:** Semi-auto pistol with blued finish and enhanced black anodized aluminum receiver. Skeletonized aluminum trigger, series 80 firing system, front strap serrations, beveled magazine well.
Price: $885.00

COLT SPECIAL COMBAT GOVERNMENT CARRY MODEL
Caliber: 45 ACP (8+1), 38 Super (9+1). **Barrel:** 5". **Weight:** NA. **Length:** NA. **Grips:** Black/silver synthetic. **Sights:** Novak front and rear night. **Features:** 1911-style semi-auto. Skeletonized three-hole trigger, slotted hammer, Smith & Alexander upswept beavertail grip palm swell safety and extended magazine well, Wilson tactical ambidextrous safety. Available in blued, hard chrome, or blue/satin nickel finish, depending on chambering.
Price: $1,676.00

CZ 75 B 9mm

CZ 75 B Decocker

CZ 75/85 Kadet

CZ 85

CZ 97 B

nut

black polycoat finish, extended beavertail, new grip geometry with checkering on front and back straps, and double or single action operation. Introduced 2005. The Shadow variant designed as an IPSC "production" division competition firearm. Includes competition hammer, competition rear sight and fiber-optic front sight, modified slide release, lighter recoil and main spring for use with "minor power factor" competition ammunition. Includes polycoat finish and slim walnut grips. Finished by CZ Custom Shop. Imported from the Czech Republic by CZ-USA.
Price: SP-01 9mm Para., black polymer, 19+1 . . . . **$850.00**

CZ 75 B AUTO PISTOL
Caliber: 9mm Para., 40 S&W, 10-shot magazine. **Barrel:** 4.7". **Weight:** 34.3 oz. **Length:** 8.1" overall. **Grips:** High impact checkered plastic. **Sights:** Square post front, rear adjustable for windage; 3-dot system. **Features:** Single action/double action design; firing pin block safety; choice of black polymer, matte or high-polish blue finishes. All-steel frame. B-SA is a single action with a drop-free magazine. Imported from the Czech Republic by CZ-USA.
Price: 75 B, black polymer, 16-shot magazine **$597.00**
Price: 75 B, dual-tone or satin nickel **$617.00**
Price: 40 S&W, black polymer, 12-shot magazine **$615.00**
Price: 40 S&W, glossy blue, dual-tone, satin nickel **$669.00**
Price: 75 B-SA, 9mm Para./40 S&W, single action **$609.00**

CZ 75 BD Decocker
Similar to the CZ 75B except has a decocking lever in place of the safety lever. All other specifications are the same. Introduced 1999. Imported from the Czech Republic by CZ-USA.
Price: 9mm Para., black polymer **$609.00**

CZ 75 B Compact Auto Pistol
Similar to the CZ 75 B except has 14-shot magazine in 9mm Para., 3.9" barrel and weighs 32 oz. Has removable front sight, non-glare ribbed slide top. Trigger guard is squared and serrated; combat hammer. Introduced 1993. Imported from the Czech Republic by CZ-USA.
Price: 9mm Para., black polymer **$631.00**
Price: 9mm Para., dual tone or satin nickel **$651.00**
Price: 9mm Para. D PCR Compact, alloy frame **$651.00**

CZ 75 Champion Pistol
Similar to the CZ 75 B except has a longer frame and slide, rubber grip to accommodate new heavy-duty magazine. Ambidextrous thumb safety, extended magazine release; three-port compensator. Blued slide and stain nickel frame finish. Introduced 2005. Imported from the Czech Republic by CZ-USA.
Price: 40 S&W, 12-shot mag. **$1,739.00**

CZ 75 Tactical Sport
Similar to the CZ 75 B except the CZ 75 TS is a competition ready pistol designed for IPSC standard division (USPSA limited division). Fixed target sights, tuned single-action operation, lightweight polymer match trigger with adjustments for take-up and overtravel, competition hammer, extended magazine catch, ambidextrous manual safety, checkered walnut grips, polymer magazine well, two tone finish. Introduced 2005. Imported from the Czech Republic by CZ-USA.
Price: 9mm Para., 20-shot mag. **$1,338.00**
Price: 40 S&W, 16-shot mag. **$1,338.00**

CZ 75 SP-01 Pistol
Similar to NATO-approved CZ 75 Compact P-01 model. Features an integral 1913 accessory rail on the dust cover, rubber grip panels,

CZ 75 SP-01 Phantom
Similar to the CZ 75 B. 9mm Luger, 19-round magazine, weighs 26 oz. and features a polymer frame with accessory rail, and a forged steel slide with a weight-saving scalloped profile. Two interchangeable grip inserts are included to accommodate users with different-sized hands.
Price: **$695.00**

CZ 85 B/85 Combat Auto Pistol
Same gun as the CZ 75 except has ambidextrous slide release and safety levers; non-glare, ribbed slide top; squared, serrated trigger guard; trigger stop to prevent overtravel. Introduced 1986. The CZ 85 Combat features a fully adjustable rear sight, extended magazine release, ambidextrous slide stop and safety catch, drop free magazine and overtravel adjustment. Imported from the Czech Republic by CZ-USA.
Price: 9mm Para., black polymer **$628.00**
Price: Combat, black polymer **$702.00**
Price: Combat, dual-tone, satin nickel **$732.00**

CZ 75 KADET AUTO PISTOL
Caliber: 22 LR, 10-shot magazine. **Barrel:** 4.88". **Weight:** 36 oz. **Grips:** High impact checkered plastic. **Sights:** Blade front, fully adjustable rear. **Features:** Single action/double action mechanism; all-steel construction. Introduced 1999. Kadet conversion kit consists of barrel, slide, adjustable sights, and magazine to convert the centerfire 75 to rimfire. Imported from the Czech Republic by CZ-USA.
Price: Black polymer **$689.00**
Price: Kadet conversion kit **$412.00**

CZ 83 DOUBLE-ACTION PISTOL
Caliber: 32 ACP, 380 ACP, 12-shot magazine. **Barrel:** 3.8". **Weight:** 26.2 oz. **Length:** 6.8" overall. **Grips:** High impact checkered plastic. **Sights:** Removable square post front, rear adjustable for windage; 3-dot system. **Features:** Single action/double action; ambidextrous magazine release and safety. Blue finish; non-glare ribbed slide top. Imported from the Czech Republic by CZ-USA.
Price: Glossy blue, 32 ACP or 380 ACP **$495.00**
Price: Satin Nickel **$522.00**

CZ 97 B AUTO PISTOL
Caliber: 45 ACP, 10-shot magazine. **Barrel:** 4.85". **Weight:** 40 oz. **Length:** 8.34" overall. **Grips:** Checkered walnut. **Sights:** Fixed. **Features:** Single action/double action; full-length slide rails; screw-in barrel bushing; linkless barrel; all-steel construction; chamber loaded indicator; dual transfer bars. Introduced 1999. Imported from the Czech Republic by CZ-USA.
Price: Black polymer **$779.00**
Price: Glossy blue **$799.00**

Dan Wesson Pointman

Dan Wesson DW RZ-10

Desert Baby Eagle

Desert Eagle Mark XIX

EAA Witness

CZ 97 BD Decocker

Similar to the CZ 97 B except has a decocking lever in place of the safety lever. Tritium night sights. Rubber grips. All other specifications are the same. Introduced 1999. Imported from the Czech Republic by CZ-USA.
Price: 9mm Para., black polymer $874.00

CZ 2075 RAMI/RAMI P AUTO PISTOL

Caliber: 9mm Para., 40 S&W. **Barrel:** 3". **Weight:** 25 oz. **Length:** 6.5" overall. **Grips:** Rubber. **Sights:** Blade front with dot, white outline rear drift adjustable for windage. **Features:** Single-action/double-action; alloy or polymer frame, steel slide; has laser sight mount. Imported from the Czech Republic by CZ-USA.
Price: 9mm Para., alloy frame, 10 and 14-shot magazines . . . $671.00
Price: 40 S&W, alloy frame, 8-shot magazine $671.00
Price: RAMI P, polymer frame, 9mm Para., 40 S&W $612.00

CZ P-01 AUTO PISTOL

Caliber: 9mm Para., 14-shot magazine. **Barrel:** 3.85". **Weight:** 27 oz. **Length:** 7.2" overall. **Grips:** Checkered rubber. **Sights:** Blade front with dot, white outline rear drift adjustable for windage. **Features:** Based on the CZ 75, except with forged aircraft-grade aluminum alloy frame. Hammer forged barrel, decocker, firing-pin block, M3 rail, dual slide serrations, squared trigger guard, re-contoured trigger, lanyard loop on butt. Serrated front and back strap. Introduced 2006. Imported from the Czech Republic by CZ-USA.
Price: CZ P-01 . . . .$672.00

DAN WESSON FIREARMS POINTMAN SEVEN AUTO PISTOL

Caliber: 10mm, 40 S&W, 45 ACP. **Barrel:** 5". **Grips:** Diamond checkered cocobolo. **Sights:** Bo-Mar style adjustable target sight. **Weight:** 38 oz. **Features:** Stainless-steel frame and serrated slide. Series 70-style 1911, stainless-steel frame, forged stainless-steel slide. One-piece match-grade barrel and bushing. 20-LPI checkered mainspring housing, front and rear slide cocking serrations, beveled magwell, dehorned by hand. Lowered and flared ejection port, Ed Brown slide stop and memory groove grip safety, tactical extended thumb safety. Commander-style match hammer, match grade sear, aluminum trigger with stainless bow, Wolff springs. Introduced 2000. Made in U.S.A. by Dan Wesson Firearms, distributed by CZ-USA.
Price: 45 ACP, 7+1 . . . . $1,158.00
Price: 10mm, 8+1 . . . . $1,191.00
Price: 40 S&W, stainless $1,189.00
Price: 45 ACP, Desert Tan $1,269.00

Dan Wesson Commander Classic Bobtail Auto Pistols

Similar to Pointman Seven, a Commander-sized frame with 4.25" barrel. Available with stainless finish, fixed night sights. Introduced 2005.

Made in U.S.A. by Dan Wesson Firearms, distributed by CZ-USA.
Price: 45 ACP, 7+1, 33 oz. $1,191.00
Price: 10mm, 8+1, 33 oz., stainless $1,224.00
Price: 10mm, 33 oz. two-tone $1,530.00

DAN WESSON DW RZ-10 AUTO PISTOL

Caliber: 10mm, 9-shot. **Barrel:** 5". **Grips:** Diamond checkered cocobolo. **Sights:** Bo-Mar style adjustable target sight. **Weight:** 38.3 oz. **Length:** 8.8" overall. **Features:** Stainless-steel frame and serrated slide. Series 70-style 1911, stainless-steel frame, forged stainless-steel slide. Commander-style match hammer. Reintroduced 2005. Made in U.S.A. by Dan Wesson Firearms, distributed by CZ-USA.
Price: 10mm, 8+1 . . . . $1,191.00

Dan Wesson DW RZ-10 Sportsman

Similar to the RZ-10 Auto except with 8-shot magazine. Weighs 36 oz., length is 8.8" overall.
Price: $1,448.00

Dan Wesson DW RZ-45 Heritage

Similar to the RZ-10 Auto except in 45 ACP with 7-shot magazine. Weighs 36 oz., length is 8.8" overall.
Price: 10mm, 8+1 . . . . $1,141.00

DESERT EAGLE MARK XIX PISTOL

Caliber: 357 Mag., 9-shot; 44 Mag., 8-shot; 50 AE, 7-shot. **Barrel:** 6", 10", interchangeable. **Weight:** 357 Mag.-62 oz.; 44 Mag.-69 oz.; 50 AE-72 oz. **Length:** 10.25" overall (6" bbl.). **Grips:** Polymer; rubber available. **Sights:** Blade on ramp front, combat-style rear. Adjustable available. **Features:** Interchangeable barrels; rotating three-lug bolt; ambidextrous safety; adjustable trigger. Military epoxy finish. Satin, bright nickel, chrome, brushed, matte or black-oxide finishes available. 10" barrel extra. Imported from Israel by Magnum Research, Inc.
Price: Black-6, 6" barrel $1,475.00
Price: Black-10, 10" barrel $1,575.00
Price: Component System Package, 3 barrels,
carrying case, from $2,801.00

DESERT BABY MICRO DESERT EAGLE PISTOL

Caliber: 380 ACP, 6-rounds. **Barrel:** 2.22". **Weight:** 14 oz. **Length:** 4.52" overall. **Grips:** NA. **Sights:** Fixed low-profile. **Features:** Small-frame DAO pocket pistol. Steel slide, aluminum alloy frame, nickel-teflon finish.
Price: $535.00

DESERT BABY EAGLE PISTOLS

Caliber: 9mm Para., 40 S&W, 45 ACP, 10- or 15-round magazines. **Barrel:** 3.64", 3.93", 4.52". **Weight:** 26.8 to 39.8 oz. **Length:** 7.25" to 8.25" overall. **Grips:** Polymer. **Sights:** Drift-adjustable rear, blade front. **Features:** Steel frame and slide; slide safety; decocker. Reintroduced in 1999. Imported from Israel by Magnum Research, Inc.
Price: $619.00

EAA Zastava EZ

Ed Brown Classic Custom

Ed Brown Kobra

Ed Brown Kobra Carry

Ed Brown Executive

EAA WITNESS FULL SIZE AUTO PISTOL

Caliber: 9mm Para., 38 Super, 18-shot magazine; 40 S&W, 10mm, 15-shot magazine; 45 ACP, 10-shot magazine. **Barrel:** 4.50". **Weight:** 35.33 oz. **Length:** 8.10" overall. **Grips:** Checkered rubber. **Sights:** Undercut blade front, open rear adjustable for windage. **Features:** Double-action/single-action trigger system; round trigger guard; frame-mounted safety. Introduced 1991. Polymer frame introduced 2005. Imported from Italy by European American Armory.
Price: 9mm Para., 38 Super, 10mm, 40 S&W, 45 ACP, full-size steel frame, Wonder finish $514.00
Price: 45/22 22 LR, full-size steel frame, blued $472.00
Price: 9mm Para., 40 S&W, 45 ACP, full-size polymer frame .$472.00

EAA WITNESS COMPACT AUTO PISTOL

Caliber: 9mm Para., 40 S&W, 10mm, 12-shot magazine; 45 ACP, 8-shot magazine. **Barrel:** 3.6". **Weight:** 30 oz. **Length:** 7.3" overall. Otherwise similar to Full Size Witness. Polymer frame introduced 2005. Imported from Italy by European American Armory.
Price: 9mm Para., 10mm, 40 S&W, 45 ACP, steel frame, Wonder finish $514.00
Price: 9mm Para., 40 S&W, 45 ACP, polymer frame $472.00

EAA WITNESS-P CARRY AUTO PISTOL

Caliber: 10mm, 15-shot magazine; 45 ACP, 10-shot magazine. **Barrel:** 3.6". **Weight:** 27 oz. **Length:** 7.5" overall. Otherwise similar to Full Size Witness. Polymer frame introduced 2005. Imported from Italy by European American Armory.
Price: 10mm, 45 ACP, polymer frame, from $598.00

EAA ZASTAVA EZ PISTOL

Caliber: 9mm Para., 15-shot magazine; 40 S&W, 11-shot magazine; 45 ACP, 10-shot magazine. **Barrel:** 3.5" or 4." **Weight:** 30-33 oz. **Length:** 7.25" to 7.5" overall. **Features:** Ambidextrous decocker, slide release and magazine release; three dot sight system, aluminum frame, steel slide, accessory rail, full-length claw extractor, loaded chamber indicator. M88 compact has 3.6" barrel, weighs 28 oz. Introduced 2008. Imported by European American Armory.
Price: 9mm Para. or 40 S&W, blued $547.00
Price: 9mm Para. or 40 S&W, chromed $587.00
Price: 45 ACP, chromed $587.00
Price: M88, from $292.00

ED BROWN CLASSIC CUSTOM

Caliber: 45 ACP, 7 shot. **Barrel:** 5". **Weight:** 40 oz. **Grips:** Cocobolo wood. **Sights:** Bo-Mar adjustable rear, dovetail front. **Features:** Single-action, M1911 style, custom made to order, stainless frame and slide available. Special mirror-finished slide.
Price: Model CC-BB, blued **$3,155.00**
Price: Model CC-SB, blued and stainless **$3,155.00**
Price: Model CC-SS, stainless **$3,155.00**

ED BROWN KOBRA AND KOBRA CARRY

Caliber: 45 ACP, 7-shot magazine. **Barrel:** 5" (Kobra); 4.25" (Kobra Carry). **Weight:** 39 oz. (Kobra); 34 oz. (Kobra Carry). **Grips:** Hogue exotic wood. **Sights:** Ramp, front; fixed Novak low-mount night sights, rear. **Features:** Has snakeskin pattern serrations on forestrap and mainspring housing, dehorned edges, beavertail grip safety.
Price: Kobra K-BB, blued **$2,195.00**
Price: Kobra K-SB, stainless and blued **$2,195.00**
Price: Kobra K-SS, stainless **$2,195.00**
Price: Kobra Carry blued, blued/stainless, or stainless from **$2,445.00**

Ed Brown Executive Pistols

Similar to other Ed Brown products, but with 25-lpi checkered frame and mainspring housing.
Price: Elite blued, blued/stainless, or stainless, from **$2,395.00**
Price: Carry blued, blued/stainless, or stainless, from **$2,645.00**
Price: Target blued, blued/stainless, or stainless (2006) from **$2,595.00**

Ed Brown Special Forces Pistol

Similar to other Ed Brown products, but with ChainLink treatment on forestrap and mainspring housing. Entire gun coated with Gen III finish. "Square cut" serrations on rear of slide only. Dehorned. Introduced 2006.
Price: From **$2,195.00**

Ed Brown Special Forces Carry Pistol

Similar to the Special Forces basic models. Features a 4.25" Commander model slide, single stack commander Bobtail frame. Weighs approx. 35 oz. Fixed dovetail 3-dot night sights with high visibility white outlines.
Price: From **$2,445.00**

Prices given are believed to be accurate at time of publication however, many factors affect retail pricing so exact prices are not possible.

Ed Brown Special Forces

Excel Arms Accelerator MP-22

Firestorm 45 Gov't

Glock 17C

Firestorm Mini

Glock 22

Glock 26

EXCEL ARMS ACCELERATOR MP-17/MP-22 PISTOLS
Caliber: 17 HMR, 22 WMR, 9-shot magazine. **Barrel:** 8.5" bull barrel. **Weight:** 54 oz. **Length:** 12.875" overall. **Grips:** Textured black composition. **Sights:** Fully adjustable target sights. **Features:** Made from 17-4 stainless steel, comes with aluminum rib, integral Weaver base, internal hammer, firing-pin block. American made, lifetime warranty. Comes with two 9-round stainless steel magazines and a California-approved cable lock. 22 WMR Introduced 2006. Made in U.S.A. by Excel Arms.
Price: $433.00
Price: Camo finishes (2008) $520.00

FIRESTORM AUTO PISTOLS
Caliber: 22 LR, 32 ACP, 10-shot magazine; 380 ACP, 7-shot magazine; 9mm Para., 40 S&W, 10-shot magazine; 45 ACP, 7-shot magazine. **Barrel:** 3.5". **Weight:** From 23 oz. **Length:** From 6.6" overall. **Grips:** Rubber. **Sights:** 3-dot. **Features:** Double action. Distributed by SGS Importers International.
Price: 22 LR, matte or duotone, from $309.95
Price: 380, matte or duotone, from $311.95
Price: Mini Firestorm 9mm Para., matte, duotone, nickel, from $395.00
Price: Mini Firestorm 40 S&W, matte, duotone, nickel, from . . $395.00
Price: Mini Firestorm 45 ACP, matte, duotone, chrome, from .$402.00

GLOCK 17/17C AUTO PISTOL
Caliber: 9mm Para., 17/19/33-shot magazines. **Barrel:** 4.49". **Weight:** 22.04 oz. (without magazine). **Length:** 7.32" overall. **Grips:** Black polymer. **Sights:** Dot on front blade, white outline rear adjustable for windage. **Features:** Polymer frame, steel slide; double-action trigger with "Safe Action" system; mechanical firing pin safety, drop safety; simple takedown without tools; locked breech, recoil operated action. ILS designation refers to Internal Locking System. Adopted by Austrian armed forces 1983. NATO approved 1984. Imported from Austria by Glock, Inc.
Price: Fixed sight $690.00

GLOCK 19/19C AUTO PISTOL
Caliber: 9mm Para., 15/17/19/33-shot magazines. **Barrel:** 4.02". **Weight:** 20.99 oz. (without magazine). **Length:** 6.85" overall. Compact version of Glock 17. Pricing the same as Model 17. Imported from Austria by Glock, Inc.
Price: Fixed sight $699.00
Price: 19C Compensated (fixed sight) $675.00

GLOCK 20/20C 10MM AUTO PISTOL
Caliber: 10mm, 15-shot magazines. **Barrel:** 4.6". **Weight:** 27.68 oz.

(without magazine). **Length:** 7.59" overall. **Features:** Otherwise similar to Model 17. Imported from Austria by Glock, Inc. Introduced 1990.
Price: Fixed sight, from $700.00

GLOCK MODEL 20 SF SHORT FRAME PISTOL
Caliber: 10mm. **Barrel:** 4.61" with hexagonal rifling. **Weight:** 27.51 oz. **Length:** 8.07" overall. **Sights:** Fixed. **Features:** Otherwise similar to Model 20 but with short-frame design, extended sight radius.
Price: $664.00

GLOCK 21/21C AUTO PISTOL
Caliber: 45 ACP, 13-shot magazines. **Barrel:** 4.6". **Weight:** 26.28 oz. (without magazine). **Length:** 7.59" overall. **Features:** Otherwise similar to Model 17. Imported from Austria by Glock, Inc. Introduced 1991. SF version has tactical rail, smaller diameter grip, 10-round magazine capacity. Introduced 2007.
Price: Fixed sight, from $700.00

GLOCK 22/22C AUTO PISTOL
Caliber: 40 S&W, 15/17-shot magazines. **Barrel:** 4.49". **Weight:** 22.92 oz. (without magazine). **Length:** 7.32" overall. **Features:** Otherwise similar to Model 17, including pricing. Imported from Austria by Glock, Inc. Introduced 1990.
Price: Fixed sight, from $641.00

GLOCK 23/23C AUTO PISTOL
Caliber: 40 S&W, 13/15/17-shot magazines. **Barrel:** 4.02". **Weight:** 21.16 oz. (without magazine). **Length:** 6.85" overall. **Features:** Otherwise similar to Model 22, including pricing. Compact version of Glock 22. Imported from Austria by Glock, Inc. Introduced 1990.
Price: Fixed sight $641.00
Price: 23C Compensated (fixed sight) $694.00

GLOCK 26 AUTO PISTOL
Caliber: 9mm Para. 10/12/15/17/19/33-shot magazines. **Barrel:** 3.46". **Weight:** 19.75 oz. **Length:** 6.29" overall. Subcompact version of Glock 17. Pricing the same as Model 17. Imported from Austria by Glock, Inc.
Price: Fixed sight $690.00

Glock 35

Glock 30

Glock 31

Heckler & Koch
USP45

Heckler & Koch
USP Compact

GLOCK 27 AUTO PISTOL
Caliber: 40 S&W, 9/11/13/15/17-shot magazines. **Barrel:** 3.46". **Weight:** 19.75 oz. (without magazine). **Length:** 6.29" overall. **Features:** Otherwise similar to Model 22, including pricing. Subcompact version of Glock 22. Imported from Austria by Glock, Inc. Introduced 1996.
Price: Fixed sight **$750.00**

GLOCK 29 AUTO PISTOL
Caliber: 10mm, 10/15-shot magazines. **Barrel:** 3.78". **Weight:** 24.69 oz. (without magazine). **Length:** 6.77" overall. **Features:** Otherwise similar to Model 20, including pricing. Subcompact version of Glock 20. Imported from Austria by Glock, Inc. Introduced 1997.
Price: Fixed sight **$672.00**

GLOCK MODEL 29 SF SHORT FRAME PISTOL
Caliber: 10mm. **Barrel:** 3.78" with hexagonal rifling. **Weight:** 24.52 oz. **Length:** 6.97" overall. **Sights:** Fixed. **Features:** Otherwise similar to Model 29 but with short-frame design, extended sight radius.
Price: **$660.00**

GLOCK 30 AUTO PISTOL
Caliber: 45 ACP, 9/10/13-shot magazines. **Barrel:** 3.78". **Weight:** 23.99 oz. (without magazine). **Length:** 6.77" overall. **Features:** Otherwise similar to Model 21, including pricing. Subcompact version of Glock 21. Imported from Austria by Glock, Inc. Introduced 1997. SF version has tactical rail, octagonal rifled barrel with a 1:15.75 rate of twist, smaller diameter grip, 10-round magazine capacity. Introduced 2008.
Price: Fixed sight **$700.00**

GLOCK 31/31C AUTO PISTOL
Caliber: 357 Auto, 15/17-shot magazines. **Barrel:** 4.49". **Weight:** 23.28 oz. (without magazine). **Length:** 7.32" overall. **Features:** Otherwise similar to Model 17. Imported from Austria by Glock, Inc.
Price: Fixed sight, from **$641.00**

GLOCK 32/32C AUTO PISTOL
Caliber: 357 Auto, 13/15/17-shot magazines. **Barrel:** 4.02". **Weight:** 21.52 oz. (without magazine). **Length:** 6.85" overall. **Features:** Otherwise similar to Model 31. Compact. Imported from Austria by Glock, Inc.
Price: Fixed sight **$669.00**

GLOCK 33 AUTO PISTOL
Caliber: 357 Auto, 9/11/13/15/17-shot magazines. **Barrel:** 3.46". **Weight:** 19.75 oz. (without magazine). **Length:** 6.29" overall. **Features:** Otherwise similar to Model 31. Subcompact. Imported from Austria by Glock, Inc.
Price: Fixed sight, from **$641.00**

GLOCK 34 AUTO PISTOL
Caliber: 9mm Para. 17/19/33-shot magazines. **Barrel:** 5.32". **Weight:** 22.9 oz. **Length:** 8.15" overall. Competition version of Glock 17 with extended barrel, slide, and sight radius dimensions. Imported from Austria by Glock, Inc.
Price: Adjustable sight, from **$648.00**

GLOCK 35 AUTO PISTOL
Caliber: 40 S&W, 15/17-shot magazines. **Barrel:** 5.32". **Weight:** 24.52 oz. (without magazine). **Length:** 8.15" overall. **Features:** Otherwise similar to Model 22. Competition version of Glock 22 with extended barrel, slide, and sight radius dimensions. Imported from Austria by Glock, Inc. Introduced 1996.
Price: Adjustable sight **$648.00**

GLOCK 36 AUTO PISTOL
Caliber: 45 ACP, 6-shot magazines. **Barrel:** 3.78". **Weight:** 20.11 oz. (without magazine). **Length:** 6.77" overall. **Features:** Single-stack magazine, slimmer grip than Glock 21/30. Subcompact. Imported from Austria by Glock, Inc. Introduced 1997.
Price: Adjustable sight **$616.00**

GLOCK 37 AUTO PISTOL
Caliber: 45 GAP, 10-shot magazines. **Barrel:** 4.49". **Weight:** 25.95 oz. (without magazine). **Length:** 7.32" overall. **Features:** Otherwise similar to Model 17. Imported from Austria by Glock, Inc. Introduced 2005.
Price: Fixed sight, from **$562.00**

GLOCK 38 AUTO PISTOL
Caliber: 45 GAP, 8/10-shot magazines. **Barrel:** 4.02". **Weight:** 24.16 oz. (without magazine). **Length:** 6.85" overall. **Features:** Otherwise similar to Model 37. Compact. Imported from Austria by Glock, Inc.
Price: Fixed sight **$614.00**

GLOCK 39 AUTO PISTOL
Caliber: 45 GAP, 6/8/10-shot magazines. **Barrel:** 3.46". **Weight:** 19.33 oz. (without magazine). **Length:** 6.3" overall. **Features:** Otherwise similar to Model 37. Subcompact. Imported from Austria by Glock, Inc.
Price: Fixed sight **$614.00**

HECKLER & KOCH USP AUTO PISTOL
Caliber: 9mm Para., 15-shot magazine; 40 S&W, 13-shot magazine; 45 ACP, 12-shot magazine. **Barrel:** 4.25-4.41". **Weight:** 1.65 lbs. **Length:** 7.64-7.87" overall. **Grips:** Non-slip stippled black polymer. **Sights:** Blade front, rear adjustable for windage. **Features:** New HK design with polymer frame, modified Browning action with recoil reduction system, single control lever. Special "hostile environment" finish on all metal parts. Available in SA/DA, DAO, left- and right-hand versions. Introduced 1993. 45 ACP Introduced 1995. Imported from Germany by Heckler & Koch, Inc.
Price: USP 45 . . . .**$919.00**
Price: USP 40 and USP 9mm **$859.00**

Prices given are believed to be accurate at time of publication however, many factors affect retail pricing so exact prices are not possible.

**Heckler & Koch
USP45 Compact**

**Heckler & Koch
USP45 Tactical**

**Heckler & Koch Mark
23 Special Operations**

Hi-Point C-9

HECKLER & KOCH USP COMPACT AUTO PISTOL
Caliber: 9mm Para., 13-shot magazine; 40 S&W and .357 SIG, 12-shot magazine; 45 ACP, 8-shot magazine. Similar to the USP except the 9mm Para., 357 SIG, and 40 S&W have 3.58" barrels, measure 6.81" overall, and weigh 1.47 lbs. (9mm Para.). Introduced 1996. 45 ACP measures 7.09" overall. Introduced 1998. Imported from Germany by Heckler & Koch, Inc.
Price: USP Compact 45 . . . .**$959.00**
Price: USP Compact 9mm Para., 40 S&W **$879.00**

HECKLER & KOCH USP45 TACTICAL PISTOL
Caliber: 40 S&W, 13-shot magazine; 45 ACP, 12-shot magazine. **Barrel:** 4.90-5.09". **Weight:** 1.9 lbs. **Length:** 8.64" overall. **Grips:** Non-slip stippled polymer. **Sights:** Blade front, fully adjustable target rear. **Features:** Has extended threaded barrel with rubber O-ring; adjustable trigger; extended magazine floorplate; adjustable trigger stop; polymer frame. Introduced 1998. Imported from Germany by Heckler & Koch, Inc.
Price: USP Tactical 45 . . . .**$1,239.00**
Price: USP Tactical 40 . . . .**$1,179.00**

HECKLER & KOCH USP COMPACT TACTICAL PISTOL
Caliber: 45 ACP, 8-shot magazine. Similar to the USP Tactical except measures 7.72" overall, weighs 1.72 lbs. Introduced 2006. Imported from Germany by Heckler & Koch, Inc.
Price: USP Compact Tactical **$1,179.00**

HECKLER & KOCH MARK 23 SPECIAL OPERATIONS PISTOL
Caliber: 45 ACP, 12-shot magazine. **Barrel:** 5.87". **Weight:** 2.42 lbs. **Length:** 9.65" overall. **Grips:** Integral with frame; black polymer. **Sights:** Blade front, rear drift adjustable for windage; 3-dot. **Features:** Civilian version of the SOCOM pistol. Polymer frame; double action; exposed hammer; short recoil, modified Browning action. Introduced 1996. Imported from Germany by Heckler & Koch, Inc.
Price: **$2,139.00**

HECKLER & KOCH P2000 AUTO PISTOL
Caliber: 9mm Para., 13-shot magazine; 40 S&W and .357 SIG, 12-shot magazine. **Barrel:** 3.62". **Weight:** 1.5 lbs. **Length:** 7" overall. **Grips:** Interchangeable panels. **Sights:** Fixed Patridge style, drift adjustable for windage, standard 3-dot. **Features:** Incorporates features of HK USP Compact pistol, including Law Enforcement Modification (LEM) trigger, double-action hammer system, ambidextrous magazine release, dual slide-release levers, accessory mounting rails, recurved, hook trigger guard, fiber-reinforced polymer frame, modular grip with exchangeable back straps, nitro-carburized finish, lock-out safety device. Introduced 2003. Imported from Germany by Heckler & Koch, Inc.
Price: **$879.00**
Price: P2000 LEM DAO, 357 SIG, intr. 2006 . . . .**$879.00**
Price: P2000 SA/DA, 357 SIG, intr. 2006 . . . .**$879.00**

HECKLER & KOCH P2000 SK AUTO PISTOL
Caliber: 9mm Para., 10-shot magazine; 40 S&W and .357 SIG, 9-shot magazine. **Barrel:** 3.27". **Weight:** 1.3 lbs. **Length:** 6.42" overall. **Sights:** Fixed Patridge style, drift adjustable. **Features:** Standard accessory rails, ambidextrous slide release, polymer frame, polygonal bore profile. Smaller version of P2000. Introduced 2005. Imported from Germany by Heckler & Koch, Inc.
Price: **$919.00**

HI-POINT FIREARMS MODEL 9MM COMPACT PISTOL
Caliber: 9mm Para., 8-shot magazine. **Barrel:** 3.5". **Weight:** 25 oz.

Length: 6.75" overall. **Grips:** Textured plastic. **Sights:** Combat-style adjustable 3-dot system; low profile. **Features:** Single-action design; frame-mounted magazine release; polymer frame. Scratch-resistant matte finish. Introduced 1993. Comps are similar except they have a 4" barrel with muzzle brake/compensator. Compensator is slotted for laser or flashlight mounting. Introduced 1998. Made in U.S.A. by MKS Supply, Inc.
Price: C-9 9mm **$155.00**

Hi-Point Firearms Model 380 Polymer Pistol
Similar to the 9mm Compact model except chambered for 380 ACP, 8-shot magazine, adjustable 3-dot sights. Weighs 25 oz. Polymer frame. Action locks open after last shot. Includes 10-shot and 8-shot magazine; trigger lock. Introduced 1998. Comps are similar except they have a 4" barrel with muzzle compensator. Introduced 2001. Made in U.S.A. by MKS Supply, Inc.
Price: CF-380 . . . .**$135.00**

HI-POINT FIREARMS 40SW/POLY AND 45 AUTO PISTOLS
Caliber: 40 S&W, 8-shot magazine; 45 ACP (9-shot). **Barrel:** 4.5". **Weight:** 32 oz. **Length:** 7.72" overall. **Sights:** Adjustable 3-dot. **Features:** Polymer frames, last round lock-open, grip mounted magazine release, magazine disconnect safety, integrated accessory rail, trigger lock. Introduced 2002. Made in U.S.A. by MKS Supply, Inc.
Price: 40SW-B **$186.00**
Price: 45 ACP **$186.00**

HIGH STANDARD VICTOR 22 PISTOL
Caliber: 22 Long Rifle (10 rounds) or .22 Short (5 rounds). **Barrel:** 4.5"-5.5". **Weight:** 45 oz.-46 oz. **Length:** 8.5"-9.5" overall. **Grips:** Freestyle wood. **Sights:** Frame mounted, adjustable. **Features:** Semi-auto with drilled and tapped barrel, tu-tone or blued finish.
Price: **$845.00**

High Standard 10X Custom 22 Pistol
Similar to the Victor model but with precision fitting, black wood grips, 5.5" barrel only. High Standard Universal Mount, 10-shot magazine, barrel drilled and tapped, certificate of authenticity. Overall length is 9.5". Weighs 44 oz. to 46 oz. From High Standard Custom Shop.
Price: **$1,095.00**

HIGH STANDARD SUPERMATIC TROPHY 22 PISTOL
Caliber: 22 Long Rifle (10 rounds) or .22 Short (5 rounds/Citation version), not interchangable. **Barrel:** 5.5", 7.25". **Weight:** 44 oz., 46 oz. **Length:** 9.5", 11.25" overall. **Grips:** Wood. **Sights:** Adjustable. **Features:** Semi-auto with drilled and tapped barrel, tu-tone or blued finish with gold accents.
Price: 5.5" **$845.00**

Kahr K9094C

Kahr M9093

Kahr PM4543

Kahr KT9093-Novak

Kahr TP4543

High Standard Olympic Military 22 Pistol
Similar to the Supermatic Trophy model but in 22 Short only with 5.5" bull barrel, five-round magazine, aluminum alloy frame, adjustable sights. Overall length is 9.5", weighs 42 oz.
Price: **$875.00**

High Standard Supermatic Citation Series 22 Pistol
Similar to the Supermatic Trophy model but with heavier trigger pull, 10" barrel, and nickel accents. 22 Short conversion unit available. Overall length 14.5", weighs 52 oz.
Price: **$895.00**

HIGH STANDARD SUPERMATIC TOURNAMENT 22 PISTOL
Caliber: 22 LR. **Barrel:** 5.5" bull barrel. **Weight:** 44 oz. **Length:** 9.5" overall. **Features:** Limited edition; similar to High Standard Victor model but with rear sight mounted directly to slide.
Price: **$835.00**

HIGH STANDARD SPORT KING 22 PISTOL
Caliber: 22 LR. **Barrel:** 4.5" or 6.75" tapered barrel. **Weight:** 40 oz. to 42 oz. **Length:** 8.5" to 10.75". **Features:** Sport version of High Standard Supermatic. Two-tone finish, fixed sights.
Price: **$725.00**

KAHR K SERIES AUTO PISTOLS
Caliber: K9: 9mm Para., 7-shot; K40: 40 S&W, 6-shot magazine. **Barrel:** 3.5". **Weight:** 25 oz. **Length:** 6" overall. **Grips:** Wraparound textured soft polymer. **Sights:** Blade front, rear drift adjustable for windage; bar-dot combat style. **Features:** Trigger-cocking double-action mechanism with passive firing pin block. Made of 4140 ordnance steel with matte black finish. Contact maker for complete price list. Introduced 1994. Made in U.S.A. by Kahr Arms.
Price: K9093C K9, matte stainless steel **$855.00**
Price: K9093NC K9, matte stainless steel w/tritium
    night sights **$985.00**
Price: K9094C K9 matte blackened stainless steel **$891.00**
Price: K9098 K9 Elite 2003, stainless steel **$932.00**
Price: K4043 K40, matte stainless steel **$855.00**
Price: K4043N K40, matte stainless steel w/tritium
    night sights **$985.00**
Price: K4044 K40, matte blackened stainless steel **$891.00**
Price: K4048 K40 Elite 2003, stainless steel **$932.00**

Kahr MK Series Micro Pistols
Similar to the K9/K40 except is 5.35" overall, 4" high, with a 3.08" barrel. Weighs 23.1 oz. Has snag-free bar-dot sights, polished feed ramp, dual recoil spring system, DA-only trigger. Comes with 5-round flush baseplate and 6-shot grip extension magazine. Introduced 1998. Made in U.S.A. by Kahr Arms.
Price: M9093 MK9, matte stainless steel **$855.00**
Price: M9093N MK9, matte stainless steel, tritium
    night sights **$958.00**
Price: M9098 MK9 Elite 2003, stainless steel **$932.00**
Price: M4043 MK40, matte stainless steel **$855.00**
Price: M4043N MK40, matte stainless steel, tritium
    night sights **$958.00**
Price: M4048 MK40 Elite 2003, stainless steel **$932.00**

KAHR P SERIES PISTOLS
Caliber: 380 ACP, 9x19, 40 S&W, 45 ACP. Similar to K9/K40 steel frame pistol except has polymer frame, matte stainless steel slide. Barrel length 3.5"; overall length 5.8"; weighs 17 oz. Includes two 7-shot magazines, hard polymer case, trigger lock. Introduced 2000. Made in U.S.A. by Kahr Arms.

Price: KP9093 9mm Para. **$739.00**
Price: KP4043 40 S&W **$739.00**
Price: KP4543 45 ACP **$805.00**
Price: KP3833 380 ACP (2008) **$649.00**

KAHR PM SERIES PISTOLS
Caliber: 9x19, 40 S&W, 45 ACP. Similar to P-Series pistols except has smaller polymer frame (Polymer Micro). Barrel length 3.08"; overall length 5.35"; weighs 17 oz. Includes two 7-shot magazines, hard polymer case, trigger lock. Introduced 2000. Made in U.S.A. by Kahr Arms.
Price: PM9093 PM9 . . . . **$786.00**
Price: PM4043 PM40 . . . . **$786.00**
Price: PM4543 (2007) **$855.00**

KAHR T SERIES PISTOLS
Caliber: T9: 9mm Para., 8-shot magazine; T40: 40 S&W, 7-shot magazine. **Barrel:** 4". **Weight:** 28.1-29.1 oz. **Length:** 6.5" overall. **Grips:** Checkered Hogue Pau Ferro wood grips. **Sights:** Rear: Novak low profile 2-dot tritium night sight, front tritium night sight. **Features:** Similar to other Kahr makes, but with longer slide and barrel upper, longer butt. Trigger cocking DAO; lock breech; "Browning-type" recoil lug; passive striker block; no magazine disconnect. Comes with two magazines. Introduced 2004. Made in U.S.A. by Kahr Arms.
Price: KT9093 T9 matte stainless steel **$831.00**
Price: KT9093-NOVAK T9, "Tactical 9," Novak night sight . . . **$968.00**
Price: KT4043 40 S&W **$831.00**

KAHR TP SERIES PISTOLS
Caliber: TP9: 9mm Para., 7-shot magazine; TP40: 40 S&W, 6-shot magazine. Barrel: 4". **Weight:** 19.1-20.1 oz. **Length:** 6.5-6.7" overall. **Grips:** Textured polymer. Similar to T-series guns, but with polymer frame, matte stainless slide. Comes with two magazines. TP40s introduced 2006. Made in U.S.A. by Kahr Arms.
Price: TP9093 TP9 . . . . **$697.00**
Price: TP9093-Novak TP9 (Novak night sights) **$838.00**
Price: TP4043 TP40 . . . . **$697.00**
Price: TP4043-Novak (Novak night sights) **$838.00**
Price: TP4543 (2007) **$697.00**
Price: TP4543-Novak (4.04 barrel, Novak night sights) **$838.00**

Prices given are believed to be accurate at time of publication however, many factors affect retail pricing so exact prices are not possible.

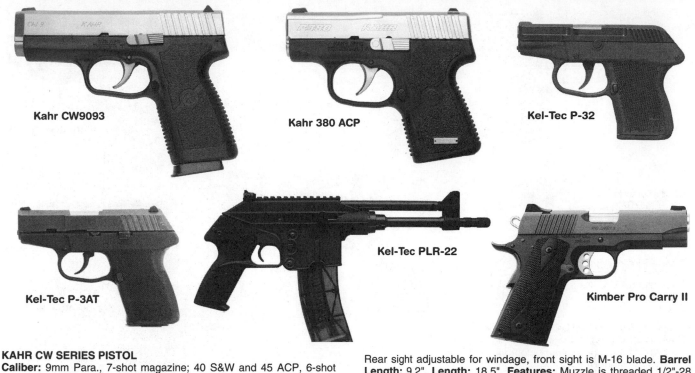

Kahr CW9093

Kahr 380 ACP

Kel-Tec P-32

Kel-Tec P-3AT

Kel-Tec PLR-22

Kimber Pro Carry II

KAHR CW SERIES PISTOL
Caliber: 9mm Para., 7-shot magazine; 40 S&W and 45 ACP, 6-shot magazine. **Barrel:** 3.5-3.64". **Weight:** 17.7-18.7 oz. **Length:** 5.9-6.36" overall. **Grips:** Textured polymer. Similar to P-Series, but CW Series have conventional rifling, metal-injection-molded slide stop lever, no front dovetail cut, one magazine. CW40 introduced 2006. Made in U.S.A. by Kahr Arms.
Price: CW9093 CW9 . . . .$549.00
Price: CW4043 CW40 . . . .$549.00
Price: CW4543 45 ACP (2008) $606.00

KAHR 380 ACP PISTOL
Caliber: 380 ACP, 6+1. **Barrel:** 2.5" Lothar Walther. **Weight:** 11.3 oz. **Length:** 4.9" overall. **Features:** DAO semi-auto with black polymer frame and grips, stainless steel slide.
Price: $649.00

KEL-TEC P-11 AUTO PISTOL
Caliber: 9mm Para., 10-shot magazine. **Barrel:** 3.1". **Weight:** 14 oz. **Length:** 5.6" overall. **Grips:** Checkered black polymer. **Sights:** Blade front, rear adjustable for windage. **Features:** Ordnance steel slide, aluminum frame. Double-action-only trigger mechanism. Introduced 1995. Made in U.S.A. by Kel-Tec CNC Industries, Inc.
Price: From $333.00

KEL-TEC PF-9 PISTOL
Caliber: 9mm Para.; 7 rounds. **Weight:** 12.7 oz. **Sights:** Rear sight adjustable for windage and elevation. **Barrel Length:** 3.1". **Length:** 5.85". **Features:** Barrel, locking system, slide stop, assembly pin, front sight, recoil springs and guide rod adapted from P-11. Trigger system with integral hammer block and the extraction system adapted from P-3AT. MIL-STD-1913 Picatinny rail. Made in U.S.A. by Kel-Tec CNC Industries, Inc.
Price: From $333.00

KEL-TEC P-32 AUTO PISTOL
Caliber: 32 ACP, 7-shot magazine. **Barrel:** 2.68". **Weight:** 6.6 oz. **Length:** 5.07" overall. **Grips:** Checkered composite. **Sights:** Fixed. **Features:** Double-action-only mechanism with 6-lb. pull; internal slide stop. Textured composite grip/frame. Now available in 380 ACP. Made in U.S.A. by Kel-Tec CNC Industries, Inc.
Price: From $318.00

KEL-TEC P-3AT PISTOL
Caliber: 380 ACP; 7-rounds. **Weight:** 7.2 oz. **Length:** 5.2". **Features:** Lightest 380 ACP made; aluminum frame, steel barrel.
Price: From $324.00

KEL-TEC PLR-16 PISTOL
Caliber: 5.56mm NATO; 10-round magazine. **Weight:** 51 oz. **Sights:** Rear sight adjustable for windage, front sight is M-16 blade. **Barrel Length:** 9.2". **Length:** 18.5". **Features:** Muzzle is threaded 1/2"-28 to accept standard attachments such as a muzzle brake. Except for the barrel, bolt, sights, and mechanism, the PLR-16 pistol is made of high-impact glass fiber reinforced polymer. Gas-operated semi-auto. Conventional gas-piston operation with M-16 breech locking system. MIL-STD-1913 Picatinny rail. Made in U.S.A. by Kel-Tec CNC Industries, Inc.
Price: Blued $665.00

Kel-Tec PLR-22 Pistol
Semi-auto pistol chambered in 22 LR; based on centerfire PLR-16 by same maker. Blowback action, 26-round magazine. Open sights and picatinny rail for mounting accessories; threaded muzzle. Overall length is 18.5", weighs 40 oz.
Price: $390.00

KIMBER CUSTOM II AUTO PISTOL
Caliber: 45 ACP. **Barrel:** 5". **Weight:** 38 oz. **Length:** 8.7" overall. **Grips:** Checkered black rubber, walnut, rosewood. **Sights:** Dovetailed front and rear, Kimber low profile adj. or fixed sights. **Features:** Slide, frame and barrel machined from steel or stainless steel. Match grade barrel, chamber and trigger group. Extended thumb safety, beveled magazine well, beveled front and rear slide serrations, high ride beavertail grip safety, checkered flat mainspring housing, kidney cut under trigger guard, high cut grip, match grade stainless steel barrel bushing, polished breech face, Commander-style hammer, lowered and flared ejection port, Wolff springs, bead blasted black oxide or matte stainless finish. Introduced in 1996. Made in U.S.A. by Kimber Mfg., Inc.
Price: Custom II $828.00
Price: Custom II Walnut (double-diamond
    walnut grips) $872.00

Kimber Stainless II Auto Pistols
Similar to Custom II except has stainless steel frame. 9mm Para. chambering and 45 ACP with night sights introduced 2008. Also chambered in 38 Super. Target version also chambered in 10mm.
Price: Stainless II 45 ACP $964.00
Price: Stainless II 9mm Para. (2008) $983.00
Price: Stainless II 45 ACP w/night sights (2008) $1,092.00
Price: Stainless II Target 45 ACP (stainless, adj. sight) $942.00

Kimber Pro Carry II Auto Pistol
Similar to Custom II, has aluminum frame, 4" bull barrel fitted directly to the slide without bushing. Introduced 1998. Made in U.S.A. by Kimber Mfg., Inc.
Price: Pro Carry II, 45 ACP. $888.00
Price: Pro Carry II, 9mm $929.00
Price: Pro Carry II w/night sights $997.00

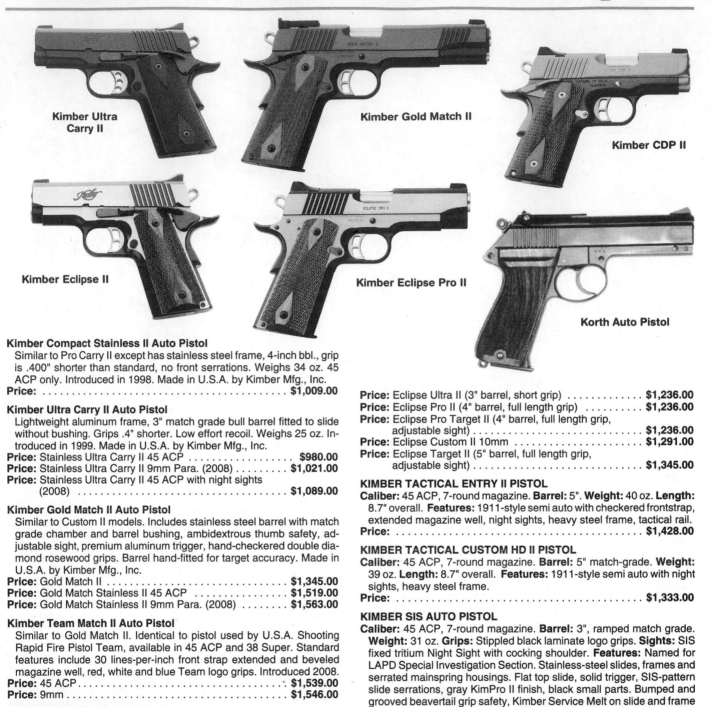

Kimber Ultra Carry II

Kimber Gold Match II

Kimber CDP II

Kimber Eclipse II

Kimber Eclipse Pro II

Korth Auto Pistol

Kimber Compact Stainless II Auto Pistol

Similar to Pro Carry II except has stainless steel frame, 4-inch bbl., grip is .400" shorter than standard, no front serrations. Weighs 34 oz. 45 ACP only. Introduced in 1998. Made in U.S.A. by Kimber Mfg., Inc.
Price: **$1,009.00**

Kimber Ultra Carry II Auto Pistol

Lightweight aluminum frame, 3" match grade bull barrel fitted to slide without bushing. Grips .4" shorter. Low effort recoil. Weighs 25 oz. Introduced in 1999. Made in U.S.A. by Kimber Mfg., Inc.
Price: Stainless Ultra Carry II 45 ACP **$980.00**
Price: Stainless Ultra Carry II 9mm Para. (2008) **$1,021.00**
Price: Stainless Ultra Carry II 45 ACP with night sights
(2008) **$1,089.00**

Kimber Gold Match II Auto Pistol

Similar to Custom II models. Includes stainless steel barrel with match grade chamber and barrel bushing, ambidextrous thumb safety, adjustable sight, premium aluminum trigger, hand-checkered double diamond rosewood grips. Barrel hand-fitted for target accuracy. Made in U.S.A. by Kimber Mfg., Inc.
Price: Gold Match II **$1,345.00**
Price: Gold Match Stainless II 45 ACP **$1,519.00**
Price: Gold Match Stainless II 9mm Para. (2008) **$1,563.00**

Kimber Team Match II Auto Pistol

Similar to Gold Match II. Identical to pistol used by U.S.A. Shooting Rapid Fire Pistol Team, available in 45 ACP and 38 Super. Standard features include 30 lines-per-inch front strap extended and beveled magazine well, red, white and blue Team logo grips. Introduced 2008.
Price: 45 ACP. **$1,539.00**
Price: 9mm **$1,546.00**

Kimber CDP II Series Auto Pistol

Similar to Custom II, but designed for concealed carry. Aluminum frame. Standard features include stainless steel slide, fixed Meprolight tritium 3-dot (green) dovetail-mounted night sights, match grade barrel and chamber, 30 LPI front strap checkering, two-tone finish, ambidextrous thumb safety, hand-checkered double diamond rosewood grips. Introduced in 2000. Made in U.S.A. by Kimber Mfg., Inc.
Price: Ultra CDP II 9mm Para. (2008) **$1,359.00**
Price: Ultra CDP II 45 ACP **$1,318.00**
Price: Compact CDP II 45 ACP **$1,318.00**
Price: Pro CDP II 45 ACP. **$1,318.00**
Price: Custom CDP II (5" barrel, full length grip) **$1,318.00**

Kimber Eclipse II Series Auto Pistol

Similar to Custom II and other stainless Kimber pistols. Stainless slide and frame, black oxide, two-tone finish. Gray/black laminated grips. 30 lpi front strap checkering. All models have night sights; Target versions have Meprolight adjustable Bar/Dot version. Made in U.S.A. by Kimber Mfg., Inc.

Price: Eclipse Ultra II (3" barrel, short grip) **$1,236.00**
Price: Eclipse Pro II (4" barrel, full length grip) **$1,236.00**
Price: Eclipse Pro Target II (4" barrel, full length grip,
adjustable sight) **$1,236.00**
Price: Eclipse Custom II 10mm **$1,291.00**
Price: Eclipse Target II (5" barrel, full length grip,
adjustable sight) **$1,345.00**

KIMBER TACTICAL ENTRY II PISTOL

Caliber: 45 ACP, 7-round magazine. **Barrel:** 5". **Weight:** 40 oz. **Length:** 8.7" overall. **Features:** 1911-style semi auto with checkered frontstrap, extended magazine well, night sights, heavy steel frame, tactical rail.
Price: **$1,428.00**

KIMBER TACTICAL CUSTOM HD II PISTOL

Caliber: 45 ACP, 7-round magazine. **Barrel:** 5" match-grade. **Weight:** 39 oz. **Length:** 8.7" overall. **Features:** 1911-style semi auto with night sights, heavy steel frame.
Price: **$1,333.00**

KIMBER SIS AUTO PISTOL

Caliber: 45 ACP, 7-round magazine. **Barrel:** 3", ramped match grade. **Weight:** 31 oz. **Grips:** Stippled black laminate logo grips. **Sights:** SIS fixed tritium Night Sight with cocking shoulder. **Features:** Named for LAPD Special Investigation Section. Stainless-steel slides, frames and serrated mainspring housings. Flat top slide, solid trigger, SIS-pattern slide serrations, gray KimPro II finish, black small parts. Bumped and grooved beavertail grip safety, Kimber Service Melt on slide and frame edges, ambidextrous thumb safety, stainless steel KimPro Tac-Mag magazine. Rounded mainspring housing and frame on Ultra version. Introduced 2007. Made in U.S.A. by Kimber Mfg., Inc.
Price: SIS Ultra (2008) **$1,427.00**
Price: SIS Pro (2008) **$1,427.00**
Price: SIS Custom **$1,427.00**
Price: Custom/RL **$1,522.00**

KORTH USA PISTOL SEMI-AUTO

Caliber: 9mm Para., 9x21. **Barrel:** 4", 4.5". **Weight:** 39.9 oz. **Grips:** Walnut, Palisander, Amboinia, Ivory. **Sights:** Fully adjustable. **Features:** DA/SA, 2 models available with either rounded or combat-style trigger guard, recoil-operated, locking block system, forged steel. Available finishes: High polish blue plasma, high polish or matted silver plasma, gray pickled finish, or high polish blue. "Schalldampfer Modell" has special threaded 4.5" barrel and thread protector for a suppressor, many deluxe options available, 10-shot mag. From Korth USA.
Price: From **$15,000.00**

Prices given are believed to be accurate at time of publication however, many factors affect retail pricing so exact prices are not possible.

Olympic Arms
Matchmaster 5

North American
Arms Guardian

Olympic Arms
Matchmaster 6

Olympic Arms
Enforcer

Olympic Arms Big Deuce

Olympic Arms Cohort

NORTH AMERICAN ARMS GUARDIAN DAO PISTOL
Caliber: 25 NAA, 32 ACP, 380 ACP, 32 NAA, 6-shot magazine. **Barrel:** 2.49". **Weight:** 20.8 oz. **Length:** 4.75" overall. **Grips:** Black polymer. **Sights:** Low profile fixed. **Features:** Double-action only mechanism. All stainless steel construction. Introduced 1998. Made in U.S.A. by North American Arms.
Price: From **$402.00**

OLYMPIC ARMS MATCHMASTER 5 1911 PISTOL
Caliber: 45 ACP, 7-shot magazine. **Barrel:** 5" stainless steel. **Weight:** 40 oz. **Length:** 8.75" overall. **Grips:** Smooth walnut with laser-etched scorpion icon. **Sights:** Ramped blade, LPA adjustable rear. **Features:** Matched frame and slide, fitted and head-spaced barrel, complete ramp and throat jobs, lowered and widened ejection port, beveled mag well, hand-stoned-to-match hammer and sear, lightweight long-shoe over-travel adjusted trigger, shaped and tensioned extractor, extended thumb safety, wide beavertail grip safety and full-length guide rod. Made in U.S.A. by Olympic Arms, Inc.
Price: **$903.00**

OLYMPIC ARMS MATCHMASTER 6 1911 PISTOL
Caliber: 45 ACP, 7-shot magazine. **Barrel:** 6" stainless steel. **Weight:** 44 oz. **Length:** 9.75" overall. **Grips:** Smooth walnut with laser-etched scorpion icon. **Sights:** Ramped blade, LPA adjustable rear. **Features:** Matched frame and slide, fitted and head-spaced barrel, complete ramp and throat jobs, lowered and widened ejection port, beveled mag well, hand-stoned-to-match hammer and sear, lightweight long-shoe over-travel adjusted trigger, shaped and tensioned extractor, extended thumb safety, wide beavertail grip safety and full length guide rod. Made in U.S.A. by Olympic Arms, Inc.
Price: **$973.00**

OLYMPIC ARMS ENFORCER 1911 PISTOL
Caliber: 45 ACP, 6-shot magazine. **Barrel:** 4" bull stainless steel. **Weight:** 35 oz. **Length:** 7.75" overall. **Grips:** Smooth walnut with etched black widow spider icon. **Sights:** Ramped blade front, LPA adjustable rear. **Features:** Compact Enforcer frame. Bushingless bull barrel with triplex counter-wound self-contained recoil system. Matched frame and slide, fitted and head-spaced barrel, complete ramp and throat jobs, lowered and widened ejection port, beveled mag well, hand-stoned-to-match hammer and sear, lightweight longshoe over-travel adjusted trigger, shaped and tensioned extractor, extended thumb safety, wide

beavertail grip safety and full length guide rod. Made in U.S.A. by Olympic Arms.
Price: **$1,033.50**

OLYMPIC ARMS COHORT PISTOL
Caliber: 45 ACP, 7-shot magazine. **Barrel:** 4" bull stainless steel. **Weight:** 36 oz. **Length:** 7.75" overall. **Grips:** Fully checkered walnut. **Sights:** Ramped blade front, LPA adjustable rear. **Features:** Full size 1911 frame. Bushingless bull barrel with triplex counter-wound self-contained recoil system. Matched frame and slide, fitted and head-spaced barrel, complete ramp and throat jobs, lowered and widened ejection port, beveled mag well, hand-stoned-to-match hammer and sear, lightweight long-shoe over-travel adjusted trigger, shaped and tensioned extractor, extended thumb safety, wide beavertail grip safety and full length guide rod. Made in U.S.A. by Olympic Arms.
Price: **$973.70**

OLYMPIC ARMS BIG DEUCE PISTOL
Caliber: 45 ACP, 7-shot magazine. **Barrel:** 6" stainless steel. **Weight:** 44 oz. **Length:** 9.75" overall. **Grips:** Double diamond checkered exotic cocobolo wood. **Sights:** Ramped blade front, LPA adjustable rear. **Features:** Carbon steel parkerized slide with satin bead blast finish full size frame. Matched frame and slide, fitted and head-spaced barrel, complete ramp and throat jobs, lowered and widened ejection port, beveled mag well, hand-stoned-to-match hammer and sear, lightweight long-shoe over-travel adjusted trigger, shaped and tensioned extractor, extended thumb safety, wide beavertail grip safety and full length guide rod. Made in U.S.A. by Olympic Arms.
Price: **$1,033.50**

OLYMPIC ARMS WESTERNER SERIES 1911 PISTOLS
Caliber: 45 ACP, 7-shot magazine. **Barrel:** 4", 5", 6" stainless steel. **Weight:** 35-43 oz. **Length:** 7.75-9.75" overall. **Grips:** Smooth ivory laser-etched Westerner icon. **Sights:** Ramped blade, LPA adjustable rear. **Features:** Matched frame and slide, fitted and head-spaced barrel, complete ramp and throat jobs, lowered and widened ejection port, beveled mag well, hand-stoned-to-match hammer and sear, lightweight long-shoe over-travel adjusted trigger, shaped and tensioned extractor, extended thumb safety, wide beavertail grip safety and full length guide rod. Entire pistol is fitted and assembled, then disassembled and subjected to the color case hardening process. Made in U.S.A. by Olympic Arms, Inc.
Price: Constable, 4" barrel, 35 oz. **$1,163.50**
Price: Westerner, 5" barrel, 39 oz. **$1,033.50**
Price: Trail Boss, 6" barrel, 43 oz. **$1,103.70**

Olympic Arms Constable

Olympic Arms Westerner

Olympic Arms Trail Boss

Olympic Arms Journeyman

Olympic Arms OA-93

Olympic Arms Street Deuce

Olympic Arms Whitney Wolverine

OLYMPIC ARMS SCHUETZEN PISTOL WORKS 1911 PISTOLS
Caliber: 45 ACP, 7-shot magazine. **Barrel:** 4", 5.2", bull stainless steel. **Weight:** 35-38 oz. **Length:** 7.75-8.75" overall. **Grips:** Double diamond checkered exotic cocobolo wood. **Sights:** Ramped blade, LPA adjustable rear. **Features:** Carbon steel parkerized slide with satin bead blast finish full size frame. Matched frame and slide, fitted and head-spaced barrel, complete ramp and throat jobs, lowered and widened ejection port, beveled mag well, hand-stoned-to-match hammer and sear, lightweight long-shoe over-travel adjusted trigger, shaped and tensioned extractor, extended thumb safety, wide beavertail grip safety and full length guide rod. Custom made by Olympic Arms Schuetzen Pistol Works. Parts are hand selected and fitted by expert pistolsmiths. Several no-cost options to choose from. Made in U.S.A. by Olympic Arms Schuetzen Pistol Works.
Price: Journeyman, 4" bull barrel, 35 oz. **$1,293.50**
Price: Street Deuce, 5.2" bull barrel, 38 oz. **$1,293.50**

OLYMPIC ARMS OA-93 AR PISTOL
Caliber: 5.56 NATO. **Barrel:** 6.5" button-rifled stainless steel. **Weight:** 4.46 lbs. **Length:** 17" overall. **Sights:** None. **Features:** Olympic Arms integrated recoil system on the upper receiver eliminates the buttstock, flat top upper, free floating tubular match handguard, threaded muzzle with flash suppressor. Made in U.S.A. by Olympic Arms, Inc.
Price: **$1,202.50**

OLYMPIC ARMS K23P AR PISTOL
Caliber: 5.56 NATO. **Barrel:** 6.5" button-rifled chrome-moly steel. **Length:** 22.25" overall. **Weight:** 5.12 lbs. **Sights:** Adjustable A2 rear, elevation adjustable front post. **Features:** A2 upper with rear sight, free floating tubular match handguard, threaded muzzle with flash

suppressor, receiver extension tube with foam cover, no bayonet lug. Made in U.S.A. by Olympic Arms, Inc. Introduced 2007.
Price: **$973.70**

OLYMPIC ARMS K23P-A3-TC AR PISTOL
Caliber: 5.56 NATO. **Barrel:** 6.5" button-rifled chrome-moly steel. **Length:** 22.25" overall. **Weight:** 5.12 lbs. **Sights:** Adjustable A2 rear, elevation adjustable front post. **Features:** Flat-top upper with detachable carry handle, free floating FIRSH rail handguard, threaded muzzle with flash suppressor, receiver extension tube with foam cover, no bayonet lug. Made in U.S.A. by Olympic Arms, Inc. Introduced 2007.
Price: **$1,118.20**

OLYMPIC ARMS WHITNEY WOLVERINE PISTOL
Caliber: 22 LR, 10-shot magazine. **Barrel:** 4.625" stainless steel. **Weight:** 19.2 oz. **Length:** 9" overall. **Grips:** Black checkered with fire/safe markings. **Sights:** Ramped blade front, dovetail rear. **Features:** Polymer frame with natural ergonomics and ventilated rib. Barrel with 6-groove 1x16 twist rate. All metal magazine shell. Made in U.S.A. by Olympic Arms.
Price: **$291.00**

PARA USA PXT 1911 SINGLE-ACTION SINGLE-STACK AUTO PISTOLS
Caliber: 38 Super, 9mm Para., 45 ACP. **Barrel:** 3.5", 4.25", 5". **Weight:** 28-40 oz. **Length:** 7.1-8.5" overall. **Grips:** Checkered cocobolo, textured composition, Mother of Pearl synthetic. **Sights:** Blade front, low-profile Novak Extreme Duty adjustable rear. High visibility 3-dot system. **Features:** Available with alloy, steel or stainless steel frames. Skeletonized trigger, spurred hammer. Manual thumb, grip and firing pin lock safeties. Full-length guide rod. PXT designates new Para Power Extractor throughout the line. Introduced 2004. Made in U.S.A. by Para USA.
Price: 1911 SSP 9mm Para. (2008) **$959.00**
Price: 1911 SSP 45 ACP (2008) **$959.00**

PARA USA PXT 1911 SINGLE-ACTION HIGH-CAPACITY AUTO PISTOLS
Caliber: 9mm Para., 45 ACP, 10/14/18-shot magazines. **Barrel:** 3", 5". **Weight:** 34-40 oz. **Length:** 7.1-8.5" overall. **Grips:** Textured composition. **Sights:** Blade front, low-profile Novak Extreme Duty adjustable rear or fixed sights. High visibility 3-dot system. **Features:** Available with alloy, steel or stainless steel frames. Skeletonized match trigger, spurred hammer, flared ejection port. Manual thumb, grip and firing pin lock safeties. Full-length guide rod. Introduced 2004. Made in U.S.A. by Para USA.
Price: PXT P14-45 Gun Rights (2008), 14+1, 5" barrel **$1,149.00**
Price: P14-45 (2008), 14+1, 5" barrel **$919.00**

Prices given are believed to be accurate at time of publication however, many factors affect retail pricing so exact prices are not possible.

Para Todd Jarrett

Para LDA

Para Warthog

Para Slim-Hawg

Para Nite Hawg

Phoenix Arms HP22

Para USA PXT Limited Pistols
Similar to the PXT-Series pistols except with full-length recoil guide system; fully adjustable rear sight; tuned trigger with over-travel stop; beavertail grip safety; competition hammer; front and rear slide serrations; ambidextrous safety; lowered ejection port; ramped match-grade barrel; dove-tailed front sight. Introduced 2004. Made in U.S.A. by Para USA.
Price: Todd Jarrett 40 S&W, 16+1, stainless **$1,729.00**

Para USA LDA Single-Stack Auto Pistols
Similar to LDA-series with double-action trigger mechanism. Coco-bolo and polymer grips. Available in 45 ACP. Introduced 1999. Made in U.S.A. by Para USA.
Price: SSP, 8+1, 5" barrel **$899.00**

Para USA LDA Hi-Capacity Auto Pistols
Similar to LDA-series with double-action trigger mechanism. Polymer grips. Available in 9mm Para., 40 S&W, 45 ACP. Introduced 1999. Made in U.S.A. by Para USA.
Price: High-Cap 45, 14+1 . . . . **$1,279.00**

PARA USA WARTHOG
Caliber: 9mm Para., 45 ACP, 6, 10, or 12-shot magazines. **Barrel:** 3". **Weight:** 24 to 31.5 oz. **Length:** 6.5". **Grips:** Varies by model. **Features:** Single action. Big Hawg (2008) is full-size .45 ACP on lightweight alloy frame, 14+1, match grade ramped barrel, Power extractor, three white-dot fixed sights. Made in U.S.A. by Para USA.
Price: Slim-Hawg (2006) single stack .45 ACP,
stainless, 6+1 . . . . **$1,099.00**
Price: Nite Hawg .45 ACP, black finish, 10+1 . . . . **$1,099.00**
Price: Warthog .45 ACP, Regal finish, 10+1 . . . . **$959.00**
Price: Warthog Stainless **$1,069.00**
Price: Big Hawg (2008) **$959.00**

PHOENIX ARMS HP22, HP25 AUTO PISTOLS
Caliber: 22 LR, 10-shot (HP22), 25 ACP, 10-shot (HP25). **Barrel:** 3". **Weight:** 20 oz. **Length:** 5.5" overall. **Grips:** Checkered composition. **Sights:** Blade front, adjustable rear. **Features:** Single action, exposed hammer; manual hold-open; button magazine release. Available in satin nickel, matte blue finish. Introduced 1993. Made in U.S.A. by Phoenix Arms.
Price: With gun lock **$130.00**
Price: HP Range kit with 5" bbl., locking case and accessories
(1 Mag) **$171.00**
Price: HP Deluxe Range kit with 3" and 5" bbls.,
2 mags, case **$210.00**

PICUDA .17 MACH-2 GRAPHITE PISTOL
Caliber: 17 HM2, 22 LR, 10-shot magazine. **Barrel:** 10" graphite barrel, "French grey" anodizing. **Weight:** 3.2 pounds. **Length:** 20.5" overall. **Grips:** Barracuda nutmeg laminated pistol stock. **Sights:** None, integral

scope base. **Features:** MLP-1722 receiver, target trigger, match bolt kit. Introduced 2008. Made in U.S.A. by Magnum Research, Inc.
Price: **$699.00**

ROCK RIVER ARMS BASIC CARRY AUTO PISTOL
Caliber: 45 ACP. **Barrel:** NA. **Weight:** NA. **Length:** NA. **Grips:** Rosewood, checkered. **Sights:** dovetail front sight, Heinie rear sight. **Features:** NM frame with 20-, 25- or 30-LPI checkered front strap, 5-inch slide with double serrations, lowered and flared ejection port, throated NM Kart barrel with NM bushing, match Commander hammer and match sear, aluminum speed trigger, dehorned, Parkerized finish, one magazine, accuracy guarantee. 3.5 lb. Trigger pull. Introduced 2006. RRA Service Auto 9mm has forged NM frame with beveled mag well, fixed target rear sight and dovetail front sight, KKM match 1:32 twist 9mm Para. barrel with supported ramp. Guaranteed to shoot 1-inch groups at 25 yards with quality 9mm Para. 115-124 grain match ammunition. Intr. 2008. Made in U.S.A. From Rock River Arms.
Price: Basic Carry PS2700 . . . . **$1,600.00**
Price: Limited Match PS2400 . . . . **$2,185.00**
Price: RRA Service Auto 9mm Para. PS2715 . . . . **$1,790.00**

ROCK RIVER ARMS LAR-15/LAR-9 PISTOLS
Caliber: .223/5.56mm NATO chamber 4-shot magazine. **Barrel:** 7", 10.5" Wilson chrome moly, 1:9 twist, A2 flash hider, 1/2-28 thread. **Weight:** 5.1 lbs. (7" barrel), 5.5 lbs. (10.5" barrel). **Length:** 23" overall. **Stock:** Hogue rubber grip. **Sights:** A2 front. **Features:** Forged A2 or A4 upper, single stage trigger, aluminum free-float tube, one magazine. Similar 9mm Para. LAR-9 also available. From Rock River Arms, Inc.
Price: LAR-15 7" A2 AR2115 . . . . **$955.00**
Price: LAR-15 10.5" A4 AR2120 . . . . **$945.00**
Price: LAR-9 7" A2 9MM2115 . . . . **$1,125.00**

ROHRBAUGH R9 SEMI-AUTO PISTOL
Caliber: 9mm Parabellum, 380 ACP. **Barrel:** 2.9". **Weight:** 12.8 oz. **Length:** 5.2" overall. **Features:** Very small double-action-only semi-auto pocket pistol. Stainless steel slide with matte black aluminum frame. Available with or without sights. Available with all-black (Stealth) and partial Diamond Black (Stealth Elite) finish.
Price: $1,149.00

RUGER SR9 AUTOLOADING PISTOL
Caliber: 9mm Para. **Barrel:** 4.14". **Weight:** 26.25, 26.5 oz. **Grips:** Glass-filled nylon in two color options—black or OD Green, w/flat or arched reversible backstrap. **Sights:** Adjustable 3-dot, built-in Picatinny-style rail. **Features:** Semi-DA, 6 configurations, striker-fired, through-hardened stainless steel slide, brushed or blackened stainless slide with black grip frame or blackened stainless slide with OD Green grip frame, ambi manual 1911-style safety, ambi mag release, mag disconnect, loaded chamber indicator, Ruger camblock design to absorb recoil, two 10 or 17-shot mags. Intr. 2008. Made in U.S.A. by Sturm, Ruger & Co.
Price: SR9 (17-Round), SR9-10 (SS) **$525.00**
Price: KBSR9 (17-Round), KBSR9-10 (Blackened SS) **$565.00**
Price: KODBSR9 (17-Round), KODBSR9-10
(OD Green Grip) **$565.00**

Ruger SR9

Ruger LCP

Ruger P90

Ruger KP944D

Ruger KP9515

Ruger KP512 MKIII

Ruger
KP45HMKIII

Ruger Mark III Hunter

RUGER LCP
Caliber: .380 ACP. **Barrel:** 2.75" **Weight:** 9.4 oz. **Grips:** Glass-filled nylon. **Sights:** Fixed. **Features:** SA, one configuration, ultra-light compact carry pistol in Ruger's smallest pistol frame, through-hardened stainless steel slide, blued finish, lock breach design, 6-shot mag. Intr. 2008. Made in U.S.A. by Sturm, Ruger & Co.
Price: LCP. **$347.00**

RUGER P90 MANUAL SAFETY MODEL AUTOLOADING PISTOL
Caliber: 45 ACP, 8-shot magazine. **Barrel:** 4.50". **Weight:** 33.5 oz. **Length:** 7.75" overall. **Grips:** Grooved black synthetic composition. **Sights:** Square post front, square notch rear adjustable for windage, both with white dot. **Features:** Double action; ambidextrous slide-mounted safety-levers. Stainless steel only. Introduced 1991.
Price: KP90 with extra mag, loader, case and gunlock **$617.00**
Price: P90 (blue) **$574.00**

Ruger KP944 Autoloading Pistol
Sized midway between full-size P-Series and compact KP94. 4.2" barrel, 7.5" overall length, weighs about 34 oz. KP94 manual safety model. Slide gripping grooves roll over top of slide. KP94 has ambidextrous safety-levers; Stainless slide, barrel, alloy frame. Also blue. Includes hard case and lock, spare magazine. Introduced 1994. Made in U.S.A. by Sturm, Ruger & Co.
Price: P944, blue, manual safety, .40 cal. **$541.00**
Price: KP944 (40-caliber) (manual safety-stainless) **$628.00**

RUGER P95 AUTOLOADING PISTOL
Caliber: 9mm, 15-shot magazine. **Barrel:** 3.9". **Weight:** 30 oz. **Length:** 7.25" overall. **Grips:** Grooved; integral with frame. **Sights:** Blade front, rear drift adjustable for windage; 3-dot system. **Features:** Molded polymer grip frame, stainless steel or chrome-moly slide. Suitable for +P+ ammunition. Safety model, decocker. Introduced 1996. Made in U.S.A. by Sturm, Ruger & Co. Comes with lockable plastic case, spare magazine, loader and lock, Picatinny rails.
Price: KP95PR15 safety model, stainless steel **$424.00**
Price: P95PR15 safety model, blued finish **$395.00**
Price: P95PR 10-round model, blued finish **$393.00**
Price: KP95PR 10-round model, stainless steel. **$424.00**

RUGER 22 CHARGER PISTOL
Caliber: .22 LR. **Barrel:** 10". **Weight:** 3.5 lbs (w/out bi-pod). **Stock:** Black Laminate. **Sights:** None. **Features:** Rimfire Autoloading, one configuration, 10/22 action, adjustable bi-pod, new mag release for easier removal, precision-rifled barrel, black matte finish, combination Weaver-style and tip-off scope mount, 10-shot mag. Intr. 2008. Made in U.S.A. by Sturm, Ruger & Co.
Price: CHR22-10. . . . .**$380.00**

RUGER MARK III STANDARD AUTOLOADING PISTOL
Caliber: 22 LR, 10-shot magazine. **Barrel:** 4.5", 4.75", 5.5", 6", or 6-7/8". **Weight:** 33 oz. (4.75" bbl.). **Length:** 9" (4.75" bbl.). **Grips:**

Checkered composition grip panels. **Sights:** Fixed, fiber-optic front, fixed rear. **Features:** Updated design of original Standard Auto and Mark II series. Hunter models have lighter barrels. Target models have cocobolo grips; bull, target, competition, and hunter barrels; and adjustable sights. Introduced 2005.
Price: MKIII4, MKIII6 (blued) **$352.00**
Price: MKIII512 (blued bull barrel) **$417.00**
Price: KMKIII512 (stainless bull barrel) **$527.00**
Price: MKIII678 (blued) **$417.00**
Price: KMKIII678GC (stainless slabside barrel) **$606.00**
Price: KMKIII678H (stainless fluted barrel) **$620.00**
Price: KMKIII45HCL (Crimson Trace Laser Grips, intr. 2008) . **$787.00**
Price: KMKIII454 (2009) **$620.00**

Ruger 22/45 Mark III Pistol
Similar to other 22 Mark III autos except has Zytel grip frame that matches angle and magazine latch of Model 1911 45 ACP pistol. Available in 4" standard, 4.5", 5.5", 6-7/8" bull barrels. Comes with extra magazine, plastic case, lock. Introduced 1992. Hunter introduced 2006.
Price: P4MKIII, 4" bull barrel, adjustable sights **$326.00**
Price: P45GCMKIII, 4.5" bull barrel, fixed sights **$324.00**
Price: P512MKIII (5.5" blued bull barrel, adj. sights) **$326.00**
Price: KP512MKIII (5.5" stainless bull barrel, adj. sights **$435.00**
Price: Hunter KP45HMKIII 4.5" barrel (2007), KP678HMKIII,
6-7/8" stainless fluted bull barrel, adj. sights **$532.00**

Sabre Defence Sphinx 9mm

Sabre Defence Sphinx 45 ACP

SIG SAUER 1911 TTT

SIG SAUER 1911 Compact Nitron

SIG SAUER 1911 Blackwater

SIG SAUER P220

SABRE DEFENCE SPHINX PISTOLS

Caliber: 9mm Para., 45 ACP., 10-shot magazine. **Barrel:** 4.43". **Weight:** 39.15 oz. **Length:** 8.27" overall. **Grips:** Textured polymer. **Sights:** Fixed Trijicon Night Sights. **Features:** CNC engineered from stainless steel billet; grip frame in stainless steel, titanium or high-strength aluminum. Integrated accessory rail, high-cut beavertail, decocking lever. Made in Switzerland. Imported by Sabre Defence Industries.
Price: 45 ACP (2007) **$2,990.00**
Price: 9mm Para. Standard, titanium w/decocker **$2,700.00**

SEECAMP LWS 32/380 STAINLESS DA AUTO

Caliber: 32 ACP, 380 ACP Win. Silvertip, 6-shot magazine. **Barrel:** 2", integral with frame. **Weight:** 10.5 oz. **Length:** 4-1/8" overall. **Grips:** Glass-filled nylon. **Sights:** Smooth, no-snag, contoured slide and barrel top. **Features:** Aircraft quality 17-4 PH stainless steel. Inertia-operated firing pin. Hammer fired double-action-only. Hammer automatically follows slide down to safety rest position after each shot, no manual safety needed. Magazine safety disconnector. Polished stainless. Introduced 1985. From L.W. Seecamp.
Price: 32 . . . . **$446.25**
Price: 380 . . . . **$795.00**

SIG SAUER 250 COMPACT AUTO PISTOL

Caliber: 9mm Para. (16-round magazine), 357 SIG, 40 S&W and 45 ACP. **Barrel:** NA. **Weight:** 24.6 oz. **Length:** 7.2" overall. **Grips:** Interchangeable polymer. **Sights:** Siglite night sights. **Features:** Modular design allows for immediate change in caliber and size; subcompact, compact and full. Six different grip combinations for each size. Introduced 2008. From Sig Sauer, Inc.
Price: P250 . . . . **$750.00**

SIG SAUER 1911 PISTOLS

Caliber: 45 ACP, 8-shot magazine. **Barrel:** 5". **Weight:** 40.3 oz. **Length:** 8.65" overall. **Grips:** Checkered wood grips. **Sights:** Novak night sights. Blade front, drift adjustable rear for windage. **Features:** Single-action 1911. Hand-fitted dehorned stainless-steel frame and slide; match-grade barrel, hammer/sear set and trigger; 25-lpi front strap checkering, 20-lpi mainspring housing checkering. Beavertail grip safety with speed bump, extended thumb safety, firing pin safety and hammer intercept notch. Introduced 2005. XO series has contrast sights, Ergo Grip XT textured polymer grips. Target line features adjustable target night sights, match barrel, custom wood grips, non-railed frame in stainless or Nitron finishes. TTT series is two-tone 1911 with Nitron slide and black controls on stainless frame. Includes burled maple grips, adjustable combat night sights. STX line available from Sig Sauer Custom Shop; two-tone 1911, non-railed, Nitron slide, stainless frame, burled maple grips. Polished cocking serrations, flat-top slide, magwell. Carry line has Novak night sights, lanyard attachment point,
gray diamondwood or rosewood grips, 8+1 capacity. Compact series has 6+1 capacity, 7.7" OAL, 4.25" barrel, slim-profile wood grips, weighs 30.3 oz. RCS line (Compact SAS) is Customs Shop version with anti-snag dehorning. Stainless or Nitron finish, Novak night sights, slim-profile gray diamondwood or rosewood grips. 6+1 capacity. 1911 C3 (2008) is a 6+1 compact .45 ACP, rosewood custom wood grips, two-tone and Nitron finishes. Weighs about 30 ounces unloaded, lightweight alloy frame. Length is 7.7". From SIG SAUER, Inc.
Price: Nitron **$1,200.00**
Price: Stainless **$1,170.00**
Price: XO Black **$1,005.00**
Price: Target Nitron (2006) **$1,230.00**
Price: TTT (2006) **$1,290.00**
Price: STX (2006) **$1,455.00**
Price: Carry Nitron (2006) **$1,200.00**
Price: Compact Nitron **$1,200.00**
Price: RCS Nitron **$1,305.00**
Price: C3 (2008) **$1,200.00**
Price: Platinum Elite **$1,275.00**
Price: Blackwater (2009) **$1,290.00**

SIG SAUER P220 AUTO PISTOLS

Caliber: 45 ACP, (7- or 8-shot magazine). **Barrel:** 4.4". **Weight:** 27.8 oz. **Length:** 7.8" overall. **Grips:** Checkered black plastic. **Sights:** Blade front, drift adjustable rear for windage. Optional Siglite night sights. **Features:** Double action. Stainless-steel slide, Nitron finish, alloy frame, M1913 Picatinny rail; safety system of decocking lever, automatic firing pin safety block, safety intercept notch, and trigger bar disconnector. Squared combat-type trigger guard. Slide stays open after last shot. Introduced 1976. P220 SAS Anti-Snag has dehorned stainless steel slide, front Siglite Night Sight, rounded trigger guard, dust cover, Custom Shop wood grips. Equinox line is Custom Shop product with Nitron stainless-steel slide with a black hard-anodized alloy frame, brush-polished flats and nickel accents. Truglo tritium fiber-optic front sight, rear Siglite night sight, gray laminated wood grips with checkering and stippling. From SIG SAUER, Inc.
Price: P220 Two-Tone, matte-stainless slide,
    black alloy frame **$1,110.00**
Price: P220 Elite Stainless (2008) **$1,350.00**
Price: P220 Two-Tone SAO, single action (2006), from . . . **$1,086.00**
Price: P220 DAK (2006) **$853.00**
Price: P220 Equinox (2006) **$1,200.00**
Price: P220 Elite Dark (2009) **$1,200.00**
Price: P220 Elite Dark, threaded barrel (2009) **$1,305.00**

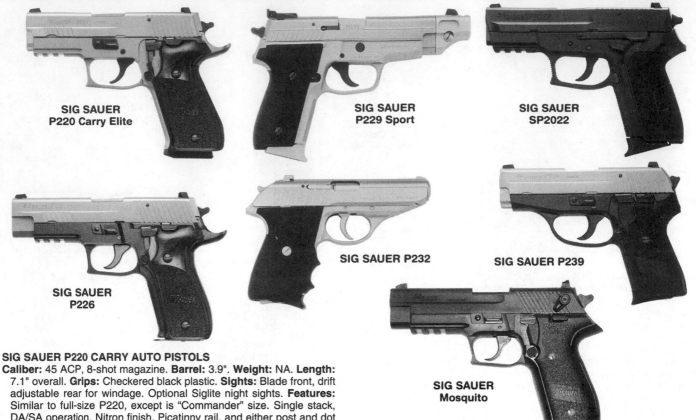

**SIG SAUER
P220 Carry Elite**

**SIG SAUER
P229 Sport**

**SIG SAUER
SP2022**

**SIG SAUER
P226**

SIG SAUER P232

SIG SAUER P239

**SIG SAUER
Mosquito**

SIG SAUER P220 CARRY AUTO PISTOLS
Caliber: 45 ACP, 8-shot magazine. **Barrel:** 3.9". **Weight:** NA. **Length:** 7.1" overall. **Grips:** Checkered black plastic. **Sights:** Blade front, drift adjustable rear for windage. Optional Siglite night sights. **Features:** Similar to full-size P220, except is "Commander" size. Single stack, DA/SA operation, Nitron finish, Picatinny rail, and either post and dot contrast or 3-dot Siglite night sights. Introduced 2005. Many variations availble. From SIG SAUER, Inc.
Price: P220 Carry, from . . . . **$975.00**; w/night sights **$1,050.00**
Price: P220 Carry Elite Stainless (2008) **$1,350.00**

SIG SAUER P229 DA Auto Pistol
Similar to the P228 except chambered for 9mm Para. (10- or 15-round magazines), 40 S&W, 357 SIG (10- or 12-round magazines). Has 3.86" barrel, 7.1" overall length and 3.35" height. Weight is 32.4 oz. Introduced 1991. Frame made in Germany, stainless steel slide assembly made in U.S.; pistol assembled in U.S. Many variations available. From SIG SAUER, Inc.
Price: P229, from . . . . **$975.00**; w/night sights **$1,050.00**
Price: P229 Platinum Elite (2008). **$1,275.00**

SIG SAUER SP2022 PISTOLS
Caliber: 9mm Para., 357 SIG, 40 S&W, 10-, 12-, or 15-shot magazines. **Barrel:** 3.9". **Weight:** 30.2 oz. **Length:** 7.4" overall. **Grips:** Composite and rubberized one-piece. **Sights:** Blade front, rear adjustable for windage. Optional Siglite night sights. **Features:** Polymer frame, stainless steel slide; integral frame accessory rail; replaceable steel frame rails; left- or right-handed magazine release, two interchangeable grips. From SIG SAUER, Inc.
Price: SP2009, Nitron finish **$613.00**

SIG SAUER P226 Pistols
Similar to the P220 pistol except has 4.4" barrel, measures 7.7" overall, weighs 34 oz. Chambered in 9mm, 357 SIG, or 40 S&W. X-Five series has factory tuned single-action trigger, 5" slide and barrel, ergonomic wood grips with beavertail, ambidextrous thumb safety and stainless slide and frame with magwell, low-profile adjustable target sights, front cocking serrations and a 25-meter factory test target. Many variations available. From SIG SAUER, Inc.
Price: P226, from **$975.00**
Price: P226 Blackwater Tactical (2009) **$1,300.00**

SIG SAUER P232 PERSONAL SIZE PISTOL
Caliber: 380 ACP, 7-shot. **Barrel:** 3.6". **Weight:** 17.6-22.4 oz. **Length:** 6.6" overall. **Grips:** Checkered black composite. **Sights:** Blade front, rear adjustable for windage. **Features:** Double action/single action or DAO. Blow-back operation, stationary barrel. Introduced 1997. From SIG SAUER, Inc.
Price: P232, from **$660.00**

SIG SAUER P239 PISTOL
Caliber: 9mm Para., 8-shot, 357 SIG 40 S&W, 7-shot magazine. **Barrel:** 3.6". **Weight:** 25.2 oz. **Length:** 6.6" overall. **Grips:** Checkered black composite. **Sights:** Blade front, rear adjustable for windage. Optional Siglite night sights. **Features:** SA/DA or DAO; blackened stainless steel slide, aluminum alloy frame. Introduced 1996. Made in U.S.A. by SIG SAUER, Inc.
Price: P239, from **$840.00**

SIG SAUER MOSQUITO PISTOL
Caliber: 22 LR, 10-shot magazine. **Barrel:** 3.9". **Weight:** 24.6 oz. **Length:** 7.2" overall. **Grips:** Checkered black composite. **Sights:** Blade front, rear adjustable for windage. **Features:** Blowback operated, fixed barrel, polymer frame, slide-mounted ambidextrous safety. Introduced 2005. Made in U.S.A. by SIG SAUER, Inc.
Price: Mosquito, from **$375.00**

SMITH & WESSON M&P AUTO PISTOLS
Caliber: 9mm Para., 40 S&W, 357 Auto. **Barrel:** 4.25". **Weight:** 24.25 oz. **Length:** 7.5" overall. **Grips:** One-piece Xenoy, wraparound with straight backstrap. **Sights:** Ramp dovetail mount front; tritium sights optional; Novak Lo-mount Carry rear. **Features:** Zytel polymer frame, embedded stainless steel chassis; stainless steel slide and barrel, stainless steel structural components, black Melonite finish, reversible magazine catch, 3 interchangeable palmswell grip sizes, universal rail, sear deactivation lever, internal lock system, magazine disconnect. Ships with 2 magazines. Internal lock models available. Overall height: 5.5"; width: 1.2"; sight radius: 6.4". Introduced November 2005. 45 ACP version introduced 2007, 10+1 or 14+1 capacity. **Barrel:** 4.5". **Length:** 8.05". **Weight:** 29.6 ounces. **Features:** Picatinny-style equipment rail; black or bi-tone, dark-earth-brown frame. Bi-tone M&P45 includes ambidextrous, frame-mounted thumb safety, take down tool with lanyard attachment. Compact 9mm Para./357 SIG/40 S&W versions introduced 2007. Compacts have 3.5" barrel, OAL 6.7". 10+1 or 12+1 capacity. **Weight:** 21.7 ounces. **Features:** Picatinny-style equipment rail. Made in U.S.A. by Smith & Wesson.
Price: Full Size, from. **$719.00**
Price: Compacts, from **$719.00**
Price: Midsize, from **$758.00**
Price: Crimson Trace Lasergrip models, from **$988.00**
Price: Thumb-safety M&P models, from **$719.00**

Prices given are believed to be accurate at time of publication however, many factors affect retail pricing so exact prices are not possible.

Smith & Wesson
M&P

Smith &
Wesson M&P
Compact

Smith & Wesson
M&P 45 Bi-Tone

Smith & Wesson
908

Smith & Wesson
4013TSW

Smith & Wesson 3913
LadySmith

Smith & Wesson SW1911

Smith & Wesson SW1911
Sub-Compact Pro Series

SMITH & WESSON MODEL 908 AUTO PISTOL

Caliber: 9mm Para., 8-shot magazine. **Barrel:** 3.5". **Weight:** 24 oz. **Length:** 6-13/16". **Grips:** One-piece Xenoy, wraparound with straight backstrap. **Sights:** Post front, fixed rear, 3-dot system. **Features:** Aluminum alloy frame, matte blue carbon steel slide; bobbed hammer; smooth trigger. Introduced 1996. Made in U.S.A. by Smith & Wesson.
Price: Model 908, black matte finish **$679.00**
Price: Model 908S, stainless matte finish **$679.00**
Price: Model 908S Carry Combo, with holster **$703.00**

SMITH & WESSON MODEL 4013TSW AUTO

Caliber: 40 S&W, 9-shot magazine. **Barrel:** 3.5". **Weight:** 26.8 oz. **Length:** 6 3/4" overall. **Grips:** Xenoy one-piece wraparound. **Sights:** Novak 3-dot system. **Features:** Traditional double-action system; stainless slide, alloy frame; fixed barrel bushing; ambidextrous decocker; reversible magazine catch, equipment rail. Introduced 1997. Made in U.S.A. by Smith & Wesson.
Price: Model 4013TSW **$1,027.00**

SMITH & WESSON MODEL 910 DA AUTO PISTOL

Caliber: 9mm Para., 10-shot magazine. **Barrel:** 4". **Weight:** 28 oz. **Length:** 7-3/8" overall. **Grips:** One-piece Xenoy, wraparound with straight backstrap. **Sights:** Post front with white dot, fixed 2-dot rear. **Features:** Alloy frame, blue carbon steel slide. Slide-mounted decocking lever. Introduced 1995.
Price: **$648.00**

SMITH & WESSON MODEL 3913 TRADITIONAL DOUBLE ACTIONS

Caliber: 9mm Para., 8-shot magazine. **Barrel:** 3.5". **Weight:** 24.8 oz. **Length:** 6.75" overall. **Grips:** One-piece Delrin wraparound, textured surface. **Sights:** Post front with white dot, Novak LoMount Carry with two dots. **Features:** TSW has aluminum alloy frame, stainless slide. Bobbed hammer with no half-cock notch; smooth .304" trigger with rounded edges. Straight backstrap. Equipment rail. Extra magazine included. Introduced 1989. The 3913-LS Ladysmith has frame that is upswept at the front, rounded trigger guard. Comes in frosted stainless steel with matching gray grips. Grips are ergonomically correct for a woman's hand. Novak LoMount Carry rear sight adjustable for windage. Extra magazine included. Introduced 1990.
Price: 3913TSW **$924.00**
Price: 3913-LS **$909.00**

SMITH & WESSON MODEL SW1911 PISTOLS

Caliber: 45 ACP, 8 rounds. **Barrel:** 5". **Weight:** 39 oz. **Length:** 8.7". **Grips:** Wood or rubber. **Sights:** Novak Lo-Mount Carry, white dot front. **Features:** Large stainless frame and slide with matte finish, single-side external safety. No. 108284 has adjustable target rear sight, ambidextrous safety levers, 20-lpi checkered front strap, comes with two 8-round magazines. DK model (Doug Koenig) also has oversized magazine well, Doug Koenig speed hammer, flat competition speed

trigger with overtravel stop, rosewood grips with Smith & Wesson silver medallions, oversized magazine well, special serial number run. No. 108295 has olive drab Crimson Trace lasergrips. No. 108299 has carbon-steel frame and slide with polished flats on slide, standard GI recoil guide, laminated double-diamond walnut grips with silver Smith & Wesson medallions, adjustable target sights. Tactical Rail No. 108293 has a Picatinny rail, black Melonite finish, Novak Lo-Mount Carry Sights, scandium alloy frame. Tactical Rail Stainless introduced 2006. SW1911PD gun is Commander size, scandium-alloy frame, 4.25" barrel, 8" OAL, 28.0 oz., non-reflective black matte finish. Gunsite edition has scandium alloy frame, beveled edges, solid match aluminum trigger, Herrett's logoed tactical oval walnut stocks, special serial number run, brass bead Novak front sight. SC model has 4.25" barrel, scandium alloy frame, stainless-steel slide, non-reflective matte finish.
Price: From **$1,130.00**
Price: Crimson Trace Laser Grips **$1,493.00**

SMITH & WESSON MODEL 1911 SUB-COMPACT PRO SERIES

Caliber: 45 ACP, 7 + 1-shot magazine. **Barrel:** 3". **Weight:** 24 oz. **Length:** 6-7/8". **Grips:** Fully stippled synthetic. **Sights:** Dovetail white dot front, fixed white 2-dot rear. **Features:** Scandium frame with stainless steel slide, matte black finish throughout. Oversized external extractor, 3-hole curved trigger with overtravel stop, full-length guide rod, and cable lock. Introduced 2009.
Price: **$1,264.00**

Springfield Armory EMP

Springfield Armory XD

Springfield Armory XD

Springfield Armory XD 45 ACP Extended

Springfield Armory XD 45 ACP

Springfield Armory 1911A1 Standard

SMITH & WESSON ENHANCED SIGMA SERIES DAO PISTOLS
Caliber: 9mm Para., 40 S&W; 10-, 16-shot magazine. **Barrel:** 4". **Weight:** 24.7 oz. **Length:** 7.25" overall. **Grips:** Integral. **Sights:** White dot front, fixed rear; 3-dot system. Tritium night sights available. **Features:** Ergonomic polymer frame; low barrel centerline; internal striker firing system; corrosion-resistant slide; Teflon-filled, electroless-nickel coated magazine, equipment rail. Introduced 1994. Made in U.S.A. by Smith & Wesson.
Price: From $482.00

SMITH & WESSON MODEL CS9 CHIEF'S SPECIAL AUTO
Caliber: 9mm Para., 7-shot magazine. **Barrel:** 3". **Weight:** 20.8 oz. **Length:** 6.25" overall. **Grips:** Hogue wraparound rubber. **Sights:** White dot front, fixed 2-dot rear. **Features:** Traditional double-action trigger mechanism. Alloy frame, stainless slide. Ambidextrous safety. Introduced 1999. Made in U.S.A. by Smith & Wesson.
Price: Stainless $782.00

SMITH & WESSON MODEL CS45 CHIEF'S SPECIAL AUTO
Caliber: 45 ACP, 6-shot magazine. **Weight:** 23.9 oz. **Features:** Introduced 1999. Made in U.S.A. by Smith & Wesson.
Price: From $787.00

SPRINGFIELD ARMORY EMP ENHANCED MICRO PISTOL
Caliber: 9mm Para., 40 S&W; 9-round magazine. **Barrel:** 3" stainless steel match grade, fully supported ramp, bull. **Weight:** 26 oz. **Length:** 6.5" overall. **Grips:** Thinline cocobolo hardwood. **Sights:** Fixed low profile combat rear, dovetail front, 3-dot tritium. **Features:** Two 9-round stainless steel magazines with slam pads, long aluminum match-grade trigger adjusted to 5 to 6 lbs., forged aluminum alloy frame, black hardcoat anodized; dual spring full-length guide rod, forged satin-finish stainless steel slide. Introduced 2007. From Springfield Armory.
Price: 9mm Para. Compact Bi-Tone $1,329.00
Price: 40 S&W Compact Bi-Tone (2008) $1,329.00

SPRINGFIELD ARMORY XD POLYMER AUTO PISTOLS
Caliber: 9mm Para., 40 S&W, 45 ACP. **Barrel:** 3", 4", 5". **Weight:** 20.5-31 oz. **Length:** 6.26-8" overall. **Grips:** Textured polymer. **Sights:** Varies by model; Fixed sights are dovetail front and rear steel 3-dot units. **Features:** Three sizes in X-Treme Duty (XD) line: Sub-Compact (3" barrel), Service (4" barrel), Tactical (5" barrel). Three ported models available. Ergonomic polymer frame, hammer-forged barrel, no-tool disassembly, ambidextrous magazine release, visual/tactile loaded chamber indicator, visual/tactile striker status indicator, grip safety, XD gear system included. Introduced 2004. XD 45 introduced 2006. Compact line introduced 2007. Compacts ship with one extended magazine (13) and one compact magazine (10). From Springfield Armory.
Price: Sub-Compact OD Green 9mm Para./40 S&W, fixed sights $543.00
Price: Compact 45 ACP, 4" barrel, Bi-Tone finish (2008) $589.00
Price: Compact 45 ACP, 4" barrel, OD green frame, stainless slide (2008) $653.00
Price: Service Black 9mm Para./40 S&W, fixed sights $543.00
Price: Service Dark Earth 45 ACP, fixed sights $571.00
Price: Service Black 45 ACP, external thumb safety (2008). . .$571.00
Price: V-10 Ported Black 9mm Para./40 S&W $573.00
Price: Tactical Black 45 ACP, fixed sights $616.00
Price: Service Bi-Tone 40 S&W, Trijicon night sights (2008) . .$695.00

SPRINGFIELD ARMORY GI 45 1911A1 AUTO PISTOLS
Caliber: 45 ACP; 6-, 7-, 13-shot magazines. **Barrel:** 3", 4", 5". **Weight:** 28-36 oz. **Length:** 5.5-8.5" overall. **Grips:** Checkered double-diamond walnut, "U.S" logo. **Sights:** Fixed GI style. **Features:** Similar to WWII GI-issue 45s at hammer, beavertail, mainspring housing. From Springfield Armory.
Price: GI .45 4" Champion Lightweight, 7+1, 28 oz. $619.00
Price: GI .45 5" High Capacity, 13+1, 36 oz. $676.00
Price: GI .45 5" OD Green, 7+1, 36 oz. $619.00
Price: GI .45 3" Micro Compact, 6+1, 32 oz. $667.00

SPRINGFIELD ARMORY MIL-SPEC 1911A1 AUTO PISTOLS
Caliber: 38 Super, 9-shot magazines; 45 ACP, 7-shot magazines. **Barrel:** 5". **Weight:** 35.6-39 oz. **Length:** 8.5-8.625" overall. **Features:** Similar to GI 45s. From Springfield Armory.
Price: Mil-Spec Parkerized, 7+1, 35.6 oz. $715.00
Price: Mil-Spec Stainless Steel, 7+1, 36 oz. $784.00
Price: Mil-Spec 38 Super, 9+1, 39 oz. $775.00

Springfield Armory Custom Loaded Champion 1911A1 Pistol
Similar to standard 1911A1, slide and barrel are 4". 7.5" OAL. Available in 45 ACP only. Novak Night Sights. Delta hammer and cocobolo grips. Parkerized or stainless. Introduced 1989.
Price: Stainless, 34 oz. $1,031.00
Price: Lightweight, 28 oz. $989.00

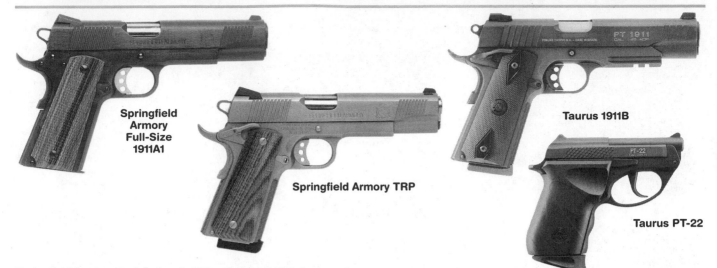

Springfield
Armory
Full-Size
1911A1

Springfield Armory TRP

Taurus 1911B

Taurus PT-22

Springfield Armory Custom Loaded Ultra Compact Pistol
Similar to 1911A1 Compact, shorter slide, 3.5" barrel, 6+1, 7" OAL. Beavertail grip safety, beveled magazine well, fixed sights. Videki speed trigger, flared ejection port, stainless steel frame, blued slide, match grade barrel, rubber grips. Introduced 1996. From Springfield Armory.
Price: Stainless Steel **$1,031.00**

SPRINGFIELD ARMORY CUSTOM LOADED MICRO-COMPACT 1911A1 PISTOL
Caliber: 45 ACP, 6+1 capacity. **Barrel:** 3" 1:16 LH. **Weight:** 24-32 oz. **Length:** 4.7". **Grips:** Slimline cocobolo. **Sights:** Novak LoMount tritium. Dovetail front. **Features:** Aluminum hard-coat anodized alloy frame, forged steel slide, forged barrel, ambi-thumb safety, Extreme Carry Bevel dehorning. Lockable plastic case, 2 magazines.
Price: Lightweight Bi-Tone **$992.00**

SPRINGFIELD ARMORY CUSTOM LOADED LONG SLIDE 1911A1 PISTOL
Caliber: 45 ACP, 7+1 capacity. **Barrel:** 6" 1:16 LH. **Weight:** 41 oz. **Length:** 9.5". **Grips:** Slimline cocobolo. **Sights:** Dovetail front; fully adjustable target rear. **Features:** Longer sight radius, 7.9".
Price: Bi-Tone Operator w/light rail **$1,189.00**

Springfield Armory Tactical Response Loaded Pistols
Similar to 1911A1 except 45 ACP only, checkered front strap and mainspring housing, Novak Night Sight combat rear sight and matching dove-tailed front sight, tuned, polished extractor, oversize barrel link; lightweight speed trigger and combat action job, match barrel and bushing, extended ambidextrous thumb safety and fitted beavertail grip safety. Checkered cocobolo wood grips, comes with two Wilson 7-shot magazines. Frame is engraved "Tactical" both sides of frame with "TRP." Introduced 1998. TRP-Pro Model meets FBI specifications for SWAT Hostage Rescue Team. From Springfield Armory.
Price: 45 TRP Service Model, black Armory Kote finish, fixed Trijicon night sights **$1,741.00**

TAURUS MODEL 800 SERIES
Caliber: 9mm Para., 40 S&W, 45 ACP. **Barrel:** 4". **Weight:** 32 oz. **Length:** 8.25". **Grips:** Checkered. **Sights:** Novak. **Features:** DA/SA. Blue and Stainless Steel finish. Introduced in 2007. Imported from Brazil by Taurus International.
Price: 809B, 9mm Para., Blue, 17+1 . . . . **$623.00**

TAURUS MODEL 1911
Caliber: 45 ACP, 8+1 capacity. **Barrel:** 5". **Weight:** 33 oz. **Length:** 8.5". **Grips:** Checkered black. **Sights:** Heinie straight 8. **Features:** SA. Blue, stainless steel, duotone blue, and blue/gray finish. Standard/picatinny rail, standard frame, alloy frame, and alloy/picatinny rail. Introduced in 2007. Imported from Brazil by Taurus International.
Price: 1911B, Blue **$719.00**
Price: 1911SS, Stainless Steel **$816.00**
Price: 1911SS-1, Stainless Steel **$847.00**
Price: 1911 DT, Duotone Blue **$795.00**

TAURUS MODEL 917
Caliber: 9mm Para., 19+1 capacity. **Barrel:** 4.3". **Weight:** 32.2 oz. **Length:** 8.5". **Grips:** Checkered rubber. **Sights:** Fixed. **Features:** SA/

DA. Blue and stainless steel finish. Medium frame. Introduced in 2007. Imported from Brazil by Taurus International.
Price: 917B-20, Blue **$542.00**
Price: 917SS-20, Stainless Steel **$559.00**

TAURUS MODEL PT-22/PT-25 AUTO PISTOLS
Caliber: 22 LR, 8-shot (PT-22); 25 ACP, 9-shot (PT-25). **Barrel:** 2.75". **Weight:** 12.3 oz. **Length:** 5.25" overall. **Grips:** Smooth rosewood or mother-of-pearl. **Sights:** Fixed. **Features:** Double action. Tip-up barrel for loading, cleaning. Blue, nickel, duo-tone or blue with gold accents. Introduced 1992. Made in U.S.A. by Taurus International.
Price: PT-22B or PT-25B, checkered wood grips **$248.00**

Taurus Model 22PLY Small Polymer Frame Pistols
Similar to Taurus Models PT-22 and PT-25 but with lightweight polymer frame. Features include 22 LR (9+1) or 25 ACP (8+1) chambering. 2.33" tip-up barrel, matte black finish, extended magazine with finger lip, manual safety. Overall length is 4.8". Weighs 10.8 oz.
Price: . . . . **TO BE ANNOUNCED**

TAURUS MODEL 24/7
Caliber: 9mm Para., 40 S&W, 45 ACP. **Barrel:** 4". **Weight:** 27.2 oz. **Length:** 7-1/8". **Grips:** "Ribber" rubber-finned overlay on polymer. **Sights:** Adjustable. **Features:** SA/DA; accessory rail, four safeties, blue or stainless finish. One-piece guide rod, flush-fit magazine, flared bushingless barrel, Picatinny accessory rail, manual safety, user changeable sights, loaded chamber indicator, tuned ejector and lowered port, one piece guide rod and flat wound captive spring. Introduced 2003. Long Slide models have 5" barrels, measure 8-1/8" overall, weigh 27.2 oz. Imported from Brazil by Taurus International.
Price: 40BP, 40 S&W, blued, 10+1 or 15+1 . . . . **$452.00**
Price: 24/7-PRO Standard Series: 4" barrel; stainless, duotone or blued finish **$452.00**
Price: 24/7-PRO Compact Series: 3.2" barrel; stainless, titanium or blued finish **$467.00**
Price: 24/7-PRO Long Slide Series: 5.2" barrel; matte stainless, blued or stainless finish **$506.00**
Price: 24/7PLS, 5" barrel, chambered in 9mm Parabellum, 38 Super and 40 S&W **$506.00**

Taurus Model 2045 Large Frame Pistol
Similar to Taurus Model 24/7 but chambered in 45 ACP only. Features include polymer frame, blued or matte stainless steel slide, 4.2" barrel, ambidextrous "memory pads" to promote safe finger position during loading, ambi three-position safety/decocker. Picatinny rail system, fixed sights. Overall length is 7.34". Weighs 31.5 oz.
Price: **$577.00**

TAURUS MODEL 58 PISTOL
Caliber: 380 ACP (19+1). **Barrel:** 3.25". **Weight:** 18.7 oz. **Length:** 6.125" overall. **Grips:** Polymer. **Sights:** Fixed. **Features:** SA/DA semi-auto. Scaled-down version of the full-size Model 92; steel slide, alloy frame, frame-mounted ambi safety, blued or stainless finish, and extended magazine.
Price: 58HCB **$602.00**
Price: 58HCSS **$617.00**

Taurus 92

Taurus 99SS

Taurus 100

Taurus 132
Millennium Pro

Taurus 138
Millennium Pro

Taurus 140
Millennium Pro

Taurus 738 TCP

TAURUS MODEL 92 AUTO PISTOL

Caliber: 9mm Para., 10- or 17-shot mags. **Barrel:** 5". **Weight:** 34 oz. **Length:** 8.5" overall. **Grips:** Checkered rubber, rosewood, mother-of-pearl. **Sights:** Fixed notch rear. 3-dot sight system. Also offered with micrometer-click adjustable night sights. **Features:** Double action, ambidextrous 3-way hammer drop safety, allows cocked & locked carry. Blue, stainless steel, blue with gold highlights, stainless steel with gold highlights, forged aluminum frame, integral key-lock. .22 LR conversion kit available. Imported from Brazil by Taurus International.
Price: 92B **$542.00**
Price: 92SS **$559.00**

Taurus Model 99 Auto Pistol

Similar to Model 92, fully adjustable rear sight.
Price: 99B **$559.00**

Taurus Model 90-Two Semi-Auto Pistol

Similar to Model 92 but with one-piece wraparound grips, automatic disassembly lathc, internal recoil buffer, addition slide serrations, picatinny rail with removable cover, 10- and 17-round magazine (9mm) or 10- and 12-round magazines (40 S&W). Overall length is 8.5". Weight is 32.5 oz.
Price: **$725.00**

TAURUS MODEL 100/101 AUTO PISTOL

Caliber: 40 S&W, 10- or 11-shot mags. **Barrel:** 5". **Weight:** 34 oz. **Length:** 8.5". **Grips:** Checkered rubber, rosewood, mother-of-pearl. **Sights:** 3-dot fixed or adjustable; night sights available. **Features:** Single/double action with three-position safety/decocker. Reintroduced in 2001. Imported by Taurus International.
Price: 100B **$542.00**

TAURUS MODEL 111 MILLENNIUM PRO AUTO PISTOL

Caliber: 9mm Para., 10- or 12-shot mags. **Barrel:** 3.25". **Weight:** 18.7 oz. **Length:** 6-1/8" overall. **Grips:** Checkered polymer. **Sights:** 3-dot fixed; night sights available. Low profile, 3-dot combat. **Features:** Double action only, polymer frame, matte stainless or blue steel slide, manual safety, integral key-lock. Deluxe models with wood grip inserts.
Price: 111BP, 111BP-12. . . . .**$419.00**
Price: 111PTi titanium slide **$592.00**

TAURUS 132 MILLENNIUM PRO AUTO PISTOL

Caliber: 32 ACP, 10-shot mag. **Barrel:** 3.25". **Weight:** 18.7 oz. **Grips:** Polymer. **Sights:** 3-dot fixed; night sights available. **Features:** Double-action-only, polymer frame, matte stainless or blue steel slide, manual safety, integral key-lock action. Introduced 2001.
Price: 132BP. **$419.00**

TAURUS 138 MILLENNIUM PRO SERIES

Caliber: 380 ACP, 10- or 12-shot mags. **Barrel:** 3.25". **Weight:** 18.7 oz. **Grips:** Polymer. **Sights:** Fixed 3-dot fixed. **Features:** Double-action-only, polymer frame, matte stainless or blue steel slide, manual safety, integral key-lock.
Price: 138BP. **$419.00**

TAURUS 140 MILLENNIUM PRO AUTO PISTOL

Caliber: 40 S&W, 10-shot mag. **Barrel:** 3.25". **Weight:** 18.7 oz. **Grips:** Checkered polymer. **Sights:** 3-dot fixed; night sights available. **Features:** Double action only; matte stainless or blue steel slide, black polymer frame, manual safety, integral key-lock action. From Taurus International.
Price: 140BP **$436.00**

TAURUS 145 MILLENNIUM PRO AUTO PISTOL

Caliber: 45 ACP, 10-shot mag. **Barrel:** 3.27". **Weight:** 23 oz. **Stock:** Checkered polymer. **Sights:** 3-dot fixed; night sights available. **Features:** Double-action only, matte stainless or blue steel slide, black polymer frame, manual safety, integral key-lock. Compact model is 6+1 with a 3.25" barrel, weighs 20.8 oz. From Taurus International.
Price: 145BP, blued **$436.00**
Price: 145SSP, stainless, ...**$453.00**

Taurus Model 609Ti-Pro

Similar to other Millennium Pro models but with titanium slide. Chambered in 9mm Parabellum. Weighs 19.7 oz. Overall length is 6.125". Features include 13+1 capacity, 3.25" barrel, checkered polymer grips, and Heinie Straight-8 sights.
Price: **$608.00**

TAURUS MODEL 738 TCP COMPACT PISTOL

Caliber: 380 ACP, 6+1 (standard magazine) or 8+1 (extended magazine). **Barrel:** 3.3". **Weight:** 9 oz. (titanium slide) to 10.2 oz. **Length:** 5.19". **Sights:** Low-profile fixed. **Features:** Lightweight DAO semi-auto with polymer frame; blued (738B), stainless (738SS) or titanium (738Ti) slide; concealed hammer; ambi safety; loaded chamber indicator.
Price: . . . .**$623.00 to $686.00**

TAURUS MODEL 911B AUTO PISTOL

Caliber: 9mm Para., 10-shot mag. **Barrel:** 4". **Weight:** 28.2 oz. **Length:** 7" overall. **Grips:** Checkered rubber, rosewood, mother-of-pearl. **Sights:** Fixed, 3-dot blue or stainless; night sights optional. **Features:** Double action, semi-auto ambidextrous 3-way hammer drop safety, allows cocked & locked carry. Blue, stainless steel, blue with gold highlights, or stainless steel with gold highlights, forged aluminum frame, integral key-lock.
Price: From **$584.00**

Prices given are believed to be accurate at time of publication however, many factors affect retail pricing so exact prices are not possible.

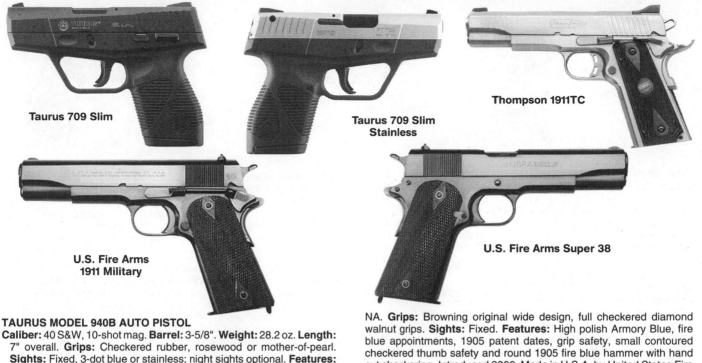

Taurus 709 Slim

Taurus 709 Slim Stainless

Thompson 1911TC

U.S. Fire Arms 1911 Military

U.S. Fire Arms Super 38

TAURUS MODEL 940B AUTO PISTOL
Caliber: 40 S&W, 10-shot mag. **Barrel:** 3-5/8". **Weight:** 28.2 oz. **Length:** 7" overall. **Grips:** Checkered rubber, rosewood or mother-of-pearl. **Sights:** Fixed, 3-dot blue or stainless; night sights optional. **Features:** Double action, semi-auto ambidextrous 3-way hammer drop safety, allows cocked & locked carry. Blue, stainless steel, blue with gold highlights, or stainless steel with gold highlights, forged aluminum frame, integral key-lock.
Price: From $584.00

TAURUS MODEL 945B/38S SERIES
Caliber: 45 ACP, 8-shot mag. **Barrel:** 4.25". **Weight:** 28.2/29.5 oz. **Length:** 7.48" overall. **Grips:** Checkered rubber, rosewood or mother-of-pearl. **Sights:** Fixed, 3-dot; night sights optional. **Features:** Double-action with ambidextrous 3-way hammer drop safety allows cocked & locked carry. Forged aluminum frame, 945C has ported barrel/slide. Blue, stainless, blue with gold highlights, stainless with gold highlights, integral key-lock. Introduced 1995. 38 Super line based on 945 frame introduced 2005. 38S series is 10+1, 30 oz., 7.5" overall. Imported by Taurus International.
Price: From $625.00

TAURUS MODEL 709 "SLIM"
Caliber: 9mm Parabellum, 7+1. **Barrel:** 3.2". **Weight:** 10 oz. **Length:** 6.2" overall. **Grips:** Checkered polymer. **Sights:** Fixed. **Features:** Semi-auto pistol, single/double action. Streamlined profile, choice of blued (709B) or stainless (709SS) slide.
Price: $436.00

THOMPSON CUSTOM 1911A1 AUTOMATIC PISTOL
Caliber: 45 ACP, 7-shot magazine. **Barrel:** 4.3". **Weight:** 34 oz. **Length:** 8" overall. **Grips:** Checkered laminate grips with a Thompson bullet logo inlay. **Sights:** Front and rear sights are black with serrations and are dovetailed into the slide. **Features:** Machined from 420 stainless steel, matte finish. Thompson bullet logo on slide. Flared ejection port, angled front and rear serrations on slide, 20-lpi checkered mainspring housing and frontstrap. Adjustable trigger, combat hammer, stainless steel full-length recoil guide rod, extended beavertail grip safety; extended magazine release; checkered slide-stop lever. Made in U.S.A. by Kahr Arms.
Price: 1911TC, 5", 39 oz., 8.5" overall, stainless frame $813.00

THOMPSON TA5 1927A-1 LIGHTWEIGHT DELUXE PISTOL
Caliber: 45 ACP, 50-round drum magazine. **Barrel:** 10.5" 1:16 right-hand twist. **Weight:** 94.5 oz. **Length:** 23.3" overall. **Grips:** Walnut, horizontal foregrip **Sights:** Blade front, open rear adjustable. **Features:** Based on Thompson machine gun design. Introduced 2008. Made in U.S.A. by Kahr Arms.
Price: TA5 (2008) $1,237.00

U.S. FIRE ARMS 1910 COMMERCIAL MODEL AUTOMATIC PISTOL
Caliber: 45 ACP, 7-shot magazine. **Barrel:** 5". **Weight:** NA. **Length:** NA. **Grips:** Browning original wide design, full checkered diamond walnut grips. **Sights:** Fixed. **Features:** High polish Armory Blue, fire blue appointments, 1905 patent dates, grip safety, small contoured checkered thumb safety and round 1905 fire blue hammer with hand cut checkering. Introduced 2006. Made in U.S.A. by United States Fire Arms Mfg. Co.
Price: $1,895.00

U.S. FIRE ARMS 1911 MILITARY MODEL AUTOMATIC PISTOL
Caliber: 45 ACP, 7-shot magazine. **Barrel:** 5". **Weight:** NA. **Length:** NA. **Grips:** Browning original wide design, full checkered diamond walnut grips. **Sights:** Fixed. **Features:** Military polish Armory Blue, fire blue appointments, 1905 patent dates, grip safety, small contoured checkered thumb safety and round 1905 fire blue hammer with hand cut checkering. Introduced 2006. Made in U.S.A. by United States Fire Arms Mfg. Co.
Price: $1,895.00

U.S. FIRE ARMS SUPER 38 AUTOMATIC PISTOL
Caliber: 38 Auto, 9-shot magazine. **Barrel:** 5". **Weight:** NA. **Length:** NA. **Grips:** Browning original wide design, full checkered diamond walnut grips. **Sights:** Fixed. **Features:** Armory blue, fire blue appointments, 1913 patent date, grip safety, small contoured checkered thumb safety and spur 1911 hammer with hand cut checkering. Supplied with two Super 38 Auto. mags. Super .38 roll mark on base. Introduced 2006. Made in U.S.A. by United States Fire Arms Mfg. Co.
Price: $1,895.00

U.S. FIRE ARMS ACE .22 LONG RIFLE AUTOMATIC PISTOL
Caliber: 22 LR, 10-shot magazine. **Barrel:** 5". **Weight:** NA. **Length:** NA. **Grips:** Browning original wide design, full checkered diamond walnut grips. **Sights:** Fixed. **Features:** Armory blue commercial finish, fire blue appointments, 1913 patent date, grip safety, small contoured checkered thumb safety and spur 1911 hammer with hand cut checkering. Supplied with two magazines. Ace roll mark on base. Introduced 2006. Made in U.S.A. by United States Fire Arms Mfg. Co.
Price: $1,995.00

WALTHER PPS PISTOL
Caliber: 9mm Para., 40 S&W. 6-, 7-, 8-shot magazines for 9mm Para.; 5-, 6-, 7-shot magazines for 40 S&W. **Barrel:** 3.2". **Weight:** 19.4 oz. **Length:** 6.3" overall. **Stocks:** Stippled black polymer. **Sights:** Picatinny-style accessory rail, 3-dot low-profile contoured sight. **Features:** PPS-"Polizeipistole Schmal," or Police Pistol Slim. Measures 1.04 inches wide. Ships with 6- and 7-round magazines. Striker-fired action, flat slide stop lever, alternate backstrap sizes. QuickSafe feature decocks striker assembly when backstrap is removed. Loaded chamber indicator. First Edition model, limited to 1,000 units, has anthracite grey finish, aluminum gun case. Introduced 2008. Made in U.S.A. by Smith & Wesson.
Price: $713.00
Price: First Edition. $665.00

Walther PPK/S

Walther P99

Walther P22

WALTHER PPK/S AMERICAN AUTO PISTOL

Caliber: 32 ACP, 380 ACP, 7-shot magazine. **Barrel:** 3.27". **Weight:** 23-1/2 oz. **Length:** 6.1" overall. Stocks: Checkered plastic. **Sights:** Fixed, white markings. **Features:** Double action; manual safety blocks firing pin and drops hammer; chamber loaded indicator on 32 and 380; extra finger rest magazine provided. Made in the United States. Introduced 1980. Made in U.S.A. by Smith & Wesson.
Price: **$605.00**

WALTHER P99 AUTO PISTOL

Caliber: 9mm Para., 9x21, 40 S&W, 10-shot magazine. **Barrel:** 4". **Weight:** 25 oz. **Length:** 7" overall. **Grips:** Textured polymer. **Sights:** Blade front (comes with three interchangeable blades for elevation adjustment), micrometer rear adjustable for windage. **Features:** Double-action mechanism with trigger safety, decock safety, internal striker safety; chamber loaded indicator; ambidextrous magazine release levers; polymer frame with interchangeable backstrap inserts. Comes with two magazines. Introduced 1997. Made in U.S.A. by Smith & Wesson.
Price: From.....................................**$799.00**

WALTHER P22 PISTOL

Caliber: 22 LR. **Barrel:** 3.4", 5". **Weight:** 19.6 oz. (3.4"), 20.3 oz. (5"). **Length:** 6.26", 7.83". **Grips:** NA. **Sights:** Interchangeable white dot, front, 2-dot adjustable, rear. **Features:** A rimfire version of the Walther P99 pistol, available in nickel slide with black frame, or green frame with black slide versions. Made in U.S.A. by Smith & Wesson.
Price: From **$362.00**

WILSON COMBAT ELITE PROFESSIONAL

Caliber: 9mm Para., 38 Super, 40 S&W; 45 ACP, 8-shot magazine. **Barrel:** Compensated 4.1" hand-fit, heavy flanged cone match grade. **Weight:** 36.2 oz. **Length:** 7.7" overall. **Grips:** Cocobolo. **Sights:** Combat Tactical yellow rear tritium inserts, brighter green tritium front insert. **Features:** High-cut front strap, 30-lpi checkering on front strap and flat mainspring housing, High-Ride Beavertail grip safety. Dehorned, ambidextrous thumb safety, extended ejector, skeletonized ultralight hammer, ultralight trigger, Armor-Tuff finish on frame and slide. Introduced 1997. Made in U.S.A. by Wilson Combat.
Price: From **$2,600.00**

Prices given are believed to be accurate at time of publication however, many factors affect retail pricing so exact pricing are not possible.

Includes models suitable for several forms of competition and other sporting purposes.

Baer 1911 Ultimate Master

Colt Special Combat Government

Baer 1911 Bullseye Wadcutter

Competitor Single Shot

CZ 75 Champion

BAER 1911 ULTIMATE MASTER COMBAT PISTOL

Caliber: 38 Super, 400 Cor-Bon 45 ACP (others available), 10-shot magazine. **Barrel:** 5", 6"; Baer NM. **Weight:** 37 oz. **Length:** 8.5" overall. **Grips:** Checkered cocobolo. **Sights:** Baer dovetail front, low-mount Bo-Mar rear with hidden leaf. **Features:** Full-house competition gun. Baer forged NM blued steel frame and double serrated slide; Baer triple port, tapered cone compensator; fitted slide to frame; lowered, flared ejection port; Baer reverse recoil plug; full-length guide rod; recoil buff; beveled magazine well; Baer Commander hammer, sear; Baer extended ambidextrous safety, extended ejector, checkered slide stop, beavertail grip safety with pad, extended magazine release button; Baer speed trigger. Made in U.S.A. by Les Baer Custom, Inc.
Price: 45 ACP Compensated **$2,790.00**
Price: 38 Super Compensated **$2,940.00**

BAER 1911 NATIONAL MATCH HARDBALL PISTOL

Caliber: 45 ACP, 7-shot magazine. **Barrel:** 5". **Weight:** 37 oz. **Length:** 8.5" overall. **Grips:** Checkered walnut. **Sights:** Baer dovetail front with under-cut post, low-mount Bo-Mar rear with hidden leaf. **Features:** Baer NM forged steel frame, double serrated slide and barrel with stainless bushing; slide fitted to frame; Baer match trigger with 4-lb. pull; polished feed ramp, throated barrel; checkered front strap, arched mainspring housing; Baer beveled magazine well; lowered, flared ejection port; tuned extractor; Baer extended ejector, checkered slide stop; recoil buff. Made in U.S.A. by Les Baer Custom, Inc.
Price: **$1,890.00**

Baer 1911 Bullseye Wadcutter Pistol

Similar to National Match Hardball except designed for wadcutter loads only. Polished feed ramp and barrel throat; Bo-Mar rib on slide; full length recoil rod; Baer speed trigger with 3-1/2-lb. pull; Baer deluxe hammer and sear; Baer beavertail grip safety with pad; flat mainspring housing checkered 20 lpi. Blue finish; checkered walnut grips. Made in U.S.A. by Les Baer Custom, Inc.
Price: From **$1,890.00**

BF CLASSIC PISTOL

Caliber: Customer orders chamberings. **Barrel:** 8-15" Heavy Match Grade with 11-degree target crown. **Weight:** Approx 3.9 lbs. **Length:** From 16" overall. **Grips:** Thumbrest target style. **Sights:** Bo-Mar/Bond ScopeRib I Combo with hooded post front adjustable for height and width, rear notch available in .032", .062", .080" and .100" widths; 1/2-MOA clicks. **Features:** Hand fitted and headspaced, drilled and tapped for scope mount. Etched receiver; gold-colored trigger. Introduced 1988. Made in U.S.A. by E. Arthur Brown Co. Inc.
Price: **$699.00**

COLT GOLD CUP TROPHY PISTOL

Caliber: 45 ACP, 8-shot + 1 magazine. **Barrel:** 5". **Weight:** NA. **Length:** 8.5". **Grips:** Checkered rubber composite with silver-plated medallion. **Sights:** (O5070X) Dovetail front, Champion rear; (O5870CS) Patridge Target Style front, Champion rear. **Features:** Adjustable aluminum trigger, Beavertail grip safety, full length recoil spring and target recoil spring, available in blued finish and stainless steel.
Price: O5070X **$1,022.00**
Price: O5870CS **$1,071.00**

COLT SPECIAL COMBAT GOVERNMENT

Caliber: 45 ACP, 38 Super. **Barrel:** 5". **Weight:** 39 oz. **Length:** 8.5". **Grips:** Rosewood w/double diamond checkering pattern. **Sights:** Clark dovetail, front; Bo-Mar adjustable, rear. **Features:** A competition-ready pistol with enhancements such as skeletonized trigger, upswept grip safety, custom tuned action, polished feed ramp. Blue or satin nickel finish. Introduced 2003. Made in U.S.A. by Colt's Mfg. Co.
Price: **$1,676.00**

COMPETITOR SINGLE-SHOT PISTOL

Caliber: 22 LR through 50 Action Express, including belted magnums. **Barrel:** 14" standard; 10.5" silhouette; 16" optional. **Weight:** About 59 oz. (14" bbl.). **Length:** 15.12" overall. **Grips:** Ambidextrous; synthetic (standard) or laminated or natural wood. **Sights:** Ramp front, adjustable rear. **Features:** Rotary cannon-type action cocks on opening; cammed ejector; interchangeable barrels, ejectors. Adjustable single stage trigger, sliding thumb safety and trigger safety. Matte blue finish. Introduced 1988. From Competitor Corp., Inc.
Price: 14", standard calibers, synthetic grip **$660.00**

CZ 75 CHAMPION COMPETITION PISTOL

Caliber: 9mm Para., 40 S&W, 16-shot mag. **Barrel:** 4.4". **Weight:** 2.5 lbs. **Length:** 9.4" overall. **Grips:** Black rubber. **Sights:** Blade front, fully adjustable rear. **Features:** Single-action trigger mechanism; three-port compensator (40 S&W, 9mm Para. have two port) full-length guide rod; extended magazine release; ambidextrous safety; flared magazine well; fully adjustable match trigger. Introduced 1999. Imported from the Czech Republic by CZ-USA.
Price: Dual-tone finish **$1,691.00**

EAA Witness Gold Team

Freedom Arms 83 22 Silhouette Class

Hammerli SP 20

High Standard Trophy

High Standard Victor

EAA WITNESS ELITE GOLD TEAM AUTO
Caliber: 9mm Para., 9x21, 38 Super, 40 S&W, 45 ACP. **Barrel:** 5.1".
Weight: 44 oz. **Length:** 10.5" overall. **Grips:** Checkered walnut,
competition-style. **Sights:** Square post front, fully adjustable rear.
Features: Triple-chamber cone compensator; competition SA trigger;
extended safety and magazine release; competition hammer; beveled
magazine well; beavertail grip. Hand-fitted major components. Hard
chrome finish. Match-grade barrel. From E.A.A. Custom Shop.
Introduced 1992. Limited designed for IPSC Limited Class competition.
Features include full-length dust-cover frame, funneled magazine
well, interchangeable front sights. Stock (2005) designed for IPSC
Production Class competition. Match introduced 2006. Made in Italy,
imported by European American Armory.
Price: Gold Team **$1,902.00**
Price: Limited, 4.5" barrel, 18+1 capacity **$1,219.00**
Price: Stock, 4.5" barrel, hard-chrome finish **$930.00**
Price: Match, 4.75" barrel, two-tone finish **$632.00**

FREEDOM ARMS MODEL 83 22 FIELD GRADE SILHOUETTE CLASS
Caliber: 22 LR, 5-shot cylinder. **Barrel:** 10". **Weight:** 63 oz. **Length:**
15.5" overall. **Grips:** Black micarta. **Sights:** Removable Patridge
front blade; Iron Sight Gun Works silhouette rear, click adjustable for
windage and elevation (optional adj. front sight and hood). **Features:**
Stainless steel, matte finish, manual sliding-bar safety system; dual
firing pins, lightened hammer for fast lock time, pre-set trigger stop.
Introduced 1991. Made in U.S.A. by Freedom Arms.
Price: Silhouette Class **$1,860.00**

FREEDOM ARMS MODEL 83 CENTERFIRE SILHOUETTE MODELS
Caliber: 357 Mag., 41 Mag., 44 Mag.; 5-shot cylinder. **Barrel:** 10",
9" (357 Mag. only). **Weight:** 63 oz. (41 Mag.). **Length:** 15.5", 14.5"
(357 only). **Grips:** Pachmayr Presentation. **Sights:** Iron Sight Gun
Works silhouette rear sight, replaceable adjustable front sight blade
with hood. **Features:** Stainless steel, matte finish, manual sliding-bar
safety system. Made in U.S.A. by Freedom Arms.
Price: Silhouette Models, from **$1,741.65**

HAMMERLI SP 20 TARGET PISTOL
Caliber: 22 LR, 32 S&W. **Barrel:** 4.6". **Weight:** 34.6-41.8 oz. **Length:**
11.8" overall. **Grips:** Anatomically shaped synthetic Hi-Grip available
in five sizes. **Sights:** Integral front in three widths, adjustable rear with
changeable notch widths. **Features:** Extremely low-level sight line;
anatomically shaped trigger; adjustable JPS buffer system for different
recoil characteristics. Receiver available in red, blue, gold, violet or
black. Introduced 1998. Imported from Switzerland by Larry's Guns
of Maine.
Price: Hammerli 22 LR **$1,539.00**

HIGH STANDARD SUPERMATIC TROPHY TARGET PISTOL
Caliber: 22 LR, 9-shot mag. **Barrel:** 5.5" bull or 7.25" fluted. **Weight:** 44-
46 oz. **Length:** 9.5-11.25" overall. **Stock:** Checkered hardwood with
thumbrest. **Sights:** Undercut ramp front, frame-mounted micro-click
rear adjustable for windage and elevation; drilled and tapped for scope
mounting. **Features:** Gold-plated trigger, slide lock, safety-lever and
magazine release; stippled front grip and backstrap; adjustable trigger
and sear. Barrel weights optional. From High Standard Manufacturing
Co., Inc.
Price: 5.5" barrel, adjustable sights **$795.00**
Price: 7.25", adjustable sights **$845.00**

HIGH STANDARD VICTOR TARGET PISTOL
Caliber: 22 LR, 10-shot magazine. **Barrel:** 4.5" or 5.5" polished blue;
push-button takedown. **Weight:** 46 oz. **Length:** 9.5" overall. **Stock:**
Checkered walnut with thumbrest. **Sights:** Undercut ramp front,
micro-click rear adjustable for windage and elevation. Also available
with scope mount, rings, no sights. **Features:** Stainless steel frame.
Full-length vent rib. Gold-plated trigger, slide lock, safety-lever and
magazine release; stippled front grip and backstrap; polished blue
slide; adjustable trigger and sear. Comes with barrel weight. From High
Standard Manufacturing Co., Inc.
Price: 4.5" or 5.5" barrel, vented sight rib,
    universal scope base **$795.00**

KIMBER SUPER MATCH II
Caliber: 45 ACP, 8-shot magazine. **Barrel:** 5". **Weight:** 38 oz. **Length:**
8.7" overall. **Grips:** Rosewood double diamond. **Sights:** Blade front,
Kimber fully adjustable rear. **Features:** Guaranteed shoot 1" group
at 25 yards. Stainless steel frame, black KimPro slide; two-piece
magazine well; premium aluminum match-grade trigger; 30 lpi front
strap checkering; stainless match-grade barrel; ambidextrous safety;
special Custom Shop markings. Introduced 1999. Made in U.S.A. by
Kimber Mfg., Inc.
Price: **$2,225.00**

Prices given are believed to be accurate at time of publication however, many factors affect retail pricing so exact prices are not possible.

Kimber Super Match II

Smith & Wesson Model 22A

Ruger MKIII512

Springfield Armory 1911A1 Trophy Match

STI Executive

KIMBER RIMFIRE TARGET
Caliber: 22 LR, 10-shot magazine. **Barrel:** 5". **Weight:** 23oz. **Length:** 8.7" overall. **Grips:** Rosewood, Kimber logo, double diamond checkering, or black synthetic double diamond. **Sights:** Blade front, Kimber fully adjustable rear. **Features:** Bumped beavertail grip safety, extended thumb safety, extended magazine release button. Serrated flat top slide with flutes, machined aluminum slide and frame, matte black or satin silver finishes, 30 lines-per-inch checkering on frontstrap and under trigger guard; aluminum trigger, test target, accuracy guarantee. No slide lock-open after firing the last round in the magazine. Introduced 1999. Made in U.S.A. by Kimber Mfg., Inc.
Price: $833.00

RUGER MARK III TARGET MODEL AUTOLOADING PISTOL
Caliber: 22 LR, 10-shot magazine. **Barrel:** 5.5" to 6-7/8". **Weight:** 41 to 45 oz. **Length:** 9.75" to 11-1/8" overall. **Grips:** Checkered cocobolo/laminate. **Sights:** .125" blade front, micro-click rear, adjustable for windage and elevation, loaded chamber indicator; integral lock, magazine disconnect. Plastic case with lock included. Mark II series introduced 1982, discontinued 2004. Mark III introduced 2005.
Price: MKIII512 (bull barrel, blued) $417.00
Price: KMKIII512 (bull barrel, stainless) $527.00
Price: MKIII678 (blued Target barrel, 6-7/8") $417.00
Price: KMKIII070GC (stainless slabside barrel) $606.00
Price: KMKIII678H (stainless fluted barrel) $620.00
Price: KMKIII45HCL (Crimson Trace Laser Grips, intr. 2008) .$787.00
Price: KMKIII45H (2009) $620.00

SMITH & WESSON MODEL 41 TARGET
Caliber: 22 LR, 10-shot clip. **Barrel:** 5.5", 7". **Weight:** 41 oz. (5.5" barrel). **Length:** 10.5" overall (5.5" barrel). **Grips:** Checkered walnut with modified thumbrest, usable with either hand. **Sights:** 1/8" Patridge on ramp base; micro-click rear adjustable for windage and elevation. **Features:** 3/8" wide, grooved trigger; adjustable trigger stop drilled and tapped.
Price: S&W Bright Blue, either barrel $1,288.00

SMITH & WESSON MODEL 22A PISTOLS
Caliber: 22 LR, 10-shot magazine. **Barrel:** 4", 5.5" bull. **Weight:** 28-39 oz. **Length:** 9.5" overall. **Grips:** Dymondwood with ambidextrous thumbrests and flared bottom or rubber soft touch with thumbrest. **Sights:** Patridge front, fully adjustable rear. **Features:** Sight bridge with Weaver-style integral optics mount; alloy frame, stainless barrel and slide; blue/black finish. Introduced 1997. The 22S is similar to the Model 22A except has stainless steel frame. Introduced 1997. Made in U.S.A. by Smith & Wesson.
Price: from $308.00
Price: Realtree APG camo finish (2008) $356.00

SPRINGFIELD ARMORY LEATHAM LEGEND TGO SERIES PISTOLS
Three models of 5" barrel, 45 ACP 1911 pistols built for serious competition. TGO 1 has deluxe low mount Bo-Mar rear sight, Dawson fiber optics front sight, 3.5 lb. trigger pull.
Price: TGO 1 . . . . $3,095.00

Springfield Armory Trophy Match Pistol
Similar to Springfield Armory's Full Size model, but designed for bullseye and action shooting competition. Available with a Service Model 5" frame with matching slide and barrel in 5" and 6" lengths. Fully adjustable sights, checkered frame front strap, match barrel and bushing. In 45 ACP only. From Springfield Inc.
Price: $1,573.00

STI EAGLE 5.0, 6.0 PISTOL
Caliber: 9mm Para., 9x21, 38 & 40 Super, 40 S&W, 10mm, 45 ACP, 10-shot magazine. **Barrel:** 5", 6" bull. **Weight:** 34.5 oz. **Length:** 8.62" overall. **Grips:** Checkered polymer. **Sights:** STI front, Novak or Heinie rear. **Features:** Standard frames plus 7 others; adjustable match trigger; skeletonized hammer; extended grip safety with locator pad. Introduced 1994. Made in U.S.A. by STI International.
Price: . . . . (5.0 Eagle) $1,940.12, (6.0 Eagle), $1,049.98

STI EXECUTIVE PISTOL
Caliber: 40 S&W. **Barrel:** 5" bull. **Weight:** 39 oz. **Length:** 8-5/8". **Grips:** Gray polymer. **Sights:** Dawson fiber optic, front; STI adjustable rear. **Features:** Stainless mag. well, front and rear serrations on slide. Made in U.S.A. by STI.
Price: $2,464.00

STI TROJAN
Caliber: 9mm Para., 38 Super, 40 S&W, 45 ACP. **Barrel:** 5", 6". **Weight:** 36 oz. **Length:** 8.5". **Grips:** Rosewood. **Sights:** STI front with STI adjustable rear. **Features:** Stippled front strap, flat top slide, one-piece steel guide rod.
Price: (Trojan 5") $1,110.00
Price: (Trojan 6", not available in 38 Super) $1,419.60

Includes models suitable for hunting and competitive courses of fire, both police and international.

Charter Arms Bulldog

Charter Arms Off Duty

Charter Arms Undercover

Charter Arms Mag Pup

Comanche III

EAA Windicator

CHARTER ARMS BULLDOG REVOLVER
Caliber: 44 Special. **Barrel:** 2.5". **Weight:** NA. **Sights:** Blade front, notch rear. **Features:** 6-round cylinder, soft-rubber pancake-style grips, shrouded ejector rod, wide trigger and hammer spur. American made by Charter Arms, distributed by MKS Supply.
Price: Blued $455.00
Price: Stainless $465.00
Price: Target Bulldog, 4" barrel, 23 oz. $459.00

CHARTER ARMS OFF DUTY REVOLVER
Caliber: 38 Spec. **Barrel:** 2". **Weight:** 12.5 oz. **Sights:** Blade front, notch rear. **Features:** 5-round cylinder, aluminum casting, DAO. American made by Charter Arms, distributed by MKS Supply.
Price: Aluminum $438.00

CHARTER ARMS UNDERCOVER REVOLVER
Caliber: **Barrel:** 2". **Weight:** 12 oz. **Sights:** Blade front, notch rear. **Features:** 6-round cylinder. American made by Charter Arms, distributed by MKS Supply.
Price: Blued $438.00

CHARTER ARMS UNDERCOVER SOUTHPAW REVOLVER
Caliber: 38 Spec. +P. **Barrel:** 2". **Weight:** 12 oz. **Sights:** NA. **Features:** Cylinder release is on the right side and the cylinder opens to the right side. Exposed hammer for both single and double-action firing. 5-round cylinder. American made by Charter Arms, distributed by MKS Supply.
Price: Blued $469.00

CHARTER ARMS MAG PUG REVOLVER
Caliber: 357 Mag. **Barrel:** 2.2". **Weight:** 23 oz. **Sights:** Blade front, notch rear. **Features:** Five-round cylinder. American made by Charter Arms, distributed by MKS Supply.
Price: Blued or stainless $409.00

CHARTER ARMS PINK LADY REVOLVER
Caliber: 32 H&R Magnum, 38 Special +P. **Barrel:** 2". **Weight:** 12 oz. **Grips:** Rubber Pachmayr-style. **Sights:** Fixed. **Features:** Snubnose, five-round cylinder. Pink anodized aluminum alloy frame.
Price: $438.00
Price: Lavender Lady, lavender frame $438.00
Price: Goldfinger, gold anodized frame, matte black barrel
and cylinder assembly $438.00

CHARTER ARMS SOUTHPAW REVOLVER
Caliber: 38 Special +P. **Barrel:** 2". **Weight:** 12 oz. **Grips:** Rubber Pachmayr-style. **Sights:** NA. **Features:** Snubnose, five-round cylinder, matte black aluminum alloy frame with stainless steel cylinder. Cylinder latch and crane assembly are on right side of frame for convenience to left-hand shooters.
Price: $469.00

COMANCHE I, II, III DA REVOLVERS
Caliber: 22 LR, 9 shot. 38 Spec., 6 shot. 357 Mag, 6 shot. **Barrel:** 6", 22

LR; 2" and 4", 38 Spec.; 2" and 3", 357 Mag. **Weight:** 39 oz. **Length:** 10.8" overall. **Grips:** Rubber. **Sights:** Adjustable rear. **Features:** Blued or stainless. Distributed by SGS Importers.
Price: I Blue $236.95
Price: I Alloy $258.95
Price: II 38 Spec., 3" bbl., 6-shot, stainless, intr. 2006 . . . . . .$236.95
Price: II 38 Spec., 4" bbl., 6-shot, stainless $219.95
Price: III 357 Mag. 3" bbl., 6-shot, blue $253.95
Price: III 357 Mag. 4" bbl., 6-shot, blue $274.95

EAA WINDICATOR REVOLVERS
Caliber: 38 Spec., 6-shot; 357 Mag., 6-shot. **Barrel:** 2", 4". **Weight:** 30 oz. (4"). **Length:** 8.5" overall (4" bbl.). **Grips:** Rubber with finger grooves. **Sights:** Blade front, fixed or adjustable on rimfires; fixed only on 32, 38. **Features:** Swing-out cylinder; hammer block safety; blue finish. Introduced 1991. Imported from Germany by European American Armory.
Price: 38 Spec. 2" barrel, alloy frame $277.00
Price: 38 Spec. 4" barrel, alloy frame $292.00
Price: 357 Mag. 2" barrel, steel frame $292.00
Price: 357 Mag. 4" barrel, steel frame $311.00

KORTH USA REVOLVERS
Caliber: 22 LR, 22 WMR, 32 S&W Long, 38 Spec., 357 Mag., 9mm Para. **Barrel:** 3", 4", 5.25", 6". **Weight:** 36-52 oz. Grips, Combat, Sport: Walnut, Palisander, Amboinia, Ivory. Grips, Target: German Walnut, matte with oil finish, adjustable ergonomic competition style. **Sights:** Adjustable Patridge (Sport) or Baughman (Combat), interchangeable and adjustable rear w/Patridge front (Target) in blue and matte. **Features:** DA/SA, 3 models, over 50 configurations, externally adjustable trigger stop and weight, interchangeable cylinder, removable wide-milled trigger shoe on Target model. Deluxe models are highly engraved editions. Available finishes include high polish blue finish, plasma coated in high polish or matted silver, gold, blue, or charcoal. Many deluxe options available. 6-shot. From Korth USA.
Price: From $8,000.00
Price: Deluxe Editions, from $12,000.00

Prices given are believed to be accurate at time of publication however, many factors affect retail pricing so exact prices are not possible.

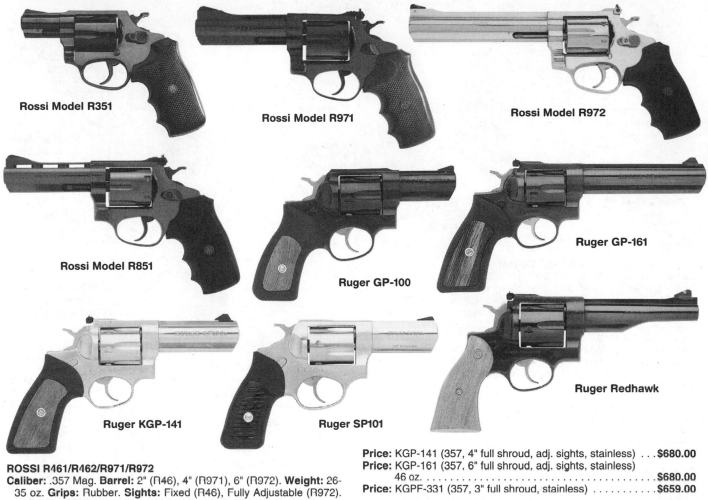

Rossi Model R351

Rossi Model R971

Rossi Model R972

Rossi Model R851

Ruger GP-100

Ruger GP-161

Ruger KGP-141

Ruger SP101

Ruger Redhawk

ROSSI R461/R462/R971/R972
Caliber: .357 Mag. **Barrel:** 2" (R46), 4" (R971), 6" (R972). **Weight:** 26-35 oz. **Grips:** Rubber. **Sights:** Fixed (R46), Fully Adjustable (R972). **Features:** DA/SA, 4 models available, +P rated frame, blue carbon or high polish stainless steel, patented Taurus Security System, 6-shot.
Price: From **$352.00**

ROSSI MODEL R351/R352/R851 REVOLVERS
Caliber: .38 Spec. **Barrel:** 2" (R35), 4" (R851). **Weight:** 24-32 oz. **Grips:** Rubber. **Sights:** Fixed (R35), Fully Adjustable (R851). **Features:** DA/SA, 3 models available, +P rated frame, blue carbon or high polish stainless steel, patented Taurus Security System, 5-shot (R35) 6-shot (R851).
Price: From **$352.00**

ROSSI MODEL R971/R972 REVOLVERS
Caliber: 357 Mag. +P, 6-shot. **Barrel:** 4", 6". **Weight:** 32 oz. **Length:** 8.5" or 10.5" overall. **Grips:** Rubber. **Sights:** Blade front, adjustable rear. **Features:** Single/double action. Patented key-lock Taurus Security System; forged steel frame. Introduced 2001. Made in Brazil by Amadeo Rossi. Imported by BrazTech/Taurus.
Price: Model R971 (blued finish, 4" bbl.) **$406.00**
Price: Model R972 (stainless steel finish, 6" bbl.) **$460.00**

Rossi Model 851
Similar to Model R971/R972, chambered for 38 Spec. +P. Blued finish, 4" barrel. Introduced 2001. Made in Brazil by Amadeo Rossi. From BrazTech/Taurus.
Price: **$352.00**

RUGER GP100 REVOLVERS
Caliber: 38 Spec. +P, 357 Mag., 6-shot. **Barrel:** 3" full shroud, 4" full shroud, 6" full shroud. **Weight:** 3" full shroud-36 oz., 4" full shroud-38 oz. **Sights:** Fixed; adjustable on 4" full shroud, all 6" barrels. **Grips:** Ruger Santoprene Cushioned Grip with Goncalo Alves inserts. **Features:** Uses action, frame features of both the Security-Six and Redhawk revolvers. Full length, short ejector shroud. Satin blue and stainless steel.
Price: GP-141 (357, 4" full shroud, adj. sights, blue) **$616.00**
Price: GP-161 (357, 6" full shroud, adj. sights, blue), 46 oz. . . **$616.00**

Price: KGP-141 (357, 4" full shroud, adj. sights, stainless) . . . **$680.00**
Price: KGP-161 (357, 6" full shroud, adj. sights, stainless)
46 oz. **$680.00**
Price: KGPF-331 (357, 3" full shroud, stainless) **$659.00**

RUGER SP101 REVOLVERS
Caliber: 327 Federal, 6-shot; 38 Spec. +P, 357 Mag., 5-shot. **Barrel:** 2.25", 3-1/16". **Weight:** (38 & 357 mag models) 2.25"-25 oz.; 3-1/16"-27 oz. **Sights:** Adjustable on 327, fixed on others. **Grips:** Ruger Cushioned Grip with inserts. **Features:** Compact, small frame, double-action revolver. Full-length ejector shroud. Stainless steel only. Introduced 1988.
Price: KSP-321X (2.25", 357 Mag.) **$589.00**
Price: KSP-331X (3-1/16", 357 Mag.) **$589.00**
Price: KSP-821X (2.25", 38 Spec.) **$589.00**
Price: KSP-32731X (3-1/16", 327 Federal, intr. 2008) **$589.00**
Price: KSP-321X-LG (Crimson Trace Laser Grips, intr. 2008) . **$839.00**

Ruger SP101 Double-Action-Only Revolver
Similar to standard SP101 except double-action-only with no single-action sear notch. Spurless hammer, floating firing pin and transfer bar safety system. Available with 2.25" barrel in 357 Mag. Weighs 25 oz., overall length 7". Natural brushed satin, high-polish stainless steel. Introduced 1993.
Price: KSP321XL (357 Mag.) **$589.00**
Price: KSP321XL-LG (357 Mag., Crimson Trace Laser Grips, intr. 2008) **$839.00**

RUGER REDHAWK
Caliber: 44 Rem. Mag., 45 Colt, 6-shot. **Barrel:** 4", 5.5", 7.5". **Weight:** About 54 oz. (7.5" bbl.). **Length:** 13" overall (7.5" barrel). **Grips:** Square butt cushioned grip panels. **Sights:** Interchangeable Patridge-type front, rear adjustable for windage and elevation. **Features:** Stainless steel, brushed satin finish, blued ordnance steel. 9.5" sight radius. Introduced 1979.
Price: KRH-44, stainless, 7.5" barrel **$861.00**
Price: KRH-44R, stainless 7.5" barrel w/scope mount **$915.00**
Price: KRH-445, stainless 5.5" barrel **$861.00**
Price: KRH-444, stainless 4" barrel (2007) **$861.00**
Price: KRH-45-4, Hogue Monogrip, 45 Colt (2008) **$861.00**

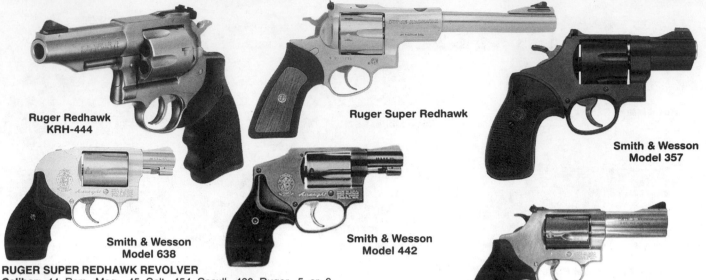

Ruger Redhawk KRH-444

Ruger Super Redhawk

Smith & Wesson Model 357

Smith & Wesson Model 638

Smith & Wesson Model 442

Smith & Wesson Model 60 Chief's Special

RUGER SUPER REDHAWK REVOLVER
Caliber: 44 Rem. Mag., 45 Colt, 454 Casull, 480 Ruger, 5 or 6-shot. **Barrel:** 2.5", 5.5", 7.5", 9.5". **Weight:** About 54 oz. (7.5" bbl.). **Length:** 13" overall (7.5" barrel). **Grips:** Hogue Tamer Monogrip. **Features:** Similar to standard Redhawk except has heavy extended frame with Ruger Integral Scope Mounting System on wide topstrap. Wide hammer spur lowered for better scope clearance. Incorporates mechanical design features and improvements of GP-100. Ramp front sight base has Redhawk-style Interchangeable Insert sight blades, adjustable rear sight. Satin stainless steel and low-glare stainless finishes. Introduced 1987.
Price: KSRH-2454, 2.5" 454 Casull/45 Colt, Hogue Tamer
Monogrip, Alaskan Model **$992.00**
Price: KSRH-7, 7.5" 44 Mag, Ruger grip **$915.00**
Price: KSRH-7454, 7.5" 45 Colt/454 Casull **$992.00**
Price: KSRH-9, 9" 44 Mag, Ruger grip **$915.00**
Price: KSRH-9480-5, 9.5", 480 Ruger, intr. 2008 . . . . **$963.00**
Price: KSRH-2, 2.5" 44 Mag, Alaskan Model, intr. 2008 . . . . . **$992.00**

SMITH & WESSON MODEL 14 CLASSIC
Caliber: 38 Spec. +P, 6-shot. **Barrel:** 6". **Weight:** 35 oz. **Length:** 11.5". **Grips:** Wood. **Sights:** Pinned Patridge front, micro adjustable rear. **Features:** Recreation of the vintage Model 14 revolver. Carbon steel frame and cylinder with blued finish.
Price: **$995.00**
Price: Model 14 150253, nickel finish $1,074.00

SMITH & WESSON M&P REVOLVERS
Caliber: 38 Spec., 357 Mag., 5 rounds (Centennial), 8 rounds (large frame). **Barrel:** 1.87" (Centennial), 5" (large frame). **Weight:** 13.3 oz. (Centennial), 36.3 oz. (large frame). **Length:** 6.31" overall (small frame), 10.5" (large frame). **Grips:** Synthetic. **Sights:** Integral U-Notch rear, XS Sights 24/7 Tritium Night. **Features:** Scandium alloy frame, stainless steel cylinder, matte black finish. Made in U.S.A. by Smith & Wesson.
Price: M&P 340, double action **$869.00**
Price: M&P 340CT, Crimson Trace Lasergrips. $1,122.00
Price: M&P R8 large frame. $1,311.00

SMITH & WESSON NIGHT GUARD REVOLVERS
Caliber: 357 Mag., 38 Spec. +P, 5-, 6-, 7-, 8-shot. **Barrel:** 2.5 or 2.75" (45 ACP). **Weight:** 24.2 oz. (2.5" barrel). **Length:** 7.325" overall (2.5" barrel). **Grips:** Pachmayr Compac Custom. **Sights:** XS Sight 24/7 Standard Dot Tritium front, Cylinder & Slide Extreme Duty fixed rear. **Features:** Scandium alloy frame, stainless PVD cylinder, matte black finish. Introduced 2008. Made in U.S.A. by Smith & Wesson.
Price: Model 310, 10mm/40 S&W (interchangeable), 2.75" barrel,
large-frame snubnose $1,153.00
Price: Model 315, 38 Special +P, 2.5" barrel,
medium-frame snubnose **$995.00**
Price: Model 325, 45 ACP, 2.75" barrel, large-frame
snubnose $1,153.00
Price: Model 327, 38/357, 2.5" barrel, large-frame
snubnose $1,153.00
Price: Model 329, 44 Magnum/38 Special (interchangeable),
2.5" barrel, large-frame snubnose $1,153.00

Price: Model 357, 41 Magnum, 2.75" barrel, large-frame
snubnose $1,153.00
Price: Model 386, 357 Magnum/44 Special +P (interchangeable),
2.5" barrel, medium-frame snubnose. $1,074.00
Price: Model 396, 44 Special, 2.5" barrel, medium-frame
snubnose $1,074.00

SMITH & WESSON J-FRAME REVOLVERS
The smallest S&W wheelguns come in a variety of chamberings, barrel lengths, and materials, as noted in the individual model listings.

SMITH & WESSON 60LS/642LS LADYSMITH REVOLVERS
Caliber: .38 Spec. +P, 357 Mag., 5-shot. **Barrel:** 1-7/8" (642LS); 2-1/8" (60LS) **Weight:** 14.5 oz. (642LS); 21.5 oz. (60LS); **Length:** 6.6" overall (60LS); . **Grips:** Wood. **Sights:** Black blade, serrated ramp front, fixed notch rear. **Features:** 60LS model has a Chiefs Special-style frame. 642LS has Centennial-style frame, frosted matte finish, smooth combat wood grips. Introduced 1996. Comes in a fitted carry/storage case. Introduced 1989. Made in U.S.A. by Smith & Wesson.
Price: From **$782.00**

SMITH & WESSON MODEL 63
Caliber: 22 LR, 8-shot. **Barrel:** 5". **Weight:** 28.8 oz. **Length:** 9.5" overall. **Grips:** Black rubber. **Sights:** Black ramp front sight, adjustable black blade rear sight. **Features:** Stainless steel construction throughout. Made in U.S.A. by Smith & Wesson.
Price: **$845.00**

SMITH & WESSON MODEL 442/637/638/642 AIRWEIGHT REVOLVERS
Caliber: 38 Spec. +P, 5-shot. **Barrel:** 1-7/8". **Weight:** 15 oz. (37, 442); 20 oz. (3); 21.5 oz.; **Length:** 6-3/8" overall. **Grips:** Soft rubber. **Sights:** Fixed, serrated ramp front, square notch rear. **Features:** Aluminum-alloy frames. Models 37, 637; Chiefs Special-style frame with exposed hammer. Introduced 1996. Models 442, 642; Centennial-style frame, enclosed hammer. Model 638, Bodyguard style, shrouded hammer. Comes in a fitted carry/storage case. Introduced 1989. Made in U.S.A. by Smith & Wesson.
Price: From **$600.00**

SMITH & WESSON MODEL 60 CHIEF'S SPECIAL
Caliber: 357 Mag., 38 Spec. +P, 5-shot. **Barrel:** 2-1/8", 3" or 5". **Weight:** 22.5 oz. (2-1/8" barrel). **Length:** 6-5/8" overall (2-1/8" barrel). **Grips:** Rounded butt synthetic grips. **Sights:** Fixed, serrated ramp front, square notch rear. **Features:** Stainless steel construction, satin finish, internal lock. Introduced 1965. The 5"-barrel model has target semi-lug barrel, rosewood grip, red ramp front sight, adjustable rear sight. Made in U.S.A. by Smith & Wesson.
Price: 2-1/8" barrel, intr. 2005 . . . . **$798.00**
Price: 3" barrel, 7.5" OAL, 24 oz. **$830.00**

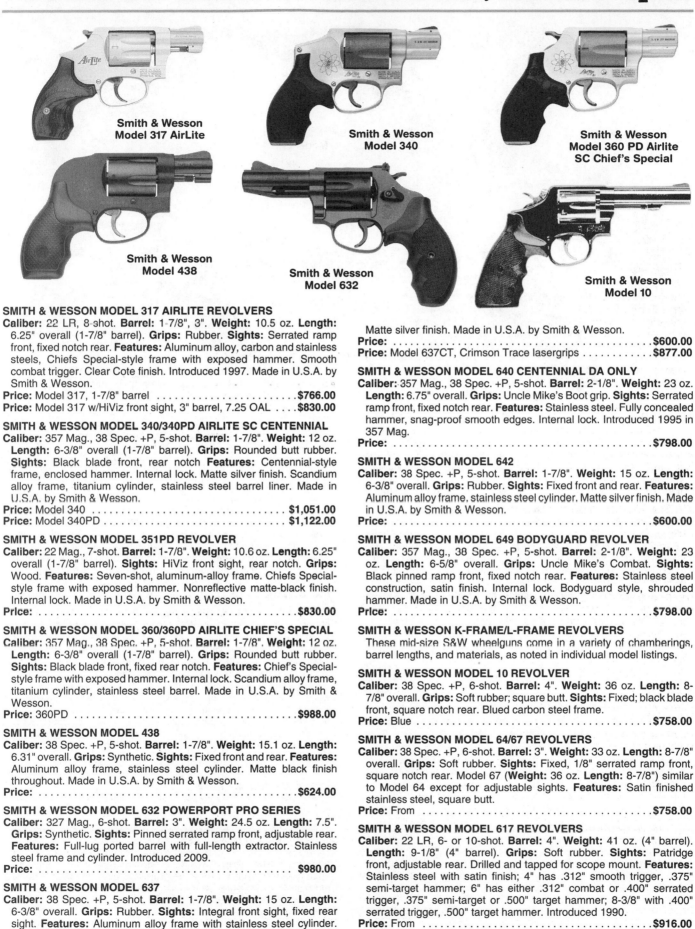

Smith & Wesson
Model 317 AirLite

Smith & Wesson
Model 340

Smith & Wesson
Model 360 PD Airlite
SC Chief's Special

Smith & Wesson
Model 438

Smith & Wesson
Model 632

Smith & Wesson
Model 10

SMITH & WESSON MODEL 317 AIRLITE REVOLVERS
Caliber: 22 LR, 8-shot. **Barrel:** 1-7/8", 3". **Weight:** 10.5 oz. **Length:** 6.25" overall (1-7/8" barrel). **Grips:** Rubber. **Sights:** Serrated ramp front, fixed notch rear. **Features:** Aluminum alloy, carbon and stainless steels, Chiefs Special-style frame with exposed hammer. Smooth combat trigger. Clear Cote finish. Introduced 1997. Made in U.S.A. by Smith & Wesson.
Price: Model 317, 1-7/8" barrel **$766.00**
Price: Model 317 w/HiViz front sight, 3" barrel, 7.25 OAL **$830.00**

SMITH & WESSON MODEL 340/340PD AIRLITE SC CENTENNIAL
Caliber: 357 Mag., 38 Spec. +P, 5-shot. **Barrel:** 1-7/8". **Weight:** 12 oz. **Length:** 6-3/8" overall (1-7/8" barrel). **Grips:** Rounded butt rubber. **Sights:** Black blade front, rear notch **Features:** Centennial-style frame, enclosed hammer. Internal lock. Matte silver finish. Scandium alloy frame, titanium cylinder, stainless steel barrel liner. Made in U.S.A. by Smith & Wesson.
Price: Model 340 . . . . **$1,051.00**
Price: Model 340PD **$1,122.00**

SMITH & WESSON MODEL 351PD REVOLVER
Caliber: 22 Mag., 7-shot. **Barrel:** 1-7/8". **Weight:** 10.6 oz. **Length:** 6.25" overall (1-7/8" barrel). **Sights:** HiViz front sight, rear notch. **Grips:** Wood. **Features:** Seven-shot, aluminum-alloy frame. Chiefs Special-style frame with exposed hammer. Nonreflective matte-black finish. Internal lock. Made in U.S.A. by Smith & Wesson.
Price: **$830.00**

SMITH & WESSON MODEL 360/360PD AIRLITE CHIEF'S SPECIAL
Caliber: 357 Mag., 38 Spec. +P, 5-shot. **Barrel:** 1-7/8". **Weight:** 12 oz. **Length:** 6-3/8" overall (1-7/8" barrel). **Grips:** Rounded butt rubber. **Sights:** Black blade front, fixed rear notch. **Features:** Chief's Special-style frame with exposed hammer. Internal lock. Scandium alloy frame, titanium cylinder, stainless steel barrel. Made in U.S.A. by Smith & Wesson.
Price: 360PD **$988.00**

SMITH & WESSON MODEL 438
Caliber: 38 Spec. +P, 5-shot. **Barrel:** 1-7/8". **Weight:** 15.1 oz. **Length:** 6.31" overall. **Grips:** Synthetic. **Sights:** Fixed front and rear. **Features:** Aluminum alloy frame, stainless steel cylinder. Matte black finish throughout. Made in U.S.A. by Smith & Wesson.
Price: **$624.00**

SMITH & WESSON MODEL 632 POWERPORT PRO SERIES
Caliber: 327 Mag., 6-shot. **Barrel:** 3". **Weight:** 24.5 oz. **Length:** 7.5". **Grips:** Synthetic. **Sights:** Pinned serrated ramp front, adjustable rear. **Features:** Full-lug ported barrel with full-length extractor. Stainless steel frame and cylinder. Introduced 2009.
Price: **$980.00**

SMITH & WESSON MODEL 637
Caliber: 38 Spec. +P, 5-shot. **Barrel:** 1-7/8". **Weight:** 15 oz. **Length:** 6-3/8" overall. **Grips:** Rubber. **Sights:** Integral front sight, fixed rear sight. **Features:** Aluminum alloy frame with stainless steel cylinder.

Matte silver finish. Made in U.S.A. by Smith & Wesson.
Price: **$600.00**
Price: Model 637CT, Crimson Trace lasergrips **$877.00**

SMITH & WESSON MODEL 640 CENTENNIAL DA ONLY
Caliber: 357 Mag., 38 Spec. +P, 5-shot. **Barrel:** 2-1/8". **Weight:** 23 oz. **Length:** 6.75" overall. **Grips:** Uncle Mike's Boot grip. **Sights:** Serrated ramp front, fixed notch rear. **Features:** Stainless steel. Fully concealed hammer, snag-proof smooth edges. Internal lock. Introduced 1995 in 357 Mag.
Price: **$798.00**

SMITH & WESSON MODEL 642
Caliber: 38 Spec. +P, 5-shot. **Barrel:** 1-7/8". **Weight:** 15 oz. **Length:** 6-3/8" overall. **Grips:** Rubber. **Sights:** Fixed front and rear. **Features:** Aluminum alloy frame, stainless steel cylinder. Matte silver finish. Made in U.S.A. by Smith & Wesson.
Price: **$600.00**

SMITH & WESSON MODEL 649 BODYGUARD REVOLVER
Caliber: 357 Mag., 38 Spec. +P, 5-shot. **Barrel:** 2-1/8". **Weight:** 23 oz. **Length:** 6-5/8" overall. **Grips:** Uncle Mike's Combat. **Sights:** Black pinned ramp front, fixed notch rear. **Features:** Stainless steel construction, satin finish. Internal lock. Bodyguard style, shrouded hammer. Made in U.S.A. by Smith & Wesson.
Price: **$798.00**

SMITH & WESSON K-FRAME/L-FRAME REVOLVERS
These mid-size S&W wheelguns come in a variety of chamberings, barrel lengths, and materials, as noted in individual model listings.

SMITH & WESSON MODEL 10 REVOLVER
Caliber: 38 Spec. +P, 6-shot. **Barrel:** 4". **Weight:** 36 oz. **Length:** 8-7/8" overall. **Grips:** Soft rubber; square butt. **Sights:** Fixed; black blade front, square notch rear. Blued carbon steel frame.
Price: Blue **$758.00**

SMITH & WESSON MODEL 64/67 REVOLVERS
Caliber: 38 Spec. +P, 6-shot. **Barrel:** 3". **Weight:** 33 oz. **Length:** 8-7/8" overall. **Grips:** Soft rubber. **Sights:** Fixed, 1/8" serrated ramp front, square notch rear. Model 67 (**Weight:** 36 oz. **Length:** 8-7/8") similar to Model 64 except for adjustable sights. **Features:** Satin finished stainless steel, square butt.
Price: From **$758.00**

SMITH & WESSON MODEL 617 REVOLVERS
Caliber: 22 LR, 6- or 10-shot. **Barrel:** 4". **Weight:** 41 oz. (4" barrel). **Length:** 9-1/8" (4" barrel). **Grips:** Soft rubber. **Sights:** Patridge front, adjustable rear. Drilled and tapped for scope mount. **Features:** Stainless steel with satin finish; 4" has .312" smooth trigger, .375" semi-target hammer; 6" has either .312" combat or .400" serrated trigger, .375" semi-target or .500" target hammer; 8-3/8" with .400" serrated trigger, .500" target hammer. Introduced 1990.
Price: From **$916.00**

Smith & Wesson
Model 686 SSR

Smith & Wesson
Model 21

Smith & Wesson
Model 329

Smith & Wesson
Model 625

Smith & Wesson
Model 329

Smith & Wesson Model 500

Smith & Wesson
Model 460V

SMITH & WESSON MODELS 620 REVOLVERS

Caliber: 38 Spec. +P; 357 Mag., 7 rounds. **Barrel:** 4". **Weight:** 37.5 oz. **Length:** 9.5". **Grips:** Rubber. **Sights:** Integral front blade, fixed rear notch on the 619; adjustable white-outline target style rear, red ramp front on 620. **Features:** Replaces Models 65 and 66. Two-piece semi-lug barrel. Satin stainless frame and cylinder. Made in U.S.A. by Smith & Wesson.
Price: **$893.00**

SMITH & WESSON MODEL 686/686 PLUS REVOLVERS

Caliber: 357 Mag., 38 S&W Special; 6 rounds. **Barrel:** 2.5", 4", 6". **Weight:** 35 oz. (2.5" barrel). **Length:** 7.5", (2.5" barrel). **Grips:** Rubber. **Sights:** White outline adjustable rear, red ramp front. **Features:** Satin stainless frame and cylinder. Plus series guns have 7-shot cylinders. Introduced 1996. Powerport (PP) has Patridge front, adjustable rear sight. Introduced early 1980s. Stock Service Revolver (SSR) intr. 2007. **Capacity:** 6. **Barrel:** 4". **Sights:** Interchangeable front, adjustable rear. **Grips:** Wood. **Finish:** Satin stainless frame and cylinder. **Weight:** 38.3 oz. **Features:** Chamfered charge holes, custom barrel w/recessed crown, bossed mainspring. High-hold ergonomic grip. Made in U.S.A. by Smith & Wesson.
Price: 686 . . . .**$909.00**
Price: Plus, 7 rounds **$932.00**
Price: PP, 6" barrel, 6 rounds, 11-3/8" OAL **$877.00**
Price: SSR **$1,059.00**

SMITH & WESSON N-FRAME REVOLVERS

These large-frame S&W wheelguns come in a variety of chamberings, barrel lengths, and materials, as noted in the individual model listings.

SMITH & WESSON MODEL 21

Caliber: 44 Special, 6-round. Barrel: 4" tapered. **Weight:** NA. **Length:** NA. **Grips:** Smooth wood. **Sights:** Pinned half-moon service front; service rear. **Features:** Carbon steel frame, blued finish.
Price: **$924.00**

SMITH & WESSON MODEL 29 CLASSIC

Caliber: 44 Mag, 6-round. **Barrel:** 6.5". **Weight:** 48.5 oz. **Length:** 12". **Grips:** Altamont service walnut. **Sights:** Adjustable white-outline rear, red ramp front. **Features:** Carbon steel frame, polished-blued or nickel finish. Has integral key lock safety feature to prevent accidental discharges. Alo available with 3" barrel. Original Model 29 made famous by "Dirty Harry" character created in 1971 by Clint Eastwood.
Price: **$1240.00**

SMITH & WESSON MODEL 329PD AIRLITE REVOLVERS

Caliber: 44 Spec., 44 Mag., 6-round. **Barrel:** 4". **Weight:** 26 oz. **Length:** 9.5". **Grips:** Wood. **Sights:** Adj. rear, HiViz orange-dot front. **Features:** Scandium alloy frame, blue/black finish.
Price: From **$1,264.00**

SMITH & WESSON MODEL 625/625JM REVOLVERS

Caliber: 45 ACP, 6-shot. **Barrel:** 4", 5". **Weight:** 43 oz. (4" barrel). **Length:** 9-3/8" overall (4" barrel). **Grips:** Soft rubber; wood optional. **Sights:** Patridge front on ramp, S&W micrometer click rear adjustable for windage and elevation. **Features:** Stainless steel construction with .400" semi-target hammer, .312" smooth combat trigger; full lug barrel. Glass beaded finish. Introduced 1989. "Jerry Miculek" Professional (JM) Series has .265"-wide grooved trigger, special wooden Miculek Grip, five full moon clips, gold bead Patridge front sight on interchangeable front sight base, bead blast finish. Unique serial number run. Mountain Gun has 4" tapered barrel, drilled and tapped, Hogue Rubber Monogrip, pinned black ramp front sight, micrometer click-adjustable rear sight, satin stainless frame and barrel, weighs 39.5 oz.
Price: 625JM **$1,074.00**

SMITH & WESSON MODEL 629 REVOLVERS

Caliber: 44 Magnum, 44 S&W Special, 6-shot. **Barrel:** 4", 5", 6.5". **Weight:** 41.5 oz. (4" bbl.). **Length:** 9-5/8" overall (4" bbl.). **Grips:** Soft rubber; wood optional. **Sights:** 1/8" red ramp front, white outline rear, internal lock, adjustable for windage and elevation. Classic similar to standard Model 629, except Classic has full-lug 5" barrel, chamfered front of cylinder, interchangeable red ramp front sight with adjustable white outline rear, Hogue grips with S&W monogram, drilled and tapped for scope mounting. Factory accurizing and endurance packages. Introduced 1990. Classic Power Port has Patridge front sight and adjustable rear sight. Model 629CT has 5" barrel, Crimson Trace Hoghunter Lasergrips, 10.5" OAL, 45.5 oz. weight. Introduced 2006.
Price: From **$1,035.00**

SMITH & WESSON X-FRAME REVOLVERS

These extra-large X-frame S&W wheelguns come in a variety of chamberings, barrel lengths, and materials, as noted in individual model listings.

SMITH & WESSON MODEL S&W500 (163565)

Caliber: 500 S&W Mag., 5 rounds. **Barrel:** 6.5". **Weight:** 60.7 oz. **Length:** 12.875". **Grips:** Synthetic. **Sights:** Red Ramp front sights, adjustable white outline rear. **Features:** Similar to other S&W500 models but with integral compensator and half-length ejector shroud. Made in U.S.A. by Smith & Wesson.
Price: From **$1,375.00**

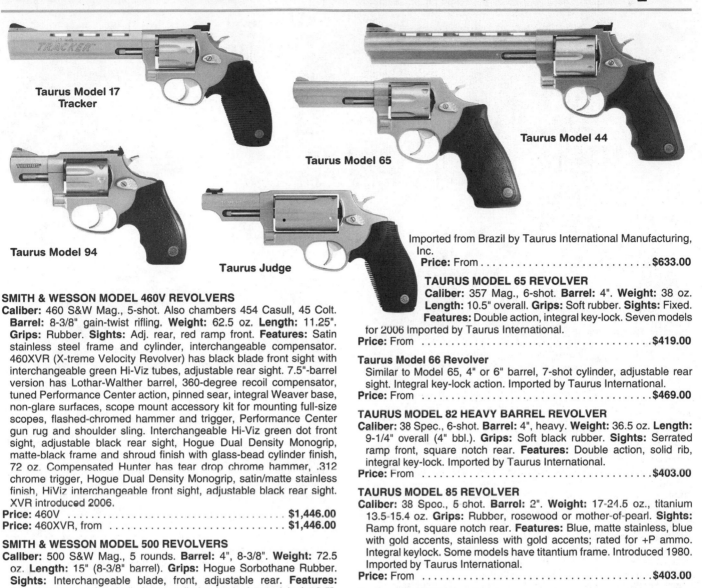

Taurus Model 17 Tracker

Taurus Model 65

Taurus Model 44

Taurus Model 94

Taurus Judge

SMITH & WESSON MODEL 460V REVOLVERS

Caliber: 460 S&W Mag., 5-shot. Also chambers 454 Casull, 45 Colt. **Barrel:** 8-3/8" gain-twist rifling. **Weight:** 62.5 oz. **Length:** 11.25". **Grips:** Rubber. **Sights:** Adj. rear, red ramp front. **Features:** Satin stainless steel frame and cylinder, interchangeable compensator. 460XVR (X-treme Velocity Revolver) has black blade front sight with interchangeable green Hi-Viz tubes, adjustable rear sight. 7.5"-barrel version has Lothar-Walther barrel, 360-degree recoil compensator, tuned Performance Center action, pinned sear, integral Weaver base, non-glare surfaces, scope mount accessory kit for mounting full-size scopes, flashed-chromed hammer and trigger, Performance Center gun rug and shoulder sling. Interchangeable Hi-Viz green dot front sight, adjustable black rear sight, Hogue Dual Density Monogrip, matte-black frame and shroud finish with glass-bead cylinder finish, 72 oz. Compensated Hunter has tear drop chrome hammer, .312 chrome trigger, Hogue Dual Density Monogrip, satin/matte stainless finish, HiViz interchangeable front sight, adjustable black rear sight. XVR introduced 2006.
Price: 460V **$1,446.00**
Price: 460XVR, from **$1,446.00**

SMITH & WESSON MODEL 500 REVOLVERS

Caliber: 500 S&W Mag., 5 rounds. **Barrel:** 4", 8-3/8". **Weight:** 72.5 oz. **Length:** 15" (8-3/8" barrel). **Grips:** Hogue Sorbothane Rubber. **Sights:** Interchangeable blade, front, adjustable rear. **Features:** Recoil compensator, ball detent cylinder latch, internal lock. 6.5"-barrel model has orange-ramp dovetail Millett front sight, adjustable black rear sight, Hogue Dual Density Monogrip, .312" chrome trigger with over-travel stop, chrome tear-drop hammer, glassbead finish. 10.5"-barrel model has red ramp front sight, adjustable rear sight, .312" chrome trigger with overtravel stop, chrome tear drop hammer with pinned sear, hunting sling. Compensated Hunter has .400 orange ramp dovetail front sight, adjustable black blade rear sight, Hogue Dual Density Monogrip, glassbead finish w/black clear coat. Made in U.S.A. by Smith & Wesson.
Price: From **$1,375.00**

SUPER SIX CLASSIC BISON BULL

Caliber: 45-80 Government, 6-shot. **Barrel:** 10" octagonal with 1:14 twist. **Weight:** 6 lbs. **Length:** 17.5"overall. **Grips:** NA. **Sights:** Ramp front sight with dovetailed blade, click-adjustable rear. **Features:** Manganese bronze frame. Integral scope mount, manual crossbolt safety.
Price: .... **Appx. $1,100.00**

TAURUS MODEL 17 "TRACKER"

Caliber: 17 HMR, 7-shot. **Barrel:** 6.5". **Weight:** 45.8 oz. **Grips:** Rubber. **Sights:** Adjustable. **Features:** Double action, matte stainless, integral key-lock.
Price: From **$453.00**

TAURUS MODEL 44 REVOLVER

Caliber: 44 Mag., 6-shot. **Barrel:** 4", 6.5", 8-3/8". **Weight:** 44-3/4 oz. **Grips:** Rubber. **Sights:** Adjustable. **Features:** Double-action. Integral key-lock. Introduced 1994. New Model 44S12 has 12" vent rib barrel.

Imported from Brazil by Taurus International Manufacturing, Inc.
Price: From **$633.00**

TAURUS MODEL 65 REVOLVER

Caliber: 357 Mag., 6-shot. **Barrel:** 4". **Weight:** 38 oz. **Length:** 10.5" overall. **Grips:** Soft rubber. **Sights:** Fixed. **Features:** Double action, integral key-lock. Seven models for 2006 Imported by Taurus International.
Price: From **$419.00**

Taurus Model 66 Revolver

Similar to Model 65, 4" or 6" barrel, 7-shot cylinder, adjustable rear sight. Integral key-lock action. Imported by Taurus International.
Price: From **$469.00**

TAURUS MODEL 82 HEAVY BARREL REVOLVER

Caliber: 38 Spec., 6-shot. **Barrel:** 4", heavy. **Weight:** 36.5 oz. **Length:** 9-1/4" overall (4" bbl). **Grips:** Soft black rubber. **Sights:** Serrated ramp front, square notch rear. **Features:** Double action, solid rib, integral key-lock. Imported by Taurus International.
Price: From **$403.00**

TAURUS MODEL 85 REVOLVER

Caliber: 38 Spec., 5-shot. **Barrel:** 2". **Weight:** 17-24.5 oz., titanium 13.5-15.4 oz. **Grips:** Rubber, rosewood or mother-of-pearl. **Sights:** Ramp front, square notch rear. **Features:** Blue, matte stainless, blue with gold accents, stainless with gold accents; rated for +P ammo. Integral keylock. Some models have titantium frame. Introduced 1980. Imported by Taurus International.
Price: From **$403.00**

Taurus 851 & 651 Revolvers

Small frame SA/DA revolvers similar to Taurus Model 85 but with Centennial-style concealed-hammer frame. Chambered in 38 Special +P (Model 851) or 357 Magnum (Model 651). Features include five-shot cylinder; 2" barrel; fixed sights; blue, matte blue, titanium or stainless finish; Taurus security lock. Overall length is 6.5". Weighs 15.5 oz. (titanium) to 25 oz. (blued and stainless).
Price: From **$411.00**

TAURUS MODEL 94 REVOLVER

Caliber: 22 LR, 9-shot cylinder; 22 Mag, 8-shot cylinder **Barrel:** 2", 4", 5". **Weight:** 18.5-27.5 oz. **Grips:** Soft black rubber. **Sights:** Serrated ramp front, click-adjustable rear. **Features:** Double action, integral key-lock. Introduced 1989. Imported by Taurus International.
Price: From **$369.00**

TAURUS MODEL 4510 JUDGE

Caliber: 3" .410/45 LC, 2.5" .410/45 LC. **Barrel:** 3", 6.5" (blued finish). **Weight:** 35.2 oz., 22.4 oz. **Length:** 7.5". **Grips:** Ribber. **Sights:** Fiber Optic. **Features:** DA/SA. Matte Stainless and Ultra-Lite Stainless finish. Introduced in 2007. Imported from Brazil by Taurus International.
Price: 4510T TrackerSS Matte Stainless **$569.00**
Price: 4510TKR-3B Judge **$558.00**
Price: 4510TKR-SSR, ported barrel, tactical rail **$608.00**

TAURUS RAGING BULL MODEL 416

Caliber: 41 Magnum, 6-shot. **Barrel:** 6.5". **Weight:** 61.9 oz. **Grips:** Rubber. **Sights:** Adjustable. **Features:** Double-action, ported, ventilated rib, matte stainless, integral key-lock.
Price: **$706.00**

Prices given are believed to be accurate at time of publication however, many factors affect retail pricing so exact prices are not possible.

Taurus 444
Ultra-Lite

Taurus Model
605

Taurus Model 444
Raging Bull

Taurus Model 608

Taurus
Model 651

Taurus
Model 650

Taurus Model 970 Tracker

TAURUS MODEL 425 TRACKER REVOLVERS
Caliber: 357 Mag., 7-shot; 41 Mag., 5-shot.
Barrel: 4" and 6". **Weight:** 28.8-40 oz. (titanium) 24.3-28. (6"). **Grips:** Rubber. **Sights:** Fixed front, adjustable rear. **Features:** Double-action stainless steel, Shadow Gray or Total Titanium; vent rib (steel models only); integral key-lock action. Imported by Taurus International.
Price: From $569.00

TAURUS MODEL 444 ULTRA-LIGHT
Caliber: 44 Mag, 5-shot. **Barrel:** 4". **Weight:** 28.3 oz. **Length:** 9.8"overall. **Grips:** Cushioned inset rubber. **Sights:** Fixed red-fiber optic front, adjustable rear. **Features:** UltraLite titanium blue finish, titanium/alloy frame built on Raging Bull design. Smooth trigger shoe, 1.760" wide, 6.280" tall. Barrel rate of twist 1:16", 6 grooves. Introduced 2005. Imported by Taurus International.
Price: $666.00

TAURUS MODEL 416/444/454 RAGING BULL REVOLVERS
Caliber: 41 Mag., 44 Mag., 454 Casull. **Barrel:** 2.25" (454 Casull only), 5", 6.5", 8-3/8". **Weight:** 53-63 oz. **Length:** 12" overall (6.5" barrel). **Grips:** Soft black rubber. **Sights:** Patridge front, adjustable rear. **Features:** Double-action, ventilated rib, ported, integral key-lock. Introduced 1997. Imported by Taurus International.
Price: From $641.00

TAURUS MODEL 605 REVOLVER
Caliber: 357 Mag., 5-shot. **Barrel:** 2". **Weight:** 24 oz. **Grips:** Rubber. **Sights:** Fixed. **Features:** Double-action, blue or stainless or titanium, concealed hammer models DAO, porting optional, integral key-lock. Introduced 1995. Imported by Taurus International.
Price: From $403.00

TAURUS MODEL 608 REVOLVER
Caliber: 357 Mag. 38 Spec., 8-shot. **Barrel:** 4", 6.5", 8-3/8". **Weight:** 44-57 oz. **Length:** 9-3/8" overall. **Grips:** Soft black rubber. **Sights:** Adjustable. **Features:** Double-action, integral key-lock action. Available in blue or stainless. Introduced 1995. Imported by Taurus International.
Price: From $584.00

TAURUS MODEL 617 REVOLVER
Caliber: 357 Mag., 7-shot. **Barrel:** 2". **Weight:** 28.3 oz. **Length:** 6.75" overall. **Grips:** Soft black rubber. **Sights:** Fixed. **Features:** Double-action, blue, Shadow Gray, bright spectrum blue or matte stainless steel, integral key-lock. Available with porting, concealed hammer. Introduced 1998. Imported by Taurus International.
Price: $436.00

TAURUS MODEL 650 CIA REVOLVER
Caliber: 357 Mag., 5-shot. **Barrel:** 2". **Weight:** 24.5 oz. **Grips:** Rubber. **Sights:** Ramp front, square notch rear. **Features:** Double-action

only, blue or matte stainless steel, integral key-lock, internal hammer. Introduced 2001. From Taurus International.
Price: From $411.00

TAURUS MODEL 651 PROTECTOR REVOLVER
Caliber: 357 Mag., 5-shot. **Barrel:** 2". **Weight:** 17-24.5 oz. **Grips:** Rubber. **Sights:** Fixed. **Features:** Concealed single-action/double-action design. Shrouded cockable hammer, blue, matte stainless, Shadow Gray, Total Titanium, integral key-lock. Made in Brazil. Imported by Taurus International Manufacturing, Inc.
Price: From $411.00

Taurus Model 731 Revolver
Similar to the Taurus Model 605, except in .32 Magnum.
Price: $469.00

TAURUS MODEL 817 ULTRA-LITE REVOLVER
Caliber: 38 Spec., 7-shot. **Barrel:** 2". **Weight:** 21 oz. **Length:** 6.5" overall. **Grips:** Soft rubber. **Sights:** Fixed. **Features:** Double-action, integral key-lock. Rated for +P ammo. Introduced 1999. Imported from Brazil by Taurus International.
Price: From $436.00

TAURUS MODEL 850 CIA REVOLVER
Caliber: 38 Spec., 5-shot. **Barrel:** 2". **Weight:** 17-24.5 oz. **Grips:** Rubber, mother-of-pearl. **Sights:** Ramp front, square notch rear. **Features:** Double-action only, blue or matte stainless steel, rated for +P ammo, integral key-lock, internal hammer. Introduced 2001. From Taurus International.
Price: From $411.00

TAURUS MODEL 941 REVOLVER
Caliber: 22 LR (Mod. 94), 22 WMR (Mod. 941), 8-shot. **Barrel:** 2", 4", 5". **Weight:** 27.5 oz. (4" barrel). **Grips:** Soft black rubber. **Sights:** Serrated ramp front, rear adjustable. **Features:** Double-action, integral key-lock. Introduced 1992. Imported by Taurus International.
Price: From $386.00

TAURUS MODEL 970/971 TRACKER REVOLVERS
Caliber: 22 LR (Model 970), 22 Magnum (Model 971); 7-shot. **Barrel:** 6". **Weight:** 53.6 oz. **Grips:** Rubber. **Sights:** Adjustable. **Features:** Double barrel, heavy barrel with ventilated rib; matte stainless finish, integral key-lock. Introduced 2001. From Taurus International.
Price: $453.00
Price: Model 17SS6, chambered in 17 HMR $453.00

Prices given are believed to be accurate at time of publication however, many factors affect retail pricing so exact prices are not possible.

Both classic six-shooters and modern adaptations for hunting and sport.

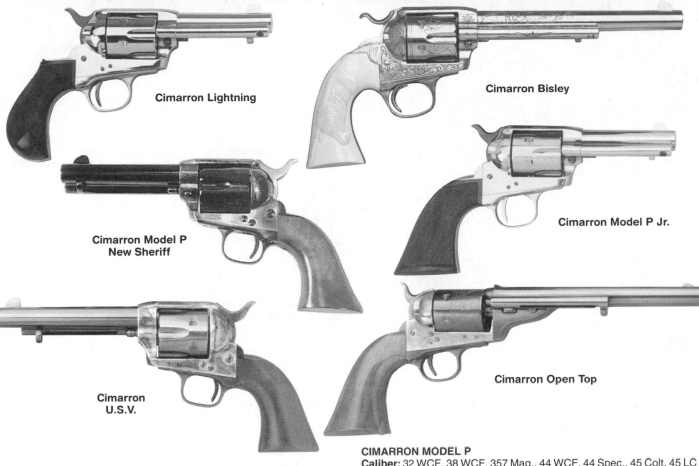

Cimarron Lightning

Cimarron Bisley

Cimarron Model P Jr.

Cimarron Model P
New Sheriff

Cimarron Open Top

Cimarron
U.S.V.

BERETTA STAMPEDE SINGLE-ACTION REVOLVER
Caliber: 357 Mag, 45 Colt, 6-shot. **Barrel:** 4.75", 5.5", 7.5", blued. **Weight:** 36.8 oz. (4.75" barrel). **Length:** 9.5" overall (4.75" barrel). **Grips:** Wood, walnut, black polymer. **Sights:** Blade front, notch rear. **Features:** Transfer-bar safety. Introduced 2003. Stampede Inox (2004) is stainless steel with black polymer grips. Compact Stampede Marshall (2004) has birdshead-style walnut grips, 3.5" barrel, color-case-hardened frame, blued barrel and cylinder. Manufactured for Beretta by Uberti.
Price: Nickel, 45 Colt **$630.00**
Price: Blued, 45 Colt, 357 Mag, 4.75", 5-1/2" **$575.00**
Price: Deluxe, 45 Colt, 357 Mag. 4.75", 5-1/2" **$675.00**
Price: Marshall, 45 Colt, 357 Mag. 3.5" **$575.00**
Price: Bisley nickel, 4.75", 5.5" **$775.00**
Price: Bisley, 4.75", 5.5" **$675.00**
Price: Stampede Deluxe, 45 Colt 7.5" **$775.00**
Price: Stampede Blued, 45 Colt 7.5" **$575.00**
Price: Marshall Old West, 45 Colt 3.5" **$650.00**

CHARTER ARMS DIXIE DERRINGER
Caliber: 22 LR, 22 Magnum, 22 LR/Magnum convertible. **Barrel:** 1-1/8". **Weight:** 6 oz. **Grips:** NA. **Sights:** NA. **Features:** Single-action minigun, five-round cylinder, hammer block safety, stainless steel construction.
Price: **$469.00**

CIMARRON LIGHTNING SA
Caliber: 22 LR, 32-20, 32 H&R, 38 Colt. **Barrel:** 3.5", 4.75", 5.5". **Grips:** Smooth or checkered walnut. **Sights:** Blade front. **Features:** Replica of the Colt 1877 Lightning DA. Similar to Cimarron Thunderer, except smaller grip frame to fit smaller hands. Standard blue, charcoal blue or nickel finish with forged, old model, or color case hardened frame. Introduced 2001. From Cimarron F.A. Co.
Price: From **$480.70**

CIMARRON MODEL P
Caliber: 32 WCF, 38 WCF, 357 Mag., 44 WCF, 44 Spec., 45 Colt, 45 LC and 45 ACP. **Barrel:** 4.75", 5.5", 7.5". **Weight:** 39 oz. **Length:** 10" overall (4" barrel). **Grips:** Walnut. **Sights:** Blade front, fixed or adjustable rear. **Features:** Uses "old model" black powder frame with "Bullseye" ejector or New Model frame. Imported by Cimarron F.A. Co.
Price: from **$494.09**
Price: Laser Engraved, from **$879.00**
Price: New Sheriff, from **$494.09**

Cimarron Bisley Model Single-Action Revolvers
Similar to 1873 Model P, special grip frame and trigger guard, knurled wide-spur hammer, curved trigger. Available in 357 Mag., 44 WCF, 44 Spl., 45 Colt. Introduced 1000. Imported by Cimarron F.A. Co.
Price: From **$574.43**

CIMARRON MODEL "P" JR.
Caliber: 32-20, 32 H&R, **Barrel:** 3.5", 4.75", 5.5". **Grips:** Checkered walnut. **Sights:** Blade front. **Features:** Styled after 1873 Colt Peacemaker, except 20 percent smaller. Blue finish with color case-hardened frame; Cowboy action. Introduced 2001. From Cimarron F.A. Co.
Price: **$400.36**

CIMARRON U.S.V. ARTILLERY MODEL SINGLE-ACTION
Caliber: 45 Colt. **Barrel:** 5.5". **Weight:** 39 oz. **Length:** 11.5" overall. **Grips:** Walnut. **Sights:** Fixed. **Features:** U.S. markings and cartouche, case-hardened frame and hammer; 45 Colt only. Imported by Cimarron F.A. Co.
Price: **$547.65**

CIMARRON 1872 OPEN TOP REVOLVER
Caliber: 38, 44 Special, 44 Colt, 44 Russian, 45 LC, 45 S&W Schofield. **Barrel:** 5.5" and 7.5". **Grips:** Walnut. **Sights:** Blade front, fixed rear. **Features:** Replica of first cartridge-firing revolver. Blue, charcoal blue, nickel or Original finish; Navy-style brass or steel Army-style frame. Introduced 2001 by Cimarron F.A. Co.
Price: **$467.31**

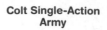

Cimarron Thunderer

Colt Single-Action Army

EAA Bounty Hunter

EMF 1875 Outlaw

EMF 1890 Police

CIMARRON THUNDERER REVOLVER
Caliber: 357 Mag., 44 WCF, 45 Colt, 6-shot. **Barrel:** 3.5", 4.75", with ejector. **Weight:** 38 oz. (3.5" barrel). **Grips:** Smooth or checkered walnut. **Sights:** Blade front, notch rear. **Features:** Thunderer grip. Introduced 1993. Imported by Cimarron F.A. Co.
Price: Stainless. **$534.26**

COLT SINGLE-ACTION ARMY REVOLVER
Caliber: 357 Mag., 38 Spec., .32/20, 44-40, 45 Colt, 6-shot. **Barrel:** 4.75", 5.5", 7.5". **Weight:** 40 oz. (4.75" barrel). **Length:** 10.25" overall (4.75" barrel). **Grips:** Black Eagle composite. **Sights:** Blade front, notch rear. **Features:** Available in full nickel finish with nickel grip medallions, or Royal Blue with color case-hardened frame. Reintroduced 1992. Sheriff's Model and Frontier Six introduced 2008.
Price: P1540, 32-20, 4.75" barrel, color case-hardened/blued
   finish **$1,290.00**
Price: P1656, 357 Mag., 5.5" barrel, nickel finish **$1,490.00**
Price: P1876, 45 LC, 7.5" barrel, nickel finish **$1,490.00**
Price: P2830S SAA Sheriff's, 3" barrel, 45 LC (2008) **$1,290.00**
Price: P2950FSS Frontier Six Shooter, 5.5" barrel, 44-40
   (2008) **$1,350.00**

EAA BOUNTY HUNTER SA REVOLVERS
Caliber: 22 LR/22 WMR, 357 Mag., 44 Mag., 45 Colt, 6-shot. **Barrel:** 4.5", 7.5". **Weight:** 2.5 lbs. **Length:** 11" overall (4-5/8" barrel). **Grips:** Smooth walnut. **Sights:** Blade front, grooved topstrap rear. **Features:** Transfer bar safety; 3-position hammer; hammer forged barrel. Introduced 1992. Imported by European American Armory.
Price: Blue or case-hardened, from **$392.00**
Price: Nickel **$432.00**
Price: 22 LR/22 WMR, blue **$292.00**
Price: As above, nickel **$325.00**

EMF MODEL 1873 FRONTIER MARSHAL
Caliber: 357 Mag., 45 Colt. **Barrel:** 4.75", 5-1/2", 7.5". **Weight:** 39 oz. **Length:** 10.5" overall. **Sights:** Blade front, notch rear. **Features:** Bright brass trigger guard and backstrap, color case-hardened frame, blued barrel and cylinder. Introduced 1998. Imported from Italy.
Price: **$485.00**

EMF HARTFORD SINGLE-ACTION REVOLVERS
Caliber: 357 Mag., 32-20, 38-40, 44-40, 44 Spec., 45 Colt. **Barrel:** 4.75", 5.5", 7.5". **Weight:** 45 oz. **Length:** 13" overall (7.5" barrel). **Grips:** Smooth walnut. **Sights:** Blade front, fixed rear. **Features:** Identical to the original Colts. All major parts serial numbered using original Colt-style lettering, numbering. Bullseye ejector head and color case-hardening on old model frame and hammer. Introduced 1990. Imported by E.M.F. Co.
Price: Old Model **$489.90**
Price: Case-hardened New Model frame **$489.90**

EMF Great Western II Express Single-Action Revolver
Same as the regular model except uses grip of the Colt Lightning revolver. Barrel lengths of 4.75". Introduced 2006. Imported by E.M.F. Co.
Price: Stainless, Ultra Ivory grips **$715.00**
Price: Walnut grips **$690.00**

EMF 1875 OUTLAW REVOLVER
Caliber: 357 Mag., 44-40, 45 Colt. **Barrel:** 7.5", 9.5". **Weight:** 46 oz. **Length:** 13.5" overall. **Grips:** Smooth walnut. **Sights:** Blade front, fixed groove rear. **Features:** Authentic copy of 1875 Remington with firing pin in hammer; color case-hardened frame, blue cylinder, barrel, steel backstrap and trigger guard. Also available in nickel, factory engraved. Imported by E.M.F. Co.
Price: All calibers **$479.90**
Price: Laser Engraved **$684.90**

EMF 1890 Police Revolver
Similar to the 1875 Outlaw except has 5.5" barrel, weighs 40 oz., with 12.5" overall length. Has lanyard ring in butt. No web under barrel. Calibers: 45 Colt. Imported by E.M.F. Co.
Price: **$489.90**

EMF 1873 GREAT WESTERN II
Caliber: .357, 45 LC, 44/40. **Barrel:** 4 3/4", 5.5", 7.5". **Weight:** 36 oz. **Length:** 11" (5.5"). **Grips:** Walnut. **Sights:** Blade front, notch rear. **Features:** Authentic reproduction of the original 2nd generation Colt single-action revolver. Standard and bone case hardening. Coil hammer spring. Hammer-forged barrel.
Price: 1873 Californian **$520.00**
Price: 1873 Custom series, bone or nickel, ivory-like grips . .**$689.90**
Price: 1873 Stainless steel, ivory-like grips **$589.90**

Prices given are believed to be accurate at time of publication however, many factors affect retail pricing so exact prices are not possible.

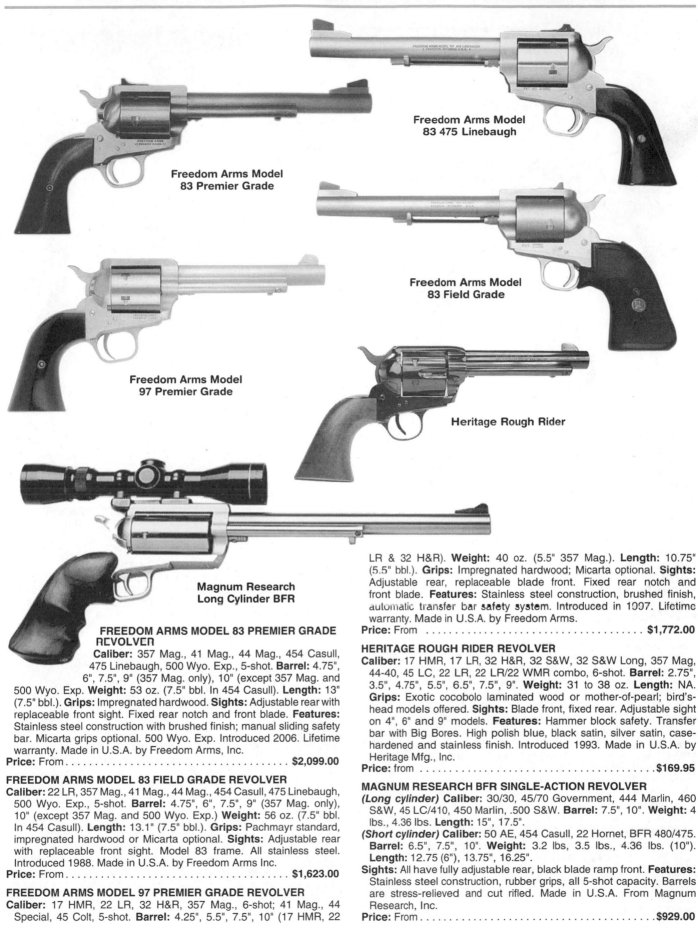

Freedom Arms Model
83 475 Linebaugh

Freedom Arms Model
83 Premier Grade

Freedom Arms Model
83 Field Grade

Freedom Arms Model
97 Premier Grade

Heritage Rough Rider

Magnum Research
Long Cylinder BFR

FREEDOM ARMS MODEL 83 PREMIER GRADE REVOLVER
Caliber: 357 Mag., 41 Mag., 44 Mag., 454 Casull, 475 Linebaugh, 500 Wyo. Exp., 5-shot. **Barrel:** 4.75", 6", 7.5", 9" (357 Mag. only), 10" (except 357 Mag. and 500 Wyo. Exp. **Weight:** 53 oz. (7.5" bbl. In 454 Casull). **Length:** 13" (7.5" bbl.). **Grips:** Impregnated hardwood. **Sights:** Adjustable rear with replaceable front sight. Fixed rear notch and front blade. **Features:** Stainless steel construction with brushed finish; manual sliding safety bar. Micarta grips optional. 500 Wyo. Exp. Introduced 2006. Lifetime warranty. Made in U.S.A. by Freedom Arms, Inc.
Price: From **$2,099.00**

FREEDOM ARMS MODEL 83 FIELD GRADE REVOLVER
Caliber: 22 LR, 357 Mag., 41 Mag., 44 Mag., 454 Casull, 475 Linebaugh, 500 Wyo. Exp., 5-shot. **Barrel:** 4.75", 6", 7.5", 9" (357 Mag. only), 10" (except 357 Mag. and 500 Wyo. Exp.) **Weight:** 56 oz. (7.5" bbl. In 454 Casull). **Length:** 13.1" (7.5" bbl.). **Grips:** Pachmayr standard, impregnated hardwood or Micarta optional. **Sights:** Adjustable rear with replaceable front sight. Model 83 frame. All stainless steel. Introduced 1988. Made in U.S.A. by Freedom Arms Inc.
Price: From **$1,623.00**

FREEDOM ARMS MODEL 97 PREMIER GRADE REVOLVER
Caliber: 17 HMR, 22 LR, 32 H&R, 357 Mag., 6-shot; 41 Mag., 44 Special, 45 Colt, 5-shot. **Barrel:** 4.25", 5.5", 7.5", 10" (17 HMR, 22 LR & 32 H&R). **Weight:** 40 oz. (5.5" 357 Mag.). **Length:** 10.75" (5.5" bbl.). **Grips:** Impregnated hardwood; Micarta optional. **Sights:** Adjustable rear, replaceable blade front. Fixed rear notch and front blade. **Features:** Stainless steel construction, brushed finish, automatic transfer bar safety system. Introduced in 1997. Lifetime warranty. Made in U.S.A. by Freedom Arms.
Price: From **$1,772.00**

HERITAGE ROUGH RIDER REVOLVER
Caliber: 17 HMR, 17 LR, 32 H&R, 32 S&W, 32 S&W Long, 357 Mag., 44-40, 45 LC, 22 LR, 22 LR/22 WMR combo, 6-shot. **Barrel:** 2.75", 3.5", 4.75", 5.5", 6.5", 7.5", 9". **Weight:** 31 to 38 oz. **Length:** NA. **Grips:** Exotic cocobolo laminated wood or mother-of-pearl; bird's-head models offered. **Sights:** Blade front, fixed rear. Adjustable sight on 4", 6" and 9" models. **Features:** Hammer block safety. Transfer bar with Big Bores. High polish blue, black satin, silver satin, case-hardened and stainless finish. Introduced 1993. Made in U.S.A. by Heritage Mfg., Inc.
Price: from **$169.95**

MAGNUM RESEARCH BFR SINGLE-ACTION REVOLVER
(Long cylinder) **Caliber:** 30/30, 45/70 Government, 444 Marlin, 460 S&W, 45 LC/410, 450 Marlin, .500 S&W. **Barrel:** 7.5", 10". **Weight:** 4 lbs., 4.36 lbs. **Length:** 15", 17.5".
(Short cylinder) **Caliber:** 50 AE, 454 Casull, 22 Hornet, BFR 480/475. **Barrel:** 6.5", 7.5", 10". **Weight:** 3.2 lbs., 3.5 lbs., 4.36 lbs. (10"). **Length:** 12.75 (6"), 13.75", 16.25".
Sights: All have fully adjustable rear, black blade ramp front. **Features:** Stainless steel construction, rubber grips, all 5-shot capacity. Barrels are stress-relieved and cut rifled. Made in U.S.A. From Magnum Research, Inc.
Price: From **$929.00**

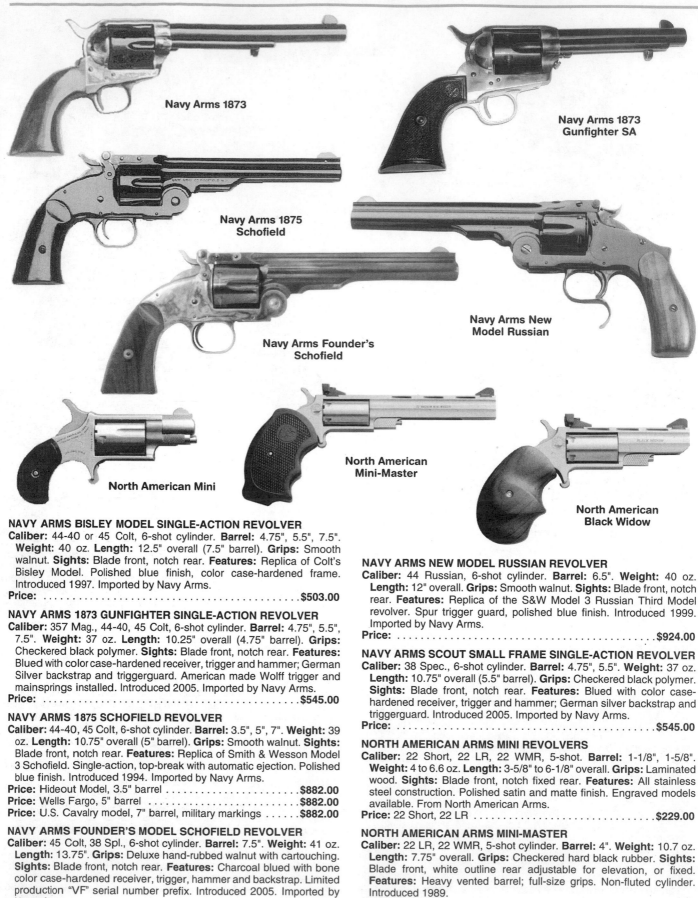

Navy Arms 1873

Navy Arms 1873 Gunfighter SA

Navy Arms 1875 Schofield

Navy Arms New Model Russian

Navy Arms Founder's Schofield

North American Mini

North American Mini-Master

North American Black Widow

NAVY ARMS BISLEY MODEL SINGLE-ACTION REVOLVER
Caliber: 44-40 or 45 Colt, 6-shot cylinder. **Barrel:** 4.75", 5.5", 7.5". **Weight:** 40 oz. **Length:** 12.5" overall (7.5" barrel). **Grips:** Smooth walnut. **Sights:** Blade front, notch rear. **Features:** Replica of Colt's Bisley Model. Polished blue finish, color case-hardened frame. Introduced 1997. Imported by Navy Arms.
Price: $503.00

NAVY ARMS 1873 GUNFIGHTER SINGLE-ACTION REVOLVER
Caliber: 357 Mag., 44-40, 45 Colt, 6-shot cylinder. **Barrel:** 4.75", 5.5", 7.5". **Weight:** 37 oz. **Length:** 10.25" overall (4.75" barrel). **Grips:** Checkered black polymer. **Sights:** Blade front, notch rear. **Features:** Blued with color case-hardened receiver, trigger and hammer; German Silver backstrap and triggerguard. American made Wolff trigger and mainsprings installed. Introduced 2005. Imported by Navy Arms.
Price: $545.00

NAVY ARMS 1875 SCHOFIELD REVOLVER
Caliber: 44-40, 45 Colt, 6-shot cylinder. **Barrel:** 3.5", 5", 7". **Weight:** 39 oz. **Length:** 10.75" overall (5" barrel). **Grips:** Smooth walnut. **Sights:** Blade front, notch rear. **Features:** Replica of Smith & Wesson Model 3 Schofield. Single-action, top-break with automatic ejection. Polished blue finish. Introduced 1994. Imported by Navy Arms.
Price: Hideout Model, 3.5" barrel $882.00
Price: Wells Fargo, 5" barrel $882.00
Price: U.S. Cavalry model, 7" barrel, military markings $882.00

NAVY ARMS FOUNDER'S MODEL SCHOFIELD REVOLVER
Caliber: 45 Colt, 38 Spl., 6-shot cylinder. **Barrel:** 7.5". **Weight:** 41 oz. **Length:** 13.75". **Grips:** Deluxe hand-rubbed walnut with cartouching. **Sights:** Blade front, notch rear. **Features:** Charcoal blued with bone color case-hardened receiver, trigger, hammer and backstrap. Limited production "VF" serial number prefix. Introduced 2005. Imported by Navy Arms.
Price: $924.00

NAVY ARMS NEW MODEL RUSSIAN REVOLVER
Caliber: 44 Russian, 6-shot cylinder. **Barrel:** 6.5". **Weight:** 40 oz. **Length:** 12" overall. **Grips:** Smooth walnut. **Sights:** Blade front, notch rear. **Features:** Replica of the S&W Model 3 Russian Third Model revolver. Spur trigger guard, polished blue finish. Introduced 1999. Imported by Navy Arms.
Price: $924.00

NAVY ARMS SCOUT SMALL FRAME SINGLE-ACTION REVOLVER
Caliber: 38 Spec., 6-shot cylinder. **Barrel:** 4.75", 5.5". **Weight:** 37 oz. **Length:** 10.75" overall (5.5" barrel). **Grips:** Checkered black polymer. **Sights:** Blade front, notch rear. **Features:** Blued with color case-hardened receiver, trigger and hammer; German silver backstrap and triggerguard. Introduced 2005. Imported by Navy Arms.
Price: $545.00

NORTH AMERICAN ARMS MINI REVOLVERS
Caliber: 22 Short, 22 LR, 22 WMR, 5-shot. **Barrel:** 1-1/8", 1-5/8". **Weight:** 4 to 6.6 oz. **Length:** 3-5/8" to 6-1/8" overall. **Grips:** Laminated wood. **Sights:** Blade front, notch fixed rear. **Features:** All stainless steel construction. Polished satin and matte finish. Engraved models available. From North American Arms.
Price: 22 Short, 22 LR $229.00

NORTH AMERICAN ARMS MINI-MASTER
Caliber: 22 LR, 22 WMR, 5-shot cylinder. **Barrel:** 4". **Weight:** 10.7 oz. **Length:** 7.75" overall. **Grips:** Checkered hard black rubber. **Sights:** Blade front, white outline rear adjustable for elevation, or fixed. **Features:** Heavy vented barrel; full-size grips. Non-fluted cylinder. Introduced 1989.
Price: Fixed sight $284.00
Price: Adjustable sight $314.00

Prices given are believed to be accurate at time of publication however, many factors affect retail pricing so exact prices are not possible.

Ruger New Model Blackhawk 50th Anniversary

Ruger Bisley Single-Action

Ruger New Model Blackhawk

Ruger Super Blackhawk Hunter

Ruger New Bearcat

Ruger New Vaquero

North American Arms Black Widow Revolver

Similar to Mini-Master, 2" heavy vent barrel. Built on 22 WMR frame. Non-fluted cylinder, black rubber grips. Available with Millett Low Profile fixed sights or Millett sight adjustable for elevation only. Overall length 5-7/8", weighs 8.8 oz. From North American Arms.
Price: Adjustable sight, 22 LR or 22 WMR **$299.00**
Price: Fixed sight, 22 LR or 22 WMR **$269.00**

NORTH AMERICAN ARMS "THE EARL" SINGLE-ACTION REVOLVER

Caliber: 22 Magnum with 22 LR accessory cylinder, 5-shot cylinder. **Barrel:** 4" octagonal. **Weight:** 6.8 oz. **Length:** 7-3/4" overall. **Grips:** Wood. **Sights:** Barleycorn front and fixed notch rear. **Features:** Single-action mini-revolver patterned after 1858-style Remington percussion revolver. Includes a spur trigger and a faux loading lever that serves as cylinder pin release.
Price: . . . .**$289.00** (22 Magnum only); **$324.00** (convertible)

RUGER NEW MODEL SINGLE SIX & NEW MODEL .32 H&R SINGLE SIX REVOLVERS

Caliber: 17 HMR, 22 LR, 22 Mag. **Barrel:** 4-5/8", 5.5", 6.5", 7.5", 9.5". 6-shot. **Grips:** Rosewood, black laminate. **Sights:** Adjustable or fixed. **Features:** Blued or stainless metalwork, short grips available, convertible models available. Introduced 2003 in 17 HMR.
Price: 17 HMR (blued) **$519.00**
Price: 22 LR/22 Mag., from **$506.00**

RUGER NEW MODEL BLACKHAWK/BLACKHAWK CONVERTIBLE

Caliber: 30 Carbine, 357 Mag./38 Spec., 41 Mag., 45 Colt, 6-shot. **Barrel:** 4-5/8", 5.5", 6.5", 7.5" (30 carbine and 45 Colt). **Weight:** 36 to 45 oz. **Lengths:** 10-3/8" to 13.5". **Grips:** Rosewood or black checkered. **Sights:** 1/8" ramp front, micro-click rear adjustable for windage and elevation. **Features:** Rosewood grips, Ruger transfer bar safety system, independent firing pin, hardened chrome-moly steel frame, music wire springs through-out. Case and lock included. Convertibles come with extra cylinder.
Price: 30 Carbine, 7.5" (BN31, blued) **$541.00**
Price: 357 Mag. (blued or satin stainless), from **$541.00**
Price: 41 Mag. (blued) **$541.00**
Price: 45 Colt (blued or satin stainless), from **$541.00**
Price: 357 Mag./9mm Para. Convertible (BN34XL, BN36XL) **$617.00**
Price: 45 Colt/45 ACP Convertible (BN44X, BN455XL) **$617.00**

Ruger Bisley Single-Action Revolver

Similar to standard Blackhawk, hammer is lower with smoothly curved, deeply checkered wide spur. The trigger is strongly curved with wide smooth surface. Longer grip frame. Adjustable rear sight, ramp-style front. Unfluted cylinder and roll engraving, adjustable sights. Chambered for 44 Mag. and 45 Colt; 7.5" barrel; overall length 13.5"; weighs 48-51 oz. Plastic lockable case. Orig. fluted cylinder introduced 1985; discontinued 1991. Unfluted cylinder introduced 1986.
Price: RB-44W (44 Mag), RB45W (45 Colt) **$683.00**

RUGER NEW MODEL SUPER BLACKHAWK

Caliber: 44 Mag., 6-shot. Also fires 44 Spec. **Barrel:** 4-5/8", 5.5", 7.5", 10.5" bull. **Weight:** 45-55 oz. **Length:** 10.5" to 16.5". **Grips:** Rosewood. **Sights:** 1/8" ramp front, micro-click rear adjustable for windage and elevation. **Features:** Ruger transfer bar safety system, fluted or unfluted cylinder, steel grip and cylinder frame, round or square back trigger guard, wide serrated trigger, wide spur hammer. With case and lock.
Price: Blue, 4-5/8", 5.5", 7.5" (S-458N, S-45N, S-47N) **$650.00**
Price: Blue, 10.5" bull barrel (S-411N) **$667.00**
Price: Stainless, 4-5/8", 5.5", 7.5" (KS-458N, KS-45N, KS-47N) **$667.00**
Price: Stainless, 10.5" bull barrel (KS-411N) **$694.00**
Price: Super Blackhawk 50th Anniversary: Gold highlights, ornamentation; commemorates 50-year anniversary of Super Blackhawk **$729.00**

RUGER NEW MODEL SUPER BLACKHAWK HUNTER

Caliber: 44 Mag., 6-shot. **Barrel:** 7.5", full-length solid rib, unfluted cylinder. **Weight:** 52 oz. **Length:** 13-5/8". **Grips:** Black laminated wood. **Sights:** Adjustable rear, replaceable front blade. **Features:** Reintroduced Ultimate SA revolver. Includes instruction manual, high-impact case, set 1" medium scope rings, gun lock, ejector rod as standard.
Price: Hunter model, satin stainless, 7.5" (KS-47NHNN) **$781.00**
Price: Hunter model, Bisley frame, satin stainless 7.5" (KS-47NHB) **$781.00**

RUGER NEW VAQUERO SINGLE-ACTION REVOLVER

Caliber: 357 Mag., 45 Colt, 6-shot. **Barrel:** 4-5/8", 5.5", 7.5". **Weight:** 39-45 oz. **Length:** 10.5" overall (4-5/8" barrel). **Grips:** Rubber with Ruger medallion. **Sights:** Fixed blade front, fixed notch rear. **Features:** Transfer bar safety system and loading gate interlock. Blued model color case-hardened finish on frame, rest polished and blued. Engraved model available. Gloss stainless. Introduced 2005.
Price: 357 Mag., blued or stainless **$659.00**
Price: 45 Colt, blued or stainless **$659.00**
Price: 357 Mag., 45 Colt, ivory grips, 45 oz. (2009) **$729.00**

Taurus Gaucho 357

Taurus Gaucho 45

Uberti 1873 Cattleman

Uberti Bisley

Uberti 1875 Outlaw

Ruger New Model Bisley Vaquero
Similar to New Vaquero but with Bisley-style hammer and grip frame. Chambered in 357 and 45 Colt. Features include a 5.5" barrel, simulated ivory grips, fixed sights, six-shot cylinder. Overall length is 11.12", weighs 45 oz.
Price: $729.00

RUGER NEW BEARCAT SINGLE-ACTION
Caliber: 22 LR, 6-shot. **Barrel:** 4". **Weight:** 24 oz. **Length:** 9" overall. **Grips:** Smooth rosewood with Ruger medallion. **Sights:** Blade front, fixed notch rear. **Features:** Reintroduction of the Ruger Bearcat with slightly lengthened frame, Ruger transfer bar safety system. Available in blue only. Rosewood grips. Introduced 1996 (blued), 2003 (stainless). With case and lock.
Price: SBC-4, blued $501.00
Price: KSBC-4, satin stainless $540.00

STI TEXICAN SINGLE-ACTION REVOLVER
Caliber: 45 Colt, 6-shot. **Barrel:** 5.5", 4140 chrome-moly steel by Green Mountain Barrels. 1:16 twist, air gauged to .0002". Chamber to bore alignment less than .001". Forcing cone angle, 3 degrees. **Weight:** 36 oz. **Length:** 11". **Grips:** "No crack" polymer. **Sights:** Blade front, fixed notch rear. **Features:** Parts made by ultra-high speed or electron discharge machined processes from chrome-moly steel forgings or bar stock. Competition sights, springs, triggers and hammers. Frames, loading gates, and hammers are color case hardened by Turnbull Restoration. Frame, back strap, loading gate, trigger guard, cylinders made of 4140 re-sulphurized Maxell 3.5 steel. Hammer firing pin (no transfer bar). S.A.S.S. approved. Introduced 2008. Made in U.S.A. by STI International.
Price: 5.5" barrel $1,299.99

TAURUS SINGLE-ACTION GAUCHO REVOLVERS
Caliber: 38 Spl, 357 Mag, 44-40, 45 Colt, 6-shot. **Barrel:** 4.75", 5.5", 7.5", 12". **Weight:** 36.7-37.7 oz. **Length:** 13". **Grips:** Checkered black polymer. **Sights:** Blade front, fixed notch rear. **Features:** Integral transfer bar; blue, blue with case hardened frame, matte stainless and the hand polished "Sundance" stainless finish. Removable cylinder, half-cock notch. Introduced 2005. Imported from Brazil by Taurus International.
Price: S/A-357-B, 357 Mag., Sundance blue finish,
    5.5" barrel $520.00
Price: S/A-357-S/S7, 357 Mag., polished stainless,
    7.5" barrel $536.00
Price: S/A-45-B7 . . . .$520.00

UBERTI 1851-1860 CONVERSION REVOLVERS
Caliber: 38 Spec., 45 Colt, 6-shot engraved cylinder. **Barrel:** 4.75", 5.5", 7.5", 8" **Weight:** 2.6 lbs. (5.5" bbl.). **Length:** 13" overall (5.5" bbl.). **Grips:** Walnut. **Features:** Brass backstrap, trigger guard; color case-hardened frame, blued barrel, cylinder. Introduced 2007. Imported from Italy by Stoeger Industries.
Price: 1851 Navy $519.00
Price: 1860 Army $549.00

UBERTI 1871-1872 OPEN TOP REVOLVERS
Caliber: 38 Spec., 45 Colt, 6-shot engraved cylinder. **Barrel:** 4.75", 5.5", 7.5". **Weight:** 2.6 lbs. (5.5" bbl.). **Length:** 13" overall (5.5" bbl.). **Grips:** Walnut. **Features:** Blued backstrap, trigger guard; color case-hardened frame, blued barrel, cylinder. Introduced 2007. Imported from Italy by Stoeger Industries.
Price: $499.00

UBERTI 1873 CATTLEMAN SINGLE-ACTION
Caliber: 45 Colt; 6-shot fluted cylinder. **Barrel:** 4.75", 5.5", 7.5". **Weight:** 2.3 lbs. (5.5" bbl.). **Length:** 11" overall (5.5" bbl.). **Grips:** Styles: Frisco (pearl styled); Desperado (buffalo horn styled); Chisholm (checkered walnut); Gunfighter (black checkered), Cody (ivory styled), one-piece walnut. **Sights:** Blade front, groove rear. **Features:** Steel or brass backstrap, trigger guard; color case-hardened frame, blued barrel, cylinder. NM designates New Model plunger style frame; OM designates Old Model screw cylinder pin retainer. Imported from Italy by Stoeger Industries.
Price: 1873 Cattleman Frisco $789.00
Price: 1873 Cattleman Desperado (2006) $789.00
Price: 1873 Cattleman Chisholm (2006) $539.00
Price: 1873 Cattleman NM, blued 4.75" barrel $479.00
Price: 1873 Cattleman NM, Nickel finish, 7.5" barrel $609.00
Price: 1873 Cattleman Cody. $789.00

UBERTI 1873 CATTLEMAN BIRD'S HEAD SINGLE ACTION
Caliber: 357 Mag., 45 Colt; 6-shot fluted cylinder **Barrel:** 3.5", 4", 4.75", 5.5". **Weight:** 2.3 lbs. (5.5" bbl.). **Length:** 10.9" overall (5.5" bbl.). **Grips:** One-piece walnut. **Sights:** Blade front, groove rear. **Features:** Steel or brass backstrap, trigger guard; color case-hardened frame, blued barrel, cylinder. Imported from Italy by Stoeger Industries.
Price: 1873 Cattleman Bird's Head OM 3.5" barrel $539.00

UBERTI 1873 BISLEY SINGLE-ACTION REVOLVER
Caliber: 357 Mag., 45 Colt (Bisley); 22 LR and 38 Spec. (Stallion), both with 6-shot fluted cylinder. **Barrel:** 4.75", 5.5", 7.5". **Weight:** 2 to 2.5 lbs. **Length:** 12.7" overall (7.5" barrel). **Grips:** Two-piece walnut. **Sights:** Blade front, notch rear. **Features:** Replica of Colt's Bisley Model. Polished blue finish, color case-hardened frame. Introduced 1997. Imported by Stoeger Industries.
Price: 1873 Bisley, 7.5" barrel $569.00

Prices given are believed to be accurate at time of publication however, many factors affect retail pricing so exact prices are not possible.

U.S. Fire Arms Single Action Army Revolver

U.S. Fire Arms Single Action Flattop Target

U.S. Fire Arms Single Action Bisley

U.S. Fire Arms Single Action Omni-Potent

U.S. Fire Arms United States Pre-War

U.S. Fire Arms Rodeo Cowboy Action

UBERTI 1873 BUNTLINE AND REVOLVER CARBINE SINGLE-ACTION

Caliber: 357 Mag., 44-40, 45 Colt; 6-shot fluted cylinder **Barrel:** 18". **Length:** 22.9" to 34". **Grips:** Walnut pistol grip or rifle stock. **Sights:** Fixed or adjustable. **Features:** Imported from Italy by Stoeger Industries.
Price: 1873 Revolver Carbine, 18" barrel, 34" OAL **$729.00**
Price: 1873 Catttleman Buntline Target, 18" barrel, 22.9" OAL **$639.00**

UBERTI OUTLAW, FRONTIER, AND POLICE REVOLVERS

Caliber: 45 Colt, 6-shot fluted cylinder. **Barrel:** 5.5", 7.5". **Weight:** 2.5 to 2.8 lbs. **Length:** 10.8" to 13.6" overall. **Grips:** Two-piece smooth walnut. **Sights:** Blade front, notch rear. **Features:** Cartridge version of 1858 Remington percussion revolver. Nickel and blued finishes. Imported by Stoeger Industries.
Price: 1875 Outlaw nickel finish **$629.00**
Price: 1875 Frontier, blued finish **$539.00**
Price: 1890 Police, blued finish **$549.00**

UBERTI 1870 SCHOFIELD-STYLE TOP BREAK REVOLVER

Caliber: 38, 44 Russian, 44-40, 45 Colt, 6-shot cylinder. **Barrel:** 3.5", 5", 7". **Weight:** 2.4 lbs. (5" barrel) **Length:** 10.8" overall (5" barrel). **Grips:** Two-piece smooth walnut or pearl. **Sights:** Blade front, notch rear. **Features:** Replica of Smith & Wesson Model 3 Schofield. Single-action, top break with automatic ejection. Polished blue finish (first model). Introduced 1994. Imported by Stoeger Industries.
Price: No. 3-2nd Model, nickel finish $1,369.00

U.S. FIRE ARMS SINGLE-ACTION REVOLVER

Caliber: 45 Colt (standard); 32 WCF, 38 WCF, 38 Spec., 44 WCF, 44 Special, 6-shot cylinder. **Barrel:** 4.75", 5.5", 7.5". **Weight:** 37 oz.

Length: NA. **Grips:** Hard rubber. **Sights:** Blade front, notch rear. **Features:** Recreation of original guns; 3" and 4" have no ejector. Available with all-blue, blue with color case-hardening, or full nickel-plate finish. Other models include Custer Battlefield Gun ($1,625, 7.5" barrel), Flattop Target ($1,625), Sheriff's Model ($875, with barrel lengths starting at 2"), Snubnose ($1,475, barrel lengths 2", 3", 4"), Omni-Potent Six-Shooter and Omni-Target Six-Shooter (from $1,625), Bisley ($1,350, introduced 2006). Made in U.S.A. by United States Fire Arms Mfg. Co.
Price: Blue/cased-colors $875.00
Price: Nickel $1,220.00

U.S. FIRE ARMS RODEO COWBOY ACTION REVOLVER

Caliber: 45 Colt, **Barrel:** 4.75", 5.5". **Grips:** Rubber. **Features:** Historically correct Armory bone case hammer, blue satin finish, transfer bar safety system, correct solid firing pin. Entry level basic cowboy SASS gun. Other models include the Gunslinger ($1,145). 2006 version includes brown-rubber stocks.
Price: $550.00
Price: New Rodeo 2 (2007) $605.00

U.S. FIRE ARMS U.S. PRE-WAR

Caliber: 45 Colt (standard); 32 WCF, 38 WCF, 38 Spec., 44 WCF, 44 Special. **Barrel:** 4.75", 5.5", 7.5". **Grips:** Hard rubber. **Features:** Armory bone case/Armory blue finish standard, cross-pin or black powder frame. Introduced 2002. Made in U.S.A. by United States Firearms Mfg. Co.
Price: $1,270.00

Specially adapted single-shot and multi-barrel arms.

Bond Arms Texas Defender

Bond Arms Century 2000 Defender

Cobra Big Bore

Cobra Standard Derringer

Comanche Super Single Shot

Downsizer WSP Single Shot

BOND ARMS TEXAS DEFENDER DERRINGER
Caliber: From 22 LR to 45 LC/.410 shotshells. **Barrel:** 3". **Weight:** 20 oz. **Length:** 5". **Grips:** Rosewood. **Sights:** Blade front, fixed rear. **Features:** Interchangeable barrels, stainless steel firing pins, cross-bolt safety, automatic extractor for rimmed calibers. Stainless steel construction, brushed finish. Right or left hand.
Price: $399.00
Price: Interchangeable barrels, 22 LR thru 45 LC, 3" $139.00
Price: Interchangeable barrels, 45 LC, 3.5" .....$159.00 to $189.00

BOND ARMS RANGER
Caliber: 45 LC/.410 shotshells. **Barrel:** 4.25". **Weight:** 23.5 oz. **Length:** 6.25". **Features:** Similar to Snake Slayer except no trigger guard. Intr. 2008. From Bond Arms.
Price: $649.00

BOND ARMS CENTURY 2000 DEFENDER
Caliber: 45 LC/.410 shotshells. **Barrel:** 3.5". **Weight:** 21 oz. **Length:** 5.5". **Features:** Similar to Defender series.
Price: $420.00

BOND ARMS COWBOY DEFENDER
Caliber: From 22 LR to 45 LC/.410 shotshells. **Barrel:** 3". **Weight:** 19 oz. **Length:** 5.5". **Features:** Similar to Defender series. No trigger guard.
Price: $399.00

BOND ARMS SNAKE SLAYER
Caliber: 45 LC/.410 shotshell (2.5" or 3"). **Barrel:** 3.5". **Weight:** 21 oz. **Length:** 5.5". **Grips:** Extended rosewood. **Sights:** Blade front, fixed rear. **Features:** Single-action; interchangeable barrels; stainless steel firing pin. Introduced 2005.
Price: $469.00

BOND ARMS SNAKE SLAYER IV
Caliber: 45 LC/410 shotshell (2.5" or 3"). **Barrel:** 4.25". **Weight:** 22 oz. **Length:** 6.25". **Grips:** Extended rosewood. **Sights:** Blade front, fixed rear. **Features:** Single-action; interchangeable barrels; stainless steel firing pin. Introduced 2006.
Price: $499.00

CHARTER ARMS DIXIE DERRINGERS
Caliber: 22 LR, 22 WMR. **Barrel:** 1.125". **Weight:** 6 oz. **Length:** 4" overall. **Grips:** Black polymer **Sights:** Blade front, fixed notch rear. **Features:** Stainless finish. Introduced 2006. Made in U.S.A. by Charter Arms, distributed by MKS Supply.
Price: $215.00

COBRA BIG BORE DERRINGERS
Caliber: 22 WMR, 32 H&R Mag., 38 Spec., 9mm Para., 380 ACP. **Barrel:** 2.75". **Weight:** 14 oz. **Length:** 4.65" overall. **Grips:** Textured black or white synthetic or laminated rosewood. **Sights:** Blade front, fixed notch rear. **Features:** Alloy frame, steel-lined barrels, steel breech block. Plunger-type safety with integral hammer block. Black, chrome or satin finish. Introduced 2002. Made in U.S.A. by Cobra Enterprises of Utah, Inc.
Price: $165.00

COBRA LONG-BORE DERRINGERS
Caliber: 22 WMR, 38 Spec., 9mm Para. **Barrel:** 3.5". **Weight:** 16 oz. **Length:** 5.4" overall. **Grips:** Black or white synthetic or rosewood. **Sights:** Fixed. **Features:** Chrome, satin nickel, or black Teflon finish. Introduced 2002. Made in U.S.A. by Cobra Enterprises of Utah, Inc.
Price: $165.00

COBRA STANDARD SERIES DERRINGERS
Caliber: 22 LR, 22 WMR, 25 ACP, 32 ACP. **Barrel:** 2.4". **Weight:** 9.5 oz. **Length:** 4" overall. **Grips:** Laminated wood or pearl. **Sights:** Blade front, fixed notch rear. **Features:** Choice of black powder coat, satin nickel or chrome finish. Introduced 2002. Made in U.S.A. by Cobra Enterprises of Utah, Inc.
Price: $145.00

COMANCHE SUPER SINGLE-SHOT PISTOL
Caliber: 45 LC, .410 **Barrel:** 10". **Sights:** Adjustable. **Features:** Blue finish, not available for sale in CA, MA. Distributed by SGS Importers International, Inc.
Price: $200.00

MAXIMUM SINGLE-SHOT PISTOL
Caliber: 22 LR, 22 Hornet, 22 BR, 22 PPC, 223 Rem., 22-250, 6mm BR, 6mm PPC, 243, 250 Savage, 6.5mm-35M, 270 MAX, 270 Win., 7mm TCU, 7mm BR, 7mm-35, 7mm INT-R, 7mm-08, 7mm Rocket, 7mm Super-Mag., 30 Herrett, 30 Carbine, 30-30, 308 Win., 30x39, 32-20, 350 Rem. Mag., 357 Mag., 357 Maximum, 358 Win., 375 H&H, 44 Mag., 454 Casull. **Barrel:** 8.75", 10.5", 14". **Weight:** 61 oz. (10.5" bbl.); 78 oz. (14" bbl.) **Length:** 15", 18.5" overall (with 10.5" and 14" bbl., respectively). **Grips:** Smooth walnut stocks and forend. Also available with 17" finger groove grip. **Sights:** Ramp front, fully adjustable open rear. **Features:** Falling block action; drilled and tapped for M.O.A. scope mounts; integral grip frame/receiver; adjustable trigger; Douglas barrel (interchangeable). Introduced 1983. Made in U.S.A. by M.O.A. Corp.
Price: Stainless receiver, blue barrel $839.00
Price: Stainless receiver, stainless barrel $937.00

Prices given are believed to be accurate at time of publication however, many factors affect retail pricing so exact prices are not possible.

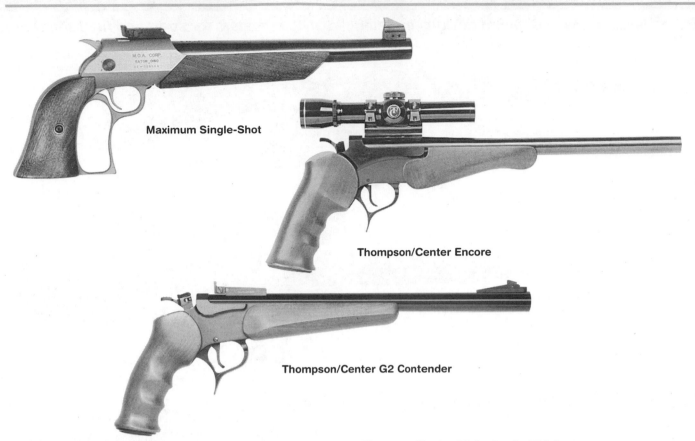

Maximum Single-Shot

Thompson/Center Encore

Thompson/Center G2 Contender

THOMPSON/CENTER ENCORE PISTOL
Caliber: 22-250, 223, 204 Ruger, 6.8 Rem., 260 Rem., 7mm-08, 243, 308, 270, 30-06, 375 JDJ, 204 Ruger, 44 Mag., 454 Casull, 480 Ruger, 444 Marlin single shot, 450 Marlin with muzzle tamer, no sights. **Barrel:** 12", 15", tapered round. **Weight:** NA. **Length:** 21" overall with 12" barrel. **Grips:** American walnut with finger grooves, walnut forend. **Sights:** Blade on ramp front, adjustable rear, or none. **Features:** Interchangeable barrels; action opens by squeezing the trigger guard; drilled and tapped for scope mounting; blue finish. Announced 1996. Made in U.S.A. by Thompson/Center Arms.
Price: $615.00

Thompson/Center G2 Contender Pistol
A second generation Contender pistol maintaining the same barrel interchangeability with older Contender barrels and their corresponding forends (except Herrett forend). The G2 frame will not accept old-style grips due to the change in grip angle. Incorporates an automatic hammer block safety with built-in interlock. Features include trigger adjustable for overtravel, adjustable rear sight; ramp front sight blade, blued steel finish.
Price: $600.00

Both classic arms and recent designs in American-style repeaters for sport and field shooting.

Armalite M15A2

Armalite AR-10A4

Armalite AR-180B

ARMALITE M15A2 CARBINE

Caliber: 223 Rem., 30-round magazine. **Barrel:** 16" heavy chrome lined; 1:9" twist. **Weight:** 7 lbs. **Length:** 35-11/16" overall. **Stock:** Green or black composition. **Sights:** Standard A2. **Features:** Upper and lower receivers have push-type pivot pin; hard coat anodized; A2-style forward assist; M16A2-type raised fence around magazine release button. Made in U.S.A. by ArmaLite, Inc.
Price: Green $1,150.00
Price: Black. $1,150.00

ARMALITE AR-10A4 SPECIAL PURPOSE RIFLE

Caliber: 308 Win., 10- and 20-round magazine. **Barrel:** 20" chrome-lined, 1:11.25" twist. **Weight:** 9.6 lbs. **Length:** 41" overall. **Stock:** Green or black composition. **Sights:** Detachable handle, front sight, or scope mount available; comes with international style flattop receiver with Picatinny rail. **Features:** Forged upper receiver with case deflector. Receivers are hard-coat anodized. Introduced 1995. Made in U.S.A. by ArmaLite, Inc.
Price: Green $1,557.00
Price: Black. $1,557.00

ArmaLite AR-10A2

Utilizing the same 20" double-lapped, heavy barrel as the ArmaLite AR10A4 Special Purpose Rifle. Offered in 308 Win. only. Made in U.S.A. by ArmaLite, Inc.
Price: AR-10A2 rifle or carbine $1,561.00

ARMALITE AR-10B RIFLE

Caliber: 308 Win. **Barrel:** 20" chrome lined. **Weight:** 9.5 lbs. **Length:** 41". **Stock:** Synthetic. **Sights:** Rear sight adjustable for windage, small and large apertures. **Features:** Early-style AR-10. Lower and upper receivers made of forged aircraft alloy. Brown Sudanese-style furniture, elevation scale window. Charging handle in carry handle. Made in U.S.A. by Armalite.
Price: $1,699.00

ARSENAL, INC. SLR-107F

Caliber: 7.62x39mm. **Barrel:** 16.25". **Weight:** 7.3 lbs. **Stock:** Left-side folding polymer stock. **Sights:** Adjustable rear. **Features:** Stamped receiver, 24mm flash hider, bayonet lug, accessory lug, stainless steel heat shield, two-stage trigger. Introduced 2008. Made in U.S.A. by Arsenal, Inc.
Price: SLR-107FR, includes scope rail. $1,035.00

ARSENAL, INC. SLR-107CR

Caliber: 7.62x39mm. **Barrel:** 16.25". **Weight:** 6.9 lbs. **Stock:** Left-side folding polymer stock. **Sights:** Adjustable rear. **Features:** Stamped receiver, front sight block/gas block combination, 500-meter rear sight, cleaning rod, stainless steel heat shield, scope rail, and removable muzzle attachment. Introduced 2007. Made in U.S.A. by Arsenal, Inc.
Price: SLR-107CR $1,200.00

ARSENAL, INC. SLR-106CR

Caliber: 5.56 NATO. **Barrel:** 16.25", Steyr chrome-lined barrel, 1:7 twist rate. **Weight:** 6.9 lbs. **Stock:** Black polymer folding stock with cutout for scope rail. Stainless-steel heatshield handguard. **Sights:** 500-meter rear sight and rear sight block calibrated for 5.56 NATO. Warsaw Pact scope rail. **Features:** Uses Arsenal, Bulgaria, Mil-Spec receiver, two-stage trigger, hammer and disconnector. Polymer magazines in 5- and 10-round capacity in black and green, with Arsenal logo. Others are 30-round black waffles, 20- and 30-round versions in clear/smoke waffle, featuring the "10" in a double-circle logo of Arsenal, Bulgaria. Ships with 5-round magazine, sling, cleaning kit in a tube, 16" cleaning rod, oil bottle. Introduced 2007. Made in U.S.A. by Arsenal, Inc.
Price: SLR-106CR $1,200.00

AUTO-ORDNANCE 1927A-1 THOMPSON

Caliber: 45 ACP. **Barrel:** 16.5". **Weight:** 13 lbs. **Length:** About 41" overall (Deluxe). **Stock:** Walnut stock and vertical forend. **Sights:** Blade front, open rear adjustable for windage. **Features:** Recreation of Thompson Model 1927. Semi-auto only. Deluxe model has finned barrel, adjustable rear sight and compensator; Standard model has plain barrel and military sight. From Auto-Ordnance Corp.
Price: Deluxe $1,420.00
Price: Lightweight model (9.5 lbs.) $1,145.00

Prices given are believed to be accurate at time of publication however, many factors affect retail pricing so exact prices are not possible.

Auto-Ordnance 1927A-1 Thompson

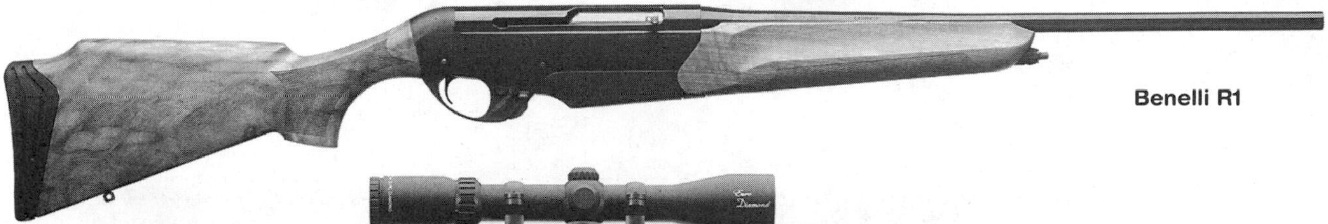

Benelli R1

Benelli R1 APG Camo

Barrett Model 82A-1

Beretta CX4 Carbine

Auto-Ordnance Thompson M1/M1-C

Similar to the 1927 A-1 except is in the M-1 configuration with side cocking knob, horizontal forend, smooth unfinned barrel, sling swivels on butt and forend. Matte-black finish. Introduced 1985.
Price: M1 semi-auto carbine **$1,334.00**
Price: M1-C lightweight semi-auto **$1,065.00**

Auto-Ordnance 1927 A-1 Commando

Similar to the 1927 A-1 except has Parkerized finish, black-finish wood butt, pistol grip, horizontal forend. Comes with black nylon sling. Introduced 1998. Made in U.S.A. by Auto-Ordnance Corp.
Price: T1-C **$1,393.00**

BARRETT MODEL 82A-1 SEMI-AUTOMATIC RIFLE

Caliber: 50 BMG, 10-shot detachable box magazine. **Barrel:** 29". **Weight:** 28.5 lbs. **Length:** 57" overall. **Stock:** Composition with energy-absorbing recoil pad. **Sights:** Scope optional. **Features:** Semi-automatic, recoil operated with recoiling barrel. Three-lug locking bolt; muzzle brake. Adjustable bipod. Introduced 1985. Made in U.S.A. by Barrett Firearms.
Price: From **$8,900.00**

BENELLI R1 RIFLE

Caliber: 300 Win. Mag., 300 WSM, 270 WSM (24" barrel); 30-06 Spfl., 308 Win. (22" barrel); 300 Win. Mag., 30-06 Spfl., (20" barrel). **Weight:** 7.1 lbs. **Length:** 43.75" to 45.75". **Stock:** Select satin walnut or synthetic. **Sights:** None. **Features:** Auto-regulating gas-operated system, three-lug rotary bolt, interchangeable barrels, optional recoil pads. Introduced 2003. Imported from Italy by Benelli USA.
Price: Synthetic with ComforTech gel recoil pad **$1,549.00**
Price: Satin walnut **$1,379.00**
Price: APG HD camo, 30-06 (2008) **$1,689.00**

BERETTA CX4/PX4 STORM CARBINE

Caliber: 9mm Para., 40 S&W, 45 ACP. **Weight:** 5.75 lbs. **Barrel Length:** 16.6", chrome lined, rate of twist 1:16 (40 S&W) or 1:10 (9mm Para.). **Length:** NA. **Stock:** Black synthetic. **Sights:** NA. **Features:** Introduced 2005. Imported from Italy by Beretta USA.
Price: **$900.00**

Browning Mark II Safari

Browning BAR Shorttrac Mossy Oak

Browning BAR LongTrac Digital Green

Browning Lightweight Stalker

Browning Lightweight Stalker

BROWNING BAR SAFARI AND SAFARI W/BOSS SEMI-AUTO RIFLES

Caliber: Safari: 243 Win., 25-06 Rem., 270 Win., 7mm Rem. Mag.., 30-06 Spfl., 308 Win., 300 Win. Mag., 338 Win. Mag. Safari w/BOSS: 270 Win., 7mm Rem. Mag., 30-06 Spfl., 300 Win. Mag., 338 Win. Mag., plus 270 WSM, 7mm WSM, 300 WSM. **Barrel:** 22-24" round tapered. **Weight:** 7.4-8.2 lbs. **Length:** 43-45" overall. **Stock:** French walnut pistol grip stock and forend, hand checkered. **Sights:** No sights. **Features:** Has new bolt release lever; removable trigger assembly with larger trigger guard; redesigned gas and buffer systems. Detachable 4-round box magazine. Scroll-engraved receiver is tapped for scope mounting. BOSS barrel vibration modulator and muzzle brake system available. Mark II Safari introduced 1993. Imported from Belgium by Browning.
Price: BAR MK II Safari, from **$1,109.00**
Price: BAR Safari w/BOSS, from **$1,229.00**

BROWNING BAR SHORTTRAC/LONGTRAC AUTO RIFLES

Caliber: (ShortTrac models) 270 WSM, 7mm WSM, 300 WSM, 243 Win., 308 Win., 325 WSM; (LongTrac models) 270 Win., 30-06 Spfl., 7mm Rem. Mag., 300 Win. Mag. **Barrel:** 23". **Weight:** 6 lbs. 10 oz. to 7 lbs. 4 oz. **Length:** 41.5" to 44". **Stock:** Satin-finish walnut, pistol-grip, fluted forend. **Sights:** Adj. rear, bead front standard, no sights on BOSS models (optional). **Features:** Designed to handle new WSM chamberings. Gas-operated, blued finish, rotary bolt design (LongTrac models).
Price: BAR ShortTrac, 243 Win., 308 Win. from **$1,079.00**
Price: BAR ShortTrac Left-Hand, intr. 2007, from **$1,129.00**

Price: BAR ShortTrac Mossy Oak New Break-up
. . . . **$1,249.00 to $1,349.00**
Price: BAR LongTrac Left Hand, 270 Win., 30-06 Spfl.,
from **$1,129.00**
Price: BAR LongTrac, from. **$1,079.00**
Price: BAR LongTrac Mossy Oak Break Up, intr. 2007,
from **$1,249.00**
Price: Bar LongTrac, Digital Green camo (2009)
. . . . **$1,247.00 to $1,347.00**

BROWNING BAR STALKER AUTO RIFLES

Caliber: 243 Win., 308 Win., 270 Win., 30-06 Spfl., 270 WSM, 7mm WSM, 300 WSM, 300 Win. Mag., 338 Win. Mag. **Barrel:** 20-24". **Weight:** 7.1-7.75 LBS. **Length:** 41-45" overall. **Stock:** Black composite stock and forearm. **Sights:** Hooded front and adjustable rear. **Features:** Gas-operated action with seven-lug rotary bolt; dual action bars; 2-, 3- or 4-shot magazine (depending on cartridge). Introduced 2001. Imported by Browning.
Price: BAR ShortTrac or LongTrac Stalker, from **$1,119.00**
Price: BAR Lightweight Stalker, from **$1,099.00**

BUSHMASTER SUPERLIGHT CARBINES

Caliber: 223 Rem., 30-shot magazine. **Barrel:** 16", heavy; 1:9" twist. **Weight:** 6.25 lbs. **Length:** 31.25-34.5" overall. **Stock:** 6-position telestock or Stubby (7.25" length). **Sights:** Fully adjustable M16A2 sight system. **Features:** Adapted from original G.I. pencil-barrel profile. Chrome-lined barrel with manganese phosphate finish. "Shorty" handguards. Has forged aluminum receivers with pushpin. Made in U.S.A. by Bushmaster Firearms, Inc.
Price: From **$1, 250.00**

Prices given are believed to be accurate at time of publication however, many factors affect retail pricing so exact prices are not possible.

**Bushmaster XM15
E2S Carbine**

Bushmaster Varminter

Bushmaster XM15 E2S Dissipator Carbine
Similar to the XM15 E2S Shorty carbine except has full-length "Dissipator" handguards. Weighs 7.6 lbs.; 34.75" overall; forged aluminum receivers with push-pin style takedown. Made in U.S.A. by Bushmaster Firearms, Inc.
Price: From **$1,240.00**

Bushmaster XM15 E25 AK Shorty Carbine
Similar to the XM15 E2S Shorty except has 14.5" barrel with an AK muzzle brake permanently attached giving 16" barrel length. Weighs 7.3 lbs. Introduced 1999. Made in U.S.A. by Bushmaster Firearms, Inc.
Price: From **$1,215.00**

Bushmaster M4 Post-Ban Carbine
Similar to the XM15 E2S except has 14.5" barrel with Mini Y compensator, and fixed telestock. MR configuration has fixed carry handle.
Price: **$1,190.00**

BUSHMASTER VARMINTER RIFLE
Caliber: 223 Rem., 5-shot. **Barrel:** 24", 1:9" twist, fluted, heavy, stainless. **Weight:** 8.75 lbs. **Length:** 42.25". **Stock:** Rubberized pistol grip. **Sights:** 1/2" scope risers. **Features:** Gas-operated, semi-auto, two-stage trigger, slotted free floater forend, lockable hard case.
Price: **$1,360.00**
Price: Bushmaster Predator: 20" 1:8 barrel, 223 Rem. **$1,245.00**
Price: Bushmaster Stainless Varmint Special: Same as
Varminter but with 24" stainless barrel **$1,277.00**

BUSHMASTER 6.8 SPC CARBINE
Caliber: 6.8 SPC, 26-shot mag. **Barrel:** 16" M4 profile. **Weight:** 6.57 lbs. **Length:** 32.75" overall. **Features:** Semi-auto AR-style with Izzy muzzle brake, six-position telestock. Available in A2 (fixed carry handle) or A3 (removable carry handle) configuration.
Price: **$1,500.00**

BUSHMASTER ORC CARBINE
Caliber: 5.56/223. **Barrel:** 16" M4 profile. **Weight:** 6 lbs. **Length:** 32.5" overall. **Features:** AR-style carbine with chrome-lined barrel, fixed carry handle, receiver-length picatinny optics rail, heavy oval M4-style handguards.
Price: **$1,085.00**

BUSHMASTER 11.5" BARREL CARBINE
Caliber: 5.56/223, 30-shot mag. **Barrel:** 11.5". **Weight:** 6.46 lbs. or 6.81 lbs. **Length:** 31.625" overall. **Features:** AR-style carbine with chrome-lined barrel with permanently attached BATF-approved 5.5" flash suppressor, fixed or removable carry handle, optional optics rail.
Price: **$1,215.00**

BUSHMASTER HEAVY-BARRELED CARBINE
Caliber: 5.56/223. **Barrel:** 16". **Weight:** 6.93 lbs. to 7.28 lbs. **Length:** 32.5" overall. **Features:** AR-style carbine with chrome-lined heavy profile vanadium steel barrel, fixed or removable carry handle, six-position telestock.
Price: **$1,215.00**

BUSHMASTER MODULAR CARBINE
Caliber: 5.56/223, 30-shot mag. **Barrel:** 16". **Weight:** 7.3 lbs. **Length:** 36.25" overall. **Features:** AR-style carbine with chrome-lined chrome-moly vanadium steel barrel, skeleton stock or six-position telestock, clamp-on front sight and detachable flip-up dual aperature rear.
Price: **$1,745.00**

BUSHMASTER CARBON 15 TOP LOADER RIFLE
Caliber: 5.56/223, internal 10-shot mag. **Barrel:** 16" chrome-lined M4 profile. **Weight:** 5.8 lbs. **Length:** 32.75" overall. **Features:** AR-style carbine with standard A2 front sight, dual aperture rear sight, receiver-length optics rail, lightweight carbon fiber receiver, six-position telestock. Will not accept detachable box magazines.
Price: **$1,070.00**

BUSHMASTER CARBON 15 FLAT-TOP CARBINE
Caliber: 5.56/223, 30-shot mag. **Barrel:** 16" M4 profile. **Weight:** 5.77 lbs. **Length:** 32.75" overall. **Features:** AR-style carbine Izzy flash suppressor, AR-type front sight, dual aperture flip, lightweight carbon composite receiver with receiver-length optics rail.
Price: **$1,155.00**
Price: Carbon 15 9mm, chambered in 9mm Parabellum . . . **$1,025.00**

BUSHMASTER 450 RIFLE AND CARBINE
Caliber: 450 Bushmaster. **Barrel:** 20" (rifle), 16" (carbine), five-round mag. **Weight:** 8.3 lbs. (rifle), 8.1 lbs. (carbine). **Length:** 39.5" overall (rifle), 35.25" overall (carbine). **Features:** AR-style with chrome-lined chrome-moly barrel, synthetic stock, Izzy muzzle brake.
Price: **$1,350.00**

BUSHMASTER GAS PISTON RIFLE
Caliber: 223, 30-shot mag. **Barrel:** 16". **Weight:** 7.46 lbs. **Length:** 32.5" overall. **Features:** Semi-auto AR-style with telescoping stock, carry handle, piston assembly rather than direct gas impingement.
Price: **$1,795.00**

BUSHMASTER TARGET RIFLE
Caliber: 5.56/223, 30-shot mag. **Barrel:** 20" or 24" heavy or standard. **Weight:** 8.43 lbs. to 9.29 lbs. **Length:** 39.5" or 43.5" overall. **Features:** Semi-auto AR-style with chrome-lined or stainless steel 1:9 barrel, fixed or removable carry handle, manganese phosphate finish.
Price: **$1,195.00**

BUSHMASTER M4A3 TYPE CARBINE
Caliber: 5.56/223, 30-shot mag. **Barrel:** 16". **Weight:** 6.22 to 6.7 lbs. **Length:** 31" to 32.5" overall. **Features:** AR-style carbine with chrome-moly vanadium steel barrel, Izzy-type flash-hider, six-position telestock, various sight options, standard or multi-rail handguard, fixed or removable carry handle.
Price: **$1,270.00**
Price: Patrolman's Carbine: Standard mil-style sights **$1,270.00**
Price: State Compliance Carbine: Compliant with various state regulations **$1,270.00**

Century International AES-10 Hi-Cap with bipod

Century International WASR-10 Hi-Cap

Century International WASR-2 Hi-Cap

Century International M70AB2 Sporter

CENTURY INTERNATIONAL AES-10 HI-CAP RIFLE
Caliber: 7.62x39mm. 30-shot magazine. **Barrel:** 23.2". **Weight:** NA. **Length:** 41.5" overall. **Stock:** Wood grip, forend. **Sights:** Fixed-notch rear, windage-adjustable post front. **Features:** RPK-style, accepts standard double-stack AK-type mags. Side-mounted scope mount, integral carry handle, bipod. Imported by Century Arms Int'l.
Price: AES-10, from $450.00

CENTURY INTERNATIONAL GP WASR-10 HI-CAP RIFLE
Caliber: 7.62x39mm. 30-shot magazine. **Barrel:** 16.25", 1:10 right-hand twist. **Weight:** 7.2 lbs. **Length:** 34.25" overall. **Stock:** Wood laminate or composite, grip, forend. **Sights:** Fixed-notch rear, windage-adjustable post front. **Features:** Two 30-rd. detachable box magazines, cleaning kit, bayonet. Version of AKM rifle; U.S.-parts added for BATFE compliance. Threaded muzzle, folding stock, bayonet lug, compensator, Dragunov stock available. Made in Romania by Cugir Arsenal. Imported by Century Arms Int'l.
Price: GP WASR-10, from $350.00

CENTURY INTERNATIONAL WASR-2 HI-CAP RIFLE
Caliber: 5.45x39mm. 30-shot magazine. **Barrel:** 16.25". **Weight:** 7.5 lbs. **Length:** 34.25" overall. **Stocks:** Wood laminate. **Sights:** Fixed-notch rear, windage-adjustable post front. **Features:** 1 30-rd. detachable box magazine, cleaning kit, sling. WASR-3 HI-CAP chambered in 223 Rem. Imported by Century Arms Int'l.
Price: GP WASR-2/3, from $250.00

CENTURY INTERNATIONAL M70AB2 SPORTER RIFLE
Caliber: 7.62x39mm. 30-shot magazine. **Barrel:** 16.25". **Weight:** 7.5 lbs. **Length:** 34.25" overall. **Stocks:** Metal grip, wood forend. **Sights:** Fixed-notch rear, windage-adjustable post front. **Features:** 2 30-rd. double-stack magazine, cleaning kit, compensator, bayonet lug and bayonet. Paratrooper-style Kalashnikov with under-folding stock. Imported by Century Arms Int'l.
Price: M70AB2, from $480.00

COLT MATCH TARGET MODEL RIFLE
Caliber: 223 Rem., 5-shot magazine. **Barrel:** 16.1" or 20". **Weight:** 7.1 to 8.5 lbs. **Length:** 34.5" to 39" overall. **Stock:** Composition stock, grip, forend. **Sights:** Post front, rear adjustable for windage and elevation. **Features:** 5-round detachable box magazine, flash suppressor, sling swivels. Forward bolt assist included. Introduced 1991. Made in U.S.A. by Colt's Mfg. Co., Inc.
Price: Match Target HBAR MT6601 . . . .$1,182.00

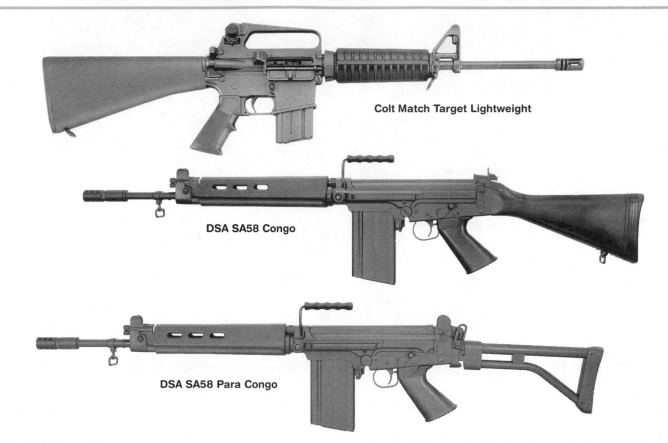

Colt Match Target Lightweight

DSA SA58 Congo

DSA SA58 Para Congo

Colt Match Target M4
Similar to above but with carbine-length barrel.
Price: . . . . **NA**

DPMS PANTHER ARMS AR-15 RIFLES
Caliber: 223 Rem., 7.62x39. **Barrel:** 16" to 24". **Weight:** 7.75 to 11.75 lbs. **Length:** 34.5" to 42.25" overall. **Stock:** Black Zytel composite. **Sights:** Square front post, adjustable A2 rear. **Features:** Steel or stainless steel heavy or bull barrel; hardcoat anodized receiver; aluminum free-float tube handguard; many options. From DPMS Panther Arms.
Price: Panther Bull Twenty (20" stainless bull bbl.) **$920.00**
Price: Arctic Panther. **$1,099.00**
Price: Panther Classic **$799.00**
Price: Panther Bull Sweet Sixteen (16" stainless bull bbl.) . . .**$885.00**
Price: DCM Panther (20" stainless heavy bbl., n.m. sights) **$1,099.00**
Price: Panther 7.62x39 (20" steel heavy bbl.) **$859.00**

DPMS PANTHER ARMS CLASSIC AUTO RIFLE
Caliber: 5.56x45mm. **Barrel:** Heavy 16" to 20" w/flash hider. **Weight:** 7 to 9 lbs. **Length:** 34-11/16" to 38-7/16". **Sights:** Adj. rear and front. **Stock:** Black Zytel w/trap door assembly. **Features:** Gas operated rotating bolt, mil spec or Teflon black finish.
Price: Panther A2 Tactical 16" **$814.00**
Price: Panther Lite 16 . . . .**$725.00**
Price: Panther Carbine **$799.00**
Price: Panther The Agency Rifle. **$1,999.00**

DSA Z4 GTC CARBINE WITH C.R.O.S.
Caliber: 5.56 NATO **Barrel:** 16" 1:9 twist M4 profile fluted chrome lined heavy barrel with threaded Vortec flash hider. **Weight:** 7.6 lbs. **Stock:** 6 position collapsible M4 stock, Predator P4X free float tactical rail. **Sights:** Chrome lined Picatinny gas block w/removable front sight. **Features:** The Corrosion Resistant Operating System incorporates the new P.O.F. Gas Trap System with removable gas plug eliminates problematic features of standard AR gas system, Forged 7075T6 DSA lower receiver. Introduced 2006. Made in U.S.A. by DSA, Inc.
Price: **$1,800.00**

DSA CQB MRP, STANDARD MRP
Caliber: 5.56 NATO **Barrel:** 16" or 18" 1:7 twist chrome-lined or stainless steel barrel with A2 flash hider **Stock:** 6 position collapsible M4 stock. **Features:** LMT 1/2" MRP upper receiver with 20.5" Standard quad rail or 16.5" CQB quad rail, LMT-enhanced bolt with dual extractor springs, free float barrel, quick change barrel system, forged 7075T6 DSA lower receiver. EOTech and vertical grip additional. Introduced 2006. Made in U.S.A. by DSA, Inc.
Price: CQB MRP w/16" chrome-lined barrel **$2,420.00**
Price: CQB MRP w/16" stainless steel barrel **$2,540.00**
Price: Standard MRP w/16" chrome-lined barrel **$2,620.00**
Price: Standard MRP w/16" or 18" stainless steel barrel . . . **$2,740.00**

DSA STD CARBINE
Caliber: 5.56 NATO. **Barrel:** 16" 1:9 twist D4 w/A2 flash hider. **Weight:** 6.25 lbs. **Length:** 31". **Stock:** A2 buttstock, D4 handguard w/heatshield. **Sights:** Forged A2 front sight with lug. **Features:** Forged 7075T6 DSA lower receiver, forged A2 or flattop upper receiver. Introduced 2006. Made in U.S.A. by DSA, Inc.
Price: A2 or Flattop STD Carbine **$1,025.00**
Price: With LMT SOPMOD stock **$1,267.00**

DSA 1R CARBINE
Caliber: 5.56 NATO. **Barrel:** 16" 1:9 twist D4 w/A2 flash hider. **Weight:** 6.25 lbs. **Length:** Variable. **Stock:** 6 position collapsible M4 stock, D4 handguard w/heatshield. **Sights:** Forged A2 front sight with lug. **Features:** Forged 7075T6 DSA lower receiver, forged A2 or flattop upper receiver. Introduced 2006. Made in U.S.A. by DSA, Inc.
Price: A2 or Flattop 1R Carbine **$1,055.00**
Price: With VLTOR ModStock **$1,175.00**

DSA XM CARBINE
Caliber: 5.56 NATO. **Barrel:** 11.5" 1:9 twist D4 with 5.5" permanently attached flash hider. **Weight:** 6.25 lbs. **Length:** Variable. **Stock:** Collapsible, Handguard w/heatshield. **Sights:** Forged A2 front sight with lug. **Features:** Forged 7075T6 DSA lower receiver, forged A2 upper receiver. Introduced 2006. Made in U.S.A. by DSA, Inc.
Price: **$1,055.00**

DSA STANDARD
Caliber: 5.56 NATO. **Barrel:** 20" 1:9 twist heavy barrel w/A2 flash hider. **Weight:** 6.25 lbs. **Length:** 38-7/16". **Stock:** A2 buttstock, A2 handguard w/heatshield. **Sights:** Forged A2 front sight with lug. **Features:** Forged 7075T6 DSA lower receiver, forged A2 or flattop upper receiver. Introduced 2006. Made in U.S.A. by DSA, Inc.
Price: A2 or Flattop Standard **$1,025.00**

DSA SA58 Gray Wolf

DSA SA58 Predator

DSA SA58 T48

DSA SA58 G1

DSA DCM RIFLE
Caliber: 223 Wylde Chamber. **Barrel:** 20" 1:8 twist chrome moly match grade Badger Barrel. **Weight:** 10 lbs. **Length:** 39.5". **Stock:** DCM freefloat handguard system, A2 buttstock. **Sights:** Forged A2 front sight with lug. **Features:** NM two stage trigger, NM rear sight, forged 7075T6 DSA lower receiver, forged A2 upper receiver. Introduced 2006. Made in U.S.A. by DSA, Inc.
Price: **$1,520.00**

DSA S1
Caliber: 223 Rem. Match Chamber. **Barrel:** 16", 20" or 24" 1:8 twist stainless steel bull barrel. **Weight:** 8.0, 9.5 and 10 lbs. **Length:** 34.25", 38.25" and 42.25". **Stock:** A2 buttstock with free float aluminum handguard. **Sights:** Picatinny gas block sight base. **Features:** Forged 7075T6 DSA lower receiver, Match two stage trigger, forged flattop upper receiver, fluted barrel optional. Introduced 2006. Made in U.S.A. by DSA, Inc.
Price: **$1,155.00**

DSA SA58 CONGO, PARA CONGO
Caliber: 308 Win. **Barrel:** 18" w/short Belgian short flash hider. **Weight:** 8.6 lbs. (Congo); 9.85 lbs. (Para Congo). **Length:** 39.75" **Stock:** Synthetic w/military grade furniture (Congo); Synthetic with non-folding steel para stock (Para Congo). **Sights:** Elevation adjustable protected post front sight, windage adjustable rear peep (Congo); Belgian type Para Flip Rear (Para Congo). **Features:** Fully-adjustable gas system, high-grade steel upper receiver with carry handle. Made in U.S.A. by DSA, Inc.
Price: Congo. **$1,850.00**
Price: Para Congo **$2,095.00**

DSA SA58 GRAY WOLF
Caliber: 308 Win. **Barrel:** 21" match-grade bull w/target crown. **Weight:** 13 lbs. **Length:** 41.75". **Stock:** Synthetic. **Sights:** Elevation-adjustable post front sight, windage-adjustable match rear peep. **Features:** Fully-adjustable gas system, high-grade steel upper receiver, Picatinny scope mount, DuraCoat finish. Made in U.S.A. by DSA, Inc.
Price: **$2,120.00**

DSA SA58 PREDATOR
Caliber: 243 Win., 260 Rem., 308 Win. **Barrel:** 16" and 19" w/target crown. **Weight:** 9 to 9.3 lbs. **Length:** 36.25" to 39.25". **Stock:** Green synthetic. **Sights:** Elevation-adjustable post front; windage-adjustable match rear peep. **Features:** Fully-adjustable gas system, high-grade steel upper receiver, Picatinny scope mount, DuraCoat solid and camo finishes. Made in U.S.A. by DSA, Inc.
Price: 243 Win., 260 Rem. **$1,695.00**
Price: 308 Win. **$1,640.00**

DSA SA58 T48
Caliber: 308 Win. **Barrel:** 21" with Browning long flash hider. **Weight:** 9.3 lbs. **Length:** 44.5". **Stock:** European walnut. **Sights:** Elevation-adjustable post front, windage adjustable rear peep. **Features:** Gas-operated semi-auto with fully adjustable gas system, high grade steel upper receiver with carry handle. DuraCoat finishes. Made in U.S.A. by DSA, Inc.
Price: **$1,995.00**

Prices given are believed to be accurate at time of publication however, many factors affect retail pricing so exact prices are not possible.

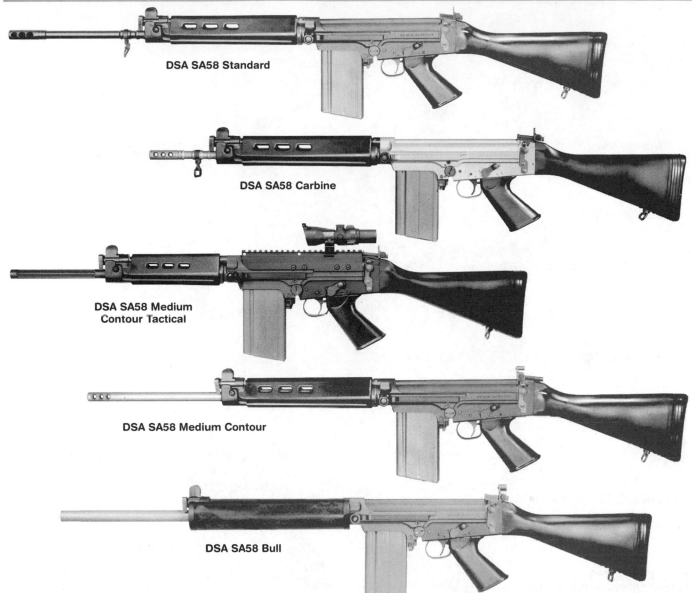

DSA SA58 Standard

DSA SA58 Carbine

DSA SA58 Medium Contour Tactical

DSA SA58 Medium Contour

DSA SA58 Bull

DSA SA58 G1

Caliber: 308 Win. **Barrel:** 21" with quick-detach flash hider. **Weight:** 10.65 lbs. **Length:** 44". **Stock:** Steel bipod cut handguard with hardwood stock and synthetic pistol grip. **Sights:** Elevation-adjustable post front, windage adjustable rear peep. **Features:** Gas-operated semi-auto with fully adjustable gas system, high grade steel upper receiver with carry handle, original GI steel lower receiver with GI bipod. DuraCoat finishes. Made in U.S.A. by DSA, Inc.
Price: **$1,850.00**

DSA SA58 STANDARD

Caliber: 308 Win. **Barrel:** 21" bipod cut w/threaded flash hider. **Weight:** 8.75 lbs. **Length:** 43". **Stock:** Synthetic, X-Series or optional folding para stock. **Sights:** Elevation-adjustable post front, windage-adjustable rear peep. **Features:** Fully adjustable short gas system, high grade steel or 416 stainless upper receiver. Made in U.S.A. by DSA, Inc.
Price: High-grade steel **$1,595.00**
Price: Folding para stock **$1,845.00**

DSA SA58 CARBINE

Caliber: 308 Win. **Barrel:** 16.25" bipod cut w/threaded flash hider. **Weight:** 8.35 lbs. **Length:** 37.5". **Stock:** Synthetic, X-Series or optional folding para stock. **Sights:** Elevation-adjustable post front, windage-adjustable rear peep. **Features:** Fully adjustable short gas system, high grade steel or 416 stainless upper receiver. Made in U.S.A. by DSA, Inc.
Price: High-grade steel **$1,595.00**
Price: Stainless steel **$1,850.00**

DSA SA58 TACTICAL CARBINE

Caliber: 308 Win. **Barrel:** 16.25" fluted with A2 flash hidor. **Weight:** 8.25 lbs. **Length:** 36.5". **Stock:** Synthetic, X-Series or optional folding para stock. **Sights:** Elevation-adjustable post front, windage-adjustable match rear peep. **Features:** Shortened fully adjustable short gas system, high grade steel or 416 stainless upper receiver. Made in U.S.A. by DSA, Inc.
Price: High-grade steel **$1,595.00**
Price: Stainless steel **$1,850.00**

DSA SA58 MEDIUM CONTOUR

Caliber: 308 Win. **Barrel:** 21" w/threaded flash hider. **Weight:** 9.75 lbs. **Length:** 43". **Stock:** Synthetic military grade. **Sights:** Elevation-adjustable post front, windage-adjustable match rear peep. **Features:** Gas-operated semi-auto with fully adjustable gas system, high grade steel receiver. Made in U.S.A. by DSA, Inc.
Price: **$1,595.00**

DSA SA58 BULL BARREL RIFLE

Caliber: 308 Win. **Barrel:** 21". **Weight:** 11.1 lbs. **Length:** 41.5". **Stock:** Synthetic, free floating handguard. **Sights:** Elevation-adjustable windage-adjustable post front, match rear peep. **Features:** Gas-operated semi-auto with fully adjustable gas system, high grade steel or stainless upper receiver. Made in U.S.A. by DSA, Inc.
Price: **$1,745.00**
Price: Stainless steel **$1,995.00**

CENTERFIRE RIFLES—Autoloaders

DSA SA58 OSW

Excel Arms Accelerator

Heckler & Koch USC

Hi-Point Carbine

Les Baer Flattop

DSA SA58 MINI OSW
Caliber: 308 Win. **Barrel:** 11" or 13" w/ A2 flash hider. **Weight:** 9 to 9.35 lbs. **Length:** 32.75" to 35". **Stock:** Fiberglass reinforced short synthetic handguard, para folding stock and synthetic pistol grip. **Sights:** Adjustable post front, para rear sight. **Features:** Semi-auto or select fire with fully adjustable short gas system, optional FAL rail handguard, SureFire Vertical Foregrip System, EOTech HOLOgraphic Sight and ITC cheekrest. Made in U.S.A. by DSA, Inc.
Price: $1,845.00

EXCEL ARMS ACCELERATOR RIFLES
Caliber: 17 HMR, 22 WMR, 17M2, 22 LR, 9-shot magazine. **Barrel:** 18" fluted stainless steel bull barrel. **Weight:** 8 lbs. **Length:** 32.5" overall. **Grips:** Textured black polymer. **Sights:** Fully adjustable target sights. **Features:** Made from 17-4 stainless steel, aluminum shroud w/ Weaver rail, manual safety, firing-pin block, last-round bolt-hold-open feature. Four packages with various equipment available. American made, lifetime warranty. Comes with one 9-round stainless steel magazine and a California-approved cable lock. Introduced 2006. Made in U.S.A. by Excel Arms.
Price: MR-17 17 HMR. $488.00
Price: MR-22 22 WMR $523.00

HECKLER & KOCH USC CARBINE
Caliber: 45 ACP, 10-shot magazine. **Barrel:** 16". **Weight:** 8.6 lb. **Length:** 35.4" overall. **Stock:** Skeletonized polymer thumbhole. **Sights:** Blade front with integral hood, fully adjustable diopter. **Features:** Based on German UMP submachine gun. Blowback operation; almost entirely constructed of carbon fiber-reinforced polymer. Free-floating heavy target barrel. Introduced 2000. From H&K.
Price: $1,249.00

HI-POINT 9MM CARBINE
Caliber: 9mm Para., 40 S&W, 10-shot magazine. **Barrel:** 16.5" (17.5" for 40 S&W). **Weight:** 4.5 lbs. **Length:** 31.5" overall. **Stock:** Black polymer, camouflage. **Sights:** Protected post front, aperture rear. Integral scope mount. **Features:** Grip-mounted magazine release. Black or chrome finish. Sling swivels. Available with laser or red dot sights. Introduced 1996. Made in U.S.A. by MKS Supply, Inc.
Price: 995-B (black) $220.00
Price: 995-CMO (camo) $235.00

LES BAER CUSTOM ULTIMATE AR 223 RIFLES
Caliber: 223. **Barrel:** 18", 20", 22", 24". **Weight:** 7.75 to 9.75 lb. **Length:** NA. **Stock:** Black synthetic. **Sights:** None furnished; Picatinny-style flattop rail for scope mounting. **Features:** Forged receiver; Ultra single-stage trigger (Jewell two-stage trigger optional); titanium firing pin; Versa-Pod bipod; chromed National Match carrier; stainless steel, hand-lapped and cryo-treated barrel; guaranteed to shoot 1/2 or 3/4 MOA, depending on model. Made in U.S.A. by Les Baer Custom Inc.
Price: Super Varmint Model $2,390.00
Price: Super Match Model (introduced 2006) $2,490.00
Price: M4 Flattop model $2,360.00
Price: Police Special 16" (2008) $1,690.00
Price: IPSC Action Model $2,640.00

Prices given are believed to be accurate at time of publication however, many factors affect retail pricing so exact prices are not possible.

Les Baer IPSC

Olympic Arms K9 Carbine

Olympic Arms K3B

Olympic Arms Plinker Plus AR15

LR 300 RIFLES
Caliber: 5.56 NATO, 30-shot magazine. **Barrel:** 16.5"; 1:9" twist. **Weight:** 7.4-7.8 lbs. **Length:** NA. **Stock:** Folding. **Sights:** YHM flip front and rear. **Features:** Flattop receive, full length top picatinny rail. Phantom flash hider, multi sling mount points, field strips with no tools. Made in U.S.A. from Z-M Weapons.
Price: AXL, AXLT **$2,139.00**
Price: NXL **$2,208.00**

MERKEL MODEL SR1 SEMI-AUTOMATIC RIFLE
Caliber: 308 Win., 300 Win Mag. **Features:** Streamlined profile, checkered walnut stock and forend, 19.7- (308) or 20-8" (300 SM) barrel, two- or five-shot detachable box magazine. Adjustable front and rear iron sights with Weaver-style optics rail included. Imported from Germany by Merkel USA.
Price: **$1,595.00**

OLYMPIC ARMS K9, K10, K40, K45 PISTOL-CALIBER AR15 CARBINES
Caliber: 9mm Para., 10mm, 40 S&W, 45 ACP; 32/10-shot modified magazines. **Barrel:** 16" button rifled stainless steel, 1x16 twist rate. **Weight:** 6.73 lbs. **Length:** 31.625" overall. **Stock:** A2 grip, M4 6-point collapsible stock. **Features:** A2 upper with adjustable rear sight, elevation adjustable front post, bayonet lug, sling swivel, threaded muzzle, flash suppressor, carbine length handguards. Made in U.S.A. by Olympic Arms, Inc.
Price: K9GL, 9mm Para., Glock lower **$1,092.00**
Price: K10, 10mm, modified 10-round Uzi magazine **$1,006.20**
Price: K40, 40 S&W, modified 10-round Uzi magazine **$1,006.20**
Price: K45, 45 ACP, modified 10-round Uzi magazine **$1,006.20**

OLYMPIC ARMS K3B SERIES AR15 CARBINES
Caliber: 5.56 NATO, 30-shot magazines. **Barrel:** 16" button rifled chrome-moly steel, 1x9 twist rate. **Weight:** 5-7 lbs. **Length:** 31.75" overall. **Stock:** A2 grip, M4 6-point collapsible buttstock. **Features:** A2 upper with adjustable rear sight, elevation adjustable front post, bayonet lug, sling swivel, threaded muzzle, flash suppressor, carbine length handguards. Made in U.S.A. by Olympic Arms, Inc.
Price: K3B base model, A2 upper. **$815.00**
Price: K3B-M4 M4 contoured barrel & handguards **$1,038.70**
Price: K3B-M4-A3-TC A3 upper, M4 barrel, FIRSH rail handguard. **$1,246.70**
Price: K3B-CAR 11.5" barrel with 5.5" permanent flash suppressor **$968.50**
Price: K3B-FAR 16" featherweight contoured barrel **$1,006.20**

OLYMPIC ARMS PLINKER PLUS AR15 MODELS
Caliber: 5.56 NATO, 30-shot magazine. Barrel 16" or 20" button-rifled chrome-moly steel, 1x9 twist. **Weight:** 7.5-8.5 lbs. **Length:** 35.5"-39.5" overall. **Stock:** A2 grip, A2 buttstock with trapdoor. **Sights:** A1 windage rear, elevation-adjustable front post. **Features:** A1 upper, fiberlite handguards, bayonet lug, threaded muzzle and flash suppressor. Made in U.S.A. by Olympic Arms, Inc.
Price: Plinker Plus. **$713.70**
Price: Plinker Plus 20 . . . . **$843.70**

Olympic Arms Plinker Plus 20

Ruger Mini-14/5 Ranch

Ruger Mini-14 ATI Stock

Ruger Mini-14 Tactical

REMINGTON MODEL R-15 MODULAR REPEATING RIFLE
Caliber: 223 and 30 Rem. AR, five-shot magazine. **Barrel:** 18" (carbine), 22", 24". **Weight:** 6.75 to 7.75 lbs. **Length:** 36.25" to 42.25". **Stock:** Camo. **Features:** AR-style with optics rail, aluminum alloy upper and lower.
Price: R-15 Hunter: 30 Rem. AR, 22" barrel, Realtree AP HD camo **$1,225.00**
Price: R-15 VTR Byron South Edition: 223, 18" barrel, Advantage MAX-1 HD camo **$1,772.00**
Price: R-15 VTR SS Varmint: Same as Byron South Edition but with 24" stainless steel barrel **$1,412.00**
Price: R-15 VTR Thumbhole: Similar to R-15 Hunter but with thumbhole stock **$1,412.00**
Price: R-15 VYR Predator: 204 Ruger or .223, 22" barrel . . **$1,225.00**
Price: R-15 Predator Carbine: Similar to above but with 18" barrel **$1,225.00**

REMINGTON MODEL R-25 MODULAR REPEATING RIFLE
Caliber: 243, 7mm-08, 308 Win., four-shot magazine. **Barrel:** 20" chrome-moly. **Weight:** 7.75 lbs. **Length:** 38.25" overall. **Features:** AR-style semi-auto with single-stage trigger, aluminum alloy upper and lower, Mossy Oak Treestand camo finish overall.
Price: **$1,567.00**

REMINGTON MODEL 750 WOODSMASTER
Caliber: 243 Win., 270 Win., 308 Win., 30-06 Spfl., 35 Whelen. 4-shot magazine. **Barrel:** 22" round tapered. **Weight:** 7.5 lbs. **Length:** 42.6" overall. **Stock:** Restyled American walnut forend and stock with machine-cut checkering. Satin finish. **Sights:** Gold bead front sight on ramp; step rear sight with windage adjustable. **Features:** Replaced wood-stocked Model 7400 line introduced 1981. Gas action, SuperCell recoil pad. Positive cross-bolt safety. Carbine chambered in 308 Win., 30-06 Spfl., 35 Whelen. Receiver tapped for scope mount. Introduced 2006. Made in U.S.A. by Remington Arms Co.
Price: 750 Woodsmaster **$879.00**

Price: 750 Woodsmaster Carbine (18.5" bbl.) **$879.00**
Price: 750 Synthetic stock (2007) **$773.00**

ROCK RIVER ARMS STANDARD A2 RIFLE
Caliber: 45 ACP. **Barrel:** NA. **Weight:** 8.2 lbs. **Length:** NA. **Stock:** Thermoplastic. **Sights:** Standard AR-15 style sights. **Features:** Two-stage, national match trigger; optional muzzle brake. Pro-Series Government package includes side-mount sling swivel, chrome-lined 1:9 twist barrel, mil-spec forged lower receiver, Hogue rubber grip, NM two-stage trigger, 6-position tactical CAR stock, Surefire M73 quad rail handguard, other features. Made in U.S.A. From Rock River Arms.
Price: Standard A2 AR1280 . . . . **$945.00**
Price: Pro-Series Government Package GOVT1001 (2008) **$2,290.00**
Price: Elite Comp AR1270 (2008) **$1,145.00**

RUGER MINI-14 RANCH RIFLE AUTOLOADING RIFLE
Caliber: 223 Rem., 5-shot detachable box magazine. **Barrel:** 18.5". Rifling twist 1:9". **Weight:** 6.75 to 7 lbs. **Length:** 37.25" overall. **Stock:** American hardwood, steel reinforced, or synthetic. **Sights:** Protected blade front, fully adjustable Ghost Ring rear. **Features:** Fixed piston gas-operated, positive primary extraction. New buffer system, redesigned ejector system. Ruger S100RM scope rings included on Ranch Rifle. Heavier barrels added in 2008, 20-round magazine added in 1009.
Price: Mini-14/5, Ranch Rifle, blued, scope rings **$855.00**
Price: K-Mini-14/5, Ranch Rifle, stainless, scope rings **$921.00**
Price: K-Mini-6.8/5P, All-Weather Ranch Rifle, stainless, synthetic stock (2008) **$921.00**
Price: Mini-14 Target Rifle: laminated thumbhole stock, heavy crowned 22" stainless steel barrel, other refinements **$1,066.00**
Price: Mini-14 ATI Stock: Tactical version of Mini-14 but with six-position collapsible stock or folding stock, grooved pistol grip. multiple picatinny optics/accessory rails . . **$872.00**
Price: Mini-14 Tactical Rifle: Similar to Mini-14 but with 16-21" barrel with flash hider, black synthetic stock, adjustable sights **$894.00**

Sabre Defence Competition Extreme

Sabre Defence M5 Tactical

Sabre Defence Heavy Bench Target

Sabre Defence Varmint

Ruger NRA Mini-14 Rifle
Similar to the Mini-14 Ranch Rifle except comes with two 20-round magazines and special Black Hogue OverMolded stock with NRA gold-tone medallion in grip cap. Special serial number sequence (NRA8XXXXX). For 2008 only.
Price: M-14/20C-NRA.......................... **$1,035.00**
Price: M-14/5C-NRA (5-round magazines)............. **$1,035.00**

Ruger Mini Thirty Rifle
Similar to the Mini-14 Ranch Rifle except modified to chamber the 7.62x39 Russian service round. **Weight:** 6.75 lbs. Has 6-groove barrel with 1:10" twist, Ruger Integral Scope Mount bases and protected blade front, fully adjustable Ghost Ring rear. Detachable 5-shot staggered box magazine. Stainless w/synthetic stock. Introduced 1987.
Price: Stainless, scope rings **$921.00**

SABRE DEFENCE SABRE RIFLES
Caliber: 5.56 NATO, 6.5 Grendel, 30-shot magazines. **Barrel:** 20" 410 stainless steel, 1x8 twist rate; or 18" vanadium alloy, chrome-lined barrel with Sabre Gill-Brake. **Weight:** 6.77 lbs. **Length:** 31.75" overall. **Stock:** SOCOM 3-position stock with Samson M-EX handguards. **Sights:** Flip-up front and rear sights. **Features:** Fluted barrel, Harris bipod, and two-stage match trigger, Ergo Grips; upper and matched lower CNC machined from 7075-T6 forgings. SOCOM adjustable stock, Samson tactical handguards, M4 contour barrels available in 14.5" and 16" are made of MIL-B-11595 vanadium alloy and chrome lined. Introduced 2002. From Sabre Defence Industries.
Price: 6.5 Grendel, from **$1,409.00**
Price: Competition Extreme, 20" barrel, from **$2,189.00**
Price: Competition Deluxe, from **$2,299.00**
Price: Competition Special, 5.56mm, 18" barrel, from **$1,899.00**
Price: SPR Carbine, from **$2,499.00**
Price: M4 Tactical, from **$1,969.00**
Price: M4 Carbine, 14.5" barrel, from **$1,399.00**
Price: M4 Flat-top Carbine, 16" barrel, from **$1,349.00**
Price: M5 Flat-top, 16" barrel, from **$1,399.00**
Price: M5 Tactical, 14.5" barrel, from **$2,099.00**
Price: M5 Carbine, from **$1,309.00**
Price: Precision Marksman, 20" barrel, from **$2,499.00**
Price: A4 Rifle, 20" barrel, from **$1,349.00**
Price: A3 National Match, 20" barrel **$1,699.00**
Price: Heavy Bench Target, 24" barrel, from **$1,889.00**
Price: Varmint, 20" barrel **$1,709.00**

SIG 556 Classic

SIG 556 DMR

SIG 556 SCM

SIG 556 SWAT

SIG 556 AUTOLOADING RIFLE

Caliber: 223 Rem., 30-shot detachable box magazine. **Barrel:** 16". Rifling twist 1:9". **Weight:** 6.8 lbs. **Length:** 36.5" overall. **Stock:** Polymer, folding style. **Sights:** Flip-up front combat sight, adjustable for windage and elevation. **Features:** Based on SG 550 series rifle. Two-position adjustable gas piston operating rod system, accepts standard AR magazines. Polymer forearm, three integrated Picatinny rails, forward mount for right- or left-side sling attachment. Aircraft-grade aluminum alloy trigger housing, hard-coat anodized finish; two-stage trigger, ambidextrous safety, 30-round polymer magazine, battery compartments, pistol-grip rubber-padded watertight adjustable butt stock with sling-attachment points. SIG 556 SWAT model has flat-top Picatinny railed receiver, tactical quad rail. SIG 556 HOLO sight options include front combat sight, flip-up rear sight, and red-dot style holographic sighting system with four illuminated reticle patterns. DMR

features a 24" military grade cold hammer-forged heavy contour barrel, 5.56mm NATO, target crown. Imported by Sig Sauer, Inc.

Price: SIG 556 . . . . **$2,099.00**
Price: SIG 556 HOLO (2008) **$1,832.00**
Price: SIG 556 DMR (2008) **$2,400.00**
Price: SIG 556 SWAT **$2,000.00**
Price: SIG 556 SCM **$1,838.00**

SMITH & WESSON M&P15 RIFLES

Caliber: 5.56mm NATO/223, 30-shot steel magazine. **Barrel:** 16", 1:9 **Weight:** 6.74 lbs., w/o magazine. **Length:** 32-35" overall. **Stock:** Black synthetic. **Sights:** Adjustable post front sight, adjustable dual aperture rear sight. **Features:** 6-position telescopic stock, thermo-set M4 handguard. 14.75" sight radius. 7-lbs. (approx.) trigger pull. 7075 T6 aluminum upper, 4140 steel barrel. Chromed barrel bore, gas key, bolt carrier. Hard-coat black-anodized receiver and barrel finish. Introduced 2006. Made in U.S.A. by Smith & Wesson.

Price: M&P15 No. 811000 . . . . **$1,406.00**
Price: M&P15T No. 811001, free float modular rail forend . **$1,888.00**
Price: M&P15A No. 811002, folding battle rear sight **$1,422.00**
Price: M&P15A No. 811013, optics ready compliant (2008). **$1,169.00**

Springfield M1A

Winchester Super X

SMITH & WESSON MODEL M&P15VTAC VIKING TACTICS MODEL
Caliber: 223 Remington/5.56 NATO, 30-round magazine. **Barrel:** 16". **Weight:** 6.5 lbs. **Length:** 35" extended, 32" collapsed, overall. **Features:** Six-position CAR stock. Surefire flash-hider and G2 light with VTAC light mount; VTAC/JP handguard; JP single-stage match trigger and speed hammer; three adjustable picatinny rails; VTAC padded two-point adjustable sling.
Price: $2,196.00

SMITH & WESSON M&P15PC CAMO
Caliber: 223 Rem/5.56 NATO, A2 configuration, 10-round mag. **Barrel:** 20" stainless with 1:8 twist. **Weight:** 8.2 lbs. **Length:** 38.5" overall. **Features:** AR-style, no sights but integral front and rear optics rails. Two-stage trigger, aluminum lower. Finished in Realtree Advantage Max-1 camo.
Price: $2,046.00

SPRINGFIELD ARMORY M1A RIFLE
Caliber: 7.62mm NATO (308), 5- or 10-shot box magazine. **Barrel:** 25-1/16" with flash suppressor, 22" without suppressor. **Weight:** 9.75 lbs. **Length:** 44.25" overall. **Stock:** American walnut with walnut-colored heat-resistant fiberglass handguard. Matching walnut handguard available. Also available with fiberglass stock. **Sights:** Military, square blade front, full click-adjustable aperture rear. **Features:** Commercial equivalent of the U.S. M-14 service rifle with no provision for automatic firing. From Springfield Armory
Price: SOCOM 16 . . . . $1,855.00
Price: SOCOM II, from $2,090.00
Price: Scout Squad, from $1,726.00
Price: Standard M1A, from $1,608.00
Price: Loaded Standard, from $1,759.00
Price: National Match, from $2,249.00
Price: Super Match (heavy premium barrel) about $2,818.00
Price: Tactical, from $3,780.00

STONER SR-15 M-5 RIFLE
Caliber: 223. **Barrel:** 20". **Weight:** 7.6 lbs. **Length:** 38" overall. **Stock:** Black synthetic. **Sights:** Post front, fully adjustable rear (300-meter sight). **Features:** Modular weapon system; two-stage trigger. Black finish. Introduced 1998. Made in U.S.A. by Knight's Mfg.
Price: $1,695.00

STONER SR-25 CARBINE
Caliber: 7.62 NATO, 10-shot steel magazine. **Barrel:** 16" free-floating **Weight:** 7.75 lbs. **Length:** 35.75" overall. **Stock:** Black synthetic. **Sights:** Integral Weaver-style rail. Scope rings, iron sights optional. **Features:** Shortened, non-slip handguard; removable carrying handle. Matte black finish. Introduced 1995. Made in U.S.A. by Knight's Mfg. Co.
Price: $3,345.00

WILSON COMBAT TACTICAL RIFLES
Caliber: 5.56mm NATO, accepts all M-16/AR-15 Style Magazines, includes one 20-round magazine. **Barrel:** 16.25", 1:9 twist, match-grade fluted. **Weight:** 6.9 lbs. **Length:** 36.25" overall. **Stock:** Fixed or collapsible. **Features:** Free-float ventilated aluminum quad-rail handguard, Mil-Spec parkerized barrel and steel components, anodized receiver, precision CNC-machined upper and lower receivers, 7075 T6 aluminum forgings. Single stage JP Trigger/ Hammer Group, Wilson Combat Tactical Muzzle Brake, nylon tactical rifle case. M-4T version has flat-top receiver for mounting optics, OD green furniture, 16.25" match-grade M-4 style barrel. SS-15 Super Sniper Tactical Rifle has 1-in-8 twist, heavy 20" match-grade fluted stainless steel barrel. Made in U.S.A by Wilson Combat.
Price: UT-15 Tactical Carbine. $1,785.00
Price: M4-TP Tactical Carbine $1,575.00
Price: SS-15P Super Sniper $1,795.00

WINCHESTER SUPER X RIFLE
Caliber: 270 WSM, 30-06 Spfl., 300 Win. Mag., 300 WSM, 4-shot steel magazine. **Barrel:** 22", 24", 1:10", blued. **Weight:** 7.25 lbs. **Length:** up to 41-3/8". **Stock:** Walnut, 14-1/8"x 7/8"x 1.25". **Sights:** None. **Features:** Gas operated, removable trigger assembly, detachable box magazine, drilled and tapped, alloy receiver, enlarged trigger guard, crossbolt safety. Reintroduced 2008. Made in U.S.A. by Winchester Repeating Arms.
Price: Super X Rifle, from $949.00

Both classic arms and recent designs in American-style repeaters for sport and field shooting.

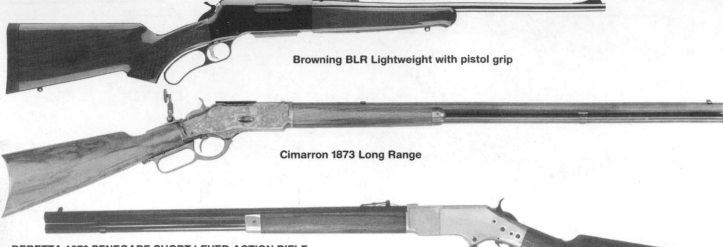

Browning BLR Lightweight with pistol grip

Cimarron 1873 Long Range

Cimarron 1866
Winchester Replica

BERETTA 1873 RENEGADE SHORT LEVER-ACTION RIFLE
Caliber: 45 Colt, 357 Magnum. **Barrel:** 20" round or 24-1/2" octagonal. **Features:** Blued finish, checkered walnut buttstock and forend, adjustable rear sight and fixed blade front, ten-round tubular magazine.
Price: $1,350.00

BERETTA GOLD RUSH SLIDE-ACTION RIFLE AND CARBINE
Caliber: 357 Magnum, 45 Colt. **Barrel:** 20" round or 24-1/2"octagonal. **Features:** External replica of old Colt Lightning Magazine Rifle. Case-hardened receiver, walnut buttstock and forend, crescent buttplate, 13-round (rifle) or 10-round (carbine) magazine. Available as Standard Carbine, Standard Rifle, or Deluxe Rifle.
Price: Standard Carbine $1,375.00
Price: Standard Rifle $1,425.00
Price: Deluxe Rifle $11,950.00

BROWNING BLR RIFLES
Action: Lever action with rotating bolt head, multiple-lug breech bolt with recessed bolt face, side ejection. Rack-and-pinion lever. Flush-mounted detachable magazines, with 4+1 capacity for magnum cartridges, 5+1 for standard rounds. **Barrel:** Button-rifled chrome-moly steel with crowned muzzle. **Stock:** Buttstocks and forends are American walnut with grip and forend checkering. Recoil pad installed. **Trigger:** Wide-groove design, trigger travels with lever. Half-cock hammer safety; fold-down hammer. **Sights:** Gold bead on ramp front; low-profile square-notch adjustable rear. **Features:** Blued barrel and receiver, high-gloss wood finish. Receivers are drilled and tapped for scope mounts, swivel studs included. Action lock provided. Introduced 1996. Imported from Japan by Browning.

BROWNING BLR LIGHTWEIGHT W/PISTOL GRIP, SHORT AND LONG ACTION; LIGHTWEIGHT '81, SHORT AND LONG ACTION
Calibers: Short Action, 20" Barrel: 22-250 Rem., 243 Win., 7mm-08 Rem., 308 Win., 358, 450 Marlin. Calibers: Short Action, 22" Barrel: 270 WSM, 7mm WSM, 300 WSM, 325 WSM. Calibers: Long Action 22" Barrel: 270 Win., 30-06. Calibers: Long Action 24" Barrel: 7mm Rem. Mag., 300 Win. Mag. **Weight:** 6.5-7.75 lbs. **Length:** 40-45" overall. **Stock:** New checkered pistol grip and Schnabel forearm. Lightweight '81 differs from Pistol Grip models with a Western-style straight grip stock and banded forearm. Lightweight w/Pistol Grip Short Action and Long Action introduced 2005. Model '81 Lightning Long Action introduced 1996.
Price: Lightweight w/Pistol Grip Short Action, from $879.00
Price: Lightweight w/Pistol Grip Long Action $929.00
Price: Lightweight '81 Short Action $839.00
Price: Lightweight '81 Long Action $889.00
Price: Lightweight '81 Takedown Short Action, intr. 2007, from $949.00
Price: Lightweight '81 Takedown Long Action, intr. 2007, from $999.00

CHARLES DALY MODEL 1892 LEVER-ACTION RIFLES
Caliber: 45 Colt; 5-shot magazine with removable plug. **Barrel:** 24.25" octagonal. **Weight:** 6.8 lbs. **Length:** 42" overall. **Stock:** Two-piece

American walnut, oil finish. **Sights:** Post front, adjustable open rear. **Features:** Color case-hardened receiver, lever, buttplate, forend cap. Introduced 2007. Imported from Italy by K.B.I., Inc.
Price: 1892 Rifle $1,094.00
Price: Take Down Rifle $1,249.00

CIMARRON 1860 HENRY RIFLE CIVIL WAR MODEL
Caliber: 44 WCF, 45 LC; 12-shot magazine. **Barrel:** 24" (rifle). **Weight:** 9.5 lbs. **Length:** 43" overall (rifle). **Stock:** European walnut. **Sights:** Bead front, open adjustable rear. **Features:** Brass receiver and buttplate. Uses original Henry loading system. Copy of the original rifle. Charcoal blue finish optional. Introduced 1991. Imported by Cimarron F.A. Co.
Price: From $1,444.78

CIMARRON 1866 WINCHESTER REPLICAS
Caliber: 38 Spec., 357, 45 LC, 32 WCF, 38 WCF, 44 WCF. **Barrel:** 24" (rifle), 20" (short rifle), 19" (carbine), 16" (trapper). **Weight:** 9 lbs. **Length:** 43" overall (rifle). **Stock:** European walnut. **Sights:** Bead front, open adjustable rear. **Features:** Solid brass receiver, buttplate, forend cap. Octagonal barrel. Copy of the original Winchester '66 rifle. Introduced 1991. Imported by Cimarron F.A. Co.
Price: 1866 Sporting Rifle, 24" barrel, from $1,096.64
Price: 1866 Short Rifle, 20" barrel, from $1,096.64
Price: 1866 Carbine, 19" barrel, from $1,123.42
Price: 1866 Trapper, 16" barrel, from $1,069.86

CIMARRON 1873 SHORT RIFLE
Caliber: 357 Mag., 38 Spec., 32 WCF, 38 WCF, 44 Spec., 44 WCF, 45 Colt. **Barrel:** 20" tapered octagon. **Weight:** 7.5 lbs. **Length:** 39" overall. **Stock:** Walnut. **Sights:** Bead front, adjustable semi-buckhorn rear. **Features:** Has half "button" magazine. Original-type markings, including caliber, on barrel and elevator and "Kings" patent. From Cimarron F.A. Co.
Price: $1,203.76

CIMARRON 1873 DELUXE SPORTING RIFLE
Similar to the 1873 Short Rifle except has 24" barrel with half-magazine.
Price: $1,324.70

CIMARRON 1873 LONG RANGE RIFLE
Caliber: 44 WCF, 45 Colt. **Barrel:** 30", octagonal. **Weight:** 8.5 lbs. **Length:** 48" overall. **Stock:** Walnut. **Sights:** Blade front, semi-buckhorn ramp rear. Tang sight optional. **Features:** Color case-hardened frame; choice of modern blue-black or charcoal blue for other parts. Barrel marked "Kings Improvement." From Cimarron F.A. Co.
Price: $1,284.10

CENTERFIRE RIFLES—Lever & Slide

Dixie 1873

Marlin 336C

Marlin 338MXLR

DIXIE ENGRAVED 1873 SPORTING RIFLE
Caliber: 44-40, 13-shot magazine. **Barrel:** 24.25", tapered octagon. **Weight:** 8.25 lbs. **Length:** 43.25" overall. **Stock:** Walnut. **Sights:** Blade front, adjustable rear. **Features:** Engraved frame polished bright (casehardened on plain). Replica of Winchester 1873. Made in Italy. From Dixie Gun Works.
Price: Plain, blued rifle in .44/40, .45 LC, .32/20, .38/40. . . . **$ 1,050.00**

DIXIE 1873 DELUXE SPORTING RIFLE
Caliber: .44-40, .45 LC, .32-20 and .38-40, 13-shot magazine. **Barrel:** 24.25", tapered octagon. **Weight:** 8.25 lbs. **Length:** 43.25" overall. **Stock:** Walnut. Checkered pistol grip buttstock and forearm. **Sights:** Blade front, adjustable rear. **Features:** Color caschardened frame. Engraved frame polished bright. Replica of Winchester 1873. Made in Italy. From Dixie Gun Works.
Price: . . . .**$ 1,050.00 to $ 1,100.00**

DIXIE LIGHTNING RIFLE AND CARBINE
Caliber: .44-40 or .45 LC, 10-shot magazine. **Barrel:** 26" round or octagon, 1:16" or 1:36" twist. **Weight:** 7.25 lbs. **Length:** 43" overall. **Stock:** Walnut. **Sights:** Blade front, open adjustable rear. **Features:** Checkered forearm, blued steel furniture. Made by Pedersoli in Italy. Imported by Dixie Gun Works.
Price: **$1,095.00**
Price: Carbine **$1,225.00**

EMF 1860 HENRY RIFLE
Caliber: 44-40 or 45 Colt. **Barrel:** 24". **Weight:** About 9 lbs. **Length:** About 43.75" overall. **Stock:** Oil-stained American walnut. **Sights:** Blade front, rear adjustable for elevation. **Features:** Reproduction of the original Henry rifle with brass frame and buttplate, rest blued. Imported by EMF.
Price: Brass frame **$1,149.90**
Price: Casehardened frame **$1,229.90**

EMF 1866 YELLOWBOY LEVER ACTIONS
Caliber: 38 Spec., 44-40, 45 LC. **Barrel:** 19" (carbine), 24" (rifle). **Weight:** 9 lbs. **Length:** 43" overall (rifle). **Stock:** European walnut. **Sights:** Bead front, open adjustable rear. **Features:** Solid brass frame, blued barrel, lever, hammer, buttplate. Imported from Italy by EMF.
Price: Rifle **$1,044.90**
Price: Border Rifle, Short **$969.90**

EMF MODEL 1873 LEVER-ACTION RIFLE
Caliber: 32/20, 357 Mag., 38/40, 44-40, 45 Colt. **Barrel:** 18", 20", 24", 30". **Weight:** 8 lbs. **Length:** 43.25" overall. **Stock:** European walnut. **Sights:** Bead front, rear adjustable for windage and elevation. **Features:** Color case-hardened frame (blue on carbine). Imported by EMF.
Price: **$1,099.90**

EMF MODEL 1873 REVOLVER CARBINE
Caliber: 357 Mag., 45 Colt. **Barrel:** 18". **Weight:** 4 lbs., 8 oz. **Length:**

43-3/4" overall. **Stock:** One-piece walnut. **Sights:** Blade front, notch rear. **Features:** Color case-hardened frame, blue barrel, backstrap and trigger guard. Introduced 1998. Imported from Italy by EMF.
Price: Standard . . . . **$979.90 to $1,040.00**

HENRY BIG BOY LEVER-ACTION CARBINE
Caliber: 357 Magnum, 44 Magnum, 45 Colt, 10-shot tubular magazine. **Barrel:** 20" octagonal, 1:38 right-hand twist. **Weight:** 8.68 lbs. **Length:** 38.5" overall. **Stock:** Straight-grip American walnut, brass buttplate. **Sights:** Marbles full adjustable semi-buckhorn rear, brass bead front. **Features:** Brasslite receiver not tapped for scope mount. Made in U.S.A. by Henry Repeating Arms.
Price: H006 44 Magnum, walnut, blued barrel **$899.95**
Price: H006DD Deluxe 44 Magnum, engraved receiver. . . . **$1,995.95**

Henry .30/30 Lever-Action Carbine
Same as the Big Boy except has straight grip American walnut, 30-30 only, 6-shot. Receivers are drilled and tapped for scope mount. Made in U.S.A. by Henry Repeating Arms.
Price: H009 Blued receiver, round barrel **$749.95**
Price: H009B Brass receiver, octagonal barrel. **$969.95**

MARLIN MODEL 336C LEVER-ACTION CARBINE
Caliber: 30-30 or 35 Rem., 6-shot tubular magazine. **Barrel:** 20" Micro-Groove. **Weight:** 7 lbs. **Length:** 38.5" overall. **Stock:** Checkered American black walnut, capped pistol grip. Mar-Shield finish; rubber buttpad; swivel studs. **Sights:** Ramp front with Wide-Scan hood, semi-buckhorn folding rear adjustable for windage and elevation. **Features:** Hammer-block safety. Receiver tapped for scope mount, offset hammer spur; top of receiver sandblasted to prevent glare. Includes safety lock.
Price: **$530.00**

Marlin Model 336SS Lever-Action Carbine
Same as the 336C except receiver, barrel and other major parts are machined from stainless steel. 30-30 only, 6-shot; receiver tapped for scope. Includes safety lock.
Price: **$650.00**

Marlin Model 336W Lever-Action Rifle
Similar to the Model 336C except has walnut-finished, cut-checkered Maine birch stock; blued steel barrel band has integral sling swivel; no front sight hood; comes with padded nylon sling; hard rubber buttplate. Introduced 1998. Includes safety lock. Made in U.S.A. by Marlin.
Price: **$452.00**
Price: With 4x scope and mount **$495.00**

Marlin Model XLR Lever-Action Rifles
Similar to Model 336C except has an 24" stainless barrel with Ballard-type cut rifling, stainless steel receiver and other parts, laminated hardwood stock with pistol grip, nickel-plated swivel studs. Chambered for 30-30 Win. with Hornady spire-pointed Flex-Tip cartridges. Includes safety lock. Introduced 2006. Similar models chambered for 308 Marlin Express introduced in 2007
Price: Model 336XLR **$816.00**

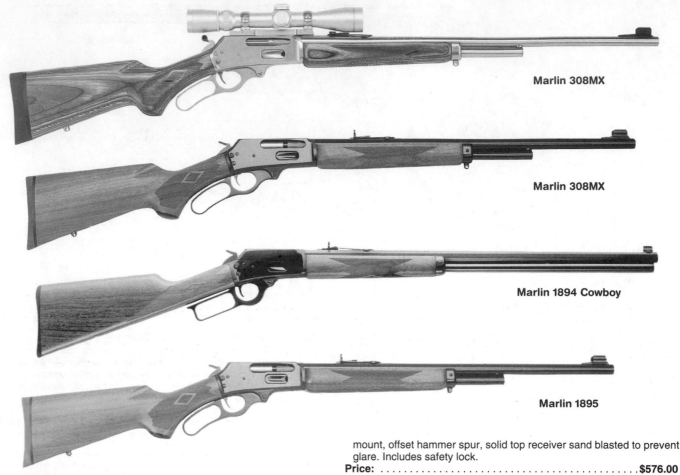

Marlin 308MX

Marlin 308MX

Marlin 1894 Cowboy

Marlin 1895

MARLIN MODEL 338MXLR
Caliber: 338 Marlin Express. Barrel: 24" stainless steel. Weight: 7.5 lbs. Length: 42.5" overall. Features: Stainless steel receiver, lever and magazine tube. Black/gray laminated checkered stock and forend. Hooded ramp front sight and adjustable semi-buckhorn rear; drilled and tapped for scope mounts. Receiver-mounted crossbolt safety.
Price: Model 338MXLR $806.00
Price: Model 308MXLR: 308 Marlin Express $806.00
Price: Model 338MX: Similar to Model 338MXLR but with
    blued metal and walnut stock and forend $611.00
Price: Model 308MX: 308 Marlin Express $611.00

MARLIN MODEL 444 LEVER-ACTION SPORTER
Caliber: 444 Marlin, 5-shot tubular magazine. Barrel: 22" deep cut Ballard rifling. Weight: 7.5 lbs. Length: 40.5" overall. Stock: Checkered American black walnut, capped pistol grip, rubber rifle buttpad. Mar-Shield finish; swivel studs. Sights: Hooded ramp front, folding semi-buckhorn rear adjustable for windage and elevation. Features: Hammer-block safety. Receiver tapped for scope mount; offset hammer spur. Includes safety lock.
Price: $619.00

Marlin Model 444XLR Lever-Action Rifle
Similar to Model 444 except has an 24" stainless barrel with Ballard-type cut rifling, stainless steel receiver and other parts, laminated hardwood stock with pistol grip, nickel-plated swivel studs. Chambered for 444 Marlin with Hornady Evolution spire-pointed Flex-Tip cartridges. Includes safety lock. Introduced 2006.
Price: (Model 444XLR) $816.00

MARLIN MODEL 1894 LEVER-ACTION CARBINE
Caliber: 44 Spec./44 Mag., 10-shot tubular magazine. Barrel: 20" Ballard-type rifling. Weight: 6 lbs. Length: 37.5" overall. Stock: Checkered American black walnut, straight grip and forend. Mar-Shield finish. Rubber rifle buttpad; swivel studs. Sights: Wide-Scan hooded ramp front, semi-buckhorn folding rear adjustable for windage and elevation. Features: Hammer-block safety. Receiver tapped for scope

mount, offset hammer spur, solid top receiver sand blasted to prevent glare. Includes safety lock.
Price: $576.00

Marlin Model 1894C Carbine
Similar to the standard Model 1894 except chambered for 38 Spec./357 Mag. with full-length 9-shot magazine, 18.5" barrel, hammer-block safety, hooded front sight. Introduced 1983. Includes safety lock.
Price: $576.00

MARLIN MODEL 1894 COWBOY
Caliber: 357 Mag., 44 Mag., 45 Colt, 10-shot magazine. Barrel: 20" tapered octagon, deep cut rifling. Weight: 7.5 lbs. Length: 41.5" overall. Stock: Straight grip American black walnut, hard rubber buttplate, Mar-Shield finish. Sights: Marble carbine front, adjustable Marble semi-buckhorn rear. Features: Squared finger lever; straight grip stock; blued steel forend tip. Designed for Cowboy Shooting events. Introduced 1996. Includes safety lock. Made in U.S.A. by Marlin.
Price: $822.00

Marlin Model 1894SS
Similar to Model 1894 except has stainless steel barrel, receiver, lever, guard plate, magazine tube and loading plate. Nickel-plated swivel studs.
Price: $704.00

MARLIN MODEL 1895 LEVER-ACTION RIFLE
Caliber: 45-70 Govt., 4-shot tubular magazine. Barrel: 22" round. Weight: 7.5 lbs. Length: 40.5" overall. Stock: Checkered American black walnut, full pistol grip. Mar-Shield finish; rubber buttpad; quick detachable swivel studs. Sights: Bead front with Wide-Scan hood, semi-buckhorn folding rear adjustable for windage and elevation. Features: Hammer-block safety. Solid receiver tapped for scope mounts or receiver sights; offset hammer spur. Includes safety lock.
Price: $619.00

Marlin Model 1895G Guide Gun Lever-Action Rifle
Similar to Model 1895 with deep-cut Ballard-type rifling; straight-grip walnut stock. Overall length is 37", weighs 7 lbs. Introduced 1998. Includes safety lock. Made in U.S.A. by Marlin.
Price: $630.00

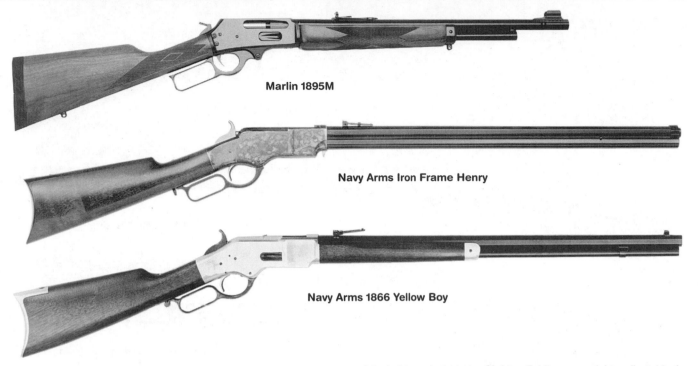

Marlin 1895M

Navy Arms Iron Frame Henry

Navy Arms 1866 Yellow Boy

Marlin Model 1895GS Guide Gun
Similar to Model 1895G except receiver, barrel and most metal parts are machined from stainless steel. Chambered for 45-70 Govt., 4-shot, 18.5" barrel. Overall length is 37", weighs 7 lbs. Introduced 2001. Includes safety lock. Made in U.S.A. by Marlin.
Price: **$752.00**

Marlin Model 1895 SBLR
Similar to Model 1895GS Guide Gun but with stainless steel barrel (18.5"), receiver, large loop lever and magazine tube. Black/gray laminated buttstock and forend, XS ghost ring rear sight, hooded ramp front sight, receiver/barrel-mounted top rail for mounting accessory optics. Chambered in 45-70 Government. Overall length is 42.5", weighs 7.5 lbs.
Price: **$979.00**

Marlin Model 1895 Cowboy Lever-Action Rifle
Similar to Model 1895 except has 26" tapered octagon barrel with Ballard-type rifling, Marble carbine front sight and Marble adjustable semi-buckhorn rear sight. Receiver tapped for scope or receiver sight. Overall length is 44.5", weighs about 8 lbs. Introduced 2001. Includes safety lock. Made in U.S.A. by Marlin.
Price: **$785.00**

Marlin Model 1895XLR Lever-Action Rifle
Similar to Model 1895 except has an 24" stainless barrel with Ballard-type cut rifling, stainless steel receiver and other parts, laminated hardwood stock with pistol grip, nickel-plated swivel studs. Chambered for 45-70 Government with Hornady Evolution spire-pointed Flex-Tip cartridges. Includes safety lock. Introduced 2006.
Price: (Model 1895MXLR) **$816.00**

Marlin Model 1895M Lever-Action Rifle
Similar to Model 1895G except has an 18.5" barrel with Ballard-type cut rifling. Chambered for 450 Marlin. Includes safety lock.
Price: (Model 1895M) **$678.00**

Marlin Model 1895MXLR Lever-Action Rifle
Similar to Model 1895M except has an 24" stainless barrel with Ballard-type cut rifling, stainless steel receiver and other parts, laminated hardwood stock with pistol grip, nickel-plated swivel studs. Chambered for 450 Marlin with Hornady Evolution spire-pointed Flex-Tip cartridges. Includes safety lock. Introduced 2006.
Price: (Model 1895MXLR) **$874.00**

MOSSBERG 464 LEVER ACTION RIFLE
Caliber: 30-30 Win., 6-shot tubular magazine. **Barrel:** 20" round. **Weight:** 6.7 lbs. **Length:** 38.5" overall. **Stock:** Hardwood, quick detachable swivel studs. **Sights:** Folding rear sight, adjustable for windage and elevation. **Features:** Blued receiver and barrel, receiver drilled and tapped, two-position top-tang safety. Available with straight grip or semi-pistol grip. Introduced 2008. From O.F. Mossberg & Sons, Inc.
Price: **$497.00**

NAVY ARMS 1874 SHARPS #2 CREEDMORE RIFLE
Caliber: .45-70 Govt. **Barrel:** 30" octagon. **Weight:** 10 lbs. **Length:** 48" overall. **Sights:** Soule target grade rear tang sight, front globe with 12 inserts. **Features:** Highly polished nickel receiver and action, double-set triggers. From Navy Arms.
Price: Model SCR072 (2008) **$1,816.00**

NAVY ARMS MILITARY HENRY RIFLE
Caliber: 44-40 or 45 Colt, 12-shot magazine. **Barrel:** 24.25". **Weight:** 9 lbs., 4 oz. **Stock:** European walnut. **Sights:** Blade front, adjustable ladder-type rear. **Features:** Brass frame, buttplate, rest blued. Replica of the model used by cavalry units in the Civil War. Has full-length magazine tube, sling swivels; no forend. Imported from Italy by Navy Arms.
Price: **$1,199.00**

Navy Arms Iron Frame Henry
Similar to the Military Henry Rifle except receiver is blued or color case-hardened steel. Imported by Navy Arms.
Price: Blued **$1,247.00**

NAVY ARMS 1866 YELLOW BOY RIFLE
Caliber: 38 Spec., 44-40, 45 Colt, 12-shot magazine. **Barrel:** 20" or 24", full octagon. **Weight:** 8.5 lbs. **Length:** 42.5" overall. **Stock:** Walnut. **Sights:** Blade front, adjustable ladder-type rear. **Features:** Brass frame, forend tip, buttplate, blued barrel, lever, hammer. Introduced 1991. Imported from Italy by Navy Arms.
Price: Yellow Boy Rifle, 24.25" barrel **$915.00**
Price: Yellow Boy Carbine, 19" barrel **$882.00**

NAVY ARMS 1873 WINCHESTER-STYLE RIFLE
Caliber: 357 Mag., 44-40, 45 Colt, 12-shot magazine. **Barrel:** 24.25". **Weight:** 8.25 lbs. **Length:** 43" overall. **Stock:** European walnut. **Sights:** Blade front, buckhorn rear. **Features:** Color case-hardened frame, rest blued. Full-octagon barrel. Imported by Navy Arms.
Price: **$1,047.00**
Price: 1873 Carbine, 19" barrel **$1,024.00**
Price: 1873 Sporting Rifle (octagonal bbl., checkered walnut stock and forend) **$1,183.00**
Price: 1873 Border Model, 20" octagon barrel **$1,047.00**
Price: 1873 Deluxe Border Model **$1,183.00**

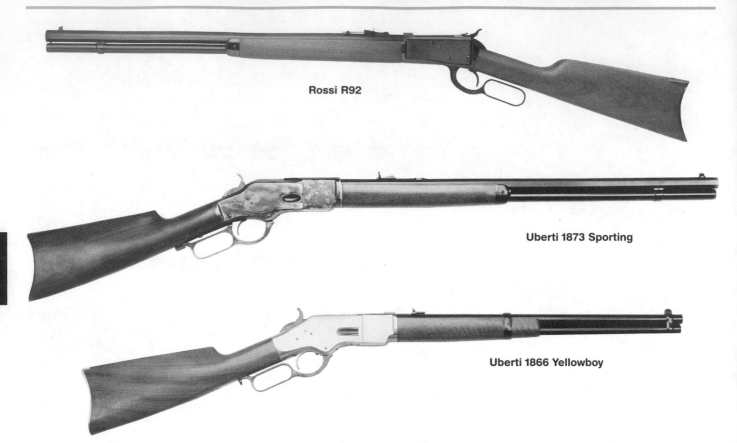

Rossi R92

Uberti 1873 Sporting

Uberti 1866 Yellowboy

PUMA MODEL 92 RIFLES AND CARBINES

Caliber: 17 HMR (XP and Scout models, only; intr. 2008), 38 Spec./357 Mag., 44 Mag., 45 Colt, 454 Casull, 480 Ruger (.44-40 in 20" octagonal barrel). **Barrel:** 16" and 20" round; 20" and 24" octagonal. 1:30" rate of twist (exc. 17 HMR is 1:9"). **Weight:** 7.7 lbs. **Stock:** Walnut stained hardwood. **Sights:** Blade front, V rear, buckhorn sights sold separately. **Features:** Finishes available in blue/blue, blue/case colored and stainless/stainless with matching crescent butt plates. .454 and .480 calibers have rubber recoil pads. Full-length magazines, thumb safety. Large lever loop or HiViz sights available on select models. Magazine capacity is 12 rounds with 24" bbl.; 10 rounds with 20" barrel; 8 rounds in 16" barrel. Introduced in 2002. Scout includes long-eye-relief scope, rail, elevated cheekpiece, intr. 2008. XP chambered in 17 HMR, 38 Spec./357 Mag. and 44 Mag., loads through magazine tube or loading gate, intr. 2008. Imported from Brazil by Legacy Sports International.
Price: From $959.00
Price: Scout Model, w/2.5x32 Nikko-Stirling Nighteater
    scope, intr. 2008, from $739.00
Price: XP Model, tube feed magazine, intr. 2008, from $613.00

REMINGTON MODEL 7600/7615 PUMP ACTION

Caliber: 243 Win., 270 Win., 30-06 Spfl., 308; 223 Rem. (7615 only). **Barrel:** 22" round tapered. **Weight:** 7.5 lbs. **Length:** 42.6" overall. **Stock:** Cut-checkered walnut pistol grip and forend, Monte Carlo with full cheekpiece. Satin or high-gloss finish. Also, black synthetic. **Sights:** Gold bead front sight on matted ramp, open step adjustable sporting rear. **Features:** Redesigned and improved version of the Model 760. Detachable 4-shot clip. Cross-bolt safety. Receiver tapped for scope mount. Introduced 1981. Model 7615 Tactical chambered in 223 Rem. **Features:** Knoxx SpecOps NRS (Non Recoil Suppressing) adjustable stock, parkerized finish, 10-round detachable magazine box, sling swivel studs. Introduced 2007.
Price:7600 Wood $792.00
Price:7600 Synthetic. $665.00
Price: 7615 Ranch Carbine $955.00
Price: 7615 Camo Hunter. $1,009.00
Price: 7615 Tactical 223 Rem., 16.5" barrel, 10-rd.
    magazine (2008). $932.00

ROSSI R92 LEVER-ACTION CARBINE

Caliber: 38 Special/357 Mag., 44 Mag., 44-40 Win., 45 Colt, 454 Casull. **Barrel:** 16" or 20" with round barrel, 20" or 24" with octagon barrel. **Weight:** 4.8 lbs. to 7 lbs. **Length:** 34" to 41.5". **Features:** Blued or stainless finish. Various options available in selected chamberings (large lever loop, fiber optic sights, cheekpiece, etc.).
Price: From $499.00

TAURUS THUNDERBOLT PUMP ACTION

Caliber: 38/.357, 45 Long Colt, 12 or 14 rounds. **Barrel:** 26" blue or polished stainless. **Weight:** 8.1 lbs. **Length:** 43" overall. **Stock:** Hardwood stock and forend. Gloss finish. **Sights:** Longhorn adjustable rear. Introduced 2004. Imported from Brazil by Taurus International.
Price: C45BR (blued) $705.00
Price: C45SSR (stainless) $813.00

TRISTAR SHARPS 1874 SPORTING RIFLE

Caliber: 45-70 Govt. **Barrel:** 28", 32", 34" octagonal. **Weight:** 9.75 lbs. **Length:** 44.5" overall. **Stock:** Walnut. **Sights:** Dovetail front, adjustable rear. **Features:** Cut checkering, case colored frame finish.
Price: $1,099.00

UBERTI 1873 SPORTING RIFLE

Caliber: 357 Mag., 44-40, 45 Colt. **Barrel:** 19" to 24.25". **Weight:** Up to 8.2 lbs. **Length:** Up to 43.3" overall. **Stock:** Walnut, straight grip and pistol grip. **Sights:** Blade front adjustable for windage, open rear adjustable for elevation. **Features:** Color case-hardened frame, blued barrel, hammer, lever, buttplate, brass elevator. Imported by Stoeger Industries.
Price: 1873 Carbine, 19" round barrel $1,199.00
Price: 1873 Short Rifle, 20" octagonal barrel $1,249.00
Price: 1873 Special Sporting Rifle, 24.25" octagonal barrel **$1,379.00**

UBERTI 1866 YELLOWBOY CARBINE, SHORT RIFLE, RIFLE

Caliber: 38 Spec., 44-40, 45 Colt. **Barrel:** 24.25", octagonal. **Weight:** 8.2 lbs. **Length:** 43.25" overall. **Stock:** Walnut. **Sights:** Blade front adjustable for windage, rear adjustable for elevation. **Features:** Frame, buttplate, forend cap of polished brass, balance charcoal blued. Imported by Stoeger Industries.
Price: 1866 Yellowboy Carbine, 19" round barrel. $1,079.00
Price: 1866 Yellowboy Short Rifle, 20" octagonal barrel . . . $1,129.00
Price: 1866 Yellowboy Rifle, 24.25" octagonal barrel $1,129.00

Prices given are believed to be accurate at time of publication however, many factors affect retail pricing so exact prices are not possible.

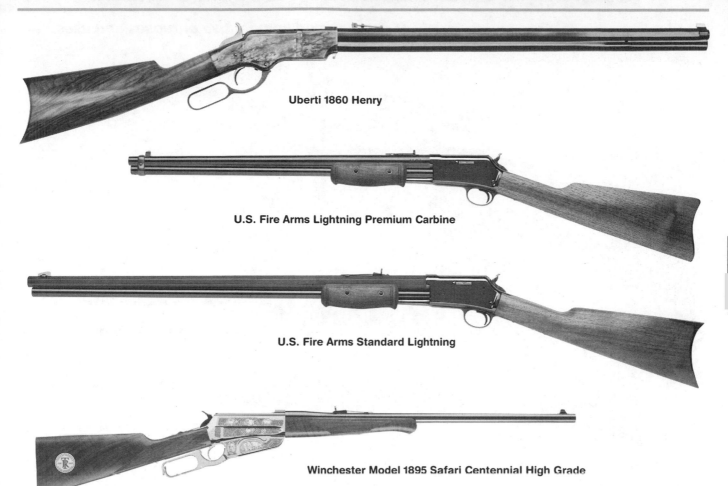

Uberti 1860 Henry

U.S. Fire Arms Lightning Premium Carbine

U.S. Fire Arms Standard Lightning

Winchester Model 1895 Safari Centennial High Grade

UBERTI 1860 HENRY RIFLE
Caliber: 44-40, 45 Colt. **Barrel:** 24.25", half-octagon. **Weight:** 9.2 lbs. **Length:** 43.75" overall. **Stock:** American walnut. **Sights:** Blade front, rear adjustable for elevation. Imported by Stoeger Industries.
Price: 1860 Henry Trapper, 18.5" barrel, brass frame **$1,329.00**
Price: 1860 Henry Rifle Iron Frame, 24.25" barrel **$1,419.00**

UBERTI LIGHTNING RIFLE
Caliber: 357 Mag., 45 Colt, 10+1. **Barrel:** 20" to 24.25". **Stock:** Walnut. Finish: Blue or case-hardened. Introduced 2006. Imported by Stoeger Industries.
Price: 1875 Lightning Rifle, 24.25" barrel **$1,259.00**
Price: 1875 Lightning Short Rifle, 20" barrel **$1,259.00**
Price: 1875 Lightning Carbine, 20" barrel **$1,179.00**

UBERTI SPRINGFIELD TRAPDOOR RIFLE
Caliber: 4-70, single shot. **Barrel:** 22" or 32.5". **Stock:** Walnut. Finish: Blue and case-hardened. Introduced 2006. Imported by Stoeger Industries.
Price: Springfield Trapdoor Carbine, 22" barrel **$1,429.00**
Price: Springfield Trapdoor Army, 32.5" barrel **$1,669.00**

U.S. FIRE ARMS STANDARD LIGHTNING MAGAZINE RIFLE
Caliber: 45 Colt, 44 WCF, 44 Spec., 38 WCF, 15-shot. **Barrel:** 26". Stock: Oiled walnut. Finish: High polish blue. Nickel finish also available. Introduced 2002. Made in U.S.A. by United States Fire-Arms Manufacturing Co.
Price: Round barrel. **$1,480.00**
Price: Octagonal barrel, checkered forend **$1,750.00**
Price: Half-round barrel, checkered forend **$1,995.00**
Price: Premium Carbine, 20" round barrel **$1,480.00**
Price: Baby Carbine, 20" special taper barrel **$1,995.00**
Price: Deluxe Lightning **$2,559.00**

WINCHESTER MODEL 1895 SAFARI CENTENNIAL HIGH GRADE
Caliber: 405 Win. **Barrel:** 24" blued round, four-round box mag. **Weight:** 8 lbs. **Length:** NA. **Features:** Patterned after original Winchester Model 1895. Commemorates Theodore Roosevelt's 1909 African safari. Checkered walnut forend and buttstock with inlaid "TR" medallion, engraved and silvered receiver.
Price: **$1,749.00**
Price: Custom Grade: Jeweled hammer, fancier wood and angraving, gold-filled highlights and numerous accessories. Production limited to 100 sets **$3,649.00**

Includes models for a wide variety of sporting and competitive purposes and uses.

Barrett Model 95

Blaser R93 Classic

Browning A-Bolt Hunter

Browning A-Bolt Target

BARRETT MODEL 95 BOLT-ACTION RIFLE

Caliber: 50 BMG, 5-shot magazine. **Barrel:** 29". **Weight:** 23.5 lbs. **Length:** 45" overall. **Stock:** Energy-absorbing recoil pad. **Sights:** Scope optional. **Features:** Bolt-action, bullpup design. Disassembles without tools; extendable bipod legs; match-grade barrel; muzzle brake. Introduced 1995. Made in U.S.A. by Barrett Firearms Mfg., Inc.
Price: From **$6,500.00**

BLASER R93 BOLT-ACTION RIFLE

Caliber: 22-250 Rem., 243 Win., 6.5x55, 270 Win., 7x57, 7mm-08 Rem., 308 Win., 30-06 Spfl., 257 Wby. Mag., 7mm Rem. Mag., 300 Win. Mag., 300 Wby. Mag., 338 Win. Mag., 375 H&H, 416 Rem. Mag. **Barrel:** 22" (standard calibers), 26" (magnum). **Weight:** 7 lbs. **Length:** 40" overall (22" barrel). **Stock:** Two-piece European walnut. **Sights:** None furnished; drilled and tapped for scope mounting. **Features:** Straight pull-back bolt action with thumb-activated safety slide/cocking mechanism; interchangeable barrels and bolt heads. Introduced 1994. Imported from Germany by Blaser USA.
Price: R93 Prestige, wood grade 3. . . . . **$3,275.00**
Price: R93 Luxus **$4,460.00**
Price: R93 Professional **$2,950.00**
Price: R93 Grand Luxe **$8,163.00**
Price: R93 Attache **$6,175.00**

BROWNING A-BOLT RIFLES

Common Features: Short-throw (60°) fluted bolt, three locking lugs, plunger-type ejector; adjustable trigger is grooved. Chrome-plated trigger sear. Hinged floorplate, detachable box magazine. Slide tang safety. Receivers are drilled and tapped for scope mounts, swivel studs included. Barrel is free-floating and glass-bedded, recessed muzzle. Safety is top-tang sliding button. Engraving available for bolt sleeve or rifle body. Introduced 1985. Imported from Japan by Browning.

BROWNING A-BOLT HUNTER

Calibers: 22" Barrel: 223 Rem., 22-250 Rem., 243 Win., 270 Win., 30-06 Spfl., 7mm-08 Rem., 308 Win. **Barrel:** 270 WSM, 7mm WSM, 300 WSM, 325 WSM (intr. 2005). **Calibers:** 24" Barrel: 25-06 Rem. **Calibers:** 26" Barrel: 7mm Rem. Mag., 300 Win. Mag., 338 Win. Mag. **Weight:** 6.25-7.2 lbs. **Length:** 41.25-46.5" overall. **Stock:** Sporter-style walnut; checkered grip and forend. **Metal Finish:** Low-luster blueing.
Price: Hunter, left-hand, from **$819.00**

BROWNING A-BOLT HUNTER FLD

Caliber: 23" Barrel: 270 WSM, 7mm WSM, 300 WSM, 325 WSM (intr. 2005). **Weight:** 6.6 lbs. **Length:** 42.75" overall. **Features:** FLD has low-luster blueing and select Monte Carlo stock with right-hand palm swell, double-border checkering. Otherwise similar to A-Bolt Hunter.
Price: FLD. **$899.00**

Browning A-Bolt Target

Similar to A-Bolt Hunter but with 28" heavy bull blued barrel, blued receiver, satin finish gray laminated stock with adjustable comb and semi-beavertail forend. Chambered in 223, 308 Winchester and 300 WSM. Available also with stainless receiver and barrel.
Price: From **$1,269.00**
Price: Stainless, from **$1,489.00**

Prices given are believed to be accurate at time of publication however, many factors affect retail pricing so exact prices are not possible.

Browning A-Bolt Stainless Target

Browning A-Bolt Medallion

Browning A-Bolt White Gold Medallion

Browning A-Bolt Stainless Stalker

Browning A-Bolt Composite Stalker

BROWNING A-BOLT MOUNTAIN TI
Caliber: 223 WSSM, 243 WSSM, 25 WSSM (all added 2005); 270 WSM, 7mm WSM, 300 WSM. **Barrel:** 22" or 23". **Weight:** 5.25-5.5 lbs. **Length:** 41.25-42.75" overall. **Stock:** Lightweight fiberglass Bell & Carlson model in Mossy-Oak New Break Up camo. Metal Finish: Stainless barrel, titanium receiver. **Features:** Pachmayr Decelerator recoil pad. Introduced 1999.
Price: From **$1,819.00**

BROWNING A-BOLT MICRO HUNTER AND MICRO HUNTER LEFT-HAND
Calibers: 20" Barrel: 22-250 Rem., 243 Win., 308 Win., 7mm-08. 22" Barrel: 22 Hornet, 270 WSM, 7mm WSM, 300 WSM, 325 WSM (2005). **Weight:** 6.25-6.4 lbs. **Length:** 39.5-41.5" overall. **Features:** Classic walnut stock with 13.3" LOP. Otherwise similar to A-Bolt Hunter.
Price: Micro Hunter, from **$759.00**
Price: Micro Hunter left-hand, from **$799.00**

BROWNING A-BOLT MEDALLION
Calibers: 22" Barrel: 223 Rem., 22-250 Rem., 243 Win., 308 Win., 270 Win., 280 Rem., 30-06.; 23" Barrel: 270 WSM, 7mm WSM, 300 WSM, 325 WSM (intr. 2005); 24" Barrel: 25-06 Rem.; 26" Barrel: 7mm Rem. Mag., 300 Win. Mag., 338 Win. Mag., 375 H&H. **Weight:** 6.25-7.1 lbs. **Length:** 41.25-46.5" overall. **Stock:** Select walnut stock, glossy finish, rosewood grip and forend caps, checkered grip and forend. Metal Finish: Engraved high-polish blued receiver.
Price: Medallion, from. **$909.00**
Price: Medallion WSM **$959.00**
Price: Medallion w/BOSS, intr. 1987, from **$1,009.00**

BROWNING A-BOLT WHITE GOLD MEDALLION, RMEF WHITE GOLD, WHITE GOLD MEDALLION W/BOSS
Calibers: 22" Barrel: 270 Win., 30-06. Calibers: 23" Barrel: 270 WSM, 7mm WSM, 300 WSM, 325 WSM (intr. 2005). Calibers: 26" Barrel: 7mm Rem. Mag., 300 Win. Mag. **Weight:** 6.4-7.7 lbs. **Length:** 42.75-

46.5" overall. **Stock:** select walnut stock with brass spacers between rubber recoil pad and between the rosewood gripcap and forend tip; gold-filled barrel inscription; palm-swell pistol grip, Monte Carlo comb, 22 lpi checkering with double borders. **Metal Finish:** Engraved high-polish stainless receiver and barrel. BOSS version chambered in 270 Win. and 30-06 (22" barrel) and 7mm Rem. Mag. and 300 Win. Mag. (26" barrel). Introduced 1988. RMEF version has engraved gripcap, continental cheekpiece; gold engraved, stainless receiver and bbl. Introduced 2004.
Price: White Gold Medallion, from **$1,309.00**
Price: Rocky Mt. Elk Foundation White Gold, 325 WSM,
intr. 2007 . . . . **$1,399.00**

BROWNING A-BOLT STAINLESS STALKER, STAINLESS STALKER LEFT-HAND
Calibers: 22" Barrel: 223 Rem., 243 Win., 270 Win., 280 Rem., 7mm-08 Rem., 30-06 Spfl., 308 Win. Calibers: 23" Barrel: 270 WSM, 7mm WSM, 300 WSM, 325 WSM (intr. 2005). Calibers: 24" Barrel: 25-06 Rem. Calibers: 26" Barrel: 7mm Rem. Mag., 300 Win. Mag., 338 Win. Mag., 375 H&H. **Weight:** 6.1-7.2 lbs. **Length:** 40.9-46.5" overall. **Features:** Similar to the A-Bolt Hunter model except receiver and barrel are made of stainless steel; other exposed metal surfaces are finished silver-gray matte. Graphite-fiberglass composite textured stock. No sights are furnished, except on 375 H&H, which comes with open sights. Introduced 1987.
Price: Stainless Stalker left-hand, from **$1,029.00**
Price: Stainless Stalker w/Boss, from. **$1,119.00**

BROWNING A-BOLT COMPOSITE STALKER
Calibers: 22 Barrel: 270 Win., 30-06 Sprg.; 23" Barrel: 270 WSM, 7mm WSM, 300 WSM, 325 WSM; 24" Barrel: 25-06 Rem.; 26" Barrel: 7mm Rem. Mag., 300 Win. Mag., 338 Win. Mag. **Weight:** 6.6-7.3 lbs. **Length:** 42.5-46.5" overall. **Features:** Similar to the A-Bolt Stainless Stalker except has black composite stock with textured finish and matte-blued finish on all exposed metal surfaces except bolt sleeve. No sights are furnished.
Price: Composite Stalker w/BOSS, from **$869.00**
Price: Stainless Stalker **$1,009.00**
Price: Stainless Stalker w/Boss, from. **$1,079.00**

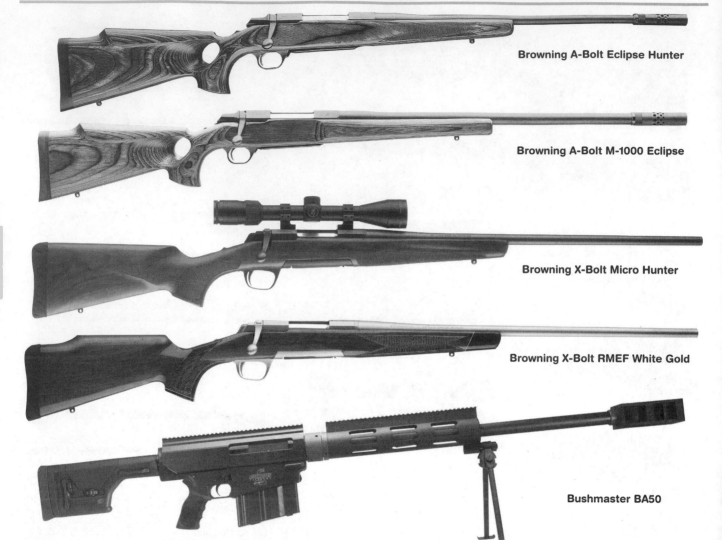

Browning A-Bolt Eclipse Hunter

Browning A-Bolt M-1000 Eclipse

Browning X-Bolt Micro Hunter

Browning X-Bolt RMEF White Gold

Bushmaster BA50

BROWNING A-BOLT ECLIPSE HUNTER W/BOSS, M-1000 ECLIPSE W/BOSS, M-1000 ECLIPSE WSM, STAINLESS M-1000 ECLIPSE WSM

Calibers: 22" Barrel: 270 Win., 30-06. Calibers: 26" Barrel: 7mm Rem. Mag., 300 Win. Mag., 270 WSM, 7mm WSM, 300 WSM. **Weight:** 7.5-9.9 lbs. **Length:** 42.75-46.5" overall. **Features:** All models have gray/black laminated thumbhole stock. Introduced 1996. Two versions have BOSS barrel vibration modulator and muzzle brake. Hunter has sporter-weight barrel. M-1000 Eclipses have long actions and heavy target barrels, adjustable triggers, bench-style forends, 3-shot magazines. Introduced 1997.
Price: Eclipse Hunter w/BOSS, from $1,259.00
Price: M-1000 Eclipse, from $1,169.00
Price: M-1000 Eclipse w/BOSS, from $1,259.00
Price: Stainless M-1000 Eclipse WSM, from $1,399.00
Price: Stainless M-1000 Eclipse w/BOSS, from $1,489.00

BROWNING X-BOLT HUNTER

Calibers: 223, 22-250, 243 Win., 25-06 Rem., 270 Win., 270 WSM, 280 Rem., 30-06 Spfl., 300 Win. Mag., 300 WSM, 308 Win., 325 WSM, 338 Win. Mag., 375 H&H Mag., 7mm Rem. Mag., 7mm WSM, 7mm-08 Rem. **Barrels:** 22", 23", 24", 26", varies by model. Matte blued or stainless free-floated barrel, recessed muzzle crown. **Weight:** 6.3-7 lbs. **Stock:** Hunter and Medallion models have wood stocks; Composite Stalker and Stainless Stalker models have composite stocks. Inflex Technology recoil pad. **Sights:** None, drilled and tapped receiver, X-Lock scope mounts. **Features:** Adjustable three-lever Feather Trigger system, polished hard-chromed steel components, factory pre-set at 3.5 lbs., alloy trigger housing. Bolt unlock button, detachable rotary magazine, 60-degree bolt lift, three locking lugs, top-tang safety, sling swivel studs. Medallion has metal engraving, gloss finish walnut stock, rosewood fore-end grip and pistol grip cap. Introduced 2008. From Browning.

Browning X-Bolt Micro Hunter

Similar to Browning X-Bolt Hunter but with compact dimensions (13-15/16 length of pull, 41-1/4 overall length).
Price: Standard chamberings $839.00
Price: Magnum $869.00

Browning X-Bolt Varmint Stalker

Similar to Browning X-Bolt Stalker but with medium-heavy free-floated barrel, target crown, composite stock. Chamberings available: 223, 22-250, 243 Winchester and 308 Winchester only.
Price: $1,019.00

Browning X-Bolt RMEF White Gold

Similar to X-Bolt Medallion but with gold-engraved matte stainless finish and Rocky Mountain Elk Foundation grip cap. Chambered in 325 WSM only.
Price: $1,399.00

Browning X-Bolt RMEF Special Hunter

Similar to above but with matte blued finish without gold highlights.
Price: $919.00

BUSHMASTER BA50 BOLT-ACTION RIFLE

Caliber: 50 Browning BMG. **Barrel:** 30" (rifle), 22" (carbine), 10-round mag. **Weight:** 30 lbs. (rifle), 27 lbs. (carbine). **Length:** 58" overall (rifle), 50" overall (carbine). **Features:** Free-floated Lother Walther barrel with muzzle brake, Magpul PRS adjustable stock.
Price: $4,895.00

Cooper Model 21 Bolt

CZ 527 Lux

CZ 527 FS

CZ 527 American

CARBON ONE BOLT-ACTION RIFLE
Caliber: 22-250 to 375 H&H. **Barrel:** Up to 28". **Weight:** 5.5 to 7.25 lbs. **Length:** Varies. **Stock:** Synthetic or wood. **Sights:** None furnished. **Features:** Choice of Remington, Browning or Winchester action with free-floated Christensen graphite/epoxy/steel barrel, trigger pull tuned to 3 to 3.5 lbs. Made in U.S.A. by Christensen Arms.
Price: Carbon One Hunter Rifle, 6.5 to 7 lbs. **$1,775.00**
Price: Carbon One Custom, 5.5 to 6.5 lbs., Shilen trigger . . **$3,900.00**
Price: Carbon Extreme **$2,450.00**

CENTURY INTERNATIONAL M70 SPORTER DOUBLE-TRIGGER BOLT ACTION RIFLE
Caliber: 22-250 Rem., 270 Win., 300 Win. Mag., 308 Win., 24" barrel. **Weight:** 7.95 lbs. **Length:** 44.5". **Sights:** Flip-up U-notch rear sight, hooded blade front sight. **Features:** Mauser M98-type action; 5-rd fixed box magazine. 22-250 has hinged floorplate. Monte Carlo stock, oil finish. Adjustable trigger on double-trigger models. 300 Win. Mag. Has 3 rd. fixed box magazine. 308 Win. holds 5 rounds. 300 and 308 have buttpads. Manufactured by Zastava in Yugoslavia, imported by Century International.
Price: M70 Sporter Double-Trigger. **$500.00**
Price: M70 Sporter Double-Trigger 22-250 . . . .**$475.00**
Price: M70 Sporter Single-Trigger .300 Win. Mag. **$475.00**
Price: M70 Sporter Single/Double Trigger 308 Win. **$500.00**

CHEYTAC M-200
Caliber: 408 CheyTac, 7-round magazine. **Barrel:** 30". **Length:** 55", stock extended. **Weight:** 27 lbs. (steel barrel); 24 lbs. (carbon fiber barrel). **Stock:** Retractable. **Sights:** None, scope rail provided. **Features:** CNC-machined receiver, attachable Picatinny rail M-1913, detachable barrel, integral bipod, 3.5-lb. trigger pull, muzzle brake. Made in U.S. by CheyTac, LLC.
Price: **$13,795.00**

COOPER MODEL 21 BOLT-ACTION RIFLE
Caliber: 17 Rem., 19-223, Tactical 20, .204 Ruger, 222 Rem, 222 Rem. Mag., 223 Rem, 223 Rem A.I., 6x45, 6x47. **Barrel:** 22" or 24" in Classic configurations, 24"-26" in Varminter configurations. **Weight:** 6.5-8.0 lbs., depending on type. **Stock:** AA-AAA select claro walnut, 20 lpi checkering. **Sights:** None furnished. **Features:** Three front locking-lug bolt-action single shot. Action: 7.75" long, Sako extractor. Button ejector. Fully adjustable single-stage trigger. Options include wood upgrades, case-color metalwork, barrel fluting, custom LOP, and many others.
Price: From **$1,395.00**

COOPER MODEL 22 BOLT-ACTION RIFLE
Caliber: 22-250 Rem., 22-250 Rem. AI, 25-06 Rem., 25-06 Rem. AI, 243 Win., 243 Win. AI, 220 Swift, 250/3000 AI, 257 Roberts, 257 Roberts AI, 7mm-08 Rem., 6mm Rem., 260 Rem., 6 x 284, 6.5 x 284, 22 BR, 6mm BR, 308 Win. **Barrel:** 24" or 26" stainless match in Classic configurations. 24" or 26" in Varminter configurations. **Weight:** 7.5 to 8.0 lbs. depending on type. **Stock:** AA-AAA select claro walnut, 20 lpi checkering. **Sights:** None furnished. **Features:** Three front locking-lug bolt-action single shot. Action: 8.25" long, Sako style extractor. Button ejector. Fully adjustable single-stage trigger. Options include wood upgrades, case-color metalwork, barrel fluting, custom LOP, and many others.
Price: From **$1,495.00**

COOPER MODEL 38 BOLT-ACTION RIFLE
Caliber: 17 Squirrel, 17 He Bee, 17 Ackley Hornet, 17 Mach IV, 19 Calhoon, 20 VarTarg, 221 Fireball, 22 Hornet, 22 K-Hornet, 22 Squirrel, 218 Bee, 218 Mashburn Bee. **Barrel:** 22" or 24" in Classic configurations, 24" or 26" in Varminter configurations. **Weight:** 6.5-8.0 lbs. depending on type. **Stock:** AA-AAA select claro walnut, 20 lpi checkering. **Sights:** None furnished. **Features:** Three front locking-lug bolt-action single shot. Action: 7" long, Sako style extractor. Button ejector. Fully adjustable single-stage trigger. Options include wood upgrades, case-color metalwork, barrel fluting, custom LOP, and many others.
Price: From **$1,395.00**

CZ 527 LUX BOLT-ACTION RIFLE
Caliber: 204 Ruger, 22 Hornet, 222 Rem., 223 Rem., detachable 5-shot magazine. **Barrel:** 23.5"; standard or heavy barrel. **Weight:** 6 lbs., 1 oz. **Length:** 42.5" overall. **Stock:** European walnut with Monte Carlo. **Sights:** Hooded front, open adjustable rear. **Features:** Improved mini-Mauser action with non-rotating claw extractor; single set trigger; grooved receiver. Imported from the Czech Republic by CZ-USA.
Price: Brown laminate stock **$718.00**
Price: Model FS, full-length stock, cheekpiece **$827.00**

CZ 527 American Bolt-Action Rifle
Similar to the CZ 527 Lux except has classic-style stock with 18 lpi checkering; free-floating barrel; recessed target crown on barrel. No sights furnished. Introduced 1999. Imported from the Czech Republic by CZUSA.
Price: From **$751.00**

Dakota 76 Traveler

Dakota 76 Classic

Dakota Longbow

CZ 550 AMERICAN CLASSIC BOLT-ACTION RIFLE

Caliber: 22-250 Rem., 243 Win., 6.5x55, 7x57, 7x64, 308 Win., 9.3x62, 270 Win., 30-06. **Barrel:** free-floating barrel; recessed target crown. **Weight:** 7.48 lbs. **Length:** 44.68" overall. **Stock:** American classic-style stock with 18 lpi checkering or FS (Mannlicher). **Sights:** No sights furnished. **Features:** Improved Mauser-style action with claw extractor, fixed ejector, square bridge dovetailed receiver; single set trigger. Introduced 1999. Imported from the Czech Republic by CZ-USA.

Price: FS (full stock) $894.00
Price: American, from $827.00

CZ 550 Safari Magnum/American Safari Magnum Bolt-Action Rifles

Similar to CZ 550 American Classic. Chambered for 375 H&H Mag., 416 Rigby, 458 Win. Mag., 458 Lott. Overall length is 46.5"; barrel length 25"; weighs 9.4 lbs., 9.9 lbs (American). Hooded front sight, express rear with one standing, two folding leaves. Imported from the Czech Republic by CZ-USA.

Price: $1,179.00
Price: American $1,261.00
Price: American Kevlar $1,714.00

CZ 550 Varmint Bolt-Action Rifle

Similar to CZ 550 American Classic. Chambered for 308 Win. and 22-250. Kevlar, laminated stocks. Overall length is 46.7"; barrel length 25.6"; weighs 9.1 lbs. Imported from the Czech Republic by CZ-USA.

Price: $841.00
Price: Kevlar $1,037.00
Price: Laminated $966.00

CZ 550 Magnum H.E.T. Bolt-Action Rifle

Similar to CZ 550 American Classic. Chambered for 338 Lapua, 300 Win. Mag., 300 RUM. Overall length is 52"; barrel length 28"; weighs 14 lbs. Adjustable sights, satin blued barrel. Imported from the Czech Republic by CZ-USA.

Price: $3,673.00

CZ 550 Ultimate Hunting Bolt-Action Rifle

Similar to CZ 550 American Classic. Chambered for 300 Win Mag. Overall length is 44.7"; barrel length 23.6"; weighs 7.7 lbs. Imported from the Czech Republic by CZ-USA.

Price: $4,242.00

CZ 750 SNIPER RIFLE

Caliber: 308 Winchester, 10-shot magazine. **Barrel:** 26". **Weight:** 11.9 lbs. **Length:** 48" overall. **Stock:** Polymer thumbhole. **Sights:** None furnished; permanently attached Weaver rail for scope mounting. **Features:** 60-degree bolt throw; oversized trigger guard and bolt handle for use with gloves; full-length equipment rail on forend; fully adjustable trigger. Introduced 2001. Imported from the Czech Republic by CZ-USA.

Price: $2,404.00

DAKOTA 76 TRAVELER TAKEDOWN RIFLE

Caliber: 257 Roberts, 25-06 Rem., 7x57, 270 Win., 280 Rem., 30-06 Spfl., 338-06, 35 Whelen (standard length); 7mm Rem. Mag., 300 Win. Mag., 338 Win. Mag., 416 Taylor, 458 Win. Mag. (short magnums); 7mm, 300, 330, 375 Dakota Magnums. **Barrel:** 23". **Weight:** 7.5 lbs. **Length:** 43.5" overall. **Stock:** Medium fancy-grade walnut in classic style. Checkered grip and forend; solid buttpad. **Sights:** None furnished; drilled and tapped for scope mounts. **Features:** Threadless disassembly. Uses modified Model 76 design with many features of the Model 70 Winchester. Left-hand model also available. Introduced 1989. African chambered for 338 Lapua Mag., 404 Jeffery, 416 Rigby, 416 Dakota, 450 Dakota, 4-round magazine, select wood, two stock cross-bolts. 24" barrel, weighs 9-10 lbs. Ramp front sight, standing leaf rear. Introduced 1989. Made in U.S.A. by Dakota Arms, Inc.

Price: Classic $6,095.00
Price: Safari $7,895.00
Price: African $9,495.00

DAKOTA 76 CLASSIC BOLT-ACTION RIFLE

Caliber: 257 Roberts, 270 Win., 280 Rem., 30-06 Spfl., 7mm Rem. Mag., 338 Win. Mag., 300 Win. Mag., 375 H&H, 458 Win. Mag. **Barrel:** 23". **Weight:** 7.5 lbs. **Length:** 43.5" overall. **Stock:** Medium fancy grade walnut in classic style. Checkered pistol grip and forend; solid buttpad. **Sights:** None furnished; drilled and tapped for scope mounts. **Features:** Has many features of the original Winchester Model 70. One-piece rail trigger guard assembly; steel gripcap. Model 70-style trigger. Many options available. Left-hand rifle available at same price. Introduced 1988. From Dakota Arms, Inc.

Price: From $4,595.00

DAKOTA LONGBOW T-76 TACTICAL RIFLE

Caliber: 300 Dakota Magnum, 330 Dakota Magnum, 338 Lapua Magnum. **Barrel:** 28", .950" at muzzle **Weight:** 13.7 lbs. **Length:** 50" to 52" overall. **Stock:** Ambidextrous McMillan A-2 fiberglass, black or olive green color; adjustable cheekpiece and buttplate. **Sights:** None furnished. Comes with Picatinny one-piece optical rail. **Features:** Uses the Dakota 76 action with controlled-round feed; three-position firing pin block safety, claw extractor; Model 70-style trigger. Comes with bipod, case tool kit. Introduced 1997. Made in U.S.A. by Dakota Arms, Inc.

Price: $4,795.00

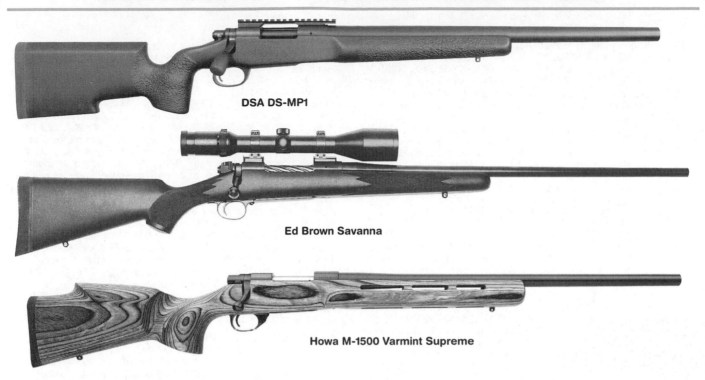

DSA DS-MP1

Ed Brown Savanna

Howa M-1500 Varmint Supreme

DAKOTA MODEL 97 BOLT-ACTION RIFLE
Caliber: 22-250 to 330. **Barrel:** 22" to 24". **Weight:** 6.1 to 6.5 lbs. **Length:** 43" overall. **Stock:** Fiberglass. **Sights:** Optional. **Features:** Matte blue finish, black stock. Right-hand action only. Introduced 1998. Made in U.S.A. by Dakota Arms, Inc.
Price: From $3,395.00

DAKOTA PREDATOR RIFLE
Caliber: 17 VarTarg, 17 Rem., 17 Tactical, 20 VarTarg, 20 Tactical, .20 PPC, 204 Ruger, 221 Rem Fireball, 222 Remington, 22 PPC, 223 Rem., 6mm PPC, 6.5 Grendel. **Barrel:** 22" match grade stainless;. **Weight:** NA. **Length:** NA. **Stock:** Special select walnut, sporter-style stock, 23 lpi checkering on forend and grip. **Sights:** None furnished. Drilled and tapped for scope mounting. **Features:** 13-5/8" LOP, 1/2" black presentation pad, 11" recessed target crown. Serious Predator includes XXX walnut varmint style stock w/semi-beavertail forend, stainless receiver. All-Weather Predator includes varmint style composite stock w/semi-beavertail forend, stainless receiver. Introduced 2007. Made in U.S.A. by Dakota Arms, Inc.
Price: Classic $4,295.00
Price: Serious $3,295.00
Price: All-Weather $1,995.00

DSA DS-MP1
Caliber: 308 Win. match chamber. **Barrel:** 22", 1:10 twist, hand-lapped stainless-steel match-grade Badger Barrel with recessed target crown. **Weight:** 11.5 lbs. **Length:** 41.75". **Stock:** Black McMillan A5 pillar bedded in Marine-Tex with 13.5" length of pull. **Sights:** Tactical Picatinny rail. **Features:** Action, action threads and action bolt locking shoulder completely trued, Badger Ordnance precision ground heavy recoil lug, machined steel Picatinny rail sight mount, trued action threads, action bolt locking shoulder, bolt face and lugs, 2.5-lb. trigger pull, barrel and action finished in Black DuraCoat, guaranteed to shoot 1/2 MOA at 100 yards with match-grade ammo. Introduced 2006. Made in U.S.A. by DSA, Inc.
Price: $2,800.00

EAA/ZASTAVA M-93 BLACK ARROW RIFLE
Caliber: 50 BMG. **Barrel:** 36". **Weight:** 7 to 8.5 lbs. **Length:** 60". **Stock:** Synthetic. **Sights:** Scope rail and iron sights. **Features: Features:** Mauser action, developed in early 1990s by Zastava Arms Factory. Fluted heavy barrel with recoil reducing muzzle brake, self-leveling and adjustable folding integral bipod, back up iron sights, heavy duty carry handle, detachable 5 round box magazine, and quick detachable scope mount. Imported by EAA. Imported from Russia by EAA Corp.
Price: $6,986.25

ED BROWN HUNTING SERIES RIFLES
Caliber: Many calibers available. **Barrel:** 24" (Savanna, Express, Varmint); 23-24" (Damara); 22" (Compact Varmint). **Weight:** 8 to 8.5 lbs. (Savanna); 6.2 to 6.9 lbs. (Damara); 9 lbs. (Express); 10 lbs. (Varmint), 8.75 lbs. (Compact Varmint). **Stock:** Fully glass-bedded McMillan fiberglass sporter. **Sights:** None furnished. Talley scope mounts utilizing heavy-duty 8-40 screws. **Features:** Custom action with machined steel trigger guard and hinged floor plate.
Price: Savanna $3,895.00
Price: Damara . . . . $3,995.00 to $4,095.00
Price: Express $4,995.00
Price: Varmint & Compact Varmint $3,895.00

ED BROWN MODEL 704 BUSHVELD
Caliber: 338 Win. Mag., 375 H&H, 416 Rem. Mag., 458 Win. Mag., 458 Lott and all Ed Brown Savanna long action calibers. **Barrel:** 24" medium or heavy weight. **Weight:** 8.25 lbs. **Stock:** Fully bedded McMillan fiberglass with Monte Carlo style cheekpiece, Pachmayr Decelerator recoil pad. **Sights:** None furnished. Talley scope mounts utilizing heavy-duty 8-40 screws. **Features:** Stainless steel barrel, additional calibers: iron sights.
Price: From $2,995.00

ED BROWN MODEL 704 EXPRESS
Caliber: 375 H&H, 416 Rem, 458 Lott, other calibers available. **Barrel:** 24" #4 Stainless barrel with black Gen III coating for superior rust protection. **Weight:** 9 lbs. **Stocks:** Hand-bedded McMillan fiberglass stock. Monte Carlo style with cheek piece and full 1" thick Pachmayr Decel recoil pad. **Sights:** Adjustable iron sights. **Features:** Ed Brown controlled feed action. A special dropped box magazine ensures feeding and allows a full four-round capacity in the magazine, plus one in the chamber. Barrel band is standard for lower profile when carrying the rifle through heavy brush.
Price: From $3,695.00

HOWA M-1500 RANCHLAND COMPACT
Caliber: 223 Rem., 22-250 Rem., 243 Win., 308 Win. and 7mm-08. **Barrel:** 20" #1 contour, blued finish. **Weight:** 7 lbs. **Stock:** Hogue Overmolded in black, OD green, Coyote Sand colors. 13.87" LOP. **Sights:** None furnished; drilled and tapped for scope mounting. **Features:** Three-position safety, hinged floor plate, adjustable trigger, forged one-piece bolt, M-16 style extractor, forged flat-bottom receiver. Also available with Nikko-Stirling Nighteater 3-9x42 riflescope. Introduced in 2008. Imported from Japan by Legacy Sports International.
Price: Rifle Only, (2008) $479.00
Price: Rifle with 3-9x42 Nighteater scope (2008) $599.00

Prices given are believed to be accurate at time of publication however, many factors affect retail pricing so exact prices are not possible.

CENTERFIRE RIFLES—Bolt-Action

HOWA M-1500 THUMBHOLE SPORTER
Caliber: 204, 223 Rem., 22-250 Rem., 243 Win., 6.5x55 (2008) 25-06 Rem., 270 Win., 7mm Rem. Mag., 308 Win., 30-06 Spfl., 300 Win. Mag., 338 Win. Mag., 375 Ruger. Similar to Camo Lightning except stock. **Weight:** 7.6 to 7.7 lbs. **Stock:** S&K laminated wood in nutmeg (brown/black) or pepper (grey/black) colors, raised comb with forward taper, flared pistol grip and scalloped thumbhole. **Sights:** None furnished; drilled and tapped for scope mounting. **Features:** Three-position safety, hinged floor plate, adjustable trigger, forged one-piece bolt, M-16 style extractor, forged flat-bottom receiver. Introduced in 2001. Imported from Japan by Legacy Sports International.
Price: Blue/Nutmeg, standard calibers . . . . **$649.00 to $669.00**
Price: Stainless/Pepper, standard calibers . . . . . . **$749.00 to $769.00**

HOWA M-1500 VARMINTER SUPREME AND THUMBHOLE VARMINTER SUPREME
Caliber: 204, 223 Rem., 22-250 Rem., 243 Win., 308 Win. **Stock:** Varminter Supreme: Laminated wood in nutmeg (brown), pepper (grey) colors, raised comb and rollover cheekpiece, full pistol grip with palm-filling swell and broad beavertail forend with six vents for barrel cooling. Thumbhole Varminter Supreme similar, adds a high, straight comb, more vertical pistol grip. **Sights:** None furnished; drilled and tapped for scope mounting. **Features:** Three-position safety, hinged floor plate, adjustable trigger, forged one-piece bolt, M-16 style extractor, forged flat-bottom receiver, hammer forged bull barrel and recessed muzzle crown; overall length, 43.75", 9.7 lbs. Introduced 2001. Barreled actions imported by Legacy Sports International; stocks by S&K Gunstocks.
Price: Varminter Supreme, Blue/Nutmeg **$679.00**
Price: Varminter Supreme, Stainless/Pepper **$779.00**
Price: Thumbhole Varminter Supreme, Blue/Nutmeg. **$679.00**
Price: Thumbhole Varminter Supreme, Stainless/Pepper **$779.00**

HOWA CAMO LIGHTNING M-1500
Caliber: 204, 223 Rem., 22-250 Rem., 243 Win., 25-06 Rem., 270 Win., 308 Win., 30-06 Spfl., 300 Win. Mag., 338 Win. Mag., 7mm Rem. Mag. **Barrel:** 22" standard calibers; 24" magnum calibers; #2 and #6 contour; blue and stainless. **Weight:** 7.6 to 9.3 lbs. **Length:** 42" to 44.5" overall. **Stock:** Synthetic with molded cheek piece, checkered grip and forend. **Sights:** None furnished; drilled and tapped for scope mounting. **Features:** Three-position safety, hinged floor plate, adjustable trigger, forged one-piece bolt, M-16 style extractor, forged flat bottom receiver. Introduced in 1993. Barreled actions imported by Legacy Sports International.
Price: Blue, #2 barrel, standard calibers **$377.00**
Price: Stainless, #2 barrel, standard calibers **$479.00**
Price: Blue, #2 barrel, magnum calibers. **$390.00**
Price: Stainless, #2 barrel, magnum calibers **$498.00**
Price: Blue, #6 barrel, standard calibers **$425.00**
Price: Stainless, #6 barrel, standard calibers **$498.00**

HOWA/HOGUE M-1500
Caliber: 204, 223 Rem., 22-250 Rem., 243 Win., 6.5x5 (2008) 25-06 Rem., 270 Win., 308 Win., 30-06 Spfl., 300 Win. Mag., 338 Win. Mag., 7mm Rem. Mag., 375 Ruger (2008). **Barrel:** Howa barreled action; stainless or blued, 22" #2 contour. **Weight:** 7.4 to 7.6 lbs. **Stock:** Hogue Overmolded, black, or OD green; ambidextrous palm swells. **Sights:** None furnished; drilled and tapped for scope mounting. **Length:** 42" to 44.5" overall. **Features:** Three-position safety, hinged floor plate, adjustable trigger, forged one-piece bolt, M-16 style extractor, forged flat bottom receiver, aluminum pillar bedding and free-floated barrels. Introduced in 2006. Available w/3-10x42 Nikko-Stirling Nighteater scope, rings, bases (2008). from Imported from Japan by Legacy Sports International.
Price: Blued, rifle only . . . . **$479.00 to $499.00**
Price: Blue, rifle with scope package (2008) . . . . . **$599.00 to $619.00**
Price: Stainless, rifle only . . . . **$625.00 to $675.00**

HOWA/HOGUE M-1500 COMPACT HEAVY BARREL VARMINTER
Chambered in 223 Rem., 308 Win., has 20" #6 contour heavy barrel, recessed muzzle crown. **Stock:** Hogue Overmolded, black, or OD green; ambidextrous palm swells. **Sights:** None furnished; drilled and tapped for scope mounting. **Length:** 44.0" overall. **Features:** Three-position safety, hinged floor plate, adjustable trigger, forged one-piece bolt, M-16 style extractor, forged flat bottom receiver, aluminum pillar bedding and free-floated barrels. **Weight:** 9.3 lbs. Introduced 2008. Imported from Japan by Legacy Sports International.
Price: From **$559.00**

HOWA/AXIOM M-1500
Caliber: 204, 223 Rem., 22-250 Rem., 243 Win., 6.5x55 (2008), 25-06 Rem. (2008), 270 Win., 308 Win., 30-06 Spfl., 7mm Rem, 300 Win. Mag., 338 Win. Mag., 375 Ruger standard barrel; 204, 223 Rem., 243 Win. and 308 Win. heavy barrel. **Barrel:** Howa barreled action, 22" contour standard barrel, 20" #6 contour heavy barrel, and 24" #6 contour heavy barrel. **Weight:** 8.6-10 lbs. **Stock:** Knoxx Industries Axiom V/S synthetic, black or camo. Adjustable length of pull from 11.5" to 15.5". **Sights:** None furnished; drilled and tapped for scope mounting. **Features:** Three-position safety, adjustable trigger, hinged floor plate, forged receiver with large recoil lug, forged one-piece bolt with dual locking lugs Introduced in 2007. Standard-barrel scope packages come with 3-10x42 Nikko-Stirling Nighteater scope, rings, bases (2008). Heavy barrels come with 4-16x44 Nikko-Stirling scope. Imported from Japan by Legacy Sports International.
Price: Axiom Standard Barrel, black stock, from **$699.00**
Price: Axiom 20" and 24" Varminter, black or camo stock, from **$799.00**
Price: Axiom 20" and 24" Varminter, camo stock w/scope (2008), from **$819.00**

HOWA M-1500 ULTRALIGHT 2-N-1 YOUTH
Caliber: 223 Rem., 22-250 Rem., 243 Win., 308 Win., 7mm-08. **Barrel:** 20" #1 contour, blued. **Weight:** 6.8 lbs. **Length:** 39.25" overall. **Stock:** Hogue Overmolded in black, 12.5" LOP. Also includes adult-size Hogue Overmolded in OD green. **Sights:** None furnished; drilled and tapped for scope mounting. **Features:** Bolt and receiver milled to reduce weight, three-position safety, hinged floor plate, adjustable trigger, forged one-piece bolt, M-16 style extractor, forged flat-bottom receiver. Scope package includes 3-9x42 Nikko-Stirling riflescope with bases and rings. Imported from Japan by Legacy Sports International.
Price: Blue, Youth Rifle. **$539.00**
Price: w/Scope package (2008) **$589.00**

H-S PRECISION PRO-SERIES BOLT-ACTION RIFLES
Caliber: 30 chamberings, 3- or 4-round magazine. **Barrel:** 20", 22", 24" or 26", sporter contour Pro-Series 10X match-grade stainless steel barrel. Optional muzzle brake on 30 cal. or smaller. **Weight:** 7.5 lbs. **Length:** NA. **Stock:** Pro-Series synthetic stock with full-length bedding block chassis system, sporter style. **Sights:** None; drilled and tapped for bases. **Features:** Accuracy guarantee: up to 30 caliber, 1/2 minute of angle (3 shots at 100 yards), test target supplied. Stainless steel action, stainless steel floorplate with detachable magazine, matte black Teflon finish. Made in U.S.A. by H-S Precision, Inc.
Price: SPR **$2,680.00**
Price: SPL Lightweight (2008) **$2,825.00**

KEL-TEC RFB
Caliber: 7.62 NATO (308 Win.). **Barrels:** 18" to 32". **Weight:** 11.3 lbs. (unloaded). **Length:** 40" overall. **Features:** Gas-operated semi-auto bullpup-style, forward-ejecting. Fully ambidextrous controls, adjustable trigger mechanism, no open sights, four-sided picatinny forend. Accepts standard FAL-type magazines. Production of the RFB has been delayed due to redesign but was expected to begin first quarter 2009.
Price: **$1,800.00**

KENNY JARRETT BOLT-ACTION RIFLE
Caliber: 223 Rem., 243 Improved, 243 Catbird, 7mm-08 Improved, 280 Remington, .280 Ackley Improved, 7mm Rem. Mag., 284 Jarrett, 30-06 Springfield, 300 Win. Mag., .300 Jarrett, 323 Jarrett, 338 Jarrett, 375 H&H, 416 Rem., 450 Rigby., other modern cartridges. **Barrel:** NA. **Weight:** NA. **Length:** NA. **Stock:** NA. **Features:** Tri-Lock receiver. Talley rings and bases. Accuracy guarantees and custom loaded ammunition.
Price: Signature Series. **$7,640.00**
Price: Wind Walker **$7,380.00**
Price: Original Beanfield (customer's receiver) **$5,380.00**
Price: Professional Hunter **$10,400.00**
Price: SA/Custom **$6,630.00**

Prices given are believed to be accurate at time of publication however, many factors affect retail pricing so exact prices are not possible.

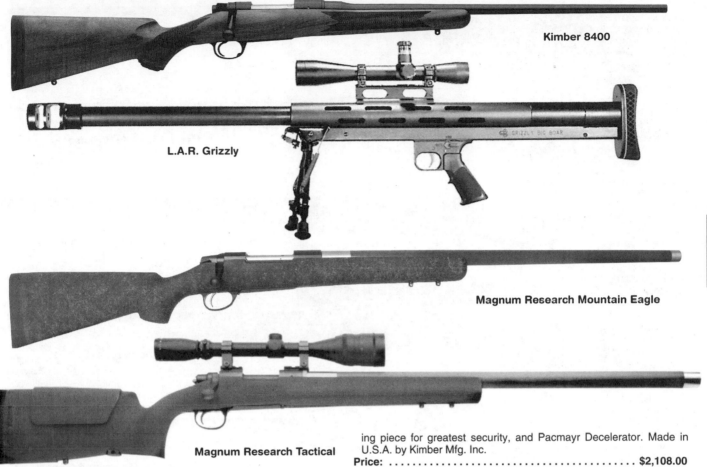

Kimber 8400

L.A.R. Grizzly

Magnum Research Mountain Eagle

Magnum Research Tactical

KIMBER MODEL 8400 BOLT-ACTION RIFLE

Caliber: 25-06 Rem., 270 Win., 7mm, 30-06 Spfl., 300 Win. Mag., 338 Win. Mag., or 325 WSM, 4 shot. **Barrel:** 24". **Weight:** 6 lbs. 3 oz. to 6 lbs 10 oz. **Length:** 43.25". **Stock:** Claro walnut or Kevlar-reinforced fiberglass. **Sights:** None; drilled and tapped for bases. **Features:** Mauser claw extractor, two-position wing safety, action bedded on aluminum pillars and fiberglass, free-floated barrel, match grade adjustable trigger set at 4 lbs., matte or polished blue or matte stainless finish. Introduced 2003. Sonora model (2008) has brown laminated stock, hand-rubbed oil finish, chambered in 25-06 Rem., 30-06 Spfl., and 300 Win. Mag. Weighs 8.5 lbs., measures 44.50" overall length. Front swivel stud only for bipod. Stainless steel bull barrel, 24" satin stainless steel finish. Made in U.S.A. by Kimber Mfg. Inc.

Price: Classic **$1,172.00**
Price: Classic Select Grade, French walnut stock (2008). . . **$1,359.00**
Price: SuperAmerica, AAA walnut stock. **$2,240.00**
Price: Sonora **$1,359.00**
Price: Police Tactical, synthetic stock, fluted barrel
(300 Win. Mag only) **$2,575.00**

Kimber Model 8400 Caprivi Bolt-Action Rifle

Similar to 8400 bolt rifle, but chambered for .375 H&H and 458 Lott, 4-shot magazine. Stock is Claro walnut or Kevlar-reinforced fiberglass. Features twin steel crossbolts in stock, AA French walnut, pancake cheekpiece, 24 lines-per-inch wrap-around checkering, ebony forend tip, hand-rubbed oil finish, barrel-mounted sling swivel stud, 3-leaf express sights, Howell-type rear sling swivel stud and a Pachmayr Decelerator recoil pad in traditional orange color. Introduced 2008. Made in U.S.A. by Kimber Mfg. Inc.

Price: **$3,196.00**

Kimber Model 8400 Talkeetna Bolt-Action Rifle

Similar to 8400 bolt rifle, but chambered in .375 H&H, 4-shot magazine. Weighs 8 lbs, overall length is 44.5". Stock is synthetic. Features free-floating match grade barrel with tapered match grade chamber and target crown, three-position wing safety acts directly on the cock-

ing piece for greatest security, and Pacmayr Decelerator. Made in U.S.A. by Kimber Mfg. Inc.

Price: **$2,108.00**

KIMBER MODEL 84M BOLT-ACTION RIFLE

Caliber: 22-250 Rem., 204 Ruger, 223 Rem., 243 Win., 260 Rem., 7mm-08 Rem., 308 Win., 5-shot. **Barrel:** 22", 24", 26". **Weight:** 5 lbs., 10 oz. to 10 lbs. **Length:** 41" to 45". **Stock:** Claro walnut, checkered with steel gripcap; synthetic or gray laminate. **Sights:** None; drilled and tapped for bases. **Features:** Mauser claw extractor, three-position wing safety, action bedded on aluminum pillars, free-floated barrel, match-grade trigger set at 4 lbs., matte blue finish. Includes cable lock. Introduced 2001. Montana (2008) has synthetic stock, Pachmayr Decelerator recoil pad, stainless steel 22" sporter barrel. Made in U.S.A. by Kimber Mfg. Inc.

Price: Classic (243 Win., 260, 7mm-08 Rem., 308) **$1,114.00**
Price: Varmint (22-250) **$1,224.00**
Price: Montana **$1,276.00**
Price: Classic Stainless, matte stainless steel receiver
and barrel (243 Win., 7mm-08, 308 Win.) **$1,156.00**

L.A.R. GRIZZLY 50 BIG BOAR RIFLE

Caliber: 50 BMG, single shot. **Barrel:** 36". **Weight:** 30.4 lbs. **Length:** 45.5" overall. **Stock:** Integral. Ventilated rubber recoil pad. **Sights:** None furnished; scope mount. **Features:** Bolt-action bullpup design, thumb and bolt stop safety. All-steel construction. Introduced 1994. Made in U.S.A. by L.A.R. Mfg., Inc.

Price: From **$2,350.00**

MAGNUM RESEARCH MOUNTAIN EAGLE MAGNUMLITE RIFLES

Caliber: 22-250 Rem., 223 Rem., 280 Rem., 7mm WSM, 30-06 Spfl., 308 Win., 300 WSM, 300 Win. Mag., 3-shot magazine. **Barrel:** 24" sport taper graphite; 26" bull barrel graphite. **Weight:** 7.1-9.2 lbs. **Length:** 44.5-48.25" overall (adjustable on Tactical model). **Stock:** Hogue OverMolded synthetic, H-S Precision Tactical synthetic, H-S Precision Varmint synthetic. **Sights:** None. **Features:** Remington Model 700 receiver. Introduced in 2001. From Magnum Research, Inc.

Price: MLR3006ST24 Hogue stock **$2,295.00**
Price: MLR7MMBST24 Hogue stock **$2,295.00**
Price: MLRT22250 H-S Tactical stock, 26" bull barrel **$2,400.00**
Price: MLRT300WI Tactical **$2,400.00**

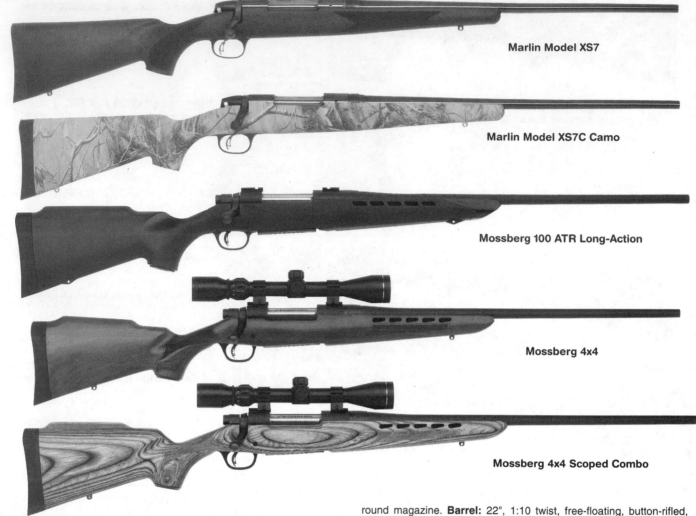

Marlin Model XS7

Marlin Model XS7C Camo

Mossberg 100 ATR Long-Action

Mossberg 4x4

Mossberg 4x4 Scoped Combo

MARLIN XL7 BOLT ACTION RIFLE

Caliber: 25-06 Rem. 270 Win., 30-06 Spfl., 4-shot magazine. **Barrel:** 22" 1:10" right-hand twist, recessed barrel crown. **Weight:** 6.5 lbs. **Length:** 42.5" overall. **Stock:** Black synthetic or Realtree APG-HD camo, Soft-Tech recoil pad, pillar bedded. **Sights:** None. **Features:** Pro-Fire trigger is user adjustable down to 2.5 lbs. Fluted bolt, steel sling swivel studs, high polished blued steel, checkered bolt handle, molded checkering, one-piece scope base. Introduced in 2008. From Marlin Firearms, Inc.
Price: Black Synthetic...................................$326.00
Price: Camouflaged $356.00

Marlin XS7 Short-Action Bolt-Action Rifle

Similar to Model XL7 but chambered in 7mm-08, 243 Winchester and 308 Winchester.
Price: .... NA
Price: XS7Y Youth $341.00
Price: XS7C Camo, Realtree APG HD camo stock $341.00

MERKEL KR1 BOLT-ACTION RIFLE

Caliber: 223 Rem., 243 Rem., 6.5x55, 7mm-08, 308 Win., 270 Win., 30-06, 9.3x62, 7mm Rem. Mag., 300 Win. Mag., 270 WSM, 300 WSM, 338 Win. Mag. **Features:** Short lock, short bolt movement, take-down design with interchangeable barrel assemblies, three-position safety, detachable box magazine, fine trigger with set feature, checkered walnut pistol-grip semi-schnable stock. Adjustable iron sights with quick release mounts. Imported from Germany by Merkel USA.
Price: $1,995.00
Price: Model KR1 Stutzen Antique: 20.8" barrel, case-colored receiver, Mannlicher-style stock $3,395.00

MOSSBERG 100 ATR BOLT-ACTION RIFLE

Caliber: 243 Win. (2006), 270 Win., 308 Win. (2006), 30-06 Spfl., 4-round magazine. **Barrel:** 22", 1:10 twist, free-floating, button-rifled, recessed muzzle crown. **Weight:** 6.7 to 7.75 lbs. **Length:** 42"-42.75" overall. **Stock:** Black synthetic, walnut, Mossy Oak New Break Up camo, Realtree AP camo. **Sights:** Factory-installed Weaver-style scope bases; scoped combos include 3x9 factory-mounted, bore-sighted scopes. **Features:** Marinecote and matte blue metal finishes, free gun lock, side lever safety. Introduced 2005. Night Train (2008) comes with Picatinny rail and factory-mounted 4-16x50mm variable scope. From O.F. Mossberg & Sons, Inc.
Price: Short-Action 243 Win., wood stock, matte blue, from. . . $424.00
Price: Long-Action 270 Win., Mossy Oak New Break Up camo, matte blue, from $424.00
Price: Scoped Combo 30-06 Spfl., Walnut-Dura-Wood stock, Marinecote finish, from $481.00
Price: Bantam Short Action 308 Win., 20" barrel $471.00
Price: Night Train Short-Action Scoped Combo (2008) $567.00

MOSSBERG 4X4 BOLT-ACTION RIFLE

Caliber: 25-06 Rem, 270 Win., 30-06 Spfl., 7mm Rem. Mag., .300 Win. Mag., .338 Win. Mag., detachable box magazine, 4 rounds standard, 3 rounds magnum. **Barrel:** 24", 1:10 twist, free-floating, button-rifled, recessed muzzle crown. **Weight:** 7+ lbs. **Length:** 42" overall. **Stock:** Skeletonized synthetic laminate (2008); black synthetic, laminated, select American black walnut. **Sights:** Factory-installed Weaver-style scope bases. **Features:** Marinecote and matte blue metal finishes, free gun lock, side lever safety. Scoped combos include factory-mounted, bore-sighted 3-9x40mm variable. Introduced 2007. From O.F. Mossberg & Sons, Inc.
Price: 25-06 Rem., walnut stock, matte blue, from $505.00
Price: 300 Win. Mag., synthetic laminate stock (2008), from . $505.00
Price: 4X4 Classic Stock Synthetic: Black synthetic stock and Marinecote metal surfaces $654.00
Price: 4X4 Scoped Combo: Matte blue finish and 3x9 scope $654.00
Price: 4X4 Classic Walnut Stock: Checkered walnut stock .. $654.00

Remington 700 CDL

Remington 700 CDL SF

Remington 700 BDL

Remington 700 SPS Varmint

Remington Model 700 LSS

REMINGTON MODEL 700 CDL CLASSIC DELUXE RIFLE
Caliber: 223 Rem., 243 Win., 25-06 Rem., 270 Win., 7mm-08 Rem., 7mm Rem. Mag., 7mm Rem. Ultra Mag., 30-06 Spfl., 300 Rem. Ultra Mag., 300 Win. Mag., 35 Whelen. **Barrel:** 24" or 26" round tapered. **Weight:** 7.4 to 7.6 lbs. **Length:** 43.6" to 46.5" overall. **Stock:** Straight-comb American walnut stock, satin finish, checkering, right-handed cheek piece, black fore-end tip and grip cap, sling swivel studs. **Sights:** None. **Features:** Satin blued finish, jeweled bolt body, drilled and tapped for scope mounts. Hinged-floorplate magazine capacity: 4, standard calibers; 3, magnum calibers. SuperCell recoil pad, cylindrical receiver, integral extractor. Introduced 2004. CDL SF (stainless fluted) chambered for 260 Rem., 257 Wby. Mag., 270 Win., 270 WSM, 7mm-08 Rem., 7mm Rem. Mag., 30-06 Spfl., 300 WSM. Left-hand versions introduced 2008 in six calibers. Made in U.S. by Remington Arms Co., Inc.

Price: Standard Calibers: 24" barrel **$959.00**
Price: Magnum Calibers: 26" barrel **$987.00**
Price: CDL SF (2007), from **$1,100.00**
Price: CDL LH (2008), from **$987.00**
Price: CDL High Polish Blued (2008), from **$959.00**
Price: CDL SF (2009), 257 Roberts . . . . **NA**

REMINGTON MODEL 700 BDL RIFLE
Caliber: 243 Win., 270 Win., 7mm Rem. Mag. 30-06 Spfl., 300 Rem Ultra Mag. **Barrel:** 22, 24, 26" round tapered. **Weight:** 7.25-7.4 lbs. **Length:** 41.6-46.5" overall. **Stock:** Walnut. Gloss-finish pistol grip stock with skip-line checkering, black forend tip and gripcap with white line spacers. Quick-release floorplate. **Sights:** Gold bead ramp front; hooded ramp, removable step-adjustable rear with windage screw. **Features:** Side safety, receiver tapped for scope mounts, matte receiver top, quick detachable swivels.

Price: 243 Win., 270 Win., 30-06 . . . . **$927.00**
Price: 7mm Rem. Mag. 300 Rem Ultra Mag. **$955.00**

REMINGTON MODEL 700 SPS RIFLES
Caliber: 17 Rem. Fireball, 204 Ruger, 22-250 Rem., 6.8 Rem SPC, 223 Rem., 243 Win., 270 Win. 270 WSM, 7mm-08 Rem., 7mm Rem. Mag., 7mm Rem. Ultra Mag., 30-06 Spfl., 308 Win., 300 WSM, 300 Win. Mag., 300 Rem. Ultra Mag. **Barrel:** 20", 24" or 26" carbon steel. **Weight:** 7 to 7.6 lbs. **Length:** 39.6" to 46.5" overall. **Stock:** Black synthetic, sling swivel studs, SuperCell recoil pad. **Sights:** None. Introduced 2005. SPS Stainless replaces Model 700 BDL Stainless Synthetic. **Barrel:** Bead-blasted 416 stainless steel. **Features:** Plated internal fire control component. SPS DM features detachable box magazine. Buckmaster Edition versions feature Realtree Hardwoods HD camouflage and Buckmasters logo engraved on floorplate. SPS Varmint includes X-Mark Pro trigger, 26" heavy contour barrel, vented beavertail forend, dual front sling swivel studs. Made in U.S. by Remington Arms Co., Inc.

Price: SPS, from **$639.00**
Price: SPS DM (2005) **$672.00**
Price: SPS Youth, 20" barrel (2007) 243 Win., 7mm-08 . . . . . . **$604.00**
Price: SPS Varmint (2007) **$665.00**
Price: SPS Stainless, (2005), from **$732.00**
Price: SPS Buckmasters Youth (2008), 243 Win. **$707.00**
Price: SPS Youth LH (2008), 243 Win., 7mm-08 . . . . **$620.00**
Price: SPS Varmint LH (2008) **$692.00**
Price: SPS Synthetic Left-Hand . . . . **NA**

REMINGTON MODEL 700 MOUNTAIN LSS RIFLES
Caliber: 270 Win., 280 Rem., 7mm-08 Rem., 30-06. **Barrel:** 22" satin stainless steel. **Weight:** 6.6 lbs. **Length:** 41.6" to 42.5" overall. **Stock:** Brown laminated, sling swivel studs, SuperCell recoil pad, black forend tip. **Sights:** None. **Barrel:** Bead-blasted 416 stainless steel, lightweight contour. Made in U.S. by Remington Arms Co., Inc.
Price: **$1,052.00**

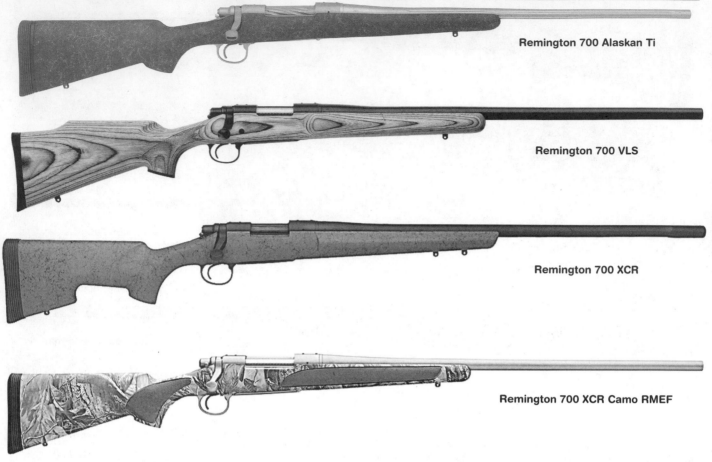

Remington 700 Alaskan Ti

Remington 700 VLS

Remington 700 XCR

Remington 700 XCR Camo RMEF

REMINGTON MODEL 700 ALASKAN TI
Caliber: 25-06 Rem., 270 Win., 270 WSM, 280 Rem., 7mm-08 Rem., 7mm Rem. Mag., 30-06 Spfl., 300 WSM, 300 Win. Mag. **Barrel:** 24" round tapered. **Weight:** 6 lbs. **Length:** 43.6" to 44.5" overall. **Stock:** Bell & Carlson carbon-fiber synthetic, sling swivel studs, SuperCell gel recoil pad. **Sights:** None. **Features:** Formerly Model 700 Titanium, introduced 2001. Titanium receiver, spiral-cut fluted bolt, skeletonized bolt handle, X-Mark Pro trigger, satin stainless finish. Drilled and tapped for scope mounts. Hinged-floorplate magazine capacity: 4, standard calibers; 3, magnum calibers. Introduced 2007. Made in U.S. by Remington Arms Co., Inc.
Price: From **$2,225.00**

REMINGTON MODEL 700 VLS/VLSS TH RIFLES
Caliber: 204 Ruger, 223 Rem., 22-250 Rem., 243 Win., 308 Win. **Barrel:** 26" heavy contour barrel (0.820" muzzle O.D.), concave target-style barrel crown **Weight:** 9.4 lbs. **Length:** 45.75" overall. **Stock:** Brown laminated stock, satin finish, with beavertail forend, gripcap, rubber buttpad. **Sights:** None. **Features:** Introduced 1995. VLSS TH (varmint laminate stock stainless) thumbhole model introduced 2007. Made in U.S. by Remington Arms Co., Inc.
Price: VLS **$979.00**
Price: VL SS TH **$1,085.00**

REMINGTON MODEL 700 VSSF-II/SENDERO SF II RIFLES
Caliber: 17 Rem. Fireball, 204 Ruger, 220 Swift, 223 Rem., 22-250 Rem., 308 Win. **Barrel:** satin blued 26" heavy contour (0.820" muzzle O.D.). VSSF has satin-finish stainless barreled action with 26" fluted barrel. **Weight:** 8.5 lbs. **Length:** 45.75" overall. **Stock:** H.S. Precision composite reinforced with aramid fibers, black (VSSF-II) Contoured beavertail fore-end with ambidextrous finger grooves, palm swell, and twin front tactical-style swivel studs. **Sights:** None. **Features:** Aluminum bedding block, drilled and tapped for scope mounts, hinged floorplate magazines. Introduced 1994. Sendero model is similar to VSSF-II except chambered for 264 Win. Mag., 7mm Rem. Mag., 7mm Rem. Ultra Mag., 300 Win. Mag., 300 Rem. Ultra Mag. Polished stainless barrel. Introduced 1996. Made in U.S. by Remington Arms Co., Inc.

Price: VSSF-II **$1,332.00**
Price: Sendero SF II **$1,359.00**

REMINGTON MODEL 700 XCR RIFLE
Caliber: 25-06 Rem., 270 Win., 270 WSM, 7mm-08 Rem., 7mm Rem. Mag., 7mm Rem Ultra Mag., 30-06 Spfl., 300 WSM, 300 Win. Mag., 300 Rem. Ultra Mag., 338 Rem. Ultra Mag., 338 Win. Mag., 375 H&H Mag., 375 Rem. Ultra Mag. **Barrel:** 24" standard caliber; 26" magnum. **Weight:** 7.4 to 7.6 lbs. **Length:** 43.6" to 46.5" overall. **Stock:** Black synthetic, SuperCell recoil pad, rubber overmolded grip and forend. **Sights:** None. **Features:** XCR (Xtreme Conditions Rifle) includes TriNyte Corrosion Control System; drilled and tapped for scope mounts. 375 H&H Mag., 375 Rem. Ultra Mag. chamberings come with iron sights. Introduced 2005. XCR Tactical model introduced 2007. **Features:** Bell & Carlson OD green tactical stock, beavertail forend, recessed thumbhook behind pistol grip, TriNyte coating over stainless steel barrel, LTR fluting. Chambered in 223 Rem., 300 Win. Mag., 308 Win. 700XCR Left Hand introduced 2008 in 270 Win., 7mm Rem. Mag., 30-06 Spfl., 300 Rem Ultra Mag. Made in U.S. by Remington Arms Co., Inc.
Price: From **$1,065.00**
Price: XCR Tactical (2007) **$1,407.00**
Price: XCR Left Hand (2008) **$1,092.00**
Price: XCR Compact Tactical (2008), 223 Rem., 308 Win. . **$1,434.00**

Remington Model 700 XCR Camo RMEF
Similar to Model 700 XCR but with stainless barrel and receiver, AP HD camo stock, TriNyte coating overall, 7mm Remington Ultra Mag chambering.
Price: **$1,199.00**

REMINGTON 700 XHR EXTREME HUNTING RIFLE
Caliber: 243 Win., 25-06, 270 Win., 7mm-08, 7mm Rem. Mag., 300 Win. Mag, 7mm Rem. Ultra Mag. **Barrel:** 24", 25", or 26" triangular magnum-contour counterbored. **Weight:** 7-1/4 to 7-5/8 lbs. **Length:** 41-5/8 to 46-1/2 overall. **Features:** Adjustable trigger, synthetic stock finished in Realtree AG HD camo, satin black oxide finish on exposed metal surfaces, hinged floorplate, SuperCell recoil pad.
Price: . . . . **$879.00 to $927.00**

CENTERFIRE RIFLES—Bolt-Action

Remington 700 XHR

Remington 700 Target Tactical

Remington 700 Varmint SF

Remington 770

Remington Seven CDL

REMINGTON MODEL 700 XCR TARGET TACTICAL RIFLE
Caliber: 308 Win. **Barrel:** 26" triangular counterbored, 1:11-1/2 rifling. **Weight:** 11.75 lbs. **Length:** 45-3/4" overall. **Features:** Textured green Bell & Carlson varmint/tactical stock with adjustable comb and length of pull, adjustable trigger, satin black oxide finish on exposed metal surfaces, hinged floorplate, SuperCell recoil pad, matte blue on exposed metal surfaces.
Price: **$1,407.00**

REMINGTON MODEL 700 VTR VARMINT/TACTICAL RIFLE
Caliber: 17 Rem. Fireball, 204 Ruger, 22-250, 223 Rem., 243 Win., 308 Win. **Barrel:** 22" triangular counterbored. **Weight:** 7.5 lbs. **Length:** 41-5/8" overall. **Features:** Olive drab overmolded or Digital Tiger TSP Desert Camo stock with vented semi-beavertail forend, tactical-style dual swivel mounts for bipod, matte blue on exposed metal surfaces.
Price: **$1,972.00**
Price: VTR Desert Recon, Digital Desert Camo stock,
    223 and 308 Win. only **$1,972.00**

REMINGTON MODEL 700 VARMINT SF RIFLE
Caliber: 17 Rem. Fireball, 204 Ruger, 22-250, 223, 220 Swift. **Barrel:** 26" stainless steel fluted. **Weight:** 8.5 lbs. **Length:** 45.75". **Features:** Synthetic stock with ventilated forend, stainless steel/triggerguard/floorplate, dual tactical swivels for bipod attachment.
Price: **$825.00**

30-06 Spfl., 300 Win. Mag. **Barrel:** 22" or 24", button rifled. **Weight:** 8.5 lbs. **Length:** 42.5" to 44.5" overall. **Stock:** Black synthetic. **Sights:** Bushnell Sharpshooter 3-9x scope mounted and bore-sighted. **Features:** Upgrade of Model 710 introduced 2001. Unique action locks bolt directly into barrel; 60-degree bolt throw; 4-shot dual-stack magazine; all-steel receiver. Introduced 2007. Made in U.S.A. by Remington Arms Co.
Price: **$460.00**
Price: Youth, 243 Win. **$460.00**
Price: Stainless Camo (2008), stainless barrel, nickel-plated bolt,
    Realtree camo stock **$540.00**

REMINGTON MODEL SEVEN CDL/CDL MAGNUM
Caliber: 17 Rem. Fireball, 243 Win., 260 Rem., 270 WSM, 7mm-08 Rem., 308 Win., 300 WSM, 350 Rem. Mag. **Barrel:** 20"; 22" magnum. **Weight:** 6.5 to 7.4 lbs. **Length:** 39.25" to 41.25" overall. **Stock:** American walnut, SuperCell recoil pad, satin finished. **Sights:** None. **Features:** Satin finished carbon steel barrel and action, 3- or 4-round magazine, hinged magazine floorplate. Furnished with iron sights and sling swivel studs, drilled and tapped for scope mounts. CDL versions introduced 2007. Made in U.S.A. by Remington Arms Co.
Price: CDL **$959.00**
Price: CDL Magnum **$1,01200**
Price: Predator (2008) **$825.00**
Price: 25th Anniversary (2008), 7mm-08 . . . . **$969.00**

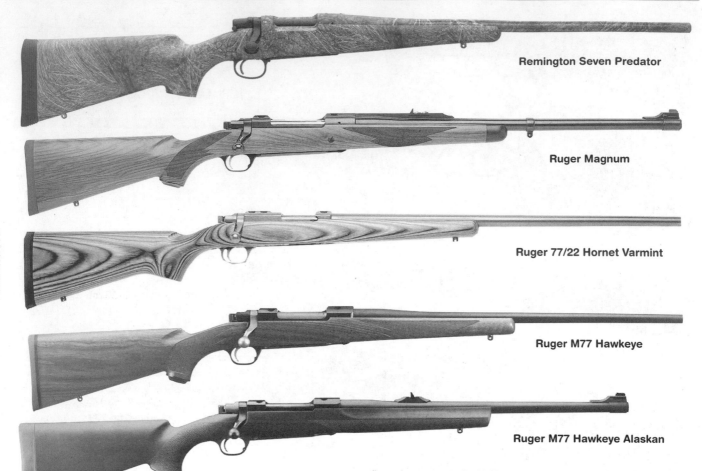

Remington Seven Predator

Ruger Magnum

Ruger 77/22 Hornet Varmint

Ruger M77 Hawkeye

Ruger M77 Hawkeye Alaskan

REMINGTON MODEL 798/799 BOLT-ACTION RIFLES
Caliber: 243 Win., 270 Win., 7mm Rem. Mag., 308 Win., .30-06 Spfl., .300 Win. Mag., .375 H&H Mag., .458 Win. Mag. **Barrel:** 20" to 26". **Weight:** 7.75 lbs. **Length:** 39.5" to 42.5" overall. **Stock:** Brown or green laminated, 1-inch rubber butt pad. **Sights:** None. Receiver drilled and tapped for standard Mauser 98 (long- and short-action) scope mounts. **Features:** Model 98 Mauser action (square-bridge Mauser 98). Claw extractor, sporter style 2-position safety, solid steel hinged floorplate magazine. Introduced 2006. Made in U.S.A. by Remington Arms Co.
Price: Model 798 SPS, black synthetic stock (2008), from.... **$527.00**
Price: Model 798 Satin Walnut Stock (2008), from......... **$648.00**
Price: Model 798 Safari Grade (2008), from............. **$1,141.00**
Price: Model 799, from........................... **$648.00**

RUGER MAGNUM RIFLE
Caliber: 375 H&H, 416 Rigby, 458 Lott. **Barrel:** 23". **Weight:** 9.5 to 10.25 lbs. **Length:** 44". **Stock:** AAA Premium Grade Circassian walnut with live-rubber recoil pad, metal gripcap, and studs for mounting sling swivels. **Sights:** Blade, front; V-notch rear express sights (one stationary, two folding) drift-adjustable for windage. **Features:** Floorplate latch secures the hinged floorplate against accidental dumping of cartridges; one-piece bolt has a non-rotating Mauser-type controlled-feed extractor; fixed-blade ejector.
Price: M77RSM MKII **$2,334.00**

RUGER COMPACT MAGNUMS
Caliber: .338 RCM, .300 RCM; 3-shot magazine. **Barrel:** 20". **Weight:** 6.75 lbs. **Length:** 39.5-40" overall. **Stock:** American walnut and black synthetic; stainless steel and Hawkeye Matte blued finishes. **Sights:** Adjustable Williams "U" notch rear sight and brass bead front sight. **Features:** Based on a shortened .375 Ruger case, the .300 and .338 RCMs match the .300 and .338 Win. Mag. in performance; RCM stock is 1/2 inch shorter than standard M77 Hawkeye stock; LC6 trigger; steel

floor plate engraved with Ruger logo and "Ruger Compact Magnum"; Red Eagle recoil pad; Mauser-type controlled feeding; claw extractor; 3-position safety; hammer-forged steel barrels; Ruger scope rings. Walnut stock includes extensive cut-checkering and rounded profiles. Intr. 2008. Made in U.S.A. by Sturm, Ruger & Co.
Price: HM77RCM (walnut/Hawkeye matte blued) **$995.00**
Price: HKM77PRCM (synthetic/SS) **$995.00**

RUGER 77/22 BOLT-ACTION RIFLE
Caliber: 22 Hornet, 6-shot rotary magazine. **Barrel:** 20" or 24". **Weight:** About 6.25 to 7.5 lbs. **Length:** 39.5" to 43.5" overall. **Stock:** Checkered American walnut, black rubber buttpad; brown laminate. **Sights:** None. **Features:** Same basic features as rimfire model except slightly lengthened receiver. Uses Ruger rotary magazine. Three-position safety. Comes with 1" Ruger scope rings. Introduced 1994.
Price: 77/22-RH (rings only, no sights) **$754.00**
Price: K77/22-VHZ Varmint, laminated stock, no sights **$836.00**

RUGER M77 HAWKEYE RIFLES
Caliber: 204 Ruger, 223 Rem., 22-250 Rem., 243 Win., 257 Roberts, 25-06 Rem., 270 Win., 280 Rem., 7mm/08, 7mm Rem. Mag., 308 Win., 30-06 Spfl., 300 Win. Mag., 338 Win. Mag., 338 Federal, 358 Win. Mag., 416 Ruger, 375 Ruger, 300 Ruger Compact Magnum, 338 Ruger Compact Magnum; 4-shot magazine, except 3-shot magazine for magnums; 5-shot magazine for 204 Ruger and 223 Rem. **Barrel:** 22", 24". **Weight:** 6.75 to 8.25 lbs. **Length:** 42-44.4" overall. **Stock:** American walnut. **Sights:** None furnished. Receiver has Ruger integral scope mount base, Ruger 1" rings. **Features:** Includes Ruger LC6 trigger, new red rubber recoil pad, Mauser-type controlled feeding, claw extractor, 3-position safety, hammer-forged steel barrels, Ruger scope rings. Walnut stock includes wrap-around cut checkering on the forearm and, more rounded contours on stock and top of pistol grips. Matte stainless version features synthetic stock. Hawkeye Alaskan and African chambered in 375 Ruger. Alaskan features matte-black finish, 20" barrel, Hogue OverMolded synthetic stock. African has 23" blued barrel, checkered walnut stock, left-handed model. 375's have windage-adjustable shallow "V" notch rear sight, white bead front sights. Introduced 2007. Left-hand models available 2008.

Prices given are believed to be accurate at time of publication however, many factors affect retail pricing so exact prices are not possible.

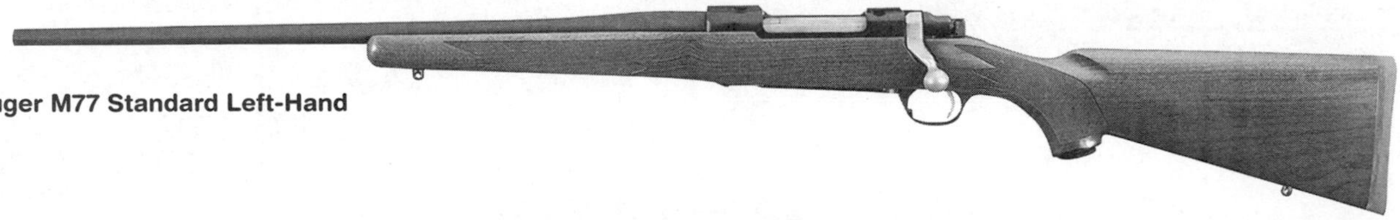

Ruger M77 Standard Left-Hand

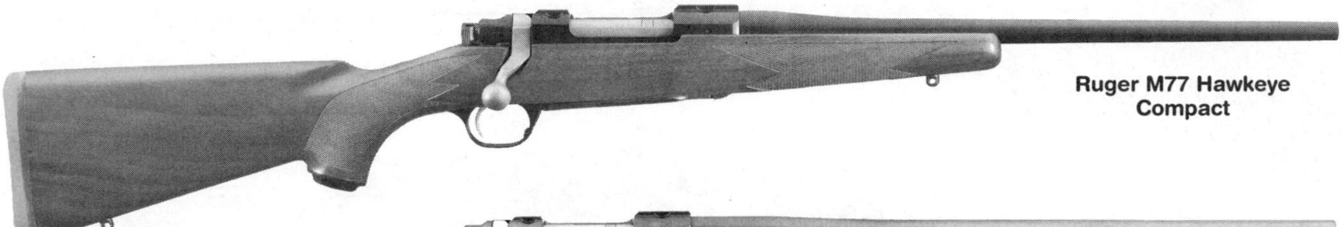

Ruger M77 Hawkeye Compact

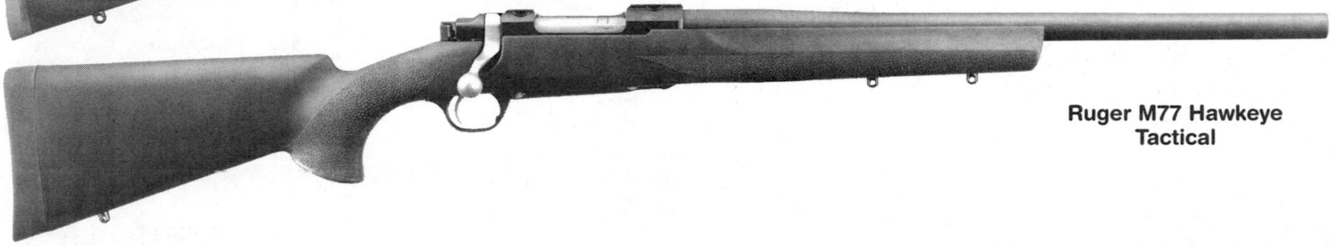

Ruger M77 Hawkeye Tactical

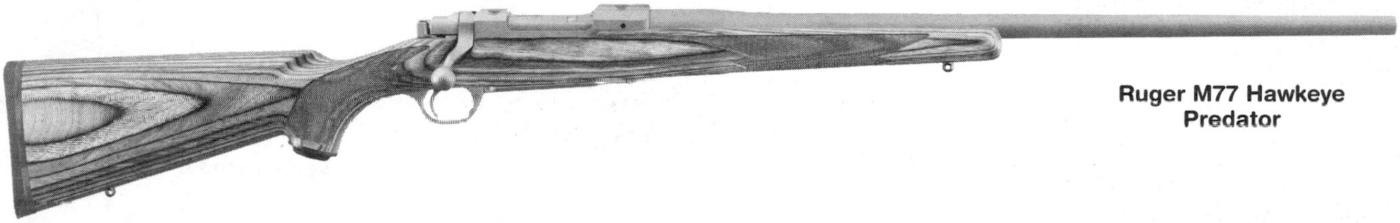

Ruger M77 Hawkeye Predator

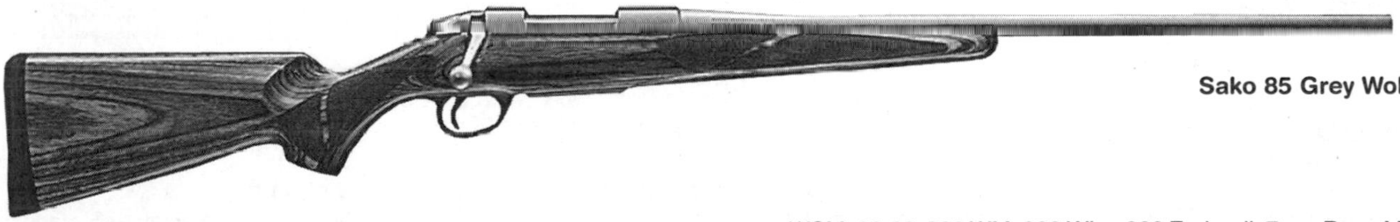

Sako 85 Grey Wolf

RUGER M77 HAWKEYE RIFLES *(cont.)*
Price: Standard, right- and left-hand. **$803.00**
Price: All-Weather. **$803.00**
Price: Laminate, left-hand **$862.00**
Price: Ultra Light. **$862.00**
Price: All-Weather Ultra Light **$803.00**
Price: Compact **$803.00**
Price: Laminate Compact **$862.00**
Price: Compact Magnum **$899.00**
Price: African **$1,079.00**
Price: Alaskan **$1,079.00**
Price: Sporter **$862.00**
Price: Tactical **$1,138.00**
Price: Predator **$935.00**
Price: International **$939.00**

RUGER M77VT TARGET RIFLE
Caliber: 22-250 Rem., 223 Rem., 204 Ruger, 243 Win., 25-06 Rem., 308 Win. **Barrel:** 26" heavy stainless steel with target grey finish. **Weight:** 9 to 9.75 lbs. **Length:** Approx. 45.75" to 46.75" overall. **Stock:** Laminated American hardwood with beavertail forend, steel swivel studs; no checkering or gripcap. **Sights:** Integral scope mount bases in receiver. **Features:** Ruger diagonal bedding system. Ruger steel 1" scope rings supplied. Fully adjustable trigger. Steel floorplate and trigger guard. New version introduced 1992.
Price: KM77VT MKII **$935.00**

SAKO A7 AMERICAN BOLT-ACTION RIFLE
Caliber: 22-250, 243 Win., 25-06, 260 Rem., 270 Win., 270 WSM, 300 WSM, 30-06, 300 WM, 308 Win., 338 Federall, 7mm Rem. Mag., 7mm-08. **Barrel:** 22-7/16" standard, 24-3/8" magnum. **Weight:** 6 lbs. 3 oz. to 6 lbs. 13 oz. **Length:** 42-5/16" to 44-5/16" overall. **Features:** Blued or stainless barrel and receiver, black composite stock with sling swivels and recoil pad, two-position safety, adjustable trigger, detachable 3+1 box magazine.
Price: From. . . . . **$850.00** (blued); **$950.00** (stainless)

SAKO TRG-42 BOLT-ACTION RIFLE
Caliber: 338 Lapua Mag. and 300 Win. Mag. **Barrel:** 27-1/8". **Weight:** 11.25 lbs. **Length:** NA. **Stock:** NA. **Sights:** NA. **Features:** 5-shot magazine, fully adjustable stock and competition trigger. Imported from Finland by Beretta USA.
Price: **$2,775.00**

SAKO MODEL 85 BOLT-ACTION RIFLES
Caliber: 22-250 Rem., 243 Win., 25-06 Rem., 260, 6.5x55mm, 270 Win., 270 WSM, 7mm-08 Rem., 308 Win., 30-06; 7mm WSM, 300 WSM, 338 Federal. **Barrel:** 22.4", 22.9", 24.4". **Weight:** 7.75 lbs. **Length:** NA. **Stock:** Polymer, laminated or high-grade walnut, straight comb, shadow-line cheekpiece. **Sights:** None furnished. **Features:** Controlled-round feeding, adjustable trigger, matte stainless or nonreflective satin blue. Quad model is polymer/stainless with four interchangeable barrels in 22 LR, 22 WMR 17 HMR and 17 Mach 2; 50-degree bolt-lift, ambidextrous palm-swell, adjustable butt-pad. Introduced 2006. Imported from Finland by Beretta USA.
Price: Sako 85 Hunter, walnut/blued **$1,700.00**
Price: Sako 85 Grey Wolf, laminated/stainless **$1,575.00**
Price: Sako 85 Quad, polymer/stainless **$925.00**
Price: Sako 85 Quad Combo, four barrels **$2,175.00**

Sako 85 Finnlight

Sako 75 Hunter

Sako 75 Deluxe

Sako 75 Varmint

Savage Model 12FV

Sako 85 Finnlight
Similar to Model 85 but chambered in 243 Win., 25-06, 260 Rem., 270 Win., 270 WSM, 300 WSM, 30-06, 300 WM, 308 Win., 6.5x55mm, 7mm Rem Mag., 7mm-08. Weighs 6 lbs., 3 oz. to 6 lbs. 13 oz. Stainless steel barrel and receiver, black synthetic stock.
Price: **$1,600.00**

SAKO 75 HUNTER BOLT-ACTION RIFLE
Caliber: 223 Rem., 22-250 Rem., 243 Win., 25-06 Rem., 260, 270 Win., 270 WSM, 280 Rem., 300 Win. Mag., 30-06; 7mm-08 Rem., 308 Win., 270 Wby. Mag., 7mm Rem. Mag., 7mm STW, 7mm Wby. Mag., 300 Wby. Mag., 338 Win. Mag., 340 Wby. Mag., 375 H&H. **Barrel:** 22", standard calibers; 24", 26" magnum calibers. **Weight:** About 6 lbs. **Length:** NA. **Stock:** European walnut with matte lacquer finish. **Sights:** None furnished; dovetail scope mount rails. **Features:** New design with three locking lugs and a mechanical ejector, key locks firing pin and bolt, cold hammer-forged barrel is free-floating, two-position safety, hinged floorplate or detachable magazine that can be loaded from the top, short 70-degree bolt lift. Five action lengths. Introduced 1997. Imported from Finland by Beretta USA.
Price: From **$1,375.00**

Sako 75 Deluxe Rifle
Similar to 75 Hunter except select wood rosewood gripcap and forend tip. Available in 17 Rem., 222, 223 Rem., 25-06 Rem., 243 Win., 7mm-08 Rem., 308 Win., 25-06 Rem., 270 Win., 280 Rem., 30-06; 270 Wby. Mag., 7mm Rem. Mag., 7mm STW, 7mm Wby. Mag., 300 Win. Mag., 300 Wby. Mag., 338 Win. Mag., 340 Wby. Mag., 375 H&H, 416 Rem. Mag. Introduced 1997. Imported from Finland by Beretta USA.
Price: From **$2,175.00**

Sako 75 Varmint Rifle
Similar to Model 75 Hunter except chambered only for 17 Rem., 222 Rem., 223 Rem., 22-250 Rem., 22 PPC and 6mm PPC, 24" heavy

barrel with recessed crown; set trigger; beavertail forend. Introduced 1998. Imported from Finland by Beretta USA.
Price: **$1,850.00**

SAVAGE MODEL 25 BOLT ACTION RIFLES
Caliber: 204 Ruger, 223 Rem., 4-shot magazine. **Barrel:** 24", medium-contour fluted barrel with recessed target crown, free-floating sleeved barrel, dual pillar bedding. **Weight:** 8.25 lbs. **Length:** 43.75" overall. **Stock:** Brown laminate with beavertail-style forend. **Sights:** Weaver-style bases installed. **Features:** Diameter-specific action built around the 223 Rem. bolthead dimension. Three locking lugs, 60-degree bolt lift, AccuTrigger adjustable from 2.5 to 3.25 lbs. Model 25 Classic Sporter has satin lacquer American walnut with contrasting forend tip, wraparound checkering, 22" blued barrel. **Weight:** 7.15 lbs. **Length:** 41.75". Introduced 2008. Made in U.S.A. by Savage Arms, Inc.
Price: Model 25 Lightweight Varminter **$641.00**
Price: Model 25 Lightweight Varminter Thumbhole **$691.00**
Price: Model 25 Classic Sporter **$672.00**

SAVAGE CLASSIC SERIES MODEL 14/114 RIFLES
Caliber: 204 Ruger, 223 Rem., 22-250 Rem., 243 Win., 7mm-08 Rem., 308 Win., 270 WSM, 300 WSM (short action Model 14), 2- or 4-shot magazine; 270 Win., 7mm Rem. Mag., 30-06 Spfl., 300 Win. Mag. (long action Model 114), 3- or 4-shot magazine. **Barrel:** 22" or 24". **Weight:** 7 to 7.5 lbs. **Length:** 41.75" to 43.75" overall (Model 14); 43.25" to 45.25" overall (Model 114). **Stock:** Satin lacquer American walnut with ebony forend, wraparound checkering, Monte Carlo Comb and cheekpiece. **Sights:** None furnished. Receiver drilled and tapped for scope mounting. **Features:** AccuTrigger, high luster blued barreled action, hinged floorplate. From Savage Arms, Inc.
Price: Model 14 or 114 Classic, from **$826.00**
Price: Model 14 or 114 American Classic, detachable box
magazine, from **$779.00**
Price: Model 14 or 114 Euro Classic, oil finish, from **$875.00**
Price: Model 14 Left Hand, 250 Savage and 300 Savage only **$779.00**

Prices given are believed to be accurate at time of publication however, many factors affect retail pricing so exact prices are not possible.

Savage Model 116FSAK

Savage Model 111F

Savage Model 11FCNS

SAVAGE MODEL 12 SERIES VARMINT RIFLES

Caliber: 204 Ruger, 223 Rem., 22-250 Rem. 4-shot magazine. **Barrel:** 26" stainless barreled action, heavy fluted, free-floating and button-rifled barrel. **Weight:** 10 lbs. **Length:** 46.25" overall. **Stock:** Dual pillar bedded, low profile, laminated stock with extra-wide beavertail forend. **Sights:** None furnished; drilled and tapped for scope mounting. **Features:** Recessed target-style muzzle. AccuTrigger, oversized bolt handle, detachable box magazine, swivel studs. Model 112BVSS has heavy target-style prone laminated stock with high comb, Wundhammer palm swell, internal box magazine. Model 12FVSS has black synthetic stock, additional chamberings in 308 Win., 270 WSM, 300 WSM. Model 12FV has blued receiver. Model 12BTCSS has brown laminate vented thumbhole stock. Made in U.S.A. by Savage Arms, Inc.

Price: Model 12 Varminter, from **$991.00**
Price: Model 12BVSS **$899.00**
Price: Model 12FVSS, from **$815.00**
Price: Model 12FV **$658.00**
Price: Model 12BTCSS (2008) **$1,041.00**
Price: Model 12 Long Range (2008) **$1,239.00**
Price: Model 12 LRPV, single-shot only with right bolt/left port or left load/right eject receiver **$1,273.00**

SAVAGE MODEL 16/116 WEATHER WARRIORS

Caliber: 204 Ruger, 223 Rem., 22-250 Rem., 243 Win., 7mm-08 Rem., 308 Win., 270 WSM, 7mm WSM, 300 WSM (short action Model 16), 2- or 4-shot magazine; 270 Win., 7mm Rem. Mag., 30-06 Spfl., 300 Win. Mag., 338 Win. Mag. (long action Model 114), 3- or 4-shot magazine. **Barrel:** 22", 24"; stainless steel with matte finish, free-floated barrel. **Weight:** 6.5 to 6.75 lbs. **Length:** 41.75" to 43.75" overall (Model 16); 42.5" to 44.5" overall (Model 116). **Stock:** Graphite/fiberglass filled composite. **Sights:** None furnished; drilled and tapped for scope mounting. **Features:** Quick-detachable swivel studs; laser-etched bolt. Left-hand models available. Model 116FSS introduced 1991; 116FSAK introduced 1994. Made in U.S.A. by Savage Arms, Inc.

Price: Model 16FHSS or 116FHSS, hinged floorplate magazine, from **$755.00**
Price: Model 16FLHSS or 116FLHSS, left hand models, from **$755.00**
Price: Model 16FSS or 116FSS, internal box magazine, from **$678.00**
Price: Model 16FCSS or 116FCSS, detachable box magazine, from **$755.00**
Price: Model 16FHSAK or 116FHSAK, adjustable muzzle brake **$822.00**

SAVAGE MODEL 10GXP3, 110GXP3 PACKAGE GUNS

Caliber: 223 Rem., 22-250 Rem., 243 Win., 7mm-08 Rem., 300 WSM (10GXP3). 25-06 Rem., 270 Win., 30-06 Spfl., 7mm Rem.

Mag., 300 Win. Mag., 300 Rem. Ultra Mag. (110GXP3). **Barrel:** 22" 24", 26". **Weight:** 7.5 lbs. average. **Length:** 43" to 47". **Stock:** Walnut Monte Carlo with checkering. **Sights:** 3-9x40mm scope, mounted & bore sighted. **Features:** Blued, free floating and button rifled, internal box magazines, swivel studs, leather sling. Left-hand available.

Price: AccuTrigger, from **$669.00**

SAVAGE MODEL 11FXP3, 111FXP3, 111FCXP3, 11FYXP3 (YOUTH) PACKAGE GUNS

Caliber: 223 Rem., 22-250 Rem., 243 Win., 308 Win., 300 WSM (11FXP3). 270 Win., 30-06 Spfl., 25-06 Rem., 7mm Rem. Mag., 300 Win. Mag., 300 Rem. Ultra Mag. (11FCXPE & 111FXP3). **Barrel:** 22" to 26". **Weight:** 6.5 lbs. **Length:** 41" to 47". **Stock:** Synthetic checkering, dual pillar bed. **Sights:** 3-9X40mm scope, mounted & bore sighted. **Features:** Blued, free floating and button rifled, Top loading internal box mag (except 111FXCP3 has detachable box magazine). Nylon sling and swivel studs. Some left-hand available.

Price: Model 11FXP3, from **$640.00**
Price: Model 111FCXP3 . . . . **$519.00**
Price: Model 11FYXP3, 243 Win., 12.5" pull (youth) **$519.00**
Price: Model 11FLYXP3 Youth: Left-handed configuration of Model 11FYXP3 Youth **$640.00**

SAVAGE MODEL 16FXP3, 116FXP3 SS ACTION PACKAGE GUNS

Caliber: 223 Rem., 243 Win., 308 Win., 300 WSM, 270 Win., 30-06 Spfl., 7mm Rem. Mag., 300 Win. Mag., 338 Win. Mag., 375 H&H, 7mm S&W, 7mm Rem. Ultra Mag., 300 Rem. Ultra Mag. **Barrel:** 22", 24", 26". **Weight:** 6.75 lbs. average. **Length:** 41" to 46". **Stock:** Synthetic checkering, dual pillar bed. **Sights:** 3-9X40mm scope, mounted & bore sighted. **Features:** Free floating and button rifled. Internal box magazine, nylon sling and swivel studs.

Price: From **$736.00**

SAVAGE MODEL 11/111 HUNTER SERIES BOLT ACTIONS

Caliber: 223 Rem., 22-250 Rem., 243 Win., 7mm-08 Rem., 308 Win., 270 WSM, 7mm WSM, 300 WSM (short action Model 11), 2- or 4-shot magazine; 25-06 Rem., 270 Win., 7mm Rem. Mag., 30-06 Spfl., 300 Win. Mag., (long action Model 111), 3- or 4-shot magazine. **Barrel:** 22" or 24"; blued free-floated barrel. **Weight:** 6.5 to 6.75 lbs. **Length:** 41.75" to 43.75" overall (Model 11); 42.5" to 44.5" overall (Model 111). **Stock:** Graphite/fiberglass filled composite or hardwood. **Sights:** Ramp front, open fully adjustable rear; drilled and tapped for scope mounting. **Features:** Three-position top tang safety, double front locking lugs. Introduced 1994. Made in U.S.A. by Savage Arms, Inc.

Price: Model 11FL or 111FL **$564.00**
Price: Model 11FL or 111FL, left hand models, from **$564.00**
Price: Model 11FCNS or 111FCNS, detachable box magazine, from **$591.00**

CENTERFIRE RIFLES—Bolt-Action

Savage Model 10 BAS

Savage Model 10 BAT/S

Savage Model 10FP

Savage Model 10FCP

Savage Model 10 Precision Carbine

Savage Model 10 Predator

SAVAGE MODEL 11/111 HUNTER SERIES BOLT ACTIONS *(cont.)*
Price: Model 11FLNS or 111FLNS $564.00
Price: Model 11G or 111G, hardwood stock, from $582.00
Price: Model 11BTH or 111BTH, laminate thumbhole stock
   (2008) $779.00
Price: Model 11FNS Model FLNS $591.00
Price: Model 11FHNS or 111FHNS. $656.00
Price: Model 11FYCAK Youth $691.00
Price: Model 11GNS or 111GNS $618.00
Price: Model 11GLNS or 111GLSN $618.00
Price: Model 11GCNS or 111GCNS $659.00

SAVAGE MODEL 10 BAS LAW ENFORCEMENT BOLT-ACTION RIFLE
Caliber: 380 Win. **Barrel:** 24" fluted heavy with muzzle brake. **Weight:** 13.4 lbs. **Length:** NA. **Features:** Bolt-action repeater based on Model 10 action but with M4-style collapsible buttstock, pistolgrip with palm swell, all-aluminum Accustock, picatinny rail for mounting optics.
Price: $1,852.00
Price: 10 BAT/S, multi-adjustable buttstock $1,991.00

SAVAGE MODEL 10FP/110FP LAW ENFORCEMENT SERIES RIFLES
Caliber: 223 Rem., 308 Win. (Model 10), 4-shot magazine; 25-06 Rem., 300 Win. Mag., (Model 110), 3- or 4-shot magazine. **Barrel:** 24"; matte blued free-floated heavy barrel and action. **Weight:** 6.5 to 6.75 lbs. **Length:** 41.75" to 43.75" overall (Model 10); 42.5" to 44.5" overall (Model 110). **Stock:** Black graphite/fiberglass composition, pillar-bedded, positive checkering. **Sights:** None furnished. Receiver drilled and tapped for scope mounting. **Features:** Black matte finish on all metal parts. Double swivel studs on the forend for sling and/or bipod mount. Right- or left-hand. Model 110FP introduced 1990. Model 10FP introduced 1998. Model 10FCPXP has HS Precision black synthetic tactical stock with molded alloy bedding system, Leupold 3.5-10x40mm black matte scope with Mil Dot reticle, Farrell Picatinny Rail Base, flip-open lens covers, 1.25" sling with QD swivels, Harris bipod, Storm heavy duty case. Made in U.S.A. by Savage Arms, Inc.
Price: Model 10FP, 10FLP (left hand), 110FP $649.00
Price: Model 10FP folding Choate stock. $896.00
Price: Model 10FCP McMillan, McMillan fiberglass tactical
   stock $1,178.00
Price: Model 10FCP-HS HS Precision, HS Precision tactical
   stock $984.00
Price: Model 10FPXP-HS Precision $2,715.00
Price: Model 10FCP $866.00
Price: Model 10FLCP, left-hand model, standard stock
   or Accu-Stock $866.00
Price: Model 110FCP $866.00
Price: Model 10 Precision Carbine, 20" medium contour barrel,
   synthetic camo Accu-Stock, 223/308 . . . . $829.00
Price: Model 10 FCM Scout $646.00

Savage Model 110-50th Anniversary Rifle
Same action as 110-series rifles, except offered in 300 Savage, limited edition of 1,000 rifles. Has high-luster blued barrel and action, unique checkering pattern, high-grade hinged floorplate, scroll pattern on receiver, 24-karat gold-plated double barrel bands, 24-karat gold-plated AccuTrigger, embossed recoil pad. Introduced 2008. Made in U.S.A. from Savage Arms, Inc.
Price: Model 110 50th Anniversary. $1,724.00

Prices given are believed to be accurate at time of publication however, many factors affect retail pricing so exact prices are not possible.

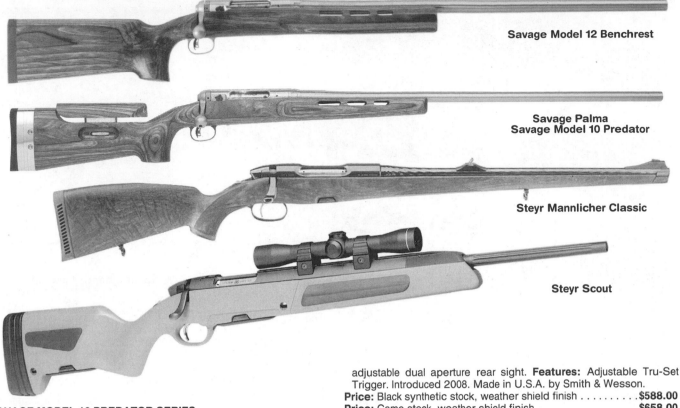

Savage Model 12 Benchrest

Savage Palma
Savage Model 10 Predator

Steyr Mannlicher Classic

Steyr Scout

SAVAGE MODEL 10 PREDATOR SERIES
Caliber: 223, 22-250, 243, 204 Ruger. **Barrel:** 22", medium-contour. **Weight:** 7.25 lbs. **Length:** 43"overall. **Stock:** Synthetic with rounded forend and oversized bolt handle. **Features:** Entirely covered in either Mossy Oak Brush or Realtree Hardwoods Snow pattern camo. Also features AccuTrigger, detachable box magazine.
Price: **$806.00**

Savage Model 10XP Predator Hunting Bolt-Action Rifle Package
Similar to Model 10 but chambered in 223, 204, 22-250 or 243 Win. Includes 4-12x40 scope, 22" barrel, AccuTrigger, choice of Realtree Snow or Mossy Oak Brush camo overall.
Price: **$839.00**

SAVAGE MODEL 12 PRECISION TARGET SERIES BENCHREST RIFLE
Caliber: 308 Win, 6.5x284 Norman, 6mm Norma BR. **Barrel:** 29" ultra-heavy. **Weight:** 12.75 lbs. **Length:** 50" overall. **Stock:** Gray laminate. Features: New Left-Load, Right-Eject target action, Target AccuTrigger adjustable from approx 6 oz to 2.5 lbs, oversized bolt handle, stainless extra-heavy free-floating and button-rifled barrel.
Price: **$1,375.00**

Savage Model 12 Precision Target Palma Rifle
Similar to Model 12 Benchrest but in 308 Palma only, 30" barrel, multi-adjustable stock, weighs 13.3 lbs.
Price: **$1,798.00**

Savage Model 12 F Class Target Rifle
Similar to Model 12 Benchrest but in 6.5x284 Norma, 6 Norma BR, 30" barrel, weighs 11.5 lbs.
Price: **$1,341.00**

Savage Model 12 F/TR Target Rifle
Similar to Model 12 Benchrest but in 308 Win. only, 30" barrel, weighs 12.65 lbs.
Price: **$1,265.00**

SMITH & WESSON I-BOLT RIFLES
Caliber: 25-06 Rem., 270 Win., 30-06 Win. (4-round magazine), 7mm Rem. Mag., 300 Win. Mag. (3-round magazine). **Barrel:** 23", 1:10" right-hand twist, 1:9" right-hand twist for 7mm Mag. Thompson/Center barrel. Blued and stainless. **Weight:** 6.75 lbs. **Stock:** Black synthetic, Realtree AP camo, walnut. Length of pull, 13-5/8", drop at comb, 7/8". Monte Carlo cheekpiece. **Sights:** Adjustable post front sight,

adjustable dual aperture rear sight. **Features:** Adjustable Tru-Set Trigger. Introduced 2008. Made in U.S.A. by Smith & Wesson.
Price: Black synthetic stock, weather shield finish **$588.00**
Price: Camo stock, weather shield finish **$658.00**

STEVENS MODEL 200 BOLT-ACTION RIFLES
Caliber: 223, 22-250, 243, 7mm-08, 308 Win. (short action) or 25-06, 270 Win., 30-06, 7mm Rem. Mag., 300 Win Mag. **Barrel:** 22" (short action) or 24" (long action blued). **Weight:** 6.5 lbs. **Length:** 41.75" overall. **Stock:** Black synthetic or camo. **Sights:** None. **Features:** Free-floating and button-rifled barrel, top loading internal box magazine, swivel studs.
Price: . . . . **$399.00** (standard); **$439.00** (camo)
Price: Model 200XP Long or Short Action
Package Rifle with 4x12 scope. **$449.00**
Price: Model 200XP Camo, camo stock **$499.00**

STEYR MANNLICHER CLASSIC RIFLE
Caliber: 222 Rem., 223 Rem., 243 Win., 25-06 Rem., 308 Win., 6.5x55, 6.5x57, 270 Win., 270 WSM, 7x64 Brenneke, 7mm-08 Rem., 7.5x55, 30-06 Spfl., 9.3x62, 6.5x68, 7mm Rem. Mag., 300 WSM, 300 Win. Mag., 8x68S, 4-shot magazine. **Barrel:** 23.6" standard; 26" magnum; 20" full stock standard calibers. **Weight:** 7 lbs. **Length:** 40.1" overall. **Stock:** Hand-checkered fancy European oiled walnut with standard forend. **Sights:** Ramp front adjustable for elevation, V-notch rear adjustable for windage. **Features:** Single adjustable trigger; 3-position roller safety with "safe-bolt" setting; drilled and tapped for Steyr factory scope mounts. Introduced 1997. Imported from Austria by Steyr Arms, Inc.
Price: Half stock, standard calibers **$3,799.00**
Price: Full stock, standard calibers. **$4,199.00**

Steyr Pro Hunter Rifle
Similar to the Classic Rifle except has ABS synthetic stock with adjustable butt spacers, straight comb without cheekpiece, palm swell, Pachmayr 1" swivels. Special 10-round magazine conversion kit available. Introduced 1997. Imported from Austria by Steyr Arms, Inc.
Price: From **$1,500.00**

STEYR SCOUT BOLT-ACTION RIFLE
Caliber: 308 Win., 5-shot magazine. **Barrel:** 19", fluted. **Weight:** NA. **Length:** NA. **Stock:** Gray Zytel. **Sights:** Pop-up front & rear, Leupold M8 2.5x28 IER scope on Picatinny optic rail with Steyr mounts. **Features:** luggage case, scout sling, two stock spacers, two magazines. Introduced 1998. Imported from Austria by Steyr Arms, Inc.
Price: From **$2,199.00**

Thompson/Center Icon

Tikka T3 Hunter

Weatherby Mark V Lazermark

STEYR SSG 69 PII BOLT-ACTION RIFLE
Caliber: 22-250 Rem., 243 Win., 308 Win., detachable 5-shot rotary magazine. **Barrel:** 26". **Weight:** 8.5 lbs. **Length:** 44.5" overall. **Stock:** Black ABS Cycolac with spacers for length of pull adjustment. **Sights:** Hooded ramp front adjustable for elevation, V-notch rear adjustable for windage. **Features:** Sliding safety; NATO rail for bipod; 1" swivels; Parkerized finish; single or double-set triggers. Imported from Austria by Steyr Arms, Inc.
Price: **$1,889.00**

THOMPSON/CENTER ICON BOLT-ACTION RIFLE
Caliber: 22-250 Rem., 243 Win., 308 Win., 30TC, 3-round box magazine. **Barrel:** 24", button rifled. **Weight:** 7.5 lbs. **Length:** 44.5" overall. **Stock:** Walnut, 20-lpi grip and forend cut checkering with ribbon detail. **Sights:** None; integral Weaver style scope mounts. **Features:** Interchangeable bolt handle, 60-degree bolt lift, Interlok Bedding System, 3-lug bolt with T-Slot extractor, cocking indicator, adjustable trigger, preset to 3 to 3.5 lbs of pull. Introduced 2007. From Thompson/Center Arms.
Price: **$1,025.00**

Thompson/Center ICON Precision Hunter Rifle
Similar to the basic ICON model. Available in 204 Ruger, 223 Rem., 22-250 Rem., 243 Win. and 308 Win. 22" heavy barrel, blued finish, varminter-style stock. Introduced 2009.
Price: **$1,149.00**

THOMPSON/CENTER VENTURE BOLT-ACTION RIFLE
Caliber: 270 Win., 7mm Rem. Mag., 30-06 Springfield, 300 Win. Mag., 3-round magazine. **Barrel:** 24". **Weight:** NA. **Length:** NA. **Stock:** Composite. **Sights:** NA. **Features:** Nitride fat bolt design, externally adjustable trigger, two-position safety, textured grip. Introduced 2009.
Price: **$489.00**

TIKKA T3 HUNTER
Caliber: 223 Rem., 22-250 Rem., 243 Win., 308 Win., 25-06 Rem., 270 Win., 30-06 Spfl., 300 Win. Mag., 338 Win. Mag., 270 WSM, 300 WSM, 6.5x55 Swedish Mauser, 7mm Rem. Mag. **Stock:** Walnut. **Sights:** None furnished. **Barrel:** 22-7/16", 24-3/8". **Features:** Detachable magazine, aluminum scope rings. Introduced 2005. Imported from Finland by Beretta USA.
Price: **$675.00**

Tikka T3 Stainless Synthetic
Similar to the T3 Hunter except stainless steel, synthetic stock. Available in 243 Win., 2506, 270 Win., 308 Win., 30-06 Spfl., 270 WSM, 300 WSM, 7mm Rem. Mag., 300 Win. Mag., 338 Win. Mag. Introduced 2005. Imported from Finland by Beretta USA.
Price: **$700.00**

Tikka T3 Lite Bolt-Action Rifle
Similar to the T3 Hunter, available in 223 Rem., 22-250 Rem., 308 Win., 243 Win., 25-06 Rem., 270 Win., 270 WSM, 30-06 Sprg., 300 Win Mag., 300 WSM, 338 Federal, 338 Win Mag., 7mm Rem. Mag., 7mm-08 Rem. Barrel lengths vary from 22-7/16" to 24-3/8". Made in Finland by Sako. Imported by Beretta USA.
Price: **$695.00**
Price: Stainless steel synthetic **$600.00**
Price: Stainless steel synthetic, left-hand **$700.00**

Tikka T3 Varmint/Super Varmint Rifle
Similar to the T3 Hunter, available in 223 Rem., 22-250 Rem., 308 Win. Length is 23-3/8" (Super Varmint). Made in Finland by Sako. Imported by Beretta USA.
Price: **$900.00**
Price: Super Varmint **$1,425.00**

ULTRA LIGHT ARMS BOLT-ACTION RIFLES
Caliber: 17 Rem. to 416 Rigby. **Barrel:** Douglas, length to order. **Weight:** 4.75 to 7.5 lbs. **Length:** Varies. **Stock:** Kevlar graphite composite, variety of finishes. **Sights:** None furnished; drilled and tapped for scope mounts. **Features:** Timney trigger, hand-lapped action, button-rifled barrel, hand-bedded action, recoil pad, sling-swivel studs, optional Jewell trigger. Made in U.S.A. by New Ultra Light Arms.
Price: Model 20 (short action) **$3,000.00**
Price: Model 24 (long action) **$3,100.00**
Price: Model 28 (magnum action) **$3,400.00**
Price: Model 40 (300 Wby. Mag., 416 Rigby) **$3,400.00**
Price: Left-hand models, add **$100.00**

WEATHERBY MARK V BOLT-ACTION RIFLES
Caliber: Deluxe version comes in all Weatherby calibers plus 243 Win., 270 Win., 7mm-08 Rem., 30-06 Spfl., 308 Win. **Barrel:** 24", 26", 28". **Weight:** 6.75 to 10 lbs. **Length:** 44" to 48.75" overall. **Stock:** Walnut, Monte Carlo with cheekpiece; high luster finish; checkered pistol grip and forend; recoil pad. **Sights:** None furnished. **Features:** 4 models with Mark V action and wood stocks; other common elements include cocking indicator; adjustable trigger; hinged floorplate, thumb safety; quick detachable sling swivels. Ultramark has hand-selected exhibition-grade walnut stock, maplewood/ebony spacers, 20-lpi checkering. Chambered for 257 and 300 Wby Mags. Lazermark same as Mark V Deluxe except stock has extensive oak leaf pattern laser carving on pistol grip and forend; chambered in Wby. Magnums—257, 270 Win., 7mm., 300, 340, with 26" barrel. Introduced 1981. Sporter is same as the Mark V Deluxe without the embellishments. Metal has low-luster blue, stock is Claro walnut with matte finish, Monte Carlo comb, recoil pad. Chambered for these Wby. Mags: 257, 270 Win., 7mm, 300, 340. Other chamberings: 7mm Rem. Mag., 300 Win. Introduced 1993. Six Mark V models come with synthetic stocks. Ultra Lightweight rifles weigh 5.75 to 6.75 lbs.; 24", 26" fluted stainless barrels with recessed

Prices given are believed to be accurate at time of publication however, many factors affect retail pricing so exact prices are not possible.

CENTERFIRE RIFLES—Bolt-Action

Weatherby Mark V Sporter

Weatherby Mark V Synthetic

Weatherby Mark V Accumark

Weatherby Mark V SVR

target crown; Bell & Carlson stock with CNC-machined aluminum bedding plate and tan "spider web" finish, skeletonized handle and sleeve. Available in 243 Win., Wby. Mag., 25-06 Rem., 270 Win., 7mm-08 Rem., 7mm Rem. Mag., 280 Rem, 308 Win., 30-06 Spfl., 300 Win. Mag. Wby. Mag chamberings: 240, 257, 270 Win., 7mm, 300. Introduced 1998. Accumark uses Mark V action with heavy-contour 26" and 28" stainless barrels with black oxidized flutes, muzzle diameter of .705". No sights, drilled and tapped for scope mounting. Stock is composite with matte gel-coat finish, full length aluminum bedding Hasblock. Weighs 8.5 lbs. Chambered for these Wby. Mags: 240 (2007), 257, 270, 7mm, 300, 340, 338-378, 30-378. Other chamberings: 22-250 (2007), 243 Win. (2007), 25-06 Rem. (2007), 270 Win. (2007), 308 Win.(2007), 7mm Rem. Mag., 300 Win. Mag. Introduced 1996. SVM (Super VarmintMaster) has 26" fluted stainless barrel, spiderweb-pattern tan laminated synthetic stock, fully adjustable trigger. Chambered for 223 Rem., 22-250 Rem., 243. Mark V Synthetic has lightweight injection-molded synthetic stock with raised Monte Carlo comb, checkered grip and forend, custom floorplate release. Weighs 6.5-8.5 lbs., 24-28" barrels. Available in 22-250 Rem., 243 Win., 25-06 Rem., 270 Win., 7mm-08 Rem., 7mm Rem., Mag, 280 Rem., 308 Win., 30-06 Spfl., 308 Win., 300 Win. Mag., 375 H&H Mag, and these Wby. Magnums: 240, 257, 270 Win., 7mm, 300, 30-378, 338-378, 340. Introduced 1997. Fibermark composites are similar to other Mark V models except has black Kevlar and fiberglass composite stock and bead-bead-blast blue or stainless finish. Chambered for 9 standard and magnum calibers. Introduced 1983; reintroduced 2001. SVR comes with 22" button-rifled chrome-moly barrel, .739 muzzle diameter. Composite stock w/bedding block, gray spiderweb pattern. Made in U.S.A. From Weatherby.

Price: Mark V Deluxe	**$2,199.00**
Price: Mark V Ultramark	**$2,979.00**
Price: Mark V Lazermark	**$2,479.00**
Price: Mark V Sporter	**$1,499.00**
Price: Mark V SVM	**$1,959.00**
Price: Mark V Ultra Lightweight	**$1,879.00**
Price: Mark V Ultra Lightweight LH	**$1,911.00**
Price: Mark V Accumark	**$1,879.00**
Price: Mark V Synthetic	**$1,209.00**
Price: Mark V Fibermark Composite	**$1,449.00**
Price: Mark V SVR Special Varmint Rifle	**$1,259.00**

WEATHERBY VANGUARD BOLT-ACTION RIFLES

Caliber: 257, 300 Wby Mags; 223 Rem., 22-250 Rem., 243 Win., 25-06 Rem. (2007), 270 Win., 270 WSM, 7mm Rem. Mag., 308 Win., 30-06 Spfl., 300 Win. Mag., 300 WSM, 338 Win. Mag. **Barrel:** 24" barreled action, matte black. **Weight:** 7.5 to 8.75 lbs. **Length:** 44" to 46-3/4" overall. **Stock:** Raised comb, Monte Carlo, injection-molded composite stock. **Sights:** None furnished. **Features:** One-piece forged, fluted bolt body with three gas ports, forged and machined receiver, adjustable trigger, factory accuracy guarantee. Vanguard Stainless has 410-Series stainless steel barrel and action, bead blasted matte metal finish. Vanguard Deluxe has raised comb, semi-fancy grade Monte Carlo walnut stock with maplewood spacers, rosewood forend and grip cap, polished action with high-gloss-blued metalwork. Vanguard Synthetic Package includes Vanguard Synthetic rifle with Bushnell Banner 3-9x40mm scope mounted and boresighted, Leupold Rifleman rings and bases, Uncle Mikes nylon sling, and Plano PRO-MAX Injection-molded case. Sporter has Monte Carlo walnut stock with satin urethane finish, fineline diamond point checkering, contrasting rosewood forend tip, matte-blued metalwork. Sporter SS metalwork is 410 Series bead-blasted stainless steel. Vanguard Youth/Compact has 20" No. 1 contour barrel, short action, scaled-down non-reflective matte black hardwood stock with 12.5" length of pull and full-size, injection-molded composite stock. Chambered for 223 Rem., 22-250 Rem., 243 Win., 7mm-08 Rem., 308 Win. Weighs 6.75 lbs.; OAL 38.9". Sub-MOA Matte and Sub-MOA Stainless models have pillar-bedded Fiberguard composite stock (Aramid, graphite unidirectional fibers and fiberglass) with 24" barreled action; matte black metalwork, Pachmayr Decelerator recoil pad. Sub-MOA Stainless metalwork is 410 Series bead-blasted stainless steel. Sub-MOA Varmint guaranteed to shoot 3-shot group of .99" or less when used with specified Weatherby factory or premium (non-Weatherby calibers) ammunition. Hand-laminated, tan Monte Carlo composite stock with black spiderwebbing; CNC-machined aluminum bedding block, 22" No. 3 contour barrel, recessed target crown. Varmint Special has tan injection-molded Monte Carlo composite stock, pebble grain finish, black spiderwebbing. 22" No. 3 contour barrel (.740 muzzle dia.), bead blasted matte black finish, recessed target crown. Made in U.S.A. From Weatherby.

Price: Vanguard Synthetic	$399.00
Price: Vanguard Stainless	$709.00
Price: Vanguard Deluxe, 7mm Rem. Mag., 300 Win. Mag. (2007)	$989.00
Price: Vanguard Synthetic Package, 25-06 Rem. (2007)	$552.00
Price: Vanguard Sporter	$689.00
Price: Vanguard Sporter SS	$869.00
Price: Vanguard Youth/Compact	$649.00
Price: Vanguard Sub-MOA Matte, 25-06 Rem. (2007)	$929.00
Price: Vanguard Sub-MOA Stainless, 270 WSM	$1,079.00
Price: Vanguard Sub-MOA Varmint, 204 Ruger (2007)	$1,009.00

Winchester Model 70
Extreme Weather SS

Winchester Model 70
Super Grade

Winchester Model 70
Coyote Light

Winchester Model 70
Featherweight

Winchester Model 70
Sporter

Winchester Model 70
Ultimate Shadow

WINCHESTER MODEL 70 BOLT-ACTION RIFLES

Caliber: Varies by model. **Barrel:** Blued, or free-floating, fluted stainless hammer-forged barrel, 22", 24", 26". Recessed target crown. **Weight:** 6.75 to 7.25 lbs. **Length:** 41 to 45.75 " overall. **Stock:** Walnut (three models) or Bell and Carlson composite; textured charcoal-grey matte finish, Pachmayr Decelerator recoil pad. **Sights:** None. **Features:** Claw extractor, three-position safety, M.O.A. three-lever trigger system, factory-set at 3.75 lbs. Super Grade features fancy grade walnut stock, contrasting black fore-end tip and pistol grip cap, and sculpted shadowline cheekpiece. Featherweight Deluxe has angled-comb walnut stock, Schnabel fore-end, satin finish, cut checkering. Sporter Deluxe has satin-finished walnut stock, cut checkering, sculpted cheekpiece. Extreme Weather SS has composite stock, drop @ comb, 0.5"; drop @ heel, 0.5". Introduced 2008. Made in U.SA. from Winchester Repeating Arms.
Price: Extreme Weather SS, 270 Win., 270 WSM, 30-06 Spfl., 300 Win. Mag., 300 WSM, 308 Win., 325 WSM, 243 Winchester, 7mm WSM, from **$1,069.00**
Price: Super Grade, 30-06 Sprg., 300 Win. Mag., 270 WSM, 300 WSM, 270 Winchester, from **$1,139.00**
Price: Featherweight Deluxe, 243 Win., 270 Win., 270 WSM, 30-06 Spfl., 300 Win. Mag., 300 WSM, 308 Win., 325 WSM, 7mm-08 Rem., from **$999.00**
Price: Sporter Deluxe, 270 Win., 270 WSM, 30-06 Spfl., 300 Win. Mag., 300 WSM, 325 WSM, from **$999.00**

WINCHESTER MODEL 70 COYOTE LIGHT

Caliber: 22-250, 243 Winchester, 308 Winchester, 270 WSM, 300 WSM and 325 WSM, five-shot magazine (3-shot in 270 WSM, 300 WSM and 325 WSM). **Barrel:** 22" fluted stainless barrel (24" in 270 WSM, 300 WSM and 325 WSM). **Weight:** 7.5 lbs. **Length:** NA. **Features:** Composite Bell and Carlson stock, Pachmayr Decelerator pad. Controlled round feeding. No sights but drilled and tapped for mounts.
Price: **$1,099.00**

WINCHESTER MODEL 70 FEATHERWEIGHT

Caliber: 22-250, 243, 7mm-08, 308, 270 WSM, 7mm WSM, 300 WSM, 325 WSM, 25-06, 270, 30-06, 7mm Rem. Mag., 300 Win. Mag., 338 Win. Mag. Capacity 5 rounds (short action) or 3 rounds (long action). **Barrel:** 22" blued barrel (24" in magnum chamberings). **Weight:** 6-1/2 to 7-1/4 lbs. **Length:** NA. **Features:** Satin-finished checkered Grade I walnut stock, controlled round feeding. Pachmayr Decelerator pad. No sights but drilled and tapped for scope mounts.
Price: Short action **$799.00**
Price: Long action and magnum) **$839.00**

WINCHESTER MODEL 70 SPORTER

Caliber: 270 WSM, 7mm WSM, 300 WSM, 325 WSM, 25-06, 270, 30-06, 7mm Rem. Mag., 300 Win. Mag., 338 Win. Mag. Capacity 5 rounds (short action) or 3 rounds (long action). **Barrel:** 22", 24" or 26" blued. **Weight:** 6-1/2 to 7-1/4 lbs. **Length:** NA. **Features:** Satin-finished checkered Grade I walnut stock with sculpted cheekpiece, controlled round feeding. Pachmayr Decelerator pad. No sights but drilled and tapped for scope mounts.
Price: Short action **$799.00**
Price: Long action and magnum) **$839.00**

WINCHESTER MODEL 70 ULTIMATE SHADOW

Caliber: 243, 308, 270 WSM, 7mm WSM, 300 WSM, 325 WSM, 270, 30-06, 7mm Rem. Mag., 300 Win. Mag. Capacity 5 rounds (short action) or 3 rounds (long action). **Barrel:** 22" matte stainless (24" or 26" in magnum chamberings). **Weight:** 6-1/2 to 7-1/4 lbs. **Length:** NA. **Features:** Synthetic stock with WinSorb recoil pad, controlled round feeding. Pachmayr Decelerator pad. No sights but drilled and tapped for scope mounts.
Price: Standard **$739.00**
Price: Magnum **$769.00**

Prices given are believed to be accurate at time of publication however, many factors affect retail pricing so exact prices are not possible.

Ballard No. 7

ARMALITE AR-50 RIFLE
Caliber: 50 BMG **Barrel:** 31". **Weight:** 33.2 lbs. **Length:** 59.5" **Stock:** Synthetic. **Sights:** None furnished. **Features:** A single-shot bolt-action rifle designed for long-range shooting. Available in left-hand model. Made in U.S.A. by Armalite.
Price: **$3,359.00**

BALLARD 1875 1 1/2 HUNTER RIFLE
Caliber: NA. **Barrel:** 26-30". **Weight:** NA **Length:** NA. **Stock:** Hand-selected classic American walnut. **Sights:** Blade front, Rocky Mountain rear. **Features:** Color case-hardened receiver, breechblock and lever. Many options available. Made in U.S.A. by Ballard Rifle & Cartridge Co.
Price: **$3,250.00**

BALLARD 1875 #3 GALLERY SINGLE SHOT RIFLE
Caliber: NA. **Barrel:** 24-28" octagonal with tulip. **Weight:** NA. **Length:** NA. **Stock:** Hand-selected classic American walnut. **Sights:** Blade front, Rocky Mountain rear. **Features:** Color case-hardened receiver, breechblock and lever. Many options available. Made in U.S.A. by Ballard Rifle & Cartridge Co.
Price: **$3,300.00**

BALLARD 1875 #4 PERFECTION RIFLE
Caliber: 22 LR, 32-40, 38-55, 40-65, 40-70, 45-70 Govt., 45-90, 45-110, 50-70, 50-90. **Barrel:** 30" or 32" octagon, standard or heavyweight. **Weight:** 10.5 lbs. (standard) or 11.75 lbs. (heavyweight bbl.). **Length:** NA. **Stock:** Smooth walnut. **Sights:** Blade front, Rocky Mountain rear. **Features:** Rifle or shotgun-style buttstock, straight grip action, single or double-set trigger, "S" or right lever, hand polished and lapped Badger barrel. Made in U.S.A. by Ballard Rifle & Cartridge Co.
Price: **$3,950.00**

BALLARD 1875 #7 LONG RANGE RIFLE
Caliber: 32-40, 38-55, 40-65, 40-70 SS, 45-70 Govt., 45-90, 45-110. **Barrel:** 32", 34" half-octagon. **Weight:** 11.75 lbs. **Length:** NA. **Stock:** Walnut; checkered pistol grip shotgun butt, ebony forend cap. **Sights:** Globe front. **Features:** Designed for shooting up to 1000 yards. Standard or heavy barrel; single or double-set trigger; hard rubber or steel buttplate. Introduced 1999. Made in U.S.A. by Ballard Rifle & Cartridge Co.
Price: From **$3,600.00**

BALLARD 1875 #8 UNION HILL RIFLE
Caliber: 22 LR, 32-40, 38-55, 40-65 Win., 40-70 SS. **Barrel:** 30" half-octagon. **Weight:** About 10.5 lbs. **Length:** NA. **Stock:** Walnut; pistol grip butt with cheekpiece. **Sights:** Globe front. **Features:** Designed for 200-yard offhand shooting. Standard or heavy barrel; double-set triggers; full loop lever; hook Schuetzen buttplate. Introduced 1999. Made in U.S.A. by Ballard Rifle & Cartridge Co.
Price: From **$4,175.00**

BALLARD MODEL 1885 LOW WALL SINGLE SHOT RIFLE
Caliber: NA. **Barrel:** 24-28". **Weight:** NA. **Length:** NA. **Stock:** Hand-selected classic American walnut. **Sights:** Blade front, sporting rear. **Features:** Color case hardened receiver, breech block and lever. Many options available. Made in U.S.A. by Ballard Rifle & Cartridge Co.
Price: **$3,300.00**

BALLARD MODEL 1885 HIGH WALL STANDARD SPORTING SINGLE SHOT RIFLE
Caliber: 17 Bee, 22 Hornet, 218 Bee, 219 Don Wasp, 219 Zipper, 22 Hi-Power, 225 Win., 25-20 WCF, 25-35 WCF, 25 Krag, 7mmx57R, 30-30, 30-40 Krag, 303 British, 33 WCF, 348 WCF, 35 WCF, 35-30/30, 9.3x74R, 405 WCF, 50-110 WCF, 500 Express, 577 Express. **Barrel:** Lengths to 34". **Weight:** NA. **Length:** NA. **Stock:** Straight-grain American walnut. **Sights:** Buckhorn or flattop rear, blade front. **Features:** Faithful copy of original Model 1885 High Wall; parts interchange with original rifles; variety of options available. Introduced 2000. Made in U.S.A. by Ballard Rifle & Cartridge Co.
Price: **$3,300.00**

BALLARD MODEL 1885 HIGH WALL SPECIAL SPORTING SINGLE SHOT RIFLE
Caliber: NA. **Barrel:** 28-30" octagonal. **Weight:** NA. **Length:** NA. **Stock:** Hand-selected classic American walnut. **Sights:** Blade front, sporting rear. **Features:** Color case hardened receiver, breech block and lever. Many options available. Made in U.S.A. by Ballard Rifle & Cartridge Co.
Price: **$3,600.00**

BARRETT MODEL 99 SINGLE SHOT RIFLE
Caliber: 50 BMG. **Barrel:** 33". **Weight:** 25 lbs. **Length:** 50.4" overall. **Stock:** Anodized aluminum with energy-absorbing recoil pad. **Sights:** None furnished; integral M1913 scope rail. **Features:** Bolt action; detachable bipod; match-grade barrel with high-efficiency muzzle brake. Introduced 1999. Made in U.S.A. by Barrett Firearms.
Price: From **$4,000.00**

BROWN MODEL 97D SINGLE SHOT RIFLE
Caliber: 17 Ackley Hornet through 45-70 Govt. **Barrel:** Up to 26", air gauged match grade. **Weight:** About 5 lbs., 11 oz. **Stock:** Sporter style with pistol grip, cheekpiece and Schnabel forend. **Sights:** None furnished; drilled and tapped for scope mounting. **Features:** Falling block action gives rigid barrel-receiver matting; polished blue/black finish. Hand-fitted action. Many options. Made in U.S.A. by E. Arthur Brown Co., Inc.
Price: From **$999.00**

BROWNING MODEL 1885 HIGH WALL SINGLE SHOT RIFLE
Caliber: 22-250 Rem., 30-06 Spfl., 270 Win., 7mm Rem. Mag., 454 Casull, 45-70 Govt. **Barrel:** 28". **Weight:** 8 lbs., 12 oz. **Length:** 43.5" overall. **Stock:** Walnut with straight grip, Schnabel forend. **Sights:** None furnished; drilled and tapped for scope mounting. **Features:** Replica of J.M. Browning's high-wall falling block rifle. Octagon barrel with recessed muzzle. Imported from Japan by Browning. Introduced 1985.
Price: **$1,260.00**

C. SHARPS ARMS MODEL 1875 TARGET & SPORTING RIFLE
Caliber: 38-55, 40-65, 40-70 Straight or Bottlenecks, 45-70, 45-90. **Barrel:** 30" heavy tapered round. **Weight:** 11 lbs. **Length:** NA. **Stock:** American walnut. **Sights:** Globe with post front sight. **Features:** Long Range Vernier tang sight with windage adjustments. Pistol grip stock with cheek rest; checkered steel buttplate. Introduced 1991. From C. Sharps Arms Co.
Price: Without sights **$1,325.00**
Price: With blade front & Buckhorn rear barrel sights **$1,420.00**
Price: With standard Tang & Globe w/post & ball front sights **$1,615.00**
Price: With deluxe vernier Tang & Globe w/spirit level & aperture sights **$1,730.00**
Price: With single set trigger, add **$125.00**

CENTERFIRE RIFLES—Single Shot

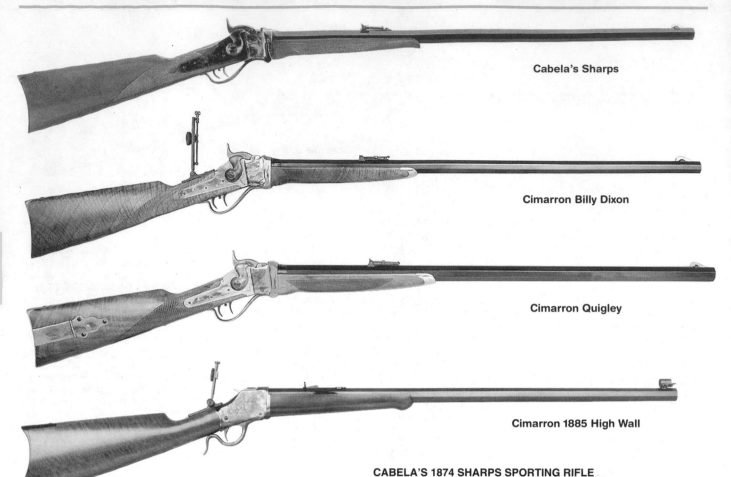

Cabela's Sharps

Cimarron Billy Dixon

Cimarron Quigley

Cimarron 1885 High Wall

C. Sharps Arms 1875 Classic Sharps
Similar to New Model 1875 Sporting Rifle except 26", 28" or 30" full octagon barrel, crescent buttplate with toe plate, Hartford-style forend with cast German silver nose cap. Blade front sight, Rocky Mountain buckhorn rear. Weighs 10 lbs. Introduced 1987. From C. Sharps Arms Co.
Price: **$1,670.00**

C. SHARPS ARMS 1874 BRIDGEPORT SPORTING RIFLE
Caliber: 38-55 TO 50-3.25. **Barrel:** 26", 28", 30" tapered octagon. **Weight:** 10.5 lbs. **Length:** 47". **Stock:** American black walnut; shotgun butt with checkered steel buttplate; straight grip, heavy forend with Schnabel tip. **Sights:** Blade front, buckhorn rear. Drilled and tapped for tang sight. **Features:** Double-set triggers. Made in U.S.A. by C. Sharps Arms.
Price: **$1,895.00**

C. SHARPS ARMS NEW MODEL 1885 HIGHWALL RIFLE
Caliber: 22 LR, 22 Hornet, 219 Zipper, 25-35 WCF, 32-40 WCF, 38-55 WCF, 40-65, 30-40 Krag, 40-50 ST or BN, 40-70 ST or BN, 40-90 ST or BN, 45-70 Govt. 2-1/10" ST, 45-90 2-4/10" ST, 45-100 2-6/10" ST, 45-110 2-7/8" ST, 45-120 3-1/4" ST. **Barrel:** 26", 28", 30", tapered full octagon. **Weight:** About 9 lbs., 4 oz. **Length:** 47" overall. **Stock:** Oil-finished American walnut; Schnabel-style forend. **Sights:** Blade front, buckhorn rear. Drilled and tapped for optional tang sight. **Features:** Single trigger; octagonal receiver top; checkered steel buttplate; color case-hardened receiver and buttplate, blued barrel. Many options available. Made in U.S.A. by C. Sharps Arms Co.
Price: From **$1,750.00**

C. SHARPS ARMS CUSTOM NEW MODEL 1877 LONG RANGE TARGET RIFLE
Caliber: 44-90 Sharps/Rem., 45-70 Govt., 45-90, 45-100 Sharps. **Barrel:** 32", 34" tapered round with Rigby flat. **Weight:** About 10 lbs. **Stock:** Walnut checkered. Pistol grip/forend. **Sights:** Classic long range with windage. **Features:** Custom production only.
Price: From **$7,250.00**

CABELA'S 1874 SHARPS SPORTING RIFLE
Caliber: 45-70. **Barrel:** 32", tapered octabon. **Weight:** 10.5 lbs. **Length:** 49.25" overall. **Stock:** Checkered walnut. **Sights:** Blade front, open adjustable rear. **Features:** Color case-hardened receiver and hammer, rest blued. Introduced 1995. Imported by Cabela's.
Price: 45-70 . . . . **$1,399.99**
Price: Quigley Sharps, 45-70 Govt., 45-120, 45-110 . . . . . . **$1,699.99**

CIMARRON BILLY DIXON 1874 SHARPS SPORTING RIFLE
Caliber: 40-40, 50-90, 50-70, 45-70 Govt. **Barrel:** 32" tapered octagonal. **Weight:** NA. **Length:** NA. **Stock:** European walnut. **Sights:** Blade front, Creedmoor rear. **Features:** Color case-hardened frame, blued barrel. Hand-checkered grip and forend; hand-rubbed oil finish. Introduced 1999. Imported by Cimarron F.A. Co.
Price: From **$1,987.70**

CIMARRON QUIGLEY MODEL 1874 SHARPS SPORTING RIFLE
Caliber: 45-110, 50-70, 50-40, 45-70 Govt., 45-90, 45-120. **Barrel:** 34" octagonal. **Weight:** NA. **Length:** NA. **Stock:** Checkered walnut. **Sights:** Blade front, adjustable rear. **Features:** Blued finish; double-set triggers. From Cimarron F.A. Co.
Price: From **$2,156.70**

CIMARRON SILHOUETTE MODEL 1874 SHARPS SPORTING RIFLE
Caliber: 45-70 Govt. **Barrel:** 32" octagonal. **Weight:** NA. **Length:** NA. **Stock:** Walnut. **Sights:** Blade front, adjustable rear. **Features:** Pistol-grip stock with shotgun-style buttplate; cut-rifled barrel. From Cimarron F.A. Co.
Price: **$1,597.70**

CIMARRON MODEL 1885 HIGH WALL RIFLE
Caliber: 38-55, 40-65, 45-70 Govt., 45-90, 45-120, 30-40 Krag, 348 Winchester. **Barrel:** 30" octagonal. **Weight:** NA. **Length:** NA. **Stock:** European walnut. **Sights:** Bead front, semi-buckhorn rear. **Features:** Replica of the Winchester 1885 High Wall rifle. Color case-hardened receiver and lever, blued barrel. Curved buttplate. Optional double-set triggers. Introduced 1999. Imported by Cimarron F.A. Co.
Price: From **$1,002.91**
Price: With pistol grip, from **$1,136.81**

Prices given are believed to be accurate at time of publication however, many factors affect retail pricing so exact prices are not possible.

Dakota Single Shot

H&R Ultra Varmint

H&R CR-45LC

H&R Ultra Hunter

Price: Ultra Hunter Rifle, 26" bull barrel in 25-06 Rem.,
laminated stock $357.00
Price: Ultra Varmint Rifle, 22" bull barrel in 223 Rem.,
laminated stock $357.00

DAKOTA MODEL 10 SINGLE SHOT RIFLE

Caliber: Most rimmed and rimless commercial calibers. **Barrel:** 23".
Weight: 6 lbs. **Length:** 39.5" overall. **Stock:** Medium fancy grade
walnut in classic style. Checkered grip and forend. **Sights:** None
furnished. Drilled and tapped for scope mounting. **Features:** Falling
block action with underlever. Top tang safety. Removable trigger plate
for conversion to single set trigger. Introduced 1990. Made in U.S.A.
by Dakota Arms.
Price: From **$4,695.00**
Price: Action only **$1,875.00**
Price: Magnum action only **$1,875.00**

EMF PREMIER 1874 SHARPS RIFLE

Caliber: 45/70, 45/110, 45/120. **Barrel:** 32", 34". **Weight:** 11-13 lbs.
Length: 49", 51" overall. **Stock:** Pistol grip, European walnut. **Sights:**
Blade front, adjustable rear. **Features:** Superb quality reproductions
of the 1874 Sharps Sporting Rifles; casehardened locks; double-set
triggers; blue barrels. Imported from Pedersoli by EMF.
Price: Business Rifle. **$1,199.90**
Price: "Quigley", Patchbox, heavy barrel **$1,799.90**
Price: Silhouette, pistol-grip **$1,499.90**
Price: Super Deluxe Hand Engraved **$3,500.00**

HARRINGTON & RICHARDSON ULTRA VARMINT/ULTRA HUNTER RIFLES

Caliber: 204 Ruger, 22 WMR, 22-250 Rem., 223 Rem., 243 Win., 25-
06 Rem., 30-06. **Barrel:** 22" to 26" heavy taper. **Weight:** About 7.5
lbs. **Stock:** Laminated birch with Monte Carlo comb or skeletonized
polymer. **Sights:** None furnished. Drilled and tapped for scope
mounting. **Features:** Break-open action with side-lever release,
positive ejection. Scope mount. Blued receiver and barrel. Swivel studs.
Introduced 1993. Ultra Hunter introduced 1995. From H&R 1871, Inc.
Price: Ultra Varmint Fluted, 24" bull barrel, polymer stock **$406.00**

HARRINGTON & RICHARDSON/NEW ENGLAND FIREARMS STAINLESS ULTRA HUNTER WITH THUMBHOLE STOCK

Caliber: 45-70 Govt. **Barrel:** 24". **Weight:** 8 lbs. **Length:** 40". **Features:**
Stainless steel barrel and receiver with scope mount rail, hammer
extension, cinnamon laminate thumbhole stock.
Price: **$439.00**

HARRINGTON & RICHARDSON/NEW ENGLAND FIREARMS HANDI-RIFLE/SLUG GUN COMBOS

Chamber: 44 Mag./12-ga. rifled slug and 357 Mag./20-ga. rifled slug.
Barrel: Rifle barrel 22" for both calibers; shotgun barrels 28" (12 ga.)
and 40" (20 ga.) fully rifled. **Weight:** 7-8 lbs. **Length:** 38" overall (both
rifle chamberings). **Features:** Single-shot break-open rifle/shotgun
combos (one rifle barrel, one shotgun barrel per combo). Rifle barrels
are not interchangeable; shotgun barrels are interchangeable. Stock
is black matte high-density polymer with sling swivel studs, molded
checkering and recoil pad. No iron sights; scope rail included.
Price: **$362.00**

HARRINGTON & RICHARDSON CR-45LC

Caliber: 45 Colt. **Barrel:** 20". **Weight:** 6.25 lbs. **Length:** 34"overall.
Features: Single-shot break-open carbine. Cut-checkered American
black walnut with case-colored crescent steel buttplate, open sights,
case-colored receiver.
Price: **$407.00**

HARRINGTON & RICHARDSON BUFFALO CLASSIC RIFLE

Caliber: 45-70 Govt. **Barrel:** 32" heavy. **Weight:** 8 lbs. **Length:** 46"
overall. **Stock:** Cut-checkered American black walnut. **Sights:** Williams
receiver sight; Lyman target front sight with 8 aperture inserts. **Features:**
Color case-hardened Handi-Rifle action with exposed hammer; color
case-hardened crescent buttplate; 19th century checkering pattern.
Introduced 1995. Made in U.S.A. by H&R 1871, Inc.
Price: Buffalo Classic Rifle **$449.00**

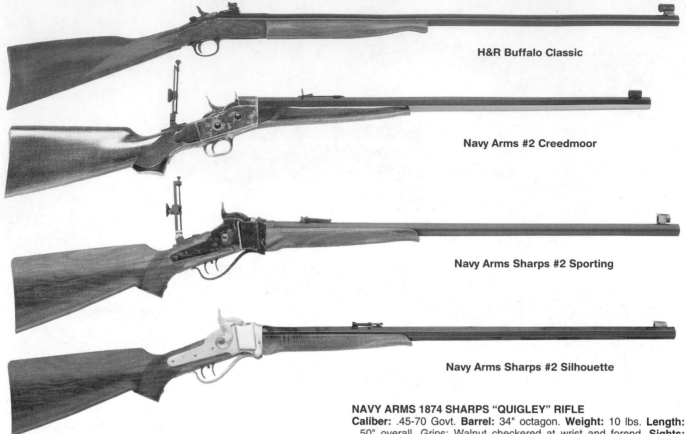

H&R Buffalo Classic

Navy Arms #2 Creedmoor

Navy Arms Sharps #2 Sporting

Navy Arms Sharps #2 Silhouette

KRIEGHOFF HUBERTUS SINGLE-SHOT RIFLE
Caliber: 222, 243 Win., 270 Win., 308 Win., 30-06 Spfl., 5.6x50R Mag., 5.6x52R, 6x62R Freres, 6.5x57R, 6.5x65R, 7x57R, 7x65R, 8x57JRS, 8x75RS, 9.3x74R, 7mm Rem. Mag., 300 Win. Mag. **Barrel:** 23.5". **Weight:** 6.5 lbs. **Length:** 40.5. **Stock:** High-grade walnut. **Sights:** Blade front, open rear. **Features:** Break-open loading with manual cocking lever on top tang; takedown; extractor; Schnabel forearm; many options. Imported from Germany by Krieghoff International Inc.
Price: Hubertus single shot, from $5,995.00
Price: Hubertus, magnum calibers $6,995.00

MEACHAM HIGHWALL SILHOUETTE OR SCHUETZEN RIFLE
Caliber: any rimmed cartridge. **Barrel:** 26-34". **Weight:** 8-15 lbs. **Sights:** none. Tang drilled for Win. base, 3/8 dovetail slot front. **Stock:** Fancy eastern walnut with cheekpiece; ebony insert in forearm tip. **Features:** Exact copy of 1885 Winchester. With most Winchester factory options available, including double set triggers. Introduced 1994. Made in U.S.A. by Meacham T&H Inc.
Price: From $4,999.00

MERKEL K1 MODEL LIGHTWEIGHT STALKING RIFLE
Caliber: 243 Win., 270 Win., 7x57R, 308 Win., 30-06 Spfl., 7mm Rem. Mag., 300 Win. Mag., 9.3x74R. **Barrel:** 23.6". **Weight:** 5.6 lbs. unscoped. **Stock:** Satin-finished walnut, fluted and checkered; sling-swivel studs. **Sights:** None (scope base furnished). **Features:** Franz Jager single-shot break-open action, cocking/uncocking slide-type safety, matte silver receiver, selectable trigger pull weights, integrated, quick detach 1" or 30mm optic mounts (optic not included). Imported from Germany by Merkel USA.
Price: Jagd Stutzen Carbine $3,795.00

MERKEL K-2 CUSTOM SINGLE-SHOT "WEIMAR" STALKING RIFLE
Caliber: 308 Win., 30-06 Spfl., 7mm Rem. Mag., 300 Win. Mag. **Features:** Franz Jager single-shot break-open action, cocking.uncocking slide safety, deep relief engraved hunting scenes on silvered receiver, octagin barrel, deluxe walnut stock. Includes front and reare adjustable iron sights, scope rings. Imported from Germany by Merkel USA.
Price: Jagd Stutzen Carbine $15,595.00

NAVY ARMS 1874 SHARPS "QUIGLEY" RIFLE
Caliber: .45-70 Govt. **Barrel:** 34" octagon. **Weight:** 10 lbs. **Length:** 50" overall. **Grips:** Walnut checkered at wrist and forend. **Sights:** High blade front, full buckhorn rear. **Features:** Color case-hardened receiver, trigger, military patchbox, hammer and lever. Double-set triggers, German silver gripcap. Reproduction of rifle from "Quigley Down Under" movie.
Price: Model SQR045 (20087) $2,026.00

NAVY ARMS 1874 SHARPS #2 CREEDMOOR RIFLE
Caliber: 45/70. **Barrel:** 30" tapered round. **Stock:** Walnut. **Sights:** Front globe, "soule" tang rear. **Features:** Nickel receiver and action. Lightweight sporting rifle.
Price: $1,816.00

Navy Arms Sharps Sporting Rifle
Same as the Navy Arms Sharps Plains Rifle except has pistol grip stock. Introduced 1997. Imported by Navy Arms.
Price: 45-70 Govt. only $1,711.00
Price: #2 Sporting with case-hardened receiver $1,739.00
Price: #2 Silhouette with full octagonal barrel $1,739.00

NAVY ARMS 1885 HIGH WALL RIFLE
Caliber: 45-70 Govt.; others available on special order. **Barrel:** 28" round, 30" octagonal. **Weight:** 9.5 lbs. **Length:** 45.5" overall (30" barrel). **Stock:** Walnut. **Sights:** Blade front, vernier tang-mounted peep rear. **Features:** Replica of Winchester's High Wall designed by Browning. Color case-hardened receiver, blued barrel. Introduced 1998. Imported by Navy Arms.
Price: 28", round barrel, target sights $1,120.00
Price: 30" octagonal barrel, target sights $1,212.00

NAVY ARMS 1873 SPRINGFIELD CAVALRY CARBINE
Caliber: 45-70 Govt. **Barrel:** 22". **Weight:** 7 lbs. **Length:** 40.5" overall. **Stock:** Walnut. **Sights:** Blade front, military ladder rear. **Features:** Blued lockplate and barrel; color case-hardened breechblock; saddle ring with bar. Replica of 7th Cavalry gun. Officer's Model Trapdoor has single-set trigger, bone case-hardened buttplate, trigger guard and breechblock. Deluxe walnut stock hand-checkered at the wrist and forend. German silver forend cap and rod tip. Adjustable rear peep target sight. Authentic flip-up 'Beech' front target sight. Imported by Navy Arms.
Price: Model STC073 . . . . $1,261.00
Price: Officer's Model Trapdoor (2008) $1,648.00

Prices given are believed to be accurate at time of publication however, many factors affect retail pricing so exact prices are not possible.

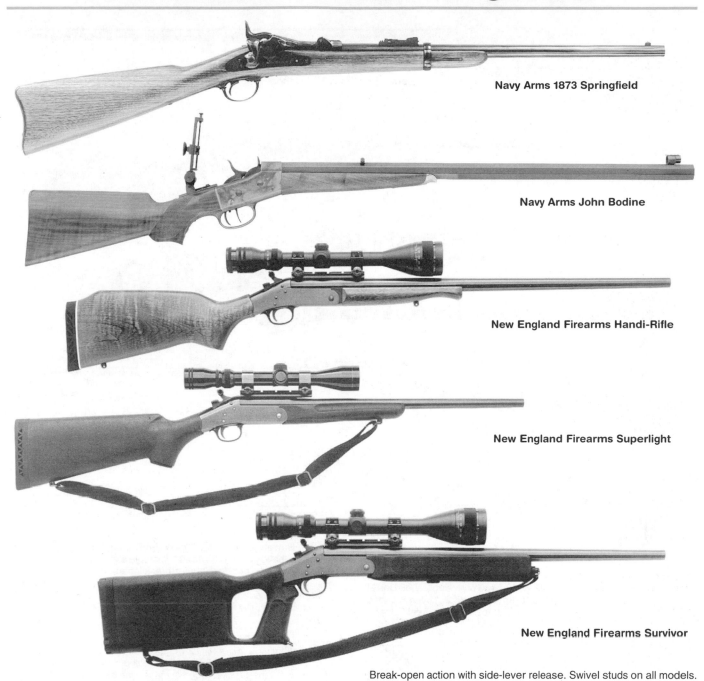

Navy Arms 1873 Springfield

Navy Arms John Bodine

New England Firearms Handi-Rifle

New England Firearms Superlight

New England Firearms Survivor

NAVY ARMS "JOHN BODINE" ROLLING BLOCK RIFLE
Caliber: 45-70 Govt. **Barrel:** 30" heavy octagonal. **Stock:** Walnut. **Sights:** Globe front, "soule" tang rear. **Features:** Double-set triggers.
Price: **$1,928.00**
Price: (#2 with deluxe nickel finished receiver) **$1,928.00**

NAVY ARMS 1874 SHARPS NO. 3 LONG RANGE RIFLE
Caliber: 45-70 Govt. **Barrel:** 34" octagon. **Weight:** 10 lbs., 14 oz. **Length:** 51.2". **Stock:** Deluxe walnut. **Sights:** Globe target front and match grade rear tang. **Features:** Shotgun buttplate, German silver forend cap, color case hardened receiver. Imported by Navy Arms.
Price: **$2,432.00**

NEW ENGLAND FIREARMS HANDI-RIFLE
Caliber: 204 Ruger, 22 Hornet, 223 Rem., 243 Win., 30-30, 270 Win., 280 Rem., 7mm-08 Rem., 308 Win., 7.62x39 Russian, 30-06 Spfl., 357 Mag., 35 Whelen, 44 Mag., 45-70 Govt., 500 S&W. **Barrel:** From 20" to 26", blued or stainless. **Weight:** 5.5 to 7 lbs. **Stock:** Walnut-finished hardwood or synthetic. **Sights:** Vary by model, but most have ramp front, folding rear, or are drilled and tapped for scope mount. **Features:**

Break-open action with side-lever release. Swivel studs on all models. Blue finish. Introduced 1989. From H&R 1871, Inc.
Price: Various cartridges. **$292.00**
Price: 7.62x39 Russian, 35 Whelen, intr. 2006 . . . . **$292.00**
Price: Youth, 37" OAL, 11.75" LOP, 6.75 lbs. **$292.00**
Price: Handi-Rifle/Pardner combo, 20 ga. synthetic, intr. 2006 . . . . **$325.00**
Price: Handi-Rifle/Pardner Superlight, 20 ga., 5.5 lbs., intr. 2006 . . . . **$325.00**
Price: Synthetic **$302.00**
Price: Stainless **$364.00**
Price: Superlight, 20" barrel, 35.25" OAL, 5.5 lbs. **$302.00**

NEW ENGLAND FIREARMS SURVIVOR RIFLE
Caliber: 223 Rem., 308 Win., .410 shotgun, 45 Colt, single shot. **Barrel:** 20" to 22". **Weight:** 6 lbs. **Length:** 34.5" to 36" overall. **Stock:** Black polymer, thumbhole design. **Sights:** None furnished; scope mount provided. **Features:** Receiver drilled and tapped for scope mounting. Stock and forend have storage compartments for ammo, etc.; comes with integral swivels and black nylon sling. Introduced 1996. Made in U.S.A. by H&R 1871, Inc.
Price: Blue or nickel finish. **$304.00**

Remington No. 1 Mid-Range

Rossi Single Shot

Rossi Matched Pairs

Ruger No. 1-B

Ruger K1-B-BBZ

NEW ENGLAND FIREARMS SPORTSTER/VERSA PACK RIFLE
Caliber: 17M2, 17 HMR, 22 LR, 22 WMR, .410 bore single shot. **Barrel:** 20" to 22". **Weight:** 5.4 to 7 lbs. **Length:** 33" to 38.25" overall. **Stock:** Black polymer. **Sights:** Adjustable rear, ramp front. **Features:** Receiver drilled and tapped for scope mounting. Made in U.S.A. by H&R 1871, Inc.
Price: Sportster 17M2, 17 HMR **$193.00**
Price: Sportster **$161.00**
Price: Sportster Youth **$161.00**

REMINGTON MODEL SPR18 SINGLE SHOT RIFLES
Caliber: 223 Rem., 243 Win., 270 Win., .30-06 Spfl., 308 Win., 7.62x39mm. **Barrel:** 23.5" chrome-lined hammer forged, all steel receiver, spiral-cut fluting. **Weight:** 6.75 lbs. **Stock:** Walnut stock and fore-end, swivel studs. **Sights:** adjustable, with 11mm scope rail. **Length:** 39.75" overall. **Features:** Made in U.S. by Remington Arms Co., Inc.
Price: Blued/walnut (2008) **$277.00**
Price: Nickel/walnut (2008).......................... **$326.00**

REMINGTON NO. 1 ROLLING BLOCK MID-RANGE SPORTER
Caliber: 45-70 Govt. **Barrel:** 30" round. **Weight:** 8.75 lbs. **Length:** 46.5" overall. **Stock:** American walnut with checkered pistol grip and forend. **Sights:** Beaded blade front, adjustable center-notch buckhorn rear. **Features:** Recreation of the original. Polished blue metal finish. Many options available. Introduced 1998. Made in U.S.A. by Remington.
Price: **$2,927.00**
Price: Silhouette model with single-set trigger, heavy barrel **$3,366.00**

ROSSI SINGLE-SHOT RIFLES
Caliber: 17, 223 Rem., 243 Win., 270 Win., .30-06, 308 Win., 7.62x39,

22-250. **Barrel:** 22" (Youth), 23". **Weight:** 6.25-7 lbs. Stocks: Wood, Black Synthetic (Youth). **Sights:** Adjustable sights, drilled and tapped for scope. **Features:** Single-shot break open, 13 models available, positive ejection, internal transfer bar mechanism, manual external safety, trigger block system, Taurus Security System, Matte blue finish, youth models available.
Price: **$238.00**

ROSSI MATCHED PAIRS
Gauge/Caliber: 12, 20, .410, 22 Mag, 22 LR, 17 HMR, 223 Rem, 243 Win., 270 Win., .30-06, 308Win., .50 (black powder). **Barrel:** 23", 28". **Weight:** 5-6.3 lbs. Stocks: Wood or black synthetic. **Sights:** Bead front on shotgun barrel, fully adjustable front and rear on rifle barrel, drilled and tapped for scope, fully adjustable fiber optic sights (black powder). **Features:** Single-shot break open, 27 models available, internal transfer bar mechanism, manual external safety, blue finish, trigger block system, Taurus Security System, youth models available.
Price: Rimfire/Shotgun, from.......................... **$178.00**
Price: Centerfire/Shotgun **$299.00**
Price: Black Powder Matched Pair, from **$262.00**

RUGER NO. 1-B SINGLE SHOT
Caliber: 223 Rem., 204 Ruger, 25-06 Rem., 270 Win., 30-06 Spfl., 7mm Rem. Mag., 300 Win. Mag., 308 Win. **Barrel:** 26" round tapered with quarter-rib; with Ruger 1" rings. **Weight:** 8.25 lbs. **Length:** 42.25" overall. **Stock:** Walnut, two-piece, checkered pistol grip and semi-beavertail forend. **Sights:** None, 1" scope rings supplied for integral mounts. **Features:** Under-lever, hammerless falling block design has auto ejector, top tang safety.
Price: 1-B **$1,093.00**
Price: K1-B-BBZ stainless steel, laminated stock 25-06 Rem., 7mm Rem. Mag., 270, 300 Win. Mag., 243 Win., 30-06 .... **$1,186.00**

Prices given are believed to be accurate at time of publication however, many factors affect retail pricing so exact prices are not possible.

CENTERFIRE RIFLES—Single Shot

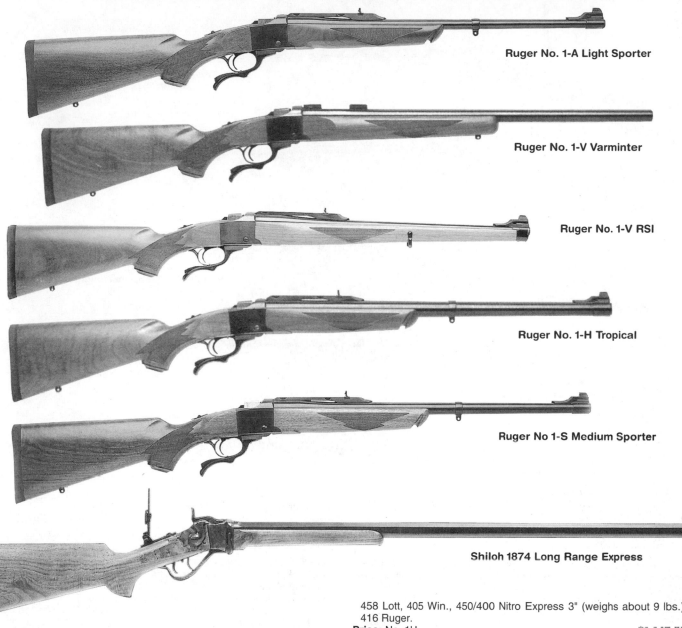

Ruger No. 1-A Light Sporter

Ruger No. 1-V Varminter

Ruger No. 1-V RSI

Ruger No. 1-H Tropical

Ruger No 1-S Medium Sporter

Shiloh 1874 Long Range Express

RUGER NO. 1-A LIGHT SPORTER
Caliber: 243 Win., 270 Win., 7x57, 30-06, 300 Ruger Compact Magnum. **Weight:** 7.25 lbs. Similar to the No. 1-B Standard Rifle except has lightweight 22" barrel, Alexander Henry-style forend, adjustable folding leaf rear sight on quarter-rib, dovetailed ramp front with gold bead.
Price: No. 1A $1,147.00

Ruger No. 1-V Varminter
Similar to the No. 1-B Standard Rifle except has 24" heavy barrel. Semi-beavertail forend, barrel ribbed for target scope block, with 1" Ruger scope rings. Calibers 204 Ruger (26" barrel), 22-250 Rem., 223 Rem., 25-06 Rem. Weight about 9 lbs.
Price: No. 1-V $1,147.00

Ruger No. 1 RSI International
Similar to the No. 1-B Standard Rifle except has lightweight 20" barrel, full-length International-style forend with loop sling swivel, adjustable folding leaf rear sight on quarter-rib, ramp front with gold bead. Calibers 30-06 Spfl., 270 and 7x57. Weight is about 7.25 lbs.
Price: No. 1 RSI $1,186.00

Ruger No. 1-H Tropical Rifle
Similar to the No. 1-B Standard Rifle except has Alexander Henry forend, adjustable folding leaf rear sight on quarter-rib, ramp front with dovetail gold bead, 24" heavy barrel. Calibers 375 H&H, 416 Rigby,

458 Lott, 405 Win., 450/400 Nitro Express 3" (weighs about 9 lbs.), 416 Ruger.
Price: No. 1H $1,147.00

Ruger No. 1-S Medium Sporter
Similar to the No. 1-B Standard Rifle except has Alexander Henry-style forend, adjustable folding leaf rear sight on quarter-rib, ramp front sight base and dovetail-type gold bead front sight. Calibers include 9.3x74R, 45-70 Govt. with 22" barrel, 338 Ruger Compact Magnum, 375 Ruger, 460 S&W Magnum, 480 Ruger/475 Linebaugh. Weighs about 7.25 lbs.
Price: No. 1-S $1,147.00
Price: K1-S-BBZ, S/S, 45-70 Govt. $1,186.00

SHILOH RIFLE CO. SHARPS 1874 LONG RANGE EXPRESS
Caliber: 40-50 BN, 40-70 BN, 40-90 BN, 45-70 Govt. ST, 45-90 ST, 45-110 ST, 50-70 ST, 50-90 ST, 38-55, 40-70 ST, 40-90 ST. **Barrel:** 34" tapered octagon. **Weight:** 10.5 lbs. **Length:** 51" overall. **Stock:** Oil-finished walnut (upgrades available) with pistol grip, shotgun-style butt, traditional cheek rest, Schnabel forend. **Sights:** Customer's choice. **Features:** Re-creation of the Model 1874 Sharps rifle. Double-set triggers. Made in U.S.A. by Shiloh Rifle Mfg. Co.
Price: $1,902.00
Price: Sporter Rifle No. 1 (similar to above except with 30" barrel, blade front, buckhorn rear sight) $1,902.00
Price: Sporter Rifle No. 3 (similar to No. 1 except straight-grip stock, standard wood) $1,800.00

Shiloh 1874 Quigley

Shiloh 1874 Saddle

Shiloh 1874 Montana Roughrider

Shiloh 1874 Creedmoor

Thompson/Center Encore

SHILOH RIFLE CO. SHARPS 1874 QUIGLEY
Caliber: 45-70 Govt., 45-110. **Barrel:** 34" heavy octagon. **Stock:** Military-style with patch box, standard grade American walnut. **Sights:** Semi buckhorn, interchangeable front and midrange vernier tang sight with windage. **Features:** Gold inlay initials, pewter tip, Hartford collar, case color or antique finish. Double-set triggers.
Price: **$3,298.00**

SHILOH RIFLE CO. SHARPS 1874 SADDLE RIFLE
Caliber: 38-55, 40-50 BN, 40-65 Win., 40-70 BN, 40-70 ST, 40-90 BN, 40-90 ST, 44-77 BN, 44-90 BN, 45-70 Govt. ST, 45-90 ST, 45-100 ST, 45-110 ST, 45-120 ST, 50-70 ST, 50-90 ST. **Barrel:** 26" full or half octagon. **Stock:** Semi fancy American walnut. Shotgun style with cheekrest. **Sights:** Buckhorn and blade. **Features:** Double-set trigger, numerous custom features can be added.
Price: **$1,852.00**

SHILOH RIFLE CO. SHARPS 1874 MONTANA ROUGHRIDER
Caliber: 38-55, 40-50 BN, 40-65 Win., 40-70 BN, 40-70 ST, 40-90 BN, 40-90 ST, 44-77 BN, 44-90 BN, 45-70 Govt. ST, 45-90 ST, 45-100 ST, 45-110 ST, 45-120 ST, 50-70 ST, 50-90 ST. **Barrel:** 30" full or half octagon. **Stock:** American walnut in shotgun or military style. **Sights:** Buckhorn and blade. **Features:** Double-set triggers, numerous custom features can be added.
Price: **$1,902.00**

SHILOH RIFLE CO. SHARPS CREEDMOOR TARGET
Caliber: 38-55, 40-50 BN, 40-65 Win., 40-70 BN, 40-70 ST, 40-90 BN, 40-90 ST, 44-77 BN, 44-90 BN, 45-70 Govt. ST, 45-90 ST, 45-100 ST, 45-110 ST, 45-120 ST, 50-70 ST, 50-90 ST. **Barrel:** 32", half round-half octagon. **Stock:** Extra fancy American walnut. Shotgun style with pistol grip. **Sights:** Customer's choice. **Features:** Single trigger, AA

finish on stock, polished barrel and screws, pewter tip.
Price: **$2,743.00**

THOMPSON/CENTER ENCORE RIFLE
Caliber: 22-250 Rem., 223 Rem., 243 Win., 204 Ruger, 6.8 Rem. Spec., 25-06 Rem., 270 Win., 7mm-08 Rem., 308 Win., 30-06 Spfl., 7mm Rem. Mag., 300 Win. Mag. **Barrel:** 24", 26". **Weight:** 6 lbs., 12 oz. (24" barrel). **Length:** 38.5" (24" barrel). **Stock:** American walnut. Monte Carlo style; Schnabel forend or black composite. **Sights:** Ramp-style white bead front, fully adjustable leaf-type rear. **Features:** Interchangeable barrels; action opens by squeezing trigger guard; drilled and tapped for T/C scope mounts; polished blue finish. Introduced 1996. Made in U.S.A. by Thompson/Center Arms.
Price: .... **$604.00 to $663.00**
Price: Extra barrels **$277.00**

Thompson/Center Stainless Encore Rifle
Similar to blued Encore except stainless steel with blued sights, black composite stock and forend. Available in 22-250 Rem., 223 Rem., 7mm-08 Rem., 30-06 Spfl., 308 Win. Introduced 1999. Made in U.S.A. by Thompson/Center Arms.
Price: .... **$680.00 to $738.00**

THOMPSON/CENTER ENCORE "KATAHDIN" CARBINE
Caliber: 45-70 Govt., 450 Marlin. **Barrel:** 18" with muzzle tamer. **Stock:** Composite.
Price: **$619.00**

Thompson/Center G2 Contender Rifle
Similar to the G2 Contender pistol, but in a compact rifle format. Weighs 5.5 lbs. Features interchangeable 23" barrels, chambered for 17 HMR, 22 LR, 223 Rem., 30/30 Win. and 45/70 Govt.; plus a 45 cal. muzzleloading barrel. All of the 16.25" and 21" barrels made for the old-style Contender will fit. Introduced 2003. Made in U.S.A. by Thompson/Center Arms.
Price: .... **$622.00 to $637.00**

Prices given are believed to be accurate at time of publication however, many factors affect retail pricing so exact prices are not possible.

Thompson/Center Encore "Katahdin"

Thompson/Center Contender

Traditions 1874 Sharps Deluxe

Traditions 1874 Sharps Sporting Deluxe

Uberti 1885 High-Wall Single Shot

TRADITIONS 1874 SHARPS DELUXE RIFLE
Caliber: 45-70 Govt. **Barrel:** 32" octagonal; 1:18" twist. **Weight:** 11.67 lbs. **Length:** 48.8" overall. **Stock:** Checkered walnut with German silver nose cap and steel buttplate. **Sights:** Globe front, adjustable Creedmore rear with 12 inserts. **Features:** Color case-hardened receiver; double-set triggers. Introduced 2001. Imported from Pedersoli by Traditions.
Price: **$1,545.00**

Traditions 1874 Sharps Sporting Deluxe Rifle
Similar to Sharps Deluxe but custom silver engraved receiver, European walnut stock and forend, satin finish, set trigger, fully adjustable.
Price: **$2,796.00**

Traditions 1874 Sharps Standard Rifle
Similar to 1874 Sharps Deluxe except has blade front and adjustable buckhorn-style rear sight. Weighs 10.67 pounds. Introduced 2001. Imported from Pedersoli by Traditions.
Price: **$1,324.00**

TRADITIONS ROLLING BLOCK SPORTING RIFLE
Caliber: 45-70 Govt. **Barrel:** 30" octagonal; 1:18" twist. **Weight:** 11.67 lbs. **Length:** 46.7" overall. **Stock:** Walnut. **Sights:** Blade front, adjustable rear. **Features:** Antique silver, color case-hardened receiver, drilled and tapped for tang/globe sights; brass buttplate and trigger guard. Introduced 2001. Imported from Pedersoli by Traditions.
Price: **$1,029.00**

UBERTI 1874 SHARPS SPORTING RIFLE
Caliber: 45-70 Govt. **Barrel:** 30", 32", 34" octagonal. **Weight:** 10.57 lbs. with 32" barrel. **Length:** 48.9" with 32" barrel. **Stock:** Walnut. **Sights:** Dovetail front, Vernier tang rear. **Features:** Cut checkering, case-colored finish on frame, buttplate, and lever. Imported by Stoeger Industries.
Price: Standard Sharps (2006), 30" barrel **$1,459.00**
Price: Special Sharps (2006) 32" barrel **$1,729.00**
Price: Deluxe Sharps (2006) 34" barrel **$2,749.00**
Price: Down Under Sharps (2006) 34" barrel **$2,249.00**
Price: Long Range Sharps (2006) 34" barrel **$2,279.00**
Price: Buffalo Hunters Sharps, 32" barrel **$2,219.00**
Price: Calvary Carbine Sharps, 22" barrel **$1,569.00**
Price: Sharps Extra Deluxe, 32" barrel (2009) **$4,199.00**
Price: Sharps Hunter, 28" barrel **$1,459.00**

UBERTI 1885 HIGH-WALL SINGLE-SHOT RIFLES
Caliber: 45-70 Govt., 45-90, 45-120 single shot. **Barrel:** 28" to 23". **Weight:** 9.3 to 9.9 lbs. **Length:** 44.5" to 47" overall. **Stock:** Walnut stock and forend. **Sights:** Blade front, fully adjustable open rear. **Features:** Based on Winchester High-Wall design by John Browning. Color case-hardened frame and lever, blued barrel and buttplate. Imported by Stoeger Industries.
Price: 1885 High-Wall, 28" round barrel **$969.00**
Price: 1885 High-Wall Sporting, 30" octagonal barrel **$1,029.00**
Price: 1885 High-Wall Special Sporting, 32" octagonal barrel **$1,179.00**

Designs for sporting and utility purposes worldwide.

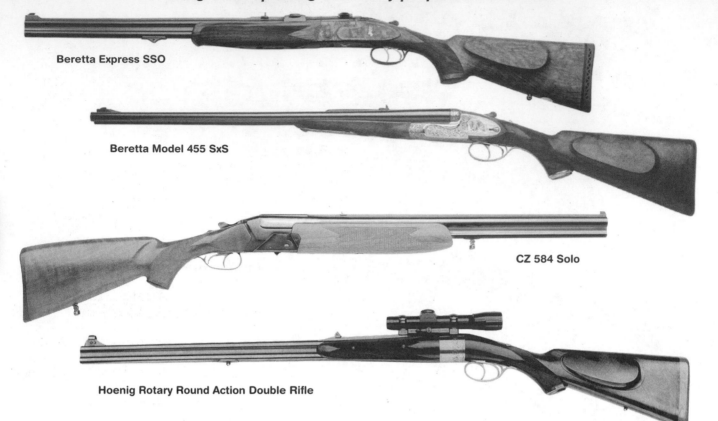

Beretta Express SSO

Beretta Model 455 SxS

CZ 584 Solo

Hoenig Rotary Round Action Double Rifle

BERETTA EXPRESS SSO O/U DOUBLE RIFLES
Caliber: 375 H&H, 458 Win. Mag., 9.3x74R. **Barrel:** 25.5". **Weight:** 11 lbs. **Stock:** European walnut with hand-checkered grip and forend. **Sights:** Blade front on ramp, open V-notch rear. **Features:** Sidelock action with color case-hardened receiver (gold inlays on SSO6 Gold). Ejectors, double triggers, recoil pad. Introduced 1990. Imported from Italy by Beretta U.S.A.
Price: SSO6 . . . . **$21,000.00**
Price: SSO6 Gold **$23,500.00**

BERETTA MODEL 455 SXS EXPRESS RIFLE
Caliber: 375 H&H, 458 Win. Mag., 470 NE, 500 NE 3", 416 Rigby. **Barrel:** 23.5" or 25.5". **Weight:** 11 lbs. **Stock:** European walnut with hand-checkered grip and forend. **Sights:** Blade front, folding leaf V-notch rear. **Features:** Sidelock action with easily removable sideplates; color case-hardened finish (455), custom big game or floral motif engraving (455EELL). Double triggers, recoil pad. Introduced 1990. Imported from Italy by Beretta U.S.A.
Price: Model 455 . . . . **$36,000.00**
Price: Model 455EELL **$47,000.00**

CZ 584 SOLO COMBINATION GUN
Caliber/Gauge: 7x57R; 12, 2-3/4" chamber. **Barrel:** 24.4". **Weight:** 7.37 lbs. **Length:** 45.25" overall. **Stock:** Circassian walnut. **Sights:** Blade front, open rear adjustable for windage. **Features:** Kersten-style double lump locking system; double-trigger Blitz-type mechanism with drop safety and adjustable set trigger for the rifle barrel; auto safety, dual extractors; receiver dovetailed for scope mounting. Imported from the Czech Republic by CZ-USA.
Price: **$851.00**

CZ 589 STOPPER OVER/UNDER GUN
Caliber: 458 Win. Magnum. **Barrels:** 21.7". **Weight:** 9.3 lbs. **Length:** 37.7" overall. **Stock:** Turkish walnut with sling swivels. **Sights:** Blade front, fixed rear. **Features:** Kersten-style action; Blitz-type double trigger; hammer-forged, blued barrels; satin-nickel, engraved receiver. Introduced 2001. Imported from the Czech Republic by CZ USA.
Price: **$2,999.00**
Price: Fully engraved model **$3,999.00**

DAKOTA DOUBLE RIFLE
Caliber: 470 Nitro Express, 500 Nitro Express. **Barrel:** 25". **Stock:** Exhibition-grade walnut. **Sights:** Express-style. **Features:** Round action; selective ejectors; recoil pad; Americase. From Dakota Arms Inc.
Price: **$25,000.00**

GARBI EXPRESS DOUBLE RIFLE
Caliber: 7x65R, 9.3x74R, 375 H&H. **Barrel:** 24.75". **Weight:** 7.75 to 8.5 lbs. **Length:** 41.5" overall. **Stock:** Turkish walnut. **Sights:** Quarter-rib with express sight. **Features:** Side-by-side double; H&H-pattern sidelock ejector with reinforced action, chopper lump barrels of Boehler steel; double triggers; fine scroll and rosette engraving, or full coverage ornamental; coin-finished action. Introduced 1997. Imported from Spain by Wm. Larkin Moore.
Price: **$25,000.00**

HOENIG ROTARY ROUND ACTION DOUBLE RIFLE
Caliber: Most popular calibers from 225 Win. to 9.3x74R. **Barrel:** 22" to 26". **Stock:** English Walnut; to customer specs. **Sights:** Swivel hood front with button release (extra bead stored in trap door gripcap), express-style rear on quarter-rib adjustable for windage and elevation; scope mount. **Features:** Round action opens by rotating barrels, pulling forward. Inertia extractor system, rotary safety blocks strikers. Single lever quick-detachable scope mount. Simple takedown without removing forend. Introduced 1997. Made in U.S.A. by George Hoenig.
Price: **$19,980.00**

HOENIG ROTARY ROUND ACTION COMBINATION
Caliber: 28 ga. **Barrel:** 26". **Weight:** 7 lbs. **Stock:** English Walnut to customer specs. **Sights:** Front ramp with button release blades. Foldable aperture tang sight windage and elevation adjustable. Quarter-rib with scope mount. **Features:** Round action opens by rotating barrels, pulling forward. Inertia extractor; rotary safety blocks strikers. Simple takedown without removing forend. Made in U.S.A. by George Hoenig.
Price: **$25,000.00**

Prices given are believed to be accurate at time of publication however, many factors affect retail pricing so exact prices are not possible.

DRILLINGS, COMBINATION / DOUBLE GUNS

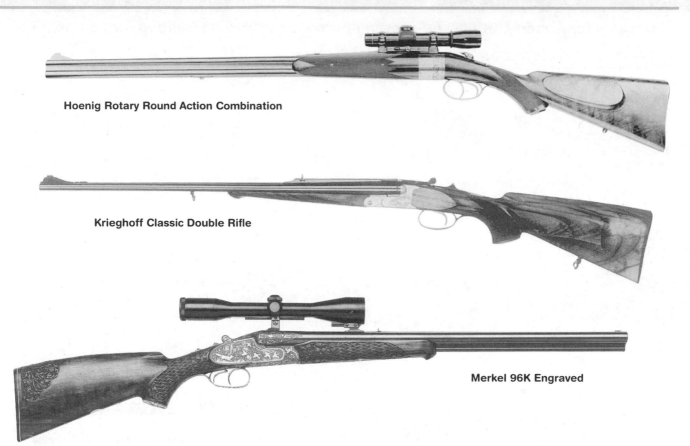

Hoenig Rotary Round Action Combination

Krieghoff Classic Double Rifle

Merkel 96K Engraved

KRIEGHOFF CLASSIC DOUBLE RIFLE
Caliber: 7x57R, 7x65R, 308 Wln., 30-06 Spfl., 8x57 JRS, 8x75RS, 9.3x74R, 375NE, 500/416NE, 470NE, 500NE. **Barrel:** 23.5". **Weight:** 7.3 to 8 lbs; 10-11 lbs. Big 5. **Stock:** High grade European walnut. Standard model has conventional rounded cheekpiece, Bavaria model has Bavarian-style cheekpiece. **Sights:** Bead front with removable, adjustable wedge (375 H&H and below), standing leaf rear on quarter-rib. **Features:** Boxlock action; double triggers; short opening angle for fast loading; quiet extractors; sliding, self-adjusting wedge for secure bolting; Purdey-style barrel extension; horizontal firing pin placement. Many options available. Introduced 1997. Imported from Germany by Krieghoff International.
Price: With small Arabesque engraving **$8,950.00**
Price: With engraved sideplates **$12,300.00**
Price: For extra barrels **$5,450.00**
Price: Extra 20-ga., 28" shotshell barrels **$3,950.00**

Krieghoff Classic Big Five Double Rifle
Similar to the standard Classic except available in 375 Flanged Mag. N.E., 500/416 NE, 470 NE, 500 NE. Has hinged front trigger, non-removable muzzle wedge (models larger than 375 caliber), Universal Trigger System, Combi Cocking Device, steel trigger guard, specially weighted stock bolt for weight and balance. Many options available. Introduced 1997. Imported from Germany by Krieghoff International. Imperial Model introduced 2006.
Price: **$11,450.00**
Price: With engraved sideplates **$14,800.00**

LEBEAU-COURALLY EXPRESS RIFLE SXS
Caliber: 7x65R, 8x57JRS, 9.3x74R, 375 H&H, 470 N.E. **Barrel:** 24" to 26". **Weight:** 7.75 to 10.5 lbs. **Stock:** Fancy French walnut with cheekpiece. **Sights:** Bead on ramp front, standing left express rear on quarter-rib. **Features:** Holland & Holland-type sidelock with automatic ejectors; double triggers. Built to order only. Imported from Belgium by Wm. Larkin Moore.
Price: **$50,000.00**

MERKEL DRILLINGS
Caliber/Gauge: 12, 20, 3" chambers, 16, 2-3/4" chambers; 22 Hornet, 5.6x50R Mag., 5.6x52R, 222 Rem., 243 Win., 6.5x55, 6.5x57R, 7x57R, 7x65R, 308 Win., 30-06 Spfl., 8x57JRS, 9.3x74R, 375 H&H. **Barrel:** 25.6". **Weight:** 7.9 to 8.4 lbs. depending upon caliber. **Stock:** Oil-finished walnut with pistol grip; cheekpiece on 12-, 16-gauge. **Sights:** Blade front, fixed rear. **Features:** Double barrel locking lug with Greener cross bolt; scroll-engraved, case-hardened receiver; automatic trigger safety; Blitz action; double triggers. Imported from Germany by Merkel USA.
Price: Model 96K (manually cocked rifle system), from **$8,495.00**
Price: Model 96K engraved (hunting series on receiver) . . . **$9,795.00**

MERKEL BOXLOCK DOUBLE RIFLES
Caliber: 5.6x52R, 243 Winchester, 6.5x55, 6.5x57R, 7x57R, 7x65R, 308 Win., 30-06 Springfield, 8x57 IRS, 9.3x74R. **Barrel:** 23.6". **Weight:** 7.7 oz. **Length:** NA. **Stock:** Walnut, oil finished, pistol grip. **Sights:** Fixed 100 meter. **Features:** Anson & Deely boxlock action with cocking indicators, double triggers, engraved color case-hardened receiver. Introduced 1995. Imported from Germany by Merkel USA.
Price: Model 140-2, from **$11,995.00**
Price: Model 141 Small Frame SXS Rifle; built on smaller
frame, chambered for 7mm Mauser, 30-06, or
9.3x74R **$8,195.00**
Price: Model 141 Engraved; fine hand-engraved hunting
scenes on silvered receiver **$9,495.00**

RIZZINI EXPRESS 90L DOUBLE RIFLE
Caliber: 30-06 Spfl., 7x65R, 9.3x74R. **Barrel:** 24". **Weight:** 7.5 lbs. **Length:** 40" overall. **Stock:** Select European walnut with satin oil finish; English-style cheekpiece. **Sights:** Ramp front, quarter-rib with express sight. **Features:** Color case-hardened boxlock action; automatic ejectors; single selective trigger; polished blue barrels. Extra 20 gauge shotgun barrels available. Imported for Italy by Wm. Larkin Moore.
Price: With case **$3,850.00**

Designs for hunting, utility and sporting purposes, including training for competition.

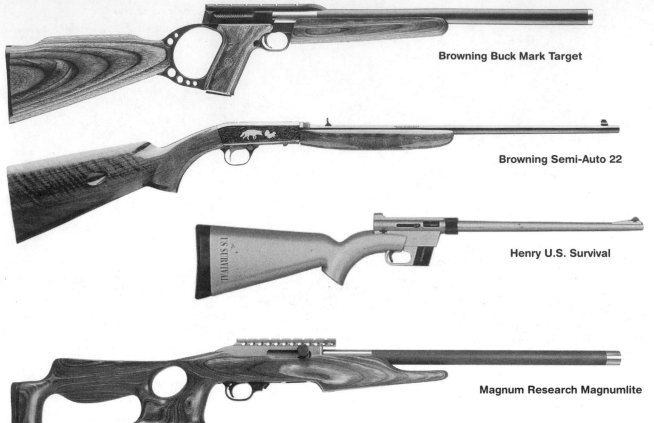

Browning Buck Mark Target

Browning Semi-Auto 22

Henry U.S. Survival

Magnum Research Magnumlite

BROWNING BUCK MARK SEMI-AUTO RIFLES

Caliber: 22 LR, 10+1. Action: A rifle version of the Buck Mark Pistol; straight blowback action; machined aluminum receiver with integral rail scope mount; manual thumb safety. **Barrel:** Recessed crowns. **Stock:** Stock and forearm with full pistol grip. **Features:** Action lock provided. Introduced 2001. Four model name variations for 2006, as noted below. **Sights:** FLD Target, FLD Carbon, and Target models have integrated scope rails. Sporter has Truglo/Marble fiber optic sights. Imported from Japan by Browning.
Price: FLD Target, 5.5 lbs., bull barrel, laminated stock **$659.00**
Price: Target, 5.4 lbs., blued bull barrel, wood stock **$639.00**
Price: Sporter, 4.4 lbs., blued sporter barrel w/sights **$639.00**

BROWNING SA-22 SEMI-AUTO 22 RIFLES

Caliber: 22 LR, 11+1. **Barrel:** 16.25". **Weight:** 5.2 lbs. **Length:** 37" overall. **Stock:** Checkered select walnut with pistol grip and semi-beavertail forend. **Sights:** Gold bead front, folding leaf rear. **Features:** Engraved receiver with polished blue finish; cross-bolt safety; tubular magazine in buttstock; easy takedown for carrying or storage. The Grade VI is available with either grayed or blued receiver with extensive engraving with gold-plated animals: right side pictures a fox and squirrel in a woodland scene; left side shows a beagle chasing a rabbit. On top is a portrait of the beagle. Stock and forend are of high-grade walnut with a double-bordered cut checkering design. Introduced 1987. Imported from Japan by Browning.
Price: Grade I, scroll-engraved blued receiver **$619.00**
Price: Grade VI BL, gold-plated engraved blued receiver . . **$1,329.00**

CZ 513 RIFLE

Caliber: 22 LR, 5-shot magazine. **Barrel:** 20.9". **Weight:** 5.7 lbs. **Length:** 39" overall. **Stock:** Beechwood. **Sights:** Tangent iron. **Features:** Simplified version of the CZ 452, no checkering on stock, simple non-adjustable trigger. Imported from the Czech Republic by CZ-USA.
Price: **$328.00**

HENRY U.S. SURVIVAL RIFLE AR-7 22

Caliber: 22 LR, 8-shot magazine. **Barrel:** 16" steel lined. **Weight:** 2.25 lbs. **Stock:** ABS plastic. **Sights:** Blade front on ramp, aperture rear. **Features:** Takedown design stores barrel and action in hollow stock. Light enough to float. Silver, black or camo finish. Comes with two magazines. Introduced 1998. From Henry Repeating Arms Co.
Price: H002S Silver finish **$245.00**
Price: H002B Black finish **$245.00**
Price: H002C Camo finish **$310.00**

KEL-TEC SU-22CA

Caliber: 22 LR. **Features:** Blowback action, cross bolt safety, adjustable front and rear sights with integral picatinny rail. Threaded muzzle, 26-round magazine.
Price: . . . . **Appx. $400.00**

MAGNUM RESEARCH MAGNUMLITE RIFLES

Caliber: 22 WMR, 17 HMR, 22 LR 17M2, 10-shot magazine. **Barrel:** 17" graphite. **Weight:** 4.45 lbs. **Length:** 35.5" overall. **Stock:** Hogue OverMolded synthetic or walnut. **Sights:** Integral scope base. **Features:** Magnum Lite graphite barrel, French grey anodizing, match bolt, target trigger. 22 LR/17M2 rifles use factory Ruger 10/22 magazines. 4-5 lbs. average trigger pull. Graphite carbon-fiber barrel weighs approx. 13.04 ounces in 22 LR, 1:16 twist. Introduced: 2007. From Magnum Research, Inc.
Price: MLR22H 22 LR. **$640.00**

MARLIN MODEL 60 AUTO RIFLE

Caliber: 22 LR, 14-shot tubular magazine. **Barrel:** 19" round tapered. **Weight:** About 5.5 lbs. **Length:** 37.5" overall. **Stock:** Press-checkered, walnut-finished Maine birch with Monte Carlo, full pistol grip; Mar-Shield finish. **Sights:** Ramp front, open adjustable rear. **Features:** Matted receiver is grooved for scope mount. Manual bolt hold-open; automatic last-shot bolt hold-open. Model 60C is similar except has hardwood Monte Carlo stock with Mossy Oak Break-Up camouflage pattern. From Marlin.
Price: **$179.00**
Price: With 4x scope **$186.00**
Price: Model 60C camo **$211.00**

Prices given are believed to be accurate at time of publication however, many factors affect retail pricing so exact prices are not possible.

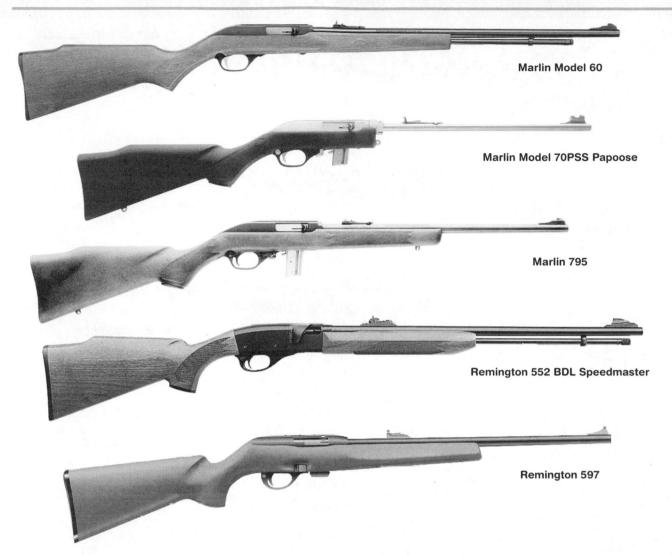

Marlin Model 60

Marlin Model 70PSS Papoose

Marlin 795

Remington 552 BDL Speedmaster

Remington 597

Marlin Model 60SS Self-Loading Rifle

Same as the Model 60 except breech bolt, barrel and outer magazine tube are made of stainless steel; most other parts are either nickel-plated or coated to match the stainless finish. Monte Carlo stock is of black/gray Maine birch laminate, and has nickel-plated swivel studs, rubber buttpad. Introduced 1993. From Marlin.

Price: **$283.00**

MARLIN 70PSS PAPOOSE STAINLESS RIFLE

Caliber: 22 LR, 7-shot magazine. **Barrel:** 16.25" stainless steel, Micro-Groove rifling. **Weight:** 3.25 lbs. **Length:** 35.25" overall. **Stock:** Black fiberglass-filled synthetic with abbreviated forend, nickel-plated swivel studs, molded-in checkering. **Sights:** Ramp front with orange post, cut-away Wide Scan hood; adjustable open rear. Receiver grooved for scope mounting. **Features:** Takedown barrel; cross-bolt safety; manual bolt hold-open; last shot bolt hold-open; comes with padded carrying case. Introduced 1986. Made in U.S.A. by Marlin.

Price: **$284.00**

MARLIN MODEL 795 AUTO RIFLE

Caliber: 22. **Barrel:** 18" with 16-groove Micro-Groove rifling. Ramp front sight, adjustable rear. Receiver grooved for scope mount. **Stock:** Black synthetic, hardwood, synthetic thumbhole, solid pink, pink camo, or Mossy Oak New Break-up camo finish. **Features:** 10-round magazine, last shot hold-open feature. Introduced 1997. SS is similar to Model 795 except stainless steel barrel. Most other parts nickel-plated. Adjustable folding semi-buckhorn rear sights, ramp front high-visibility post and removable cutaway wide scan hood. Made in U.S.A. by Marlin Firearms Co.

Price: 795 . . . . **$157.00**
Price: 795SS **$227.00**

MOSSBERG MODEL 702 PLINKSTER AUTO RIFLE

Caliber: 22 LR, 10-round detachable magazine. **Barrel:** 18" free-floating. **Weight:** 4.1 to 4.6 lbs. **Sights:** Adjustable rifle. Receiver grooved for scope mount. **Stock:** Solid pink or pink marble finish synthetic. **Features:** Ergonomically placed magazine release and safety buttons, crossbolt safety, free gun lock. Made in U.S.A. by O.F. Mossberg & Sons, Inc.

Price: Pink Plinkster (2008) **$199.00**

REMINGTON MODEL 552 BDL DELUXE SPEEDMASTER RIFLE

Caliber: 22 S (20), L (17) or LR (15) tubular magazine. **Barrel:** 21" round tapered. **Weight:** 5.75 lbs. **Length:** 40" overall. **Stock:** Walnut. Checkered grip and forend. **Sights:** Big game. **Features:** Positive cross-bolt safety, receiver grooved for tip-off mount.

Price: **$593.00**
Price: Smoothbore model (2007) **$633.00**

REMINGTON 597 AUTO RIFLE

Caliber: 22 LR, 10-shot clip; 22 WMR, 8-shot clip. **Barrel:** 20". **Weight:** 5.5 lbs. **Length:** 40" overall. **Stock:** Black synthetic. **Sights:** Big game. **Features:** Matte black finish, nickel-plated bolt. Receiver is grooved and drilled and tapped for scope mounts. Introduced 1997. Made in U.S.A. by Remington.

Price: Synthetic Scope Combo (2007) **$239.00**
Price: Model 597 Magnum **$492.00**
Price: Model 597 w/Mossy Oak Blaze Pink or Orange,
22 LR (2008) **$260.00**
Price: Model 597 Stainless TVP, 22 LR (2008) **$552.00**
Price: Model 597 TVP: Skeletonized laminated stock with
undercut forend, optics rail **$552.00**
Price: Model 597 FLX: Similar to Model 597, Blaze/Pink camo
but with FLX Digital Camo stock **$260.00**

Remington 597 FLX

Ruger 10/22 Deluxe Sporter

Ruger 10/22 Target

RUGER 10/22 AUTOLOADING CARBINE

Caliber: 22 LR, 10-shot rotary magazine. **Barrel:** 18.5" round tapered. **Weight:** 5 lbs. **Length:** 37.25" overall. **Stock:** American hardwood with pistol grip and barrel band or synthetic. **Sights:** Brass bead front, folding leaf rear adjustable for elevation. **Features:** Detachable rotary magazine fits flush into stock, cross-bolt safety, receiver tapped and grooved for scope blocks or tip-off mount. Scope base adaptor furnished with each rifle.
Price: Model 10/22-RB (black matte) **$269.00**
Price: Model 10/22-CRR Compact RB (black matte), 2006 . . . **$307.00**

Ruger 10/22 Deluxe Sporter
Same as 10/22 Carbine except walnut stock with hand checkered pistol grip and forend; straight buttplate, no barrel band, has sling swivels.
Price: Model 10/22-DSP **$355.00**

Ruger 10/22-T Target Rifle
Similar to the 10/22 except has 20" heavy, hammer-forged barrel with tight chamber dimensions, improved trigger pull, laminated hardwood stock dimensioned for optical sights. No iron sights supplied. Introduced 1996. Made in U.S.A. by Sturm, Ruger & Co.
Price: 10/22-T **$485.00**
Price: K10/22-T, stainless steel **$533.00**

Ruger K10/22-RPF All-Weather Rifle
Similar to the stainless K10/22/RB except has black composite stock of thermoplastic polyester resin reinforced with fiberglass; checkered grip and forend. Brushed satin, natural metal finish with clear hardcoat finish. Weighs 5 lbs., measures 37" overall. Introduced 1997. From Sturm, Ruger & Co.
Price: **$318.00**

SAVAGE MODEL 64G AUTO RIFLE

Caliber: 22 LR, 10-shot magazine. **Barrel:** 20", 21". **Weight:** 5.5 lbs. **Length:** 40", 41". **Stock:** Walnut-finished hardwood with Monte Carlo-type comb, checkered grip and forend. **Sights:** Bead front, open adjustable rear. Receiver grooved for scope mounting. **Features:** Thumb-operated rotating safety. Blue finish. Side ejection, bolt hold-open device. Introduced 1990. Made in Canada, from Savage Arms.
Price: From **$187.00**

THOMPSON/CENTER 22 LR CLASSIC RIFLE

Caliber: 22 LR, 8-shot magazine. **Barrel:** 22" match-grade. **Weight:** 5.5 pounds. **Length:** 39.5" overall. **Stock:** Satin-finished American walnut with Monte Carlo-type comb and pistol gripcap, swivel studs. **Sights:** Ramp-style front and fully adjustable rear, both with fiber optics. **Features:** All-steel receiver drilled and tapped for scope mounting; barrel threaded to receiver; thumb-operated safety; trigger guard safety lock included. New 22 Classic Benchmark TGT target rifle variant has 18" heavy barrel, brown laminated target stock, blued with matte finish, 10-shot magazine and no sights; drilled and tapped.
Price: T/C 22 LR Classic (blue) **$396.00**
Price: T/C 22 LR Classic Benchmark **$505.00**

Classic and modern models for sport and utility, including training.

Browning BL-22

Henry Lever-Action 22

Henry Golden Boy 22

Henry Pump-Action 22

Marlin Model 39A

BROWNING BL-22 RIFLES

Action: Short-throw lever action, side ejection. Rack-and-pinion lever. Tubular magazines, with 15+1 capacity for 22 LR. **Barrel:** Recessed muzzle. **Stock:** Walnut, two-piece straight grip Western style. Trigger: Half-cock hammer safety; fold-down hammer. **Sights:** Bead post front, folding-leaf rear. Steel receiver grooved for scope mount. **Weight:** 5-5.4 lbs. **Length:** 36.75-40.75" overall. **Features:** Action lock provided. Introduced 1996. FLD Grade II Octagon has octagonal 24" barrel, silver nitride receiver with scroll engraving, gold-colored trigger. FLD Grade I has satin-nickel receiver, blued trigger, no stock checkering. FLD Grade II has satin-nickel receivers with scroll engraving; gold-colored trigger, cut checkering. Both introduced 2005. Grade I has blued receiver and trigger, no stock checkering. Grade II has gold-colored trigger, cut checkering, blued receiver with scroll engraving. Imported from Japan by Browning.

Price: BL-22 Grade I/II, from. **$529.00**
Price: BL-22 FLD Grade I/II, from **$569.00**
Price: BL-22 FLD, Grade II Octagon **$839.00**

HENRY LEVER-ACTION RIFLES

Caliber: 22 Long Rifle (15 shot), 22 Magnum (11 shots), 17 HMR (11 shots). **Barrel:** 18.25" round. **Weight:** 5.5 to 5.75 lbs. **Length:** 34" overall (22 LR). **Stock:** Walnut. **Sights:** Hooded blade front, open adjustable rear. **Features:** Polished blue finish; full-length tubular magazine; side ejection; receiver grooved for scope mounting. Introduced 1997. Made in U.S.A. by Henry Repeating Arms Co.

Price: H001 Carbine 22 LR. **$325.00**
Price: H001L Carbine 22 LR, Large Loop Lever. **$340.00**
Price: H001Y Youth model (33" overall, 11-round 22 LR) **$325.00**
Price: H001M 22 Magnum, 19.25" octagonal barrel, deluxe
 walnut stock **$475.00**
Price: H001V 17 HMR, 20" octagonal barrel, Williams Fire
 Sights **$549.95**

Henry Lever Octagon Frontier Model

Same as Lever rifles except chambered in 17 HMR, 22 Short/22 Long/22 LR, 22 Magnum; 20" octagonal barrel **Sights:** Marbles full adjustable semi-buckhorn rear, brass bead front. Weighs 6.25 lbs. Made in U.S.A. by Henry Repeating Arms Co.

Price: H001T Lever Octagon **$425.00**
Price: H001TM Lever Octagon 22 Magnum **$539.95**

HENRY GOLDEN BOY 22 LEVER-ACTION RIFLE

Caliber: 17 HMR, 22 LR (16-shot), 22 Magnum. **Barrel:** 20" octagonal. **Weight:** 6.25 lbs. **Length:** 38" overall. **Stock:** American walnut. **Sights:** Blade front, open rear. **Features:** Brasslite receiver, brass buttplate, blued barrel and lever. Introduced 1998. Made in U.S.A. from Henry Repeating Arms Co.

Price: H004 22 LR **$515.00**
Price: H004M 22 Magnum **$595.00**
Price: H004V 17 HMR **$615.00**
Price: H004DD 22 LR Deluxe, engraved receiver **$1,200.00**

HENRY PUMP-ACTION 22 PUMP RIFLE

Caliber: 22 LR, 15-shot. **Barrel:** 18.25". **Weight:** 5.5 lbs. **Length:** NA. **Stock:** American walnut. **Sights:** Bead on ramp front, open adjustable rear. **Features:** Polished blue finish; receiver grooved for scope mount; grooved slide handle; two barrel bands. Introduced 1998. Made in U.S.A. from Henry Repeating Arms Co.

Price: H003T 22 LR **$515.00**
Price: H003TM 22 Magnum **$595.00**

MARLIN MODEL 39A GOLDEN LEVER-ACTION RIFLE

Caliber: 22, S (26), L (21), LR (19), tubular magazine. **Barrel:** 24" Micro-Groove. **Weight:** 6.5 lbs. **Length:** 40" overall. **Stock:** Checkered American black walnut; Mar-Shield finish. Swivel studs; rubber buttpad. **Sights:** Bead ramp front with detachable Wide-Scan hood, folding rear semi-buckhorn adjustable for windage and elevation. **Features:** Hammer block safety; rebounding hammer. Takedown action, receiver tapped for scope mount (supplied), offset hammer spur, gold-colored steel trigger. From Marlin Firearms.

Price: **$593.00**

Remington Model 572 BDL Feluxe Fieldmaster

Ruger Model 96/22

Taurus 62R

MOSSBERG MODEL 464 RIMFIRE LEVER-ACTION RIFLE
Caliber: 22 LR. **Barrel:** 20" round blued. **Weight:** 5.6 lbs. **Length:** 35-3/4" overall. **Features:** Adjustable sights, straight grip stock, 124-shot tubular magazine, plain hardwood straight stock and forend.
Price: . . . . **NA; apparently not yet in production**

REMINGTON 572 BDL DELUXE FIELDMASTER PUMP RIFLE
Caliber: 22 S (20), L (17) or LR (15), tubular magazine. **Barrel:** 21" round tapered. **Weight:** 5.5 lbs. **Length:** 40" overall. **Stock:** Walnut with checkered pistol grip and slide handle. **Sights:** Big game. **Features:** Cross-bolt safety; removing inner magazine tube converts rifle to single shot; receiver grooved for tip-off scope mount.
Price: $607.00

RUGER MODEL 96 LEVER-ACTION RIFLE
Caliber: 22 WMR, 9 rounds; 17 HMR, 9 rounds. **Barrel:** 18.5". **Weight:** 5.25 lbs. **Length:** 37-3/8" overall. **Stock:** Hardwood. **Sights:** Gold bead front, folding leaf rear. **Features:** Sliding cross button safety, visible cocking indicator; short-throw lever action. Introduced 1996. Made in U.S.A. by Sturm, Ruger & Co.
Price: 96/22M, 22 WMR or 17 HMR. $451.00

TAURUS MODEL 62 PUMP RIFLE
Caliber: 22 LR, 12- or 13-shot. **Barrel:** 16.5" or 23" round. **Weight:** 72 oz. to 80 oz. **Length:** 39" overall. **Stock:** Premium hardwood. **Sights:** Adjustable rear, bead blade front, optional tang. **Features:** Blue, case hardened or stainless, bolt-mounted safety, pump action, manual firing pin block, integral security lock system. Imported from Brazil by Taurus International.
Price: From $299.00

Taurus Model 72 Pump Rifle
Same as Model 62 except chambered in 22 Magnum or 17 HMR; 16.5" barrel holds 10-12 shots, 23" barrel holds 11-13 shots. Weighs 72 oz. to 80 oz. Introduced 2001. Imported from Brazil by Taurus International.
Price: From $329.00

Includes models for a variety of sports, utility and competitive shooting.

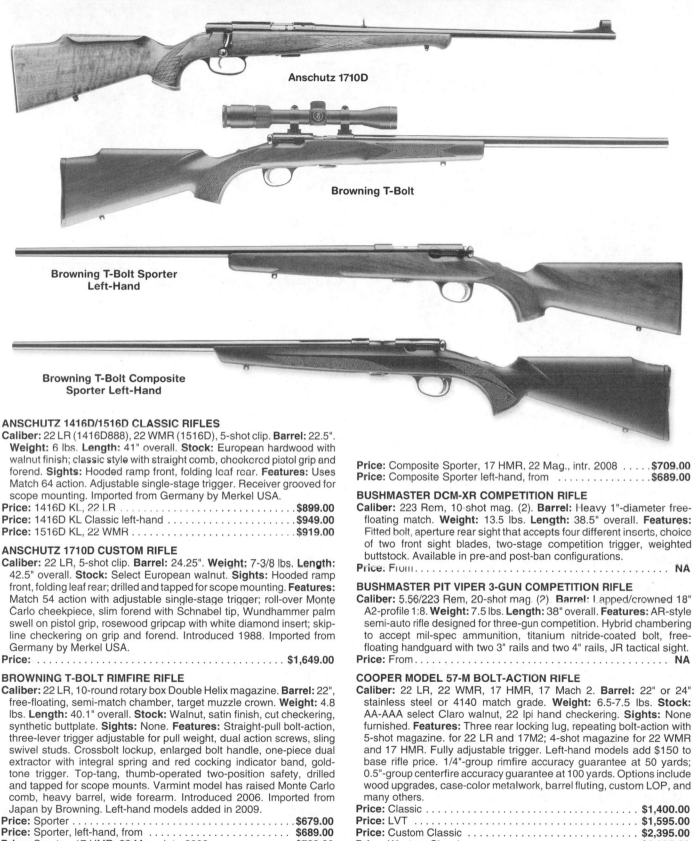

Anschutz 1710D

Browning T-Bolt

Browning T-Bolt Sporter
Left-Hand

Browning T-Bolt Composite
Sporter Left-Hand

ANSCHUTZ 1416D/1516D CLASSIC RIFLES
Caliber: 22 LR (1416D888), 22 WMR (1516D), 5-shot clip. **Barrel:** 22.5". **Weight:** 6 lbs. **Length:** 41" overall. **Stock:** European hardwood with walnut finish; classic style with straight comb, checkered pistol grip and forend. **Sights:** Hooded ramp front, folding leaf rear. **Features:** Uses Match 64 action. Adjustable single-stage trigger. Receiver grooved for scope mounting. Imported from Germany by Merkel USA.
Price: 1416D KL, 22 LR **$899.00**
Price: 1416D KL Classic left-hand **$949.00**
Price: 1516D KL, 22 WMR **$919.00**

ANSCHUTZ 1710D CUSTOM RIFLE
Caliber: 22 LR, 5-shot clip. **Barrel:** 24.25". **Weight:** 7-3/8 lbs. **Length:** 42.5" overall. **Stock:** Select European walnut. **Sights:** Hooded ramp front, folding leaf rear; drilled and tapped for scope mounting. **Features:** Match 54 action with adjustable single-stage trigger; roll-over Monte Carlo cheekpiece, slim forend with Schnabel tip, Wundhammer palm swell on pistol grip, rosewood gripcap with white diamond insert; skip-line checkering on grip and forend. Introduced 1988. Imported from Germany by Merkel USA.
Price: **$1,649.00**

BROWNING T-BOLT RIMFIRE RIFLE
Caliber: 22 LR, 10-round rotary box Double Helix magazine. **Barrel:** 22", free-floating, semi-match chamber, target muzzle crown. **Weight:** 4.8 lbs. **Length:** 40.1" overall. **Stock:** Walnut, satin finish, cut checkering, synthetic buttplate. **Sights:** None. **Features:** Straight-pull bolt-action, three-lever trigger adjustable for pull weight, dual action screws, sling swivel studs. Crossbolt lockup, enlarged bolt handle, one-piece dual extractor with integral spring and red cocking indicator band, gold-tone trigger. Top-tang, thumb-operated two-position safety, drilled and tapped for scope mounts. Varmint model has raised Monte Carlo comb, heavy barrel, wide forearm. Introduced 2006. Imported from Japan by Browning. Left-hand models added in 2009.
Price: Sporter **$679.00**
Price: Sporter, left-hand, from **$689.00**
Price: Sporter, 17 HMR, 22 Mag., intr. 2008. . . . .**$709.00**
Price: Target/Varmint, intr. 2007 . . . .**$709.00**
Price: Composite Target/Varmint, intr. 2008 . . . .**$709.00**
Price: Composite Target/Varmint left-hand, from **$689.00**

Price: Composite Sporter, 17 HMR, 22 Mag., intr. 2008 . . . . .**$709.00**
Price: Composite Sporter left-hand, from **$689.00**

BUSHMASTER DCM-XR COMPETITION RIFLE
Caliber: 223 Rem, 10-shot mag. (2). **Barrel:** Heavy 1"-diameter free-floating match. **Weight:** 13.5 lbs. **Length:** 38.5" overall. **Features:** Fitted bolt, aperture rear sight that accepts four different inserts, choice of two front sight blades, two-stage competition trigger, weighted buttstock. Available in pre-and post-ban configurations.
Price: From . . . . **NA**

BUSHMASTER PIT VIPER 3-GUN COMPETITION RIFLE
Caliber: 5.56/223 Rem, 20-shot mag. (?). **Barrel:** Lapped/crowned 18" A2-profile 1:8. **Weight:** 7.5 lbs. **Length:** 38" overall. **Features:** AR-style semi-auto rifle designed for three-gun competition. Hybrid chambering to accept mil-spec ammunition, titanium nitride-coated bolt, free-floating handguard with two 3" rails and two 4" rails, JR tactical sight.
Price: From . . . . **NA**

COOPER MODEL 57-M BOLT-ACTION RIFLE
Caliber: 22 LR, 22 WMR, 17 HMR, 17 Mach 2. **Barrel:** 22" or 24" stainless steel or 4140 match grade. **Weight:** 6.5-7.5 lbs. **Stock:** AA-AAA select Claro walnut, 22 lpi hand checkering. **Sights:** None furnished. **Features:** Three rear locking lug, repeating bolt-action with 5-shot magazine. for 22 LR and 17M2; 4-shot magazine for 22 WMR and 17 HMR. Fully adjustable trigger. Left-hand models add $150 to base rifle price. 1/4"-group rimfire accuracy guarantee at 50 yards; 0.5"-group centerfire accuracy guarantee at 100 yards. Options include wood upgrades, case-color metalwork, barrel fluting, custom LOP, and many others.
Price: Classic **$1,400.00**
Price: LVT **$1,595.00**
Price: Custom Classic **$2,395.00**
Price: Western Classic **$3,295.00**
Price: TRP-3 (22 LR only, benchrest style) **$1,395.00**
Price: Jackson Squirrel Rifle **$1,595.00**
Price: Jackson Hunter (synthetic) **$1,495.00**

Cooper Model 57 Classic

Cooper Custom Classic

CZ 452 Lux

CZ 452 Varmint

CZ 452 American Classic

Marlin 917V

CZ 452 LUX BOLT-ACTION RIFLE
Caliber: 22 LR, 22 WMR, 5-shot detachable magazine. **Barrel:** 24.8". **Weight:** 6.6 lbs. **Length:** 42.63" overall. **Stock:** Walnut with checkered pistol grip. **Sights:** Hooded front, fully adjustable tangent rear. **Features:** All-steel construction, adjustable trigger, polished blue finish. Imported from the Czech Republic by CZ-USA.
Price: 22 LR, 22 WMR $427.00

CZ 452 Varmint Rifle
Similar to the Lux model except has heavy 20.8" barrel; stock has beavertail forend; weighs 7 lbs.; no sights furnished. Available in 22 LR, 22 WMR, 17HMR, 17M2. Imported from the Czech Republic by CZ-USA.
Price: From $497.00

CZ 452 American Bolt-Action Rifle
Similar to the CZ 452 M 2E Lux except has classic-style stock of Circassian walnut; 22.5" free-floating barrel with recessed target crown; receiver dovetail for scope mounting. No open sights furnished. Introduced 1999. Imported from the Czech Republic by CZ-USA.
Price: 22 LR, 22 WMR $463.00

DAVEY CRICKETT SINGLE SHOT RIFLE
Caliber: 22 LR, 22 WMR, single shot. **Barrel:** 16-1/8". **Weight:** About 2.5 lbs. **Length:** 30" overall. **Stock:** American walnut. **Sights:** Post on ramp front, peep rear adjustable for windage and elevation. **Features:** Drilled and tapped for scope mounting using special Chipmunk base ($13.95). Engraved model also available. Made in U.S.A. Introduced 1982. Formerly Chipmunk model. From Keystone Sporting Arms.
Price: From $220.00

HENRY ACU-BOLT RIFLE
Caliber: 22, 22 Mag., 17 HMR; single shot. **Barrel:** 20". **Weight:** 4.15 lbs. **Length:** 36". **Stock:** One-piece fiberglass synthetic. **Sights:** Scope mount and 4x scope included. **Features:** Stainless barrel and receiver, bolt-action.
Price: H007 22 LR, ... $399.95

HENRY "MINI" BOLT ACTION 22 RIFLE
Caliber: 22 LR, single shot youth gun. **Barrel:** 16" stainless, 8-groove rifling. **Weight:** 3.25 lbs. **Length:** 30", LOP 11.5". **Stock:** Synthetic, pistol grip, wraparound checkering and beavertail forearm. **Sights:** William Fire sights. **Features:** One-piece bolt configuration manually operated safety.
Price: H005 22 LR, black fiberglass stock $249.95
Price: H005S 22 LR, orange fiberglass stock $249.95

MARLIN MODEL 917 BOLT-ACTION RIFLES
Caliber: 17 HMR, 4- and 7-shot clip. **Barrel:** 22". **Weight:** 6 lbs., stainless 7 lbs. **Length:** 41". **Stock:** Checkered walnut Monte Carlo SS, laminated black/grey. **Sights:** No sights but receiver grooved. **Features:** Swivel studs, positive thumb safety, red cocking indicator, safety lock, SS 1" brushed aluminum scope rings.
Price: 917 .... $240.00
Price: 917VS Stainless steel barrel $287.00
Price: 917VT Laminated thumbhole stock (2008), from ... $382.00
Price: 917VST, stainless-finish metal, gray/black laminated thumbhole stock $426.00
Price: 917VSF, fluted barrel $397.00
Price: 917VS-CF, carbon fiber-patterned stock $358.00

Marlin Model 915YN "Little Buckaroo"

Marlin 983T

MARLIN MODEL 915YN "LITTLE BUCKAROO"
Caliber: 22 S, L, LR, single shot. **Barrel:** 16.25" Micro-Groove. **Weight:** 4.25 lbs. **Length:** 33.25" overall. **Stock:** One-piece walnut-finished, press-checkered Maine birch with Monte Carlo; Mar-Shield finish. **Sights:** Ramp front, adjustable open rear. **Features:** Beginner's rifle with thumb safety, easy-load feed throat, red cocking indicator. Receiver grooved for scope mounting. Introduced 1989.
Price: **$203.00**
Price: 915YS (stainless steel with fire sights) **$227.00**

MARLIN MODEL 982 BOLT-ACTION RIFLE
Caliber: 22 WMR. **Barrel:** 22" Micro-Groove. **Weight:** 6 lbs. **Length:** 41" overall. **Stock:** Walnut Monte Carlo genuine American black walnut with swivel studs; full pistol grip; classic cut checkering; rubber rifle butt pad; tough Mar-Shield finish. **Sights:** Adjustable semi-buckhorn folding rear, ramp front sight with brass bead and Wide-Scan front sight hood. **Features:** 7-shot clip, thumb safety, red cocking indicator, receiver grooved for scope mount. 982S has stainless steel front breech bolt, barrel, receiver and bolt knob. All other parts are either stainless steel or nickel-plated. Has black Monte Carlo stock of fiberglass-filled polycarbonate with molded-in checkering, nickel-plated swivel studs. Introduced 2005. Made in U.S.A. by Marlin Firearms Co.
Price: 982VS (heavy stainless barrel, 7 lbs). **$309.00**
Price: 982VS-CF (carbon fiber stock). **$350.00**

Marlin Model 925M Bolt-Action Rifles
Similar to the Model 982 except chambered for 22 WMR. Has 7-shot clip magazine, 22" Micro-Groove barrel, checkered walnut-finished Maine birch stock. Introduced 1989.
Price: 925M. **$234.00**
Price: 925RM, black fiberglass-filled synthetic stock **$220.95**

MARLIN MODEL 983 BOLT-ACTION RIFLE
Caliber: 22 WMR. **Barrel:** 22"; 1:16" twist. **Weight:** 6 lbs. **Length:** 41" overall. **Stock:** Walnut Monte Carlo with sling swivel studs, rubber buttpad. **Sights:** Ramp front with brass bead, removable hood; adjustable semi-buckhorn folding rear. **Features:** Thumb safety, red cocking indicator, receiver grooved for scope mount. 983S is same as the Model 983 except front breech bolt, striker knob, trigger stud, cartridge lifter stud and outer magazine tube are of stainless steel; other parts are nickel-plated. Introduced 1993. 983T has a black Monte Carlo fiberglass-filled synthetic stock with sling swivel studs. Introduced 2001. Made in U.S.A. by Marlin Firearms Co.
Price: 983 . . . . **$308.00**
Price: 983S (stainless barrel) **$337.00**
Price: 983T (fiberglass stock) **$245.00**

MEACHAM LOW-WALL RIFLE
Caliber: Any rimfire cartridge. **Barrel:** 26-34". **Weight:** 7-15 lbs. **Sights:** none. Tang drilled for Win. base, 3/8" dovetail slot front. **Stock:** Fancy eastern walnut with cheekpiece; ebony insert in forearm tip. Features: Exact copy of 1885 Winchester. With most Winchester factory options available including double set triggers. Introduced 1994. Made in U.S.A. by Meacham T&H Inc.
Price: From **$4,999.00**

MOSSBERG MODEL 817 VARMINT BOLT-ACTION RIFLE
Caliber: 17 HMR, 5-round magazine. **Barrel:** 21"; free-floating bull barrel, recessed muzzle crown. **Weight:** 4.9 lbs. (black synthetic), 5.2 lbs. (wood). **Stock:** Black synthetic or wood; length of pull, 14.25". **Sights:** Factory-installed Weaver-style scope bases. **Features:**

Blued or brushed chrome metal finishes, crossbolt safety, gun lock. Introduced 2008. Made in U.S.A. by O.F. Mossberg & Sons, Inc.
Price: Black synthetic stock, chrome finish (2008) **$279.00**

MOSSBERG MODEL 801/802 BOLT RIFLES
Caliber: 22 LR, 10-round detachable magazine. **Barrel:** 18" free-floating. **Weight:** 4.1 to 4.6 lbs. **Sights:** Adjustable rifle. Receiver grooved for scope mount. **Stock:** Solid pink or pink marble finish synthetic. **Features:** Ergonomically placed magazine release and safety buttons, crossbolt safety, free gun lock. 801 Half Pint has 12.25" length of pull, 16" barrel, and weighs 4 lbs. Hardwood stock; removable magazine plug. Made in U.S.A. by O.F. Mossberg & Sons, Inc.
Price: Pink Plinkster (2008) **$199.00**
Price: Half Pint (2008). **$199.00**

NEW ENGLAND FIREARMS SPORTSTER SINGLE-SHOT RIFLES
Caliber: 22 LR, 22 WMR, 17 HMR, single-shot. **Barrel:** 20". **Weight:** 5.5 lbs. **Length:** 36.25" overall. **Stock:** Black polymer. **Sights:** None furnished; scope mount included. **Features:** Break open, side-lever release; automatic ejection; recoil pad; sling swivel studs; trigger locking system. Introduced 2001. Made in U.S.A. by New England Firearms.
Price: **$149.00**
Price: Youth model (20" barrel, 33" overall, weighs 5-1/3 lbs.) **$149.00**
Price: Sportster 17 HMR **$180.00**

NEW ULTRA LIGHT ARMS 20RF BOLT-ACTION RIFLE
Caliber: 22 LR, single shot or repeater. **Barrel:** Douglas, length to order. **Weight:** 5.25 lbs. **Length:** Varies. **Stock:** Kevlar/graphite composite, variety of finishes. **Sights:** None furnished; drilled and tapped for scope mount. **Features:** Timney trigger, hand-lapped action, button-rifled barrel, hand-bedded action, recoil pad, sling-swivel studs, optional Jewell trigger. Made in U.S.A. by New Ultra Light Arms.
Price: 20 RF single shot **$1,300.00**
Price: 20 RF repeater **$1,350.00**

REMINGTON MODEL FIVE SERIES
Caliber: 17 HMR, 22 LR, 22 WMR. **Barrel:** 16.5" (Youth), 22". **Barrel:** Carbon-steel, hammer-forged barrel, 1:16 twist, polished blue finish. **Weight:** 5.5 to 6.75 lbs. **Stock:** Hardwood, laminate, European Walnut. **Length:** 35.25" to 40.75" overall. **Features:** Detachable, steel magazine box with five-round capacity; steel trigger guard; chrome-plated bolt body; single stage trigger with manual two-position safety; buttplate; sling swivel studs (excluding Youth version); adjustable big game-style rifle sights; and dovetail-style receiver. Introduced 2006. Model Five Youth (22 LR) has 12.4-inch length of pull, 16.5-inch barrel, single-shot adapter. Model Five Laminate has weather-resistant brown laminate stock. Model Five European Walnut has classic satin-finish stock. Made in U.S.A. by Remington.
Price: Model Five Youth, 22 LR (2008). **$237.00**
Price: Model Five Laminate, 17 HMR (2008), 22 LR, 22 WMR **$363.00**
Price: Model Five European Walnut, 22 LR (2008) **$279.00**

ROSSI MATCHED PAIR SINGLE-SHOT RIFLE/SHOTGUN
Caliber: 17 HMR, 22 LR, 22 Mag. **Barrel:** 18.5" or 23". **Weight:** 6 lbs. **Stock:** Hardwood (brown or black finish). **Sights:** Fully adjustable front and rear. **Features:** Break-open breech, transfer-bar manual safety, includes matched 410-, 20 or 12 gauge shotgun barrel with bead front sight. Introduced 2001. Imported by BrazTech/Taurus.
Price: S121280RS **$160.00**
Price: S121780RS **$200.00**
Price: S122280RS **$160.00**
Price: S201780RS **$200.00**

Rossi Matched Pair

Ruger 77/17

Savage Mark I-G

Savage Mark II-BV

RUGER K77/22 VARMINT RIFLE
Caliber: 22 LR, 10-shot, 22 WMR, 9-shot detachable rotary magazine. **Barrel:** 24", heavy. **Weight:** 7.25 lbs. **Length:** 43.25" overall. **Stock:** Laminated hardwood with rubber buttpad, quick-detachable swivel studs. **Sights:** None furnished. Comes with Ruger 1" scope rings. **Features:** Stainless steel or blued finish. Three-position safety, dual extractors. Stock has wide, flat forend. Introduced 1993.
Price: K77/22VBZ, 22 LR **$836.00**
Price: K77/22VMBZ, 22 WMR **$836.00**

RUGER 77/22 RIMFIRE BOLT-ACTION RIFLE
Caliber: 22 LR, 10-shot rotary magazine; 22 WMR, 9-shot rotary magazine. **Barrel:** 20". **Weight:** About 6 lbs. **Length:** 39.25" overall. **Stock:** Checkered American walnut, laminated hardwood, or synthetic stocks, stainless sling swivels. **Sights:** Plain barrel with 1" Ruger rings. **Features:** Mauser-type action uses Ruger's rotary magazine. Three-position safety, simplified bolt stop, patented bolt locking system. Uses the dual-screw barrel attachment system of the 10/22 rifle. Integral scope mounting system with 1" Ruger rings. Blued model introduced 1983. Stainless steel and blued with synthetic stock introduced 1989.
Price: 77/22R (no sights, rings, walnut stock). **$754.00**
Price: K77/22RP (stainless, no sights, rings, synthetic stock) .**$754.00**
Price: 77/22RM (22 WMR, blued, walnut stock) **$754.00**
Price: K77/22RMP (22 WMR, stainless, synthetic stock) **$754.00**

RUGER 77/17 RIMFIRE BOLT-ACTION RIFLE
Caliber: 17 HMR (9-shot rotary magazine. **Barrel:** 22" to 24". **Weight:** 6.5-7.5 lbs. **Length:** 41.25-43.25" overall. **Stock:** Checkered American walnut, laminated hardwood; stainless sling swivels. **Sights:** Plain barrel with 1" Ruger rings. **Features:** Mauser-type action uses Ruger's rotary magazine. Three-position safety, simplified bolt stop, patented bolt locking system. Uses the dual-screw barrel attachment system of the 10/22 rifle. Integral scope mounting system with 1" Ruger rings. Introduced 2002.

Price: 77/17-RM (no sights, rings, walnut stock) **$754.00**
Price: K77/17-VMBBZ (Target grey bbl, black laminate stock) **$836.00**

SAVAGE MARK I-G BOLT-ACTION RIFLE
Caliber: 22 LR, single shot. **Barrel:** 20.75". **Weight:** 5.5 lbs. **Length:** 39.5" overall. **Stock:** Walnut-finished hardwood with Monte Carlo-type comb, checkered grip and forend. **Sights:** Bead front, open adjustable rear. Receiver grooved for scope mounting. **Features:** Thumb-operated rotating safety. Blue finish. Rifled or smooth bore. Introduced 1990. Made in Canada, from Savage Arms Inc.
Price: Mark I-G, rifled or smooth bore, right- or left-handed . . .**$226.00**
Price: Mark I-GY (Youth), 19" barrel, 37" overall, 5 lbs. **$226.00**

SAVAGE MARK II BOLT-ACTION RIFLE
Caliber: 22 LR, 10-shot magazine. **Barrel:** 20.5". **Weight:** 5.5 lbs. **Length:** 39.5" overall. **Stock:** Walnut-finished hardwood with Monte Carlo-type comb, checkered grip and forend. **Sights:** Bead front, open adjustable rear. Receiver grooved for scope mounting. **Features:** Thumb-operated rotating safety. Blue finish. Introduced 1990. Made in Canada, from Savage Arms, Inc.
Price: Mark II-BV. **$342.00**
Price: Mark II-GY (youth), 19" barrel, 37" overall, 5 lbs. **$226.00**
Price: Mark II-GL, left-hand **$226.00**
Price: Mark II-F, 17 HM2 . . . .**$202.00**
Price: Mark II XP Camo Scope Package (2008). **$400.00**
Price: Mark II Classic T, thumbhole walnut stock (2008) **$559.00**
Price: Mark II BTV: laminated thumbhole vent stock,
AccuTrigger, blued receiver and bull barrel **$393.00**
Price: Mark II BVTS: stainless barrel/receiver;
available in right- or left-hand (BTVLS) configuration
. . . . **$393.00** (standard); **$441.00** (left hand)

Savage Mark II-FSS Stainless Rifle
Similar to the Mark II except has stainless steel barreled action and black synthetic stock with positive checkering, swivel studs, and 20.75" free-floating and button-rifled barrel with detachable magazine. Weighs 5.5 lbs. Introduced 1997. Imported from Canada by Savage Arms, Inc.
Price: **$273.00**

Prices given are believed to be accurate at time of publication however, many factors affect retail pricing so exact prices are not possible.

Savage Model 93G

Savage Model 93FSS

Savage Model 93FVSS

Savage Model 93R17BTV

Savage Model 93R17XP
Snow Camo

SAVAGE MODEL 93G MAGNUM BOLT-ACTION RIFLE
Caliber: 22 WMR, 5-shot magazine. **Barrel:** 20.75". **Weight:** 5.75 lbs. **Length:** 39.5" overall. **Stock:** Walnut-finished hardwood with Monte Carlo-type comb, checkered grip and forend. **Sights:** Bead front, adjustable open rear. Receiver grooved for scope mount. **Features:** Thumb-operated rotary safety. Blue finish. Introduced 1994. Made in Canada, from Savage Arms.
Price: Model 93G **$260.00**
Price: Model 93F (as above with black graphite/fiberglass
    stock) **$241.00**
Price: Model 93 Classic, American walnut stock (2008)...... **$566.00**
Price: Model 93 Classic T, American walnut thumbhole stock
    (2008) **$604.00**

Savage Model 93FSS Magnum Rifle
  Similar to Model 93G except stainless steel barreled action and black synthetic stock with positive checkering. Weighs 5.5 lbs. Introduced 1997. Imported from Canada by Savage Arms, Inc.
Price: **$306.00**

Savage Model 93FVSS Magnum Rifle
  Similar to Model 93FSS Magnum except 21" heavy barrel with recessed target-style crown, satin-finished stainless barreled action, black graphite/fiberglass stock. Drilled and tapped for scope mount-

ing, comes with Weaver-style bases. Introduced 1998. Imported from Canada by Savage Arms, Inc.
Price: **$347.00**

Savage Model 93R17 Bolt-Action Rifles
  Similar to Model 93G Magnum but chambered in 17 HMR. Features include standard synthetic, hardwood or walnut stock or thumbhole stock with cheekpiece, 21" or 22" barrel, no sights, detachable box magazine.
Price: Model 93R17BTV: Laminted ventilated thumbhole
    stock, blued barrel/receiver **$393.00**
Price: Model 93R17BV: Standard brown laminate stock,
    heavy barrel **$342.00**
Price: Model 93R17GV: Checkered hardwood stock **$278.00**
Price: Model 93R17GLV: Left-hand configuration **$278.00**
Price: Model 93R17 Classic T: Checkered walnut thumbhole
    stock with unvented forend, blued barrel/receiver **$559.00**
Price: Model 93R17 Classic: Standard walnut stock **$559.00**
Price: Model 93R17BTVS: Laminated thumbhole vent stock,
    stainless steel barrel and receiver **$441.00**
Price: Model 93R17BLTVS: Left-hand **$441.00**
Price: Model 93R17BVSS: Similar to Model 93R17BTVS but
    with gray laminated non-thumbhole stock **$411.00**
Price: Model 93R17FVS: Black synthetic stock, AccuTrigger,
    blued or stainless heavy barrel **$347.00**

Savage Model 30G Stevens "Favorite"

Savage Cub G Youth

Winchester Wildcat Bolt Action 22

SAVAGE MODEL 30G STEVENS "FAVORITE"
Caliber: 22 LR, 22 WMR Model 30GM, 17 HMR Model 30R17. **Barrel:** 21". **Weight:** 4.25 lbs. **Length:** 36.75". **Stock:** Walnut, straight grip, Schnabel forend. **Sights:** Adjustable rear, bead post front. **Features:** Lever action falling block, inertia firing pin system, Model 30G half octagonal barrel, Model 30GM full octagonal barrel.
Price: Model 30G **$344.00**
Price: Model 30 Takedown **$360.00**

SAVAGE CUB T MINI YOUTH
Caliber: 22 S, L, LR; 17 Mach 2. **Barrel:** 16". **Weight:** 3.5 lbs. **Length:** 33". **Stock:** Walnut finished hardwood thumbhole stock. **Sights:** Bead post, front; peep, rear. **Features:** Mini single-shot bolt action, free-floating button-rifled barrel, blued finish. From Savage Arms.

Price: Cub T Thumbhole, walnut stained laminated **$266.00**
Price: Cub T Pink Thumbhole (2008) **$280.00**

WINCHESTER WILDCAT BOLT ACTION 22
Caliber: 22 S, L, LR; one 5-round and three 10-round magazines. **Barrel:** 21". **Weight:** 6.5 lbs. **Length:** 38-3/8". **Stock:** Checkered hardwood stock, checkered black synthetic Winchester buttplate, Schnabel fore-end. **Sights:** Bead post, front; buckhorn rear. **Features:** Steel sling swivel studs, blued finish. Wildcat Target/Varmint rifle has .866" diameter bull barrel. Receiver drilled, tapped, and grooved for bases. Adjustable trigger, dual front steel swivel studs. Reintroduced 2008. From Winchester Repeating Arms.
Price: **$259.00**
Price: Wildcat/Varmint **$309.00**

**Includes models for classic American and ISU target competition
and other sporting and competitive shooting.**

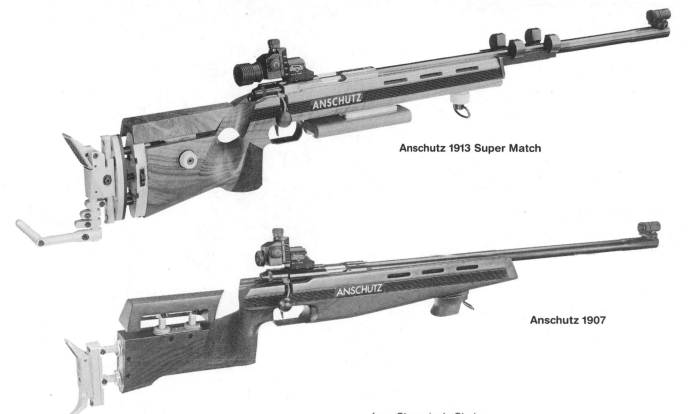

Anschutz 1913 Super Match

Anschutz 1907

ANSCHUTZ 1903 MATCH RIFLE
Caliber: 22 LR, single shot. **Barrel:** 21.25". **Weight:** 8 lbs. **Length:** 43.75" overall. **Stock:** Walnut-finished hardwood with adjustable cheekpiece; stippled grip and forend. **Sights:** None furnished. **Features:** Uses Anschutz Match 64 action. A medium weight rifle for intermediate and advanced Junior Match competition. Available from Champion's Choice.
Price: Right-hand **$965.00**

ANSCHUTZ 64-MP R SILHOUETTE RIFLE
Caliber: 22 LR, 5-shot magazine. **Barrel:** 21.5", medium heavy; 7/8" diameter. **Weight:** 8 lbs. **Length:** 39.5" overall. **Stock:** Walnut-finished hardwood, silhouette-type. **Sights:** None furnished. **Features:** Uses Match 64 action. Designed for metallic silhouette competition. Stock has stippled checkering, contoured thumb groove with Wundhammer swell. Two-stage #5098 trigger. Slide safety locks sear and bolt. Introduced 1980. Available from Champion's Choice.
Price: 64-MP R **$950.00**
Price: 64-S BR Benchrest (2008) **$1,175.00**

Anschutz 2007 Match Rifle
Uses same action as the Model 2013, but has a lighter barrel. European walnut stock in right-hand, true left-hand or extra-short models. Sights optional. Available with 19.6" barrel with extension tube, or 26", both in stainless or blue. Introduced 1998. Available from Champion's Choice.
Price: Right-hand, blue, no sights. **$2,410.90**

ANSCHUTZ 1827BT FORTNER BIATHLON RIFLE
Caliber: 22 LR, 5-shot magazine. **Barrel:** 21.7". **Weight:** 8.8 lbs. with sights. **Length:** 40.9" overall. **Stock:** European walnut with cheekpiece, stippled pistol grip and forend. **Sights:** Optional globe front specially designed for Biathlon shooting, micrometer rear with hinged snow cap. **Features:** Uses Super Match 54 action and nine-way adjustable trigger; adjustable wooden buttplate, biathlon butthook, adjustable hand-stop rail. Uses Anschutz/Fortner system straight-pull bolt action, blued or stainless steel barrel. Introduced 1982. Available

from Champion's Choice.
Price: Nitride finish with sights, about **$2,895.00**

ANSCHUTZ SUPER MATCH SPECIAL MODEL 2013 RIFLE
Caliber: 22 LR, single shot. **Barrel:** 25.9". **Weight:** 13 lbs. **Length:** 41.7" to 42.9". **Stock:** Adjustable aluminum. **Sights:** None furnished. **Features:** 2313 aluminum-silver/blue stock, 500mm barrel, fast lock time, adjustable cheek piece, heavy action and muzzle tube, w/ handstop and standing riser block. Introduced in 1997. Available from Champion's Choice.
Price: Right-hand **$3,195.00**

ANSCHUTZ 1912 SPORT RIFLE
Caliber: 22 LR. **Barrel:** 26" match. **Weight:** 11.4 lbs. **Length:** 41.7" overall. **Stock:** Non-stained thumbhole stock adjustable in length with adjustable butt plate and cheek piece adjustment. Flat forend raiser block 4856 adjustable in height. Hook butt plate. **Sights:** None furnished. **Features:** "Free rifle" for women. Smallbore model 1907 with 1912 **stock:** Match 54 action. Delivered with: Hand stop 6226, forend raiser block 4856, screw driver, instruction leaflet with test target. Available from Champion's Choice.
Price: **$2,595.00**

Anschutz 1913 Super Match Rifle
Same as the Model 1911 except European walnut International-type stock with adjustable cheekpiece, or color laminate, both available with straight or lowered forend, adjustable aluminum hook buttplate, adjustable hand stop, weighs 13 lbs., 46" overall. Stainless or blue barrel. Available from Champion's Choice.
Price: Right-hand, blue, no sights, walnut stock **$2,695.00**

Anschutz 1907 Standard Match Rifle
Same action as Model 1913 but with 7/8" diameter 26" barrel (stainless or blue). Length is 44.5" overall, weighs 10.5 lbs. Choice of stock configurations. Vented forend. Designed for prone and position shooting ISU requirements; suitable for NRA matches. Also available with walnut flat-forend stock for benchrest shooting. Available from Champion's Choice.
Price: Right-hand, blue, no sights. **$1,655.00**

Armalite AR-10(T)

Armalite AR-10 338 Federal

Bushmaster A2

Bushmaster DCM-XR

ARMALITE AR-10(T) RIFLE
Caliber: 308 Win., 10-shot magazine. **Barrel:** 24" target-weight Rock 5R custom. **Weight:** 10.4 lbs. **Length:** 43.5" overall. **Stock:** Green or black composition; N.M. fiberglass handguard tube. **Sights:** Detachable handle, front sight, or scope mount available. Comes with international-style flattop receiver with Picatinny rail. **Features:** National Match two-stage trigger. Forged upper receiver. Receivers hard-coat anodized. Introduced 1995. Made in U.S.A. by ArmaLite, Inc.
Price: Black **$1,912.00**
Price: AR-10, 338 Federal **$1,912.00**

ARMALITE M15A4(T) EAGLE EYE RIFLE
Caliber: 223 Rem., 10-round magazine. **Barrel:** 24" heavy stainless; 1:8" twist. **Weight:** 9.2 lbs. **Length:** 42-3/8" overall. **Stock:** Green or black butt, N.M. fiberglass handguard tube. **Sights:** One-piece international-style flattop receiver with Weaver-type rail, including case deflector. **Features:** Detachable carry handle, front sight and scope mount (30mm or 1") available. Upper and lower receivers have push-type pivot pin, hard coat anodized. Made in U.S.A. by ArmaLite, Inc.
Price: Green or black furniture **$1,296.00**

ARMALITE M15 A4 CARBINE 6.8 & 7.62X39
Caliber: 6.8 Rem, 7.62x39. **Barrel:** 16" chrome-lined with flash suppressor. **Weight:** 7 lbs. **Length:** 26.6". **Features:** Front and rear picatinny rails for mounting optics, two-stage tactical trigger, anodized aluminum/phosphate finish.
Price: **$1,107.00**

BLASER R93 LONG RANGE SPORTER 2 RIFLE
Caliber: 308 Win., 10-shot detachable box magazine. **Barrel:** 24". **Weight:** 10.4 lbs. **Length:** 44" overall. **Stock:** Aluminum with synthetic lining. **Sights:** None furnished; accepts detachable scope mount. **Features:** Straight-pull bolt action with adjustable trigger; fully adjustable stock; quick takedown; corrosion resistant finish. Introduced 1998. Imported from Germany by Blaser USA.
Price: **$3,848.00**

BUSHMASTER A2/A3 TARGET RIFLE
Caliber: 5.56mm, 223 Rem., 30-round magazine **Barrel:** 20", 24". **Weight:** 8.43 lbs. (A2); 8.78 lbs. (A3). **Length:** 39.5" overall (20" barrel). **Stock:** Black composition; A2 type. **Sights:** Adjustable post front, adjustable aperture rear. **Features:** Patterned after Colt M-16A2. Chrome-lined barrel with manganese phosphate exterior. Available in stainless barrel. Made in U.S.A. by Bushmaster Firearms Co.
Price: (A3 type) **$1,135.00**

BUSHMASTER DCM-XR COMPETITION RIFLE
Caliber: 5.56mm, 223 Rem., 10-round magazine. **Barrel:** 20" extra-heavy (1" diameter) barrel with 1.8" twist for heavier competition bullets. **Weight:** About 12 lbs. with balance weights. **Length:** 38.5". **Stock:** NA. **Sights:** A2 rear sight. **Features:** Has special competition rear sight with interchangeable apertures, extra-fine 1/2- or 1/4-MOA windage and elevation adjustments; specially ground front sight post in choice of three widths. Full-length handguards over free-floater barrel tube. Introduced 1998. Made in U.S.A. by Bushmaster Firearms, Inc.
Price: A2 . . . . **$1,150.00**
Price: A3 . . . . **$1,250.00**

Prices given are believed to be accurate at time of publication however, many factors affect retail pricing so exact prices are not possible.

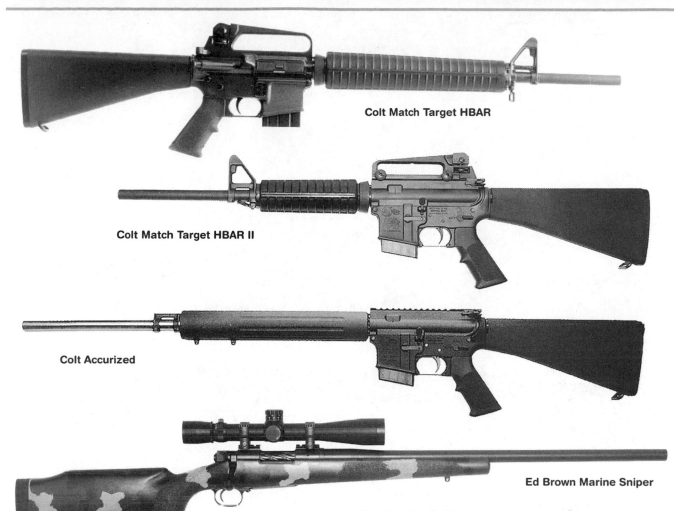

Colt Match Target HBAR

Colt Match Target HBAR II

Colt Accurized

Ed Brown Marine Sniper

BUSHMASTER VARMINTER RIFLE
Caliber: 5.56mm. **Barrel:** 24", fluted. **Weight:** 8.4 lbs. **Length:** 42.25" overall. **Stock:** Black composition, A2 type. **Sights:** None furnished; upper receiver has integral scope mount base. **Features:** Chrome-lined .950" extra heavy barrel with counter-bored crown, manganese phosphate finish, free-floating aluminum handguard, forged aluminum receivers with push-pin takedown, hard anodized mil-spec finish. Competition trigger optional. Made in U.S.A. by Bushmaster Firearms, Inc.
Price: **$1,360.00**

COLT MATCH TARGET HBAR & M4 RIFLES
Caliber: 223 Rem. **Barrel:** 20". **Weight:** 8 lbs. **Length:** 39" overall. **Stock:** Synthetic. **Sights:** Front: elevation adj. post; rear: 800-meter, aperture adj. for windage and elevation. **Features:** Heavy barrel, rate of rifling twist 1:7. Introduced 1991. Made in U.S.A. by Colt. M4 variant has 16.1" barrel.
Price: Model MT6601, MT6601C **$1,183.00**
Price: Model 6400C **$1,289.00**

Colt Match Target Competition HBAR Rifle
Similar to the Match Target except has removable carry handle for scope mounting, 1:9" rifling twist, 9-round magazine. Weighs 8.5 lbs. Introduced 1991.
Price: Model MT6700C **$1,250.00**

Colt Match Target Competition HBAR II Rifle
Similar to the Match Target Competition HBAR except has 16:1" barrel, overall length 34.5", and weighs 7.1 lbs. Introduced 1995.
Price: Model MT6731 . . . . **$1,172.00**

Colt Accurized Rifle
Similar to the Match Target Model except has 24" barrel. Features flat-top receiver for scope mounting, stainless steel heavy barrel, tubular handguard, and free-floating barrel. Matte black finish. Weighs 9.25 lbs. Made in U.S.A. by Colt's Mfg. Co., Inc.
Price: Model CR6724 . . . . **$1,334.00**

EAA/HW 660 MATCH RIFLE
Caliber: 22 LR. **Barrel:** 26". **Weight:** 10.7 lbs. **Length:** 45.3" overall. **Stock:** Match-type walnut with adjustable cheekpiece and buttplate. **Sights:** Globe front, match aperture rear. **Features:** Adjustable match trigger; stippled pistol grip and forend; forend accessory rail. Introduced 1991. Imported from Germany by European American Armory.
Price: About **$999.00**
Price: With laminate stock **$1,159.00**

ED BROWN MODEL 704, M40A2 MARINE SNIPER
Caliber: 308 Win., 30-06 Springfield. **Barrel:** Match-grade 24". **Weight:** 9.25 lbs. **Stock:** Hand bedded McMillan GP fiberglass tactical stock with recoil pad in special Woodland Camo molded-in colors. **Sights:** None furnished. Leupold Mark 4 30mm scope mounts with heavy-duty screws. **Features:** Steel trigger guard, hinged floor plate, three position safety.
Price: From **$3,695.00**

OLYMPIC ARMS SM SERVICEMATCH AR15 RIFLES
Caliber: 223 Rem. minimum SAAMI spec, 30-shot magazine. **Barrel:** 20" broach-cut Ultramatch stainless steel 1x8 twist rate. **Weight:** 10 lbs. **Length:** 39.5" overall. **Stock:** A2 grip, A2 buttstock with trapdoor. **Sights:** A2 NM rear, elevation adjustable front post. **Features:** DCM-ready AR15, free-floating handguard looks standard, A2 upper, threaded muzzle, flash suppressor. Premium model adds pneumatic recoil buffer, Bob Jones interchangeable sights, two-stage trigger and Turner Saddlery sling. Made in U.S.A. by Olympic Arms, Inc.
Price: SM-1, 20" DCM ready **$1,272.70**
Price: SM-1P, Premium 20" DCM ready **$1,727.70**

Olympic Arms SM-1

Olympic Arms SM-1P

Olympic Arms UM-1

Olympic Arms ML-1

OLYMPIC ARMS UM ULTRAMATCH AR15 RIFLES

Caliber: 223 Rem. minimum SAAMI spec, 30-shot magazine. **Barrel:** 20" or 24" bull broach-cut Ultramatch stainless steel 1x10 twist rate. **Weight:** 8-10 lbs. **Length:** 38.25" overall. **Stock:** A2 grip, A2 buttstock with trapdoor. **Sights:** None, flat-top upper and gas block with rails. **Features:** Flat top upper, free floating tubular match handguard, Picatinny gas block, crowned muzzle, factory trigger job and "Ultramatch" pantograph. Premium model adds pneumatic recoil buffer, Harris S-series bipod, hand selected premium receivers and William Set Trigger. Made in U.S.A. by Olympic Arms, Inc.
Price: UM-1, 20" Ultramatch **$1,332.50**
Price: UM-1P **$1,805.70**

OLYMPIC ARMS ML-1/ML-2 MULTIMATCH AR15 CARBINES

Caliber: 223 Rem. minimum SAAMI spec, 30-shot magazine. **Barrel:** 16" broach-cut Ultramatch stainless steel 1x10 twist rate. **Weight:** 7-8 lbs. **Length:** 34-36" overall. **Stock:** A2 grip and varying buttstock. **Sights:** None. **Features:** The ML-1 includes A2 upper with adjustable rear sight, elevation adjustable front post, free floating tubular match handguard, bayonet lug, threaded muzzle, flash suppressor and M4 6-point collapsible buttstock. The ML-2 includes bull diameter barrel, flat top upper, free floating tubular match handguard, Picatinny gas block, crowned muzzle and A2 buttstock with trapdoor. Made in U.S.A. by Olympic Arms, Inc.
Price: ML-1 or ML-2 . . . . **$1,188.20**

OLYMPIC ARMS K8 TARGETMATCH AR15 RIFLES

Caliber: 5.56 NATO, 223 WSSM, 243 WSSM, .25 WSSM 30/7-shot magazine. **Barrel:** 20", 24" bull button-rifled stainless/chrome-moly steel 1x9/1x10 twist rate. **Weight:** 8-10 lbs. **Length:** 38"-42" overall. **Stock:** A2 grip, A2 buttstock with trapdoor. **Sights:** None. **Features:** Barrel has satin bead-blast finish; flat-top upper, free-floating tubular match handguard, Picatinny gas block, crowned muzzle and "Targetmatch" pantograph on lower receiver. K8-MAG model uses Winchester Super Short Magnum cartridges. Includes 24" bull chrome-moly barrel, flat-top upper, free-floating tubular match handguard, Picatinny gas block, crowned muzzle and 7-shot magazine. Made in U.S.A. by Olympic Arms, Inc.
Price: K8 . . . .**$908.70**
Price: K8-MAG **$1,363.70**

COMPETITION RIFLES—Centerfire & Rimfire

Remington 40-XB Rangemaster

Sako TRG-22

Springfield Armory M1A Super Match

Springfield Armory M1A/M-21

REMINGTON 40-XB RANGEMASTER TARGET CENTERFIRE
Caliber: 15 calibers from 220 Swift to 300 Win. Mag. **Barrel:** 27.25".
Weight: 11.25 lbs. **Length:** 47" overall. **Stock:** American walnut,
laminated thumbhole or Kevlar with high comb and beavertail forend
stop. Rubber non-slip buttplate. **Sights:** None. Scope blocks installed.
Features: Adjustable trigger. Stainless barrel and action. Receiver
drilled and tapped for sights. Model 40-XB Tactical (2008) chambered in
308 Win., comes with guarantee of 0.75 inch maximum 5 shot groups
at 100 yards. **Weight:** 10.25 lbs. Includes Teflon-coated stainless
button-rifled barrel, 1:14 twist, 27.25 inch long, three longitudinal flutes.
Bolt-action repeater, adjustable 40-X trigger and precision machined
aluminum bedding block. Stock is H-S Precision Pro Series synthetic
tactical stock, black with green web finish, vertical pistol grip. From
Remington Custom Shop.
Price: 40-XB KS, aramid fiber stock, single shot **$2,780.00**
Price: 40-XB KS, aramid fiber stock, repeater **$2,634.00**
Price: 40-XB Tactical 308 Win. (2008) **$2,927.00**
Price: 40-XB Thumbhole Repeater. **$2,927.00**

REMINGTON 40-XBBR KS
Caliber: Five calibers from 22 BR to 308 Win. **Barrel:** 20" (light varmint
class), 24" (heavy varmint class). **Weight:** 7.25 lbs. (light varmint
class); 12 lbs. (heavy varmint class). **Length:** 38" (20" bbl.), 42"
(24"bbl.). **Stock:** Aramid fiber. **Sights:** None. Supplied with scope
blocks. **Features:** Unblued benchrest with stainless steel barrel, trigger
adjustable from 1-1/2 lbs. to 3.5 lbs. Special two-oz. trigger extra cost.
Scope and mounts extra.
Price: Single shot **$3,806.00**

REMINGTON 40-XC KS TARGET RIFLE
Caliber: 7.62 NATO, 5-shot. **Barrel:** 24", stainless steel. **Weight:** 11 lbs.
without sights. **Length:** 43.5" overall. **Stock:** Aramid fiber. **Sights:**

None furnished. **Features:** Designed to meet the needs of competitive
shooters. Stainless steel barrel and action.
Price: **$3,000.00**

REMINGTON 40-XR CUSTOM SPORTER
Caliber: 22 LR, 22 WM. **Barrel:** 24" stainless steel, no sights. **Weight:**
9.75 lbs. **Length:** 40". **Features:** Model XR-40 Target rifle action. Many
options available in stock, decoration or finish.
Price: Single shot **$4,391.00**
Price: 40-XRBR KS, bench rest 22 LR **$2,927.00**

SAKO TRG-22 BOLT-ACTION RIFLE
Caliber: 308 Win., 10-shot magazine. **Barrel:** 26". **Weight:** 10.25 lbs.
Length: 45.25" overall. **Stock:** Reinforced polyurethane with fully
adjustable cheekpiece and buttplate. **Sights:** None furnished. Optional
quick-detachable, one-piece scope mount base, 1" or 30mm rings.
Features: Resistance-free bolt, free-floating heavy stainless barrel,
60-degree bolt lift. Two-stage trigger is adjustable for length, pull,
horizontal or vertical pitch. Introduced 2000. Imported from Finland
by Beretta USA.
Price: TRG-22 folding stock **$4,560.00**

SPRINGFIELD ARMORY M1A SUPER MATCH
Caliber: 308 Win. **Barrel:** 22", heavy Douglas Premium. **Weight:** About
11 lbs. **Length:** 44.31" overall. **Stock:** Heavy walnut competition stock
with longer pistol grip, contoured area behind the rear sight, thicker
butt and forend, glass bedded. **Sights:** National Match front and rear.
Features: Has figure-eight-style operating rod guide. Introduced 1987.
From Springfield Armory.
Price: About **$2,479.00**

Springfield Armory M1A/M-21 Tactical Model Rifle
Similar to M1A Super Match except special sniper stock with adjustable cheekpiece and rubber recoil pad. Weighs 11.6 lbs. From Springfield Armory.
Price: **$2,975.00**

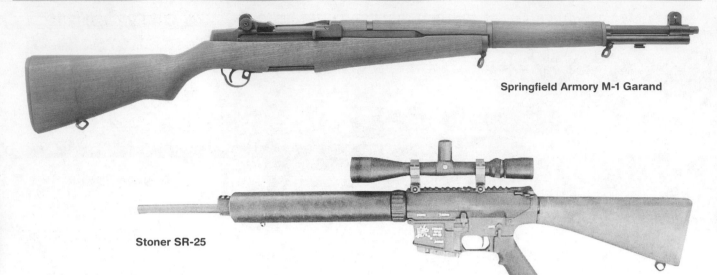

Springfield Armory M-1 Garand

Stoner SR-25

SPRINGFIELD ARMORY M-1 GARAND AMERICAN COMBAT RIFLES
Caliber: 30-06 Spfl., 308 Win., 8-shot. **Barrel:** 24". **Weight:** 9.5 lbs. **Length:** 43.6". **Stock:** American walnut. **Sights:** Military square post front, military aperture, MOA adjustable rear. **Features:** Limited production, certificate of authenticity, all new receiver, barrel and stock with remaining parts USGI mil-spec. Two-stage military trigger.
Price: About **$2,479.00**

STONER SR-15 MATCH RIFLE
Caliber: 223. **Barrel:** 20". **Weight:** 7.9 lbs. **Length:** 38" overall. **Stock:** Black synthetic. **Sights:** None furnished; flattop upper receiver for scope mounting. **Features:** Short Picatinny rail, two-stage match trigger. Introduced 1998. Made in U.S.A. by Knight's Mfg. Co.
Price: **$1,650.00**

STONER SR-25 MATCH RIFLE
Caliber: 7.62 NATO, 10-shot steel magazine, 5-shot optional. **Barrel:** 24" heavy match; 1:11.25" twist. **Weight:** 10.75 lbs. **Length:** 44" overall. **Stock:** Black synthetic AR-15A2 design. Full floating forend of mil-spec synthetic attaches to upper receiver at a single point. **Sights:** None furnished. Has integral Weaver-style rail. Rings and iron sights optional. **Features:** Improved AR-15 trigger, AR-15-style seven-lug rotating bolt. Introduced 1993. Made in U.S.A. by Knight's Mfg. Co.
Price: **$3,345.00**
Price: SR-25 Lightweight Match (20" medium match target
contour barrel, 9.5 lbs., 40" overall) **$3,345.00**

TIME PRECISION 22 RF BENCH REST RIFLE
Caliber: 22 LR, single shot. **Barrel:** Shilen match-grade stainless. **Weight:** 10 lbs. with scope. **Length:** NA. **Stock:** Fiberglass. Pillar bedded. **Sights:** None furnished. **Features:** Shilen match trigger removable trigger bracket, full-length steel sleeve, aluminum receiver. Introduced 2008. Made in U.S.A. by Time Precision.
Price: **$2,200.00**

Includes a wide variety of sporting guns and guns suitable for various competitions.

Benelli Legacy

Benelli M2 20 gauge Realtree APG HD

Benelli M2 20 gauge Realtree APG HD

Benelli M4

Benelli Montefeltro

BENELLI LEGACY SHOTGUN

Gauge: 12, 20, 2-3/4" and 3" chamber. **Barrel:** 24", 26", 28" (Full, Mod., Imp. Cyl., Imp. Mod., cylinder choke tubes). Mid-bead sight. **Weight:** 5.8 to 7.4 lbs. **Length:** 49-5/8" overall (28" barrel). **Stock:** Select AA European walnut with satin finish. **Features:** Uses the rotating bolt inertia recoil operating system with a two-piece steel/aluminum etched receiver (bright on lower, blue upper). Drop adjustment kit allows the stock to be custom fitted without modifying the stock. Introduced 1998. Ultralight model has gloss-blued finish receiver. Weight is 6.0 lbs., 24" barrel, 45.5" overall length. WeatherCoat walnut stock. Introduced 2006. Imported from Italy by Benelli USA, Corp.

Price: Legacy $1,689.00
Price: Sport (2008) $2,269.00

BENELLI ULTRA LIGHT SHOTGUN

Gauge: 12, 20, 3" chamber. **Barrel:** 28". Mid-bead sight. **Weight:** 5.2 to 6 lbs. **Features:** Similar to Legacy line. Drop adjustment kit allows the stock to be custom fitted without modifying the stock. WeatherCoat walnut stock. Lightened receiver, shortened magazine tube, carbon-fiber rib and grip cap. Introduced 2008. Imported from Italy by Benelli USA, Corp.

Price: 12 gauge. $1,539.00

BENELLI M2 FIELD SHOTGUNS

Gauge: 20 ga., 12 ga., 3" chamber. **Barrel:** 21", 24", 26", 28". **Weight:** 5.4 to 7.2 lbs. **Length:** 42.5 to 49.5" overall. **Stock:** Synthetic, Advantage Max-4 HD, Advantage Timber HD, APG HD. **Sights:** Red bar. **Features:** Uses the Inertia Driven bolt mechanism. Vent rib. Comes with set of five choke tubes. Imported from Italy by Benelli USA.

Price: Synthetic ComforTech gel recoil pad $1,319.00
Price: Camo ComforTech gel recoil pad. $1,335.00

Price: Satin walnut $1,229.00
Price: Rifled slug synthetic $1,380.00
Price: Camo turkey model w/SteadyGrip stock $1,429.00
Price: Realtree APG HD ComforTech stock (2007) $1,429.00
Price: Realtree APG HD ComforTech 20 ga. (2007) $1,429.00
Price: Realtree APG HD LH ComforTech (2007) $1,429.00
Price: Realtree APG HD ComforTech Slug (2007). $1,429.00
Price: Realtree APG HD w/SteadyGrip stock (2007) $1,429.00
Price: Black Synthetic Grip Tight 20 ga. (2007) $1,319.00

BENELLI M4 TACTICAL SHOTGUN

Gauge: 12 ga., 3" chamber. **Barrel:** 18.5". **Weight:** 7.8 lbs. **Length:** 40" overall. **Stock:** Synthetic. **Sights:** Ghost Ring rear, fixed blade front. **Features:** Auto-regulating gas-operated (ARGO) action, choke tube, Picatinny rail, standard and collapsible stocks available, optional LE tactical gun case. Introduced 2006. Imported from Italy by Benelli USA.

Price: Pistol grip stock, black synthetic. $1,699.00
Price: Desert camo pistol grip (2007) $1,829.00

BENELLI MONTEFELTRO SHOTGUNS

Gauge: 12 and 20 ga. Full, Imp. Mod., Mod., Imp. Cyl., Cyl. choke tubes. **Barrel:** 24", 26", 28". **Weight:** 5.3 to 7.1 lbs. **Stock:** Checkered walnut with satin finish. **Length:** 43.6 to 49.5" overall. **Features:** Uses the Inertia Driven rotating bolt system with a simple inertia recoil design. Finish is blue. Introduced 1987.

Price: 24", 26", 28" $1,219.00
Price: Left hand. $1,229.00
Price: 20 ga. $1,219.00
Price: 20 ga. short stock (LOP: 12.5") $1,120.00
Price: Silver (AA walnut; nickel-blue receiver) $1,649.00
Price: Silver 20 ga. $1,649.00

Benelli Super Black Eagle II Realtree APG HD Slug

Benelli Super Black Eagle II

Beretta 3901 Citizen

Beretta UGB

BENELLI SUPER BLACK EAGLE II SHOTGUNS
Gauge: 12, 3-1/2" chamber. **Barrel:** 24", 26", 28" (Cyl. Imp. Cyl., Mod., Imp. Mod., Full choke tubes). **Weight:** 7.1 to 7.3 lbs. **Length:** 45.6 to 49.6" overall. **Stock:** European walnut with satin finish, polymer, or camo. Adjustable for drop. **Sights:** Red bar front. **Features:** Uses Benelli inertia recoil bolt system. Vent rib. Advantage Max-4 HD, Advantage Timber HD camo patterns. Features ComforTech stock. Introduced 1991. Left-hand models available. Imported from Italy by Benelli USA.
Price: Satin walnut, non-ComforTech **$1,549.00**
Price: Camo stock, ComforTech gel recoil pad **$1,759.00**
Price: Black Synthetic stock **$1,649.00**
Price: Max-4 HD Camo stock **$1,759.00**
Price: Timber HD turkey model w/SteadyGrip stock. **$1,680.00**
Price: Realtree APG HD w/ComforTech stock (2007) **$1,759.00**
Price: Realtree APG HD LH ComforTech stock (2007) **$1,759.00**
Price: Realtree APG HD Slug Gun (2007) **$1,730.00**

BENELLI CORDOBA SHOTGUN
Gauge: 20; 12; 3" chamber. **Barrel:** 28" and 30", ported, 10mm sporting rib. **Weight:** 7.2 to 7.3 lbs. **Length:** 49.6 to 51.6". **Features:** Designed for high-volume sporting clays and Argentina dove shooting. Inertia-driven action, Extended Sport CrioChokes, 4+1 capacity. Ported. Imported from Italy by Benelli USA.
Price: Black synthetic GripTight ComforTech stock **$1,869.00**
Price: Black synthetic GripTight ComforTech stock, 20 ga.,
(2007) **$1,869.00**
Price: Max-4 HD ComforTech stock (2007) **$2,039.00**

BENELLI SUPERSPORT & SPORT II SHOTGUNS
Gauge: 20; 12; 3" chamber. **Barrel:** 28" and 30", ported, 10mm sporting rib. **Weight:** 7.2 to 7.3 lbs. **Length:** 49.6 to 51.6". **Stock:** Carbon fiber, ComforTech (Supersport) or walnut (Sport II). **Sights:** Red bar front, metal midbead. Sport II is similar to the Legacy model except has nonengraved dual tone blue/silver receiver, ported wide-rib barrel, adjustable buttstock, and functions with all loads. Walnut stock with satin finish. Introduced 1997. **Features:** Designed for high-volume sporting clays. Inertia-driven action, Extended CrioChokes, 4+1

capacity. Ported. Imported from Italy by Benelli USA.
Price: Carbon fiber ComforTech stock **$1,979.00**
Price: Carbon fiber ComforTech stock, 20 ga. (2007) **$1,979.00**
Price: Sport II 20 ga. (2007) **$1,699.00**

BERETTA 3901 SHOTGUNS
Gauge: 12, 20 gauge; 3" chamber, semi-auto. **Barrel:** 26", 28". **Weight:** 6.55 lbs. (20 ga.), 7.2 lbs. (12 ga.). **Length:** NA. **Stock:** Wood, X-tra wood (special process wood enhancement), and polymer. **Features:** Based on A390 shotgun introduced in 1996. Mobilchokes, removable trigger group. 3901 Target RL uses gas operating system; Sporting style flat rib with steel front bead and mid-bead, walnut stock and forearm, satin matte finish, adjustable LOP from 12P13", adjustable for cast on/off, Beretta's Memory System II to adjust the parallel comb. Weighs 7.2 lbs. 3901 Citizen has polymer stock. 3901 Statesman has basic wood and checkering treatment. 3901 Ambassador has X-tra wood stock and fore end; high-polished receiver with engraving, Gel-Tek recoil pad, optional TruGlo fiber-optic front sight. 3901 Rifled Slug Shotgun has black high-impact synthetic stock and fore end, 24" barrel, 1:28 twist, Picatinny cantilever rail. Introduced 2006. Made in U.S. by Beretta USA.
Price: 3901 Target RL **$900.00**
Price: 3901 Citizen, synthetic or wood, from **$750.00**
Price: 3901 Statesman **$900.00**
Price: 3901 Rifled Slug Shotgun **$800.00**

BERETTA UGB25 XCEL SEMI-AUTO SHOTGUN
Gauge: 12, 2-3/4" chambers. **Barrel:** 28", 30", 32"; competition-style interchangeable vent rib; Optima choke tubes. **Weight:** 7.7-9 lbs. **Stock:** High-grade walnut with oil finish; hand-checkered grip and forend, adjustable. **Features:** Break-open semiautomatic. High-resistance fiberglass-reinforced technopolymer trigger plate, self-lubricating firing mechanism. Rounded alloy receiver, polished sides, external cartridge carrier and feeding port, bottom eject. two technopolymer recoil dampers on breech bolt, double recoil dampers located in the receiver, Beretta Recoil Reduction System, recoil-absorbing Beretta Gel Tek recoil pad. Optima-Bore barrel with a lengthened forcing cone, Optimachoke and Extended Optimachoke tubes. Steel-shot capable, interchangeable aluminum alloy top rib. Introduced 2006. Imported from Italy by Beretta USA.
Price: **$3,875.00**

Prices given are believed to be accurate at time of publication however, many factors affect retail pricing so exact prices are not possible.

SHOTGUNS—Autoloaders

Beretta AL391 Urika Sporting

Beretta AL391 Urika Gold Sporting

Beretta A391 Xtrema2 3.5

BERETTA AL391 TEKNYS SHOTGUNS
Gauge: 12, 20 gauge; 3" chamber, semi-auto. **Barrel:** 26", 28". **Weight:** 5.9 lbs. (20 ga.), 7.3 lbs. (12 ga.). **Length:** NA. **Stock:** X-tra wood (special process wood enhancement). **Features:** Flat 1/4 rib, TruGlo Tru-Bead sight, recoil reducer, stock spacers, overbored bbls., flush choke tubes. Comes with fitted, lined case.
Price: From **$2,050.00**

BERETTA AL391 URIKA AND URIKA 2 AUTO SHOTGUNS
Gauge: 12, 20 gauge; 3" chamber. **Barrel:** 22", 24", 26", 28", 30"; five Mobilchoke choke tubes. **Weight:** 5.95 to 7.28 lbs. **Length:** Varies by model. **Stock:** Walnut, black or camo synthetic; shims, spacers and interchangeable recoil pads allow custom fit. **Features:** Self-compensating gas op-eration handles full range of loads; recoil re-ducer in receiver; enlarged trigger guard; re-duced-weight receiver, barrel and forend; hard-chromed bore. Introduced 2000. AL391 Urika 2 (2007) has self-cleaning action, X-Tra Grain stock finish. AL391 Urika 2 Gold has higher-grade select oil-finished wood stock, upgraded engrav-ing (gold-filled gamebirds on field models, gold-filled laurel leaf on competition version). Kick-Off recoil reduction system available in Syn-thetic, Realtree Advantage Max-4 and AP models. Imported from Italy by Beretta USA.
Price: Urika 2 X-tra Grain, from **$1,400.00**
Price: Urika 2 Gold, from **$1,550.00**
Price: Urika 2 Synthetic **$975.00**
Price: Urika 2 Realtree AP Kick-Off, ... **$1,350.00**

BERETTA A391 XTREMA2 3.5 AUTO SHOTGUNS
Gauge: 12 ga. 3.5" chamber. **Barrel:** 24", 26", 28". **Weight:** 7.8 lbs. **Stock:** Synthetic. **Features:** Semi-auto goes with two-lug rotating bolt and self-compensating gas valve, extended tang, cross bolt safety, self-cleaning, with case.
Price: From **$1,250.00**

BREDA GRIZZLY
Gauge: 12, 3.5" chamber. **Barrel:** 28". **Weight:** 7.2 lbs. **Stock:** Black synthetic or Advantage Timber with matching metal parts. **Features:** Chokes tubes are Mod., IC, Full; inertia-type action, four-round magazine. Imported from Italy by Legacy Sports International.
Price: Blued/black (2008) **$1,826.00**
Price: Advantage Timber Camo (2008) **$2,121.00**

BREDA XANTHOS
Gauge: 12, 3" chamber. **Barrel:** 28". **Weight:** 6.5 lbs. **Stock:** High grade walnut. **Features:** Chokes tubes are Mod., IC, Full; inertia-type action, four-round magazine, spark engraving with hand-engraved details and hand-gilding figures on receiver. Blued, Grey or Chrome finishes. Imported from Italy by Legacy Sports International.
Price: Blued (2007) **$2,309.00**

Price: Grey (2007) **$2,451.00**
Price: Chrome (2007) **$3,406.00**

BREDA ECHO
Gauge: 12, 20. 3" chamber. **Barrel:** 28". **Weight:** 6.0-6.5 lbs. **Stock:** Walnut. **Features:** Chokes tubes are Mod., IC, Full; inertia-type action, four-round magazine, blue, grey or nickel finishes, modern engraving, fully checkered pistol grip. Imported from Italy by Legacy Sports International.
Price: Blued, 12 ga. (2008) **$1,897.00**
Price: Grey, 12 ga. (2008) **$1,969.00**
Price: Nickel, 12 ga. (2008) **$2,214.00**
Price: Nickel, 20 ga. (2008) **$2,214.00**

BREDA ALTAIR
Gauge: 12, 20. 3" chamber. **Barrel:** 28". **Weight:** 5.7-6.1 lbs. **Stock:** Oil-rubbed walnut. **Features:** Chokes tubes are Mod., IC, Full; gas-actuated action, four-round magazine, blued finish, lightweight frame. Imported from Italy by Legacy Sports International.
Price: Blued, 12 ga. (2008) **$1,320.00**
Price: Grey, 20 ga. (2008) **$1,320.00**

BROWNING GOLD AUTO SHOTGUNS
Gauge: 12, 3" or 3-1/2" chamber; 20, 3" chamber. **Barrel:** 12 ga.-26", 28", 30", Invector Plus choke tubes; 20 ga.-26", 30", Invector choke tubes. **Weight:** 7 lbs., 9 oz. (12 ga.), 6 lbs., 12 oz. (20 ga.). **Length:** 46.25" overall (20 ga., 26" barrel). **Stock:** 14"x1.5"x2-1/3"; select walnut with gloss finish; palm swell grip. **Features:** Self-regulating, self-cleaning gas system shoots all loads; lightweight receiver with special non-glare deep black finish; large reversible safety button; large rounded trigger guard, gold trigger. The 20 gauge has slightly smaller dimensions; 12 gauge have back-bored barrels, Invector Plus tube system. Introduced 1994. Gold Evolve shotguns have new rib design, HiViz sights. Imported by Browning.
Price: Gold Evolve Sporting, 12 ga., 2-3/4" chamber **$1,326.00**
Price: Gold Superlite Hunter, 12 or 20 ga., 26" or
28" barrel, 6.6 lbs. **$1,161.00**

BROWNING GOLD NWTF TURKEY SERIES AND MOSSY OAK SHOTGUNS
Gauge: 12, 10, 3-1/2" chamber. Similar to the Gold Hunter except has specialized camouflage patterns, including National Wild Turkey Federation design. Includes extra-full choke tube and HiViz fiber-optic sights on some models and Dura-Touch coating. Camouflage patterns include Mossy Oak New Break-Up (NBU) or Mossy Oak New Shadow Grass (NSG). NWTF models include NWTF logo on stock. Introduced 2001. From Browning.
Price: NWFT Gold Ultimate Turkey, 24" barrel, 12 ga.
3-1/2" chamber **$1,513.00**
Price: NWFT Gold 10 Gauge, 24" barrel, 3-1/2" chamber . . **$1,639.00**

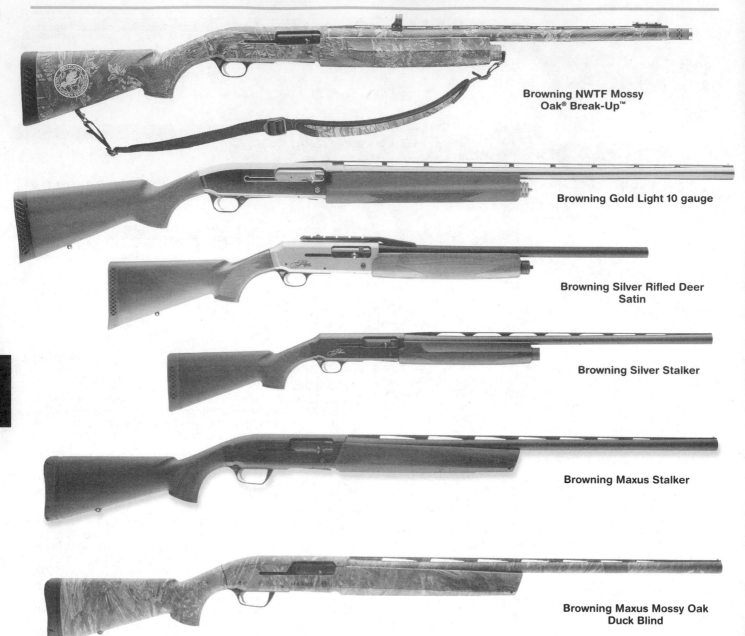

Browning NWTF Mossy Oak® Break-Up™

Browning Gold Light 10 gauge

Browning Silver Rifled Deer Satin

Browning Silver Stalker

Browning Maxus Stalker

Browning Maxus Mossy Oak Duck Blind

BROWNING GOLD GOLDEN CLAYS AUTO SHOTGUNS
Gauge: 12, 2-3/4" chamber. **Barrel:** 28", 30", Invector Plus choke tubes. **Weight:** about 7.75 lbs. **Length:** From 47.75 to 50.5". **Stock:** Select walnut with gloss finish; palm swell grip, shim adjustable. **Features:** Ported barrels, "Golden Clays" models feature gold inlays and engraving. Imported by Browning.
Price: Gold "Golden Clays" Sporting Clays, intr. 2005 . . . . . **$1,941.00**

Browning Gold Light 10 Gauge Auto Shotgun
Similar to the Gold Hunter except has an alloy receiver that is 1 lb. lighter than standard model. Offered in 26" or 28" bbls. With Mossy Oak Break-Up or Shadow Grass coverage; 5-shot magazine. Weighs 9 lbs., 10 oz. (28" bbl.). Introduced 2001. Imported by Browning.
Price: Camo model only **$1,509.00**

BROWNING SILVER AUTO SHOTGUNS
Gauge: 12, 3" or 3-1/2" chamber; 20, 3" chamber. **Barrel:** 12 ga.-26", 28", 30", Invector Plus choke tubes. **Weight:** 7 lbs., 9 oz. (12 ga.), 6 lbs., 7 oz. (20 ga.). **Stock:** Satin finish walnut. **Features:** Active Valve gas system, semi-humpback receiver. Invector Plus tube system, three choke tubes. Imported by Browning.
Price: Silver Hunter, 12 ga., 3.5" chamber **$1,239.00**
Price: Silver Hunter, 20 ga., 3" chamber, intr. 2008 . . . . **$1,079.00**

Price: Silver Micro, 20 ga., 3" chamber, intr. 2008 . . . . **$1,079.00**
Price: Silver Sporting, 12 ga., 2-3/4" chamber,
intr. 2009 . . . . **$1,199.00**
Price: Silver Sporting Micro, 12 ga., 2-3/4" chamber,
intr. 2008. . . . . **$1,199.00**
Price: Silver Rifled Deer, Mossy Oak New Break-Up,
12 ga., 3" chamber, intr. 2008 . . . . **$1,319.00**
Price: Silver Rifled Deer Stalker, 12 ga., 3" chamber,
intr. 2008. . . . . **$1,169.00**
Price: Silver Rifled Deer Satin, satin-finished aluminum
alloy receiver and satin-finished walnut buttstock
and forend **$1,229.00**
Price: Silver Stalker, black composite buttstock and forend **$1,179.00**

BROWNING MAXUS
Gauge: 12; 3" or 3.5" chambers. **Barrel:** 26" or 28". **Weight:** 6-7/8 lbs. **Length:** 47.25" to 49.25". **Stock:** Composite with close radius pistol grip. **Features:** Aluminum receiver, lightweight profile barrel with vent rib, Vector Pro lengthened forcing cone, DuraTouch Armor Coating overall. Handles shorter shells interchangeably.
Price: Stalker, matte black finish overall, 3-1/2" **$1,379.00**
Price: Stalker, matte black finish overall, 3" **$1,199.00**
Price: Mossy Oak Duck Blind overall, 3-1/2" **$1,499.00**
Price: Mossy Oak Duck Blind overall, 3" **$1,339.00**

Prices given are believed to be accurate at time of publication however, many factors affect retail pricing so exact prices are not possible.

SHOTGUNS—Autoloaders

Charles Daly Field Pump

Charles Daly Maxi-Mag Field Hunter VR-MC

Charles Daly Superior II

Escort Model AS

Franchi 48AL Deluxe

CHARLES DALY FIELD SEMI-AUTO SHOTGUNS
Gauge: 12, 20, 28. **Barrel:** 22", 24", 26", 28" or 30". **Stock:** Synthetic black, Realtree Hardwoods or Advantage Timber. **Features:** Interchangeable barrels handle all loads including steel shot. Slug model has adjustable sights. Maxi-Mag is 3.5" chamber.
Price: Field Hunter, from **$489.00**

CHARLES DALY SUPERIOR II SEMI-AUTO SHOTGUNS
Gauge: 12, 20, 28. **Barrel:** 26", 28" or 30". **Stock:** Select Turkish walnut. **Features:** Factory ported interchangeable barrels; wide vent rib on Trap and Sport models; fluorescent red sights.
Price: Superior II Hunter, from **$649.00**
Price: Superior II Sport **$709.00**
Price: Superior II Trap. **$739.00**

ESCORT SEMI-AUTO SHOTGUNS
Gauge: 12, 20; 3" or 3.5" chambers. **Barrel:** 22" (Youth), 26" and 28". **Weight:** 6.7-7.8 lbs. **Stock:** Polymer in black, Shadow Grass® or Obsession® camo finish, Turkish walnut, select walnut. **Sights:** Optional HiViz Spark front. **Features:** Black-chrome or dipped-camo metal parts, top of receiver dovetailed for sight mounts, gold plated trigger, trigger guard safety, magazine cut-off. Three choke tubes (IC, M, F) except the Waterfowl/Turkey Combo, which adds a .665 turkey choke to the standard three. Waterfowl/Turkey combo is two-barrel set, 24"/26" and 26"/28". Several models have Trio recoil pad. Models are: AS, AS Select, AS Youth, AS Youth Select, PS, PS Spark and Waterfowl/Turkey. Introduced 2002. Camo introduced 2003. Youth, Slug and Obsession camo introduced 2005. Imported from Turkey by Legacy Sports International.
Price: . . . . **$425.00 to $589.00**

FRANCHI INERTIA I-12 SHOTGUN
Gauge: 12, 3" chamber. **Barrel:** 24", 26", 28" (Cyl., IC, Mod., IM, F choke tubes). **Weight:** 7.5 to 7.7 lbs. **Length:** 45" to 49". **Stock:** 14-3.8" LOP, satin walnut with checkered grip and forend, synthetic, Advantage Timber HD or Max-4 camo patterns. **Features:** Inertia-Driven action. AA walnut stock. Red bar front sight, metal mid sight. Imported from Italy by Benelli USA.
Price: Synthetic. **$839.00**
Price: Camo **$949.00**
Price: Satin walnut **$949.00**

FRANCHI MODEL 720 SHOTGUNS
Gauge: 20, 3" chamber. **Barrel:** 24", 26", 28" w/(IC, Mod., F choke tubes). **Weight:** 5.9 to 6.1 lbs. **Length:** 43.25" to 49". **Stock:** WeatherCoat finish walnut, Max-4 and Timber HD camo. **Sights:** Front bead. **Features:** Made in Italy and imported by Benelli USA.
Price: **$1,049.00**
Price: Walnut, 12.5" LOP, 43.25" OAL **$999.00**

FRANCHI 48AL FIELD AND DELUXE SHOTGUNS
Gauge: 20 or 28, 2-3/4" chamber. **Barrel:** 24", 26", 28" (Full, Cyl., Mod., choke tubes). **Weight:** 5.4 to 5.7 lbs. **Length:** 42.25" to 48". **Stock:** Walnut with checkered grip and forend. **Features:** Long recoil-operated action. Chrome-lined bore; cross-bolt safety. Imported from Italy by Benelli USA.
Price: AL Field 20 ga. **$839.00**
Price: AL Deluxe 20 ga., A grade walnut **$1,099.00**
Price: AL Field 28 ga. **$999.00**

FRANCHI 720 COMPETITION SHOTGUN
Gauge: 20; 4+1. **Barrel:** 28" ported; tapered target rib and bead front sight. **Weight:** 6.2 lbs. **Stock:** Walnut with WeatherCoat. **Features:** Gas-operated, satin nickel receiver.
Price: **$1,149.00**

Prices given are believed to be accurate at time of publication however, many factors affect retail pricing so exact prices are not possible.

SHOTGUNS—Autoloaders

Remington Model 105 CTi

Remington Model 1100 G3

HARRINGTON & RICHARDSON EXCELL AUTO 5 SHOTGUNS
Gauge: 12, 3" chamber. **Barrel:** 22", 24", 28", four screw-in choke tubes (IC, M, IM, F). **Weight:** About 7 lbs. **Length:** 42.5" to 48.5" overall, depending on barrel length. **Stock:** American walnut with satin finish; cut checkering; ventilated buttpad. Synthetic stock or camo-finish. **Sights:** Metal bead front or fiber-optic front and rear. **Features:** Ventilated rib on all models except slug gun. Imported by H&R 1871, Inc.
Price: Synthetic, black, 28" barrel, 48.5" OAL $415.00
Price: Walnut, checkered grip/forend, 28" barrel, 48.5" OAL . .$461.00
Price: Waterfowl, camo finish. $521.00
Price: Turkey, camo finish, 22" barrel, fiber optic sights. $521.00
Price: Combo, synthetic black stock, with slug barrel. $583.00

LANBER SEMI-AUTOMATIC SHOTGUNS
Gauge: 12, 3". **Barrel:** 26", 28", chrome-moly alloy steel, welded, ventilated top and side ribs. **Weight:** 6.8 lbs. **Length:** 48-3/8". **Stock:** Walnut, oiled finish, laser checkering, rubber buttplate. **Sights:** Fiber-optic front. **Features:** Extractors or automatic ejectors, control and unblocking button. Rated for steel shot. Lanber Polichokes. Imported by Lanber USA.
Price: Model 2533. . . . .$635.00

MOSSBERG 930 AUTOLOADER
Gauge: 12, 3" chamber, 4-shot magazine. **Barrel:** 24", 26", 28", over-bored to 10-gauge bore dimensions; factory ported, Accu-Choke tubes. **Weight:** 7.5 lbs. **Length:** 44.5" overall (28" barrel). **Stock:** Walnut or synthetic. Adjustable stock drop and cast spacer system. **Sights:** "Turkey Taker" fiber-optic, adjustable windage and elevation. Front bead fiber-optic front on waterfowl models. **Features:** Self-regulating gas system, dual gas-vent system and piston, EZ-Empty magazine button, cocking indicator. Interchangeable Accu-Choke tube set (IC, Mod, Full) for waterfowl and field models. XX-Full turkey Accu-Choke tube included with turkey models. Ambidextrous thumb-operated safety, Uni-line stock and receiver. Receiver drilled and tapped for scope base attachment, free gun lock. Introduced 2008. From O.F. Mossberg & Sons, Inc.
Price: Turkey, from. $545.00
Price: Waterfowl, from $545.00
Price: Combo, from $604.00
Price: Field, from. $568.00
Price: Slugster, from. $539.00
Price: Turkey Pistolgrip; full pistolgrip stock, matte black or Mossy Oak Obsession camo finish overall $628.00
Price: Tactical; 18.5" tactical barrel, black synthetic stock and matte black finish. $653.00
Price: Road Blocker; includes muzzle brake $697.00
Price: SPX; no muzzle brake, M16-style front sight, ghost ring rear sight, full pistolgrip stock, eight-round extended magazine $667.00
Price: SPX; conventional synthetic stock $700.00
Price: Home Security/Field Combo; 18.5" Cylinder bore barrel and 28" ported Field barrel; black synthetic stock and matte black finish $604.00

MOSSBERG MODEL 935 MAGNUM AUTOLOADING SHOTGUNS
Gauge: 12; 3" and 3.5" chamber, interchangeable. **Barrel:** 22", 24", 26", 28". **Weight:** 7.25 to 7.75 lbs. **Length:** 45" to 49" overall. **Stock:** Synthetic. **Features:** Gas-operated semi-auto models in blued or camo finish. Fiber optics sights, drilled and tapped receiver, interchangeable Accu-Mag choke tubes.
Price: 935 Magnum Turkey: Realtree Hardwoods, Mossy Oak New Break-up or Mossy Oak Obsession camo overall, 24" barrel $732.00
Price: 935 Magnum Turkey Pistolgrip; full pistolgrip stock . .$831.00
Price: 935 Magnum Grand Slam: 22" barrel, Realtree Hardwoods or Mossy Oak New Break-up camo overall $747.00
Price: 935 Magnum Flyway: 28" barrel and Advantage Max-4 camo overall $781.00
Price: 935 Magnum Waterfowl: 26"or 28" barrel, matte black, Mossy Oak New Break-up, Advantage Max-4 or Mossy Oak Duck Blind cam overall . . . .$613.00 to $725.00
Price: 935 Magnum Slugster: 24" fully rifled barrel, rifle sights, Realtree AP camo overall $747.00
Price: 935 Magnum Turkey/Deer Combo: interchangeable 24" Turkey barrel, Mossy Oak New Break-up camo overall $807.00
Price: 935 Magnum Waterfowl/Turkey Combo: 24" Turkey and 28" Waterfowl barrels, Mossy Oak New Break-up finish overall $807.00

REMINGTON MODEL 105 CTI SHOTGUN
Gauge: 12, 3" chamber, 4-shot magazine. **Barrel:** 26", 28" (IC, Mod., Full ProBore chokes). **Weight:** 7 lbs. **Length:** 46.25" overall (26" barrel). **Stock:** Walnut with satin finish. Checkered grip and forend. **Sights:** Front bead. **Features:** Aircraft-grade titanium receiver body, skeletonized receiver with carbon fiber shell. Bottom feed and eject, target grade trigger, R3 recoil pad, FAA-approved lockable hard case, .735" overbored barrel with lengthened forcing cones. TriNyte coating; carbon/aramid barrel rib. Introduced 2006.
Price: $1,559.00

REMINGTON MODEL SPR453 SHOTGUN
Gauge: 12; 3.5" chamber, 4+1 capacity. **Barrel:** 24", 26", 28" vent rib. **Weight:** 8 to 8.25 lbs. **Stock:** Black synthetic. **Features:** Matte finish, dual extractors, four extended screw-in SPR choke tubes (improved cylinder, modified, full and super-full turkey). Introduced 2006. From Remington Arms Co.
Price: Black synthetic $497.00

REMINGTON MODEL 11-87 SPORTSMAN SHOTGUNS
Gauge: 12, 20, 3" chamber. **Barrel:** 26", 28", RemChoke tubes. Standard contour, vent rib. **Weight:** About 7.75 to 8.25 lbs. **Length:** 46" to 48" overall. **Stock:** Black synthetic or Mossy Oak Break Up Mossy Oak Duck Blind, and Realtree Hardwoods HD and AP Green HD camo finishes. **Sights:** Single bead front. **Features:** Matte-black metal finish, magazine cap swivel studs. Sportsman Deer gun has 21-inch fully rifled barrel, cantilever scope mount.
Price: Sportsman Camo (2007), 12 or 20 ga. $879.00
Price: Sportsman black synthetic, 12 or 20 ga. $772.00
Price: Sportsman Deer FR Cantilever, 12 or 20 ga. $892.00
Price: Sportsman Youth Synthetic 20 ga., (2008). $772.00
Price: Sportsman Youth Camo 20 ga., (2008) $879.00
Price: Sportsman Super Magnum 12 ga., 28" barrel (2008). .$825.00
Price: Sportsman Super Magnum Shurshot Turkey 12 ga., (2008) $972.00
Price: Sportsman Super Magnum Waterfowl 12 ga., (2008) . .$959.00
Price: Sportsman Compact Synthetic; black synthetic but with reduced overall dimensions $772.00

Prices given are believed to be accurate at time of publication however, many factors affect retail pricing so exact prices are not possible.

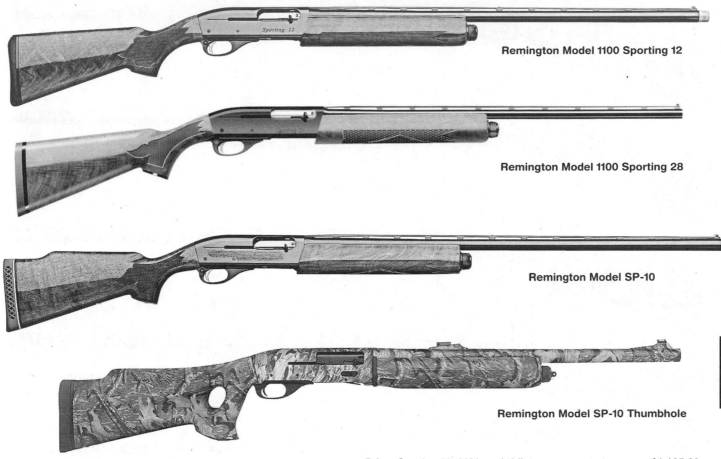

Remington Model 1100 Sporting 12

Remington Model 1100 Sporting 28

Remington Model SP-10

Remington Model SP-10 Thumbhole

REMINGTON MODEL 1100 G3 SHOTGUN

Gauge: 20, 12; 3" chamber. **Barrel:** 26", 28". **Weight:** 6.75-7.6 lbs. **Stock:** Realwood semi-Fancy carbon fiber laminate stock, high gloss finish, machine cut checkering. **Features:** Gas operating system, pressure compensated barrel, solid carbon-steel engraved receiver, titanium coating. Action bars, trigger and extended carrier release, action bar sleeve, action spring, locking block, hammer, sear and magazine tube have nickel-plated, Teflon coating. R3 recoil pad, overbored (.735" dia.) vent rib barrels, ProBore choke tubes. 20 gauge have Rem Chokes. Comes with lockable hard case. Introduced 2006.

Price: G3, 12 or 20 ga. **$1,239.00**
Price: G3 Left Hand, 12 ga. 28" barrel (2008) **$1,329.00**

REMINGTON MODEL 1100 TARGET SHOTGUNS

Gauge: .410 bore, 28, 20, 12. **Barrel:** 26", 27", 28", 30" light target contoured vent rib barrel with twin bead target sights. **Stock:** Semifancy American walnut stock and forend, cut checkering, high gloss finish. **Features:** Gold-plated trigger. Four extended choke tubes: Skeet, Improved Cylinder, Light Modified and Modified. 1100 Tournament Skeet (20 and 12 gauge) receiver is roll-marked with "Tournament Skeet." 26" light contour, vent rib barrel has twin bead sights, Extended Target Choke Tubes (Skeet and Improved Cylinder). Model 1100 Premier Sporting (2008) has polished nickel receiver, gold accents, light target contoured vent rib Rem Choke barrels. Wood is semi-fancy American walnut stock and forend, high-gloss finish, cut checkering, sporting clays-style recoil pad. Gold trigger, available in 12, 20, 28 and .410 bore options, Briley extended choke tubes, Premier Sporting hard case. Competition model (12 gauge) has overbored (0.735" bore diameter) 30" barrel. **Weight:** 8 lbs. 10mm target-style rib with twin beads. Extended ProBore choke tubes in Skeet, Improved Cylinder, Light-Modified, Modified and Full. Semi-fancy American walnut stock and forend. Classic Trap model has polished blue receiver with scroll engraving, gold accents, 30" low-profile, light-target contoured vent rib barrel with standard .727" dimensions. Comes with specialized Rem Choke trap tubes: Singles (.027"), Mid Handicap (.034"), and Long Handicap (.041"). Monte Carlo stock of semi-fancy American walnut, deep-cut checkering, high-gloss finish.

Price: Sporting 12, 28" barrel, 8 lbs. **$1,105.00**
Price: Sporting 20, 28" barrel, 7 lbs. **$1,105.00**
Price: Sporting 28, 27" barrel, 6.75 lbs. **$1,159.00**
Price: Sporting 410, 27" barrel, 6.75 lbs. **$1,159.00**
Price: Classic Trap, 12 ga. 30" barrel, ... **$1,159.00**
Price: Premier Sporting (2008), from **$1,359.00**
Price: Competition, standard stock, 12 ga. 30" barrel **$1,692.00**
Price: Competition, adjustable comb **$1,692.00**

Remington Model 1100 TAC-4

Similar to Model 1100 but with 18" or 22" barrel with ventilated rib; 12 gauge 2-3/4"only; standard black synthetic stock or Knoxx SpecOps SpeedFeed IV pistolgrip stock; RemChoke tactical choke tube; matte black finish overall. Length is 42-1/2" and weighs 7-3/4 lbs.
Price: **$945.00**

REMINGTON MODEL SP-10 MAGNUM SHOTGUN

Gauge: 10, 3-1/2" chamber, 2-shot magazine. **Barrel:** 23", 26", 30" (full and mod. RemChokes). **Weight:** 10.75 to 11 lbs. **Length:** 47.5" overall (26" barrel). **Stock:** Walnut with satin finish (30" barrel) or camo synthetic (26" barrel). Checkered grip and forend. **Sights:** Twin bead. **Features:** Stainless steel gas system with moving cylinder; 3/8" vent rib. Receiver and barrel have matte finish. Brown recoil pad. Comes with padded Cordura nylon sling. Introduced 1989. SP-10 Magnum Camo has buttstock, forend, receiver, barrel and magazine cap covered with Mossy Oak Duck Blind Obsession camo finish; bolt body and trigger guard have matte black finish. RemChoke tube, 26" vent rib barrel with mid-rib bead and Bradley-style front sight, swivel studs and quick-detachable swivels, non-slip Cordura carrying sling. Introduced 1993.
Price: SP-10 Magnum, satin finish walnut stock **$1,772.00**
Price: SP-10 Magnum Full Camo **$1,932.00**
Price: SP-10 Magnum Waterfowl **$1,945.00**

SAIGA AUTOLOADING SHOTGUN

Gauge: 12, 20, .410; 3" chamber. **Barrel:** 19", 24". **Weight:** 7.9 lbs. **Length: Stock:** Black synthetic. **Sights:** Fixed or adjustable leaf. **Features:** Magazine fed, 2- or 5-round capacity. Imported from Russia by Russian American Armory Co.
Price: **$347.95**

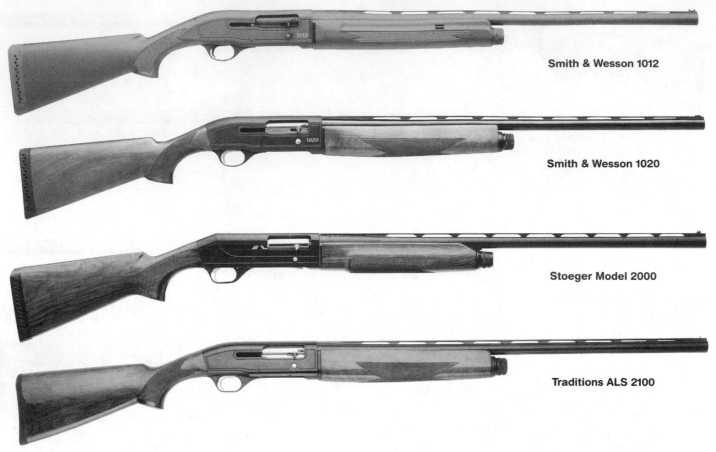

Smith & Wesson 1012

Smith & Wesson 1020

Stoeger Model 2000

Traditions ALS 2100

SMITH & WESSON 1000/1020/1012 SUPER SEMI-AUTO SHOTGUNS

Gauge: 12, 20; 3" in 1000; 3-1/2" chamber in Super. **Barrel:** 24", 26", 28", 30". **Stock:** Walnut. Synthetic finishes are satin, black, Realtree MAX-4, Realtree APG. **Sights:** TruGlo fiber-optic. **Features:** 29 configurations. Gas operated, dual-piston action; chrome-lined barrels, five choke tubes, shim kit for adjusting stock. 20-ga. models are Model 1020 or Model 1020SS (short stock). Lifetime warranty. Introduced 2007. Imported from Turkey by Smith & Wesson.
Price: From **$623.00**

STOEGER MODEL 2000 SHOTGUNS

Gauge: 12, 3" chamber, set of five choke tubes (C, IC, M, F, XFT). **Barrel:** 24", 26", 28", 30". **Stock:** Walnut, synthetic, Timber HD, Max-4. **Sights:** Red bar front. **Features:** Inertia-recoil. Minimum recommended load: 3 dram, 1-1/8 oz. Imported by Benelli USA.
Price: Walnut **$499.00**
Price: Synthetic. **$499.00**
Price: Max-4 . . . . **$549.00**
Price: Black synthetic pistol grip (2007) **$499.00**
Price: APG HD camo pistol grip (2007), 18.5" barrel **$549.00**

TRISTAR VIPER SEMI-AUTOMATIC SHOTGUNS

Gauge: 12, 20; shoots 2-3/4" or 3" interchangeably. **Barrel:** 26", 28" barrels (carbon fiber only of-fered in 12-ga. 28" and 20-ga. 26"). **Stock:** Wood, black synthetic, Mossy Oak Duck Blind camouflage, faux carbon fiber finish (2008) with the new Comfort Touch technology. **Features:** Magazine cut-off, vent rib with matted sight plane, brass front bead (camo models have fiber-optic front sight), five round magazine-shot plug included, and 3 Beretta-style choke tubes (IC, M, F). Viper synthetic, Viper camo have swivel studs. Five-year warranty. Viper Youth models have shortened length of pull and 24" barrel. Imported by Tristar Sporting Arms Ltd.
Price: From **$469.00**
Price: Camo models (2008), from **$569.00**

TRADITIONS ALS 2100 SERIES SEMI-AUTOMATIC SHOTGUNS

Gauge: 12, 3" chamber; 20, 3" chamber. **Barrel:** 24", 26", 28" (Imp. Cyl., Mod. and Full choke tubes). **Weight:** 5 lbs., 10 oz. to 6 lbs., 5 oz. **Length:** 44" to 48" overall. **Stock:** Walnut or black composite. **Features:** Gas-operated; vent rib barrel with Beretta-style threaded muzzle. Introduced 2001 by Traditions.
Price: Field Model (12 or 20 ga., 26" or 28" bbl., walnut stock) **$479.00**
Price: Youth Model (12 or 20 ga., 24" bbl., walnut stock) **$479.00**
Price: (12 or 20 ga., 26" or 28" barrel, composite stock) **$459.00**

Traditions ALS 2100 Turkey Semi-Automatic Shotgun

Similar to ALS 2100 Field Model except chambered in 12 gauge, 3" only with 26" barrel and Mossy Oak Break Up camo finish. Weighs 6 lbs.; 46" overall.
Price: **$519.00**

Traditions ALS 2100 Waterfowl Semi-Automatic Shotgun

Similar to ALS 2100 Field Model except chambered in 12 gauge, 3" only with 28" barrel and Advantage Wetlands camo finish. Weighs 6.25 lbs.; 48" overall. Multi chokes.
Price: **$529.00**

Traditions ALS 2100 Hunter Combo

Similar to ALS 2100 Field Model except 2 barrels, 28" vent rib and 24" fully rifled deer. Weighs 6 to 6.5 lbs.; 48" overall. Choice TruGlo adj. sights or fixed cantilever mount on rifled barrel. Multi chokes.
Price: Walnut, rifle barrel **$609.00**
Price: Walnut, cantilever. **$629.00**
Price: Synthetic. **$579.00**

Traditions ALS 2100 Slug Hunter Shotgun

Similar to ALS 2100 Field Model, 12 ga., 24" barrel, overall length 44"; weighs 6.25 lbs. Designed specifically for the deer hunter. Rifled barrel has 1 in 36" twist. Fully adjustable fiber-optic sights.
Price: Walnut, rifle barrel **$529.00**
Price: Synthetic, rifle barrel. **$499.00**
Price: Walnut, cantilever. **$549.00**
Price: Synthetic, cantilever **$529.00**

Traditions ALS 2100 Home Security Shotgun

Similar to ALS 2100 Field Model, 12 ga., 20" barrel, overall length 40", weighs 6 lbs. Can be reloaded with one hand while shouldered and ontarget. Swivel studs installed in stock.
Price: **$399.00**

Prices given are believed to be accurate at time of publication however, many factors affect retail pricing so exact prices are not possible.

Winchester Super X3 Waterfowl

Winchester X2 NWTF Turkey

Winchester Super X2 Sporting Clays

VERONA MODEL 401 SERIES SEMI-AUTO SHOTGUNS
Gauge: 12. **Barrel:** 26", 28". **Weight:** 6.5 lbs. **Stock:** Walnut, black composite. **Sights:** Red dot. **Features:** Aluminum receivers, gas-operated, 2-3/4" or 3" Magnum shells without adj. or Mod., 4 screw-in chokes and wrench included. Sling swivels, gold trigger. Blued barrel. Imported from Italy by Legacy Sports International.
Price: **$1,199.00**
Price: 406 Series **$1,199.00**

WINCHESTER SUPER X3 SHOTGUNS
Gauge: 12, 3" and 3.5" chambers. **Barrel:** 26", 28", .742" back-bored; Invector Plus choke tubes. **Weight:** 7 to 7.25 lbs. **Stock:** Composite, 14.25"x1.75"x2". Mossy Oak New Break-Up camo with Dura-Touch Armor Coating. Pachmayr Decelerator buttpad with hard heel insert, customizable length of pull. **Features:** Alloy magazine tube, gunmetal grey Perma-Cote UT finish, self-adjusting Active Valve gas action, lightweight recoil spring system. Electroless nickel-plated bolt, three choke tubes, two length-of-pull stock spacers, drop and cast adjustment spacers, sling swivel studs. Introduced 2006. Made in Belgium, assembled in Portugal by U.S. Repeating Arms Co.
Price: Composite . . . . **$1,119.00 to $1,239.00**
Price: Cantilever Deer. **$1,179.00**
Price: Waterfowl w/Mossy Oak Brush camo, intr. 2007 . . . . **$1,439.00**
Price: Field model, walnut stock, Intr. 2007 . . . . **$1,439.00**
Price: Gray Shadow **$1,299.00**
Price: All-Purpose Field **$1,439.00**

Price: Classic Field **$1,159.00**
Price: NWTF Cantiliever Extreme Turkey **$1,499.00**

WINCHESTER SUPER X3 FLANIGUN EXHIBITION/SPORTING
Similar to X3 but .742" backbored barrel, red-toned receiver, black Dura-Touch Armor Coated synthetic stock.
Price: **$1,459.00**

WINCHESTER SUPER X2 AUTO SHOTGUNS
Gauge: 12, 3", 3-1/2" chamber. **Barrel:** Belgian, 24", 26", 28"; Invector Plus choke tubes. **Weight:** 7-1/4 to 7.5 lbs. **Stock:** 14.25"x1.75"x2". Walnut or black synthetic. **Features:** Gas-operated action shoots all loads without adjustment; vent rib barrels; 4-shot magazine. Introduced 1999. Assembled in Portugal by U.S. Repeating Arms Co.
Price: Universal Hunter T **$1,252.00**
Price: NWTF Turkey, 3-1/2", Mossy Oak Break-Up camo . . **$1,236.00**
Price: Universal Hunter Model **$1,252.00**

Winchester Super X2 Sporting Clays Auto Shotguns
Similar to the Super X2 except has two gas pistons (one for target loads, one for heavy 3" loads), adjustable comb system and high-post rib. Back-bored barrel with Invector Plus choke tubes. Offered in 28" and 30" barrels. Introduced 2001. From U.S. Repeating Arms Co.
Price: Super X2 sporting clays **$999.00**
Price: Signature red stock. **$1,015.00**
Price: Practical MK I, composite stock, TruGlo sights **$1,116.00**

Includes a wide variety of sporting guns and guns suitable for competitive shooting.

Benelli Nova Pump

Benelli Nova Pump Slug

Browning BPS Trap

Browning BPS Rifled Deer
Mossy Oak New Break-Up

Browning BPS Micro Trap

BENELLI SUPERNOVA PUMP SHOTGUNS
Gauge: 12; 3.5" chamber. **Barrel:** 24", 26", 28". **Length:** 45.5-49.5". **Stock:** Synthetic; Max-4 , Timber, APG HD (2007). **Sights:** Red bar front, metal midbead. **Features:** 2-3/4", 3" chamber (3-1/2" 12 ga. only). Montefeltro rotating bolt design with dual action bars, magazine cut-off, synthetic trigger assembly, adjustable combs, shim kit, choice of buttstocks. 4-shot magazine. Introduced 2006. Imported from Italy by Benelli USA.
Price: Synthetic ComforTech $499.00
Price: Camo ComforTech $599.00
Price: SteadyGrip . . . .$599.00 to $619.00
Price: Tactical, Ghost Ring sight. . . . .$459.00 to $499.00
Price: Rifled Slug ComforTech, synthetic stock (2007) $670.00
Price: Tactical desert camo pistol grip, 18" barrel (2007). $589.00

BENELLI NOVA PUMP SHOTGUNS
Gauge: 12, 20. **Barrel:** 24", 26", 28". **Stock:** Black synthetic, Max-4, Timber and APG HD. **Sights:** Red bar. **Features:** 2-3/ 4", 3" chamber (3-1/2" 12 ga. only). Montefeltro rotating bolt design with dual action bars, magazine cut-off, synthetic trigger assembly, 4-shot magazine. Introduced 1999. Field & Slug Combo has 24" barrel and rifled bore; open rifle sights; synthetic stock; weighs 8.1 lbs. Imported from Italy by Benelli USA.
PrPrice: Max-4 HD camo stock $499.00
Price: H₂0 model, black synthetic, matte nickel finish. $599.00
Price: APG HD stock , 20 ga. (2007) $529.00
Price: Tactical, 18.5" barrel, Ghost Ring sight $429.00
Price: Black synthetic youth stock, 20 ga. $429.00
Price: APG HD stock (2007), 20 ga. $529.00

BROWNING BPS PUMP SHOTGUNS
Gauge: 10, 12, 3-1/2" chamber; 12, 16, or 20, 3" chamber (2-3/4" in target guns), 28, 2-3/4" cham-ber, 5-shot magazine, .410, 3" chamber. **Barrel:** 10 ga.-24" Buck Special, 28", 30", 32" Invector; 12, 20 ga.-22", 24", 26", 28", 30", 32" (Imp. Cyl., Mod. or Full), .410-26" barrel. (Imp. Cyl., Mod.

and Full choke tubes.) Also available with Invector choke tubes, 12 or 20 ga.; Upland Special has 22" barrel with Invector tubes. BPS 3" and 3-1/2" have back-bored barrel. **Weight:** 7 lbs., 8 oz. (28" barrel). **Length:** 48.75" overall (28" barrel). **Stock:** 14.25"x1.5"x2.5". Select walnut, semi-beavertail forend, full pistol grip stock. **Features:** All 12 gauge 3" guns except Buck Special and game guns have back-bored barrels with Invector Plus choke tubes. Bottom feeding and ejection, receiver top safety, high post vent rib. Double action bars eliminate binding. Vent rib barrels only. All 12 and 20 gauge guns with 3" chamber available with fully engraved receiver flats at no extra cost. Each gauge has its own unique game scene. Introduced 1977. Stalker is same gun as the standard BPS except all exposed metal parts have a matte blued finish and the stock has a black finish with a black recoil pad. Available in 10 ga. (3-1/2") and 12 ga. with 3" or 3-1/2" chamber, 22", 28", 30" barrel with In-vector choke system. Introduced 1987. Rifled Deer Hunter is similar to the standard BPS except has newly designed receiver/magazine tube/barrel mounting system to eliminate play, heavy 20.5" barrel with rifle-type sights with adjustable rear, solid receiver scope mount, "rifle" stock dimensions for scope or open sights, sling swivel studs. Gloss or matte finished wood with checkering, polished blue metal. Introduced 1992. Imported from Japan by Browning.
Price: Stalker (black syn. stock), 12 ga., from $549.00
Price: Rifled Deer Hunter (22" rifled bbl., cantilever mount),
    intr. 2007. . . . .$699.00
Price: Trap, intr. 2007. . . . .$729.00
Price: Hunter, 16 ga., intr. 2008 . . . .$569.00
Price: Upland Special, 16 ga., intr. 2008 . . . .$569.00
Price: Mossy Oak New Breakup, 3", 12 ga. only $679.00
Price: Mossy Oak New Breakup, 3-1/2", 12 ga. only $799.00
Price: Mossy Oak Duck Blind finish overall, 3" $679.00
Price: Mossy Oak Duck Blind finish overall, 3-1/2" $799.00
Price: Rifled Deer Mossy Oak New Break-Up, 12 ga. $719.00
Price: Rifled Deer Mossy Oak New Break-Up, 20 ga. $839.00
Price: Micro Trap, similar to BPS Trap but with compact
    dimensions (13-3/4" length of pull, 48-1/4" overall
    length), 12 gauge only $729.00

Prices given are believed to be accurate at time of publication however, many factors affect retail pricing so exact prices are not possible.

SHOTGUNS—Slide & Lever Actions

Browning BPS 10 gauge Mossy Oak Shadow Grass

Browning BPS 10 gauge

Charles Daly Maxi-Mag Turkey

Escort AimGuard

Escort Field Hunter

Browning BPS 10 Gauge Camo Pump Shotgun
Similar to the standard BPS except completely covered with Mossy Oak Shadow Grass camouflage. Available with 26" and 28" barrel. Introduced 1999. Imported by Browning
Price: $799.00

Browning BPS NWTF Turkey Series Pump Shotgun
Similar to the standard BPS except has full coverage Mossy Oak Break-Up camo finish on synthetic stock, forearm and exposed metal parts. Offered in 12 gauge, 3" or 3-1/2" chamber; 24" bbl. has extra-full choke tube and HiViz fiber-optic sights. Introduced 2001. From Browning.
Price: 12 ga., 3-1/2" chamber $859.00
Price: 12 ga., 3" chamber $709.00

Browning BPS Micro Pump Shotgun
Similar to the BPS Stalker except 20 ga. only, 22" Invector barrel, stock has pistol grip with recoil pad. Length of pull is 13.25"; weighs 6 lbs., 12 oz. Introduced 1986.
Price: $569.00

CHARLES DALY FIELD PUMP SHOTGUNS
Gauge: 12, 20. **Barrel:** Interchangeable 18.5", 24", 26", 28", 30" multi-choked. **Weight:** NA. **Stock:** Synthetic, various finishes, recoil pad. **Receiver:** Machined aluminum. **Features:** Field Tactical and Slug models come with adustable sights; Youth models may be upgraded to full size. Imported from Turkey by K.B.I., Inc.
Price: Field Tactical $274.00
Price: Field Hunter $499.00
Price: Field Hunter, Realtree Hardwood $289.00
Price: Field Hunter Advantage $289.00

CHARLES DALY MAXI-MAG PUMP SHOTGUNS
Gauge: 12 gauge, 3-1/2". **Barrel:** 24", 26", 28"; multi-choke system. **Weight:** NA. **Stock:** Synthetic black, Realtree Hardwoods, or Advantage Timber receiver, aluminum alloy. **Features:** Handles 2-3/4", 3" and 3-1/2" loads. Interchangeable ported barrels; Turkey package includes sling, HiViz sights, XX Full choke. Imported from Turkey by K.B.I., Inc.
Price: Field Hunter $329.00
Price: Field Hunter Advantage $319.00
Price: Field Hunter Hardwoods $319.00
Price: Field Hunter Turkey $434.00

EMF OLD WEST PUMP (SLIDE ACTION) SHOTGUN
Gauge: 12. **Barrel:** 20". **Weight:** 7 lbs. **Length:** 39-1/2" overall. **Stock:** Smooth walnut with cushioned pad. **Sights:** Front bead. **Features:** Authentic reproduction of Winchester 1897 pump shotgun; blue receiver and barrel; standard modified choke. Introduced 2006. Imported from China for EMF by TTN.
Price: $449.90

ESCORT PUMP SHOTGUNS
Gauge: 12, 20; 3" chamber. **Barrel:** 18" (AimGuard and MarineGuard), 22" (Youth Pump), 26", and 28" lengths. **Weight:** 6.7-7.0 lbs. **Stock:** Polymer in black, Shadow Grass® camo or Obsession® camo finish. Two adjusting spacers included. Youth model has Trio recoil pad. **Sights:** Bead or Spark front sights, depending on model. AimGuard and MarineGuard models have blade front sights. **Features:** Black-chrome or dipped camo metal parts, top of receiver dovetailed for sight mounts, gold plated trigger, trigger guard safety, magazine cut-off. Three choke tubes (IC, M, F) except AimGuard/MarineGuard which are cylinder bore. Models include: FH, FH Youth, AimGuard and Marine Guard. Introduced in 2003. Imported from Turkey by Legacy Sports International.
Price: . . . .$389.00 to $469.00

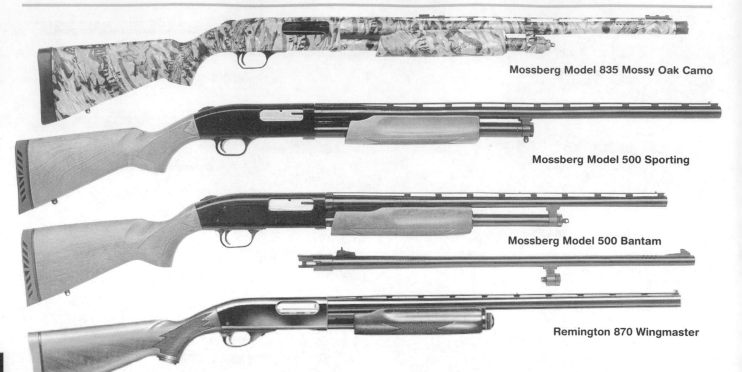

Mossberg Model 835 Mossy Oak Camo

Mossberg Model 500 Sporting

Mossberg Model 500 Bantam

Remington 870 Wingmaster

HARRINGTON & RICHARDSON PARDNER PUMP FIELD GUN FULL-DIP CAMO

Gauge: 12, 20; 3" chamber. **Barrel:** 28" fully rifled. **Weight:** 7.5 lbs. **Length:** 48-1/8" overall. **Stock:** Synthetic or hardwood. **Sights:** NA. **Features:** Steel receiver, double action bars, cross-bolt safety, easy take-down, vent rib, screw-in Modified choke tube. Ventilated recoil pad and grooved forend with Realtree APG-HDTM full camo dip finish.

Price: Full camo version $278.00

IAC MODEL 87W-1 LEVER-ACTION SHOTGUN

Gauge: 12; 2-3/4" chamber only. **Barrel:** 20" with fixed Cylinder choke. **Weight:** NA. **Length:** NA. **Stock:** American walnut. **Sights:** Bead front. **Features:** Modern replica of Winchester Model 1887 lever-action shotgun. Includes five-shot tubular magazine, pivoting split-lever design to meet modern safety requirements. Imported by Interstate Arms Corporation.

Price: $429.95

ITHACA GUN COMPANY DEERSLAYER III SLUG SHOTGUN

Gauge: 12, 20; 3" chamber. **Barrel:** 26" fully rifled, heavy fluted with 1:28 twist for 12 ga.; 1:24 for 20 ga. **Weight:** 8.14 lbs. to 9.5 lbs. with scope mounted. **Length:** 45.625" overall. **Stock:** Fancy black walnut stock and forend. **Sights:** NA. **Features:** Updated, slug-only version of the classic Model 37. Bottom ejection, blued barrel and receiver.

Price: $1,189.00

ITHACA GUN COMPANY MODEL 37 28 GAUGE SHOTGUN

Gauge: 28. **Barrel:** 26" or 28". **Weight:** NA. **Length:** NA. **Stock:** Black walnut stock and forend. **Sights:** NA. **Features:** Scaled down receiver with traditional Model 37 bottom ejection and easy takedown. Available in Fancy "A," Fancy "AA," and Fancy "AAA" grades with increasingly elaborate receiver engraving and decoration. Special order only.

Price: Fancy "A" grade $999.00

MOSSBERG MODEL 835 ULTI-MAG PUMP SHOTGUNS

Gauge: 12, 3-1/2" chamber. **Barrel:** Ported 24" rifled bore, 24", 28", Accu-Mag choke tubes for steel or lead shot. **Weight:** 7.75 lbs. **Length:** 48.5" overall. **Stock:** 14"x1.5"x2.5". Dual Comb. Cut-checkered hardwood or camo synthetic; both have recoil pad. **Sights:** White bead front, brass mid-bead; fiber-optic rear. **Features:** Shoots 2-3/4", 3" or 3-1/2" shells. Back-bored and ported barrel to reduce recoil, improve patterns. Ambidextrous thumb safety, twin extractors, dual slide bars. Mossberg Cablelock included. Introduced 1988.

Price: Thumbhole Turkey $674.00
Price: Tactical Turkey $636.00
Price: Synthetic Thumbhole Turkey, from $493.00

Price: Turkey, from $487.00
Price: Waterfowl, from $437.00
Price: Combo, from $559.00

MOSSBERG MODEL 500 SPORTING PUMP SHOTGUNS

Gauge: 12, 20, .410, 3" chamber. **Barrel:** 18.5" to 28" with fixed or Accu-Choke, plain or vent rib. **Weight:** 6-1/4 lbs. (.410), 7-1/4 lbs. (12). **Length:** 48" overall (28" barrel). **Stock:** 14"x1.5"x2.5". Walnut-stained hardwood, black synthetic, Mossy Oak Advantage camouflage. Cut-checkered grip and forend. **Sights:** White bead front, brass mid-bead; fiber-optic. **Features:** Ambidextrous thumb safety, twin extractors, disconnecting safety, dual action bars. Quiet Carry forend. Many barrels are ported. From Mossberg.

Price: Turkey............................$410.00
Price: Waterfowl, from $406.00
Price: Combo, from............................$391.00
Price: Field, from............................$354.00
Price: Slugster, from............................$354.00

Mossberg Model 500 Bantam Pump Shotgun

Same as the Model 500 Sporting Pump except 12 or 20 gauge, 22" vent rib Accu-Choke barrel with choke tube set; has 1" shorter stock, reduced length from pistol grip to trigger, reduced forend reach. Introduced 1992.

Price: $354.00
Price: Super Bantam (2008), from $338.00

NEW ENGLAND PARDNER PUMP SHOTGUN

Gauge: 12 ga., 3". **Barrel:** 28" vent rib, screw-in Modified choke tube. **Weight:** 7.5 lbs. **Length:** 48.5". **Stock:** American walnut, grooved forend, ventilated recoil pad. **Sights:** Bead front. **Features:** Machined steel receiver, double action bars, five-shot magazine.

Price: $200.00

REMINGTON MODEL 870 WINGMASTER SHOTGUNS

Gauge: 12, 20, 28 ga., .410 bore. **Barrel:** 25", 26", 28", 30" (RemChokes). **Weight:** 7-1/4 lbs. **Length:** 46", 48". **Stock:** Walnut, hardwood. **Sights:** Single bead (Twin bead Wingmaster). **Features:** Light contour barrel. Double action bars, cross-bolt safety, blue finish. LW is 28 gauge and .410-bore only, 25" vent rib barrel with RemChoke tubes, high-gloss wood finish. Limited Edition Model 870 Wingmaster 100th Anniversary Commemorative Edition (2008 only) is 12 gauge with gold centennial logo, "100 Years of Remington Pump Shotguns" banner. Gold-plated trigger, American B Grade walnut stock and forend, high-gloss finish, fleur-de-lis checkering.

Price: Wingmaster, walnut, blued $785.00
Price: LW .410-bore $839.00
Price: 100th Anniversary (2008), 12 ga., 28" barrel $1,035.00

Prices given are believed to be accurate at time of publication however, many factors affect retail pricing so exact prices are not possible.

SHOTGUNS—Slide & Lever Actions

Remington Model 870 Windmaster LW

Remington Model 870 Marine Magnum

Remington Model 870 Express Deer Gun

Remington Model 870 Express Turkey Gun

Remington Model 870 Express Youth Turkey Gun

Remington Model 870 Express Compact Camo

Remington Model 870 Marine Magnum Shotgun

Similar to 870 Wingmaster except all metal plated with electroless nickel, black synthetic stock and forend. Has 18" plain barrel (cyl.), bead front sight, 7-shot magazine. Introduced 1992. XCS version with TriNyte corrosion control introduced 2007.

Price: **$772.00**

Remington Model 870 Classic Trap Shotgun

Similar to Model 870 Wingmaster except has 30" vent rib, light contour barrel, singles, mid- and long-handicap choke tubes, semi-fancy American walnut stock, high-polish blued receiver with engraving. Chamber 2.75". From Remington Arms Co.

Price: **$1,039.00**
Price: XCS (2007) **$899.00**

Remington Model 870 Express Shotguns

Similar to Model 870 Wingmaster except laminate, syn-thetic black, or camo stock with solid, black recoil pad and pressed checkering on grip and forend. Out-side metal surfaces have black oxide finish. Comes with 26" or 28" vent rib barrel with mod. RemChoke tube. ShurShot Turkey (2008) has ShurShot synthetic pistol-grip thumbhole design, extended forend, Mossy Oak Obsession camouflage, matte black met-al finish, 21" vent rib barrel, twin beads, Turkey Extra Full Rem Choke tube. Receiver drilled and tapped for mounting optics. ShurShot FR CL

(Fully Rifled Cantilever, 2008) includes compact 23" fully-rifled barrel with integrated cantilever scope mount.

Price: 12 and 20 ga., laminate or synthetic right-hand stock . . **$383.00**
Price: 12 or 20 ga., laminate or synthetic left-hand stock **$409.00**
Price: Express Synthetic, 12 ga., 18" barrel (2007) **$383.00**
Price: Express Synthetic, 20 ga., 7 round capacity, from **$385.00**
Price: Express Synthetic Deer FR 12 ga., rifle sights **$425.00**
Price: Express Laminate Deer FR 12 ga., rifle sights **$416.00**
Price: Express Synthetic or Laminate Turkey 12 ga.,
21" barrel **$388.00**
Price: Express Camo Turkey 12 ga., 21" barrel **$445.00**
Price: Express Combo Turkey/Deer Camo 12 ga. **$612.00**
Price: Express Synthetic Youth Combo 20 ga. **$543.00**
Price: Express Magnum ShurShot Turkey (2008) **$492.00**
Price: Express Magnum ShurShot FR CL (2008) **$500.00**
Price: Express ShurShot Synthetic Cantilever; 12 or 20 ga.
with ShurShot stock and cantilever scope mount **$532.00**
Price: Express Compact Deer; 20 ga., similar to 870 Express
Laminate Deer but with smaller dimensions **$395.00**
Price: Express Compact Pink Camo; 20 ga. **$429.00**
Price: Express Compact Synthetic; matte black synthetic
stock **$383.00**
Price: Express Compact Camo; camo buttstock and forend . **$429.00**
Price: Express Compact Jr.; Shorter barrel and LOP **$383.00**

Remington Model 870 Express
Super Magnum

Remington Model 870 Express Tactical

Remington Model 870 Express Tactical
with Ghost Ring Sights

Remington Model 870 SPS Shurshot
Synthetic Super Slug

Remington Model 870 Express Super Magnum Shotgun
Similar to Model 870 Express except 28" vent rib barrel with 3-1/2" chamber, vented recoil pad. Introduced 1998. Model 870 Express Super Magnum Waterfowl (2008) is fully camouflaged with Mossy Oak Duck Blind pattern, 28-inch vent rib Rem Choke barrel, "Over Decoys" Choke tube (.007") fiber-optic HiViz single bead front sight; front and rear sling swivel studs, padded black sling.
Price: **$431.00**
Price: Super Magnum synthetic, 26" **$431.00**
Price: Super Magnum turkey camo (full-coverage
RealTree Advantage camo), 23" **$564.00**
Price: Super Magnum combo (26" with Mod. RemChoke
and 20" fully rifled deer barrel with 3" chamber
and rifle sights; wood stock) **$577.00**
Price: Super Magnum Waterfowl (2008). **$577.00**

Remington Model 870 Special Purpose Shotguns (SPS)
Similar to the Model 870 Express synthetic, chambered for 12 ga. 3" and 3-1/2" shells, has Realtree Hardwoods HD or APG HD camo-synthetic stock and metal treatment, TruGlo fiber-optic sights. Intro-duced 2001. SPS Max Gobbler introduced 2007. Knoxx SpecOps adjustable stock, Williams Fire Sights fiber-optic sights, R3 recoil pad, Realtree APG HD camo. Drilled and tapped for Weaver-style rail
Price: SPS 12 ga. 3" **$671.00**
Price: SPS Super Mag Max Gobbler (2007). **$819.00**

Price: SPS Super Mag Max Turkey ShurShot 3-1/2" (2008) . . **$644.00**
Price: SPS Synthetic ShurShot FR Cantilever 3" (2008) **$671.00**

Remington Model 870 Express Tactical
Similar to Model 870 but in 12 gauge only (2-2/4" and 3" interchange-ably) with 18.5" barrel, Tactical RemChoke extended/ported choke tube, black synthetic buttstock and forend, extended magazine tube, gray powdercoat finish overall. 38.5" overall length, weighs 7.5 lbs.
Price: **$372.00**
Price: Model 870 TAC Desert Recon; desert camo stock and
sand-toned metal surfaces **$692.00**
Price: Model 870 Express Tactical with Ghost Ring Sights; Top-
mounted accessories rail and XS ghost ring rear sight **$505.00**

REMINGTON MODEL 870 SPS SHURSHOT SYNTHETIC SUPER SLUG
Gauge: 12; 2-3/4" and 3" chamber, interchangeable. **Barrel:** 25.5" extra-heavy, fully rifled pinned to receiver. **Weight:** 7-7/8 lbs. **Length:** 47" overall. **Features:** Pump-action model based on 870 platform. SuperCell recoil pad. Drilled and tapped for scope mounts with Weaver rail included. Matte black metal surfaces, Mossy Oak Treestand Shurshot buttstock and forend.
Price: . . . . **NA**
Price: 870 SPS ShurShot Synthetic Cantilever; cantilever scope mount
and Realtree Hardwoods camo buttstock and forend . **$532.00**
Price: 870 SPS ShurShot Synthetic Turkey; adjustable sights and APG
HD camo buttstock and forend **$532.00**

Prices given are believed to be accurate at time of publication however, many factors affect retail pricing so exact prices are not possible.

Remington Model 887 Nitro Mag Pump

Remington Model 887 Nitro Mag Pump Waterfowl

Winchester Super X Pump Black Shadow Field

Winchester Super X Pump Defender

REMINGTON MODEL 887 NITRO MAG PUMP SHOTGUN
Gauge: 12; 3.5", 3", and 2-3/4" chambers. **Barrel:** 28". **Features:** Pump-action model based on the Model 870. Interchangeable shells, black matte ArmoLokt rustproof coating throughout. SuperCell recoil pad. Solid rib and Hi-Viz front sight with interchangeable light tubes. Black synthetic stock with contoured grip panels.
Price: **$399.00**
Price: Model 887 Nitro Mag Waterfowl, Advantage
Max-4 camo overall **$532.00**

STOEGER MODEL P350 SHOTGUNS
Gauge: 12, 3.5" chamber, set of five choke tubes (C, IC, M, IM, XF). **Barrel:** 18.5",24", 26", 28". **Stock:** Black synthetic, Timber HD, Max-4 HD, APG HD camos. **Sights:** Red bar front. **Features:** Inertia-recoil, mercury recoil reducer, pistol grip stocks. Imported by Benelli USA.
Price: Synthetic. **$329.00**
Price: Max-4, Timber HD **$429.00**
Price: Black synthetic pistol grip (2007) **$329.00**
Price: APG HD camo pistol grip (2007) **$429.00**

WINCHESTER SUPER X PUMP SHOTGUNS
Gauge: 12, 3" chambers. **Barrel:** 18"; 26" and 28" barrels are .742" back-bored, chrome plated; Invector Plus choke tubes. **Weight:** 7 lbs. **Stock:** Walnut or composite. **Features:** Rotary bolt, four lugs, dual steel action bars. Walnut Field has gloss-finished walnut stock and forearm, cut checkering. Black Shadow Field has composite stock and forearm, non-glare matte finish barrel and receiver. Speed Pump Defender has composite stock and forearm, chromed plated, 18" cylinder choked barrel, non-glare metal surfaces, five-shot magazine, grooved forearm. Weight, 6.5 lbs. Reintroduced 2008. Made in U.S.A. from Winchester Repeating Arms Co.
Price: Black Shadow Field **$359.00**
Price: Defender. **$319.00**

Includes a variety of game guns and guns for competitive shooting.

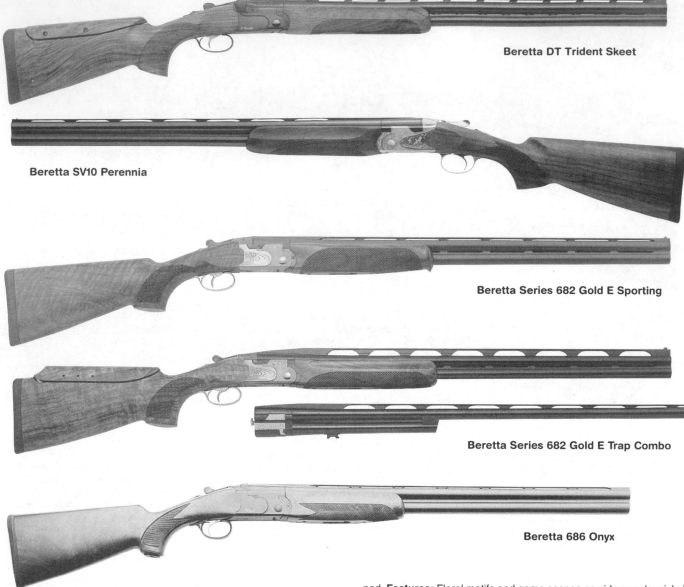

Beretta DT Trident Skeet

Beretta SV10 Perennia

Beretta Series 682 Gold E Sporting

Beretta Series 682 Gold E Trap Combo

Beretta 686 Onyx

BERETTA DT10 TRIDENT SHOTGUNS
Gauge: 12, 2-3/4", 3" chambers. **Barrel:** 28", 30", 32", 34"; competition-style vent rib; fixed or Optima choke tubes. **Weight:** 7.9 to 9 lbs. **Stock:** High-grade walnut stock with oil finish; hand-checkered grip and forend, adjustable stocks available. **Features:** Detachable, adjustable trigger group, raised and thickened receiver, forend iron has adjustment nut to guarantee wood-to-metal fit. Introduced 2000. Imported from Italy by Beretta USA.
Price: DT10 Trident Trap, adjustable stock. **$7,400.00**
Price: DT10 Trident Skeet **$7,900.00**
Price: DT10 Trident Sporting, from. **$6,975.00**

BERETTA SV10 PERENNIA O/U SHOTGUN
Gauge: 12, 3" chambers. **Barrel:** 26", 28", 30". Optima-Bore profile, polished blue. Bore diameter 18.6mm (0.73 in.) Self-adjusting dual conical longitudinal locking lugs, oversized monobloc bearing shoulders, replaceable hinge pins. Ventilated top rib, 6x6mm. Long guided extractors, automatic ejection or mechanical extraction. Optimachoke tubes. **Weight:** 7.3 lbs. **Stock:** Quick take-down stock with pistol grip or English straight stock. Kick-off recoil reduction system available on request on Q-Stock. **Length of pull:** 14.7", drop at comb, 1.5", drop at heel, 2.36" or 1.38"/2.17". Semibeavertail forend with elongated forend lever. New checkering pattern, matte oil finish, rubber

pad. **Features:** Floral motifs and game scenes on side panels; nickel-based protective finish, arrowhead-shaped sideplates, solid steel alloy billet. Kick-Off recoil reduction mechanism available on select models. Fixed chokes on request, removable trigger group, titanium single selective trigger. Manual or automatic safety, newly designed safety and selector lever. Gel-Tek recoil pad available on re-quest. Polypropylene case, 5 chokes with spanner, sling swivels, plastic pad, Beretta gun oil. In-troduced 2008. Imported from Italy by Beretta USA.
Price: From **$3,250.00**

BERETTA SERIES 682 GOLD E SKEET, TRAP, SPORTING O/U SHOTGUNS
Gauge: 12, 2-3/4" chambers. **Barrel:** skeet-28"; trap-30" and 32", Imp. Mod. & Full and Mobilchoke; trap mono shotguns-32" and 34" Mobilchoke; trap top single guns-32" and 34" Full and Mobilchoke; trap combo sets-from 30" O/U, to 32" O/U, 34" top single. **Stock:** Close-grained walnut, hand checkered. **Sights:** White Bradley bead front sight and center bead. **Features:** Receiver has Greystone gunmetal gray finish with gold accents. Trap Monte Carlo stock has deluxe trap recoil pad. Various grades available. Imported from Italy by Beretta USA.
Price: 682 Gold E Trap with adjustable stock. **$4,425.00**
Price: 682 Gold E Trap Unsingle **$4,825.00**
Price: 682 Gold E Sporting. **$4,075.00**
Price: 682 Gold E Skeet, adjustable stock **$4,425.00**

Prices given are believed to be accurate at time of publication however, many factors affect retail pricing so exact prices are not possible.

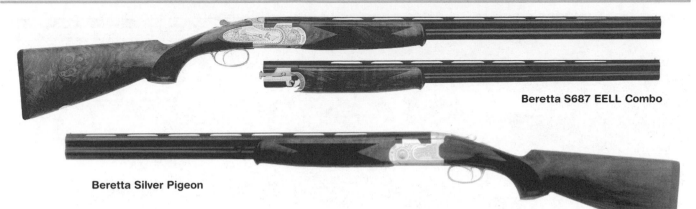

Beretta S687 EELL Combo

Beretta Silver Pigeon

Beretta Silver Pigeon II

Browning Cynergy Classic Field Grade III

Browning Cynergy Classic Field Grade VI

BERETTA 686 ONYX O/U SHOTGUNS
Gauge: 12, 20, 28; 3", 3.5" chambers. **Barrel:** 26", 28" (Mobilchoke tubes). **Weight:** 6.8-6.9 lbs. **Stock:** Checkered American walnut. **Features:** Intended for the beginning sporting clays shooter. Has wide, vented target rib, radiused recoil pad. Polished black finish on receiver and barrels. Introduced 1993. Imported from Italy by Beretta U.S.A.
Price: White Onyx. **$1,975.00**
PPrice: White Onyx Sporting **$2,175.00**

BERETTA SILVER PIGEON O/U SHOTGUNS
Gauge: 12, 20, 28, 3" chambers (2-3/4" 28 ga.). .410 bore, 3" chamber. **Barrel:** 26", 28". **Weight:** 6.8 lbs. **Stock:** Checkered walnut. **Features:** Interchangeable barrels (20 and 28 ga.), single selective gold-plated trigger, boxlock action, auto safety, Schnabel forend.
Price: Silver Pigeon S. **$2,400.00**
Price: Silver Pigeon II **$3,150.00**
Price: Silver Pigeon III **$3,275.00**
Price: Silver Pigeon IV **$3,200.00**
Price: Silver Pigeon V. **$3,675.00**

BERETTA ULTRALIGHT O/U SHOTGUNS
Gauge: 12, 2-3/4" chambers. **Barrel:** 26", 28", Mobilchoke tubes. **Weight:** About 5 lbs., 13 oz. **Stock:** Select American walnut with checkered grip and forend. **Features:** Low-profile aluminum alloy receiver with titanium breech face insert. Electroless nickel receiver with game scene engraving. Single selective trigger; automatic safety. Introduced 1992. Ultralight Deluxe except has matte electroless nickel finish receiver with gold game scene engraving; matte oil-finished, select walnut stock and forend. Imported from Italy by Beretta U.S.A.
Price: **$2,075.00**
Price: Ultralight Deluxe **$2,450.00**

BERETTA COMPETITION SHOTGUNS
Gauge: 12, 20, 28, and .410 bore, 2-3/4", 3" and 3-1/2" chambers. **Barrel:** 26" and 28" (Mobilchoke tubes). **Stock:** Close-grained walnut. **Features:** Highly-figured, American walnut stocks and forends, and a unique, weather-resistant finish on barrels. Silver designates standard 686, 687 models with silver receivers; 686 Silver Pigeon has enhanced engraving pattern, Schnabel forend; Gold indicates higher grade 686EL, 687EL models with full sideplates. Imported from Italy by Beretta U.S.A.
Price: S687 EELL Gold Pigeon Sporting (D.R. engraving). . **$7,675.00**

BILL HANUS 16-GAUGE BROWNING CITORI M525 FIELD
Gauge: 16. **Barrel:** 26" and 28". **Weight:** 6-3/4 pounds. **Stock:** 1-1/2" x 2-3/8" x 14-1/4" and cast neutral. Adjusting for cast-on for left-handed shooters or cast-off for right-handed shooters, $300 extra. Oil finish. **Features:** Full pistol grip with a graceful Schnable forearm and built on a true 16-gauge frame. Factory supplies three Invector choke tubes: IC-M-F and Bill Hanus models come with two Briley-made skeet chokes for close work over dogs and clay-target games.
Price: **$1,795.00**

BROWNING CYNERGY O/U SHOTGUNS
Gauge: 12, 20, 28. **Barrel:** 26", 28", 30", 32". **Stock:** Walnut or composite. **Sights:** White bead front most models; HiViz Pro-Comp sight on some models; mid bead. **Features:** Mono-Lock hinge, recoil-reducing interchangeable Inflex recoil pad, silver nitride receiver; striker-based trigger, ported barrel option. Models include: Cynergy Sporting, Adjustable Comb; Cynergy Sporting Composite CF; Cynergy Field, Composite; Cynergy Classic Sporting; Cynergy Classic Field; Cynergy Camo Mossy Oak New Shadow Grass; Cynergy Camo Mossy

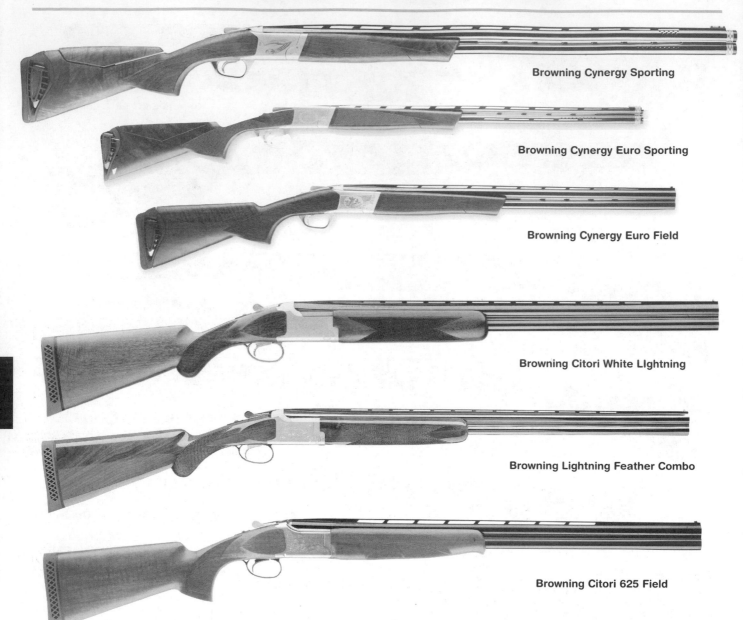

Browning Cynergy Sporting

Browning Cynergy Euro Sporting

Browning Cynergy Euro Field

Browning Citori White LIghtning

Browning Lightning Feather Combo

Browning Citori 625 Field

BROWNING CYNERGY O/U SHOTGUNS *(cont.)*

Oak New Break-Up; and Cynergy Camo Mossy Oak Brush. Imported from Japan by Browning.
Price: Cynergy Classic Field, 12 ga., from $2,399.00
Price: Cynergy Classic Field Grade III, similar to Cynergy
Classic Field but with full coverage high-relief
engraving on reciever and top lever, gloss finish
Grade III/IV walnut., from $3,499.00
Price: Cyergy Classic Field Grade VI, similar to Cynergy
Classic Field Grade III but with more extensive,
gold-highlighted engraving, from $5,229.00
Price: Cynergy Classic Sporting, from $3,499.00
Price: Cynergy Euro Sporting, 12 ga.; 28", 30",
or 32" barrels $3,719.00
Price: Cynergy Euro Sporting Composite 12 ga. $3,499.00
Price: Cynergy Euro Sporting, adjustable comb, intr. 2006 . $4,079.00
Price: Cynergy Feather, 12 ga. intr. 2007. . . . . $2,579.00
Price: Cynergy Feather, 20, 28 ga., .410, intr. 2008. . . . . . . $2,599.00
Price: Cynergy Euro Sporting, 20 ga., intr. 2008 . . . . $3,739.00
Price: Cynergy Euro Field, Invector Plus tubes in 12
and 20 gauge, standard Invector tubes on
28 gauge and 410 . . . . $2,509.00

BROWNING CITORI O/U SHOTGUNS

Gauge: 12, 20, 28 and .410. **Barrel:** 26", 28" in 28 and .410. Offered with Invector choke tubes. All 12 and 20 gauge models have back-bored barrels and Invector Plus choke system. **Weight:** 6 lbs., 8 oz. (26" .410) to 7 lbs., 13 oz. (30" 12 ga.). **Length:** 43" overall (26" bbl.). **Stock:** Dense walnut, hand checkered, full pistol grip, beavertail forend. Field-type recoil pad on 12 ga. field guns and trap and skeet models. **Sights:** Medium raised beads, German nickel silver. **Features:** Barrel selector integral with safety, automatic ejectors, three-piece takedown. Citori 625 Field (intr. 2008) includes Vector Pro extended forcing cones, new wood checkering patterns, silver-nitride finish with high-relief engraving, gloss oil finish with Grade II/III walnut with radius pistol grip, Schnabel forearm, 12 gauge, three Invector Plus choke tubes. Citori 625 Sporting (intr. 2008) includes standard and adjustable combs, 32", 30", and 28" barrels, five Diamond Grade extended Invector Plus choke tubes. Triple Trigger System allows adjusting length of pull and choice of wide checkered, narrow smooth, and wide smooth canted trigger shoe. HiViz Pro-Comp fiber-optic front sights. Imported from Japan by Browning.
Price: Lightning, from $1,763.00
Price: White Lightning, from $1,836.00
Price: Superlight Feather $2,098.00
Price: Lightning Feather, combo 20 and 28 ga. $1,869.00
Price: 625 Field, 12, 20 or 28 ga. and .410. Weighs
6 lbs. 12 oz. to 7 lbs. 14 oz. $2,339.00
Price: 625 Sporting, 12, 20 or 28 ga. and .410,
standard comb, intr. 2008. . . . . $3,329.00
Price: 625 Sporting, 12 ga., adj. comb, intr. 2008. . . . . $3,639.00

SHOTGUNS—Over/Unders

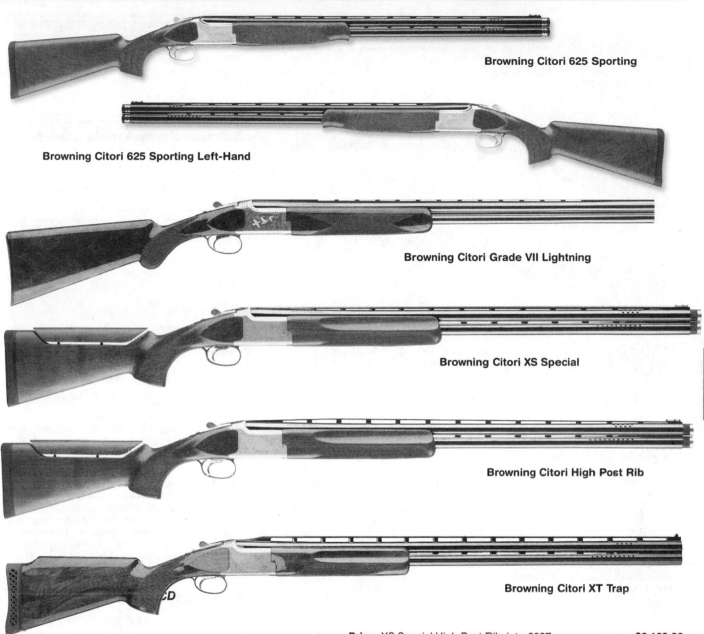

Browning Citori 625 Sporting

Browning Citori 625 Sporting Left-Hand

Browning Citori Grade VII Lightning

Browning Citori XS Special

Browning Citori High Post Rib

Browning Citori XT Trap

Browning Citori High Grade Shotguns
Similar to standard Citori except has engraved hunting scenes and gold inlays, high-grade, hand-oiled walnut stock and forearm. Introduced 2000. From Browning.
Price: Grade IV Lightning, engraved gray receiver,
introduced 2005, from **$2,999.00**
Price: Grade VII Lightning, engraved gray or blue receiver,
introduced 2005, from **$4,769.00**
Price: GTS High Grade, intr. 2007 . . . . **$4,309.00**

Browning Citori XS Sporting O/U Shotguns
Similar to the standard Citori except available in 12, 20, 28 or .410 with 28", 30", 32" ported barrels with various screw-in choke combinations: S (Skeet), C (Cylinder), IC (Improved Cylinder), M (Modified), and IM (Improved Modified). Has pistol grip stock, rounded or Schnabel forend. Weighs 7.1 lbs. to 8.75 lbs. Introduced 2004. Ultra XS Prestige (intr. 2008) has silver-nitride finish receiver with gold accented, high-relief Ultra XS Special engraving. Also, single selective trigger, hammer ejectors, gloss oil finish walnut stock with right-hand palm swell, adjustable comb, Schnabel forearm. Comes with five Invector-Plus Midas Grade choke tubes.
Price: XS Special, 12 ga.; 30", 32" barrels **$3,169.00**
Price: XS Skeet, 12 or 20 ga. **$2,829.00**

Price: XS Special High Post Rib, intr. 2007 . . . . **$3,169.00**
Price: Ultra XS Prestige, intr. 2008 . . . . **$4,759.00**

Browning Citori XT Trap O/U Shotgun
Similar to the Citori XS Special except has engraved silver nitride receiver with gold highlights, vented side barrel rib. Available in 12 gauge with 30" or 32" barrels, Invector-Plus choke tubes, adjustable comb and buttplate. Introduced 1999. Imported by Browning.
Price: XT Trap. **$2,639.00**
Price: XT Trap w/adjustable comb **$2,959.00**
Price: XT Trap Gold w/adjustable comb, introduced 2005 . . **$4,899.00**

CHARLES DALY MODEL 206 O/U SHOTGUN
Gauge: 12, 3" chambers. **Barrel:** 26", 28", 30", chrome-moly steel. **Weight:** 8 lbs. **Stock:** Check-ered select Turkish walnut stocks. **Features:** Single selective trigger, extractors or selective automatic ejectors. Sporting model has 10mm ventilated rib and side ventilated ribs. Trap model comes with 10mm top rib and side ventilated ribs and includes a Monte Carlo Trap buttstock. Both competition ribs have mid-brass bead and front fluorescent sights. Five Multi-Choke tubes. Introduced 2008. Imported from Turkey by K.B.I., Inc.
Price: Field, 26" or 28", extractors **$759.00**
Price: Field, 26" or 28", auto-eject **$884.00**
Price: Sporting, 28" or 30" ported, ... **$999.00**
Price: Trap, 28" or 30" ported, ... **$1,064.00**

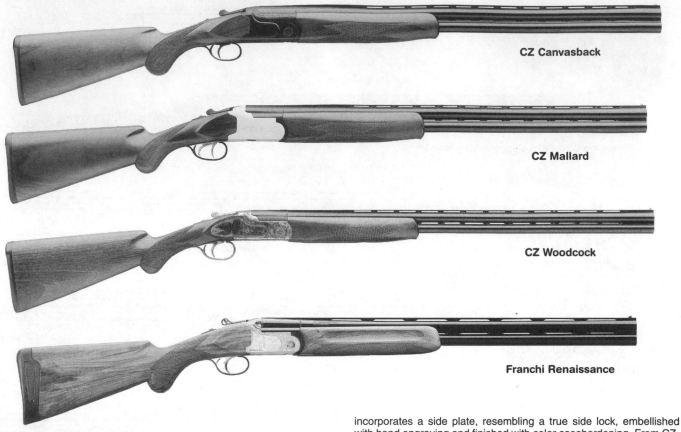

CZ Canvasback

CZ Mallard

CZ Woodcock

Franchi Renaissance

CZ SPORTING OVER/UNDER
Gauge: 12, 3" chambers. **Barrel:** 30", 32" chrome-lined, back-bored with extended forcing cones. **Weight:** 9 lbs. **Length:** NA. **Stock:** Neutral cast stock with an adjustable comb, trap style forend, pistol grip and ambidextrous palm swells. #3 grade Circassian walnut. At lowest position, drop at comb: 1-5/8"; drop at heel: 2-3/8"; length of pull: 14-1/2". **Features:** Designed for Sporting Clays and FITASC competition. Hand engraving, satin black-finished receiver. Tapered rib with center bead and a red fiber-optic front bead, 10 choke tubes with wrench, single selective trigger, automatic ejectors, thin rubber pad with slick plastic top. Introduced 2008. From CZ-USA.
Price: $2,509.00

CZ CANVASBACK
Gauge: 12, 20, 3" chambers. **Barrel:** 26", 28". **Weight:** 7.3 lbs. **Length:** NA. **Stock:** Round-knob pistol grip, Schnabel forend, Turkish walnut. **Features:** Single selective trigger, set of 5 screw-in chokes, black chrome finished receiver. From CZ-USA.
Price: $819.00

CZ MALLARD
Gauge: 12, 20, 28, .410, 3" chambers. **Barrel:** 26". **Weight:** 7.7 lbs. **Length:** NA. **Stock:** Round-knob pistol grip, Schnabel forend, Turkish walnut. **Features:** Double triggers and extractors, coin finished receiver. From CZ-USA.
Price: $562.00

CZ REDHEAD
Gauge: 12, 20, 3" chambers. **Barrel:** 28". **Weight:** 7.4 lbs. **Length:** NA. **Stock:** Round-knob pistol grip, Schnabel forend, Turkish walnut. **Features:** Single selective triggers and extractors (12 & 20 ga.), screw-in chokes (12, 20, 28 ga.) choked IC and Mod (.410), coin finished receiver, multi chokes. From CZ-USA.
Price: $965.00

CZ WOODCOCK
Gauge: 12, 20, 28, .410, 3" chambers. **Barrel:** 26". **Weight:** 7.7 lbs. **Length:** NA. **Stock:** Round-knob pistol grip, Schnabel forend, Turkish walnut. **Features:** Single selective triggers and extractors (auto ejectors on 12 & 20 ga.), screw-in chokes (12, 20, 28 ga.) choked IC and Mod (.410), coin finished receiver, multi chokes. The sculptured frame incorporates a side plate, resembling a true side lock, embellished with hand engraving and finished with color casehardening. From CZ-USA.
Price: $1,246.00

ESCORT OVER/UNDER SHOTGUNS
Gauge: 12, 3" chamber. **Barrel:** 28". **Weight:** 7.4 lbs. **Stock:** Walnut or select walnut with Trio recoil pad; synthetic stock with adjustable comb. Three adjustment spacers. **Sights:** Bronze front bead. **Features:** Blued barrels, blued or nickel receiver. Trio recoil pad. Five interchangeable chokes (SK, IC, M, IM, F); extractors or ejectors (new, 2008), barrel selector. Hard case available. Introduced 2007. Imported from Turkey by Legacy Sports International.
Price: $599.00

FRANCHI RENAISSANCE AND RENAISSANCE SPORTING O/U SHOTGUNS
Gauge: 12, 20, 28, 3" chamber. **Barrel:** 26", 28". **Weight:** 5.0 to 6.0 lbs. **Length:** 42-5/8" to 44-5/8". **Stock:** 14.5" LOP, European oil-finished walnut with standard grade A grade, and AA grade choices. Prince of Wales grip. **Features:** TSA recoil pad, interchangeable chokes, hard case. Introduced 2006. *Sporting model:* **Gauge:** 12 , 3". **Barrel:** 30" ported. **Weight:** 7.9 lbs. **Length:** 46 5/8". **Stock:** 14.5" LOP, A-grade European oil-finished walnut. **Features:** TSA recoil pad, adjustable comb, lengthened forcing cones, extended choke tubes (C, IC, M and wrench), hard case. Introduced 2007. Imported from Italy by Benelli USA.
Price: Field $1,729.00
Price: Classic $1,899.00
Price: Elite. $2,399.00
Price: Sporting $2,249.00

KIMBER MARIAS O/U SHOTGUN
Gauge: 20, 16; 3". **Barrel:** 26", 28", 30". **Weight:** 6.5 lbs. **Length:** NA. **Stock:** Turkish walnut stocks, 24-lpi checkering, oil finish. **LOP:** 14.75". **Features:** Hand-detachable back-action sidelock, bone-charcoal case coloring. Hand-engraving on receiver and locks, Belgian rust blue barrels, chrome lined. Five thinwall choke tubes, automatic ejectors, ventilated rib. Gold line cocking indicators on locks. Grade I has 28" barrels, Prince of Wales stock in grade three Turkish walnut in either 12 or 20 gauge. Grade II shas grade four Turkish walnut stocks, 12 gauge in Prince of Wales and 20 with either Prince of Wales or English profiles. Introduced 2008. Imported from Italy by Kimber Mfg., Inc.
Price: Grade II. $5,799.00

Prices given are believed to be accurate at time of publication however, many factors affect retail pricing so exact prices are not possible.

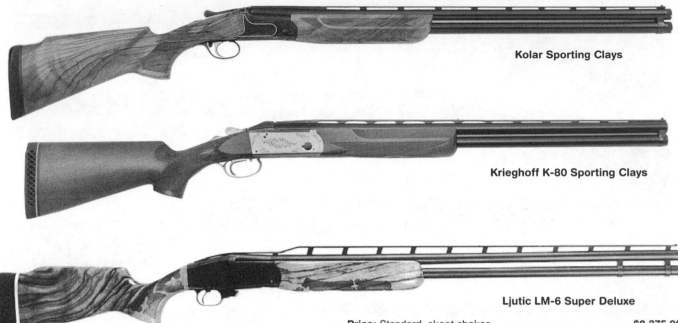

Kolar Sporting Clays

Krieghoff K-80 Sporting Clays

Ljutic LM-6 Super Deluxe

KOLAR SPORTING CLAYS O/U SHOTGUNS
Gauge: 12, 2-3/4" chambers. **Barrel:** 30", 32", 34"; extended choke tubes. **Stock:** 14-5/8"x2.5"x1-7/8"x1-3/8". French walnut. Four stock versions available. **Features:** Single selective trigger, detachable, adjustable for length; overbored barrels with long forcing cones; flat tramline rib; matte blue finish. Made in U.S. by Kolar.
Price: Standard..................................... **$9,595.00**
Price: Prestige.................................... **$14,190.00**
Price: Elite Gold................................. **$16,590.00**
Price: Legend.................................... **$17,090.00**
Price: Select..................................... **$22,590.00**
Price: Custom................................ **Price on request**

Kolar AAA Competition Trap O/U Shotgun
Similar to the Sporting Clays gun except has 32" O/U /34" Unsingle or 30" O/U /34" Unsingle barrels as an over/under, unsingle, or combination set. Stock dimensions are 14.5"x2.5"x1.5"; American or French walnut; step parallel rib standard. Contact maker for full listings. Made in U.S.A. by Kolar.
Price: Over/under, choke tubes, standard.............. **$9,595.00**
Price: Combo (30"/34", 32"/34"), standard............. **$12,595.00**

Kolar AAA Competition Skeet O/U Shotgun
Similar to the Sporting Clays gun except has 28" or 30" barrels with Kolarite AAA sub gauge tubes; stock of American or French walnut with matte finish; flat tramline rib; under barrel adjustable for point of impact. Many options available. Contact maker for complete listing. Made in U.S.A. by Ko-lar.
Price: Standard, choke tubes...................... **$10,995.00**
Price: Standard, choke tubes, two-barrel set.......... **$12,995.00**

KRIEGHOFF K-80 SPORTING CLAYS O/U SHOTGUN
Gauge: 12. **Barrel:** 28", 30", 32", 34" with choke tubes. **Weight:** About 8 lbs. **Stock:** #3 Sporting stock designed for gun-down shooting. **Features:** Standard receiver with satin nickel finish and classic scroll engraving. Selective mechanical trigger adjustable for position. Choice of tapered flat or 8mm parallel flat barrel rib. Free-floating barrels. Aluminum case. Imported from Germany by Krieghoff International, Inc.
Price: Standard grade with five choke tubes, from....... **$9,395.00**

KRIEGHOFF K-80 SKEET O/U SHOTGUNS
Gauge: 12, 2-3/4" chambers. **Barrel:** 28", 30", 32", (skeet & skeet), optional choke tubes). **Weight:** About 7.75 lbs. **Stock:** American skeet or straight skeet stocks, with palm-swell grips. Walnut. **Features:** Satin gray receiver finish. Selective mechanical trigger adjustable for position. Choice of ventilated 8mm parallel flat rib or ventilated 8-12mm tapered flat rib. Introduced 1980. Imported from Germany by Krieghoff International, Inc.

Price: Standard, skeet chokes..................... **$8,375.00**
Price: Skeet Special (28", 30", 32" tapered flat rib, skeet & skeet choke tubes)............................ **$9,100.00**

KRIEGHOFF K-80 TRAP O/U SHOTGUNS
Gauge: 12, 2-3/4" chambers. **Barrel:** 30", 32" (Imp. Mod. & Full or choke tubes). **Weight:** About 8.5 lbs. **Stock:** Four stock dimensions or adjustable stock available; all have palm-swell grips. Checkered European walnut. **Features:** Satin nickel receiver. Selective mechanical trigger, adjustable for position. Ventilated step rib. Introduced 1980. Imported from Germany by Krieghoff International, Inc.
Price: K-80 O/U (30", 32", Imp. Mod. & Full), from....... **$8,850.00**
Price: K-80 Unsingle (32", 34", Full), standard, from..... **$10,080.00**
Price: K-80 Combo (two-barrel set), standard, from...... **$13,275.00**

Krieghoff K-20 O/U Shotgun
Similar to the K-80 except built on a 20-gauge frame. Designed for skeet, sporting clays and field use. Offered in 20, 28 and .410; 28", 30" and 32" barrels. Imported from Germany by Krieghoff International Inc.
Price: K-20, 20 gauge, from........................ **$9,575.00**
Price: K-20, 28 gauge, from........................ **$9,725.00**
Price: K-20, .410, from............................ **$9,725.00**

LEBEAU-COURALLY BOSS-VEREES O/U SHOTGUN
Gauge: 12, 20, 2-3/4" chambers. **Barrel:** 25" to 32". **Weight:** To customer specifications. **Stock:** Exhibition-quality French walnut. **Features:** Boss-type sidelock with automatic ejectors; single or double triggers; chopper lump barrels. A custom gun built to customer specifications. Imported from Belgium by Wm. Larkin Moore.
Price: From..................................... **$96,000.00**

LJUTIC LM-6 SUPER DELUXE O/U SHOTGUNS
Gauge: 12. **Barrel:** 28" to 34", choked to customer specs for live birds, trap, international trap. **Weight:** To customer specs. **Stock:** To customer specs. Oil finish, hand checkered. **Features:** Custom-made gun. Hollow-milled rib, pull or release trigger, push-button opener in front of trigger guard. From Ljutic Industries.
Price: Super Deluxe LM-6 O/U..................... **$19,995.00**
Price: Over/Under combo (interchangeable single barrel, two trigger guards, one for single trigger, one for doubles)............................. **$27,995.00**
Price: Extra over/under barrel sets, 29"-32"............ **$6,995.00**

MARLIN L. C. SMITH O/U SHOTGUNS
Gauge: 12, 20. **Barrel:** 26", 28". **Stock:** Checkered walnut w/recoil pad. **Length:** 45". **Weight:** 7.25 lbs. **Features:** 3" chambers; 3 choke tubes (IC, Mod., Full), single selective trigger, selective automatic ejectors; vent rib; bead front sight. Imported from Italy by Marlin. Introduced 2005.
Price: LC12-OU (12 ga., 28" barrel)................. **$1,254.00**
Price: LC20-OU (20 ga., 26" barrel, 6.25 lbs., OAL 43")... **$1,254.00**

SHOTGUNS—Over/Unders

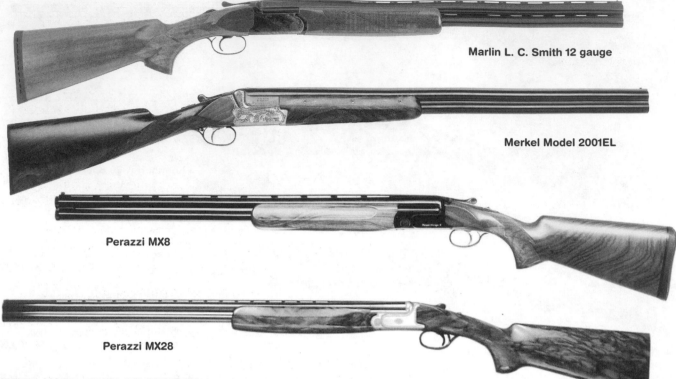

Marlin L. C. Smith 12 gauge

Merkel Model 2001EL

Perazzi MX8

Perazzi MX28

MERKEL MODEL 2001EL O/U SHOTGUN
Gauge: 12, 20, 3" chambers, 28, 2-3/4" chambers. **Barrel:** 12-28"; 20, 28 ga.-26.75". **Weight:** About 7 lbs. (12 ga.). **Stock:** Oil-finished walnut; English or pistol grip. **Features:** Self-cocking Blitz boxlock action with cocking indicators; Kersten double cross-bolt lock; silver-grayed receiver with engraved hunting scenes; coil spring ejectors; single selective or double triggers. Imported from Germany by Merkel USA.
Price: **$9,995.00**
Price: Model 2001EL Sporter; full pistol grip stock **$9,995.00**

Merkel Model 2000CL O/U Shotgun
Similar to Model 2001EL except scroll-engraved case-hardened receiver; 12, 20, 28 gauge. Imported from Germany by Merkel USA.
Price: **$8,495.00**
Price: Model 2016 CL; 16 gauge **$8,495.00**

PERAZZI MX8/MX8 SPECIAL TRAP, SKEET O/U SHOTGUNS
Gauge: 12, 2-3/4" chambers. **Barrel:** Trap: 29.5" (Imp. Mod. & Extra Full), 31.5" (Full & Extra Full). Choke tubes optional. Skeet: 27-5/8" (skeet & skeet). **Weight:** About 8.5 lbs. (trap); 7 lbs., 15 oz. (skeet). **Stock:** Interchangeable and custom made to customer specs. **Features:** Has detachable and interchangeable trigger group with flat V springs. Flat 7/16" vent rib. Many options available. Imported from Italy by Perazzi U.S.A., Inc.
Price: MX Trap Single. **$10,934.00**

Perazzi MX8 Special Skeet O/U Shotgun
Similar to the MX8 Skeet except has adjustable four-position trigger, skeet stock dimensions. Imported from Italy by Perazzi U.S.A., Inc.
Price: From **$11,166.00**

PERAZZI MX8 O/U SHOTGUNS
Gauge: 12, 2-3/4" chambers. **Barrel:** 28-3/8" (Imp. Mod. & Extra Full), 29.5" (choke tubes). **Weight:** 7 lbs., 12 oz. **Stock:** Special specifications. **Features:** Has single selective trigger; flat 7/16" x 5/16" vent rib. Many options available. Imported from Italy by Perazzi U.S.A., Inc.
Price: Standard. **$12,532.00**
Price: Sporting **$11,166.00**
Price: Trap Double Trap (removable trigger group) **$15,581.00**
Price: Skeet **$12,756.00**
Price: SC3 grade (variety of engraving patterns) . . . . . . **$23,000.00+**
Price: SCO grade (more intricate engraving, gold inlays). **$39,199.00+**

Perazzi MX8/20 O/U Shotgun
Similar to the MX8 except has smaller frame and has a removable

trigger mechanism. Available in trap, skeet, sporting or game models with fixed chokes or choke tubes. Stock is made to customer specifications. Introduced 1993. Imported from Italy by Perazzi U.S.A., Inc.
Price: From **$11,731.00**

PERAZZI MX12 HUNTING O/U SHOTGUNS
Gauge: 12, 2-3/4" chambers. **Barrel:** 26.75", 27.5", 28-3/8", 29.5" (Mod. & Full); choke tubes available in 27-5/8", 29.5" only (MX12C). **Weight:** 7 lbs., 4 oz. **Stock:** To customer specs; interchangeable. **Features:** Single selective trigger; coil springs used in action; Schnabel forend tip. Imported from Italy by Perazzi U.S.A., Inc.
Price: From **$11,166.00**
Price: MX12C (with choke tubes). From **$11,960.00**

Perazzi MX20 Hunting O/U Shotguns
Similar to the MX12 except 20 ga. frame size. Non-removable trigger group. Available in 20, 28, .410 with 2-3/4" or 3" chambers. 26" standard, and choked Mod. & Full. Weight is 6 lbs., 6 oz. Imported from Italy by Perazzi U.S.A., Inc.
Price: **$11,166.00**
Price: MX20C (as above, 20 ga. only, choke tubes). From **$11,960.00**

PERAZZI MX10 O/U SHOTGUN
Gauge: 12, 2-3/4" chambers. **Barrel:** 29.5", 31.5" (fixed chokes). **Weight:** NA. **Stock:** Walnut; cheekpiece adjustable for elevation and cast. **Features:** Adjustable rib; vent side rib. Externally selective trigger. Available in single barrel, combo, over/under trap, skeet, pigeon and sporting models. Introduced 1993. Imported from Italy by Perazzi U.S.A., Inc.
Price: MX200410 . . . . **$18,007.00**

PERAZZI MX28, MX410 GAME O/U SHOTGUN
Gauge: 28, 2-3/4" chambers, .410, 3" chambers. **Barrel:** 26" (Imp. Cyl. & Full). **Weight:** NA. **Stock:** To customer specs. **Features:** Made on scaled-down frames proportioned to the gauge. Introduced 1993. Imported from Italy by Perazzi U.S.A., Inc.
Price: From **$22,332.00**

PIOTTI BOSS O/U SHOTGUN
Gauge: 12, 20. **Barrel:** 26" to 32", chokes as specified. **Weight:** 6.5 to 8 lbs. **Stock:** Dimensions to customer specs. Best quality figured walnut. **Features:** Essentially a custom-made gun with many options. Introduced 1993. Imported from Italy by Wm. Larkin Moore.
Price: From **$69,000.00**

Prices given are believed to be accurate at time of publication however, many factors affect retail pricing so exact prices are not possible.

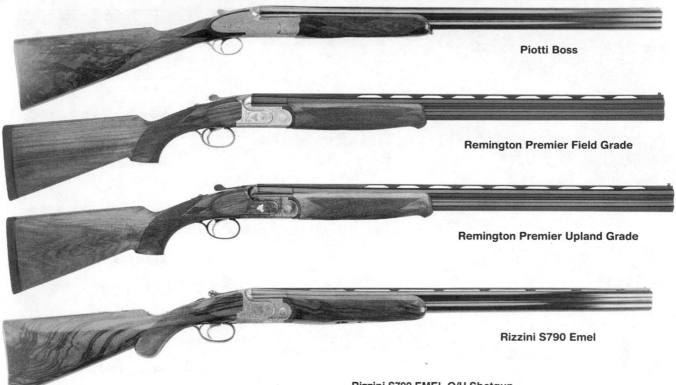

Piotti Boss

Remington Premier Field Grade

Remington Premier Upland Grade

Rizzini S790 Emel

POINTER OVER/UNDER SHOTGUN
Gauge: 12, 20, 28, .410, 3" chambers. **Barrel:** 28", blued. **Weight:** 6.1 to 7.6 lbs. **Stock:** Turkish Walnut. **Sights:** Fiber-optic front, bronze mid-bead. Choke: IC/M/F. **Features:** Engraved nickel receiver, automatic ejectors, fitted hard plastic case. Clays model has oversized fiber-optic front sight and palm swell pistol grip. Introduced 2007. Imported from Turkey by Legacy Sports International.
Price: ....$1,299.00 to $1,499.00

REMINGTON PREMIER OVER/UNDER SHOTGUNS
Gauge: 12, 20, 28, 3" chambers; 28, 2-3/4" chambers. **Barrel:** 26", 28", 30" in 12 gauge; overbored (.735), polished blue; 7mm vent rib. **Sights:** Ivory front bead, steel mid bead. **Weight:** 6.5 to 7.5 lbs. **Stock:** Walnut, cut checkering, Schnabel forends. Checkered pistol grip, checkered forend, satin finish, rubber butt pad. Right-hand palm swell. **Features:** Single selective mechanical trigger, selective automatic ejectors; serrated free-floating vent rib. Five flush mount ProBore choke tubes for 12s and 20s; 28-gauge equipped with 3 flush mount ProBore choke tubes. Hard case included. Introduced 2006. Made in Italy, imported by Remington Arms Co.
Price: Premier Field, nickel-finish receiver, from **$2,086.00**
Price: Premier Upland, case-colored receiver finish, from .. **$2,226.00**
Price: Premier Competition STS (2007) **$2,540.00**
Price: Premier Competition STS Adj. Comb (2007) **$2,890.00**

REMINGTON SPR310 OVER/UNDER SHOTGUNS
Gauge: 12, 20, 28, .410 bore, 3" chambers; 28, 2-3/4" chambers. **Barrel:** 26", 28", 29.5"; blued chrome-lined. **Weight:** 7.25 to 7.5 lbs. **Stock:** Checkered walnut stock and forend, 14.5" LOP; 1.5" drop at comb; 2.5" drop at heel. **Features:** Nickel finish or blued receiver. Single selective mechanical trigger, selective automatic ejectors; serrated free-floating vent rib. SC-4 choke tube set on most models. Sporting has ported barrels, right-hand palm swell, target forend, wide rib. Introduced 2008. Imported by Remington Arms Co.
Price: SPR310, from.................................**$598.00**
Price: SPR310 Sporting **$770.00**

RIZZINI S790 EMEL O/U SHOTGUN
Gauge: 20, 28, .410. **Barrel:** 26", 27.5" (Imp. Cyl. & Imp. Mod.). **Weight:** About 6 lbs. **Stock:** 14"x1.5"x2-1/8". Extra fancy select walnut. **Features:** Boxlock action with profuse engraving; automatic ejectors; single selective trigger; silvered receiver. Comes with Nizzoli leather case. Introduced 1996. Imported from Italy by Wm. Larkin Moore & Co.
Price: From **$14,600.00**

Rizzini S792 EMEL O/U Shotgun
Similar to S790 EMEL except dummy sideplates with extensive engraving coverage. Nizzoli leather case. Introduced 1996. Imported from Italy by Wm. Larkin Moore & Co.
Price: From **$15,500.00**

RIZZINI UPLAND EL O/U SHOTGUN
Gauge: 12, 16, 20, 28, .410. **Barrel:** 26", 27.5", Mod. & Full, Imp. Cyl. & Imp. Mod. choke tubes. **Weight:** About 6.6 lbs. **Stock:** 14.5"x1-1/2"x2.25". **Features:** Boxlock action; single selective trigger; ejectors; profuse engraving on silvered receiver. Comes with fitted case. Introduced 1996. Imported from Italy by Wm. Larkin Moore & Co.
Price: From **$5,200.00**

Rizzini Artemis O/U Shotgun
Same as Upland EL model except dummy sideplates with extensive game scene engraving. Fancy European walnut stock. Fitted case. Introduced 1996. Imported from Italy by Wm. Larkin Moore & Co.
Price: From **$3.260.00**

RIZZINI S782 EMEL O/U SHOTGUN
Gauge: 12, 2-3/4" chambers. **Barrel:** 26", 27.5" (Imp. Cyl. & Imp. Mod.). **Weight:** About 6.75 lbs. **Stock:** 14.5"x1.5"x2.25". Extra fancy select walnut. **Features:** Boxlock action with dummy sideplates, extensive engraving with gold inlaid game birds, silvered receiver, automatic ejectors, single selective trigger. Nizzoli leather case. Introduced 1996. Imported from Italy by Wm. Larkin Moore & Co.
Price: From **$18,800.00**

RUGER RED LABEL O/U SHOTGUNS
Gauge: 12, 20, 3" chambers; 28 2-3/4" chambers. **Barrel:** 26", 28", 30" in 12 gauge. **Weight:** About 7 lbs. (20 ga.); 7.5 lbs. (12 ga.). **Length:** 43" overall (26" barrels). **Stock:** 14"x1.5"x2.5". Straight grain American walnut. Checkered pistol grip or straight grip, checkered forend, rubber butt pad. **Features:** Stainless steel receiver. Single selective mechanical trigger, selective automatic ejectors; serrated free-floating vent rib. Comes with two skeet, one Imp. Cyl., one Mod., one Full choke tube and wrench. Made in U.S. by Sturm, Ruger & Co.
Price: Red Label with pistol grip stock **$1,956.00**
Price: English Field with straight-grip stock **$1,956.00**
Price: Sporting clays (30" bbl.) **$1,956.00**

Ruger Engraved Red Label O/U Shotgun
Similar to Red Label except scroll engraved receiver with 24-carat gold game bird (pheasant in 12 gauge, grouse in 20 gauge, woodcock in 28 gauge). Introduced 2000.
Price: Engraved Red Label, pistol grip only **$2,180.00**

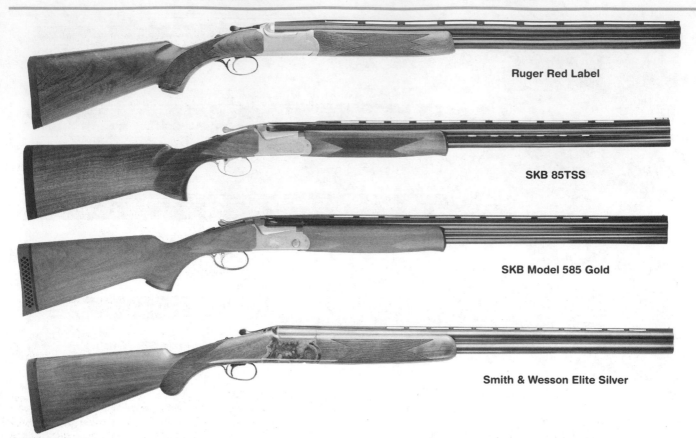

Ruger Red Label

SKB 85TSS

SKB Model 585 Gold

Smith & Wesson Elite Silver

SAVAGE MILANO O/U SHOTGUNS
Gauge: 12, 20, 28, and 410, 2-3/4" (28 ga.) and 3" chambers. **Barrel:** 28"; chrome lined, elongated forcing cones, automatic ejectors. 12, 20, and 28 come with 3 Interchokes (F-M-IC); 410 has fixed chokes (M-IC). **Weight:** 12 ga., 7.5 lbs; 20, 28 gauge, .410, 6.25 lbs. **Length:** NA. **Stock:** Satin finish Turkish walnut stock with laser-engraved checkering, solid rubber recoil pad, Schnabel forend. **Features:** Single selective, mechanical set trigger, fiber-optic front sight with brass mid-rib bead. Introduced 2006. Imported from It-aly by Savage Arms, Inc.
Price: $1,714.00

SKB MODEL GC7 O/U SHOTGUNS
Gauge: 12 or 20, 3"; 28, 2-3/4"; .410, 3". **Barrel:** 26", 28", Briley internal chokes. **Weight:** NA. **Length:** NA. **Stock:** Grade II and Grade III American black walnut, high-gloss finish, finger-groove forend. **Sights:** Top ventilated rib, sloped with matte surface (Game). **Features:** Low-profile boxlock action; Greener crossbolt locking action, silver-nitride finish; automatic ejec-tors, single selective trigger. Introduced 2008. Imported from Japan by SKB Shotguns, Inc.
Price: GC7 Game Bird Grade 1, from $1,569.00
Price: GC7 Clays Grade 1, from $1,679.00

SKB MODEL 85TSS O/U SHOTGUNS
Gauge: 12, 20, .410: 3"; 28, 2-3/4". **Barrel:** Chrome lined 26", 28", 30", 32" (w/choke tubes). **Weight:** 7 lbs., 7 oz. to 8 lbs., 14 oz. **Stock:** Hand-checkered American walnut with matte finish, Schnabel or grooved forend. Target stocks available in various styles. **Sights:** HiViz competition sights. **Features:** Low profile boxlock action with Greener-style cross bolt; single selective trigger; manual safety. Back-bored barrels with lengthened forcing cones. Introduced 2004. Imported from Japan by SKB Shotguns, Inc.
Price: Sporting Clays, Skeet, fixed comb, from $2,199.00
Price: Sporting clays, Skeet, adjustable comb, from $2,429.00
Price: Trap, standard or Monte Carlo $2,329.00
Price: Trap adjustable comb $2,529.00
Price: Trap Unsingle (2007) $2,799.00

SKB MODEL 585 O/U SHOTGUNS
Gauge: 12 or 20, 3"; 28, 2-3/4"; .410, 3". **Barrel:** 12 ga.-26", 28", (InterChoke tubes); 20 ga.-26", 28" (InterChoke tubes); 28-26", 28" (InterChoke tubes); .410-26", 28" (InterChoke tubes). **Weight:** 6.6 to 8.5 lbs. **Length:** 43" to 51-3/8" overall. **Stock:** 14-1/8"x1.5"x2-3/16".

Hand checkered walnut with matte finish. **Sights:** Metal bead front (field). **Features:** Boxlock action; silver nitride finish; manual safety, automatic ejectors, single selective trigger. All 12-gauge barrels are back-bored, have lengthened forcing cones and longer choke tube system. Introduced 1992. Imported from Japan by SKB Shotguns, Inc.
Price: Field $1,699.00
Price: Two-barrel field set, 12 & 20 . . . . $2,749.00
Price: Two-barrel field set, 20 & 28 or 28 & .410 . . . . $2,829.00

SMITH & WESSON ELITE SILVER SHOTGUNS
Gauge: 12, 3" chambers. **Barrel:** 26", 28", 30", rust-blued chopper-lump. **Weight:** 7.8 lbs. **Length:** 46-48". **Sights:** Ivory front bead, metal mid-bead. **Stock:** AAA (grade III) Turkish walnut stocks, hand-cut checkering, satin finish. **Features:** Smith & Wesson-designed trigger-plate action, hand-engraved receivers, bone-charcoal case hardening, lifetime warranty. Five choke tubes. Introduced 2007. Made in Turkey, imported by Smith & Wesson.
Price: $2,380.00

STEVENS MODEL 512 GOLD WING SHOTGUNS
Gauge: 12, 20, 28, .410; 2-3/4" and 3" chambers. **Barrel:** 26", 28". **Weight:** 6 to 8 lbs. **Sights:** NA. **Features:** Five screw-in choke tubes with 12, 20, and 28 gauge; .410 has fixed M/IC chokes. Black chrome, sculpted receiver with a raised gold pheasant, laser engraved trigger guard and forend latch. Turkish walnut stock finished in satin lacquer and beautifully laser engraved with fleur-de-lis checkering on the side panels, wrist and Schnabel forearm.
Price: $649.00

STOEGER CONDOR O/U SHOTGUNS
Gauge: 12, 20, 2-3/4" 3" chambers; 16, .410. **Barrel:** 22", 24", 26", 28", 30". **Weight:** 5.5 to 7.8 lbs. **Sights:** Brass bead. **Features:** IC, M, or F screw-in choke tubes with each gun. Oil finished hardwood with pistol grip and forend. Auto safety, single trigger, automatic extractors.
Price: Condor, 12, 20, 16 ga. or .410 . . . . $399.00
Price: Condor Supreme (w/mid bead), 12 or 20 ga. $599.00
Price: Condor Combo, 12 and 20 ga. Barrels, from $549.00
Price: Condor Youth, 20 ga. or .410 . . . . $399.00
Price: Condor Competition, 12 or 20 ga. $599.00
Price: Condor Combo, 12/20 ga., RH or LH (2007) $829.00
Price: Condor Outback, 12 or 20 ga., 20" barrel $369.00

Prices given are believed to be accurate at time of publication however, many factors affect retail pricing so exact prices are not possible.

SHOTGUNS—Over/Unders

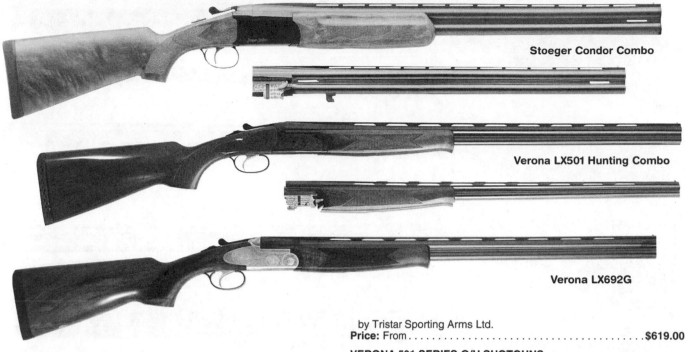

Stoeger Condor Combo

Verona LX501 Hunting Combo

Verona LX692G

TRADITIONS CLASSIC SERIES O/U SHOTGUNS

Gauge: 12, 3"; 20, 3"; 16, 2-3/4"; 28, 2-3/4"; .410, 3". **Barrel:** 26" and 28". **Weight:** 6 lbs., 5 oz. to 7 lbs., 6 oz. **Length:** 43" to 45" overall. **Stock:** Walnut. **Features:** Single-selective trigger; chrome-lined barrels with screw-in choke tubes; extractors (Field Hunter and Field I models) or automatic ejectors (Field II and Field III models); rubber butt pad; top tang safety. Imported from Fausti of Italy by Traditions.
Price: Field Hunter: Blued receiver; 12 or 20 ga.; 26" bbl. has IC and Mod. tubes, 28" has mod. and full tubes $669.00
Price: Field I: Blued receiver; 12, 20, 28 ga. or .410; fixed chokes (26" has I.C. and mod., 28" has mod. and full) . .$619.00
Price: Field II: Coin-finish receiver; 12, 16, 20, 28 ga. or .410; gold trigger; choke tubes $789.00
Price: Field III: Coin-finish receiver; gold engraving and trigger; 12 ga.; 26" or 28" bbl.; choke tubes $999.00
Price: Upland II: Blued receiver; 12 or 20 ga.; English-style straight walnut stock; choke tubes $839.00
Price: Upland III: Blued receiver, gold engraving; 20 ga.; high-grade pistol grip walnut stock; choke tubes $1,059.00
Price: Upland III: Blued, gold engraved receiver, 12 ga. Round pistol grip stock, choke tubes $1,059.00
Price: Sporting Clay II: Silver receiver; 12 ga.; ported barrels with skeet, i.c., mod. and full extended tubes $959.00
Price: Sporting Clay III: Engraved receivers, 12 and 20 ga., walnut stock, vent rib, extended choke tubes $1,189.00

TRADITIONS MAG 350 SERIES O/U SHOTGUNS

Gauge: 12, 3-1/2". **Barrel:** 24", 26" and 28". **Weight:** 7 lbs. to 7 lbs., 4 oz. **Length:** 41" to 45" overall. **Stock:** Walnut or composite with Mossy Oak Break-Up or Advantage Wetlands camouflage. **Features:** Black matte, engraved receiver; vent rib; automatic ejectors; single selective trigger; three screw-in choke tubes; rubber recoil pad; top tang safety. Imported from Fausti of Italy by Traditions.
Price: (Mag Hunter II: 28" black matte barrels, walnut stock, includes I.C., Mod. and Full tubes) $799.00
Price: (Turkey II: 24" or 26" camo barrels, Break-Up camo stock, includes Mod., Full and X-Full tubes) $889.00
Price: (Waterfowl II: 28" camo barrels, Advantage Wetlands camo stock, includes IC, Mod. and Full tubes) $899.00

TRISTAR HUNTER EX O/U SHOTGUN

Gauge: 12, 20, 28, .410. **Barrel:** 26", 28". **Weight:** 5.7 lbs. (.410); 6.0 lbs. (20, 28), 7.2-7.4 lbs. (12). Chrome-lined steel mono-block bar-rel, five Beretta-style choke tubes (SK, IC, M, IM, F). **Length:** NA. **Stock:** Walnut, cut checkering. 14.25"x1.5"x2-3/8". **Sights:** Brass front sight. **Features:** All have extractors, engraved receiver, sealed actions, self-adjusting locking bolts, single selective trigger, ventilated rib. 28 ga. and .410 built on true frames. Five-year warranty. Imported from Italy

by Tristar Sporting Arms Ltd.
Price: From $619.00

VERONA 501 SERIES O/U SHOTGUNS

Gauge: 12, 20, 28, .410 (3" chambers). **Barrel:** 28". **Weight:** 6-7 lbs. **Stock:** Enhanced walnut with Scottish net type checkering and oiled finish. **Features:** Select fire single trigger, automatic ejectors, chromed barrels with X-CONE system to reduce felt recoil, and ventilated rubber butt pad. Introduced 1999. Imported from Italy by Legacy Sports International.
Price: Combos 20/28, 28/.410 . . . . $1,599.00

Verona 702 Series O/U Shotguns

Same as 501 series model except with deluxe nickel receiver.
Price: $1,699.00

Verona LX692 Gold Hunting O/U Shotguns

Similar to Verona 501 except engraved, silvered receiver with false sideplates showing gold inlaid bird hunting scenes on three sides; Schnabel forend tip; hand-cut checkering; black rubber butt pad. Available in 12 and 20 gauge only, five Interchoke tubes. Introduced 1999. Imported from Italy by B.C. Outdoors.
Price: $1,295.00
Price: LX692G Combo 28/.410 . . . . $2,192.40

Verona LX680 Sporting O/U Shotgun

Similar to Verona 501 except engraved, silvered receiver; ventilated middle rib; beavertail forend; hand-cut checkering; available in 12 or 20 gauge only with 2-3/4" chambers. Introduced 1999. Imported from Italy by B.C. Outdoors.
Price: $1,159.68

Verona LX680 Skeet/Sporting/Trap O/U Shotgun

Similar to Verona 501 except skeet or trap stock dimensions; beavertail forend, palm swell on pistol grip; ventilated center barrel rib. Introduced 1999. Imported from Italy by B.C. Outdoors.
Price: $1,736.96

Verona LX692 Gold Sporting O/U Shotgun

Similar to Verona LX680 except false sideplates have gold-inlaid bird hunting scenes on three sides; red high-visibility front sight. Introduced 1999. Imported from Italy by B.C. Outdoors.
Price: Skeet/sporting. $1,765.12
Price: Trap (32" barrel, 7-7/8 lbs.) $1,594.80

VERONA LX680 COMPETITION TRAP O/U SHOTGUNS

Gauge: 12. **Barrel:** 30" O/U, 32" single bbl. **Weight:** 8-3/8 lbs. combo, 7 lbs. single. **Stock:** Walnut. **Sights:** White front, mid-rib bead. **Features:** Interchangeable barrels switch from OU to single configurations. 5 Briley chokes in combo, 4 in single bbl. extended forcing cones, ported barrels 32" with raised rib. By B.C. Outdoors.
Price: Trap Single (LX680TGTSB) $1,736.96
Price: Trap Combo (LX680TC) $2,553.60

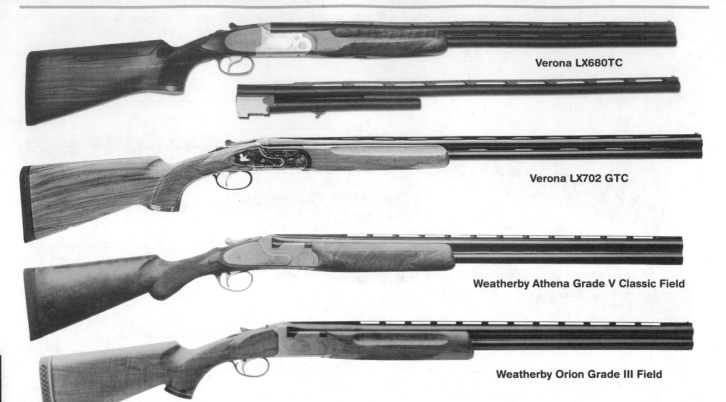

Verona LX680TC

Verona LX702 GTC

Weatherby Athena Grade V Classic Field

Weatherby Orion Grade III Field

VERONA LX702 GOLD TRAP COMBO O/U SHOTGUNS

Gauge: 20/28, 2-3/4" chamber. **Barrel:** 30". **Weight:** 7 lbs. **Stock:** Turkish walnut with beavertail forearm. **Sights:** White front bead. **Features:** 2-barrel competition gun. Color case-hardened side plates and receiver with gold inlaid pheasant. Vent rib between barrels. 5 Interchokes. Imported from Italy by B.C. Outdoors.
Price: Combo **$2,467.84**
Price: 20 ga. **$1,829.12**

Verona LX702 Skeet/Trap O/U Shotguns

Similar to Verona LX702. Both are 12 gauge and 2-3/4" chamber. Skeet has 28" barrel and weighs 7.75 lbs. Trap has 32" barrel and weighs 7-7/8 lbs. By B.C. Outdoors.
Price: Skeet **$1,829.12**
Price: Trap **$1,829.12**

WEATHERBY ATHENA GRADE V AND GRADE III CLASSIC FIELD O/U SHOTGUNS

Gauge: Grade III and Grade IV: 12, 20, 3" chambers. 28, 2-3/4" chambers. Grade V: 12, 20, 3" chambers. **Barrel:** 26", 28" monobloc, IMC multi-choke tubes. Modified Greener crossbolt action. Matte ventilated top rib with brilliant front bead. **Weight:** 12 ga., 7.25 to 8 lbs.; 20 ga. 6.5 to 7.25 lbs. **Length:** 43" to 45". **Stock:** Rounded pistol grip, slender forend, Old English recoil pad. Grade V has oil-finished AAA American Claro walnut with 20-lpi checkering. Grade III has AA Claro walnut with oil finish, fine-line checkering. **Features:** Silver nitride/gray receivers; Grade III has hunting scene engraving. Grade IV has chrome-plated false sideplates featuring single game scene gold plate overlay. Grade V has rose and scroll engraving with gold-overlay upland game scenes. Top levers engraved with gold Weatherby flying "W". Introduced 1999. Imported from Japan by Weatherby.
Price: Grade III **$2,599.00**
Price: Grade IV **$2,799.00**
Price: Grade V **$3,999.00**

WEATHERBY ORION D'ITALIA O/U SHOTGUNS

Gauge: 12, 20, 3" chambers; 28, 2-3/4" chamber. **Barrel:** 26", 28", IMC multi-choke tubes. Matte ventilated top rib with brilliant bead front sight. **Weight:** 6-1/2 to 8 lbs. **Stock:** 14.25"x1.5"x2.5". American walnut, checkered grip and forend. Old English recoil pad. **Features:** All models have a triggerguard that features Weatherby's "Flying W" engraved with gold fill. D'Italia I available in 12 and 20 gauge, 26" and 28" barrels. Walnut stock with high lustre urethane finish. Metalwork is blued to high lustre finishand has a gold-plated trigger for corrosion protection. D'Italia II available in 12, 20 and 28 gauge with 26" and 28" barrels. Fancy grade walnut stock, hard chrome receiver with sculpted frameheads, elaborate game and floral engraving pattern, and matte vent mid & top rib with brilliant front bead sight. D'Italia III available in 12 and 20 gauge with 26" and 28" barrels. Hand-selected, oil-finished walnut stock wtih 20 LPI checkering, intricate engraving and gold plate game scene overlay, and damascened monobloc barrel and sculpted frameheads. D'Italia SC available in 12 gauge only with barrel lengths of 28", 30", and 32", weighs 8 lbs. Features satin, oil-finished walnut stock that is adjustable for cheek height with target-style pistol grip and Schnaubel forend, shallow receiver aligns hands for improved balance and pointability, ported barrels reduce muzzle jump, and fiber optic front sight for quick targer acquisition. Introduced 1998. Imported from Japan by Weatherby.
Price: D'Italia I **$1,699.00**
Price: D'Italia II **$1,899.00**
Price: D'Italia III **$2,199.00**
Price: D'Italia SC **$2,599.00**

WINCHESTER SELECT MODEL 101 O/U SHOTGUNS

Gauge: 12, 2-3/4", 3" chambers. **Barrel:** 28", 30", 32", ported, Invector Plus choke system. **Weight:** 7 lbs. 6 oz. to 7 lbs. 12. oz. **Stock:** Checkered high-gloss grade II/III walnut stock, Pachmayr Decelerator sporting pad. **Features:** Chrome-plated chambers; back-bored barrels; tang barrel selec-tor/safety; Signature extended choke tubes. Model 101 Field comes with solid brass bead front sight, three tubes, engraved receiver. Model 101 Sporting has adjustable trigger, 10mm runway rib, white mid-bead, Tru-Glo front sight, 30" and 32" barrels. Camo version of Model 101 Field comes with full-coverage Mossy Oak Duck Blind pattern. Model 101 Pigeon Grade Trap has 10mm steel runway rib, mid-bead sight, interchangeable fiber-optic front sight, porting and vented side ribs, adjustable trigger shoe, fixed raised comb or adjustable comb, Grade III/IV walnut, 30" or 32" barrels, molded ABS hard case. Reintroduced 2008. From Winchester Repeating Arms. Co.
Price: Model 101 Field **$1,739.00**
Price: Model 101 Deluxe Field **$1,659.00**
Price: Model 101 Sporting **$2,139.00**
Price: Model 101 Pigeon Grade Trap, intr. 2008 . . . . **$2,299.00**
Price: Model 101 Pigeon Grade Trap w/adj. comb,
intr. 2008. . . . . **$2,429.00**
Price: Model 101 Light (2009) **$1,999.00**
Price: Model 101 Pigeon Sporting (2009) **$2,579.00**

Prices given are believed to be accurate at time of publication however, many factors affect retail pricing so exact prices are not possible.

Variety of models for utility and sporting use, including some competitive shooting.

Bill Hanus Birdgun

CZ Bobwhite

CZ Ringneck

CZ Hammer Coach

ARRIETA SIDELOCK DOUBLE SHOTGUNS

Gauge: 12, 16, 20, 28, .410. **Barrel:** Length and chokes to customer specs. **Weight:** To customer specs. **Stock:** To customer specs. Straight English with checkered butt (standard), or pistol grip. Select European walnut with oil finish. **Features:** Essentially custom gun with myriad options. H&H pattern hand-detachable sidelocks, selective automatic ejectors, double triggers (hinged front) standard. Some have selfopening action. Finish and engraving to customer specs. Imported from Spain by Quality Arms, Inc.

Price: Model 557	$4,500.00
Price: Model 570	$5,350.00
Price: Model 578	$5,880.00
Price: Model 600 Imperial	$7,995.00
Price: Model 601 Imperial Tiro	$9,160.00
Price: Model 801	$14,275.00
Price: Model 802	$14,275.00
Price: Model 803	$9,550.00
Price: Model 871	$6,670.00
Price: Model 872	$17,850.00
Price: Model 873	$16,275.00
Price: Model 874	$13,125.00
Price: Model 875	$19,850.00
Price: Model 931	$20,895.00

AYA MODEL 4/53 SHOTGUNS

Gauge: 12, 16, 20, 28, 410. **Barrel:** 26", 27", 28", 30". **Weight:** To customer specifications. **Length:** To customer specifications. **Features:** Hammerless boxlock action; double triggers; light scroll engraving; automatic safety; straight grip oil finish walnut stock; checkered butt. Made in Spain. Imported by New England Custom Gun Service, Lt.

Price:	$2,999.00
Price: No. 2	$4,799.00
Price: No. 2 Rounded Action	$5,199.00

BERETTA 471 SIDE-BY-SIDE SHOTGUNS

Gauge: 12, 20; 3" chamber. **Barrel:** 24", 26", 28"; 6mm rib. **Weight:** 6.5 lbs. **Stock:** English or pistol stock, straight butt for various types of recoil pads. Beavertail forend. English stock with recoil pad in red or black rubber, or in walnut and splinter forend. Select European walnut, checkered, oil finish. **Features:** Optima-Choke Extended Choke Tubes. Automatic ejection or mechanical extraction. Firing-pin block safety,

manual or automatic, open top-lever safety. Introduced 2007. Imported from Italy by Beretta U.S.A.

Price: Silver Hawk........................ $3,750.00

BILL HANUS NOBILE III BY FABARM

Gauge: 20. **Barrel:** 28" Tribor® barrels with 3" chambers and extra-long 82mm (3-1/4") internal choke tubes. **Weight:** 5.75 lbs. **Stock:** Upgraded walnut 1-1/2"x2-1/4"x14-3/8", with 1/4" cast-off to a wood butt plate. Altering to 1/4" cast-on for left-handed shooters, $300 extra. **Features:** Tribor® barrels feature extra-long forcing cones along with over-boring, back-boring and extra-long (82mm vs 50mm) choke tubes which put more pellets in the target area. Paradox®-rifled choke tube for wider patterns at short-range targets. Adjustable for automatic ejectors or manual extraction. Adjustable opening tension. Fitted leather case.

Price: $3,395.00

CONNECTICUT SHOTGUN MANUFACTURING COMPANY RBL SIDE-BY-SIDE SHOTGUN

Gauge: 12, 16, 20, 28. **Barrel:** 26", 28", 30", 32". **Weight:** NA. **Length:** NA. **Stock:** NA. **Features:** Round-action SXS shotguns made in the USA. Scaled frames, five TruLock choke tubes. Deluxe fancy grade walnut buttstock and forend. Quick Change recoil pad in two lengths. Various dimensions and options available depending on gauge.

Price: 12 gauge	$2,950.00
Price: 20 gauge	$2,799.00
Price: 28 gauge	$3,650.00

CZ BOBWHITE AND RINGNECK SHOTGUNS

Gauge: 12, 20, 28, .410. (5 screw-in chokes in 12 and 20 ga. and fixed chokes in IC and Mod in .410). **Barrel:** 20". **Weight:** 6.5 lbs. **Length:** NA. **Stock:** Sculptured Turkish walnut with straight English-style grip and double triggers (Bobwhite) or conventional American pistol grip with a single trigger (Ringneck). Both are hand checkered 20 lpi. **Features:** Both color case-hardened shotguns are hand engraved.

Price: Bobwhite	$789.00
Price: Ringneck	$1,036.00

CZ HAMMER COACH SHOTGUNS

Gauge: 12, 3" chambers. **Barrel:** 20". **Weight:** 6.7 lbs. **Length:** NA. **Stock:** NA. **Features:** Following in the tradition of the guns used by the stagecoach guards of the 1880's, this cowboy gun features double triggers, 19th century color case-hardening and fully functional external hammers.

Price: $904.00

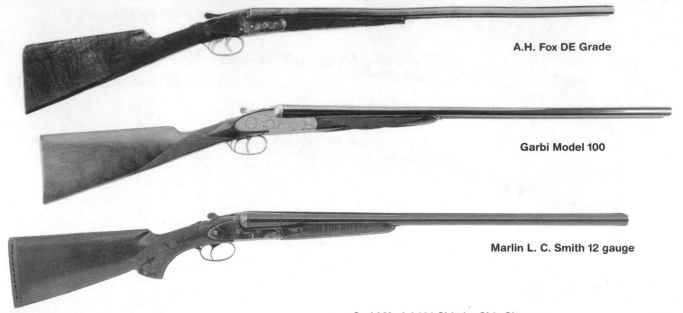

A.H. Fox DE Grade

Garbi Model 100

Marlin L. C. Smith 12 gauge

DAKOTA PREMIER GRADE SHOTGUN
Gauge: 12, 16, 20, 28, .410. **Barrel:** 27". **Weight:** NA. **Length:** NA. **Stock:** Exhibition-grade English walnut, hand-rubbed oil finish with straight grip and splinter forend. **Features:** French grey finish; 50 percent coverage engraving; double triggers; selective ejectors. Finished to customer specifications. Made in U.S. by Dakota Arms.
Price: From **$14,950.00**

Dakota Legend Shotgun
Similar to Premier Grade except has special selection English walnut, full-coverage scroll engraving, oak and leather case. Made in U.S. by Dakota Arms.
Price: From **$19,000.00**

EMF OLD WEST HAMMER SHOTGUN
Gauge: 12. **Barrel:** 20". **Weight:** 8 lbs. **Length:** 37" overall. **Stock:** Smooth walnut with steel butt place. **Sights:** Large brass bead. **Features:** Colt-style exposed hammers rebounding type; blued receiver and barrels; cylinder bore. Introduced 2006. Imported from China for EMF by TTN.
Price: **$474.90**

FOX, A.H., SIDE-BY-SIDE SHOTGUNS
Gauge: 16, 20, 28, .410. **Barrel:** Length and chokes to customer specifications. Rust-blued Chromox or Krupp steel. **Weight:** 5-1/2 to 6.75 lbs. **Stock:** Dimensions to customer specifications. Hand-checkered Turkish Circassian walnut with hand-rubbed oil finish. Straight, semi or full pistol grip; splinter, Schnabel or beavertail forend; traditional pad, hard rubber buttplate or skeleton butt. **Features:** Boxlock action with automatic ejectors; double or Fox single selective trigger. Scalloped, rebated and color case-hardened receiver; hand finished and handengraved. Grades differ in engraving, inlays, grade of wood, amount of hand finishing. Introduced 1993. Made in U.S. by Connecticut Shotgun Mfg.
Price: CE Grade **$14,500.00**
Price: XE Grade **$16,000.00**
Price: DE Grade **$19,000.00**
Price: FE Grade **$24,000.00**
Price: 28/.410 CE Grade **$16,500.00**
Price: 28/.410 XE Grade **$18,000.00**
Price: 28/.410 DE Grade **$21,000.00**
Price: 28/.410 FE Grade **$26,000.00**

GARBI MODEL 100 DOUBLE SHOTGUN
Gauge: 12, 16, 20, 28. **Barrel:** 26", 28", choked to customer specs. **Weight:** 5-1/2 to 7.5 lbs. **Stock:** 14.5"x2.25"x1.5". European walnut. Straight grip, checkered butt, classic forend. **Features:** Sidelock action, automatic ejectors, double triggers standard. Color case-hardened action, coin finish optional. Single trigger; beavertail forend, etc. optional. Five additional models available. Imported from Spain by Wm. Larkin Moore.
Price: From **$4,850.00**

Garbi Model 101 Side-by-Side Shotgun
Similar to the Garbi Model 100 except hand engraved with scroll engraving; select walnut stock; better overall quality than the Model 100. Imported from Spain by Wm. Larkin Moore.
Price: From **$6,250.00**

Garbi Model 103 A & B Side-by-Side Shotguns
Similar to the Garbi Model 100 except has Purdey-type fine scroll and rosette engraving. Better overall quality than the Model 101. Model 103B has nickel-chrome steel barrels, H&H-type easy opening mechanism; other mechanical details remain the same. Imported from Spain by Wm. Larkin Moore.
Price: Model 103A. From **$14,100.00**
Price: Model 103B. From **$21,600.00**

Garbi Model 200 Side-by-Side Shotgun
Similar to the Garbi Model 100 except has heavy-duty locks, magnum proofed. Very fine Continen-tal-style floral and scroll engraving, well figured walnut stock. Other mechanical features remain the same. Imported from Spain by Wm. Larkin Moore.
Price: **$17,100.00**

KIMBER VALIER SIDE-BY-SIDE SHOTGUN
Gauge: 20, 16, 3" chambers. **Barrels:** 26" or 28", IC and M. **Weight:** 6 lbs. 8 oz. **Stock:** Turkish walnut, English style. **Features:** Sidelock design, double triggers, 50-percent engraving; 24 lpi checkering; auto-ejectors (extractors only on Grade I). Color case-hardened sidelocks, rust blue barrels. Imported from Turkey by Kimber Mfg., Inc.
Price: Grade II **$4,999.00**

LEBEAU-COURALLY BOXLOCK SIDE-BY-SIDE SHOTGUN
Gauge: 12, 16, 20, 28, .410-bore. **Barrel:** 25" to 32". **Weight:** To customer specifications. **Stock:** French walnut. **Features:** Anson & Deely-type action with automatic ejectors; single or double triggers. Custom gun built to customer specifications. Imported from Belgium by Wm. Larkin Moore.
Price: From **$25,500.00**

LEBEAU-COURALLY SIDELOCK SIDE-BY-SIDE SHOTGUN
Gauge: 12, 16, 20, 28, .410-bore. **Barrel:** 25" to 32". **Weight:** To customer specifications. **Stock:** Fancy French walnut. **Features:** Holland & Holland-type action with automatic ejectors; single or double triggers. Custom gun built to customer specifications. Imported from Belgium by Wm. Larkin Moore.
Price: From **$56,000.00**

MARLIN L. C. SMITH SIDE-BY-SIDE SHOTGUN
Gauge: 12, 20, 28, .410. **Stock:** Checkered walnut w/recoil pad. **Features:** 3" chambers, single trigger, selective automatic ejectors; 3 choke tubes (IC, Mod., Full); solid rib, bead front sight. Imported from Italy by Marlin. Introduced 2005.
Price: LC12-DB (28" barrel, 43" OAL, 6.25 lbs) **$1,962.00**
Price: LC28-DB (26" barrel, 41" OAL, 6 lbs) **$1,484.00**

Prices given are believed to be accurate at time of publication however, many factors affect retail pricing so exact prices are not possible.

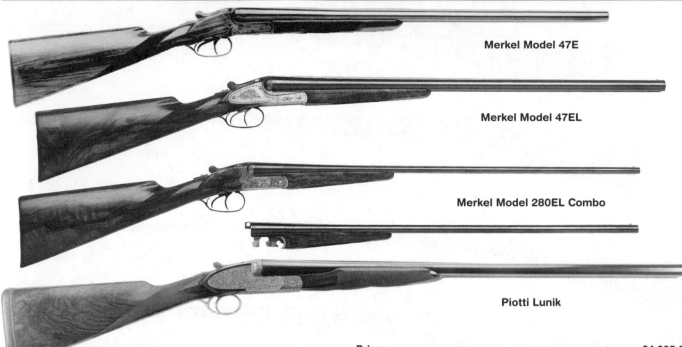

Merkel Model 47E

Merkel Model 47EL

Merkel Model 280EL Combo

Piotti Lunik

MERKEL MODEL 47E, 147E SIDE-BY-SIDE SHOTGUNS
Gauge: 12, 3" chambers, 16, 2.75" chambers, 20, 3" chambers. **Barrel:** 12, 16 ga.-28"; 20 ga.-26.75" (Imp. Cyl. & Mod., Mod. & Full). **Weight:** About 6.75 lbs. (12 ga.). **Stock:** Oil-finished walnut; straight English or pistol grip. **Features:** Anson & Deeley-type boxlock action with single selective or double triggers, automatic safety, cocking indicators. Color case-hardened receiver with standard arabesque engraving. Imported from Germany by Merkel USA.
Price: Model 47E (H&H ejectors) **$4,595.00**
Price: Model 147E (as above with ejectors) **$5,795.00**

Merkel Model 47EL, 147EL Side-by-Side Shotguns
Similar to Model 47E except H&H style sidelock action with cocking indicators, ejectors. Silver-grayed receiver and sideplates have arabesque engraving, engraved border and screws (Model 47E), or fine hunting scene engraving (Model 147E). Limited edition. Imported from Germany by Merkel USA.
Price: Model 47EL **$7,195.00**
Price: Model 147EL **$7,695.00**

Merkel Model 280EL, 360EL Shotguns
Similar to Model 47E except smaller frame. Greener cross bolt with double under-barrel locking lugs, fine engraved hunting scenes on silver-grayed receiver, luxury-grade wood, Anson and Deely boxlock action. H&H ejectors, single-selective or double triggers. Introduced 2000. Imported from Germany by Merkel USA.
Price: Model 280EL (28 gauge, 28" barrel, Imp. Cyl. and
Mod. chokes) **$7,695.00**
Price: Model 360EL (.410, 28" barrel, Mod. and
Full chokes) **$7,695.00**
Price: Model 280EL Combo **$11,195.00**

MERKEL MODEL 280SL and 360SL Shotguns
Similar to Model 280EL and 360EL except has sidelock action, double triggers, English-style arabesque engraving. Introduced 2000. Imported from Germany by Merkel USA.
Price: Model 280SL (28 gauge, 28" barrel, Imp. Cyl.
and Mod. chokes) **$10,995.00**
Price: Model 360SL (.410, 28" barrel, Mod. and
Full chokes) **$10,995.00**

MERKEL MODEL 1620 SIDE-BY-SIDE SHOTGUN
Gauge: 16. **Features:** Greener crossbolt with double under-barrel locking lugs, scroll-engraved case-hardened receiver, Anson and Deely boxlock aciton, Holland & Holland ejectors, English-style stock, single selective or double triggers, or pistol grip stock with single selective trgger. Imported from Germany by Merkel USA.

Price: **$4,995.00**
Price: Model 1620E; silvered, engraved receiver **$5,995.00**
Price: Model 1620 Combo; 16- and 20-gauge two-barrel set **$7,695.00**
Price: Model 1620EL; upgraded wood **$7,695.00**
Price: Model 1620EL Combo; 16- and 20-gauge two-barrel
set **$11,195.00**

PIOTTI KING NO. 1 SIDE-BY-SIDE SHOTGUN
Gauge: 12, 16, 20, 28, .410. **Barrel:** 25" to 30" (12 ga.), 25" to 28" (16, 20, 28, .410). To customer specs. Chokes as specified. **Weight:** 6.5 lbs. to 8 lbs. (12 ga. to customer specs.). **Stock:** Dimensions to customer specs. Finely figured walnut; straight grip with checkered butt with classic splinter forend and hand-rubbed oil finish standard. Pistol grip, beavertail forend. **Features:** Holland & Holland pattern sidelock action, automatic ejectors. Double trigger; non-selective single trigger optional. Coin finish standard; color case-hardened optional. Top rib; level, file-cut; concave, ventilated optional. Very fine, full coverage scroll engraving with small floral bouquets. Imported from Italy by Wm. Larkin Moore.
Price: From **$38,300.00**

Piotti Lunik Side-by-Side Shotgun
Similar to the Piotti King No. 1 in overall quality. Has Renaissance-style large scroll engraving in relief. Best quality Holland & Holland-pattern sidelock ejector double with chopper lump (demi-bloc) barrels. Other mechanical specifications remain the same. Imported from Italy by Wm. Larkin Moore.
Price: From **$39,900.00**

PIOTTI PIUMA SIDE-BY-SIDE SHOTGUN
Gauge: 12, 16, 20, 28, .410. **Barrel:** 25" to 30" (12 ga.), 25" to 28" (16, 20, 28, .410). **Weight:** 5-1/2 to 6-1/4 lbs. (20 ga.). **Stock:** Dimensions to customer specs. Straight grip stock with walnut checkered butt, classic splinter forend, hand-rubbed oil finish are standard; pistol grip, beavertail forend, satin luster finish optional. **Features:** Anson & Deeley boxlock ejector double with chopper lump barrels. Level, file-cut rib, light scroll and rosette engraving, scalloped frame. Double triggers; single non-selective optional. Coin finish standard, color case-hardened optional. Imported from Italy by Wm. Larkin Moore.
Price: From **$19,200.00**

REMINGTON SPR210 SIDE-BY-SIDE SHOTGUNS
Gauge: 12, 20, 28, .410 bore, 3" chambers; 28, 2-3/4" chambers. **Barrel:** 26", 28", blued chrome-lined. **Weight:** 6.75 to 7 lbs. **Stock:** checkered walnut stock and forend, 14.5" LOP; 1.5" drop at comb; 2.5" drop at heel. **Features:** Nickel or blued receiver. Single selective mechanical trigger, selective automatic ejectors; SC-4 choke tube set on most models. Steel receiver/mono block, auto tang safety, rubber recoil pad. Introduced 2008. Imported by Remington Arms Co.
Price: SPR210, from **$479.00**

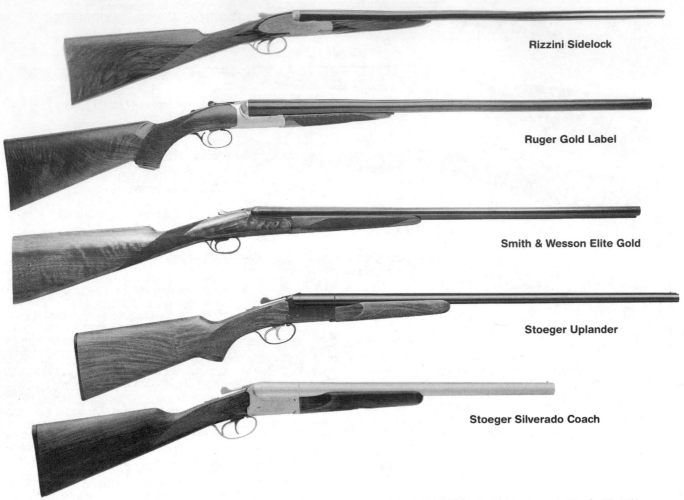

Rizzini Sidelock

Ruger Gold Label

Smith & Wesson Elite Gold

Stoeger Uplander

Stoeger Silverado Coach

REMINGTON SPR220 SIDE-BY-SIDE SHOTGUNS
Gauge: 12, 20, 2-3/4" or 3" chambers. **Barrel:** 20", 26", blued chrome-lined. **Weight:** 6.25 to 7 lbs. Otherwise similar to SPR210 except has double trigger/extractors. Introduced 2008. Imported by Remington Arms Co.
Price: SPR220, from $342.00

RIZZINI SIDELOCK SIDE-BY-SIDE SHOTGUN
Gauge: 12, 16, 20, 28, .410. **Barrel:** 25" to 30" (12, 16, 20 ga.), 25" to 28" (28, .410). To customer specs. Chokes as specified. **Weight:** 6.5 lbs. to 8 lbs. (12 ga. to customer specs). **Stock:** Dimensions to customer specs. Finely figured walnut; straight grip with checkered butt with classic splinter forend and hand-rubbed oil finish standard. Pistol grip, beavertail forend. **Features:** Sidelock action, auto ejectors. Double triggers or non-selective single trigger standard. Coin finish standard. Imported from Italy by Wm. Larkin Moore.
Price: 12, 20 ga. From $106,000.00
Price: 28, .410 bore. From $95,000.00

RUGER GOLD LABEL SIDE-BY-SIDE SHOTGUN
Gauge: 12, 3" chambers. **Barrel:** 28" with skeet tubes. **Weight:** 6.5 lbs. **Length:** 45". **Stock:** American walnut straight or pistol grip. **Sights:** Gold bead front, full length rib, serrated top. **Features:** Spring-assisted break-open, SS trigger, auto eject. Five interchangeable screw-in choke tubes, combination safety/barrel selector with auto safety reset.
Price: $3,226.00

SMITH & WESSON ELITE GOLD SHOTGUNS
Gauge: 20, 3" chambers. **Barrel:** 26", 28", 30", rust-blued chopper-lump. **Weight:** 6.5 lbs. **Length:** 43.5-45.5". **Sights:** Ivory front bead, metal mid-bead. **Stock:** AAA (grade III) Turkish walnut stocks, hand-cut checkering, satin finish. English grip or pistol grip. **Features:** Smith & Wesson-designed trigger-plate action, hand-engraved receivers, bone-charcoal case hardening, lifetime warranty. Five choke tubes.

Introduced 2007. Made in Turkey, imported by Smith & Wesson.
Price: $2,380.00

STOEGER UPLANDER SIDE-BY-SIDE SHOTGUNS
Gauge: 16, 28, 2-3/4" chambers. 12, 20, .410, 3" chambers. **Barrel:** 22", 24", 26", 28". **Weight:** 7.3 lbs. **Sights:** Brass bead. **Features:** Double trigger, IC & M fixed choke tubes with gun.
Price: With fixed or screw-in chokes. $369.00
Price: Supreme, screw-in chokes, 12 or 20 ga. $489.00
Price: Youth, 20 ga. or .410, 22" barrel, double trigger $369.00
Price: Combo, 20/28 ga. or 12/20 ga. $649.00

STOEGER COACH GUN SIDE-BY-SIDE SHOTGUNS
Gauge: 12, 20, 2-3/4", 3" chambers. **Barrel:** 20". **Weight:** 6.5 lbs. **Stock:** Brown hardwood, classic beavertail forend. **Sights:** Brass bead. **Features:** IC & M fixed chokes, tang auto safety, auto extractors, black plastic buttplate. Imported by Benelli USA.
Price: Supreme blued finish $469.00
Price: Supreme blued barrel, stainless receiver $469.00
Price: Silverado Coach Gun with English synthetic stock. $469.00

TRADITIONS ELITE SERIES SIDE-BY-SIDE SHOTGUNS
Gauge: 12, 3"; 20, 3"; 28, 2-3/4"; .410, 3". **Barrel:** 26". **Weight:** 5 lbs., 12 oz. to 6.5 lbs. **Length:** 43" overall. **Stock:** Walnut. **Features:** Chrome-lined barrels; fixed chokes (Elite Field III ST, Field I DT and Field I ST) or choke tubes (Elite Hunter ST); extractors (Hunter ST and Field I models) or automatic ejectors (Field III ST); top tang safety. Imported from Fausti of Italy by Traditions.
Price: Elite Field I DT C 12, 20, 28 ga. or .410; IC and Mod. fixed chokes (F and F on .410); double triggers . . $789.00 to $969.00
Price: Elite Field I ST C 12, 20, 28 ga. or .410; same as DT but with single trigger . . . . $969.00 to $1,169.00
Price: Elite Field III ST C 28 ga. or .410; gold-engraved receiver; high-grade walnut stock $2,099.00
Price: Elite Hunter ST C 12 or 20 ga.; blued receiver; IC and Mod. choke tubes $999.00

Prices given are believed to be accurate at time of publication however, many factors affect retail pricing so exact prices are not possible.

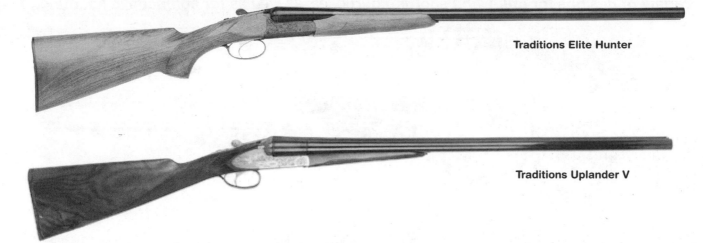

Traditions Elite Hunter

Traditions Uplander V

TRADITIONS UPLANDER SERIES SIDE-BY-SIDE SHOTGUNS
Gauge: 12, 3"; 20, 3". **Barrel:** 26", 28". **Weight:** 6-1/4 lbs. to 6.5 lbs. **Length:** 43" to 45" overall. **Stock:** Walnut. **Features:** Barrels threaded for choke tubes (Improved Cylinder, Modified and Full); top tang safety, extended trigger guard. Engraved silver receiver with side plates and lavish gold inlays. Imported from Fausti of Italy by Traditions.
Price: Uplander III Silver 12, 20 ga. $2,699.00
Price: Uplander V Silver 12, 20 ga. $3,199.00

TRISTAR BRITTANY CLASSIC SIDE-BY-SIDE SHOTGUN
Gauge: 12, 16, 20, 28, .410, 3" chambers. **Barrel:** 27", chrome lined, three Beretta-style choke tubes (IC, M, F). **Weight:** 6.3 to 6.7 lbs. **Stock:** Rounded pistol grip, satin oil finish. **Features:** Engraved case-colored one-piece frame, auto se-lective ejectors, single selective trigger, solid raised barrel rib, top tang safety. Imported from Spain by Tristar Sporting Arms Ltd.
Price: From. $1,419.00

WEATHERBY SBS ATHENA D'ITALIA SIDE-BY-SIDE SHOTGUNS
Gauge: D'Italia: 12, 20, 2-3/4" or 3" chambers, 28, 2-3/4" chambers. **Barrel:** 26" on 20 and 28 gauges; 28" on 12 ga. Chrome-lined, lengthened forcing cones, backbored. **Weight:** 6.75 to 7.25 lbs. **Length:** 42.5" to 44.5". **Stock:** Walnut, 20-lpi laser cut checkering, "New Scottish" pattern. **Features:** All come with foam-lined take-down case. Machined steel receiver, hardened and chromed with coin finish, engraved triggerguard with roll-formed border. D'Italia has double triggers, brass front bead. PG is identical to D'Italia, except for rounded pistol grip and semi-beavertail forearm. Deluxe features sculpted frameheads, Bolino-style engraved game scene with floral engraving. AAA Fancy Turkish walnut, straight grip, 24-lpi hand checkering, hand-rubbed oil finish. Single mechanical trigger; right barrel fires first. Imported from Italy by Weatherby.
Price: SBS Athena D'Italia SBS $3,129.00
Price: SBS Athena D'Italia PG SBS $3,799.00

Variety of designs for utility and sporting purposes, as well as for competitive shooting.

Browning BT-99 Trap

H&R Model 928 Ultra Slug Hunter Deluxe

H&R Tamer

H&R Ultra Lite Slug Hunter

H&R Topper Deluxe

BERETTA DT10 TRIDENT TRAP TOP SINGLE SHOTGUN
Gauge: 12, 3" chamber. **Barrel:** 34"; five Optima Choke tubes (Full, Full, Imp. Modified, Mod. and Imp. Cyl.). **Weight:** 8.8 lbs. **Stock:** High-grade walnut; adjustable. **Features:** Detachable, adjustable trigger group; Optima Bore for improved shot pattern and reduced recoil; slim Optima Choke tubes; raised and thickened receiver for long life. Introduced 2000. Imported from Italy by Beretta USA.
Price: **$7,400.00**

BROWNING BT-99 TRAP O/U SHOTGUNS
Gauge: 12. **Barrel:** 30", 32", 34". **Stock:** Walnut; standard or adjustable. **Weight:** 7 lbs. 11 oz. to 9 lbs. **Features:** Back-bored single barrel; interchangeable chokes; beavertail forearm; extractor only; high rib.
Price: BT-99 w/conventional comb, 32" or 34" barrels **$1,529.00**
Price: BT-99 w/adjustable comb, 32" or 34" barrels **$1,839.00**
Price: BT-99 Golden Clays w/adjustable comb, 32" or
34" barrels **$3,989.00**
Price: BT-99 Grade III, 32" or 34" barrels, intr. 2008 ...... **$2,369.00**

HARRINGTON & RICHARDSON ULTRA SLUG HUNTER/TAMER SHOTGUNS
Gauge: 12, 20 ga., 3" chamber, .410. **Barrel:** 20" to 24" rifled. **Weight:** 6 to 9 lbs. **Length:** 34.5" to 40". **Stock:** Hardwood, laminate, or polymer with full pistol grip; semi-beavertail forend. **Sights:** Gold bead front. **Features:** Break-open action with side-lever release, automatic ejector. Introduced 1994. From H&R 1871, LLC.

Price: Ultra Slug Hunter, blued, hardwood **$273.00**
Price: Ultra Slug Hunter Youth, blued, hardwood, 13-1/8"
LOP. **$273.00**
Price: Ultra Slug Hunter Deluxe, blued, laminated **$273.00**
Price: Tamer .410 bore, stainless barrel, black polymer stock . **$173.00**

HARRINGTON & RICHARDSON ULTRA LITE SLUG HUNTER
Gauge: 12, 20 ga., 3" chamber. **Barrel:** 24" rifled. **Weight:** 5.25 lbs. **Length:** 40". **Stock:** Hardwood with walnut finish, full pistol grip, recoil pad, sling swivel studs. **Sights:** None; base included. **Features:** Youth Model, available in 20 ga. has 20" rifled barrel. Deluxe Model has checkered laminated stock and forend. From H&R 1871, LLC.
Price: **$194.00**

Harrington & Richardson Ultra Slug Hunter Thumbhole Stock
Similar to the Ultra Lite Slug Hunter but with laminated thumbhole stock and weighs 8.5 lbs.
Price: .... **NA**

HARRINGTON & RICHARDSON TOPPER MODELS
Gauge: 12, 16, 20, .410, up to 3.5" chamber. **Barrel:** 22 to 28". **Weight:** 5-7 lbs. **Stock:** Polymer, hardwood, or black walnut. **Features:** Satin nickel frame, blued barrel. Reintroduced 1992. From H&R 1871, LLC.
Price: Deluxe Classic, 12/20 ga., 28" barrel w/vent rib **$225.00**
Price: Topper Deluxe 12 ga., 28" barrel, black hardwood **$179.00**
Price: Topper 12, 16, 20 ga., .410, 26" to 28", black
hardwood **$153.00**
Price: Topper Junior 20 ga., .410, 22" barrel, hardwood **$160.00**
Price: Topper Junior Classic, 20 ga., .410, checkered
hardwood **$160.00**

SHOTGUNS—Bolt Actions & Single Shot

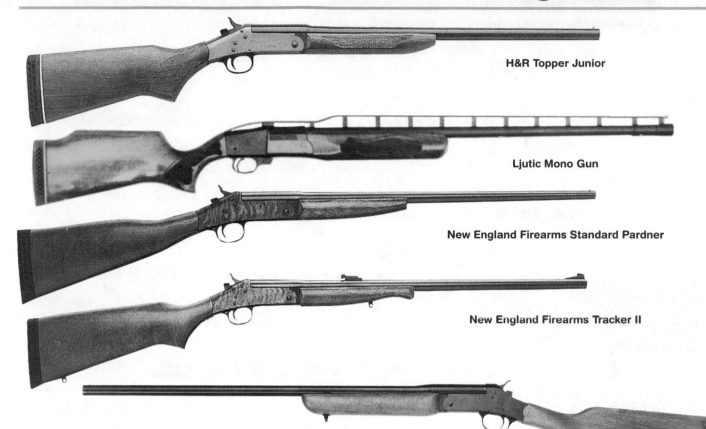

H&R Topper Junior

Ljutic Mono Gun

New England Firearms Standard Pardner

New England Firearms Tracker II

Rossi Single-Shot

Harrington & Richardson Topper Trap Gun
Similar to other Topper Models but with select checkered walnut stock and forend wtih fluted comb and full pistol grip; 30" barrel with two white beads and screw-in chokes (Improved Modified Extended included); deluxe Pachmayr trap recoil pad.
Price: $360.00

KRIEGHOFF K-80 SINGLE BARREL TRAP GUN
Gauge: 12, 2-3/4" chamber. **Barrel:** 32" or 34" Unsingle. Fixed Full or choke tubes. **Weight:** About 8-3/4 lbs. **Stock:** Four stock dimensions or adjustable stock available. All hand-checkered European walnut. **Features:** Satin nickel finish. Selective mechanical trigger adjustable for finger position. Tapered step vent rib. Adjustable point of impact.
Price: Standard grade Full Unsingle, from $10,080.00

KRIEGHOFF KX-5 TRAP GUN
Gauge: 12, 2-3/4" chamber. **Barrel:** 32", 34"; choke tubes. **Weight:** About 8.5 lbs. **Stock:** Factory adjustable stock. European walnut. **Features:** Ventilated tapered step rib. Adjustable position trigger, optional reloace trigger. Fully adjustable rib. Satin gray electroless nickel receiver. Fitted aluminum case. Imported from Germany by Krieghoff International, Inc.
Price: $5,395.00

LJUTIC MONO GUN SINGLE BARREL SHOTGUN
Gauge: 12 only. **Barrel:** 34", choked to customer specs; hollow-milled rib, 35.5" sight plane. **Weight:** Approx. 9 lbs. **Stock:** To customer specs. Oil finish, hand checkered. **Features:** Custom gun. Pull or release trigger; removable trigger guard contains trigger and hammer mechanism; Ljutic pushbutton opener on front of trigger guard. From Ljutic Industries.
Price: Std., med. or Olympic rib, custom bbls., fixed choke.. $7,495.00
Price: Stainless steel mono gun $8,495.00

Ljutic LTX Pro 3 Deluxe Mono Gun
Deluxe, lightweight version of the Mono gun with high quality wood, upgrade checkering, special rib height, screw-in chokes, ported and cased.
Price: $8,995.00
Price: Stainless steel model $9,995.00

NEW ENGLAND FIREARMS PARDNER AND TRACKER II SHOTGUNS
Gauge: 10, 12, 16, 20, 28, .410, up to 3.5" chamber for 10 and 12 ga.

16, 28, 2-3/4" chamber. **Barrel:** 24" to 30". **Weight:** Varies from 5 to 9.5 lbs. **Length:** Varies from 36" to 48". **Stock:** Walnut-finished hardwood with full pistol grip, synthetic, or camo finish. **Sights:** Bead front on most. **Features:** Transfer bar ignition; break-open action with side-lever release. Introduced 1987. From New England Firearms.
Price: Pardner, all gauges, hardwood stock, 26" to 32"
blued barrel, Mod. or Full choke $140.00
Price: Pardner Youth, hardwood stock, straight grip,
22" blued barrel $149.00
Price: Pardner Screw-In Choke model, intr. 2006 . . . . $164.00
Price: Turkey model, 10/12 ga., camo finish
or black . . . . $192.00 to $259.00
Price: Youth Turkey, 20 ga., camo finish or black $192.00
Price: Waterfowl, 10 ga., camo finish or hardwood $227.00
Price: Tracker II slug gun, 12/20 ga., hardwood $196.00

REMINGTON SPR100 SINGLE-SHOT SHOTGUNS
Gauge: 12, 20, .410 bore, 3" chambers. **Barrel:** 24", 26", 28", 29.5", blued chrome-lined. **Weight:** 6.25 to 6.5 lbs. **Stock:** Walnut stock and forend. **Features:** Nickel or blued receiver. Cross-bolt safety, cocking indicator, titanium-coated trigger, selectable ejector or extractor. Introduced 2008. Imported by Remington Arms Co.
Price: SPR100, from $479.00

ROSSI SINGLE-SHOT SHOTGUNS
Gauge: 12, 20, .410. **Barrel:** 22" (Youth), 28". **Weight:** 3.75-5.25 lbs. **Stocks:** Wood. **Sights:** Bead front sight, fully adjustable fiber optic sight on Slug and Turkey. **Features:** Single-shot break open, 8 models available, positive ejection, internal transfer bar mechanism, trigger block system, Taurus Security System, blued finish, Rifle Slug has ported barrel.
Price: From $117.00

ROSSI TUFFY SHOTGUN
Gauge: .410. **Barrel:** 18-1/2". **Weight:** 3 lbs. **Length:** 29.5" overall. **Features:** Single-shot break-open model with black synthetic thumbhole stock in blued or stainless finish.
Price: . . . . Appx. $150.00

Rossi Tuffy

Rossi Matched Pair

Tar-Hunt RSG-20 Mountaineer

Thompson/Center Encore Rifled Slug

Thompson/Center Encore Turkey

ROSSI MATCHED PAIRS
Gauge/Caliber: 12, 20, .410, .22 Mag, .22LR, .17HMR, .223 Rem, .243 Win, .270 Win, .30-06, .308 Win, .50 (black powder). **Barrel:** 23", 28". **Weight:** 5-6.3 lbs. **Stocks:** Wood or black synthetic. **Sights:** Bead front on shotgun barrel, fully adjustable front and rear on rifle barrel, drilled and tapped for scope, fully adjustable fiber optic sights (black powder). **Features:** Single-shot break open, 27 models available, internal transfer bar mechanism, manual external safety, blue finish, trigger block system, Taurus Security System, youth models available.
Price: Rimfire/Shotgun, from **$160.00**
Price: Centerfire/Shotgun **$271.95**
Price: Black Powder Matched Pair, from **$262.00**

ROSSI MATCHED SET
Gauge/Caliber: 12, 20, .22 LR, .17 HMR, .243 Win, .270 Win, .50 (black powder). **Barrel:** 33.5". **Weight:** 6.25-6.3 lbs. **Stocks:** Wood. **Sights:** Bead front on shotgun barrel, fully adjustable front and rear on rifle barrel, drilled and tapped for scope, fully adjustable fiber optic sights (black powder). **Features:** Single-shot break open, 4 models available, internal transfer bar mechanism, manual external safety, blue finish, trigger block system, Taurus Security System, youth models available.
Price: From **$374.00**

TAR-HUNT RSG-12 PROFESSIONAL RIFLED SLUG GUN
Gauge: 12, 2-3/4" or 3" chamber, 1-shot magazine. **Barrel:** 23", fully rifled with muzzle brake. **Weight:** 7.75 lbs. **Length:** 41.5" overall. **Stock:** Matte black McMillan fiberglass with Pachmayr Decelerator pad. **Sights:** None furnished; comes with Leupold windage or Weaver bases. **Features:** Uses rifle-style action with two locking lugs; two-position safety; Shaw barrel; single-stage, trigger; muzzle brake.

Many options available. All models have area-controlled feed action. Introduced 1991. Made in U.S. by Tar-Hunt Custom Rifles, Inc.
Price: 12 ga. Professional model **$2,585.00**
Price: Left-hand model add. **$110.00**

Tar-Hunt RSG-16 Elite Shotgun
Similar to RSG-12 Professional except 16 gauge; right- or left-hand versions.
Price: **$2,585.00**

Tar-Hunt RSG-20 Mountaineer Slug Gun
Similar to the RSG-12 Professional except chambered for 20 gauge (2-3/4" and 3" shells); 23" Shaw rifled barrel, with muzzle brake; two-lug bolt; one-shot blind magazine; matte black finish; McMillan fiberglass stock with Pachmayr Decelerator pad; receiver drilled and tapped for Rem. 700 bases. Right- or left-hand versions. Weighs 6.5 lbs. Introduced 1997. Made in U.S. by Tar-Hunt Custom Rifles, Inc.
Price: **$2,585.00**

THOMPSON/CENTER ENCORE RIFLED SLUG GUN
Gauge: 20, 3" chamber. **Barrel:** 26", fully rifled. **Weight:** About 7 lbs. **Length:** 40.5" overall. **Stock:** Walnut with walnut forearm. **Sights:** Steel; click-adjustable rear and ramp-style front, both with fiber optics. **Features:** Encore system features a variety of rifle, shotgun and muzzle-loading rifle barrels interchangeable with the same frame. Break-open design operates by pulling up and back on trigger guard spur. Composite stock and forearm available. Introduced 2000.
Price: **$684.00**

THOMPSON/CENTER ENCORE TURKEY GUN
Gauge: 12 ga. **Barrel:** 24". **Features:** All-camo finish, high definition Realtree Hardwoods HD camo.
Price: **$763.00**

Designs for utility, suitable for and adaptable to competitions and other sporting purposes.

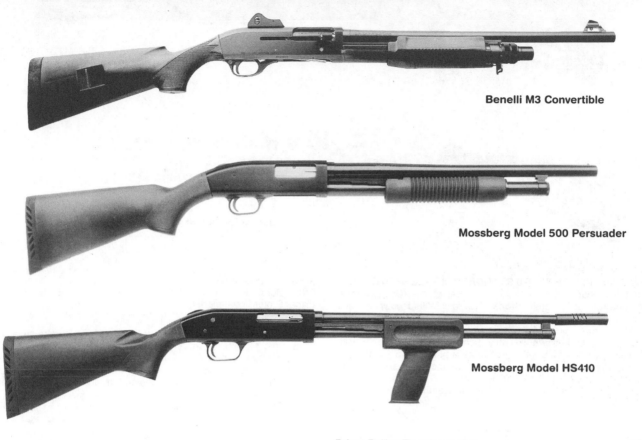

Benelli M3 Convertible

Mossberg Model 500 Persuader

Mossberg Model HS410

BENELLI M3 CONVERTIBLE SHOTGUN
Gauge: 12, 2-3/4", 3" chambers, 5-shot magazine. **Barrel:** 19.75" (Cyl.). **Weight:** 7 lbs., 4oz. **Length:** 41" overall. **Stock:** High-impact polymer with sling loop in side of butt; rubberized pistol grip on stock. **Sights:** Open rifle, fully adjustable. Ghost ring and rifle type. **Features:** Combination pump/auto action. Alloy receiver with inertia recoil rotating locking lug bolt; matte finish; automatic shell release lever. Introduced 1989. Imported by Benelli USA. Price with pistol grip, open rifle sights.
Price: With ghost ring sights, pistol grip stock **$1,489.00**

BENELLI M2 TACTICAL SHOTGUN
Gauge: 12, 2-3/4", 3" chambers, 5-shot magazine. **Barrel:** 18.5" IC, M, F choke tubes. **Weight:** 6.7 lbs. **Length:** 39.75" overall. **Stock:** Black polymer. **Sights:** Rifle type ghost ring system, tritium night sights optional. **Features:** Semi-auto intertia recoil action. Cross-bolt safety; bolt release button; matte-finish metal. Introduced 1993. Imported from Italy by Benelli USA.
Price: With rifle sights **$1,159.00**
Price: With ghost ring sights, standard stock **$1,269.00**
Price: With ghost ring sights, pistol grip stock **$1,269.00**
Price: With rifle sights, pistol grip stock **$1,159.00**
Price: ComforTech stock, rifle sights **$1,269.00**
Price: Comfortech Stock, Ghost Ring. **$1,379.00**

MOSSBERG MODEL 500 SPECIAL PURPOSE SHOTGUNS
Gauge: 12, 20, .410, 3" chamber. **Barrel:** 18.5", 20" (Cyl.). **Weight:** 7 lbs. **Stock:** Walnut-finished hardwood or black synthetic. **Sights:** Metal bead front. **Features:** Available in 6- or 8-shot models. Top-mounted safety, double action slide bars, swivel studs, rubber recoil pad. Blue, Parkerized, Marinecote finishes. Mossberg Cablelock included. From Mossberg. The HS410 Home Security model chambered for .410 with 3" chamber; has pistol grip forend, thick recoil pad, muzzle brake and has special spreader choke on the 18.5" barrel. Overall length is 37.5", weight is 6.25 lbs. Blue finish; synthetic field stock. Mossberg Cablelock and video included. Mariner model has Marinecote metal finish to resist rust and corrosion. Synthetic field stock; pistol grip kit included. 500 Tactical 6-shot has black synthetic tactical stock. Introduced 1990.

Price: Rolling Thunder, 6-shot **$471.00**
Price: Tactical Cruiser, 18.5" barrel **$434.00**
Price: Persuader/Cruiser, 6 shot, from **$394.00**
Price: Persuader/Cruiser, 8 shot, from **$394.00**
Price: HS410 Home Security **$404.00**
Price: Mariner 6 or 9 shot, from **$538.00**
Price: Tactical 6 shot, from **$509.00**

MOSSBERG MODEL 590 SPECIAL PURPOSE SHOTGUN
Gauge: 12, 3" chamber, 9 shot magazine. **Barrel:** 20" (Cyl.). **Weight:** 7.25 lbs. **Stock:** Synthetic field or Speedfeed. **Sights:** Metal bead front or Ghost Ring. **Features:** Top-mounted safety, double slide action bars. Comes with heat shield, bayonet lug, swivel studs, rubber recoil pad. Blue, Parkerized or Marinecote finish. Mossberg Cablelock included. From Mossberg.
Price: Synthetic stock, from **$471.00**
Price: Speedfeed stock, from **$552.00**

REMINGTON MODEL 870 AND MODEL 1100 TACTICAL SHOTGUNS
Gauge: 870: 12, 2-3/4 or 3" chamber; 1100: 2-3/4". **Barrel:** 18", 20", 22" (Cyl or IC). **Weight:** 7.5-7.75 lbs. **Length:** 38.5-42.5" overall. **Stock:** Black synthetic, synthetic Speedfeed IV full pistol-grip stock, or Knoxx Industries SpecOps stock w/recoil-absorbing spring-loaded cam and adjustable length of pull (12" to 16", 870 only). **Sights:** Front post w/ dot only on 870; rib and front dot on 1100. **Features:** R3 recoil pads, LimbSaver technology to reduce felt recoil, 2-, 3- or 4-shot extensions based on barrel length; matte-olive-drab barrels and receivers. Model 1100 Tactical is available with Speedfeed IV pistol grip stock or standard black synthetic stock and forend. Speedfeed IV model has an 18" barrel with two-shot extension. Standard synthetic-stocked version is equipped with 22" barrel and four-shot extension. Introduced 2006. From Remington Arms Co.
Price: 870, Speedfeed IV stock, 3" chamber,
38.5" overall, from **$587.00**
Price: 870, SpecOps stock, 3" chamber, 38.5" overall, from . . **$587.00**
Price: 1100, synthetic stock, 2-3/4" chamber, 42.5" overall . . . **$945.00**
Price: 870 TAC Desert Recon (2008), 18" barrel, 2-shot **$692.00**

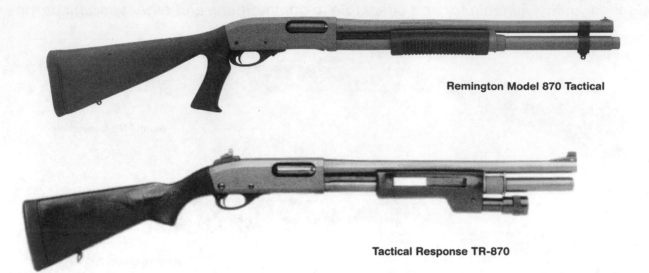

Remington Model 870 Tactical

Tactical Response TR-870

TACTICAL RESPONSE TR-870 STANDARD MODEL SHOTGUNS
Gauge: 12, 3" chamber, 7-shot magazine. **Barrel:** 18" (Cyl.). **Weight:** 9 lbs. **Length:** 38" overall. **Stock:** Fiberglass-filled polypropolene with non-snag recoil absorbing butt pad. Nylon tactical forend houses flashlight. **Sights:** Trak-Lock ghost ring sight system. Front sight has Tritium insert. **Features:** Highly modified Remington 870P with Parkerized finish. Comes with nylon three-way adjustable sling, high visibility non-binding follower, high performance magazine spring, Jumbo Head safety, and Side Saddle extended 6-shot shell carrier on left side of receiver. Introduced 1991. From Scattergun Technologies, Inc.

Price: Standard model **$1,050.00**
Price: Border Patrol model, from **$1,050.00**
Price: Professional model, from **$1,070.00**

TRISTAR COBRA PUMP
Gauge: 12, 3". **Barrel:** 28". **Weight:** 6.7 lbs. Three Beretta-style choke tubes (IC, M, F). **Length:** NA. **Stock:** Matte black synthetic stock and forearm. **Sights:** Vent rib with matted sight plane. **Features:** Five-year warranty. Cobra Tactical Pump Shotgun magazine holds 7, return spring in forearm, 20" barrel, Cylinder choke. Introduced 2008. Imported by Tristar Sporting Arms Ltd.
Price: Tactical **$349.00**

Prices given are believed to be accurate at time of publication however, many factors affect retail pricing so exact prices are not possible.

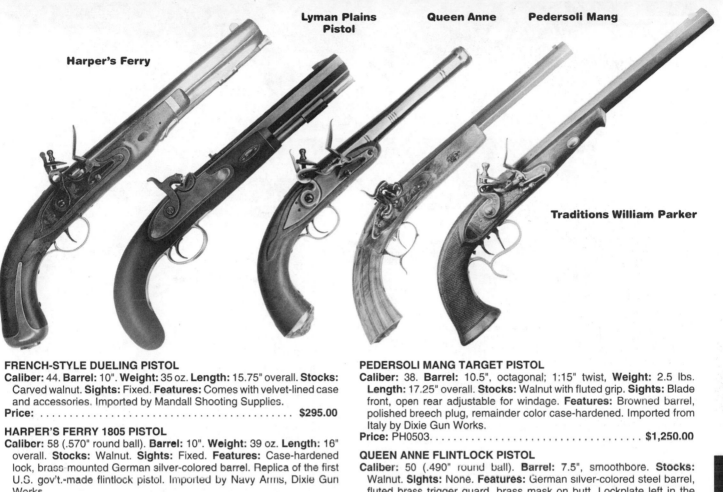

Harper's Ferry

Lyman Plains Pistol

Queen Anne

Pedersoli Mang

Traditions William Parker

FRENCH-STYLE DUELING PISTOL
Caliber: 44. **Barrel:** 10". **Weight:** 35 oz. **Length:** 15.75" overall. **Stocks:** Carved walnut. **Sights:** Fixed. **Features:** Comes with velvet-lined case and accessories. Imported by Mandall Shooting Supplies.
Price: **$295.00**

HARPER'S FERRY 1805 PISTOL
Caliber: 58 (.570" round ball). **Barrel:** 10". **Weight:** 39 oz. **Length:** 16" overall. **Stocks:** Walnut. **Sights:** Fixed. **Features:** Case-hardened lock, brass-mounted German silver-colored barrel. Replica of the first U.S. gov't.-made flintlock pistol. Imported by Navy Arms, Dixie Gun Works.
Price: Dixie Gun Works RH0225 . . . . **$495.00**
Price: Dixie Kit FH0411 . . . . **$395.00**

KENTUCKY FLINTLOCK PISTOL
Caliber: 45, 50, 54. **Barrel:** 10.4". **Weight:** 37-40 oz. **Length:** 15.4" overall. **Stocks:** Walnut. **Sights:** Fixed. **Features:** Specifications, including caliber, weight and length may vary with importer. Case-hardened lock, blued barrel; available also as brass barrel flintlock Model 1821. Imported by The Armoury.
Price: Single cased set (Navy Arms) **$375.00**

KENTUCKY PERCUSSION PISTOL
Similar to Flint version but percussion lock. Imported by The Armoury, Navy Arms, CVA (50-cal.).
Price: . . . . **$129.95 to $225.00**
Price: Steel barrel (Armoury) **$179.00**
Price: Single cased set (Navy Arms) **$355.00**
Price: Double cased set (Navy Arms) **$600.00**

LE PAGE PERCUSSION DUELING PISTOL
Caliber: .45. **Barrel:** 10.25" octagon, rifled. **Weight:** 36-41 oz. **Length:** 16.9" overall. **Stocks:** Walnut, fluted butt. **Sights:** Blade front, open style rear. **Features:** Double set trigger. Bright barrel, brass furniture (silver plated). Imported by Dixie Gun Works
Price: PH0310 . . . .**$525.00**

LYMAN PLAINS PISTOL
Caliber: 50 or 54. **Barrel:** 8"; 1:30" twist, both calibers. **Weight:** 50 oz. **Length:** 15" overall. **Stocks:** Walnut half-stock. **Sights:** Blade front, square notch rear adjustable for windage. **Features:** Polished brass trigger guard and ramrod tip, color case-hardened coil spring lock, springloaded trigger, stainless steel nipple, blackened iron furniture. Hooked patent breech, detachable belt hook. Introduced 1981. From Lyman Products.
Price: Finished **$349.95**
Price: Kit **$289.95**

PEDERSOLI MANG TARGET PISTOL
Caliber: 38. **Barrel:** 10.5", octagonal; 1:15" twist, **Weight:** 2.5 lbs. **Length:** 17.25" overall. **Stocks:** Walnut with fluted grip. **Sights:** Blade front, open rear adjustable for windage. **Features:** Browned barrel, polished breech plug, remainder color case-hardened. Imported from Italy by Dixie Gun Works.
Price: PH0503 . . . . **$1,250.00**

QUEEN ANNE FLINTLOCK PISTOL
Caliber: 50 (.490" round ball). **Barrel:** 7.5", smoothbore. **Stocks:** Walnut. **Sights:** None. **Features:** German silver-colored steel barrel, fluted brass trigger guard, brass mask on butt. Lockplate left in the white. Made by Pedersoli in Italy. Introduced 1983. Imported by Dixie Gun Works.
Price: RH0211 . . . . **$375.00**
Price: Kit FH0421 . . . . **$295.00**

TRADITIONS KENTUCKY PISTOL
Caliber: 50. **Barrel:** 10"; octagon with 7/8" flats; 1:20" twist. **Weight:** 40 oz. **Length:** 15" overall. **Stocks:** Stained beech. **Sights:** Blade front, fixed rear. **Features:** Bird's-head grip; brass thimbles; color case-hardened lock. Percussion only. Introduced 1995. From Traditions.
Price: Finished **$209.00**
Price: Kit **$174.00**

TRADITIONS TRAPPER PISTOL
Caliber: 50. **Barrel:** 9.75"; 7/8" flats; 1:20" twist. **Weight:** 2.75 lbs. **Length:** 16" overall. **Stocks:** Beech. **Sights:** Blade front, adjustable rear. **Features:** Double-set triggers; brass buttcap, trigger guard, wedge plate, forend tip, thimble. From Traditions.
Price: Percussion **$286.00**
Price: Flintlock **$312.00**
Price: Kit **$149.00**

TRADITIONS VEST-POCKET DERRINGER
Caliber: 31. **Barrel:** 2.25"; brass. **Weight:** 8 oz. **Length:** 4.75" overall. **Stocks:** Simulated ivory. **Sights:** Bead front. **Features:** Replica of riverboat gamblers' derringer; authentic spur trigger. From Traditions.
Price: **$165.00**

TRADITIONS WILLIAM PARKER PISTOL
Caliber: 50. **Barrel:** 10-3/8"; 15/16" flats; polished steel. **Weight:** 37 oz. **Length:** 17.5" overall. **Stocks:** Walnut with checkered grip. **Sights:** Brass blade front, fixed rear. **Features:** Replica dueling pistol with 1:20" twist, hooked breech. Brass wedge plate, trigger guard, cap guard; separate ramrod. Double-set triggers. Polished steel barrel, lock. Imported by Traditions.
Price: **$381.00**

Army 1860

Baby Dragoon 1848

Dixie Wyatt Earp

Le Mat Revolver

New Model 1858 Army Percussion

ARMY 1860 PERCUSSION REVOLVER
Caliber: 44, 6-shot. **Barrel:** 8". **Weight:** 40 oz. **Length:** 13-5/8" overall. **Stocks:** Walnut. **Sights:** Fixed. **Features:** Engraved Navy scene on cylinder; brass trigger guard; case-hardened frame, loading lever and hammer. Some importers supply pistol cut for detachable shoulder stock, have accessory stock available. Imported by Cabela's (1860 Lawman), EMF, Navy Arms, The Armoury, Cimarron, Dixie Gun Works (half-fluted cylinder, not roll engraved), Euroarms of America (brass or steel model), Armsport, Traditions (brass or steel), Uberti U.S.A. Inc., United States Patent Fire-Arms.
Price: Dixie Gun Works RH0125 . . . . **$240.00**
Price: Brass frame (EMF) **$215.00**
Price: Single cased set (Navy Arms) **$300.00**
Price: Double cased set (Navy Arms) **$490.00**
Price: 1861 Navy: Same as Army except 36-cal., 7.5" bbl.,
weighs 41 oz., cut for shoulder stock; round cylinder
(fluted available), from Cabela's, CVA (brass frame, 44 cal.),
United States Patent Fire-Arms . . . . **$99.95 to $385.00**
Price: Steel frame kit (EMF) **$240.00**
Price: Colt Army Police, fluted cyl., 5.5", 36-cal. (Cabela's) . **$229.99**
Price: With nickeled frame, barrel and backstrap,
gold-tone fluted cylinder, trigger and hammer,
simulated ivory grips (Traditions) **$199.00**

BABY DRAGOON 1848, 1849 POCKET, WELLS FARGO
Caliber: 31. **Barrel:** 3", 4", 5", 6"; seven-groove; RH twist. **Weight:** About 21 oz. **Stocks:** Varnished walnut. **Sights:** Brass pin front, hammer notch rear. **Features:** No loading lever on Baby Dragoon or Wells Fargo models. Unfluted cylinder with stagecoach holdup scene; cupped cylinder pin; no grease grooves; one safety pin on cylinder and slot in hammer face; straight (flat) mainspring. From Armsport, Cimarron F.A. Co., Dixie Gun Works, EMF, Uberti U.S.A. Inc.
Price: 5.5" barrel, 1849 Pocket with loading lever (Dixie) **$250.00**
Price: 4" (Uberti USA Inc.) **$275.00**

DIXIE WYATT EARP REVOLVER
Caliber: 44. **Barrel:** 12", octagon. **Weight:** 46 oz. **Length:** 18" overall. **Stocks:** One-piece hardwood. **Sights:** Fixed. **Features:** Highly polished brass frame, backstrap and trigger guard; blued barrel and cylinder; case-hardened hammer, trigger and loading lever. Navy-size shoulder stock requires minor fitting. From Dixie Gun Works.
Price: RH0130 . . . . **$187.50**

LE MAT REVOLVER
Caliber: 44/20 ga. **Barrel:** 6.75" (revolver); 4-7/8" (single shot). **Weight:** 3 lbs., 7 oz. **Length:** 14" overall. **Stocks:** Hand-checkered walnut.

Sights: Post front, hammer notch rear. **Features:** Exact reproduction with all-steel construction; 44-cal. 9-shot cylinder, 20-gauge single barrel; color case-hardened hammer with selector; spur trigger guard; ring at butt; lever-type barrel release. From Navy Arms.
Price: Cavalry model (lanyard ring, spur trigger guard) **$750.00**
Price: Army model (round trigger guard, pin-type barrel
release) **$750.00**
Price: Naval-style (thumb selector on hammer) **$750.00**

NEW MODEL 1858 ARMY PERCUSSION REVOLVER
Caliber: 36 or 44, 6-shot. **Barrel:** 6.5" or 8". **Weight:** 38 oz. **Length:** 13.5" overall. **Stocks:** Walnut. **Sights:** Blade front, groove-in-frame rear. **Features:** Replica of Remington Model 1858. Also available from some importers as Army Model Belt Revolver in 36-cal., a shortened and lightened version of the 44. Target Model (Uberti U.S.A. Inc., Navy Arms) has fully adjustable target rear sight, target front, 36 or 44. Imported by Cimarron F.A. Co., CVA (as 1858 Army, brass frame, 44 only), Navy Arms, The Armoury, EMF, Euroarms of America (engraved, stainless and plain), Armsport, Traditions (44 only), Uberti U.S.A. Inc.
Price: Steel frame, Dixie RH0220 . . . . **$315.00**
Price: Steel frame kit (Euroarms) . . . . **$115.95 to $150.00**
Price: Stainless steel Model 1858 (Euroarms, Uberti U.S.A. Inc.,
Navy Arms, Armsport, Traditions) . . . . . . **$169.95 to $380.00**
Price: Target Model, adjustable rear sight (Cabela's, Euroarms, Uberti
U.S.A. Inc., Stone Mountain Arms) . . . . **$95.95 to $399.00**
Price: Brass frame (CVA, Cabela's, Traditions,
Navy Arms) . . . . **$79.95 to $199.99**
Price: Buffalo model, 44-cal. (Cabela's) **$119.99**
Price: Hartford model, steel frame, cartouche (EMF) **$225.00**
Price: Improved Conversion (Cimarron) **$492.00**

NAVY MODEL 1851 PERCUSSION REVOLVER
Caliber: 36, 44, 6-shot. **Barrel:** 7.5". **Weight:** 44 oz. **Length:** 13" overall. **Stocks:** Walnut finish. **Sights:** Post front, hammer notch rear. **Features:** Brass backstrap and trigger guard; some have 1st Model squareback trigger guard, engraved cylinder with navy battle scene; case-hardened frame, hammer, loading lever. Imported by The Armoury, Cabela's, Cimarron F.A. Co., Navy Arms, EMF, Dixie Gun Works, Euroarms of America, Armsport, CVA (44-cal. only), Traditions (44 only), Uberti U.S.A. Inc., United States Patent Fire-Arms.
Price: Brass frame (Dixie Gun Works RH0100) **$275.00**
Price: Steel frame (Dixie Gun Works RH0210) **$200.00**
Price: Engraved model (Dixie Gun Works RH0110) **$275.00**
Price: Confederate Navy (Cabela's) **$139.99**
Price: Hartford model, steel frame, German silver trim,
cartouche (EMF) **$190.00**
Price: Man With No Name Conversion (Cimarron, 2006) . . . **$480.00**

BLACKPOWDER REVOLVERS

Pocket Police 1862

North American Companion

Rogers & Spencer

Spiller & Burr

Walker

NORTH AMERICAN COMPANION PERCUSSION REVOLVER
Caliber: 22. **Barrel:** 1-1/8". **Weight:** 5.1 oz. **Length:** 4.5" overall. **Stocks:** Laminated wood. **Sights:** Blade front, notch fixed rear. **Features:** All stainless steel construction. Uses standard #11 percussion caps. Comes with bullets, powder measure, bullet seater, leather clip holster, gun rag. Long Rifle or Magnum frame size. Introduced 1996. Made in U.S. by North American Arms.
Price: Long Rifle frame **$215.00**

North American Super Companion Percussion Revolver
Similar to the Companion except has larger frame. Weighs 7.2 oz., has 1-5/8" barrel, measures 5-7/16" overall. Comes with bullets, powder measure, bullet seater, leather clip holster, gun rag. Introduced 1996. Made in U.S. by North American Arms.
Price: **$230.00**

POCKET POLICE 1862 PERCUSSION REVOLVER
Caliber: 36, 5-shot. **Barrel:** 4.5", 5.5", 6.5", 7.5". **Weight:** 26 oz. **Length:** 12" overall (6.5" bbl.). **Sights:** Fixed. **Features:** Round tapered barrel; half-fluted and rebated cylinder; case-hardened frame, loading lever and hammer; silver or brass trigger guard and backstrap. Imported by Dixie Gun Works, Navy Arms (5.5" only), Uberti U.S.A. Inc. (5.5", 6.5" only), United States Patent Fire-Arms and Cimarron F.A. Co.
Price: Dixie Gun Works RH0422 . . . . **$315.00**
Price: Hartford model, steel frame, cartouche (EMF) **$300.00**

ROGERS & SPENCER PERCUSSION REVOLVER
Caliber: 44. **Barrel:** 7.5". **Weight:** 47 oz. **Length:** 13.75" overall. **Stocks:** Walnut. **Sights:** Cone front, integral groove in frame for rear. **Features:** Accurate reproduction of a Civil War design. Solid frame; extra large nipple cut-out on rear of cylinder; loading lever and cylinder easily removed for cleaning. From Dixie Gun Works, Euroarms of America (standard blue, engraved, burnished, target models), Navy Arms.
Price: Dixie Gun Works RH1320 . . . . **$425.00**
Price: Nickel-plated **$215.00**
Price: Engraved (Euroarms) **$430.00**
Price: Target version (Euroarms) . . . . **$239.00 to $270.00**
Price: Burnished London Gray (Euroarms) . . . . . **$245.00 to $370.00**

SHERIFF MODEL 1851 PERCUSSION REVOLVER
Caliber: 36, 44, 6-shot. **Barrel:** 5". **Weight:** 40 oz. **Length:** 10.5" overall. **Stocks:** Walnut. **Sights:** Fixed. **Features:** Brass backstrap and trigger guard; engraved navy scene; case-hardened frame, hammer, loading lever. Imported by EMF.
Price: Steel frame **$169.95**
Price: Brass frame **$140.00**

SPILLER & BURR REVOLVER
Caliber: 36 (.375" round ball). **Barrel:** 7", octagon. **Weight:** 2.5 lbs. **Length:** 12.5" overall. **Stocks:** Two-piece walnut. **Sights:** Fixed. **Features:** Reproduction of the C.S.A. revolver. Brass frame and trigger guard. Also available as a kit. From Dixie Gun Works, Navy Arms.
Price: **$232.50**

UBERTI 1847 WALKER REVOLVERS
Caliber: 44 6-shot engraved cylinder. **Barrel:** 9" 7 grooves. **Weight:** 4.5 lbs. **Length:** 15.7" overall. **Stocks:** One-piece hardwood. **Sights:** Fixed. **Features:** Copy of Sam Colt's first commercially-made revolving pistol, loading lever available, no trigger guard. Case-hardened hammer. Blued finish. Made in Italy by Uberti, imported by Benelli USA.
Price: **$429.00**

UBERTI 1848 DRAGOON AND POCKET REVOLVERS
Caliber: 44 6-shot engraved cylinder. **Barrel:** 7.5" 7 grooves. **Weight:** 4.1 lbs. **Stocks:** One-piece walnut. **Sights:** Fixed. **Features:** Copy of

Eli Whitney's design for Colt using Walker parts. Blued barrel, backstrap, and trigger guard. Made in Italy by Uberti, imported by Benelli USA.
Price: 1848 Whitneyville Dragoon, 7.5" barrel . . . **$429.00**
Price: 1848 Dragoon, 1st-3rd models, 7.5" barrel . **$409.00**
Price: 1848 Baby Dragoon, 4" barrel **$339.00**

UBERTI 1858 NEW ARMY REVOLVERS
Caliber: 44 6-shot engraved cylinder. **Barrel:** 8" 7 grooves. **Weight:** 2.7 lbs. **Length:** 13.6". **Stocks:** Two-piece walnut. **Sights:** Fixed. **Features:** Blued or stainless barrel, backstrap; brass trigger guard. Made in Italy by Uberti, imported by Benelli USA.
Price: 1858 New Army Stainless 8" barrel **$429.00**
Price: 1858 New Army 8" barrel **$349.00**
Price: 1858 Target Carbine 18" barrel **$549.00**
Price: 1862 Pocket Navy 5.5" barrel, 36 caliber **$349.00**
Price: 1862 Police 5.5" barrel, 36 caliber **$349.00**

UBERTI 1861 NAVY PERCUSSION REVOLVER
Caliber: 36, 6-shot. **Barrel:** 7.5", 7-groove, round. **Weight:** 2 lbs., 6 oz. **Length:** 13". **Stocks:** One-piece walnut. **Sights:** German silver blade front sight. **Features:** Rounded trigger guard, "creeping" loading lever, fluted or round cylinder, steel backstrap, trigger guard, cut for stock. Imported by Cimarron F.A. Co., Uberti U.S.A. Inc., Dixie Gun Works.
Price: Dixie RH0420 . . . . **$295.00**

1862 POCKET NAVY PERCUSSION REVOLVER
Caliber: 36, 5-shot. **Barrel:** 5.5", 6.5", octagonal, 7-groove, LH twist. **Weight:** 27 oz. (5.5" barrel). **Length:** 10.5" overall (5.5" bbl.). **Stocks:** One-piece varnished walnut. **Sights:** Brass pin front, hammer notch rear. **Features:** Rebated cylinder, hinged loading lever, brass or silver-plated backstrap and trigger guard, color-cased frame, hammer, loading lever, plunger and latch, rest blued. Has original-type markings. From Cimarron F.A. Co., Uberti U.S.A. Inc., Dixie Gun Works.
Price: With brass backstrap, trigger guard **$250.00**

WALKER 1847 PERCUSSION REVOLVER
Caliber: 44, 6-shot. **Barrel:** 9". **Weight:** 84 oz. **Length:** 15.5" overall. **Stocks:** Walnut. **Sights:** Fixed. **Features:** Case-hardened frame, loading lever and hammer; iron backstrap; brass trigger guard; engraved cylinder. Imported by Cabela's, Cimarron F.A. Co., Navy Arms, Uberti U.S.A. Inc., EMF, Cimarron, Traditions, United States Patent Fire-Arms.
Price: Dixie RH0200 . . . . **$385.00**
Price: Dixie Kit RH0400 . . . . **$300.00**
Price: Hartford model, steel frame, cartouche (EMF) **$350.00**

Cabela's Traditional Hawken

ARMOURY R140 HAWKEN RIFLE
Caliber: 45, 50 or 54. **Barrel:** 29". **Weight:** 8.75 to 9 lbs. **Length:** 45.75" overall. **Stock:** Walnut, with cheekpiece. **Sights:** Dovetailed front, fully adjustable rear. **Features:** Octagon barrel, removable breech plug; double set triggers; blued barrel, brass stock fittings, color case-hardened percussion lock. From Armsport, The Armoury.
Price: .... **$225.00 to $245.00**

BOSTONIAN PERCUSSION RIFLE
Caliber: 45. **Barrel:** 30", octagonal. **Weight:** 7.25 lbs. **Length:** 46" overall. **Stock:** Walnut. **Sights:** Blade front, fixed notch rear. **Features:** Color case-hardened lock, brass trigger guard, buttplate, patchbox. Imported from Italy by EMF.
Price: **$285.00**

CABELA'S BLUE RIDGE RIFLE
Caliber: 32, 36, 45, 50, .54. **Barrel:** 39", octagonal. **Weight:** About 7.75 lbs. **Length:** 55" overall. **Stock:** American black walnut. **Sights:** Blade front, rear drift adjustable for windage. **Features:** Color case-hardened lockplate and cock/hammer, brass trigger guard and buttplate, double set, double-phased triggers. From Cabela's.
Price: Percussion **$569.99**
Price: Flintlock **$599.99**

CABELA'S TRADITIONAL HAWKEN
Caliber: 50, 54. **Barrel:** 29". **Weight:** About 9 lbs. **Stock:** Walnut. **Sights:** Blade front, open adjustable rear. **Features:** Flintlock or percussion. Adjustable double-set triggers. Polished brass furniture, color case-hardened lock. Imported by Cabela's.
Price: Percussion, right-hand or left-hand **$339.99**
Price: Flintlock, right-hand **$399.99**

CABELA'S KODIAK EXPRESS DOUBLE RIFLE
Caliber: 50, 54, 58, 72. **Barrel:** Length NA; 1:48" twist. **Weight:** 9.3 lbs. **Length:** 45.25" overall. **Stock:** European walnut, oil finish. **Sights:** Fully adjustable double folding-leaf rear, ramp front. **Features:** Percussion. Barrels regulated to point of aim at 75 yards; polished and engraved lock, top tang and trigger guard. From Cabela's.
Price: 50, 54, 58 calibers **$929.99**
Price: 72 caliber **$959.99**

COOK & BROTHER CONFEDERATE CARBINE
Caliber: 58. **Barrel:** 24". **Weight:** 7.5 lbs. **Length:** 40.5" overall. **Stock:** Select walnut. **Features:** Re-creation of the 1861 New Orleans-made artillery carbine. Color case-hardened lock, browned barrel. Buttplate, trigger guard, barrel bands, sling swivels and nosecap of polished brass. From Euroarms of America.
Price: **$563.00**
Price: Cook & Brother rifle (33" barrel) **$606.00**

CVA OPTIMA ELITE BREAK-ACTION RIFLE
Caliber: 45, 50. **Barrel:** 28" fluted. **Weight:** 8.8 lbs. **Stock:** Ambidextrous solid composite in standard or thumbhole. **Sights:** Adj. fiber-optic. **Features:** Break-action, stainless No. 209 breech plug, aluminum loading rod, cocking spur, lifetime warranty.
Price: CR4002 (50-cal., blued/Realtree HD) **$398.95**
Price: CR4002X (50-cal., stainless/Realtree HD) **$456.95**
Price: CR4003X (45-cal., stainless/Realtree HD) **$456.95**
Price: CR4000T (50-cal), blued/black fiber grip thumbhole) . **$366.95**
Price: CR4000 (50-cal., blued/black fiber grip) **$345.95**
Price: CR4002T (50-cal., blued/Realtree HD thumbhole) ... **$432.95**
Price: CR4002S (50-cal., stainless/Realtree HD thumbhole) **$422.95**
Price: CR4000X (50-cal., stainless/black fiber grip thumbhole) **$451.95**
Price: CR4000S (50-cal., stainless steel/black fiber grip) ... **$400.95**

CVA Optima 209 Magnum Break-Action Rifle
Similar to Optima Elite but with 26" bbl., nickel or blue finish, 50 cal.
Price: PR2008N (nickel/Realtree HD thumbhole) **$345.95**
Price: PR2004N (nickel/Realtree) **$322.95**
Price: PR2000 (blued/black) **$229.95**
Price: PR2006N (nickel/black) **$273.95**

CVA Wolf 209 Magnum Break-Action Rifle
Similar to Optima 209 Mag but with 24 barrel, weighs 7 lbs, and in 50-cal. only.
Price: PR2101N (nickel/camo) **$253.95**
Price: PR2102 (blued/camo). **$231.95**
Price: PR2100 (blued/black) **$180.95**
Price: PR2100N (nickel/black) **$202.95**
Price: PR2100NS (nickel/black scoped package) **$277.95**
Price: PR2100S (blued/black scoped package) **$255.95**

CVA APEX
Caliber: 45, 50. **Barrel:** 27", 1:28 twist. **Weight:** 8 lbs. **Length:** 42". **Stock:** Synthetic. **Features:** Ambi stock with rubber grip panels in black or Realtree APG camo, crush-zone recoil pad, reversible hammer spur, quake claw sling, lifetime warranty.
Price: CR4010S (50-cal., stainless/black) **$576.95**
Price: CR4011S (45-cal., stainless/black) **$576.95**
Price: CR4012S (50-cal., stainless/Realtree HD) **$651.95**
Price: CR4013S (45-cal., stainless/Realtree HD) **$651.95**

CVA ACCURA
Similar to Apex but weighs 7.3 lbs., in stainless steel or matte blue finish, cocking spur.
Price: PR3106S (50-cal, stainless steel/Realtree APG thumbhole) **$495.95**
Price: PR3107S (45-cal., stainless steel/Realtree APG thumbhole) **$495.95**
Price: PR 3104S (50-cal., stainless steel/black fibergrip thumbhole) **$438.95**
Price: PR3100 (50-cal., blued/black fibergrip) **$345.95**
Price: PR3100S (50-cal., stainless steel/black fibergrip) ... **$403.95**
Price: PR3102S (50-cal., stainless steel/Realtree APG) **$460.95**

CVA BUCKHORN 209 MAGNUM
Caliber: 50. **Barrel:** 24". **Weight:** 6.3 lbs. **Sights:** Illuminator fiber-optic. **Features:** Grip-dot stock, thumb-actuated safety; drilled and tapped for scope mounts.
Price: Black stock, blue barrel **$145.00**

CVA KODIAK MAGNUM RIFLE
Caliber: 50. No. 209 primer ignition. **Barrel:** 28"; 1:28" twist. **Stock:** Ambidextrous black or Mossy Oak® camo. **Sights:** Fiber-optic. **Features:** Blue or nickel finish, recoil pad, lifetime warranty. From CVA.
Price: Mossy Oak® camo; nickel barrel **$300.00**
Price: Stainless steel/black fibergrip **$288.95**
Price: Blued/black fibergrip. **$229.95**

DIXIE EARLY AMERICAN JAEGER RIFLE
Caliber: 54. **Barrel:** 27.5" octagonal; 1:24" twist. **Weight:** 8.25 lbs. **Length:** 43.5" overall. **Stock:** American walnut; sliding wooden patchbox on butt. **Sights:** Notch rear, blade front. **Features:** Flintlock or percussion. Browned steel furniture. Imported from Italy by Dixie Gun Works.
Price: Flintlock FR0838. .... **$695.00**
Price: Percussion PR0835, case-hardened **$695.00**
Price: Kit **$775.00**

Dixie Sharps New Model 1859 Military

Euroarms 1861 Springfield

Gonic Model 93 Thumbhole

DIXIE DELUXE CUB RIFLE
Caliber: 32, 36, 40, 45. **Barrel:** 28" octagon. **Weight:** 6.25 lbs. **Length:** 44" overall. **Stock:** Walnut. **Sights:** Fixed. **Features:** Short rifle for small game and beginning shooters. Brass patchbox and furniture. Flint or percussion, finished or kit. From Dixie Gun Works
Price: Deluxe Cub (45-cal.) **$525.00**
Price: Deluxe Cub (flint) **$530.00**
Price: Super Cub (50-cal) **$530.00**
Price: Deluxe Cub (32-cal. flint) **$725.00**
Price: Deluxe Cub (36-cal. flint) **$725.00**
Price: Deluxe Cub kit (32-cal. percussion) **$550.00**
Price: Deluxe Cub kit (36-cal. percussion) **$550.00**
Price: Deluxe Cub (45-cal. percussion) **$675.00**
Price: Super Cub (percussion) **$450.00**
Price: Deluxe Cub (32-cal. percussion) **$675.00**
Price: Deluxe Cub (36-cal. percussion) **$675.00**

DIXIE PEDERSOLI 1857 MAUSER RIFLE
Caliber: 54. **Barrel:** 39-3/8". **Weight:** 9.5 lbs. **Length:** 54.75" overall. **Stock:** European walnut with oil finish, sling swivels. **Sights:** Fully adjustable rear, lug front. **Features:** Percussion (musket caps). Armory bright finish with color case-hardened lock and barrel tang, engraved lockplate, steel ramrod. Introduced 2000. Imported from Italy by Dixie Gun Works.
Price: PR1330. . . . . **$995.00**

DIXIE SHARPS NEW MODEL 1859 MILITARY RIFLE
Caliber: 54. **Barrel:** 30", 6-groove; 1:48" twist. **Weight:** 9 lbs. **Length:** 45.5" overall. **Stock:** Oiled walnut. **Sights:** Blade front, ladder-style rear. **Features:** Blued barrel, color case-hardened barrel bands, receiver, hammer, nosecap, lever, patchbox cover and buttplate. Introduced 1995. Imported from Italy by Dixie Gun Works.
Price: PR0862. . . . . **$1,100.00**
Price: Carbine (22 barrel, 7-groove, 39-1/4" overall,
     weighs 8 lbs.) **$925.00**

DIXIE U.S. MODEL 1816 FLINTLOCK MUSKET
Caliber: .69. **Barrel:** 42", smoothbore. **Weight:** 9.75 lbs. **Length:** 56 7/8" overall. **Stock:** Walnut w/oil finish. **Sights:** Blade front. **Features:** All metal finished "National Armory Bright," three barrel bands w/springs, steel ramrod w/button-shaped head. Imported by Dixie Gun Works.
Price: FR0305. . . . . **$1,200.00**
Price: PR0257, Percussion conversion **$995.00**

EMF 1863 SHARPS MILITARY CARBINE
Caliber: 54. **Barrel:** 22", round. **Weight:** 8 lbs. **Length:** 39" overall. **Stock:** Oiled walnut. **Sights:** Blade front, military ladder-type rear. **Features:** Color case-hardened lock, rest blued. Imported by EMF.
Price: **$759.90**

EUROARMS VOLUNTEER TARGET RIFLE
Caliber: 451. **Barrel:** 33" (two-band), 36" (three-band). **Weight:** 11 lbs.

(two-band). **Length:** 48.75" overall (two-band). **Stock:** European walnut with checkered wrist and forend. **Sights:** Hooded bead front, adjustable rear with interchangeable leaves. **Features:** Alexander Henry-type rifling with 1:20" twist. Color case-hardened hammer and lockplate, brass trigger guard and nosecap, remainder blued. Imported by Euroarms of America, Dixie Gun Works.
Price: PR1031. . . . . **$925.00**

EUROARMS 1861 SPRINGFIELD RIFLE
Caliber: 58. **Barrel:** 40". **Weight:** About 10 lbs. **Length:** 55.5" overall. **Stock:** European walnut. **Sights:** Blade front, three-leaf military rear. **Features:** Reproduction of the original three-band rifle. Lockplate marked "1861" with eagle and "U.S. Springfield." White metal. Imported by Euroarms of America.
Price: **$730.00**

EUROARMS ZOUAVE RIFLE
Caliber: 54, 58 percussion. **Barrel:** 33". **Weight:** 9.5 lbs. Overall **length:** 49". **Features:** One-piece solid barrel and bolster. For 54 caliber, .535 R.B., .540 minnie. For 58 caliber .575 R.B., .577 minnie. 1863 issue. Made in Italy. Imported by Euroarms of America.
Price: **$469.00**

EUROARMS HARPERS FERRY RIFLE
Caliber: 58 flintlock. **Barrel:** 35". **Weight:** 9 lbs. Overall **length:** 59.5". **Features:** Antique browned barrel. Barrel .575 RB. .577 minnie. 1803 issue. Made in Italy. Imported by Euroarms of America.
Price: **$735.00**

GONIC MODEL 93 M/L RIFLE
Caliber: 45, 50. **Barrel:** 26"; 1:24" twist. **Weight:** 6.5 to 7 lbs. **Length:** 43" overall. **Stock:** American hardwood with black finish. **Sights:** Adjustable or aperture rear, hooded post front. **Features:** Adjustable trigger with side safety; unbreakable ramrod; comes with A. Z. scope bases installed. Introduced 1993. Made in U.S. by Gonic Arms, Inc.
Price: Model 93 Standard (blued barrel). **$720.00**
Price: Model 93 Standard (stainless brl., 50 cal. only) **$782.00**

Gonic Model 93 Deluxe M/L Rifle
Similar to the Model 93 except has classic-style walnut or gray laminated wood stock. Introduced 1998. Made in U.S. by Gonic Arms, Inc.
Price: Blue barrel, sights, scope base, choice of stock. **$902.00**
Price: Stainless barrel, sights, scope base, choice of stock (50 cal. only) **$964.00**

Gonic Model 93 Mountain Thumbhole M/L Rifles
Similar to the Model 93 except has high-grade walnut or gray laminate stock with extensive hand-checkered panels, Monte Carlo cheekpiece and beavertail forend; integral muzzle brake. Introduced 1998. Made in U.S. by Gonic Arms, Inc.
Price: Blued or stainless **$2,700.00**

Prices given are believed to be accurate at time of publication however, many factors affect retail pricing so exact prices are not possible.

Harper's Ferry 1803

J.P. Murray

Kentucky Flintlock

HARPER'S FERRY 1803 FLINTLOCK RIFLE
Caliber: 54 or 58. **Barrel:** 35". **Weight:** 9 lbs. **Length:** 59.5" overall. **Stock:** Walnut with cheekpiece. **Sights:** Brass blade front, fixed steel rear. **Features:** Brass trigger guard, sideplate, buttplate; steel patchbox. Imported by Euroarms of America, Navy Arms (54-cal. only), and Dixie Gun Works.
Price: 54-cal. (Navy Arms) **$625.00**
Price: 54-cal. (Dixie Gun Works), FR0171 . . . . **$995.00**
Price: 54-cal. (Euroarms) **$809.00**

HAWKEN RIFLE
Caliber: 45, 50, 54 or 58. **Barrel:** 28", blued, 6-groove rifling. **Weight:** 8.75 lbs. **Length:** 44" overall. **Stock:** Walnut with cheekpiece. **Sights:** Blade front, fully adjustable rear. **Features:** Coil mainspring, double-set triggers, polished brass furniture. From Armsport and EMF.
Price: . . . . **$220.00 to $345.00**

J.P. HENRY TRADE RIFLE
Caliber: 54. **Barrel:** 34"; 1" flats. **Weight:** 8.5 lbs. **Length:** 45" overall. **Stock:** Premium curly maple. **Sights:** Silver blade front, fixed buckhorn rear. **Features:** Brass buttplate, side plate, trigger guard and nosecap; browned barrel and lock; L&R Large English percussion lock; single trigger. Made in U.S. by J.P. Gunstocks, Inc.
Price: **$965.50**

J.P. MURRAY 1862-1864 CAVALRY CARBINE
Caliber: 58 (.577" Minie). **Barrel:** 23". **Weight:** 7 lbs., 9 oz. **Length:** 39" overall. **Stock:** Walnut. **Sights:** Blade front, rear drift adjustable for windage. **Features:** Blued barrel, color case-hardened lock, blued swivel and band springs, polished brass buttplate, trigger guard, barrel bands. From Dixie Gun Works.
Price: Dixie Gun Works PR0173. . . . . **$750.00**

KENTUCKY FLINTLOCK RIFLE
Caliber: 44, 45, or 50. **Barrel:** 35". **Weight:** 7 lbs. **Length:** 50" overall. **Stock:** Walnut stained, brass fittings. **Sights:** Fixed. **Features:** Available in carbine model also, 28" bbl. Some variations in detail, finish. Kits also available from some importers. Imported by The Armoury.
Price: About . . . . **$217.95 to $345.00**

Kentucky Percussion Rifle
Similar to Flintlock except percussion lock. Finish and features vary with importer. Imported by The Armoury and CVA.
Price: About **$259.95**
Price: 45 or 50 cal. (Navy Arms) **$425.00**
Price: Kit, 50 cal. (CVA) **$189.95**

KNIGHT SHADOW RIFLE
Caliber: 50. **Barrel:** 26". **Weight:** 7 lbs., 12 oz. **Length:** 42" overall. **Stock:** Checkered with recoil pad, swivel studs, Realtree APG HD. or black composite. **Sights:** Fully adjustable, metallic fiber-optic. **Features:** Bolt-action in-line system uses #209 shotshell primer for ignition; primer is held in plastic drop-in Primer Disc. Available in blued or stainless steel. Made in U.S. by Knight Rifles (Modern Muzzleloading).
Price: Blued/black **$289.99**
Price: Stainless/black **$329.99**
Price: Realtree APG HD camo (2009) **$329.99**

KNIGHT ROLLING BLOCK RIFLE
Caliber: 50, 52. **Barrel:** 27"; 1:28" twist. **Weight:** 8 lbs. **Length:** 43.5" overall. **Stock:** Brown Sandstone laminate, checkered, recoil pad, sling swivel studs. **Sights:** Fully adjustable, metallic fiber-optic. **Features:** Uses #209 shotshell primer, comes in stainless steel or blued, with walnut or black composite stock. Made in U.S. by Knight Rifles (Modern Muzzleloading).
Price: 50 Stainless/black. **$419.99**
Price: 50 Blued/black **$329.99**
Price: 50 Stainless/Realtree (2009) **$459.99**
Price: 50 Stainless/Brown Sandstone (2009) **$438.88**
Price: 52 Stainless/Next G-1 . . . . **$459.99**

KNIGHT LONG RANGE HUNTER
Caliber: 50. **Barrel:** 27" custom fluted; 1:28" twist. **Weight:** 8 lbs. 6 oz. **Length:** 45.5" overall. **Stock:** Cast-off design thumbhole, checkered, recoil pad, sling swivel studs, in Forest Green or Sandstone. **Sights:** Fully-adjustable, metallic fiber-optic. **Features:** Full plastic jacket ignition system. Made in U.S. by Knight Rifles (Modern Muzzleloading).
Price: SS Forest Green. **$769.99**
Price: SS Forest Green Thumbhole **$799.99**

KNIGHT EXTREME
Caliber: 50, 52. **Barrel:** 26", fluted stainess, 1:28" twist. **Weight:** 7 lbs. 14 oz to 8 lbs. **Length:** 45" overall. **Stock:** Stainless steel laminate, blued walnut, black composite thumbhole with blued or SS, Realtree Hardwoods Green HD with thumbhole. **Sights:** Fully adjustable metallic fiber-optics. **Features:** Full plastic jacket ignition system. Made in U.S. by Knight Rifles (Modern Muzzleloading).
Price: 50 SS/Realtree (2009) **$529.99**
Price: 52 SS/black (2009) **$229.94**
Price: 50 SS/black **$459.99**
Price: 50 SS/black w/thumbhole **$489.99**
Price: 50 SS/brown **$569.99**

KNIGHT BIGHORN
Caliber: 50. **Barrel:** 26"; 1:28" twist. **Weight:** 7 lbs. 3 oz. **Length:** 44.5" overall. **Stock:** Realtree Advantage MAX-1 HD or black composite thumbhole, checkered with recoil pad, sling swivel studs. **Sights:** Fully adjustable metallic fiber-optic. **Features:** Uses 4 different ignition systems (included): #11 nipple, musket nipple, bare 208 shotgun primer and 209 Extreme shotgun primer system (Extreme weatherproof full plastic jacket system); one-piece removable hammer assembly. Made in U.S. by Knight Rifles (Modern Muzzleloading).
Price: Stainless/Realtree w/thumbhole (2009) **$459.99**
Price: Stainless/black **$419.99**
Price: Stainless/black w/thumbhole **$439.99**

Prices given are believed to be accurate at time of publication however, many factors affect retail pricing so exact prices are not possible.

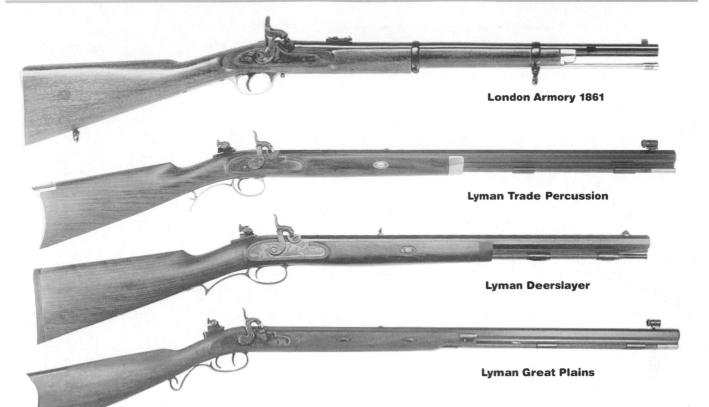

London Armory 1861

Lyman Trade Percussion

Lyman Deerslayer

Lyman Great Plains

KNIGHT 52 MODELS

Caliber: 52. **Barrel:** 26";1:26" twist (composite), 27" 1:28" twist (G-1 camo). **Weight:** 8 lbs. **Length:** 43.5" (G-1 camo); 45" (composite) overall. **Stock:** Standard black composite or Next G-1, checkered with recoil pad, sling swivel studs. **Sights:** Fully adjustable metallic fiber-optic. **Features:** PowerStem breech plug. Made in U.S. by Knight Rifles (Modern Muzzleloading).
Price: Stainless/black (2009) **$299.94**
Price: Stainless/Next G-1 . . . . **$459.99**

LONDON ARMORY 1861 ENFIELD MUSKETOON

Caliber: 58, Minie ball. **Barrel:** 24", round. **Weight:** 7 to 7.5 lbs. **Length:** 40.5" overall. **Stock:** Walnut, with sling swivels. **Sights:** Blade front, graduated military-leaf rear. **Features:** Brass trigger guard, nosecap, buttplate; blued barrel, bands, lockplate, swivels. Imported by Euroarms of America, Navy Arms.
Price: . . . . **$300.00 to $521.00**
Price: Kit . . . . **$365.00 to $402.00**

LONDON ARMORY 2-BAND 1858 ENFIELD

Caliber: .577" Minie, .575" round ball. **Barrel:** 33". **Weight:** 10 lbs. **Length:** 49" overall. **Stock:** Walnut. **Sights:** Folding leaf rear adjustable for elevation. **Features:** Blued barrel, color case-hardened lock and hammer, polished brass buttplate, trigger guard, nosecap. From Navy Arms, Euroarms of America, Dixie Gun Works.
Price: PR0330 . . . . **$650.00**

LONDON ARMORY 3-BAND 1853 ENFIELD

Caliber: 58 (.577" Minie, .575" round ball, .580" maxi ball). **Barrel:** 39". **Weight:** 9.5 lbs. **Length:** 54" overall. **Stock:** European walnut. **Sights:** Inverted "V" front, traditional Enfield folding ladder rear. **Features:** Re-creation of the famed London Armory Company Pattern 1853 Enfield Musket. One-piece walnut stock, brass buttplate, trigger guard and nosecap. Lockplate marked "London Armoury Co." and with a British crown. Blued Baddeley barrel bands. From Euroarms of America, Navy Arms.
Price: About . . . . **$350.00 to $606.00**

LYMAN TRADE RIFLE

Caliber: 50, 54. **Barrel:** 28" octagon;1:48" twist. **Weight:** 10.8 lbs. **Length:** 45" overall. **Stock:** European walnut. **Sights:** Blade front, open rear adjustable for windage or optional fixed sights. **Features:** Fast twist rifling for conical bullets. Polished brass furniture with blue steel parts, stainless steel nipple. Hook breech, single trigger, coil spring percussion lock. Steel barrel rib and ramrod ferrules. Introduced 1980. From Lyman.
Price: 50-cal. percussion **$474.95**
Price: 50-cal. flintlock **$499.95**
Price: 54-cal. percussion **$474.95**
Price: 54-cal. flintlock **$499.95**

LYMAN DEERSTALKER RIFLE

Caliber: 50, 54. **Barrel:** 24", octagonal; 1:48" rifling. **Weight:** 10.4 lbs. **Stock:** Walnut with black rubber buttpad. **Sights:** Lyman #37MA beaded front, fully adjustable fold-down Lyman #16A rear. **Features:** Stock has less drop for quick sighting. All metal parts are blackened, with color case-hardened lock; single trigger. Comes with sling and swivels. Available in flint or percussion. Introduced 1990. From Lyman.
Price: 50-cal. flintlock **$529.95**
Price: 50-, 54-cal., flintlock, left-hand **$569.95**
Price: 54 cal. flintlock **$529.95**
Price: 50-, 54 cal. percussion **$487.95**
Price: 50-, 54-cal. stainless steel **$609.95**

LYMAN GREAT PLAINS RIFLE

Caliber: 50, 54. **Barrel:** 32"; 1:60" twist. **Weight:** 11.6 lbs. **Stock:** Walnut. **Sights:** Steel blade front, buckhorn rear adjustable for windage and elevation and fixed notch primitive sight included. **Features:** Blued steel furniture. Stainless steel nipple. Coil spring lock, Hawken-style trigger guard and double-set triggers. Round thimbles recessed and sweated into rib. Steel wedge plates and toe plate. Introduced 1979. From Lyman.
Price: Percussion **$654.95**
Price: Flintlock **$699.95**
Price: Percussion kit **$519.95**
Price: Flintlock kit **$574.95**
Price: Left-hand percussion **$669.95**
Price: Left-hand flintlock **$709.95**

Lyman Great Plains Hunter Model

Similar to Great Plains model except 1:32" twist shallow-groove barrel and comes drilled and tapped for Lyman 57GPR peep sight.
Price: Percussion **$654.95**
Price: Flintlock **$699.95**
Price: Left-hand percussion **$669.95**

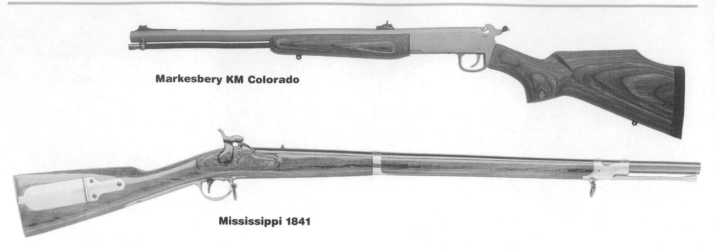

Markesbery KM Colorado

Mississippi 1841

MARKESBERY KM BLACK BEAR M/L RIFLE

Caliber: 36, 45, 50, 54. **Barrel:** 24"; 1:26" twist. **Weight:** 6.5 lbs. **Length:** 38.5" overall. **Stock:** Two-piece American hardwood, walnut, black laminate, green laminate, black composition, X-Tra or Mossy Oak® Break-up™ camouflage. **Sights:** Bead front, open fully adjustable rear. **Features:** Interchangeable barrels; exposed hammer; Outer-Line Magnum ignition system uses small rifle primer or standard No. 11 cap and nipple. Blue, black matte, or stainless. Made in U.S. by Markesbery Muzzle Loaders.

Price: American hardwood walnut, blue finish $536.63
Price: American hardwood walnut, stainless $553.09
Price: Black laminate, blue finish $539.67
Price: Black laminate, stainless $556.27
Price: Black composite, blue finish $532.65
Price: Black composite, stainless $549.93
Price: Green laminate, blue finish $539.00
Price: Green laminate, stainless $556.27

Markesbery KM Brown Bear Rifle

Similar to KM Black Bear except one-piece thumbhole stock with Monte Carlo comb. Stock in Crotch Walnut composite, green or black laminate, black composite or X-Tra or Mossy Oak® Break-Up™ camouflage. Made in U.S. by Markesbery Muzzle Loaders, Inc.

Price: Black composite, blue finish $658.83
Price: Crotch Walnut, blue finish $658.83
Price: Walnut wood $662.81
Price: Black wood $662.81
Price: Black laminated wood $662.81
Price: Green laminated wood $662.81
Price: Black composite, stainless $676.11
Price: Crotch Walnut composite, stainless $676.11
Price: Walnut wood, stainless $680.07
Price: Black wood, stainless $680.07
Price: Black laminated wood, stainless $680.07
Price: Green laminate, stainless $680.07

Markesbery KM Grizzly Bear Rifle

Similar to KM Black Bear except thumbhole buttstock with Monte Carlo comb. Stock in Crotch Walnut composite, green or black laminate, black composite or X-Tra or Mossy Oak® Break-Up camouflage. Made in U.S. by Markesbery Muzzle Loaders, Inc.

Price: Black composite, blue finish $642.96
Price: Crotch Walnut, blue finish $642.96
Price: Walnut wood $646.93
Price: Black wood $646.93
Price: Black laminate wood $646.93
Price: Green laminate wood $646.93
Price: Black composite, stainless $660.98
Price: Crotch Walnut composite, stainless $660.98
Price: Black laminate wood, stainless $664.20
Price: Green laminate wood, stainless $664.20
Price: Walnut wood, stainless $664.20
Price: Black wood, stainless $664.20

Markesbery KM Polar Bear Rifle

Similar to KM Black Bear except one-piece stock with Monte Carlo comb. Stock in American Hard-wood walnut, green or black laminate, black composite, or X-Tra or Mossy Oak® Break-Up™ camouflage.

Interchangeable barrel system, Outer-Line ignition system, cross-bolt double safety. Available in 36, 45, 50, 54 caliber. Made in U.S. by Markesbery Muzzle Loaders, Inc.

Price: American Hardwood walnut, blue finish $539.01
Price: Black composite, blue finish $536.63
Price: Black laminate, blue finish $541.17
Price: Green laminate, blue finish $541.17
Price: American Hardwood walnut, stainless $556.27
Price: Black composite, stainless $556.04
Price: Black laminate, stainless $570.56
Price: Green laminate, stainless $570.56

MARKESBERY KM COLORADO ROCKY MOUNTAIN RIFLE

Caliber: 36, 45, 50, 54. **Barrel:** 24"; 1:26" twist. **Weight:** 6.5 lbs. **Length:** 38.5" overall. **Stock:** American hardwood walnut, green or black laminate. **Sights:** Firesight bead on ramp front, fully adjustable open rear. **Features:** Replicates Reed/Watson rifle of 1851. Straight grip stock with or without two barrel bands, rubber recoil pad, large-spur hammer. Made in U.S. by Markesbery Muzzle Loaders, Inc.

Price: American hardwood walnut, blue finish $545.92
Price: Black or green laminate, blue finish $548.30
Price: American hardwood walnut, stainless $563.17
Price: Black or green laminate, stainless $566.34

MDM BUCKWACKA IN-LINE RIFLES

Caliber: 45 Nitro Mag., 50. **Barrel:** 23", 25". **Weight:** 7 to 7.75 lbs. **Stock:** Black, walnut, laminated and camouflage finishes. **Sights:** Williams Fire Sight blade front, Williams fully adjustable rear with ghost-ring peep aperture. **Features:** Break-open action; Incinerating Ignition System incorporates 209 shotshell primer directly into breech plug; 50-caliber models handle up to 150 grains of Pyrodex; synthetic ramrod; transfer bar safety; stainless or blued finish. Made in U.S. by Millennium Designed Muzzleloaders Ltd.

Price: 45 Nitro, stainless steel, walnut stock $399.95
Price: 45 Nitro, stainless steel, Mossy Oak Break-up stock . $465.95
Price: 45 Nitro, blued action, walnut stock $369.95
Price: 45 Nitro, blued action, Mossy Oak Break-up stock . . . $425.95
Price: 50-cal., stainless steel, walnut stock $399.95
Price: 50-cal., stainless steel, Mossy Oak Break-up stock . . $465.95
Price: 50-cal., blued action, walnut stock $369.95
Price: 50-cal., blued action, Mossy Oak Break-up stock $435.95
Price: 50-cal., Youth-Ladies, blued action, walnut stock $369.95
Price: 50-cal., Youth-Ladies, stainless steel, walnut stock . . $399.95

MDM M2K In-Line Rifle

Similar to Buckwacka except adjustable trigger and double-safety mechanism designed to prevent misfires. Made in U.S. by Millennium Designed Muzzleloaders Ltd.

Price: . . . . $529.00 to $549.00

MISSISSIPPI 1841 PERCUSSION RIFLE

Caliber: 54, 58. **Barrel:** 33". **Weight:** 9.5 lbs. **Length:** 48-5/8" overall. **Stock:** One-piece European walnut full stock with satin finish. **Sights:** Brass blade front, fixed steel rear. **Features:** Case-hardened lockplate marked "U.S." surmounted by American eagle. Two barrel bands, sling swivels. Steel ramrod with brass end, browned barrel. From Navy Arms, Dixie Gun Works, Euroarms of America.

Price: Dixie Gun Works PR0870 . . . . $825.00

BLACKPOWDER MUSKETS & RIFLES

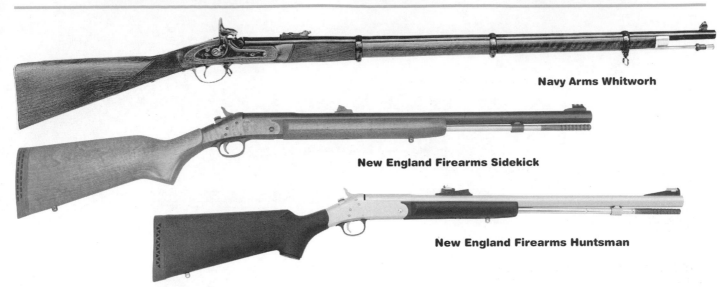

Navy Arms Whitworh

New England Firearms Sidekick

New England Firearms Huntsman

NAVY ARMS 1861 MUSKETOON
Caliber: 58. **Barrel:** 39". **Weight:** NA. **Length:** NA. **Stock:** NA. **Sights:** Front is blued steel base and blade, blued steel lip-up rear adjustable for elevation. **Features:** Brass nosecap, triggerguard, buttplate, blued steel barrel bands, color case-hardened lock with engraved lockplate marked "1861 Enfield" ahead of hammer & crown over "PH" on tail. Barrel is marked "Parker Hale LTD Birmingham England." Imported by Navy Arms.
Price: **$900.00**

NAVY ARMS PARKER-HALE 1853 THREE-BAND ENFIELD
Caliber: 58. **Barrel:** 39", tapered, round, blued. **Weight:** NA. **Length:** 55-1/4" overall. **Stock:** Walnut. **Sights:** Front is blued steel base and blade, blued steel lip-up rear adjustable for elevation. **Features:** Meticulously reproduced based on original gauges and patterns. Features brass nosecap, triggerguard, buttplate, blued steel barrel bands, color case-hardened lock with engraved lockplate marked "Parker-Hale" ahead of hammer & crown over "PH" on tail. Barrel is marked "Parker Hale LTD Birmingham England." From Navy Arms.
Price: Finished rifle **$1,050.00**

Navy Arms Parker-Hale 1858 Two-Band Enfield
Similar to the Three-band Enfield with 33" barrel, 49" overall length. Engraved lockplate marked "1858 Enfield" ahead of hammer & crown over "PH" on tail. Barrel is marked "Parker Hale LTD Birmingham England."
Price: **$1,050.00**

NAVY ARMS PARKER-HALE VOLUNTEER RIFLE
Caliber: 451. **Barrel:** 32", 1:20" twist. **Weight:** 9.5 lbs. **Length:** 49" overall. **Stock:** Walnut, checkered wrist and forend. **Sights:** Globe front, adjustable ladder-type rear. **Features:** Recreation of the type of gun issued to volunteer regiments during the 1860s. Rigby-pattern rifling, patent breech, detented lock. Stock is glass beaded for accuracy. Engfaved lockplate marked "Alex Henry" & crown on tail, barrel marked "Parker Hale LTD Birmingham England" and "Alexander Henry Rifling .451" Imported by Navy Arms.
Price: **$1,400.00**

NAVY ARMS PARKER-HALE WHITWORTH MILITARY TARGET RIFLE
Caliber: 45. **Barrel:** 36". **Weight:** 9.25 lbs. **Length:** 52.5" overall. **Stock:** Walnut. Checkered at wrist and forend. **Sights:** Hooded post front, open step-adjustable rear. **Features:** Faithful reproduction of Whitworth rifle. Trigger has detented lock, capable of fine adjustments without risk of the sear nose catching on the half-cock notch and damaging both parts. Engraved lockplate marked "Whitworth" ahead of hammer & crown on tail. Barrel marked "Parker Hale LTD Birmingham England" in one line on front of sight and "Sir Joseph Whitworth's Rifling .451" on left side. Introduced 1978. Imported by Navy Arms.
Price: **$1,550.00**

NAVY ARMS BROWN BESS MUSKET
Caliber: 75, smoothbore. **Barrel:** 41.8". **Weight:** 9 lbs., 5 oz. **Length:** 41.8" overall. **Features:** Brightly polished steel and brass, one-piece

walnut stock. Signature of gunsmith William Grice and the date 1762, the crown and alphabetical letters GR (Georgius Rex). Barrel is made of steel, satin finish; the walnut stock is oil finished. From Navy Arms.
Price: **$1,100.00**

NAVY ARMS COUNTRY HUNTER
Caliber: 50. **Barrel:** 28.4", 6-groove, 1:34 twist. **Weight:** 6 lbs. **Length:** 44" overall. **Features:** Matte finished barrel. From Navy Arms.
Price: **$450.00**

NAVY ARMS PENNSYLVANIA RIFLE
Caliber: 32, 45. **Barrel:** 41.6". **Weight:** 7 lbs. 12 oz. to 8 lbs. 6 oz. **Length:** 56.1" overall. **Features:** Extra long rifle finished wtih rust brown color barrel and one-piece oil finished walnut stock. Adjustable double-set trigger. Vertically adjustable steel front and rear sights. From Navy Arms.
Price: **$675.00**

NEW ENGLAND FIREARMS SIDEKICK
Caliber: 50, 209 primer ignition. **Barrel:** 26" (magnum). **Weight:** 6.5 lbs. **Length:** 41.25". **Stock:** Black matte polymer or hardwood. **Sights:** Adjustable fiber-optic open, tapped for scope mounts. **Features:** Single-shot based on H&R break-open action. Uses No. 209 shotgun primer held in place by special primer carrier. Telescoping brass ramrod. Introduced 2004.
Price: Wood stock, blued frame, black-oxide barrel) **$216.00**
Price: Stainless barrel and frame, synthetic stock) **$310.00**

NEW ENGLAND FIREARMS HUNTSMAN
Caliber: 50, 209 primer ignition. **Barrel:** 22" to 26". **Weight:** 5.25 to 6.5 lbs. **Length:** 40" to 43". **Stock:** Black matte polymer or hardwood. **Sights:** Fiber-optic open sights, tapped for scope mounts. **Features:** Break-open action, transfer-bar safety system, breech plug removable for cleaning. Introduced 2004.
Price: Stainless Huntsman **$306.00**
Price: Huntsman **$212.00**
Price: Pardner Combo 12 ga./50 cal muzzleloader **$259.00**
Price: Tracker II Combo 12 ga. rifled slug barrel /50 cal. **$288.00**
Price: Handi-Rifle Combo 243/50 cal. **$405.00**

New England Firearms Stainless Huntsman
Similar to Huntsman, but with matte nickel finish receiver and stainless bbl. Introduced 2003. From New England Firearms.
Price: **$381.00**

PACIFIC RIFLE MODEL 1837 ZEPHYR
Caliber: 62. **Barrel:** 30", tapered octagon. **Weight:** 7.75 lbs. **Length:** NA. **Stock:** Oil-finished fancy walnut. **Sights:** German silver blade front, semi-buckhorn rear. Options available. **Features:** Improved underhammer action. First production rifle to offer Forsyth rifle, with narrow lands and shallow rifling with 1:14" pitch for high-velocity round balls. Metal finish is slow rust brown with nitre blue accents. Optional sights, finishes and integral muzzle brake available. Introduced 1995. Made in U.S. by Pacific Rifle Co.
Price: From **$995.00**

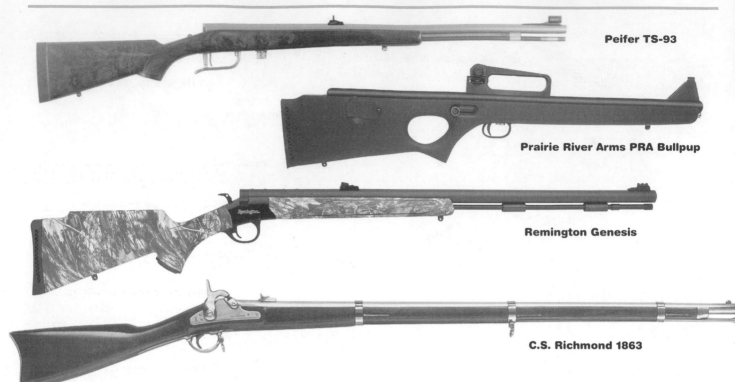

Peifer TS-93

Prairie River Arms PRA Bullpup

Remington Genesis

C.S. Richmond 1863

Pacific Rifle Big Bore African Rifles

Similar to the 1837 Zephyr except in 72-caliber and 8-bore. The 72-caliber is available in standard form with 28" barrel, or as the African with flat buttplate, checkered upgraded wood; weight is 9 lbs. The 8-bore African has dual-cap ignition, 24" barrel, weighs 12 lbs., checkered English walnut, engraving, gold inlays. Introduced 1998. Made in U.S. by Pacific Rifle Co.

Price: 72-caliber, from **$1,150.00**
Price: 8-bore, from **$2,500.00**

PEIFER MODEL TS-93 RIFLE

Caliber: 45, 50. **Barrel:** 24" Douglas premium; 1:20" twist in 45; 1:28" in 50. **Weight:** 7 lbs. **Length:** 43.25" overall. **Stock:** Bell & Carlson solid composite, with recoil pad, swivel studs. **Sights:** Williams bead front on ramp, fully adjustable open rear. Drilled and tapped for Weaver scope mounts with dovetail for rear peep. **Features:** In-line ignition uses #209 shotshell primer; fast lock time; fully enclosed breech; adjustable trigger; automatic safety; removable primer holder. Blue or stainless. Made in U.S. by Peifer Rifle Co. Introduced 1996.

Price: Blue, black stock. **$730.00**
Price: Blue, wood or camouflage composite stock, or
   stainless with black composite stock **$803.00**
Price: Stainless, wood or camouflage composite stock **$876.00**

PRAIRIE RIVER ARMS PRA BULLPUP RIFLE

Caliber: 50. **Barrel:** 28"; 1:28" twist. **Weight:** 7.5 lbs. **Length:** 31.5" overall. **Stock:** Hardwood or black all-weather. **Sights:** Blade front, open adjustable rear. **Features:** Bullpup design thumbhole stock. Patented internal percussion ignition system. Left-hand model available. Dovetailed for scope mount. Introduced 1995. Made in U.S. by Prairie River Arms, Ltd.

Price: 4140 alloy barrel, hardwood stock **$199.00**
Price: All Weather stock, alloy barrel **$205.00**

REMINGTON GENESIS MUZZLELOADER

Caliber: 50. **Barrel:** 28", 1-in-28" twist, blued, camo, or stainless fluted. **Weight:** 7.75 lbs. **Length:** NA. **Stock:** Black synthetic, Mossy Oak New Break-Up, Realtree Hardwoods HD. **Sights:** Williams fiber-optic sights, drilled and tapped for scope mounts. **Features:** TorchCam action, 209 primer, up to 150-grain charges. Over-travel hammer, crossbolt safety with ambidextrous HammerSpur (right- and left-handed operation). Buckmasters version has stainless fluted barrel with a Realtree Hardwoods HD camo stock, laser-engraved Buckmasters logo. Aluminum anodized ramrod with jag, front and rear swivel studs, removable 7/16" breech plug; optimized for use with Remington

Kleanbore 209 Muzzleloading Primers. Introduced 2006. Made in U.S. by Remington Arms Co.

Price: Genesis ML, black synthetic, carbon matte blued **$237.00**
Price: Genesis MLS Overmold synthetic, stainless satin **$307.00**
Price: Genesis ML Camo Mossy Oak Break-Up full camo . . . **$349.00**
Price: Genesis ML Camo Mossy Oak Break-Up matte blue . **$293.00**
Price: Genesis MLS Camo, Mossy Oak Break-up,
   stainless satin **$342.00**
Price: Genesis ML SF Synthetic Thumbhole **$349.00**
Price: Genesis ML SF Synthetic Thumbhole, stainless satin . **$405.00**
Price: Genesis ML SF Buckmasters (2007) **$363.00**
Price: Genesis ML SF laminate thumbhole, stainless satin . . **$538.00**

RICHMOND, C.S., 1863 MUSKET

Caliber: 58. **Barrel:** 40". **Weight:** 11 lbs. **Length:** 56.25" overall. **Stock:** European walnut with oil finish. **Sights:** Blade front, adjustable folding leaf rear. **Features:** Reproduction of the three-band Civil War musket. Sling swivels attached to trigger guard and middle barrel band. Lockplate marked "1863" and "C.S. Richmond." All white metal. Brass buttplate and forend cap. Imported by Euroarms of America, Navy Arms, and Dixie Gun Works.

Price: Euroarms **$730.00**
Price: Dixie Gun Works PR0846 . . . . **$1,050.00**
Price: Navy Arms **$1,005.00**

ROCKY MOUNTAIN HAWKEN

Caliber: NA. **Barrel:** 34-11/16". **Weight:** 10 lbs. **Length:** 52" overall. **Stock:** Walnut or maple. **Sights:** Blade front, drift adjustable rear. **Features:** Percussion, double set trigger, casehard-ened furniture, hook breech, brown barrel. Made by Pedersoli in Italy. Imported by Dixie Gun Works.

Price: Maple Stock PR3430 . . . . **$925.00**
Price: Walnut Stock PR3435 . . . . **$875.00**

ROSSI MUZZLELOADERS

Caliber: .50. **Barrel:** 20", 23". **Weight:** 5-6.3 lbs. **Stocks:** Wood. **Sights:** Fully adjustable fiber optic sights. **Features:** Black powder break open, 2 models available, manual external safety, Taurus Security System, blue or stainless finish, youth models available. From Rossi USA.

Price: **$209.00**
Price: Youth Size (2008). **$269.00**
Price: S50MB **$179.95**
Price: S50SM **$229.95**
Price: S45YBM (2009) **$195.95**
Price: S45YSM (2009) **$242.95**
Price: S50YBN (2009) **$195.95**
Price: S50YSM (2009) **$242.95**

BLACKPOWDER MUSKETS & RIFLES

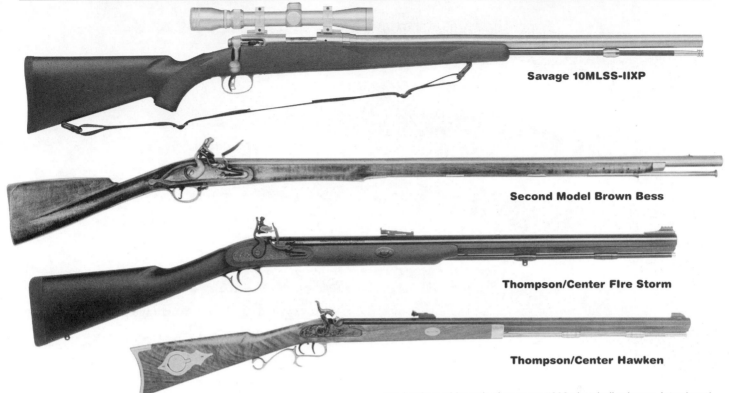

Savage 10MLSS-IIXP

Second Model Brown Bess

Thompson/Center Fire Storm

Thompson/Center Hawken

SAVAGE MODEL 10ML MUZZLELOADER RIFLE SERIES
Caliber: 50. **Barrel:** 24", 1:24 twist, blue or stainless. **Weight:** 7.75 lbs. **Stock:** Black synthetic, Realtree Hardwood JD Camo, brown laminate. **Sights:** Green adjustable rear, Red FiberOptic front. **Features:** XP Models scoped, no sights, designed for smokeless powder, #209 primer ignition. Removeable breech plug and vent liner.
Price: Model 10ML-II. $531.00
Price: Model 10ML-II Camo $569.00
Price: Model 10MLSS-II Camo $628.00
Price: Model 10MLBSS-II $667.00
Price: Model 10ML-IIXP $569.00
Price: Model 10MLSS-IIXP $628.00

SECOND MODEL BROWN BESS MUSKET
Caliber: 75, uses .735" round ball. **Barrel:** 42", smoothbore. **Weight:** 9.5 lbs. **Length:** 59" overall. **Stock:** Walnut (Navy); walnut-stained hardwood (Dixie). **Sights:** Fixed. **Features:** Polished barrel and lock with brass trigger guard and buttplate. Bayonet and scabbard available. From Navy Arms, Dixie Gun Works.
Price: Finished . . . . $475.00 to $950.00
Price: Kit, Dixie Gun Works, FR0825 . . . . $875.00
Price: Carbine (Navy Arms) $835.00
Price: Dixie Gun Works FR0810 . . . . $995.00

THOMPSON/CENTER TRIUMPH MAGNUM MUZZLELOADER
Caliber: 50. **Barrel:** 28" Weather Shield coated. **Weight:** NA. **Length:** NA. **Stock:** Black composite or Realtree AP HD Camo. **Sights:** NA. **Features:** QLA 209 shotshell primer ignition. Introduced 2007. Made in U.S. by Thompson/Center Arms.
Price: $457.00

Thompson/Center Bone Collector
Similar to the Triumph Magnum but with added Flex Tech technology and Energy Burners to a shorter stock. Also added is Thompson/Center's premium fluted barrel with Weather Shield and their patented Power Rod.
Price: $708.00

THOMPSON/CENTER ENCORE 209X50 MAGNUM
Caliber: 50. **Barrel:** 26"; interchangeable with centerfire calibers. **Weight:** 7 lbs. **Length:** 40.5" overall. **Stock:** American walnut butt and forend, or black composite. **Sights:** TruGlo fiber-optic front and rear. **Features:** Blue or stainless steel. Uses the stock, frame and forend of the Encore centerfire pistol; break-open design using trigger guard spur; stainless steel universal breech plug; uses #209 shotshell primers. Introduced 1998. Made in U.S. by Thompson/Center Arms.
Price: Stainless with camo stock $772.00
Price: Blue, walnut stock and forend $678.00
Price: Blue, composite stock and forend $637.00
Price: Stainless, composite stock and forend $713.00
Price: All camo Realtree Hardwoods $729.00

THOMPSON/CENTER FIRE STORM RIFLE
Caliber: 50. **Barrel:** 26"; 1:28" twist. **Weight:** 7 lbs. **Length:** 41.75" overall. **Stock:** Black synthetic with rubber recoil pad, swivel studs. **Sights:** Click-adjustable steel rear and ramp-style front, both with fiber-optic inserts. **Features:** Side hammer lock is the first designed for up to three 50-grain Pyrodex pellets; patented Pyrodex Pyramid breech directs ignition fire 360 degrees around base of pellet. Quick Load Accurizor Muzzle System; aluminum ramrod. Flintlock only. Introduced 2000. Made in U.S. by Thompson/Center Arms.
Price: Blue finish, flintlock model with 1:48" twist for round balls, conicals $436.00
Price: SST, flintlock $488.00

THOMPSON/CENTER HAWKEN RIFLE
Caliber: 50. **Barrel:** 28" octagon, hooked breech. **Stock:** American walnut. **Sights:** Blade front, rear adjustable for windage and elevation. **Features:** Solid brass furniture, double-set triggers, button rifled barrel, coil-type mainspring. From Thompson/Center Arms.
Price: Percussion model $590.00
Price: Flintlock model $615.00

THOMPSON/CENTER OMEGA
Caliber: 50". **Barrel:** 28", fluted. **Weight:** 7 lbs. **Length:** 42" overall. **Stock:** Composite or laminated. **Sights:** Adjustable metal rear sight with fiber-optics; metal ramp front sight with fiber-optics. **Features:** Drilled and tapped for scope mounts. Thumbhole stock, sling swivel studs. From T/C..
Price: $777.00

TRADITIONS BUCKSKINNER CARBINE
Caliber: 50. **Barrel:** 21"; 15/16" flats, half octagon, half round; 1:20" or 1:66" twist. **Weight:** 6 lbs. **Length:** 37" overall. **Stock:** Beech or black laminated. **Sights:** Beaded blade front, fiber-optic open rear click adjustable for windage and elevation or fiber-optics. **Features:** Uses V-type mainspring, single trigger. Non-glare hardware; sling swivels. From Traditions.
Price: Flintlock $249.00
Price: Flintlock, laminated stock $303.00

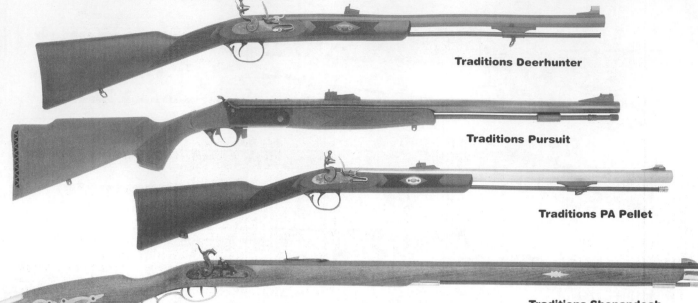

Traditions Deerhunter

Traditions Pursuit

Traditions PA Pellet

Traditions Shenandoah

TRADITIONS DEERHUNTER RIFLE SERIES
Caliber: 32, 50 or 54. **Barrel:** 24", octagonal; 15/16" flats; 1:48" or 1:66" twist. **Weight:** 6 lbs. **Length:** 40" overall. **Stock:** Stained hardwood or All-Weather composite with rubber buttpad, sling swivels. **Sights:** Lite Optic blade front, adjustable rear fiber-optics. **Features:** Flint or percussion with color case-hardened lock. Hooked breech, oversized trigger guard, blackened furniture, PVC ramrod. All-Weather has composite stock and C-nickel barrel. Drilled and tapped for scope mounting. Imported by Traditions, Inc.
Price: Percussion, 50-cal.; blued barrel; 1:48" twist **$228.00**
Price: Flintlock, 50 caliber only; 1:48" twist **$278.00**
Price: 50-cal., synthetic/blued **$224.00**
Price: Flintlock, 50-cal., synthetic/blued **$256.00**
Price: Redi-Pak, 50 cal. flintlock **$308.00**
Price: Flintlock, left-handed hardwood, 50 cal. **$337.00**
Price: 50-cal., hardwood/blued **$264.00**

TRADITIONS PURSUIT BREAK-OPEN MUZZLELOADER
Caliber: 45, 54 and 12 gauge. **Barrel:** 28", tapered, fluted; blued, stainless or Hardwoods Green camo. **Weight:** 8.25 lbs. **Length:** 44" overall. **Stock:** Synthetic black or Hardwoods Green. **Sights:** Steel fiber-optic rear, bead front. Introduced 2004 by Traditions, Inc.
Price: Steel, blued, 45 or 50 cal., synthetic stock **$279.00**
Price: Steel, nickel, 45 or 50 cal., synthetic stock **$309.00**
Price: Steel, nickel w/Hardwoods Green stock **$359.00**
Price: Matte blued; 12 ga., synthetic stock **$369.00**
Price: Matte blued; 12 ga. w/Hardwoods Green stock **$439.00**
Price: Lightweight model, blued, synthetic stock **$199.00**
Price: Lightweight model, blued, Mossy Oak® Break-Up™ Camo stock **$239.00**
Price: Lightweight model, nickel, Mossy Oak® Break-Up™ Camo stock **$279.00**

TRADITIONS EVOLUTION LONG DISTANCE BOLT-ACTION BLACKPOWDER RIFLE
Caliber: 45, 50 percussion. **Barrel:** 26", fluted with porting. **Sights:** Steel fiber-optic. **Weight:** 7 to 7.25 lbs. **Length:** 45" overall. **Features:** Bolt-action, cocking indicator, thumb safety, aluminum ramrod, sling studs. Wide variety of stocks and metal finishes. Introduced 2004 by Traditions, Inc.
Price: 50-cal. synthetic stock **$314.00**
Price: 45-cal. synthetic stock **$259.00**
Price: 50-cal. AW/Adv. Timber HD **$370.00**
Price: 50-cal. synthetic black/blued **$293.00**

TRADITIONS PA PELLET FLINTLOCK
Caliber: 50. **Barrel:** 26", blued, nickel. **Weight:** 7 lbs. **Stock:** Hardwood, synthetic and synthetic break-up. **Sights:** Fiber-optic. **Features:** Removeable breech plug, left-hand model with hardwood stock. 1:48" twist.
Price: Hardwood, blued **$343.00**
Price: Hardwood left, blued **$378.00**

TRADITIONS HAWKEN WOODSMAN RIFLE
Caliber: 50. **Barrel:** 28"; 15/16" flats. **Weight:** 7 lbs., 11 oz. **Length:** 44.5" overall. **Stock:** Walnut-stained hardwood. **Sights:** Beaded blade front, hunting-style open rear adjustable for windage and elevation. **Features:** Percussion only. Brass patchbox and furniture. Double triggers. From Traditions.
Price: 50-cal. nickel/black laminate **$299.95**
Price: 50-cal Percussion **$396.00**
Price: 50-cal., left-hand **$415.00**
Price: 50-cal., flintlock **$434.00**

TRADITIONS KENTUCKY RIFLE
Caliber: 50. **Barrel:** 33.5"; 7/8" flats; 1:66" twist. **Weight:** 7 lbs. **Length:** 49" overall. **Stock:** Beech; inletted toe plate. **Sights:** Blade front, fixed rear. **Features:** Full-length, two-piece stock; brass furniture; color case-hardened lock. From Traditions.
Price: **$364.00**

TRADITIONS PENNSYLVANIA RIFLE
Caliber: 50. **Barrel:** 40.25"; 7/8" flats; 1:66" twist, octagon. **Weight:** 9 lbs. **Length:** 57.5" overall. **Stock:** Walnut. **Sights:** Blade front, adjustable rear. **Features:** Brass patchbox and ornamentation. Double-set triggers. From Traditions.
Price: Flintlock **$720.00**
Price: Percussion **$664.00**

TRADITIONS SHENANDOAH RIFLE
Caliber: 36, 50. **Barrel:** 33.5" octagon; 1:66" twist. **Weight:** 7 lbs., 3 oz. **Length:** 49.5" overall. **Stock:** Walnut. **Sights:** Blade front, buckhorn rear. **Features:** V-type mainspring; double-set trigger; solid brass buttplate, patchbox, nosecap, thimbles, trigger guard. Introduced 1996. From Traditions.
Price: Flintlock **$588.00**
Price: Percussion **$551.00**
Price: 36 cal. flintlock, 1:48" twist **$618.00**
Price: 36 cal. percussion, 1:48" twist **$558.00**

TRADITIONS TENNESSEE RIFLE
Caliber: 50. **Barrel:** 24", octagon; 15/16" flats; 1:66" twist. **Weight:** 6 lbs. **Length:** 40.5" overall. **Stock:** Stained beech. **Sights:** Blade front, fixed rear. **Features:** One-piece stock has inletted brass furniture, cheekpiece; double-set trigger; V-type mainspring. Flint or percussion. From Traditions.
Price: Flintlock **$484.00**
Price: Percussion **$439.00**

Prices given are believed to be accurate at time of publication however, many factors affect retail pricing so exact prices are not possible.

BLACKPOWDER MUSKETS & RIFLES

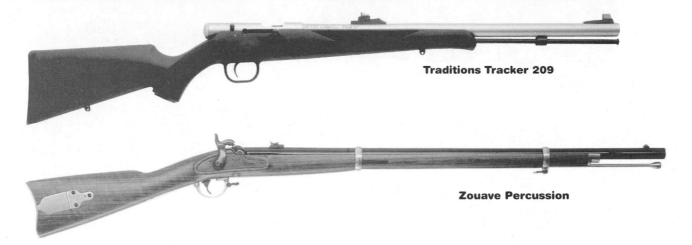

Traditions Tracker 209

Zouave Percussion

TRADITIONS TRACKER 209 IN-LINE RIFLES
Caliber: 45, 50. **Barrel:** 22" blued or C-nickel finish; 1:28" twist, 50 cal. 1:20" 45 cal. **Weight:** 6 lbs., 4 oz. **Length:** 41" overall. **Stock:** Black, Advantage Timber® composite, synthetic. **Sights:** Lite Optic blade front, adjustable rear. **Features:** Thumb safety; adjustable trigger; rubber butt pad and sling swivel studs; takes 150 grains of Pyrodex pellets; one-piece breech system takes 209 shotshell primers. Drilled and tapped for scope. From Traditions.
Price: (Black composite or synthetic stock, 22" blued barrel) . **$161.00**
Price: (Black composite or synthetic stock, 22" C-nickel barrel) **$184.00**
Price: (Advantage Timber® stock, 22" C-nickel barrel) **$249.00**
Price: (Redi-Pak, black stock and blued barrel, powder flask, capper, ball starter, other accessories) **$219.00**
Price: (Redi-Pak, synthetic stock and blued barrel, with scope) **$265.00**

ULTRA LIGHT ARMS MODEL 209 MUZZLELOADER
Caliber: 45 or 50. **Barrel:** 24" button rifled; 1:32" twist. **Weight:** Under 5 lbs. **Stock:** Kevlar/Graphite **Features:** Recoil pad, sling swivels included. Some color options available. Adj. Timney trigger, positive primer extraction.
Price: **$1,300.00**

WHITE MODEL 97 WHITETAIL HUNTER RIFLE
Caliber: 45, 50. **Barrel:** 22", 1:20" twist (45 cal.); 1:24" twist (50 cal.). **Weight:** 7.7 lbs. **Length:** 40" overall. **Stock:** Black laminated or black composite. **Sights:** Marble TruGlo fully adjustable, steel rear with white diamond, red bead front with high-visibility inserts. **Features:** In-line ignition with FlashFire one-piece nipple and breech plug that uses standard or magnum No. 11 caps, fully adjustable trigger, double safety system, aluminum ramrod; drilled and tapped for scope. Hard case. Made in U.S.A. by Split Fire Sporting Goods.
Price: Whitetail w/laminated or composite stock. **$499.95**
Price: Adventurer w/26" stainless barrel & thumbhole stock) **$699.95**
Price: Odyssey w/24" carbon fiber wrapped barrel & thumbhole stock **$1,299.95**

WHITE MODEL 98 ELITE HUNTER RIFLE
Caliber: 45, 50. **Barrel:** 24", 1:24" twist (50 cal.) **Weight:** 8.6 lbs. **Length:** 43.5" overall. **Stock:** Black laminate wtih swivel studs. **Sights:** TruGlo fully adjustable, steel rear with white diamond, red bead front with high-visibility inserts. **Features:** In-line ignition with FlashFire one-piece nipple and breech plug that uses standard or magnum No. 11 caps, fully adjustable trigger, double safety system, aluminum ramrod, drilled and tapped for scope, hard gun case. Made in U.S.A. by Split Fire Sporting Goods.
Price: Composite or laminate wood stock. **$499.95**

White Thunderbolt Rifle
Similar to the Elite Hunter but is designed to handle 209 shotgun primers only. Has 26" stainless steel barrel, weighs 9.3 lbs. and is 45.5" long. Composite or laminate stock. Made in U.S.A. by Split Fire Sporting Goods.
Price: **$599.95**

WHITE MODEL 2000 BLACKTAIL HUNTER RIFLE
Caliber: 50. **Barrel:** 22", 1:24" twist (50 cal.). **Weight:** 7.6 lbs. **Length:** 39-7/8" overall. **Stock:** Black laminated with swivel studs with laser engraved deer or elk scene. **Sights:** TruGlo fully adjustable, steel rear with white diamond, red bead front with high-visibility inserts. **Features:** Teflon finished barrel, in-line ignition with FlashFire one-piece nipple and breech plug that uses standard or magnum No. 11 caps, fully adjustable trigger, double safety system, aluminum ramrod, drilled and tapped for scope. Hard gun case. Made in U.S.A. by Split Fire Sporting Goods.
Price: Laminate wood stock, w/laser engraved game scene . **$599.95**

WHITE LIGHTNING II RIFLE
Caliber: 45 and 50 percussion. **Barrel:** 24", 1:32" twist. **Sights:** Adj. rear. **Stock:** Black polymer. **Weight:** 6 lbs. **Features:** In-line, 209 primer ignition system, blued or nickel-plated bbl., adj. trigger, Delrin ramrod, sling studs, recoil pad. Made in U.S.A. by Split Fire Sporting Goods.
Price: **$299.95**

WHITE ALPHA RIFLE
Caliber: 45, 50 percussion. **Barrel:** 27" tapered, stainless. **Sights:** Marble TruGlo rear, fiber-optic front. **Stock:** Laminated. **Features:** Lever action rotating block, hammerless; adj. trigger, positive safety. All stainless metal, including trigger. Made in U.S.A. by Split Fire Sporting Goods.
Price: **$449.95**

WINCHESTER APEX SWING-ACTION MAGNUM RIFLE
Caliber: 45, 50. **Barrel:** 28". **Stock:** Mossy Oak® Camo, Black Fleck. **Sights:** Adj. fiber-optic. **Weight:** 7 lbs., 12 oz. **Overall length:** 42". **Features:** Monte Carlo cheekpiece, swing-action design, external hammer.
Price: Mossy Oak®/stainless **$489.95**
Price: Black Fleck/stainless **$449.95**
Price: Full Mossy Oak® **$469.95**
Price: Black Fleck/blued **$364.95**

WINCHESTER X-150 BOLT-ACTION MAGNUM RIFLE
Caliber: 45, 50. **Barrel:** 26". **Stock:** Hardwoods or Timber HD, Black Fleck, Break-Up™. **Weight:** 8 lbs., 3 oz. **Sights:** Adj. fiber-optic. **Features:** No. 209 shotgun primer ignition, stainless steel bolt, stainless fluted bbl.
Price: Mossy Oak®, Timber, Hardwoods/stainless. **$349.95**
Price: Black Fleck/stainless **$299.95**
Price: Mossy Oak®, Timber, Hardwoods/blued **$279.95**
Price: Black Fleck/blued **$229.95**

ZOUAVE PERCUSSION RIFLE
Caliber: 58, 59. **Barrel:** 32.5". **Weight:** 9.5 lbs. **Length:** 48.5" overall. **Stock:** Walnut finish, brass patchbox and buttplate. **Sights:** Fixed front, rear adjustable for elevation. **Features:** Color case-hardened lockplate, blued barrel. From Navy Arms, Dixie Gun Works, EMF, Euroarms of America.
Price: Dixie Gun Works PR0853 (58) **$525.00**

Knight TK2000

CABELA'S BLACKPOWDER SHOTGUNS
Gauge: 10, 12, 20. **Barrel:** 10-ga., 30"; 12-ga., 28.5" (Extra-Full, Mod., Imp. Cyl. choke tubes); 20-ga., 27.5" (Imp. Cyl. & Mod. fixed chokes). **Weight:** 6.5 to 7 lbs. **Length:** 45" overall (28.5" barrel). **Stock:** American walnut with checkered grip; 12- and 20-gauge have straight stock, 10-gauge has pistol grip. **Features:** Blued barrels, engraved, color case-hardened locks and hammers, brass ramrod tip. From Cabela's.
Price: 10-gauge **$849.99**
Price: 12-gauge **$719.99**
Price: 20-gauge **$659.99**

DIXIE MAGNUM PERCUSSION SHOTGUN
Gauge: 10, 12, 20. **Barrel:** 30" (Imp. Cyl. & Mod.) in 10-gauge; 28" in 12-gauge. **Weight:** 6.25 lbs. **Length:** 45" overall. **Stock:** Hand-checkered walnut, 14" pull. **Features:** Double triggers; light hand engraving; case-hardened locks in 12-gauge, polished steel in 10-gauge; sling swivels. From Dixie Gun Works.
Price: 12 ga. PS0930 . . . . **$825.00**
Price: 12-ga. Kit PS0940 . . . . **$725.00**
Price: 20-ga. PS0334 . . . . **$825.00**
Price: 10-ga. PS1030 . . . . **$900.00**
Price: 10-ga. kit PS1040 . . . . **$725.00**
Price: Coach Gun, 12 ga. 20" bbl PS0914 . . . . **$800.00**

KNIGHT TK2000 NEXT G-1 CAMO MUZZLELOADING SHOTGUN
Gauge: 12. **Barrel:** 26", extra-full choke tube. **Weight:** 7 lbs., 7 oz. **Length:** 45" overall. **Stock:** Synthetic black or Realtree Hardwoods; recoil pad; swivel studs. **Sights:** Fully adjustable rear, blade front with fiber-optics. **Features:** Receiver drilled and tapped for scope mount; in-line ignition; adjustable trigger; removable breech plug; double safety system; Imp. Cyl. choke tube available. Made in U.S. by Knight Rifles (Modern Muzzleloading)
Price: **$379.99**

NAVY ARMS SIDE-BY-SIDE SHOTGUN
Caliber: 12 smoothbore. **Barrel:** 28.5". **Weight:** 7 lbs. **Length:** 44.3" overall. **Features:** English model reproduction has checkered walnut stock, slightly choked and inside choked blued barrels, engraved locks. From Navy Arms.
Price: **$910.00**

WHITE TOMINATOR SHOTGUN
Caliber: 12. **Barrel:** 25" blue, straight, tapered stainless steel. **Weight:** NA. **Length:** NA. **Stock:** Black laminated or black wood. **Sights:** Drilled and tapped for easy scope mounting. **Features:** Interchangeable choke tubes. Custom vent rib with high visibility front bead. Double safeties. Fully adjustable custom trigger. Recoil pad and sling swivel studs. Made in U.S.A. by Split Fire Sporting Goods.
Price: **$349.95**

**Benjamin & Sheridan
EB17/EB22**

ARS HUNTING MASTER AR6 AIR PISTOL
Caliber: .22 (.177 + 20 special order). **Barrel:** 12" rifled. **Weight:** 3 lbs. **Length:** 18.25 overall. **Power:** NA. **Grips:** Indonesian walnut with checkered grip. **Sights:** Adjustable rear, blade front. **Features:** 6 shot repeater with rotary magazine, single or double action, receiver grooved for scope, hammer block and trigger block safeties.
Price: **$659.00**

BEEMAN P1 MAGNUM AIR PISTOL
Caliber: .177, 20. **Barrel:** 8.4". **Weight:** 2.5 lbs. **Length:** 11" overall. **Power:** Top lever cocking; spring-piston. **Grips:** Checkered walnut. **Sights:** Blade front, square notch rear with click micrometer adjustments for windage and elevation. Grooved for scope mounting. **Features:** Dual power for .177 and 20 cal.; low setting gives 350-400 fps; high setting 500-600 fps. All Colt 45 auto grips fit gun. Dry-firing feature for practice. Optional wood shoulder stock. Imported by Beeman.
Price: . . . . **$499.95 to $525.95**

BEEMAN P3 PNEUMATIC AIR PISTOL
Caliber: .177. **Barrel:** NA. **Weight:** 1.7 lbs. **Length:** 9.6" overall. **Power:** Single-stroke pneumatic; overlever barrel cocking. **Grips:** Reinforced polymer. **Sights:** Front and rear fiber-optic sights. **Features:** Velocity 410 fps. Polymer frame; automatic safety; two-stage trigger; built-in muzzle brake.
Price: **$245.95**
Price: With scope **$335.95**

BEEMAN/FEINWERKBAU P44
Caliber: .177, single shot. **Barrel:** 0.17". **Weight:** 2.10 lbs. **Length:** 16.54" overall. **Power:** Pre-charged pneumatic. **Grips:** Walnut grip. **Sights:** front and rear sights. **Features:** 500 fps, sighting line adjustable from 360 to 395mm, adjustable 3-d grip in 3 sizes, adjustable match trigger, delivered in special transport case.
Price: **$2,575.95**
Price: Left-hand model **$2,655.95**

BEEMAN/FEINWERKBAU P56
Caliber: .177, 5-shot magazine. **Barrel:** 8.81". **Weight:** 2.43 lbs. **Length:** 16.54" overall. **Power:** Pre-charged pneumatic. **Grips:** Walnut Morini grip. **Sights:** front and rear sights. **Features:** 500 fps, match-adjustable trigger, adjustable rear sight, front sight accepts interchangeable inserts, delivered in special transport case.
Price: **$2,654.00**

BEEMAN/FWB 103 AIR PISTOL
Caliber: .177. **Barrel:** 10.1", 12-groove rifling. **Weight:** 2.5 lbs. **Length:** 16.5" overall. **Power:** Single-stroke pneumatic, underlever cocking. **Grips:** Stippled walnut with adjustable palm shelf. **Sights:** Blade front, open rear adjustable for windage and elevation. Notch size adjustable for width. Interchangeable front blades. **Features:** Velocity 510 fps. Fully adjustable trigger. Cocking effort 2 lbs. Imported by Beeman.
Price: Right-hand **$2,110.00**
Price: Left-hand **$2,350.00**

BEEMAN HW70A AIR PISTOL
Caliber: .177. **Barrel:** 6-1/4", rifled. **Weight:** 38 oz. **Length:** 12-3/4" overall. **Power:** Spring, barrel cocking. **Grips:** Plastic, with thumbrest. **Sights:** Hooded post front, square notch rear adjustable for windage and elevation. Comes with scope base. **Features:** Adjustable trigger, 31-lb. cocking effort, 440 fps MV; automatic barrel safety. Imported by Beeman.
Price: **$289.95**

BENJAMIN & SHERIDAN CO2 PISTOLS
Caliber: .22, single shot. **Barrel:** 6-3/8", brass. **Weight:** 1 lb. 12 oz. **Length:** 9" overall. **Power:** 12-gram CO_2 cylinder. **Grips:** American Hardwood. **Sights:** High ramp front, fully adjustable notched rear. **Features:** Velocity to 500 fps. Turnbolt action with cross-bolt safety. Gives about 40 shots per CO_2 cylinder. Black or nickel finish. Made in U.S. by Crosman Corp.
Price: EB22 (.22) **$118.59**

BENJAMIN & SHERIDAN PNEUMATIC PELLET PISTOLS
Caliber: .177, .22, single shot. **Barrel:** 9-3/8", rifled brass. **Weight:** 2 lbs., 8 oz. **Length:** 12.25" overall. **Power:** Underlever pnuematic, hand pumped. **Grips:** American Hardwood. **Sights:** High ramp front, fully adjustable notch rear. **Features:** Velocity to 525 fps (variable). Bolt action with cross-bolt safety. Choice of black or nickel finish. Made in U.S. by Crosman Corp.
Price: Black finish, HB17 (.177), HB22 (.22) **$133.59**

CROSMAN C11
Caliber: .177, 18-shot BB or pellet. **Weight:** 1.4 lbs. **Length:** 8.5". **Power:** 12g CO_2. **Sights:** Fixed. **Features:** Compact semi-automatic BB pistol. Velocity up to 480 fps. Under barrel weaver style rail.
Price: **$52.99**

CROSMAN 2240
Caliber: .22. **Barrel:** Rifled steel. **Weight:** 1 lb. 13 oz. **Length:** 11.125". **Power:** CO_2. **Grips:** NA. **Sights:** Blade front, rear adjustable. **Features:** Ergonomically designed ambidextrous grip fits the hand for perfect balance and comfort with checkering and a thumbrest on both grip panels. From Crosman.
Price: **$57.83**

CROSMAN 3576 REVOLVER
Caliber: .177, pellets. **Barrel:** Rifled steel. **Weight:** 2 lbs. **Length:** 11.38". **Power:** CO_2. **Grips:** NA. **Sights:** Blade front, rear adjustable. **Features:** Semi-auto 10-shot with revolver styling and finger-molded grip design, 6" barrel for increased accuracy. From Crosman.
Price: **$52.59**

CROSMAN MODEL 1088 REPEAT AIR PISTOL
Caliber: .177, 8-shot pellet clip. **Barrel:** Rifled steel. **Weight:** 17 oz. **Length:** 7.75" overall. **Power:** CO_2 Powerlet. **Grips:** Checkered black plastic. **Sights:** Fixed blade front, adjustable rear. **Features:** Velocity about 430 fps. Single or double semi-automatic action. From Crosman.
Price: **$60.99**

CROSMAN PRO77
Caliber: .177, 17-shot BB. **Weight:** 1.31 lbs. **Length:** 6.75". **Power:** 12g CO_2. **Sights:** Fixed. **Features:** Compact pistol with realistic recoil. Under the barrel weaver style rail. Velocity up to 325 fps.
Price: Pro77CS **$114.00**

CROSMAN T4
Caliber: .177, 8-shot BB or pellet. **Weight:** 1.32 lbs. **Length:** 8.63". **Power:** 12g CO_2. **Sights:** Fixed front, windage adjustable rear. **Features:** Shoots BBs or pellets. Easy patent-pending CO_2 piercing mechanism. Under the barrel weaver style rail.
Price: T4CS **$89.59**
Price: T4OPS, includes adjustable Red Dot sight, barrel compensator, and pressure operated tactical flashlight. Comes in foam padeed, hard sided protective case **$167.99**

DAISY POWERLINE® MODEL 15XT AIR PISTOL
Caliber: .177 BB, 15-shot built-in magazine. **Barrel:** NA. **Weight:** NA. **Length:** 7.21". **Power:** CO_2. **Grips:** NA. **Sights:** NA. **Features:** Velocity 425 fps. Made in the U.S.A. by Daisy Mfg. Co.
Price: **$50.99**
Price: With electronic point sight **$64.99**

DAISY MODEL 717 AIR PISTOL
Caliber: .177, single shot. **Weight:** 2.25 lbs. **Length:** 13-1/2" overall. **Grips:** Molded checkered woodgrain with contoured thumbrest. **Sights:** Blade and ramp front, open rear with windage and elevation adjustments. **Features:** Single pump pneumatic pistol. Rifled steel barrel. Crossbolt trigger block. Muzzle velocity 360 fps. From Daisy Mfg. Co.
Price: **$220.94**

AIRGUNS—Handguns

DAISY MODEL 747 TRIUMPH AIR PISTOL
Caliber: .177, single shot. **Weight:** 2.35 lbs. **Length:** 13-1/2" overall. **Grips:** Molded checkered woodgrain with contoured thumbrest. **Sights:** Blade and ramp front, open rear with windage and elevation adjustments. **Features:** Single pump pneumatic pistol. Lothar Walther rifled high-grade steel barrel; crowned 12 lands and grooves, right-hand twist. Precision bore sized for match pellets. Muzzle velocity 360 fps. From Daisy Mfg. Co.
Price: **$264.99**

DAISY POWERLINE® 201
Caliber: .177 BB or pellet. **Weight:** 1 lb. **Length:** 9.25" overall. **Sights:** Blade and ramp front, fixed open rear. **Features:** Spring-air action, trigger-block safety and smooth-bore steel barrel. Muzzle velocity 230 fps. From Daisy Mfg. Co.
Price: **$29.99**

DAISY POWERLINE® 693 AIR PISTOL
Caliber: .177, single shot. **Weight:** 1.10 lbs. **Length:** 7.9" overall. **Grips:** Molded checkered. **Sights:** Blade and ramp front, fixed open rear. **Features:** Semi-automoatic BB pistol with a nickel finish and smooth bore steel barrel. Muzzle veocity 400 fps. From Daisy Mfg. Co.
Price: **$76.99**

DAISY POWERLINE® 5170 CO2 PISTOL
Caliber: .177 BB. **Weight:** 1 lb. **Length:** 9.5" overall. **Sights:** Blade and ramp front, open rear. **Features:** CO2 semi-automatic action, manual trigger-block safety, upper and lower rails for mounting sights and other accessories and a smooth-bore steel barrel. Muzzle velocity 520 fps. From Daisy Mfg. Co.
Price: **$59.99**

DAISY POWERLINE® 5501 CO2 BLOWBACK PISTOL
Caliber: .177 BB. **Weight:** 1 lb. **Length:** 9.5" overall. **Sights:** Blade and ramp front, open rear. **Features:** CO2 semi-automatic blow-back action, manual trigger-block safety, and a smooth-bore steel barrel. Muzzle velocity 430 fps. From Daisy Mfg. Co.
Price: **$99.99**

EAA/BAIKAL IZH-M46 TARGET AIR PISTOL
Caliber: .177, single shot. **Barrel:** 10". **Weight:** 2.4 lbs. **Length:** 16.8" overall. **Power:** Underlever single-stroke pneumatic. **Grips:** Adjustable wooden target. **Sights:** Micrometer fully adjustable rear, blade front. **Features:** Velocity about 440 fps. Hammer-forged, rifled barrel. Imported from Russia by European American Armory.
Price: **$430.00**

GAMO P-23, P-23 LASER PISTOL
Caliber: .177, 12-shot. **Barrel:** 4.25". **Weight:** 1 lb. **Length:** 7.5". **Power:** CO2 cartridge, semi-automatic, 410 fps. **Grips:** Plastic. **Sights:** NA. **Features:** Walther PPK cartridge pistol copy, optional laser sight. Imported from Spain by Gamo.
Price: . . . . **$89.95**, (with laser) **$139.95**

GAMO PT-80, PT-80 LASER PISTOL
Caliber: .177, 8-shot. **Barrel:** 4.25". **Weight:** 1.2 lbs. **Length:** 7.2". **Power:** CO2 cartridge, semi-automatic, 410 fps. **Grips:** Plastic. **Sights:** 3-dot. **Features:** Optional laser sight and walnut grips available. Imported from Spain by Gamo.
Price: . . . . **$108.95**, (with laser) **$159.95**
Price: (with walnut grip) **$119.95**

HAMMERLI AP-40 AIR PISTOL
Caliber: .177. **Barrel:** 10". **Weight:** 2.2 lbs. **Length:** 15.5". **Power:** NA. **Grips:** Adjustable orthopedic. **Sights:** Fully adjustable micrometer. **Features:** Sleek, light, well balanced and accurate.
Price: **$1,400.00**

MAGNUM RESEARCH DESERT EAGLE
Caliber: .177, 8-shot pellet. **Barrel:** 5.7" rifled. **Weight:** 2.5 lbs. 11" overall. **Power:** 12g CO2. **Sights:** Fixed front, adjustable rear. Velocity of 425 fps. 8-shot rotary clip. Double or single action. The first .177 caliber air pistol with BLOWBACK action. Big and weighty, designed in the likeness of the real Desert Eagle.
Price: **$172.31**

MAGNUM BABY DESERT
Caliber: .177, 15-shot BB. 4" **Weight:** 1.0 lbs. 8-1/4" overall. **Power:** 12g CO2. **Sights:** Fixed front and rear. Velocity of 420 fps. Double action BB repeater. Comes with bonus Picatinny top rail and built-in bottom rail.
Price: **$41.54**

MORINI CM 162 EL MATCH AIR PISTOLS
Caliber: .177, single shot. **Barrel:** 9.4". **Weight:** 32 oz. **Length:** 16.1" overall. **Power:** Scuba air. **Grips:** Adjustable match type. **Sights:** Interchangeable blade front, fully adjustable match-type rear. **Features:** Power mechanism shuts down when pressure drops to a preset level. Adjustable electronic trigger.
Price: **$1,075.00**

PARDINI K58 MATCH AIR PISTOLS
Caliber: .177, single shot. **Barrel:** 9". **Weight:** 37.7 oz. **Length:** 15.5" overall. **Power:** Precharged compressed air; single-stroke cocking. **Grips:** Adjustable match type; stippled walnut. **Sights:** Interchangeable post front, fully adjustable match rear. **Features:** Fully adjustable trigger. Short version K-2 available. Imported from Italy by Larry's Guns.
Price: **$819.00**

RWS 9B/9N AIR PISTOLS
Caliber: .177, single shot. **Barrel:** 8". **Weight:** 2.38 lbs. **Length:** 10.4". **Power:** 550 fps. **Grips:** Right hand with thumbrest. **Sights:** Adjustable. **Features:** Spring-piston powered. Black or nickel finish.
Price: 9B/9N **$150.00**

SMITH & WESSON 586
Caliber: .177, 10-shot pellet. Rifled. **Power:** 12g CO2. **Sights:** Fixed front, adjustable rear. 10-shot rotary clip. Double or single action. Replica revolvers that duplicate both weight and handling.
Price: 4" barrel, 2.5 lbs, 400 fps **$215.34**
Price: 6" barrel, 2.8 lbs, 425 fps **$231.49**
Price: 8" barrel, 3.0 lbs, 460 fps **$247.65**
Price: S&W 686 Nickel, 6" barrel, 2.8 lbs, 425 fps **$253.03**

STEYR LP10P MATCH AIR PISTOL
Caliber: .177, single shot. **Barrel:** 9". **Weight:** 38.7 oz. **Length:** 15.3" overall. **Power:** Scuba air. **Grips:** Adjustable Morini match, palm shelf, stippled walnut. **Sights:** Interchangeable blade in 4mm, 4.5mm or 5mm widths, adjustable open rear, interchangeable 3.5mm or 4mm leaves. **Features:** Velocity about 500 fps. Adjustable trigger, adjustable sight radius from 12.4" to 13.2". With compensator. Recoil elimination.
Price: **$1,400.00**

TECH FORCE SS2 OLYMPIC COMPETITION AIR PISTOL
Caliber: .177 pellet, single shot. **Barrel:** 7.4". **Weight:** 2.8 lbs. **Length:** 16.5" overall. **Power:** Spring piston, sidelever. **Grips:** Hardwood. **Sights:** Extended adjustable rear, blade front accepts inserts. **Features:** Velocity 520 fps. Recoilless design; adjustments allow duplication of a firearm's feel. Match-grade, adjustable trigger; includes carrying case. Imported from China by Compasseco, Inc.
Price: **$295.00**

TECH FORCE 35 AIR PISTOL
Caliber: .177 pellet, single shot. **Weight:** 2.86 lbs. **Length:** 14.9" overall. **Power:** Spring-piston, underlever. **Grips:** Hardwood. **Sights:** Micrometer adjustable rear, blade front. **Features:** Velocity 400 fps. Grooved for scope mount; trigger safety. Imported from China by Compasseco, Inc.
Price: **$39.95**

Tech Force S2-1 Air Pistol
Similar to Tech Force 8 except basic grips and sights for plinking.
Price: **$29.95**

WALTHER LP300 MATCH PISTOL
Caliber: .177. **Barrel:** 236mm. **Weight:** 1.018g. **Length:** NA. **Power:** NA. **Grips:** NA. **Sights:** Integrated front with three different widths, adjustable rear. **Features:** Adjustable grip and trigger.
Price: **$1,800.00**

WALTHER PPK/S
Caliber: .177, 15-shot steel BB. 3-1/2". **Weight:** 1.2 lbs. 6-1/4" overall. **Power:** 12g CO2. **Sights:** Fixed front and rear. Velocity of 295 fps. Lookalike of one of the world's most famous pistols. Realistic recoil. Heavyweight steel construction.
Price: **$71.92**
Price: With laser sight **$94.23**
Price: With BiColor pistol, targets, shooting glasses, BBs **$84.62**

WALTHER CP99 COMPACT
Caliber: .177, 17-shot steel BB semi-auto. 3". **Weight:** 1.7 lbs. 6-1/2" overall. **Power:** 12g CO2. **Sights:** Fixed front and rear. Velocity of 345 fps. Realistic recoil, blowback action. Heavyweight steel construction. Built-in Picatinny mount.
Price: **$83.08**

Prices given are believed to be accurate at time of publication however, many factors affect retail pricing so exact prices are not possible.

AIRGUNS—Long Guns

AIRFORCE CONDOR RIFLE
Caliber: .177, .22 single shot. **Barrel:** 24" rifled. **Weight:** 6.5 lbs. **Length:** 38.75" overall. **Power:** Pre-charged pneumatic. **Stock:** NA. **Sights:** Intended for scope use, fiber-optic open sights optional. **Features:** Lothar Walther match barrel, adjustable power levels from 600-1,300 fps. 3,000 psi fill pressure. Automatic safety. Air tank volume: 490cc. An integral extended scope rail allows easy mounting of the largest airgun scopes. Operates on high-pressure air from scuba tank or hand pump. Manufactured in the U.S.A by AirForce Airguns.
Price: Gun only (.22 or .177) **$631.00**

AIRFORCE TALON AIR RIFLE
Caliber: .177, .22, single shot. **Barrel:** 18" rifled. **Weight:** 5.5 lbs. **Length:** 32.6". **Power:** Pre-charged pneumatic. **Stock:** NA. **Sights:** Intended for scope use, fiber-optic open sights optional. **Features:** Lothar Walther match barrel, adjustable power levels from 400-1,000 fps, 3,000 psi fill pressure. Automatic safety. Air tank volume: 490cc. Operates on high-pressure air from scuba tank or hand pump. Manufactured in the U.S.A. by AirForce Airguns.
Price: Gun only (.22 or .177). **$514.25**

AIRFORCE TALON SS AIR RIFLE
Caliber: .177, .22, single shot. **Barrel:** 12" rifled. **Weight:** 5.25 lbs. **Length:** 32.75". **Power:** Pre-charged pneumatic. **Stock:** NA. **Sights:** Intended for scope use, fiber-optic open sights optional. **Features:** Lothar Walther match barrel, adjustable power levels from 400-1,000 fps. 3,000 psi fill pressure. Automatic safety. Chamber in front of barrel strips away air turbulence, protects muzzle and reduces firing report. Air tank volume: 490cc. Operates on high-pressure air from scuba tank or hand pump. Manufactured in the U.S.A. by AirForce Airguns.
Price: Gun only (.22 or .177). **$535.50**

AIRROW MODEL A-8SRB STEALTH AIR RIFLE
Caliber: .177, .22, .25, 9-shot. **Barrel:** 20"; rifled. **Weight:** 6 lbs. **Length:** 34" overall. **Power:** CO2 or compressed air; variable power. **Stock:** Telescoping CAR-15-type. **Sights:** Variable 3.5-10x scope. **Features:** Velocity 1100 fps in all calibers. Pneumatic air trigger. All aircraft aluminum and stainless steel construction. Mil-spec materials and finishes. From Swivel Machine Works, Inc.
Price: About **$2,299.00**

AIRROW MODEL A-8S1P STEALTH AIR RIFLE
Caliber: #2512 16" arrow. **Barrel:** 16". **Weight:** 4.4 lbs. **Length:** 30.1" overall. **Power:** CO2 or compressed air; variable power. **Stock:** Telescoping CAR-15-type. **Sights:** Scope rings only. 7 oz. rechargeable cylinder and valve. **Features:** Velocity to 650 fps with 260-grain arrow. Pneumatic air trigger. Broadhead guard. All aircraft aluminum and stainless steel construction. Mil-spec materials and finishes. A-8S Models perform to 2,000 PSIG above or below water levels. Waterproof case. From Swivel Machine Works, Inc.
Price: **$1,699.00**

ARS HUNTING MASTER AR6 AIR RIFLE
Caliber: .22, 6-shot repeater. **Barrel:** 25-1/2". **Weight:** 7 lbs. **Length:** 41-1/4" overall. **Power:** Precompressed air from 3000 psi diving tank. **Stock:** Indonesian walnut with checkered grip; rubber buttpad. **Sights:** Blade front, adjustable peep rear. **Features:** Velocity over 1000 fps with 32-grain pellet. Receiver grooved for scope mounting. Has 6-shot rotary magazine. Imported by Air Rifle Specialists.
Price: **$580.00**

BEEMAN HW100
Caliber: .177 or .22, 14-shot magazine. **Barrel:** 21-1/2". **Weight:** 9 lbs. **Length:** 42.13" overall. **Power:** Pre-charged. **Stock:** Walnut Sporter checkering on the pistol grip & forend; walnut thumbhose with lateral finger grooves on the forend & stippling on the pistol grip. **Sights:** None. Grooved for scope mounting. **Features:** 1140 fps .177 caliber; 945 fps .22 caliber. 14-shot magazine, quick-fill cylinder. Two-stage adjustable match trigger and manual safety.
Price: .177 or .22 caliber Sport Stock **$1,649.95**
Price: .177 or .22 caliber Thumbhole Stock **$1,649.95**

BEEMAN R1 AIR RIFLE
Caliber: .177, .20 or .22, single shot. **Barrel:** 19.6", 12-groove rifling. **Weight:** 8.5 lbs. **Length:** 45.2" overall. **Power:** Spring-piston, barrel cocking. **Stock:** Walnut-stained beech; cut-checkered pistol grip; Monte Carlo comb and cheekpiece; rubber buttpad. **Sights:** Tunnel front with interchangeable inserts, open rear click-adjustable for windage and elevation. Grooved for scope mounting. **Features:** Velocity 940-1000 fps (.177), 860 fps (20), 800 fps (.22). Non-drying nylon piston and breech seals. Adjustable metal trigger. Milled steel safety. Right- or left-hand stock. Adjustable cheekpiece and buttplate at extra cost. Custom and Super Laser versions available. Imported by Beeman.
Price: Right-hand **$729.95**
Price: Left-hand **$789.95**

BEEMAN R7 AIR RIFLE
Caliber: .177, .20, single shot. **Barrel:** 17". **Weight:** 6.1 lbs. **Length:** 40.2" overall. **Power:** Spring-piston. **Stock:** Stained beech. **Sights:** Hooded front, fully adjustable micrometer click open rear. **Features:** Velocity to 700 fps (.177), 620 fps (20). Receiver grooved for scope mounting; double-jointed cocking lever; fully adjustable trigger; checkered grip. Imported by Beeman.
Price: .177 . . . . **$409.95**
Price: .20 . . . . **$429.95**

BEEMAN R9 AIR RIFLE
Caliber: .177, .20, single shot. **Barrel:** NA. **Weight:** 7.3 lbs. **Length:** 43" overall. **Power:** Spring-piston, barrel cocking. **Stock:** Stained hardwood. **Sights:** Tunnel post front, fully adjustable open rear. **Features:** Velocity to 1000 fps (.177), 800 fps (20). Adjustable Rekord trigger; automatic safety; receiver dovetailed for scope mounting. Imported from Germany by Beeman Precision Airguns.
Price: .177 . . . . **$499.95**
Price: .20 . . . . **$524.95**

BEEMAN R11 MKII AIR RIFLE
Caliber: .177, single shot. **Barrel:** 19.6". **Weight:** 8.6 lbs. **Length:** 43.5" overall. **Power:** Spring-piston, barrel cocking. **Stock:** Walnut-stained beech; adjustable buttplate and cheekpiece. **Sights:** None furnished. Has dovetail for scope mounting. **Features:** Velocity 910-940 fps. All-steel barrel sleeve. Imported by Beeman.
Price: **$679.95**

BEEMAN RX-2 GAS-SPRING MAGNUM AIR RIFLE
Caliber: .177, .20, .22, .25, single shot. **Barrel:** 19.6", 12-groove rifling. **Weight:** 8.8 lbs. **Power:** Gas-spring piston air; single stroke barrel cocking. **Stock:** Laminated wood stock. **Sights:** Tunnel front, click-adjustable rear. **Features:** Velocity adjustable to about 1200 fps. Imported by Beeman.
Price: .177, right-hand **$889.95**
Price: .20, right-hand **$909.95**
Price: .22, right-hand **$889.95**
Price: .25, right-hand **$909.95**

BEEMAN R1 CARBINE
Caliber: .177,. 20, .22 single shot. **Barrel:** 16.1". **Weight:** 8.6 lbs. **Length:** 41.7" overall. **Power:** Spring-piston, barrel cocking. **Stock:** Stained beech; Monte Carlo comb and checkpiece; cut checkered pistol grip; rubber buttpad. **Sights:** Tunnel front with interchangeable inserts, open adjustable rear; receiver grooved for scope mounting. **Features:** Velocity up to 1000 fps (.177). Non-drying nylon piston and breech seals. Adjustable metal trigger. Machined steel receiver end cap and safety. Right- or left-hand stock. Imported by Beeman.
Price: .177, 20, .22, right-hand **$749.95**

BEEMAN/FEINWERKBAU 700 P ALUMINUM OR WOOD STOCK
Caliber: .177, single shot. **Barrel:** 16.6". **Weight:** 10.8 lbs. Aluminum; 9.9 lbs. Wood. **Length:** 43.3-46.25" Aluminum; 43.7" Wood. **Power:** Pre-charged pneumatic. **Stock:** Aluminum stock P laminated hardwood. **Sights:** Tunnel front sight with interchangeable inserts, click micrometer match aperture rear sight. **Features:** Velocity 570 fps. Recoilless action. Anatomical grips can be tilted and pivoted to the barrel axis. Adjustable buttplate and cheekpiece.
Price: Aluminum 700, right, blue or silver **$3,934.95**
Price: Aluminum 700, universal **$3,069.95**

BEEMAN/FEINWERKBAU P70 FIELD TARGET
Caliber: .177, single shot. **Barrel:** 24.6". **Weight:** 10.6 lbs. **Length:** 43.3" overall. **Power:** Pre-charged pneumatic. **Stock:** Aluminum stock (red or blue) anatomical grips, buttplate & cheekpiece. **Sights:** None, receiver grooved for scope mounting. **Features:** 870 fps velocity. At 50 yards, this air rifle is capable of achieving 1/2-inch groups. Match adjustable trigger. 2001 US Field Target National Champion.
Price: P70FT, precharged, right (red or blue) **$3,819.95**
Price: P70FT, precharged, left (red or blue) **$3,964.95**

Beretta CX4 Storm

BEEMAN/HW 97 AIR RIFLE
Caliber: .177, .20, .22, single shot. **Barrel:** 17.75". **Weight:** 9.2 lbs. **Length:** 44.1" overall. **Power:** Spring-piston, underlever cocking. **Stock:** Walnut-stained beech; rubber buttpad. **Sights:** None. Receiver grooved for scope mounting. **Features:** Velocity 830 fps (.177). Fixed barrel with fully opening, direct loading breech. Adjustable trigger. Imported by Beeman Precision Airguns.
Price: .177 . . . . **$779.95**
Price: .20, .22 . . . . **$799.95**

BENJAMIN & SHERIDAN PNEUMATIC (PUMP-UP) AIR RIFLE
Caliber: .177 or .22, single shot. **Barrel:** 19-3/8", rifled brass. **Weight:** 5-1/2 lbs. **Length:** 36-1/4" overall. **Power:** Underlever pneumatic, hand pumped. **Stock:** American walnut stock and forend. **Sights:** High ramp front, fully adjustable notched rear. **Features:** Variable velocity to 800 fps. Bolt action with ambidextrous push-pull safety. Black or nickel finish. Made in the U.S. by Benjamin Sheridan Co.
Price: 392 or 397 . . . . **$249.40**

BERETTA CX4 STORM
Caliber: .177, 30-shot semi-auto. 17-1/2", rifled. **Weight:** 5.25 lbs. **Length:** 30.75" overall. **Power:** 88g CO2. **Stock:** Replica style. **Sights:** Adjustable front and rear. Blowback action. Velocity of 600 fps. Accessory rails.
Price: **$276.92**

BSA SUPERTEN MK3 AIR RIFLE
Caliber: .177, .22 10-shot repeater. **Barrel:** 17-1/2". **Weight:** 7 lbs., 8 oz. **Length:** 37" overall. **Power:** Precharged pneumatic via buddy bottle. **Stock:** Oil-finished hardwood; Monte Carlo with cheekpiece, cut checkered grip; adjustable recoil pad. **Sights:** No sights; intended for scope use. **Features:** Velocity 1000+ fps (.177), 1000+ fps (.22). Patented 10-shot indexing magazine, bolt-action loading. Left-hand version also available. Imported from U.K.
Price: **$599.95**

BSA SUPERTEN MK3 BULLBARREL
Caliber: .177, .22, .25, single shot. **Barrel:** 18-1/2". **Weight:** 8 lbs., 8 oz. **Length:** 43" overall. **Power:** Spring-air, underlever cocking. **Stock:** Oil-finished hardwood; Monte Carlo with cheekpiece, checkered at grip; recoil pad. **Sights:** Ramp front, micrometer adjustable rear. Maxi-Grip scope rail. **Features:** Velocity 950 fps (.177), 750 fps (.22), 600 fps (25). Patented rotating breech design. Maxi-Grip scope rail protects optics from recoil; automatic anti-beartrap plus manual safety. Imported from U.K.
Price: Rifle, MKII Carbine (14" barrel, 39-1/2" overall) **$349.95**

BSA MAGNUM SUPERSPORT AIR RIFLE, CARBINE
Caliber: .177, .22, .25, single shot. **Barrel:** 18-1/2". **Weight:** 6 lbs., 8 oz. **Length:** 41" overall. **Power:** Spring-air, barrel cocking. **Stock:** Oil-finished hardwood; Monte Carlo with cheekpiece, recoil pad. **Sights:** Ramp front, micrometer adjustable rear. Maxi-Grip scope rail. **Features:** Velocity 950 fps (.177), 750 fps (.22), 600 fps (25). Patented Maxi-Grip scope rail protects optics from recoil; automatic anti-beartrap plus manual tang safety. Muzzle brake standard. Imported for U.K.
Price: **$194.95**
Price: Carbine, 14" barrel, muzzle brake **$214.95**

BSA METEOR AIR RIFLE
Caliber: .177, .22, single shot. **Barrel:** 18-1/2". **Weight:** 6 lbs. **Length:** 41" overall. **Power:** Spring-air, barrel cocking. **Stock:** Oil-finished hardwood. **Sights:** Ramp front, micrometer adjustable rear. **Features:** Velocity 650 fps (.177), 500 fps (.22). Automatic anti-beartrap; manual tang safety. Receiver grooved for scope mounting. Imported from U.K.
Price: Rifle **$144.95**
Price: Carbine **$164.95**

CROSMAN MODEL POWERMASTER 664SB AIR RIFLES
Caliber: .177 (single shot pellet) or BB, 200-shot reservoir. **Barrel:** 20", rifled steel. **Weight:** 2 lbs. 15 oz. **Length:** 38-1/2" overall. **Power:**

Pneumatic; hand-pumped. **Stock:** Wood-grained ABS plastic; checkered pistol grip and forend. **Sights:** Fiber-optic front, fully adjustable open rear. **Features:** Velocity about 645 fps. Bolt action, cross-bolt safety. From Crosman.
Price: **$105.50**

CROSMAN MODEL PUMPMASTER 760 AIR RIFLES
Caliber: .177 pellets (single shot) or BB (200-shot reservoir). **Barrel:** 19-1/2", rifled steel. **Weight:** 2 lbs., 12 oz. **Length:** 33.5" overall. **Power:** Pneumatic, hand-pump. **Stock:** Walnut-finished ABS plastic stock and forend. **Features:** Velocity to 590 fps (BBs, 10 pumps). Short stroke, power determined by number of strokes. Fiber-optic front sight and adjustable rear sight. Cross-bolt safety. From Crosman.
Price: Model 760 . . . . **$40.59**

CROSMAN MODEL REPEATAIR 1077 RIFLES
Caliber: .177 pellets, 12-shot clip. **Barrel:** 20.3", rifled steel. **Weight:** 3 lbs., 11 oz. **Length:** 38.8" overall. **Power:** CO2 Powerlet. **Stock:** Textured synthetic or hardwood. **Sights:** Blade front, fully adjustable rear. **Features:** Velocity 590 fps. Removable 12-shot clip. True semi-automatic action. From Crosman.
Price: **$73.99**

CROSMAN MODEL .2260 AIR RIFLE
Caliber: .22, single shot. **Barrel:** 24". **Weight:** 4 lbs., 12 oz. **Length:** 39.75" overall. **Power:** CO2 Powerlet. **Stock:** Hardwood. **Sights:** Blade front, adjustable rear open or peep. **Features:** Variable pump power; three pumps give 395 fps, six pumps 530 fps, 10 pumps 600 fps (average). Full-size adult air rifle. From Crosman.
Price: **$83.84**

CROSMAN MODEL CLASSIC 2100 AIR RIFLE
Caliber: .177 pellets (single shot), or BB (200-shot BB reservoir). **Barrel:** 21", rifled. **Weight:** 4 lbs., 13 oz. **Length:** 39-3/4" overall. **Power:** Pump-up, pneumatic. **Stock:** Wood-grained checkered ABS plastic. **Features:** Three pumps give about 450 fps, 10 pumps about 755 fps (BBs). Cross-bolt safety; concealed reservoir holds over 200 BBs. From Crosman.
Price: Model 2100B **$62.99**

DAISY 1938 RED RYDER AIR RIFLE
Caliber: BB, 650-shot repeating action. **Barrel:** Smoothbore steel with shroud. **Weight:** 2.2 lbs. **Length:** 35.4" overall. **Stock:** Wood stock burned with Red Ryder lariat signature. **Sights:** Post front, adjustable open rear. **Features:** Walnut forend. Saddle ring with leather thong. Lever cocking. Gravity feed. Controlled velocity. From Daisy Mfg. Co.
Price: **$55.99**

DAISY MODEL 840B GRIZZLY AIR RIFLE
Caliber: .177 pellet single shot; or BB 350-shot. **Barrel:** 19", smoothbore, steel. **Weight:** 2.25 lbs. **Length:** 36.8" overall. **Power:** Single pump pneumatic. **Stock:** Molded wood-grain stock and forend. **Sights:** Ramp front, open, adjustable rear. **Features:** Muzzle velocity 320 fps (BB), 300 fps (pellet). Steel buttplate; straight pull bolt action; cross-bolt safety. Forend forms pump lever. From Daisy Mfg. Co.
Price: **$60.99**
Price: (840C in Mossy Oak Breakup Camo) **$64.99**

DAISY MODEL 4841 GRIZZLY
Caliber: .177 pellet single shot. **Barrel:** NA. **Weight:** NA. **Length:** 36.8" overall. **Power:** Single pump pneumatic. **Stock:** Composite camo. **Sights:** Blade and ramp front. **Features:** Muzzle velocity 350 fps. Fixed Daisy Model 808 scope. From Daisy Mfg. Co.
Price: **$69.99**

DAISY MODEL 105 BUCK AIR RIFLE
Caliber: .177 or BB. **Barrel:** Smoothbore steel. **Weight:** 1.6 lbs. **Length:** 29.8" overall. **Power:** Lever cocking, spring air. **Stock:** Stained solid wood. **Sights:** TruGlo fiber-optic, open fixed rear. **Features:** Velocity to 275. Crossbolt trigger block safety. From Daisy Mfg. Co.
Price: **$39.99**

DAISY AVANTI MODEL 888 MEDALIST
Caliber: .177, pellet. **Barrel:** Lothar Walther rifled high-grade steel, crowned, 12 lands and grooves, right-hand twist. Precision bore sized for match pellets. **Weight:** 6.9 lbs. **Length:** 38.5" overall. **Power:** CO2 single shot bolt. **Stock:** Sporter-style multicolored laminated hardwood. **Sights:** Hooded front with interchangeable aperture inserts; micrometer adjustable rear peep sight. **Features:** Velocity to 500. Crossbolt trigger block safety. From Daisy Mfg. Co.
Price: **$525.99**

Prices given are believed to be accurate at time of publication however, many factors affect retail pricing so exact prices are not possible.

AIRGUNS—Long Guns

Gamo Viper

Gamo Shadow Fox

DAISY AVANTI MODEL 887 GOLD MEDALIST
Caliber: 177, pellet. **Barrel:** Lothar Walther rifled high-grade steel, crowned, 12 lands and grooves, right hand twist. Precision bore sized for match pellets. **Weight:** 7.3 lbs. **Length:** 39.5" overall. **Power:** CO2 power single shot bolt. **Stock:** Laminated hardwood. **Sights:** Front globe sight with changeable aperture inserts: rear diopter sight with micrometer click adjustment for windage and elevation. **Features:** Velocity to 500. Crossbolt trigger block safety. Includes rail adapter. From Daisy Mfg. Co.
Price: **$599.99**

DAISY MODEL 853 LEGEND
Caliber: .177, pellet. **Barrel:** Lothar Walther rifled high-grade steel barrel, crowned, 12 lands and grooves, right-hand twist. Precision bore sized for match pellets. **Weight:** 5.5 lbs. **Length:** 38.5" overall. **Power:** Single-pump pneumatic, straight pull-bolt. **Stock:** Full-length, sporter-style hardwood with adjustable length. **Sights:** Hooded front with interchangeable aperture inserts; micrometer adjustable rear. **Features:** Velocity to 510. Crossbolt trigger block safety with red indicator. From Daisy Mfg. Co.
Price: **$432.00**
Price: Model 835 Legend EX; velocity to 490 .... **$432.00**

DAISY MODEL 753 ELITE
Caliber: .177, pellet. **Barrel:** Lothar Walther rifled high-grade steel barrel, crowned, 12 lands and grooves, right-hand twist. Precision bore sized for match pellets. **Weight:** 6.4 lbs. **Length:** 39.75" overall. **Power:** Recoilless single pump pneumatic, straight pull bolt. **Stock:** Full length match-style hardwood stock with raised cheek piece and adjustable length. **Sights:** Front globe sight with changeable aperture inserts, diopter rear sight with micrometer adjustable rear. **Features:** Velocity to 510. Crossbolt trigger block safety with red indicator. From Daisy Mfg. Co.
Price: **$558.99**

DAISY MODEL 105 BUCK AIR RIFLE
Caliber: .177 or BB. **Barrel:** Smoothbore steel. **Weight:** 1.6 lbs. **Length:** 29.8" overall. **Power:** Lever cocking, spring air. **Stock:** Stained solid wood. **Sights:** TruGlo fiber-optic, open fixed rear. **Features:** Velocity to 275. Cross-bolt trigger block safety. From Daisy Mfg. Co.
Price: **$39.99**

DAISY POWERLINE® TARGETPRO 953 AIR RIFLE
Caliber: .177 pellets, single shot. **Weight:** 6.40 lbs. **Length:** 39.75" overall. **Power:** Pneumatic single-pump cocking lever; straight-pull bolt. **Stock:** Full-length, match-style black composite. **Sights:** Front and rear fiber optic. **Features:** Rifled high-grade steel barrel with 1:15 twist. Max. Muzzle Velocity of 560 fps. From Daisy Mfg. Co.
Price: **$29.99**

DAISY POWERLINE® 500 BREAK BARREL
Caliber: .177 pellet, single shot. **Barrel:** Rifled steel. **Weight:** 6.6 lbs. **Length:** 45.7" overall. **Stock:** Stained solid wood. **Sights:** Truglo® fiber-optic front, micro-adjustable open rear, adjustable 4x32 riflescope. **Features:** Auto rear-button safety. Velocity to 490 fps. Made in U.S.A. by Daisy Mfg. Co.
Price: **$120.99**

DAISY POWERLINE® 800 BREAK BARREL
Caliber: .177 pellet, single shot. **Barrel:** Rifled steel. **Weight:** 6.6 lbs. **Length:** 46.7" overall. **Stock:** Black composite. **Sights:** Truglo fiber-optic front, micro-adjustable open rear, adjustable 4x32 riflescope. **Features:** Auto rear-button safety. Velocity to 800 fps. Made in U.S.A. by Daisy Mfg. Co.
Price: **$120.99**

DAISY POWERLINE® 880 AIR RIFLE
Caliber: .177 pellet or BB, 50-shot BB magazine, single shot for pellets. **Barrel:** Rifled steel. **Weight:** 3.7 lbs. **Length:** 37.6" overall. **Power:** Multi-pump pneumatic. **Stock:** Molded wood grain; Monte Carlo comb. **Sights:** Hooded front, adjustable rear. **Features:** Velocity to 685 fps. (BB). Variable power (velocity, range) increase with pump strokes; resin receiver with dovetailed scope mount. Made in U.S.A. by Daisy Mfg. Co.
Price: **$71.99**

DAISY POWERLINE® 901 AIR RIFLE
Caliber: .177. **Barrel:** Rifled steel. **Weight:** 3.7 lbs. **Length:** 37.5" overall. **Power:** Multi-pump pneumatic. **Stock:** Advanced composite. **Sights:** Fiber-optic front, adjustable rear. **Features:** Velocity to 750 fps. (BB); advanced composite receiver with dovetailed mounts for optics. Made in U.S.A. by Daisy Mfg. Co.
Price: **$83.99**

DAISY POWERLINE® 1000 BREAK BARREL
Caliber: .177 pellet, single shot. **Barrel:** Rifled steel. **Weight:** 6.6 lbs. **Length:** 46.7" overall. **Stock:** Black composite. **Sights:** Truglo® fiber-optic front, micro-adjustable open rear, adjustable 4x32 riflescope. **Features:** Auto rear-button safety. Velocity to 750 fps (BB). Made in U.S.A. by Daisy Mfg. Co.
Price: **$231.99**

EAA/BAIKAL IZH61 AIR RIFLE
Caliber: .177 pellet, 5-shot magazine. **Barrel:** 17.8". **Weight:** 6.4 lbs. **Length:** 31" overall. **Power:** Spring-piston, side-cocking lever. **Stock:** Black plastic. **Sights:** Adjustable rear, fully hooded front. **Features:** Velocity 490 fps. Futuristic design with adjustable stock. Imported from Russia by European American Armory.
Price: **$122.65**

GAMO VIPER AIR RIFLE
Caliber: .177. **Barrel:** NA. **Weight:** 7.25 lbs. **Length:** 43.5". **Power:** Single-stroke pneumatic, 1200 fps. **Stock:** Synthetic. **Sights:** 3-9x40IR scope. **Features:** 30-pound cocking effort. Imported from Spain by Gamo.
Price: **319.95**

GAMO SHADOW AIR RIFLES
Caliber: .177. **Barrel:** 18", fluted polymer bull. **Weight:** 6.1 to 7.15 lbs. **Length:** 43" to 43.3". **Power:** Single-stroke pneumatic, 850-1,000 fps. **Stock:** Tough all-weather molded synthetic. **Sights:** NA. **Features:** Single shot, manual safety,
Price: Sport **$219.95**
Price: Hunter **$219.95**
Price: Big Cat 1200 .... **$169.95**
Price: Fox **$279.95**

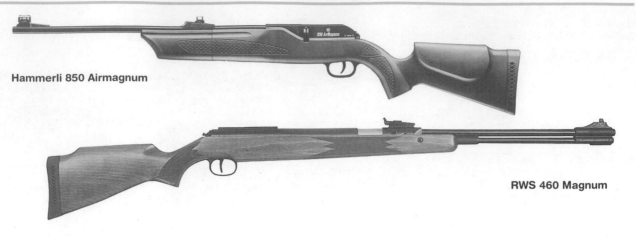

Hammerli 850 Airmagnum

RWS 460 Magnum

GAMO HUNTER AIR RIFLES
Caliber: .177. **Barrel:** NA. **Weight:** 6.5 to 10.5 lbs. **Length:** 43.5-48.5". **Power:** Single-stroke pneumatic, 850-1,000 fps. **Stock:** Wood. **Sights:** Varies by model **Features:** Adjustable two-stage trigger, rifled barrel, raised scope ramp on receiver. Realtree camo model available.
Price: Sport **$219.95**
Price: Pro **$279.95**
Price: Extreme (.177), Extreme .22 . . . . **$529.95**

GAMO WHISPER AIR RIFLES
Caliber: .177, .22. **Barrel:** 18", fluted polymer bull. **Weight:** 5.28 to 7.4 lbs. **Length:** 45.7" to 46". **Stock:** Tough all-weather molded synthetic. **Sights:** Fiber-optic front with sight guard, adjustable rear. **Features:** Single shot, manual trigger safety. Non-removable noise dampener (with up to 52 percent reduction).
Price: Whisper **$279.95**
Price: Whisper Deluxe **$319.95**
Price: Whisper VH (Varmint Hunter/Whisper in one rifle) **$329.95**
Price: Whisper .22 . . . . **$299.95**
Price: CSI Camo (.177) **$329.95**
Price: CSI Camo (.22) **$329.95**

HAMMERLI AR 50 AIR RIFLE
Caliber: .177. **Barrel:** 19.8". **Weight:** 10 lbs. **Length:** 43.2" overall. **Power:** Compressed-air. **Stock:** Anatomically-shaped universal and right-hand; match style; multi-colored laminated wood. **Sights:** Interchangeable element tunnel front, adjustable Hammerli peep rear. **Features:** Vibration-free firing release; adjustable match trigger and trigger stop; stainless air tank, built-in pressure gauge. Gives 270 shots per filling. Imported from Switzerland by SIG SAUER, Inc.
Price: **$1,653.00**

HAMMERLI MODEL 450 MATCH AIR RIFLE
Caliber: .177, single shot. **Barrel:** 19.5". **Weight:** 9.8 lbs. **Length:** 43.3" overall. **Power:** Pneumatic. **Stock:** Match style with stippled grip, rubber buttpad. Beech or walnut. **Sights:** Match tunnel front, Hammerli diopter rear. **Features:** Velocity about 560 fps. Removable sights; forend sling rail; adjustable trigger; adjustable comb. Imported from Switzerland by SIG SAUER, Inc.
Price: Beech stock **$1,355.00**
Price: Walnut stock **$1,395.00**

HAMMERLI 850 AIR MAGNUM
Caliber: .177, .22, 8-shot repeater. 23-1/2", rifled. **Weight:** 5.8 lbs. 41" overall. **Power:** 88g CO2. **Stock:** All-weather polymer, Monte Carlo, textured grip and forearm. **Sights:** Hooded fiber optic front, fiber optic adjustable rear. Velocity of 760 fps (.177), 655 (22). Blue finish. Rubber buttpad. Bolt-action. Scope compatible.
Price: .177, .22 . . . . **$235.99**

HAMMERLI STORM ELITE
Caliber: .177, single shot. 19-1/2", rifled. **Weight:** 6.8 lbs. 45-1/2" overall. **Power:** Spring-air, break-barrel cocking. **Stock:** Synthetic, burled wood look, checkered grip and forearm, cheekpiece. **Sights:** Hooded fiber optic front, fiber optic adjustable rear. Velocity of 1000 fps. 24 lbs. cocking effort. Nickel finish. Rubber buttpad. Scope compatible.
Price: **$165.90**

HAMMERLI RAZOR
Caliber: .177, .22, single shot. **Barrel:** 19", rifled. **Weight:** 17.5 lbs. **Length:** 45-1/2" overall. **Power:** Spring-air, break-barrel cocking. **Stock:** Vaporized beech wood, checkered grip and forearm, cheekpiece. Sleek curves. **Sights:** Hooded fiber optic front, fiber optic adjustable rear. **Features:** Velocity of 1000 fps (.177), 820 (.22). 35 lbs. cocking effort. Blued finish. Rubber buttpad. Scope compatible.
Price: **$219.99**

HAMMERLI NOVA
Caliber: .177, single shot. 18", rifled. **Weight:** 7.8 lbs. 45-1/2" overall. **Power:** Spring-air, under-lever cocking. **Stock:** Vaporized beech wood competition, checkered grip and forearm, cheekpiece. **Sights:** Hooded fiber optic front, fiber optic adjustable rear. **Features:** Velocity of 1000 fps. 36 lbs. cocking effort. Blued finish. Rubber buttpad. Scope compatible.
Price: **$342.00**

HAMMERLI QUICK
Caliber: .177, single shot. 18-1/4", rifled. **Weight:** 5.5 lbs. 41" overall. **Power:** Spring-air, break-barrel cocking. **Stock:** Synthetic impact proof, checkered grip and forearm, cheekpiece. **Sights:** Hooded fiber optic front, fiber optic adjustable rear. Compact, lightweight. Velocity of 620 fps. 18 lbs. cocking effort. Blued finish. Rubber buttpad. Scope compatible. Automatic safety.
Price: **$120.00**

RWS 460 MAGNUM
Caliber: .177, .22, single shot. 18-7/16", rifled. **Weight:** 8.3 lbs. 45" overall. **Power:** Spring-air, underlever cocking. **Stock:** American Sporter, checkered grip and forearm. **Sights:** Ramp front, adjustable rear. Velocity of 1350 fps (.177), 1150 (.22). 36 lbs. cocking effort. Blue finish. Rubber buttpad. Top-side loading port. Scope compatible.
Price: .177, .22 . . . . **$630.99**

RWS MODEL 34
Caliber: .177, .22, single shot. **Barrel:** 19-1/2", rifled. **Weight:** 7.3 lbs. **Length:** 45" overall. **Power:** Spring-air, break-barrel cocking. **Stock:** Wood. **Sights:** Hooded front, adjustable rear. **Features:** Velocity of 1000 fps (.177), 800 (.22). 33 lbs. cocking effort. Blued finish. Scope compatible.
Price: .177, .22 . . . . **$202.00**

RWS 34 PANTHER
Caliber: .177, .22, single shot. 19-3/4", rifled. **Weight:** 7.7 lbs. 46" overall. **Power:** Spring-air, break-barrel cocking. **Stock:** Synthetic black. **Sights:** Ramp fiber optic front, adjustable fiber optic rear. Velocity of 1000 fps (.177), 800 (.22). 33 lbs. cocking effort. Blued finish. Scope compatible. Automatic safety.
Price: .177, .22 . . . . **$192.00**

RWS 48
Caliber: .177, .22, single shot. 17", rifled, fixed. **Weight:** 9.0 lbs. 42-1/2" overall. **Power:** Spring-air, side-lever cocking. **Stock:** Wood stock. **Sights:** Adjustable front, adjustable rear. Velocity of 1100 fps (.177), 900 (.22). 39 lbs. cocking effort. Blued finish. Scope compatible. Automatic safety.
Price: .177, .22 . . . . **$330.00**

Prices given are believed to be accurate at time of publication however, many factors affect retail pricing so exact prices are not possible.

AIRGUNS—Long Guns

TECH FORCE 6 AIR RIFLE
Caliber: .177 pellet, single shot. **Barrel:** 14". **Weight:** 6 lbs. **Length:** 35.5" overall. **Power:** Spring-piston, sidelever action. **Stock:** Paratrooper-style folding, full pistol grip. **Sights:** Adjustable rear, hooded front. **Features:** Velocity 800 fps. All-metal construction; grooved for scope mounting. Imported from China by Compasseco, Inc.
Price: **$69.95**

TECH FORCE 99 AIR RIFLE
Caliber: .177, .22, single shot. **Barrel:** 18", rifled. **Weight:** 8 lbs. **Length:** 44.5" overall. **Power:** Spring piston. **Stock:** Beech wood; raised cheek piece and checkering on pistol grip and forearm, plus soft rubber recoil pad. **Sights:** Insert type front. **Features:** Velocity 1,100 fps (.177; 900 fps: .22); fixed barrel design has an underlever cocking mechanism with an anti-beartrap lock and automatic safety. Imported from China by Compasseco, Inc.
Price: 177 or .22 caliber **$152.96**

WALTHER LEVER ACTION
Caliber: .177, 8-shot lever action. **Barrel:** 19", rifled. **Weight:** 7.5 lbs. **Length:** 38" overall. **Power:** Two 12g CO2. **Stock:** Wood. **Sights:** Fixed front, adjustable rear. **Features:** Classic design. Velocity of 630 fps. Scope compatible.
Price: **$475.50**

WINCHESTER MODEL 1000SB
Caliber: .177, pellet, break-barrel spring air. **Barrel:** Rifled steel. **Weight:** 6.6 lbs. **Length:** 44.5" overall. **Stock:** Sporter style black composite. **Sights:** TRUGLO fiber optic with hooded front and micro adjustable rear. **Features:** Velocity of 1000 fps. 4 X 32 adjustable objective, fog proof/shockproof scope with crosshair reticle. From Daisy Mfg. Co.
Price: **$231.99**

WINCHESTER MODEL 1000B
Caliber: .177, pellet, break-barrel spring air. **Barrel:** Rifled steel, solid steel shroud. **Weight:** 6.6 lbs. **Length:** 44.5" overall. **Stock:** Black composite. **Sights:** TRUGLO fiber optic with hooded front and micro adjustable rear. **Features:** Velocity of 1000 fps. From Daisy Mfg. Co.
Price: **$184.99**

WINCHESTER MODEL 1000XS
Caliber: .177, pellet, break-barrel spring air. **Barrel:** Rifled steel, solid steel shroud. **Weight:** 6.6 lbs. **Length:** 46.7" overall. **Stock:** Walnut. **Sights:** Hooded front with blade and ramp, micro-adjustable rear. **Features:** Velocity of 1000 fps, uniquely designed 4 X 32 scope with adjustable objective. From Daisy Mfg. Co.
Price: **$269.99**

WINCHESTER MODEL 1000X
Caliber: .177, pellet, break-barrel spring air. **Barrel:** Rifled steel, solid steel shroud. **Weight:** 6.6 lbs. **Length:** 46.7" overall. **Stock:** Walnut. **Sights:** Hooded front with blade and ramp, micro-adjustable rear. **Features:** Velocity of 1000 fps. From Daisy Mfg. Co.
Price: **$228.99**

WINCHESTER MODEL 800XS
Caliber: .177, pellet, break-barrel spring air. **Barrel:** Rifled steel, solid steel shroud. **Weight:** 6.6 lbs. **Length:** 46.7" overall. **Stock:** Walnut. **Sights:** Hooded front with blade and ramp, micro-adjustable rear. **Features:** Velocity of 800 fps. Scope is fogproof and shockproof with fully adjustable windage and elevation and cross hair reticle. Also includes mounting rings. From Daisy Mfg. Co.
Price: **$201.99**

WINCHESTER MODEL 800X
Caliber: .177, pellet, break-barrel spring air. **Barrel:** Rifled steel, solid steel shroud. **Weight:** 6.6 lbs. **Length:** 46.7" overall. **Stock:** Walnut. **Sights:** Hooded front with blade and ramp, micro-adjustable rear. **Features:** Velocity of 800 fps. From Daisy Mfg. Co.
Price: **$164.99**

THE 2010 GUN DIGEST WEB DIRECTORY

by Holt Bodinson

The GUN DIGEST Web Directory is now in its eleventh year of publication and grows with every edition. The firearms industry is doing a remarkably good job of adapting to e-commerce. More and more firearm related businesses are striking out and creating their own discrete web pages because it's never been easier with the inexpensive software programs now available. "Home is where you hang your @." *[Editor's Note: That is, without a doubt, the worst pun I have ever heard. – DMS]*

The Internet is a dynamic environment and since our last edition, there have been numerous changes. Companies have consolidated and adopted a new owner's web site address. New companies have appeared and old companies and discussion groups have disappeared. Search engines are now more powerful than ever and seem to root out even the most obscure reference to a product name or manufacturer.

The following index of web addresses is offered to our readers as a convenient jumping-off point. Half the fun is just exploring what's out there. Considering that most of the web pages have hot links to other firearm-related web pages, the Internet trail just goes on-and-on once you've taken the initial step to go online.

Here are a few pointers:

If the website you desire is not listed, try using the full name of the company or product, typed without spaces, between www. and .com, for example, www.krause.com. Probably 95 percent of current websites are based on this simple, self-explanatory format.

Try a variety of search engines like Google, Microsoft Internet Explorer, Yahoo, Ask.com, Dogpile.com, Metacrawler, GoTo.com, HotBot, AltaVista, Lycos, Excite, InfoSeek, Looksmart, and WebCrawler while using key words such as gun, firearm, rifle, pistol, blackpowder, shooting, hunting — frankly, any word that relates to the sport. Each search engine combs through their indices in a different fashion and produces different results. Google is currently the dominant, general search engine. Accessing the various search engines is simple. Just type www.google.com for example, and you're on your way.

Welcome to the digital world of firearms. "A journey of a thousand sites begins with a single click."

WEB DIRECTORY

AMMUNITION AND COMPONENTS

A-Square Co.: www.asquarecompany.com
3-D Ammunition: www.3dammo.com
Accurate Arms Co. Inc: www.accuratepowder.com
ADCO/Nobel Sport Powder: www.adcosales.com
Aguila Ammunition: www.aguilaammo.com
Alexander Arms: www.alexanderarms.com
Alliant Powder: www.alliantpowder.com
American Ammunition: www.a-merc.com
American Derringer Co.: www.amderringer.com
American Pioneer Powder: www.americanpioneerpowder.com
Ammo Depot: www.ammodepot.com
Arizona Ammunition, Inc.: www.arizonaammunition.com
Ballistic Products, Inc.: www.ballisticproducts.com
Barnaul Cartridge Plant: www.ab.ru/~stanok
Barnes Bullets: www.barnesbullets.com
Baschieri & Pellagri: www.baschieri-pellagri.com
Beartooth Bullets: www.beartoothbullets.com
Bell Brass: www.bellbrass.com
Berger Bullets, Ltd.: www.bergerbullets.com
Berry's Mfg., Inc.: www.berrysmfg.com
Big Bore Bullets of Alaska: www.awloo.com/bbb/index.htm
Big Bore Express: www.powerbeltbullets.com
Bismuth Cartridge Co.: www.bismuth-notox.com
Black Dawge Cartridge: www.blackdawgecartridge.com
Black Hills Ammunition, Inc.: www.black-hills.com
BlackHorn209: www.blackhorn209.com
Brenneke of America Ltd.: www.brennekeusa.com
Buffalo Arms: www.buffaloarms.com
Calhoon, James, Bullets: www.jamescalhoon.com
Cartuchos Saga: www.saga.es
Cast Performance Bullet: www.castperformance.com
CCI: www.cci-ammunition.com
Centurion Ordnance: www.aguilaammo.com
Century International Arms: www.centuryarms.com
Cheaper Than Dirt: www.cheaperthandirt.com
Cheddite France: www.cheddite.com
Claybuster Wads: www.claybusterwads.com
Clean Shot Powder: www.cleanshot.com
Cole Distributing: www.cole-distributing.com
Combined Tactical Systems: www.less-lethal.com
Cor-Bon/Glaser: www.cor-bon.com
Cowboy Bullets: www.cowboybullets.com
Defense Technology Corp.: www.defense-technology.com
Denver Bullet Co.: denbullets@aol.com
Dillon Precision: www.dillonprecision.com
Dionisi Cartridge: www.dionisi.com
DKT, Inc.: www.dktinc.com
Down Range Mfg.: www.downrangemfg.com
Dynamit Nobel RWS Inc.: www.dnrws.com
Elephant/Swiss Black Powder: www.elephantblackpowder.com
Eley Ammunition: www.eleyusa.com
Eley Hawk Ltd.: www.eleyhawk.com
Environ-Metal: www.hevishot.com
Estate Cartridge: www.estatecartridge.com
Extreme Shock Munitions: www.extremeshockusa.net
Federal Cartridge Co.: www.federalpremium.com
Fiocchi of America: www.fiocchiusa.com
Fowler Bullets: www.benchrest.com/fowler
Gamebore Cartridge: www.gamebore.com
Garrett Cartridges: www.garrettcartridges.com
Gentner Bullets: www.benchrest.com/gentner/
Glaser Safety Slug, Inc.: www.corbon.com
GOEX Inc.: www.goexpowder.com
GPA: www.cartouchegpa.com
Graf & Sons: www.grafs.com

Hastings: www.hastingsammunition.com
Hawk Bullets: www.hawkbullets.com
Hevi.Shot: www.hevishot.com
Hi-Tech Ammunition: www.iidbs.com/hitech
Hodgdon Powder: www.hodgdon.com
Hornady: www.hornady.com
Hull Cartridge: www.hullcartridge.com
Huntington Reloading Products: www.huntingtons.com
Impact Bullets: www.impactbullets.com
IMR Smokeless Powders: www.imrpowder.com
International Cartridge Corp: www.iccammo.com
Israel Military Industries: www.imisammo.co.il
ITD Enterprise: www.itdenterpriseinc.com
Kent Cartridge America: www.kentgamebore.com
Knight Bullets: www.benchrest.com/knight/
Kynoch Ammunition: www.kynochammunition.com
Lapua: www.lapua.com
Lawrence Brand Shot: www.metalico.com
Lazzeroni Arms Co.: www.lazzeroni.com
Leadheads Bullets: www.proshootpro.com
Lightfield Ammunition Corp: www.lightfieldslugs.com
Lomont Precision Bullets: www.klomont.com/kent
Lost River Ballistic Technologies, Inc.: www.lostriverballistic.com
Lyman: www.lymanproducts.com
Magkor Industries: www.magkor.com
Magnum Muzzleloading Products: www.mmpsabots.com
Magnus Bullets: www.magnusbullets.com
MagSafe Ammunition: www.realpages.com/magsafeammo
Magtech: www.magtechammunition.com
Masterclass Bullet Co.: www.mastercast.com
Meister Bullets: www.meisterbullets.com
Midway USA: www.midwayusa.com
Miltex, Inc.: www.miltexusa.com
Mitchell Mfg. Co.: www.mitchellsales.com
MK Ballistic Systems: www.mkballistics.com
Mullins Ammunition: www.mullinsammunition.com
National Bullet Co.: www.nationalbullet.com
Navy Arms: www.navyarms.com
Nobel Sport: www.nobelsportammo.com
Norma: www.norma.cc
North Fork Technologies: www.northforkbullets.com
Nosler Bullets, Inc.: www.nosler.com
Old Western Scrounger: www.ows-ammunition.com
Oregon Trail/Trueshot Bullets: www.trueshotbullets.com
Pattern Control: www.patterncontrol.com
PMC: www.pmcammo.com
Polywad: www.polywad.com
PowerBelt Bullets: www.powerbeltbullets.com
PR Bullets: www.prbullet.com
Precision Ammunition: www.precisionammo.com
Precision Reloading: www.precisionreloading.com
Pro Load Ammunition: www.proload.com
Quality Cartridge: www.qual-cart.com
Rainier Ballistics: www.rainierballistics.com
Ram Shot Powder: www.ramshot.com
Reloading Specialties Inc.: www.reloadingspecialties.com
Remington: www.remington.com
Rio Ammo: www.rioammo.com
Rocky Mountain Cartridge: www.rockymountaincartridge.com
RUAG Ammotec: www.ruag.com
Samco Global Arms: www.samcoglobal.com
Schuetzen Powder: www.schuetzenpowder.com
Sellier & Bellot USA Inc.: www.sb-usa.com
Shilen: www.shilen.com
Sierra: www.sierrabullets.com
Simunition: www.simunition.com
SinterFire, Inc.: www.sinterfire.com

WEB DIRECTORY

Speer Bullets: www.speer-bullets.com
Sporting Supplies Int'l Inc.: www.ssiintl.com
Starline: www.starlinebrass.com
Swift Bullets Co.: www.swiftbullet.com
Ten-X Ammunition: www.tenxammo.com
Top Brass: www.top-brass.com
Triton Cartridge: www.a-merc.com
Trueshot Bullets: www.trueshotbullets.com
Tru-Tracer: www.trutracer.com
Ultramax Ammunition: www.ultramaxammunition.com
Vihtavuori Lapua: www.vihtavuori-lapua.com
Weatherby: www.weatherby.com
West Coast Bullets: www.westcoastbullet.com
Western Powders Inc.: www.westernpowders.com
Widener's Reloading & Shooters Supply: www.wideners.com
Winchester Ammunition: www.winchester.com
Windjammer Tournament Wads: www.windjammer-wads.com
Wolf Ammunition: www.wolfammo.com
Woodleigh Bullets: www.woodleighbullets.com.au
Zanders Sporting Goods: www.gzanders.com

CASES, SAFES, GUN LOCKS, AND CABINETS

Ace Case Co.: www.acecase.com
AG English Sales Co.: www.agenglish.com
All Americas' Outdoors: www.innernet.net/gunsafe
Alpine Cases: www.alpinecases.com
Aluma Sport by Dee Zee: www.deezee.com
American Security Products: www.amsecusa.com
Americase: www.americase.com
Assault Systems: www.elitesurvival.com
Avery Outdoors, Inc.: www.averyoutdoors.com
Bear Track Cases: www.beartrackcases.com
Boyt Harness Co.: www.boytharness.com
Bulldog Gun Safe Co.: www.gardall.com
Cannon Safe Co.: www.cannonsafe.com
CCL Security Products: www.cclsecurity.com
Concept Development Corp.: www.saf-t-blok.com
Doskocil Mfg. Co.: www.doskocilmfg.com
Fort Knox Safes: www.ftknox.com
Franzen Security Products: www.securecase.com
Frontier Safe Co.: www.frontiersafe.com
Granite Security Products: www.granitesafe.com
Gunlocker Phoenix USA Inc.: www.gunlocker.com
GunVault: www.gunvault.com
Hakuba USA Inc.: www.hakubausa.com
Heritage Safe Co.: www.heritagesafecompany.com
Hide-A-Gun: www.hide-a-gun.com
Homak Safes: www.homak.com
Hunter Company: www.huntercompany.com
Kalispel Case Line: www.kalispelcaseline.com
Knouff & Knouff, Inc.: www.kkair.com
Knoxx Industries: www.knoxx, com
Kolpin Mfg. Co.: www.kolpin.com
Liberty Safe & Security: www.libertysafe.com
New Innovative Products: www.starlightcases
Noble Security Systems Inc.: www.noble.co.ll
Phoenix USA Inc.: www.gunlocker.com
Plano Molding Co.: www.planomolding.com
Rhino Gun Cases: www.rhinoguns.com
Rhino Safe: www.rhinosafe.com
Rotary Gun Racks: www.gun-racks.com
Safe Tech, Inc.: www.safrgun.com
Saf-T-Hammer: www.saf-t-hammer.com
Saf-T-Lok Corp.: www.saf-t-lok.com
San Angelo All-Aluminum Products Inc.: sasptuld@x.netcom.com
Securecase: www.securecase.com
Shot Lock Corp.: www.shotlock.com

Smart Lock Technology Inc.: www.smartlock.com
Sportsmans Steel Safe Co.: www.sportsmansteelsafes.com
Stack-On Products Co.: www.stack-on.com
Starlight Cases: www.starlightcases.com
Sun Welding: www.sunwelding.com
Technoframes: www.technoframes.com
T.Z. Case Int'l: www.tzcase.com
Versatile Rack Co.: www.versatilegunrack.com
V-Line Industries: www.vlineind.com
Winchester Safes: www.fireking.com
Ziegel Engineering: www.ziegeleng.com
Zonetti Armor: www.zonettiarmor.com

CHOKE DEVICES, RECOIL REDUCERS, SUPPRESSORS AND ACCURACY DEVICES

Advanced Armament Corp.: www.advanced-armament.com
100 Straight Products: www.100straight.com
Answer Products Co.: www.answerrifles.com
Briley Mfg: www.briley.com
Carlson's: www.choketube.com
Colonial Arms: www.colonialarms.com
Comp-N-Choke: www.comp-n-choke.com
Gemtech: www.gem-tech.com
Hastings: www.hastingsbarrels.com
Kick's Industries: www.kicks-ind.com
LimbSaver: www.limbsaver.com
Mag-Na-Port Int'l Inc.: www.magnaport.com
Metro Gun: www.metrogun.com
Patternmaster Chokes: www.patternmaster.com
Poly-Choke: www.poly-choke.com
Sims Vibration Laboratory: www.limbsaver.com
Teague Precision Chokes: www.teague.ca
Truglo: www.truglo.com

CHRONOGRAPHS AND BALLISTIC SOFTWARE

Barnes Ballistic Program: www.barnesbullets.com
Ballisticard Systems: www.ballisticards.com
Competition Electronics: www.competitionelectronics.com
Competitive Edge Dynamics: www.cedhk.com
Hodgdon Shotshell Program: www.hodgdon.com
Lee Shooter Program: www.leeprecision.com
Load From A Disk: www.loadammo.com
Oehler Research Inc.: www.oehler-research.com
PACT: www.pact.com
ProChrony: www.competitionelectronics.com
Quickload: www.neconos.com
RCBS Load: www.rcbs.com
Shooting Chrony Inc.: www.shootingchrony.com
Sierra Infinity Ballistics Program: www.sierrabullets.com

CLEANING PRODUCTS

Accupro: www.accupro.com
Ballistol USA: www.ballistol.com
Battenfeld Technologies: www.battenfeldtechnologies.com
Birchwood Casey: www.birchwoodcasey.com
Blue Wonder: www.bluewonder.com
Bore Tech: www.boretech.com
Break-Free, Inc.: www.break-free.com
Bruno Shooters Supply: www.brunoshooters.com
Butch's Bore Shine: www.lymanproducts.com
C.J. Weapons Accessories: www.cjweapons, com
Clenzoil: www.clenzoil.com
Corrosion Technologies: www.corrosionx.com
Dewey Mfg.: www.deweyrods.com
DuraCoat: www.lauerweaponry.com
Eezox Inc.: www.xmission.com

490 GUN DIGEST®

WEB DIRECTORY

G 96: www.g96.com
Gunslick Gun Care: www.gunslick.com
Gunzilla: www.topduckproducts.com
Hollands Shooters Supply: www.hollandgun.com
Hoppes: www.hoppes.com
Hydrosorbent Products: www.dehumidify.com
Inhibitor VCI Products: www.theinhibitor.com
Iosso Products: www.iosso.com
KG Industries: www.kgcoatings.com
Kleen-Bore Inc.: www.kleen-bore.com
L&R Mfg.: www.lrultrasonics.com
Lyman: www.lymanproducts.com
Mil-Comm Products: www.mil-comm.com
Militec-1: www.militec-1.com
Mpro7 Gun Care: www.mp7.com
Old West Snake Oil: www.oldwestsnakeoil.com
Otis Technology, Inc.: www.otisgun.com
Outers: www.outers-guncare.com
Ox-Yoke Originals Inc.: www.oxyoke.com
Parker-Hale Ltd.: www.parker-hale.com
Prolix Lubricant: www.prolixlubricant.com
ProShot Products: www.proshotproducts.com
ProTec Lubricants: www.proteclubricants.com
Rusteprufe Labs: www.rusteprufe.com
Sagebrush Products: www.sagebrushproducts.com
Sentry Solutions Ltd.: www.sentrysolutions.com
Shooters Choice Gun Care: www.shooters-choice.com
Silencio: www.silencio.com
Slip 2000: www.slip2000.com
Stony Point Products: www.uncle-mikes.com
Tetra Gun: www.tetraproducts.com
The TM Solution: thetmsolution@comcast.net
Top Duck Products: www.topduckproducts.com
Ultra Bore Coat: www.ultracoatingsinc.com
World's Fastest Gun Bore Cleaner: www.michaels-oregon.com

FIREARM MANUFACTURERS AND IMPORTERS

A-Square: www.asquarecompany.com
Accuracy Int'l North America: www.accuracyinternational.org
Accuracy Rifle Systems: www.mini-14.net
Ace Custom 45's: www.acecustom45.com
Advanced Weapons Technology: www.AWT-Zastava.com
AIM: www.aimsurplus.com
AirForce Airguns: www.airforceairguns.com
Air Gun, Inc.: www.airrifle-china.com
Airguns of Arizona: www.airgunsofarizona.com
Airgun Express: www.airgunexpress.com
Alchemy Arms: www.alchemyltd.com
Alexander Arms: www.alexanderarms.com
American Derringer Corp.: www.amderringer.com
American Spirit Arms Corp.: www.gunkits.com
American Tactical Imports: www.americantactical.us
American Western Arms: www.awaguns.com
Anics Corp.: www.anics.com
Anschutz: www.anschutz-sporters.com
Answer Products Co.: www.answerrifles.com
AR-7 Industries, LLC: www.ar-7.com
Ares Defense Systems: www.aresdefense.com
Armalite: www.armalite.com
Armi Sport: www.armisport.com
Armory USA: www.globaltraders.com
Armsco: www.armsco.net
Armscorp USA Inc.: www.armscorpusa.com
Arnold Arms: www.arnoldarms.com
Arsenal Inc.: www.arsenalinc.com
Arthur Brown Co.: www.eabco.com
Atlanta Cutlery Corp.: www.atlantacutlery.com

Auction Arms: www.auctionarms.com
Autauga Arms, Inc.: www.autaugaarms.com
Auto-Ordnance Corp.: www.tommygun.com
AWA Int'l: www.awaguns.com
Axtell Rifle Co.: www.riflesmith.com
AyA: www.aya-fineguns.com
Baikal: www.baikalinc.ru/eng/
Ballard Rifles, LLC: www.ballardrifles.com
Barrett Firearms Mfg.: www.barrettrifles.com
Beeman Precision Airguns: www.beeman.com
Benelli USA Corp.: www.benelliusa.com
Benjamin Sheridan: www.crosman.com
Beretta U.S.A. Corp.: www.berettausa.com
Bernardelli: www.bernardelli
Bersa: www.bersa-llama.com
Bill Hanus Birdguns: www.billhanusbirdguns.com
Blaser Jagdwaffen Gmbh: www.blaser.de
Bleiker: www.bleiker.ch
Bluegrass Armory: www.bluegrassarmory.com
Bond Arms: www.bondarms.com
Borden's Rifles, Inc.: www.bordensrifles.com
Boss & Co.: www.bossguns.co.uk
Bowen Classic Arms: www.bowenclassicarms.com
Briley Mfg: www.briley.com
BRNO Arms: www.zbrojovka.com
Brown, David McKay: www.mckaybrown.com
Brown, Ed Products: www.brownprecision.com
Browning: www.browning.com
BRP Corp.: www.brpguns.com
BSA Guns: www.bsaguns.com
BUL Ltd.: www.bultransmark.com
Bushmaster Firearms/Quality Parts: www.bushmaster.com
BWE Firearms: www.bwefirearms.com
Caesar Guerini USA: www.gueriniusa.com
Cape Outfitters: www.doublegun.com
Carbon 15: www.professional-ordnance.com
Caspian Arms, Ltd.: www.caspianarmsltd.8m.com
Casull Arms Corp.: www.casullarms.com
Calvary Arms: www.calvaryarms.com
CDNN Investments, Inc.: www.cdnninvestments.com
Century Arms: www.centuryarms.com
Chadick's Ltd.: www.chadicks-ltd.com
Champlin Firearms: www.champlinarms.com
Chapuis Arms: www.doubleguns.com/chapuis.htm
Charles Daly: www.charlesdaly.com
Charter Arms: www.charterfirearms.com
CheyTac USA: www.cheytac.com
Christensen Arms: www.christensenarms.com
Cimarron Firearms Co.: www.cimarron-firearms.com
Clark Custom Guns: www.clarkcustomguns.com
Cobra Enterprises: www.cobrapistols.com
Cogswell & Harrison: www.cogswell.co.uk/home.htm
Colt's Mfg Co.: www.colt.com
Compasseco, Inc.: www.compasseco.com
Connecticut Valley Arms: www.cva.com
Cooper Firearms: www.cooperfirearms.com
Corner Shot: www.cornershot.com
CPA Rifles: www.singleshotrifles.com
Crosman: www.crosman.com
Crossfire, LLC: www.crossfirelle.com
C.Sharp Arms Co.: www.csharparms.com
CVA: www.cva.com
Czechpoint Int'l: www.czechpoint-usa.com
CZ USA: www.cz-usa.com
Daisy Mfg Co.: www.daisy.com
Dakota Arms Inc.: www.dakotaarms.com
Dan Wesson Firearms: www.danwessonfirearms.com

WEB DIRECTORY

Davis Industries: www.davisindguns.com
Detonics USA: www.detonicsusa.com
Diana: www.diana-airguns.de
Dixie Gun Works: www.dixiegunworks.com
Dlask Arms Corp.: www.dlask.com
D.P.M.S., Inc.: www.dpmsinc.com
D.S.Arms, Inc.: www.dsarms.com
Dumoulin: www.dumoulin-herstal.com
Dynamit Noble: www.dnrws.com
EAA Corp.: www.eaacorp.com
Eagle Imports, Inc.: www.bersa-llama.com
Ed Brown Products: www.edbrown.com
EDM Arms: www.edmarms.com
E.M.F. Co.: www.emf-company.com
Enterprise Arms: www.enterprise.com
E R Shaw: www.ershawbarrels.com
European American Armory Corp.: www.eaacorp.com
Evans, William: www.williamevans.com
Excel Arms: www.excelarms.com
Fabarm: www.fabarm.com
FAC-Guns-N-Stuff: www.gunsnstuff.com
Falcon Pneumatic Systems: www.falcon-airguns.com
Fausti Stefano: www.faustistefanoarms.com
Firestorm: www.firestorm-sgs.com
Flodman Guns: www.flodman.com
FN Herstal: www.fnherstal.com
FNH USA: www.fnhusa.com
Franchi: www.franchiusa.com
Freedom Arms: www.freedomarms.com
Galazan: www.connecticutshotgun.com
Gambo Renato: www.renatogamba.it
Gamo: www.gamo.com
Gary Reeder Custom Guns: www.reeder-customguns.com
Gazelle Arms: www.gazellearms.com
German Sport Guns: www.germansportguns.com
Gibbs Rifle Company: www.gibbsrifle.com
Glock: www.glock.com
Griffin & Howe: www.griffinhowe.com
Grizzly Big Boar Rifle: www.largrizzly.com
GSI Inc.: www.gsifirearms.com
Guerini: www.gueriniusa.com
Gunbroker.Com: www.gunbroker.com
Hammerli: www.carl-walther.com
Hatfield Gun Co.: www.hatfield-usa.com
Hatsan Arms Co.: www.hatsan.com.tr
Heckler and Koch: www.hk-usa.com
Henry Repeating Arms Co.: www.henryrepeating.com
Heritage Mfg.: www.heritagemfg.com
Heym: www.heym-waffenfabrik.de
High Standard Mfg.: www.highstandard.com
Hi-Point Firearms: www.hi-pointfirearms.com
Holland & Holland: www.hollandandholland.com
H&R 1871 Firearms: www.hr1871.com
H-S Precision: www.hsprecision.com
Hunters Lodge Corp.: www.hunterslodge.com
IAR Inc.: www.iar-arms.com
Imperial Miniature Armory: www.1800miniature.com
Interarms: www.interarms.com
International Military Antiques, Inc.: www.ima-usa.com
Inter Ordnance: www.interordnance.com
Intrac Arms International LLC: www.hsarms.com
Israel Arms: www.israelarms.com
Iver Johnson Arms: www.iverjohnsonarms.com
Izhevsky Mekhanichesky Zavod: www.baikalinc.ru
James River Mfg.: www.jamesriverarmory.com
Jarrett Rifles, Inc.: www.jarrettrifles.com
J&G Sales, Ltd.: www.jgsales.com

Johannsen Express Rifle: www.johannsen-jagd.de
Jonathan Arthur Ciener: www.22lrconversions.com
JP Enterprises, Inc.: www.jprifles.com
Kahr Arms/Auto-Ordnance: www.kahr.com
K.B.I.: www.kbi-inc.com
Kel-Tec CNC Ind., Inc.: www.kel-tec.com
Kifaru: www.kifaru.net
Kimber: www.kimberamerica.com
Knight's Armament Co.: www.knightsarmco.com
Knight Rifles: www.knightrifles.com
Korth: www.korthwaffen.de
Krebs Custom Guns: www.krebscustom.com
Krieghoff Int'l: www.krieghoff.com
KY Imports, Inc.: www.kyimports.com
K-VAR: www.k-var.com
L.A.R Mfg: www.largrizzly.com
Lazzeroni Arms Co.: www.lazzeroni.com
Legacy Sports International: www.legacysports.com
Les Baer Custom, Inc.: www.lesbaer.com
Lewis Machine & Tool Co.: www.lewismachine.net
Linebaugh Custom Sixguns: www.sixgunner.com/linebaugh
Ljutic: www.ljuticgun.com
Llama: www.bersa-llama.com
Lone Star Rifle Co.: www.lonestarrifle.com
LRB Arms: www.lrbarms.com
LWRC Int'l: www.lwrifles.com
Magnum Research: www.magnumresearch.com
Majestic Arms: www.majesticarms.com
Markesbery Muzzleloaders: www.markesbery.com
Marksman Products: www.marksman.com
Marlin: www.marlinfirearms.com
Mauser: www.mauser.com
McMillan Bros Rifle Co.: www.mcfamily.com
MDM: www.mdm-muzzleloaders.com
Meacham Rifles: www.meachamrifles.com
Merkel: www.hk-usa.com
Miller Arms: www.millerarms.com
Miltech: www.miltecharms.com
Miltex, Inc.: www.miltexusa.com
Mitchell's Mausers: www.mitchellsales.com
MK Ballistic Systems: www.mkballistics.com
M-Mag: www.mmag.com
Montana Rifle Co.: www.montanarifleman.com
Mossberg: www.mossberg.com
Navy Arms: www.navyarms.com
Nesika: www.nesika.com
New England Arms Corp.: www.newenglandarms.com
New England Custom Gun Svc, Ltd.:
   www.newenglandcustomgun.com
New England Firearms: www.hr1871.com
New Ultra Light Arms: www.newultralight.com
Nighthawk Custom: www.nighthawkcustom.com
North American Arms: www.northamericanarms.com
Nosler Bullets, Inc.: www.nosler.com
Nowlin Mfg. Inc.: www.nowlinguns.com
O.F. Mossberg & Sons: www.mossberg.com
Ohio Ordnance Works: www.ohioordnanceworks.com
Olympic Arms: www.olyarms.com
Panther Arms: www.dpmsinc.com
Para-USA: www.para-usa.com
Pedersoli Davide & Co.: www.davide-pedersoli.com
Perazzi: www.perazzi.com
Pietta: www.pietta.it
PKP Knife-Pistol: www.sanjuanenterprise.com
Power Custom: www.powercustom.com
Professional Arms: www.professional-arms.com
PTR 91, Inc.: www.ptr91.com

WEB DIRECTORY

Purdey & Sons: www.purdey.com
Remington: www.remington.com
Republic Arms Inc.: www.republicarmsinc.com
Rhineland Arms, Inc.: www.rhinelandarms.com
Rigby: www.johnrigbyandco.com
Rizzini USA: www.rizziniusa.com
Robar Companies, Inc.: www.robarguns.com
Robinson Armament Co.: www.robarm.com
Rock River Arms, Inc.: www.rockriverarms.com
Rogue Rifle Co. Inc.: www.chipmunkrifle.com
Rohrbaugh Firearms: www.rohrbaughfirearms.com
Rossi Arms: www.rossiusa.com
RPM: www.rpmxlpistols.com
Russian American Armory: www.raacfirearms.com
RUAG Ammotec: www.ruag.com
Sabatti SPA: www.sabatti.com
Sabre Defense Industries: www.sabredefense.com
Saco Defense: www.sacoinc.com
Safari Arms: www.olyarms.com
Sako: www.berettausa.com
Samco Global Arms Inc.: www.samcoglobal.com
Sarco Inc.: www.sarcoinc.com
Savage Arms Inc.: www.savagearms.com
Scattergun Technologies Inc.: www.wilsoncombat.com
Searcy Enterprises: www.searcyent.com
Shiloh Rifle Mfg.: www.shilohrifle.com
SIGARMS, Inc.: www.sigarms.com
Simpson Ltd.: www.simpsonltd.com
SKB Shotguns: www.skbshotguns.com
Smith & Wesson: www.smith-wesson.com
SOG International, Inc.: soginc@go-concepts.com
Sphinx System: www.sphinxarms.com
Springfield Armory: www.springfield-armory.com
SSK Industries: www.sskindustries.com
Stag Arms: www.stagarms.com
Steyr Arms, Inc.: www.steyrarms.com
Stoeger Industries: www.stoegerindustries.com
Strayer-Voigt Inc.: www.sviguns.com
Sturm, Ruger & Company: www.ruger-firearms.com
Tactical Rifles: www.tacticalrifles.com
Tactical Solutions: www.tacticalsol.com
Tar-Hunt Slug Guns, Inc.: www.tar-hunt.com
Taser Int'l: www.taser.com
Taurus: www.taurususa.com
Taylor's & Co., Inc.: www.taylorsfirearms.com
Tennessee Guns: www.tennesseeguns.com
TG Int'l: www.tnguns.com
The 1877 Sharps Co.: www.1877sharps.com
Thompson Center Arms: www.tcarms.com
Tikka: www.berettausa.com
TNW, Inc.: www.tnwfirearms.com
Traditions: www.traditionsfirearms.com
Tristar Sporting Arms: www.tristarsportingarms.com
Uberti: www.ubertireplicas.com
Ultralite 50: www.ultralite50.com
Ultra Light Arms: www.newultralight.com
Umarex: www.umarex.com
U.S. Firearms Mfg. Co.: www.usfirearms.com
Valkyrie Arms: www.valkyriearms.com
Vektor Arms: www.vektorarms.com
Verney-Carron: www.verney-carron.com
Volquartsen Custom Ltd.: www.volquartsen.com
Vulcan Armament: www.vulcanarmament.com
Walther USA: www.waltheramerica.com
Weatherby: www.weatherby.com
Webley and Scott Ltd.: www.webley.co.uk
Westley Richards: www.westleyrichards.com

Widley: www.widleyguns.com
Wild West Guns: www.wildwestguns.com
William Larkin Moore & Co.: www.doublegun.com
Wilson Combat: www.wilsoncombat.com
Winchester Rifles and Shotguns: www.winchesterguns.com

GUN PARTS, BARRELS, AFTER-MARKET ACCESSORIES

300 Below: www.300below.com
Accuracy International of North America:
   www.accuracyinternational.org
Accuracy Speaks, Inc.: www.accuracyspeaks.com
Accurary Systems: www.accuracysystemsinc.com
Advanced Barrel Systems: www.carbonbarrels.com
Advantage Arms: www.advantagearms.com
Aim Surplus: www.aimsurplus.com
AK-USA: www.ak-103.com
American Spirit Arms Corp.: www.gunkits.com
Amhurst-Depot: www.amherst-depot.com
AMT Gun Parts: www.amt-gunparts.com
Armatac Industries: www.armatac.com
Badger Barrels, Inc.: www.badgerbarrels.com
Bar-Sto Precision Machine: www.barsto.com
Battenfeld Technologies: www.battenfeldtechnologies.com
Bellm TC's: www.bellmtcs.com
Belt Mountain Enterprises: www.beltmountain.com
Bergara Barrels: www.bergarabarrels.com
Briley: www.briley.com
Brownells: www.brownells.com
B-Square: www.b-square.com
Buffer Technologies: www.buffertech.com
Bullberry Barrel Works: www.bullberry.com
Bulldog Barrels: www.bulldogbarrels.com
Bushmaster Firearms/Quality Parts: www.bushmaster.com
Butler Creek Corp: www.butler-creek.com
Cape Outfitters Inc.: www.capeoutfitters.com
Caspian Arms Ltd.: www.caspianarms.com
Cheaper Than Dirt: www.cheaperthandirt.com
Chesnut Ridge: www.chestnutridge.com/
Chip McCormick Corp: www.chipmccormickcorp.com
Choate Machine & Tool Co.: www.riflestock.com
Cierner, Jonathan Arthur: www.22lrconversions.com
CJ Weapons Accessories: www.cjweapons.com
Colonial Arms: www.colonialarms.com
Comp-N-Choke: www.comp-n-choke.com
Cylinder & Slide Shop: www.cylinder-slide.com
Daniel Defense: www.danieldefense.com
Dave Manson Precision Reamers.: www.mansonreamers.com
Digi-Twist: www.fmtcorp.com
Dixie Gun Works: www.dixiegun.com
Douglas Barrels: www.benchrest.com/douglas/
DPMS: www.dpmsinc.com
D.S.Arms, Inc.: www.dsarms.com
eBay: www.ebay.com
Ed Brown Products: www.edbrown.com
EFK Marketing/Fire Dragon Pistol Accessories: www.flmfire.com
E.R. Shaw: www.ershawbarrels.com
Forrest Inc.: www.gunmags.com
Fulton Armory: www.fulton-armory.com
Galazan: www.connecticutshotgun.com
Gemtech: www.gem-tech.com
Gentry, David: www.gentrycustom.com
GG&G: www.gggaz.com
Green Mountain Rifle Barrels: www.gmriflebarrel.com
Gun Parts Corp.: www.e-gunparts.com
Harris Engineering: www.harrisbipods.com
Hart Rifle Barrels: www.hartbarrels.com

WEB DIRECTORY

Hastings Barrels: www.hastingsbarrels.com
Heinie Specialty Products: www.heinie.com
Holland Shooters Supply: www.hollandgun.com
H-S Precision: www.hsprecision.com
100 Straight Products: www.100straight.com
I.M.A.: www.ima-usa.com
Jack First Gun Shop: www.jackfirstgun.com
Jarvis, Inc.: www.jarvis-custom.com
J&T Distributing: www.jtdistributing.com
John's Guns: www.johnsguns.com
John Masen Co.: www.johnmasen.com
Jonathan Arthur Ciener, Inc.: www.22lrconversions.com
JP Enterprises: www.jpar15.com
Keng's Firearms Specialities: www.versapod.com
KG Industries: www.kgcoatings.com
Kick Eez: www.kickeez.com
Kidd Triggers: www.coolguyguns.com
King's Gunworks: www.kingsgunworks.com
Knoxx Industries: www.knoxx.com
Krieger Barrels: www.kriegerbarrels.com
K-VAR Corp.: www.k-var.com
LaRue Tactical: www.laruetactical.com
Les Baer Custom, Inc.: www.lesbaer.com
Lilja Barrels: www.riflebarrels.com
Lone Star Rifle Co.: www.lonestarrifles.com
Lone Wolf Dist.: www.lonewolfdist.com
Lothar Walther Precision Tools Inc. w: ww.lothar-walther.de
M&A Parts, Inc.: www.m-aparts.com
MAB Barrels: www.mab.com.au
Majestic Arms: www.majesticarms.com
Marvel Products, Inc.: www.marvelprod.com
MEC-GAR SrL: www.mec-gar.it
Mesa Tactical: www.mesatactical.com
Michaels of Oregon Co.: www.michaels-oregon.com
North Mfg. Co.: www.rifle-barrels.com
Numrich Gun Parts Corp.: www.e-gunparts.com
Pachmayr: www.pachmayr.com
Pac-Nor Barrels: www.pac-nor.com
Para Ordinance Pro Shop: www.ltms.com
Point Tech Inc.: pointec@ibm.net
Promag Industries: www.promagindustries.com
Power Custom, Inc.: www.powercustom.com
Precision Reflex: www.pri-mounts.com
Red Star Arms: www.redstararms.com
Rocky Mountain Arms: www.rockymountainarms.com
Royal Arms Int'l: www.royalarms.com
R.W. Hart: www.rwhart.com
Sarco Inc.: www.sarcoinc.com
Scattergun Technologies Inc.: www.wilsoncombat.com
Schuemann Barrels: www.schuemann.com
Seminole Gunworks Chamber Mates: www.chambermates.com
Shilen: www.shilen.com
Sims Vibration Laboratory: www.limbsaver.com
Smith & Alexander Inc.: www.smithandalexander.com
Speed Shooters Int'l: www.shooternet.com/ssi
Sprinco USA Inc.: sprinco@primenet.com
Springfield Sporters, Inc.: www.ssporters.com
STI Int'l: www.stiguns.com
S&S Firearms: www.ssfirearms.com
SSK Industries: www.sskindustries.com
Sun Devil Mfg.: www.sundevilmfg.com
Sunny Hill Enterprises: www.sunny-hill.com
Tac Star: www.lymanproducts.com
Tactical Innovations: www.tacticalinc.com
Tapco: www.tapco.com
Trapdoors Galore: www.trapdoors.com
Triple K Manufacturing Co. Inc.: www.triplek.com

U.S.A. Magazines Inc.: www.usa-magazines.com
Verney-Carron SA: www.verney-carron.com
Volquartsen Custom Ltd.: www.volquartsen.com
W.C. Wolff Co.: www.gunsprings.com
Waller & Son: www.wallerandson.com
Weigand Combat Handguns: www.weigandcombat.com
Western Gun Parts: www.westerngunparts.com
Wilson Arms: www.wilsonarms.com
Wilson Combat: www.wilsoncombat.com
Wisner's Inc.: www.wisnerinc.com
Z-M Weapons: www.zmweapons.com/home.htm

GUNSMITHING SUPPLIES AND INSTRUCTION

American Gunsmithing Institute: www.americangunsmith.com
Battenfeld Technologies: www.battenfeldtechnologies.com
Bellm TC's: www.bellmtcs.com
Blue Ridge Machinery & Tools: www.blueridgemachinery.com
Brownells, Inc.: www.brownells.com
B-Square Co.: www.b-square.com
Clymer Mfg. Co.: www.clymertool.com
Craftguard Metal Finishing: crftgrd@aol.com
Dem-Bart: www.dembartco.com
Doug Turnbull Restoration: www.turnbullrestoration, com
Du-Lite Corp.: www.dulite.com
Dvorak Instruments: www.dvorakinstruments.com
Gradiant Lens Corp.: www.gradientlens.com
Grizzly Industrial: www.grizzly.com
Gunline Tools: www.gunline.com
Harbor Freight: www.harborfreight.com
JGS Precision Tool Mfg. LLC: www.jgstools.com
Mag-Na-Port International: www.magnaport.com
Manson Precision Reamers: www.mansonreamers.com
Midway: www.midwayusa.com
Murray State College: www.mscok.edu
Olympus America Inc.: www.olympus.com
Pacific Tool & Gauge: www.pacifictoolandgauge.com
Trinidad State Junior College: www.trinidadstate.edu

HANDGUN GRIPS

A&G Supply Co.: www.gripextender.com
Ajax Custom Grips, Inc.: www.ajaxgrips.com
Altamont Co.: www.altamontco.com
Aluma Grips: www.alumagrips.com
Badger Grips: www.pistolgrips.com
Barami Corp.: www.hipgrip.com
Blu Magnum Grips: www.blumagnum.com
Buffalo Brothers: www.buffalobrothers.com
Crimson Trace Corp.: www.crimsontrace.com
Eagle Grips: www.eaglegrips.com
Falcon Industries: www.ergogrips.net
Herrett's Stocks: www.herrettstocks.com
Hogue Grips: www.getgrip.com
Kirk Ratajesak: www.kgratajesak.com
Lett Custom Grips: www.lettgrips.com
N.C. Ordnance: www.gungrip.com
Nill-Grips USA: www.nill-grips.com
Pachmayr: www.pachmayr.com
Pearce Grips: www.pearcegrip.com
Trausch Grips Int.Co.: www.trausch.com
Tyler-T Grips: www.t-grips.com
Uncle Mike's: www.uncle-mikes.com

HOLSTERS AND LEATHER PRODUCTS

Akah: www.akah.de
Aker Leather Products: www.akerleather.com
Alessi Distributor R&F Inc.: www.alessiholsters.com

WEB DIRECTORY

Alfonso's of Hollywood: **www.alfonsogunleather.com**
Armor Holdings: **www.holsters.com**
Bagmaster: **www.bagmaster.com**
Bianchi International: **www.bianchi-intl.com**
Blackhawk Outdoors: **www.blackhawk.com**
Blackhills Leather: **www.blackhillsleather.com**
BodyHugger Holsters: **www.nikolais.com**
Boyt Harness Co.: **www.boytharness.com**
Brigade Gun Leather: **www.brigadegunleather.com**
Chimere: **www.chimere.com**
Clipdraw: **www.clipdraw.com**
Conceal It: **www.conceal-it.com**
Concealment Shop Inc.: **www.theconcealmentshop.com**
Coronado Leather Co.: **www.coronadoleather.com**
Covert Carry: **www.covertcarry.com**
Creedmoor Sports, Inc.: **www.creedmoorsports.com**
Custom Leather Wear: **www.customleatherwear.com**
Defense Security Products: **www.thunderwear.com**
Dennis Yoder: **www.yodercustomleather.com**
DeSantis Holster: **www.desantisholster.com**
Dillon Precision: **www.dillonprecision.com**
Don Hume Leathergoods, Inc.: **www.donhume.com**
Ernie Hill International: **www.erniehill.com**
Fist: **www.fist-inc.com**
Fobus USA: **www.fobusholster.com**
Front Line Ltd.: **frontlin@internet-zahav.net**
Galco: **www.usgalco.com**
Gilmore's Sports Concepts: **www.gilmoresports.com**
Gould & Goodrich: **www.gouldusa.com**
Gunmate Products: **www.gun-mate.com**
Hellweg Ltd.: **www.hellwegltd.com**
Hide-A-Gun: **www.hide-a-gun.com**
High Noon Holsters: **www.highnoonholsters.com**
Holsters.Com: **www.holsters.com**
Horseshoe Leather Products: **www.horseshoe.co.uk**
Hunter Co.: **www.huntercompany.com**
Kirkpatrick Leather Company: **www.kirkpatrickleather.com**
KNJ: **www.knjmfg.com**
Kramer Leather: **www.kramerleather.com**
Law Concealment Systems: **www.handgunconcealment.com**
Levy's Leathers Ltd.: **www.levysleathers.com**
Mernickle Holsters: **www.mernickleholsters.com**
Michaels of Oregon Co.: **www.michaels-oregon.com**
Milt Sparks Leather: **www.miltsparks.com**
Mitch Rosen Extraordinary Gunleather: **www.mitchrosen.com**
Old World Leather: **www.gun-mate.com**
Pacific Canvas & Leather Co. **paccanadleather@directway.com**
Pager Pal: **www.pagerpal.com**
Phalanx Corp.: **www.smartholster.com**
PWL: **www.pwlusa.com**
Rumanya Inc.: **www.rumanya.com**
S.A. Gunleather: **www.elpasoleather.com**
Safariland Ltd. Inc.: **www.safariland.com**
Shooting Systems Group Inc.: **www.shootingsystems.com**
Strictly Anything Inc.: **www.strictlyanything.com**
Strong Holster Co.: **www.strong-holster.com**
The Belt Co.: **www.conceal-it.com**
The Leather Factory Inc. **lflandry@flash.net**
The Outdoor Connection: **www.outdoorconnection.com**
Top-Line USA inc.: **www.toplineusa.com**
Triple K Manufacturing Co.: **www.triplek.com**
Wilson Combat: **www.wilsoncombat.com**

MISCELLANEOUS SHOOTING PRODUCTS

10X Products Group: **www.10Xwear.com**
Aero Peltor: **www.aearo.com**
American Body Armor: **www.americanbodyarmor.com**

Armor Holdings Products: **www.armorholdings.com**
Battenfeld Technologies: **www.battenfeldtechnologies.com**
Beamhit: **www.beamhit.com**
Beartooth: **www.beartoothproducts.com**
Bodyguard by S&W: **www.yourbodyguard.com**
Burnham Brothers: **www.burnhambrothers.com**
Collectors Armory: **www.collectorsarmory.com**
Dalloz Safety: **www.cdalloz.com**
Deben Group Industries Inc.: **www.deben.com**
Decot Hy-Wyd Sport Glasses: **www.sportyglasses.com**
E.A.R., Inc.: **www.earinc.com**
First Choice Armor: **www.firstchoicearmor.com**
Gunstands: **www.gunstands.com**
Howard Leight Hearing Protectors: **www.howardleight.com**
Hunters Specialities: **www.hunterspec.com**
Johnny Stewart Wildlife Calls: **www.hunterspec.com**
Merit Corporation: **www.meritcorporation.com**
Michaels of Oregon: **www.michaels-oregon.com**
MPI Outdoors: **www.mpioutdoors.com**
MTM Case-Gard: **www.mtmcase-gard.com**
North Safety Products: **www.northsafety-brea.com**
Plano Molding: **www.planomolding.com**
Pro-Ears: **www.pro-ears.com**
Second Chance Body Armor Inc.: **www.secondchance.com**
Silencio: **www.silencio.com**
Smart Lock Technologies: **www.smartlock.com**
Surefire: **www.surefire.com**
Taser Int'l: **www.taser.com**
Walker's Game Ear Inc.: **www.walkersgameear.com**

MUZZLELOADING FIREARMS AND PRODUCTS

American Pioneer Powder: **www.americanpioneerpowder.com**
Armi Sport: **www.armisport.com**
Barnes Bullets: **www.barnesbullets, com**
Black Powder Products: **www.bpiguns.com**
Buckeye Barrels: **www.buckeyebarrels.com**
Cabin Creek Muzzleloading: **www.cabincreek.net**
CVA: **www.cva.com**
Caywood Gunmakers: **www.caywoodguns.com**
Davide Perdsoli & co.: **www.davide-pedersoli.com**
Dixie Gun Works, Inc.: **www.dixiegun.com**
Elephant/Swiss Black Powder: **www.elephantblackpowder.com**
Goex Black Powder: **www.goexpowder.com**
Green Mountain Rifle Barrel Co.: **www.gmriflebarrel.com**
Gunstocks Plus: **www.gunstocksplus.com**
Harvester Bullets: **www.harvesterbullets.com**
Hornady: **www.hornady.com**
Jedediah Starr Trading Co.: **www.jedediah-starr.com**
Jim Chambers Flintlocks: **www.flintlocks.com**
Kahnke Gunworks: **www.powderandbow.com/kahnke/**
Knight Rifles: **www.knightrifles.com**
Knob Mountain Muzzleloading:
   www.knobmountainmuzzleloading.com
The leatherman: **www.blackpowderbags.com**
Log Cabin Shop: **www.logcabinshop.com**
L&R Lock Co.: **www.lr-rpl.com**
Lyman: **www.lymanproducts.com**
Magkor Industries: **www.magkor.com**
MDM Muzzleloaders: **www.mdm-muzzleloaders.com**
Middlesex Village Trading: **www.middlesexvillagetrading.com**
Millennium Designed Muzzleloaders:
   www.mdm-muzzleloaders.com
MSM, Inc.: **www.msmfg.com**
Muzzleloader Builders Supply:
   www.muzzleloadersbuilderssupply.com
Muzzleload Magnum Products: **www.mmpsabots.com**
Muzzleloading Technologies, Inc.: **www.mtimuzzleloading.com**

WEB DIRECTORY

Navy Arms: www.navyarms.com
Northwest Trade Guns: www.northstarwest.com
Nosler, Inc.: www.nosler.com
October Country Muzzleloading: www.oct-country.com
Ox-Yoke Originals Inc.: www.oxyoke.com
Pacific Rifle Co.: pacificrifle@aol.com
Palmetto Arms: www.palmetto.it
Pietta: www.pietta.it
Powerbelt Bullets: www.powerbeltbullets.com
PR Bullets: www.prbullets.com
Precision Rifle Dead Center Bullets: www.prbullet.com
R.E. Davis CVo.: www.redaviscompany.com
Remington: www.remington.com
Rightnour Mfg. Co. Inc.: www.rmcsports.com
The Rifle Shop: trshoppe@aol.com
Savage Arms, Inc.: www.savagearms.com
Schuetzen Powder: www.schuetzenpowder.com
TDC: www.tdcmfg.com
Tennessee Valley Muzzleloading: www.avsia.com/tvm
Thompson Center Arms: www.tcarms.com
Tiger Hunt Stocks: www.gunstockwood.com
Track of the Wolf: www.trackofthewolf.com
Traditions Performance Muzzleloading:
   www.traditionsfirearms.com
Vernon C. Davis & Co.: www.stonewallcreekoutfitters.com

PUBLICATIONS, VIDEOS, AND CDS

Arms and Military Press: www.skennerton.com
A&J Arms Booksellers: www.ajarmsbooksellers.com
American Cop: www.americancopmagazine.com
American Firearms Industry: www.amfire.com
American Handgunner: www.americanhandgunner.com
American Hunter: www.nrapublications.org
American Pioneer Video: www.americanpioneervideo.com
American Rifleman: www.nrapublications.org
American Shooting Magazine: www.americanshooting.com
Backwoodsman: www.backwoodsmanmag.com
Black Powder Cartridge News: www.blackpowderspg.com
Blue Book Publications: www.bluebookinc.com
Combat Handguns: www.combathandguns.com
Concealed Carry: www.uscca.us
Cornell Publications: www.cornellpubs.com
Countrywide Press: www.countrysport.com
DBI Books/Krause Publications: www.krause.com
Fouling Shot: www.castbulletassoc.org
George Shumway Publisher: www.shumwaypublisher.com
Gun List: www.gunlist.com
Gun Video: www.gunvideo.com
GUNS Magazine: www.gunsmagazine.com
Guns & Ammo: www.gunsandammomag.com
Gun Week: www.gunweek.com
Gun World: www.gunworld.com
Harris Publications: www.harrispublications.com
Heritage Gun Books: www.gunbooks.com
Krause Publications: www.krause.com
Law and Order: www.hendonpub.com
Man at Arms: www.manatarmsbooks.com
Muzzleloader: www.muzzleloadermag.com
Paladin Press: www.paladin-press.com
Precision Shooting: www.precisionshooting.com
Ray Riling Arms Books: www.rayrilingarmsbooks.com
Rifle and Handloader Magazines: www.riflemagazine.com
Safari Press Inc.: www.safaripress.com
Scurlock Publishing: www.muzzleloadingmag.com
Shoot! Magazine: www.shootmagazine.com
Shooting Illustrated: www.nrapublications.org
Shooting Industry: www.shootingindustry.com

Shooting Sports Retailer: www.shootingsportsretailer.com
Shooting Sports USA: www.nrapublications.org
Shotgun News: www.shotgunnews.com
Shotgun Report: www.shotgunreport.com
Shotgun Sports Magazine: www.shotgun-sports.com
Single Shot Rifle Journal: www.assra.com
Small Arms Review: www.smallarmsreview.com
Small Caliber News: www.smallcaliber.com
Sporting Clays Web Edition: www.sportingclays.net
Sports Afield: www.sportsafield.comm
Sportsmen on Film: www.sportsmenonfilm.com
SWAT Magazine: www.swatmag.com
The Single Shot Exchange Magazine: singleshot@earthlink.net
The Sixgunner: www.sskindustries.com
Varmint Hunter: www.varminthunter.org
VSP Publications: www.gunbooks.com

RELOADING TOOLS

Antimony Man: www.theantimonyman.com
Ballisti-Cast Mfg.: www.ballisti-cast.com
Battenfeld Technologies: www.battenfeldtechnologies.com
Bruno Shooters Supply: www.brunoshooters.com
Buffalo Arms: www.buffaloarms.com
CabineTree: www.castingstuff.com
Camdex, Inc.: www.camdexloader.com
CH/4D Custom Die: www.ch4d.com
Colorado Shooters Supply: www.hochmoulds.com
Corbin Mfg & Supply Co.: www.corbins.com
Dillon Precision: www.dillonprecision.com
Forster Precision Products: www.forsterproducts.com
GSI International, Inc.: www.gsiinternational.com
Hanned Line: www.hanned.com
Harrell's Precision: www.harrellsprec.com
Holland's Shooting Supplies: www.hollandgun.com
Hornady: www.hornady.com
Huntington Reloading Products: www.huntingtons.com
J & J Products Co.: www.jandjproducts.com
Lead Bullet Technology: www.lbtmoulds.com
Lee Precision, Inc.: www.leeprecision.com
Littleton Shotmaker: www.leadshotmaker.com
Load Data: www.loaddata.com
Lyman: www.lymanproducts.com
Magma Engineering: www.magmaengr.com
Mayville Engineering Co. (MEC): www.mecreloaders.com
Midway: www.midwayusa.com
Moly-Bore: www.molybore.com
Montana Bullet Works: www.montanabulletworks.com
MTM Case-Guard: www.mtmcase-guard.com
NECO: www.neconos.com
NEI: www.neihandtools.com
Neil Jones Custom Products: www.neiljones.com
Ponsness/Warren: www.reloaders.com
Quinetics Corp.: www.quineticscorp.com
Ranger Products:
   www.pages.prodigy.com/rangerproducts.home.htm
Rapine Bullet Mold Mfg Co.: www.bulletmoulds.com
RCBS: www.rcbs.com
Redding Reloading Equipment: www.redding-reloading.com
Russ Haydon's Shooting Supplies: www.shooters-supply.com
Sinclair Int'l Inc.: www.sinclairintl.com
Stoney Point Products Inc: www.stoneypoint.com
Thompson Bullet Lube Co.: www.thompsonbulletlube.com
Vickerman Seating Die: www.castingstuff.com
Wilson (L.E. Wilson): www.lewilson.com

RESTS: BENCH, PORTABLE, ATTACHABLE

Battenfeld Technolgies: www.battenfeldtechnologies.com

Bench Master: www.bench-master.com
B-Square: www.b-square.com
Bullshooter: www.bullshooterssightingin.com
Desert Mountain Mfg.: www.benchmasterusa.com
Harris Engineering Inc.: www.harrisbipods
Kramer Designs: www.snipepod.com
L Thomas Rifle Support: www.ltsupport.com
Level-Lok: www.levellok.com
Midway: www.midwayusa.com
Predator Sniper Styx: www.predatorsniperstyx.com
Ransom International: www.ransom-intl.com
Rotary Gun Racks: www.gun-racks.com
R.W. Hart: www.rwhart.com
Sinclair Intl, Inc.: www.sinclairintl.com
Stoney Point Products: www.uncle-mikes.com
Target Shooting: www.targetshooting.com
Varmint Masters: www.varmintmasters.com
Versa-Pod: www.versa-pod.com

SCOPES, SIGHTS, MOUNTS AND ACCESSORIES

Accumount: www.accumounts.com
Accusight: www.accusight.com
ADCO: www.shooters.com/adco/index/htm
Adirondack Opitcs: www.adkoptics.com
Advantage Tactical Sight: www.advantagetactical.com
Aimpoint: www.aimpoint.com
Aim Shot, Inc.: www.miniosprey.com
Aimtech Mount Systems: www.aimtech-mounts.com
Alpec Team, Inc.: www.alpec.com
Alpen Outdoor Corp.: www.alpenoutdoor.com
American Technologies Network, Corp.: www.atncorp.com
AmeriGlo, LLC: www.ameriglo.net
ArmaLaser: www.armalaser.com
ARMS: www.armsmounts.com
Aro-Tek, Ltd.: www.arotek.com
ATN: www.atncorp.com
Badger Ordnance: www.badgerordnance.com
Barrett: www.barrettrifles.com
Beamshot-Quarton: www.beamshot.com
BSA Optics: www.bsaoptics.com
B-Square Company, Inc.: www.b-square.com
Burris: www.burrisoptics.com
Bushnell Performance Optics: www.bushnell.com
Carl Zeiss Optical Inc.: www.zeiss.com
Carson Optical: www.carson-optical.com
CenterPoint Precision Optics: www.centerpointoptics.com
Centurion Arms: www.centurionarms.com
C-More Systems: www.cmore.com
Conetrol Scope Mounts: www.conetrol.com
Crimson Trace Corp.: www.crimsontrace.com
Crossfire L.L.C.: www.amfire.com/hesco/html
Cylinder & Slide, Inc.: www.cylinderslide.com
DCG Supply Inc.: www.dcgsupply.com
D&L Sports: www.dlsports.com
DuraSight Scope Mounting Systems: www.durasight.com
EasyHit, Inc.: www.easyhit.com
EAW: www.eaw.de
Elcan Optical Technologies:
    www.armament.com, www.elcan.com
Electro-Optics Technologies: www.eotechmdc.com/holosight
EoTech: www.eotech-inc.com
Europtik Ltd.: www.europtik.com
Fujinon, Inc.: www.fujinon.com
GG&G: www.w.gggaz.com
Gilmore Sports: www.gilmoresports.com
Gradient Lens Corp.: www.gradientlens.com
Hakko Co. Ltd.: www.hakko-japan.co.jp

Hahn Precision: www.hahn-precision.com
Hesco: www.hescosights.com
Hi-Lux Optics: www.hi-luxoptics.com
Hitek Industries: www.nightsight.com
HIVIZ: www.hivizsights.com
Hollands Shooters Supply: www.hollandguns.com
Horus Vision: www.horusvision.com
Hunter Co.: www.huntercompany.com
Innovative Weaponry, Inc.: www.ptnightsights.com
Insight: www.insighttechnology.com
Ironsighter Co.: www.ironsighter.com
ITT Night Vision: www.ittnightvision.com
Kahles: www.kahlesoptik.com
Knight's Armament: www.knightarmco.com
Kowa Optimed Inc.: www.kowascope.com
Kwik-Site Co.: www.kwiksitecorp.com
L-3 Communications-Eotech: www.l-3com.com
LaRue Tactical: www.laruetactical.com
Laser Bore Sight: www.laserboresight.com
Laser Devices Inc.: www.laserdevices.com
Lasergrips: www.crimsontrace.com
LaserLyte: www.laserlytesights.com
LaserMax Inc.: www.lasermax.com
Laser Products: www.surefire.com
Leapers, Inc.: www.leapers.com
Leatherwood: www.hi-luxoptics.com
Legacy Sports: www.legacysports.com
Leica Camera Inc.: www.leica-camera.com/usa
Leupold: www.leupold.com
Lewis Machine & Tool: www.lewismachine.net
LightForce/NightForce USA: www.nightforcescopes.com
Lyman: www.lymanproducts.com
l ynx: www.b-square.com
MaTech: www.adcofirearms.com
Marble's Outdoors: www.marblesoutdoors.com
MDS, Inc.: www.mdsincorporated.com
Meopta: www.meopta.com
Meprolight: www.kimberamerica.com
Micro Sight Co.: www.microsight.com
Millett: www.millettsights.com
Miniature Machine Corp.: www.mmcsight.com
Mini-Scout-Mount: www.amegaranges.com
Montana Vintage Arms: www.montanavintagearms.com
Moro Vision: www.morovision.com
Mounting Solutions Plus: www.mountsplus.com
NAIT: www.nait.com
Newcon International Ltd.: newconsales@newcon-optik.com
Night Force Optics: www.nightforcescopes.com
Night Optics USA, Inc.: www.nightoptics.com
Night Owl Optics: www.nightowloptics.com
Night Vision Systems: www.nightvisionsystems.com
Nikon Inc.: www.nikonusa.com
North American Integrated Technologies: www.nait.com
O.K. Weber, Inc.: www.okweber.com
Optolyth-Optic: www.optolyth.de
Osprey Optics: www.osprey-optics.com
Pentax Corp.: www.pentaxlightseeker.com
Precision Reflex: www.pri-mounts.com
Pride Fowler, Inc.: www.rapidreticle.com
Premier Reticles: www.premierreticles.com
Redfield: www.redfieldoptics.com
Rifle Electronics: www.theriflecam.com
R&R Int'l Trade: www.nightoptic.com
Schmidt & Bender: www.schmidt-bender.com
Scopecoat: www.scopecoat.com
Scopelevel: www.scopelevel.com
Segway Industries: www.segway-industries.com

WEB DIRECTORY

Shepherd Scope Ltd.: **www.shepherdscopes.com**
Sig Sauer: **www.sigsauer.com**
Sightron: **www.sightron.com**
Simmons: **www.simmonsoptics.com**
S&K: **www.scopemounts.com**
Springfield Armory: **www.springfield-armory.com**
Sure-Fire: **www.surefire.com**
Swarovski/Kahles: **www.swarovskioptik.com**
Swift Optics: **www.swiftoptics.com**
Talley Mfg. Co.: **www.talleyrings.com**
Target Scope Blocks-Steve Earl Products:
   Steven.m.earle@comcast.net
Tasco: **www.tascosales.com**
Tech Sights: **www.tech-sights.com**
Trijicon Inc.: **www.trijicon.com**
Troy Industries: **www.troyind.com**
Truglo Inc.: **www.truglo.com**
Ultimak: **www.ultimak.com**
UltraDot: **www.ultradotusa.com**
Unertl Optical Co.: **www.unertlopics.com**
US Night Vision: **www.usnightvision.com**
U.S. Optics Technologies Inc.: **www.usoptics.com**
Valdada-IOR Optics: **www.valdada.com**
Viridian Green Laser Sights: **www.viridiangreenlaser.com**
Warne: **www.warnescopemounts.com**
Weaver Mounts: **www.weaver-mounts.com**
Weaver Scopes: **www.weaveroptics.com**
Wilcox Industries Corp: **www.wilcoxind.com**
Williams Gun Sight Co.: **www.williamsgunsight.com**
Wilson Combat: **www.wilsoncombat.com**
XS Sight Systems: **www.xssights.com**
Zeiss: **www.zeiss.com**

SHOOTING ORGANIZATIONS, SCHOOLS AND RANGES

Amateur Trapshooting Assoc.: **www.shootata.com**
American Custom Gunmakers Guild: **www.acgg.org**
American Gunsmithing Institute: **www.americangunsmith.com**
American Pistolsmiths Guild: **www.americanpistol.com**
American Shooting Sports Council: **www.assc.com**
American Single Shot Rifle Assoc.: **www.assra.com**
Antique Shooting Tool Collector's Assoc.:
   www.oldshootingtools.org
Assoc. of Firearm & Tool Mark Examiners: **www.afte.org**
BATF: **www.atf.ustreas.gov**
Blackwater Lodge and Training Center:
   www.blackwaterlodge.com
Boone and Crockett Club: **www.boone-crockett.org**
Buckmasters, Ltd.: **www.buckmasters.com**
Cast Bullet Assoc.: **www.castbulletassoc.org**
Citizens Committee for the Right to Keep & Bear Arms:
   www.ccrkba.org
Civilian Marksmanship Program: **www.odcmp.com**
Colorado School of Trades: **www.gunsmith-school.com**
Cylinder & Slide Pistolsmithing Schools: **www.cylinder-slide.com**
Ducks Unlimited: **www.ducks.org**
4-H Shooting Sports Program: **www.4-hshootingsports.org**
Fifty Caliber Institute: **www.fiftycal.org**
Fifty Caliber Shooters Assoc.: **www.fcsa.org**
Firearms Coalition: **www.nealknox.com**
Front Sight Firearms Training Institute: **www.frontsight.com**
German Gun Collectors Assoc.: **www.germanguns.com**
Gun Clubs: **www.associatedgunclubs.org**
Gun Owners' Action League: **www.goal.org**
Gun Owners of America: **www.gunowners.org**
Gun Trade Asssoc. Ltd.: **www.brucepub.com/gta**
Gunsite Training Center, Inc.: **www.gunsite.com**

Handgun Hunters International: **www.sskindustries.com**
Hunting and Shooting Sports Heritage Fund:
   www.huntandshoot.org
I.C.E. Traing: **www.icetraining.com**
International Defense Pistol Assoc.: **www.idpa.com**
International Handgun Metallic Silhouette Assoc.: **www.ihmsa.org**
International Hunter Education Assoc.: **www.ihea.com**
Int'l Law Enforcement Educators and Trainers Assoc.:
   www.ileeta.com
International Single Shot Assoc.: **www.issa-schuetzen.org**
Jews for the Preservation of Firearms Ownership: **www.jpfo.org**
Mule Deer Foundation: **www.muledeer.org**
Muzzle Loaders Assoc. of Great Britain: **www.mlagb.com**
National 4-H Shooting Sports: **www.4-hshootingsports.org**
National Association of Sporting Goods Wholesalers:
   www.nasgw.org
National Benchrest Shooters Assoc.: **www.benchrest.com**
National Muzzle Loading Rifle Assoc.: **www.nmlra.org**
National Reloading Manufacturers Assoc: **www.reload-nrma.com**
National Rifle Assoc.: **www.nra.org**
National Rifle Assoc. ILA: **www.nraila.org**
National Shooting Sports Foundation: **www.nssf.org**
National Skeet Shooters Association: **www.nssa-nsca.com**
National Sporting Clays Assoc.: **www.nssa-nsca.com**
National Wild Turkey Federation: **www.nwtf.com**
NICS/FBI: **www.fbi.gov**
North American Hunting Club: **www.huntingclub.com**
Order of Edwardian Gunners (Vintagers): **www.vintagers.org**
Outdoor Industry Foundation:
   www.outdoorindustryfoundation.org
Pennsylvania Gunsmith School: **www.pagunsmith.com**
Piedmont Community College: **www.piedmontcc.edu**
Quail Unlimited: **www.qu.org**
Remington Society of America: **www.remingtonsociety.com**
Right To Keep and Bear Arms: **www.rkba.org**
Rocky Mountain Elk Foundation: **www.rmef.org**
SAAMI: **www.saami.org**
Safari Club International: **www.scifirstforhunters.org**
Scholastic Clay Target Program: **www.nssf.org/sctp**
Second Amendment Foundation: **www.saf.org**
Second Amendment Sisters: **www.2asisters.org**
Shooting Ranges Int'l: **www.shootingranges.com**
Sig Sauer Academy: **www.sigsauer.com**
Single Action Shooting Society: **www.sassnet.com**
Students for Second Amendment: **www.sf2a.org**
Suarez Training: **www.warriortalk.com**
S&W Academy and Nat'l Firearms Trng. Center:
   www.sw-academy.com
Tactical Defense Institute: **www.tdiohio.com**
Tactical Life: **www.tactical-life.com**
Ted Nugent United Sportsmen of America: **www.tnugent.com**
Thunder Ranch: **www.thunderranchinc.com**
Trapshooters Homepage: **www.trapshooters.com**
Trinidad State Junior College: **www.trinidadstate.edu**
U.S. Concealed Carry Association: **www.uscca.us**
U.S. Int'l Clay Target Assoc.: **www.usicta.com**
United States Fish and Wildlife Service: **www.fws.gov**
U.S. Practical Shooting Assoc.: **www.uspsa.org**
USA Shooting: **www.usashooting.com**
Varmint Hunters Assoc.: **www.varminthunter.org**
U.S. Sportsmen's Alliance: **www.ussportsmen.org**
Winchester Arms Collectors Assoc.:
   www.winchestercollector.com
Women Hunters: **www.womanhunters.com**
Women's Shooting Sports Foundation: **www.wssf.org**

WEB DIRECTORY

STOCKS, GRIPS, FOREARMS

Ace, Ltd.: www.aceltdusa.com
Advanced Technology: www.atigunstocks.com
Battenfeld Technologies: www.battenfeldtechnologies.com
Bell & Carlson, Inc.: www.bellandcarlson.com
Boyd's Gunstock Industries, Inc.: www.boydgunstocks.com
Butler Creek Corp: www.butler-creek.com
Cadex: www.vikingtactics.com
Calico Hardwoods, Inc.: www.calicohardwoods.com
Choate Machine: www.riflestock.com
Command Arms: www.commandarms.com
C-More Systems: www.cmore.com
D&L Sports: www.dlsports.com
Duo Stock: www.duostock.com
Elk Ridge Stocks: www.reamerrentals.com/elk_ridge.htm
FAB Tactical: www.botachtactical.com
Fajen: www.battenfeldtechnologies.com
Falcon Ergo Grip: www.ergogrips.com
Great American Gunstocks: www.gunstocks.com
Grip Pod: www.grippod.com
Gun Stock Blanks: www.gunstockblanks.com
Herrett's Stocks: www.herrettstocks.com
High Tech Specialties: www.bansnersrifle.com/hightech
Hogue Grips: www.getgrip.com
Holland's Shooting Supplies: www.hollandgun.com
Knight's Mfg. Co.: wwwknightarmco.com
Knoxx Industries: www.blackhawk.com
KZ Tactical: www.kleyzion.com
LaRue Tactical: www.laruetactical.com
Lewis Machine & Tool: www.lewismachine.net
Lone Wolf: www.lonewolfriflestocks.com
Magpul: www.magpul.com
McMIllan Fiberglass Stocks: www.mcmfamily.com
MPI Stocks: www.mpistocks.com
Precision Gun Works: www.precisiongunstocks.com
Ram-Line: www.outers-guncare.com
Richards Microfit Stocks: www.rifle-stocks.com
Rimrock Rifle Stock: www.rimrockstocks.com
Royal Arms Gunstocks: www.imt.net/~royalarms
S&K Industries: www.sandkgunstocks.com
Speedfeed, Inc.: www.speedfeedinc.com
TacStar/Pachmayr: www.tacstar.com
Tango Down: www.tangodown.com
TAPCO: www.tapco.com
Surefire: www.surefire.com
Tiger-Hunt Curly Maple Gunstocks: www.gunstockwood.com
Vltor: www.vltor.com
Wenig Custom Gunstocks Inc.: www.wenig.com
Wilcox Industries: www.wilcoxind.com
Yankee Hill: www.yhm.net

TARGETS AND RANGE EQUIPMENT

Action Target Co.: www.actiontarget.com
Advanced Interactive Systems: www.ais-sim.com
Birchwood Casey: www.birchwoodcasey.com
Bullet Proof Electronics: www.thesnipertarget.com
Caswell Meggitt Defense Systems: www.mds-caswell.com
Champion Traps & Targets: www.championtarget.com
Handloader/Victory Targets: www.targetshandloader.com
Just Shoot Me Products: www.ballistictec.com
Laser Shot: www.lasershot.com
Mountain Plains Industries: www.targetshandloader.com
MTM Products: www.mtmcase-gard.com
Natiional Target Co.: www.nationaltarget.com
Newbold Target Systems: www.newboldtargets.com
Porta Target, Inc.: www.portatarget.com

Range Management Services Inc.: www.casewellintl.com
Range Systems: www.shootingrangeproducts.com
Reactive Target Systems Inc.: chrts@primenet.com
ShatterBlast Targets: www.daisy.com
Super Trap Bullet Containment Systems: www.supertrap.com
Thompson Target Technology: www.thompsontarget.com
Tombstone Tactical Targets: www.tttargets.com
Visible Impact Targets: www.crosman.com
White Flyer: www.whiteflyer.com

TRAP AND SKEET SHOOTING EQUIPMENT AND ACCESSORIES

Auto-Sporter Industries: www.auto-sporter.com
10X Products Group: www.10Xwear.com
Claymaster Traps: www.claymaster.com
Do-All Traps, Inc.: www.doalloutdoors.com
Laporte USA: www.laporte-shooting.com
Outers: www.blount.com
Trius Products Inc.: www.triustraps.com
White Flyer: www.whiteflyer.com

TRIGGERS

American Trigger Corp.: www.americantrigger.com
Brownells: www.brownells.com
Chip McCormick Corp.: www.chipmccormickcorp.com
Huber Concepts: www.huberconcepts.com
Kidd Triggers.: www.coolguyguns.com
Shilen: www.shilen.com
Timney Triggers: www.timneytrigger.com
Williams Trigger Specialties: www.williamstriggers.com

MAJOR SHOOTING WEBSITES AND LINKS

24 Hour Campfire: www.24hourcampfire.com
Alphabetic Index of Links: www.gunsgunsguns.com
Auction Arms: www.auctionarms.com
Benchrest Central: www.benchrest.com
Big Game Hunt: www.biggamehunt.net
Bullseye Pistol: www.bullseyepistol.com
Firearms History: www.researchpress.co.uk/firearms
Glock Talk: www.glocktalk.com
Gun Broker Auctions: www.gunbroker.com
Gun Industry: www.gunindustry.com
Gun Blast: www.gunblast.com
Gun Boards: www.gunboards.com
GunsAmerica.com: www.gunsamerica.com
Guns Unified Nationally Endorsing Dignity: www.guned.com
Gun Shop Finder: www.gunshopfinder.com
GUNS and Hunting: www.gunsandhunting.com
Hunt and Shoot (NSSF): www.huntandshoot.org
Keep and Bear Arms: www.keepandbeararms.com
Leverguns: www.leverguns.com
Load Swap: www.loadswap.com
Outdoor Press Room: www.outdoorpressroom.com
Real Guns: www.realguns.com
Ruger Forum: www.rugerforum.com
SavageShooters: www.savageshooters.com
Shooters Forum: www.shootersforum.com
Shotgun Sports Resource Guide: www.shotgunsports.com
Sixgunner: www.sixgunner.com
Sniper's Hide: www.snipershide.com
Sportsman's Web: www.sportsmansweb.com
Surplus Rifles: www.surplusrifle.com
Tactical-Life: www.tactical-life.com
Wing Shoooting USA: www.wingshootingusa.org

FOR COLLECTOR • HUNTER • SHOOTER • OUTDOORSMAN
IMPORTANT NOTICE TO BOOK BUYERS

Books listed here may be bought from Ray Riling Arms Books Co., 6844 Gorsten St., Philadelphia, PA 19119, Phone 215-438-2456; FAX: 215-438-5395. E-mail: sales@rayrilingarmsbooks.com. Larry Riling is the researcher and compiler of "The Arms Library" and a seller of gun books for over 65 years. The Riling stock includes books classic and modern, many hard-to-find items, and many not obtainable elsewhere. These pages list a portion of the current stock. They offer prompt, complete service, with delayed shipments occurring only on out-of-print or out-of-stock books.

Visit our Web site at www.rayrilingarmsbooks.com and order all of your favorite titles online from our secure site.

NOTICE FOR ALL CUSTOMERS: Remittance in U.S. funds must accompany all orders. For your convenience we accept VISA, MasterCard, Discover & American Express. For shipments in the U.S., add $7.00 for the 1st book and $2.00 for each additional book for postage and insurance. Minimum order $10.00. International Orders add $13.00 for the 1st book and $5.00 for each additional book. All International orders are shipped at the buyer's risk unless an additional $5 for insurance is included. USPS does not offer insurance to all countries unless shipped Air-Mail. Please e-mail or call for pricing.

Payments in excess of order or for "Backorders" are credited or fully refunded at request. Books "As-Ordered" are not returnable except by permission and a handling charge on these of 10 percent or $2.00 per book, whichever is greater, is deducted from refund or credit. Only Pennsylvania customers must include current sales tax.

A full variety of arms books also available from Rutgers Book Center, 127 Raritan Ave., Highland Park, NJ 08904/732-545-4344; FAX: 732-545-6686 or I.D.S.A. Books, 3220 E. Galbraith Rd., Cincinnati, OH 45236. Email IDSABooks@IDSABooks.com; www.IDSABooks.com.

BALLISTICS AND HANDLOADING

ABC's of Reloading, 7th Edition, by Bill Chevalier, Iola, WI, Krause Publications, 2005. 288 pp., illustrated with 550 b&w photos. Softcover. $21.95

American Cartridge, The, by Charles Suydam, Borden Publishing Co. Alhambra, CA, 1986. 184 pp., illus. Softcover $24.95
An illustrated study of the rimfire cartridge in the United States.

Ammo and Ballistics II, by Robert W. Forker, Safari Press, Inc., Huntington Beach, CA, 2002. 298 pp., illus. Paper covers. $19.95
Ballistic data on 125 calibers and 1,400 loads out to 500 yards.

Barnes Bullets Reloading Manual Number 3, Barnes Bullets, American Fork, UT, 2003. 668 pp., illus. $29.95
Features data and trajectories on the new weight X, XBT and Solids in calibers from .22 to .50 BMG.

Black Powder, Pig Lead and Steel Silhouettes, by Paul A. Matthews, Prescott, AZ, Wolfe Publishing, 2002. 132 pp., illustrated with b&w photographs and detailed drawings and diagrams. Softcover $16.95

Cartridge Reloading Tools of the Past, by R.H. Chamberlain, and Tom Quigley, Castle Rock, WA, 1998. 167 pp., illus. Paper covers. $25.00
A detailed treatment of the extensive Winchester and ideal line of handloading tools and bullet molds, plus Remington, Marlin, Ballard, Browning, Maynard, and many others.

Cast Bullets for the Black Powder Rifle, by Paul A. Matthews, Wolfe Publishing Co., Prescott, AZ, 1996. 133 pp., illus. Paper covers. $22.50
The tools and techniques used to make your cast bullet shooting a success.

Complete Blackpowder Handbook, 5th Edition, by Sam Fadala, DBI Books, a division of Krause Publications, Iola, WI, 2006. 448 pages, with over 650 b&w photos. Paper covers. $26.95
More than 650 detailed photos illustrating new gear and demonstrating effective techniques. Written for every blackpowder enthusiast-hunters, war re-enactors, collectors, cowboy action shooters, target shooters and DIY blackpowder hobbyists.

Complete Reloading Manual, One Book / One Caliber, CA, Load Books USA, 2000. $7.95 each
Contains unabridged information from U.S. bullet and powder makers. With thousands of proven and tested loads, plus dozens of various bullet designs and different powders. Spiral bound. Available in all calibers.

Designing and Forming Custom Cartridges for Rifles and Handguns, by Ken Howell. Precision Shooting, Manchester, CT. 2002. 600 pp., illus. $59.95
The classic work in its field, out of print for the last few years and virtually unobtainable on the used book market, now returns in an exact reprint of the original. Full size (8½" x 11"), hardcovers. Dozens of cartridge drawings never published anywhere before–dozens you've never heard of (guaranteed!). Precisely drawn to the dimensions specified by the men who designed them, the factories that made them, and the authorities that set the standards. All drawn to the same format and scale (1.5x) for most, how to form them from brass. Other practical information included.

Early Gunpowder Artillery 1300-1600 by John Norris, London, The Crowood Press, 2003. 1st edition. 141 pp., with 160 b&w photos. Hardcover. New in new dust jacket. $34.95

Early Loading Tools & Bullet Molds, Pioneer Press, 1988. 88 pp., illus. Softcover. $7.50

Handbook for Shooters and Reloaders, by P.O. Ackley, Salt Lake City, UT, 1998, (Vol. I), 567 pp., illus. Includes a separate exterior ballistics chart. $24.95; (Vol. II), a new printing with specific new material. 495 pp., illus. $21.95

Handgun Stopping Power; The Definitive Study, by Marshall & Sandow. Boulder, CO, Paladin Press, 1992. 240 pp. $45.00
Offers accurate predictions of the stopping power of specific loads in calibers from 380 Auto to 45 ACP, as well as such specialty rounds as the Glaser Safety Slug, Federal Hydra-Shok, MagSafe, etc. This is the definitive methodology for predicting the stopping power of handgun loads, the first to take into account what really happens when a bullet meets a man.

Handloader's Digest: 18th Edition edited by Ken Ramage, Iola, WI, Krause Publications, 2003. 300 b&w photos, 256 pp. Softcover. $19.95

Handloader's Manual of Cartridge Conversions, Revised 3rd edition, by John Donnelly, and Bryce Towsley, Accokeek, MD, Stoeger Publications, 2004. 609pp, Hardcover. NEW $39.95
Over 900 cartridges described in detail, complete with dimensions, and accurate drawings. Includes case capacities and all physical data.

Hatcher's Notebook, by S. Julian Hatcher, Stackpole Books, Harrisburg, PA, 1992. 488 pp., illus. $39.95
A reference work for shooters, gunsmiths, ballisticians, historians, hunters and collectors.

Headstamped Cartridges and Their Variations; Volume 1, by Daniel L. Shuey, W.R.A. Co., Rockford, IL, WCF Publications, 2003. 351 pp. illustrated with b&w photos. Hardcover. $55.00

Headstamped Cartridges and Their Variations; Volume 2, by Daniel L. Shuey, W.R.A. Co., Rockford, IL, WCF Publications, 2003. 351 pp. illustrated with b&w photos. Hardcover. $55.00

History & Development of Small Arms Ammunition, Volume 1, Second Edition–With A Value Guide, Martial Long Arms, Flintlock through Rimfire, by George A. Hoyem, Missoula, MT, Armory Publications, 2005. Hardcover. New in new dust jacket. $60.00

Hornady Handbook of Cartridge Reloading, 7th Edition, edited by Larry Steadman, Hornady Mfg. Co., Grand Island, NE, 2007, 978 pages, illus. $44.95
This completely revised and updated manual contains load data for almost every cartridge available, including the latest developments like the 204 Ruger and 500 S&W. Includes tips on basic reloading, rifle and handgun load data and an illustrated glossary.

How-To's for the Black Powder Cartridge Rifle Shooter, by Paul A. Matthews, Wolfe Publishing Co., Prescott, AZ, 1995. 45 pp. Paper covers. $22.50
Covers lube recipes, good bore cleaners and over-powder wads. Tips include compressing powder charges, combating wind resistance, improving ignition and much more.

Loading the Black Powder Rifle Cartridge, by Paul A. Matthews, Wolfe Publishing Co., Prescott, AZ, 1993. 121 pp., illus. Paper covers. $22.50
Author Matthews brings the blackpowder cartridge shooter valuable information on the basics, including cartridge care, lubes and moulds, powder charges and developing and testing loads in his usual authoritative style.

Lyman 48th Reloading Handbook, No. 48. Connecticut, Lan Publishing Corporation, 2003. 48th edition. 480 pp. Softcover. $26.95

Lyman Cast Bullet Handbook, 3rd Edition, edited by C. Kenneth Ramage, Lyman Publications, Middlefield, CT, 1980. 416 pp., illus. Paper covers. $19.95
Information on more than 5000 tested cast bullet loads and 19 pages of trajectory and wind drift tables for cast bullets.

Lyman Black Powder Handbook, 2nd Edition, edited by Sam Fadala, Lyman Products for Shooters, Middlefield, CT, 2000. 239 pp., illus. Paper covers. $19.95
Comprehensive load information for the modern blackpowder shooter.

Lyman Shotshell Handbook, 5th Edition, edited by Edward A. Matunas, Lyman Products Co., Middlefield, CT, 2007. 330 pp., illus. Paper covers. $25.95
This new 5th edition covers cases, wads and primers currently offered by all leading manufacturers in all gauges from .410 to 10 gauge. In addition, the latest and also the most popular powders from Alliant, Hodgdon, Accurate, IMR, VihtaVuori, Ramshot, Winchester are included.

Make It Accurate-Get the Maximum Performance from Your Hunting Rifle, by Craig Boddington, Long Beach, CA, Safari Press, 1999. Hardcover. New in new dust jacket. $24.95

Metallic Cartridge Conversions: The History of the Guns and Modern Reproductions, by Dennis Adler, Foreword by R. L. Wilson, Iola, WI, Krause Publications, 2003. 1st edition. 208 pp. 250 color photos. Hardcover. New in new dust jacket. $39.95

Modern Exterior Ballistics, by Robert L. McCoy, Schiffer Publishing Co., Atglen, PA, 1999. 128 pp. $95.00
Advanced students of exterior ballistics and flight dynamics will find this comprehensive textbook on the subject a useful addition to their libraries.

Modern Reloading 2nd Edition, by Richard Lee, Inland Press, 2003. 623 pp., illus. $29.95
The how-to's of rifle, pistol and shotgun reloading plus load data for rifle and pistol calibers.

Mr. Single Shot's Cartridge Handbook, by Frank de Haas, Mark de Haas, Orange City, IA, 1996. 116 pp., illus. Paper covers. $22.50
This book covers most of the cartridges, both commercial and wildcat, that the author has known and used.

Norma Reloading Manual, by Norma Precision AB, 2004, 1st edition. Data for over 2,000 loads in 73 calibers. 432pp, hardcover, $34.95

Nosler Reloading Manual #5, edited by Gail Root, Nosler Bullets, Inc., Bend, OR, 2002. 516 pp., illus. $29.99
Combines information on their ballistic tip, partition and handgun bullets with traditional powders and new powders never before used, plus trajectory information from 100 to 500 yards.

Reloading for Shotgunners, 4th Edition, by Kurt D. Fackler, and M.L. McPherson, DBI Books, a division of Krause Publications, Iola, WI, 1997. 320 pp., illus. Paper covers. $19.95
Expanded reloading tables with over 11,000 loads. Bushing charts for every major press and component maker. All new presentation on all aspects of shotshell reloading by two of the top experts in the field.

Reloading Tools, Sights and Telescopes for S/S Rifles, by Gerald O. Kelver, Brighton, CO, 1982. 163 pp., illus. Softcover. $15.00

A listing of most of the famous makers of reloading tools, sights and telescopes with a brief description of the products they manufactured.

Rimfire Cartridge in the United States and Canada, Illustrated History of Rimfire Cartridges, Manufacturers, and the Products Made from 1857-1984, by John L. Barber, Thomas Publications, Gettysburg, PA 2000. 1st edition. Profusely illus. 221 pp. $50.00

The author has written an encyclopedia of rimfire cartridges from the 22 to the massive 1.00 in. Gatling. Fourteen chapters, six appendices and an excellent bibliography.

Round Ball to Rimfire: Civil War Small Arms Ammunition, Vol. 1, by Dean S. Thomas, Gettysburg, PA, Thomas Publications, 2003. 344 pp. Hardcover. $40.00

Federal Ordnance Dept., Arsenals, Smoothbores & Rifle Muskets. Detailed information on the Ordnance Department, Northern arsenals, patents, designers, & manufacturers of Federal musket ammunition.

Round Ball to Rimfire: Civil War Small Arms Ammunition, Vol. 2, by Dean S. Thomas, Gettysburg, PA, Thomas Publications, 2004. 528 pp. Hardcover. $49.95

Federal Breechloading Carbines and Rifles. Federal carbine and rifle ammunition. Detailed information on patents, designers, & manufacturers of Federal breechloaders and their ammunition.

Round Ball to Rimfire: Civil War Small Arms Ammunition, Vol. 3, by Dean S. Thomas, Gettysburg, PA, Thomas Publications, 2005. 488 pp. Hardcover. $49.95

Federal pistols, revolvers and miscellaneous essays. Detailed information on patents, designers, & manufacturers. Miscellaneous essays wrap-up the Northern side of the story.

Shotshells & Ballistics, Safari Press, 2002. 275 pp., photos. Softcover, $19.95

Accentuated with photos from the field and the range, this is a reference book unlike any other.

Sierra Reloading Manual, 5th Edition: Rifle and Handgun Manual of Reloading Data. Sedalia, MO, Sierra Bullets, 2003. Hardcover. $39.95

Speer Reloading Manual No. 13, edited by members of the Speer research staff, Omark Industries, Lewiston, ID, 1999. 621 pp., illus. $29.95

With 13 new sections containing the latest technical information and reloading trends for both novice and expert in this latest edition. More than 9,300 loads are listed, including new propellant powders from Accurate Arms, Alliant, Hodgdon and Vihtavuori.

Stopping Power: A Practical Analysis of the Latest Handgun Ammunition, by Marshall & Sanow, Paladin Press, 2002. 600+ photos, 360 pp. Softcover. $49.95

Stopping Power bases its conclusions on real-world facts from real-world gunfights. It provides the latest street results of actual police and civilian shootings in all of the major handgun calibers, from 22 LR to 45 ACP, plus more than 30 chapters of vital interest to all gun owners.

Street Stoppers, The Latest Handgun Stopping Power Street Results, by Marshall & Lanow, Boulder, CO, Paladin Press, 1996. 374 pp., illus. Softcover. $42.95

Street Stoppers is the long-awaited sequel to *Handgun Stopping Power*. It provides the latest results of real-life shootings in all of the major handgun calibers, plus more than 25 thought-provoking chapters that are vital to anyone interested in firearms, wound ballistics, and combat shooting. This book also covers the street results of the hottest new caliber to hit the shooting world in years, the 40 Smith & Wesson, plus updated street results of the latest exotic ammunition.

Understanding Firearm Ballistics, 6th Edition, by Robert A. Rinker, Mulberry House Corydon, IN, 2005. 437 pp., illus. Paper covers. New, revised and expanded. $24.95

Explains basic to advanced firearm ballistics in understandable terms.

Why Not Load Your Own?, by Col. T. Whelen, Gun Room Press, Highland Park, NJ 1996, 4th ed., rev. 237 pp., illus. $20.00

A basic reference on handloading, describing each step, materials and equipment. Includes loads for popular cartridges.

Wildcat Cartridges, "Reloader's Handbook of Wildcat Cartridge Design", by Fred Zeglin, privately printed, 2005. 1st edition. 287 Pages, Hard back book. Forward by Wayne van Zwoll. Pictorial Hardcover. $39.95

Twenty-two chapters cover wildcatting from every possible angle. History, dimensions, load data, and how to make or use reloading tool and reamers. If you're interested in reloading or wildcatting this is a must have book.

Wildcat Cartridges Volumes 1 & 2 Combination, by the editors of *Handloaders* magazine, Wolfe Publishing Co., Prescott, AZ, 1997. 350 pp., illus. Paper covers. $39.95

A profile of the most popular information on wildcat cartridges that appeared in the *Handloaders* magazine.

W.R.A. Co.; Headstamped Cartridges and their Variations; Volume 1, by Daniel Shuey, Rockford, IL, WCF Publications, 2001. 298pp illustrated with b&w photos, Hardcover, $55.00

W.R.A. Co.; Headstamped Cartridges and their Variations; Volume 2, by Daniel Shuey, Rockford, IL, WCF Publications, 2003. 351pp illustrated with b&w photos, Hardcover, $50.00

COLLECTORS

1 October 1934 SS Dienstalterliste, by the Ulric of England Research Unit San Jose, CA, R. James Bender Publishing, 1994. Reprint softcover. $29.95

10. Panzer Division: In Action in the East, West and North Africa 1939-1943, by Jean Resta and N. Moller, Canada, J.J. Fedorowicz Publishing Inc., 2003. 1st edition. Hardcover. $89.95

18th Century Weapons of the Royal Welsh Fuziliers from Flixton Hall, by Erik Goldstein, Thomas Publications, Gettysburg, PA, 2002. 1st edition. 126 pp., illustrated with b&w photos. Softcover. $19.95

.45-70 Springfield Book I, by Albert Frasca and Robert Hill, Frasca Publishing, 2000. Memorial edition. Hardback with gold embossed cover and spine. $95.00

The Memorial edition reprint of the .45-70 Springfield was done to honor Robert H. Hill who was an outstanding Springfield collector, historian, researcher, and gunsmith. Only 1,000 of these highly regarded books were printed, using the same binding and cover material as the original 1980 edition. The book is considered the bible for 45-70 Springfield Trapdoor collectors.

.45-70 Springfield Book II 1865-1893, by Albert Frasca, Frasca Publishing, Springfield, Ohio 1997, 400+ pp. and 400+ photographs which cover ALL the trapdoor Springfield models. Hardback with gold embossed cover and spine. A MUST for the trapdoor collector! $85.00

.45-70 Springfield 4th Ed. Revised & Expanded, The, by Joe Poyer and Craig Riesch, North Cape Publications, Tustin, CA, 2006. 274 pp., illus. Paper covers. $19.95

Every part and every change to that part made by the Ordnance Department is described in photos and drawings. Dimensions and finishes are listed for each part in both the text and tables.

'51 Colt Navies, by Nathan L. Swayze, The Gun Room Press, Highland Park, NJ, 1993. 243 pp., illus. $59.95

The Model 1851 Colt Navy, its variations and markings.

1862 U.S. Cavalry Tactics, by Philip St. George Cooke, Mechanicsburg, PA, Stackpole Books, 2004. 416 pp. Hardcover. New in new dust jacket. $19.89

A Collector's Guide to the '03 Springfield, by Bruce N. Canfield, Andrew Mowbray Inc., Lincoln, RI, 2004. 160 pp., illus. Paper covers. $22.00

A comprehensive guide follows the '03 through its unparalleled tenure of service. Covers all of the interesting variations, modifications and accessories of this highly collectible military rifle.

An Illustrated Guide To The '03 Springfield Service Rifle, by Bruce N. Canfield Andrew Mowbray, Inc., Pictorial Hardcover 2005. $49.95

Your ultimate guide to the military '03 Springfield! Three times as large as the author's previous best selling book on this topic. Covers all models, all manufacturers and all conflicts, including WWI, WWII and beyond. Heavily illustrated. Serial number tables, combat photos, sniper rifles and more! 240 pages, illustrated with over 450 photos.

Complete Guide To The United States Military Combat Shotguns, by Bruce N. Canfield Andrew Mowbray, Inc., 2007. 1st edition. 312 Pages. $49.95

From the famed Winchester M97 to the Mossberg and beyond! Expanded and updated covereage of American combat shotguns with three times the information found in the author's pervious best-selling book on this topic. Hundreds of detailed photographs show you the specific features that you need to recognize in order to identify fakes and assembled guns. Special, in-depth historical coverage of WWI, WWII, Korea, Vietnam and Iraq!

A Collector's Guide to United States Combat Shotguns, by Bruce N. Canfield, Andrew Mowbray Inc., Lincoln, RI, 1992. 184 pp., illus. Paper covers. $24.00

This book provides full coverage of combat shotguns, from the earliest examples right up to the Gulf War and beyond.

A Collector's Guide to Winchester in the Service, by Bruce N. Canfield, Andrew Mowbray, Inc., Lincoln, RI, 1991. 192 pp., illus. Paper covers. $24.00

The firearms produced by Winchester for the national defense. From Hotchkiss to the M14, each firearm is examined and illustrated.

A Concise Guide to the Artillery at Gettysburg, by Gregory Coco, Thomas Publications, Gettysburg, PA, 1998. 96 pp., illus. Paper covers. $10.00

Coco's book on Gettysburg is a beginner's guide to artillery and its use at the battle. It covers the artillery batteries, describing the types of cannons, shells, fuses, etc. using interesting narrative and human interest stories.

A Glossary of the Construction, Decoration and Use of Arms and Armor in All Countries and in All Times, by George Cameron Stone, Dover Publishing, New York 1999. Softcover. $39.95

An exhaustive study of arms and armor in all countries through recorded history-from the Stone Age up to WWII. With over 4,500 b&w illustrations, this Dover edition is an unabridged republication of the work originally published in 1934 by the Southworth Press, Portland, MA. A new Introduction has been specially prepared for this edition.

A Guide to American Trade Catalogs 1744-1900, by Lawrence B. Romaine, Dover Publications, New York, NY. 422 pp., illus. Paper covers. $12.95

A Guide to Ballard Breechloaders, by George J. Layman, Pioneer Press, Union City, TN, 1997. 261 pp., illus. Paper covers. $19.95

Documents the saga of this fine rifle from the first models made by Ball & Williams of Worchester, to its production by the Marlin Firearms Co., to the cessation of 19th century manufacture in 1891, and finally to the modern reproductions made in the 1990s.

A Guide to the Maynard Breechloader, by George J. Layman, George J. Layman, Ayer, MA, 1993. 125 pp., illus. Paper covers. $14.95

The first book dedicated entirely to the Maynard family of breech-loading firearms. Coverage of the arms is given from the 1850s through the 1880s.

A Guide to U.S. Army Dress Helmets 1872-1904, by Kasal and Moore, North Cape Publications, 2000. 88 pp., illus. Paper covers. $15.95

This thorough study provides a complete description of the Model 1872 and 1881 dress helmets worn by the U.S. Army.

A Study of Remington's Smoot Patent and Number Four Revolvers, by Parker Harry, Parker Ora Lee, and Joan Reisch, Foreword by Roy M. Marcot, Santa Ana, CA, Armslore Press, Graphic Publishers, 2003. 1st edition. 120 pp., profusely illus., plus 8-page color section. Softcover. $17.95

A detailed, pictorial essay on Remington's early metallic cartridge-era pocket revolvers: their design, development, patents, models, identification and variations. Includes the biography of arms inventor Wm. S. Smoot, as well as a mini-history of the Remington Arms Company.

Accoutrements of the United States Infantry, Riflemen, and Dragoons 1834-1839, by R.T. Huntington, Historical Arms Series No. 20. Canada, Museum Restoration. 58 pp. illus. Softcover. $8.95

Although the 1841 edition of the U.S. Ordnance Manual provides ample information on the equipment that was in use during the 1840s, it is evident that the patterns of equipment that it describes were not introduced until 1838 or 1839. This guide is intended to fill this gap in our knowledge by providing an overview of what we now know about the accoutrements that were issued to the regular infantryman, rifleman, and dragoon, in the 1830s with excursions into earlier and later years.

Ackermann Military Prints: Uniforms of the British and Indian Armies 1840-1855, by William Y. Carman with Robert W. Kenny Jr., Schiffer Publications, Atglen, PA, 2002. 1st edition. 176 pp., with over 160 color images. $69.95

Afrikakorps: Rommel's Tropical Army in Original Color, by Bernd Peitz, Gary Wilkins. Atglen, PA, Schiffer Publications, 2004. 1st edition. 192 pp., with over 200 color and b&w photographs. Hardcover. New in new dust jacket. $59.95

Air Guns, by Eldon G. Wolff, Duckett's Publishing Co., Tempe, AZ, 1997. 204 pp., illus. Paper covers. $35.00

Historical reference covering many makers, European and American guns, canes and more.

All About Southerners, by Lionel J. Bogut, White Star, Inc., 2002. A limited edition of 1,000 copies. Signed and numbered. 114 pp., including bibliography, and plenty of b&w photographs and detailed drawings. Hardcover. $29.95

Detailed look at the characteristics and design of the "Best Little Pistol in the World."

Allgemeine-SS The Commands, Units and Leaders of the General SS, by Mark C. Yerger, Atglen, PA, Schiffer Publications, 1997. 1st edition. Hardcover. New in new dust jacket. $49.95

Allied and Enemy Aircraft: May 1918; Not to be Taken from the Front Lines, Historical Arms Series No. 27. Canada, Museum Restoration. Softcover. $8.95

The basis for this title is a very rare identification manual published by the French government in 1918 that illustrated 60 aircraft with three or more views: French, English American, German, Italian, and Belgian, which might have been seen over the trenches of France. Each is described in a text translated from the original French. This is probably the most complete collection of illustrations of WWI aircraft that has survived.

American Beauty; The Prewar Colt National Match Government Model Pistol, by Timothy J. Mullin, Collector Grade Publications, Cobourg, Ontario, Canada. 72 pp., illus. $34.95

Includes over 150 serial numbers, and 20 spectacular color photos of factory engraved guns and other authenticated upgrades, including rare "double-carved" ivory grips.

American Civil War Artillery 1861-65: Field Artillery, by Philip Oxford Katcher, United Kingdom, Osprey Publishing, 2001. 1st edition. 48 pp. Softcover. $14.95

Perhaps the most influential arm of either army in the prosecution of the American Civil War, the artillery of both sides grew to be highly professional organizations. This book covers all the major artillery pieces employed, including the Napoleon, Parrott Rifle and Mountain Howitzer.

American Military and Naval Belts, 1812-1902, by R. Stephen Dorsey, Eugene, OR, Collectors Library, 2002. 1st edition. Hardcover. $80.00

With introduction by Norm Flayderman, this massive work is the NEW key reference on sword belts, waist belts, sabre belts, shoulder belts and cartridge belts (looped and non-looped). At over 460 pp., this 8½" x 11" book offers over 840 photos (primarily in color) and original period drawings. In addition, this work offers the first, comprehensive research on the Anson Mills woven cartridge belts, the belt-related patents and the government contracts from 1880 through 1902. This book is a "must" for all accoutrements collectors, military historians and museums.

American Military Headgear Insignia, by Michael J. O'Donnell and J. Duncan, Campbell, Alexandria, VA, O'Donnell Publishing, 2004. 1st edition. 311 pp., 703 photo figures, 4 sketches. Hardcover. New in new dust jacket. $89.95

American Military Saddle, 1776-1945, The, by R. Stephen Dorsey and Kenneth L. McPheeters, Collector's Library, Eugene, OR, 1999. 400 pp., illus. $67.00

The most complete coverage of the subject ever written on the American Military Saddle. Nearly 1,000 actual photos and official drawings, from the major public and private collections in the U.S. and Great Britain.

American Police Collectibles; Dark Lanterns and Other Curious Devices, by Matthew G. Forte, Turn of the Century Publishers, Upper Montclair, NJ, 1999. 248 pp., illus. $24.95

For collectors of police memorabilia (handcuffs, police dark lanterns, mechanical and chain nippers, rattles, billy clubs and nightsticks) and police historians.

American Thunder II: The Military Thompson Submachine Guns, by Frank Iannamico, Harmony, ME, Moose Lake Publishing, 2004, 2nd edition. Many great photographs that show detail markings and features of the various models, as well as vintage WW11 photographs showing the Thompson in action. 536 pages, Soft cover, $29.95

An Introduction to the Civil War Small Arms, by Earl J. Coates and Dean S. Thomas, Thomas Publishing Co., Gettysburg, PA, 1990. 96 pp., illus. Paper covers. $10.00

The small arms carried by the individual soldier during the Civil War.

Arming the Glorious Cause; Weapons of the Second War for Independence, by James B. Whisker, Daniel D. Hartzler and Larry W. Tantz, Old Bedford Village Press, Bedford, PA., 1998. 175 pp., illus. $45.00

A photographic study of Confederate weapons.

Arms & Accoutrements of the Mounted Police 1873-1973, by Roger F. Phillips, and Donald J. Klancher, Museum Restoration Service, Ont., Canada, 1982. 224 pp., illus. $49.95 Also, available in paperback, $29.95

A definitive history of the revolvers, rifles, machine guns, cannons, ammunition, swords, etc. used by the NWMP, the RNWMP and the RCMP during the first 100 years of the Force.

Arms and Armor in Colonial America 1526-1783, by Harold Peterson, Dover Publishing, New York, 2000. 350 pp. with over 300 illustrations, index, bibliography and appendix. Softcover. $34.95

Over 200 years of firearms, ammunition, equipment and edged weapons.

Arms and Armor in the Art Institute of Chicago, by Waltler J. Karcheski, Bulfinch, New York 1999. 128 pp., 103 color photos, 12 b&w illustrations. $50.00

The George F. Harding Collection of arms and armor is the most visited installation at the Art Institute of Chicago–a testament to the enduring appeal of swords, muskets and the other paraphernalia of medieval and early modern war. Organized both chronologically and by type of weapon, this book captures the best of this astonishing collection in 115 striking photographs-most in color–accompanied by illuminating text.

Arms Makers of Western Pennsylvania, by James B. Whisker, Old Bedford Village Press. 1st edition. Deluxe hardbound edition, 176 pp., $50.00

Printed on fine coated paper with many large photographs and detailed text describing the period, lives, tools, and artistry of the Arms Makers of Western Pennsylvania.

Arsenal of Freedom: The Springfield Armory 1890-1948, by Lt. Col. William Brophy, Andrew Mowbray, Inc., Lincoln, RI,1997. 20 pgs. of photos. 400 pp. As new, Softcover. $29.95

A year-by-year account drawn from offical records. Reports, charts, tables and line drawings.

Art of Remington Arms, by Tom Davis, Sporting Classics, 2004, 1st edition. Large format book, featuring 200 paintings by Remington Arms over the years on it's calendars, posters, shell boxes, etc. 50 full-color by Bob Kuhn alone. Hardcover. NEW $54.95

Astra Automatic Pistols, by Leonardo M. Antaris, FIRAC Publishing Co., Sterling, CO, 1989. 248 pp., illus. $55.00

Charts, tables, serial ranges, etc. The definitive work on Astra pistols.

Ballard: The Great American Single Shot Rifle, by John T. Dutcher. Denver, CO, privately printed, 2002. 1st edition. 380 pp., illustrated with b&w photos, with 8 page color insert. Hardcover. New in new dust jacket. $79.95

Basic Documents on U.S. Martial Arms, commentary by Col. B.R. Lewis, reissue by Ray Riling, Phila., PA, 1956 and 1960. Rifle Musket Model 1855. Each $10.00

The first issue rifle of musket caliber, a muzzleloader equipped with the Maynard Primer, 32 pp. Rifle Musket Model 1863. The typical Union muzzleloader of the Civil War, 26 pp. Breech-Loading Rifle Musket Model 1866. The first of our 50-caliber breechloading rifles, 12 pp. Remington Navy Rifle Model 1870. A commercial type breech-loader made at Springfield, 16 pp. Lee Straight Pull Navy Rifle Model 1895. A magazine cartridge arm of 6mm caliber, 23 pp. Breech-Loading Arms (five models) 27 pp. Ward-Burton Rifle Musket 1871, 16 pp.

Battle Colors: Insignia and Aircraft Markings of the Eighth Air Force in World War II, by Robert A. Watkins, Atglen, PA, Schiffer Publications, 2004. Hardcover. $45.00

This book is an invaluable tool for anyone with an interest in the history of the U.S. Eighth Air Force in World War II. 128 pages, with over 500 color illustrations.

Battle Colors: Insignia and Aircraft Markings of the Eighth Air Force in World War II, Vol. 2, by Robert A. Watkins, Atglen, PA, Schiffer Publications, 2006. $45.00

This work includes diagrams showing approved specifications for the size and placement of all versions of the U.S. insignia as applied to USAAF P-38, P-47 and P-51 fighter aircraft. Also included are all unit airfield location maps and order-of-battle charts for all combat air elements assigned to the 8th AAF from June 1942 through June 1945. 144 pages, with over 600 color profiles, insignia, photographs, and maps. Hardcover

Battle Weapons of the American Revolution, by George C. Neuman, Scurlock Publishing Co., Texarkana, TX, 2001. 400 pp. Illus. Softcovers. $44.95

The most extensive photographic collection of Revolutionary War weapons ever in one volume. More than 1,600 photos of over 500 muskets, rifles, swords, bayonets, knives and other arms used by both sides in America's War for Independence.

Bedford County Rifle and Its Makers, by Calvin Hetrick, Introduction by George Shumway, George Shumway Pub., 1975. 40 pp. illus. Softcover. $10.00

The author's study of the graceful and distinctive muzzle-loading rifles made in Bedford County, Pennsylvania, stands as a milestone on the long path to the understanding of America's longrifles.

Belgian Rattlesnake; The Lewis Automatic Machine Gun, by William M. Easterly, Collector Grade Publications, Cobourg, Ontario, Canada, 1998. 584 pp., illus. $79.95

The most complete account ever published on the life and times of Colonel Isaac Newton Lewis and his crowning invention, the Lewis Automatic machine gun.

Best of Holland & Holland, England's Premier Gunmaker, by Michael McIntosh and Jan G. Roosenburg. Safari Press, Inc., Long Beach, CA, 2002. 1st edition. 298 pp. Profuse color illustrations. $69.95

Holland & Holland has had a long history of not only building London's "best" guns but also providing superior guns–the ultimate gun in finish, engraving, and embellishment.

Big Guns, Civil War Siege, Seacoast, and Naval Cannon, by Edwin Olmstead, Wayne E. Stark, and Spencer C. Tucker, Museum Restoration Service, Bloomfield, Ontario, Canada, 1997. 360 pp., illus. $80.00

This book is designed to identify and record the heavy guns available to both sides by the end of the Civil War.

Blue Book of Air Guns, 6th Edition, edited by S.P. Fjestad, Blue Book Publications, Inc. Minneapolis, MN 2007. $29.95

It contains most of the popular 2007 and vintage makes and models with detailed descriptions and up-to-date pricing! There are also hundreds of b&w images, and the Color Photo Grading System™ allows readers to stop guessing at airgun condition factors.

Blue Book of Gun Values, 28th Edition, edited by S.P. Fjestad, Blue Book Publications, Inc. Minneapolis, MN 2007. $39.95

This new edition simply contains more firearm values and information than any other single publication. Expanded to 2,080 pages featuring over 100,000 firearms prices, up-to-date pricing and information on thousands of firearms, including new 2007 makes/models. Completely revised 80 page color Photo Percentage Grading System.

Blue Book of Modern Black Powder Values, 4th Edtion, by Dennis Adler, Blue Book Publications, Inc. Minneapolis, MN 2005. 271 pp., illus. 41 color photos. $24.95

This new title contains more up-to-date blackpowder values and related information than any other single publication and will keep you up-to-date on modern blackpowder models and prices, including most makes and models introduced by 2005!

Blunderbuss 1500-1900, The, by James D. Forman, Historical Arms Series No. 32. Canada, Museum Restoration, 1994. 40 pp., illus. Softcover. $8.95

An excellent and authoritative booklet giving tons of information on the Blunderbuss, a very neglected subject.

Boarders Away Volume I: With Steel-Edged Weapons & Polearms, by William Gilkerson, Andrew Mowbray, Inc. Publishers, Lincoln, RI, 1993. 331 pp. $48.00

Contains the essential 24-page chapter "War at Sea" which sets the historical and practical context for the arms discussed. Includes chapters on Early Naval Weapons, Boarding Axes, Cutlasses, Officers Fighting Swords and Dirks, and weapons at hand of Random Mayhem.

Boarders Away, Volume II: Firearms of the Age of Fighting Sail, by William Gilkerson, Andrew Mowbray, Inc. Publishers, Lincoln, RI, 1993. 331 pp., illus. $65.00

Covers the pistols, muskets, combustibles and small cannons used aboard American and European fighting ships, 1626-1826.

Boston's Gun Bible, by Boston T. Party, Ignacio, CO, Javelin Press, August 2000. Expanded edition. Softcover. $28.00

This mammoth guide for gun owners everywhere is a completely updated and expanded edition (more than 500 new pages!) of Boston T. Party's classic Boston on Guns and Courage. Boston gives new advice on which shoulder weapons and handguns to buy and why, before exploring such topics as why you should consider not getting a concealed carry permit, what guns and gear will likely be outlawed next and much more.

Bren Gun Saga, by Thomas B. Dugelby, Collector Grade Publications, Cobourg, Ontario, Canada, 1999, revised and expanded edition. 406 pp., illus. $65.95

A modern, definitive book on the Bren in this revised expanded edition, which in terms of numbers of pages and illustrations is nearly twice the size of the original.

British Board of Ordnance Small Arms Contractors 1689-1840, by De Witt Bailey, Rhyl, England, W. S. Curtis, 2000. 150 pp. $18.00

Thirty years of research in the Archives of the Ordnance Board in London has identified more than 600 of these suppliers. The names of many can be found marking the regulation firearms of the period. In the study, the contractors are identified both alphabetically and under a combination of their date period together with their specialist trade.

British Enfield Rifles, Volume 1, The SMLE MK I and MK III Rifles, by Charles R. Stratton, North Cape Pub., Tustin, CA, 1997. 150 pp., illus. Paper covers. $16.95

A systematic and thorough examination on a part-by-part basis of the famous British battle rifle that endured for nearly 70 years as the British Army's number one battle rifle.

British Enfield Rifles, Volume 2, No. 4 and No. 5 Rifles, by Charles R. Stratton, North Cape Publications, Tustin, CA, 1999. 150 pp., illus. Paper covers. $16.95

The historical background for the development of both rifles describing each variation and an explanation of all the marks, numbers and codes found on most parts.

British Enfield Rifles, Volume 4, The Pattern 1914 and U. S. Model 1917 Rifles, by Charles R. Stratton, North Cape Publications, Tustin, CA, 2000. Paper covers. $16.95

One of the least known American and British collectible military rifles is analyzed on a part by part basis. All markings and codes, refurbishment procedures and WWII upgrade are included as are the various sniper rifle versions.

British Falling Block Breechloading Rifle from 1865, by Jonathan Kirton, Tom Rowe Books, Maynardsville, TN, 2nd edition, 1997. 380 pp., illus. $70.00

Expanded edition of a comprehensive work on the British falling block rifle.

British Gun Engraving, by Douglas Tate, Safari Press, Inc., Huntington Beach, CA, 1999. 240 pp., illus. Limited, signed and numbered edition, in a slipcase. $80.00

A historic and photographic record of the last two centuries.

British Gunmakers: Volume One – London, by Nigel Brown, London, Quiller, 2004. 280 pp., 33 colour, 43 b&w photographs, line drawings. Hardcover. $99.95

British Gunmakers: Volume Two-Birmingham, Scotland, And the Regions, by Nigel Brown, London, Quiller, 2005. 1st edition. 439pp, hardcover. $99.95

With this book, read in conjunction with Volume One, the reader or scholar should be able to trace the history and likely age of any shotgun or rifle made in this region since 1800.

British Military Flintlock Rifles 1740-1840, With a Remarkable Wealth of Data about the Riflemen and Regiments that Carried These Weapons, by De Witt Bailey, Andrew Mowbray, Inc. Lincoln, RI, 2002. 1st edition. 264 pp. with over 320 photographs. Hardcover. $47.95

Pattern 1776 Rifles, the Ferguson Breechloader, the famous Baker Rifle, rifles of the Hessians and other German Mercenaries, American Loyalist rifles, rifles given to Indians, Cavalry rifles and rifled carbines, bayonets, accoutrements, ammunition and more.

British Service Rifles and Carbines 1888-1900, by Alan M. Petrillo, Excaliber Publications, Latham, NY, 1994. 72 pp., illus, Paper covers. $11.95

A complete review of the Lee-Metford and Lee-Enfield rifles and carbines.

British Single Shot Rifles, Volume 1, Alexander Henry, by Wal Winfer, Tom Rowe, Maynardsville, TN, 1998, 200 pp., illus. $50.00

Detailed study of the single shot rifles made by Henry. Illustrated with hundreds of photographs and drawings.

British Single Shot Rifles, Volume 3, Jeffery, by Wal Winfer, Rowe Publications, Rochester, N.Y., 1999. 260 pp., illus. $60.00

The Farquharsen as made by Jeffery and his competitors, Holland & Holland, Bland, Westley, Manton. Large section on the development of nitro cartridges including the 600.

British Single Shot Rifles, Volume 4; Westley Richards, by Wal Winfer, Rowe Publications, Rochester, N.Y., 2000. 265 pp., illus., photos. $60.00

In this 4th volume, Winfer covers a detailed study of the Westley Richards single shot rifles, including Monkey Tails, Improved Martini, 1872,1873, 1878,1881, 1897 Falling Blocks. He also covers Westley Richards cartridges, history and reloading information.

British Single Shot Rifles, Volume 5; Holland & Holland, by Winfer, Wal, Rochester, NY: Rowe Publications, 2004. 1st edition. ISBN: 097076085X. 218 pages. Hardcover. New in new dust jacket. (12063)

Volume 5 of the never ending study of the British single shot. One of the rarest and finest quality single shots made by any British firm is described. A large section is devoted to the cartridge developments carried on by Hollands with a large section on their Paradox cartridges.

Broad Arrow: British & Empire Factory Production, Proof, Inspection, Armourers, Unit & Issue Markings, by Ian Skennerton. Australia, Arms & Militaria Press, 2001. 140 pp., circa 80 illus. Stiff paper covers. $29.95

Thousands of service markings are illustrated and their applications described. Invaluable reference on units, also ideal for medal collectors.

Browning Dates of Manufacture, compiled by George Madis, Art and Reference House, Brownsboro, TX, 1989. 48 pp. $8.00

Gives the date codes and product codes for all models from 1824 to the present.

Browning Sporting Firearms: Dates of Manufacture, by D. R. Morse. Phoenix, AZ, Firing Pin Enterprizes, 2003. 37 pp. Softcover. New. $6.95

Covers their pistols, revolvers, rifles, shotguns and commemoratives, plus, models and serial numbers.

Browning Machine Gun Volume 1-Rifle Caliber Brownings in U.S. Service, by Dolf Goldsmith, Canada: Collector Grade Publications, 2005. 1st Edition, 552 pages, 568 illustrations. Hardcover. $79.95

This profusely illustrated history covers all models of the U.S. Browning, from the first "gas hammer" Model 1895 and the initial recoil-operated Models of 1901 and 1910, through the adoption and manufacture of the famous water-cooled heavy Model 1917 during World War I and the numerous Interwar experimental tank and aircraft guns, most of which were built up on surplus M1917 receivers.

Browning Machine Gun Volume 2-Rifle Caliber Brownings Abroad, by Dolf Goldsmith, Canada: Collector Grade Publications, 2006. 1st Edition, 392 pages, with over 486 illustrations. Hardcover, $69.95

This second volume of Dolf Goldsmith's series on Browning machine guns proves beyond doubt that the rifle-caliber Browning was simply the most popular and most-used machine gun ever designed. In some ways this book is even more engrossing than Volume I, as it describes and illustrates in considerable detail the many variations on the basic Browning which were manufactured and/or used by over twenty countries, in virtually every corner of the world, in both World Wars, in Korea and in Vietnam.

Browning–Sporting Arms of Distinction 1903-1992, by Matt Eastman, Long Beach, CA, Safari Press, 2004. 428 pp., profuse illus. Hardcover. $50.00

Bullard Firearms, by G. Scott Jamieson, Schiffer Publications, Atglen, PA 2002. 400 pp., with over 1100 color and b&w photos, charts, diagrams. Hardcover. $100.00

Bullard Firearms is the story of a mechanical genius whose rifles and cartridges were the equal of any made in America in the 1880s, yet little of substance had been written about James H. Bullard or his arms prior to 1988 when the first edition, called *Bullard Arms*, was published. This greatly expanded volume, with over 1,000 b&w and 150 color plates, most not previously published, answers many of the questions posed in the first edition. The final chapter outlines, in chart form, almost 500 Bullard rifles by serial number, caliber and type. Quick and easy to use, this book is a real benefit for collectors and dealers alike.

Burning Powder, compiled by Major D.B. Wesson, Wolfe Publishing Company, Prescott, AZ, 1992. 110 pp. Soft cover. $10.95

A rare booklet from 1932 for Smith & Wesson collectors.

Burnside Breech Loading Carbines, The, by Edward A. Hull, Andrew Mowbray, Inc., Lincoln, RI, 1986. 95 pp., illus. $16.00

No. 1 in the "Man at Arms Monograph Series." A model-by-model historical/technical examination of one of the most widely used cavalry weapons of the American Civil War based upon important and previously unpublished research.

C.S. Armory Richmond: History of the Confederate States Armory, Richmond, VA and the Stock Shop at the C.S. Armory, Macon, GA., by Paul Davies, privately printed, 2000. 368 pp., illustrated with b&w photos. Hardcover. $75.00

The American Society of Arms Collectors is pleased to recommend C.S. Armory Richmond as a useful and valuable reference for collectors and scholars in the field of antique firearms. Gives fantastic explanations of machinery, stocks, barrels, and every facet of the production process during the timeframe covered in this book.

Cacciare A Palla: Uso E Tecnologia Dell'arma Rigata, by Marco E. Nobili, Italy, Il Volo Srl, 1994. 4th Edition-1st printing. 397 pp., illustrated with b&w photographs. Hardcover. New in new dust jacket. $75.00

Call of Duty; Military Awards and Decorations of the United States of America, by John E. Strandberg, LTC and Roger James Bender, San Jose, CA, R. James Bender Publishing, 2005. (New expanded edition). 559 pp. illustrated with 1,293 photos (most in color). Hardcover. $67.95

Camouflage Uniforms of European and NATO Armies; 1945 to the Present, by J. F. Borsarello, Atglen, PA, Schiffer Publications. Over 290 color and b&w photographs, 120 pp. Softcover. $29.95

This full-color book covers nearly all of the NATO, and other European armies' camouflaged uniforms, and not only shows and explains the many patterns, but also their efficacy of design. Described and illustrated are the variety of materials tested in over 40 different armies, and includes the history of obsolete trial tests from 1945 to the present time. This book provides a superb reference for the historian, reenactor, designer, and modeler.

Camouflage Uniforms of the Waffen-SS A Photographic Reference, by Michael Beaver, Schiffer Publishing, Atglen, PA. Over 1,000 color and b&w photographs and illustrations, 296 pp. $69.95

Finally a book that unveils the shroud of mystery surrounding Waffen-SS camouflage clothing. Illustrated here, both in full color and in contemporary b&w photographs, this unparalleled look at Waffen-SS combat troops and their camouflage clothing will benefit both the historian and collector.

Canadian Colts for the Boer War, by Col. Robert D. Whittington III. Hooks, TX, Brownlee Books, 2003. A limited edition of 1,000 copies. Numbered. 5 pp. Paper covers. New. $15.00

A study of Colt Revolvers issued to the First and Second Canadian Contingents Special Service Force.

Canadian Colts for the Boer War, Part 2, Col. Robert D. by Whittington III, Hooks, TX, Brownlee Books, 2005. A limited edition of 1,000 copies. Numbered. 5 pp. Paper covers, $5.00

Canadian Gunsmiths from 1608: A Checklist of Tradesmen, by John Belton, Historical Arms Series No. 29. Canada, Museum Restoration, 1992. 40 pp., 17 illustrations. Softcover. $8.95

This checklist is a greatly expanded version of HAS No. 14, listing the names, occupation, location, and dates of more than 1,500 men and women who worked as gunmakers, gunsmiths, armorers, gun merchants, gun patent holders, and a few other gun related trades.

Canadian Militaria Directory & Sourcebook Second Edition, by Clive M. Law, Ont. Canada, Service Publications, 1998. pp. 90. Softcover. $14.95

Cap Guns, by James Dundas, Schiffer Publishing, Atglen, PA, 1996. 160 pp., illus. Paper covers. $29.95

Over 600 full-color photos of cap guns and gun accessories with a current value guide.

Carbines of the Civil War, by John D. McAulay, Pioneer Press, Union City, TN, 1981. 123 pp., illus. Paper covers. $12.95

A guide for the student and collector of the colorful arms used by the Federal cavalry.

Carbines of the U.S. Cavalry 1861-1905, by John D. McAulay, Andrew Mowbray Publishers, Lincoln, RI, 1996. $35.00

Covers the crucial use of carbines from the beginning of the Civil War to the end of the cavalry carbine era in 1905.

Cartridge Carbines of the British Army, by Alan M. Petrillo, Excalibur Publications, Latham, NY, 1998. 72 pp., illus. Paper covers. $11.95

Begins with the Snider-Enfield which was the first regulation cartridge carbine introduced in 1866 and ends with the 303 caliber No.5, Mark 1 Enfield.

Cartridges for Collectors, by Fred Datig, Pioneer Press, Union City, TN, 1999. Three volumes of 176 pp. each. Vol. 1 (Centerfire); Vol. 2 (Rimfire and Misc.) types. Volume 1, softcover only, $19.95. Volumes 2 and 3, hardcover. $19.95

Vol. 3 (Additional Rimfire, Centerfire, and Plastic). All illustrations are shown in full-scale drawings.

Civil War Arms Makers and Their Contracts, edited by Stuart C. Mowbray and Jennifer Heroux, Andrew Mowbray Publishing, Lincoln, RI, 1998. 595 pp. $39.50

A facsimile reprint of the Report by the Commissioner of Ordnance and Ordnance Stores, 1862.

Civil War Arms Purchases and Deliveries, edited by Stuart C. Mowbray, Andrew Mowbray Publishing, Lincoln, RI, 1998. 300pp., illus. $39.50

A facsimile reprint of the master list of Civil War weapons purchases and deliveries including Small Arms, Cannon, Ordnance and Projectiles.

Civil War Cartridge Boxes of the Union Infantryman, by Paul Johnson, Andrew Mowbray, Inc., Lincoln, RI, 1998. 352 pp., illus. $45.00

There were four patterns of infantry cartridge boxes used by Union forces during the Civil War. The author describes the development and subsequent pattern changes to these cartridge boxes. All updated prices, scores of new listings, and hundreds of new pictures! It's the one reference work no collector should be without. An absolute must.

Civil War Collector's Price Guide; 11th Edition, Orange, VA, Publisher's Press, 2006. 300 pps., softbound, heavily illustrated, full color cover. $37.95

Our newly released 11th edition of the popular Civil War Collector's Price Guide! Expanded to include new images and new listings.

ARMS LIBRARY

Civil War Commanders, by Dean Thomas, Thomas Publications, Gettysburg, PA. 1998. 72 pp., illus., photos. Paper covers. $9.95

138 photographs and capsule biographies of Union and Confederate officers. A convenient personalities reference guide.

Civil War Heavy Explosive Ordnance: A Guide to Large Artillery Projectiles, Torpedoes, and Mines, by Jack Bell, Denton, TX, University of North Texas Press, 2003. 1,016 b&w photos. 537 pp. Hardcover. New in new dust jacket. $50.00

Civil War Infantryman: In Camp, on the March, and in Battle, by Dean Thomas, Thomas Publications, Gettysburg, PA. 1998. 72 pp., illus. Softcovers. $12.95

Uses first-hand accounts to shed some light on the "common soldier" of the Civil War from enlistment to muster-out, including camp, marching, rations, equipment, fighting, and more.

Civil War Pistols, by John D. McAulay, Andrew Mowbray Inc., Lincoln, RI, 1992. 166 pp., illus. $38.50

A survey of the handguns used during the American Civil War.

Civil War Relic Hunting A to Z, by Robert Buttafuso, Sheridan Books, 2000. 1st edition. illus., 91 pp., b&w illustrations. Softcover. $21.95

Civil War Sharps Carbines and Rifles, by Earl J. Coates and John D. McAulay, Thomas Publications, Gettysburg, PA, 1996. 108 pp., illus. Paper covers. $12.95

Traces the history and development of the firearms including short histories of specific serial numbers and the soldiers who received them.

Civil War Small Arms of the U.S. Navy and Marine Corps, by John D. McAulay, Mowbray Publishing, Lincoln, RI, 1999. 186 pp., illus. $39.00

The first reliable and comprehensive guide to the firearms and edged weapons of the Civil War Navy and Marine Corps.

Collecting Military Headgear; A Guide to 5000 Years of Helmet History, by Robert Atglen Attard, PA, Schiffer Publications, 2004. 1st edition. Hardcover. New in new dust jacket. $69.95

Collecting Third Reich Recordings, by Stuart McKenzie, San Jose, CA, R. James Bender Publishing, 2001. 1st edition. Softcover. $29.95

Collector's Illustrated Encyclopedia of the American Revolution, by George C. Neumann and Frank J. Kravic, Rebel Publishing Co., Inc., Texarkana, TX, 1989. 286 pp., illus. $42.95

A showcase of more than 2,300 artifacts made, worn, and used by those who fought in the War for Independence.

Colonel Thomas Claiborne Jr. and the Colt Whitneyville-Walker Pistol, by Col. Robert D. Whittington III, Hooks, TX, Brownlee Books, 2005. A limited edition of 1,000 copies. Numbered. 8 pp. Paper covers. $7.50

Colonels in Blue: Union Army Colonels of the Civil War, by Roger Hunt, New York, Atglen, PA, Schiffer Publications, 2003. 1st edition. 288 pp., with over 640 b&w photographs. Hardcover. New in new dust jacket. $59.95

Colonial Frontier Guns, by T.M. Hamilton, Pioneer Press, Union City, TN, 1988. 176 pp., illus. Paper covers. $17.50

A complete study of early flint muskets of this country.

Colt 1909 Military Revolvers; The 1904 Thompson-Lagarde Report, and General John J. Pershing, by Col. Robert D. Whittington III. Hooks, TX, Brownlee Books, 2003. A limited edition of 1,000 copies. Numbered. 10 pp. Paper covers. New. $10.00

The 1904 Thompson-Lagarde Report, and General John J. Pershing.

Colt and Its Collectors Exhibition Catalog for Colt: The Legacy of A Legend, Buffalo Bill Historical Center, Cody, Wyoming. Colt Collectors Association, 2003. 1st edition. Hardcover. New in new dust jacket. $125.00

Colt and Its Collectors accompanies the upcoming special exhibition, Colt: The Legacy of a Legend, opening at the Buffalo Bill Historical Center in May 2003. Numerous essays, over 750 color photographs by Paul Goodwin.

Colt Armory, by Ellsworth Grant, Man-at-Arms Bookshelf, Lincoln, RI, 1996. 232 pp., illus. $35.00

A history of Colt's Manufacturing Company.

Colt Engraving Book, Volumes I & II, by R. L. Wilson. Privately printed, 2001. Each volume is appx. 500 pp., with 650 illustrations, most in color. $390.00

This third edition from the original texts of 1974 and 1982 has been fine-tuned and dramatically expanded, and is by far the most illuminating and complete. With over 1,200 illustrations, more than 2/3 of which are in color, this book joins the author's The Book of Colt Firearms, and Fine Colts as companion volumes. Approximately 1,000 pages in two volumes, each signed by the author, serial numbered, and strictly limited to 3000 copies. Volume I covers from the Paterson and pre-Paterson period through c.1921 (end of the Helfricht period). Volume II commences with Kornbrath, and Glahn, and covers Colt embellished arms from c.1919 through 2000.

Colt Model 1905 Automatic Pistol, by John Potocki, Andrew Mowbray Publishing, Lincoln, RI, 1998. 191 pp., illus. $28.00

Covers all aspects of the Colt Model 1905 Automatic Pistol, from its invention by the legendary John Browning to its numerous production variations.

Colt Peacemaker British Model, by Keith Cochran, Cochran Publishing Co., Rapid City, SD, 1989. 160 pp., illus. $35.00

Covers those revolvers Colt squeezed in while completing a large order of revolvers for the U.S. Cavalry in early 1874, to those magnificent cased target revolvers used in the pistol competitions at Bisley Commons in the 1890s.

Colt Peacemaker Encyclopedia, by Keith Cochran, Cochran Publishing Co., Rapid City, SD, 1986. 434 pp., illus. $60.00

A must-have book for the Peacemaker collector.

Colt Peacemaker Encyclopedia, Volume 2, by Keith Cochran, Cochran Publishing Co., SD, 1992. 416 pp., illus. $60.00

Included in this volume are extensive notes on engraved, inscribed, historical and noted revolvers, as well as those revolvers used by outlaws, lawmen, movie and television stars.

Colt Pistols, Texas, And The U.S. Army 1847-1861, by Col. Robert D. Whittington III. Hooks, TX, Brownlee Books, 2003. A limited edition of 1,000 copies. Numbered. 8 pp. Paper covers. New. $7.50

A study of the Colt pistols used in Texas by the U.S. Army between 1847-1861. A remarkable detailed report.

Colt Presentations: From the Factory Ledgers 1856-1869, by Herbert G. Houze. Lincoln, RI, Andrew Mowbray, Inc., 2003. 112 pp., 45 b&w photos. Softcover. $21.95

Samuel Colt was a generous man. He also used gifts to influence government decision makers. But after Congress investigated him in 1854, Colt needed to hide the gifts from prying eyes, which makes it very difficult for today's collectors to document the many revolvers presented by Colt and the factory. Using the original account journals of the Colt's Patent Fire Arms Manufacturing Co., renowned arms authority Herbert G. Houze finally gives us the full details behind hundreds of the most exciting Colts ever made.

Colt Single Action Army Revolver Study: New Discoveries, by Kenneth Moore, Lincoln, RI, Andrew Mowbray, Inc., 2003. 1st edition. 200 pp., with 77 photos and illustrations. Hardcover. New. $49.95

Twenty-five years after co-authoring the classic Study of the Colt Single Action Army Revolver, Ken fills in the gaps and sets the record straight. The serial number data alone will astound you. Includes, ejector models, special section on low serial numbers, U.S. Army testing data, new details about militia S.A.A.'s plus a true wealth of cartridge info.

Colt Single Action Army Revolvers: The Legend, the Romance and the Rivals, by "Doc" O'Meara, Krause Publications, Iola, WI, 2000. 160 pp., illustrated with 250 photos in b&w and a 16-page color section. $22.95

Production figures, serial numbers by year, and rarities.

Colt Single Action Army Revolvers and Alterations, by C. Kenneth Moore, Mowbray Publishers, Lincoln, RI, 1999. 112 pp., illus. $35.00

A comprehensive history of the revolvers that collectors call "Artillery Models." These are the most historical of all S.A.A. Colts, and this new book covers all the details.

Colt Single Action Army Revolvers and the London Agency, by C. Kenneth Moore, Andrew Mowbray Publishers, Lincoln, RI, 1990. 144 pp., illus. $35.00

Drawing on vast documentary sources, this work chronicles the relationship between the London Agency and the Hartford home office.

Colt Sporting Firearms: Dates of Manufacture, by D.R. Morse, Phoenix, AZ, Firing Pin Enterprizes, 2003. 82 pp. Softcover. New. $6.95

Covers their pistols, revolvers, rifles, shotguns and commemoratives, plus models and serial numbers.

Colt U.S. General Officers' Pistols, by Horace Greeley IV, Andrew Mowbray Inc., Lincoln, RI, 1990. 199 pp., illus. $38.00

These unique weapons, issued as a badge of rank to General Officers in the U.S. Army from WWII onward, remain highly personal artifacts of the military leaders who carried them. Includes serial numbers and dates of issue.

Colt Walker's, Walkers Controversy is Solved, by Col. Robert D. Whittington III. Hooks, TX, Brownlee Books, 2005. A limited edition of 1,000 copies. Numbered. 17 pp. Paper covers. New. $15.00

The truth about serial numbers on the Colt Whitneyville-Walker Pistols presented to Captain Samuel Hamilton Walker by Sam Colt and J. B. Colt on July 28th, 1847.

Colts from the William M. Locke Collection, by Frank Sellers, Andrew Mowbray Publishers, Lincoln, RI, 1996. 192 pp., illus. $55.00

This important book illustrates all of the famous Locke Colts, with captions by arms authority Frank Sellers.

Colt's Dates of Manufacture 1837-1978, by R.L. Wilson, published by Maurie Albert, Coburg, Australia; N.A. distributor Madis Books, TX, 1997. 61 pp. $8.50

An invaluable pocket guide to the dates of manufacture of Colt firearms up to 1978.

Colt's Pocket '49: Its Evolution Including the Baby Dragoon and Wells Fargo, by Robert Jordan and Darrow Watt, privately printed, Loma Mar, CA 2000. 304 pp., with 984 color photos, illus. Beautifully bound in a deep blue leather-like case. $125.00

Detailed information on all models and covers engaving, cases, accoutrements, holsters, fakes, and much more. Included is a summary booklet containing information such as serial numbers, production ranges and identifing photos. This book is a masterpiece on its subject.

Colt's SAA Post War Models, by George Garton, The Gun Room Press, Highland Park, NJ, 1995. 166 pp., illus. $39.95

Complete facts on the post-war Single Action Army revolvers. Information on calibers, production numbers and variations taken from factory records.

Combat Helmets of the Third Reich: A Study in Photographs, by Thomas Kibler, Pottsboro, TX, Reddick Enterprises, 2003. 1st edition. 96 pp., illustrated in full color. Pictorial softcover. $19.95

Combat Perspective The Thinking Man's Guide to Self-Defense, by Gabriel Suarez, Boulder, CO, Paladin Press, 2003. 1st edition. 112 pp. Softcover. $15.00

Complete Guide to United States Military Medals 1939 to Present, 6th Edition, by Colonel Frank C. Foster, Medals of America Press, Fountain Inn, SC, 2006. 168 pp., illus., photos. $29.95

Complete criteria for every Army, Navy, Marine, Air Force, Coast Guard, and Merchant Marine award since 1939. All decorations, service medals, and ribbons shown in full color and accompanied by dates and campaigns, as well as detailed descriptions on proper wear and display.

Complete Guide to the M1 Garand and the M1 Carbine, by Bruce N. Canfield, 2nd printing, Andrew Mowbray Inc., Lincoln, RI, 1999. 296 pp., illus. $39.50

Expanded and updated coverage of both the M1 Garand and the M1 Carbine, with more than twice as much information as the author's previous book on this topic.

Complete Guide to U.S. Infantry Weapons of the First War, by Bruce Canfield, Andrew Mowbray, Publisher, Lincoln, RI, 2000. 304 pp., illus. $39.95

The definitive study of the U.S. Infantry weapons used in WWI.

Complete Guide to U.S. Infantry Weapons of World War Two, by Bruce Canfield, Andrew Mowbray, Publisher, Lincoln, RI, 1995. 303 pp., illus. $39.95

A definitive work on the weapons used by the United States Armed Forces in WWII.

Confederate Belt Buckles & Plates, by Steve E. Mullinax, O'Donnell Publishing, Alexandria, VA, 1999. Expanded edition. 247 pp., illus. Hardcover. $34.00

Hundreds of crisp photographs augment this classic study of Confederate accoutrement plates.

Confederate Carbines & Musketoons Cavalry Small Arms Manufactured in and for the Southern Confederacy 1861-1865, by John M. Murphy, Santa Ana, CA, privately printed, 2002. Reprint. Hardcover. New in new dust jacket. $79.95

Confederate Rifles & Muskets: Infantry Small Arms Manufactured in the Southern Confederacy 1861-1865, by John M. Murphy. Santa Ana, CA, privately printed, 1996. Reprint. 768 pp., 8 pp. color plates, profusely illustrated. Hardcover. $119.95

ARMS LIBRARY

The first in-depth and academic analysis and discussion of the "long" longarms produced in the South by and for the Confederacy during the American Civil War. The collection of Dr. Murphy is doubtless the largest and finest grouping of Confederate longarms in private hands today.

Confederate Saddles & Horse Equipment, by Ken R. Knopp, Orange, VA, Publisher's Press, 2002. 194 pps., illus. Hardcover. $39.95

A pioneer work on the subject. After 10 years of research Ken Knopp has compiled a thorough and fascinating study of the little-known field of Confederate saddlery and equipment. An indispensable source for collectors and historians.

Cooey Firearms, Made in Canada 1919-1979, by John A. Belton, Museum Restoration, Canada, 1998. 36pp., with 46 illus. Paper covers. $8.95

More than 6 million rifles and at least 67 models were made by this small Canadian riflemaker. They have been identified from the first 'Cooey Canuck' through the last variations made by the 'Winchester-Cooey'. Each is descibed and most are illustrated in this first book on the Cooey.

Cowboy and Gunfighter Collectible, by Bill Mackin, Mountain Press Publishing Co., Missoula, MT, 1995. 178 pp., illus. Paper covers. $25.00

A photographic encyclopedia with price guide and makers' index.

Cowboy Collectibles and Western Memorabilia, by Bob Bell and Edward Vebell, Schiffer Publishing, Atglen, PA, 1992. 160 pp., illus. Paper covers. $29.95

The exciting era of the cowboy and the wild west collectibles including rifles, pistols, gun rigs, etc.

Cowboy Culture: The Last Frontier of American Antiques, by Michael Friedman, Schiffer Publishing, Ltd., West Chester, PA, 2002. 300 pp., illus. $89.95

Covers the artful aspects of the old west, the antiques and collectibles. Illustrated with clear color plates of over 1,000 items such as spurs, boots, guns, saddles, etc.

Cowboys and the Trappings of the Old West, by William Manns and Elizabeth Clair Flood, Zon International Publishing Co., Santa Fe, NM, 1997, 1st edition. 224 pp., illus. $45.00

A pictorial celebration of the cowboy dress and trappings.

Custom Firearms Engraving, by Tom Turpin, Krause Publications, Iola, WI, 1999. 208 pp., illus. $49.95

Over 200 four-color photos with more than 75 master engravers profiled. Engravers directory with addresses in the U.S. and abroad.

Daisy Air Rifles & BB Guns: The First 100 Years, by Neal Punchard. St. Paul, MN, Motorbooks, 2002. 1st edition. 10" x 10", 156 pp., 300 color. Hardcover. $29.95

Flash back to the days of your youth and recall fond memories of your Daisy. Daisy Air Rifles and BB Guns looks back fondly on the first 100 years of Daisy BB rifles and pistols, toy and cork guns, accessories, packaging, period advertising and literature.

Death From Above: The German FG42 Paratrooper Rifle, New Expanded Edition, by Blake Stevens, Collector Grade Publications, Canada, 2007. 228 pages, 278 illustrations. $59.95

This book depicts and describes seven basic models of the FG42, from the earliest prototype (the Type 'A') through the first or 'early' production series (the Type 'E') with its distinctively swept-back handgrip and intricately machined receiver, then the initial Rheinmetall redesign utilizing a stamped receiver (the Type 'F'), followed by the ultimate if extremely short-lived final series production model, the Type 'G'. Amazingly, virtually none of the Type 'G' components will interchange with their lookalike Type 'F' counterparts. This includes magazines.

Decorations, Medals, Ribbons, Badges and Insignia of the United States Navy; World War II to Present, by James G. Thompson, Medals of America Press, Fountain Inn, SC. 2005. 124 pp., illus. $29.95

The most complete guide to United States Army medals, ribbons, rank, insignia and patches from WWII to the present day. Each medal and insignia shown in full color. Includes listing of respective criteria and campaigns.

Defending the Dominion, Canadian Military Rifles, 1855-1955, by David Edgecombe. Service Publications, Ont., Canada, 2003. 168 pp., with 60+ illustrations. Hardcover. $39.95

This book contains much new information on the Canadian acquisition, use and disposal of military rifles during the most significant century in the development of small arms. In addition to the venerable Martini-Henry, there are chapters on the Winchester, Snider, Starr, Spencer, Peabody, Enfield rifles and others.

Derringer in America, Volume 1, The Percussion Period, by R.L. Wilson and L.D. Eberhart, Andrew Mowbray Inc., Lincoln, RI, 1985. 271 pp., illus. $48.00

A long awaited book on the American percussion derringer.

Derringer in America, Volume 2, the Cartridge Period, by L.D. Eberhart and R.L. Wilson, Andrew Mowbray Inc., Publishers, Lincoln, RI, 1993. 284 pp., illus. $65.00

Comprehensive coverage of cartridge derringers organized alphabetically by maker. Includes all types of derringers known by the authors to have been offered in the American market.

Devil's Paintbrush: Sir Hiram Maxim's Gun, by Dolf Goldsmith, 3rd Edition, expanded and revised, Collector Grade Publications, Toronto, Canada, 2002. 384 pp., illus. $79.95

The classic work on the world's first true automatic machine gun.

Dressed For Duty: America's Women in Uniform, 1898-1973 Volume I, by Jill Halcomb Smith, San Nose, CA, Bender Publishing, 2002. 1st edition. 480 pages-1,089 photos & illustrations (many in color), deluxe binding. Hardcover. $54.95

Dressed For Duty: America's Women in Uniform, 1898-1973 Volume II, by Jill Halcomb Smith, San Nose, CA, Bender Publishing, 2004. 1st edition. 544 pages-1,300 photos & illustrations (many in color), deluxe binding. Hardcover. $59.95

Dr. Josephus Requa Civil War Dentist and the Billinghurst-Requa Volley Gun, by John M. Hyson Jr., and Margaret Requa DeFrancisco, Museum Restoration Service, Bloomfield, Ont., Canada, 1999. 36 pp., illus. Paper covers. $8.95

The story of the inventor of the first practical rapid-fire gun to be used during the American Civil War.

Dutch Luger (Parabellum) A Complete History, by Bas J. Martens and Guus de Vries, Ironside International, Alexandria, VA, 1995. 268 pp., illus. $49.95

The history of the Luger in the Netherlands. An extensive description of the Dutch pistol and trials and the different models of the Luger in the Dutch service.

E.C. Prudhomme's Gun Engraving Review, by E. C. Prudhomme, R&R Books, Livonia, NY, 1994. 164 pp., illus. $60.00

As a source for engravers and collectors, this book is an indispensable guide to styles and techniques of the world's foremost engravers.

Eagle on U.S. Firearms, by John W. Jordan, Pioneer Press, Union City, TN, 1992. 140 pp., illus. Paper covers. $17.50

Stylized eagles have been stamped on government owned or manufactured firearms in the U.S. since the beginning of our country. This book lists and illustrates these various eagles in an informative and refreshing manner.

Emblems of Honor; Patches and Insignia of the U.S. Army from the Great War to the Early Cold War Vol. IV Armor-Cavalry-Tank Destroyer, by Kurt Keller, Constabulary, PA, privately printed, 2005. 1st edition, signed. 232 pp., with over 600 color photos. Hardcover. New in new dust jacket. $59.95

Emma Gees, by Capt. Herbert W. McBride, Mt. Ida, AR, Lancer Publishing, 2003. 224 pp., b&w photos. Softcover. $19.95

Encyclopedia of Rifles & Handguns; A Comprehensive Guide to Firearms, edited by Sean Connolly, Chartwell Books, Inc., Edison, NJ., 1996. 160 pp., illus. $26.00

Encyclopedia of United States Army Insignia and Uniforms, by William Emerson, OK, University of Oklahoma Press, 1996. Hardcover. $134.95

Enemies Foreign and Domestic, by Matthew Bracken, San Diego, CA, Steelcutter Publishing, 2003. Softcover. $19.89

Eprouvettes: A Comprehensive Study of Early Devices for the Testing of Gunpowder, by R.T.W. Kempers, Royal Armouries Museum, Leeds, England, 1999. 352 pp., illustrated with 240 b&w and 28 color plates. $125.00

Equipment of the WWII Tommy, by David Gordon, Missoula, MT, Pictorial Histories Publishing, 2004. 1st edition. Softcover. $24.95

Fifteen Years in the Hawken Lode, by John D. Baird, The Gun Room Press, Highland Park, NJ, 1976. 120 pp., illus. $24.95

A collection of thoughts and observations gained from many years of intensive study of the guns from the shop of the Hawken brothers.

Fighting Colors: The Creation of Military Aircraft Nose Art, by Gary Velasco, Paducah, KY, Turner Publishing, 2005. 1st edition. Hardcover. New in new dust jacket. $57.95

Fighting Iron, by Art Gogan, Andrew Mowbray, Inc., Lincoln, R.I., 2002. 176 pp., illus. $28.00

It doesn't matter whether you collect guns, swords, bayonets or accoutrement–sooner or later you realize that it all comes down to the metal. If you don't understand the metal, you don't understand your collection.

Fine Art of the West, by Byron Price, New York, Abbeville Press, 2004, 2nd revised edition. $75.00

A glossary and bibliography complete this first comprehensive look at one of America's most fascinating forms of artistic expression. 276 pages illustrated with color photos.

Firearm Suppressor Patents; Volume 1: United States Patents, by N.R. Parker, Foreword by Alan C. Paulson, Boulder, CO, Paladin Press, 2004. 392 pp., illus. Softcover. $45.00

Firearms from Europe, 2nd Edition, by David Noe, Larry W. Yantz, Dr. James B. Whisker, Rowe Publications, Rochester, N.Y., 2002. 192 pp., illus. $45.00

A history and description of firearms imported during the American Civil War by the United States of America and the Confederate States of America.

Firearms of the American West 1803-1865, Volume 1, by Louis A. Garavaglia and Charles Worman, University of Colorado Press, Niwot, CO, 1998. 402 pp., illus. $79.95

Traces the development and uses of firearms on the frontier during this period.

Firearms of the American West 1866-1894, Volume 2, by Louis A. Garavaglia and Charles G. Worman, University of Colorado Press, Niwot, CO, 1998. 416 pp., illus. $79.95

A monumental work that offers both technical information on all of the important firearms used in the West during this period and a highly entertaining history of how they were used, who used them, and why.

Firepower from Abroad, by Wiley Sword, Andrew Mowbray Publishing, Lincoln, R.I., 2000. 120 pp., illus. $23.00

The Confederate Enfield and the LeMat revolver and how they reached the Confederate market.

Flayderman's Guide to Antique American Firearms and Their Values, 8th Edition, edited by Norm Flayderman, Krause Publications, Iola, WI, 2001. 692 pp., illus. Paper covers. $34.95

A completely updated and new edition with more than 3,600 models and variants extensively described with all marks and specifications necessary for quick identification.

Flintlock Fowlers: The First Guns Made in America, by Tom Grinslade, Texarkana, TX: Scurlock Publishing Co., 2005. 1st edition. 248 pages. Hardcover. New in new dust jacket. $75.00 Paperback $38.00

The most complete compilation of fowlers ever in one book. Essential resource for collectors, builders and flintlock enthusiasts!

F.N. F.A.L. Assembly, Disassembly Manual 7.62mm, by Skennerton & Riling, Ray Riling Arms Books Co. Philadelphia, PA 2004. 36 pages, $5.00

Over 60 photos & line drawings. Ideal workshop reference for stripping & assembly with exploded parts drawings, specifications, service accessories, historical information and recommended reading references. Triple saddle-stitched binding with durable plastic laminated cover makes this an ideal workshop guide.

FN-FAL Rifle, et al, by Duncan Long, Paladin Press, Boulder, CO, 1999. 144 pp., illus. Paper covers. $18.95

Detailed descriptions of the basic models produced by Fabrique Nationale and the myriad variants that evolved as a result of the firearms' universal acceptance.

Freund & Bro. Pioneer Gunmakers to the West, by F.J. Pablo Balentine, Graphic Publishers, Newport Beach, CA, 1997. 380 pp., illus. $69.95

The story of Frank W. and George Freund, skilled German gunsmiths who plied their trade on the Western American frontier during the final three decades of the nineteenth century.

Full Circle: A Treatise On Roller Locking, by Blake Stevens, Collector Grade Publications, Toronto, Canada, 2006. 536 pages, with over 737 illustrations. $79.95

After the war the roller lock was taken from Germany first to France; then to Spain, and Switzerland; through Holland; and finally back "Full Circle" to Germany again, where it was used in the G3, the service rifle of the Bundeswehr, from 1959 through to the adoption of the 5.56mm G36 in 1995. The classic work on the world's first true automatic machine gun.

Fusil de Tulole in New France, 1691-1741, by Russel Bouchard, Museum Restorations Service, Bloomfield, Ontario, Canada, 1997. 36 pp., illus. Paper covers. $8.95

The development of the company and the identification of their arms.

Gas Trap Garand, by Billy Pyle, Collector Grade Publications, Cobourg, Ontario, Canada, 1999 316 pp., illus. $59.95

The in-depth story of the rarest Garands of them all, the initial 80 Model Shop rifles made under the personal supervision of John Garand himself in 1934 and 1935, and the first 50,000 plus production "gas trap" M1's manufactured at Springfield Armory between August, 1937 and August, 1940.

George Schreyer, Sr. and Jr., Gunmakers of Hanover, Pennsylvania, by George Shumway, George Shumway Publishers, York, PA, 1990. 160pp., illus. $50.00
This monograph is a detailed photographic study of almost all known surviving longrifles and smoothbore guns made by highly regarded gunsmiths George Schreyer, Sr. and George Schreyer Jr.

German and Austrian Gunmakers Trade Catalogs, by George Hoyem, Jaeger Press, 2002. This is a 252 page 11" x 8.5" case bound book with a four color dust jacket, compiled by Hans E. Pfingsten and George A. Hoyem, containing five illustrated gunmakers trade catalogues dating from 1914 to 1935, three of them export issues in German, English, French and Spanish. Hardcover. New in new dust jacket. $60.00

German Anti-Tank Weapons-Panzerbuchse, Panzerfaust and Panzerschrek: Propaganda Series Volume 5, by DeVries and Martens. Alexandria,VA, Ironside Intl., 2005. 1st edition. 152pp, illustrated with 200 high quality b&w photos, most never published before. Hardcover, $38.95

German Assault Rifle 1935-1945, The, by Peter R. Senich, Paladin Press, Boulder, CO, 1987. 328 pp., illus. $60.00
A complete review of machine carbines, machine pistols and assault rifles employed by Hitler's Wehrmacht during WWII.

German Belt Buckles 1845-1945: Buckles of the Enlisted Soldiers, by Peter Nash Atglen, PA, Schiffer Publications, 2003. 1st edition. Hardcover. New in new dust jacket. $59.95

German Camouflaged Helmets of the Second World War; Volume 1: Painted and Textured Camouflage, by Branislav Atglen Radovic, PA, Schiffer Publications, 2004. 1st edition. Hardcover. New in new dust jacket. $79.95

German Camouflaged Helmets of the Second World War; Volume 2: Wire, Netting, Covers, Straps, Interiors, Miscellaneous, by Branislav Atglen Radovic, PA, Schiffer Publications, 2004. 1st edition. Hardcover. New in new dust jacket. $79.95

German Cross in Gold-Holders of the SS and Police, by Mark Yerger, San Jose, CA, Bender Publishing, 2004. 1st edition. 432 pp., 295 photos and illustrations, deluxe binding. Hardcover. $44.95

German Cross in Gold-Holders of the SS and Police Volume 2-"Das Reich", by Mark Yerger, San Jose, CA, Bender Publishing, 2005. 1st edition. 432 pp., 295 photos and illustrations, deluxe binding. Hardcover. $44.95

German K98k Rifle, 1934-1945: The Backbone of the Wehrmacht, by Richard D. Law, Collector Grade Publications, Toronto, Canada, 1993. 336 pp., illus. $69.95
The most comprehensive study ever published on the 14,000,000 bolt-action K98k rifles produced in Germany between 1934 and 1945.

German Machine Guns, by Daniel D. Musgrave, revised edition, Ironside International Publishers, Inc. Alexandria, VA, 1992. 586 pp., 650 illus. $49.95
The most definitive book ever written on German machine guns. Covers the introduction and development of machine guns in Germany from 1899 to the rearmament period after WWII.

German Military Abbreviations, by Military Intelligence Service, Canada, Service Publications. 268 pp. Stiff paper covers. $16.95

German Paratroops: Uniforms, Insignia & Equipment of the Fallschirmjager in World War II, by Robert Atglen Kurtz, PA, Schiffer Publications, 2003. 1st edition. Hardcover. New in new dust jacket. $59.95

German Tanks of World War II in Color, by Michael Green; Thomas Anderson; Frank Schultz, St. Paul, MN, MBI Publishing Company, 2000. 1st edition. Softcover. $14.95

Government Issue: U.S. Army European Theater of Operations Collector Guide, by Henry-Paul Enjames, Philippe Charbonnier, France, Histoire & Collections, 2004. Hardcover, $49.89

Government Models, by William H.D. Goddard, Andrew Mowbray Publishing, Lincoln, RI, 1998. 296 pp., illus. $58.50
The most authoritative source on the development of the Colt model of 1911.

Grasshoppers and Butterflies, by Adrian B. Caruana, Museum Restoration Service, Alexandria Bay, N.Y., 1999. 32 pp., illus. Paper covers. $8.95
No.39 in the Historical Arms Series. The light 3 pounders of Pattison and Townsend.

Greenhill Dictionary of Guns and Gunmakers: From Colt's First Patent to the Present Day, 1836-2001, by John Walter, Greenhill Publishing, 2001, 1st edition, 576 pp., illustrated with 200 photos, 190 trademarks and 40 line drawings, Hardcover. $59.95
Covers military small arms, sporting guns and rifles, air and gas guns, designers, inventors, patentees, trademarks, brand names and monograms. A famed book of great value, truly encyclopedic in scope and sought after by firearms collectors.

Gun Powder Cans & Kegs, by Ted and David Bacyk and Tom Rowe, Rowe Publications, Rochester, NY, 1999. 150 pp., illus. $65.00
The first book devoted to powder tins and kegs. All cans and kegs in full color. With a price guide and rarity scale.

Gun Tools, Their History and Identification, by James B. Shaffer, Lee A. Rutledge and R. Stephen Dorsey, Collector's Library, Eugene, OR, 1992. 375 pp., illus. $30.00
Written history of foreign and domestic gun tools from the flintlock period to WWII.

Gun Tools, Their History and Identifications, Volume 2, by Stephen Dorsey and James B. Shaffer, Collectors' Library, OR, 1997. 396 pp., illus. Paper covers. $30.00
Gun tools from the Royal Armouries Museum in England, Pattern Room, Royal Ordnance Reference Collection in Nottingham and from major private collections.

Gunmakers of London 1350-1850 with Supplement, by Howard L. Blackmore, Museum Restoration Service, Alexandria Bay, NY, 1999. 222 pp., illus. Two volumes. Slipcased. $135.00
A listing of all the known workmen of gunmaking in the first 500 years, plus a history of the guilds, cutlers, armourers, founders, blacksmiths, etc. 260 gunmarks are illustrated. Supplement is 156 pages, and begins with an introductory chapter on "foreign" gunmakers followed by records of all the new information found about previously unidentified armourers, gunmakers and gunsmiths.

Guns of Dagenham: Lanchester, Patchett, Sterling, by Peter Laidler and David Howroyd, Collector Grade Publications, Inc., Canada, 1995. 310 pp. illus. $39.95
An in-depth history of small arms made by the Sterling Company of Dagenham, England, from 1940 until Sterling was purchased by British Aerospace in 1989 and closed.

Guns of Remington: Historic Firearms Spanning Two Centuries, compiled by Howard M. Madaus, Biplane Productions, Publisher, in cooperation with Buffalo Bill Historical Center, Cody, WY, 1998. 352 pp., illustrated with over 800 color photos. $79.95
A complete catalog of the firearms in the exhibition, "It Never Failed Me: The Arms & Art of Remington Arms Company" at the Buffalo Bill Historical Center, Cody, Wyoming.

Guns of the Third Reich, by John Walter, Pennsylvania, Stackpole Books, 2004. 1st edition. 256pp, 60 illust. Hardcover. $34.95
John Walter examines the full range of guns used by the Third Reich from the commercially successful Walter PP and PPK, to the double-action, personal defense pistols Mauser HSc and Sauer M38.

Guns of the Western Indian War, by R. Stephen Dorsey, Collector's Library, Eugene, OR, 1997. 220 pp., illus. Paper covers. $30.00
The full story of the guns and ammunition that made western history in the turbulent period of 1865-1890.

Gunsmiths of Illinois, by Curtis L. Johnson, George Shumway Publishers, York, PA, 1995. 160 pp., illus. $50.00
Genealogical information is provided for nearly 1,000 gunsmiths. Contains hundreds of illustrations of rifles and other guns, of handmade origin, from Illinois.

Gunsmiths of Manhattan, 1625-1900: A Checklist of Tradesmen, by Michael H. Lewis, Museum Restoration Service, Bloomfield, Ont., Canada, 1991. 40 pp., illus. Paper covers. $8.95
This listing of more than 700 men in the arms trade in New York City prior to about the end of the 19th century will provide a guide for identification and further research.

Gunsmiths of Maryland, by Daniel D. Hartzler and James B. Whisker, Old Bedford Village Press, Bedford, PA, 1998. 208 pp., illus. $45.00
Covers firelock Colonial period through the breech-loading patent models. Featuring longrifles.

Gunsmiths of Virginia, by Daniel D. Hartzler and James B. Whisker, Old Bedford Village Press, Bedford, PA, 1992. 206 pp., illus. $40.00
A photographic study of American longrifles.

Gunsmiths of West Virginia, by Daniel D. Hartzler and James B. Whisker, Old Bedford Village Press, Bedford, PA, 1998. 176 pp., illus. $40.00
A photographic study of American longrifles.

Gunsmiths of York County, Pennsylvania, by Daniel D. Hartzler and James B. Whisker, Old Bedford Village Press, Bedford, PA, 1998. 160 pp., illus. $40.00
Photographs and research notes on the longrifles and gunsmiths of York County, Pennsylvania.

Hand Forged for Texas Cowboys, by Kurt House, an Antonio, TX, Three Rivers Publishing, 2005. This beautifully illustrated book features color photos as well as b&w period photos, and will be a welcome addition to the library of any reader. 160 pages. Hardcover. New in new dust jacket. $69.95

Harrington & Richardson Sporting Firearms: Dates of Manufacture 1871-1991, by D.R. Morse. Phoenix, AZ, Firing Pin Enterprizes, 2003. 14 pp. Softcover. $6.95
Covers their pistols, revolvers, rifles, shotguns and commemoratives, plus models.

Hawken Rifle: Its Place in History, by Charles E. Hanson Jr., The Fur Press, Chadron, NE, 1979. 104 pp., illus. Paper covers. $15.00
A definitive work on this famous rifle.

Hi-Standard Sporting Firearms: Dates of Manufacture, by D.R. Morse. 1926-1992. Phoenix, AZ, Firing Pin Enterprizes, 2003. 22 pp. Softcover. New. $6.95
Covers their pistols, revolvers, rifles, shotguns and commemoratives, plus models and serial numbers.

High Standard: A Collector's Guide to the Hamden & Hartford Target Pistols, by Tom Dance, Andrew Mowbray, Inc., Lincoln, RI, 1991. 192 pp. Paper covers. $24.00
From Citation to Supermatic, all of the production models and specials made from 1951 to 1984 are covered according to model number or series.

History of Modern U.S. Military Small Arms Ammunition, Volume 1, 1880-1939, revised by F.W. Hackley, W.H. Woodin and E.L. Scranton, Thomas Publications, Gettysburg, PA, 1998. 328 pp., illus. $49.95
This revised edition incorporates all publicly available information concerning military small arms ammunition for the period 1880 through 1939 in a single volume.

History of Modern U.S. Military Small Arms Ammunition, Volume 2, 1940-1945, by F.W. Hackley, W.H. Woodin and E.L. Scranton, Gun Room Press, Highland Park, NJ, 1998. 297 pages, illustrated. $49.95
Based on decades of original research conducted at the National Archives, numerous military, public and private museums and libraries, as well as individual collections, this edition incorporates all publicly available information concerning military small arms ammunition for the period 1940 through 1945.

History of Smith & Wesson Firearms, by Dean Boorman, Lyons Press, New York, NY, 2002. 44 pp., illustrated in full color. Hardcover. $29.95
The definitive guide to one of the world's best-known firearms makers. Takes the story through the years of the Military and Police 38 and of the Magnum cartridge, to today's wide range of products for law-enforcement customers.

History of Winchester Rifles, by Dean Boorman, Lyons Press, New York, NY, 2001. 144 pp., illus. 150 full-color photos. $29.95
A captivating and wonderfully photographed history of one of the most legendary names in gun lore.

History of Colt Firearms, by Dean Boorman, Lyons Press, New York, NY, 2001. 144 pp., illus. $29.95
Discover the fascinating story of the world's most famous revolver, complete with more than 150 stunning full-color photographs.

Holsters and Shoulder Stocks of the World, by Anthony Vanderlinden, Greensboro, NC, Wet Dog Publications, 2005. 1st edition. Hardcover $45.95
About 500 holsters and shoulder-stocks will be documented in this first edition. Pistols are listed by make and model. The user guide references the countries that used the holsters so that collectors can instantly refer to either a pistol model or country or use. 204 pages, with over 1000 b& w photos.

Honour Bound: The Chauchat Machine Rifle, by Gerard Demaison and Yves Buffetaut, Collector Grade Publications, Inc., Cobourg, Ont., Canada, 1995. $39.95
The story of the CSRG (Chauchat) machine rifle, the most manufactured automatic weapon of WWI.

Hunting Weapons from the Middle Ages to the Twentieth Century, by Howard L. Blackmore, Dover Publications, Meneola, NY, 2000. 480 pp., illus. Paper covers. $16.95
Dealing mainly with the different classes of weapons used in sport: swords, spears, crossbows, guns, and rifles, from the Middle Ages until the present day.

Illustrations of United States Military Arms 1776-1903 and Their Inspector's Marks, compiled by Turner Kirkland, Pioneer Press, Union City, TN, 1988. 37 pp., illus. Paper covers. $7.00

Reprinted from the 1949 Bannerman catalog. Valuable information for both the advanced and beginning collector.

Imperial German Military Officers' Helmets and Headdress 1871-1918, by Thomas N.G. Stubbs, Atglen, PA, Schiffer Publications, 2003. 1st edition. Hardcover. New in new dust jacket. $79.95

Imperial Japanese Grenade Rifles and Launchers, by Gregory A. Babich and Thomas A. Keep Lemont, PA, Dutch Harlow Publishing, 2004. 1st edition. Hardcover. New in new dust jacket. $75.00

Indian Trade Relics, by Lar Hothem, Paducah, KY, Collector Books, 2003. 1st edition. 320pp. Pictorial Hardcover. $29.95

Indian War Cartridge Pouches, Boxes and Carbine Boots, by R. Stephen Dorsey, Collector's Library, Eugene, OR, 1993. 156 pp., illus. Paper covers. $20.00

The key reference work to the cartridge pouches, boxes, carbine sockets and boots of the Indian War period 1865-1890.

Individual Gear and Personal Items of the GI in Europe 1942-1945; From Pro-Kits to Pin-Up, by James Klokner, Atglen., PA, Schiffer Publications, 2005. 224 pages with over 470 color and b&w photographs. Hardcover. $59.95

This book is by far the best and most complete study available of personal items of the American soldier during World War II and truly an indispensable resource.

International Armament, with History, Data, Technical Information and Photographs of Over 800 Weapons, 2nd edition, new printing, by George B. Johnson, Alexandria, VA, Ironside International, 2002. Hardcover. New in new dust jacket. $59.95

The development and progression of modern military small arms. Over 800 photographs and illustrations with both historical and technical data. Two volumes are now bound into one book.

Jaeger Rifles, collected articles published in Muzzle Blasts, by George Shumway, York PA, 2003. Reprint. 108 pp., illus. Stiff paper covers. New. $30.00

Thirty-six articles previously published in *Muzzle Blasts* are reproduced here.

Japanese Rifles of World War Two, by Duncan O. McCollum, Excalibur Publications, Latham, NY, 1996. 64 pp., illus. Paper covers. $18.95

A sweeping view of the rifles and carbines that made up Japan's arsenal during the conflict.

Kentucky Rifle, by Captain John G.W. Dillin, George Shumway Publisher, York, PA, 1993. 221 pp., illus. $50.00

This well-known book was the first attempt to tell the story of the American longrifle. This edition retains the original text and illustrations with supplemental footnotes provided by Dr. George Shumway.

Legends and Reality of the AK, by Val Shilin and Charlie Cutshaw, Paladen Press, Boulder, CO, 2000. 192 pp., illus. Paper covers. $35.00

A behind-the-scenes look at history, design and impact of the Kalashnikov family of weapons.

Light 6-Pounder Battalion Gun of 1776, by Adrian Caruana, Museum Restoration Service, Bloomfield, Ontario, Canada, 2001. 76 pp., illus. Paper covers. $8.95

London Gun Trade, 1850-1920, by Joyce E. Gooding, Museum Restoration Service, Bloomfield, Ontario, Canada, 2001. 48 pp., illus. Paper covers. $8.95

Names, dates and locations of London gunmakers working between 1850 and 1920 are listed. Compiled from the original Kelly's post office directories of the City of London.

London Gunmakers and the English Duelling Pistol, 1770-1830, by Keith R. Dill, Museum Restoration Service, Bloomfield, Ontario, Canada, 1997. 36 pp., illus. Paper covers. $8.95

Ten gunmakers made London one of the major gunmaking centers of the world. This book examines how the design and construction of their pistols contributed to that reputation and how these characteristics may be used to date flintlock arms.

Longrifles of Pennsylvania, Volume 1, Jefferson, Clarion & Elk Counties, by Russel H. Harringer, George Shumway Publisher, York, PA, 1984. 200 pp., illus. $50.00

First in series that will treat in great detail the longrifles and gunsmiths of Pennsylvania.

M1 Garand .30 Assembly, Disassembly Manual, by Skennerton & Riling, Ray Riling Arms Books Co. Philadelphia, PA 2004. 36 pages, $5.00

With over 60 photos & line drawings. Ideal workshop reference for stripping & assembly with exploded parts drawings, specifications, service accessories, historical information and recommended reading references.

M1 Carbine .30 M1, M1A1, M2 & M3 Assembly, Disassembly Manual, by Skennerton & Riling, Ray Riling Arms Books Co. Philadelphia, PA 2004. 36 pages, $5.00

With over 60 photos & line drawings. Ideal workshop reference for stripping & assembly with exploded parts drawings, specifications, service accessories, historical information and recommended reading references.

M1 Carbine: A Revolution in Gun-Stocking, by Grafton H. Cook II and Barbara W. Cook, Lincoln, RI, Andrew Mowbray, Inc., 2002. 1st edition. 208 pp., heavily illustrated with 157 rare photographs of the guns and the men and women who made them. Softcover. $29.95

Shows you, step by step, how M1 carbine stocks were made, right through to assembly with the hardware. Also contains lots of detailed information about other military weapons, like the M1A1, the M1 Garand, the M14 and much, much more.

M1 Carbine: Design, Development, and Production, by Larry Ruth, Gun Room Press, Highland Park, NJ, 1987. 291 pp., illus. Paper $19.95

The origin, development, manufacture and use of this famous carbine of WWII.

M1 Carbine Owner's Guide, by Larry Ruth and Scott A. Duff, Scott A. Duff Publications, Export, PA, 1997. 126 pp., illus. Paper covers. $21.95

This book answers the questions M1 owners most often ask concerning maintenance activities not encounted by military users.

M1 Garand: Owner's Guide, by Scott A. Duff, Scott A. Duff Publications, Export, PA, 1998. 132 pp., illus. Paper covers. $21.95

This book answers the questions M1 owners most often ask concerning maintenance activities not encounted by military users.

M1 Garand Complete Assembly Guide, Vol 2, by Scott A. Duff, Scott A. Duff Publications, Export, PA, 2006. 162 pp., illus. Paper covers. $20.95

This book goes beyond the military manuals in depth and scope, using words It won't make you an Garand armorer, but it will make you a more knowledgeable owner.

M1 Garand: Post World War, by Scott A. Duff, Scott A. Duff Publications, Export, PA, 1990. 139 pp., illus. Softcover. $21.95

A detailed account of the activities at Springfield Armory through this period. International Harvester, H&R, Korean War production and quantities delivered. Serial numbers.

M1 Garand: World War II, by Scott A. Duff, Scott A. Duff Publications, Export, PA, 2001. 210 pp., illus. Paper covers. $34.95

The most comprehensive study available to the collector and historian on the M1 Garand of WWII.

M1 Garand 1936 to 1957, 4th Edition, Revised & Expanded, by Joe Poyer and Craig Riesch, North Cape Publications, Tustin, CA, 2006. 232 pp., illus. PC. $19.95

Describes the entire range of M1 Garand production in text and quick-scan charts.

M1 Garand Serial Numbers and Data Sheets, by Scott A. Duff, Scott A. Duff Publications, Export, PA, 1995. 101 pp., illus. Paper covers. $11.95

Provides the reader with serial numbers related to dates of manufacture and a large sampling of data sheets to aid in identification or restoration.

Machine Guns, by Ian V. Hogg, Iola, WI, Krause Publications, 2002. 1st edition. 336 pp., illustrated with b&w photos with a 16-page color section. Softcover. $29.95

A detailed history of the rapid-fire gun, 14th Century to present. Covers the development, history and specifications.

Made in the C.S.A.: Saddle Makers of the Confederacy, by Ken R. Knopp, Hattiesburg, MS, privately printed, 2003. 1st edition signed. 205 pp., illus., signed by the author. Softcover. $30.00

Maine Made Guns and Their Makers, by Dwight B. Demeritt Jr., Maine State Museum, Augusta, ME, 1998. 209 pp., illus. $55.00

An authoritative, biographical study of Maine gunsmiths.

Marksmanship in the U.S. Army, by William Emerson, Oklahoma, Univ. of Oklahoma Press, 2004 256 pages Illustrated with b&w photos. Hardcover. NEW $64.95

Marlin Firearms: A History of the Guns and the Company That Made Them, by Lt. Col. William S. Brophy, USAR, Ret., Stackpole Books, Harrisburg, PA, 1989. 672 pp., illus. $89.95

The definitive book on the Marlin Firearms Co. and their products.

Martini-Henry .450 Rifles & Carbines, by Dennis Lewis, Excalibur Publications, Latham, NY, 1996. 72 pp., illus. Paper covers. $11.95

The stories of the rifles and carbines that were the mainstay of the British soldier through the Victorian wars.

Mauser Bolt Rifles, by Ludwig Olson, F. Brownell & Son, Inc., Montezuma, IA, 1999. 364 pp., illus. $64.95

The most complete, detailed, authoritative and comprehensive work ever done on Mauser bolt rifles. Completely revised deluxe 3rd edition.

Mauser Military Rifle Markings, by Terence W. Lapin, Arlington, VA, Hyrax Publishers, LLC, 2001. 167 pp., illus. 2nd edition. Revised and expanded. Softcover. $22.95

A general guide to reading and understanding the often mystifying markings found on military Mauser rifles. Includes German Regimental markings as well as German police markings and WWII German Mauser subcontractor codes. A handy reference to take to gun shows.

Military Holsters of World War II, by Eugene J. Bender, Rowe Publications, Rochester, NY, 1998. 200 pp., illus. $49.95

A revised edition with a new price guide of the most definitive book on this subject.

Military Remington Rolling Block Rifle, The, by George Layman, Pioneer Press, TN, 1998. 146 pp., illus. Paper covers. $24.95

A standard reference for those with an interest in the Remington rolling block family of firearms.

Mortimer, the Gunmakers, 1753-1923, by H. Lee Munson, Andrew Mowbray Inc., Lincoln, RI, 1992. 320 pp., illus. $65.00

Seen through a single, dominant, English gunmaking dynasty, this fascinating study provides a window into the classical era of firearms artistry.

Mossberg Sporting Firearms: Dates of Manufacture, by D.R. Morse, Phoenix, AZ, Firing Pin Enterprizes, 2003. Softcover. $6.95

Covers their pistols, revolvers, rifles, shotguns and commemoratives, plus models and serial numbers.

MP38, 40, 40/1 & 41 Submachine Gun, by de Vries & Martens. Propaganda Photo Series, Volume II. Alexandria, VA, Ironside International, 2001. 1st edition. 150 pp., illustrated with 200 high quality b&w photos. Hardcover. $34.95

Covers all essential information on history and development, ammunition and accessories, codes and markings, and contains photos of nearly every model and accessory. Includes a unique selection of original German WWII propaganda photos, most never published before.

Navy Luger, by Joachim Gortz and John Walter, Handgun Press, Glenview, IL, 1988. 128 pp., illus. $24.95

The 9mm Pistole 1904 and the Imperial German Navy. A concise illustrated history.

New World of Russian Small Arms and Ammunition, by Charlie Cutshaw, Paladin Press, Boulder, CO, 1998. 160 pp., illus. $42.95

Detailed descriptions, specifications and first-class illustrations of the AN-94, PSS silent pistol, Bizon SMG, Saifa-12 tactical shotgun, the GP-25 grenade launcher and more cutting edge Russian weapons.

Number 5 Jungle Carbine, by Alan M. Petrillo, Excalibur Publications, Latham, NY, 1994. 32 pp., illus. Paper covers. $7.95

A comprehensive treatment of the rifle that collectors have come to call the "Jungle Carbine"–the Lee-Enfield Number 5, Mark 1.

Observations on Colt's Second Contract, November 2, 1847, by G. Maxwell Longfield and David T. Basnett, Museum Restoration Service, Bloomfield, Ontario, Canada, 1997. 36 pp., illus. Paper covers. $6.95

This study traces the history and the construction of the Second Model Colt Dragoon supplied in 1848 to the U.S. Cavalry.

Official Soviet SVD Manual, The, by Major James F. Gebhardt (Ret.), Paladin Press, Boulder, CO, 1999. 112 pp., illus. Paper covers. $22.00

Operating instructions for the 7.62mm Dragunov, the first Russian rifle developed from scratch specifically for sniping.

Ordnance Tools, Accessories & Appendages of the M1 Rifle, by Billy Pyle. Houston, TX, privately printed, 2002. 2nd edition. 206 pp., illustrated with b&w photos. Softcover $40.00

OSS Special Weapons II, by John Brunner, Williamstown, NJ, Phillips Publications, 2005, 2nd edition. 276pp. profusely illustrated with photos, some in color. Hardcover, New in New DJ. $59.95

P-08 Parabellum Luger Automatic Pistol, The, edited by J. David McFarland, Desert Publications, Cornville, AZ, 1982. 20 pp., illus. Paper covers. $11.95

Covers every facet of the Luger, plus a listing of all known Luger models.

Packing Iron, by Richard C. Rattenbury, Zon International Publishing, Millwood, NY, 1993. 216 pp., illus. $45.00

ARMS LIBRARY

The best book yet produced on pistol holsters and rifle scabbards. Over 300 variations of holster and scabbards are illustrated in large, clear plates.

Painted Steel, Steel Pots Volume 2, by Chris Armold, Bender Publishing, San Jose, CA, 2001. 384 pp.-1,053 photos, hundreds in color. $57.95

From the author of *Steel Pots: The History of America's Steel Combat Helmets* comes *Painted Steel: Steel Pots, Vol. II.* This companion volume features detailed chapters on painted and unit marked helmets of WWI and WWII, plus a variety of divisional, regimental and subordinate markings. Special full-color plates detail subordinate unit markings such as the tactical markings used by the U.S. 2nd Division in WWI.

Parker Gun Catalog 1900, by Parker Brothers, Davis, IL: Old Reliable Publishing, 1996. Reprint. One of the most attractive and sought-after of the Parker gun catalogs, this one shows the complete Parker line circa 1900. This is the only catalog which pictures EH and NH grades, and is the first to picture $50.00 VH grade. A deluxe reprint, 15pp., illustrated. Stiff Paper Covers. Fine. $10.00

Parker Gun Catalog 1910, by Parker Brothers, Davis, IL: Old Reliable Publishing, 1996. Reprint. One of the most attractive and sought-after of the Parker gun catalogs, this one shows the complete Parker line circa 1910. A deluxe reprint, 20pp., illustrated. Stiff Paper Covers. Fine. $10.00

Parker Gun Catalog 1913 (Flying Ducks), by Parker Brothers, Davis, IL: Old Reliable Publishing, 1996. 36pp., illustrated. Stiff Paper Covers. Fine. $20.00

One of the most attractive and sought-after of the Parker gun catalogs, this one shows the complete Parker line circa 1913. A deluxe reprint, it has the same embossed cover as the original "Flying Ducks" catalog.

Pattern Dates for British Ordnance Small Arms, 1718-1783, by DeWitt Bailey, Thomas Publications, Gettysburg, PA, 1997. 116 pp., illus. Paper covers. $20.00

The weapons discussed in this work are those carried by troops sent to North America between 1737 and 1783, or shipped to them as replacement arms while in America.

Percussion Ammunition Packets 1845-1888 Union, Confederate & European, by John J. Malloy, Dean S. Thomas and Terry A. White with Foreward by Norm Flayderman. Gettysburg, PA, Thomas Publications, 2003. 1st edition. 134 pp., illustrated with color photos. Hardcover. New. $75.00

Finally a means to recognize the untold variety of labeled types of ammunition box labels.

Peters & King, by Thomas D. Schiffer. Krause Publications, Iola, WI 2002. 1st edition. 256 pp., 200+ b&w photos with a 32-page color section. Hardcover. $44.95

Discover the history behind Peters Cartridge and King Powder and see how they shaped the arms industry into what it is today and why their products fetch hundreds, even thousands of dollars at auctions. Current values are provided for their highly collectible product packaging and promotional advertising premiums such as powder kegs, tins, cartridge boxes, and calendars.

Presentation and Commercial Colt Walker Pistols, by Col. Robert D. Whittington III. Hooks, TX, Brownlee Books, 2005. A limited edition of 1,000 copies. Numbered. 21 pp. Paper covers. New. $15.00

A study of events at the Whitneyville Armoury and Samuel Colt's Hartford Factory from 1 June 1847 to 29 November 1848.

Presentation and Commercial Colt Walker Pistols, 2nd Revision, by Col. Robert D. Whittington III. Hooks, TX, Brownlee Books, 2006. A limited edition of 1,000 copies. Numbered. 26 pp. Paper covers. New. $20.00

A study of events at the Whitneyville Armoury and Samuel Colt's Hartford Factory from 1 June 1847 to 29 November 1848. Updated.

Price Guide: Orders and Decorations Germany, 1871-1945, Second Edition, by Klaus Lubbe, Germany, Niemann,2004. 2nd edition. German and English text. 817 pages, over 2,000 photos. Hardcover. $104.95

It is a reference for prices as well as on the differences between the various orders, decorations, award documents, award cases of issue, and miniatures. No fantasy pieces are included, or projected orders which were never realized.

Proud Promise: French Autoloading Rifles, 1898-1979, by Jean Huon, Collector Grade Publications, Inc., Cobourg, Ont., Canada, 1995. 216 pp., illus. $39.95

The author has finally set the record straight about the importance of French contributions to modern arms design.

Purdey Gun and Rifle Makers: The Definitive History, by Donald Dallas, Quiller Press, London, 2000. 245 pp., illus. Color throughout. A limited edition of 3,000 copies. Signed and numbered. With a PURDEY book plate. $99.95

Queen Anne Pistol, 1660-1780: A History of the Turn-Off Pistol, by John W. Burgoyne, Bloomfield, Ont., Canada, Museum Restoration Service, 2002. 1st edition-Historical Arms New Series No. 1. 120 pp. Pictorial hardcover. $35.00

A detailed, fast moving, thoroughly researched text and almost 200 cross-referenced illustrations.

Recreating the 18th Century Powder Horn, by Scott and Cathy Sibley, Texarkana, TX, Scurlock Publishing, 2005. 1st edition. 91 pages. Softcover. $19.95

Scott and Cathy Sibley demonstrates every detail and secret of recreating an 18th century powder horn. New and experienced horn makers will enjoy this how-to book. Lavishly illustrated wtih full-color photos and step-by-step illustrations.

Red Shines The Sun: A Pictorial History of the Fallschirm-Infantrie, by Eric Queen. San Jose, CA, R. James Bender Publishing, 2003. 1st edition. Hardcover. $69.95

A culmination of 12 years of research, this reference work traces the history of the Army paratroopers of the Fallschirm-Infanterie from their origins in 1937, to the expansion to battalion strength in 1938, then on through operations at Wola Gulowska (Poland), and Moerdijk (Holland). This 240-page comprehensive look at their history is supported by 600 images, many of which are in full color, and nearly 90% are previously unpublished.

Reloading Tools, Sights and Telescopes for Single Shot Rifles, by Gerald O. Kelver, Brighton, CO, 1982. 163 pp., illus. Paper covers. $13.95

A listing of most of the famous makers of reloading tools, sights and telescopes with a brief description of the products they manufactured.

Remington-Lee Rifle, by Eugene F. Myszkowski, Excalibur Publications, Latham, NY, 1995. 100 pp., illus. Paper covers. $22.50

Features detailed descriptions, including serial number ranges, of each model from the first Lee magazine rifle produced for the U.S. Navy to the last Remington-Lee small bore shipped to the Cuban Rural Guard.

Remington 'America's Oldest Gunmaker', The Official Authorized History of the Remington Arms Company, by Roy Marcot. Madison, NC, Remington Arms Company, 1999. 1st edition. 312 pp., with 167 b&w illustrations, plus 291 color plates. $79.95

This is without a doubt the finest history of that firm ever to have been compiled. Based on firsthand research in the Remington company archives, it is extremely well written.

Remington Sporting Firearms: Dates of Manufacture, by D.R. Morse, Phoenix, AZ, Firing Pin Enterprizes, 2003. 43 pp. Softcover. New. $6.95

Covers their pistols, revolvers, rifles, shotguns and commemoratives, plus models and serial numbers.

Remington's Vest Pocket Pistols, by Robert E. Hatfield, Lincoln, RI, Andrew Mowbray, Inc., 2002. 117 pp. Hardcover. $29.95

While Remington Vest Pocket pistols have always been popular with collectors, very little solid information has been available about them. Inside you will find 100+ photographs, serial number data, exploded views of all four Remington Vest Pocket pistol sizes, component parts lists and a guide to disassembly and reassembly. Also includes a discussion of Vest Pocket Wire-Stocked Buggy/Bicycle rifles, plus the documented serial number story.

Revolvers of the British Services 1854-1954, by W.H.J. Chamberlain and A.W.F. Taylerson, Museum Restoration Service, Ottawa, Canada, 1989. 80 pp., illus. $27.50

Covers the types issued among many of the United Kingdom's naval, land or air services.

Rifles of the U.S. Army 1861-1906, by John D. McAulay, Andrew Mowbray, Inc., Lincoln, RI, 2003. 1st edition. Over 40 rifles covered, 278 pp., illus. Hardcover. New. $47.95

This exciting new book by renowned authority John McAulay gives the reader detailed coverage of the issue and actual field service of America's fighting rifles, both in peacetime and in war, including their military service with the infantry, artillery, cavalry and engineers. One feature that all readers will value is the impressive number of historical photos, taken during the Civil War, the Mexican War, the Indian Wars, the Spanish-American War, the Philippine Insurrection and more. Procurement information, issue details and historical background.

Ruger and his Guns, by R.L. Wilson, Book Sales, New York, NY, 2006. 358 pp., illus. $24.95

A history of the man, the company and their firearms.

Running Recon: A photo Jorney with SOG Special Ops Along the Ho Chi Minh Trail, by Frank Grecco. Boulder, CO: Paladin Press, 2006. Softcover. $50.00

Running Recon is a combination of military memoir and combat photography book. It reflects both the author's experience in Kontum, Vietnam, from April 1969 to April 1970 as part of the top-secret Studies and Observation Group (SOG) and the collective experience of SOG veterans in general.

Russell M. Catron and His Pistols, by Warren H. Buxton, Ucross Books, Los Alamos, NM, 1998. 224 pp., illus. Paper covers. $49.50

An unknown American firearms inventor and manufacturer of the mid-twentieth century. Military, commerical, ammunition.

SAFN-49 and the FAL, by Joe Poyer and Dr. Richard Feirman, North Cape Publications, Tustin, CA, 1998. 160 pp., illus. Paper covers. $14.95

The first complete overview of the SAFN-49 battle rifle, from its pre-WWII beginnings to its military service in countries as diverse as the Belgian Congo and Argentina. The FAL was a "light" version of the SAFN-49 and it became the Free World's most adopted battle rifle.

Sash Hook Smith & Wesson Revolvers, The, by Col. Robert D. Whittington III. & and Kolman A. Gabel, Hooks, TX, Brownlee Books, 2003. A limited edition of 1,000 copies. Numbered. 10 pp. Paper covers. New. $10.00

The true story of the Sash Hook Smith & Wesson Revolvers and how they came to be.

Savage Sporting Firearms: Dates of Manufacture 1907-1997, by D.R. Morse. Phoenix, AZ, Firing Pin Enterprizes, 2003. 22 pp. Softcover. New. $6.95

Covers their pistols, revolvers, rifles, shotguns and commemoratives, plus models and serial numbers.

Scottish Firearms, by Claude Blair and Robert Woosnam-Savage, Museum Restoration Service, Bloomfield, Ont., Canada, 1995. 52 pp., illus. Paper covers. $8.95

This revision of the first book devoted entirely to Scottish firearms is supplemented by a register of surviving Scottish long guns.

Sharps Firearms, by Frank Seller, Denver, CO, 1998. 358 pp., illus. $65.00

Traces the development of Sharps firearms with full range of guns made including all martial variations.

Sight Book; Winchester, Lyman, Marble, and Other Companies, by George Madis, Borwsboro,TX, Art & Reference House, 2005. 1st edition. 183 pages, with over 350 illustrations. Hardcover. $26.95

Silk and Steel: Women at Arms, by R. L. Wilson, New York, Random House, 2003. 1st edition. 300+ Striking four-color images; 8½" x 11", 320 pgs. Hardcover. New in new dust jacket. (9775). $65.00

Beginning with Artemis and Diana, goddesses of hunting, evolving through modern times, here is the first comprehensive presentation on the subject of women and firearms. No object has had a greater impact on world history over the past 650 years than the firearm, and a surprising number of women have been keen on the subject, as shooters, hunters, collectors, engravers, and even gunmakers.

SKS Carbine, by Steve Kehaya and Joe Poyer, North Cape Publications, Tustin, CA, 1997. 150 pp., illus. Paper covers. $16.95

The first comprehensive examination of a major historical firearm used through the Vietnam conflict to the diamond fields of Angola.

SKS Type 45 Carbines, by Duncan Long, Desert Publications, El Dorado, AZ, 1992. 110 pp., illus. Paper covers. $19.95

Covers the history and practical aspects of operating, maintaining and modifying this abundantly available rifle.

Slave Badges and the Slave-Hire System in Charleston, South Carolina, 1783-1865, by Harlan Greene, Harry S. Hutchins Jr., Brian E. Hutchins. Jefferson, NC, McFarland & Company, 2004. 152 pp. Hardcover, $35.00

Smith & Wesson 1857-1945, by Robert J. Neal and Roy G. Jinks, R&R Books, Livonia, NY, 1996. 434 pp., illus. $50.00

The bible for all existing and aspiring Smith & Wesson collectors.

Smith & Wesson Sporting Firearms: Dates of Manufacture, by D.R. Morse, Phoenix, AZ, Firing Pin Enterprizes, 2003. 76 pp. Softcover. $6.95

Covers their pistols, revolvers, rifles, shotguns and commemoratives, plus models and serial numbers.

Sniper Variations of the German K98k Rifle, by Richard D. Law, Collector Grade Publications, Ontario, Canada, 1997. 240 pp., illus. $47.50

Volume 2 of "Backbone of the Wehrmacht" the author's in-depth study of the German K98k rifle. This volume concentrates on the telescopic-sighted rifle of choice for most German snipers during WWII.

Southern Derringers of the Mississippi Valley, by Turner Kirkland, Pioneer Press, Tenn., 1971. 80 pp., illus., paper covers. $10.00

A guide for the collector and a much-needed study.

Soviet Russian Tokarev "TT" Pistols and Cartridges 1929-1953, by Fred Datig, Graphic Publishers, Santa Ana, CA, 1993. 168 pp., illus. $39.95

Details of rare arms and their accessories are shown in hundreds of photos. It also contains a complete bibliography and index.

Spencer Repeating Firearms, by Roy M. Marcot, New York, Rowe Publications, 2002. 316 pp.; numerous b&w photos and illustrations. Hardcover. $65.00

Springfield 1903 Rifles, by Lt. Col. William S. Brophy, USAR, Ret., Stackpole Books Inc., Harrisburg, PA, 1985. 608 pp., illus. $75.00

The illustrated, documented story of the design, development, and production of all the models, appendages, and accessories.

SS Headgear, by Kit Wilson. Johnson Reference Books, Fredericksburg, VA. 72 pp., 15 full-color plates and over 70 b&w photos. $16.50

An excellent source of information concerning all types of SS headgear, to include Allgemeine-SS, Waffen-SS, visor caps, helmets, overseas caps, M-43's and miscellaneous headgear. Also includes a guide on the availability and current values of SS headgear. This guide was compiled from auction catalogs, dealer price lists, and input from advanced collectors in the field.

SS Helmets: A Collector's Guide, Vol 1, by Kelly Hicks, Johnson Reference Books, Fredericksburg, VA. 96 pp., illus. $17.50

Deals only with SS helmets and features some very nice color close-up shots of the different SS decals used. Over 85 photographs, 27 in color. The author has documented most of the known types of SS helmets, and describes in detail all of the vital things to look for in determining the originality, style type, and finish.

SS Helmets: A Collector's Guide, Vol 2, by Kelly Hicks, Johnson Reference Books, Fredericksburg, VA. 2000. 128 pp. 107 full-color photos, 14 period photos. $25.00

Volume II contains dozen of highly detailed, full-color photos of rare and original SS and Field Police helmets, featuring both sides as well as interior view. The outstanding decal section offers detailed close-ups of original SS and Police decals and, in conjunction with Volume I, completes the documentation of virtually all types of original decal variations used between 1934 and 1945.

SS Uniforms, Insignia and Accoutrements, by A. Hayes. Schiffer Publications, Atglen, PA. 1996. 248 pp., with over 800 color and b&w photographs. $69.95

This new work explores in detailed color the complex subject of Allgemeine and Waffen-SS uniforms, insignia, and accoutrements. Hundreds of authentic items are extensively photographed in close-up to enable the reader to examine and study.

Sturmgewehr! From Firepower to Striking Power, by Hans-Dieter Handrich. Canada, Collector Grade, 2004. 1st edition. 600pp., 392 illustrations. Hardcover $79.95

Hans-Dieter spent years researching original documentation held in the military archives of Germany and elsewhere to produce the entire technical and tactical history of the design, development and fielding of the world's first mass-produced assault rifle and the revolutionary 7.92x33mm Kurz cartridge.

Sturm Ruger Sporting Firearms: Dates of Manufacture, by D.R. Morse, Phoenix, AZ, Firing Pin Enterprizes, 2003. 22 pp. Softcover, $6.95

Covers their pistols, revolvers, rifles, shotguns and commemoratives, plus models and serial numbers.

Sumptuous Flaske, by Herbert G. Houze, Andrew Mowbray, Inc., Lincoln, RI, 1989. 158 pp., illus. Softcover, $35.00

Catalog of a recent show at the Buffalo Bill Historical Center bringing together some of the finest European and American powder flasks of the 16th to 19th centuries.

Swedish Mauser Rifles, The, by Steve Kehaya and Joe Poyer, North Cape Publications, Tustin, CA, 1999. 267 pp., illus. Paper covers. $19.95

Every known variation of the Swedish Mauser carbine and rifle is described, all match and target rifles and all sniper versions. Includes serial number and production data.

System Lefaucheaux: Continuing the Study of Pinfire Cartridge Arms Including Their Role in the American Civil War, by Chris C. Curtis, Foreword by Norm Flayderman, Armslore Press, 2002. 1st edition. 312 pp., heavily illustrated with b&w photos. Hardcover. New in new dust jacket. $44.95

Thoughts on the Kentucky Rifle in its Golden Age, by Joe K. Kindig, III. York, PA, George Shumway Publisher, 2002. Annotated second edition. 561 pp.; Illustrated. This scarce title, long out of print, is once again available. Hardcover. $85.00

The definitive book on the Kentucky Rifle, illustrating 266 of these guns in 856 detailed photographs.

Tin Lids—Canadian Combat Helmets, #2 in "Up Close" Series, by Roger V. Lucy, Ottawa, Ontario, Service Publications, 2000. 2nd edition. 48 pp. Softcover. $17.95

Toys That Shoot and Other Neat Stuff, by James Dundas, Schiffer Books, Atglen, PA, 1999. 112 pp., illus. Paper covers. $24.95

Shooting toys from the twentieth century, especially 1920s to 1960s, in over 420 color photographs of BB guns, cap shooters, marble shooters, squirt guns and more. Complete with a price guide.

Trade Guns of the Hudson's Bay Company 1670-1970, Historical Arms New Series No. 2, by S. James Gooding, Bloomfield, Ont. Canada, Museum Restoration Service, 2003. 1st edition. 158 pp., thoroughly researched text. Includes bibliographical references. Pictorial hardcover. $35.00

Trapdoor Springfield, by M.D. Waite and B.D. Ernst, The Gun Room Press, Highland Park, NJ, 1983. 250 pp., illus. $39.95

The first comprehensive book on the famous standard military rifle of the 1873-92 period.

Treasures of the Moscow Kremlin: Arsenal of the Russian Tsars, A Royal Armories and the Moscow Kremlin exhibition, HM Tower of London 13, June 1998 to 11 September, 1998, BAS Printers, Over Wallop, Hampshire, England. XXII plus 192 pp. over 180 color illustrations. Text in English and Russian. $65.00

For this exhibition catalog, each of the 94 objects on display are photographed and described in detail to provide the most informative record of this important exhibition.

U.S. Army Headgear 1812-1872, by John P. Langellier and C. Paul Loane. Atglen, PA, Schiffer Publications, 2002. 167 pp., with over 350 color and b&w photos. Hardcover. $69.95

This profusely illustrated volume represents more than three decades of research in public and private collections by military historian John P. Langellier and Civil War authority C. Paul Loane.

U.S. Army Rangers & Special Forces of World War II Their War in Photographs, by Robert Todd Ross, Atglen, PA, Schiffer Publications, 2002. 216 pp., over 250 b&w and color photographs. Hardcover. $59.95

Never before has such an expansive view of WWII elite forces been offered in one volume. An extensive search of public and private archives unearthed an astonishing number of rare and never before seen images, including color. Most notable are the nearly 20 exemplary photographs of Lieutenant Colonel William O. Darby's Ranger Force in Italy, taken by Robert Capa, considered by many to be the greatest combat photographer of all time.

U.S. Guns of World War II, by Paul Davies, Gettysburg, PA, Thomas Publications, 2004. 1st edition. A record of army ordnance research and the development of small arms. Hundreds of photos. 144pp, Softcover. $17.95

U.S. Handguns of World War II: The Secondary Pistols and Revolvers, by Charles W. Pate, Andrew Mowbray, Inc., Lincoln, RI, 1998. 515 pp., illus. $39.00

This indispensable new book covers all of the American military handguns of WWII except for the M1911A1 Colt automatic.

U.S. Martial Single Shot Pistols, by Daniel D. Hartzler and James B. Whisker, Old Bedford Village Press, Bedford, PA, 1998. 128 pp., illus. $45.00

A photographic chronicle of military and semi-martial pistols supplied to the U.S. Government and the several States.

U.S. Military Arms Dates of Manufacture from 1795, by George Madis, Dallas, TX, 1995. 64 pp. Softcover. $9.95

Lists all U.S. military arms of collector interest alphabetically, covering about 250 models.

U.S. Naval Handguns, 1808-1911, by Fredrick R. Winter, Andrew Mowbray Publishers, Lincoln, RI, 1990. 128 pp., illus. $26.00

The story of U.S. Naval handguns spans an entire century—included are sections on each of the important naval handguns within the period.

U.S. Silent Service—Dolphins & Combat Insignia 1924-1945, by David Jones. Bender Publishing, San Jose, CA, 2001. 224 pp., 532 photos (most in full color). $39.95

This beautiful full-color book chronicles, with period letters and sketches, the developmental history of U.S. submarine insignia prior to 1945. It also contains many rare and never before published photographs, plus interviews with WWII submarine veterans, from enlisted men to famous skippers. All known contractors are covered plus embroidered versions, mess dress variations, the Roll of Honor, submarine combat insignia, battleflags, launch memorabilia and related submarine collectibles (postal covers, match book covers, jewelry, posters, advertising art, postcards.

Uniform and Dress Army and Navy of the Confederate States of America (Official Regulations), by Confederate States of America, Ray Riling Arms Books, Philadelphia, PA, 1960. $20.00

A portfolio containing a complete set of nine color plates especially prepared for framing, reproduced in exactly 200 sets from the very rare Richmond, VA., 1861 regulations.

Uniforms & Equipment of the Austro-Hungarian Army in World War One, by Spencer A. Coil, Atglen, PA, Schiffer Publications, 2003. 1st edition. 352 pp., with over 550 b&w and color photographs. Hardcover. New in new dust jacket. $69.95

Uniforms and Insignia of the Cossacks in the German Wehrmacht in World War II, by Peter Schuster and Harald Tiede, Atglen, PA, Schiffer Publications, 2003. 1st edition. 160 pp., illustrated with over 420 b&w and color photographs. Hardcover. New in new dust jacket. $49.95

Uniforms & Equipment of the Imperial German Army 1900-1918: A Study in Period Photographs, by Charles Woolley, Schiffer Publications, Atglen, PA, 2000. 375 pp., over 500 b&w photographs and 50 color drawings. Fully illustrated. $69.95

Features formal studio portraits of pre-war dress and wartime uniforms of all arms. Includes a 60-page full-color uniform section reproduced from rare 1914 plates.

Uniforms of the Third Reich: A Study in Photographs, by Maguire Hayes, Schiffer Publications, Atglen, PA, 1997. 200 pp., with over 400 color photographs. $69.95

This new book takes a close look at a variety of authentic WWII era German uniforms including examples from the Army, Luftwaffe, Kriegsmarine, Waffen-SS, Allgemeine-SS, Hitler youth and political leaders. Various accoutrements worn with the uniforms are also included to aid the collector.

Uniforms of the United States Army, 1774-1889, by Henry Alexander Ogden, Dover Publishing, Mineola, NY. 1998. 48 pp. of text plus 44 color plates. Softcover. $9.95

A republication of the work published by the quarter-master general, United States army in 1890. A striking collection of lithographs and a marvelous archive of military, social, and costume history portraying the gamut of U.S. Army uniforms from fatigues to full dress, between 1774 and 1889.

Uniforms of the Waffen-SS; Black Service Uniform-LAH Guard Uniform-SS Earth-Grey Service Uniform-Model 1936 Field Service Uniform-1939-1940-1941 Volume 1, by Michael D. Beaver, Schiffer Publications, Atglen, PA, 2002. 272 pp., with 500 color, and b&w photos. $79.95

This spectacular work is a heavily documented record of all major clothing articles of the Waffen-SS. Hundreds of unpublished photographs were used in production. This book is indispensable and an absolute must-have for any serious historian of WWII German uniforms.

Uniforms of the Waffen-SS; Sports and Drill Uniforms-Black Panzer Uniform-Camouflage-Concentration Camp Personnel-SD-SS Female Auxiliaries, Volume 3, by Michael D. Beaver, Schiffer Publications, Atglen, PA, 2002. 272 pp., with 500 color, and b&w photos. $79.95

Uniforms of the Waffen-SS; 1942-1943-1944-1945-Ski Uniforms-Overcoats-White Service Uniforms-Tropical Clothing, Volume 2, by Michael D. Beaver, Schiffer Publications, Atglen, PA, 2002. 272 pp., with 500 color, and b&w photos. $79.95

Uniforms, Organization, and History of the German Police, Volume I, by John R. Angolia and Hugh Page Taylor, San Jose, CA, R. James Bender Publishing, 2004. 704 pp. illustrated with b&w and color photos. Hardcover. $59.95

United States Marine Corps Uniforms, Insignia, and Personal Items of World War II, by Harlan Glenn Atglen, PA: Schiffer Publications, 2005. 1st edition. 272pp. Hardcover. NEW $79.95

Covering in detail the combat and dress uniforms of the United States Marine in World War II, this new volume is destined to become the World War II Marine Corps collector's reference! Shown in detail are the herringbone utilities that Marines wore from Guadalcanal to Okinawa, as well as Summer Service, Winter Service and Dress (Blues) uniforms.

ARMS LIBRARY

United States Martial Flintlocks, by Robert M. Reilly, Mowbray Publishing Co., Lincoln, RI, 1997. 264 pp., illus. $40.00
A comprehensive history of American flintlock longarms and handguns (mostly military) c. 1775 to c. 1840.

United States Submachine Guns: From the American 180 to the ZX-7, by Frank Iannamico, Harmony, ME, Moose Lake Publishing, 2004. 1st edition. This profusely illustrated new book covers the research and development of the submachine gun in the U.S. from World War I to the present. to1943. Many photos and charts, nearly 500 pages! Soft cover. $29.95

Variations of Colt's New Model Police and Pocket Breech Loading Pistols, by John D. Breslin, William Q. Pirie and David E. Price, Lincoln, RI, Andrew Mowbray Publishers, 2002. 1st edition. 158 pp., heavily illustrated with over 160 photographs and superb technical detailed drawings and diagrams. Pictorial hardcover. $37.95
A type-by-type guide to what collectors call small frame conversions.

Vietnam Order of Battle, by Shelby L. Stanton, William C. Westmoreland. Mechanicsburg, PA, Stackpole Books, 2003. 1st edition. 416 pp., 32 in full color, 101 pp. halftones. Hardcover. New in new dust jacket. $69.95

Visor Hats of the United States Armed Forces 1930-1950, by Joe Tonelli, Atglen, PA, Schiffer Publications, 2003. 1st edition. Hardcover. New in new dust jacket. $79.95

W.F. Cody Buffalo Bill Collector's Guide with Values, The, by James W. Wojtowicz, Collector Books, Paducah, KY, 1998. 271 pp., illus. $24.95
A profusion of colorful collectibles including lithographs, programs, photographs, books, medals, sheet music, guns, etc. and today's values.

Walther: A German Legend, by Manfred Kersten, Safari Press, Inc., Huntington Beach, CA, 2000. 400 pp., illus. $85.00
This comprehensive book covers, in rich detail, all aspects of the company and its guns, including an illustrious and rich history, the WWII years, all the pistols (models 1 through 9), the P-38, P-88, the long guns, 22 rifles, centerfires, Wehrmacht guns, and even a gun that could shoot around a corner.

Walther P-38 Pistol, by Maj. George Nonte, Desert Publications, Cornville, AZ, 1982. 100 pp., illus. Paper covers. $12.95
Complete volume on one of the most famous handguns to come out of WWII. All models covered.

Walther Pistols: Models 1 Through P99, Factory Variations and Copies, by Dieter H. Marschall, Ucross Books, Los Alamos, NM. 2000. 140 pp., with 140 b&w illustrations, index. Paper covers. $19.95
This is the English translation, revised and updated, of the highly successful and widely acclaimed German language edition. This book provides the collector with a reference guide and overview of the entire line of the Walther military, police, and self-defense pistols from the very first to the very latest. Models 1-9, PP, PPK, MP, AP, HP, P.38, P1, P4, P38K, P5, P88, P99 and the Manurhin models. Variations, where issued, serial ranges, calibers, marks, proofs, logos, and design aspects in an astonishing quantity and variety are crammed into this very well researched and highly regarded work.

Walther Models PP & PPK, 1929-1945 – Volume 1, by James L. Rankin, Coral Gables, FL, 1974. 142 pp., illus. $40.00
Complete coverage on the subject as to finish, proofmarks and Nazi Party inscriptions.

Walther Volume II, Engraved, Presentation and Standard Models, by James L. Rankin, J.L. Rankin, Coral Gables, FL, 1977. 112 pp., illus. $40.00
The new Walther book on embellished versions and standard models. Has 88 photographs, including many color plates.

Walther, Volume III, 1908-1980, by James L. Rankin, Coral Gables, FL, 1981. 226 pp., illus. $40.00
Covers all models of Walther handguns from 1908 to date, includes holsters, grips and magazines.

Winchester an American Legend, by R.L. Wilson, New York, Book Sales, 2004. Reprint. Hardcover. New in new dust jacket. $24.95

Winchester Bolt Action Military & Sporting Rifles 1877 to 1937, by Herbert G. Houze, Andrew Mowbray Publishing, Lincoln, RI, 1998. 295 pp., illus. $45.00
Winchester was the first American arms maker to commercially manufacture a bolt action repeating rifle, and this book tells the exciting story of these Winchester bolt actions.

Winchester Book, by George Madis, David Madis Gun Book Distributor, Dallas, TX, 2000. 650 pp., illus. $54.50
A new, revised 25th anniversary edition of this classic book on Winchester firearms. Complete serial ranges have been added.

Winchester Dates of Manufacture 1849-1984, by George Madis, Art & Reference House, Brownsboro, TX, 1984. 59 pp. $8.50
A most useful work, compiled from records of the Winchester factory.

Winchester Engraving, by R.L. Wilson, Beinfeld Books, Springs, CA, 1989. 500 pp., illus. $185.00
A classic reference work of value to all arms collectors.

Winchester Handbook, The, by George Madis, Art & Reference House, Lancaster, TX, 1982. 287 pp., illus. $26.95
The complete line of Winchester guns, with dates of manufacture, serial numbers, etc.

Winchester Lever Action Repeating Firearms, Vol. 1, The Models of 1866, 1873 and 1876, by Arthur Pirkle, North Cape Publications, Tustin, CA, 1995. 112 pp., illus. Paper covers. $19.95
Complete, part-by-part description, including dimensions, finishes, markings and variations throughout the production run of these fine, collectible guns.

Winchester Lever Action Repeating Rifles, Vol. 2, The Models of 1886 and 1892, by Arthur Pirkle, North Cape Publications, Tustin, CA, 1996. 150 pp., illus. Paper covers. $19.95
Describes each model on a part-by-part basis by serial number range complete with finishes, markings and changes.

Winchester Lever Action Repeating Rifles, Vol. 3, The Model of 1894, by Arthur Pirkle, North Cape Publications, Tustin, CA, 1998. 150 pp., illus. Paper covers. $19.95
The first book ever to provide a detailed description of the Model 1894 rifle and carbine.

Winchester Lever Legacy, The, by Clyde "Snooky" Williamson, Buffalo Press, Zachary, LA, 1988. 664 pp., illus. $75.00

A book on reloading for the different calibers of the Winchester lever action rifle.

Winchester Model 1876 "Centennial" Rifle, The, by Herbert G. Houze. Lincoln, RI, Andrew Mowbray, Inc., 2001. Illustrated with over 180 b&w photographs. 192 pp. Hardcover. $45.00
The first authoritative study of the Winchester Model 1876 written using the company's own records. This book dispels the myth that the Model 1876 was merely a larger version of the Winchester company's famous Model 1873 and instead traces its true origins to designs developed immediately after the American Civil War. For Winchester collectors, and those interested in the mechanics of the 19th-century arms industry, this book provides a wealth of previously unpublished information.

Winchester Pocket Guide: Identification & Pricing for 50 Collectible Rifles and Shotguns, by Ned Schwing, Iola, WI, Krause Publications, 2004. 1st edition. 224 pp., illus. Softcover. $12.95

Winchester Repeating Arms Company Its History & Development from 1865 to 1981, by Herbert G. Houze, Iola, WI, Krause Publications, 2004. 1st edition. Softcover. $34.98

Winchester Single-Shot, Volume 1; A History and Analysis, The, by John Campbell, Andrew Mowbray, Inc., Lincoln, RI, 1995. 272 pp., illus. $55.00
Covers every important aspect of this highly-collectible firearm.

Winchester Single-Shot, Volume 2; Old Secrets and New Discoveries, The, by John Campbell, Andrew Mowbray, Inc., Lincoln, RI, 2000. 280 pp., illus. $55.00
An exciting follow-up to the classic first volume.

Winchester Sporting Firearms: Dates of Manufacture, by D.R. Morse, Phoenix, AZ, Firing Pin Enterprizes, 2003. 45 pp. Softcover. $6.95
Covers their pistols, revolvers, rifles, shotguns and commemoratives, plus models and serial numbers.

Winchester-Lee Rifle, The, by Eugene Myszkowski, Excalibur Publications, Tucson, AZ 2000. 96 pp., illus. Paper covers. $22.95
The development of the Lee Straight Pull, the cartridge and the approval for military use. Covers details of the inventor and memorabilia of Winchester-Lee related material.

World War One Collectors Handbook Volumes 1 and 2, by Paul Schulz, Hayes Otoupalik and Dennis Gordon, Missoula, MT, privately printed, 2002. Two volumes in one edition. 110 pp., loaded with b&w photos. Softcover. $21.95
Covers, uniforms, insignia, equipment, weapons, souvenirs and miscellaneous. Includes price guide. For all of you Doughboy collectors, this is a must.

World War II German War Booty, A Study in Photographs, by Thomas M. Johnson, Atglen, PA, Schiffer Publications, 2003. 1st edition. 368 pp. Hardcover. New in new dust jacket. $79.95

Worldwide Webley and the Harrington and Richardson Connection, by Stephen Cuthbertson, Ballista Publishing and Distributing Ltd., Gabriola Island, Canada, 1999. 259 pp., illus. $50.00
A masterpiece of scholarship. Over 350 photographs plus 75 original documents, patent drawings, and advertisements accompany the text.

World's Great Handguns: From 1450 to the Present Day, The, by Roger Ford, Secaucus, NJ, Chartwell Books, Inc., 1997. 1st edition. 176 pp. Hardcover. New in new dust jacket. $19.95

GENERAL

331+ Essential Tips and Tricks; A How-To Guide for the Gun Collector, by Stuart Mowbray, Lincoln, RI, 2006. 1st edition, photographs. Full color, 272 pp., 357 photographs. Soft cover. $35.99
Everything from gun photography to detecting refinishes can be found in this comprehensive new reference book.

A Rifleman Went to War, by H. W. McBride, Lancer Militaria, Mt. Ida, AR, 1987. 398 pp., illus. $29.95
The classic account of practical marksmanship on the battlefields of WWI.

Action Shooting: Cowboy Style, by John Taffin, Krause Publications, Iola, WI, 1999. 320 pp., illus. $39.95
Details on the guns and ammunition. Explanations of the rules used for many events.

Advanced Muzzleloader's Guide, by Toby Bridges, Stoeger Publishing Co., So. Hackensack, NJ, 1985. 256 pp., illus. Paper covers. $14.95
The complete guide to muzzle-loading rifles, pistols and shotguns–flintlock and percussion.

Aids to Musketry for Officers & NCOs, by Capt. B.J. Friend, Excalibur Publications, Latham, NY, 1996. 40 pp., illus. Paper covers. $7.95
A facsimile edition of a pre-WWI British manual filled with useful information for training the common soldier.

Airgun Odyssey, by Steve Hanson, Manchester, CT, Precision Shooting, Inc., 2004. 1st edition. 175 pp. Pictorial softcover. $27.95

America's Great Gunmakers, by Wayne van Zwoll, Stoeger Publishing Co., So. Hackensack, NJ, 1992. 288 pp., illus. Paper covers. $16.95
This book traces in great detail the evolution of guns and ammunition in America and the men who formed the companies that produced them.

American Air Rifles, by James E. House, Krause Publications, Iola, WI, 2002. 1st edition. 208 pp., with 198 b&w photos. Softcover. $22.95
Air rifle ballistics, sights, pellets, games, and hunting caliber recommendations are thoroughly explained to help shooters get the most out of their American air rifles. Evaluation of more than a dozen American-made and American-imported air rifle models.

American and Imported Arms, Ammunition and Shooting Accessories, Catalog No. 18 of the Shooter's Bible, Stoeger, Inc., reprinted by Fayette Arsenal, Fayetteville, NC, 1988. 142 pp., illus. Paper covers. $10.95
A facsimile reprint of the 1932 Stoeger's Shooter's Bible.

American B.B. Gun: A Collector's Guide, by Arni T. Dunathan. A.S. Barnes and Co., Inc., South Brunswick, 2001. 154 pp., illustrated with nearly 200 photographs, drawings and detailed diagrams. Hardcover. $35.00

Annie Oakley of the Wild West, by Walter Havighurst, New York, Castle Books, 2000. 246 pp. Hardcover. New in new dust jacket. $10.00

Antique Guns; The Collector's Guide, by Steve Carpenteri, Accokeek, MD: Stoeger Publications, 2005. Revised edition. 260 pages, illus. plus a 32 page color section. Soft cover. New. $22.95
Covers a vast spectrum of pre-1900 firearms: those manufactured by U.S. gun makers as well as Canadian, French, German, Belgian, Spanish and other foreign firms.

Armed Response, by Massad Ayoob, and David Kenik, NY, Merril Press, 2005. These are valuable real-life lessons about preparing to face a lethal threat, winning a gunfight, and surviving the ensuing court battle that can not be found outside of expensive tactical schools. 179 pages, with b&w photos. Foreword by Massad Ayoob. Soft cover. $19.95

Arming & Equipping the United States Cavalry 1865-1902, by Dusan Farrington, Lincoln, RI: Andrew Mowbray, Inc., 2005. 1st edition. $68.95

775 photos!!! Simply packed with serial numbers, issue information, reports from the field and more! Meticulously researched and absolutely up-to-date. A complete reference to all the arms and accoutrements. And at a bargain price to boot! Hardcover. New in new dust jacket. $68.95

Arming the Glorious Cause: Weapons of the Second War for Independence, by James B. Whisker, Daniel D. Hartzler and Larry W. Yantz, R & R Books, Livonia, NY, 1998. 175 pp., illus. $45.00

A photographic study of Confederate weapons.

Arms & Armor in the Art Institute of Chicago, by Walter J. Karcheski Jr., Bulfinch Press, Boston, MA, 1995. 128 pp., illus. $35.00

Now, for the first time, the Art Institute of Chicago's arms and armor collection is presented in the visual delight of 103 color illustrations.

Arms for the Nation: Springfield Longarms, edited by David C. Clark, Scott A. Duff, Export, PA, 1994. 73 pp., illus. Paper covers. $9.95

A brief history of the Springfield Armory and the arms made there.

Arrowmaker Frontier Series Volume 1, by Roy Chandler, Jacksonville, NC, Ron Brigade Armory, 2000. 390 pp. Hardcover. New in new dust jacket. $38.95

Arsenal of Freedom, The Springfield Armory, 1890-1948: A Year-by-Year Account Drawn from Official Records, compiled and edited by Lt. Col. William S. Brophy, USAR Ret., Andrew Mowbray, Inc., Lincoln, RI, 1991. 400 pp., illus. Softcover. $29.95

A "must buy" for all students of American military weapons, equipment and accoutrements.

Art of American Arms Makers Marketing Guns, Ammunition, and Western Adventure During the Golden Age of Illustration, by Richard C., Rattenbury, Oklahoma City, OK, National Cowboy Museum, 2004. 132 pp. of color photos. Softcover. $29.95

Art of American Game Calls, by Russell E. Lewis, Paducah, KY, Collector Books, 2005. 1st edition. 176 pp. Pictorial hardcover. $24.95

Art of Blacksmithing, by Alex W. Bealer, New York, Book Sales, 1996. Revised edition. 440 pp. Hardcover. New in new dust jacket. $10.00

Art of Remington Arms, Sporting Classics, 2004, by Tom Davis. 1st edition. Hardcover. $60.00

Battle of the Bulge: Hitler's Alternate Scenarios, by Peter Tsouras, Mechanicsburg, PA, Stackpole Books, 2004. 1st edition. 256 pp., 24 b&w photos, 10 maps. Hardcover. $34.95

Belgian Rattlesnake: The Lewis Automatic Machine Gun, The, by William M. Easterly, Collector Grade Publications, Inc., Cobourg, Ont. Canada, 1998. 542 pp., illus. $79.95

A social and technical biography of the Lewis automatic machine gun and its inventors.

Benchrest Shooting Primer, The, edited by Dave Brennan, Precision Shooting, Inc., Manchester, CT, 2000. 2nd edition. 420 pp., illustrated with b&w photographs, drawings and detailed diagrams. Pictorial softcover. $24.95

The very best articles on shooting and reloading for the most challenging of all the rifle accuracy disciplines…benchrest shooting.

Black Rifle Frontier Series Volume 2, The, by Roy Chandler, Jacksonville, NC, Iron Brigade Armory, 2002. 226 pp. Hardcover. New in new dust jacket. $42.95

In 1760, inexperienced Jack Elan settles in Sherman's Valley, suffers tragedy, is captured by hostiles, escapes, and fights on. This is the "2nd" book in the Frontier Series.

Blue Book of Airguns 6th Edition, by Robert Beeman and John Allen, Minneapolis, MN, Blue Book Publications, Inc., 2007. Softcover. $29.95

Blue Book of Gun Values, 28th Edition (2007 Edition), by S.P. Fjestad, Minneapolis, MN, Blue Book Publications, Inc., 2080 pp., illus. Paper covers. $39.95

Blue Book of Modern Black Powder Values, 4th Edition, by Dennis Adler, John Allen, Minneapolis, MN, Blue Book Publications, Inc., 2004. Softcover. $24.95

Bodyguard Manual, by Leroy Thompson, Mechanicsburg,PA. Greenhill Books, 2005. 208 pages, 16 pages of plates. Soft cover. $23.95

Bodyguard Manual details the steps a protective team takes to prevent attack as well as the tactics employed when it is necessary to counter one.

British Small Arms of World War II, by Ian D. Skennerton, Arms & Militaria Press, Australia, 1988. 110 pp., 37 illus. $25.00

C Stories, by Jeff Cooper, Sycamore Island Books, 2005. 1st edition. Quite simply, CStories is Jeff Cooper at his best. illus., 316 pp. Hardcover. New in new dust jacket. $49.95

Carbine and Shotgun Speed Shooting: How to Hit Hard and Fast in Combat, by Steve Moses. Paladin Press, Boulder, CO. 2002. 96 pp., illus. Softcover $18.00

In this groundbreaking book, he breaks down the mechanics of speed shooting these weapons, from stance and grip to sighting, trigger control and more, presenting them in a concise and easily understood manner.

Cavalry Raids of the Civil War, by Col. Robert W. Black, Mechanicsburg, PA, Stackpole Books, 2004. 1st edition. 288 pp., 30 b&w drawings. Softcover. $17.95

CO2 Pistols and Rifles, by James E. House, Iola, WI, Krause Publications, 2004. 1st edition 240 pp., with 198 b&w photos. Softcover. $24.95

Combatives FM-3-25.150, by U.S. Army, Boulder, CO, Paladin Press, 2004. Photos, illus., 272 pp. Soft cover. $19.95

This exact reprint of the U.S. Army's most current field manual on hand-to-hand combat (FM 3-25.150) reflects the first major revision to the Army's close-quarters combat program in a decade. This field manual shows them how.

Complete .50-caliber Sniper Course, The, by Dean Michaelis, Paladin Press, Boulder, CO, 2000. 576 pp., illus., $60.00

The history from German Mauser T-Gewehr of WWI to the Soviet PTRD and beyond. Includes the author's Program of Instruction for Special Operations Hard-Target Interdiction Course.

Complete Guide to Game Care and Cookery, 4th Edition, The, by Sam Fadala, Krause Publications, Iola, WI, 2003. 320 pp., illus. Paper covers. $21.95

Over 500 photos illustrating the care of wild game in the field and at home with a separate recipe section providing over 400 tested recipes.

Concealed Handgun Manual, 4th Edition, The, by Chris Bird, San Antonio, TX, Privateer Publications, 2004. 332 pp., illus. Softcover, $21.95

Cowboys & the Trappings of the Old West, by William Manns & Elizabeth Clair Flood, Santa Fe, NM, ZON International Publishing Company, 1997. 224 pp., 550 colorful photos. Foreword by Roy Rogers. Hardcover. $45.00

Big & beautiful book covering: Hats, boots, spurs, chaps, guns, holsters, saddles and more. It's really a pictorial cele bration of the old time buckaroo. This exceptional book presents all the accoutrements of the cowboy life in a comprehensive tribute to the makers. The history of the craftsmen and the evolution of the gear are lavishly illustrated.

Cowgirls, Revised and Expanded 2nd Edition Early Images and Collectibles Price Guide, by Judy Crandall, Atglen, PA, Schiffer Publications, 2005. 2nd edition. Soft cover. $24.95

The First Ladies from the Great American West live again in this comprehensive pictorial chronicle.

Cowgirls: Women of the Wild West, by Elizabeth Clair Flood and William Maims, edited by Helene Helene, Santa Fe, NM, ZON International Publishing Company, 2000. 1st edition. Hardcover. New in new dust jacket. $45.00

Custom Firearms Engraving, by Tom Turpin, Krause Publications, Iola, WI, 1999. 208 pp., illus. $49.95

Provides a broad and comprehensive look at the world of firearms engraving. The exquisite styles of more than 75 master engravers are shown on beautiful examples of handguns, rifles, shotguns, and other firearms, as well as knives.

Custom Gunmakers of the 20th Century, by Michael Pretov, Manchester, CT, Precision Shooting, 2005. 168 pages, illustrated with Photos. Hardcover. $24.95 NEW.

Daisy Air Rifles & BB Guns: The First 100 Years, by Neal Punchard, St. Paul, MN, Motorbooks, 2002. 1st edition. Hardcover, 10" x 10", 156 pp., 300 color. Hardcover. $29.95

Dead On, by Tony Noblitt and Warren Gabrilska, Paladin Press, Boulder, CO, 1998. 176 pp., illus. Paper covers. $22.00

The long-range marksman's guide to extreme accuracy. ***Defensive Use of Firearms,*** by Stephen Wenger, Boulder,CO, Paladin Press, 2005. 5½" x 8½", soft cover, illus., 120 pp. Soft cover. $20.00

This concise and affordable handbook offers the reader a set of common-sense principles, tactics and techniques distilled from hundreds of hours of the author's training, which includes certification as a law-enforcement handgun, shotgun, patrol rifle and tactical shooting instructor.

Do or Die A Supplementary Manual on Individual Combat, by Lieut. Col. A.J. Drexel Biddle, U.S.M.C.R., Boulder, CO, Paladin Press, 2004. 80 pp., illus. Softcover, $15.00

Down to Earth: The 507th Parachute Infantry Regiment in Normandy: June 6-july 11 1944, by Martin Morgan ICA, Atglen, PA, Schiffer Publishing, 2004. 1st edition. 304 pp., color and b&w photos. Hardcover. New in new dust jacket. $69.95

Effective Defense: The Woman, the Plan, the Gun, by Gila Hayes, Onalaska, WA, Police Bookshelf, 2000. 2nd edition. Photos, 264 pp. Softcover. $16.95

Elmer Keith: The Other Side of a Western Legend, by Gene Brown, Precision Shooting, Inc., Manchester, CT 2002. 1st edition. 168 pp., illustrated with b&w photos. Softcover. $19.95

An updated and expanded edition of his original work, incorporating new tales and information that have come to light in the past six years. Gene Brown was a long time friend of Keith, and today is unquestionably the leading authority on Keith's books.

Encyclopedia of Native American Bows, Arrows and Quivers, by Steve Allely and Jim Hamm, The Lyons Press, N.Y., 1999. 160 pp., illus. $29.95

A landmark book for anyone interested in archery history, or Native Americans.

Exercise of Armes, The, by Jacob de Gheyn, Dover Publications, Inc., Mineola, NY, 1999. 144 pp., illus. Paper covers. $14.95

Republications of all 117 engravings from the 1607 classic military manual. A meticulously accurate portrait of uniforms and weapons of the 17th century Netherlands.

Fighting Iron: A Metals Handbook for Arms Collectors, by Art Gogan, Mowbray Publishers, Inc., Lincoln, RI, 2002. 176 pp., illus. $28.00

A guide that is easy to use, explains things in simple English and covers all of the different historical periods that we are interested in.

FBI Guide to Concealable Weapons, by the FBI, Boulder, Co, Paladin Press, 2005. As citizens responsible for our own safety, we must know everything possible about the dangers that face us, and awareness is the first, vital step in this direction. Photos, 88 pp. Soft cover. $15.00

Filipino Fighting Whip: Advanced Training Methods and Combat Applications, The, by Tom Meadows, Boulder, CO, Paladin Press, 2005. This book is a comprehensive guide for advanced training methods and combat applications as practiced and taught by the best fighters and whip practitioners in the world. 216 pp. Soft cover. $20.00

Fine Art of the West, by Byron B. Price and Christopher Lyon, New York, Abbeville Press, 2004. Hardcover. $75.00

Firearm Suppressor Patents, Volume One: United States Patents, by N.R. Parker, Boulder, CO, Paladin Press, 2004. 392 pages, illustrated. Soft cover. $45.00

This book provides never-before-published interviews with three of today's top designers as well as a special section on the evolution of cutting-edge silencer mounting systems.

Firearms Assembly Disassembly; Part 4: Centerfire Rifles (2nd Edition), by J. B. Wood, Iola, WI, Krause Publications, 2004. 2nd edition. 576 pp., 1,750 b&w photos. Softcover. $24.95

Fireworks: A Gunsight Anthology, by Jeff Cooper, Paladin Press, Boulder, CO, 1998. 192 pp., illus. Paper cover. $27.00

A collection of wild, hilarious, shocking and always meaningful tales from the remarkable life of an American firearms legend.

Force-On-Force Gunfight Training: The Interactive, Reality Based Solution, by Gabriel Suarez, Boulder,CO, Paladin Press, 2005. 105 pages, illustrated with photos. Soft cover. $15.00

Fort Robinson, Frontier Series, Volume 4, by Roy Chandler, Jacksonville, NC, Ron Brigade Armory, 2003. 1st edition. 560 pp. Hardcover. New in new dust jacket. $39.95

Frederic Remington: The Color of Night, by Nancy Anderson, Princeton University Press, 2003. 1st edition. 136 color illus, 24 halftones; 10" x 11", 208 pgs. Hardcover, New in new dust jacket. $49.95; UK $52.49

From a Stranger's Doorstep to the Kremlin Gate, by Mikhail Kalashnikov, Ironside International Publishers, Inc., Alexandria, VA, 1999. 460 pp., illus. $34.95

A biography of the most influential rifle designer of the 20th century. His AK-47 assault rifle has become the most widely used (and copied) assault rifle of this century.

Frontier Rifleman, The, by H.B. LaCrosse Jr., Pioneer Press, Union City, TN, 1989. 183 pp., illus. Softcover. $17.50

The Frontier rifleman's clothing and equipment during the era of the American Revolution, 1760-1800.

Galloping Thunder: The Stuart Horse Artillery Battalion, by Robert Trout, Mechanicsburg, PA, Stackpole Books, 2002. 1st edition. Hardcover, $39.95

Gatling Gun: 19th Century Machine Gun to 21st Century Vulcan, The, by Joseph Berk, Paladin Press, Boulder, CO, 1991. 136 pp., illus. $34.95

Here is the fascinating on-going story of a truly timeless weapon, from its beginnings during the Civil War to its current role as a state-of-the-art modern combat system.

German Artillery of World War Two, by Ian V. Hogg, Stackpole Books, Mechanicsburg, PA, 1997, 304 pp., illus. $44.95

Complete details of German artillery use in WWII.

Gone Diggin: Memoirs of a Civil War Relic Hunter, by Toby Law, Orange, VA, Publisher's Press, 2002. 1st edition signed. 151 pp., illustrated with b&w photos. $24.95

The true story of one relic hunter's life-The author kept exacting records of every relic hunt and every relic hunter he was with working with.

Gun Digest 2009, 63rd Annual Edition, edited by Ken Ramage, Iola, WI, Krause Publications, 2006. Softcover. $27.95

This all new 63rd edition continues the editorial excellence, quality, content and comprehensive cataloguing that firearms enthusiasts have come to know and expect. The most read gun book in the world for the last half century.

Gun Digest Book of Cowboy Action Shooting: Gear, Guns, Tactics, The, edited by Kevin Michalowski, Iola, WI, Krause Publications, 2005. Softcover. 288 pages, plus 200 b&w photos! $24.99

This one-of-a-kind guide offers complete coverage of the sport from the top experts and personalities in the field.

Gun Digest Book of Exploded Firearms Drawings: 975 Isometric Views, The, by Harold Murtz, Iola,WI, Krause Publications, 2005, 3rd edition. 1032pp, 975 photos. Soft cover. $34.95

This book is sure to become a must-have for gunsmiths, shooters and law enforcement officials!

Gun Digest Blackpowder Loading Manual New Expanded 4th Edition, by Sam Fadala, Iola, WI, Krause Publications, 2006. 352 pp., illus. Softcover. $27.95

All blackpowder rifle, pistol, and shotgun users should be equipped with the new information supplied in this seminal reference--complete with loading tutorial and instructive articles expertly written by author Sam Fadala. Loading techniques are covered for more than 250 different modern blackpowder firearms--the illustrations are clear and the text is expertly laid out--easily understandable to even the most novice shooter. Experts will also benefit from the tips and techniques of Sam Fadala. This is the must-have book blackpowder shooters have been craving.

Gun Digest Book of Deer Guns, The, edited by Dan Shideler, Iola, WI, Krause Publications, 2004. 1st edition Softcover, 160pp, 225 b&w photos. $14.99

An illustrated catalog section details deer rifles, shotguns, handguns and muzzleloaders, complete with current pricing information from "Modern Gun Values." A special reference section includes selected portions of the Arms Library, as well as a website directory of state game and fish departments. This practical guide is a must for any deer hunter!

Gun Digest Book of Guns for Personal Defense Arms & Accessories for Self-Defense, The, edited by Kevin Michalowski, Iola, WI, Krause Publications, 2004. 1st edition Softcover. 160pp plus 200 b&w photos! $14.99

Handgun enthusiasts or anyone looking to find out about handguns for personal defense will find everything they need to know in the pages of this comprehensive guide and reference. Readers will learn the basics of selection and use of handguns for personal defense. The book covers uses of revolvers, semi-automatic pistols, ammunition, holsters, firearms training options, buying a used gun and much more. A catalog section contains listings of currently available pistols and revolvers suitable for personal defense, complete with pricing for each.

Gun Digest Book of Sporting Clays, 3rd Edition, The, edited by Rick Sapp, Iola, WI, Krause Publications, 2005. 1st edition Softcover, 288 pages, illustrated. $19.95

New articles cover equipment selection, strategies, technical issues and more. Features a review of the 50 best clay ranges in the country -Includes a fully illustrated catalog of currently available sporting clays shotguns showing complete specifications and retail prices.

Gun Digest Book of Trap & Skeet Shooting, 4th Edition, The, edited by Rick Sapp, Iola, WI, Krause Publications, 2004. 1st edition Softcover, 256 pages, illustrated. $22.95

The book includes comprehensive coverage on choosing and fitting the right shotgun for each sport, explains the hows and whys of chokes in plain language, and provides an in-depth review of shells, loads and reloading. Valuable reference tools include the official rules for each game as well as a manufacturer's directory for guns, ammunition, clothing and accessories.

Gun Engraving, by C. Austyn, Safari Press Publication, Huntington Beach, CA, 1998. 128 pp., plus 24 pp. of color photos. $50.00

A well-illustrated book on fine English and European gun engravers. Includes a fantastic pictorial section that lists types of engravings and prices.

Gun Notes, Volume 1, by Elmer Keith, Safari Press, Huntington Beach, CA, 2002. 219 pp., illus. Softcover. $24.95

A collection of Elmer Keith's most interesting columns and feature stories that appeared in *"Guns & Ammo"* magazine from 1961 to the late 1970s.

Gun Notes, Volume 2, by Elmer Keith, Safari Press, Huntington Beach, CA, 2002. 292 pp., illus. Softcover. $24.95

Covers articles from Keith's monthly column in *"Guns & Ammo"* magazine during the period from 1971 through Keith's passing in 1982.

Guns & Shooting: A Selected Bibliography, by Ray Riling, Ray Riling Arms Books Co., Phila., PA, 1982. 434 pp., illus. Limited, numbered edition. $75.00

A limited edition of this superb bibliographical work, the only modern listing of books devoted to guns and shooting.

Guns Illustrated 2007: 39th Edition, edited by Ken Ramage, Iola, WI, Krause Publications, 2006. Softcover. $21.95

Highly informative, technical articles on a wide range of shooting topics by some of the top writers in the industry. A catalog section lists more than 3,000 firearms currently manufactured in or imported to the U.S.

Guns of the Gunfighters: Lawmen, Outlaws & TV Cowboys, by Doc O'Meara, Iola, WI, Krause Publications, 2003. 1st edition. 16-page color section, 225 b&w photos. Hardcover. $34.95

Explores the romance of the Old West, focusing on the guns that the good guys & bad guys, real & fictional characters, carried with them. Profiles of more than 50 gunslingers, half from the Old West and half from Hollywood, include a brief biography of each gunfighter, along with the guns they carried. Fascinating stories about the TV and movie celebrities of the 1950s and 1960s detail their guns and the skill–or lack thereof–they displayed.

Guns, Bullets, and Gunfighters, by Jim Cirillo, Paladin Press, Boulder, CO, 1996. 119 pp., illus. Paper covers. $16.00

Lessons and tales from a modern-day gunfighter.

Gunstock Carving: A Step-by-Step Guide to Engraving Rifles and Shotguns, by Bill Janney, East Pertsburg, PA, Fox Chapel Publishing, October 2002. 89 pp., illustrated in color. Softcover. $19.95

Learn gunstock carving from an expert. Includes step-by-step projects and instructions, patterns, tips and techniques.

Hands Off! Self Defense for Women, by Maj. Fairbairn, Boulder, CO: Paladin Press, 2004. 56 pages. Soft cover. $15.00

Paladin Press is proud to bring back a work by the inimitable self-defense master W.E. Fairbairn so that a new generation of Americans can enjoy his teachings.

Hand-To-Hand Combat: United States Naval Institute, by U.S. Navy, Boulder, CO, Paladin Press, 2003. 1st edition. 240 pp. Softcover. $25.00

Now you can own one of the classic publications in the history of U.S. military close-quarters combat training. In 11 photo-heavy chapters, Hand-to-Hand Combat covers training tips; vulnerable targets; the brutal fundamentals of close-in fighting; frontal and rear attacks; prisoner search and control techniques; disarming pistols, rifles, clubs and knives; offensive means of "liquidating an enemy"; and much more. After reading this book (originally published by the United States Naval Institute in 1943), you will see why it has long been sought by collectors and historians of hand-to-hand combat.

Hidden in Plain Sight, "A Practical Guide to Concealed Handgun Carry" (Revised 2nd Edition), by Trey Bloodworth and Mike Raley, Paladin Press, Boulder, CO, 1997, softcover, photos, 176 pp. $20.00

This invaluable guide offers the latest advice on what to look for when choosing a CCW, how to dress for comfortable, effective concealed carry, traditional and more unconventional carry modes, accessory holsters, customized clothing and accessories, accessibility data based on draw-time comparisons and new holsters on the market. Includes 40 new manufacturer listings.

HK Assault Rifle Systems, by Duncan Long, Paladin Press, Boulder, CO, 1995. 110 pp., illus. Paper covers. $27.95

The little known history behind this fascinating family of weapons tracing its beginnings from the ashes of WWII to the present time.

Holsters for Combat and Concealed Carry, by R.K. Campbell, Boulder, CO, Paladin Press, 2004. 1st edition. 144 pp. Softcover. $22.00

Hostage Rescue Manual; Tactics of the Counter-Terrorist Professionals, by Leroy Thompson, Mechanicsburg, PA. Greehnill Books, 2005. 208 pages, with 16 pages of photos. Soft cover. $23.95

Incorporating vivid photographs and diagrams of rescue units in action, the Hostage Rescue Manual is the complete reference work on counter-terrorist procedures all over the world.

Hunter's Guide to Accurate Shooting, by Wayne van Zwoll, Guilford, CT, Lyons Press, 2002. 1st edition. 288 pp. Hardcover. $29.95

Firearms expert van Zwoll explains exactly how to shoot the big-game rifle accurately. Taking into consideration every pertinent factor, he shows a step-by-step analysis of shooting and hunting with the big-game rifle.

Hunting Time: Adventures in Pursuit of North American Big Game: A Forty-Year Chronicle, The, by John E. Howard, Deforest, WI, Saint Huberts Press, 2002. 1st edition. 537 pp., illustrated with drawings. Hardcover. $29.95

From a novice's first hunt for whitetailed deer in his native Wisconsin, to a seasoned hunter's pursuit of a Boone and Crockett Club record book caribou in the northwest territories, the author carries the reader along on his forty year journey through the big game fields of North America.

Instinct Combat Shooting; Defensive Handgunning for Police, by Chuck Klein, Flushing, NY, Looseleaf Law, 2004. 54 pages. Soft cover. $22.95

Tactical tips for effective armed defense, helpful definitions and court-ready statements that help you clearly articulate and competently justify your deadly force decision-making.

Jack O'Connor Catalogue of Letters, by Ellen Enzler Herring, Agoura, CA, Trophy Room Books, 2002. 1st edition. Hardcover. 262 pages, 18 illustrations. $55.00

During a sixteen year period beginning in 1960, O'Connor exchanged many letters with his pal, John Jobson. Material from nearly three hundred of these has been assembled and edited by Ellen Enzler Herring and published in chronological order. A number of the letters have been reproduced in full or part. They offer considerable insight into the beloved gun editor and "Dean of Outdoor Writers" over and beyond what we know about him from his books.

Jane's Guns Recognition Guide: 4th Edition, by Ian Hogg, Terry Gander, NY, Harper Collins, 2005. 464 pages, illustrated. Soft cover. $24.95

This book will help you identify them all. Jane's, always known for meticulous detail in the information of military equipment, aircraft, ships and much more!

Kill or Get Killed, by Col. Rex Applegate, Paladin Press, Boulder, CO, 1996. 400 pp., illus. $49.95

The best and longest-selling book on close combat in history.

Living With Terrorism; Survival Lessons from the Streets of Jerusalem, by Howard Linett, Boulder, CO, Paladin Press, 2005. 277 pages, illustrated with photos. Soft cover. $20.00

Before these dangers become a reality in your life, read this book.

Lost Classics of Jack O'Connor, The, edited by Jim Casada, Columbia, SC, Live Oak Press, 2004. 1st edition. Hardcover. New in new dust jacket. 33 photos, 40 illus by Dan Burr; 376 pages, with illustrations and photos. $35.00

You'll find 40 of O'Connor's most fascinating stories in the Trade Edition of Lost Classics. Exciting tales with a twist of humor.

Manual for H&R Reising Submachine Gun and Semi-Auto Rifle, edited by George P. Dillman, Desert Publications, El Dorado, AZ, 1994. 81 pp., illus. Paper covers. $14.95

A reprint of the Harrington & Richardson 1943 factory manual and the rare military manual on the H&R submachine gun and semi-auto rifle.

Manufacture of Gunflints, The, by Sydney B.J. Skertchly, facsimile reprint with new introduction by Seymour de Lotbiniere, Museum Restoration Service, Ontario, Canada, 1984. 90 pp., illus. $24.50

Limited edition reprinting of the very scarce London edition of 1879.

Master Tips, by J. Winokur, Potshot Press, Pacific Palisades, CA, 1985. 96 pp., illus. Paper covers. $11.95

Basics of practical shooting.

Military and Police Sniper, The, by Mike R. Lau, Precision Shooting, Inc., Manchester, CT, 1998. 352 pp., illus. Paper covers. $34.95

Advanced precision shooting for combat and law enforcement.

Military Small Arms of the 20th Century, 7th Edition, by Ian V. Hogg and John Weeks, DBI Books, a division of Krause Publications, Iola, WI, 2000. 416 pp., illus. Paper covers. Over 800 photographs and illustrations. $24.95

Covers small arms of 46 countries.

Modern Guns Identification and Values, 16th Edition, by Steve and Russell Quertermous, Paducah, KY, Collector's Books, 2006. 1800+ illus; 8.5"x11", 575 pgs. Soft cover. $18.95

Updated edition features current market values for over 2,500 models of rifles, shotguns, & handguns. Contains model name, gauge or caliber, action, finish or stock & forearm, barrel, cylinder or magazine, sights, weight & length, & comments.

Modern Gun Values: 13th Edition, edited by Dan Shideler, Krause Publications, Iola, WI, 2006. Softcover. 680 Pages, 3,000+ b&w photos. $24.95

This all-new expanded edition helps collectors identify the firearm, evaluate condition and determine value. Detailed specifications—and current values from specialized experts—are provided for domestic and imported handguns, rifles, shotguns and commemorative firearms. Heavily illustrated. Over 7,500 arms described and valued, in three grades of condition, according to the NRA's Modern standards.

Modern Law Enforcement Weapons & Tactics, 3rd edition, by Patrick Sweeney, Iola, WI, Krause Publications, 2004. Illustrated, b&w photos, 256 pages. $22.99

Sweeney walks you through the latest gear and tactics employed by American law enforcement officers.

Modern Sporting Guns, by Christopher Austyn, Safari Press, Huntington Beach, CA, 1994. 128 pp., illus. $40.00

A discussion of the "best" English guns; round action, over-and-under, boxlocks, hammer guns, bolt action and double rifles as well as accessories.

More Tactical Reality; Why There's No Such Thing as an Advanced Gunfight, by Louis Awerbuck, Boulder, CO, Paladin Press, 2004. 144 pp. Softcover. $25.00

MP-40 Machine Gun, The, Desert Publications, El Dorado, AZ, 1995. 32 pp., illus. Paper covers. $11.95

A reprint of the hard-to-find operating and maintenance manual for one of the most famous machine guns of WWII.

Naval Percussion Locks and Primers, by Lt. J. A. Dahlgren, Museum Restoration Service, Bloomfield, Canada, 1996. 140 pp., illus. $35.00

First published as an Ordnance Memoranda in 1853, this is the finest existing study of percussion locks and primers origin and development.

Official Soviet AKM Manual, translated by Maj. James F. Gebhardt (Ret.), Paladin Press, Boulder, CO, 1999. 120 pp., illus. Paper covers. $18.00

This official military manual, available in English for the first time, was originally published by the Soviet Ministry of Defence. Covers the history, function, maintenance, assembly and disassembly, etc. of the 7.62mm AKM assault rifle.

One-Round War: U.S.M.C. Scout-Snipers in Vietnam, by Peter Senich, Paladin Press, Boulder, CO, 1996. 384 pp., illus. Paper covers $59.95

Sniping in Vietnam focusing specifically on the Marine Corps program.

Optics Digest: Scopes, Binoculars, Rangefinders, and Spotting Scopes, by Clair Rees, Long Beach, CA, Safari Press, 2005. 189 pp. Softcover. $24.95

OSS Special Operations in China, by Col. F. Mills and John W. Brunner, Williamstown, NJ, Phillips Publications, 2003. 1st edition. 550 pp., illustrated with photos. Hardcover. New in new dust jacket. $34.95

Paintball Digest The Complete Guide to Games, Gear, and Tactics, by Richard Sapp, Iola, WI, Krause Publications, 2004. 1st edition. 272 pp. Softcover. $19.99

Paleo-Indian Artifacts: Identification & Value Guide, by Lar Hothem, Paducah, KY, Collector Books, 2005. 1st edition. 379 pp. Pictorial hardcover. $29.95

Panzer Aces German Tank Commanders of WWII, by Franz Kurowski, translated by David Johnston, Mechanicsburg, PA, Stackpole Books, 2004. 1st edition. 448 pp., 50 b&w photos Softcover. $19.95

Parker Brothers: Knight of the Trigger, by Ed Muderlak, Davis, IL, Old Reliable Publishing, 2002. 223 pp. $25.00

Knight of the Trigger tells the story of the Old West when Parker's most famous gun saleman traveled the country by rail, competing in the pigeon ring, hunting with the rich and famous, and selling the "Old Reliable" Parker shotgun. The life and times of Captain Arthur William du Bray, Parker Brothers' on-the-road sales agent from 1884 to 1926, is described in a novelized version of his interesting life.

Peril in the Powder Mills: Gunpowder & Its Men, by David McMahon & Anne Kelly Lane, West Conshohocken, PA, privately printed, 2004. 1st edition. 118 pp. Softcover. $18.95

Powder Horns and their Architecture; And Decoration as Used by the Soldier, Indian, Sailor and Traders of the Era, by Madison Grant, York, PA, privately printed, 1987. 165 pp., profusely illustrated. Hardcover. $45.00

Covers homemade pieces from the late eighteenth and early nineteenth centuries.

Practically Speaking: An Illustrated Guide-The Game, Guns and Gear of the International Defensive Pistol Association, by Walt Rauch, Lafayette Hills, PA, privately printed, 2002. 1st edition. 79 pp., illustrated with drawings and color photos. Softcover. $24.95

The game, guns and gear of the International Defensive Pistol Association with real-world applications.

Present Sabers: A Popular History of the U.S. Horse Cavalry, by Allan T. Heninger, Tucson, AZ, Excalibur Publications, 2002. 1st edition. 160 pp., with 148 photographs, 45 illustrations and 4 charts. Softcover. $24.95

An illustrated history of America's involvement with the horse cavalry, from its earliest beginnings during the Revolutionary War through its demise in WWII. The book also contains several appendices, as well as depictions of the regular insignia of all the U.S. Cavalry units.

Principles of Personal Defense, by Jeff Cooper, Paladin Press, Boulder, CO, 2006. 80 pp., illus. Paper covers. $14.00

This revised edition of Jeff Cooper's classic on personal defense offers great new illustrations and a new preface while retaining the theory of individual defense behavior presented in the original book.

Queen's Rook: A Soldier's Story, by Croft Barker, Flatonia,TX, Cistern Publishing, 2004. Limited edition of 500 copies. 177 pages, with 50 never before published photographs. Soft cover. $35.00

Men of the U.S. Army were assigned to South Vietnamese Infantry companies and platoons. Many of these men were lost in a war that is still misunderstood. This is their story, written in their own words. These Americans, and the units they lived with, engaged in savage fights against Viet Cong guerillas and North Vietnamese Army Regulars in the dark, deadly jungles north of Saigon.

Quotable Hunter, The, edited by Jay Cassell and Peter Fiduccia, The Lyons Press, N.Y., 1999. 224 pp., illus. $20.00

This collection of more than three hundred memorable quotes from hunters through the ages captures the essence of the sport, with all its joys idiosyncrasies, and challenges.

Real World Self-Defense by Jerry Vancook, Boulder, CO, Paladin Press, 1999. 224 pp. Soft cover. $20.00

Presenting tactics and techniques that are basic, easy to learn and proven effective under the stress of combat, he covers unarmed defense, improvised weapons, edged weapons, firearms and more, photos, illus.

Renaissance Drill Book, by Jacob de Gheyn, edited by David J. Blackmore, Mechanicsburg, PA, Greenhill Books, 2003. 1st edition. 248 pp., 117 illustrations. Hardcover. $24.95

Jacob de Gheyn's Exercise of Armes was an immense success when first published in 1607. It is a fascinating 17th-century military manual, designed to instruct contemporary soldiers how to handle arms effectively, and correctly, and it makes for a unique glimpse into warfare as waged in the Thirty Years War and the English Civil War. In addition, detailed illustrations show the various movements and postures to be adopted during use of the pike.

Running Recon, A Photo Journey with SOG Special Ops Along the Ho Chi Minh Trail, by Frank Greco, Boulder, CO, Paladin Press, 2004. Paper covers. $50.00

Running Recon is a combination of military memoir and combat photography book. It reflects both the author's experience in Kontum, Vietnam, from April 1969 to April 1970 as part of the top-secret Studies and Observation Group (SOG) and the collective experience of SOG veterans in general. What sets it apart from other Vietnam books is its wealth of more than 700 photographs, many never before published, from the author's personal collection and those of his fellow SOG veterans.

Sharpshooting for Sport and War, by W.W. Greener, Wolfe Publishing Co., Prescott, AZ, 1995. 192 pp., illus. $30.00

This classic reprint explores the *first* expanding bullet; service rifles; shooting positions; trajectories; recoil; external ballistics; and other valuable information.

Shooter's Bible 2007 No. 98, by Wayne Van Zwoll, Stoeger Publishing, 2006. New for this edition is a special Web Directory designed to complement the regular Reference section, including the popular Gun finder index. 576 pages. Pictorial Soft cover. $24.95

Shooting Buffalo Rifles of the Old West, by Mike Venturino, MLV Enterprises, Livingston, MT, 2002. 278 pp., illustrated with b&w photos. Softcover. $30.00

This tome will take you through the history, the usage, the many models, and the actual shooting (and how to's) of the many guns that saw service on the Frontier and are lovingly called "Buffalo Rifles" today. If you love to shoot your Sharps, Ballards, Remingtons, or Springfield "Trapdoors" for hunting or competition, or simply love Old West history, your library WILL NOT be complete without this latest book from Mike Venturino!

Shooting Colt Single Actions, by Mike Venturino, MLV Enterprises, Livingston, MT, 1997. 205 pp., illus. Softcover. $25.00

A complete examination of the Colt Single Action including styles, calibers and generations, b&w photos throughout.

Shooting Lever Guns of the Old West, by Mike Venturino, MLV Enterprises, Livingston, MT, 1999. 300 pp., illus. Softcover. $27.95

Shooting the lever action type repeating rifles of our American West.

Shooting Sixguns of the Old West, by Mike Venturino, MLV Enterprises, Livingston, MT, 1997. 221 pp., illus. Paper covers. $26.50

A comprehensive look at the guns of the early West: Colts, Smith & Wesson and Remingtons, plus blackpowder and reloading specs.

Shooting to Live, by Capt. W.E. Fairbairn and Capt. E.A. Sykes, Paladin Press, Boulder, CO, 1997, 4½" x 7", soft cover, illus., 112 pp. $14.00

Shooting to Live is the product of Fairbairn's and Sykes' practical experience with the handgun. Hundreds of incidents provided the basis for the first true book on life-or-death shootouts with the pistol. Shooting to Live teaches all concepts, considerations and applications of combat pistol craft.

Small Arms of World War II, by Chris Chant, St. Paul, MN, MBI Publishing Company, 2001. 1st edition. 96 pp., single page on each weapon with photograph, description, and a specifications table. Hardcover. New. $13.95

Detailing the design and development of each weapon, this book covers the most important infantry weapons used by both Allied and Axis soldiers between 1939 and 1945. These include both standard infantry bolt-action rifles, such as the German Kar 98 and the British Lee-Enfield, plus the automatic rifles that entered service toward the end of the war, such as the Stg 43. As well as rifles, this book also features submachine guns, machine guns and handguns and a specifications table for each weapon.

Sniper Training, FM 23-10, Reprint of the U.S. Army field manual of August, 1994, Paladin Press, Boulder, CO, 1995. 352 pp., illus. Paper covers. $30.00

The most up-to-date U.S. military sniping information and doctrine.

Song of Blue Moccasin, by Roy Chandler, Jacksonville, NC, Ron Brigade Armory, 2004. 231 pp. Hardcover. New in new dust jacket. $45.00

Speak Like a Native; Professional Secrets for Mastering Foreign Languages, by Michael Janich, Boulder CO, Paladin Press, 2005. 136 pages. Soft cover. $19.00

No matter what language you wish to learn or the level of fluency you need to attain, this book can help you learn to speak like a native.

Special Operations: Weapons and Tactics, by Timothy Mullin, London, Greenhill Press, 2003. 1st edition. 176 pp., with 189 illustrations. $39.95

The tactics and equipment of Special Forces explained in full, Contains 200 images of weaponry and training. This highly illustrated guide covers the full experience of special operations training from every possible angle. There is also considerable information on nonfirearm usage, such as specialized armor and ammunition.

Standard Catalog of Firearms 2009, 19th Edition, by Dan Shideler, Iola, WI, Krause Publications, 2008. 1504 pages, 7,100+ b&w photos, plus a 16-page color section. Paper covers. $34.95

Now in its 19th year and completely updated for 2008, this edition of the world famous Standard Catalog of Firearms is bigger and better than ever. With entries for virtually all of the world's commercial firearms from the percussion era to the present day, Standard Catalog of Firearms is the only book you need to identify and price collectible rifles, handguns and shotguns. Includes: "Sleepers": Collectible firearms that are outperforming the market. Value Trends: Real-Life auction reports showing value ranges. How to buy and sell on the Internet.

Standard Catalog of Military Firearms 3rd Edition: The Collector's Price & Reference Guide, by Phillip Peterson, Iola, WI, Krause Publications, 2005. 480 pp. Softcover. $29.99

A companion volume to Standard Catalog of Firearms, this revised and expanded second edition comes complete with all the detailed information readers found useful and more. Listings beginning with the early cartridge models of the 1870s to the latest high-tech sniper rifles have been expanded to include more models, variations, historical information, and data, offering more detail for the military firearms collector, shooter, and history buff. Identification of specific firearms is easier with nearly 250 additional photographs. Plus, readers will enjoy "snap shots," small personal articles from experts relating real-life experiences with exclusive models. Revised to include every known military firearm available to the U.S. collector. Special feature articles on focused aspects of collecting and shooting.

Street Tough, Hard Core, Anything Goes, Street Fighting Fundamentals, by Phil Giles, Boulder, CO, Paladin Press, 2004. 176 pages. Soft cover. $25.00

ARMS LIBRARY

A series of intense training drills performed at full power and full speed sets the Street Tough program apart from all other self-defense regimens.

Stress Fire, Vol. 1: Stress Fighting for Police, by Massad Ayoob, Police Bookshelf, Concord, NH, 1984. 149 pp., illus. Paper covers. $11.95

Gunfighting for police, advanced tactics and techniques.

Stress Fire Gunfighting for Police Vol. 2; Advanced Combat Shotgun, by Massad Ayoob, Police Bookshelf, Concord, NH, 1997. 212 pp., illus. Paper covers. $12.95

The long-awaited second volume in Massad Ayoob's series on Advanced Gunfighting for Police. Learn to control the 12-gauge shotgun in the most rapid fire, pain-rree aimed fire from the shoulder, Speed reloads that don't fail under stress, proven jam-response techniques, keys to selecting a good shotgun.

Tactical Advantage, The, by Gabriel Suarez, Paladin Press, Boulder, CO, 1998. 216 pp., illus. Paper covers. $22.00

Learn combat tactics that have been tested in the world's toughest schools.

Tactical Marksman, by Dave M. Lauch, Paladin Press, Boulder, CO, 1996. 165 pp., illus. Paper covers. $35.00

A complete training manual for police and practical shooters.

Tim Murphy Rifleman Frontier Series Volume 3, by Roy Chandler, Jacksonville, NC, Iron Brigade Armory, 2003. 1st edition. 396 pp. Hardcover. $39.95

Tim Murphy may be our young nation's earliest recognized hero. Murphy was seized by Seneca Tribesmen during his infancy. Traded to the Huron, he was renamed and educated by Sir William Johnson, a British colonial officer. Freed during the prisoner exchange of 1764, Murphy discovered his superior ability with a Pennsylvania longrifle. An early volunteer in the Pennsylvania militia, Tim Murphy served valiantly in rifle companies including the justly famed Daniel Morgan's Riflemen. This is Murphy's story.

To Ride, Shoot Straight, and Speak the Truth, by Jeff Cooper, Paladin Press, Boulder, CO, 1997, 5½" x 8½", soft-cover, illus., 384 pp. $32.00

Combat mind-set, proper sighting, tactical residential architecture, nuclear war-these are some of the many subjects explored by Jeff Cooper in this illustrated anthology. The author discusses various arms, fighting skills and the importance of knowing how to defend oneself, and one's honor, in our rapidly changing world.

Trailriders Guide to Cowboy Action Shooting, by James W. Barnard, Pioneer Press, Union City, TN, 1998. 134 pp., plus 91 photos, drawings and charts. Paper covers. $24.95

Covers the complete spectrum of this shooting discipline, from how to dress to authentic leather goods, which guns are legal, calibers, loads and ballistics.

Traveler's Guide to the Firearms Laws of the Fifty States, 2007 Edition, by Scott Kappas, KY, Traveler's Guide, 2007, 64pp,. Softcover. $12.95

U.S. Army Hand-to-Hand Combat: FM 21-150, 1954 Edition, Boulder,CO, Paladin Press, 2005. 192 pp. illus. Soft cover. $20.00

U.S. Infantry Weapons in Combat: Personal Experiences from Wolrd War II and Korea, by Mark Goodwin w/ forward by Scott Duff, Export, PA, Scott Duff Pub., 2005.

237pp, over 50 photos and drawings. Soft cover. $23.50

The stories about U.S. infantry weapons contained in this book are the real hands-on experiences of the men who actually used them for their intended purposes.

U.S. Marine Corp Rifle and Pistol Marksmanship, 1935, reprinting of a government publication, Lancer Militaria, Mt. Ida, AR, 1991. 99 pp., illus. Paper covers. $11.95

The old corps method of precision shooting.

U.S. Marine Corps Scout/Sniper Training Manual, Lancer Militaria, Mt. Ida, AR, 1989. Softcover. $27.95

Reprint of the original sniper training manual used by the Marksmanship Training Unit of the Marine Corps Development and Education Command in Quantico, Virginia.

U.S. Marine Corps Scout-Sniper, World War II and Korea, by Peter R. Senich, Paladin Press, Boulder, CO, 1994. 236 pp., illus. $44.95

The most thorough and accurate account ever printed on the training, equipment and combat experiences of the U.S. Marine Corps Scout-Snipers.

U.S. Marine Corps Sniping, Lancer Militaria, Mt. Ida, AR, 1989. Irregular pagination. Softcover. $18.95

A reprint of the official Marine Corps FMFM1-3B.

U.S. Marine Uniforms-1912-1940, by Jim Moran, Williamstown, NJ, Phillips Publications, 2001. 174 pp., illustrated with b&w photographs. Hardcover. $49.95

Ultimate Sniper: An Advanced Training Manual for Military and Police Snipers, Updated and Expanded Edition, by Major John L. Plaster, Paladin Press, Boulder, CO, 2006. 584 pp., illus. Paper covers. $49.95

Now this revolutionary book has been completely updated and expanded for the 21st century. Through revised text, new photos, specialized illustrations, updated charts and additional information sidebars, The Ultimate Sniper once again thoroughly details the three great skill areas of sniping – marksmanship, fieldcraft and tactics.

Uniforms And Equipment of the Imperial Japanese Army in World War II, by Mike Hewitt, Atglen, PA, Schiffer Publications, 2002. 176 pp., with over 520 color and b&w photos. Hardcover. $59.95

Unrepentant Sinner, by Col. Charles Askins, Paladin Press, Boulder, CO, 2000. 322 pp., illus. $29.95

The autobiography of Colonel Charles Askins.

Vietnam Order of Battle, by Shelby L. Stanton, William C. Westmoreland, Mechanicsburg, PA, Stackpole Books, 2003. 1st edition. 416 pp., 32 in full color, 101 halftones. Hardcover. $69.95

A monumental, encyclopedic work of immense detail concerning U.S. Army and allied forces that fought in the Vietnam War from 1962 through 1973. Extensive lists of units providing a record of every Army unit that served in Vietnam, down to and including separate companies, and also including U.S. Army aviation and riverine units. Shoulder patches and distinctive unit insignia of all divisions and battalions. Extensive maps portraying unit locations at each six-month interval. Photographs and descriptions of all major types of equipment employed in the conflict. Plus much more!

Warriors; On lIving with Courage, Discipline, and Honor, by Loren Christensen, Boulder, CO, Paladin Press, 2004. 376 pages. Soft cover. $20.00

The writers who contributed to this work are a diverse mix, from soldiers, cops and SWAT officers to martial art masters to experts in the fields of workplace violence, theology and school safety. They are some of the finest warrior authors, warrior trainers and warrior scholars today. Many have faced death, survived and now teach others to do the same. Here they speak candidly on what it's like to sacrifice, to train, to protect.

"Walking Stick" Method of Self-Defence, The, by an officer of the Indian police, Boulder, CO: Paladin Press, 2004. 1st edition. 112 pages. Soft cover. $15.00

The entire range of defensive and offensive skills is discussed and demonstrated, including guards, strikes, combinations, counterattacks, feints and tricks, double-handed techniques and training drills.

Weapons of Delta Force, by Fred Pushies, St. Paul, MN, MBI Publishing Company, 2002. 1st edition. 128 pgs., 100 b&w and 100 color illustrated. Hardcover. $24.95

America's elite counter-terrorist organization, Delta Force, is a handpicked group of the U.S. Army's finest soldiers. Delta uses some of the most sophisticated weapons in the field today, and all are detailed in this book. Pistols, sniper rifles, special mission aircraft, fast attack vehicles, SCUBA and paratrooper gear, and more are presented in this fully illustrated account of our country's heroes and their tools of the trade.

Weapons of the Waffen-SS, by Bruce Quarrie, Sterling Publishing Co., Inc., 1991. 168 pp., illus. $24.95

An in-depth look at the weapons that made Hitler's Waffen-SS the fearsome fighting machine it was.

Weatherby: The Man, The Gun, The Legend, by Grits and Tom Gresham, Cane River Publishing Co., Natchitoches, LA, 1992. 290 pp., illus. $34.95

A fascinating look at the life of the man who changed the course of firearms development in America.

Winchester Era, The, by David Madis, Art & Reference House, Brownsville, TX, 1984. 100 pp., illus. $19.95

Story of the Winchester company, management, employees, etc.

Winchester Pocket Guide; Identification and Pricing for 50 Collectible Rifles and Shotguns, by Ned Schwing, Iola,WI, Krause Publications, 2004. 224 pages, illustrated. Soft cover. $12.95

The Winchester Pocket Guide also features advice on collecting, grading and pricing the collectible firearms.

With British Snipers to the Reich, by Capt. C. Shore, Lander Militaria, Mt. Ida, AR, 1988. 420 pp., illus. $29.95

One of the greatest books ever written on the art of combat sniping.

World's Machine Pistols and Submachine Guns-Vol. 2a 1964 to 1980, The, by Nelson & Musgrave, Ironside International, Alexandria, VA, 2000. 673 pp. $69.95

Containing data, history and photographs of over 200 weapons. With a special section covering shoulder stocked automatic pistols, 100 additional photos.

Wyatt Earp: A Biography of the Legend: Volume 1: The Cowtown Years, by Lee A. Silva, Santa Ana, CA, privately printed, 2002. 1st edition signed. Hardcover. New in new dust jacket. $86.95

GUNSMITHING

Accurizing the Factory Rifle, by M.L. McPhereson, Precision Shooting, Inc., Manchester, CT, 1999. 335 pp., illus. Paper covers. $44.95

A long-awaiting book, which bridges the gap between the rudimentary (mounting sling swivels, scope blocks and that general level of accomplishment) and the advanced (precision chambering, barrel fluting, and that general level of accomplishment) books that are currently available today.

Antique Firearms Assembly Disassembly: The Comprehensive Guide to Pistols, Rifles, & Shotguns, by David Chicoine, Iola, WI, Krause Publications, 2005. 528 pages, 600 b&w photos & illus. Soft cover. $29.95

Create a resource unequaled by any. Features over 600 photos of antique and rare firearms for quick identification.

Art of Engraving, The, by James B. Meek, F. Brownell & Son, Montezuma, IA, 1973. 196 pp., illus. $47.95

A complete, authoritative, imaginative and detailed study in training for gun engraving. The first book of its kind–and a great one.

Checkering and Carving of Gun Stocks, by Monte Kennedy, Stackpole Books, Harrisburg, PA, 1962. 175 pp., illus. $39.95

Revised, enlarged cloth-bound edition of a much sought-after, dependable work.

Firearms Assembly/Disassembly, Part I: Automatic Pistols, 2nd Revised Edition, The Gun Digest Book of, by J.B. Wood, DBI Books, a division of Krause Publications, Iola, WI, 1999. 480 pp., illus. Paper covers. $24.95

Covers 58 popular autoloading pistols plus nearly 200 variants of those models integrated into the text and completely cross-referenced in the index.

Firearms Assembly/Disassembly Part II: Revolvers, Revised Edition, The Gun Digest Book of, by J.B. Wood, DBI Books, a division of Krause Publications, Iola, WI, 1997. 480 pp., illus. Paper covers. $27.95

Covers 49 popular revolvers plus 130 variants. The most comprehensive and professional presentation available to either hobbyist or gunsmith.

Firearms Assembly/Disassembly Part III: Rimfire Rifles 3rd Edition, The Gun Digest Book of, by J. B. Wood, Krause Publications, Iola, WI, 2006. Softcover. 576 Pages, 1,590 b&w photos. $27.95

This redesigned volume provides comprehensive step-by-step disassembly instruction patterns for 74 rifles-nearly 200 firearms when combined with variations. All the hands-on information you need to increase accuracy and speed.

Firearms Assembly/Disassembly Part IV: Centerfire Rifles, 3rd Revised Edition, The Gun Digest Book of, by J.B. Wood, Krause Publications, Iola, WI, 2004. 480 pp., illus. Paper covers. $24.95

Covers 54 popular centerfire rifles plus 300 variants. The most comprehensive and professional presentation available to either hobbyist or gunsmith.

Firearms Assembly/Disassembly, Part V: Shotguns, Revised Edition, The Gun Digest Book of, by J.B. Wood, Krause Publications, Iola, WI, 2002. 480 pp., illus. Paper covers. $24.95

Covers 46 popular shotguns plus over 250 variants with step-by-step instructions on how to dismantle and reassemble each. The most comprehensive and professional presentation available to either hobbyist or gunsmith.

Firearms Assembly: The NRA Guide to Rifle and Shotguns, NRA Books, Wash., DC, 1980. 264 pp., illus. Paper covers. $14.95

Text and illustrations explaining the takedown of 125 rifles and shotguns, domestic and foreign.

Firearms Assembly: The NRA Guide to Pistols and Revolvers, NRA Books, Wash., DC, 1980. 253 pp., illus. Paper covers. $14.95

Text and illustrations explaining the takedown of 124 pistol and revolver models, domestic and foreign.

Firearms Bluing and Browning, by R.H. Angier, Stackpole Books, Harrisburg, PA. 151 pp., illus. $19.95

A world master gunsmith reveals his secrets of building, repairing and renewing a gun, quite literally, lock, stock and barrel. A useful, concise text on chemical coloring methods for the gunsmith and mechanic.

Guns and Gunmaking Tools of Southern Appalachia, by John Rice Irwin, Schiffer Publishing Ltd., 1983. 118 pp., illus. Paper covers. $9.95

The story of the Kentucky rifle.

Gunsmith Kinks, by F.R. (Bob) Brownell, F. Brownell & Son, Montezuma, IA, 1st ed., 1969. 496 pp., well illus. $22.98

A widely useful accumulation of shop kinks, short cuts, techniques and pertinent comments by practicing gunsmiths from all over the world.

Gunsmith Kinks 2, by Bob Brownell, F. Brownell & Son, Publishers, Montezuma, IA, 1983. 496 pp., illus. $22.95

A collection of gunsmithing knowledge, shop kinks, new and old techniques, shortcuts and general know-how straight from those who do them best–the gunsmiths.

Gunsmith Kinks 3, edited by Frank Brownell, Brownells Inc., Montezuma, IA, 1993. 504 pp., illus. $24.95

Tricks, knacks and "kinks" by professional gunsmiths and gun tinkerers. Hundreds of valuable ideas are given in this volume.

Gunsmith Kinks 4, edited by Frank Brownell, Brownells Inc., Montezuma, IA, 2001. 564 pp., illus. 332 detailed illustrations. 560+ pages with 706 separate subject headings and over 5000 cross-indexed entries. $27.75

An incredible gold mine of information.

Gunsmith Machinist, The, by Steve Acker, Village Press Publications Inc, Michigan. 2001. Hardcover, New in new dust jacket. $69.95

Gunsmith of Grenville County: Building the American Longrifle, The, by Peter Alexander, Texarkana, TX, Scurlock Publishing Co., 2002. 400 pp.in, with hundreds of illustrations, and six color photos of original rifles. Stiff paper covers. $45.00

The most extensive how-to book on building longrifles ever published. Takes you through every step of building your own longrifle, from shop set up and tools to engraving, carving and finishing.

Gunsmithing, by Roy F. Dunlap, Stackpole Books, Harrisburg, PA, 1990. 742 pp., illus. $44.95

A manual of firearm design, construction, alteration and remodeling. For amateur and professional gunsmiths and users of modern firearms.

Gunsmithing at Home: Lock, Stock and Barrel, by John Traister, Stoeger Publishing Co., Wayne, NJ, 1997. 320 pp., illus. Paper covers. $19.95

A complete step-by-step fully illustrated guide to the art of gunsmithing.

Gunsmithing Shotguns: The Complete Guide to Care & Repair, by David Henderson, New York, Globe Pequot, 2003. 1st edition. Hardcover. $24.95

Gunsmithing: Guns of the Old West: Expanded 2nd Edition, by David Chicoine, Iola, WI, Krause Publications, 2004. 446 pp.in, illus. Softcover. $29.95

This updated second edition guides collectors, cowboy action shooters, hobbyists and Old West re-enactors through repairing and improving Old West firearms. New additions include 125 high-resolution diagrams and illustrations, five new handgun models, four new long gun models, and an expanded and illustrated glossary. The book offers expanded coverage of the first edition's featured guns (over 40 original and replica models), as well as updated gunsmithing tips and advice. The step-by-step, detailed illustrations demonstrate to both amateur and advanced gunsmiths how to repair and upgrade Old West firearms.

Gunsmithing: Pistols & Revolvers: Expanded 2nd Edition, by Patrick Sweeney, Iola, WI, Krause Publications, 2004. 384 Pages, illustrated, 850 b&w photos. $24.99

Set up an efficient and organized workplace and learn what tools are needed. Then, tackle projects like installing new grips, adjusting trigger pull and sight replacement. Includes a troubleshooting guide, glossary terms and a directory of suppliers and services for most brands of handguns.

Gunsmithing: Rifles, by Patrick Sweeney, Krause Publications, Iola, WI, 1999. 352 pp., illus. Paper covers. $24.95

Tips for lever-action rifles. Building a custom Ruger 10/22. Building a better hunting rifle.

Home Gunsmithing the Colt Single Action Revolvers, by Loren W. Smith, Ray Riling Arms Books, Co., Phila., PA, 2001. 119 pp., illus. $24.95

Affords the Colt Single Action owner detailed, pertinent information on the operating and servicing of this famous and historic handgun.

How to Convert Military Rifles, Williams Gun Sight Co., Davision, MI, new and enlarged seventh edition, 1997. 76 pp., illus. Paper covers. $13.95

This latest edition updated the changes that have occured over the past thirty years. Tips, instructions and illustratons on how to convert popular military rifles as the Enfield, Mauser 96 and SKS just to name a few are presented.

Mauser M98 & M96, by R.A. Walsh, Wolfe Publishing Co., Prescott, AR, 1998. 123 pp., illus. Paper covers. $32.50

How to build your own favorite custom Mauser rifle from two of the best bolt action rifle designs ever produced–the military Mauser Model 1898 and Model 1896 bolt rifles.

Mr. Single Shot's Gunsmithing-Idea-Book, by Frank de Haas, Mark de Haas, Orange City, IA, 1996. 168 pp., illus. Paper covers. $22.50

Offers easy to follow, step-by-step instructions for a wide variety of gunsmithing procedures all reinforced by plenty of photos.

Recreating the American Longrifle, by William Buchele, et al, George Shumway Publisher, York, Pa, 5th edition, 1999. 175 pp., illus. $40.00

Includes full size plans for building a Kentucky rifle.

Story of Pope's Barrels, The, by Ray M. Smith, R&R Books, Livonia, NY, 1993. 203 pp., illus. $39.00

A reissue of a 1960 book whose author knew Pope personally. It will be of special interest to Schuetzen rifle fans, since Pope's greatest days were at the height of the Schuetzen-era before WWI.

Survival Gunsmithing, by J.B. Wood, Desert Publications, Cornville, AZ, 1986. 92 pp., illus. Paper covers. $11.95

A guide to repair and maintenance of the most popular rifles, shotguns and handguns.

Tactical 1911, The, by Dave Lauck, Paladin Press, Boulder, CO, 1998. 137 pp., illus. Paper covers. $20.00

Here is the only book you will ever need to teach you how to select, modify, employ and maintain your Colt.

HANDGUNS

.22 Caliber Handguns; A Shooter's Guide, by D.F. Geiger, Lincoln, RI, Andrew Mowbray, Inc., 2003. 1st edition. Softcover. $21.95

.380 Enfield No. 2 Revolver, The, by Mark Stamps and Ian Skennerton, I.D.S.A. Books, Piqua, OH, 1993. 124 pp., 80 illus. Paper covers. $19.95

9mm Parabellum; The History & Development of the World's 9mm Pistols & Ammunition, by Klaus-Peter Konig and Martin Hugo, Schiffer Publishing Ltd., Atglen, PA, 1993. 304 pp., illus. $39.95

Detailed history of 9mm weapons from Belguim, Italy, Germany, Israel, France, U.S.A., Czechoslovakia, Hungary, Poland, Brazil, Finland and Spain.

A Study of Colt New Army and Navy Pattern Double action Revolvers 1889-1908, by Robert Best. Privately Printed, 2005, 2nd Printing. 276 pages. Hardcover $62.00

A Study…" is a detailed look into Colt's development and production of the Double Action Swing Out Cylinder New Army and Navy series revolvers. Civilian model production, U.S. Army and Navy models and contracts, and other Government organizations using these revolvers are all covered in this book. There are over 150 photographs with 24 pages of color photos to show specific markings and manufacturing changes. Fully documented.

Advanced Master Handgunning, by Charles Stephens, Paladin Press, Boulder, CO, 1994. 72 pp., illus. Paper covers. $14.00

Secrets and surefire techniques for winning handgun competitions.

Advanced Tactical Marksman More High Performance Techniques for Police, Military, and Practical Shooters, by Dave M. Lauck. Paladin Press, Boulder, CO, 2002. 1st edition. 232 pp., photos, illus. Softcover $35.00

Lauck, one of the most respected names in high-performance shooting and gunsmithing, refines and updates his 1st book. Dispensing with overcomplicated mil-dot formulas and minute-of-angle calculations, Lauck shows you how to achieve superior accuracy and figure out angle shots, train for real-world scenarios, choose optics and accessories.

American Beauty: The Prewar Colt National Match Government Model Pistol, by Timothy Mullin, Collector Grade Publications, Canada, 1999. 72 pp., 69 illus. $34.95

69 illustrations, 20 in full color photos of factory engraved guns and other authenticated upgrades, including rare 'double-carved' ivory grips.

Automatic Pistol, The, by J.B.L. Noel, Foreword by Timothy J. Mullin, Boulder, CO, Paladin Press, 2004. 128 pp., illus. Softcover. $14.00

Ayoob Files: The Book, The, by Massad Ayoob, Police Bookshelf, Concord, NH, 1995. 223 pp., illus. Paper covers. $14.95

The best of Massad Ayoob's acclaimed series in *American Handgunner* magazine.

Big Bore Handguns, by John Taffin, Krause Publications, Iola, WI, 2002. 1st edition. 352 pp., 320 b&w photos with a 16-page color section. Hardcover. $39.95

Gives honest reviews and an inside look at shooting, hunting, and competing with the biggest handguns around. Covers handguns from major gunmakers, as well as handgun customizing, accessories, reloading, and cowboy activities. Significant coverage is also given to handgun customizing, accessories, reloading, and popular shooting hobbies including hunting and cowboy activities.

Bill Ruger's .22 Pistol: A Photographic Essay of the Ruger Rimfire Pistol, by Don Findlay, New York, Simon & Schuster, 2000. 2nd printing. Limited edition of 100 copies, signed and numbered. Hardcover, $100.00

Browning High Power Automatic Pistol (Expanded Edition), by Blake R. Stevens, Collector Grade Publications, Canada, 1996. 310 pp., with 313 illus. $49.95

An in-depth chronicle of seventy years of High Power history, from John M. Browning's original 16-shot prototypes to the present. Profusely illustrated with rare original photos and drawings from the FN Archive to describe virtually every sporting and military version of the High Power. The Expanded Edition contains 30 new pages on the interesting Argentine full-auto High Power, the latest FN 'MK3' and BDA9 pistols, plus FN's revolutionary P90 5.7x28mm Personal Defense Weapon, and more!

Browning Hi-Power Assembly, Disassembly Manual 9mm, by Skennerton & Riling, Ray Riling Arms Books Co. Philadelphia, PA, 2005. 36 pages, illustrated. $5.00

Ideal workshop reference for stripping & assembly with exploded parts drawings, specifications, service accessories, historical information and recommended reading references. Ideal workbook for shooters and collectors alike. The binding is triple saddle-stitched with a durable plastic laminated cover.

Browning Hi-Power Pistols, Desert Publications, Cornville, AZ, 1982. 20 pp., illus. Paper covers. $13.95

Covers all facets of the various military and civilian models of the Browning Hi-Power pistol.

Canadian Military Handguns 1855-1985, by Clive M. Law, Museum Restoration Service, Bloomfield, Ont., Canada, 1994. 130pp., illus. $40.00

A long-awaited and important history for arms historians and pistol collectors.

Classic Handguns of the 20th Century, by David Arnold. Iola, WI, Krause Publications, 2004. 144 pages, color photos. Softcover. $24.99

You'll need this book to find out what qualities, contributions and characteristics made each of the twenty handguns found within a "classic" in the eyes of noted gun historian and author, David W. Arnold. Join him on this most fascinating visual walk through the most significant and prolific handguns of the 20th century. From the Colt Single-Action Army Revolver and the German P08 Luger to the Walther P-38 and Beretta Model 92.

Collecting U. S. Pistols & Revolvers, 1909-1945, by J. C. Harrison. The Arms Chest, Oklahoma City, OK, 1999. 2nd edition (revised). 185 pp., illus. Spiral bound. $35.00

Valuable and detailed reference book for the collector of U.S. pistols & revolvers. Identifies standard issue original military models of the M1911, M1911A1 and M1917 Cal .45 pistols and revolvers as produced by all manufacturers from 1911 through 1945. Plus .22 Ace models, National Match models, and similar foreign military models produced by Colt or manufactured under Colt license, plus arsenal repair, refinish and lend-lease models.

Colt .45 Pistol M1911A1 Assembly, Disassembly Manual, by Skennerton & Riling, Ray Riling Arms Books Co. Philadelphia, PA, 2005. 36 pages, illustrated. $5.00

Ideal workshop reference for stripping & assembly with exploded parts drawings, specifications, service accessories, historical information and recommended reading references. Ideal workbook for shooters and collectors alike. The binding is triple saddle-stitched with a durable plastic laminated cover.

Colt .45 Auto Pistol, compiled from U.S. War Dept. Technical Manuals, and reprinted by Desert Publications, Cornville, AZ, 1978. 80 pp., illus. Paper covers. $14.95

Covers every facet of this famous pistol from mechanical training, manual of arms, disassembly, repair and replacement of parts.

Colt Single Action Army Revolver Study: New Discoveries, by Kenneth Moore, Lincoln, RI, Andrew Mowbray, Inc., 2003. 1st edition. Hardcover. $47.95

Combat Perspective; The Thinking Man's Guide to Self-Defense, by Gabriel Suarez, Boulder, CO, Paladin Press, 2003. 1st edition. 112 pp. Softcover. $15.00

In the Combat Perspective, Suarez keys in on developing your knowledge about and properly organizing your mental attitude toward combat to improve your odds of winning – not just surviving – such a fight. In this book he examines each in a logical and scientific manner, demonstrating why, when it comes to defending your life, the mental edge is at least as critical to victory as the tactical advantage.

Complete Encyclopedia of Pistols & Revolvers, by A.E. Hartnik, Knickerbocker Press, New York, NY, 2003. 272 pp., illus. $19.95

A comprehensive encyclopedia specially written for collectors and owners of pistols and revolvers.

Concealable Pocket Pistols: How to Choose and Use Small-Caliber Handguns, by Terence McLeod, Paladin Press, 2001. 1st edition. 80 pp. Softcover. $14.00

Small-caliber handguns are often maligned as too puny for serious self-defense, but millions of Americans own and carry these guns and have used them successfully to stop violent assaults. Find out what millions of Americans already know about these practical self-defense tools.

Concelealed Handgun Manual, The, 4th Edition, by Chris Bird. San Antonio, Privateer Publications, 2004. 332 pages, illus. Softcover. $21.95

If you carry a gun for personal protection, or plan to, you need to read this book. You will learn whether carrying a gun is for you, what gun to choose and how to carry it, how to stay out of trouble, when to shoot and how to shoot, gunfighting tactics, what to expect after you have shot someone, and how to apply for a concealed-carry license in 30 states, plus never-before published details of actual shooting incidents.

Confederate Lemat Revolver; Secret Weapon of the Confederacy?, The, by Doug Adams, Lincoln, RI, Andrew Mowbray, Inc.,2005. 1st edition. Nearly 200 spectacular full-color illustrations and over 70 b&w period photos, illustrations and patent drawings. 112 pages. Softcover. $29.95

This exciting new book describes LeMat's wartime adventures aboard blockade runners and alongside the famous leaders of the Confederacy, as well as exploring, as never before, the unique revolvers that he manufactured for the Southern Cause.

Darling Pepperbox: The Story of Samuel Colt's Forgotten Competitors in Bellingham, The, Mass. and Woonsocket, RI, by Stuart C. Mowbray, Lincoln, RI, Andrew Mowbray, Inc., 2004. 1st edition. 104 pp. Softcover. $19.95

Developmental Cartridge Handguns of .22 Calibre, as Produced in the United States & Abroad from 1855 to 1875, by John S. Laidacker, Atglen, PA, Schiffer Publications, 2003. Reprint. 597 pp., with over 860 b&w photos, drawings, and charts. Hardcover. $100.00

This book is a reprint edition of the late John Laidacker's personal study of early .22 Cartridge Handguns from 1855-1875. Laidacker's primary aim was to offer a quick reference to the collector, and his commentary on the wide variety of types, variations and makers, as well as detailed photography, make this a superb addition to any firearm library.

Effective Handgun Defense, by Frank James, Iola, WI, Krause Publications, 2004. 1st edition. 223 pp, illustated, softcover. NEW $19.95

Effective Handgun Defense, it's readily apparent that he'd have had no problem making his way in an urban environment either. He has a keen mind for the requirements and nuances for "concealed carry" and personal defense, and a fluid style of presenting his material that is neither awkward nor "precious."

Engraved Handguns of .22 Calibre, by John S. Laidacker, Atglen, PA, Schiffer Publications, 2003. 1st edition. 192 pp., with over 400 color and b&w photos. $69.95

Essential Guide to Handguns: Firearms Instruction for Personal Defense and Protection, by Stephen Rementer and Brian Eimer, Phd., Flushing, NY, Looseleaf law Publications, 2005. 1st edition. Over 300 pages plus illustrations. Softcover. $24.89

Farnam Method of Defensive Handgunning, The, by John S. Farnam, Police Bookshelf, 1999. 191 pp., illus. Paper covers. $24.00

A book intended to not only educate the new shooter, but also to serve as a guide and textbook for his and his instructor's training courses.

Fast and Fancy Revolver Shooting, by Ed McGivern, Anniversary Edition, Winchester Press, Piscataway, NJ, 1984. 484 pp., illus. $19.95

A fascinating volume, packed with handgun lore and solid information by the acknowledged dean of revolver shooters.

French Service Handguns: 1858-2004, by Eugene Medlin & Jean Huon, Tommy Gun Publications, 2004. 1st edition. Over 200 pages and more than 125 photographs. Hardcover, $44.95

Over 10 years in the making, this long awaited volume on French handguns is finally here. this book offers in depth coverage on everything from the 11mm Pinfire to the 9mm Parabellum-including various Lefaucheux revolvers, MAB's, Spanish pistols, and revolvers used in WWI, Uniques, plus, many photos of one-of-a-kind prototypes of the French contract Browning, Model 1935s, and 35a pistols used in WWII.

German Handguns: The Complete Book of the Pistols and Revolvers of Germany, 1869 to the Present, by Ian Hogg, Greenhill Publishing, 2001. 320 pp., 270 illustrations. Hardcover. $49.95

Ian Hogg examines the full range of handguns produced in Germany from such classics as the Luger M1908, Mauser HsC and Walther PPK, to more unusual types such as the Reichsrevolver M1879 and the Dreyse 9mm. He presents the key data (length, weight, muzzle velocity, and range) for each weapon discussed and also gives its date of introduction and service record, evaluates and discusses peculiarities, and examines in detail particular strengths and weaknesses.

Glock in Competition, by Robin Taylor, Spokane, WA, Taylor Press, 2006, 2nd edition. 248pp, Softcover. NEW $19.95

Covered topics include reloading, trigger configurations, recalls, and refits, magazine problems, modifying the Glock, choosing factory ammo, and a host of others.

Glock: The New Wave in Combat Handguns, by Peter Alan Kasler, Paladin Press, Boulder, CO, 1993. 304 pp., illus. $27.00

Kasler debunks the myths that surround what is the most innovative handgun to be introduced in some time.

Glock's Handguns, by Duncan Long, Desert Publications, El Dorado, AR, 1996. 180 pp., illus. Paper covers. $19.95

An outstanding volume on one of the world's newest and most successful firearms of the century.

Gun Digest Book of Beretta Pistols, The, by Massad Ayoob, Iola, WI, Krause Publications, 2005. 288 pages, 300+ photos help with identification. Softcover. $27.99

This new release from the publishers of Gun Digest, readers get information including caliber,weight and barrel lengths for modern pistols. A review of the accuracy and function of all models of modern Beretta pistols give active shooters details needed to make the most of this popular firearm. More than 300 photographs, coupled with articles detailing the development of design and style of these handguns, create a comprehensive must-have resource.

Gun Digest Book of Combat Handgunnery 5th Edition, The, Complete Guide to Combat Shooting, by Massad Ayoob, Iola, WI, Krause Publications, 2002. $22.95

Tap into the knowledge of an international combat handgun expert for the latest in combat handgun designs, strengths and limitations; caliber, size, power and ability; training and technique; cover, concealment and hostage situations. Unparalleled!

Gun Digest Book of the 1911, The, by Patrick Sweeney, Krause Publications, Iola, WI, 2002. 336 pp., with 700 b&w photos. Softcover. $27.95

Complete guide of all models and variations of the Model 1911. The author also includes repair tips and information on buying a used 1911.

Gun Digest Book of the 1911 2nd Edition, The, by Patrick Sweeney, Krause Publications, Iola, WI, 2006. 336 pp., with 700 b&w photos. Softcover. $27.95

Complete guide of all models and variations of the Model 1911. The author also includes repair tips and information on buying a used 1911.

Gun Digest Book of the Glock; A Comprehensive Review, Design, History and Use, The, Iola, WI, Krause Publications, 2003. 303 pp., with 500 b&w photos. Softcover. 27.95

Examine the rich history and unique elements of the most important and influential firearms design of the past 50 years, the Glock autoloading pistol. This comprehensive review of the revolutionary pistol analyzes the performance of the various models and chamberings and features a complete guide to available accessories and little-known factory options. You'll see why it's the preferred pistol for law enforcement use and personal protection.

Gun Digest Book of the SIG-Sauer, The, by Massad Ayoob, Iola, WI, Krause Publications, 2005. 1st edition 304pp. Softcover. $27.99

Noted firearms training expert Massad Ayoob takes an in-depth look at some of the finest pistols on the market. If you own a SIG-Sauer pistol, have consdered buying one or just appreciate the fine quality of these pistols, this is the book for you. Ayoob takes a practical look at each of the SIG-Sauer pistols including handling characteristics, and design and performance. Each gun in every caliber is tested and evaluated, giving you all the details you need as you choose and use your SIG-Sauer pistol.

Gun Digest Book of Smith & Wesson, The, by Patrick Sweeney, Iola, WI, Krause Publications, 2005. 1st edition. Covers all categories of Smith & Wesson Guns in both competition and law enforcement. 312pp, 500 b&w photos. Softcover, $27.99

Hand Cannons: The World's Most Powerful Handguns, by Duncan Long, Paladin Press, Boulder, CO, 1995. 208 pp., illus. Paper covers. $22.00

Long describes and evaluates each powerful gun according to their features.

Handgun Combatives, by Dave Spaulding, Flushing, NY, Looseleaf Law Publications,2005. 212pp, with 60 plus photos, softcover. NEW $22.95

Handgun Stopping Power "The Definitive Study," by Evan P. Marshall & Edwin J. Sanow, Paladin Press, Boulder, CO, 1997. 240 pp. photos. Softcover. $45.00

Dramatic first-hand accounts of the results of handgun rounds fired into criminals by cops, storeowners, cabbies and others are the heart and soul of this long-awaited book. This is the definitive methodology for predicting the stopping power of handgun loads, the first to take into account what really happens when a bullet meets a man.

Handguns 2007, 19th Edition, Ken Ramage, Iola WI, Gun Digest Books, 2006, 320pp, 500 b&w photos, Softcover. $24.99

Target shooters, handgun hunters, collectors and those who rely upon handguns for self-defense will want to pack this value-loaded and entertaining volume in their home libraries. Shooters will find the latest pistol and revolver designs and accessories, plus test reports on several models. The handgun becomes an artist's canvas in a showcase of engraving talents. The catalog section–with comprehensive specs on every known handgun in production–includes a new display of semi-custom handguns, plus an expanded, illustrated section on the latest grips, sights, scopes and other aiming devices. Offer easy access to products, services and manufacturers.

Handguns of the Armed Organizations of the Soviet Occupation Zone and German Democratic Republic, by Dieter H. Marschall, Los Alamos, NM, Ucross Books, 2000. Softcover. $29.95

Translated from German this groundbreaking treatise covers the period from May 1945 through 1996. The organizations that used these pistols are described along with the guns and holsters. Included are the P08, P38, PP, PPK, P1001, PSM, Tokarev, Makarov, (including .22 LR, cutaway, silenced, Suhl marked), Stechlin, plus Hungarian, Romanian and Czech pistols.

Heckler & Koch's Handguns, by Duncan Long, Desert Publications, El Dorado, AR, 1996. 142 pp., illus. Paper covers. $19.95

Traces the history and the evolution of H&K's pistols from the company's beginning at the end of WWII to the present.

Hidden in Plain Sight, by Trey Bloodworth & Mike Raley, Paladin Press, Boulder, CO, 2003. Paper covers. $20.00

A practical guide to concealed handgun carry.

High Standard: A Collectors Guide to the Hamden & Hartford Target Pistols, by Tom Dance, Andrew Mowbray, Inc., Lincoln, RI, 1999. 192 pp., heavily illustrated with b&w photographs and technical drawings. $24.00

From Citation to Supermatic, all of the production models and specials made from 1951 to 1984 are covered according to model number or series, making it easy to understand the evolution to this favorite of shooters and collectors.

High Standard Automatic Pistols 1932-1950, by Charles E. Petty, The Gun Room Press, Highland Park, NJ, 1989. 124 pp., illus. $19.95

A definitive source of information for the collector of High Standard arms.

Hi-Standard Pistols and Revolvers, 1951-1984, by James Spacek, Chesire, CT, 1998. 128 pp., illus. Paper covers. $14.95

Technical details, marketing features and instruction/parts manual of every model High Standard pistol and revolver made between 1951 and 1984. Most accurate serial number information available.

History of Smith & Wesson Firearms, by Dean Boorman, New York, Lyons Press, 2002. 1st edition. 144 pp., illustrated in full color. Hardcover. $29.95

The definitive guide to one of the world's best-known firearms makers. Takes the story through the years of the Military & Police .38 & of the Magnum cartridge, to today's wide range of products for law-enforcement customers.

How to Become a Master Handgunner: The Mechanics of X-Count Shooting, by Charles Stephens, Paladin Press, Boulder, CO, 1993. 64 pp., illus. Paper covers. $14.00

Offers a simple formula for success to the handgunner who strives to master the technique of shooting accurately.

How to Customize Your Glock: Step-By-Step Modifications You Can Do at Little Cost, by Robert and Morgan Boatman, Paladin Press, Boulder, CO, 2005, 1st edition. 8½" x 11", photos, 72 pp. Softcover. $20.00

This mini-"Glocksmithing" course by Glock enthusiasts Robert and Morgan Boatman first explains why you would make a specific modification and what you gain in terms of improved performance. The workbook format makes the manual simple to follow as you work on your Glock, andhigh-resolution photos illustrate each part and step precisely. Make your Glock work even more effectively for you bythinking outside the box.

Inglis Diamond: The Canadian High Power Pistol, by Clive M. Law, Collector Grade Publications, Canada, 2001. 312 pp., illus. $49.95

This definitive work on Canada's first and indeed only mass produced handgun, in production for a very brief span of time and consequently made in relatively few numbers, the venerable Inglis-made Browning High Power covers the pistol's initial history, the story of Chinese and British adoption, use post-war by Holland, Australia, Greece, Belgium, New Zealand, Peru, Brasil and other countries. All new information on the famous light-weights and the Inglis Diamond variations. Completely researched through official archives in a dozen countries. Many of the bewildering variety of markings have never been satisfactorily explained until now

Japanese Military Cartridge Handguns 1893-1945, A Revised and Expanded Edition of Hand Cannons of Imperial Japan, by Harry L. Derby III and James D. Brown, Atglen, PA, Schiffer Publications, 2003. 1st edition. Hardcover. New in new dust jacket. $79.95

When originally published in 1981, *The Hand Cannons of Imperial Japan* was heralded as one of the most readable works on firearms ever produced. To arms collectors and scholars, it remains a prized source of information on Japanese handguns, their development, and their history. In this new revised and expanded edition, original author Harry Derby has teamed with Jim Brown to provide a thorough update reflecting twenty years of additional research. An appendix on valuation has also been added, using a relative scale that should remain relevant despite inflationary pressures. For the firearms collector, enthusiast, historian or dealer, this is the most complete and up-to-date work on Japanese military handguns ever written.

Living with Glocks: The Complete Guide to the New Standard in Combat Handguns, by Robert H. Boatman, Boulder, CO, Paladin Press, 2002. 1st edition. 184 pp., illus. Hardcover. $29.95

In addition to demystifying the enigmatic Glock trigger, Boatman describes and critiques each Glock model in production. Separate chapters on the G36, the enhanced G20 and the full-auto G18 emphasize the job-specific talents of these standout models for those seeking insight on which Glock pistol might best meet their needs. And for those interested in optimizing their Glock's capabilities, this book addresses all the peripherals–holsters, ammo, accessories, silencers, modifications and conversions, training programs and more.

Living With the 1911, by Robert Boatman, Boulder, CO, Paladin Press, 2005. 144pp, softcover. NEW $25.00

Luger P'08 Pistol, 9mm Assembly, Disassembly Manual, by Skennerton & Riling, Ray Riling Arms Books Co. Philadelphia, PA, 2005. 36 pages, illustrated. $5.00

Ideal workshop reference for stripping & assembly with exploded parts drawings, specifications, service accessories, historical information and recommended reading references. The binding is triple saddle-stitched with a durable plastic laminated cover.

Luger Handbook, by Aarron Davis, Krause Publications, Iola, WI, 1997. 112 pp., illus. Paper covers. $9.95

Now you can identify any of the legendary Luger variations using a simple decision tree. Each model and variation includes pricing information, proof marks and detailed attributes in a handy, user-friendly format. Plus, it's fully indexed. Instantly identify that Luger!

Lyman Pistol and Revolver Handbook, 3rd edition, by Lyman. Middletown, CT, Lyman Products Corp, 2005. 3rd edition. 272pp, Softcover. NEW $22.95

Makarov Pistol Assembly, Disassembly Manual 9mm, by Skennerton & Riling, Ray Riling Arms Books Co. Philadelphia, PA, 2005. 36 pages, illustrated. $5.00

Ideal workshop reference for stripping & assembly with exploded parts drawings, specifications, ervice accessories, historical information and recommended reading references. The binding is triple saddle-stitched with a durable plastic laminated cover.

Mauser Self-Loading Pistol, by Belford & Dunlap, Borden Publishing Co., Alhambra, CA. Over 200 pp., 300 illus., large format. $29.95

The long-awaited book on the "Broom Handles," covering their inception in 1894 to the end of production. Complete and in detail: pocket pistols, Chinese and Spanish copies.

Mauser Broomhandle Model 1896 Pistol Assembly, Disassembly Manual, by Skennerton & Riling, Ray Riling Arms Books Co. Philadelphia, PA, 2005. 36 pages, illustrated. $5.00

Ideal workshop reference for stripping & assembly with exploded parts drawings, specifications, service accessories, historical information and recommended reading references.

Mental Mechanics of Shooting: How to Stay Calm at the Center, by Vishnu Karmakar and Thomas Whitney, Littleton, CO, Center Vision, Inc., 2001. 144 pp. Softcover. $19.95

Not only will this book help you stay free of trigger jerk, it will help you in all areas of your shooting.

Model 35 Radom Pistol, The, by Terence Lapin, Hyrax Publishers, 2004. 95 pages with b&w photos, Stiff paper covers. $18.95

Model 1911 Automatic Pistol, by Robert Campbell, Accokeek, Maryland, Stoeger Publications, 2004. Hardcover. $24.95

Modern Law Enforcement Weapons & Tactics, 3rd Edition, by Patrick Sweeney, Iola, WI, Krause Publications, 2004. 256 pp. Softcover. $22.99

Official 9mm Markarov Pistol Manual, translated into English by Major James Gebhardt, U.S. Army (Ret.), Desert Publications, El Dorado, AR, 1996. 84 pp., illus. Paper covers. $14.95

The information found in this book will be of enormous benefit and interest to the owner or a prospective owner of one of these pistols.

Operator's Tactical Pistol Shooting Manual; A Practical Guide to Combat Marksmanship, by Erik Lawrence, Linesville, PA, Blackheart Publishing, 2003. 1st edition. 233 pp. Softcover. $24.50

This manual-type book begins with the basics of safety with a pistol and progresses into advanced pistol handling. A self-help guide for improving your capabilities with a pistol at your own pace.

P08 Luger Pistol, by de Vries & Martens, Alexandria, VA, Ironside International, 2002. 152 pp., illustrated with 200 high quality b&w photos. Hardcover. $34.95

Covers all essential information on history and development, ammunition and accessories, codes and markings, and contains photos of nearly every model and accessory. Includes a unique selection of original German WWII propaganda photos, most never published before.

P-08 Parabellum Luger Automatic Pistol, edited by J. David McFarland, Desert Publications, Cornville, AZ, 1982. 20 pp., illus. Paper covers. $14.95

Covers every facet of the Luger, plus a listing of all known Luger models.

P-38 Pistol: Postwar Distributions, 1945-1990, Volume 3, by Warren Buxton, Ucross Books, Los Alamos, MN 1999, plus an addendum to Volumes 1 & 2. 272 pp. with 342 illustrations. $75.00

P-38 Pistol: The Contract Pistols, 1940-1945, Volume 2, by Warren Buxton, Ucross Books, Los Alamos, MN 1999. 256 pp. with 237 illustrations. $75.00

P-38 Pistol: The Walther Pistols, 1930-1945, Volume 1, by Warren Buxton, Ucross Books, Los Alamos, MN 1999. 328 pp. with 160 illustrations. $75.00

A limited run reprint of this scarce and sought-after work on the P-38 Pistol.

Peacemakers: Arms and Adventure in the American West, by RL Wilson. New York, Book Sales, 2004, reprint. 392pp. colored endpapers, 320 full color illustrations. Hardcover in New DJ, $24.89

Percussion Pistols and Revolvers: History, Performance and Practical Use, by Mike Cumpston and Johnny Bates, Texas, Iunivers, Inc, 2005. 1st edition. 208 pages. Softcover. $19.95

With the advent of the revolving pistols came patents that created monopolies in revolver production and the through-bored cylinder necessary for self-contained metallic cartridges. The caplock revolvers took on a separate evolution and remained state of the art long after the widespread appearance of cartridge-firing rifles and shotguns.

Pistol as a Weapon of Defence in the House and on the Road, by Jeff Cooper, Boulder, CO, Paladin Press, 2004. 1st edition. 48pp. Softcover. $9.00

Penned in 1875 and recently discovered collecting dust on a library bookshelf, this primer for the pistol is remarkably timely in its insights and observations. From a historical perspective, it contains striking parallels to the thinking and controversy that swirl about the practical use of the pistol today.

Pistols of the World; Fully Revised, 4th Edition, Iola, WI, Krause Publications, 2005. 432pp, chronicles 2,500 handguns made from 1887-2004. Stiff paper covers, $22.95

More than 1,000 listings and 20 years of coverage were added since the previous edition.

Pistols of World War I, by Robert J. Adamek, Pittsburgh, Pentagon Press, 2001. 1st edition signed and numbered. 296 pp. with illustrations and photos. Softcover. $45.00

Over 90 pistols illustrated, technical data, designers, history, proof marks. Over 25 pistol magazines illustrated with dimensions, serial number ranges. Over 35 cartridges illustrated with dimensions, manufactures, year of introduction. Weapons from 16 countries involved in WWI, statistics, quantities made, identification.

Remington Large-Bore Conversion Revolvers, by R. Phillips. Canada, Prately printed, 2005. Limited printing of 250 signed and numbered copies in leather hardcover. 126pp, with 200 illustrations. NEW $55.00

Ruger .22 Automatic Pistol, Standard/Mark I/Mark II Series, by Duncan Long, Paladin Press, Boulder, CO, 1989. 168 pp., illus. Paper covers. $16.00

The definitive book about the pistol that has served more than 1 million owners so well.

Ruger .22 Automatic Pistols: The Complete Guide for all Models from 1947 to 2003, Grand Rapids, MI, The Ruger Store, 2004. 74 pp., 66 high-resolution grayscale images. Printed in the U.S.A. with card stock cover and bright white paper. Softcover. $12.95

Includes 'rare' complete serial numbers and manufacturing dates from 1949-2004.

Ruger "P" Family of Handguns, by Duncan Long, Desert Publications, El Dorado, AZ, 1993. 128 pp., illus. Paper covers. $14.95

A full-fledged documentary on a remarkable series of Sturm Ruger handguns.

Ruger Pistol Reference Booklet 1949-1982 (Pocket Guide to Ruger Rimfire Pistols Standard and Mark I), by Don Findlay. Lubbock Tx, 2005. Softcover. 24 pages, illustrated with b&w photos. $9.95

Designed for the professional un dealer as well as the collector. Complete list of serial numbers as well as production dates. Also, includes photos of the original boxes the guns came in.

Semi-automatic Pistols in Police Service and Self Defense, by Massad Ayoob, Police Bookshelf, Concord, NH, 1990. 25 pp., illus. Softcover. $11.95

First quantitative, documented look at actual police experience with 9mm and 45 police service automatics.

Shooting Colt Single Actions, by Mike Venturino, Livingston, MT, 1997. 205 pp., illus. Paper covers. $25.00

A definitive work on the famous Colt SAA and the ammunition it shoots.

SIG Handguns, by Duncan Long, Desert Publications, El Dorado, AZ, 1995. 150 pp., illus. Paper covers. $19.95

The history of SIG/Sauer handguns, including Sig, Sig-Hammerli and Sig/Sauer variants.

Smith & Wesson's Automatics, by Larry Combs, Desert Publications, El Dorado, AZ, 1994. 143 pp., illus. Paper covers. $19.95

A must for every S&W auto owner or prospective owner.

Smith & Wesson: Sixguns of the Old West, by David Chicoine. Lincoln, RI., Andrew Mowbray, Inc., 2004. 1st edition. 480 pages, countless photos and detailed technical drawings. Hardcover. New in new dust jacket. $69.49

The Schofields, The Americans, The Russians, The New Model #3s, and The DAs.

Smith & Wesson American Model; In U.S. And Foreign Service, by Charles W. Pate, Mowbray Publishers, Lincoln, RI, 2006. 408 pp., illus. $65.00

This new book is an awesome new collector's guide to the S&W American. A huge resource on the military and western use of this classic large frame revolver.

Spanish Handguns: The History of Spanish Pistols and Revolvers, by Gene Gangarosa Jr., Stoeger Publishing Co., Accokeek, MD, 2001. 320 pp., illustrated, b&w photos. Paper covers. $21.95

Standard Catalog Of Luger, by Aaron Davis, Gun Digest Books, Iola WI, 2006. 256 pages, illustrated with photos. Paper Covers $29.99

This comprehensive identification and price guide goes a long way to giving Luger enthusiasts information to enjoy and be successful in an extremely active collector market. With Standard Catalog of Luger, firearms enthusiasts receive an unrivaled reference that includes: Reproductions of symbols and makers' marks from every model of Luger for use in accurately identifying the hundreds of Luger variations, More than 1,000 detailed photos and line illustrations demonstrating design and performance of Luger pistols, Manufacturing data and model rarity information to aid collectors when buying Lugers as an investment. Perfect for firearms collectors, gun shop owners, auction houses, museums, and appraisers.

Standard Catalog Of Smith & Wesson; 3rd Edition, by Jim Supica, & Richard Nahas, Gun Digest Books, Iola WI, 2006 384 pages, with photos, Hardcover. $39.99

Definitive Smith & Wesson identification and pricing reference, includes 350+ full-color photos for improved identification. Smith & Wesson is one of the hottest manufacturers of handguns, offering more new models than any other maker-39 new products in 2005 alone. Comprehensive coverage of Smith & Wesson firearm line including the only handgun in the world in continuous production since 1899. The 3rd Edition combines full color photos with details collectors need to identify and better appreciate all Smith & Wesson firearms.

Star Firearms, by Leonardo M. Antaris, Davenport, TA, Firac Publications Co., 2002. 1st edition. Hardcover. New in new dust jacket. $119.95

Tactical 1911, by Dave Lauck, Paladin Press, Boulder, CO, 1999. 152 pp., illus. Paper covers. $22.00

The cop's and SWAT operator's guide to employment and maintenance.

Tactical Pistol, by Gabriel Suarez, Foreword by Jeff Cooper, Paladin Press, Boulder, CO, 1996. 216 pp., illus. Paper covers. $25.00

Advanced gunfighting concepts and techniques.

Tactical Pistol Shooting; Your Guide to Tactics that Work, by Erik Lawrence. Iola, WI, Krause Publications, 2005. 1st edition. More than 250 step-by-step photos to illustrate techniques. 233pp, Softcover. NEW $18.95

Thompson/Center Contender Pistol, by Charles Tephens, Paladin Press, Boulder, CO, 1997. 58 pp., illus. Paper covers. $14.00

How to tune and time, load and shoot accurately with the Contender pistol.

U.S. Handguns of World War II, The Secondary Pistols and Revolvers, by Charles W. Pate, Mowbray Publishers, Lincoln, RI, 1997. 368 pp., illus. $39.00

This indispensable new book covers all of the American military handguns of WWII except for the M1911A1.

Walther P-38 Assembly, Disassembly Manual 9mm, by Skennerton & Riling, Ray Riling Arms Books Co. Philadelphia, PA, 2005. 36 pages, illustrated. $5.00

Ideal workshop reference for stripping & assembly with exploded parts drawings, specifications, service accessories, historical information and recommended reading references. The binding is triple saddle-stitched with a durable plastic laminated cover.

Walther Pistols: Models 1 Through P99, Factory Variations and Copies, by Dieter H. Marschall, Ucross Books, Los Alamos, NM. 2000. 140 pp., with 140 b&w illustrations, index. Paper covers. $21.95

This is the English translation, revised and updated, of the highly successful and widely acclaimed German language edition. This book provides the collector with a reference guide and overview of the entire line of the Walther military, police, and self-defense pistols from the very first to the very latest Variations, where issued, serial ranges, calibers, marks, proofs, logos, and design aspects in an astonishing quantity and variety are crammed into this very well researched and highly regarded work.

HUNTING

NORTH AMERICA

A Varmint Hunter's Odyssey, by Steve Hanson with guest chapter by Mike Johnson, Precision Shooting, Inc. Manchester, CT, 1999. 279 pp., illus. Paper covers. $39.95

A new classic by a writer who eats, drinks and sleeps varmint hunting and varmint rifles.

Advanced Black Powder Hunting, by Toby Bridges, Stoeger Publishing Co., Wayne, NJ, 1998. 288 pp., illus. Paper covers. $21.95

The first modern day publication to be filled from cover to cover with guns, loads, projectiles, accessories and the techniques to get the most from today's front loading guns.

Adventures of an Alaskan–You Can Do, by Dennis W. Confer, Foreword by Craig Boddington. Anchorage, AK, Wiley Ventures, 2003. 1st edition. 279 pp., illus. Softcover. $24.95

This book is about 45% fishing, 45% hunting, & 10% related adventures; travel, camping and boating. It is written to stimulate, encourage and motivate readers to make happy memories that they can do on an average income and to entertain, educate and inform readers of outdoor opportunities.

Aggressive Whitetail Hunting, by Greg Miller, Krause Publications, Iola, WI, 1995. 208 pp., illus. Paper covers. $14.95

Learn how to hunt trophy bucks in public forests, private farmlands and exclusive hunting grounds from one of America's foremost hunters.

Alaska Safari, by Harold Schetzle & Sam Fadala, Anchorage, AK, Great Northwest Publishing, 2002. Revised 2nd edition. 366 pp., illus. with b&w photos. Softcover. $29.95

The author has brought a wealth of information to the hunter and anyone interested in Alaska. Harold Schetzle is a great guide and has also written another book of stories of Alaska hunting taken from many, many years of hunting and guiding. The most comprehensive guide to Alaska hunting.

Alaskan Adventures-Volume I-The Early Years, by Russell Annabel, Long Beach, CA, Safari Press,2005, 2nd printing. 453pp. illus. Hardcover. New in new dust jacket. $35.00

No other writer has ever been able to capture the spirit of adventure and hunting in Alaska like Russell Annabel.

Alaskan Yukon Trophies Won and Lost, by G.O. Young, Wolfe Publishing, Prescott, AZ, 2002. Softcover. $35.00

.A classic big game hunting tale with 273 pages b&w photographs and a five-page epilogue by the publisher.

American Duck Shooting, by George Bird Grinnell, Stackpole Books, Harrisburg, PA, 1991. 640 pp., illus. Paper covers. $19.95

First published in 1901 at the height of the author's career. Describes 50 species of waterfowl, and discusses hunting methods common at the turn of the century.

Bear Hunting in Alaska: How to Hunt Brown and Grizzly Bears, by Tony Russ, Northern Publishing, 2004. 116 b&w photos, illus. 256 pgs. Soft cover. Excellent. $22.95

Teaches every skill you will need to prepare for, scout, find, select, stalk, shoot and care for one of the most sought-after trophies on earth – the Alaskan brown bear and the Alaskan Grizzly.

Bears of Alaska, by Erwin Bauer, Sasquatch Books, 2002. Soft cover. Excellent . $15.95

Best of Babcock, The, by Havilah Babcock, Introduction by Hugh Grey, The Gunnerman Press, Auburn Hills, MI, 1985. 262 pp., illus. $19.95

A treasury of memorable pieces, 21 of which have never before appeared in book form.

Blacktail Trophy Tactics, by Boyd Iverson, Stoneydale Press, Stevensville, MI, 1992. 166 pp., illus. Paper covers. $14.95

A comprehensive analysis of blacktail deer habits, describing a deer's and man's use of scents, still hunting, tree techniques, etc.

Bowhunter's Handbook, Expert Strategies and Techniques, by M.R. James with Fred Asbell, Dave Holt, Dwight Schuh and Dave Samuel, DBI Books, a division of Krause Publications, Iola, WI, 1997. 256 pp., illus. Paper covers. $19.95

Tips from the top on taking your bowhunting skills to the next level.

Buffalo Harvest, The, by Frank Mayer as told to Charles Roth, Pioneer Press, Union City, TN, 1995. 96 pp., illus. Paper covers. $12.50

The story of a hide hunter during his buffalo hunting days on the plains.

Call of the Quail: A Tribute to the Gentleman Game Bird, by Michael McIntosh, et al., Countrysport Press, Traverse City, MI, 1990. 175 pp., illus. $35.00

A new anthology on quail hunting.

Calling All Elk, by Jim Zumbo, Cody, WY, 1989. 169 pp., illus. Paper covers. $14.95

The only book on the subject of elk hunting that covers every aspect of elk vocalization.

Complete Book of Grouse Hunting, The, by Frank Woolner, The Lyons Press, New York, NY, 2000. 192 pp., illus. Paper covers. $24.95

The history, habits, and habitat of one of America's great game birds–and the methods used to hunt it.

Complete Book of Mule Deer Hunting, The, by Walt Prothero, The Lyons Press, New York, NY, 2000. 192 pp., illus. Paper covers. $24.95

Field-tested practical advice on how to bag the trophy buck of a lifetime.

Complete Book of Wild Turkey Hunting, The, by John Trout Jr., The Lyons Press, New York, NY, 2000. 192 pp., illus. Paper covers. $24.95

An illustrated guide to hunting for one of America's most popular game birds.

Complete Book of Woodcock Hunting, The, by Frank Woolner, The Lyons Press, New York, NY, 2000. 192 pp., illus. Paper covers. $24.95

A thorough, practical guide to the American woodcock and to woodcock hunting.

Complete Guide To Hunting Wild Boar in California, The, by Gary Kramer, Safari Press, 2002. 1st edition. 127 pp., 37 photos. Softcover. $15.95

Gary Kramer takes the hunter all over California, from north to south and east to west. He discusses natural history, calibers, bullets, rifles, pistols, shotguns, black powder, and bow and arrows—even recipes.

Complete Venison Cookbook from Field to Table, The, by Jim & Ann Casada, Krause Publications, Iola, WI, 1996. 208 pp., Comb-bound. $12.95

More than 200 kitchen-tested recipes make this book the answer to a table full of hungry hunters or guests.

Cougar Attacks: Encounters of the Worst Kind, by Kathy Etling, NY, Lyons Press, 2004. 1st edition. 256 pages, illustrated with b&w photos. Soft cover. $14.95

Blood-curdling encounters between the big cats of North America and their most reluctant prey, humans.

Coyote Hunting, by Phil Simonski, Stoneydale Press, Stevensville, MT, 1994. 126 pp., illus. Paper covers. $12.95

Probably the most thorough "how-to-do-it" book on coyote hunting ever written.

Dabblers & Divers: A Duck Hunter's Book, compiled by the editors of *Ducks Unlimited* magazine, Willow Creek Press, Minocqua, WI, 1997. 160 pp., illus. $39.95

A word-and-photographic portrayal of waterfowl hunter's singular intimacy with, and passion for, watery haunts and wildfowl.

Deer & Deer Hunting, by Al Hofacker, Krause Publications, Iola, WI, 1993. 208 pp., illus. $34.95

Coffee-table volume packed full of how-to-information that will guide hunts for years to come.

Dreaming the Lion, by Thomas McIntyre, Countrysport Press, Traverse City, MI, 1994. 309 pp., illus. $35.00

Reflections on hunting, fishing and a search for the wild. Twenty-three stories by ***Sports Afield*** editor, Tom McIntyre.

Eastern Cougar: Historic Accounts, Scientific Investigations, and New Evidence, by Chris Bolgiano, Mechanicsburg,PA, Stackpole Books, 2005. Soft cover. $19.95

This fascinating anthology probes America's troubled history with large predators and makes a vital contribution to the wildlife management debates of today.

Elk and Elk Hunting, by Hart Wixom, Stackpole Books, Harrisburg, PA, 1986. 288 pp., illus. $34.95

Your practical guide to fundamentals and fine points of elk hunting.

Elk Hunting Guide: Skills, Gear, and Insight, by Tom Airhart, Stackpole Books,2005. A thorough, informative guide to the growing sport of elk hunting with in-depth coverage of current equipment and gear, techniques for tracking elk and staying safe in the wilderness and advice on choosing guides and outfitters. 432pp, 71 b&w photos, 38 illus. $19.95

Elk Hunting in the Northern Rockies, by Ed Wolff, Stoneydale Press, Stevensville, MT, 1984. 162 pp., illus. $18.95

Helpful information about hunting the premier elk country of the northern Rocky Mountain states–Wyoming, Montana and Idaho.

Elk Hunting with the Experts, by Bob Robb, Stoneydale Press, Stevensville, MT, 1992. 176 pp., illus. Paper covers. $15.95

A complete guide to elk hunting in North America by America's top elk hunting expert.

Encyclopedia of Buffalo Hunters and Skinners Volume 1 A-D, by Gilbert Reminger, Pioneer Press, 2003. The first volume in the series. 286 pages, acknowledgements, introduction, preface, illustrated, maps, plates, portraits, appendices, bibliography, index. Hardcover. $35.00

Encyclopedia of Buffalo Hunters and Skinners Volume 2 E-K, by Gilbert Reminger, Pioneer Press, 2006. The 2nd volume in the series. 285 pages, 115 photos, 15 drawings/newspaper items, and 6 maps. Index, Bibliography. Hardcover. $35.00

Vol. II covers hunters and skinners, that have so far surfaced, with surnames that begin with E-K, beginning with skinner William Earl and runs through the Kuykendall brothers, Judge and John, who hunted late (1886-1888) in southeastern New Mexico.

Fair Chase in North America, by Craig Boddington, Long Beach, CA, Safari Press, 2004. 1st edition. Hardcover. New in new dust jacket. $39.95

Getting a Stand, by Miles Gilbert, Pioneer Press, Union City, TN, 1993. 204 pp., illus. Paper covers. $13.95

An anthology of 18 short personal experiences by buffalo hunters of the late 1800s, specifically from 1870-1882.

Greatest Elk; The Complete Historical and Illustrated Record of North America's Biggest Elk, by R. Selner, Safari Press, Huntington Beach, CA, 2000. 209 pp., profuse color illus. $39.95

Here is the book all elk hunters have been waiting for! This oversized book holds the stories and statistics of the biggest bulls ever killed in North America. Stunning, full-color photographs highlight over 40 world-class heads, including the old world records!

ARMS LIBRARY

Grouse and Woodcock, A Gunner's Guide, by Don Johnson, Krause Publications, Iola, WI, 1995. 256 pp., illus. Paper covers. $14.95

Find out what you need in guns, ammo, equipment, dogs and terrain.

Gunning for Sea Ducks, by George Howard Gillelan, Tidewater Publishers, Centreville, MD, 1988. 144 pp., illus. $14.95

A book that introduces you to a practically untouched arena of waterfowling.

Head Fer the Hills–Volume VI (1934-1960), by Russell Annabel, Long Beach, CA, Safari Press, 2005, Deluxe, Limited, Signed edition. 312pp., photos, drawings. Hardcover in a Slipcase. $60.00

As Tex Cobb, Russell Annabel's famous mentor and eternal companion, was famous for saying, "Head fer the hills," which is exactly what Rusty did.

Heck with Moose Hunting, The, by Jim Zumbo, Wapiti Valley Publishing Co., Cody, WY, 1996. 199 pp., illus. $17.95

Jim's hunts around the continent including encounters with moose, caribou, sheep, antelope and mountain goats.

High Pressure Elk Hunting, by Mike Lapinski, Stoneydale Press Publishing Co., Stevensville, MT, 1996. 192 pp., illus. $19.95

The secrets of hunting educated elk revealed.

Horns in the High Country, by Andy Russell, Alfred A. Knopf, NY, 1973. 259 pp., illus. Paper covers. $12.95

A many-sided view of wild sheep and their natural world.

How to Hunt, by Dave Bowring, Winchester Press, Piscataway, NJ, 1982. 208 pp., illus. Hardcover $15.00

A basic guide to hunting big game, small game, upland birds, and waterfowl.

Hunt High for Rocky Mountain Goats, Bighorn Sheep, Chamois & Tahr, by Duncan Gilchrist, Stoneydale Press, Stevensville, MT, 1992. 192 pp., illus. Paper covers. $19.95

The source book for hunting mountain goats.

Hunter's Alaska, The, by Roy F. Chandler, Iron Brigade, 2005. Hardcover. $49.95

This is a book written by Roy F. Chandler (Rocky). Rocky's Alaskan travels span half a century. Hunters hoping to hunt the "Great Land" will read exactly how it is done and what they can hope for if they ever make it into the Alaskan wilderness. This is a new publication of 2500 signed and numbered copies. Previous books, written by Rocky, about hunting Alaska have become collectors items. This book has some information from the prior books and much more "added" information.

Hunting Adventure of Me and Joe, by Walt Prothero, Safari Press, Huntington Beach, CA, 1995. 220 pp., illus. $22.50

A collection of the author's best and favorite stories.

Hunting America's Wild Turkey, by Toby Bridges, Stoeger Publishing Company, Pocomoke, MD, 2001. 256 pp., illus. $16.95

The techniques and tactics of hunting North America's largest, and most popular, woodland game bird.

Hunting Hard in Alaska, by Marc Taylor, Anchorage, AK, Biblio Distribution, 2003 Softcover. $19.95

Hunting In Alaska: A Comprehensive Guide, by Christopher Batin, Alaska Angler Pubs., 2002. 430 pages. Soft cover. $29.95

Hunting the Land of the Midnight Sun, by Alaska Professional Hunters Assoc., Safari Press, 2005. Hardcover. New in new dust jacket. $29.95

Contains contributions by Rob Holt, Gary King, Gary LaRose, Garth Larsen, Jim Shockey, Jeff Davis, and many others.

Hunting Mature Bucks, by Larry L. Weishuhn, Krause Publications, Iola, WI, 1995. 256 pp., illus. Paper covers. $14.95

One of North America's top white-tailed deer authorities shares his expertise on hunting those big, smart and elusive bucks.

Hunting Open-Country Mule Deer, by Dwight Schuh, Sage Press, Nampa, ID, 1989. 180 pp., illus. $18.95

A guide taking Western bucks with rifle and bow.

Hunting the Rockies, Home of the Giants, by Kirk Darner, Marceline, MO, 1996. 291 pp., illus. $25.00

Understand how and where to hunt Western game in the Rockies.

Hunting Western Deer, by Jim and Wes Brown, Stoneydale Press, Stevensville, MT, 1994. 174 pp., illus. Paper covers. $14.95

A pair of expert Oregon hunters provide insight into hunting mule deer and blacktail deer in the western states.

Hunting Wild Turkeys in the West, by John Higley, Stoneydale Press, Stevensville, MT, 1992. 154 pp., illus. Paper covers. $12.95

Covers the basics of calling, locating and hunting turkeys in the western states.

Hunting with the Twenty-Two, by Charles Singer Landis, R&R Books, Livonia, NY, 1994. 429 pp., illus. $35.00

A miscellany of articles touching on the hunting and shooting of small game.

In Search of the Buffalo, by Charles G. Anderson, Pioneer Press, Union City, TN, 1996. 144 pp., illus. Paper covers. $13.95

The primary study of the life of J. Wright Mooar, one of the few hunters fortunate enough to kill a white buffalo.

In the Turkey Woods, by Jerome B. Robinson, The Lyons Press, N.Y., 1998. 207 pp., illus. $24.95

Practical expert advice on all aspects of turkey hunting–from calls to decoys to guns.

Kodiak Island and its Bears, by Harry Dodge, Anchorage, Great Northwest Publishing, 2004. 364 pages, carefully indexed, thoughtfully footnoted, and lavishly illustrated. $27.50

This is the most significant volume about Kodiak Island and its bears that has been published in at least 20 years. This book now stands to become a new classic for all time.

Lost Classics of Jack O'Connor, by Jim Casada, Live Oak Press, 2004. Exciting tales with a twist of humor. 33 photos, 40 illus. by Dan Burr; 376 pages, with illustrations and photos. Hardcover. New in new dust jacket. $35.00

Montana–Land of Giant Rams, Volume 2, by Duncan Gilchrist, Outdoor Expeditions and Books, Corvallis, MT, 1992. 208 pp., illus. $34.95

The reader will find stories of how many of the top-scoring trophies were taken.

Montana–Land of Giant Rams, Volume 3, by Duncan Gilchrist, Outdoor Expeditions and Books, Corvallis, MT, 1999. 224 pp., illus. Paper covers. $19.95

All new sheep information including over 70 photos. Learn about how Montana became the "Land of Giant Rams" and what the prospects of the future are.

More Tracks: 78 Years of Mountains, People & Happiness, by Howard Copenhaver, Stoneydale Press, Stevensville, MT, 1992. 150 pp., illus. $18.95

A collection of stories by one of the back country's best storytellers about the people who shared with Howard his great adventure in the high places and wild Montana country.

Mostly Huntin', by Bill Jordan, Everett Publishing Co., Bossier City, LA, 1987. 254 pp., illus. $21.95

Jordan's hunting adventures in North America, Africa, Australia, South America and Mexico.

Mule Deer: Hunting Today's Trophies, by Tom Carpenter and Jim Van Norman, Krause Publications, Iola, WI, 1998. 256 pp., illus. Paper covers. $19.95

A tribute to both the deer and the people who hunt them. Includes info on where to look for big deer, prime mule deer habitat and effective weapons for the hunt.

Muzzleloading for Deer and Turkey, by Dave Ehrig, Stackpole Books, 2005. 475 pages, 293 b&w photos. Hardcover. New in new dust jacket. $29.95

My Health is Better in November, by Havilah Babcock, University of S. Carolina Press, Columbia, SC, 1985. 284 pp., illus. $24.95

Adventures in the field set in the plantation country and backwater streams of SC.

North American Waterfowler, The, by Paul S. Bernsen, Superior Publ. Co., Seattle, WA, 1972. 206 pp. Paper covers. $9.95

The complete inside and outside story of duck and goose shooting. Big and colorful, illustrations by Les Kouba.

Old Man and the Boy, The, by Robert Ruark, Henry Holt & Co., New York, NY, 303 pp., illus. $24.95

A timeless classic, telling the story of a remarkable friendship between a young boy and his grandfather as they hunt and fish together.

Old Man's Boy Grows Older, The, by Robert Ruark, Henry Holt & Co., Inc., New York, NY, 1993. 300 pp., illus. $24.95

The heartwarming sequel to the best-selling *The Old Man and the Boy.*

One Man, One Rifle, One Land; Hunting all Species of Big Game in North America, by J.Y. Jones, Safari Press, Huntington Beach, CA, 2000. 400 pp., illus. $59.95

Journey with J.Y. Jones as he hunts each of the big-game animals of North America–from the polar bear of the high Arctic to the jaguar of the low-lands of Mexico–with just one rifle.

Outdoor Pastimes of an American Hunter, by Theodore Roosevelt, Stackpole Books, Mechanicsburg, PA, 1994. 480 pp., illus. Paper covers. $18.95

Stories of hunting big game in the West and notes about animals pursued and observed.

Outlaw Gunner, The, by Harry M. Walsh, Tidewater Publishers, Cambridge, MD, 1973. 178 pp., illus. $22.95

A colorful story of market gunning in both its legal and illegal phases.

Pheasant Days, by Chris Dorsey, Voyageur Press, Stillwater, MN, 1992. 233 pp., illus. $24.95

The definitive resource on ringnecks. Includes everything from basic hunting techniques to the life cycle of the bird.

Pheasant Hunter's Harvest, by Steve Grooms, Lyons & Burford Publishers, New York, NY, 1990. 180 pp. $22.95

A celebration of pheasant, pheasant dogs and pheasant hunting. Practical advice from a passionate hunter.

Pheasant Tales, by Gene Hill et al, Countrysport Press, Traverse City, MI, 1996. 202 pp., illus. $39.00

Charley Waterman, Michael McIntosh and Phil Bourjaily join the author to tell some of the stories that illustrate why the pheasant is America's favorite game bird.

Pheasants of the Mind, by Datus Proper, Wilderness Adventures Press, Bozeman, MT, 1994. 154 pp., illus. $25.00

No single title sums up the life of the solitary pheasant hunter like this masterful work.

Portraits of Elk Hunting, by Jim Zumbo, Safari Press, Huntington Beach, CA, 2001. 222 pp. illus. $39.95

Zumbo has captured in photos as well as in words the essence, charisma, and wonderful components of elk hunting: back-country wilderness camps, sweaty guides, happy hunters, favorite companions, elk woods, and, of course, the majestic elk. Join Zumbo in the uniqueness of the pursuit of the magnificent and noble elk.

Precision Bowhunting: A Year-Round approach to taking Mature Whitetails, by John and Chris Eberhart, Stackpole Books, 2005. 214pp, b&w photos. Soft cover. $16.95

Packed with vital information and fresh insights, Precision Bow hunting belongs on the bookshelf of every serious bow hunter.

Proven Whitetail Tactics, by Greg Miller, Krause Publications, Iola, WI, 1997. 224 pp., illus. Paper covers. $19.95

Proven tactics for scouting, calling and still-hunting whitetail.

Quest for Dall Rams, by Duncan Gilchrist, Duncan Gilchrist Outdoor Expeditions and Books, Corvallis, MT, 1997. 224 pp., illus. Paper covers. $19.95

The most complete book of Dall sheep ever written. Covers information on Alaska and provinces with Dall sheep and explains hunting techniques, equipment, etc.

Quest for Giant Bighorns, by Duncan Gilchrist, Outdoor Expeditions and Books, Corvallis, MT, 1994. 224 pp., illus. Paper covers. $19.95

How some of the most successful sheep hunters hunt and how some of the best bighorns were taken.

Radical Elk Hunting Strategies, by Mike Lapinski, Stoneydale Press Publishing Co., Stevensville, MT, 1988. 161 pp., illus. $18.95

Secrets of calling elk in close.

Rattling, Calling & Decoying Whitetails, by Gary Clancy, edited by Patrick Durkin, Krause Publications, Iola, WI, 2000. 208 pp., illus. Paper covers. $19.95

How to consistently coax big bucks into range.

Records of North American Caribou and Moose, Craig Boddington et al, The Boone & Crockett Club, Missoula, MT, 1997. 250 pp., illus. $24.95

More than 1,800 caribou listings and more than 1,500 moose listings, organized by the state or Canadian province where they were taken.

Records of North American Elk and Mule Deer, 2nd Edition, edited by Jack and Susan Reneau, The Boone & Crockett Club, Missoula, MT, 1996. 360 pp., illus. Paper cover, $18.95; hardcover, $24.95

Updated and expanded edition featuring more than 150 trophy, field and historical photos of the finest elk and mule deer trophies ever recorded.

Records of North American Sheep, Rocky Mountain Goats and Pronghorn, edited by Jack and Susan Reneau, The Boone & Crockett Club, Missoula, MT, 1996. 400 pp., illus. Paper cover, $18.95; hardcover, $24.95

The first B&C Club records book featuring all 3941 accepted wild sheep, Rocky Mountain goats and pronghorn trophies.

Reflections on Snipe, by Worth Mathewson, illustrated by Eldridge Hardie, Camden, ME, Country Sport Press, 2003. Hardcover. 144 pp. $25.00

Reflections on Snipe is a delightful compendium of information on snipe behavior and habitats; gunning history; stories from the field; and the pleasures of hunting with good companions, whether human or canine.

Ringneck; A Tribute to Pheasants and Pheasant Hunting, by Steve Grooms, Russ Sewell and Dave Nomsen, The Lyons Press, New York, NY, 2000. 120 pp., illus. $40.00

A glorious full-color coffee-table tribute to the pheasant and those who hunt them.

Rooster! A Tribute to Pheasant Hunting, by Dale C. Spartas, Riverbend Publishing, 2003. 1st edition. 150+ glorious photos of pheasants, hunting dogs and hunting trips with family and friends. 128 pgs. Hardcover. $39.95

A very special, must-have book for the 2.3 million pheasant hunters across the country!

Rub-Line Secrets, by Greg Miller, edited by Patrick Durkin, Krause Publications, Iola, WI, 1999. 208 pp., illus. Paper covers. $19.95

Based on nearly 30 years' experience. Proven tactics for finding, analyzing and hunting big bucks' rub-lines.

Season, The, by Tom Kelly, Lyons & Burford, New York, NY, 1997. 160 pp., illus. $22.95

The delight and challenges of a turkey hunter's spring season.

Secret Strategies from North America's Top Whitetail Hunters, compiled by Nick Sisley, Krause Publications, Iola, WI, 1995. 256 pp., illus. Paper covers. $14.95

Bow and gun hunters share their success stories.

Sheep Hunting in Alaska–The Dall Sheep Hunter's Guide, by Tony Russ, Outdoor Expeditions and Books, Corvallis, MT, 1994. 160 pp., illus. Paper covers. $19.95

A how-to guide for the Dall sheep hunter.

Southern Deer & Deer Hunting, by Larry Weishuhn and Bill Bynum, Krause Publications, Iola, WI, 1995. 256 pp., illus. Paper covers. $14.95

Mount a trophy southern whitetail on your wall with this firsthand account of stalking big bucks below the Mason-Dixon line.

Spring Gobbler Fever, by Michael Hanback, Krause Publications, Iola, WI, 1996. 256 pp., illus. Paper covers. $15.95

Your complete guide to spring turkey hunting.

Stand Hunting for Whitetails, by Richard P. Smith, Krause Publications, Iola, WI, 1996. 256 pp., illus. Paper covers. $14.95

The author explains the tricks and strategies for successful stand hunting.

Successful Black Bear Hunting, by Bill Vaznis, Iola,WI, Krause Publications, 2004. 144 pages, illustrated with full color photographs and drawings. Pictorial Soft cover. $23.99

Sultan of Spring: A Hunter's Odyssey Through the World of the Wild Turkey, The, by Bob Saile, The Lyons Press, New York, NY, 1998. 176 pp., illus. $22.95

A literary salute to the magic and mysticism of spring turkey hunting.

Taking Big Bucks, by Ed Wolff, Stoneydale Press, Stevensville, MT, 1987. 169 pp., illus. $18.95

Solving the whitetail riddle.

Tales of Quails 'n Such, by Havilah Babcock, University of S. Carolina Press, Columbia, SC, 1985. 237 pp. $19.95

A group of hunting stories, told in informal style, on field experiences in the South in quest of small game.

They Left Their Tracks, by Howard Coperhaver, Stoneydale Press Publishing Co., Stevensville, MT, 1990. 190 pp., illus. $18.95

Recollections of 60 years as an outfitter in the Bob Marshall Wilderness.

To Heck with Moose Hunting, by Jim Zumbo, Wapiti Publishing Co., Cody, WY, 1996. 199 pp., illus. $17.95

Jim's hunts around the continent and even an African adventure.

Track Pack: Animal Tracks In Full Life Size, by Ed Gray, Mechanicsburg, PA, Stackpole Books, 2003. 1st edition. Spiral-bound, 34 pp. $7.95

An indispensable reference for hunters, trackers, and outdoor enthusiasts. This handy guide features the tracks of 38 common North American animals, from squirrels to grizzlies.

Trickiest Thing in Feathers, The, by Corey Ford, compiled and edited by Laurie Morrow, illustrated by Christopher Smith, Wilderness Adventures, Gallatin Gateway, MT, 1998. 208 pp., illus. $29.95

Here is a collection of Corey Ford's best wing-shooting stories, many of them previously unpublished.

Upland Equation: A Modern Bird-Hunter's Code, The, by Charles Fergus, Lyons & Burford Publishers, New York, NY, 1996. 86 pp. $18.00

A book that deserves space in every sportsman's library. Observations based on firsthand experience.

Upland Tales, edited by Worth Mathewson, Sand Lake Press, Amity, OR, 1996. 271 pp., illus. $29.95

A collection of articles on grouse, snipe and quail.

Waterfowler's World, by Bill Buckley, Ducks Unlimited, Inc., Memphis, TN, 1999. 192 pp., illustrated in color. $37.50

An unprecedented pictorial book on waterfowl and waterfowlers.

When the Duck Were Plenty, by Ed Muderlak, Safari Press, Inc., Huntington Beach, CA, 2000. 300 pp., illus. $29.95

The golden age of waterfowling and duck hunting from 1840 until 1920. An anthology.

Whitetail: Behavior Through the Seasons, by Charles J. Alsheimer, Krause Publications, Iola, WI, 1996. 208 pp., illus. $34.95

In-depth coverage of whitetail behavior presented through striking portraits of the whitetail in every season.

Whitetail: The Ultimate Challenge, by Charles J. Alsheimer, Krause Publications, Iola, WI, 1995. 228 pp., illus. Paper covers. $14.95

Learn deer hunting's most intriguing secrets–fooling deer using decoys, scents and calls–from America's premier authority.

Whitetails by the Moon, by Charles J. Alsheimer, edited by Patrick Durkin, Krause Publications, Iola, WI, 1999. 208 pp., illus. Paper covers. $19.95

Predict peak times to hunt whitetails. Learn what triggers the rut.

Wildfowler's Season, by Chris Dorsey, Lyons & Burford Publishers, New York, NY, 1998. 224 pp., illus. $37.95

Modern methods for a classic sport.

Wildfowling Tales, by William C. Hazelton, Wilderness Adventures Press, Belgrade, MT, 1999. 117 pp., illustrated with etchings by Brett Smith. In a slipcase. $50.00

Tales from the great ducking resorts of the continent.

Windward Crossings: A Treasury of Original Waterfowling Tales, by Chuck Petrie et al, Willow Creek Press, Minocqua, WI, 1999. 144 pp., 48 color art and etching reproductions. $35.00

An illustrated, modern anthology of previously unpublished waterfowl hunting (fiction and creative nonfiction) stories by America's finest outdoor journalists.

Wings of Thunder: New Grouse Hunting Revisited, by Steven Mulak, Countrysport Books, Selma, AL, 1998. 168 pp. illus. $30.00

The author examines every aspect of New England grouse hunting as it is today–the bird and its habits, the hunter and his dog, guns and loads, shooting and hunting techniques, practice on clay targets, clothing and equipment.

Woodchuck Hunter, The, by Paul C. Estey, R&R Books, Livonia, NY, 1994. 135 pp., illus. $25.00

This book contains information on woodchuck equipment, the rifle, telescopic sights and includes interesting stories.

AFRICA/ASIA/ELSEWHERE

A Bullet Well Placed; One Hunter's Adventures Around the World, by Johnny Chilton, Safari Press, 2004. 245 pages. Hardcover. New in new dust jacket. $34.95

Painting a picture of what it is actually like to be there and do it, this well-written book captures the excitement and emotions of each journey.

A Country Boy in Africa, by George Hoffman, Trophy Room Books, Agoura, CA, 1998. 267 pp., illustrated with over 100 photos. Limited, numbered edition signed by the author. $85.00

In addition to the author's long and successful hunting career, he is known for developing a most effective big game cartridge, the .416 Hoffman.

A Hunter's Africa, by Gordon Cundill, Trophy Room Books, Agoura, CA, 1998. 298 pp., over 125 photographic illustrations. Limited numbered edition signed by the author. $125.00

A good look by the author at the African safari experience-elephant, lion, spiral-horned antelope, firearms, people and events, as well as the clients that make it worthwhile.

A Hunter's Wanderings in Africa, by Frederick Courteney Selous, Alexanders Books, Alexander, NC, 2003. 504 pp., illus. $28.50

A reprinting of the 1920 London edition. A narrative of nine years spent amongst the game of the far interior of South Africa.

A Pioneering Hunter, by B Marsh, Safari Press, 2006. A limited edition of 1,000 copies. Signed and Numbered. 107. 247pp, color photos. Hardcover in a Slipcase. $65.00

Elephant cropping, buffalo tales, and colorful characters—this book has it all.

A Professional Hunter's Journey of Discovery, by Alec McCallum, Agoura, CA, Trophy Room Books, 2003. Limited edition of 1,000. Signed and numbered. 132 pp. Hardcover. New in new dust jacket. $125.00

A View From A Tall Hill: Robert Ruark in Africa, by Terry Wieland, Bristol, CT, Country Sport Press, 2004. Reprint. 432 pp., Hardcover New in new dust jacket $45.00

African Adventures and Misadventures: Escapades in East Africa with Mau Mau and Giant Forest Hogs, by William York, Long Beach, CA, Safari Press, 2003. A limited edition of 1,000 copies. Signed and numbered. 250 pp., color and b&w photos. Hardcover in a slipcase. $70.00

From his early days in Kenya when he and a companion trekked alone through the desert of the NFD and had to fend off marauding lions that ate his caravan ponies to encountering a Mau Mau terrorist who took potshots at his victims with a stolen elephant gun, the late Bill York gives an entertaining account of his life that will keep you turning the pages. As with York's previous book, the pages are loaded with interesting anecdotes, fascinating tales, and well-written prose that give insight into East Africa and its more famous characters.

African Game Trails, by Theodore Roosevelt, Peter Capstick, Series Editor, St. Martin's Press, New York, NY 1988. 583 pp., illus. $26.95

The famed safari of the noted sportsman, conservationist, and president.

African Hunter II, edited by Craig Boddington and Peter Flack, Foreword by Robin Hurt, Introduction by James Mellon, Long Beach, CA, Safari Press, 2004. 606 pp., profuse color and b&w photos. Hardcover. $135.00

James Mellon spent five years hunting in every African country open to hunting during the late 1960s and early 1970s, making him uniquely qualified to write a book of such scope and breadth. Because so much has changed in today's Africa, however, it was necessary to update the original. With over 500 full-color pages, hundreds of photographs, and updated tables on animals and where they are available, this is THE book to consult for the information on Africa today.

African Rifles & Cartridges, by John Taylor, The Gun Room Press, Highland Park, NJ, 1977. 431 pp., illus. $35.00

Experiences and opinions of a professional ivory hunter in Africa describing his knowledge of numerous arms and cartridges for big game. A reprint.

African Twilight, by Robert F. Jones, Wilderness Adventure Press, Bozeman, MT, 1994. 208 pp., illus. $36.00

Details the hunt, danger and changing face of Africa over a span of three decades.

Atkin, Grant & Lang: A Detailed History of Enduring Gunmakers (trade edition), by Don Masters, Safari Press, 2005. 316pp., color and b&w photos. Hardcover. New in new dust jacket. $69.89

The history of three makers and their several relatives making guns under their own names. In the pages of this book you can learn all the details of the gun makers: dates, premises, main employees, rises and declines in sales fortunes, as well as the many interesting historical anecdotes and insights we have come to expect from Don Masters.

Baron in Africa; The Remarkable Adventures of Werner von Alvensleben, by Brian Marsh, Foreword by Ian Player, Safari Press, Huntington Beach, CA, 2001. 288 pp., illus. $35.00

Follow his career as he hunts lion, goes after large kudu, kills a full-grown buffalo with a spear, and hunts for elephant and ivory in some of the densest brush in Africa. The adventure and the experience were what counted to this fascinating character, not the money or fame; indeed, in the end he left Mozambique with barely more than the clothes on his back. This is a must-read adventure story of one of the most interesting characters to have come out of Africa after WWII.

ARMS LIBRARY

Buffalo!, by Craig Boddington, Safari Books, 2006. 256pp, color photos, Hardcover. $39.95
Craig tells his readers where to hunt, how and when to hunt, and what will happen when they do hunt. He describes what it means to rush the herd, one of his favorite methods of hunting these worthy opponents. He tells of the great bull in Masailand that he almost got, of the perfect hunt he had in Zambia, and of the charge he experienced in Tanzania.

Buffalo, Elephant, & Bongo (trade edition): Alone in the Savannas and Rain Forests of the Cameroon, by Reinald Von Meurers, Long Beach, CA, Safari Press, 2004. Hardcover. New in new dust jacket. $39.50

Cottar: The Exception was the Rule, by Pat Cottar, Trophy Room Books, Agoura, CA, 1999. 350 pp., illus. Limited, numbered and signed edition. $135.00
The remarkable big game hunting stories of one of Kenya's most remarkable pioneers.

Dangerous Game, True Stories of Dangerous Hunting on Three Continents, The, Safari Press, 2006. A limited edition of 500 copies. Signed and Numbered. 225pp, photos. Hardcover in a Slipcase. $70.00

Death and Double Rifles, by Mark Sullivan, Nitro Express Safaris, Phoenix, AZ, 2000. 295 pp., illus. $85.00
Sullivan has captured every thrilling detail of hunting dangerous game in this lavishly illustrated book. Full of color pictures of African hunts & rifles.

Death in a Lonely Land, by Peter Capstick, St. Martin's Press, New York, NY, 1990. 284 pp., illus. $22.95
Twenty-three stories of hunting as only the master can tell them.

Death in the Dark Continent, by Peter Capstick, St. Martin's Press, New York, NY, 1983. 238 pp., illus. $22.95
A book that brings to life the suspense, fear and exhilaration of stalking ferocious killers under primitive, savage conditions, with the ever present threat of death.

Death in the Long Grass, by Peter Hathaway Capstick, St. Martin's Press, New York, NY, 1977. 297 pp., illus. $22.95
A big game hunter's adventures in the African bush.

Death in the Silent Places, by Peter Capstick, St. Martin's Press, New York, NY, 1981. 243 pp., illus. $23.95
The author recalls the extraordinary careers of legendary hunters such as Corbett, Karamojo Bell, Stigand and others.

Elephant Hunters, Men of Legend, by Tony Sanchez-Arino, Safari Press, 2005. A limited edition of 1,000 copies. Signed and Numbered. 240 pages. Hardcover in a Slipcase. $100.00
This newest book from Tony Sanchez is the most interesting ever to emerge on that intrepid and now finished breed of man: Elephant Hunters, Men of Legend.

Encounters with Lions, by Jan Hemsing, Trophy Room Books, Agoura, CA, 1995. 302 pp., illus. $75.00
Some stories fierce, fatal, frightening and even humorous of when man and lion meet.

Fodor's African Safari, From Budget to Big Spending Where and How to Find the Best Big Game Adventure in Southern and Eastern Africa, by David Bristow, Julian Harrison, Chris Swiac, New York, Fodor's, 2004. 1st edition. 190 pp. Softcover. $9.95

Frederick Selous: A Hunting Legend-Recollections By and About the Great Hunter (trade edition), by F.C. Selous (edited by James Casada), Safari Press, 2005. 187pp., illus. Hardcover. $34.95
This second book on Selous, edited by Africana expert Dr. James Casada, completes the work on the lost writings by Selous begun in Africa's Greatest Hunter.

From Mt. Kenya to the Cape: Ten Years of African Hunting, by Craig Boddington, Long Beach, CA, Safari Press, 2005. Hardcover. New in new dust jacket. $39.95
This wealth of information makes not only great reading, but the appendixes also provide tips on rifles, cartridges, equipment, and how to plan a safari.

From Sailor to Professional Hunter: The Autobiography of John Northcote, Trophy Room Books, Agoura, CA, 1997. 400 pp., illus. Limited edition, signed and numbered. $125.00
Only a handful of men can boast of having a 50-year professional hunting career throughout Africa as John Northcote has had.

Gone are the Days; Jungle Hunting for Tiger and other Game in India and Nepal 1953-1969, by Peter Byrne, Safari Press, Inc., Huntington Beach, CA, 2001. 225 pp., illus. Limited signed, numbered, slipcased. $70.00

Great Hunters: Their Trophy Rooms and Collections, Volume 1, compiled and published by Safari Press, Inc., Huntington Beach, CA, 1997. 172 pp., illustrated in color. $60.00
A rare glimpse into the trophy rooms of top international hunters. A few of these trophy rooms are museums.

Great Hunters: Their Trophy Rooms & Collections, Volume 2, compiled and published by Safari Press, Inc., Huntington Beach, CA, 1998. 224 pp., illustrated with 260 full-color photographs. $60.00
Volume Two of the world's finest, best produced series of books on trophy rooms and game collections. 46 sportsmen sharing sights you'll never forget on this guided tour.

Great Hunters: Their Trophy Rooms & Collections, Volume 3, compiled and published by Safari Press, Inc., Huntington Beach, CA, 2000. 204 pp., illustrated with 260 full-color photographs. $60.00
At last, the long-awaited third volume in the best photographic series ever published of trophy room collections is finally available. As before, each trophy room is accompanied by an informative text explaining the collection and giving you insights into the hunters who went to such great efforts to create their trophy rooms. All professionally photographed in the highest quality possible.

Great Hunters: Their Trophy Rooms & Collections, Volume 4, compiled and published by Safari Press, Inc., Huntington Beach, CA, 2005. 204 pp., illustrated with 260 full-color photographs. $60.00
At last, the long-awaited fourth volume in the best photographic series ever published of trophy room collections is finally available. Each trophy room is accompanied by an informative text explaining the collection and giving you insights into the hunters who went to such great efforts to create their trophy rooms. All professionally photographed in the highest quality possible.

Heart of an African Hunter, by Peter Flack, Long Beach, CA, Safari Press, 2005. 266 pp. illustrated with b&w photos. Hardcover. $35.00

Hemingway in Africa: The Last Safari, by Christopher Ondaatje, Overlook Press, 2004. 1st edition. 240 pp. Hardcover. New in new dust jacket. $37.50

Horn of the Hunter, by Robert Ruark, Safari Press, Long Beach, CA, 1987. 315 pp., illus. $35.00
Ruark's most sought-after title on African hunting, here in reprint.

Hunter's Tracks, by J.A. Hunter, Safari Press Publications, Huntington Beach, CA, 1999. 240 pp., illus. $24.95
This is the exciting story of John Hunter's efforts to capture the shady head man of a gang of ivory poachers and smugglers. The story is interwoven with the tale of one of East Africa's most grandiose safaris taken with an Indian maharaja.

Hunting in Ethiopia, An Anthology, by Tony Sanchez-Arino, Safari Press, Huntington Beach, CA, 1996. 350 pp., illus. Limited, signed and numbered edition. $135.00
The finest selection of hunting stories ever compiled on hunting in this great game country.

Hunting in Kenya, by Tony Sanchez-Arino, Safari Press, Inc., Huntington Beach, CA, 2000. 350 pp., illus. Limited, signed and numbered edition in a slipcase. $135.00
The finest selection of hunting stories ever compiled on hunting in this great game country make up this anthology.

Hunting in the Sudan, An Anthology, compiled by Tony Sanchez-Arino, Safari Press, Huntington Beach, CA, 1992. 350 pp., illus. Limited, signed and numbered edition in a slipcase. $125.00
The finest selection of hunting stories ever compiled on hunting in this great game country.

Hunting Instinct, The, by Phillip D. Rowter, Safari Press, Inc., Huntington Beach, CA, 2005, trade edition. Hardcover. New in new dust jacket. $29.95
Safari chronicles from the Republic of South Africa and Namibia 1990-1998.

Hunting the Dangerous Game of Africa, by John Kingsley-Heath, Sycamore Island Books, Boulder, CO, 1998. 477 pp., illus. $95.00
Written by one of the most respected, successful, and ethical P.H.'s to trek the sunlit plains of Botswana, Kenya, Uganda, Tanganyika, Somaliland, Eritrea, Ethiopia, and Mozambique. Filled with some of the most gripping and terrifying tales ever to come out of Africa.

Hunting, Settling and Remembering, by Philip H. Percival, Trophy Room Books, Agoura, CA, 1997. 230 pp., illus. Limited, numbered and signed edition. $85.00
If Philip Percival is to come alive again, it will be through this, the first edition of his easy, intricate and magical book illustrated with some of the best historical big game hunting photos ever taken.

Hunting Trips in The Land of the Dragon; Anglo and American Sportsmen in Old China, 1870-1940, by Kenneth Czech, Safari Press, 2005. Hardcover. New in new dust jacket. $34.95
The first part of this anthology takes the reader after duck, pheasant, and other upland game while the second part focuses on the large game of China and the border regions. The latter includes hunts for Manchurian tiger, tufted deer, goral, wild goat, wild yak, antelope, takin, wild sheep in the Mongolian Altai, wapiti, blue sheep, ibex, Ovis poli of the Pamir, wild sheep of the Tian Shan, brown bear, and panda--all written by such famous names as Major General Kinloch, St. George Littledale, Kermit Roosevelt, and Roy Chapman Andrews.

In the Salt, by Lou Hallamore, Trophy Room Books, Agoura, CA, 1999. 227 pp., illustrated in b&w and full color. Limited, numbered and signed edition. $125.00
A book about people, animals and the big game hunt, about being outwitted and outmaneuvered. It is about knowing that sooner or later your luck will change and your trophy will be "in the salt."

International Hunter 1945-1999, Hunting's Greatest Era, by Bert Klineburger, Sportsmen on Film, Kerrville, TX, 1999. 400 pp., illus. A limited, numbered and signed edition. $125.00
The most important book of the greatest hunting era by the world's preeminent international hunter.

Jim Corbett Collection, by Jim Corbett, Safari press, 2005. 1124 pages, illus, 5 volumes. Hardcover in a Slipcase. $100.00
The complete set of Jim Corbett's works, housed in a printed slipcase and feature the work of the internationally famous wildlife artist Guy Coheleach.

King of the Wa-Kikuyu, by John Boyes, St. Martin Press, New York, NY, 1993. 240 pp., illus. $19.95
In the 19th and 20th centuries, Africa drew to it a large number of great hunters, explorers, adventurers and rogues. Many have become legendary, but John Boyes (1874-1951) was the most legendary of them all.

Kwaheri! On the Spoor of Big Game in East Africa, by Robert von Reitnauer, Long beach, CA, Safari Press, 2005. A limited edition of 1,000 copies. Signed and Numbered. 285 pages, illustrated with photos. Hardcover in a Slipcase. $75.00
This is the story of an immense land in the days before the truly big tuskers all but disappeared. A very good read.

Last Horizons: Hunting, Fishing and Shooting on Five Continents, by Peter Capstick, St. Martin's Press, New York, NY, 1989. 288 pp., illus. $19.95
The first in a two-volume collection of hunting, fishing and shooting tales from the selected pages of *The American Hunter*, *Guns & Ammo* and *Outdoor Life*.

Last of the Ivory Hunters, by John Taylor, Safari Press, Long Beach, CA, 1990. 354 pp., illus. $29.95
Reprint of the classic book "Pondoro" by one of the most famous elephant hunters of all time.

Legends of the Field: More Early Hunters in Africa, by W.R. Foran, Trophy Room Press, Agoura, CA, 1997. 319 pp., illus. Limited edition. $100.00
This book contains the biographies of some very famous hunters: William Cotton Oswell, F.C. Selous, Sir Samuel Baker, Arthur Neumann, Jim Sutherland, W.D.M. Bell and others.

Lives of A Professional Hunting Family, by Gerard Agoura Miller, Trophy Room Books, 2003. A limited edition of 1,000 copies. Signed and numbered. 303 pp., 230 b&w photographic illustrations. Hardcover. $135.00

Lost Classics, by Robert Ruark, Safari Press, Huntington Beach, CA, 1996. 260 pp., illus. $35.00
The magazine stories that Ruark wrote in the 1950s and 1960s finally in print in book form.

Lost Wilderness; True Accounts of Hunters and Animals in East Africa, by Mohamed Ismail and Alice Pianfetti, Safari Press, Inc., Huntington Beach, CA, 2000. 216 pp., photos, illus. Limited edition signed, numbered and slipcased. $60.00

Mahonhboh, by Ron Thomson, Hartbeesport, South Africa, 1997. 312 pp., illus. Limited signed and numbered edition. $50.00
Elephants and elephant hunting in South Central Africa.

Man-Eaters of Tsavo, The, by Lt. Colonel J.H. Patterson, Peter Capstick, series editor, St. Martin's Press, New York, NY, 1986, 5th printing. 346 pp., illus. $22.95

Maneaters and Marauders, by John "Pondoro" Taylor, Long Beach, CA, Safari Press, 2005. 1st edition, Safari edition. Hardcover. New in new dust jacket. $29.95

McElroy Hunts Asia, by C.J. McElroy, Safari Press, Inc., Huntington Beach, CA, 1989. 272 pp., illus. $50.00

From the founder of SCI comes a book on hunting the great continent of Asia for big game: tiger, bear, sheep and ibex. Includes the story of the all-time record Altai Argali as well as several markhor hunts in Pakistan.

Memoirs of A Sheep Hunter, by Rashid Jamsheed, Safari Press, Inc., Huntington Beach, CA, 1996. 330 pp., illus. $70.00

The author reveals his exciting accounts of obtaining world-record heads from his native Iran, and his eventual move to the U.S. where he procured a grand-slam of North American sheep.

Memoirs of An African Hunter (Trade Edition), by Terry Irwin, Safari Press, 2005. 411pp, 95 color and 20 b&w photos, large format. Hardcover $70.00

Memories of Africa; Hunting in Zambia and Sudan, by W. Brach, Safari Press, 2005. 2005. A limited edition of 1,000 copies. Signed and Numbered. Written with an interesting flair and a true graphic perspective of the animals, people, and the hunt, this is a realistic portrayal, not Hollywood-style swaggering and gun-slinging, of hunting the magnificent wildlife of Zambia and Sudan over the last three decades. 285 pages, illustrated with photos. Hardcover in a Slipcase. $85.00

Mundjamba: The Life Story of an African Hunter, by Hugo Seia, Trophy Room Books, Agoura, CA, 1996. 400 pp., illus. Limited, numbered and signed by the author. $125.00

An autobiography of one of the most respected and appreciated professional African hunters.

My Africa: A Professional Hunter's Journey of Discovery, by Alec McCallum, Trouphy Room Books, 2003. Limited Edition: 1000. Signed and numbered. hunting. 232pp. Hardcover. New in new dust jacket. $125.00

My Wanderings Though Africa: The Life and Times of a Professional Hunter, by Mike and James Cameron, Safari Press, 2004. Deluxe, Limited, Signed edition. 208pp, b&w photos. Hardcover in a Slipcase. $75.00

This is a book for readers whose imagination carries them into a world where reality means starry skies, the call of a jackal and the moan of a lion, the smell of gun oil, and smoke from a cooking fire rising into the African night.

On Target, by Christian Le Noel, Trophy Room Books, Agoura, CA, 1999. 275 pp., illus. Limited, numbered and signed edition. $85.00

History and hunting in Central Africa.

One Long Safari, by Peter Hay, Trophy Room Books, Agoura, CA, 1998. 350 pp., with over 200 photographic illustrations and 7 maps. Limited numbered edition signed by the author. $100.00

Contains hunts for leopards, sitatunga, hippo, rhino, snakes and, of course, the general African big game bag.

Optics for the Hunter, by John Barsness, Safari Press, Inc., Huntington Beach, CA, 1999. 236 pp., illus. $24.95

An evaluation of binoculars, scopes, range finders, spotting scopes for use in the field.

Out in the Midday Shade, by William York, Safari Press, Inc., Huntington Beach, CA, 2005. Trade Edition. Hardcover. New in new dust jacket. $35.00

Path of a Hunter, The, by Gilles Tre-Hardy, Trophy Room Books, Agoura, CA, 1997. 318 pp., illus. Limited Edition, signed and numbered. $85.00

A most unusual hunting autobiography with much about elephant hunting in Africa.

Perfect Shot: Mini Edition for Africa, The, by Kevin Robertson, Long Beach, CA, Safari Press, 2004. 2nd printing Softcover. $17.95

Perfect Shot: Shot Placement for African Big Game, The, by Kevin "Doctari" Robertson, Safari Press, Inc., Huntington Beach, CA, 1999. 230 pp., illus. $65.00

The most comprehensive work ever undertaken to show the anatomical features for all classes of African game. Includes caliber and bullet selection, rifle selection and trophy handling.

Peter Capstick's Africa: A Return to the Long Grass, by Peter Hathaway Capstick, St. Martin's Press, N. Y., NY, 1987. 213 pp., illus. $35.00

A first-person adventure in which the author returns to the long grass for his own dangerous and very personal excursion.

Pondoro, by John Taylor, Safari Press, Inc., Huntington Beach, CA, 1999. 354 pp., illus. $39.95

The author is considered one of the best storytellers in the hunting book world, and Pondoro is highly entertaining. A classic African big-game hunting title.

Quotable Hunter, The, by Jay Cassell and Peter Fiduccia, The Lyons Press, N.Y., 1999. 288 pp., illus. $20.00

This collection of more than three hundred quotes from hunters through the ages captures the essence of the sport, with all its joys, idosyncrasies, and challenges.

Return to Toonaklut–The Russell Annabel Story, by Jeff Davis, Long Beach, CA, Safari Press, 2002. 248 pp., photos, illus. $34.95

Those of us who grew up after WW II cannot imagine the Alaskan frontier that Rusty Annabel walked into early in the twentieth century. The hardships, the resourcefulness, the natural beauty, not knowing what lay beyond the next horizon, all were a part of his existence. This is the story of the man behind the legend, and it is as fascinating as any of the tales Rusty Annabel ever spun for the sporting magazines.

Rifles and Cartridges for Large Game–From Deer to Bear–Advice on the Choice of A Rifle, by Layne Simpson, Long Beach, CA, Safari Press, 2002. Illustrated with 100 color photos, oversize book. 225 pp., color illus. $39.95

Layne Simpson, who has been field editor for *Shooting Times* magazine for 20 years, draws from his hunting experiences on five continents to tell you what rifles, cartridges, bullets, loads, and scopes are best for various applications, and he explains why in plain English. Developer of the popular 7mm STW cartridge, Simpson has taken big game with rifle cartridges ranging in power from the .220 Swift to the .460 Weatherby Magnum, and he pulls no punches when describing their effectiveness in the field.

Rifles for Africa; Practical Advice on Rifles and Ammunition for an African Safari, by Gregor Woods, Long Beach, CA, Safari Press, 2002. 1st edition. 430 pp., illus., photos. $39.95

Invaluable to the person who seeks advice and information on what rifles, calibers, and bullets work on African big game, be they the largest land mammals on earth or an antelope barely weighing in at 20 lbs.!

Robert Ruark's Africa, by Robert Ruark, edited by Michael McIntosh, Countrysport Press, Selma, AL, 1999. 256 pp. illustrated with 19 original etchings by Bruce Langton. $32.00

These previously uncollected works of Robert Ruark make this a classic big-game hunting book.

Safari: The Last Adventure, by Peter Capstick, St. Martin's Press, New York, NY, 1984. 291 pp., illus. $22.95

A modern comprehensive guide to the African Safari.

Safari Rifles: Double, Magazine Rifles and Cartridges for African Hunting, by Craig Boddington, Safari Press, Huntington Beach, CA, 1990. 416 pp., illus. $37.50

A wealth of knowledge on the safari rifle. Historical and present double-rifle makers, ballistics for the large bores, and much, much more.

Sands of Silence, by Peter H. Capstick, Saint Martin's Press, New York, NY, 1991. 224 pp., illus. $35.00

Join the author on safari in Nambia for his latest big-game hunting adventures.

Song of the Summits–Hunting Sheep, Ibex, and Markhor in Asia, Europe, and North America, by Jesus Yurén, Long Beach, CA, Safari Press, 2003. Limited edition. Hardcover in a slipcase. $75.00

Sunset Tales of Safariland, by Stan Bleazard, Trophy Room Books, 2006. Deluxe, Limited, Signed edition. Large 8½" x11" format, bound in sumptuous forest green gilt stamped suede binding. 274 pages. 113 b&w photographic illustrations and index. $125.00

Sunset Tales of Safariland will be of considerable interest to anyone interested in big game hunting.

Tales of the African Frontier, by J.A. Hunter, Safari Press Publications, Huntington Beach, CA, 1999. 308 pp., illus. $24.95

The early days of East Africa is the subject of this powerful John Hunter book.

Tanzania Safari: Hei Safari, by Robert DePole, Trophy Room Books, 2004. Sumptuous Burgundy gilt stamped faux suede binding, 343 pages plus 12 page index of people and places. 32 pages of black & white photographic illustrations. The reader will "see" the animals on the pages long enough to remember them forever. Hardcover. $125.00

To Heck With It–I'm Going Hunting–My First Eighteen Years as an International Big-Game Hunter–Limited Edition, by Arnold Alward with Bill Quimby, Long Beach, CA, Safari Press, 2003. Deluxe, 1st edition, limited to 1,000 signed copies. $80.00

Uganda Safaris, by Brian Herne, Winchester Press, Piscataway, NJ, 1979. 236 pp., illus. $24.95

The chronicle of a professional hunter's adventures in Africa.

Under the African Sun, by Dr. Frank Hibben, Safari Press, Inc., Huntington Beach, CA, 1999. Limited edition signed, numbered and in a slipcase. $85.00

Forty-eight years of hunting the African continent.

Under the African Sun, by Dr. Frank Hibben, Safari Press, Inc., Huntington Beach, CA, 2005. Trade edition. 305 pages illustrated with b&w and color photos. Hardcover. New in new dust jacket. $39.95

Under the Shadow of Man Eaters, by Jerry Jaleel, The Jim Corbett Foundation, Edmonton, Alberta, Canada, 1997. 152 pp., illus. A limited, numbered and signed edition. Paper covers. $35.00

The life and legend of Jim Corbett of Kumaon.

Use Enough Gun, by Robert Ruark, Safari Press, Huntington Beach, CA, 1997. 333 pp., illus. $35.00

Robert Ruark on big game hunting.

Warrior: The Legend of Col. Richard Meinertzhagen, by Peter H. Capstick, St. Martins Press, New York, NY, 1998. 320 pp., illus. $23.95

A stirring and vivid biography of the famous British colonial officer Richard Meinertzhagen, whose exploits earned him fame and notoriety as one of the most daring and ruthless men to serve during the glory days of the British Empire.

Waterfowler's World, The, by Bill Buckley, Willow Creek Press, Minocqua, WI, 1999. 176 pp., 225 color photographs. $37.50

Waterfowl hunting from Canadian prairies, across the U.S. heartland, to the wilds of Mexico, from the Atlantic to the Pacific coasts and the Gulf of Mexico.

Weatherby: Stories From the Premier Big-Game Hunters of the World, 1956-2002, The, edited by Nancy Vokins, Long Beach, CA, Safari Press, 2004. Deluxe, limited, signed edition. 434 pp., profuse color and b&w illus. Hardcover in a slipcase. $200.00

Wheel of Life–Bunny Allen, A Life of Safaris and Sex, The, by Bunny Allen, Long Beach, CA, Safari Press, 2004. 1st edition. 300 pp., illus, photos. Hardcover. $34.95

Wind, Dust & Snow-Great Rams of Asia, by Robert M. Anderson, Collectors Covey, 1997. Deluxe Limited edition of 500 copies. Signed and Numbered. 240pp profuse illus. More than 200 photos some on the greatest Asian rams ever taken by sportsmen. $150.00

A complete chronology of modern exploratory and pioneering Asian sheep-hunting expeditions from 1960 until 1996, with wonderful background history and previously untold stories.

With a Gun in Good Country, by Ian Manning, Trophy Room Books, Agoura, CA, 1996. Limited, numbered and signed by the author. $85.00

A book written about that splendid period before the poaching onslaught which almost closed Zambia and continues to the granting of her independence. It then goes on to recount Manning's experiences in Botswana, Congo, and briefly in South Africa.

Yoshi–The Life and Travels of an International Trophy Hunter, by W. Yoshimoto with Bill Quimby, Long Beach, CA, Safari Press, Inc., 2002. A limited edition of 1,000 copies, signed and numbered. 298 pp., color and b&w photos. Hardcover in a slipcase. $85.00

Watson T. Yoshimoto, a native Hawaiian, collected all 16 major varieties of the world's wild sheep and most of the many types of goats, ibex, bears, antelopes, and antlered game of Asia, Europe, North America, South America, and the South Pacific…as well as the African Big Five. Along the way he earned the respect of his peers and was awarded hunting's highest achievement, the coveted Weatherby Award.

RIFLES

'03 Springfield Rifles Era, by Clark S. Campbell, Richmond, VA, privately printed, 2003. 1st edition. 368 pp., 146 illustrations, drawn to scale by author. Hardcover. $58.00

A much-expanded version of this author's famous The '03 Springfield (1957) and The '03 Springfields (1971), representing 40 years of research into all things '03. Part I is a complete and verifiably correct study of all standardized and special-purpose models of the U.S. M1903 Springfield rifle, in both .22 and .30 calibers, including those prototypes which led to standard models, and also all standardized .30 caliber cartridges, including National and International Match, and caliber .22. Part II is the result of the author's five years as a Research and

Development Engineer with Remington Arms Co., and will be of inestimable value to anyone planning a custom sporter, whether or not based on the '03.

.303 SMLE Rifle No. 1 Assembly, Disassembly Manual, by Skennerton & Riling, Ray Riling Arms Books Co. Philadelphia, PA 2004. 36 pages, $5.00

With over 60 photos & line drawings. Ideal workshop reference for stripping & assembly with exploded parts drawings, specifications, service accessories, historical information and recommended reading references.

.303 British Rifle No. 4 Assembly, Disassembly Manual, by Skennerton & Riling, Ray Riling Arms Books Co. Philadelphia, PA 2004. 36 pages, $5.00

With over 60 photos & line drawings. Ideal workshop reference for stripping & assembly with exploded parts drawings, specifications, service accessories, historical information and recommended reading references.

.577 Snider-Enfield Rifles & Carbines; British Service Longarms, by Ian Skennerton. 1866-C.1880. Australia, Arms & Militaria Press, 2003. 1st edition. 240 pp. plus 8 color plates, 100 illustrations. Marking Ribbon. Hardcover. $39.50

The definitive study of Britain's first breech-loading rifle, at first converted from Enfield muskets, then newly made with Mk III breech. The trials, development, rifle and carbine models are detailed; new information along with descriptions of the cartridges.

1903 Springfield Assembly, Disassembly Manual .30 Model, by Skennerton & Riling, Ray Riling Arms Books Co. Philadelphia, PA 2004. 36 pages, $5.00

With over 60 photos & line drawings. Ideal workshop reference for stripping & assembly with exploded parts drawings, specifications, service accessories, historical information and recommended reading references.

1903 Springfield Rifle and Its Variations, by Joe Poyer, Tustin, CA, North Cape Publications, 2004. 466 pages, illustrated with hundreds of color and b& drawings and photos. Soft cover. $22.95

It covers the entire spectrum of the Model 1903 rifle from the rod bayonet to the M1903A4 sniper rifle.

A Master Gunmaker's Guide to Building Bolt-Action Rifles, by Bill Holmes, Boulder, CO, Paladin Press, 2003. Photos, illus., 152 pp. Softcover. $25.00

Many people today call themselves gunmakers, but very few have actually made a gun. Most buy parts wherever available and simply assemble them. During the past 50 years Bill Holmes has built from scratch countless rifles, shotguns and pistols of amazing artistry, ranging in caliber from .17 to .50.

A Potpourri of Single Shot Rifles and Actions, by Frank de Haas and Mark de Haas, Ridgeway, MO, 1993. 153 pp., illus. Paper covers. $22.50

The author's 6th book on non-bolt-action single shots. Covers more than 40 single-shot rifles in historical and technical detail.

Accurizing & Shooting Lee-Enfields, by Ian Skennerton, Australia, Arms & Militaria Press, 2005. 35pp, saddle-stitched laminated covers. ALL color photos and illustrations. Stiff paper covers. $15.00

This new full color heavily illustrated work by Ian Skennerton answers all those questions regarding the use of the Lee Enfield Rifles. Packed with detailed information covering the guns, the armourer's tools, and the sighting options for this fascinating series.

AK-47 and AK-74 Kalashnikov Rifles and Their Variations, by Joe Poyer, Tustin, CA, North Cape Publications, 2004. 1st edition. Softcover, 188 pages, Illustrated. $22.95

This is the newest book in the "Shooter's and Collector's Guide" series. Prepared with the help of members of the Kalashnikov Collectors Association, this 188 page book surveys every variation of the 7.62 AK-47 and the 5.45 AK-74 developed in the old Soviet Union on a part-to-part basis to permit easy identification of original rifles and those made from kits available from various manufacturers in different countries.

AK-47 Assembly, Disassembly Manual 7.62 X 39mm, by Skennerton & Riling, Ray Riling Arms Books Co. Philadelphia, PA 2004. 36 pages, $5.00

With over 60 photos & line drawings. Ideal workshop reference for stripping & assembly with exploded parts drawings, specifications, service accessories, historical information and recommended reading references. Ideal workbook for shooters and collectors alike. Triple saddle-stitched binding with durable plastic laminated cover makes this an ideal workshop guide.

AK-47 Assault Rifle, Desert Publications, Cornville, AZ, 1981. 150 pp., illus. Paper covers. $15.95

Complete and practical technical information on the only weapon in history to be produced in an estimated 30,000,000 units.

American Hunting Rifles: Their Application in the Field for Practical Shooting, by Craig Boddington, Safari Press, Huntington Beach, CA, 1996. 446 pp., illus. Second printing trade edition. Softcover $24.95

Covers all the hunting rifles and calibers that are needed for North America's diverse game.

American Krag Rifle and Carbine, by Joe Poyer, North Cape Publications, Tustin, CA, 2002. 1st edition. 317 pp., illustrated with hundreds of b&w drawings and photos. Softcover. $19.95

Provides the arms collector, historian and target shooter with a part by part analysis of what has been called the rifle with the smoothest bolt action ever designed. All changes to all parts are analyzed in detail and matched to serial number ranges. A monthly serial number chart by production year has been devised that will provide the collector with the year and month in which his gun was manufactured. A new and complete exploded view was produced for this book.

American Percussion Schuetzen Rifle, by J. Hamilton and T. Rowe, Rochester, NY, Rowe Publications, 2005. 1st edition. 388 pp. Hardcover. New in new dust jacket. $98.00

An Illustrated Guide to the '03 Springfield Service Rifle, by Bruce Canfield, Lincoln, RI, Andrew Mowbray, 2005. 240 pages, illustrated with over 450 photos. Pictorial Hardcover. $49.95

Your ultimate guide to the military '03 Springfield! Covers all models, all manufacturers and all conflicts, including WWI, WWII and beyond. Heavily illustrated with professional photography showing the details that separate a great collectible rifle from the rest. Serial number tables, combat photos, sniper rifles and more!

AR-15 & M-16 5.56mm Assembly, Disassembly Manual, by Skennerton & Riling, Ray Riling Arms Books Co. Philadelphia, PA 2004. 36 pages, $5.00

With over 60 photos & line drawings. Ideal workshop reference for stripping & assembly with exploded parts drawings, specifications, service accessories, historical information and recommended reading references.

AR-15 Complete Owner's Guide, Volume 1, 2nd Edition, by Walt Kuleck and Scott Duff, Export, PA, Scott A. Duff Publications, 2002. 224 pp., 164 photographs & line drawings. Softcover. $21.95

This book provides the prospective, new or experienced AR-15 owner with the in-depth knowledge he or she needs to select, configure, operate, maintain and troubleshoot his or her rifle. The Guide covers history, applications, details of components and subassemblies, operating, cleaning, maintenance, and future of perhaps the most versatile rifle system ever produced. A comprehensive Colt model number table and pre-/post-ban serial number information are included.

AR-15 Complete Assembly Guide, Volume 2, by Walt Kuleck and Clint McKee. Export, PA, Scott A. Duff Publications, 2002. 1st edition. 155 pp., 164 photographs & line drawings. Softcover. $19.95

This book goes beyond the military manuals in depth and scope, using words and pictures to clearly guide the reader through every operation required to assemble their AR-15-type rifle. You'll learn the best and easiest ways to build your rifle. It won't make you an AR-15 armorer, but it will make you a more knowledgeable owner. In short, if you build it, you'll know how to repair it.

AR-15/M16, A Practical Guide, by Duncan Long, Paladin Press, Boulder, CO, 1985. 168 pp., illus. Paper covers. $22.00

The definitive book on the rifle that has been the inspiration for so many modern assault rifles.

Argentine Mauser Rifles 1871-1959, by Colin Atglen, Webster, PA, Schiffer Publications, 2003. 1st edition. 304 pp., over 400 b&w and color photographs, drawings, and charts. Hardcover. $79.95

This is the complete story of Argentina's contract Mauser rifles from the purchase of their first Model 1871s to the disposal of the last shipment of surplus rifles received in the United States in May 2002. The Argentine Commission's relentless pursuit of tactical superiority resulted in a major contribution to the development of Mauser's now famous bolt-action system.

Art of Shooting with the Rifle, by Col. Sir H. St. John Halford, Excalibur Publications, Latham, NY, 1996. 96 pp., illus. Paper covers. $12.95

A facsimile edition of the 1888 book by a respected rifleman providing a wealth of detailed information.

Art of the Rifle, by Jeff Cooper, Paladin Press, Boulder, CO, 1997. 104 pp., illus. Paper covers $22.00

Everything you need to know about the rifle whether you use it for security, meat or target shooting.

Assault Rifle, by Maxim Popenker, and Anthony Williams, London, Crowood Press, 2005. 224 pages. Hardcover. New in new dust jacket. $34.95

Includes brief historical summary of the assault rifle, its origins and development; gun design including operating mechanisms and weapon configuration, and more. The second part includes: national military rifle programs since the end of WWII; history of developments in each country including experimental programs; and detailed descriptions of the principal service and experimental weapons.

Ballard: The Great American Single Shot Rifle, by John T Dutcher, Denver, CO, privately printed, 2002. 1st edition. 380 pp., illustrated with b&w photos, with an 8-page color insert. Hardcover. $79.95

Benchrest Actions and Triggers, by Stuart Otteson, Rohnert Park, CA, Adams-Kane Press, July 2003. Limited edition. 64 pp. Softcover. $27.95

Stuart Otteson's *Benchrest Actions and Triggers* is truly a lost classic. Benchrest Actions and Triggers is a compilation of 17 articles Mr. Otteson wrote. The articles contained are of particular interest to the benchrest crowd. Reprinted by permission of Wolfe Publishing.

Black Magic: The Ultra Accurate AR-15, by John Feamster, Precision Shooting, Manchester, CT, 1998. 300 pp., illus. $29.95

The author has compiled his experiences pushing the accuracy envelope of the AR-15 to its maximum potential. A wealth of advice on AR-15 loads, modifications and accessories for everything from NRA Highpower and Service Rifle competitions to benchrest and varmint shooting.

Black Rifle, M16 Retrospective, by R. Blake Stevens and Edward C. Ezell, Collector Grade Publications, Toronto, Canada, 1987. 416 pp., 441 illustrations and photos. $59.95

At the time of this writing, the 5.56mm NATO M16A2 rifle is heir to world wide acceptance after a quarter-century of U.S. service, longer than any other U.S. rifle in this century except the 1903 bolt-action Springfield. Its history has been far from one of calm acceptance.

Black Rifle II: The M16 into the 21st Century, by Christopher R. Bartocci, Canada, Collector Grade Publications, 2004. 408 pages, 626 illustrations. $69.95

This book chronicles all the new third- and fourth-generation rifle and carbine models which have been introduced by Colt and Diemaco since *The Black Rifle* was originally published, and describes and depicts the myriad of enhanced sights and rails systems which help make the M16s of today the most versatile, modular and effective combat weapons in the world. Includes an in-depth reference compendium of all Colt military and civilian models and components.

Blitzkrieg!–The MP40 Maschinenpistole of WWII, by Frank Iannamico, Harmony, ME, Moose Lake Publishing, 2003. 1st edition. Over 275 pp., 280 photos and documents. Softcover. $29.95

It's back, now in a new larger 8" x11" format. Lots of new information and many unpublished photos. This book includes the history and development of the German machine pistol from the MP18.I to the MP40.

Bolt Action Rifles, Expanded 4th Edition, by Frank de Haas and Wayne van Zwoll, Krause Publications, Iola, WI 2003. 696 pp., illustrated with 615 b&w photos. Softcover. $29.95

British .22RF Training Rifles, by Dennis Lewis and Robert Washburn, Excalibur Publications, Latham, NY, 1993. 64 pp., illus. Paper covers. $10.95

The story of Britain's training rifles from the early Aiming Tube models to the post-WWII trainers.

Building Double Rifles on Shotgun Actions, by W. Ellis Brown, Ft. Collins, CO, Bunduki Publishing, 2001. 1st edition. 187 pp., including index and b&w photographs. Hardcover. $55.00

Carbine .30 M1, M1A1, M2 & M3 Assembly, Disassembly Manual, by Skennerton & Riling, Ray Riling Arms Books Co. Philadelphia, PA 2004. 36 pages, over 60 photos & line drawings. $5.00

Ideal workshop reference for stripping & assembly with exploded parts drawings, specifications, service accessories, historical information and recommended reading references.

ARMS LIBRARY

Classic Sporting Rifles, by Christopher Austyn, Safari Press, Huntington Beach, CA, 1997. 128 pp., illus. $50.00
As the head of the gun department at Christie's Auction House the author examines the "best" rifles built over the last 150 years.

Collectable '03, by J.C. Harrison, The Arms Chest, Oklahoma City, OK. 1999. 2nd edition (revised). 234 pp., illustrated with drawings, Spiral bound. $35.00
Valuable and detailed reference book for the collector of the Model 1903 Springfield rifle.

Collecting Classic Bolt Action Military Rifles, by Paul S. Scarlata, Andrew Mowbray, Inc., Lincoln, RI, 2001. 280 pp., illus. $39.95
Over 400 large photographs detail key features you will need to recognize in order to identify guns for your collection. Learn the original military configurations of these service rifles so you can tell them apart from altered guns and bad restorations. The historical sections are particularly strong, giving readers a clear understanding of how and why these rifles were developed, and which troops used them.

Collecting the Garand, by J.C. Harrison, The Arms Chest, Oklahoma City, OK. 2001. 2nd edition (revised). 198 pp., illus. with pictures and drawings. Spiral bound. $35.00
Valuable and detailed reference book for the collector of the Garand.

Collecting the M1 Carbine, by J.C. Harrison, The Arms Chest, Oklahoma City, OK. 2000. 2nd edition (revised). 247 pp., illustrated with pictures and drawings. Spiral bound. $35.00
Valuable and detailed reference book for the collector of the M1 Carbine. Identifies standard issue original military models of M1 and M1A1 Models of 1942, '43, '44, and '45 carbines as produced by each manufacturer, plus arsenal repair, refinish and lend-lease.

Competitive AR15: The Mouse That Roared, by Glenn Zediker, Zediker Publishing, Oxford, MS, 1999. 286 pp., illus. Paper covers. $29.95
A thorough and detailed study of the newest precision rifle sensation.

Complete AR15/M16 Sourcebook, Revised and Updated Edition, by Duncan Long, Paladin Press, Boulder, CO, 2002. 336 pp., illus. Paper covers. $39.95
The latest development of the AR15/M16 and the many spin-offs now available, selective-fire conversion systems for the 1990s, the vast selection of new accessories.

Complete Book of the .22: A Guide to the World's Most Popular Guns, by Wayne van Zwoll, Lyons Press, 2004. 1st edition. 336 pgs. Hardcover. $26.95

Complete Guide to the M1 Garand and the M1 Carbine, by Bruce Canfield, Andrew Mowbray, Inc., Lincoln, RI, 1999. 296 pp., illus. $39.50
Covers all of the manufacturers of components, parts, variations and markings. The total story behind these guns, from their invention through WWII, Korea, Vietnam and beyond! 300+ photos show you features, markings, overall views and action shots. Thirty-three tables and charts give instant reference to serial numbers, markings, dates of issue and proper configurations. Special sections on sniper guns, National Match rifles, exotic variations, and more!

Complete M1 Garand, by Jim Thompson, Paladin Press, Boulder, CO, 1998. 160 pp., illus. Paper cover. $24.00
A guide for the shooter and collector, heavily illustrated.

Crown Jewels: The Mauser In Sweden; A Century of Accuracy and Precision, by Dana Jones, Canada, Collector Grade Publications, 2003. 1st edition. 312 pp., 691 illustrations. Hardcover. $49.95
Here is the first in-depth study of all the Swedish Mausers: the 6.5mm M/94 carbines, M/96 long rifles, M/38 short rifles, Swedish K98Ks (called the M/39 in 7.92x57mm, then, after rechambering to fire the 8x63mm machine un cartridge, the M/40); sniper rifles, and other military adaptations such as grenade launchers and artillery simulators. Also covers a wide variety of the micrometer-adjustment rear sight inserts and "diopter" receiver sights produced for the Swedish Mauser. Full chapters on bayonets and the many accessories, both military and civilian.

Defending the Dominion, Canadian Military Rifles, 1855-1955, by David Edgecombe, Ont. Canada, Service Publications, 2003. 1st edition. 168 pp., with 60+ illustrations. Hardcover. $39.95

Desperate Measures-The Last Ditch Weapons of the Nazi Voksstrurm, by Darrin Weaver, Canada, Collector Grade Publications, 2005. 424 pages, 558 illustrations. $69.50
All are covered in detail, and the book includes many previously unpublished photographs of original Volkssturm weapons, including prototypes and rare presentation examples.

F.N.-F.A.L. Auto Rifles, Desert Publications, Cornville, AZ, 1981. 130 pp., illus. Paper covers. $18.95
A definitive study of one of the free world's finest combat rifles.

FAL Rifle, by R. Blake Stevens and Jean van Rutten, Collector Grade Publications, Cobourg, Canada, 1993. 848 pp., illus. $129.95
Originally published in three volumes, this classic edition covers North American, UK and Commonwealth and the metric FAL's.

Fighting Rifle, by Chuck Taylor, Paladin Press, Boulder, CO, 1983. 184 pp., illus. Paper covers. $25.00
The difference between assault and battle rifles and auto and light machine guns.

FN-49; Last Elegant Old-World Military Rifle, by Wayne Johnson., Greensboro, NC, Wet Dog Pub. 2004. 200 pages with Over 300 quality b&w photographs. $45.95
The FN-49 The Last Elegant old World Military Rifle book contains both information on the SAFN as well as the AFN rifle.

FN-FAL Rifle, The, et al, by Duncan Long, Delta Press, El Dorado, AR, 1998. 148 pp., illus. Paper covers. $18.95
A comprehensive study of one of the classic assault weapons of all times. Detailed descriptions of the basic models plus the myriad of variants that evolved as a result of its universal acceptance.

Forty Years with the .45-70, 2nd Edition, Revised and Expanded, by Paul A. Matthews, Wolfe Publishing Co., Prescott, AZ, 1997. 184 pp., illus. Paper covers. $17.95
This book is pure gun lore of the .45-70. It not only contains a history of the cartridge, but also years of the author's personal experiences.

Garand .30 Assembly, Disassembly Manual, by Skennerton & Riling, Ray Riling Arms Books Co. Philadelphia, PA 2004. 36 pages, $5.00
With over 60 photos & line drawings. Ideal workshop reference for stripping & assembly with exploded parts drawings, specifications, service accessories, historical information and recommended reading references.

German Sniper 1914-1945, by Peter R. Senich, Paladin Press, Boulder, CO, 1997 8½" x 11", hardcover, photos, 468 pp. $79.95
The complete story of Germany's sniping arms development through both world wars. Presents more than 600 photos of Mauser 98's, Selbstladegewehr 41s and 43s, optical sights by Goerz, Zeiss, etc., plus German snipers in action. An exceptional hardcover collector's edition for serious military historians everywhere.

Great Remington 8 and Model 81 Autoloading Rifles, by John Henwood, Canada, Collector Grade Publications, 2003. 1st edition. 304 pp., 291 illustrations, 31 in color. Hardcover. $59.95

Gun Digest Book of the.22 Rimfire, by James House, Iola,WI, Krause Publications, 2005. 288pgs. Soft cover. 250 b&w photos. $24.99
The most comprehensive guide to rimfire weapons & ammo. Info on current & vintage models. Covers the history, sights & sighting, techniques for testing accuracy, options for enhancing models, & more.

Gun-Guides, AK-47 AKM All Variants, Disassembly and Reassembly Guide, by Gun Guides, 2005. 16pp, illustrations, cardstock cover. Bright white paper. Soft cover. $6.99
The complete guide for ALL models.

Gun-Guides, Colt AR15 and All Variants, Disassembly and Reassembly Guide, by Gun Guides, 2005. 16pp, illustrations, cardstock cover. Bright white paper. Soft cover. $6.99
The complete guide for ALL models.

Gun-Guides, 1911 Pistols & All Variants-Disassembly & Reassembly, by Gun Guides, 2006. 16pp, illustrations, cardstock cover. Bright white paper. Soft cover. $6.99
The complete guide for ALL models.

Gun-Guides, Glock, Disassembly and Reassembly for All Models, by Gun Guides, 2005. 16pp, illustrations, cardstock cover. Bright white paper. Soft cover. $6.99
The complete guide for ALL models.

Gun-Guides, Remington 1100, 11-87 Shotguns, Disassembly and Reassembly Guides, by Gun Guides, 2005. The complete guide for ALL models, 16pp, illustrations, Cardstock cover. Bright white paper. Soft cover. $6.99

Gun-Guides, Remington 870 Shotguns, Disassembly and Reassembly Guides, by Gun Guides, 2005. The complete guide for ALL models, 16pp, illustrations, Cardstock cover. Bright white paper. Soft cover. $6.99

Gun-Guides, Ruger .22 Automatic Pistols: The Complete Guide for All Models from 1947 to 2003, by Gun Guides, 2005. 74 pages, 66 high-resolution grayscale images. Cardstock cover. Bright white paper. $11.95
The complete guide for ALL models. Includes "rare" complete serial numbers and manufacturing dates from 1949-2004.

Gun-Guides, Ruger Single Action Revolvers, Blackhawk, Super Blackhawk, Vaquero and Bisley Models Disassembly and Reassembly Guide for All Models, 1955-2005, by Gun Guides, 2005. 16pp, illustrations, cardstock cover. Bright white paper. $6.99
The complete guide for ALL models.

Gun-Guides, Ruger 10/22 & 10/17 Carbines Complete Guide to All Models from 1964-2004, by Gun Guides, 2005. 55 pages & 66 high-resolution grayscale images. Bright white paper. Soft cover. $11.95
Easy to use: Comb binding lies open and flat on your work surface. Includes all serial numbers and manufacture dates for all models from 1964-2004!

Gun-Guides, Ruger Mini-14 Complete Guide to All Models from 1972-2003, by Gun Guides, 2005. 52pp, illustrations, cardstock cover. Bright white paper. Soft cover. $11.95
The complete guide for ALL models.

Gun-Guides, SKS Semi-Automatic Rifles, Disassembly and Reassembly Guide, by Gun Guides, 2005. 16pp, illustrations, cardstock cover. Bright white paper. Soft cover. $6.99
The complete guide for ALL models.

Handbook of Military Rifle Marks 1866-1950 (third edition), by Richard Hoffman, and Noel Schott, Maple leaf Militaria Publications, 2002. 66 pp, with illustrations, signed by the authors. Stiff paper covers. $20.00
An illustrated military rifles and marks. Officially being used as a reference tool by many law enforcement agencies including BATF, the St. Louis and Philadelphia Police Departments and the Illinois State Police.

High Performance Muzzle Loading Big Game Rifles, by Toby Bridges, Maryland, Stoeger Publications, 2004. 160 pages. Pictorial Hardcover. $24.95
Covers all aspects of in-lines including getting top performance, working up loads, choosing projectiles, scope selection, coping with muzzleloader trajectory, tips for maintaining accuracy, plus much, much more.

Historic Henry Rifle: Oliver Winchester's Famous Civil War Repeater, by Wiley Sword, Andrew Mowbray, Inc., Lincoln, RI. 2002. Softcover. $29.95
It was perhaps the most important firearm of its era. Tested and proved in the fiery crucible of the Civil War, the Henry Rifle became the forerunner of the famous line of Winchester Repeating Rifles that "Won the West." Here is the fascinating story from the frustrations of early sales efforts aimed at the government to the inspired purchase of the Henry Rifle by veteran soldiers who wanted the best weapon.

Hitler's Garands: German Self-Loading Rifles of World War II, by Darrin W. Weaver, Collector Grade Publications, Canada, 2001. 392 pp., 590 illustrations. $69.95
Hitler's Wehrmacht began WWII armed with the bolt-action K98k, a rifle only cosmetically different from that with which Imperial Germany had fought the Great War a quarter-century earlier. Then in 1940, the Heereswaffenamt (HWaA, the Army Weapons Office) issued a requirement for a new self-loading rifle.

How-To's for the Black Powder Cartridge Rifle Shooter, by Paul A. Matthews, Wolfe Publishing Co., Prescott, AZ, 1996. 136 pp., illus. Paper covers. $22.50
Practices and procedures used in the reloading and shooting of blackpowder cartridges.

Imperial Japanese Grenade Rifles and Launchers, by Greg Babisch and Thomas Keep, Lemont, PA, Dutch Harlow Publishing, 2004. 247 pages, illustrated with numerous b&w and color photos throughout. Hardcover. New in new dust jacket. $75.00
This book is a must for museums, military historians, and collectors of Imperial Japanese rifles, rifle cartridges, and ordnance.

Jaeger Rifles Collected Articles Published in Muzzle Blasts, by George Shumway, York, PA, George Shumway, 2003. 108 pp., illus. Stiff paper covers. $30.00

Johnson Rifles and Machine Guns: The Story of Melvin Maynard Johnson Jr. and his Guns, by Bruce N. Canfield, Lincoln, RI, Andrew Mowbray, Inc., 2002. 1st edition. 272 pp. with over 285 photographs. Hardcover. $49.95

The M1941 Johnson rifle is the hottest WWII rifle on the collector's market today. From invention and manufacture through issue to the troops, this book covers them all!

Kalashnikov: The Arms and the Man, A Revised and Expanded Edition of the AK47 Story, by Edward C. Ezell, Canada, Collector Grade Publications, 2002. 312 pp., 356 illustrations. Hardcover. $59.95

The original edition of The AK47 Story was published in 1986, and the events of the intervening fifteen years have provided much fresh new material. Beginning with an introduction by Dr. Kalashnikov himself, this is a most comprehensive study of the "life and times" of the AK, starting with the early history of small arms manufacture in Czarist Russia and then the Soviet Union.

Last Enfield: SA80–The Reluctant Rifle, by Steve Raw, Collector Grade Publications, Canada 2003. 1st edition. 360 pp., with 382 illustrations. Hardcover. $49.95

This book presents the entire, in-depth story of its subject firearm, in this case the controversial British SA80, right from the founding of what became the Royal Small Arms Factory (RSAF) Enfield in the early 1800s; briefly through two world wars with Enfield at the forefront of small arms production for British forces; and covering the adoption of the 7.62mm NATO cartridge in 1954 and the L1A1 rifle in 1957.

Last Steel Warrior: The U.S. M14 Rifle, by Frank Iannamico, Moose Lake Pub., 2006. With over 400 pages and 537 photos and illustrations. Soft cover. $29.95

Acclaimed gun author Frank Iannamico's latest book covers history, development and deployment of the influential M14 rifle.

Lee Enfield No. 1 Rifles, by Alan M. Petrillo, Excaliber Publications, Latham, NY, 1992. 64 pp., illus. Paper covers. $10.95

Highlights the SMLE rifles from the Mark 1-VI.

Lee Enfield Number 4 Rifles, by Alan M. Petrillo, Excalibur Publications, Latham, NY, 1992. 64 pp., illus. Paper covers. $10.95

A pocket-sized, bare-bones reference devoted entirely to the .303 WWII and Korean War vintage service rifle.

Legendary Sporting Rifles, by Sam Fadala, Stoeger Publishing Co., So. Hackensack, NJ, 1992. 288 pp., illus. Paper covers. $16.95

Covers a vast span of time and technology beginning with the Kentucky longrifle.

Li'l M1 .30 Cal. Carbine, by Duncan Long, Desert Publications, El Dorado, AZ, 1995. 203 pp., illus. Paper covers. $19.95

Traces the history of this little giant from its original creation.

Living With the Big .50, The Shooter's Guide to the World's Most Powerful Rifle, Robert Boatman, Boulder, CO, Paladin Press, 2004. 176 pp. Soft cover. $29.00

Living with the Big .50 is the most thorough book ever written on this powerhouse rifle.

M1 Carbine Owner's Manual, M1, M2 & M3 .30 Caliber Carbines, Firepower Publications, Cornville, AZ, 1984. 102 pp., illus. Paper covers. $9.95

The complete book for the owner of an M1 carbine.

M1 Carbine Owner's Guide, by Scott A. Duff, Export, PA, Scott Duff Publications, 2002. 144 pages, illustrated. $21.95

Tells you what to look for before you choose a Carbine for collecting or shooting. Identification guide with serial numbers by production quarter for approximate date of manufacture. Illustrated, complete guide to markings, nomenclature of parts, assembly, disassembly and special tools. History and identification guide with serial numbers by production quarter for approximate date of manufacture. Includes troubleshooting, maintenance, cleaning and lubrication guide.

M1 Garand .30 Assembly, Disassembly Manual, by Skennerton & Riling, Ray Riling Arms Books Co. Philadelphia, PA 2004. 36 pages, over 60 photos & line drawings. $5.00

Ideal workshop reference for stripping & assembly with exploded parts drawings, specifications, service accessories, historical information and recommended reading references.

M1 Garand Owners Guide, Vol 1, by Scott A. Duff, Export, PA, Scott Duff Publications, 2002. 126 pages, illustrated. $21.95

Makes shooting, disassembly and maintenance work easier. Contains a brief history as well as production dates and other information to help identify who made it and when. Line drawings identify the components and show their position and relationships plainly.

M1 Garand Complete Assembly Guide, Vol. 2, by Walt Kuleck, and Clint McKee, Export, PA, Scott Duff Publications, 2004. 162 pp. $21.95

You'll learn the best and easiest ways to build your rifle. It won't make you a Garand armorer, but it will make you a more knowledgeable owner. You'll be able to do more with (and to) your rifle.

M1 Garand Serial Numbers & Data Sheets, by Scott A. Duff, Scott A. Duff, Export, PA, 1995. 101 pp. Paper covers. $11.95

This pocket reference book includes serial number tables and data sheets on the Springfield Armory, gas trap rifles, gas port rifles, Winchester Repeating Arms, International Harvester and H&R Arms Co. and more.

M1 Garand: Post World War, by Scott A. Duff, Scott A. Duff Publications, Export, PA, 1990. 139 pp., illus. Softcover. $21.95

A detailed account of the activities at Springfield Armory through this period. International Harvester, H&R, Korean War production and quantities delivered. Serial numbers.

M1 Garand: World War 2, by Scott A. Duff, Scott A. Duff Publications, Export, PA, 1993. 210 pp., illus. Paper covers. $34.95

The most comprehensive study available to the collector and historian on the M1 Garand of WWII.

M14 Rifle Assembly, Disassembly Manual 7.62mm, by Skennerton & Riling, Ray Riling Arms Books Co. Philadelphia, PA 2004. 36 pages, over 60 photos & line drawings. $5.00

Ideal workshop reference for stripping & assembly with exploded parts drawings, specifications, service accessories, historical information and recommended reading references.

M14 Owner's Guide and Match Conditioning Instructions, by Scott A. Duff and John M. Miller, Duff Publications, Export, PA, 1996. 180 pp., illus. Paper covers. $19.95

Traces the history and development from the T44 through the adoption and production of the M14 rifle.

M14 Complete Assembly Guide; Vol. 2, by Walt Kuleck, and Clint McKee, Duff Publications, Export, PA, 1996. 180 pp., illus. Paper covers. $24.95

You'll learn the best and easiest ways to enhance, disassemble and assemble your rifle. It won't make you an M14/M1A armorer, but it will make you a knowledgeable owner. You'll be able to do more with (and to) your rifle.

M14 Rifle, facsimile reprint of FM 23-8, Desert Publications, Cornville, AZ, 50 pp., illus. Paper $11.95

Well illustrated and informative reprint covering the M-14 and M-14E2.

M14-Type Rifle: A Shooter's And Collector's Guide; 3rd Edition Revised and Expanded edition, by Joe Poyer, North Cape Publications, Tustin, CA, 2007. 104 pp., illus. Paper covers. $19.95

This new revised and expanded edition examines the M14 rifle and its two sniper variations on a part-by-part basis but surveys all current civilian semiautomatic M14-type rifles and components available today. It also provides as a guide for shooters who want to restore an M14 to original condition or build a superb match rifle. Included are the Chinese variations of the M14. The history of the development and use of the M14 in Vietnam, and now in Iraq and Afghanistan, is detailed. The book is fully illustrated with photos and drawings that clarify the text. Appendices provide up-to-date information on parts and supplies and gunsmithing services.

M14/M14A1 Rifles and Rifle Marksmanship, Desert Publications, El Dorado, AZ, 1995. 236 pp., illus. Paper covers. $19.95

Contains a detailed description of the M14 and M14A1 rifles and their general characteristics, procedures for disassembly & assembly, operating and functioning of the rifles.

M16/AR15 Rifle, by Joe Poyer, North Cape Publications, Tustin, CA, 1998. 150 pp., illus. Paper covers. $19.95

From its inception as the first American assault battle rifle to the firing lines of the National Matches, the M16/AR15 rifle in all its various models and guises has made a significant impact on the American rifleman.

Major Ned H. Roberts and the Schuetzen Rifle, edited by Gerald O. Kelver, Brighton, CO, 1998. 3rd edition. 122 pp., illus. $13.95

A compilation of the writings of Major Ned H. Roberts which appeared in various gun magazines.

Mannlicher Military Rifles: Straight Pull and Turn Bolt Designs, Paul Scarlata, Lincoln, RI, Andrew Mowbray, 2004. Hardcover, 168 pages 8.5 x 11, filled with black & white photos. Hardcover. NEW $32.49

Profusely illustrated with close-up photos, drawings and diagrams, this book is the most detailed examination of Mannlicher military rifles ever produced in the English language.

Mauser Military Rifles Of The World, 4th Edition, by Robert Ball, Iola, WI, Krause Publications, 2006. 448 pp., with historical data, coupled with detailed color photos. $49.95

The ultimate Mauser military rifle reference, this superior guide is packed with more models, all-color photos and Mauser history tailored to the interests and needs of firearms collectors. With more than 50 countries represented, 75 years of Mauser military rifle production is meticulously cataloged with descriptions, historical details, model specifications and markings, for easy identification by collectors.

Mauser Military Rifle Markings, 2nd Edition, Revised and Expanded, by Terence Lapin, Hyrax Publishers, Arlington, VA. 2005, 167 pages, illustrated. Softcover. $22.95

A general guide to reading and understanding the often mystifying markings found on military Mauser Rifles. Includes German Regimental markings as well as German police markings and W.W. 2 German Mauser subcontractor codes. A handy reference to take to gun shows.

Mauser Rifles & Carbines Assembly, Disassembly Manual, by Skennerton & Riling, Ray Riling Arms Books Co. Philadelphia, PA 2004. 36 pages, over 60 photos & line drawings. $5.00

Ideal workshop reference for stripping & assembly with exploded parts drawings, specifications, service accessories, historical information and recommended reading references.

Mauser Smallbore Sporting, Target and Training Rifles, by Jon Speed, Collector Grade Publications, Inc., Cobourg, Ont., Canada, 1998. 372 pp., illus. $67.50

The history of all the smallbore sporting, target and training rifles produced by the legendary Mauser-Werke of Obendorf am Neckar.

Mauser: Original-Oberndorf Sporting Rifles, by Jon Speed, Collector Grade Publications, Inc., Cobourg, Ont., Canada, 1997. 508 pp., illus. $89.95

The most exhaustive study ever published of the design origins and manufacturing history of the original Oberndorf Mauser Sporter.

MG34-MG42 German Universal Machineguns, by Folke Myrvang, Collector Grade Publications, Canada. 2002. 496 pp., 646 illustrations. $79.95

This is the first-ever COMPETE study of the MG34 & MG42. Here the author presents in-depth coverage of the historical development, fielding, tactical use of and modifications made to these remarkable guns and their myriad accessories and ancillaries, plus authoritative tips on troubleshooting.

Military Bolt Action Rifles, 1841-1918, by Donald B. Webster, Museum Restoration Service, Alexander Bay, NY, 1993. 150 pp., illus. $34.50

A photographic survey of the principal rifles and carbines of the European and Asiatic powers of the last half of the 19th century and the first years of the 20th century.

Military Rifles of Japan, 5th Edition, by F.L. Honeycutt, Julin Books, Lake Park, FL, 1999. 208 pp., illus. $42.00

A new revised and updated edition. Includes the early Murata-period markings, etc.

Mini-14, by Duncan Long, Paladin Press, Boulder, CO, 1987. 120 pp., illus. Paper covers. $17.00

History of the Mini-14, the factory-produced models, specifications, accessories, suppliers, and much more.

MKB 42, MP43, MP44 and the Sturmgewehr 44, by de Vries & Martens. Alexandria, VA, Ironside International, 2003. 1st edition. 152 pp., illustrated with 200 high quality b&w photos. Hardcover. $39.95

Covers all essential information on history and development, ammunition and accessories, codes and markings, and contains photos of nearly every model and accessory. Includes a unique selection of original German WWII propaganda photos, most never published before.

Modern Guns: Fred Adolph Genoa, by Fred Adolph, Oceanside, CA, Armory Publications, 2003. One of only a few catalogs that list 2, 3 and 4 barrel guns. 68 pages, illustrated. Stiff Paper Covers. New. $19.95

Modern Sniper Rifles, by Duncan Long, Paladin Press, Boulder, CO, 1997, 8½" x 11", soft cover, photos, illus., 120 pp. $20.00

Noted weapons expert Duncan Long describes the .22 LR, single-shot, bolt-action, semiautomatic and large-caliber rifles that can be used for sniping purposes, including the U.S. M21, Ruger Mini-14, AUG and HK-94SG1. These and other models are evaluated on the basis of their features, accuracy, reliability and handiness in the field. The author also looks at the best scopes, ammunition and accessories.

More Single Shot Rifles and Actions, by Frank de Haas and Mark de Haas, Orange City, IA, 1996. 146 pp., illus. Paper covers. $22.50

Covers 45 different single shot rifles. Includes the history plus photos, drawings and personal comments.

Mosin-Nagant Assembly, Disassembly Manual 7.62mmR, by Skennerton & Riling, Ray Riling Arms Books Co. Philadelphia, PA 2004. 36 pages, $5.00

With over 60 photos & line drawings. Ideal workshop reference for stripping & assembly with exploded parts drawings, specifications, service accessories, historical information and recommended reading references.

Mosin-Nagant Rifle, by Terence W. Lapin, North Cape Publications, Tustin, CA, 1998. 30 pp., illus. Paper covers. $19.95

The first ever complete book on the Mosin-Nagant rifle written in English. Covers every variation.

Mr. Single Shot's Book of Rifle Plans, by Frank de Haas and Mark de Haas, Orange City, IA, 1996. 85 pp., illus. Paper covers. $22.50

Contains complete and detailed drawings, plans and instructions on how to build four different and unique breech-loading single shot rifles of the author's own proven design.

Muskets of the Revolution and the French & Indian Wars; The Smoothbore Longarm in Early America, Including British, French, Dutch, German, Spanish, and American Weapons, by Bill Ahearn, Lincoln, RI, Andrew Mowbray, 2005. 248 pages, illustrated. Pictorial hardcover. $49.95

Not just a technical study of old firearms, this is a tribute to the bravery of the men who fought on both sides of that epic conflict and a celebration of the tools of freedom that have become so much a part of our national character. Includes many never-before published photos!

Neutrality Through Marksmanship: A Collector's and Shooter's Guide to Swedish Army Rifles 1867-1942, by Doug Bowser, Camellia City Military Publications, 1996. 1st edition. Stiff paper covers. $20.00

No. 4 (T) Sniper Rifle: An Armourer's Perspective, The, by Peter Laidler with Ian Skennerton, I.D.S.A. Books, Piqua, OH, 1993. 125 pp., 75 illus. Paper covers. $19.95

A reprint of the 1864 London edition. Captain Heaton was one of the great rifle shots from the earliest days of the Volunteer Movement.

Official SKS Manual, Translation by Major James F. Gebhardt (Ret.), Paladin Press, Boulder, CO, 1997. 96 pp., illus. Paper covers. $16.00

This Soviet military manual covering the widely distributed SKS is now available in English.

Official Soviet AK-47 Manual: Operating Instructions for the 5.45mm Kalashnikov Assault Rifle, and Kalashnikov Light Machine Gun, by James Gebhardt, Boulder, CO, Paladin Press, 2006. 8½" x 11", illus., 150 pp. Soft cover. $25.00

Written to teach Russian soldiers every detail of the operation and maintenance of the Kalashnikov Assault Rifle (AK-74) and Kalashnikov Light Machine Gun (RPK-74), this manual includes ballistic tables, zeroing information, combat firing instructions, data for the 5.45mm service cartridge and more.

Old German Target Arms: Alte Schiebenwaffen, by Jesse Thompson, C. Ron Dillon, Allen Hallock and Bill Loos, Rochester, NY, Tom Rowe Publications, 2003. 1st edition. 392 pp. Hardcover. $98.00

History of Schueten shooting from the middle ages through WWII. Hundreds of illustrations, most in color. History & memorabilia of the Bundesschiessen (State or National Shoots), bird target rifles, American shooters in Germany. Schutzen rifles such as matchlocks, wheellocks, flintlocks, percussion, bader, bornmuller, rifles by Buchel and more.

Old German Target Arms: Alte Schiebenwaffen Volume 2, by Jesse Thompson, C. Ron Dillon, Allen Hallock and Bill Loos, Rochester, NY, Tom Rowe Publications, 2004. 1st edition. 392 pp. Hardcover. $98.00

Old German Target Arms: Alte Schiebenwaffen Volume 3, by Jesse Thompson, C. Ron Dillon, Allen Hallock and Bill Loos, Rochester, NY, Tom Rowe Publications, 2005. 1st edition. 392 pp. Hardcover. $98.00

Ordnance Tools, Accessories & Appendages of the M1 Rifle, by Billy Pyle, Houston, TX, privately printed, 2002. 2nd edition. 206 pp., illustrated with b&w photos. Softcover. $40.00

This is the new updated second edition with over 350 pictures and drawings, of which 30 are new. Part I contains accessories, appendages, and equipment. Part II covers ammunition, grenades, and pyrotechnics. Part III shows the inspection gages. Part IV presents the ordnance tools, fixtures, and assemblies. Part V contains miscellaneous items related to the M1.

Police Rifles, by Richard Fairburn, Paladin Press, Boulder, CO, 1994. 248 pp., illus. Paper covers. $35.00

Selecting the right rifle for street patrol and special tactical situations.

Poor Man's Sniper Rifle, by D. Boone, Paladin Press, Boulder, CO, 1995. 152 pp., illus. Paper covers. $18.95

Here is a complete plan for converting readily available surplus military rifles to high-performance sniper weapons.

Precision Shooting with the M1 Garand, by Roy Baumgardner, Precision Shooting, Inc., Manchester, CT, 1999. 142 pp., illus. Paper covers. $12.95

Starts off with the ever popular ten-article series on accurizing the M1 that originally appeared in Precision Shooting in the 1993-95 era. There follows nine more Baumgardner-authored articles on the M1 Garand and finally a 1999 updating chapter.

Remington 700, by John F. Lacy, Taylor Publishing Co., Dallas, TX, 2002. 208 pp., illus. $54.95

Covers the different models, limited editions, chamberings, proofmarks, serial numbers, military models, and much more.

Remington Autoloading and Pump Action Rifles, by Eugene Myszkowski, Tucson, AZ, Excalibur Publications, 2002. 132 pp., with 162 photographs, 6 illustrations and 18 charts. Softcover. $20.95

An illustrated history of Remington's centerfire Models 760, 740, 742, 7400 and 7600. The book is thoroughly researched and features many previously unpublished photos of the rifles, their accessories and accoutrements. Also covers high grade, unusual and experimental rifles. Contains information on collecting, serial numbers and barrel codes.

Rifle Rules: Magic for the Ultimate Rifleman, by Don Paul, Kaua'i, HI, Pathfinder Publications, 2003. 1st edition. 116 pp., illus. Softcover. $14.95

A new method that shows you how to add hundreds of yards to your effective shooting ability. Ways for you to improve your rifle's accuracy which no factory can do. Illustrations & photos added to make new concepts easy.

Rifle Shooter, by G. David Tubb, Oxford, MS, Zediker Publishing, 2004. 1st edition. 416 pp softcover, 7" x 10" size, 400 photos and illustrations, very high quality printing. Softcover. $34.95

This is not just a revision of his landmark "Highpower Rifle" but an all-new, greatly expanded work that reveals David's thoughts and recommendations on all aspects of precision rifle shooting. Each shooting position and event is dissected and taken to extreme detail, as are the topics of ammunition, training, rifle design, event strategies, and wind shooting. You will learn the secrets of perhaps the greatest rifleman ever, and you'll learn how to put them to work for you!

Rifles of the U.S. Army 1861-1906, by John D. McAulay, Lincoln, RI, Andrew Mowbray, Inc., 2003. 1st edition. 278 pp., illus. Hardcover. $45.89

Rifles of the White Death (Valkoisen Kuoleman Kivaarit) A Collector's and Shooter's Guide to Finnish Military Rifles 1918-1944, by Doug Bowser, MS, Camellia City Military Publications, 1998. 1st edition. Stiff paper covers. $35.00

Rock In A Hard Place The Browning Automatic Rifle, by James L. Ballou. Collector Grade, Canada, 2004. 1st edition. 500 pages, with 751 illustrations. Hardcover $79.95

This first-ever in-depth study of the popular BAR includes clear photos of all U.S.-made military and commercial models, experimental models from Britain and France, plus offshore copies and clones from Belgium, Poland and Sweden.

Rock Island Rifle Model 1903, by C.S. Ferris, Export, PA, Scott A. Duff Publications, 2002. 177 pp., illustrated with b&w photographs. Foreword by Scott A. Duff. Softcover. $22.95

S.L.R.–Australia's F.N. F.A.L., by Ian Skennerton and David Balmer, Arms & Militaria Press, 1989. 124 pp., 100 illus. Paper covers. $24.50

Schuetzen Rifles, History and Loading, by Gerald O. Kelver, Pioneer Press, Union City, TN, 1998. 3rd edition. Illus. $13.95

Reference work on these rifles, their bullets, loading, telescopic sights, accuracy, etc. A limited, numbered ed.

Serbian and Yugoslav Mauser Rifles, by Banko Bogdanovich, Tustin, CA, North Cape Publications, 2005. 278pp. Soft cover. $19.95

In Serbian and Yugoslav Mauser Rifles, each model is discussed in its own chapter. All serial numbers are presented by year. All markings are presented and translated and all finishes and changes to all models are described in text and charts and well illustrated with both photographs and excellent drawings for clarity.

Shooting Lever Guns of the Old West, by Mike Venturino, MLV Enterprises, Livingston, MT, 1999. 300 pp., illus. Paper covers. $27.95

Shooting the lever action type repeating rifles of our American west.

Shooting the .43 Spanish Rolling Block, by Croft Barker, Flatonia, TX, Cistern Publishing, 2003. 1st edition. 137 pp. Softcover. $25.50

The source for information on .43 caliber rolling blocks. Lots of photos and text covering Remington & Oveido actions, antique cartridges, etc. Features smokless & black powder loads, rifle disassembly and maintenance, 11mm bullets. Required reading for the rolling block owner.

Shooting the Blackpowder Cartridge Rifle, by Paul A. Matthews, Wolfe Publishing Co., Prescott, AZ, 1994. 129 pp., illus. Paper covers. $22.50

A general discourse on shooting the blackpowder cartridge rifle and the procedure required to make a particular rifle perform.

Single Shot Military Rifle Handbook, by Croft Barker, Flatonia, TX, Cistern Publishing, 2005. Includes over 40 new high quality photos of vintage rifles, antique cartridges and related equipment. 130pp., many b&w photos. Soft cover. $25.50

Contains instruction on preparing authentic ammunition, shooting techniques, the uses of vintage military sights, rifle refurbishing, etc. Evolution of the single shot military rifle and the center fire cartridge is described.

Single Shot Rifles and Actions, by Frank de Haas, Orange City, IA, 1990. 352 pp., illus. Softcover. $27.00

The definitive book on over 60 single shot rifles and actions.

SKS Carbine 7.62 x 39mm Assembly, Disassembly Manual, by Skennerton & Riling, Ray Riling Arms Books Co. Philadelphia, PA 2004. 36 pages, over 60 photos & line drawings. $5.00

Ideal workshop reference for stripping & assembly with exploded parts drawings, specifications, service accessories, historical information and recommended reading references.

Small Arms Identification Series, No. 1–.303 Rifle, No. 1 S.M.L.E. Marks III and III*, by Ian Skennerton, I.D.S.A. Books, Piqua, OH, 1981. 48 pp. $10.50

Small Arms Identification Series, No. 2–.303 Rifle, No. 4 Marks I, & I*, Marks 1/2, 1/3 & 2, by Ian Skennerton, I.D.S.A. Books, Piqua, OH, 1994. 48 pp. $10.50

Small Arms Identification Series, No. 3–9mm Austen Mk I & 9mm Owen Mk I Sub-Machine Guns, by Ian Skennerton, I.D.S.A. Books, Piqua, OH, 1994. 48 pp. $10.50

Small Arms Identification Series, No. 4–.303 Rifle, No. 5 Mk I, by Ian Skennerton, I.D.S.A. Books, Piqua, OH, 1994. 48 pp. $10.50

Small Arms Identification Series, No. 5–.303-in. Bren Light Machine Gun, by Ian Skennerton, I.D.S.A. Books, Piqua, OH, 1994. 48 pp. $10.50

Springfield Rifle M1903, M1903A1, M1903A3, M1903A4, Desert Publications, Cornville, AZ, 1982. 100 pp., illus. Paper covers. $14.95

Covers every aspect of disassembly and assembly, inspection, repair and maintenance.

Still More Single Shot Rifles, by James J. Grant, Pioneer Press, Union City, TN, 1995. 211 pp., illus. $29.95

This is Volume Four in a series of single-shot rifles by America's foremost authority. It gives more in-depth information on those single-shot rifles that were presented in the first three books.

Sturm, Ruger 10/22 Rifle and .44 Magnum Carbine, by Duncan Long, Paladin Press, Boulder, CO, 1988. 108 pp., illus. Paper covers. $15.00

An in-depth look at both weapons detailing the elegant simplicity of the Ruger design. Offers specifications, troubleshooting procedures and ammunition recommendations.

Swedish Mauser Rifles, by Steve Kehaya and Joe Poyer, Tustin, CA, North Cape Publications, 2004. 2nd edition, revised. 267 pp., illus. Softcover. $19.95

Every known variation of the Swedish Mauser carbine and rifle is described including all match and target rifles and all sniper versions. Includes serial number and production data.

Swiss Magazine Loading Rifles 1869 to 1958, by Joe Poyer, Tustin, CA, North Cape Publications, 2003. 1st edition. 317 pp., illustrated with hundreds of b&w drawings and photos. Softcover. $19.95

It covers the K-31 on a part-by-part basis, as well as its predecessor models of 1889 and 1911, and the first repeating magazine rifle ever adopted by a military, the Model 1869 Vetterli rifle and its successor models. Also includes a history of the development and use of these fine rifles. Details regarding their ammunition, complete assembly/disassembly instructions as well as sections on cleaning, maintenance and trouble shooting.

Tactical Rifle, by Gabriel Suarez, Paladin Press, Boulder, CO, 1999. 264 pp., illus. Paper covers. $25.00

The precision tool for urban police operations.

Target Rifle in Australia, by J.E. Corcoran, R&R, Livonia, NY, 1996. 160 pp., illus. $40.00

A most interesting study of the evolution of these rifles from 1860-1900. British rifles from the percussion period through the early smokeless era are discussed.

Total Airguns; The Complete Guide to Huting with Air Rifles, by Peter Wadeson, London, Swan Hill Press, 2005. 300 pages, illustrated with b&w photos. Hardcover. $29.95

This book covers every aspect from choosing a rifle and scope to field craft and hunting techniques, camouflage, decoys, night shooting, and equipment maintenance. Extensive details on all air gun shooting techniques.

U.S. M1 Carbine: Wartime Production, 5th Edition, Revised and Expanded! by Craig Riesch, North Cape Publications, Tustin, CA 2007 237 pages. $19.95

The book contains 38 charts and 212 photographs, and 14 drawings. The book provides a history of the M1 Carbine's development, manufacture and use during World War II, as well as through the Korean War and the war in Vietnam. All variations of the M1 Carbine are discussed – M1, M1A1, and M2 – by manufacturer. Serial number ranges for original manufacture are included.

U.S. Rifle .30 Model 1917 and .303 BRITISH Pattern 1914 Assembly, Disassembly Manual, by Skennerton & Riling, Ray Riling Arms Books Co. Philadelphia, PA 2004. 36 pages, over 60 photos & line drawings. $5.00

Ideal workshop reference for stripping & assembly with exploded parts drawings, specifications, service accessories, historical information and recommended reading references. Ideal workbook for shooters and collectors alike. Triple saddle-stitched binding with durable plastic laminated cover makes this an ideal workshop guide.

U.S. Marine Corps AR15/M16 A2 Manual, reprinted by Desert Publications, El Dorado, AZ, 1993. 262 pp., illus. Paper covers. $16.95

A reprint of TM05538C-23&P/2, August, 1987. The A-2 manual for the Colt AR15/M16.

U.S. Marine Corps Rifle Marksmanship, by U.S. Marine Corps, Boulder, CO, Paladin Press, 2002. Photos, illus., 120 pp. Softcover. $20.00

This manual is the very latest Marine doctrine on the art and science of shooting effectively in battle. Its 10 chapters teach the versatility, flexibility and skills needed to deal with a situation at any level of intensity across the entire range of military operations. Topics covered include the proper combat mindset; cleaning your rifle under all weather conditions; rifle handling and marksmanship the Marine way; engaging targets from behind cover; obtaining a battlefield zero; engaging immediate threat, multiple and moving targets; shooting at night and at unknown distances; and much more.

U.S. Rifle M14—From John Garand to the M21, by R. Blake Stevens, Collector Grade Publications, Inc., Toronto, Canada, revised 2nd edition, 1991. 350 pp., illus. $49.50

A classic, in-depth examination of the development, manufacture and fielding of the last wood-and-metal ("lock, stock, and barrel") battle rifle to be issued to U.S. troops.

United States Rifle Model of 1917, by CS Ferris, Export, PA, Scott Duff Pubs., 2004. 213 pages, illustrated with b&w photographs. Foreword by Scott A. Duff. Soft cover. $23.95

If you are interested in the study of the United States Rifle Model of 1917 and have been disappointed by the lack of information available, then this book is for you!

Ultimate in Rifle Accuracy, by Glenn Newick, Stoeger Publishing Co., Wayne, NJ, 1999. 205 pp., illus. Paper covers. $11.95

This handbook contains the information you need to extract the best performance from your rifle.

War Baby! The U.S. Caliber 30 Carbine, Volume 1, by Larry Ruth, Collector Grade Publications, Toronto, Canada, 1992. 512 pp., illus. $69.95

Volume 1 of the in-depth story of the phenomenally popular U.S. caliber 30 carbine. Concentrates on design and production of the military 30 carbine during WWII.

War Baby Comes Home: The U.S. Caliber 30 Carbine, Volume 2, by Larry Ruth, Collector Grade Publications, Toronto, Canada, 1993. 386 pp., illus. $49.95

The triumphant completion of Larry Ruth's two-volume, in-depth series on the most popular U.S. military small arm in history.

Winchester: An American Legend, by R.L. Wilson, NY, Book Sales, 2004, reprint. 404 pages, illustrated with color and b&w photographs. Hardcover. New in new dust jacket. $29.95

Winchester Model 52: Perfection in Design, by Herbert Houze, Iola, WI, Krause Publications, 2006. Soft cover. $22.95

Herbert Houze unravels the mysteries surrounding the development of what many consider the most perfect rifle ever made. The book covers the rifle's improvements through five modifications. Users, collectors and marksmen will appreciate each variation's history, serial number sequences and authentic photos.

Winchester Model 61 Assembly, Disassembly Manual, by Skennerton & Riling, Ray Riling Arms Books Co. Philadelphia, PA 2004. 36 pages, over 60 photos & line drawings. $5.00

Ideal workshop reference for stripping & assembly with exploded parts drawings, specifications, service accessories, historical information and recommended reading references.

Winchester Model 70 Assembly, Disassembly Manual, by Skennerton & Riling, Ray Riling Arms Books Co. Philadelphia, PA 2004. 36 pages, over 60 photos & line drawings. $5.00

Ideal workshop reference for stripping & assembly with exploded parts drawings, specifications, service accessories, historical information and recommended reading references.

Winchester Model 94 Assembly, Disassembly Manual, by Skennerton & Riling, Ray Riling Arms Books Co. Philadelphia, PA 2004. 36 pages, over 60 photos & line drawings. $5.00

Ideal workshop reference for stripping & assembly with exploded parts drawings, specifications, service accessories, historical information and recommended reading references.

Winchester Slide-Action Rifles, Models 61, 62, 1890 & 1906, by Ned Schwing, Iola, WI, Krause Publications, 2004. 456 Pages, illustrated, 300 b&w photos. Soft cover. $39.95

Take a complete historical look at the favorite slide-action guns of America through Ned Schwing's eyes. Explore receivers, barrels, markings, stocks, stampings and engraving in complete detail.

Workbench AR-15 Project; A Step by Step Guide to Building Your Own Legal AR-15 Without Paperwork, The, by D.A. Hanks, Boulder, CO, Paladin Press, 2004. 80 pages, photos. Soft cover. $19.89

Hanks walks you through the entire process with clear text and detailed photos—staying legal, finishing the lower receiver, assembling all the parts and test-firing your completed rifle. For academic study only.

SHOTGUNS

A Collector's Guide to United States Combat Shotguns, by Bruce N. Canfield, Andrew Mowbray Inc., Publishers, Lincoln, RI, 1993. 184 pp., illus. Paper covers. $24.00

Full coverage of the combat shotgun, from the earliest examples to the Gulf War and beyond.

A.H. Fox: "The Finest Gun in the World," revised and enlarged edition, by Michael McIntosh, Countrysport, Inc., New Albany, OH, 1995. 408 pp., illus. $60.00

The first detailed history of one of America's finest shotguns.

Advanced Combat Shotgun: Stress Fire 2, by Massad Ayoob, Police Bookshelf, Concord, NH, 1993. 197 pp., illus. Paper covers. $14.95

Advanced combat shotgun fighting for police.

Best Guns, by Michael McIntosh, Countrysport Press, Selma, AL, 1999, revised edition. 418 pp. $45.00

Combines the best shotguns ever made in America with information on British and Continental makers.

Best of Holland & Holland, England's Premier Gunmaker, by Michael McIntosh and Jan G. Roosenburg. Long Beach, CA, Safari Press, Inc., 2002. 1st edition. 298 pp., profuse color illustrations. Hardcover. $69.95

Holland & Holland has had a long history of not only building London's "best" guns but also providing superior guns–the ultimate gun in finish, engraving, and embellishment. From the days of old in which a maharaja would order 100 fancifully engraved H&H shotguns for his guests to use at his duck shoot to the recent elaborately decorated sets depicting the Apollo 11 moon landing or the history of the British Empire, all of these guns represent the zenith in the art and craft of gunmaking and engraving. Never before have so many superlative guns from H&H– or any other maker for that matter–been displayed in one book.

Better Shot, by Ken Davies, Quiller Press, London, England, 1992. 136 pp., illus. $39.95

Step-by-step shotgun techniques with Holland and Holland.

Black's Buyer's Directory 2007 Wing & Clay, by James Black, Grand View Media, 2006. Soft cover. $17.95

1,637 companies in 62 sections providing shotgun related products and services worldwide. Destinations: 1,412 hunting destinations, 1,279 sporting clays, trap and skeet clubs state by state.

Breaking Clays, by Chris Batha, Stackpole Books, Mechanicsburg, PA, 2005. Hardcover. $29.95

This clear and concise book offers a distillation of the best tips and techniques that really work to improve your scores and give you the knowledge to develop to your full shooting potential

Browning Auto-5 Shotguns: The Belgian FN Production, by H. M. Shirley Jr. and Anthony Vanderlinden, Geensboro, NC, Wet Dog Publications, 2003. Limited edition of 2,000 copies, signed by the author. 233 pp., plus index. Over 400 quality b&w photographs and 24 color photographs. Hardcover $59.95

This is the first book devoted to the history, model variations, accessories and production dates of this legendary gun. This publication is to date the only reference book on the Auto-5 (A-5) shotgun prepared entirely with the extensive cooperation and support of Browning, FN Herstal, the Browning Firearms Museum and the Liege Firearms Museum.

Browning-Sporting Arms of Distinction 1903-1992, by Matt Eastman, Safari Press, 2005. Hardcover. $50.00

Finally, the history of the Browning family, the inventions, the company, and Browning's association with Colt, Winchester, Savage, and others is detailed in this all-inclusive book, which is profusely illustrated with hundreds of pictures and charts.

Cogswell & Harrison; Two Centuries of Gunmaking, by G. Cooley and J. Newton, Safari Press, Long Beach, CA, 2000. 128 pp., 30 color photos, 100 b&w photos. $39.95

The authors have gathered a wealth of fascinating historical and technical material that will make the book indispensable, not only to many thousands of "Coggie" owners worldwide, but also to anyone interested in the general history of British gunmaking.

Defensive Shotgun, The, by Louis Awerbuck, S.W.A.T. Publications, Cornville, AZ, 1989. 77 pp., illus. Softcover. $14.95

Cuts through the myths concerning the shotgun and its attendant ballistic effects.

Ducks Unlimited Guide to Shotgunning, The, by Don Zutz, Willow Creek Press, Minocqua, WI, 2000. 166 pg. Illustrated. $24.50

This book covers everything from the grand old guns of yesterday to today's best shotguns and loads, from the basic shotgun fit and function to expert advice on ballistics, chocks, and shooting techniques.

Fine European Gunmakers: Best Continental European Gunmakers & Engravers, by M. Nobili, Long Beach, CA, Safari Press, 2002. 250 pp., illustated in color. $69.95

Many experts argue that Continental gunmakers produce guns equally as good or better than British makers. Marco Nobili's new work showcases the skills of the best craftsmen from continental Europe. The book covers the histories of the individual firms and looks at the guns they currently build, tracing the developments of their most influential models.

Firearms Assembly/Disassembly, Part V: Shotguns, 2nd Edition, The Gun Digest Book of, by J.B. Wood, Krause Publications, Iola, WI, 2002. 560 pp., illus. $24.95

Covers 54 popular shotguns plus over 250 variants. The most comprehensive and professional presentation available to either hobbyist or gunsmith.

Game Shooting, by Robert Churchill, Countrysport Press, Selma, AL, 1998. 258 pp., illus. $30.00

The basis for every shotgun instructional technique devised and the foundation for all wingshooting and the game of sporting clays.

Greatest Hammerless Repeating Shotgun Ever Built: The Model 12 Winchester 1912-1964 by David Riffle, 1995. Color illustrations. 195 large detailed b&w photos, 298 pgs. Pictorial hardcover. $54.95

This offers an extremely well written and detailed year-by-year study of the gun, its details, inventors, makers, engravers, and star shooters.

Greener Story, by Graham Greener, Safari Press, Long Beach, CA, 2000. 231 pp., color and b&w illustrations. $69.95

The history of the Greener gunmakers and their guns.

Gunsmithing Shotguns: The Complete Guide to Care & Repair, by David Henderson, New York, Globe Pequot, 2003. 1st edition, b&w photos & illus; 6" x 9", 256 pp., illus. Hardcover. $24.95

An overview designed to provide insight, ideas and techniques that will give the amateur gunsmith the confidence and skill to work on his own guns. General troubleshooting, common problems, stocks and woodworking, soldering and brazing, barrel work and more.

Heyday of the Shotgun, by David Baker, Safari Press, Inc., Huntington Beach, CA, 2000. 160 pp., illus. $39.95

The art of the gunmaker at the turn of the last century when British craftsmen brought forth the finest guns ever made.

Holland & Holland: The "Royal" Gunmaker, by Donald Dallas, London, Safari Press, 2004. 1st edition. 311 pp. Hardcover. $75.00

Donald Dallas tells the fascinating story of Holland & Holland from its very beginnings, and the history of the family is revealed for the first time. The terrific variety of the firm's guns and rifles is described in great detail and set within the historical context of their eras. The book is profusely illustrated with 112 color and 355 b&w photographs, mostly unpublished. In addition many rare guns and rifles are described and illustrated.

House of Churchill, by Don Masters, Safari Press, Long Beach, CA, 2002. 512 pp., profuse color and b&w illustrations. $79.95

This marvelous work on the house of Churchill contains serial numbers and dates of manufacture of its guns from 1891 forward, price lists from 1895 onward, a complete listing of all craftsmen employed at the company, as well as the prices realized at the famous Dallas auction where the "last" production guns were sold. It was written by Don Masters, a long-time Churchill employee, who is keeping the flame of Churchill alive.

Italian Gun, by Steve Smith and Laurie Morrow, Wilderness Adventures, Gallatin Gateway, MT, 1997. 325 pp., illus. $49.95

The first book ever written entirely in English for American enthusiasts who own, aspire to own, or simply admire Italian guns.

Ithaca Featherlight Repeater; The Best Gun Going, by Walter C. Snyder, Southern Pines, NC, 1998. 300 pp., illus. $89.95

Describes the complete history of each model of the legendary Ithaca Model 37 and Model 87 Repeaters from their conception in 1930 throught 1997.

Ithaca Gun Company from the Beginning, by Walter C. Snyder, Cook & Uline Publishing Co., Southern Pines, NC, 2nd edition, 1999. 384 pp., illustrated in color and b&w. $90.00

The entire family of Ithaca Gun Company products is described along with new historical information and the serial number/date of manufacturing listing has been improved.

Little Trapshooting Book, by Frank Little, Shotgun Sports Magazine, Auburn, CA, 1994. 168 pp., illus. Paper covers. $19.95

Packed with know-how from one of the greatest trapshooters of all time.

Mental Training for the Shotgun Sports, by Michael J. Keyes, Shotgun Sports, Auburn, CA, 1996. 160 pp., illus. Paper covers. $29.95

The most comprehensive book ever published on what it takes to shoot winning scores at trap, skeet and sporting clays.

More Shotguns and Shooting, by Michael McIntosh, Countrysport Books, Selma, AL, 1998. 256 pp., illus. $30.00

From specifics of shotguns to shooting your way out of a slump, it's McIntosh at his best.

Mossberg Shotguns, by Duncan Long, Delta Press, El Dorado, AR, 2000. 120 pp., illus. $24.95

This book contains a brief history of the company and its founder, full coverage of the pump and semiautomatic shotguns, rare products and a care and maintenance section.

Mysteries of Shotgun Patterns, by George G. Oberfell and Charles E. Thompson, Ray Riling Arms Books, Philadelphia, PA, 2005. 164 pp., illus. Paper covers. $25.00

Shotgun ballistics for the hunter in non-technical language.

Parker Gun, by Larry Baer, Gun Room Press, Highland Park, NJ, 1993. 195 pp., illustrated with b&w and color photos. $35.00

Covers in detail, production of all models on this classic gun. Many fine specimens from great collections are illustrated.

Parker Guns 'The Old Reliable'-A Concise HIsory of the Famous American Shotgun Manufacturing Co., by Ed Muderlak, Long Beach, CA, Safari Press, 2004 results. A must-have for the American shotgun enthusiast. Hardcover. New in new dust jacket. $48.50

Parker Gun Identification & Serialization, by S.P. Fjestad, Minneapolis, MN, Blue Book Publications, 2002. 1st edition. Softcover. $34.95

This new 608-page publication is the only book that provides an easy reference for Parker shotguns manufactured between 1866-1942. Included is a comprehensive 46-page section on Parker identification, with over 100 detailed images depicting serialization location and explanation, various Parker grades, extra features, stock configurations, action types, and barrel identification.

Parker Story: Volumes 1 & 2, by Bill Mullins, "et al." The Double Gun Journal, East Jordan, MI, 2000. 1,025 pp. of text and 1,500 color and monochrome illustrations. Hardbound in a gold-embossed cover. $295.00

The most complete and attractive "last word" on America's preeminent double gun maker. Includes tables showing the number of guns made by gauge, barrel length and special features for each grade.

Pigeon Shooter: The Complete Guide to Modern Pigeon Shooting, by Jon Batley, London, Swan Hill press, 2005. Hardcover. $29.95

Covering everything from techniques to where and when to shoot. This updated edition contains all the latest information on decoys, hides, and the new pigeon magnets as well as details on the guns and equipment required and invaluable hands-on instruction.

Purdey Gun and Rifle Makers: The Definitive History, by Donald Dallas, Quiller Press, London 2000. 245 pp., illus. Signed and numbered. Limited edition of 3,000 copies. With a PURDEY bookplate. $100.00

Re-Creating the Double Barrel Muzzle Loading Shotgun, by William R. Brockway, York, PA, George Shumway, 2003. Revised 2nd edition. 175 pp., illus. Includes full size drawings. Softcover. $40.00

This popular book, first published in 1985 and out of print for over a decade, has been updated by the author. This book treats the making of double guns of classic style, and is profusely illustrated, showing how to do it all. Many photos of old and contemporary shotguns.

Reloading for Shotgunners, 4th Edition, by Kurt D. Fackler and M.L. McPherson, DBI Books, a division of Krause Publications, Iola, WI, 1997. 320 pp., illus. Paper covers. $19.95

Expanded reloading tables with over 11,000 loads. Bushing charts for every major press and component maker. All new presentation on all aspects of shotshell reloading by two of the top experts in the field.

Remington Double Shotguns, by Charles G. Semer, Denver, CO, 1997. 617 pp., illus. $60.00

This book deals with the entire production and all grades of double shotguns made by Remington during the period of their production 1873-1910.

Shotgun Encyclopedia, The, by John Taylor, Safari Press, Inc., Huntington Beach, CA, 2000. 260 pp., illus. $34.95

A comprehensive reference work on all aspects of shotguns and shotgun shooting.

Shotgun Technicana, by Michael McIntosh and David Trevallion, Camden, ME, Down East Books, 2002. 272 pp., with 100 illustrations. Hardcover $28.00

Everything you wanted to know about fine double shotguns by the nation's foremost experts.

Shotgun–A Shooting Instructor's Handbook, by Michael Yardley, Long Beach, CA, Safari Press, 2002. 272 pp., b&w photos, line drawings. Hardcover. $29.95

This is one of the very few books intended to be read by shooting instructors and other advanced shooters. There is practical advice on gun fit, and on gun and cartridge selection.

Shotgunning: The Art and the Science, by Bob Brister, Winchester Press, Piscataway, NJ, 1976. 321 pp., illus. $18.95

Hundreds of specific tips and truly novel techniques to improve the field and target shooting of every shotgunner.

Shotguns and Shooting, by Michael McIntosh, Countrysport Press, New Albany, OH, 1995. 258 pp., illus. $30.00

The art of guns and gunmaking, this book is a celebration no lover of fine doubles should miss.

Shotguns & Shotgunning, by Layne Simpson, Iola, WI, Krause Publications, 2003. 1st edition. High-quality color photography 224 pp., color illus. Hardcover. $36.95

This is the most comprehensive and valuable guide on the market devoted exclusively to shotguns. Part buyer's guide, part technical manual, and part loving tribute, shooters and hunters of all skill levels will enjoy this comprehensive reference tool.

Spanish Best: The Fine Shotguns of Spain, 2nd Edition, by Terry Wieland, Down East Books, Traverse City, MI, 2001. 364 pp., illus. $60.00

A practical source of information for owners of Spanish shotguns and a guide for those considering buying a used shotgun.

Streetsweepers: The Complete Book of Combat Shotguns, Revised and Updated Edition, by Duncan Long, Boulder Co, Paladin Press, 2004. illus., 224 pp. Soft cover. $35.00

Including how to choose the right gauge and shot, decipher the terminology and use special-purpose rounds such as flechettes and tear-gas projectiles; and gives expert instruction on customizing shotguns, telling you what you must know about the assault weapon ban before you choose or modify your gun.

Successful Shotgunning; How to Build Skill in the Field and Take More Birds in Competition, by Peter F. Blakeley, Mechanicsburg, PA, Stackpole Books, 2003. 1st edition. 305 pp., illustrated with 119 b&w photos & 4-page color section with 8 photos. Hardcover. $24.95

Successful Shotgunning focuses on wing-shooting and sporting clays techniques.

Tactical Shotgun, The, by Gabriel Suzrez, Paladin Press, Boulder, CO, 1996. 232 pp., illus. Paper covers. $25.00

The best techniques and tactics for employing the shotgun in personal combat.

Trapshooting is a Game of Opposites, by Dick Bennett, Shotgun Sports, Inc., Auburn, CA, 1996. 129 pp., illus. Paper covers. $19.95

Discover everything you need to know about shooting trap like the pros.

U.S. Winchester Trench and Riot Guns and Other U.S. Military Combat Shotguns, by Joe Poyer, North Cape Publications, Tustin, CA, 1992. 124 pp., illus. Paper covers. $15.95

A detailed history of the use of military shotguns, and the acquisition procedures used by the U.S. Army's Ordnance Department in both world wars.

Uncle Dan Lefever, Master Gunmaker: Guns of Lasting Fame, by Robert W. Elliott, privately printed, 2002. Profusely illustrated with b&w photos, with a 45-page color section. 239 pp. Handsomely bound, with gilt titled spine and top cover. Hardcover. $60.00

Winchester Model 12 Assembly, Disassembly Manual, by Skennerton & Riling, Ray Riling Arms Books Co. Philadelphia, PA 2004. 36 pages, over 60 photos & line drawings. $5.00

Ideal workshop reference for stripping & assembly with exploded parts drawings, specifications, service accessories, historical information and recommended reading references. Ideal workbook for shooters and collectors alike. Triple saddle-stitched binding with durable plastic laminated cover makes this an ideal workshop guide.

Winchester Model Twelve, by George Madis, Art and Reference House, Dallas, TX, 1982. 176 pp., illus. $26.95

A definitive work on this famous American shotgun.

Winchester Model 97 Assembly, Disassembly Manual, by Skennerton & Riling, Ray Riling Arms Books Co. Philadelphia, PA 2004. 36 pages, over 60 photos & line drawings. $5.00

Ideal workshop reference for stripping & assembly with exploded parts drawings, specifications, service accessories, historical information and recommended reading references. Ideal workbook for shooters and collectors alike. Triple saddle-stitched binding with durable plastic laminated cover makes this an ideal workshop guide.

World's Fighting Shotguns, by Thomas F. Swearengen, T.B.N. Enterprises, Alexandria, VA, 1998. 500 pp., illus. $59.95

The complete military and police reference work from the shotgun's inception to date, with up-to-date developments.

A

A. Uberti S.p.A., Via Artigiana 1, Gardone Val Trompia, Brescia 25063, ITALY, P: 011 390308341800, F: 011 390308341801, www. ubertireplicas.it
Firearms

A.R.M.S., Inc./Atlantic Research Marketing Systems, Inc., 230 W. Center St., West Bridgewater, MA 02379, P: 508-584-7816, F: 508-588-8045, www.armsmounts.com
Scopes, Sights and Accessories

AA & E Leathercraft, 107 W. Gonzales St., Yoakum, TX 77995, P: 800-331-9092, F: 361-293-9127, www.tandybrands.com
Bags & Equipment Cases; Custom Manufacturing; Hunting Accessories; Knives/ Knife Cases; Leathergoods; Shooting Range Equipment; Sports Accessories

ACIGI / Fujiiryoki, 4399 Ingot St., Fremong, CA 94538, P: 888-816-0888, F: 510-651-6188, www.fujichair.com
Wholesaler/Distributor

ACR Electronics, Inc., 5757 Ravenswood Rd., Ft. Lauderdale, FL 33312, P: 800-432-0227, F: 954-983-5087, www.acrelectronics.com
Backpacking; Hunting Accessories; Lighting Products; Sports Accessories; Survival Kits/ First Aid; Training and Safety Equipment

Accro-Met, Inc., 3406 Westwood Industrial Drive, Monroe, NC 28110, P: 800-543-4755, F: 704-283-2112, www.accromet.com
Gun Barrels; Wholesaler/Distributor

Accu-Fire, Inc., P.O. Box 121990, Arlington, TX 76012, P: 888 MUZZLEMATE, F: 817-303-4505
Firearms Maintenance Equipment

Accu-Shot/B&T Industries, LLC, P.O. Box 771071, Wichita, KS 67277, P: 316-721-3222, F: 316-721-1021, www.accu-shot.com
Gun Grips & Stocks; Hunting Accessories; Law Enforcement; Scopes, Sights & Accessories; Shooting Range Equipment; Sports Accessories; Training and Safety Equipment

Accuracy International North America, Inc., 35100 North State Highway, Mingus, TX 76463-6405, P: 907-440-4024, www. accuracyinternational.org
Firearms; Firearms Maintenance Equipment; Law Enforcement; Magazines, Cartridge; Scopes, Sights & Accessories; Wholesaler/ Distributor

AccuSharp Knife Sharpeners/Fortune Products, Inc., 205 Hickory Creek Road, Marble Falls, TX 78654, P: 800-742-7797, F: 800-600-5373, www.accusharp.com
Archery; Camping; Cooking Equipment/ Accessories; Cutlery; Hunting Accessories; Knives/Knife Cases; Sharpeners; Sports Accessories

Action Target, P.O. Box 636, Provo, UT 84603-0636, P: 888-377-8033, F: 801-377-8096, www.actiontarget.com
Law Enforcement; Shooting Range Equipment; Targets; Training & Safety Equipment

AcuSport Corp., One Hunter Place, Bellefontaine, OH 43311, P: 800-543-3150, www.acusport.com
Ammunition; Black Powder Accessories; Firearms; Hunting Accessories; Online Services; Retailer Services; Scopes, Sights & Accessories; Wholesaler/Distributor

Adams Arms/Retrofit Piston Systems, 255 Hedden Court, Palm Harbor, FL 34681, P: 727-853-0550, F: 727-353-0551, www. arisfix.com

ADCO Arms Co., Inc., 4 Draper St., Woburn, MA 01801, P: 800-775-3687, F: 781-935-1011, www.adcosales.com
Ammunition; Firearms; Paintball Accessories, Scopes, Sights & Accessories

ADS, Inc., Pinehurst Centre, 477 Viking Dr., Suite 350, Virginia Beach, VA 23452, P: 800-948-9433, F: 757-481-2039, www. adstactical.com

ADSTAR, Inc., 1390 Jerusalem Ave., North Merrick, NY 11566, P: 516-483-1800, F: 516-483-2590
Emblems & Decals; Outdoor Art, Jewelry, Sculpture

Advanced Armament Corp., 1434 Hillcrest Rd., Norcross, GA 30093, P: 770-925-9988, F: 770-925-9989, www.advanced-armament. com
Firearms; Hearing Protection; Law Enforcement

Advanced Engineered Systems, Inc., 14328 Commercial Parkway, South Beloit, IL 61080, P: 815-624-7797, F: 815-624-8198, www.advengsys.com
Ammunition; Custom Manufacturing

Advanced Technology International, 2733 W. Carmen Ave., Milwaukee, WI 53209, P: 800-925-2522, F: 414-664-3112, www. atigunstocks.com
Books/Industry Publications; Gun Grips & Stocks; Gun Parts/Gunsmithing; Hunting Accessories; Law Enforcement; Scopes, Sights & Accessories

Advanced Training Systems, 4524 Highway 61 North, St. Paul, MN 55110, P: 651-429-8091, F: 651-429-8702, www.duelatron.com
Law Enforcement; Shooting Range Equipment; Targets; Training & Safety Equipment

Advantage® Camouflage, P.O. Box 9638, Columbus, GA 31908, P: 800-992-9968, F: 706-569-9346, www.advantagecamo.com
Camouflage

Advantage Tactical Sight/WrenTech Industries, LLC, 7 Avenida Vista Grande B-7, Suite 510, Sante Fe, NM 87508, F: 310-316-6413 or 505-466-1811, F: 505-466-4735, www. advantagetactical.com
Scopes, Sights & Accessories

Adventure Action Gear/+VENTURE Heated Clothing, 5932 Bolsa Ave., Suite 103, Huntington Beach, CA 92649, P: 310-412-1070, F: 610-423-5257, www.ventureheat. com
Men & Women's Clothing; Export/Import Specialists; Footwear; Gloves, Mitts, Hats; Sports Accessories; Vehicles, Utility & Rec.; Wholesaler/Distributor

Adventure Lights, Inc., 444 Beaconsfield Blvd., Suite 201, Beaconsfield, Quebec H9W 4C1, CANADA, P: 514-694-8477, F: 514-694-2353

Adventure Medical Kits, P.O. Box 43309, Oakland, CA 94624, P: 800-324-3517, F: 510-261-7419, www.adventuremedicalkits. com
Backpacking; Books/Industry Publications; Camping; Custom Manufacturing; Hunting Accessories; Sports Accessories; Survival Kits/ First Aid; Training & Safety Equipment

AE Light/Div. of Allsman Enterprises, LLC, P.O. Box 1869, Rogue River, OR 97537, P: 541-471-8988, F: 888-252-1473, www.aelight. com
Camping; Custom Manufacturing; Hunting Accessories; Law Enforcement; Lighting Products; Wholesale/Distributor

AES Optics, 201 Corporate Court, Senatobia, MS 38668, P: 800-416-0866, F: 662-301-4739, www.aesoutdoors.com
Eyewear

Aetco, Inc., 2825 Metropolitan Place, Pomona, CA 91767, P: 800-982-5258, F: 800-451-2434, www.aetcoinc.com
Firearms; Hearing Protection; Holsters; Law Enforcement; Leathergoods; Lighting Products; Training & Safety Equipment; Wholesaler/Distributor

Africa Sport Hunting Safaries, 11265 E. Edison St., Tucson, AZ 85749, P: 520-440-5384, F: 520-885-8032, www. africasporthuntingsafaris.com
Archery; Outdoor Art, Jewelry, Sculpture; Outfitter; Tours/Travel

AFTCO Bluewater/Al Agnew, 17351 Murphy Ave., Irvine, CA 92614, P: 949-660-8757, F: 949-660-7067, www.aftcobluewater.com

Aftermath Miami/Stunt Studios, 3911 Southwest 47th Ave., Suite 914, Davie, FL 33314, P: 954-581-5822, F: 954-581-3165, www.aftermathairsoft.com
Airsoft Guns & Accessories

Aguila Ammunition/Centurion Ordnance, Inc., 11611 Rainbow Ridge, Holotoo, TX 78023, P: 210-695-4602, F: 210-695-4603, www. aguilaammo.com
Ammunition

Aimpoint, Inc., 14103 Mariah Court, Chantilly, VA 20151, 877-246-7646, F: 703-263-9463, www.aimpoint.com
Scopes, Sights & Accessories

AimShot/Osprey International, Inc., 25 Hawks Farm Rd., White, GA 30184, P: 888-448-3247, F: 770-387-0114, www.aimshot.com, www.miniosprey.com
Archery; Binoculars; Holsters; Hunting Accessories; Law Enforcement; Lighting Products; Scopes, Sights & Accessories; Wholesaler/Distributor

Aimtech Mount Systems, P.O. Box 223, Thomasville, GA 31799-0223, P: 229-226-4313, F: 229-227-0222, www.aimtech-mounts.com
Hunting Accessories; Scopes, Sights & Accessories

Air Gun, Inc., 9320 Harwin Dr., Houston, TX 77036, P: 800-456-0022, F: 713-780-4831, www.airrifle-china.com
Airguns; Ammunition; Hunting Accessories; Scopes, Sights & Accessories; Wholesaler/ Distributor

AirForce Airguns, P.O. Box 2478, Fort Worth, TX 76113, P: 877-247-4867, F: 817-451-1613, www.airforceairguns.com
Airguns; Hunting Accessories; Law Enforcement; Scopes, Sights & Accessories

Aitec Co., Ltd., Export Dept., Rm. 817, Crystal Beach ok, Jung Dong Haeundae-Gu Busan, 612 010, SOUTH KOREA, P: 011 82517416497, F: 011 82517462194, www. aitec.co.kr
Lighting Products

Ajax Custom Grips, Inc./Ajax Shooter Supply, 9130 Viscount Row, Dallas, TX 75247, P: 800-527-7537, F: 214-630-4942, www. ajaxgrips.com
Gun Grips & Stocks; Gun Parts/Gunsmithing; Holsters; Law Enforcement; Lighting Products; Magazines, Cartridge; Wholesaler/Distributor

MANUFACTURER'S AND PRODUCT DIRECTORY

AKDAL/Ucyildiz Arms Ind./Blow & Voltran, Bostanci Cd. Uol Sk. No: 14/A, Y. Dudullu-Umraniye, Istanbul, 34775, TURKEY, P: 011-90 216527671011, F: 011-90 2165276705, www.akdalarms.com, www.voltranarms.com
Airguns; Firearms

Aker International Inc., 2248 Main St., Suite 6, Chula Vista, CA 91911, P: 800-645-AKER, F: 888-300-AKER, www.akerleather.com
Holsters; Hunting Accessories; Law Enforcement; Leathergoods

Al Mar Knives, P.O. Box 2295, Tualatin, OR 97062, P: 503-670-9080, www.almarknives.com
Custom Manufacturing, Knives/Knife Cases

Alexander Arms, U.S. Army Radford Arsenal, Radford, VA 24141, P: 540-639-8356, F: 540-639-8353, www.alexanderarms.com
Ammunition; Firearms; Magazine, Cartridges; Reloading

All-Star Apparel, 6722 Vista Del Mar Ave., Suite C. La Jolla, CA 92037, P: 858-205-7827, F: 858-225-3544, www.all-star.ws
Camouflage; Men & Women's Clothing; Gloves, Mitts, Hats

All Weather Outerwear, 34 35th St., Brooklym, NY 11232, P: 800-965-6550, F: 718-788-2205
Camouflage; Men's Clothing

AllClear, LLC dba Auspit Rotisserie BBQ's, 2050 Russett Way, Carson City, NV 89703, P: 775-468-5665, F: 775-546-6091, www.auspitbbq.com

Allen Company, 525 Burbank St., P.O. Box 445, Broomfield, CO 80020, P: 800-876-8600, F: 303-466-7437, www.allencompany.net
Archery; Black Powder Accessories; Eyewear; Gun Cases; Hearing Protection; Hunting Accessories; Scopes, Sights & Accessories; Shooting Range Equipment

Alliant Powder/ATK Commercial Products, Route 114, Building 229, P.O. Box 6, Radford, VA 24143, P: 800-276-9337, F: 540-639-8496, www.alliantpowder.com
Reloading

Alot Enterprise Company, Ltd., 1503 Eastwood Centre, 5 A Kung Ngam Village Rd., Shaukeiwan, HONG KONG, P: 011 85225199728, F: 011 85225190122, www.alothk.com
Binoculars; Compasses; Eyewear; Hunting Accessories; Photographic Equipment; Scopes, Sights, & Accessories; Sports Accessories; Telescopes

Alpen Outdoor Corp., 10329 Dorset St., Rancho Cucamonga, CA 91730, P: 877-987-8379, F: 909-987-8661, www.alpenoutdoor.com
Backpacking; Binoculars; Camping; Hunting Accessories; Scopes, Sights & Accessories; Shooting Range Equipment; Sports Accessories, Wholesaler/Distributor

Alpine Archery, P.O. Box 319, Lewiston, ID 83501, P: 208-746-4717, F: 208-746-1635

ALPS Mountaineering, 1 White Pine, New Haven, MO 63068, P: 800-344-2577, F: 573-459-2044, www.alpsouthdoorz.com
Backpacking; Camouflage; Camping; Hunting Accessories; Sports Accessories

ALS Technologies, Inc., 1103 Central Blvd., P.O. Box 525, Bull Shoals, AR 72619, P: 877-902-4257, F: 870-445-8746, www.alslesslethal.com
Ammunition; Firearms; Gun Parts/Gunsmithing; Law Enforcement; Training & Safety Equipment

Alta Industries, 1460 Cader Lane, Petaluma, CA 94954, P: 707-347-2900, F: 707-347-2950, www.altaindustries.com

Altama Footwear, 1200 Lake Hearn Dr., Suite 475, Atlanta, GA 30319, P: 800-437-9888, F: 404-260-2889, www.altama.com
Footwear; Law Enforcement

Altamont Co., 291 N. Church St., P.O. Box 309, Thomasboro, IL 61878, P: 800-626-5774, F: 217-643-7973, www.altamontco.com
Gun Grips & Stocks

AlumaGrips, 2851 N. 34th Place, Mesa, AZ 85213, P: 602-690-5459, F: 480-807-3955
Firearms Maintenance Equipment; Gun Grips & Stocks; Gun Parts/Gunsmithing; Law Enforcement

AmChar Wholesale, Inc., 100 Airpark Dr., Rochester, NY 14624, P: 585-328-3951, F: 585-328-3749, www.amchar.com

American COP Magazine/FMG Publications, 12345 World Trade Dr., San Diego, CA 92128, P: 800-537-3006, F: 858-605-0247, www.americancopmagazine.com
Books/Industry Publications; Law Enforcement; Videos

American Cord & Webbing Co., Inc., 88 Century Dr., Woonsocket, RI 02895, P: 401-762-5500, F: 401-762-5514, www.acw1.com
Archery; Backpacking; Bags & Equipment Cases; Custom Manufacturing; Law Enforcement; Pet Supplies

American Defense Systems, Inc., 230 Duffy Ave., Hicksville, NY 11801, P: 516-390-5300, F: 516-390-5308, www.adsiarmor.com
Custom Manufacturing; Shooting Range Equipment; Training & Safety Equipment

American Furniture Classics/Div. of Dawson Heritage Furniture, P.O. Box 111, Webb City, MO 64870, P: 888-673-9080, F: 417-673-9081, www.americanfurnitureclassics.com
Gun Cabinets/Racks/Safes; Gun Cases; Home Furnishings

American Gunsmithing Institute (AGI), 1325 Imola Ave. West, P.O. Box 504, Napa, CA 94559, P: 800-797-0867, F: 707-253-7149, www.americangunsmith.com
Books/Industry Publications; Computer Software; Firearms Maintenance Equipment; Gun Parts/Gunsmithing; Videos

American Pioneer Powder, Inc., 20423 State Road 7, Suite F6-268, Boca Raton, FL 33498, P: 888-756-7693, F: 888-766-7693, www.americanpioneerpowder.com
Black Powder/Smokeless Powder; Reloading

American Plastics/SEWIT, 1225 N. MacArthur Drive, Suite 200, Tracy, CA 95376, P: 209-834-0287, F: 209-834-0924, www.americanplastics.com
Backpacking; Bags & Equipment Cases; Export/Import Specialists; Gun Cases; Holsters; Hunting Accessories; Survival Kits/First Aid; Wholesaler/Distributor

American Security Products Co., 11925 Pacific Ave., Fontana, CA 92337, P: 800-421-6142, F: 951-685-9685, www.amsecusa.com
Gun Cabinets/Racks/Safes

American Tactical Imports, 100 Airpark Dr., Rochester, NY 14624, P: 585-328-3951, F: 585-328-3749

American Technologies Network, Corp./ATN, Corp., 1341 San Mateo Ave., South San Francisco, CA 94080, P: 800-910-2862, F: 650-875-0129, www.atncorp.com
Binoculars; Law Enforcement; Lighting Products; Photographic Equipment; Scopes, Sights & Accessories; Telescopes

Americase, Inc., 1610 E. Main St., Waxahachie, TX 75165, P: 800-972-2737, F: 972-937-8373, www.americase.com
Bags & Equipment Cases; Custom Manufacturing; Gun Cases; Hunting Accessories

AmeriGlo, 5579-B Chamblee Dunwoody Rd., Suite 214, Atlanta, GA 30338, P: 770-390-0554, F: 770-390-9781, www.ameriglo.com
Camping; Law Enforcement; Lighting Products; Scopes, Sights & Accessories; Survival Kits/First Aid; Training & Safety Equipment

Ameristep, 901 Tacoma Court, Clio, MI 48420, P: 800-374-7837, F: 810-686-7121, www.ameristep.com
Archery; Blinds; Hunting Accessories; Training & Safety Equipment; Treestands

Ammo-Loan Worldwide, 815 D, Lewiston, ID 83501, P: 208-746-7012, F: 208-746-1703

Ammo-Up, 10601 Theresa Dr., Jacksonville, FL 32246, P: 800-940-2688, F: 904-645-5918, www.ammoupusa.com
Shooting Range Equipment

AMT/Auto Mag Co./C.G., Inc., 5200 Mitchelldale, Suite E17, Houston, TX 77092, P: 713-686-3232, F: 713-681-5665

Anglers Book Supply/Hunters & Shooters Book & DVD Catalog, 1380 W. 2nd Ave., Eugene, OR 97402, P: 800-260-3869, F: 541-342-1785, www.anglersbooksupply.com
Books/Industry Publications; Computer Software; Videos; Wholesaler/Distributor

ANXO-Urban Body Armor Corp., 7359 Northwest 34 St., Miami, FL 33122, P: 866-514-ANXO, F: 305-593-5498, www.urbanbodyarmor.com
Men & Women's Clothing; Custom Manufacturing; Law Enforcement

Apple Creek Whitetails, 14109 Cty. Rd. VV, Gillett, WI 54124, P: 920-598-0154, F: 920-855-1773, www.applecreekwhitetails.com

ARC/ArcticShield, Inc./X-System, 1700 West Albany, Suite A, Broken Arrow, OK 74012, P: 877-974-4353, F: 918-258-8790, www.arcoutdoors.com
Footwear; Hunting Accessories; Scents & Lures; Sports Accessories

Arc'Teryx, 100-2155 Dollarton Hwy., North Vancouver, British Columbia V7H 3B2, CANADA, P: 604-960-3001, F: 604-904-3692, www.arcteryx.com
Backpacking; Camouflage; Men's Clothing; Custom Manufacturing; Gloves, Mitts, Hats; Law Enforcement; Outfitter

Arctic Adventures, 19950 Clark Graham, Baie D'urfe, Quebec H9X 3R8, CANADA, P: 800-465-9474, F: 514-457-9834, www.arcticadventures.ca
Outfitter

Ares Defense Systems, Inc., P.O. Box 10667, Blacksburg, VA 24062, P: 540-639-8633, F: 540-639-8634, www.aresdefense.com
Firearms; Gun Parts/Gunsmithing; Law Enforcement; Lighting Products; Magazines, Cartridge; Scopes, Sights & Accessories; Shooting Range Equipment; Survival Kits/First Aid

Argentina Ducks & Doves LLC, P.O. Box 129, Pittsview, AL 36871, P: 334-

MANUFACTURER'S
AND PRODUCT DIRECTORY

855-9474, F: 334-855-9474, www.
argentinaducksanddoves.com
Outfitter; Tours/Travel

ArmaLite, Inc., 745 S. Hanford St., Geneseo, IL
61254, P: 309-944-6939, F: 309-944-6949,
www.armalite.com
Firearms; Firearms Maintenance Equipment

Armament Technology, Inc./ELCAN Optical
Technologies, 3045 Robie St., Suite 113,
Halifax, Nova Scotia B3K 4P6, CANADA,
P: 902-454-6384, F: 902-454-4641, www.
armament.com
*International Exhibitors; Law Enforcement;
Scopes, Sights & Accessories; Telescopes;
Wholesaler/Distributor*

Armatix GmbH, Feringastrabe. 4, Unterfohring,
D 85774, GERMANY, P: 011 498999228140,
F: 011 498999228228, www.armatix.de

Armi Sport di Chiappa Silvia e C. SNC-Chiappa
Firearms, Via Milano, 2, Azzano Mella (Bs),
25020, ITALY, P: 011-39 0309749065, F:
011-39 0309749232, www.chiappafirearms.
com
*Black Powder Accessories; Firearms;
International Exhibitors*

Armor Express, 1554 E. Torch Lake Dr., P.O.
Box 21, Central Lake, MI 49622, P: 866-357-
3845, F: 231-544-6734, www.armorexpress.
com
Law Enforcement

Armorshield USA, LLC, 30 ArmorShield Dr.,
Stearns, KY 42647, P: 800-386-9455, F:
800-392-9455, www.armorshield.net
Law Enforcement

Arms Corp. of the Philippines/Armscor
Precision International, Armscorp Ave., Bgy
Fortune, Marikina City, 1800, PHILIPPINES,
P: 011 6329416243, F: 011 6329420682,
www.armscor.com.ph
*Airguns; Ammunition; Bags & Equipment
Cases; Custom Manufacturing; Firearms; Gun
Barrels; Gun Parts/Gunsmithing; International
Exhibitors*

Arms Tech, Ltd., 5025 North Central Ave., Suite
459, Phoenix, AZ 85012, P: 602-272-9045,
F: 602-272-1922, www.armstechltd.com
Firearms; Law Enforcement

Arno Bernard Custom Knives, 19 Duiker St.,
Bethlehem, 9700, SOUTH AFRICA, P: 011
27583033196, F: 011 27583033196

Arrieta, Morkaiko, 5, Elgoibar, (Guipuzcoa)
20870, SPAIN, P: 011-34 943743150, F:
011-34 943743154, www.arrietashotguns.
com
Firearms

Arrow Precision, LLC, 2750 W. Gordon St.,
Allentown, PA 18104, P: 610-437-7138, F:
610-437-7139, www.arrow-precision.com
*Archery; Crossbows & Accessories; Paintballs,
Guns & Accessories*

ARS Business Solutions, LLC, 940 Industrial
Dr., Suite 107, Sauk Rapids, MN 56379, P:
800-547-7120, www.arss.com
Computer Software; Retailer Services

Arsenal, Inc., 3300 S. Decatur Blvd., Suite
10632, Las Vegas, NV 89102, P: 888-539-
2220, F: 702-643-8860, www.arsenalinc.com
Firearms

Artistic Plating Co., 405 W. Cherry St.,
Milwaukee, WI 53212, P: 414-271-8138, F:
414-271-5541, www.artisticplating.net
*Airguns; Ammunition; Archery; Cutlery;
Firearms; Game Calls; Gun Barrels; Reloading*

ARY, Inc., 10301 Hickman Mills Dr., Suite 110,
Kansas City, MO 64137, P: 800-821-7849, F:
816-761-0055, www.aryinc.com
Cutlery; Knives/Knife Cases

ASAT Outdoors, LLC, 307 E. Park Ave., Suite
207A, Anaconda, MT 59711, P: 406-563-
9336, F: 406-563-7315
*Archery; Blinds; Camouflage; Men's Clothing;
Gloves, Mitts, Hats; Hunting Accessories; Law
Enforcement; Paintball Accessories*

Ashbury International Group, Inc., P.O.
Box 8024, Charlottesville, VA 22906, P:
434-296-8600, F: 434-296-9260, www.
ashburyintlgroup.com
*Camouflage; Firearms; Law Enforcement;
Scopes, Sights & Accessories; Wholesaler/
Distributor*

Asociacion Armera, P. I Azitain, 2-J, P.O. Box
277, Eibar, Guipúzcoa 20600, SPAIN, P: 011
34943208493, F: 011 34943700966, www.
a-armera.com
Associations/Agencies

ASP, Inc., 2511 E. Capitol Dr., Appleton, WI
54911, P: 800-236-6243, F: 800-236-8601,
www.asp-usa.com
*Law Enforcement; Lighting Products; Training
& Safety Equipment*

A-Square Company/A-Square of South Dakota,
LLC, 302 Antelope Dr., Chamberlain, SD
57325, P: 605-234-0500, F: 605-234-0510,
www.asquareco.com
*Ammunition; Books/Industry Publications;
Firearms; Reloading*

Astra Radio Communications, 2238 N. Glassell
St., Suite D, Orange, CA 92865, P: 714-637-
2828, F: 714-637-2669, www.arcmics.com
Two-Way Radios

Atak Arms Ind., Co. Ltd., Imes San. Sit.
A Blok 107, Sk. No: 70, Y. Dudullu,
Umraniye, Istanbul, 34775 TURKEY, P:
+902164203996, F: +902164203998, www.
atakarms.com
Airguns; Firearms; Training & Safety Equipment

Atascosa Wildlife Supply, 1204 Zanderson
Ave., Jourdanton, TX 78026, P: 830-769-
9711, F: 830-769-1001

ATK/ATK Commercial Products, 900 Ehlen Dr.,
Anoka, MN 55303, P: 800-322-2342, F: 763-
323-2506, www.atk.com
*Ammunition; Binoculars; Clay Targets;
Firearms Maintenance Equipment; Reloading;
Scopes, Sights & Accessories; Shooting
Range Equipment; Targets*

ATK /ATK Law Enforcement, 2299 Snake River
Ave., Lewiston, ID 83501, P: 800-627-3640,
F: 208-798-3392, www.atk.com
*Ammunition; Bags & Equipment Cases;
Binoculars; Firearms Maintenance Equipment;
Reloading; Scopes, Sights & Accessories*

Atlanco, 1125 Hayes Industrial Dr., Marietta,
GA 30062-2471, P: 800-241-9414, F: 770-
427-9011, www.truspec.com
*Camouflage; Men's Clothing; Custom
Manufacturing; Law Enforcement; Wholesaler/
Distributor*

Atlanta Cutlery Corp., 2147 Gees Mill Rd.,
Conyers, GA 30013, P: 800-883-8838, F:
770-760-8993, www.atlantacutlery.com
*Custom Manufacturing; Cutlery; Firearms;
Holsters; Knives/Knife Cases; Leathergoods;
Wholesaler/Distributor*

Atlas Glove Consumer Products/LFS, Inc., 851
Coho Way, Bellingham, WA 98225, P: 800-
426-8860, F: 888-571-8175, www.lfsinc.
com/atlasoutdoor

Gloves, Mitts, Hats

Atsko, 2664 Russel St., Orangeburg, SC
29115, P: 800-845-2728, F: 803-531-2139,
www.atsko.com
*Archery; Backpacking; Camouflage; Camping;
Custom Manufacturing; Hunting Accessories;
Scents & Lures*

AuctionArms.com, Inc., 3031 Alhambra Dr.,
Suite 101, Cameron Park, CA 95682, P: 877-
GUN-AUCTION, F: 530-676-2497, www.
auctionarms.com
*Airguns; Archery; Black Powder Accessories;
Black Powder/Smokeless Powder; Camping;
Firearms; Online Services*

Autumnwood Wool Outfitters, Inc., 828 Upper
Pennsylvania Ave., Bangor, PA 18013, P:
610-588-5744, F: 610-588-4868, www.
autumnwoodoutfitters.com

Avon Protection Systems, 1369 Brass Mill
Rd., Suite A, Belcamp, MD 21017, P: 888-
286-6440, F: 410-273-0126, www.avon-
protection.com
Law Enforcement; Training & Safety Equipment

A-Way Hunting Products (MI), 3230 Calhoun
Rd., P.O. Box 492, Beaverton, MI, 48612,
P: 989-435-3879, F: 989-435-8960, www.
awayhunting.com
Decoys; Game Calls; Scents & Lures; Videos

AWC Systems Technology, 1515 W. Deer
Valley Rd., Suite A-105, Phoenix, AZ 85027,
P: 623-780-1050, F: 800-897-5708, www.
awcsystech.com

AyA-Aguirre Y Aranzabal, Avda. Otaola, 25-3a
Planta, Eibar, (Guipúzcoa) 20600, SPAIN, P:
011-34-943-820437, F: 011-34-943-200133,
www.aya-fineguns.com
Firearms

B

B-Square/Div. Armor Holdings, Inc., 8909
Forum Way, Fort Worth, TX 76140, P: 800-
433-2909, F: 817-926-7012

BAM Wuxi Bam Co., Ltd., No 37 Zhongnan
Rd., Wuxi, JiangSu 214024, CHINA, P: 011-
86 51085432361, FL 011-86 51085401258,
www.china-bam.com
*Airguns; Gun Cases; Scopes, Sights &
Accessories*

BCS International, 1819 St. George St., Green
Bay, WI 54302, P: 888-965-3700, F: 888-
965-3701
*Bags & Equipment Cases; Camouflage; Men &
Women's Clothing; Export/Import Specialists;
Leathergoods*

B.E. Meyers, 14540 Northeast 91st St.,
Redmond, WA 98052, P: 800-327-5648, F:
425-867-1759, www.bemeyers.com
Custom Manufacturing; Law Enforcement

B & F System, Inc., The, 3920 S. Walton Walker
Blvd., Dallas, TX 75236, P: 214-333-2111, F:
214-333-2137, www.bnfusa.com
*Binoculars; Cooking Equipment/Accessories;
Cutlery; Gloves, Mitts, Hats; Leathergoods;
Scopes, Sights & Accessories; Telescopes;
Wholesaler/Distributor*

BOGgear, LLC, 111 W. Cedar Lane, Suite A,
Payson, AZ 85541, P: 877-264-7637, F: 505-
292-9130, www.boggear.com
*Binoculars; Firearms; Hunting Accessories;
Law Enforcement; Outfitter; Photographic
Equipment; Shooting Range Equipment;
Training & Safety Equipment*

MANUFACTURER'S AND PRODUCT DIRECTORY

BSA Optics, 3911 S.W. 47th Ave., Suite 914, Ft. Lauderdale, FL 33314, P: 954-581-2144, F: 954-581-3165, www.bsaoptics.com
Binoculars; Scopes, Sights & Accessories; Sports Accessories; Telescopes

B.S.N. Technology Srl, Via Guido Rossa, 46/52, Cellatica (Bs), 25060, ITALY, P: 011 390302522436, F: 011 390302520946, www.bsn.it
Ammunition; Gun Barrels; Reloading

Bad Boy, Inc., 102 Industrial Dr., Batesville, AR 72501, P: 870-698-0090, F: 870-698-2123

Bad Boy Enterprises, LLC/Bad Boy Buggies, 2 River Terminal Rd., P.O. Box 19087, Natchez, MS 39122, P: 866-678-6701, F: 601-442-6707, www.badboybuggies.com
Vehicles, Utility & Rec

Badger Barrels, Inc., 8330 196 Ave., P.O. Box 417, Bristol, WI 53104, P: 262-857-6950, F: 262-857-6988, www.badgerbarrelsinc.com
Gun Barrels

Badger Ordnance, 1141 Swift St., North Kansas City, MO 64116, P: 816-421-4956, F: 816-421-4958, www.badgerordnance.com
Custom Manufacturing; Firearms; Firearms Maintenance Equipment; Gun Parts/Gunsmithing; Law Enforcement; Magazines, Cartridge; Scopes, Sights & Accessories; Telescopes

Badland Beauty, LLC, P.O. Box 151507, Lufkin, TX 75915, P: 936-875-5522, F: 936-875-5525, www.badlandbeauty.com
Women's Clothing

BAE Systems/Mobility & Protection Systems, 13386 International Parkway, Jacksonville, FL 32218, P: 904-741-5600, F: 904-741-9996, www.baesystems.com
Bags & Equipment Cases; Black Powder/Smokeless Powder; Gloves, Mitts, Hats; Holsters; Hunting Accessories; Law Enforcement; Scopes, Sights & Accessories; Training & Safety Equipment

Bandera/Cal-Bind, 1315 Fernbridge Dr., Fortuna, CA 95540, P: 866-226-3378, F: 707-725-1156, www.banderausa.com
Archery; Hunting Accessories; Leathergoods; Sports Accessories; Wholesaler/Distributor

Barbour, Inc., 55 Meadowbrook Dr., Milford, NH 03055-4613, P: 800-338-3474, F: 603-673-6510, www.barbour.com
Bags & Equipment Cases; Men & Women's Clothing; Footwear; Gloves, Mitts, Hats; Leathergoods

Bardin & Marsee Publishing, 1112 N. Shadesview Terrace, Birmingham, AL 35209, P: 205-453-4361, F: 404-474-3086, www.theoutdoorbible.com
Books/Industry Publications

Barnaul Cartridge Plant CJSC, 28 Kulagina St., Barnaul, 656002, RUSSIAN FEDERATION, P: 011 0073852774391, F: 011 0073852771608, www.ab.ru/~stanok
Ammunition

Barnes Bullets, Inc., P.O. Box 620, Mona, UT 84645, P: 801-756-4222, F: 801-756-2465, www.barnesbullets.com
Black Powder Accessories; Computer Software; Custom Manufacturing; Hunting Accessories; Law Enforcement; Recoil Protection Devices & Services; Reloading

Barnett Outdoors, LLC, 13447 Byrd Dr., P.O. Box 934, Odessa, FL 33556, P: 800-237-4507, F: 813-920-5400, www.barnettcrossbows.com

Archery; Crossbows & Accessories; Sports Accessories

Baron Technology, Inc./Baron Engraving, 62 Spring Hill Rd., Trumbull, CT 06611, P: 203-452-0515, F: 203-452-0663, www.baronengraving.com
Custom Manufacturing; Cutlery; Firearms; Gun Parts/Gunsmithing; Knives/Knife Cases; Law Enforcement; Outdoor Art, Jewelry, Sculpture; Sports Accessories

Barrett Firearms Mfg., Inc., P.O. Box 1077, Murfreesboro, TN 37133, P: 615-896-2938, F: 615-896-7313, www.barrettrifles.com
Firearms

Barska Optics, 1721 Wright Ave., La Verne, CA 91750, P: 909-445-8168, F: 909-445-8169, www.barska.com

Bates Footwear/Div. Wolverine World Wide, Inc., 9341 Courtland Dr., Rockford, MI 49351, P: 800-253-2184, F: 616-866-5658, www.batesfootwear.com
Footwear; Law Enforcement

Battenfeld Technologies, Inc., 5885 W. Van Horn Tavern Rd., Columbia, MO 65203, P: 877-509-9160, F: 573-446-6606, www.battenfeldtechnologies.com
Firearms Maintenance Equipment; Gun Grips & Stocks; Gun Parts/Gunsmithing; Hearing Protection; Recoil Protection Devices & Services; Reloading; Shooting Range Equipment; Targets

Battle Lake Outdoors, 203 W. Main, P.O. Box 548, Clarissa, MN 56440, P: 800-243-0465, F: 218-756-2426, www.battlelakeoutdoors.com
Archery; Backpacking; Bags & Equipment Cases; Black Powder Accessories; Camping; Gun Cases; Hunting Accessories; Law Enforcement

Batz Corp., 1524 Highway 291 North, P.O. Box 130, Prattsville, AR 72129, P: 800-637-7627, F: 870-699-4420, www.batzusa.com
Backpacking; Camping; Custom Manufacturing; Hunting Accessories; Knives/Knife Cases; Lighting Products; Pet Supplies; Retail Packaging

Bayco Products, Inc., 640 S. Sanden Blvd., Wylie, TX 75098, P: 800-233-2155, F: 469-326-9401, www.baycoproducts.com

Beamshot-Quarton USA, Inc., 5805 Callaghan Rd., Suite 102, San Antonio, TX 78228, P: 800-520-8435, F: 210-735-1326, www.beamshot.com
Airguns; Archery; Crossbows & Accessories; Hunting Accessories; Law Enforcement; Lighting Products; Paintball Accessories; Scopes, Sights & Accessories

Bear & Son Cutlery, Inc., 1111 Bear Blvd. SW, Jacksonville, AL 36265, P: 800-844-3034, F: 256-435-9348, www.bearandsoncutlery.com
Cutlery; Hunting Accessories; Knives/Knife Cases

Bear Valley Outfitters, P.O. Box 2294, Swan River, Manitoba R0L-1Z0 CANADA, P: 204-238-4342, F: 204-238-4342, www.bearvalleyoutfitters.com

Beeman Precision Airguns, 5454 Argosy Ave., Huntington Beach, CA 92649, P: 714-890-4800, F: 714-890-4808, www.beeman.com
Airguns; Ammunition; Gun Cases; Holsters; Lubricants; Scopes, Sights & Accessories; Targets

Beijing Defense Co., Ltd., 18 B, Unit One, No. 1 Building, Linghangguoji, Guangqumen Nanxiao St., Chongwen District, Beijing,

100061, CHINA, P: 011 861067153626, F: 011 861067152121, www.tacticalgear.com
Backpacking; Bags & Equipment Cases; Gun Cases; Holsters; Training & Safety Equipment

Bell and Carlson, Inc., 101 Allen Rd., Dodge City, KS 67801, P: 620-225-6688, F: 620-225-9095, www.bellandcarlson.com
Camouflage; Custom Manufacturing; Gun Grips & Stocks; Gun Parts/Gunsmithing; Hunting Accessories; Shooting Range Equipment

Bell-Ranger Outdoor Apparel, 1538 Crescent Dr., P.O. Box 14307, Augusta, GA, 30909, P: 800-241-7618, F: 706-738-3608, www.bellranger.com
Camouflage; Men & Women's Clothing; Hunting Accessories

Benchmade Knife Company, Inc., 300 Beavercreek Rd., Oregon City, OR 97045, P: 800-800-7427, F: 503-655-7922, www.benchmade.com
Knives/Knife Cases; Men's Clothing

Benelli Armi S.p.A./Benelli USA, 17603 Indian Head Hwy., Accokeek, MD 20607, P: 301-283-6981, F: 301-283-6986, www.benelli.it, www.benelliusa.com
Firearms

Beretta/Law Enforcement and Defense, 17601 Beretta Dr., Accokeek, MD 20607, P: 800-545-9567, F: 301-283-5111, www.berettale.com
Firearms; Gun Parts/Gunsmithing; Holsters; Law Enforcement; Lighting Products

Beretta U.S.A. Corp., 17601 Beretta Dr., Accokeek, MD 20607, P: 800-636-3420, F: 253-484-3775

Bergan, LLC, 27600 Hwy. 125, Monkey Island, OK 74331, P: 866-217-9606. F: 918-257-8950, www.berganexperience.com
Pet Products

Berger Bullets, 4275 N. Palm St., Fullerton, CA 92835, P: 714-447-5456, F: 714-447-5478, www.bergerbullets.com
Ammunition; Custom Manufacturing; Reloading

Berry's Manufacturing, Inc., 401 N. 3050 East, St. George, UT 84790, P: 800-269-7373, F: 435-634-1683, www.berrysmfg.com
Ammunition; Custom Manufacturing; Export/Import Specialists; Gun Cases; Reloading; Wholesaler/Distributor

Beta Company, The, 2137B Flintstone Dr., Tucker, GA 30084, P: 800-669-2382, F: 770-270-0599, www.betaco.com
Law Enforcement; Magazines, Cartridge

Beyond Clothing/Beyond Tactical, 1025 Conger St., Suite 8, Eugene, OR 97402, P: 800-775-2279, F: 703-997-6581, www.beyondtactical.com
Backpacking; Camouflage; Men & Women's Clothing; Custom Manufacturing; Law Enforcement

BFAST, LLC, 10 Roff Ave., Palasades Park, NJ 07650, P: 973-706-8210, F: 201-943-3546, www.firearmsafetynet.com
Law Enforcement; Shooting Range Equipment; Sports Accessories; Training & Safety Equipment

Bianchi International, 3120 E. Mission Blvd. Ontario, CA 91761, P: 800-347-1200, F: 800-366-1669, www.bianchi-intl.com
Backpacking; Bags & Equipment Cases; Gun Cases; Holsters; Hunting Accessories; Knives/Knife Cases; Leathergoods; Sports Accessories

Big Game Treestands, 1820 N. Redding Ave., P.O. Box 382, Windom, MN 56101, P: 800-268-5077, F: 507-831-4350, www.biggametreestands.com
Blinds; Hunting Accessories; Shooting Range Equipment; Treestands

Big Sky Carvers/Montana Silversmiths, 308 E. Main St., P.O. Box 507, Manhattan, MT 59741, P: 406-284-3193, F: 406-284-4028, www.bigskycarvers.com
Decoys; Home Furnishings; Lighting Products; Outdoor Art, Jewelry, Sculpture; Watches; Wholesaler/Distributor

Big Sky Racks, Inc., 25A Shawnee Way, Bozeman, MT 58715, P: 800-805-8716, F: 406-585-7378, www.bigskyracks.com
Gun Cabinets, Racks, Safes; Gun Locks; Hunting Accessories

BigFoot Bag/PortaQuip, 1215 S. Grant Ave., Loveland, CO 80537, P: 877-883-0200, F: 970-663-5415, www.bigfootbag.com
Bags & Equipment Cases; Camping; Hunting Accessories; Law Enforcement; Paintball Accessories; Sports Accessories; Tours & Travel

Bill's Sewing Machine Co., 301 Main Avenue East, Hildebran, NC 28637, P: 828-397-6941, F: 828-397-6193, www.billsewing.com

Bill Wiseman & Co., Inc., 18456 Hwy. 6 South, College Station, TX 77845, P: 979-690-3456, F: 979-690-0156, www.billwisemanandco.com
Firearms; Gun Barrels; Gun Parts/Gunsmithing

BioPlastics Co., 34655 Mills Rd., North Ridgeville, OH 44039, P: 440-327-0485, F: 440-327-3666, www.bioplastics.us

Birchwood Casey, 7900 Fuller Rd., Eden Prairie, MN 55344, P: 800-328-6156, F: 952-937-7979, www.birchwoodcasey.com
Black Powder Accessories; Camping; Firearms Maintenance Equipment; Gun Cases; Gun Parts/Gunsmithing; Hunting Accessories; Lubricants; Targets

Bison Designs, 735 S. Lincoln St., Longmont, CO 80501, P: 800-536-2476, F: 303-678-9988, www.bisondesigns.com
Backpacking; Men & Women's Clothing; Pet Supplies; Survival Kits/First Aid; Training & Safety Equipment; Wholesaler/Distributor

Black Hills Ammunition, P.O. Box 3090, Rapid City, SD 57709, P: 605-348-5150, F: 605-348-9827, www.black-hills.com
Ammunition

Black Hills Shooters Supply, Inc., 2875 Creek Dr., Rapid City, SD 57703, P: 800-289-2506, F: 800-289-4570, www.bhshooters.com
Reloading; Wholesaler/Distributor

Black Powder Products Group, 5988 Peachtree Corners East, Norcross, GA 30071, P: 800-320-8767, F: 770-242-8546, www.bpiguns.com
Black Powder Accessories; Firearms; Firearms Maintenance Equipment; Hunting Accessories; Scopes, Sights & Accessories

BlackHawk Products Group, 6160 Commander Pkwy., Norfolk, VA 23502, P: 800-694-5263, F: 757-436-3088, www.blackhawk.com
Bags & Equipment Cases; Men's Clothing; Gloves, Mitts, Hats; Holsters; Hunting Accessories; Knives/Knife Cases; Law Enforcement; Recoil Protection Devices & Services

Blackheart International, LLC, RR3, Box 115, Philippi, WV 26416, P: 877-244-8166, F: 304-457-1281, www.bhigear.com

Ammunition; Gun Parts/Gunsmithing; Holsters; Law Enforcement; Magazines, Cartridge; Scopes, Sights & Accessories; Survival Kits/First Aid; Training & Safety Equipment

Blackwater, P.O. Box 1029, Moyock, NC 27958, P: 252-435-2488, F: 252-435-6388, www.blackwaterusa.com
Bags & Equipment Cases; Men's Clothing; Custom Manufacturing; Gun Cases; Holsters; Law Enforcement; Targets; Training & Safety Equipment

Blade-Tech Industries, 2506 104th St. Court S, Suite A, Lakewood, WA 98499, P: 253-581-4347, F: 253-589-0282, www.blade-tech.com
Bags & Equipment Cases; Custom Manufacturing; Cutlery; Holsters; Hunting Accessories; Knives/Knife Cases; Law Enforcement; Sports Accessories

Blaser Jagdwaffen GmBH, Ziegelstadel 1, Isny, 88316, GERMANY, P: 011 4907562702348, F: 011 4907562702343, www.blaser.de
Firearms; Gun Barrels; Gun Cases; Gun Grips & Stocks; Hunting Accessories

Blauer Manufacturing Co. 20 Aberdeen St., Boston, MA 02215, P: 800-225-6715, www.blauer.com
Law Enforcement; Men & Women's Clothing

Blue Book Publications, Inc., 8009 34th Ave. S, Suite 175, Minneapolis, MN 55425, P: 800 877 4867, F: 062 863 1486, www.bluebookinc.com
Books/Industry Publications; Computer Software

Blue Force Gear, Inc., P.O. Box 853, Pooler, GA 31322, P: 877-430-2583, F: 912-964-7701, www.blueforcegear.com
Bags & Equipment Cases; Hunting Accessories; Law Enforcement; Scopes, Sights & Accessories; Sports Accessories

Blue Ridge Knives, 166 Adwolfe Rd., Marion, VA 24354, P: 276-783-6143, F: 276-783-9298, www.blueridgeknives.com
Binoculars; Cutlery; Export/Import Specialists; Knives/Knife Cases; Lighting Products; Scopes, Sights & Accessories; Sharpeners; Wholesaler/Distributor

Blue Stone Safety Products Co., Inc., 2950 W. 63rd St., Chicago, IL 60629, P: 773-776-9472, F: 773-776-9472, www.wolverineholsters.com
Holsters; Law Enforcement

Bluegrass Armory, 145 Orchard St., Richmond, KY 40475, P: 859-625-0874, F: 859-625-0874, www.bluegrassarmory.com
Firearms

Bluestar USA, Inc., 111 Commerce Center Drive, Suite 303, P.O. Box 2903, Huntersville, NC 28078, P: 877-948-7827, F: 704-875-6714, www.bluestar-hunting.com
Archery; Crossbows & Accessories; Hunting Accessories; Law Enforcement; Training & Safety Equipment; Wholesaler/Distributor

BlueWater Ropes/Yates Gear, Inc., 2608 Hartnell Ave., Suite 6, Redding, CA 96002, P: 800-YATES-16, F: 530-222-4640, www.yatesgear.com
Law Enforcement; Training & Safety Equipment; Wholesaler/Distributor

Bobster Eyewear, 12220 Parkway Centre Dr., Suite B, Poway, CA 92064, P: 800-603-2662, F: 858-715-0066, www.bobster.com
Eyewear; Hunting Accessories; Law Enforcement; Shooting Range Equipment; Sports Accessories; Training & Safety Equipment

Body Specs Sunglasses & Goggles, 22846 Industrial Place, Grass Valley, CA 95949, P: 800-824-5907, F: 530-268-1751, www.bodyspecs.com
Eyewear; Law Enforcement; Shooting Range Equipment; Training & Safety Equipment

Bogs Footwear/The Combs Co., 16 Oakway Center, Eugene, OR 97401, P: 800-485-2070, F: 541-484-1345, www.bogsfootwear.com or www.raftersfootwear.com
Footwear

Boker USA, Inc., 1550 Balsam St., Lakewood, CO 80214, P: 800-992-6537, F: 303-462-0668, www.bokerusa.com
Cutlery; Knives/Knife Cases

Border Crossing Scents, 8399 Bristol Rd., Davison, MI 48423, P: 888-653-2759, F: 810-653-2809, www.bordercrossingscents.com
Scents & Lures

Boss Buck, Inc., 210 S. Hwy. 175, Seagoville, TX 75159, P: 972-287-1216, F: 972-287-1892, www.bossbuck.com
Blinds; Feeder Equipment; Hunting Accessories; Scents & Lures; Treestands

Boston Leather, Inc., 1801 Eastwood Dr., P.O. Box 1213, Sterling, IL 61081, P: 800-733-1492, F: 800-856-1650, www.bostonleather.com
Bags & Equipment Cases; Custom Manufacturing; Gun Cases; Holsters; Knives/Knife Cases; Law Enforcement; Leathergoods; Pet Supplies

Boyds' Gunstock Industries, Inc., 25376 403rd Ave., Mitchell, SD 57301, P: 605-996-5011, F: 605-996-9878, www.boydsgunstocks.com
Custom Manufacturing; Firearms Maintentance Equipment; Gun Grips & Stocks; Gun Parts/Gunsmithing; Hunting Accessories; Shooting Range Equipment

Boyt Harness/Bob Allen Sportswear, 1 Boyt Dr., Osceola, IA 50213, P: 800-685-7020, www.boytharness.com
Gun Cases; Hunting Accessories; Law Enforcement; Men & Women's Clothing; Pet Supplies; Shooting Accessories

BraeVal, 23 E. Main St., Torrington, CT 06790, P: 860-482-7260, F: 860-482-7247, www.braeval.net
Men's Clothing

Brass Magnet, 5910 S. University Blvd., Suite C 18-330, Greenwood Village, CO 80121, P: 303-347-2636, F: 360-364-2636

Brazos Walking Sticks, 6408 Gholson Rd., Waco, TX 76705, P: 800-880-7119, F: 254-799-7199, www.brazos-walking-sticks.com
Canes; Walking Sticks

Breaching Technologies, Inc., P.O. Box 701468, San Antonio, TX 78270, P: 866-552-7427, F: 210-590-5193, www.breachingtechnologies.com
Law Enforcement; Training & Safety Equipment

Break-Free, 13386 International Parkway, Jacksonville, FL 32218, P: 800-433-2909, F: 800-588-0339, www.break-free.com
Law Enforcement; Lubricants

Brenneke™ of America, L.P., P.O. Box 1481, Clinton, IA 52733, P: 800-753-9733, F: 563-244-7421, www.brennekeusa.com
Ammunition

Brenzovich Firearms & Training Center/dba BFTC, 22301 Texas 20, Fort Hancock, TX 79839, P: 877-585-3775, F: 915-764-2030, www.brenzovich.com

Airguns; Ammunition; Archery; Black Powder Accessories; Export/Import Specialists; Firearms; Training & Safety Equipment; Wholesaler/Distributor

Brigade Quartermasters, Ltd., 1025 Cobb International Dr., Kennesaw, GA 30152, P: 770-428-1248, F: 720-426-7211

Briley Manufacturing, Inc., 1230 Lumpkin Rd., Houston, TX 77043, P: 800-331-5718, F: 713-932-1043
Chokes, Gun Accessories, Gunsmithing

Brite-Strike Technologies, 26 Wapping Rd., Jones River Industrial Park, Kingston, MA 02364, P: 781-585-5509, F: 781-585-5332, www.brite-strike.com
Law Enforcement; Lighting Products

Broco, Inc., 10868 Bell Ct., Rancho Cucamonga, CA 91730, P: 800-845-7259, F: 800-845-7259, www.brocoinc.com
Law Enforcement

Brookwood/Fine Uniform Co., 1125 E. Broadway, Suite 51, Glendale, CA 91205, P: 626-443-3736, F: 626-444-1551, www.brookwoodbags.com
Archery; Backpacking; Bags & Equipment Cases; Camping; Gun Cases; Hunting Accessories; Knives/Knife Cases; Shooting Range Equipment

Brookwood Companies, Inc., 25 W. 45th St., 11th Floor, New York, NY 10036, P: 800-426-5468, F: 646-472-0294, www.brookwoodcos.com

Brownells/Brownells MIL/LE Supply Group, 200 S. Front St., Montezuma, IA 50171, P: 800-741-0015, F: 800-264-3068, www.brownells.com
Export/Import Specialists; Firearms Maintenance Equipment; Gun Grips & Stocks; Gun Parts/Gunsmithing; Lubricants; Magazines, Cartridge; Scopes, Sights & Accessories; Wholesaler/Distributor

Browning, 1 Browning Place, Morgan, UT 84050, P: 801-876-2711, F: 801-876-3331, www.browning.com

Browning Archery, 2727 N. Fairview Ave., Tucson, AZ 85705, P: 520-838-2000, F: 520-838-2019, www.browning-archery.com
Archery

Browning Footwear, 107 Highland St., Martinsburg, PA 16662, P: 800-441-4319, F: 814-793-9272, www.browningfootwear.com
Footwear

Browning Hosiery/Carolina Hosiery, 2316 Tucker St., Burlington, NC 27215, P: 336-226-5581, F: 336-226-9721, www.browninghosiery.com
Men & Women's Clothing, Footwear

Browning Off Road/Polaris Industries, 2100 Hwy. 55, Medina, MN 55340, P: 763-542-0500, F: 763-542-2317, www.browningoffroad.com
Vehicles, Utility & Rec

Browning Outdoor Health and Safety Products, 1 Pharmacal Way, Jackson, WI 53037, P: 800-558-6614, F: 262-677-9006, www.browningsupplies.com
Survival Kits/First Aid

Browning Signature Automotive/Signature Products Group, 2550 S. Decker Lake Blvd. Suite 1, Salt Lake City, UT 84119, P: 801-237-0184, F: 801-237-0118, www.spgcompany.com
Emblems & Decals

Bruce Foods/Cajun Injector, Inc., P.O. Box 1030, New Iberia, LA 70562, P: 337-365-8101, F: 337-364-3742, www.brucefoods.com
Camping; Cooking Equipment/Accessories; Food; Online Services

Brunton, 2255 Brunton Ct., Riverton, WY 82501, P: 307-857-4700, F: 307-857-4703, www.brunton.com
Backpacking, Binoculars, Camping, Scopes

Buck Gardner Calls, LLC, 2129 Troyer Ave., Building 249, Suite 104, Memphis, TN 38114, P: 901-946-2996, F: 901-946-8747, www.buckgardner.com
Duck Calls & Accessories; Cooking

Buck Knives, Inc., 660 S. Lochsa St., Post Falls, ID 83854, P: 800-326-2825, www.buckknives.com
Backpacking; Camping; Custom Manufacturing; Cutlery; Hunting Accessories; Knives/Knife Cases; Law Enforcement; Sharpeners

Buckaroo-Stoo/BVM Productions, 2253 Kingsland Ave., Bronx, NY 10469, P: 877-286-4599, F: 718-652-3014, www.buckaroostoo.com
Scents & Lures

Buck Stop Lure Company, Inc., 3600 Grow Rd., P.O. Box 636, Stanton, MI 48888, P: 800-477-2368, F: 989-762-5124, www.buckstopscents.com
Archery; Books/Industry Publications; Hunting Accessories; Pet Supplies; Scents & Lures; Videos

Buck Wear, Inc., 2900 Cowan Ave., Baltimore, MD 21223, P: 800-813-7708, F: 410-646-7700, www.buckwear.com
Men & Women's Clothing

Buffalo Tools/Sportsman Series, 1220 N. Price Rd., St. Louis, MO 63132, P: 800-568-6657, F: 636-537-1055, www.buffalotools.com
Cooking Equipment/Accessories; Export/Import Specialists; Wholesaler/Distributor

Buffer Technologies, P.O. Box 105047, Jefferson City, MO 65110, P: 877-628-3337, F: 573-634-8522, www.buffertech.com
Gun Parts/Gunsmithing; Law Enforcement; Magazines, Cartridge; Recoil Protection Devices & Services

Bug Band, 127 Riverside Dr., Cartersville, GA 30120, P: 800-473-9467, F: 678-721-9279, www.bugband.com
Archery; Backpacking; Camping; Hunting Accessories; Law Enforcement; Outfitter; Survival Kits/First Aid; Wholesaler/Distributor

Bul, Ltd., 10 Rival St., Tel Aviv, 67778, ISRAEL, P: 011 97236392911, F: 011 97236874853, www.bultransmark.com
Firearms; Gun Barrels; Gun Parts/Gunsmithing; Law Enforcement

Bulldog Barrels, LLC, 106 Isabella St., 4 North Shore Center, Suite 110, Pittsburgh, PA 15212, P: 866-992-8553, F: 412-322-1912, www.bulldogbarrels.com
Firearms; Gun Barrels; Gun Parts/Gunsmithing

Bulldog Cases, 830 Beauregard Ave., Danville, VA 24541, P: 800-843-3483, F: 434-793-7504
Bags & Equipment Cases; Camouflage; Gun Cases; Holsters

Bulldog Equipment, 3706 SW 30th Ave., Hollywood, FL 33312, P: 954-581-5510 or 954-448-5221, F: 954-581-4221, www.bulldogequipment.us
Backpacking; Bags & Equipment Cases; Custom Manufacturing; Gloves, Mitts, Hats; Gun Cases; Law Enforcement; Outfitter

Bulls and Beavers, LLC, P.O. Box 2870, Sun Valley, ID 83353, P: 208-726-8217, www.bullsandbeavers.com

Burn Machine, LLC, The, 26305 Glendale, Suite 200, Redford, MI 48239, P: 800-380-6527, F: 313-794-4355, www.theburnmachine.com
Sports Accessories; Training & Safety Equipment; Wholesaler/Distributor

Burris Company, Inc., 331 E. 8th St., Greeley, CO 80631, P: 970-356-1670, F: 970-356-8702, www.burrisoptics.com
Binoculars; Scopes, Sights & Accessories; Targets

Bushido Tactical, LLC, P.O. Box 721289, Orlando, FL 32972, P: 407-454-4256, F: 407-286-4416, www.bushidotactical.com
Law Enforcement; Training

Bushnell Law Enforcement/Bushnell Outdoor Products, 9200 Cody St., Overland Park, KS 66214, P: 800-423-3537, F: 800-548-0446, www.unclemikesle.com
Binoculars; Firearms Maintenance Equipment; Gloves, Mitts, Hats; Gun Cases; Holsters; Law Enforcement; Lubricants; Scopes, Sights & Accessories

Business Control Systems Corp., 1173 Green St., Iselin, NJ 08830, P: 800-233-5876, F: 732-283-1192, www.businesscontrol.com
Archery; Computer Software; Firearms; Law Enforcement; Retailer Services; Shooting Range Equipment; Wholesaler/Distributor

Butler Creek Corp./Bushnell Outdoor Accessories, 9200 Cody St., Overland Park, KS 66214, P: 800-423-3537, F: 800-548-0446, www.butlercreek.com
Firearms Maintenance Equipment; Gun Barrels; Gun Grips & Stocks; Hunting Accessories; Leathergoods; Scopes, Sights & Accessories

C

CAM Commerce Solutions, 17075 Newhope St., Fountain Valley, CA 92708, 866-840-4443, F: 702-564-3206, www.camcommerce.com
Computer Software

CASL Industries/Tanglefree/Remington, P.O. Box 1280, Clayton, CA 94517, P: 877-685-5055, F: 925-685-6055, www.tanglefree.com or www.caslinindustries.com
Bags & Equipment Cases; Blinds; Camouflage; Decoys; Gun Cases; Hunting Accessories

CAS Hanwei, 650 Industrial Blvd., Sale Creek, TN 37373-9797, P: 800-635-9366, F: 423-332-7248, www.cashanwei.com
Custom Manufacturing; Cutlery; Knives/Knife Cases; Leathergoods; Wholesaler/Distributor

CCF Race Frames LLC, P.O. Box 29009, Richmond, VA 23242, P: 804-622-4277, F: 804-740-9599, www.ccfraceframes.com
Firearms; Firearms Maintenance Equipment; Gun Parts/Gunsmithing; Law Enforcement

CCI Ammunition/ATK Commercial Products, 2299 Snake River Ave., Lewiston, ID 83501, P: 800-256-8685, F: 208-798-3392, www.cci-ammunition.com
Ammunition

CGTech, 9000 Research Dr., Irvine, CA 92618, P: 949-753-1050, F: 949-753-1053, www.cgtech.com
Computer Software; Custom Manufacturing

CJ Weapons Accessories, 317 Danielle Ct., Jefferson City, MO 65109, P: 800-510-5919, F: 573-634-2355, www.cjweapons.com

Firearms Maintenance Equipment; Gun Parts/Gunsmithing; Hunting Accessories; Law Enforcement; Magazines, Cartridge; Shooting Range Equipment; Sports Accessories; Wholesaler/Distributor

CMMG, Inc., 620 County Rd. 118, P.O. Box 369, Fayette, MO 65248, P: 660-248-2293, F: 660-248-2290, www.cmmginc.com
Firearms; Law Enforcement; Magazines, Cartridge

CTI Industries Corp., 22160 N. Pepper Rd., Barrington, IL 60010, P: 866-382-1707, F: 800-333-1831, www.zipvac.com
Archery; Backpacking; Bags & Equipment Cases; Camping; Cooking Equipment/Accessories; Custom Manufacturing; Food; Hunting Accessories

CVA, 5988 Peachtree Corners East, Norcross, GA 30071, P: 800-320-8767, F: 770-242-8546
Black Powder Accessories; Firearms; Firearms Maintenance Equipment; Gun Barrels

CZ-USA/Dan Wesson, 3327 N. 7th St., Kansas city, KS 66115, P: 800-955-4486, F: 913-321-4901, www.cz-usa.com
Firearms

Cablz, 411 Meadowbrook Lane, Birmingham, AL 35213, P: 205-222-4477, F: 205-870-8847

Caesar Guerini USA, 700 Lake St., Cambridge, MD 21613, P: 866-901-1131, F: 410-901-1137, www.gueriniusa.com
Firearms

CALVI S.p.A., Via Iv Novembre, 2, Merate (LC), 23807, ITALY, P: 011 3903999851, F: 011 390399985240, www.calvi.it
Custom Manufacturing; Firearms; Gun Barrels; Gun Locks; Gun Parts/Gunsmithing

Camdex, Inc., 2330 Alger, Troy, MI 48083, P: 248-528-2300, F: 248-528-0989, www.camdexloader.com
Reloading

Camelbak Products, 2000 S. McDowell Blvd., Petaluma, CA 94954, P: 800-767-8725, F: 707-665-3844, www.camelbak.com
Backpacking; Bags & Equipment Cases; Gloves, Mitts, Hats; Holsters; Law Enforcement

Camerons Products/CM International, Inc., 2547 Durango Dr., P.O. Box 60220, Colorado Springs, CO 80960, P: 888-563-0227, F: 719-390-0946, www.cameronsproducts.com
Backpacking; Camping; Cooking Equipment/Accessories; Hunting Accessories; Retailer Services; Tours/Travel; Wholesaler/Distributor

Camfour, Inc., 65 Westfield Industrial Park Rd., Westfield, MA 01085, P: 800-FIREARM, F: 413-568-9663, www.camfour.com
Ammunition; Black Powder Accessories; Computer Software; Export/Import Specialists; Firearms; Hunting Accessories; Law Enforcement; Wholesaler/Distributor

Cammenga Corp., 100 Aniline Ave. N, Suite 258, Holland, MI 49424, P: 616-392-7999, F: 616-392-9432, www.cammenga.com
Magazines, Cartridge; Reloading; Training & Safety Equipment

Camo Unlimited, 1021 B Industrial Park Dr., Marietta, GA 30062, P: 866-448-CAMO, F: 770-420-2299, www.camounlimited.com
Blinds; Camouflage; Hunting Accessories; Paintball Accessories

C-More Systems, 7553 Gary Rd., P.O. Box 1750, Manassas, VA 20109, P: 888-265-8266, F: 703-361-5881, www.cmore.com

Airguns; Archery; Crossbows & Accessories; Custom Manufacturing; Firearms; Hunting Accessories; Law Enforcement; Scopes, Sights & Accessories; Shooting Range Equipment

CamoSpace.com, P.O. Box 125, Rhodesdale, MD 21659, P: 410-310-0380, F: 410-943-8849

Camouflage Face Paint, 2832 Southeast Loop 820, Fort Worth, TX 76140, P: 877-625-3879, F: 817-615-8670, www.camofacepaint.com
Archery; Camouflage; Custom Manufacturing; Export/Import Specialists; Hunting Accessories; Online Services; Paintball Accessories; Wholesaler/Distributor

Camowraps, 429 South St., Slidell, LA 70460, P: 866-CAMO-MAN, F: 985-661-1447, www.camowraps.com
Camouflage; Custom Manufacturing; Emblems & Decals; Printing Services

Camp Chef, 675 North 600 West, P.O. Box 4057, Logan, UT 84321, P: 800-783-8347, F: 435-752-1592, www.campchef.com
Cooking Equipment/Accessories

Camp Technologies, LLC/Div. DHS Technologies, LLC, 33 Kings Hwy., Orangeburg, NY 10962, P: 866-969-2400, F: 845-365-2114, www.camprtv.com
Backpacking; Camping; Hunting Accessories; Law Enforcement; Outfitter; Sports Accessories; Vehicles, Utility & Rec

CampCo/Smith & Wesson Watches HUMVEE/UZI, 4625 W. Jefferson Blvd., Los Angeles, CA 90016, P: 888-9-CAMPCO, F: 323-766-2424, www.campco.com
Backpacking; Binocular; Camping; Compasses; Knives/Knife Cases; Law Enforcement; Lighting Products; Wholesaler/Distributor

Canal Street Cutlery Co., 30 Canal St., Ellenville, NY 12428, P: 845-647-5900, F: 845-647-1456, www.canalstreetcutlery.com
Cutlery; Knives/Knife Cases

Cannon Safe, Inc., 216 S. 2nd Ave., Building 932, San Bernardino, CA 92408, P: 800-242-1055, F: 909-382-0707, www.cannonsafe.com
Gun Cabinets/Racks/Safes; Gun Locks

Careco Multimedia, Inc., 5717 Northwest Pkwy., Suite 104, San Antonio, TX 78249, P: 800-668-8081, F: 251-948-3011, www.americanaoutdoors.com, www.outdooraction.com, www.fishingandhuntingtexas.com
Online Services; Videos; Wholesaler/Distributor

Carl Zeiss Optronics GmbH, Gloelstr. 3-5, Wetzlar, 35576, GERMANY, P: 011 4964414040, F: 011 496441404510, www.zeiss.com/optronics
Law Enforcement; Scopes, Sights & Accessories; Shooting Range Equipment; Targets; Telescopes

Carl Zeiss Sports Optics/Zeiss, 13005 N. Kingston Ave., Chester, VA 23836, P: 800-441-3005, F: 804-530-8481, www.zeiss.com/sports
Binoculars; Scopes, Sights & Accessories

Carlson's Choke Tubes, 720 S. Second St., P.O. Box 162, Atwood, KS 67730, P: 785-626-3700, F: 785-626-3999, www.choketube.com
Custom Manufacturing; Firearms Maintenance Equipment; Game Calls; Gun Parts/Gunsmithing; Hunting Accessories; Scopes, Sights & Accessories; Shooting Range Equipment

Carson Optical, 35 Gilpin Ave., Hauppauge, NY 11788, P: 800-967-8427, F: 631-427-6749, www.carsonoptical.com
Binoculars; Export/Import Specialists; Scopes, Sights & Accessories; Telescopes

Cartuchos Saga, Pda. Caparrela s/n, Lleida, 25192, SPAIN, P: 011 34973275000, F: 011 34973275008
Ammunition

Case Cutlery (W.R. Case & Sons Cutlery Co.), Owens Way, Bradford, PA 16701, P: 800-523-6350, F: 814-358-1736, www.wrcase.com
Cutlery; Knives/Knife Cases; Sharpeners

Caspian Arms, Ltd., 75 Cal Foster Dr., Wolcott, VT 05680, P: 802-472-6454, F: 802-472-6709, www.caspianarms.com
Firearms; Gun Parts/Gunsmithing; Law Enforcement

Cass Creek International, LLC, 1881 Lyndon Blvd., Falconer, NY 14733, P: 800-778-0389, F: 716-665-6536, www.casscrock.com
Game Calls; Hunting Accessories

Cejay Engineering, LLC/InfraRed Combat Marking Beacons, 2129 Gen Booth Blvd., Suite 103-284, Virginia Beach, VA 23454, P: 603-880-8501, F: 603-880-8502, www.cejayeng.com
Lighting Products

Celestron, 2835 Columbia St., Torrance, CA 90503, P: 310-328-9560, F: 310-212-5835, www.celestron.com
Binoculars; Scopes, Sights & Accessories; Telescopes

Center Mass, Inc., 6845 Woonsocket, Canton, MI 48187, P: 800-794-1216, F: 734-416-0650, www.centermassinc.com
Bags & Equipment Cases; Emblems & Decals; Hunting Accessories; Law Enforcement; Men's Clothing; Shooting Range Equipment; Targets; Training & Safety Equipment

Century International Arms, Inc., 430 S. Congress Dr., Suite 1, DelRay Beach, FL 33445, P: 800-527-1252, F: 561-265-4520, www.centuryarms.com
Ammunition; Firearms; Firearms Maintenance Equipment; Gun Parts/Gunsmithing; Law Enforcement; Magazines, Cartridge; Scopes, Sights & Accessories; Wholesaler/Distributor

Cequre Composite Technologies, 5995 Shier-Rings Rd., Suite A, Dublin, OH 43016, P: 614-526-0095, F: 614-526-0098, www.wearmor.com
Custom Manufacturing; Law Enforcement; Shooting Range Equipment; Targets

Cerakote/NIC Industries, Inc., 7050 Sixth St., White City, OR 97503, P: 866-774-7628, F: 541-830-6518, www.nicindustries.com
Camouflage; Custom Manufacturing; Firearms; Firearms Maintenance Equipment; Knives/Knife Cases; Law Enforcement; Lubricants; Paintball Guns

Champion Traps and Targets/ATK Commercial Products, N5549 Cty. Trunk Z, Onalaska, WI 54650, P: 800-635-7656, F: 763-323-3890, www.championtargetr.com
Clay Targets; Hearing Protection; Shooting Range Equipment; Targets

Chapin International, P.O. Box 549, Batavia, NY 14020, P: 800-444-3140, F: 585-813-0118, www.chapinmfg.com
Feeder Equipment

Chapman Innovations, 343 W. 400 South, Salt Lake City, UT 84101, P: 801-415-0024, F: 801-415-2001, www.carbonx.com

MANUFACTURER'S AND PRODUCT DIRECTORY

Gloves, Mitts, Hats; Law Enforcement; Men & Women's Clothing

Charter Arms/MKS Supply, Inc., 8611A North Dixie Dr., Dayton, OH 45414, P: 866-769-4867, F: 937-454-0503, www. charterfirearms.com
Firearms

Cheddite France, 99 Route de Lyon, P.O. Box 112, Bourg-les-Valence, 26500, FRANCE, P: 011 33475564545, F: 011 33475563587, www.cheddite.com
Ammunition

Chengdu Lis Business, 4-3-9, 359 Shuhan Rd., Chengdu, SICH 610036, CHINA, P: 0110862887541867, F: 011 862887578686, www.lisoptics.com
Binoculars; Compasses; Cutlery; Lighting Products; Scopes, Sights & Accessories; Telescopes

CheyTac Associates, LLC, 363 Sunset Dr., Arco, ID 83213, P: 256-325-0622, F: 208-527-3328, www.cheytac.com
Ammunition; Computer Software; Custom Manufacturing; Firearms; Law Enforcement; Training & Safety Equipment

Chiappa Firearms-Armi Sport di Chiappa Silvia e C. SNC, Via Milano, 2, Azzano Mella (Bs), 25020, ITALY, P: 011 390309749065, F: 011 390309749232, www.chiappafirearms.com
Black Powder Accessories; Firearms

China Shenzhen Aimbond Enterprises Co., Ltd., 19D, Building No. 1, China Phoenix Building, No. 2008, Shennan Rd., Futian District, Shenzhen, Guangdong 518026, CHINA, P: 011 8675582522730812, F: 011 8675583760022, www.sino-optics.com
Binoculars; Eyewear; Firearms Maintenance Equipment; Hunting Accessories; Lighting Products; Scopes, Sights & Accessories; Telescopes

Chip McCormick Custom, LLC, 105 Sky King Dr., Spicewood, TX 78669, P: 800-328-2447, F: 830-693-4975, www.cmcmags.com
Gun Parts/Gunsmithing; Magazines, Cartridge

Choate Machine & Tool, 116 Lovers Lane, Bald Knob, AR 72010, P: 800-972-6390, F: 501-724-5873, www.riflestock.com
Gun Grips & Stocks; Law Enforcement

Chongqing Dontop Optics Co., Ltd., No. 5 Huangshan Ave. Middle Beibu New District, Chongqing, 401121, CHINA, P: 011 862386815057, F: 011 862386815100, www.dontop.com
Binoculars; Custom Manufacturing; Scopes, Sights & Accessories; Shooting Range Equipment; Telescopes

Chongqing Jizhou Enterprise Co., Ltd., Rm 8-1, Block A3, Jiazhou Garden, Chongqing, Yubei 401147, CHINA, P: 011 862367625115, F: 011 862367625121, www.cqjizhou.com
Binoculars; Compasses; Scopes, Sights & Accessories; Telescopes

Chonwoo Corp./Chonwoo Case & Cover (Tianjin) Co., Ltd., 4-6, SamJun-Dong Songpa-gu, Seoul, 138-837, SOUTH KOREA, P: 011 8224205094, F: 011 8224236154, www.chonwoo.co.kr
Backpacking; Bags & Equipment Cases; Gun Cases; Holsters; Hunting Accessories; Knives/Knife Cases; Leathergoods

Chris Reeve Knives, 2949 S. Victory View Way, Boise, ID 83709, P: 208-375-0367, F: 208-375-0368, www.chrisreeve.com
Backpacking; Camping; Cutlery; Hunting Accessories; Knives/Knife Cases; Law Enforcement; Sports Accessories

Christensen Arms, 192 E. 100 North, Fayette, UT 84630, P: 888-517-8855, F: 435-528-5773, www.christensenarms.com
Custom Manufacturing; Firearms; Gun Barrels

Christie & Christie Enterprises, Inc., 404 Bolivia Blvd., Bradenton, FL 34207, P: 440-413-0031, F: 440-428-5551
Gun Grips & Stocks; Gun Parts/Gunsmithing; Magazines, Cartridge; Scopes, Sights & Accessories; Wholesaler/Distributor

Cimarron Firearms Co., 105 Winding Oaks Rd., P.O. Box 906, Fredericksburg, TX 78624, P: 830-997-9090, F: 830-997-0802, www. cimarron-firearms.com
Black Powder Accessories; Firearms; Gun Cases; Gun Grips & Stocks; Gun Parts/ Gunsmithing; Holsters; Leathergoods; Wholesaler/Distributor

Citadel (Cambodia) Pt., Ltd., Nr 5 Str 285 Tuol Kork, Phnom Penh, BP 440, CAMBODIA, P: 011 85512802676, F: 011 85523880015, www.citadel.com.kh
Cutlery

Clark Textile Co./ASF Group, 624 S. Grand Ave., San Pedro, CA 90731, P: 310-831-2334, F: 310-831-2335, www.asfgroup.com
Camouflage; Printing Services

Classic Accessories, 22640 68th Ave. S, Kent, WA 98032, P: 800-854-2315, F: 253-395-3991, www.classicaccessories.com
Bags & Equipment Cases; Camouflage; Gun Cases; Hunting Accessories; Pet Supplies; Wholesaler/Distributor

Classic Old West Styles, 1712 Texas Ave., El Paso, TX 79901, P: 800-595-COWS, F: 915-587-0616, www.cows.com
Custom Manufacturing; Holsters; Hunting Accessories; Leathergoods; Men's Clothing; Outfitter; Sports Accessories; Wholesaler/ Distributor

Claude Dozorme Cutlery, Z.A. de Racine-B.P. 19, La Monnerie, 63650, FRANCE, P: 011 33473514106, F: 011 33473514851, www. dozorme-claude.fr
Cutlery

Claybuster Wads/Harvester Muzzleloading, 635 Bob Posey St., Henderson, KY 42420, P: 800-922-6287, F: 270-827-4972, www. claybusterwads.com
Black Powder Accessories; Reloading

Clever SRL, Via A. Da Legnago, 9/A, I-37141 Ponteflorio, Verona, ITALY, P: 011 390458840770, F: 011 390458840380, www. clevervr.com
Ammunition

Cliff Weil, Inc., 8043 Industrial Park Rd., Mechanicsville, VA 23116, P: 800-446-9345, F: 804-746-2595, www.cliffweil.com
Eyewear

Club Red, Inc./Bone Collector by Michael Waddell, 4645 Church Rd., Cumming, GA 30028, P: 888-428-1630, F: 678-947-1445, www.clubredinc.com
Emblems & Decals; Men & Women's Clothing

Clymer Precision, 1605 W. Hamlin Rd., Rochester Hills, MI 48309, P: 877-REAMERS, F: 248-853-1530, www. clymertool.com
Black Powder Accessories; Books/Industry Publications; Custom Manufacturing; Firearms Maintenance Equipment; Gun Parts/ Gunsmithing; Law Enforcement; Reloading

CMere Deer®, 205 Fair Ave., P.O. Box 1336, Winnsboro, LA, 71295, P: 866-644-8600, F: 318-435-3885, www.cmeredeer.com

Scents & Lures

Coastal Boot Co., Inc. 2821 Center Port Circle, Pompano Beach, FL 33064, P: 954-782-3244, F: 954-782-4342, www.coastalboot. com
Footwear

Coast Products/LED Lenser, 8033 NE Holman St., Portland, OR 97218, P: 800-426-5858, F: 503-234-4422, www.coastportland.com
Camping; Compasses; Cutlery; Knives/Knife Cases; Law Enforcement; Lighting Products; Sharpeners

Cobra Enterprises of Utah, Inc., 1960 S. Milestone Dr., Suite F, Salt Lake City, UT 84104, P: 801-908-8300, F: 801-908-8301, www.cobrapistols.net
Firearms

Codet Newport Corp./Big Bill Work Wear, 924 Crawford Rd., Newport, VT 05855, P: 800-992-6338, F: 802-334-8268, www.bigbill. com
Backpacking; Bags & Equipment Cases; Camouflage; Camping; Footwear; Gloves, Mitts, Hats; Men's Clothing

Cold Steel Inc., 3036 Seaborg Ave., Suite A, Ventura, CA 93003, P: 800-255-4716, F: 805-642-9727, www.coldsteel.com
Cutlery; Knives/Knife Cases; Law Enforcement; Sports Accessories; Videos

Collector's Armoury, Ltd., P.O. Box 1050, Lorton, VA 22199, P: 800-336-4572, F: 703-493-9424, www.collectorsarmoury.com
Black Powder Accessories; Books/Industry Publications; Cutlery; Firearms; Holsters; Home Furnishings; Training & Safety Equipment; Wholesaler/Distributor

Colonial Arms, Inc. 1504 Hwy. 31 S, P.O. Box 250, Bay Minette, AL 36507, P: 800-949-8088, F: 251-580-5006, www.colonialarms. com
Firearms; Firearms Maintenance Equipment; Gun Barrels; Gun Parts/Gunsmithing; Hunting Accessories; Lubricants; Recoil Protection Devices & Services; Wholesaler/Distributor

Colt's Manufacturing Co., LLC, P.O. Box 1868, Hartford, CT 06144, P: 800-962-COLT, F: 860-244-1449, www.coltsmfg.com
Custom Manufacturing; Firearms; Gun Parts/ Gunsmithing; Law Enforcement

Columbia River Knife and Tool, 18348 SW 126th Pl., Tualatin, OR 97062, P: 800-891-3100, F: 503-682-9680, www.crkt.com
Knives/Knife Cases; Sharpeners

Columbia Sportswear Co., 14375 NW Science Park Dr., Portland, OR 97229, P: 800-547-8066, F: 503-985-5800, www.columbia.com
Bags & Equipment Cases; Binoculars; Footwear; Gloves, Mitts, Hats; Men & Women's Clothing; Pet Supplies; Scopes, Sights & Accessories

Combined Tactical Systems, 388 Kinsman Rd., P.O. Box 506, Jamestown, PA 16134, P: 724-932-2177, F: 724-932-2166, www.less-lethal.com
Law Enforcement

Compass Industries, Inc., 104 E. 25th St., New York, NW 10010, P: 800-221-9904, F: 212-353-0826, www.compassindustries.com
Binoculars; Camping; Compasses; Cutlery; Export/Import Specialists; Eyewear; Hunting Accessories; Wholesaler/Distributor

Competition Electronics, 3469 Precision Dr., Rockford, IL 61109, P: 815-874-8001, F: 815-874-8181, www.competitionelectronics. com

Firearms Maintenance Equipment; Reloading; Shooting Range Equipment; Training & Safety Equipment

Condor Outdoor Products, 1866 Business Center Dr., Duarte, CA 91010, P: 800-552-2554, F: 626-303-3383, www.condoroutdoor.com
Backpacking; Bags & Equipment Cases; Camouflage; Footwear; Gun Cases; Holsters; Wholesaler/Distributor

Condor Tool & Knife, Inc., 6309 Marina Dr., Orlando, FL 32819, P: 407-876-0886, F: 407-876-0994, www.condortk.com
Archery; Camping; Custom Manufacturing; Cutlery; Gun Cases; Hunting Accessories; Knives/Knife Cases; Leathergoods

Connecticut Shotgun Mfg. Co., 100 Burritt St., New Britain, CT 06053, P: 800-515-4867, F: 860-832-8707, www.connecticutshotgun.com
Firearms; Firearms Maintenance Equipment; Gun Cabinets/Racks/Safes; Gun Cases; Gun Parts/Gunsmithing; Hunting Accessories; Knives/Knife Cases; Scopes, Sights & Accessories

Consorzio Armaioli Bresciani, Via Matteotti, 325, Gardone V.T., Brescia 25063, ITALY, P: 011 39030821752, F: 011 39030831425, www.armaiolibresciani.org
Firearms; Gun Parts/Gunsmithing; Videos

Consorzio Cortellinai Maniago SRL, Via Della Repubblica, 21, Maniago, PN 33085, ITALY, P: 011 39042771185, F: 011 390427700440, www.consorziocoltellinai.it
Camping; Cutlery; Hunting Accessories; Knives/Knife Cases; Law Enforcement

Convert-A-Ball Distributing, Inc., 955 Ball St., P.O. Box 199, Sidney, NE 69162, P: 800-543-1732, F: 308-254-7194, www.convert-a-ball.net
Camping; Vehicles, Utility & Rec

Cooper Firearms of MT, Inc./Cooper Arms, 4004 Hwy. 93 North, P.O. Box 114, Stevensville, MT 59870, P: 406-777-0373, F: 406-777-5228, www.cooperfirearms.com
Custom Manufacturing; Firearms

CopShoes.com/MetBoots.com, 6655 Poss Rd., San Antonio, TX 78238, P: 866-280-0400, F: 210-647-1401, www.copshoes.com
Footwear; Hunting Accessories; Law Enforcement

Cor-Bon/Glaser/Div. Dakota Ammo Inc., 1311 Industry Rd., P.O. Box 369, Sturgis, SD 57785, P: 605-347-4544, F: 605-347-5055, www.corbon.com
Ammunition

Cornell Hunting Products, 114 Woodside Dr., Honea Path, SC 29654, P: 864-369-9587, F: 864-369-9587, www.cornellhuntinproducts.com
Backpacking; Game Calls; Hunting Accessories; Wholesaler/Distributor

Corsivia, Poligono El Campillo, Calle Alemania, 59-61, Zuera, (Zaragoza) 50800, SPAIN, P: 011 34976680075, F: 011 34976680124, www.corsivia.com
Clay Targets

Counter Assault Pepper Sprays/Bear Deterrent, Law Enforcement & Personal Defense, 120 Industrial Court, Kalispell, MT 59901, P: 800-695-3394. F: 406-257-6674, www.counterassault.com
Archery; Backpacking; Camping; Hunting Accessories; Law Enforcement; Sports Accessories; Survival Kits/First Aid; Training & Safety Equipment

Crackshot Corp., 2623 E 36th St. N, Tulsa, OK 74110, P: 800-667-1753, F: 918-838-1271, www.crackshotcorp.com
Archery; Backpacking; Camping; Footwear; Hunting Accessories; Men & Women's Clothing; Training & Safety Equipment

Creative Castings/Les Douglas, 12789 Olympic View Rd. NW, Silverdale, WA 98383, P: 800-580-6516, F: 800-580-0495, www.wildlifepins.com
Custom Manufacturing; Emblems & Decals; Outdoor Art, Jewelry, Sculpture; Pet Supplies; Retailer Services; Watches; Wholesaler/Distributor

Creative Pet Products, P.O. Box 39, Spring Valley, WI 54767, P: 888-436-4566, F: 877-269-6911, www.petfirstaidkits.com
Gloves, Mitts, Hats; Pet Supplies; Survival Kits/First Aid; Training & Safety Equipment

Crest Ultrasonics Corp., P.O. Box 7266, Trenton, NJ 08628, P: 800-273-7822, F: 877-254-7939, www.crest-ultrasonics.com
Custom Manufacturing; Firearms Maintenance Equipment; Gun Parts/Gunsmithing; Law Enforcement; Lubricants; Shooting Range Equipment; Wholesaler/Distributor

Crimson Trace Holdings, LLC/Lasergrips, 9780 SW Freeman Dr., Wilsonville, OR 97070, P: 800-442-2406, F: 503-783-5334, www.crimsontrace.com
Firearms; Gun Grips & Stocks; Hunting Accessories; Law Enforcement; Scopes, Sights & Accessories; Training & Safety Equipment

Critter Cribs, P.O. Box 48545, Fort Worth, TX 76148, P: 877-611-2742, F: 866-351-3291, www.crittercribs.com
Camouflage; Hunting Accessories; Law Enforcement; Pet Supplies

Crooked Horn Outfitters, 26315 Trotter Dr., Tehachapi, CA 93561, P: 877-722-5872, F: 661-822-9100, www.crookedhorn.com
Archery; Bags & Equipment Cases; Binoculars; Hunting Accessories

Crosman Corp., Inc., Routes 5 and 20, East Bloomfield, NY 14443, P: 800-724-7486, F: 585-657-5405, www.crosman.com
Airguns; Airsoft; Ammunition; Archery; Crossbows & Accessories; Scopes, Sights & Accessories; Shooting Range Equipment; Targets

Crye Precision, LLC, 63 Flushing Ave., Suite 252, Brooklyn, NY 11205, P: 718-246-3838, F: 718-246-3833, www.cryeprecision.com
Bags & Equipment Cases; Camouflage; Custom Manufacturing; Law Enforcement; Men's Clothing

Cuppa, 3131 Morris St. N, St. Petersburg, FL 33713, P: 800-551-6541, F: 727-820-9212, www.cuppa.net
Custom Manufacturing; Emblems & Decals; Law Enforcement; Outdoor Art, Jewelry, Sculpture; Retailer Services

Custom Leather, 460 Bingemans Centre Dr., Kitchener, Ontario N2B 3X9, CANADA, P: 800-265-4504, F: 519-741-2072, www.customleather.com
Custom Manufacturing; Gun Cases; Hunting Accessories; Leathergoods

Cutting Edge Tactical, 166 Mariners Way, Moyock, NC 27958, P: 800-716-9425, F: 252-435-2284, www.cuttingedgetactical.com
Bags & Equipment Cases; Binoculars; Eyewear; Footwear; Gun Grips & Stocks; Law Enforcement; Lighting Products; Training & Safety Equipment

Cybrics, Ltd., No 68, Xing Yun Rd., Jin San Industrial Area, Yiwu, Zhejiang 322011, CHINA, P: 011 8657985556142, F: 011 8657985556210, www.cybrics.eu
Bags & Equipment Cases; Camouflage; Gloves, Mitts, Hats; Men & Women's Clothing

Cygnus Law Enforcement Group, 1233 Janesville Ave., Fort Atkinson, WI 53538, P: 800-547-7377, F: 303-322-0627, www.officer.com
Law Enforcement

Cylinder & Slide, Inc., 245 E. 4th St., Fremont, NE 68025, P: 800-448-1713, F: 402-721-0263, www.cylinder-slide.com
Firearms; Gun Barrels; Gun Grips & Stocks; Gun Parts/Gunsmithing; Magazines, Cartridge; Scopes, Sights & Accessories; Wholesaler/Distributor

D

DAC Technologies/GunMaster, 12120 Colonel Glenn Rd., Suite 6200, Little Rock, AR 72210, P: 800-920-0098, F: 501-661-9108, www.dactec.com
Black Powder Accessories; Camping; Cooking Equipment/Accessories; Firearms Maintenance Equipment; Gun Cabinets/Racks/Safes; Gun Locks; Hunting Accessories; Wholesaler/Distributor

DMT-Diamond Machine Technology, 84 Hayes Memorial Dr., Marlborough, MA 01752, P: 800-666-4368, F: 508-485-3924, www.dmtsharp.com
Archery; Cooking Equipment/Accessories; Cutlery; Hunting Accessories; Knives/Knife Cases; Sharpeners; Sports Accessories; Taxidermy

D & K Mfg., Co., Inc., 5180 US Hwy. 380, Bridgeport, TX 76426, P: 800-553-1028, F: 940-683-0248, www.d-k.net
Bags & Equipment Cases; Custom Manufacturing; Emblems & Decals; Law Enforcement; Leathergoods

D.S.A., Inc., 27 W. 990 Industrial Ave. (60010), P.O. Box 370, Lake Barrington, IL 60011, P: 847-277-7258, F: 847-277-7263, www.dsarms.com
Ammunition; Books/Industry Publications; Firearms; Gun Grips & Stocks; Gun Parts/Gunsmithing; Law Enforcement; Magazines, Cartridge; Scopes, Sights & Accessories

Daisy Manufacturing Co./Daisy Outdoors Products, 400 W. Stribling Dr., P.O. Box 220, Rogers, AR 72756, P: 800-643-3458, F: 479-636-0573, www.daisy.com
Airguns; Airsoft; Ammunition; Clay Targets; Eyewear; Scopes, Sights & Accessories; Targets; Training & Safety Equipment

Dakota Arms, Inc., 1310 Industry Rd., Sturgis, SD 57785, P: 605-347-4686, F: 605-347-4459, www.dakotaarms.com
Ammunition; Custom Manufacturing; Export/Import Specialists; Firearms; Gun Cases; Gun Grips & Stocks; Gun Parts/Gunsmithing; Reloading

Damascus Protective Gear, P.O. Box 543, Rutland, VT, 05702, P: 800-305-2417, F: 805-639-0610, www.damascusgear.com
Archery; Custom Manufacturing; Gloves, Mitts, Hats; Law Enforcement; Leathergoods

Danalco, Inc., 1020 Hamilton Rd., Suite G, Duarte, CA 91010, P: 800-868-2629, F: 800-216-9938, www.danalco.com

MANUFACTURER'S AND PRODUCT DIRECTORY

Footwear; Gloves, Mitts, Hats

Dan's Whetstone Co., Inc./Washita Mountain Whetstone Co., 418 Hilltop Rd., Pearcy, AR 71964, P: 501-767-1616, F: 501-767-9598, www.danswhetstone.com
Black Powder Accessories; Camping; Cutlery; Gun Parts/Gunsmithing; Hunting Accessories; Knives/Knife Cases; Sharpeners; Sports Accessories

Daniel Defense, Inc., 6002 Commerce Blvd., Suite 109, Savannah, GA 31408, P: 866-554-4867, F: 912-964-4237, www.danieldefense.com
Firearms

Danner, Inc., 17634 NE Airport Way, Portland, OR 97230, P: 800-345-0430, F: 503-251-1119
Footwear

Darkwoods Blind, LLC, 1209 SE 44th, Suite 2, Oklahoma City, OK 73129, P: 405-520-6754, F: 405-677-2262, www.darkwoodsblind.com
Archery; Blinds; Camouflage; Custom Manufacturing; Firearms; Hunting Accessories; Outfitter; Vehicles, Utility & Rec

Darn Tough Vermont, 364 Whetstone Dr., P.O. Box 307, Northfield, VT 05663, P: 877-DARNTUFF, F: 802-485-6140, www.darntough.com
Backpacking; Camping; Footwear; Hunting Accessories; Men & Women's Clothing

Davidson's, 6100 Wilkinson Dr., Prescott, AZ, 86301, P: 800-367-4867, F: 928-776-0344, www.galleryofguns.com
Ammunition; Firearms; Law Enforcement; Magazines, Cartridge; Online Services; Scopes, Sights & Accessories; Wholesaler/Distributor

Day Six Outdoors, 1150 Brookstone Centre Parkway, Columbus, GA 31904, P: 877-DAY-SIX0, F: 706-323-0178, www.day6outdoors.com
Feeder Equipment; Wildlife Management

Del Norte Outdoors, P.O. Box 5046, Santa Maria, CA 93456, P: 805-474-1793, F: 805-474-1793, www.delnorteoutdoors.com
Archery; Hunting Accessories; Sports Accessories

Del-Ton, Inc., 218B Aviation Pkwy., Elizabethtown, NC 28337, P: 910-645-2172, F: 910-645-2244, www.del-ton.com
Firearms; Gun Barrels; Gun Parts/Gunsmithing; Law Enforcement; Wholesaler/Distributor

DeLorme, Two DeLorme Dr., Yarmouth, ME 04096, P: 800-335-6763, F: 800-575-2244, www.delorme.com
Books/Industry Publications; Computer Software; Hunting Accessories; Sports Accessories; Tours/Travel

Demyan, 10, 2nd Donskoy Ln., Moscow, 119071, RUSSIAN FEDERATION, P: 011 74959847629, F: 011 74959847629, www.demyan.info
Airguns; Firearms

Dengta Sinpraise Weaving & Dressing Co., Ltd., Tai Zihe District, Wangshuitai Pangjiahe, Liao Yang, LiaoNing Province 111000, CHINA, P: 011 964193305888, F: 011 864193990566, www.sinpraise-hunting.com
Camouflage; Camping; Men & Women's Clothing; Sports Accessories

DeSantis Holster and Leather Goods Co., 431 Bayview Ave., Amityville, NY 11701, P: 800-424-1236, F: 631-841-6320, www.desantisholster.com
Bags & Equipment Cases; Gun Cases; Holsters; Hunting Accessories; Law Enforcement; Leathergoods

Desert Tactical Arms, P.O. Box 65816, Salt Lake City, UT 84165, P: 801-975-7272, F: 801-908-6425, www.deserttacticalarms.com
Firearms; Law Enforcement

Desiccare, Inc., 3400 Pomona Blvd., Pomona, CA 91768, P: 800-446-6650, F: 909-444-9045, www.desiccare.com
Food; Footwear; Gun Cabinets/Racks/Safes; Leathergoods; Scents & Lures

Diamondback Tactical, 23040 N. 11th Ave., Bldg. 1, Phoenix, AZ 85027, P: 800-735-7030, F: 623-583-0674, www.diamondbacktactical.com
Law Enforcement

Diana/Mayer & Grammelspacher GmbH & Co. KG, Karlstr, 34, Rastatt, 76437, GERMANY, P: 011 4972227620, F: 011 49722276278, www.diana-airguns.de
Airguns; Scopes, Sights & Accessories

Dillon Precision Products, Inc., 8009 E. Dillon's Way, Scottsdale, AZ 85260, P: 800-223-4570, F: 480-998-2786, www.dillonprecision.com
Bags & Equipment Cases; Feeder Equipment; Hearing Protection; Holsters; Hunting Accessories; Reloading

Dimension 3D Printing, 7655 Commerce Way, Eden Prairie, MN 55344, P: 888-480-3548, F: 952-294-3715, www.dimensionprinting.com
Computer Software; Custom Manufacturing; Gun Parts/Gunsmithing; Hunting Accessories; Scopes, Sights & Accessories

Ding Zing Chemical Products Co., Ltd., No. 8-1 Pei-Lin Rd., Hsiao-Kang Dist., Kaohsiung, 812, TAIWAN, P: 011 88678070166, F: 011 88678071616, www.dingzing.com
Backpacking; Bags & Equipment Cases; Camping; Custom Manufacturing; Footwear; Gloves, Mitts, Hats; Men & Women's Clothing; Sports Accessories

Directex, 304 S. Leighton Ave., Anniston, AL 36207, P: 800-845-3603, F: 256-235-2275, www/directex.net
Archery; Backpacking; Bags & Equipment Cases; Custom Manufacturing; Export/Import Specialists; Gun Cases; Holsters; Hunting Accessories

Dixie Gun Works, Inc., 1412 W. Reelfoot Ave., P.O. Box 130, Union City, TN 38281, P: 800-238-6785, F: 731-885-0440, www.dixiegunworks.com
Black Powder Accessories; Book/Industry Publications; Firearms; Gun Parts/Gunsmithing; Hunting Accessories; Knives/Knife Cases

DNZ Products, LLC/Game Reaper & Freedom Reaper Scope Mounts, 2710 Wilkins Dr., Sanford, NC 27330, P: 919-777-9608, F: 919-777-9609, www.dnzproducts.com
Black Powder Accessories; Custom Manufacturing; Gun Parts/Gunsmithing; Hunting Accessories; Scopes, Sights & Accessories

Do-All Traps, LLC/dba Do-All Outdoors, 216 19th Ave. N, Nashville, TN 37203, P: 800-252-9247, F: 800-633-3172, www.doalloutdoors.com
Clay Targets; Gun Cases; Hunting Accessories; Outdoor Art, Jewelry, Sculpture; Recoil Protection Devices & Services; Shooting Range Equipment; Targets; Taxidermy

Doc's Deer Farm and Scents, 2118 Niles-Cortland Rd., Cortland, OH 44420, P: 330-638-9507, F: 330-638-2772, www.docsdeerscents.com
Archery; Hunting Accessories; Scents & Lures

Docter Optic/Imported by Merkel USA, 7661 Commerce Lane, Trussville, AL 35173, P: 800-821-3021, F: 205-655-7078, www.merkel-usa.com
Binoculars; Scopes, Sights & Accessories

Dogtra Co., 22912 Lockness Ave., Torrance, CA, 90501, P: 888-811-9111, F: 310-534-9111, www.dogtra.com
Hunting Accessories; Pet Supplies; Training & Safety Equipment

Dokken Dog Supply, Inc., 4186 W. 85th St., Northfield, MN 55057, P: 507-744-2616, F: 507-744-5575, www.deadfowltrainer.com
Hunting Accessories; Pet Supplies; Scents & Lures; Training & Safety Equipment

DoubleStar/J&T Distributing, P.O. Box 430, Winchester, KY 40391, P: 888-736-7725, F: 859-745-4638, www.jtdistributing.com
Firearms; Firearms Maintenance Equipment; Gun Barrels; Gun Parts/Gunsmithing; Magazines, Cartridge; Wholesaler/Distributor

Down Range Mfg., LLC, 4170 N. Gun Powder Circle, Hastings, NE 68901, P: 402-463-3415, F: 402-463-3452, www.downrangemfg.com
Ammunition; Clay Targets; Custom Manufacturing; Reloading

Down Wind Scents, LLC, P.O. Box 549, Severna Park, MD 21146, P: 410-647-8451, F: 410-647-7828, www.downwindscents.com
Archery; Firearms Maintenance Equipment; Hunting Accessories; Lubricants; Scents & Lures

DPMS Firearms, LLC, 3312 12th St. SE, St. Cloud, MN 56304, P: 800-578-3767, F: 320-258-4449, www.dpmsinc.com
Firearms; Scopes, Sights & Accessories

Dri Duck Traders, 7007 College Blvd., Suite 700, Overland Park, KS 66221, P: 866-852-8222, F: 913-234-6280, www.driducktraders.com
Camouflage; Men & Women's Clothing

DriFire, LLC, 3151 Williams Rd., Suite E, Columbus, GA 31909, P: 866-266-4035, F: 706-507-7556, www.drifire.com
Camouflage; Men & Women's Clothing; Training & Safety Equipment

DryGuy, LLC, P.O. Box 1102, Mercer Island, WA 98040, P: 888-330-9452, F: 206-232-9830, www.maxxdry.com
Backpacking; Bags & Equipment Cases; Camping; Footwear; Gloves, Mitts, Hats; Hunting Accessories; Sports Accessories; Wholesaler/Distributor

Du-Lite Corp., 171 River Rd., Middletown, CT 06457, P: 860-347-2505, F: 860-344-9404, www.du-lite.com
Gunsmithing; Lubricants

Duck Commander Co., Inc./Buck Commander Co., Inc., 1978 Brownlee Rd., Calhoun, LA 71225, P: 318-396-1126, F: 318-396-1127, www.duckcommander.com, www.buckcommander.com
Camping; Emblems & Decals; Food; Game Calls; Gun Cases; Hunting Accessories, Men & Women's Clothing; Videos

Ducks Unlimited, Inc., One Waterfowl Way, Memphis, TN 38120, P: 800-45-DUCKS, F: 901-758-3850, www.ducks.org

Books/Industry Publications; Camouflage; Decoys; Firearms; Hunting Accessories; Outdoor Art, Jewelry, Sculpture; Wildlife Management

Duk-Inn-Blind, 49750 Alpine Dr., Macomb, MI 48044, P: 586-855-7494, F: 603-626-4672
Blinds; Camouflage; Hunting Accessories; Wholesaler/Distributor

Dummies Unlimited, Inc., 2435 Pine St., Pomona, CA 91767, P: 866-4DUMMIES, F: 909-392-7510, F: 909-392-7510, www.dummiesunlimited.com
Law Enforcement; Shooting Range Equipment; Targets; Training & Safety Equipment

Duostock Designs, Inc., P.O. Box 32, Welling, OK 74471, P: 866-386-7865, F: 918-431-3182, www.duostock.com
Firearms; Gun Grips & Stocks; Law Enforcement; Recoil Protection Devices & Services

Durasight Scope Mounting Systems, 5988 Peachtree Corners East, Norcross, GA 30071, P: 800-321-8767, F: 770-242-8546, www.durasight.com
Scopes, Sights & Accessories

Dynamic Research Technologies, LLC, 405 N. Lyon St., Grant City, MO 64456, P: 660-564-2331, F: 660-564-2103, www.drtammo.com
Ammunition; Reloading

E

E-Z Mount Corp., 1706 N. River Dr., San Angelo, TX 76902, P: 800-292-3756, F: 325-658-4951, www.ezmountcorp@zipnet.us
Gun Cabinets/Racks/Safes

E-Z Pull Trigger, 932 W. 5th St., Centralia, IL 62801, P: 618-532-6964, F: 618-532-5154, www.ezpulltriggerassist.com
Firearms; Gun Parts/Gunsmithing; Hunting Accessories

E.A.R., Inc./Insta-Mold Div., P.O. Box 18888, Boulder, CO 80303, P: 800-525-2690, F: 303-447-2637, www.earinc.com
Eyewear; Hearing Protection; Law Enforcement; Shooting Range Equipment; Wholesaler/Distributor

ER Shaw/Small Arms Mfg., 5312 Thoms Run Rd., Bridgeville, PA 15017, P: 412-221-4343, F: 412-221-4303, www.ershawbarrels.com
Custom Manufacturing; Firearms; Gun Barrels

ECS Composites, 3560 Rogue River Hwy., Grants Pass, OR 97527, P: 541-476-8871, F: 541-474-2479, www.transitcases.com
Custom Manufacturing; Gun Cases; Law Enforcement; Sports Accessories

EMCO Supply, Inc./Red Rock Outdoor Gear, 2601 Dutton Ave., Waco, TX 76711, P: 800-342-4654, F: 254-662-0045
Backpacking; Bags & Equipment Cases; Blinds; Camouflage; Compasses; Game Calls; Hunting Accessories; Law Enforcement

E.M.F. Co., Inc./Purveyors of Fine Firearms Since 1956, 1900 E. Warner Ave., Suite 1-D, Santa Ana, CA 92705, P: 800-430-1310, F: 800-508-1824, www.emf-company.com
Black Powder Accessories; Firearms; Gun Parts/Gunsmithing; Holsters; Leathergoods; Wholesaler/Distributor

EOTAC, 1940 Old Dunbar Rd., West Columbia, SC 29172, P: 803-744-9930, F: 803-744-9933, www.eotac.com
Tactical Clothing

ESS Goggles, P.O. Box 1017, Sun Valley, ID 83353, P: 877-726-4072, F: 208-726-4563
Eyewear; Hunting Accessories; Law Enforcement; Shooting Range Equipment; Training & Safety Equipment

ETL/Secure Logic, 2351 Tenaya Dr., Modesto, CA 95354, P: 800-344-3242, F: 209-529-3854, www.securelogiconline.com
Firearms; Gun Cabinets/Racks/Safes; Training & Safety Equipment

EZ 4473/American Firearms Software, 5955 Edmond St., Las Vegas, NV 89118, P: 702-364-9022, F: 702-364-9063, www.ez4473.com
Computer Software; Retailer Services

EZE-LAP® Diamond Products, 3572 Arrowhead Dr., Carson City, NV 89706, P: 800-843-4815, F: 775-888-9555, www.eze-lap.com
Camping; Cooking Equipment/Accessories; Cutlery; Gun Parts/Gunsmithing; Hunting Accessories; Sharpeners; Sports Accessories

Eagle Grips, Inc., 460 Randy Rd., Carol Stream, IL, 60188, P: 800-323-6144, F: 630-260-0486, www.eaglegrips.com
Gun Grips & Stocks

Eagle Imports, Inc., 1750 Brielle Ave., Suite B-1, Wanamassa, NJ 07712, P: 732-493-0333, F: 732-493-0301, www.bersafirearmsusa.com
Export/Import Specialists; Firearms; Holsters; Magazines, Cartridge; Wholesaler/Distributor

Eagle Industries Unlimited, Inc., 1000 Biltmore Dr., Fenton, MO 63026, P: 888-343-7547, F: 636-349-0321, www.eagleindustries.com
Backpacking; Bags & Equipment Cases; Camping; Gun Cases; Holsters; Hunting Accessories; Law Enforcement; Sports Accessories

Eagle Seed Co., 8496 Swan Pond Rd., P.O. Box 308, Weiner, AR 72479, P: 870-684-7377, F: 870-684-2225, www.eagleseed.com
Custom Manufacturing; Retail Packaging; Wholesaler/Distributor; Wildlife Management

Ear Phone Connection, 25139 Avenue Stanford, Valencia, CA 91355, P: 888-372-1888, F: 661-775-5622, www.earphoneconnect.com
Airsoft; Hearing Protection; Law Enforcement; Paintball Accessories; Two-Way Radios

EarHugger Safety Equipment, Inc., 1819 N. Main St., Suite 8, Spanish Fork, UT 84660, P: 800-236-1449, F: 801-371-8901, www.earhuggersafety.com
Law Enforcement

Easy Loop Lock, LLC, 8049 Monetary Dr., Suite D-4, Riviera Beach, FL 33404, P: 561-304-4990, F: 561-337-4655, www.ellock.com
Camping; Gun Locks; Hunting Accessories; Sports Accessories; Wholesaler/Distributor

E-Z Mount Corp., 1706 N. River Dr., San Angelo, TX 76902, P: 800-292-3756, F: 325-658-4951, www.ezmountcorp@zipnet.us
Gun Cabinets/Racks/Safes

E-Z Pull Trigger, 932 W. 5th St., Centralia, IL 62801, P: 618-532-6964, F: 618-532-5154, www.ezpulltriggerassist.com
Firearms; Gun Parts/Gunsmithing; Hunting Accessories

Eberlestock, P.O. Box 862, Boise, ID 83701, P: 877-866-3047, F: 240-526-2632, www.eberlestock.com
Archery; Backpacking; Bags & Equipment Cases; Gun Grips & Stocks; Hunting Accessories; Law Enforcement

Ed Brown Products, Inc., P.O. Box 492, Perry, MO 63462, P: 573-565-3261, F: 573-565-2791, www.edbrown.com
Computer Software; Custom Manufacturing; Firearms; Gun Barrels; Gun Parts/Gunsmithing; Magazines, Cartridge; Scopes, Sights & Accessories

EdgeCraft Corp./Chefs Choice, 825 Southwood Rd., Avondale, PA 19311, P: 800-342-3255, F: 610-268-3545, www.edgecraft.com
Cooking Equipment/Accessories; Custom Manufacturing; Cutlery; Export/Import Specialists; Hunting Accessories; Knives/Knife Cases; Sharpeners

Edgemaker Co., The/(formerly) The Jennex Co., 3902 Funston St., Toledo, OH 43612, P: 800-531-EDGE, F: 419-478-0833, www.edgemaker.com
Camping; Cutlery; Hunting Accessories; Sharpeners; Sports Accessories; Wholesaler/Distributor

El Paso Saddlery, 2025 E. Yandell, El Paso, TX 79903, P: 915-544-2233, F: 915-544-2535, www.epsaddlery.com
Holsters; Leathergoods

Elastic Products/Industrial Opportunities, Inc., 2586 Hwy. 19, P.O. Box 1649, Andrews, NC 28901, P: 800-872-4264, F: 828-321-4784, www.elasticproducts.com
Camouflage; Custom Manufacturing; Hunting Accessories; Men's Clothing

ELCAN Optical Technologies, 1601 N. Plano Rd., Richardson, TX 75081, P: 877-TXELCAN, F: 972-344-8260, www.elcan.com
Binoculars; Custom Manufacturing; Law Enforcement; Scopes, Sights & Accessories

Elder Hosiery Mills, Inc., 139 Homewood Ave., P.O. Box 2377, Burlington, NC 27217, P: 800-745-0267, F: 336-226-5846, www.elderhosiery.com
Footwear

Eley Limited/Eley Hawk Limited, Selco Way, First Ave., Minworth Industrial Estate, Minworth, Sutton Coldfield, West Midlands B76 1BA, UNITED KINGDOM, P: 011 4401213134567, F: 011-4401213134568, www.eleyammunition.com, www.eleyhawkltd.com
Ammunition

Elite First Aid, Inc., 700 E. Club Blvd., Durham, NC 27704, P: 800-556-2537, F: 919-220-6071, www.elite1staid.com
Backpacking; Camping; Cooking Equipment/Accessories; Hunting Accessories; Sports Accessories; Survival Kits/First Aid; Wholesaler/Distributor

Elite Iron, LLC, 1345 Thunders Trail, Bldg. D, Potomac, MT 59823, P: 406-244-0234, F: 406-244-0135, www.eliteiron.net
Law Enforcement; Scopes, Sights & Accessories

Elite Survival Systems, 310 W. 12th St., P.O. Box 245, Washington, MO 63090, P: 866-340-2778, F: 636-390-2977, www.elitesurvival.com
Backpacking; Bags & Equipment Cases; Custom Manufacturing; Footwear; Gun Cases; Holsters; Knives/Knife Cases; Law Enforcement

Ellett Brothers, 267 Columbia Ave., P.O. Box 128, Chapin, SC 29036, P: 800-845-3711, F: 800-323-3006, www.ellettbrothers.com
Ammunition; Archery; Black Powder Accessories; Firearms; Hunting Accessories;

MANUFACTURER'S AND PRODUCT DIRECTORY

Leathergoods; Scopes, Sights & Accessories; Wholesaler/Distributor

Ellington-Rush, Inc./Cough Silencer/SlingStix, 170 Private Dr., Lula, GA 30554, P: 706-677-2394, F: 706-677-3425, www.coughsilencer.com, www.slingstix.com
Archery; Black Powder Accessories; Game Calls; Hunting Accessories; Law Enforcement; Shooting Range Equipment

Elvex Corp., 13 Trowbridge, Bethel, CT 06801, P: 800-888-6582, F: 203-791-2278, www.elvex.com
Eyewear; Hearing Protection; Hunting Accessories; Law Enforcement; Men's Clothing; Paintball Accessories

Emerson Knives, Inc., 2730 Monterey St., Suite 101, Torrance, CA 90503, P: 310-212-7455, F: 310-212-7289, www.emersonknives.com
Camping; Cutlery; Knives/Knife Cases; Men & Women's Clothing; Wholesaler/Distributor

Empire Pewter Manufacturing, P.O. Box 15, Amsterdam, NY 12010, P: 518-843-0048, F: 518-843-7050
Custom Manufacturing; Emblems & Decals; Outdoor Art, Jewelry, Sculpture

Energizer Holdings, 533 Maryville University Dr., St. Louis, MO 63141, P: 314-985-2000, F: 314-985-2207, www.energizer.com
Backpacking; Camping; Hunting Accessories; Law Enforcement; Lighting Products; Sports Accessories; Survival Kits/First Aid; Training & Safety Equipment

Enforcement Technology Group, Inc., 400 N. Broadway, 4th Floor, Milwaukee, WI 53202, P: 800-873-2872, F: 414-276-1533, www.etgi.us
Custom Manufacturing; Law Enforcement; Online Services; Shooting Range Equipment; Training & Safety Equipment; Wholesaler/Distributor

Entreprise Arms, Inc., 5321 Irwindale Ave., Irwindale, CA 91706-2025, P: 626-962-8712, F: 626-962-4692, www.entreprise.com
Firearms; Gun Parts/Gunsmithing

Environ-Metal, Inc./Hevishot®, 1307 Clark Mill Rd., P.O. Box 834, Sweet Home, OR 97386, P: 541-367-3522, F: 541-367-3552, www.hevishot.com
Ammunition; Law Enforcement; Reloading

EOTAC, 1940 Old Dunbar Rd., West Columbia, SC 29172, P: 888-672-0303, F: 803-744-9933, www.eotac.com
Gloves, Mitts, Hats; Men's Clothing

Epilog Laser, 16371 Table Mountain Pkwy., Golden, CO 80403, P: 303-277-1188, F: 303-277-9669, www.epiloglaser.com

Essential Gear, Inc./eGear, 171 Wells St., Greenfield, MA 01301, P: 800-582-3861, F: 413-772-8947, www.essentialgear.com
Backpacking; Camping; Hunting Accessories; Law Enforcement; Lighting Products; Sports Accessories; Survival Kits/First Aid; Training & Safety Equipment

European American Armory Corp., P.O. Box 560746, Rockledge, FL 32956, P: 321-639-4842, F: 321-639-7006, www.eaacorp.com
Airguns; Firearms

Evans Sports, Inc., 801 Industrial Dr., P.O. Box 20, Houston, MO 65483, P: 800-748-8318, F: 417-967-2819, www.evanssports.com
Ammunition; Bags & Equipment Cases; Camping; Custom Manufacturing; Gun Cabinets/Racks/Safes; Hunting Accessories; Retail Packaging; Sports Accessories

Evolved Habitats, 2261 Morganza Hwy., New Roads, LA 70760, P: 225-638-4016, F: 225-638-4009, www.evolved.com
Archery; Export/Import Specialists; Hunting Accessories; Pet Supplies; Scents & Lures; Wildlife Management

Extendo Bed Co., 223 Roedel Ave., Caldwell, ID 83605, P: 800-752-0706, F: 208-286-0925, www.extendobed.com
Law Enforcement; Training & Safety Equipment

Extreme Dimension Wildlife Calls, LLC, 208 Kennebec Rd., Hampden, ME 04444, P: 866-862-2825, F: 207-862-3925, www.phantomcalls.com
Game Calls

Extreme Shock USA, 182 Camp Jacob Rd., Clintwood, VA 24228, P: 877-337-6772, F: 276-926-6092, www.extremeshockusa.net
Ammunition; Law Enforcement; Lubricants; Reloading

ExtremeBeam Tactical, 2275 Huntington Dr., Suite 872, San Marino, CA 91108, P: 626-372-5898, F: 626-609-0640, www.extremebeamtactical.com
Camping; Law Enforcement; Lighting Products; Outfitter

Exxel Outdoors, Inc., 14214 Atlanta Dr., Laredo, TX 78045, P: 956-724-8933, F: 956-725-2516, www.prestigemfg.com
Camping; Export/Import Specialists; Men's Clothing

F

F&W Media/Krause Publications, 700 E. State St., Iola, WI 54990, P: 800-457-2873, F: 715-445-4087, www.krausebooks.com
Books/Industry Publications; Videos

F.A.I.R. Srl, Via Gitti, 41, Marcheno, 25060, ITALY, P: 011 39030861162, F: 011 390308610179, www.fair.it
Firearms; Gun Barrels; Gun Parts/Gunsmithing; Hunting Accessories

F.A.P. F. LLI Pietta SNC, Via Mandolossa, 102, Gussago, Brescia 25064, ITALY, P: 011 390303737098, F: 011 390303737100, www.pietta.it
Black Powder Accessories; Firearms; Gun Cases; Gun Grips & Stocks; Gun Parts/Gunsmithing; Holsters

F.I.A.V. L. Mazzacchera SPA, Via S. Faustino, 62, Milano, 20134, ITALY, P: 011 390221095411, F: 011 390221095530, www.flav.it
Gun Parts/Gunsmithing

FMG Publications/Shooting Industry Magazine, 12345 World Trade Dr., San Diego, CA 92128, P: 800-537-3006, F: 858-605-0247, www.shootingindustry.com
Books/Industry Publications; Videos

FNH USA, P.O. Box 697, McLean, VA 22101, P: 703-288-1292, F: 703-288-1730, www.fnhusa.com
Ammunition; Firearms; Law Enforcement; Training & Safety Equipment

F.T.C. (Friedheim Tool), 1433 Roosevelt Ave., National City, CA 91950, 619-474-3600, F: 619-474-1300, www.ftcsteamers.com
Firearms Maintenance Equipment

Fab Defense, 43 Yakov Olamy St., Moshav Mishmar Hashiva, 50297, ISRAEL, P: 011 972039603399, F: 011 972039603312, www.fab-defense.com
Gun Grips & Stocks; Law Enforcement; Targets

FailZero, 7825 SW Ellipse Way, Stuart, FL 34997, P: 772-223-6699, F: 772-223-9996
Gun Parts/Gunsmithing

Falcon Industries, P.O. Box 1690, Edgewood, NM 87015, P: 877-281-3783, F: 505-281-3991, www.ergogrips.net
Gun Grips & Stocks; Gun Parts/Gunsmithing; Law Enforcement; Scopes, Sights & Accessories; Sports Accessories

Fasnap® Corp., 3500 Reedy Dr., Elkhart, IN 46514, P: 800-624-2058, F: 574-264-0802, www.fasnap.com
Backpacking; Bags & Equipment Cases; Gun Cases; Holsters; Hunting Accessories; Knives/Knife Cases; Leathergoods; Wholesaler/Distributor

Faulk's Game Call Co., Inc., 616 18th St., Lake Charles, LA 70601, P: 337-436-9726, FL 337-494-7205, www.faulkcalls.com
Game Calls

Fausti Stefano s.r.l., Via Martiri dell'Indipendenza 70, Marcheno (BS), 25060, ITALY, P: 011 390308960220, F: 011 390308610155, www.faustistefanoarms.com
Firearms

Feather Flage "Ducks In A Row Camo"/B & D Garments, LLC, P.O. Box 5326, Lafayette, LA 70502, P: 866-DUK-CAMO, F: 337-896-8137, www.featherflage.com
Camouflage; Wholesaler/Distributor

Federal Premium Ammunition/ATK Commercial Products, 900 Ehlen Dr., Anoka, MN 55303, P: 800-322-2342, F: 763-323-2506, www.federalpremium.com
Ammunition

Feijuang International Corp., 4FI-1/7, No. 177 Min-Sheng West Road, Taipei, TAIWAN, P: 011 886225520169, F: 011 886225578359
Blinds; Camping; Compasses; Eyewear; Hearing Protection; Hunting Accessories; Sports Accessories

Fenix Flashlights, LLC/4Sevens, LLC, 4896 N. Royal Atlanta Dr., Suite 305, Tucker, GA 30084, P: 866-471-0749, F: 866-323-9544, www.4sevens.com
Backpacking; Camping; Law Enforcement; Lighting Products

FenixLightUS/Casualhome Worldwide, Inc., 29 William St., Amityville, NY 11701, P: 877-FENIXUS, F: 631-789-2970, www.fenixlightus.com
Camping; Law Enforcement; Lighting Products; Scopes, Sights & Accessories; Shooting Range Equipment; Wholesaler/Distributor

Field & Stream Watches, 12481 NW 44th St., Coral Springs, FL 33065, P: 954-509-1476, F: 954-509-1479, www.tfg24gold.com
Camping; Hunting Accessories; Outfitter; Sports Accessories; Watches; Wholesaler/Distributor

Filson, 1555 4th Ave. S, Seattle, WA 98134, P: 800-297-1897, F: 206-624-4539, www.filson.com
Bags & Equipment Cases; Footwear; Gloves, Mitts, Hats; Gun Cases; Hunting Accessories; Leathergoods; Men & Women's Clothing

Final Approach/Bushnell Outdoor Accessories, 9200 Cody, Overland Park, KS 66214, P: 800-423-3537, F: 913-752-3539, www.kolpin-outdoors.com
Bags & Equipment Cases; Blinds; Decoys; Gun Cases; Hunting Accessories; Videos

MANUFACTURER'S
AND PRODUCT DIRECTORY

Fiocchi of America, Inc., 6930 N. Fremont Rd., Ozark, MO 65721, P: 800-721-AMMO, 417-725-1039, www.fiocciusa.com
Ammunition; Reloading

First Choice Armor & Equipment, Inc., 209 Yelton St., Spindale, NC 28160, P: 800-88-ARMOR, F: 866-481-4929, www.firstchoicearmor.com
Law Enforcement; Training & Safety Equipment

First-Light USA, LLC, 320 Cty. Rd. 1100 North, Seymour, IL 61875, P: 877-454-4450, F: 877-454-4420, www.first-light-usa.com
Backpacking; Camping; Firearms; Law Enforcement; Lighting Products; Survival Kits/ First Aid; Training & Safety Equipment

Flambeau, Inc., P.O. Box 97, Middlefield, OH 44062, P: 440-632-1631, F: 440-632-1581, www.flambeauoutdoors.com
Bags & Equipment Cases; Crossbows & Accessories; Custom Manufacturing; Decoys; Game Calls; Gun Cases

Fleming & Clark, Ltd., 3013 Honeysuckle Dr., Spring Hill, TN 37174, P: 800-373-6710, F: 931-487-9972, www.flemingandclark.com
Bags & Equipment Cases; Footwear; Gun Cases; Hunting Accessories; Knives/Knife Cases; Leathergoods; Men's Clothing; Wholesaler/Distributor

Flitz International, Ltd., 821 Mohr Ave., Waterford, WI 53185, P: 800-558-8611, F: 262-534-2991, www.flitz.com
Black Powder Accessories; Firearms Maintenance Equipment; Gun Barrels; Gun Grips & Stocks; Gun Parts/Gunsmithing; Knives/Knife Cases; Lubricants; Scopes, Sights & Accessories

Fobus Holsters/CAA-Command Arms Accessories, 780 Haunted Lane, Bensalem, PA 19020, P: 267-803-1517, F: 267-803-1002, www.fobusholsters.com, www.commandarms.com
Bags & Equipment Cases; Firearms; Gun Cases; Gun Grips & Stocks; Gun Parts/ Gunsmithing; Holsters; Law Enforcement; Scopes, Sights & Accessories

Foiles Migrators, Inc., 101 N. Industrial Park Dr., Pittsfield, IL 62363, P: 866-83-GEESE, F: 217-285-5995, www.foilesstraitmeat.com
Game Calls; Hunting Accessories

FoodSaver/Jarden Consumer Solutions, 24 Latour Ln., Little Rock, AR 72223, P: 501-821-0138, F: 501-821-0139, www.foodsaver.com
Backpacking; Camping; Cooking Equipment/ Accessories; Food; Hunting Accessories

Force One, LLC, 520 Commercial Dr., Fairfield, OH 45014, P: 800-462-7880, F: 513-939-1166, www.forceonearmor.com
Custom Manufacturing; Law Enforcement

Forster Products, Inc., 310 E. Lanark Ave., Lanark, IL 61046, P: 815-493-6360, F: 815-493-2371, www.forsterproducts.com
Black Powder Accessories; Custom Manufacturing; Firearms Maintenance Equipment; Gun Parts/Gunsmithing; Lubricants; Reloading; Scopes, Sights & Accessories

Fort Knox Security Products, 993 N. Industrial Park Rd., Orem, UT 84057, P: 800-821-5216, F: 801-226-5493, www.ftknox.com
Custom Manufacturing; Gun Cabinets/Racks/ Safes; Home Furnishings; Hunting Accessories

Foshan City Nanhai Weihong Mold Products Co., Ltd./Xinwei Photo Electricity Industrial Co., Ltd., Da Wo District, Dan Zhao Town, Nanhai, Foshan City, GuangZhou, 528216,

CHINA, P: 011 8675785444666, F: 011 8675785444111, www.weihongmj.net
Binoculars; Scopes, Sights & Accessories

Fox Knives Oreste Frati SNC, Via La Mola, 4, Maniago, Pordenone 33085, ITALY, P: 011 39042771814, F: 011 390427700514, www.foxcutlery.com
Camouflage; Camping; Cutlery; Hunting Accessories; Knives/Knife Cases; Law Enforcement; Wholesaler/Distributor

Fox Outdoor Products, 2040 N. 15th Ave., Melrose Park, IL 60160, P: 800-523-4332, F: 708-338-9210, www.foxoutdoor.com
Bags & Equipment Cases; Camouflage; Eyewear; Gun Cases; Holsters; Law Enforcement; Men's Clothing; Wholesaler/ Distributor

FoxFury Personal Lighting Solutions, 2091 Elevado Hill Dr., Vista, CA 92084, P: 760-945-4231, F: 760-758-6283, www.foxfury.com
Backpacking; Camping; Hunting Accessories; Law Enforcement; Lighting Products; Paintball Accessories; Sports Accessories; Training & Safety Equipment

FOXPRO, Inc., 14 Fox Hollow Dr., Lewistown, PA 17044, P: 866-463-6977, F: 717-247-3594, www.gofoxpro.com
Archery; Decoys; Game Calls; Hunting Accessories

Foxy Huntress, 17 Windsor Ridge, Frisco, TX 75034, P: 866-370-1343, F: 972-370-1343, www.foxyhuntress.com
Camouflage; Women's Clothing

Franchi, 17603 Indian Head Hwy., Accokeek, MD 20607, P: 800-264-4962, www.franchiusa.com
Firearms

Franklin Sports, Inc./Uniforce Tactical Division, 17 Campanelli Pkwy., Stoughton, MA 02072, P: 800-225-8647, F: 781-341-3220, www.uniforcetactical.com
Camouflage; Eyewear; Gloves, Mitts, Hats; Law Enforcement; Leathergoods; Men's Clothing; Wholesaler/Distributor

Franzen Security Products, Inc., 680 Flinn Ave., Suite 35, Moorpark, CA 93021, P: 800-922-7656, F: 805-529-0446, www.securecase.com
Bags & Equipment Cases; Custom Manufacturing; Gun Cases; Gun Locks; Hunting Accessories; Law Enforcement; Shooting Range Equipment; Training & Safety Equipment

Fraternal Blue Line, P.O. Box 260199, Boston, MA 02126, P: 617-212-1288, F: 617-249-0857, www.fraternalblueline.org
Custom Manufacturing; Emblems & Decals; Law Enforcement; Men & Women's Clothing; Wholesaler/Distributor

Freedom Arms, Inc., 314 Hwy. 239, Freedom, WY 83120, P: 800-833-4432, F: 800-252-4867, www.freedomarms.com
Firearms; Gun Cases; Holsters; Scopes, Sights & Accessories

Freelinc, 266 W. Center St., Orem, UT 84057, P: 866-467-1199, F: 801-672-3003, www.freelinc.com
Law Enforcement

Frogg Toggs, 131 Sundown Drive NW, P.O. Box 609, Arab, AL 35016, P: 800-349-1835, F: 256-931-1585, www.froggtoggs.com
Backpacking; Camouflage; Footwear; Hunting Accessories; Men & Women's Clothing

Front Line/Army Equipment, Ltd., 6 Platin St., Rishon-Le-Zion, 75653, ISRAEL, P: 011 97239519460, F: 011 97239519463, www.front-line.co.il
Bags & Equipment Cases; Gun Cases; Holsters

Frost Cutlery Co., 6861 Mountain View Rd., Ooltewah, TN 37363, P: 800-251-7768, F: 423-894-9576, www.frostcutlery.com
Camping; Cooking Equipment/Accessories; Cutlery; Hunting Accessories; Knives/Knife Cases; Retail Packaging; Sharpeners; Wholesaler/Distributor

Fujinon, Inc., 10 High Point Dr., Wayne, NJ 07470, P: 973-633-5600, F: 973-694-8299, www.fujinon.jp.com
Binoculars; Scopes, Sights & Accessories

Fusion Tactical, 4200 Chino Hills Pkwy., Suite 820-143, Chino Hills, CA 91709, P: 909-393-9450, F: 909-606-6834
Custom Manufacturing; Retail Packaging; Sports Accessories; Training & Safety Equipment

G

G24 Innovations, Ltd., Solar Power, Westloog Environmental Centre, Cardiff, CF3 2EE, UNITED KINGDON, 011 442920837340, F: 011 443930837341, www.g24i.com
Bags & Equipment Cases; Camping; Custom Manufacturing; Lighting Products

G96 Products Co., Inc., 85-5th Ave., Bldg. 6, P.O. Box 1684, Paterson, NJ 07544, P: 877-332-0035, F: 973-684-3848, www.g96.com
Black Powder Accessories; Firearms Maintenance Equipment; Lubricants

GG&G, 3602 E. 42nd Stravenue, Tucson, AZ 85713, P: 800-380-2540, F: 520-748-7583, www.gggaz.com
Custom Manufacturing; Firearms; Gun Barrels; Gun Grips & Stocks; Gun Parts/Gunsmithing; Law Enforcement; Lighting Products; Scopes, Sights & Accessories

G.A. Precision, 1141 Swift St., N. Kansas City, MO 64116, P: 816-221-1844, F: 816-421-4958, www.gaprecision.net
Firearms

G.G. Telecom, Inc./Spypoint, 555 78 Rd., Suite 353, Swanton, VT 05488, CANADA, P: 888-SPYPOINT, F: 819-604-1644, www.spy-point.com
Hunting Accessories; Photographic Equipment

G-LOX, 520 Sampson St., Houston, TX 77003, P: 713-228-8944, F: 713-228-8947, www.g-lox.com
Archery; Gun Cabinets/Racks/Safes; Gun Locks; Hunting Accessories; Shooting Range Equipment

GSM Products/Walker Game Ear, 3385 Roy Orr Blvd., Grand Prairie, TX 75050, P: 877-269-8490, F: 760-450-1014, www.gsmoutdoors.com
Archery; Feeder Equipment; Hearing Protection; Hunting Accessories; Lighting Products; Scopes, Sights & Accessories; Wildlife Management

GT Industrial Products, 10650 Irma Dr., Suite 1, Northglenn, CO 80233, P: 303-280-5777, F: 303-280-5778, www.gt-ind.com
Camping; Hunting Accessories; Lighting Products; Survival Kits/First Aid

Galati Gear/Galati International, 616 Burley Ridge Rd., P.O. Box 10, Wesco, MO 65586, P: 877-425-2847, F: 573-775-4308, www.galatigear.com, www.galatiinternational.com

MANUFACTURER'S AND PRODUCT DIRECTORY

Bags & Equipment Cases; Cutlery; Gun Cases; Holsters; Knives/Knife Cases; Law Enforcement; Sports Accessories

Galileo, 13872 SW 119th Ave., Miami, FL 33186, P: 800-548-3537, F: 305-234-8510, www.galileosplace.com
Binoculars; Photographic Equipment; Scopes, Sights & Accessories; Telescopes

Gamebore Cartridge Co., Ltd., Great Union St., Hull, HU9 1AR, UNITED KINGDOM, P: 011 441442223707, F: 011 4414823252225, www.gamebore.com
Ammunition; Cartridges

Gamehide–Core Resources, 12257C Nicollet Ave. S, Burnsville, MN 55337, P: 888-267-3591, F: 952-895-8845, www.gamehide.com
Archery; Camouflage; Custom Manufacturing; Export/Import Specialists; Gloves, Mitts, Hats; Hunting Accessories; Men & Women's Clothing

Gamo USA Corp., 3911 SW 47th Ave., Suite 914, Fort Lauderdale, FL 33314, P: 954-581-5822, F: 954-581-3165, www.gamousa.com
Airguns; Ammunition; Hunting Accessories; Online Services; Scopes, Sights & Accessories; Targets

Garmin International, 1200 E. 151st St., Olathe, KS 66062, P: 913-397-8200, F: 913-397-8282, www.garmin.com
Backpacking; Camping; Compasses; Computer Software; Hunting Accessories; Sports Accessories; Two-Way Radios; Vehicles, Utility & Rec

Garrett Metal Detectors, 1881 W. State St., Garland, TX 75042, P: 972-494-6151, F: 972-494-1881, www.garrett.com
Law Enforcement; Sports Accessories

Geissele Automatics, LLC, 1920 W. Marshall St., Norristown, PA 19403, P: 610-272-2060, F: 610-272-2069, www.ar15trigger.com
Firearms; Gun Parts/Gunsmithing

Gemstar Manufacturing, 1515 N. 5th St., Cannon Falls, MN 55009, P: 800-533-3631, F: 507-263-3129
Bags & Equipment Cases; Crossbows & Accessories; Custom Manufacturing; Gun Cases; Law Enforcement; Paintball Accessories; Sports Accessories; Survival Kits/First Aid

Gemtech, P.O. Box 140618, Boise, ID 83714, P: 208-939-7222, www.gem-tech.com
Firearms; Hearing Protection; Law Enforcement; Training & Safety Equipment; Wildlife Management

General Inspection, LLC, 10585 Enterprise Dr., Davisburg, MI 48350, P: 888-817-6314, F: 248-625-0789, www.geninsp.com
Ammunition; Custom Manufacturing

General Starlight Co., 250 Harding Blvd. W, P.O. Box 32154, Richmond Hill, Ontario L4C 9S3, CANADA, P: 905-850-0990, www.electrooptic.com
Binoculars; Law Enforcement; Photographic Equipment; Scopes, Sights & Accessories; Telescopes; Training & Safety Equipment; Wholesaler/Distributor

Generation Guns–(G2) ICS, No. 6, Lane 205, Dongihou Rd., Shengang Township, Taichung County, 429, TAIWAN, P: 011 886425256461, F: 011 886425256484, www.icsbb.com
Airsoft; Sports Accessories

Gerber Legendary Blades, 14200 SW 72nd Ave., Portland, OR 97224, P: 800-443-4871, F: 307-857-4702, www.gerbergear.com

Knives/Knife Cases; Law Enforcement; Lighting Products

Gerstner & Sons, Inc., 20 Gerstner Way, Dayton, OH 45402, P: 937-228-1662, F: 937-228-8557, www.gerstnerusa.com
Bags & Equipment Cases; Custom Manufacturing; Gun Cabinets/Racks/Safes; Gun Cases; Home Furnishings; Knives/Knife Cases; Shooting Range Equipment

GH Armor Systems, 1 Sentry Dr., Dover, TN 37058, P: 866-920-5940, F: 866-920-5941, www.gharmorsystems.com
Custom Manufacturing; Law Enforcement; Men & Women's Clothing

Giant International/Motorola Consumer Products, 3495 Piedmont Rd., Suite 920, Bldg. Ten, Atlanta, GA 30305, P: 800-638-5119, F: 678-904-6030, www.giantintl.com
Backpacking; Camouflage; Camping; Hunting Accessories; Training & Safety Equipment; Two-Way Radios

Ginsu Outdoors, 118 E. Douglas Rd., Walnut Ridge, AR 72476, P: 800-982-5233, F: 870-886-9142, www.ginsuoutdoors.com
Cutlery; Hunting Accessories; Knives/Knife Cases

Girsan–Yavuz 16, Batlama Deresi Mevkii Sunta Sok. No 19, Giresun, 28200, TURKEY, P: 011 905332160201, F: 011 904542153928, www.yavuz16.com
Firearms; Gun Parts/Gunsmithing

Glacier Glove, 4890 Aircenter Circle, Suite 210, Reno, NV 89502, P: 800-728-8235, F: 775-825-6544, www.glacierglove.com
Gloves, Mitts, Hats; Hunting Accessories; Men's Clothing

Glendo Corp./GRS Tools, 900 Overlander Rd., P.O. Box 1153, Emporia, KS 66801, P: 800-835-3519, F: 620-343-9640, www.glendo.com
Books/Industry Publications; Custom Manufacturing; Lighting Products; Scopes, Sights & Accessories; Videos; Wholesaler/Distributor

Glock, Inc., 6000 Highlands Pkwy., Smyrna, GA 30082, P: 770-432-1202, F: 770-433-8719, www.glock.com, www.teamglock.com, www.glocktraining.com, www.gssfonline.com
Firearms; Gun Parts/Gunsmithing; Holsters; Knives/Knife Cases; Law Enforcement; Men & Women's Clothing; Retailer Services

Goex, Inc., P.O. Box 659, Doyline, LA 71023, P: 318-382-9300, F: 318-382-9303, www.goexpowder.com
Ammunition; Black Powder/Smokeless Powder

Gold House Hardware (China), Ltd., Rm 12/H, 445 Tian He Bei Rd., Guangzhou, 510620, CHINA, P: 011 862038801911, F: 011 862038808485, www.ghhtools.com
Camping; Cutlery; Gun Cases; Hunting Accessories; Knives/Knife Cases; Scopes, Sights & Accessories; Targets

Goldenrod Dehumidifiers, 3600 S. Harbor Blvd., Oxnard, CA 93035, P: 800-451-6797, F: 805-985-1534, www.goldenroddehumidifiers.com
Gun Cabinets/Racks/Safes

Golight, Inc., 37146 Old Hwy. 17, Culbertson, NE 69024, P: 800-557-0098, F: 308-278-2525, www.golight.com
Camping; Hunting Accessories; Law Enforcement; Lighting Products; Vehicles, Utility & Rec

Gore & Associates, Inc., W.L., 295 Blue Ball Rd., Elkton, MD 21921, P: 800-431-GORE, F: 410-392-9057, www.gore-tex.com
Footwear; Gloves, Mitts, Hats; Law Enforcement; Men & Women's Clothing

Gould & Goodrich, Inc., 709 E. McNeil St., Lillington, NC, 27546, P: 800-277-0732, FL 910-893-4742, www.gouldusa.com
Holsters; Law Enforcement; Leathergoods

Grabber/MPI Outdoors, 5760 N. Hawkeye Ct. SW, Grand Rapids, MI 49509, P: 800-423-1233, F: 616-940-7718, www.warmers.com
Archery; Backpacking; Camouflage; Camping; Footwear; Gloves, Mitts, Hats; Hunting Accessories; Survival Kits/First Aid

Gradient Lens Corp., 207 Tremont St., Rochester, NY 14608, P: 800-536-0790, F: 585-235-6645, www.gradientlens.com
Firearms Maintenance Equipment; Gun Barrels; Gun Parts/Gunsmithing; Scopes, Sights & Accessories; Shooting Range Equipment

Grand View Media Group, 200 Croft St., Suite 1, Birmingham, AL 35242, P: 888-431-2877, F: 205-408-3798, www.gvmg.com
Books/Industry Publications

Granite Security Products, Inc., 4801 Esco Dr., Fort Worth, TX 76140, P: 817-561-9095, F: 817-478-3056, www.winchestersafes.com
Gun Cabinets/Racks/Safes

Gransfors Bruks, Inc., P.O. Box 818, Summerville, SC 29484. P: 843-875-0240, F: 843-821-2285
Custom Manufacturing; Law Enforcement; Men's Clothing; Wholesaler/Distributor

Grant Adventures Int'l., 9815 25th St. E, Parrish, FL 34219, P: 941-776-3029, F: 941-776-1092
Archery; Outfitter

Grauer Systems, 38 Forster Ave., Mount Vernon, NY 10552, P: 415-902-4721, www.grauerbarrel.com
Firearms; Gun Barrels; Gun Grips & Stocks; Law Enforcement; Lighting Products; Scopes, Sights & Accessories

Graves Recoil Systems, LLC/Mallardtone, LLC, 9115 Crows Nest Dr., Pine Bluff, AR 71603, P: 870-534-3000, F: 870-534-3000, www.stockabsorber.com
Black Powder Accessories; Firearms; Game Calls; Hunting Accessories; Recoil Protection Devices & Services; Wholesaler/Distributor

Great American Tool Co., Inc./Gatco Sharpeners/Timberline Knives, 665 Hertel Ave., Buffalo, NY 14207, P: 800-548-7427, F: 716-877-2591, www.gatcosharpeners.com
Cutlery; Knives/Knife Cases; Sharpeners

Green Supply, Inc., 3059 Audrain Rd., Suite 581, Vandalia, MO 63382, P: 800-424-4867, F: 573-594-2211, www.greensupply.com
Ammunition; Camping; Computer Software; Firearms; Hunting Accessories; Online Services; Retailer Services; Scopes, Sights & Accessories; Wholesaler/Distributor

Grip On Tools, 4628 Amash Industrial Dr., Wayland, MI 49348, P: 616-877-0000, F: 616-877-4346

Grizzly Industrial, 1821 Valencia St., Bellingham, WA 98229, P: 800-523-4777, F: 800-438-5901, www.grizzly.com
Firearms Maintenance Equipment; Gun Cabinets/Racks/Safes; Gun Parts/Gunsmithing

Grohmann Knives, Ltd., 116 Water St., P.O. Box 40, Pictou, Nova Scotia B0K 1H0,

CANADA, P: 888-7-KNIVES, F: 902-485-5872, www.grohmannknives.com
Backpacking; Camping; Cooking Equipment/ Accessories; Custom Manufacturing; Cutlery; Hunting Accessories; Knives/Knife Cases; Sharpeners

GrovTec US, Inc., 16071 SE 98t Ave., Clackamas, OR, 97015, P: 503-557-4689, F: 503-557-4936, www.grovtec.com
Custom Manufacturing; Firearms Maintenance Equipment; Gun Parts/Gunsmithing; Holsters

Guay Guay Trading Co., Ltd., 11F-3, No. 27, Lane 169, Kangning St., Shijr City, Taipei County 221, TAIWAN, P: 011 886226922000, F: 011 886226924000, www.guay2.com
Airsoft

Gun Grabber Products, Inc., 3417 E. 54th St., Texarkana, AR 71854, P: 877-486-4722, F: 870-774-2111, www.gungrab.com
Gun Cabinets/Racks/Safes; Hunting Accessories

Gun Video, 4585 Murphy Canyon Rd., San Diego, CA 92123, P: 800-942-8273, F: 858-569-0505, www.gunvideo.com
Books/Industry Publications; Gun Parts/ Gunsmithing; Law Enforcement; Training & Safety Equipment; Videos

GunBroker.com, P.O. Box 2511, Kennesaw, GA 30156, P: 720-223-2083, F: 720-223-0164, www.gunbroker.com
Airguns; Computer Software; Firearms; Gun Parts/Gunsmithing; Hunting Accessories; Online Services; Reloading; Retailer Services

GunMate Products/Bushnell Outdoor Accessories, 9200 Cody, Overland Park, KS 66214, P: 800-423-3537, F: 800-548-0446, www.unclemikes.com
Gun Cases; Holsters; Hunting Accessories; Leathergoods

Gunslick Gun Care/ATK Commercial Products, N5549 Cty. Trunk Z, Onalaska, WI 54650, P: 800-635-7656, F: 763-323-3890, www.gunslick.com
Firearms Maintenance Equipment; Lubricants

GunVault, Inc., 216 S. 2nd Ave., Bldg. 932, San Bernardino, CA 92408, P: 800-222-1055, F: 909-382-2042, www.gunvault.com
Gun Cabinets/Racks/Safes; Gun Cases; Gun Locks

H

HKS Products, Inc., 7841 Foundation Dr., Florence, KY 41042, P: 800-354-9814, F: 859-342-5865, www.hksspeedloaders.com
Hunting Accessories; Law Enforcement

H & C Headware/Capco Sportswear, 5945 Shiloh Rd., Alpharetta, GA 30005, P: 800-381-3331, F: 800-525-2613, www.kccaps.com
Camouflage

H & M Metal Processing, 1850 Front St., Cuyanoga Falls, OH 44221, P: 330-928-9021, F: 330-928-5472, www.handmmetal.com
Airguns; Archery; Black Powder Accessories; Custom Manufacturing; Firearms Maintenance Equipment; Gun Barrels; Gun Parts/ Gunsmithing

Haas Outdoors, Inc./Mossy Oak, P.O. Box 757, West Point, MS 39773, P: 662-494-8859, F: 662-509-9397

H-S Precision, Inc., 1301 Turbine Dr., Rapid City, SD 57703, P: 605-341-3006, F: 605-342-8964, www.hsprecision.com

Firearms; Gun Barrels; Gun Grips & Stocks; Law Enforcement; Magazines, Cartridge; Shooting Range Equipment

Haix®-Schuhe Produktions-u. Vertriebs GmbH, Aufhofstrasse 10, Mainburg, Bavaria 84048, GERMANY, P: 011 49875186250, F: 011 498751862525, www.haix.com
Footwear; Law Enforcement; Leathergoods

Haix North America, Inc., 157 Venture Ct., Suite 11, Lexington, KY 40511, P: 866-344-4249, F: 859-281-0113, www.haix.com
Footwear; Law Enforcement; Leathergoods

Haley Vines Outdoor Collection Badland Beauty, P.O. Box 150308, Lufkin, TX 75915, P: 936-875-5522, F: 936-875-5525, www.haleyvines.com
Bags & Equipment Cases; Gloves, Mitts, Hats; Wholesaler/Distributor; Women's Clothing

Hallmark Dog Training Supplies, 3054 Beechwood Industrial Ct., P.O. Box 97, Hubertus, WI 53033, P: 800-OK4DOGS, F: 262-628-4434, www.hallmarkdogsupplies.com
Custom Manufacturing; Hunting Accessories; Pet Supplies; Scents & Lures; Videos; Wholesaler/Distributor

Halys, 1205 W. Cumberland, Corbin, KY 40701, P: 606-528-7490, F: 606-528-7497, www.halysgear.com
Custom Manufacturing; Men & Women's Clothing; Wholesaler/Distributor

Hammerhead Ind./Gear Keeper, 1501 Goodyear Ave., Ventura, CA 93003, P: 888-588-9981, F: 805-658-8833, www.gearkeeper.com
Backpacking; Camping; Compasses; Game Calls; Hunting Accessories; Law Enforcement; Lighting Products; Sports Accessories

HangZhou Fujie Outdoor Products, Inc., Qinyuanyashe, Shenghuoguan, Suite 1108, 163# Jichang Rd., Hanzhou, ZHJG 310004, CHINA, P: 011 8657181635196, F: 011 8657187718232, www.hangzhou-outdoor.com
Footwear; Gloves, Mitts, Hats; Gun Cases; Men & Women's Clothing

Hardigg Storm Case, 147 N. Main St., South Deerfield, MA 01373, P: 800-542-7344, F: 413-665-8330
Bags & Equipment Cases; Gun Cases

Harris Engineering, Inc., 999 Broadway, Barlow, KY 42024, P: 270-334-3633, F: 270-334-3000
Hunting Accessories; Shooting Range Equipment; Sports Accessories

Harris Publications, Inc./Harris Tactical Group, 1115 Broadway, 8th Floor, New York, NY 10010, P: 212-807-7100, F: 212-807-1479, www.tactical-life.com
Airguns; Books/Industry Publications; Cutlery; Firearms; Knives/Knife Cases; Law Enforcement; Paintball Guns; Retailer Services

Hastings, 717 4th St., P.O. Box 135, Clay Center, KS 67432, P: 785-632-3169, F: 785-632-6554, www.hastingsammunition.com
Ammunition; Firearms; Gun Barrels

Hatsan Arms Co., Izmir-Ankara Karayolu 26. Km. No. 289, OSB Kemalpasa, Izmir, 35170, TURKEY, P: 011 902328789100, F: 011 902328789723, www.hatsan.com.tr
Airguns; Firearms; Scopes, Sights & Accessories

Havalon Knives/Havels Inc., 3726 Lonsdale St., Cincinnati, OH 45227, P: 800-638-4770, F: 513-271-4714, www.havalon.com

Hunting Accessories; Knives/Knife Cases

Havaser Turizm, Ltd., Nargileci Sokak No. 4, Mercan, Eminonu, 34450, TURKEY, P: 011 90212135452, F: 011 902125128079
Firearms

Hawke Sport Optics, 6015 Highview Dr., Suite G, Fort Wayne, IN 46818, P: 877-429-5347, F: 260-918-3443, www.hawkeoptics.com
Airguns; Binoculars; Computer Software; Crossbows & Accessories; Scopes, Sights & Accessories

Haydel's Game Calls, 5018 Hazel Jones Rd., Bossier City, LA 71111, P: 800-HAYDELS, F: 888-310-3711, www.haydels.com
Archery; Emblems & Decals; Game Calls; Gun Parts/Gunsmithing; Hunting Accessories; Videos

Health Enterprises, 90 George Leven Dr., N. Attleboro, MA 02760, P: 800-633-4243, F: 508-695-3061, www.healthenterprises.com
Hearing Protection

Heat Factory, Inc., 2390 Oak Ridge Way, Vista, CA 92081, P: 800-993-4328, F: 760-727-8721, www.heatfactory.com
Archery; Backpacking; Camping; Footwear; Gloves, Mitts, Hats; Hunting Accessories, Men & Women's Clothing

Heatmax, Inc., 505 Hill Rd., Dalton, GA 30721, P: 800-432-8629, F: 706-226-2195, www.heatmax.com
Archery; Backpacking; Camping; Footwear; Hunting Accessories; Law Enforcement; Pet Supplies; Sports Accessories

Heckler & Koch, Inc., 5675 Transport Blvd., Columbus, GA 31907, P: 706-568-1906, F: 706-568-9151, www.hk-usa.com
Firearms

Helly Hansen Pro (US), Inc., 3703 I St. NW, Auburn, WA 98001, P: 866-435-5902, F: 253-333-8359, www.hellyhansen.com
Men's Clothing

Hen & Rooster Cutlery, 6861 Mountain View Rd., Ooltewah, TN 37363, P: 800-251-7768, F: 423-894-9576, www.henandrooster.com
Camping; Cooking Equipment/Accessories; Cutlery; Hunting Accessories; Retail Packaging; Wholesaler/Distributor

Hendon Publishing Co./Law and Order/Tactical Response Magazines, 130 Waukegan Rd., Suite 202, Deerfield, IL 60015, P: 800-843-9764, F: 847-444-3333, www.hendonpub.com
Books/Industry Publications; Law Enforcement

Heritage Manufacturing, Inc., 4600 NW 135th St., Opa Locka, FL 33054, P: 305-685-5966, F: 305-687-6721, www.heritagemfg.com
Firearms

Heros Pride, P.O. Box 10033, Van Nuys, CA 91410, P: 888-492-9122, F: 888-492-9133, www.herospride.com
Custom Manufacturing; Emblems & Decals; Law Enforcement; Men & Women's Clothing; Wholesaler/Distributor

Hi-Point Firearms/MKS Supply, Inc., 8611-A N. Dixie Dr., Dayton, OH 45414, P: 877-425-4867, F: 937-454-0503, www.hi-pointfirearms.com
Firearms; Holsters; Law Enforcement; Magazines, Cartridge

Hiatt Thompson Corp., 7200 W. 66th St., Bedford Park, IL 60638, P: 708-496-8585, F: 708-496-8618, www.handcuffsusa.com
Law Enforcement

HideAway/Remington Packs/Cerf Bros. Bag Co., 2360 Chaffee Dr., St. Louis, MO 63146,

MANUFACTURER'S AND PRODUCT DIRECTORY

P: 800-237-3224, F: 314-291-5588, www.
cerfbag.com
*Backpacking; Bags & Equipment Cases;
Camouflage; Camping; Gun Cases;
Wholesaler/Distributor*

High Standard Mfg., Co./F.I., Inc. ATM–
AutoMag, 5200 Mitchelldale, Suite E17,
Houston, TX 77092, P: 800-272-7816, F:
713-681-5665, www.highstandard.com
*Firearms; Gun Barrels; Gun Grips & Stocks;
Gun Parts/Gunsmithing; Lubricants;
Magazines, Cartridge*

Highgear/Highgear USA, Inc., 145 Cane Creek
Industrial Park Rd., Suite 200, Fletcher, NC
28732, P: 888-295-4949, F: 828-681-5320,
www.highgear.com
*Camping; Compasses; Hunting Accessories;
Lighting Products; Sports Accessories;
Survival Kits/First Aid*

Hillman Ltd., No. 62, Tzar Samuil St.,
Sofia, Sofia 1000, BULGARIA, P: 011
35929882981, F: 011 35929882981, www.
hillman.bg
*Backpacking; Camouflage; Footwear; Gloves,
Mitts, Hats; Gun Cases; Hunting Accessories;
Men & Women's Clothing*

HitchSafe Key Vault, 18424 Hwy. 99,
Lynnwood, WA 98037, P: 800-654-1786, F:
206-523-9876, www.hitchsafe.com
*Gun Cabinets/Racks/Safes; Gun Locks;
Hunting Accessories; Outfitter; Sports
Accessories; Vehicles, Utility & Rec*

HiViz Shooting Systems/North Pass, Ltd.,
1941 Heath Pkwy., Suite 1, Fort Collins, CO
80524, P: 800-589-4315, F: 970-416-1208,
www.hivizsights.com
*Black Powder Accessories; Gun Parts/
Gunsmithing; Hunting Accessories; Paintball
Accessories; Recoil Protection Devices &
Services; Scopes, Sights & Accessories;
Sports Accessories*

Hobie Cat Co./Hobie Fishing/Hobie Kayaks,
4925 Oceanside Blvd., Oceanside, CA
92056, P: 760-758-9100, F: 760-758-1841,
www.hobiecat.com
*Bags & Equipment Cases; Camping; Hunting
Accessories; Sports Accessories; Tours/Travel*

Hodgdon Powder Co., 6231 Robinson,
Shawnee Mission, KS 66202, P: 913-362-
9455, F: 913-362-1307, www.hodgdon.com
*Black Powder/Smokeless Powder; Books/
Industry Publications; Reloading*

Hog Wild, LLC, 221 SE Main St., Portland, OR
97214, P: 888-231-6465, F: 503-233-0960,
www.hogwildtoys.com
Sports Accessories; Watches

Hogue, Inc., 550 Linne Rd., Paso Robles, CA
93447, P: 805-239-1440, F: 805-239-2553,
www.hogueinc.com
Gun Grips & Stocks; Holsters

Homak Manufacturing Co., Inc., 1605 Old Rt.
18, Suite 4-36, Wampum, PA 16157, P: 800-
874-6625, F: 724-535-1081, www.homak.
com
*Custom Manufacturing; Gun Cabinets/Racks/
Safes; Gun Cases; Gun Locks; Hunting
Accessories; Reloading; Retail Packaging*

HongKong Meike Digital Technology Co., Ltd.,
No. 12 Jiaye Rd. Pinghu St., Longgang
District, Shenzhen, GNGD 518111,
CHINA, P: 011 8613424151607, F: 011
8675528494339, www.mkgrip.com
Scopes, Sights & Accessories

Hope Global, 50 Martin St., Cumberland, RI
02864, P: 401-333-8990, F: 401-334-6442,
www.hopeglobal.com

*Custom Manufacturing; Footwear; Hunting
Accessories; Law Enforcement; Pet Supplies;
Scopes, Sights & Accessories; Shooting
Range Equipment; Sports Accessories*

Hoppe's/Bushnell Outdoor Accessories, 9200
Cody, Overland Park, KS 66214, P: 800-221-
9035, F: 800-548-0446, www.hoppes.com
*Black Powder Accessories; Firearms
Maintenance Equipment; Hearing Protection;
Law Enforcement; Lubricants; Shooting Range
Equipment*

Horizon Manufacturing Ent., Inc./RackEm
Racks, P.O. Box 7174, Buffalo Grove, IL
60089, P: 877-722-5369 (877-RACKEM-9),
F: 866-782-1550, www.rackems.com
*Airguns; Custom Manufacturing; Firearms;
Firearms Maintenance Equipment; Footwear;
Gloves, Mitts, Hats; Gun Cabinets/Racks/
Safes; Holsters; Hunting Accessories; Law
Enforcement; Shooting Range Equipment*

Hornady Manufacturing Co., 3625 Old Potash
Hwy., P.O. Box 1848, Grand Island, NE
68803, P: 308-382-1390, F: 308-382-5761,
www.hornady.com
*Ammunition; Black Powder Accessories;
Lubricants; Reloading*

Horus Vision, LLC, 659 Huntington Ave., San
Bruno, CA 94066, P: 650-588-8862, F: 650-
588-6264, www.horusvision.com
*Computer Software; Law Enforcement;
Scopes, Sights & Accessories; Targets;
Watches*

Howard Leight by Sperian, 900 Douglas
Pike, Smithfield, RI 02917, P: 866-
786-2353, F: 401-233-7641, www.
howardleightshootingsports.com, www.
sperianprotection.com
*Eyewear; Hearing Protection; Hunting
Accessories; Sports Accessories; Training &
Safety Equipment*

Huanic Corp., No. 67 Jinye Rd., Hi-tech
Zone, Xi'an, SHNX 710077, CHINA, P: 011
862981881001, F: 011 862981881011, www.
huanic.com
*Hunting Accessories; Scopes, Sights &
Accessories; Shooting Range Equipment;
Targets*

Hubertus Solingen Cutlery, 147 Wuppertaler
Strasse, Solingen, D-42653, GERMANY, P:
011 49212591994, F: 011 49212591992,
www.hubertus-solingen.de
*Custom Manufacturing; Cutlery; Knives/Knife
Cases; Survival Kits/First Aid*

Hunter Co., Inc./Hunter Wicked Optics, 3300
W. 71st Ave., Westminster, CO 80030, P:
800-676-4868, F: 303-428-3980, www.
huntercompany.com
*Binoculars; Custom Manufacturing; Gun
Cases; Holsters; Hunting Accessories; Knives/
Knife Cases; Leathergoods; Scopes, Sights &
Accessories*

Hunter Dan, 64 N. US 231, P.O. Box 103,
Greencastle, IN 46135, P: 888-241-4868, F:
765-655-1440, www.hunterdan.com
*Archery; Home Furnishings; Hunting
Accessories; Outdoor Art, Jewelry, Sculpture;
Sports Accessories; Training & Safety
Equipment*

Hunter's Edge, LLC, 270 Whigham Dairy Rd.,
Bainbridge, GA 39817, P: 888-455-0970, F:
912-248-6219, www.hunters-edge.com
*Archery; Camouflage; Decoys; Game Calls;
Gloves, Mitts, Hats; Hunting Accessories;
Men's Clothing; Scents & Lures*

Hunter's Specialties, 6000 Huntington Ct. NE,
Cedar Rapids, IA 52402, P: 800-728-0321,
F: 319-395-0326, www.hunterspec.com
*Archery; Blinds; Camouflage; Game Calls;
Gloves, Mitts, Hats; Hunting Accessories;
Scents & Lures; Videos*

Hunterbid.com/Chiron, Inc., 38 Crosby Rd.,
Dover, NH 03820, P: 603-433-8908, F: 603-
431-4072, www.hunterbid.com
Gun Grips & Stocks; Gun Parts/Gunsmithing

Hunting's-A-Drag, 42 Maple St., Rifton, NY
12471, P: 845-658-8557, F: 845-658-8569,
www.gamesled.com
Hunting Accessories

Huntington Die Specialties, 601 Oro Dam Blvd.,
P.O. Box 991, Oroville, CA 95965, P: 866-
RELOADS, F: 530-534-1212, huntingtons.
com
*Black Powder Accessories; Books/Industry
Publications; Reloading; Wholesaler/Distributor*

HyperBeam, 1504 Sheepshead Bay Rd., Suite
300, Brooklyn, NY 11236, P: 888-272-4620,
F: 718-272-1797, www.nightdetective.com
*Binoculars; Hunting Accessories; Law
Enforcement; Lighting Products; Photographic
Equipment; Scopes, Sights & Accessories;
Shooting Range Equipment; Telescopes*

Hyskore/Power Aisle, Inc., 193 West Hills Rd.,
Huntington Station, NY 11746, P: 631-673-
5975, F: 631-673-5976, www.hyskore.com
*Custom Manufacturing; Export/Import
Specialists; Eyewear; Firearms Maintenance
Equipment; Gun Cabinets/Racks/Safes;
Hearing Protection; Shooting Range
Equipment*

I

I.C.E., 68 Route 125, Kingston, NH 03848,
P: 603-347-3005, F: 603-642-9291, www.
icesigns.com
Retailer Services

ICS, No. 6, Lane 205, Dongzou Rd., Taichung,
Shangang 429, TAIWAN, P: 011-88
6425256461, F: 011-88 6425256484, icsbb.
com
*Airguns; Sports Accessories; Training & Safety
Equipment*

IHC, Inc., 12400 Burt Rd., Detroit, MI 48228,
P: 800-661-4642, F: 313-535-3220, www.
ihccorp.com
*Archery; Backpacking; Camping; Crossbows
& Accessories; Firearms; Lighting Products;
Magazines, Cartridge; Scopes, Sights &
Accessories*

i-SHOT/S.E.R.T. System, 16135 Kennedy St.,
Woodbridge, VA 22191, P: 703-670-8001, F:
703-940-9148, www.ishot-inc.com
*Bags & Equipment Cases; Custom
Manufacturing; Firearms; Law Enforcement;
Training & Safety Equipment; Wholesaler/
Distributor*

Icebreaker, Inc., P.O. Box 236, Clarkesville, GA
30523, P: 800-343-BOOT, F: 706-754-0423,
www.icebreakerinc.com
*Camouflage; Footwear; Gloves, Mitts, Hats;
Hunting Accessories*

Impact Gel Sports, P.O. Box 128, Melrose, WI
54642, P: 608-488-3630, F: 608-488-3633,
www.impactgel.com
Footwear

Import Merchandiser's Inc./MasterVision Cap
Lights, N-11254 Industrial Lane, P.O. Box
337, Elcho, WI 54428, P: 715-275-5132, F:
715-275-5176, www.mastervisionlight.com

MANUFACTURER'S AND PRODUCT DIRECTORY

Camping; Custom Manufacturing; Gloves, Mitts, Hats; Hunting Accessories; Lighting Products; Sports Accessories

IMR Powder Co., 6231 Robinson, Shawnee Mission, KS 66202, P: 913-362-9455, F: 913-362-1307, www.imrpowder.com
Black Powder/Smokeless Powder; Reloading

Indo-US Mim Tec. Pvt., Ltd., 315 Eisenhower Pkwy., Suite 211, Ann Arbor, MI 48108, P: 734-327-9842, F: 734-327-9873, www.mimindia.com
Airguns; Archery; Crossbows & Accessories; Gun Locks; Gun Parts/Gunsmithing; Knives/Knife Cases; Paintball Guns; Scopes, Sights & Accessories

Industrial Revolution/Light My Fire USA, 9225 151st Ave. NE, Redmond, WA 98052, P: 888-297-6062, F: 425-883-0036, www.industrialrev.com
Camping; Cooking Equipment/Accessories; Cutlery; Knives/Knife Cases; Lighting Products; Photographic Equipment; Survival Kits/First Aid; Wholesaler/Distributor

Indusys Techologies Belgium SPRL (UFA–Belgium), 22 Pas Bayard, Tavier, Liege B-4163, BELGIUM, P: 011 3243835234, F: 011 3243835189, www.indusys.be
Ammunition; Reloading; Shooting Range Equipment; Training & Safety Equipment

Innovative Plastech, Inc., 1260 Kingsland Dr., Batavia, IL 60510, P: 630-232-1808, F: 630-232-1978
Custom Manufacturing; Retail Packaging; Sports Accessories

INOVA/Emissive Energy Corp., 135 Circuit Dr., North Kingstown, RI 02852, P: 401-294-2030, F: 401-294-2050, www.inovalight.com
Backpacking; Camping; Hunting Accessories; Law Enforcement; Lighting Products; Sports Accessories; Survival Kits/First Aid; Training & Safety Equipment

Insight Tech-Gear, 23 Industrial Dr., Londonderry, NH 03053, P: 877-744-4802, F: 603-668-1084, www.insighttechgear.com
Hunting Accessories; Law Enforcement; Lighting Products; Paintball Accessories; Scopes, Sights & Accessories; Training & Safety Equipment

Instant Armor, Inc., 350 E. Easy St., Suite 1, Simi Valley, CA 93065, P: 805-526-3046, F: 805-526-9213, www.instantarmor.com
Law Enforcement

Instrument Technology, Inc., P.O. Box 381, Westfield, MA 10186, P: 413-562-3606, F: 413-568-9809, www.scopes.com
Law Enforcement

InterMedia Outdoors, Inc., 512 7th Ave., 11th Floor, New York, NY 10018, P: 212-852-6600, F: 212-302-4472, www.imoutdoorsmedia.com
Books/Industry Publications

International Cartridge Corp., 2273 Route 310, Reynoldsville, PA 15851, P: 877-422-5332, F: 814-938-6821, www.iccammo.com
Ammunition; Law Enforcement; Reloading; Shooting Range Equipment; Training & Safety Equipment

International Supplies/Seahorse Protective Cases, 945 W. Hyde Park, Inglewood, CA 90302, P: 800-999-1984, F: 310-673-5988, www.internationalsupplies.com
Bags & Equipment Cases; Export/Import Specialists; Eyewear; Gun Cases; Lighting Products; Photographic Equipment; Retailer Services; Wholesaler/Distributor

Interstate Arms Corp., 6 Dunham Rd., Billerica, MA 01821, P: 800-243-3006, F: 978-671-0023, www.interstatearms.com
Firearms

Iosso Products, 1485 Lively Blvd., Elk Grove, IL 60007, P: 888-747-4332, F: 847-437-8478, www.iosso.com
Black Powder Accessories; Crossbows & Accessories; Firearms Maintenance Equipment; Gun Parts/Gunsmithing; Hunting Accessories; Law Enforcement; Lubricants; Reloading

Iowa Rotocast Plastics, Inc., 1712 Moellers Dr., P.O. Box 320, Decorah, IA 52101, P: 800-553-0050, F: 563-382-3016, www.irpoutdoors.com
Backpacking; Blinds; Camping; Custom Manufacturing; Emblems & Decals; Printing Services; Sports Accessories; Wholesaler/Distributor

Irish Setter, 314 Main St., Red Wing, MN 55066, P: 888-SETTER-0, www.irlshsetterboots.com
Footwear; Men's Clothing

Ironclad Performance Wear, 2201 Park Place, Suite 101, El Segundo, CA 90245, P: 888-314-3197, F: 310-643-0300
Camouflage; Gloves, Mitts, Hats; Hunting Accessories; Leathergoods; Men & Women's Clothing; Sports Accessories

Itasca by C.O. Lynch Enterprises, 2655 Fairview Ave. N, Roseville, MN 55113, P: 800-225-2565, F: 651-633-9095, www.itascacol.com
Footwear

Ithaca Gun Co., LLC, 420 N. Warpole St., Upper Sandusky, OH 43351, P: 877-648-4222, F: 419-294-3230, www.ithacagun.com
Firearms

ITT, 7635 Plantation Rd., Roanoke, VA 24019, P: 800-448-8678, F: 540-366-9015, www.nightvision.com
Binoculars; Scopes, Sights & Accessories

ITW Military Products, 195 E. Algonquin Rd., Des Plaines, IL 60016, P: 203-240-7110, F: 847-390-8727, www.itwmilitaryproducts.com
Backpacking; Bags & Equipment Cases; Camouflage; Cooking Equipment/Accessories; Custom Manufacturing; Law Enforcement

Iver Johnson Arms Inc./Manufacturing Research, 1840 Baldwin St., Suite 10, Rockledge, FL 32955, P: 321-636-3377, F: 321-632-7745, www.iverjohnsonarms.com
Firearms; Gun Parts/Gunsmithing; Training & Safety Equipment

J

J.F. Griffin Publishing, LLC, 430 Main St., Suite 5, Williamstown, MA 01267, P: 413-884-1001, F: 413-884-1039, www.jfgriffin.com
Books/Industry Publications

JBP Holsters/Masters Holsters, 10100 Old Bon Air Pl., Richmond, VA 23235, P: 804-320-5653, F: 804-320-5653, www.jbpholsters.com
Gun Cases; Holsters; Hunting Accessories; Law Enforcement; Leathergoods; Sports Accessories; Training & Safety Equipment; Wholesaler/Distributor

JGS Precision Tool Mfg., LLC, 60819 Selander Rd., Coos Bay, OR 97420, P: 541-267-4331, F: 541-267-5996, www.jgstools.com
Firearms Maintenance Equipment; Gun Parts/Gunsmithing

J & J Armory/Dragon Skin/Pinnacle Armor, 1344 E. Edinger Ave., Santa Ana, CA 92705, P: 866-9-ARMORY, F: 714-558-4817, www.jandjarmory.com
Firearms; Law Enforcement; Training & Safety Equipment

J & J Products Co., 9134 Independence Ave., Chatsworth, CA 91311, P: 626-571-8084, F: 626-571-8704, www.jandjproducts.com
Custom Manufacturing; Hunting Accessories; Recoil Protection Devices & Services; Reloading; Retail Packaging; Sports Accessories

J & K Outdoor Products, Inc., 3864 Cty. Rd. Q, Wisconsin Rapids, WI 54495, P: 715-424-5757, F: 715-424-5757, www.jkoutdoorproducts.com
Archery; Hunting Accessories; Law Enforcement; Paintball Accessories; Scopes, Sights & Accessories

J-Tech (Steady Flying Enterprise Co., Ltd.), 1F, No. 235 Ta You Rd., Sung Shang, Taipei, 105, TAIWAN, P: 011 886227663986, F: 011 886287874836, www.tacticaljtech.com
Backpacking; Custom Manufacturing; Gloves, Mitts, Hats; Gun Cases; Holsters; Law Enforcement; Lighting Products; Wholesaler/Distributor

Jaccard Corp., 3421 N. Benzing Rd., Orchard Park, NY 14127, P: 866-478-7373, F: 716-825-5319, www.jaccard.com
Cooking Equipment/Accessories

Jack Brittingham's World of Hunting Adventure, 609-A E. Clinton Ave., Athens, TX 75751, P: 800-440-4515, F: 903-677-2126, www.jackbrittingham.com
Hunting Accessories; Training & Safety Equipment; Videos; Wildlife Management

Jack Link's Beef Jerky, One Snackfood Ln., P.O. Box 397, Minong, WI 54859, P: 800-346-6896, F: 715-466-5986, www.linksnacks.com
Custom Manufacturing

Jackite, Inc., 2868 W. Landing Rd., Virginia Beach, VA 23456, P: 877-JACKITE, F: 877-JACKFAX, www.jackite.com
Decoys; Hunting Accessories; Outdoor Art, Jewelry, Sculpture; Wholesaler/Distributor

Jackson Rifles X-Treme Shooting Products, LLC, Glenswinton, Parton, Castle Douglas, SCOTLAND DG7 3NL, P: 011 441644470223, F: 011 441644470227, www.jacksonrifles.com
Firearms; Gun Barrels; Gun Parts/Gunsmithing; Wholesaler/Distributor

Jacob Ash Holdings, Inc., 301 Munson Ave., McKees Rocks, PA 15136, P: 800-245-6111, F: 412-331-6347, www.jacobash.com
Camouflage; Gloves, Mitts, Hats; Hunting Accessories; Law Enforcement; Leathergoods; Men & Women's Clothing; Sports Accessories

James River Manufacturing, Inc./James River Armory, 3601 Commerce Dr., Suite 110, Baltimore, MD 21227, P: 410-242-6991, F: 410-242-6995, www.jamesriverarmory.com
Firearms

Japan Optics, Ltd., 2-11-29, Ukima, Kita-ku, Tokyo, 115-0051, JAPAN, P: 011 81359146680, F: 011 81353722232
Scopes, Sights & Accessories

Jeff's Outfitters, 599 Cty. Rd. 206, Cape Girardeau, MO 63701, P: 573-651-3200, F: 573-651-3207, www.jeffsoutfitters.com
Bags & Equipment Cases; Custom Manufacturing; Gun Cases; Hunting

MANUFACTURER'S AND PRODUCT DIRECTORY

Accessories; Knives/Knife Cases; Leathergoods; Scopes, Sights & Accessories

Jest Textiles, Inc./Bucksuede, 13 Mountainside Ave., Mahwah, NJ 07430, P: 800-778-7918, F: 866-899-4951, www.jesttex.com
Bags & Equipment Cases; Camouflage; Custom Manufacturing; Export/Import Specialists; Gloves, Mitts, Hats; Home Furnishings; Men & Women's Clothing

John Marshall Design, LLC, P.O. Box 46105, Baton Rouge, LA 70895, P: 800-697-2698, F: 225-275-5900
Camouflage; Home Furnishings; Men & Women's Clothing

John's Guns/A Dark Horse Arms Co., 1041 FM 1274, Coleman, TX 76834.P: 325-382-4885, F: 325-382-4887, www.darkhorsearms.com
Custom Manufacturing; Firearms; Hearing Protection; Law Enforcement

Johnston Brothers, 623 Meeting St., Bldg. B, P.O. Box 21810, Charleston, SC 29413, P: 800-257-2595, F: 800-257-2534
Bags & Equipment Cases; Firearms Maintenance Equipment; Gun Cases

Jonathan Arthur Ciener, Inc., 8700 Commerce St., Cap Canaveral, FL 32920, P: 321-868-2200, F: 321-868-2201, www.22lrconversions.com
Firearms; Gun Barrels; Gun Parts/Gunsmithing; Hunting Accessories; Magazines, Cartridge; Recoil Protection Devices & Services; Shooting Range Equipment; Training & Safety Equipment

Jordan Outdoor Enterprises, Ltd., P.O. Box 9638, Columbus, GA 31908, P: 800-992-9968, F: 706-569-9346, www.realtree.com
Camouflage; Videos

Joseph Chiarello & Co., Inc./NSSF Endorsed Insurance Program, 31 Parker Rd., Elizabeth, NJ 07208, P: 800-526-2199, F: 908-352-8512, www.guninsurance.com
Insurance; Retailer Services

Joy Enterprises, 1862 Dr., ML King Jr. Blvd., Port Commerce Center III, Riviera Beach, FL 33404, P: 800-500-FURY, F: 561-863-3277, www.joyenterprises.com
Binoculars; Camping; Compasses; Cutlery; Knives/Knife Cases; Law Enforcement; Sharpeners; Sports Accessories

JP Enterprises, Inc., P.O. Box 378, Hugo, NN 55038, P: 651-426-9196, F: 651-426-2472, www.jprifles.com
Firearms; Gun Parts/Gunsmithing; Recoil Protection Devices & Services; Scopes, Sights & Accessories

JS Products, Inc./Snap-on, 5440 S. Procyon Ave., Las Vegas, NV 89118, P: 702-362-7011, F: 702-362-5084
Lighting Products

K

KA Display Solutions, Inc., P.O. Box 99, 512 Blackman Blvd. W, Wartrace, TN 37183, P: 800-227-9540, F: 931-389-6686, www.kadsi.com
Custom Manufacturing; Gun Cabinets/Racks/Safes; Gun Cases; Home Furnishings; Knives/Knife Cases; Retailer Services; Scopes, Sights & Accessories

K.B.I., Inc./Charles Daly, P.O. Box 6625, Harrisburg, PA 17112, P: 866-325-9486, F: 717-540-8567, www.charlesdaly.com
Ammunition; Export/Import Specialists; Firearms; Hunting Accessories; Law Enforcement; Scopes, Sights & Accessories

Ka-Bar Knives, Inc., 200 Homer St., Olean, NY 14760, P: 800-282-0130, FL 716-790-7188, www.ka-bar.com
Knives/Knife Cases; Law Enforcement

KDF, Inc., 2485 St. Hwy. 46 N, Seguin, TX 78155, P: 800-KDF-GUNS; F: 830-379-8144
Firearms; Gun Grips & Stocks; Recoil Protection Devices & Services; Scopes, Sights & Accessories

KDH Defense Systems, Inc., 401 Broad St., Johnstown, PA 15906, P: 814-536-7701, F: 814-536-7716, www.kdhdefensesystems.com
Law Enforcement

KNJ Manufacturing, LLC, 757 N. Golden Key, Suite D, Gilbert, AZ 85233, P: 800-424-6606, F: 480-497-8480, www.knjmfg.com
Bags & Equipment Cases; Custom Manufacturing; Gun Cases; Holsters; Hunting Accessories; Law Enforcement; Wholesaler/Distributor

KNS Precision, Inc., 112 Marschall Creek Rd., Fredericksburg, TN 78624, P: 830-997-0000, F: 830-997-1443, www.knsprecisioninc.com
Firearms; Gun Grips & Stocks; Gun Parts/Gunsmithing; Law Enforcement; Lighting Products; Scopes, Sights & Accessories; Training & Safety Equipment; Wholesaler/Distributor

KP Industries, Inc., 3038 Industry St., Suite 108, Oceanside, CA 92054, P: 800-956-3377, F: 760-722-9884, www.kpindustries.com
Export/Import Specialists; Law Enforcement; Outfitter; Paintball Accessories; Shooting Range Equipment; Sports Accessories; Training & Safety Equipment

K-VAR Corp., 3300 S. Decatur Blvd., Suite 10601, Las Vegas, NV 89102, P: 702-364-8880, F: 702-307-2303, www.k-var.com
Firearms Maintenance Equipment; Gun Barrels; Gun Grips & Stocks; Magazines, Cartridge; Scopes, Sights & Accessories

Kahr Arms, 130 Goddard Memorial Dr., Worcester, MA 01603, P: 508-795-3919, FL 508-795-7046, www.kahr.com
Firearms; Holsters; Law Enforcement

Kakadu Traders Australia, 12832 NE Airport Way, Portland, OR 97230, P: 800-852-5288, F: 503-255-7819, www.kakaduaustralia.com
Bags & Equipment Cases; Camouflage; Men & Women's Clothing; Wholesaler/Distributor

Kalispel Case Line/Cortona Shotguns, 418641 SR 20, P.O. Box 267, Cusick, WA 99119, P: 509-445-1121, F: 509-445-1082, www.kalispelcaseline.com
Archery; Bags & Equipment Cases; Export/Import Specialists; Firearms; Gun Cases; Law Enforcement; Wholesaler/Distributor

Katz Knives, 10924 Mukilteo Speedway, Suite 287, Mukilteo, WA 98275, P: 800-848-7084, F: 480-786-9338, www.katzknives.com
Backpacking; Camping; Custom Manufacturing; Cutlery; Knives/Knife Cases; Sharpeners; Wholesaler/Distributor

Kel-Tec CNC Ind., Inc., 1475 Cox Rd., Cocoa, FL 32926, P: 321-631-0068, F: 321-631-1169, www.kel-tec-cnc.com
Firearms

Kelbly's, Inc., 7222 Dalton Fox Lk. Rd., North Lawrence, OH 44666, P: 330-683-4674, F: 330-682-7349, www.kelbly.com
Firearms; Scopes, Sights & Accessories

Kenetrek Boots, 237 Quail Run Rd., Suite A, Bozeman, MT, 59718, P: 800-232-6064, F: 406-585-5548, www.kenetrek.com
Footwear; Men's Clothing

Keng's Firearms Specialty, Inc./Versa-Pod/Champion Gun Sights, 875 Wharton Dr. SW, P.O. Box 44405, Atlanta, GA 30336, P: 800-848-4671, F: 404-505-8445, www.versapod.com
Gun Grips & Stocks; Hunting Accessories; Scopes, Sights & Accessories

KenMar Products, 411 Cameron Rd., Mattawa, Ontario P0H 1V0, CANADA, P: 866-456-5959, F: 705-744-6540, www.kenmarproducts.com
Camouflage; Gun Cases; Hunting Accessories; Leathergoods; Men's Clothing; Scents & Lures; Sports Accessories

Kent Cartridge, 727 Hite Rd., P.O. Box 849, Kearneysville, WV, 25430, P: 888-311-5368, F: 304-725-0454, www.kentgamebore.com
Ammunition

Kenyon Consumer Products/KCP Acquisition, LLC, 141 Fairgrounds Rd., West Kingston, RI 02892, P: 800-537-0024, F: 401-782-4870, www.kenyonconsumer.com
Backpacking; Camping; Law Enforcement; Men & Women's Clothing

Kernel Game Call, 13231 Champion Forest Dr., Suite 201, Houston, TX 77069, P: 830-928-2140, F: 830-792-6215
Feeder Equipment; Game Calls

Kershaw Knives, 18600 SW Teton Ave., Tualatin, OR 97062, P: 800-325-2891, F: 503-682-7168, www.kershawknives.com
Cutlery; Knives/Knife Cases

Kestrel Pocket Weather Meters, 21 Creek Circle, Boothwyn, PA 19061, P: 800-784-4221, F: 610-447-1577, www.kestrelweather.com
Backpacking; Camping; Crossbows & Accessories; Hunting Accessories; Law Enforcement; Shooting Range Equipment; Sports Accessories; Training & Safety Equipment

Keyes Hunting Gear, P.O. Box 1047, Pagosa Springs, CO 81147, P: 317-442-8132, F: 317-770-2127, www.keyeshuntinggear.com
Archery; Backpacking; Bags & Equipment Cases; Camouflage; Camping; Hunting Accessories; Men & Women's Clothing

Keystone Sporting Arms, LLC, 155 Sodom Rd., Milton, PA 17847, P: 800-742-0455, F: 570-742-1455, www.crickett.com
Airsoft; Books/Industry Publications; Firearms; Gun Grips & Stocks; Hunting Accessories; Shooting Range Equipment; Targets; Training & Safety Equipment

KG Industries, LLC, 16790 US Hwy. 63 S, Bldg. 2, Hayward, WI 54843, P: 800-348-9558, F: 715-934-3570, www.kgcoatings.com
Camouflage; Custom Manufacturing; Firearms; Firearms Maintenance Equipment; Gun Barrels; Knives/Knife Cases; Law Enforcement; Lubricants

Kick-EEZ Products, 1819 Schurman Way, Suite 106, Woodland, WA 98674, P: 877-KICKEEZ, F: 360-225-9702, www.kickeezproducts.com
Black Powder Accessories; Clay Targets; Gun Grips & Stocks; Gun Parts/Gunsmithing; Hunting Accessories; Recoil Protection Devices & Services; Targets

Kiesler Distributor of Lewis Machine & Tool Co., 2802 Sable Mill Rd., Jeffersonville, IN 47130,

MANUFACTURER'S AND PRODUCT DIRECTORY

P: 800-444-2950, F: 812-284-6651, www.kiesler.com
Firearms

Kilgore Flares Co., LLC, 155 Kilgore Dr., Toone, TN 38381, P; 731-228-5371, F: 731-228-4173, www.kilgoreflares.com
Ammunition

Kimar Srl/Chiappa Firearms, Via Milano, 2, Azzano Mella, 25020, ITALY, P: 011 390309749065, F: 011 390309749232, www.kimar.com
Airguns; Firearms; Pet Supplies; Training & Safety Equipment

Kimber Mfg., Inc./Meprolight, Inc., One Lawton St., Yonkers, NY 10705, P: 888-243-4522, F: 406-758-2223
Firearms; Law Enforcement

Kingman Training/Kingman Group, 14010 Live Oak Ave., Baldwin Park, CA 91706, P: 888-KINGMAN, F: 626-851-8530, www.kingmantraining.com
Bags & Equipment Cases; Eyewear; Gun Cases; Men's Clothing; Paintball Accessories, Guns & Paintballs

Kingport Industries, LLC, 1303 Shermer Rd., Northbrook, IL 60062, P: 866-303-5463, F: 847-446-5663, www.kingportindustries.com
Bags & Equipment Cases; Custom Manufacturing; Export/Import Specialists; Leathergoods; Wholesaler/Distributor

King's Outdoor World, 1450 S. Blackhawk Blvd., P.O. Box 307, Mt. Pleasant, UT 84647, P: 800-447-6897, F: 435-462-7436, www.kingoutdoorworld.com
Camouflage; Custom Manufacturing; Hunting Accessories; Men's Clothing; Wholesaler/Distributor

Kitasho Co., Ltd./Kanetsune, 5-1-11 Sakae-Machi, Seki-City, Gifu-Pref, 501 3253 JAPAN, P: 11 81575241211, FL 011 81575241210, www.kanetsune.com
Knives/Knife Cases

Knight Rifles/Div. Modern Muzzleloading, 715B Summit Dr., Decatur, AL 52544, P: 800-696-1703, F: 256-260-8951, www.knightrifles.com
Firearms

Knight's Manufacturing Co., 701 Columbia Blvd., Titusville, FL 32780, P: 321-607-9900, F: 321-383-2143, www.knightarmco.com
Firearms; Scopes, Sights & Accessories

Kolpin Outdoors/Bushness Outdoor Accessories, 9200 Cody, Overland Park, KS 66214, P: 800-423-3537, F: 800-548-0446, www.kolpin-outdoors.com
Firearms Maintenance Equipment; Gun Cases; Hunting Accessories

Konus USA Corp., 7530 NW 79th St., Miami, FL 33166, P: 305-884-7618, F: 305-884-7620, www.konususa.com
Binoculars; Compasses; Eyewear; Scopes, Sights & Accessories; Sports Accessories; Telescopes; Watches

Kowa Optimed, Inc., 20001 S. Vermont Ave., Torrance CA 90502, P: 800-966-5692, F: 310-327-4177, www.kowa-usa.com
Binoculars; Scopes, Sights & Accessories; Telescopes

Krause Publications/F&W Media, 700 E. State St., Iola, WI 54990, P: 888-457-2873, F: 715-445-4087, www.krausebooks.com
Books/Industry Publications; Videos

Krieger Barrels, Inc., 2024 Mayfield Rd., Richfield, WI 53076, P: 262-628-8558, F: 262-628-8748, www.kriegerbarrels.com

Gun Barrels

Kriss-TDI, 2697 International Dr., Pkwy. 4, 140, Virginia Beach, VA 23452, P: 202-821-1089, F: 202-821-1094, www.kriss-tdi.com
Firearms; Law Enforcement; Magazines, Cartridge

Kroll International, 51360 Danview Tech Ct., Shelby TWP, MI 48315, P: 800-359-6912, F: 800-359-9721, www.krollcorp.com
Bags & Equipment Cases; Footwear; Gloves, Mitts, Hats; Holsters; Hunting Accessories; Knives/Knife Cases; Law Enforcement; Wholesaler/Distributor

Kruger Optical, LLC, 141 E. Cascade Ave., Suite 208, P.O. Box 532, Sisters, OR 97759, P: 541-549-0770, F: 541-549-0769, www.krugeroptical.com
Binoculars; Scopes, Sights & Accessories

Kunming Yuanda Optical Co., Ltd./Norin Optech Co. Ltd., 9/F Huihua Bldg. No. 80 Xianlie, Zhong Rd., Guangzhou, 51007, CHINA, P: 011 862037616375, F: 011 862037619210, www.norin-optech.com
Binoculars; Compasses; Scopes, Sights & Accessories; Sports Accessories; Telescopes

Kutmaster/Div. Utica Cutlery Co., 820 Noyes St., Utica, NY 13503, P: 800-888-4223, F: 315-733-6602, www.kutmaster.com
Backpacking; Camping; Cooking Equipment & Accessories; Cutlery; Hunting Accessories; Knives/Knife Cases; Sports Accessories; Survival Kits/First Aid

Kwik-Site Co./Ironsighter Co., 5555 Treadwell, Wayne, MI 48184, P: 734-326-1500, F: 734-326-4120, www.kwiksitecorp.com
Black Powder Accessories; Firearms Maintenance Equipment; Hunting Accessories; Scopes, Sights & Accessories; Sporting Accessories

L

L.P.A. Srl di Ghilardi, Via Vittorlo Alfieri, 26, Gardone V.T., 25063, ITALY, P: 011 390308911481, F: 011 390308910951, www.lpasights.com
Black Powder Accessories; Gun Parts/Gunsmithing; Scopes, Sights & Accessories

L-3 Communications-Eotech, 1201 E. Ellsworth Rd., Ann Arbor, MI 48108, P: 734-741-8868, F: 734-741-8221, www.l-3com.com/eotech
Law Enforcement; Scopes, Sights & Accessories

L-3 Electro-Optical Systems, 3414 Herrmann Dr., Garland, TX 75041, P: 866-483-9972, F: 972-271-2195, www.l3nightvision.com
Law Enforcement; Scopes, Sights & Accessories

L.A. Lighter, Inc./Viclight, 19805 Harrison Ave., City of Industry, CA 91789, P: 800-499-4708, F: 909-468-1859, www.lalighter.com
Camping; Cooking Equipment/Accessories; Lighting Products; Sports Accessories; Training & Safety Equipment; Wholesaler/Distributor

L.A.R. Manufacturing, 4133 W. Farm Rd., West Jordan, UT 84088, P: 801-280-3505, F: 801-280-1972, www.largrizzly.com
Firearms

La Crosse Technology, Ltd., 2809 Losey Blvd. S, La Crosse, WI 54601, P: 800-346-9544, F: 608-796-1020, www.lacrossetechnology.com
Sports Accessories; Wholesaler/Distributor

LEM Products, 109 May Dr., Harrison, OH 45030, P: 513-202-1188, F: 513-202-9494, www.lemproducts.com
Books/Industry Publications; Cooking Equipment/Accessories; Cutlery; Knives/Knife Cases; Sharpeners; Videos; Wholesaler/Distributor

L&R Ultrasonics, 577 Elm St., Kearny, NJ 07032, P: 201-991-5330, F: 201-991-5870, www.lrultrasonics.com
Decoys; Firearms; Firearms Maintenance Equipment; Gun Parts/Gunsmithing; Lubricants; Reloading; Shooting Range Equipment

LRB Arms, 96 Cherry Lane, Floral Park, NY 11001, P: 516-327-9061, F: 516-327-0246, www.lrbarms.com
Firearms; Wholesaler/Distributor

LRI–Photon Micro Light, 20448 Hwy. 36, Blachly, OR 97412, P: 541-925-3741, F: 541-925-3751, www.laughingrabbitinc.com
Backpacking; Camping; Hunting Accessories; Law Enforcement; Lighting Products; Sports Accessories; Survival Kits/First Aid; Training & Safety Equipment

Lachausee/New Lachaussée, UFA Belgium, Rue de Tige, 13, Herstal, Liège B 4040, BELGIUM, P: 011 3242488811, F: 011 3242488800, www.lachaussee.com
Ammunition; Firearms Maintenance Equipment; Reloading; Shooting Range Equipment

Lakeside Machine, LLC, 1213 Industrial St., Horseshoe Bend, AR 72512, P: 870-670-4999, F: 870-670-4998, www.lakesideguns.com
Custom Manufacturing; Firearms; Hunting Accessories; Law Enforcement

Lanber, Zubiaurre 3, P.O. Box 3, Zaldibar, (Vizcaya) 48250, SPAIN, P: 011 34946827702, F: 011 34946827999, www.lanber.com
Firearms

Lancer Systems, 7566 Morris Ct., Suite 300, Allentown, PA, 18106, P: 610-973-2614, F: 610-973-2615, www.lancer-systems.com
Custom Manufacturing; Gun Parts/Gunsmithing; Magazines, Cartridge

Landmark Outdoors/Yukon Advanced Optics/Sightmark/Mobile Hunter/Trophy Score/Amacker, 201 Regency Pkwy., Mansfield, TX 76063, P: 877-431-3579, F: 817-453-8770, www.landmarkoutdoors.com
Airsoft; Binoculars; Custom Manufacturing; Feeder Equipment; Hunting Accessories; Law Enforcement; Paintball Accessories; Scopes, Sights & Accessories; Shooting Range Equipment; Treestands; Wholesaler/Distributor

Lanigan Performance Products/KG Industries, 10320 Riverburn Dr., Tampa, FL 33467, P: 813-651-5400, F: 813-991-6156, www.thesacskit.com
Gun Parts/Gunsmithing

Lansky Sharpeners, P.O. Box 50830, Henderson, NV 89016, P: 716-877-7511, F: 716-877-6955, www.lansky.com
Archery; Camping; Cooking Equipment/Accessories; Cutlery; Hunting Accessories; Knives/Knife Cases; Law Enforcement; Sharpeners

Lapua/Vihtavuori, 123 Winchester Dr., Sedalia, MO 65301, P: 660-826-3232, F: 660-826-3232, www.lapua.com
Ammunition; Books/Industry Publications; Reloading; Videos

LaRue Tactical, 850 CR 177, Leander, TX 78641, P: 512-259-1585, F: 512-259-1588, www.laruetactical.com
Custom Manufacturing; Scopes, Sights & Accessories; Targets

Laser Ammo, Ltd., #7 Bar Kochva St., Rishon Lezion, 75353, ISRAEL, P: 682-286-3311, www.laser-ammo.com
Ammunition; Firearms; Law Enforcement; Scopes, Sights & Accessories; Shooting Range Equipment; Training & Safety Equipment

Laser Devices, Inc., 2 Harris Ct., Suite A-4, Monterey, CA 93940, P: 800-235-2162, F: 831-373-0903, www.laserdevices.com
Holsters; Law Enforcement; Lighting Products; Scopes, Sights & Accessories; Shooting Range Equipment; Sports Accessories; Targets; Training & Safety Equipment

Laser Shot, Inc., 4214 Bluebonnet Dr., Stafford, TX 77477, P: 281-240-8241, F: 281-240-8241
Law Enforcement; Training & Safety Equipment

LaserLyte, 101 Airpark Rd., Cottonwood, AZ 86326, P: 928-649-3201, F: 928-649-3970, www.laserlyte.com
Hunting Accessories; Scopes, Sights & Accessories

LaserMax, Inc., 3495 Winton Place Bldg. B, Rochester, NY 14623, P: 800-527-3703, F: 585-272-5427, www.lasermax.com
Airsoft; Crossbows & Accessories; Firearms; Law Enforcement; Paintball Accessories; Scopes, Sights & Accessories; Shooting Range Equipment; Training & Safety Equipment

Lauer Custom Weaponry/Duracoat Products, 3601 129th St., Chippewa Falls, WI 54729, P: 800-830-6677, F: 715-723-2950, www.lauerweaponry.com
Camouflage; Custom Manufacturing; Firearms; Hunting Accessories; Law Enforcement; Lubricants; Magazines, Cartridge; Scopes, Sights & Accessories

Law Enforcement Targets, Inc., 8802 W. 35 W. Service Dr. NE, Blaine, MN 55449, P: 800-779-0182, F: 651-645-5360, www.letargets.com
Eyewear; Gun Cabinets/Racks/Safes; Gun Grips & Stocks; Hearing Protection; Law Enforcement; Targets; Training & Safety Equipment

Law Officer Magazine/Div. Elsevier Public Safety/Elsevier, 525 B St., Suite 1900, San Diego, CA 92101, P: 800-266-5367, F: 619-699-6396, www.lawofficer.com
Books/Industry Publications; Law Enforcement

Lawman Leather Goods, P.O. Box 30115, Las Vegas, NV 89173, P: 877-44LAWMAN, F: 702-227-0036, www.lawmanleathergoods.com
Black Powder Accessories; Books/Industry Publications; Holsters; Law Enforcement; Leathergoods; Wholesaler/Distributor

Lazzeroni Arms Co., 1415 S. Cherry Ave., Tuscon, AZ 85713, P: 888-4-WARBIRD, F: 520-624-6202, www.lazzeroni.com
Ammunition; Firearms

Leapers, Inc., 32700 Capitol St., Livonia, MI 48150, P: 734-542-1500, F: 734-542-7095, www.leapers.com
Airguns; Airsoft; Bags & Equipment Cases; Gun Cases; Holsters; Law Enforcement; Lighting Products; Scopes, Sights & Accessories

Leatherman Tool Group, Inc., 12106 NE Ainsworth Circle, Portland, OR 97220, P: 800-847-8665, F: 503-253-7830, www.leatherman.com
Backpacking; Hunting Accessories; Knives/Knife Cases; Lighting Products; Sports Accessories

Leatherwood/Hi-Lux Optics/Hi-Lux, Inc., 3135 Kashiwa St., Torrance, CA 90505, P: 888-445-8912, F: 310-257-8096, www.hi-luxoptics.com
Binoculars; Scopes, Sights & Accessories; Telescopes

Legacy Sports International, 4750 Longley Lane, Suite 208, Reno, NV 89502, P: 775-828-0555, F: 775-828-0565, www.legacysports.com
Firearms; Gun Cabinets/Racks/Safes; Gun Cases; Scopes, Sights & Accessories

Leica Sport Optics/Leica Camera Inc., 1 Peart Ct., Unit A, Allendale, NJ 07401, P: 800-222-0118, F: 201-955-1686, www.leica-camera.com/usa
Binoculars; Photographic Equipment; Scopes, Sights & Accessories

LensPen–Parkside Optical, 650-375 Water St., Vancouver, British Columbia V6B 5C6, CANADA, P: 877-608-0868, F: 604-681-6194, www.lenspens.com
Binoculars; Hunting Accessories; Law Enforcement; Photographic Equipment; Scopes, Sights & Accessories; Sports Accessories; Telescopes

Les Baer Custom, Inc., 1804 Iowa Dr., Leclaire, IA 52753, P: 563-289-2126, F: 563-289-2132, www.lesbaer.com
Custom Manufacturing; Export/Import Specialists; Firearms; Gun Barrels; Gun Parts/Gunsmithing

Leupold & Stevens, Inc., 14400 NW Greenbriar Pkwy. 9700, P.O. Box 688, Beaverton, OR 97006, P: 503-646-9171, F: 503-526-1478, www.leupold.com
Binoculars; Lighting Products; Scopes, Sights & Accessories

Level Lok Shooting System/Div. Brutis Enterprises Inc., 105 S. 12th St., Pittsburgh, PA 15203, P: 888-461-7468, F: 412-488-5440, www.levellok.com
Binoculars; Firearms; Gun Grips & Stocks; Hunting Accessories; Photographic Equipment; Scopes, Sights & Accessories; Shooting Range Equipment; Sports Accessories

Levy's Leathers Limited, 190 Disraeli Freeway, Winnipeg, Manitoba R3B 2Z4, CANADA, P: 800-565-0203, F: 888-329-5389, www.levysleathers.com
Archery; Bags & Equipment Cases; Hunting Accessories; Knives/Knife Cases; Leathergoods

Lew Horton Distributing Co., Inc., 15 Walkup Dr., P.O. Box 5023, Westboro, MA 01581, P: 800-446-7866, F: 508-366-5332, www.lewhorton.com
Ammunition; Firearms; Hunting Accessories; Knives/Knife Cases; Law Enforcement; Magazines, Cartridge; Scopes, Sights & Accessories; Wholesaler/Distributor

Lewis Machine & Tool, 1305 11th St. W, Milan, IL 61264, P: 309-787-7151, F: 309-787-7193, www.lewismachine.net
Firearms

Liberty Mountain, 4375 W. 1980 S, Suite 100, Salt Lake City, UT 84104, P: 800-366-2666, F: 801-954-0766, www.libertymountain.com
Backpacking; Camping; Cooking Equipment/Accessories; Gloves, Mitts, Hats; Knives/Knife Cases; Lighting Products; Survival Kits/First Aid; Wholesaler/Distributor

Liberty Safe & Security Products, Inc., 1199 W. Utah Ave., Payson, UT 84651, P: 800-247-5625, F: 801-465-5880, www.libertysafe.com
Firearms Maintenance Equipment; Gun Cabinets/Racks/Safes; Gun Locks; Home Furnishings; Hunting Accessories; Law Enforcement; Sports Accessories; Training & Safety Equipment

Light My Fire USA, 9225 151st Ave. NE, Redmond, WA 98052, P: 888-297-6062, F: 425-883-0036
Camping; Cooking Equipment/Accessories; Knives/Knife Cases; Survival Kits/First Aid

Lightfield Ammunition Corp., P.O. Box 162, Adelphia, NJ 07710, P: 732-462-9200, F: 732-780-2437, www.lightfieldslugs.com
Ammunition

LightForce USA, Inc/NightForce Optics, 1040 Hazen Ln., Orofino, ID 83544, P: 800-732-9824, F: 208-476-9817, www.nightforceoptics.com
Law Enforcement; Lighting Products; Scopes, Sights & Accessories; Telescopes

LimbSaver, 50 W. Rose Nye Way, Shelton, WA 98584, P: 877-257-2761, F: 360-427-4025, www.limbsaver.com
Archery; Crossbows & Accessories; Hunting Accessories; Men's Clothing; Paintball Accessories; Recoil Protection Devices & Services; Scopes, Sights & Accessories

Linton Cutlery Co., Ltd., 7F, No. 332, Yongji Rd., Sinyi District, Taipei, 110, TAIWAN, P: 011 886227090905, F: 011 886227003978, www.linton-cutlery.com
Cutlery; Export/Import Specialists; Hunting Accessories; Law Enforcement; Sports Accessories; Wholesaler/Distributor

Linville Knife and Tool Co., P.O. Box 71, Bethania, NC 27010, P: 336-923-2062
Cutlery; Gun Grips & Stocks; Knives/Knife Cases

Lipseys, P.O. Box 83280, Baton Rouge, LA 70884, P: 800-666-1333, FL 225-755-3333, www.lipseys.com
Black Powder Accessories; Firearms; Holsters; Hunting Accessories; Magazines, Cartridge; Online Services; Scopes, Sights & Accessories; Wholesaler/Distributor

Little Giant Ladders, 1198 N. Spring Creek Pl., Springville, UT 84663, P: 800-453-1192, F: 801-489-1130, www.littlegiantladders.com
Law Enforcement; Training & Safety Equipment

Little Sportsman, Inc., 315 N. 400 W, P.O. Box 715, Fillmore, UT 84631, P: 435-743-4400, F: 435-846-2132, www.littlesportsman.com
Books/Industry Publications

LockSAF/VMR Capital Group, 2 Gold St., Suite 903, New York, NY 10038, P: 877-568-5625, F: 877-893-4502, www.locksaf.com
Gun Cabinets/Racks/Safes

Loksak, Inc. (formerly Watchful Eye), P.O. Box 980007, Park City, UT 84098, P: 800-355-1126, F: 435-940-0956, www.loksak.com
Bags & Equipment Cases

Lone Wolf Distributors, Inc., 57 Shepard Rd., P.O. Box 3549, Oldtown, ID 83822, P: 888-279-2077, F: 208-437-1098, www.lonewolfdist.com
Books/Industry Publications; Firearms Maintenance Equipment; Gun Barrels; Gun

MANUFACTURER'S AND PRODUCT DIRECTORY

Parts/Gunsmithing; Holsters; Scopes, Sights & Accessories; Videos; Wholesaler/Distributor

Lone Wolf Knives, 9373 SW Barber St., Suite A, Wilsonville, OR 97070, P: 503-431-6777, F: 503-431-6776, www.lonewolfknives.com
Archery; Backpacking; Camouflage; Camping; Cutlery; Hunting Accessories; Knives/Knife Cases; Law Enforcement

Long Perng Co., Ltd., #16, Hejiang Rd., Chung Li Industrial Zone, Chung Li City, Taoyuan Hsien, 320, TAIWAN, P: 011 88634632468, F: 011 88634631948, www.longperng.com.tw
Binoculars; Scopes, Sights & Accessories; Telescopes

Longleaf Camo, 1505 Airport Rd., Flowood, MS 39232, P: 866-751-2266, F: 601-719-0713, www.longleafcamo.com
Camouflage; Footwear; Gloves, Mitts, Hats; Men & Women's Clothing

Loon Lake Decoy Co., Inc., 170 Industrial Ct., Wabasha, MN 55981, P: 800-555-2696, F: 612-565-4871, www.loonlakedecoycompany.com
Custom Manufacturing; Decoys; Home Furnishings; Hunting Accessories; Lighting Products; Outdoor Art, Jewelry, Sculpture; Wholesaler/Distributor

Lorpen North America, Inc., 100 Ironside Crescent, Suite 8, Toronto, Ontario M1X 1M9, CANADA, P: 888-224-9781, F: 416-335-8201, www.lorpen.com
Footwear

Lothar Walther Precision Tools, Inc., 3425 Hutchinson Rd., Cumming, GA 30040, P: 770-889-9998, F: 770-889-4919, www.lothar-walther.com
Custom Manufacturing; Export/Import Specialists; Gun Barrels

Lou's Police Distributor, 7815 W. 4th Ave., Hialeah, FL 33014, P: 305-822-5362, F: 305-822-9603, www.louspolice.com
Ammunition; Firearms; Gun Grips & Stocks; Hearing Protection; Holsters; Law Enforcement; Scopes, Sights & Accessories; Wholesaler/Distributor

LouderThanWords.US/Heirloom Precision, LLC, 2118 E. 5th St., Tempe, AZ 85281, P: 480-804-1911, www.louderthanwords.us
Firearms; Gun Parts/Gunsmithing; Holsters

Lowa Boots, 86 Viaduct Rd., Stamford, CT 06907, P: 888-335-5692, F: 203-353-0311, www.lowaboots.com
Footwear; Men & Women's Clothing

Lowrance–Navico, Eagle–Navico, 12000 E. Skelly Dr., Tulsa, OK 74128, P: 800-352-1356, F: 918-234-1707, www.lowrance.com
Archery; Backpacking; Camping; Hunting Accessories; Law Enforcement; Sports Accessories; Survival Kits/First Aid; Vehicles, Utility & Rec

Lowy Enterprises, Inc., 1970 E. Gladwick St., Rancho Dominguez, CA 90220, P: 310-763-1111, F: 310-763-1112, www.lowyusa.com
Backpacking; Bags & Equipment Cases; Custom Manufacturing; Law Enforcement; Outfitter; Paintball Accessories; Sports Accessories; Wholesaler/Distributor

Luggage-USA, Inc./L A Luggage, 710 Ducommun St., Los Angeles, CA 90012, P: 888-laluggage, F: 213-626-0800, www.luggage-usa.com
Backpacking; Bags & Equipment Cases; Camouflage; Camping; Export/Import Specialists; Gun Cases; Leathergoods; Wholesaler/Distributor

Lumberjack Tools, 9304 Wolf Pack Terrace, Colorado Springs, CO 80920, P: 719-282-3043, F: 719-282-3046, www.lumberjacktools.com
Camping; Crossbows & Accessories; Firearms; Home Furnishings; Hunting Accessories; Taxidermy; Treestands; Wholesaler/Distributor

Luminox Watch Co., 2301 Kerner Blvd., Suite A, San Rafael, CA 94901, P: 415-455-9500, F: 415-482-8215, www.luminox.com
Backpacking; Camping; Custom Manufacturing; Hunting Accessories; Law Enforcement, Outdoor Art, Jewelry, Sculpture; Sports Accessories; Watches

LWRC International, LLC, 815 Chesapeake Dr., Cambridge, MD 21613, P: 410-901-1348, F: 410-228-1799, www.lwrifles.com
Ammunition; Custom Manufacturing; Firearms; Firearms Maintenance Equipment; Gun Barrels; Gun Parts/Gunsmithing; Law Enforcement; Magazines, Cartridge

Lyalvale Express Limited, Express Estate, Whittington, Lichfield, WS13 8XA, UNITED KINGDOM, P: 011-44 1543434400, F: 011-44 1543434420, www.lyalvaleexpress.com
Ammunition

Lyman-Pachmayr-Trius Products/TacStar-A-Zoom-Butchs-Uni-Dot, 475 Smith St., Middletown, CT 06457, P: 800-225-9626, F: 860-632-1699, www.lymanproducts.com
Black Powder Accessories; Books/Industry Publications; Firearms; Firearms Maintenance Equipment; Gun Parts/Gunsmithing; Reloading; Scopes, Sights & Accessories; Shooting Range Equipment

Lyons Press, 246 Goose Ln., Guilford, CT 06437, P: 800-243-0495, F: 800-820-2329, www.glovepequot.com
Books/Industry Publications; Wholesaler/Distributor

M

MDM/Millennium Designed Muzzleloaders, Ltd., RR 1, Box 405, Maidstone, VT 05905, P: 802-676-331, F: 802-676-3322, www.mdm-muzzleloaders.com
Ammunition; Black Powder Accessories; Black Powder/Smokeless Powder; Custom Manufacturing; Firearms Maintenance Equipment; Gun Barrels; Gun Cases; Scopes, Sights & Accessories

MDS Inc., 3429 Stearns Rd., Valrico, FL 33596, P: 800-435-9352, F: 813-684-5953, www.mdsincorporated.com
Firearms Maintenance Equipment; Gun Parts/Gunsmithing; Law Enforcement

MFI, 563 San Miguel, Liberty, KY 42539, P: 606-787-0022, F: 606-787-0059, www.mfiap.com
Custom Manufacturing; Export/Import Specialists; Firearms; Gun Grips & Stocks; Gun Parts/Gunsmithing; Scopes, Sights & Accessories; Sports Accessories; Wholesaler/Distributor

MGI, 102 Cottage St., Bangor, ME 04401, P: 207-945-5441, F: 207-945-4010, www.mgimilitary.com
Firearms; Gun Barrels; Law Enforcement

MGM–Mike Gibson Manufacturing, 17891 Karcher Rd., Caldwell, ID 83607, P: 888-767-7371, F: 208-454-0666, www.mgmtargets.com
Clay Targets; Custom Manufacturing; Firearms; Gun Cabinets/Racks/Safes; Shooting Range Equipment; Targets; Training & Safety Equipment

MG Arms, Inc., 6030 Treaschwig Rd., Spring, TX 77373, P: 281-821-8282, F: 281-821-6387, www.mgarmsinc.com
Ammunition; Custom Manufacturing; Firearms; Gun Grips & Stocks; Wholesaler/Distributor

MPI Outdoors/Grabber, 5760 N. Hawkeye Ct., Grand Rapids, MI 49509, P: 800-423-1233, F: 616-977-7718, www.warmers.com
Backpacking; Camouflage; Camping; Cooking Equipment/Accessories; Gloves, Mitts, Hats; Hunting Accessories; Lighting Products; Survival Kits/First Aid

MPRI, 10220 Old Columbia Rd., Suites A & B, Columbia, MD 21046, P: 800-232-6448, F: 410-309-1506, www.mpri.com
Ammunition; Gun Barrels; Law Enforcement; Shooting Range Equipment; Targets; Training & Safety Equipment

MPT Industries, 6-B Hamilton Business Park, 85 Franklin Rd., Dover, NJ 07801, P: 973-989-9220, F: 973-989-9234, www.mptindustries.com
Airguns; Camping; Firearms; Firearms Maintenance Equipment; Lubricants; Paintball Guns; Sports Accessories

M-Pro 7 Gun Care/Bushnell Outdoor Accessories, 9200 Cody, Overland Park, KS 66214, P: 800-845-2444, F: 800-548-0446, www.mpro7.com
Black Powder Accessories; Firearms Maintenance Equipment; Gun Parts/Gunsmithing; Hunting Accessories; Law Enforcement; Lubricants

M-Pro 7 Gun Care, 225 W. Deer Valley Rd., Suite 4, Phoenix, AZ 85027, P: 888-YES-4MP7, F: 623-516-0414, www.mpro7.com
Black Powder Accessories; Firearms Maintenance Equipment; Gun Parts/Gunsmithing; Hunting Accessories; Law Enforcement; Lubricants

MSA, 121 Gamma Dr., Pittsburgh, PA 15238, P: 800-672-2222, F: 412-967-3373
Bags & Equipment Cases; Eyewear; Hearing Protection; Law Enforcement; Survival Kits/First Aid; Training & Safety Equipment

MSA Safety Works, 121 Gamma Dr., Pittsburgh, PA 15238, P: 800-969-7562, F: 800-969-7563, www.msasafetyworks.com
Eyewear; Hearing Protection; Shooting Range Equipment; Training & Safety Equipment

MT2, LLC/Metals Treatment Technologies, 14045 W. 66th Ave., Arvada, CO 80004, P: 888-435-6645, F: 303-456-5998, www.mt2.com
Firearms Maintenance Equipment; Shooting Range Equipment

MTM Case-Gard Co., P.O. Box 13117, Dayton, OH 45413, P: 800-543-0548, F: 937-890-1747, www.mtmcase-gard.com
Bags & Equipment Cases; Black Powder Accessories; Camping; Firearms Maintenance Equipment; Gun Cases; Hunting Accessories; Reloading; Targets

Mace Security International, 160 Benmont Ave., Bennington, VT 05201, P: 800-255-2634, F: 802-753-1209, www.mace.com
Archery; Camping; Hunting Accessories; Law Enforcement; Sports Accessories; Training & Safety Equipment

Mag Instrument, Inc./Maglite, 2001 S. Hellman Ave., Ontario, CA 91761, P: 800-289-6241, F: 775-719-4586, www.maglite.com
Backpacking; Camping; Hunting Accessories; Lighting Products; Sports Accessories;

MANUFACTURER'S AND PRODUCT DIRECTORY

Survival Kits/First Aid; Training & Safety Equipment

Magellan Navigation, 471 El Camino Real, Santa Clara, CA 94050, P: 408-615-5100, F: 408-615-5200, www.magellangps.com
Backpacking; Camping; Compasses; Computer Software; Hunting Accessories; Sports Accessories; Vehicles, Utility & Rec

Maglula, Ltd., P.O. Box 302, Rosh Ha'ayin, 48103, ISRAEL, P: 011 97239030902, F: 011 97239030902, www.maglula.com
Firearms Maintenance Equipment; Gun Parts/Gunsmithing; Magazines, Cartridge; Shooting Range Equipment

Magnum USA, 4801 Stoddard Rd., Modesto, CA 95356, P: 800-521-1698, F: 209-545-2079, www.magnumboots.com
Footwear; Law Enforcement; Men's Clothing

Magnum Research, Inc., 7110 University Ave. NE, Minneapolis, MN 55432, P: 800-772-6168, F: 763-574-0109, www.magnumresearch.com
Firearms

Magnum Tents, P.O. Box 18127, Missoula, MT 59808, P: 877-836-8226, F: 877-836-8226, www.magnumtents.com
Camping; Hunting Accessories

Magpul Industries Corp., P.O. Box 17697, Boulder, CO 80308, P: 877-462-4785, F: 303-828-3469, www.magpul.com
Firearms; Gun Grips & Stocks; Gun Parts/Gunsmithing; Law Enforcement; Videos

Magtech Ammunition Co., Inc., 248 Apollo Dr., Suite 180, Lino Lakes, MN 55014, P: 800-466-7191, F: 763-235-4004, www.magtechammunition.com
Ammunition; Export/Import Specialists; Law Enforcement; Reloading; Shooting Range Equipment; Wholesaler/Distributor

Mahco, Inc., 1202 Melissa Dr., Bentonville, AR 72712, P: 479-273-0052, F: 479-271-9248
Bags & Equipment Cases; Binoculars; Camouflage; Camping; Hunting Accessories; Knives/Knife Cases; Scopes, Scopes, Sights & Accessories

Majestic Arms, Ltd., 101-A Ellis St., Staten Island, NY 10307, P: 718-356-6765, F: 718-356-6835, www.majesticarms.com
Firearms; Gun Barrels; Gun Parts/Gunsmithing

Mako Group, 74 Rome St., Farmingdale, NY 11735, P: 631-880-3396, F: 631-880-3397, www.themakogroup.com
Custom Manufacturing; Gun Grips & Stocks; Law Enforcement; Lighting Products; Scopes, Sights & Accessories; Targets; Training & Safety Equipment; Wholesaler/Distributor

Mancom Manufacturing Inc., 1335 Osprey Dr., Ancaster, Ontario L9G 4V5, CANADA, P: 888-762-6266, F: 905-304-6137, www.mancom.ca
Custom Manufacturing; Law Enforcement; Shooting Range Equipment; Training & Safety Equipment

Manners Composite Stocks, 1209 Swift, North Kansas City, MO 64116, P: 816-283-3334, www.mannerstock.com
Custom Manufacturing; Firearms Maintenance Equipment; Gun Grips & Stocks; Law Enforcement; Shooting Range Equipment

Dave Manson Precision Reamers/Div. Loon Lake Precision, Inc., 8200 Embury Rd., Grand Blanc, MI 48439, P: 810-953-0732, F: 810-953-0735, www.mansonreamers.com
Black Powder Accessories; Custom Manufacturing; Firearms Maintenance Equipment; Gun Barrels; Gun Parts/

Gunsmithing; Recoil Protection Devices & Services; Reloading

Mantis Knives/Famous Trails, 1580 N. Harmony Circle, Anaheim, CA 92807, P: 877-97-SCOPE, F: 714-701-9672, www.mantisknives.com
Binoculars; Camping; Hunting Accessories; Knives/Knife Cases; Law Enforcement; Photographic Equipment; Scopes, Sights & Accessories; Wholesaler/Distributor

Manzella Productions, 80 Sonwil Dr., Buffalo, NY 14225, P: 716-681-8880, F: 716-681-6888
Hunting Accessories; Law Enforcement

Marbles, 420 Industrial Park, Gladstone, MI 49837, P: 906-428-3710, F: 906-428-3711, www.marblescutlery.com
Compasses; Cutlery; Scopes, Sights & Accessories; Sharpeners

Marlin Firearms/H&R, 100 Kenna Dr., P.O. Box 248, North Haven, CT 06473, P: 888-261-1179, F: 336-548-8736, www.marlinfirearms.com
Firearms

Marvel Precision, LLC, P.O. Box 127, Cortland, NE 68331, P: 800-295-1987, F: 402-791-2246, www.marvelprecision.com
Firearms; Wholesaler/Distributor

Masen Co., Inc., John, 1305 Jelmak St., Grand Prairie, TX 75050, P: 972-970-3691, F: 972-970-3691, www.johnmasen.com
Firearms Maintenance Equipment; Gun Grips & Stocks; Gun Parts/Gunsmithing; Magazines, Cartridge; Online Services; Scopes, Sights & Accessories; Wholesaler/Distributor

Maserin Coltellerie SNC, Via dei Fabbri, 19, Maniago, 33085, ITALY, P: 011 39042771335, F: 011 390427700690, www.maserin.com
Cutlery; Hunting Accessories; Knives/Knife Cases; Law Enforcement; Sports Accessories

Master Cutlery, Inc., 700 Penhorn Ave., Secausus, NJ 07094, P: 888-271-7228, F: 888-271-7228, www.mastercutlery.com
Airsoft; Crossbows & Accessories; Custom Manufacturing; Cutlery

Masterbuilt Manufacturing, Inc., 1 Masterbuilt Ct., Columbus, GA 31907, P: 800-489-1581, F: 706-327-5632, www.masterbuilt.com
Camping; Cooking Equipment/Accessories; Hunting Accessories; Vehicles, Utility & Rec

Matterhorn Footwear/Cove Shoe Co., HH Brown Work & Outdoor Group, 107 Highland St., Martinsburg, PA 16662, P: 800-441-4319, F: 814-793-9272, www.matterhornboot.com
Footwear; Law Enforcement; Training & Safety Equipment

Matz Abrasives/Stagecoach, 1209 W. Chestnut St., Burbank, CA 91506, P: 818-840-8042, F: 818-840-8340, www.matzrubber.com
Black Powder Accessories; Custom Manufacturing; Firearms Maintenance Equipment; Gun Grips & Stocks; Gun Parts/Gunsmithing; Hunting Accessories; Recoil Protection Devices & Services

Maurice Sporting Goods, Inc., 1910 Techny Rd., Northbrook, IL 60065, P: 866-477-3474, F: 847-715-1419, www.maurice.net
Archery; Camping; Firearms Maintenance Equipment; Game Calls; Gloves, Mitts, Hats; Hunting Accessories; Sports Accessories; Wholesaler/Distributor

Maxit Designs, Inc., P.O. Box 1052, Carmichael, CA 95609, P: 800-556-2948, F: 916-489-7031, www.maxit-inc.com
Footwear; Gloves, Mitts, Hats; Men & Women's Clothing

Maxpedition Hard-Use Gear/Edgygear, Inc., P.O. Box 5008, Palos Verdes, CA 90274, P: 877-629-5556, F: 310-515-5950, www.maxpedition.com
Backpacking; Bags & Equipment Cases; Gun Cases; Holsters; Hunting Accessories; Knives/Knife Cases; Law Enforcement; Sports Accessories

MaxPro Police & Armor, 4181 W. 5800 N, Mountain Green, UT 84050, P: 801-876-3616, F: 801-876-2746, www.maxpropolice.com
Training & Safety Equipment

Mayville Engineering Co. (MEC), 800 Horicon St., Suite 1, Mayville, WI 53050, P: 800-797-4MEC, F: 920-387-5802, www.mecreloaders.com
Reloading

McConkey, Inc./ATV Backpacker Cart, P.O. Box 1362, Seeley Lake, MT 59868, P: 308-641-1085, F: 866-758-9896, www.atvbackpackercart.com
Ammunition; Backpacking; Camping; Hunting Accessories; Sports Accessories; Vehicles, Utility & Rec; Wholesaler/Distributor

McGowan Manufacturing Co., 4854 N. Shamrock Pl., Suite 100, Tucson, AZ 85705, P: 800-342-4810, F: 520-219-9759, www.mcgowanmfg.com
Archery; Camping; Cooking Equipment/Accessories; Crossbows & Accessories; Cutlery; Hunting Accessories; Knives/Knife Cases; Sharpeners

McKeon Products, Inc./Mack's Hearing Protection, 25460 Guenther, Warren, MI 48091, P: 586-427-7560, F: 586-427-7204, www.macksearplugs.com
Camping; Hearing Protection; Hunting Accessories; Sports Accessories; Training & Safety Equipment

McMillan Fiberglass Stocks, 1638 W. Knudsen Dr., Suite A, Phoenix, AZ 85027, P: 877-365-6148, F: 623-581-3825, www.mcmillanusa.com
Firearms; Gun Grips & Stocks

McNett Corp., 1411 Meador Ave., Bellingham, WA 98229, P: 360-671-2227, F: 360-671-4521, www.mcnett.com
Backpacking; Camouflage; Camping; Hunting Accessories; Knives/Knife Cases; Lubricants; Paintball Accessories; Sports Accessories

Mcusta Knives/Mcusta Knives USA, P.O. Box 22901, Portland, OR 97269, P: 877-714-5487, F: 503-344-4631, www.mcustausa.com
Cooking Equipment/Accessories; Cutlery; Hunting Accessories; Knives/Knife Cases; Law Enforcement; Sports Accessories; Wholesaler/Distributor

Mead Industries, Inc., 411 Walnut St., P.O. Box 402, Wood River, NE 68883, P: 308-583-2875, F: 308-583-2002
Ammunition

MEC-GAR SRL, Via Mandolossa, 102/a, Gussago, Brescia, 25064, ITALY, P: 011 390303735413, F: 011 390303733687, www.mec-gar.it
Gun Parts/Gunsmithing; Law Enforcement; Magazine, Cartridge

Medalist/Performance Sports Apparel, 1047 Macarthur Rd., Reading PA, 19605, P: 800-

MANUFACTURER'S AND PRODUCT DIRECTORY

543-8952, F: 610-373-5400, www.medalist. com
Camouflage; Hunting Accessories; Men & Women's Clothing

Meggitt Training Systems/Caswell, 296 Brogdon Rd., Suwanee, GA 30024, P: 800-813-9046, F: 678-288-1515, www. meggitttrainingsystems.com
Custom Manufacturing; Law Enforcement; Shooting Range Equipment; Targets; Training & Safety Equipment

Meissenberg Designs, 7583 MT Hwy. 35, Bigfork, MT 59911, P: 877-974-7446, F: 866-336-2571, www.oldwoodsigns.com
Home Furnishings; Printing Services

Medota Products, Inc., 120 Bridgepoint Way, Suite B, South St. Paul, MN 55075, P: 800-224-1121, F: 651-457-9085, www. mendotaproducts.com
Custom Manufacturing; Hunting Accessories; Pet Supplies; Training & Safety Equipment

Meopta USA, Inc., 50 Davids Dr., Hauppauge, NY, 11788, P: 800-828-8928, F: 631-436-5920, www.meopta.com
Binoculars; Scopes, Sights & Accessories; Telescopes

Meprolight, 2590 Montana Hwy. 35, Suite B, Kalispell, MT 59901, P: 406-758-2222, F: 406-758-2223
Scopes, Sights & Accessories

Meprolight, Ltd., 58 Hazait St., Or-Akiva Industrial Park, Or-Akiva, 30600, ISRAEL, P: 011 97246244111, F: 011 97246244123, www.meprolight.com
Binoculars; Firearms; Gun Parts/Gunsmithing; Hunting Accessories; Law Enforcement; Lighting Products; Scopes, Sights & Accessories; Telescopes

Mercury Luggage Mfg. Co./Code Alpha Tactical Gear, 4843 Victory St., Jacksonville, FL 32207, P: 800-874-1885, F: 904-733-9671, www.mercuryluggage.com
Bags & Equipment Cases; Camouflage; Custom Manufacturing; Export/Import Specialists; Law Enforcement

Merkel USA, 7661 Commerce Ln., Trussville, AL 35173, P: 800-821-3021, F: 205-655-7078, www.merkel-usa.com
Binoculars; Firearms; Scopes, Sights & Accessories

Mesa Tactical, 1760 Monrovia Ave., Suite A14, Costa Mesa, CA 92627, P: 949-642-3337, F: 949-642-3339, www.mesatactical.com
Gun Grips & Stocks; Law Enforcement; Scopes, Sights & Accessories

Metal Ware Corp./Open Country, 1700 Monroe St., P.O. Box 237, Two Rivers, WI 54241, P: 800-624-2949, F: 920-794-3161, www. opencountrycampware.com
Backpacking; Camping; Cooking Equipment/ Accessories; Sports Accessories

Meyerco, 4481 Exchange Service Dr., Dallas, TX 75236, P: 214-467-8949, F: 214-467-9241, www.meyercousa.com
Bags & Equipment Cases; Camping; Cutlery; Gun Cases; Hunting Accessories; Knives/Knife Cases; Law Enforcement; Sharpeners

Mick Lacy Game Calls, 628 W. Main St., Princeville, IL 61559, P: 800-681-1070, F: 309-385-1068, www.micklacygamecalls.com
Game Calls; Hunting Accessories

Microsonic, 2960 Duss Ave., Ambridge, PA 15003, P: 724-266-9480, F: 724-266-9482, www.microsonic-inc.com
Hearing Protection

Microtech Knives, Inc./Microtech Small Arms Research, Inc., 300 Chestnut St., Bradford, PA 16701, P: 814-363-9260, F: 814-363-9284, www.msarinc.com
Custom Manufacturing; Cutlery; Firearms; Knives/Knife Cases; Law Enforcement; Sports Accessories

Midland Radio Corp., 5900 Parretta Dr., Kansas City, MO, 64120, P: 816-241-8500, F: 816-241-5713, www.midlandradio.com
Hunting Accessories; Sports Accessories; Training & Safety Equipment; Two-Way Radios

Midwest Industries, Inc., 828 Philip Dr., Suite 2, Waukesha, WI 53186, P: 262-896-6780, F: 262-896-6756, www.midwestindustriesinc. com
Gun Cases; Gun Parts/Gunsmithing; Law Enforcement; Lubricants; Magazines, Cartridge; Scopes, Sights & Accessories

Midwest Quality Gloves, Inc., 835 Industrial Rd., P.O. Box 260, Chillicothe, MO 64601, P: 800-821-3028, F: 660-646-6933, www. midwestglove.com
Archery; Camouflage; Gloves, Mitts, Hats; Hunting Accessories; Men's Clothing

Mil-Comm Products Co., Inc., 2 Carlton Ave., East Rutherford, NJ 07073, P: 888-947-3273, F: 201-935-6059, www.mil-comm.com
Black Powder Accessories; Firearms Maintenance Equipment; Gun Cabinets/Racks/ Safes; Gun Locks; Gun Parts/Gunsmithing; Law Enforcement; Lubricants; Paintball Guns

Mil-Spec Plus/Voodoo Tactical, 435 W. Alondra Blvd., Gardena, CA 90248, P: 310-324-8855, F: 310-324-6909, www.majorsurplus.com
Bags & Equipment Cases; Eyewear; Footwear; Gloves, Mitts, Hats; Gun Cases; Law Enforcement

Mil-Tac Knives & Tools, P.O. Box 642, Wylie, TX 75098, P: 877-MIL-TAC6, F: 972-412-2208, www.mil-tac.com
Cutlery; Eyewear; Gloves, Mitts, Hats; Gun Parts/Gunsmithing; Hunting Accessories; Knives/Knife Cases; Law Enforcement; Survival Kits/First Aid

Militaria, Inc., Rt. 2, P.O. Box 166, Collins, GA 30421, P: 912-693-6411, F: 912-693-2060
Books/Industry Publications; Emblems & Decals; Firearms Maintenance Equipment; Lubricants; Wholesaler/Distributor

Military Outdoor Clothing, Inc., 1917 Stanford St., Greenville, TX 75401, P: 800-662-6430, F: 903-454-2433, www. militaryoutdoorclothing.com
Bags & Equipment Cases; Camouflage; Gloves, Mitts, Hats; Law Enforcement; Men & Women's Clothing

Milkor USA, Inc., 3735 N. Romero Rd., Suite 2M, Tucson, AZ 85705, P: 520-888-0103, F: 520-888-0122, www.milkorusainc.com
Firearms

Millett Sights/Bushnell Outdoor Products, 6200 Cody, Overland Park, KS 66214, P: 888-276-5945, F: 800-548-0446, www.millettsights. com
Black Powder Accessories; Gun Parts/ Gunsmithing; Hunting Accessories; Law Enforcement; Scopes, Sights & Accessories

Minox USA, 438 Willow Brook Rd., Merdien, NH 03770, P: 866-469-3080, F: 603-469-3471, www.minox.com
Binoculars

Mocean, 1635 Monrovia Ave., Costa Mesa, CA 92627, P: 949-646-1701, F: 949-646-1590, www.mocean.net
Custom Manufacturing; Law Enforcement; Men & Women's Clothing; Wholesaler/ Distributor

MOJO Outdoors, 2984 New Monroe Rd., P.O. Box 8460, Monroe, LA 71211, P: 318-283-7777, F: 318-283-1127, www.mojooutdoors. com
Decoys

Molehill Mt. Equipment, Inc., 416 Laskspur St., Suite A, Ponderay, ID 83852, P: 800-804-0820, F: 208-263-3056, www.molehillmtn. com
Camouflage; Camping; Footwear; Gloves, Mitts, Hats; Men & Women's Clothing

Montana Canvas, 110 Pipkin Way, Belgrade, MT 59714, P: 800-235-6518, F: 406-388-1039, www.montanacanvas.com
Camping; Hunting Accessories

Montana Decoys, P.O. Box 2377, Colstrip, MT 59323, P: 888-332-6998, F: 406-748-3471, www.montantadecoy.com
Decoys

Montana Rifle Co./Montana Rifleman, Inc., 3172 Montana Hwy. 35, Kalispell, MT 59901, P: 406-755-4867, F: 406-755-9449, www. montanarifle.com
Custom Manufacturing; Firearms; Gun Barrels; Gun Parts/Gunsmithing

Moore Texas Hunting, 108 S. Ranch House Rd., Suite 800, Aledo, TX 76008, P: 817-688-1774, F: 817-441-1606, www. mooretexashunting.com
Custom Manufacturing; Hunting Accessories; Sports Accessories; Wholesaler/Distributor

MoroVision Night Vision, Inc., P.O. Box 342, Dana Point, CA 92629, P: 800-424-8222, F: 949-488-3361, www.morovision.com
Binoculars; Camping; Hunting Accessories; Law Enforcement; Lighting Products; Photographic Equipment; Scopes, Sights & Accessories; Wholesaler/Distributor

Morton Enterprises, 35 Pilot Ln., Great Cacapon, WV, 25422, P: 877-819-7280, www.uniquecases.com
Bags & Equipment Cases; Custom Manufacturing; Gun Cases; Hunting Accessories; Law Enforcement; Sports Accessories

Mossy Oak, P.O. Box 757, West Point, MS 39773, P: 662-494-8859, F: 662-494-8837, www.mossyoak.com
Books; Camouflage; Home Furnishings; Hunting Accessories; Men & Women's Clothing; Videos

Mostly Signs, 12993 Los Nietos Rd., Sante Fe Springs, CA 90670, P: 888-667-8595, F: 800-906-9855, www.mostlysigns.com
Home Furnishings; Wholesaler/Distributor

Moteng, Inc., 12220 Parkway Centre Dr., Poway, CA 92064, P: 800-367-5900, F: 800-367-5903, www.moteng.com
Camping; Cutlery; Knives/Knife Cases; Law Enforcement; Lighting Products; Online Services; Training & Safety Equipment; Wholesaler/Distributor

Mothwing Camo/Gameday Camo, P.O. Box 2019, Calhoun, GA 30703, P: 800-668-4946, F: 706-625-2484, www.mothwing.com
Camouflage; Men & Women's Clothing; Vehicles, Utility & Rec

Moultrie Products, LLC, 150 Industrial Rd., Alabaster, AL 35007, P: 800-653-3334, F: 205-664-6706, www.moultriefeeders.com
Feeder Equipment; Photographic Equipment; Wildlife Management

Mountain Corp./Mountain Life, 59 Optical Ave., P.O. Box 686, Keene, NH 03431, P: 800-545-9684, F: 603-355-3702, www. themountain.com
Law Enforcement; Men & Women's Clothing; Outfitter; Retail Packaging; Wholesaler/ Distributor

Mountain House/Oregon Freeze Dry, 525 25th SW, Albany, OR 97321, P: 800-547-0244, F: 541-812-6601, www.mountainhouse.com
Backpacking; Camping; Hunting Accessories

Mounting Solutions Plus, 10655 SW 185 Terrace, Miami, FL 33157, P: 800-428-9394, F: 305-232-1247, www.mountsplus.com
Scopes, Sights & Accessories; Wholesaler/ Distributor

MTM-Multi Time Machine, Inc., 1225 S. Grand Ave., Los Angeles, CA 90015, P: 213-741-0808, F: 213-741-0840, www. specialopswatch.com
Archery; Backpacking; Camouflage; Hunting Accessories; Law Enforcement; Sports Accessories; Watches

Mud River Dog Products, 355 E. Hwy. 264, Suite D, Bethel Heights, AR 72764, P: 479-927-2447, F: 479-927-2667, www. mudriverdogproducts.com
Bags & Equipment Cases; Blinds; Camping; Custom Manufacturing; Hunting Accessories; Men's Clothing; Pet Supplies, Vehicles, Utility & Rec

Muela, Ctra. N-420, KM 165, 500, Argamasilla De Calatrava, (Ciudad Real) 13440, SPAIN, P: 011 34926477093, F: 011 34926477237, www.mmuela.com
Knives/Knife Cases

Muller Prinsloo Knives, P.O. Box 2263, Bethlehem, 9700, SOUTH AFRICA, P: 011 27824663885, F: 011 27583037111
Knives/Knife Cases

Mystery Ranch, 34156 E. Frontage Rd., Bozeman, MT 59715, P: 406-585-1428, F: 406-585-1792, www.mysteryranch.com
Backpacking; Bags & Equipment Cases; Camping; Law Enforcement; Photographic Equipment

N

Nantong Universal Optical Instruments Co., Ltd., No. 1 Pingchao Industrial Garden, Nantong, Jiangsu 226361, CHINA, P: 011 8651386726888, F: 011 8651386718158, www.zoscn.com
Airguns; Binoculars; Gun Cases; Gun Locks; Scopes, Sights & Accessories; Wholesaler/ Distributor

National Emblem, Inc., 17036 S. Avalon Blvd., Carson, CA 90746, P: 800-877-6185, F: 310-515-5966, www.nationalemblem.com
Custom Manufacturing; Emblems & Decals; Gloves, Mitts, Hats

National Geographic Maps, P.O. Box 4357, Evergreen, CO 80437, P: 800-962-1643, F: 800-626-8676, www.nationalgeographic. com/map
Archery; Backpacking; Books/Industry Publications; Camping; Compasses; Computer Software; Sports Accessories

National Muzzle Loading Rifle Association, P.O. Box 67, Friendship, IN 47021, P: 812-667-5131, F: 812-667-5137, www.nmlra.org

National Rifle Association, 11250 Waples Mill Rd., Fairfax, VA 22030, P: 800-672-3888, F: 703-267-3810, www.nra.org

National Wild Turkey Federation, 770 Augusta Rd., P.O. Box 530, Edgefield, SC 29824, P: 800-843-6983, F: 803-637-0034, www.nwtf. org

Nation's Best Sports, 4216 Hahn Blvd., Fort Worth, TX 76117, P: 817-788-0034, F: 817-788-8542, www.nationsbestsports.com
Retailer Services

Nature Coast Laser Creations, 9185 Mercedes Terrace N, Crystal River, FL 34428, P: 352-564-0794, www.laserautotags.com
Custom Manufacturing; Emblems & Decals; Hunting Accessories; Outdoor Art, Jewelry, Sculpture; Paintball Accessories; Sports Accessories; Vehicles, Utility & Rec

N-Vision Optics, 220 Reservior St., Suite 26, Neenham, MA 02494, P: 781-505-8360, F: 781-998-5656, www.nvisionoptics.com
Binoculars; Law Enforcement; Scopes, Sights & Accessories

Navy Arms Co./Forgett Militaria, 219 Lawn St., Martinsburg, WV 25405, P: 304-262-1651, F: 304-262-1658, www.navyarms.com
Firearms

Nester Hosiery, Inc., 1400 Carter St., Mount Airy, NC 27030, P: 888-871-1507, F: 336-789-0626, www.nesteroutdoorsocks.com
Backpacking; Camping; Custom Manufacturing; Footwear; Hunting Accessories; Men & Women's Clothing; Sports Accessories

New Century Science & Tech, Inc., 10302 Olney St., El Monte, CA 91731, P: 866-627-8278, F: 626-575-2478, www.ncstar.com
Binoculars; Crossbows & Accessories; Custom Manufacturing; Export/Import Specialists; Firearms Maintenance Equipment; Gun Cases; Lighting Products; Scopes, Sights & Accessories

New Ultra Light Arms, 214 Price St., P.O. Box 340, Granville, WV 26534, P: 304-292-0600, FL 304-292-9662, www.newultralight.com
Firearms

Newcon Optik, 105 Sparks Ave., Toronto M2H 2S5, CANADA, P: 877-368-6666, F: 416-663-9065, www.newcon-optik.com
Binoculars; Hunting Accessories; Law Enforcement; Paintballs; Photographic Equipment; Scopes, Sights & Accessories; Shooting Range Equipment

Nextorch, Inc., 2401 Viewcrest Ave., Everett, WA 98203, P: 425-290-3092, www.nextorch. com
Hunting Accessories; Knives/Knife Cases; Lighting Products

Night Optics USA, Inc., 5122 Bolsa Ave., Suite 101, Huntington Beach, CA 92649, P: 800-30-NIGHT, F: 714-899-4485, www. nightoptics.com
Binoculars; Camping; Hunting Accessories; Law Enforcement; Scopes, Sights & Accessories; Training & Safety Equipment; Wholesaler/Distributor; Wildlife Management

Night Owl Optics/Bounty Hunter/Fisher Research Labs, 1465-H Henry Brennan, El Paso, TX 79936, P: 800-444-5994, F: 915-633-8529, www.nightowloptics.com
Binoculars; Camping; Hunting Accessories; Law Enforcement; Photographic Equipment; Scopes, Sights & Accessories; Sports Accessories; Telescopes

Night Vision Depot, P.O. Box 3415, Allentown, PA 18106, P: 610-395-9743, F: 610-395-9744, www.nvdepot.com

Binoculars; Hunting Accessories; Law Enforcement; Lighting Products; Scopes, Sights & Accessories; Wholesaler/Distributor

Night Vision Systems (NVS), 542 Kemmerer Ln., Allentown, PA 18104, P: 800-797-2849, F: 610-391-9220, www.nighvisionsystems. com
Law Enforcement; Scopes, Sights & Accessories

Nighthawk Custom, 1306 W. Trimble, Berryville, AR 72616, P: 877-268-4867, F: 870-423-4230, www.nighthawkcustom.com
Firearms; Gun Grips & Stocks; Gun Parts/ Gunsmithing; Hearing Protection; Holsters

Nikon, Inc., 1300 Walt Whitman Rd., Melville, NY 11747, P: 631-547-4200, FL 631-547-4040, www.nikonhunting.com
Binoculars; Hunting Accessories; Scopes, Sights & Accessories

Ningbo Electric and Consumer Goods I/E. Corp., 17/F, Lingqiao Plaza, 31 Yaohang Street, Ningbo, Zhejiang, 315000 CHINA P: 011 8657487194807; F: 011 8657487296214

Nite Ize, Inc., 5660 Central Ave., Boulder, CO 80301, P: 800-678-6483, F: 303-449-2013, www.niteize.com
Bags & Equipment Cases; Camping; Custom Manufacturing; Holsters; Lighting Products; Pet Supplies

Nite Lite Co., 3801 Woodland Heights Rd., Suite 100, Little Rock, AR 72212, P: 800-648-5483, F: 501-227-4892, www. huntsmart.com
Game Calls; Hunting Accessories; Lighting Products; Men's Clothing; Pet Supplies; Scents & Lures; Scopes, Sights & Accessories; Training & Safety Equipment

Nitrex Optics/ATK Commercial Products, N5549 Cty. Tk. Z, Onalaska, WI 54650, P: 800-635-7656, F: 763-323-3890, www. nitrexoptics.com
Binoculars; Scopes, Sights & Accessories

NiViSys Industries LLC, 400 S. Clark Dr., Suite 105, Tempe, AZ 85281, P: 480-970-3222, F: 480-970-3555, www.nivisys.com
Binoculars; Law Enforcement; Lighting Products; Photographic Equipment; Scopes, Sights & Accessories; Wholesaler/Distributor

Norica Laurona, Avda. Otaola, 16, Eibar, (Guipúzcoa) 20600, P: 011 34943207445, F: 011 34943207449, www.norica.es, www. laurona.com
Airguns; Ammunition; Firearms; Hearing Protection; Hunting Accessories; Knives/Knife Cases; Scopes, Sights & Accessories

Norma Precision AB/RUAG Ammotec, Jagargatan, Amotfors, S-67040, SWEDEN, P: 044-46-571-31500, F: 011-46-571-31540, www.norma.cc
Ammunition; Custom Manufacturing; Reloading

North American Arms, Inc., 2150 S. 950 E, Provo, UT 84606, P: 800-821-5783, F: 801-374-9998, www.northamericanarms.com
Firearms

North American Hunter, 12301 Whitewater Dr., Minnetonka, MN 55343, P: 800-688-7611, F: 952-936-9169, www.huntingclub.com
Books/Industry Publications

Northern Lights Tactical, P.O. 10272, Prescott, AZ 86304, P: 310-376-4266, F: 310-798-9278, www.northernlightstactical.com
Archery; Hunting Accessories; Law Enforcement; Paintball Accessories; Shooting

MANUFACTURER'S AND PRODUCT DIRECTORY

Range Equipment; Targets; Training & Safety Equipment; Vehicles, Utility & Rec

Northridge International, Inc., 23679 Calabasas Rd., Suit 406, Calabasas, CA 91302, P: 661-269-2269, www.northridgeinc.com
Camouflage; Compasses; Cutlery; Firearms; Firearms Maintenance Equipment; Gun Barrels; Gun Cases; Survival Kits/First Aid

Northwest Territorial Mint, P.O. Box 2148, Auburn, WA 98071, P: 800-344-6468, F: 253-735-2210, www.nwtmint.com
Custom Manufacturing; Emblems & Decals; Knives/Knife Cases; Outdoor Art, Jewelry, Sculpture

Northwest Tracker, Inc., 6205 NE 63rd St., Vancouver, WA 98661, P: 360-213-0363, F: 360-693-2212, www.trackeroutpost.com
Gun Cabinets/Racks/Safes; Gun Cases; Hunting Accessories; Treestands

Nosler, Inc., 107 SW Columbia, P.O. Box 671, Bend, OR 97709, P: 800-285-3701, F: 800-766-7537, www.nosler.com
Ammunition; Black Powder Accessories; Books/Industry Publications; Firearms; Reloading

Not Your Daddy's, 7916 High Heath, Knoxville, TN 37919, P: 865-806-8496, F: 865-690-4555
Gun Cases

Nova Silah Sanayi, Ltd., Merkez Mah. Kultur Cad. No: 22/14, Duzce, TURKEY, P: 011-90 2125140279, F: 011-90 2125111999
Firearms

Novatac, Inc., 300 Carlsbad Village Dr., Suite 108A-100, Carlsbad, CA 92008, P: 760-730-7370, FL 760-730-7375, www.novatac.com
Backpacking; Camping; Hunting Accessories; Law Enforcement; Lighting Products; Survival Kits/First Aid; Training & Safety Equipment

NRA FUD, 11250 Waples Mill Rd., Fairfax, VA 22030, P: 703-267-1300, F: 703-267-3800, www.nrafud.com
Decoys; Hunting Accessories; Wholesaler/Distributor

NTA Enterprise, Inc./Huntworth/Thermologic, R J Casey Industrial Park, Columbus Ave., Pittsburgh, PA 15233, P: 877-945-6837, F: 412-325-7865, www.thermologicgear.com
Archery; Backpacking; Camouflage; Gloves, Mitts, Hats; Hunting Accessories; Men & Women's Clothing; Sports Accessories

Numrich Gun Parts Corp./Gun Parts Corp., 226 Williams Ln., P.O. Box 299, West Hurley, NY 12491, P: 866-686-7424, F: 877-GUN-PART, www.e-gunparts.com
Firearms Maintenance Equipment; Gun Barrels; Gun Cases; Gun Grips & Stocks; Gun Parts/Gunsmithing; Hunting Accessories; Magazines, Cartridge; Scopes, Sights & Accessories

Nutri-Vet, LLC, 495 N. Dupont Ave., Boise, ID 83713, P: 877-728-8668, F: 208-377-1941, www.nutri-vet.com
Pet Supplies

Nuwai International Co., Ltd./Nuwai LED Flashlight, 11 FL., 110 Li Gong St., Bei, Tou Taipei, 11261, TAIWAN, P: 011 886228930199, F: 011 886228930198, www.nuwai.com
Camping; Lighting Products; Outfitter

Nylok Corp., 15260 Hallmark Dr., Macomb, MI 48042, P: 586-786-0100, FL 810-780-0598
Custom Manufacturing; Gun Parts/Gunsmithing; Lubricants

O

O'Keeffe's Co., 251 W. Barclay Dr., P.O. Box 338, Sisters, OR 97759, P: 800-275-2718, F: 541-549-1486, www.okeeffescompany.com
Archery; Backpacking; Camping; Footwear; Outfitter; Sports Accessories; Survival Kits/First Aid

O.F. Mossberg & Sons, Inc., 7 Grasso Ave., North Haven, CT 06473, P: 203-230-5300, F: 203-230-5420, www.mossberg.com
Firearms; Gun Barrels; Hunting Accessories; Law Enforcement

Oakley, Inc., One Icon, Foothill Ranch, CA 92610, P: 800-525-4334, F: 858-459-4336, www.usstandardissue.com
Eyewear; Footwear

Odyssey Automotive Specialty, 317 Richard Mine Rd., Wharton, MJ 07885, P: 800-535-9441, F: 973-328-2601, www.odysseyauto.com
Custom Manufacturing; Gun Cabinets/Racks/Safes; Gun Cases; Law Enforcement; Vehicles, Utility & Rec

Oehler Research, Inc., P.O. Box 9135, Austin, TX 78766, P: 800-531-5125, F: 512-327-6903, www.oehler-research.com
Ammunition; Computer Software; Hunting Accessories; Reloading; Shooting Range Equipment; Targets

Oklahoma Leather Products/Don Hume Leathergoods, 500 26th NW, Miami, OK 74354, P: 918-542-6651, F: 918-542-6653, www.oklahomaleatherproducts.com
Black Powder Accessories; Custom Manufacturing; Cutlery; Holsters; Hunting Accessories; Knives/Knife Cases; Law Enforcement; Leathergoods

Old Western Scrounger, Inc., 50 Industrial Pkwy., Carson City, NV 89706, P: 800-UPS-AMMO, F: 775-246-2095, www.ows-ammunition.com
Ammunition; Reloading

Olivon Manufacturing Co., Ltd./Olivon-Worldwide, 600 Tung Pu Rd., Shanghai, China, Shanghai, Jiangsu, CHINA, P: 604-764-7731, F: 604-909-4951, www.olivonmanufacturing.com
Bag & Equipment Cases; Binoculars; Gun Cabinets/Racks/Safes; Gun Cases; Hunting Accessories; Scopes, Sights & Accessories; Telescopes

Olympic Arms, Inc., 624 Old Pacific Hwy. SE, Olympia, WA 98513, P: 800-228-3471, F: 360-491-3447, www.olyarms.com
Firearms; Gun Barrels; Gun Grips & Stocks; Gun Parts/Gunsmithing; Law Enforcement; Training & Safety Equipment

On-Target Productions, Inc., 6722 River Walk Dr., Valley City, OH 44280, P: 330-483-6183, F: 330-483-6183, www.ontargetdvds.com
Videos

On Time Wildlife Feeders, 110 E. Railroad Ave., Ruston, LA 71270, P:318-225-1834, F: 315-225-1101

One Shot, 6871 Main St., Newtown, OH 45244, P: 513-233-0885, F: 513-233-0887

Ontario Knife Co./Queen Cutlery Co./Ontario Knife Co., 26 Empire St., P.O. Box 145, Franklinville, NY 14737, P: 800-222-5233, F: 800-299-2618, www.ontarioknife.com
Camping; Custom Manufacturing; Cutlery; Hunting Accessories; Knives/Knife Cases; Law Enforcement; Training & Safety Equipment

Op. Electronics Co., Ltd., 53 Shing-Ping Rd. 5/F, Chungli, 320, TAIWAN, P: 011 88634515131, F: 011 88634615130, www.digi-opto.com
Scopes, Sights & Accessories; Training & Safety Equipment

Opti-Logic Corp., 201 Montclair St., P.O. Box 2002, Tullahoma, TN 37388, P: 888-678-4567, F: 931-455-1229, www.opti-logic.com
Archery; Binoculars; Crossbows & Accessories; Hunting Accessories; Law Enforcement; Scopes, Sights & Accessories

Optisan Corp., Taipei World Trade Center 4B06, 5, Hsin Yi Rd., Section 5, Taipei, 110, TAIWAN, P: 011 8675785799936, F: 011 862081117707
Bags & Equipment Cases; Binoculars; Lighting Products; Photographic Equipment; Scopes, Sights & Accessories; Telescopes

Optolyth/Sill Optics GmbH & Co KG, Johann-Höllfritsch-Straße 13, Wendelstein, 90530, GERMANY, P: 011 499129902352, F: 011 499129902323, www.optolyth.de
Binoculars; Scopes, Sights & Accessories

Original Footwear Co., 4213 Technology Dr., Modesto, CA 95356, P: 888-476-7700, F: 209-545-2739, www.originalswat.com
Footwear; Law Enforcement; Wholesaler/Distributor

Original Muck Boot Co., 1136 2nd St., Rock Island, IL 61201, P: 800-790-9296, F: 800-267-6809, www.muckbootcompany.com
Footwear

Osprey International Inc./AimShot, 25 Hawks Farm Rd., White, GA 30184, P: 888-448-3247, F: 770-387-0114, www.osprey-optics.com
Binoculars; Hunting Accessories; Law Enforcement; Lighting Products; Scopes, Sights & Accessories; Wholesaler/Distributor

Otis Technology, Inc., 6987 Laura St., P.O. Box 582, Lyon Falls, NY 13368, P: 800-OTISGUN, F: 315-348-4332, www.otisgun.com
Black Powder Accessories; Firearms Maintenance Equipment; Gun Parts/Gunsmithing; Hunting Accessories; Lubricants; Paintball Accessories; Scopes, Sights & Accessories; Training & Safety Equipment

Otte Gear, 332 Bleecker St., Suite E10, New York, NY 10014, P: 212-604-0304, F: 773-439-5237, www.ottegear.com
Backpacking; Camouflage; Camping; Gloves, Mitts, Hats; Men's Clothing

Otter Outdoors, 411 W. Congress, Maple Lake, MN 55358, P: 877-466-8837, F: 320-963-6192, www.otteroutdoors.com
Blinds; Custom Manufacturing; Hunting Accessories; Sports Accessories; Vehicles, Utility & Rec

Outdoor Cap Co., 1200 Melissa Ln., P.O. Box 210, Bentonville, AR 72712, P: 800-279-3216, F: 800-200-0329, www.outdoorcap.com
Camouflage; Custom Manufacturing; Gloves, Mitts, Hats; Hunting Accessories; Men & Women's Clothing

Outdoor Connection, 424 Neosho, Burlington, NS 66839, P: 888-548-0636, F: 620-364-5563, www.outdoor-connection.com
Outfitter; Tours/Travel

Outdoor Connection, Inc., 7901 Panther Way, Waco, TX 76712, P: 800-533-6076, F: 866-533-6076, www.outdoorconnection.com
Bags & Equipment Cases; Camouflage; Gun Cases; Gun Parts/Gunsmithing; Hunting

MANUFACTURER'S
AND PRODUCT DIRECTORY

Accessories; Retail Packaging; Shooting Range Equipment; Sports Accessories

Outdoor Edge Cutlery Corp., 4699 Nautilus Ct. S, Suite 503, Boulder, CO 80301, P: 800-447-3343, F: 303-530-7020, www.outdooredge.com
Cutlery; Hunting Accessories; Sharpeners

Outdoor Kids Club Magazine, P.O. Box 35, Greenville, OH 45331, P: 937-417-0903, www.outdoorkidsclub.com
Books/Industry Publications

Outdoor Research, 2203 First Ave. S, Seattle, WA 98134, P: 888-467-4327, F: 206-467-0374, www.outdoorresearch.com/gov
Gloves, Mitts, Hats; Law Enforcement

OutdoorSportsMarketingCenter.com, 95 Old Stratton Chase, Atlanta, GA 30328, P: 256-653-5087, F: 404-943-1634, www.outdoorsportsmarketingcenter.com
Books/Industry Publications; Computer Software; Emblems & Decals; Online Services; Printing Services; Retail Packaging; Retailer Services

Outers Gun Care/ATK Commercial Products, N5549 Cty. Tk. Z, Onalaska, WI 54650, P: 800-635-7656, F: 763-323-3890, www.outers-guncare.com
Firearms Maintenance Equipment; Lubricants

Over The Hill Outfitters/Adventures Beyond, 4140 Cty. Rd. 234, Durango, CO 81301, P: 970-385-7656, www.overthehilloutfitters.com
Outfitter

Ozonics, 107A This Way, P.O. Box 598, Lake Jackson, TX 77566, P: 979-285-2400, F: 979-297-7744, www.ozonicshunting.com
Scents & Lures

P

PMC/Poongsan, 60-1, Chungmoro - 3ka, Chung-Gu, Seoul 100-705, C.P.O. Box 3537, Seoul, SOUTH KOREA, P: 011 92234065628, F: 011 92234065415, www.pmcammo.com
Ammunition; Law Enforcement

PSC, Pendleton Safe Co., 139 Lee Byrd Rd., Loganville, GA 30052, P: 770-466-6661, F: 678-990-7888
Gun Safes

PSI, LLC, 2 Klarides Village Dr., Suite 336, Seymour, CT 06483, P: 203-262-6484, F: 203-262-6562, www.precisionsalesintl.com
Gun Parts/Gunsmithing; Law Enforcement; Magazines, Cartridge; Scopes, Sights & Accessories

P.S. Products, Inc./Personal Security Products, 414 S. Pulaski St., Suite 1, Little Rock, AR 72201, P: 877-374-7900, F: 501-374-7800, www.psproducts.com
Custom Manufacturing; Export/Import Specialists; Holsters; Law Enforcement; Sports Accessories; Wholesaler/Distributor

Pacific Solution, 14225 Telephone Ave., Suite D, Chino, CA 91710, P: 909-465-9858, F: 909-465-9878
Cutlery; Hunting Accessories; Knives/Knife Cases; Wholesaler/Distributor

Pacific Sun Marketing, 14505 N. 5th St., Bellevue, WA 98007, P: 425-653-3900, F: 425-653-3908
Home Furnishings; Hunting Accessories; Outdoor Art, Jewelry, Sculpture

Pacific Tool & Gauge, Inc., 598 Avenue C, P.O. Box 2549, White City, OR 97503, P:

541-826-5808, F: 541-826-5304, www.pacifictoolandgauge.com
Black Powder Accessories; Books/Industry Publications; Custom Manufacturing; Firearms Maintenance Equipment; Gun Parts/Gunsmithing; Law Enforcement; Reloading

Palco Sports Airsoft, 8575 Monticello Ln. N, Maple Grove, MN 55369-4546, P: 800-882-4656, F: 763-559-2286, www.palcosports.com
Airguns; Airsoft; Crossbows & Accessories; Paintball Guns & Accessories; Sports Accessories

Panthera Outdoors, LLC, 1555 Wedgefield Dr., Rock Hill, SC 29732, P: 276-673-5278

Para USA, Inc., 10620 Southern Loop Blvd., Charlotte, NC 28134-7381, P: 866-661-1911, www.para-usa.com
Firearms

Paragon Luggage, 1111-A Bell Ave., Tustin, CA 92780, P: 714-258-8698, F: 714-258-0018

Paramount Apparel, Inc., 1 Paramount Dr., P.O. Box 98, Bourbon, MO 65441, P: 800-255-4287, F: 800-428-0215, www.paramountoutdoors.com
Camouflage; Custom Manufacturing; Gloves, Mitts, Hats; Hunting Accessories; Men & Women's Clothing; Retailer Services; Sports Accessories

Parker-Hale, Bedford Rd., Petersfield, Hampshire GU32 3XA, UNITED KINGDOM, P: 011-44 1730268011, F: 011-44 1730260074, www.parker-hale.co.uk
Firearms Maintenance Equipment; Law Enforcement; Lubricants

Parmatech Corp., 2221 Pine View Way, Petaluma, CA 94954, P: 800-709-1555, F: 707-778-2262, www.parmatech.com
Custom Manufacturing; Gun Parts/Gunsmithing

Parris Manufacturing, 1825 Pickwick St., P.O. Box 338, Savannah, TN 38372, P: 800-530-7308, F: 731-925-1139, www.parrismfgco.com
Airguns; Archery; Binoculars; Camouflage; Crossbows & Accessories; Wholesaler/Distributor

Passport Sports, Inc., 3545 N. Courtenay Pkwy., P.O. Box 540638, Merritt Island, FL 32953, P: 321-459-0005, F: 321-459-3482, www.passport-holsters.com
Bags & Equipment Cases; Custom Manufacturing; Gun Cases; Holsters; Leathergoods

Patriot3, Inc., P.O. Box 278, Quantico, VA 22134, P: 888-288-0911, F: 540-891-5654, www.patriot3.com
Law Enforcement

Patriot Ordnance Factory, 23623 N. 67th Ave., Glendale, AZ 85310, P: 623-561-9572, F: 623-321-1680, www.pof-usa.com
Custom Manufacturing; Firearms; Gun Barrels; Gun Parts/Gunsmithing; Hunting Accessories; Law Enforcement

PBC, 444 Caribbean Dr., Lakeland, FL 33803, P: 954-304-5948, www.pbccutlery.com
Cutlery; Knives/Knife Cases

Peacekeeper International, 2435 Pine St., Pomona, CA 91767, P: 909-596-6699, F: 909-596-8899, www.peacekeeperproducts.com
Holsters; Law Enforcement; Leathergoods; Targets; Training & Safety Equipment

Peak Beam Systems, Inc., 3938 Miller Rd., P.O. Box 1127, Edgemont, PA 19028, P:

610-353-8505, F: 610-353-8411, www.peakbeam.com
Law Enforcement; Lighting Products

Peca Products, Inc., 471 Burton St., Beloit, WI 53511, P: 608-299-1615, F: 608-229-1827, www.pecaproducts.com
Custom Manufacturing; Firearms Maintenance Equipment; Hunting Accessories; Law Enforcement; Photographic Equipment; Scopes, Sights & Accessories; Sports Accessories; Wholesaler/Distributor

Pedersoli 2 SRL, Via Artigiani, 13, Gardone V.T. 25063, ITALY, P: 011 390308915000, F: 011 390308911019, www.davide-pedersoli.com
Black Powder Accessories; Firearms; Gun Grips & Stocks

Pedersoli Davide & C. SNC, Via Artigiani, 57, Gardone V.T., Brescia 25063, ITALY, P: 011 39308915000, F: 011 39308911019, www.davide-pedersoli.com
Black Powder Accessories; Cutlery; Firearms; Knives/Knife Cases

Peerless Handcuff Co., 95 State St., Springfield, MA 01103, P: 800-732-3705, F: 413-734-5467, www.peerless.net
Law Enforcement

Peet Shoe Dryer, Inc./Peet Dryer, 919 St. Maries River Rd., P.O. Box 618, St. Maries, ID 83861, 800-222-PEET (7338), F: 800-307-4582, www.peetdryer.com
Footwear; Gloves, Mitts, Hats; Hunting Accessories

Pelican Products, Inc., 23215 Early Ave., Torrance, CA 90505, P: 800-473-5422, F: 310-326-3311
Archery; Backpacking; Bags & Equipment Cases; Camping; Crossbows & Accessories; Gun Cases; Hunting Accessories; Paintball Accessories

Peltor, 5457 W. 79th St., Indianapolis, IN 46268, P: 800-327-3431, F: 800-488-8007, www.aosafety.com
Eyewear; Hearing Protection; Shooting Range Equipment; Two-Way Radios

PentagonLight, 151 Mitchell Ave., San Francisco, CA 94080, P: 800-PENTA-15, F: 650-877-9555, www.pentagonlight.com
Holsters; Hunting Accessories; Law Enforcement; Lighting Products; Sports Accessories; Survival Kits/First Aid; Wholesaler/Distributor

Pentax Imaging Co., 600 12th St., Suite 300, Golden, CO 80401, P: 800-877-0155, F: 303-460-1628, www.pentaxsportoptics.com
Binoculars; Photographic Equipment; Scopes, Sights & Accessories

Perazzi U.S.A., Inc., 1010 W. Tenth St., Azusa, CA 91702, P: 626-334-1234, F: 626-334-0344
Firearms

Perfect Fit, 39 Stetson Rd., Ruite 222, P.O. Box 439, Corinna, ME 04928, P: 800-634-9208, F: 800-222-0417, www.perfectfitusa.com
Custom Manufacturing; Emblems & Decals; Law Enforcement; Leathergoods; Training & Safety Equipment; Wholesaler/Distibutor

Permalight (Asia) Co., Ltd./Pila Flashlights, 4/F, Waga Commercial Centre, 99 Wellington St., Central HONG KONG, P: 011 85228150616, F: 011 85225423269, www.pilatorch.com
Camping; Firearms; Hunting Accessories; Law Enforcement; Lighting Products; Training & Safety Equipment; Wholesaler/Distributor

MANUFACTURER'S
AND PRODUCT DIRECTORY

Pete Rickard Co., 115 Walsh Rd., Cobleskill, NY 12043, P: 518-234-2731, F: 518-234-2454, www.peterickard.com
Archery; Game Calls; Hunting Accessories; Leathergoods; Lubricants; Pet Supplies; Scents & Lures; Shooting Range Equipment

Petzl America, Freeport Center M-7, P.O. Box 160447, Clearfield, UT 84016, P: 877-807-3805, F: 801-926-1501, www.petzl.com
Gloves, Mitts, Hats; Law Enforcement; Lighting Products; Training & Safety Equipment

Phalanx Corp., 4501 N. Dixie Hwy., Boca Raton, FL 33431, P: 954-360-0000, F: 561-417-0500, www.smartholster.com
Gun Locks; Holsters; Law Enforcement; Training & Safety Equipment

Phillips Plastics, 1201 Hanley Rd., Hudson, WI 54016, P: 877-508-0252, F: 715-381-3291, www.phillipsplastics.com
Custom Manufacturing

Phoebus Tactical Flashlights/Phoebus Manufacturing, 2800 Third St., San Francisco, CA 94107, P: 415-550-0770, F: 415-550-2655, www.phoebus.com
Lighting Products

Photop Suwtech, Inc., 2F, Building 65, 421 Hong Cao Rd., Shanghai, 200233, CHINA, P: 011 862164853978, F: 011 862164850389, www.photoptech.com
Law Enforcement; Lighting Products; Scopes, Sights & Accessories

Pine Harbor Holding Co., Inc., P.O. Box 336, Chippewa Falls, WI 54729, P: 715-726-8714, F: 715-726-8739
Blinds; Camouflage; Decoys; Hunting Accessories

Pinnacle Ammunition Co., 111 W. Port Plaza, Suite 600, St. Louis, MO 63146, P: 888-702-2660, F: 314-293-1943, www.pinnacleammo.com
Ammunition

PistolCam, Inc., 1512 Front St., Keeseville, NY 12944, P: 518-834-7093, F: 518-834-7061, www.pistolcam.com
Firearms; Gun Parts/Gunsmithing; Law Enforcement; Photographic Equipment; Scopes, Sights & Accessories; Videos

Plano Molding Co., 431 E. South St., Plano, IL 60545, P: 800-226-9868, F: 630-552-9737, www.planomolding.com
Archery; Bags & Equipment Cases; Firearms Maintenance Equipment; Gun Cases; Hunting Accessories

Plotmaster Systems, Ltd., 111 Industrial Blvd., P.O. Box 111, Wrightsville, GA 31096, P: 888-629-4263, F: 478-864-9109, www.theplotmaster.com
Feeder Equipment; Wholesaler/Distributor; Wildlife Management

PlotSpike Wildlife Seeds/Ragan and Massey, Inc., 100 Ponchatoula Pkwy., Ponchatoula, LA 70454, P: 800-264-5281, F: 985-386-5565, www.plotspike.com
Scents & Lures; Wildlife Management

Plymouth Engineered Shapes, 201 Commerce Ct., Hopkinsville, KY 42240, P: 800-718-7590, F: 270-886-6662, www.plymouth.com/engshapes.aspx
Crossbows & Accessories; Firearms; Gun Barrels; Gun Parts/Gunsmithing

Point Blank Body Armor/PACA Body Armor, 2102 SW 2 St., Pompano Beach, FL 33069, P: 800-413-5155, F: 954-414-8118, www.pointblankarmor.com, www.pacabodyarmor.com
Law Enforcement

Point Tech, Inc., 160 Gregg St., Suite 1, Lodi, NJ 07644, P: 201-368-0711, F: 201-368-0133
Firearms; Gun Barrels; Gun Parts/Gunsmithing

Polaris USA, Inc./Signal Mobile USA, 4511 N. O'Connor Rd., Suite 1150, Irving, TX 75062, P: 817-719-1086, F: 817-887-0807, www.polarisvision.com, www.ezsignal.com

Police and Security News, 1208 Juniper St., Quakertown, PA 18951, P: 215-538-1240, F: 215-538-1208, www.policeandsecuritynews.com
Books/Industry Publications; Law Enforcement

Police Magazine/Police Recruit Magazine, 3520 Challenger St., Torrance, CA 90503, P: 480-367-1101, F: 480-367-1102, www.policemag.com
Books/Industry Publications; Law Enforcement

PoliceOne.com, 200 Green St., Second Floor, San Francisco, CA 94111, P: 800-717-1199, F: 480-854-7079, www.policeone.com
Law Enforcement

Port-A-Cool, 709 Southview Circle, P.O. Box 2167, Center, TX 75935, P: 800-695-2942, F: 936-598-8901
Camouflage; Custom Manufacturing; Sports Accessories; Training & Safety Equipment

Portman Security Systems Ltd., 330 W. Cummings Park, Woburn, MA 01801, P: 781-935-9288, F: 781-935-9188, www.portmansecurity.com
Custom Manufacturing; Firearms Maintenance Equipment; Gun Parts/Gunsmithing; Law Enforcement; Pet Supplies; Scopes, Sights & Accessories; Vehicles, Utility & Rec

PowerBelt Bullets, 5988 Peachtree Corners E, Norcross, GA 30071, P: 800-320-8767, F: 770-242-8546, www.powerbeltbullets.com
Ammunition; Black Powder Accessories

PowerFlare, 6489 Camden Ave., Suite 108, San Jose, CA 95120, P: 877-256-6907, F: 408-268-5431, www.powerflare.com
Lighting Products; Survival Kits/First Aid; Training & Safety Equipment; Wholesaler/Distributor

PowerTech, Inc./Smith & Wesson Flashlights, 360 E. South St., Collierville, TN 38017, P: 901-850-9393, F: 901-850-9797, www.powertechinc.com
Camping; Hunting Accessories; Law Enforcement; Lighting Products; Sports Accessories

Practical Air Rifle Training Systems, LLC, P.O. Box 174, Pacific, MO 63069, P: 314-271-8465, F: 636-271-8465, www.smallarms.com
Airguns; Custom Manufacturing; Law Enforcement; Shooting Range Equipment; Targets; Training & Safety Equipment

Precision Ammunition, LLC, 5402 E. Diana St., Tampa, FL 33610, P: 888-393-0694, F: 813-626-0078, www.precisionammo.com
Ammunition; Law Enforcement; Reloading

Precision Metalsmiths, Inc., 1081 E. 200th St., Cleveland, OH 44117, P: 216-481-8900, F: 216-481-8903, www.precisionmetalsmiths.com
Archery; Custom Manufacturing; Firearms; Gun Barrels; Gun Locks; Gun Parts/Gunsmithing; Knives/Knife Cases; Scopes, Sights & Accessories

Precision Reflex, Inc., 710 Streine Dr., P.O. Box 95, New Bremen, OH 45869, P: 419-629-2603, F: 419-629-2173, www.pri-mounts.com
Custom Manufacturing; Firearms; Gun Barrels; Law Enforcement; Magazines, Cartridge; Scopes, Sights & Accessories

Predator, Inc., 2605 Coulee Ave., La Crosse, WI 54601, P: 800-430-3305, F: 608-787-0667, www.predatorcamo.com
Archery; Backpacking; Blinds; Camouflage; Men's Clothing

Predator International, 4401 S. Broadway, Suite 201, Englewood, CO 80113, P: 877-480-1636, F: 303-482-2987, www.predatorpellets.com
Airguns; Airsoft; Ammunition

Predator Sniper Products, 102 W. Washington St., P.O. Box 743, St. Francis, KS 67756, P: 785-332-2731, F: 785-332-8943, www.predatorsniperstyx.com
Custom Manufacturing; Game Calls; Hunting Accessories; Shooting Range Equipment; Wholesaler/Distributor

Predator Trailcams LLC, 10609 W. Old Hwy. 10 R.D., Saxon, WI 54559, P: 715-893-5001, F: 715-893-5005, www.predatortrailcams.com
Archery; Firearms; Hunting Accessories; Outfitter; Photographic Equipment; Sports Accessories; Wildlife Management

Premier Reticles, 175 Commonwealth Ct., Winchester, VA 22602, P: 540-868-2044, F: 540-868-2045 www.premierreticles.com
Scopes, Sights & Accessories; Telescopes

Premierlight, 35 Revenge Rd., Unit 9, Lordswood, Kent ME5 8DW, UNITED KINGDOM, P: 011-44-1634-201284, F: 011-44-1634-201286, www.premierlight-uk.com
Backpacking; Camping; Hunting Accessories; Law Enforcement; Lighting Products; Sports Accessories; Training & Safety Equipment; Wholesaler/Distributor

Prestige Apparel Mfg. Co./Exxel Outdoors, 300 American Blvd., Haleyville, AL 35565, P: 800-221-7452, F: 205-486-9882, www.exxel.com
Camouflage; Camping; Custom Manufacturing; Export/Import Specialists; Gloves, Mitts, Hats; Men's Clothing; Wholesaler/Distributor

Primary Weapons Systems, 800 E. Citation Ct., Suite C, Boise, ID 83716, P: 208-344-5217, F: 208-344-5395, www.primaryweapons.com
Firearms; Firearms Maintenance Equipment; Gun Parts/Gunsmithing; Law Enforcement; Recoil Protection Devices & Services

Primax Hunting Gear Ltd., Rm. 309, 3/F Jiali Mansion, 39-5#, Xingning Rd., Ningbo, Zhejiang 315040, CHINA, P: 011 8657487894016, F: 011 8657487894017, www.primax-hunting.com
Backpacking; Bags & Equipment Cases; Blinds; Camping; Compasses; Gun Cases; Hunting Accessories; Scopes, Sights & Accessories

Primos Hunting Calls, 604 First St., Flora, MS 39071, P: 800-523-2395, F: 601-879-9324, www.primos.com
Archery; Blinds; Camouflage; Decoys; Game Calls; Hunting Accessories; Scents & Lures; Videos

Princeton Tec, P.O. Box 8057, Trenton, NJ 08650, P: 800-257-9080, FL 609-298-9601, www.princetontec.com
Backpacking; Camping; Cooking Equipment/Accessories; Lighting Products; Photographic Equipment; Sports Accessories; Training & Safety Equipment

MANUFACTURER'S AND PRODUCT DIRECTORY

Pro-Iroda Industries, Inc., No. 68, 32nd Rd., Taichung Industrial Park, Taichung, 407, TAIWAN, P: 888-66-IRODA, F: 440-247-4630, www.pro-iroda.com
Archery; Camping; Cooking Equipment/ Accessories; Custom Manufacturing

Pro-Shot Products, P.O. Box 763, Taylorville, IL 62568, P: 217-824-9133, F: 217-824-8861, www.proshotproducts.com
Black Powder Accessories; Firearms Maintenance Equipment; Lubricants

Pro-Systems Spa, Via al Corbé 63, ITALY, P: 011 390331576887, F: 011 390331576295, www.pro-systems.it, www.pro-systems.us
Law Enforcement

Pro Ears/Benchmaster, 101 Ridgeline Dr., Westcliffe, CO 81252, P: 800-891-3660, F: 719-783-4162, www.pro-ears.com
Crossbows & Accessories; Custom Manufacturing; Hearing Protection; Hunting Accessories; Law Enforcement; Shooting Range Equipment; Sports Accessories; Training & Safety Equipment

Pro Line Manufacturing Co., 186 Parish Dr., Wayne, NJ 07470, P: 800-334-4612, F: 973-692-0999, www.prolineboots.com
Camouflage; Footwear; Leathergoods; Wholesaler/Distributor

Professionals Choice/G&A Investments, Inc., 2615 Fruitland Ave., Vernon, CA 90058, P: 323-589-2775, F: 323-589-3511, www.theprofessionalschoice.net
Firearms Maintenance Equipment; Gun Parts/Gunsmithing; Lubricants; Wholesaler/ Distributor

Proforce Equipment, Inc./Snugpak USA, 2201 NW 102nd Place, Suite 1, Miami, FL 33172, P: 800-259-5962, F: 800-664-5095, www.proforceequipment.com
Backpacking; Camping; Hunting Accessories; Knives/Knife Cases; Law Enforcement; Men's Clothing; Survival Kits/First Aid; Watches

Prois Hunting Apparel for Women, 28000B W. Hwy. 50, Gunnison, CO 81230, P: 970-641-3355, F: 970-641-6602, www.proishunting.com
Camouflage; Hunting Accessories; Women's Clothing

ProMag Industries, Inc./Archangel Manufacturing, LLC, 10654 S. Garfield Ave., South Gate, CA 90280, P: 800-438-2547, F: 562-861-6377, www.promagindustries.com
Gun Grips & Stocks; Gun Parts/Gunsmithing; Law Enforcement; Magazines, Cartridge; Retail Packaging; Scopes, Sights & Accessories

Promatic, Inc., 7803 W. Hwy. 116, Gower, MO 64454, UNITED KINGDOM, P: 888-767-2529, F: 816-539-0257, www.promatic.biz
Airguns; Clay Targets; Shooting Range Equipment; Targets; Training & Safety Equipment

Propper International Sales, 520 Huber Park Ct., St. Charles, MO 63304, P: 800-296-9690, F: 877-296-9690, www.propper.com
Camouflage; Law Enforcement; Men's Clothing

Protective Products International, 1649 NW 136th Ave., Sunrise, FL 33323, P: 800-509-9111, F: 954-846-0555, www.body-armor.com
Custom Manufacturing; Export/Import Specialists; Law Enforcement; Men & Women's Clothing; Training & Safety Equipment; Vehicles, Utility & Rec

Pumo GmbH IP Solingen, An den Eichen 20-22, Solingen, HMBG 42699, GERMANY, P: 011 492851589655, F: 011 492851589660, www.pumaknives.de
Custom Manufacturing; Cutlery; Hunting Accessories; Knives/Knife Cases; Sharpeners

Pyramex Safety Products, 281 Moore Lane, Collierville, TN 38017, P: 800-736-8673, F: 877-797-2639, www.pyramexsafety.com
Eyewear; Hearing Protection; Training & Safety Equipment

Pyramyd Air, 26800 Fargo Ave., Suite L, Bedford, OH 44146, P: 888-262-4867, F: 216-896-0896, www.pyramydair.com
Airguns, Airsoft

Q

Quail Unlimited, 31 Quail Run, Edgefield, SC 29824, P: 803-637-5731, F: 803-637-5303, www.qu.org
Books/Industry Publications; Firearms; Hunting Accessories; Men & Women's Clothing; Outdoor Art, Jewelry, Sculpture; Wildlife Management

Quake Industries, Inc., 732 Cruiser Ln., Belgrade, MT 59714, P: 770-449-4687, F: 406-388-8810, www.quakeinc.com
Archery; Crossbows & Accessories; Custom Manufacturing; Hunting Accessories; Scopes, Sights & Accessories; Sports Accessories; Treestands

Quaker Boy, Inc., 5455 Webster Rd., Orchard Park, NY 14127, P: 800-544-1600, F: 716-662-9426, www.quakerboy.com
Camouflage; Game Calls; Gloves, Mitts, Hats; Hunting Accessories; Targets; Videos

Quality Cartridge, P.O. Box 445, Hollywood, MD 20636, P: 301-373-3719, F: 301-373-3719, www.qual-cart.com
Ammunition; Custom Manufacturing; Reloading

Quality Deer Management Assoc., 170 Whitetail Way, P.O. Box 160, Bogart, GA 30622, P: 800-209-3337, F: 706-353-0223, www.qdma.com
Books/Industry Publications; Men & Women's Clothing; Videos; Wholesaler/Distributor; Wildlife Management

Quantico Tactical Supply, 109 N. Main St., Raeford, NC 28376, P: 910-875-1672, F: 910-875-3797, www.quanticotactical.com
Eyewear; Firearms; Footwear; Holsters; Knives/Knife Cases; Law Enforcement; Survival Kits/First Aid

Quayside Publishing Group, 400 1st Ave. N, Suite 300, Minneapolis, MN 55401, P: 800-328-0590, F: 612-344-8691, www.creativepub.com
Books/Industry Publications

Quiqlite, Inc., 6464 Hollister Ave., Suite 4, Goleta, CA 93117, P: 866-496-2606, F: 800-910-5711, www.quiqlite.com
Backpacking; Camping; Hunting Accessories; Law Enforcement; Lighting Products; Reloading; Training & Safety Equipment

R

R & R Racing, Inc., 45823 Oak St., Lyons, OR 97358, P: 503-551-7283, F: 503-859-4711, www.randrracingonline.com
Custom Manufacturing; Hearing Protection; Shooting Range Equipment; Targets; Training & Safety Equipment; Wholesaler/Distributor

R & W Rope Warehouse, 39 Tarkiln Pl., P.O. Box 50420, New Bedford, MA 02745, P: 800-260-8599, F: 508-995-1114, www.rwrope.com
Backpacking; Camouflage; Camping; Custom Manufacturing; Hunting Accessories; Law Enforcement; Pet Supplies; Training & Safety Equipment

Rackulator, Inc., P.O. Box 248, Golden Valley, ND 58541, P: 888-791-4213, F: 701-983-4625, www.rackulator.com
Hunting Accessories

Radians, 7580 Bartlett Corp. Dr., Bartlett, TN 38133, P: 877-723-4267, F: 901-266-2558, www.radiansinc.com
Camouflage; Eyewear; Footwear; Gloves, Mitts, Hats; Hearing Protection; Hunting Accessories; Sports Accessories; Training & Safety Equipment

Raine, Inc., 6401 S. Madison Ave., Anderson, IN 46013, P: 800-826-5354, F: 765-622-7691, www.raineinc.com
Bags & Equipment Cases; Camping; Custom Manufacturing; Holsters; Knives/Knife Cases; Law Enforcement; Two-Way Radios

Rainer Ballistics, 4500 15th St. E, Tacoma, WA 98424, P: 800-638-8722, F: 253-922-7854, www.rainierballistics.com
Ammunition; Reloading; Wholesaler/Distributor

Ram Mounting Systems, 8410 Dallas Ave. S, Seattle, WA 98108, P: 206-763-8361, F: 206-763-9615, www.ram-mount.com
Hunting Accessories; Law Enforcement; Sports Accessories; Vehicles, Utility & Rec

Ramba, Via Giorgio La Pira, 20 Flero (Bs), Brescia 25020, ITALY, P: 011 390302548522, F: 011 390302549749, www.ramba.it
Ammunition; Reloading

Ranch Products, P.O. Box 145, Malinta, OH 43535, P: 419-966-2881, F: 313-565-8536, www.ranchproducts.com
Gun Parts/Gunsmithing; Scopes, Sights & Accessories

Rancho Trinidad, 4803 Fountainhead, Houston, TX 77066, P: 210-487-1640, F: 210-487-1640, www.ranchotrinidad.com
Outfitter; Tours/Travel

Randolph Engineering, Inc., 26 Thomas Patten Dr., Randolph, MA 02368, P: 800-541-1405, F: 781-986-0337, www.randolphusa.com
Eyewear

Range Systems, 5121 Winnetka Ave. N, Suite 150, New Hope, MN 55428, P: 888-999-1217, F: 763-537-6657, www.range-systems.com
Eyewear; Law Enforcement; Shooting Range Equipment; Targets; Training & Safety Equipment

Ranger/Xtratuf/NEOS Footwear, 1136 2nd St., Rock Island, IL 61201, P: 800-790-9296, F: 800-267-6809, www.npsusa.com
Footwear

Rapid Dominance Corp., 2121 S. Wilmington Ave., Compton, CA 90220, P: 800-719-5260, F: 310-608-3648, www.rapiddominance.com
Bags & Equipment Cases; Gloves, Mitts, Hats; Men's Clothing; Wholesaler/Distributor

Rat Cutlery Co., 60 Randall Rd., Gallant, AL 35972, P: 865-933-8436, F: 256-570-0175, www.ratcutlery.com
Backpacking; Camping; Cutlery; Knives/Knife Cases; Law Enforcement; Survival Kits/First Aid; Tours/Travel; Training & Safety Equipment

Rattlers Brand/Boyt Harness Co., One Boyt Dr., Osceola, IA 50213, P: 800-550-2698, F: 641-342-2703, www.rattlersbrand.com
Camouflage; Sports Accessories

MANUFACTURER'S AND PRODUCT DIRECTORY

Raza Khalid & Co., 14/8, Haji Pura, P.O. Box 1632, Sailkot, Punjab 51310, PAKISTAN, P: 011 92523264232, F: 011 92523254932, www.razakhalid.com
Bags & Equipment Cases; Gloves, Mitts, Hats; Gun Cases; Hunting Accessories; Law Enforcement; Paintball Accessories; Pet Supplies; Shooting Range Equipment

RBR Tactical Armor, Inc., 3113 Aspen Ave., Richmond, VA 23228, P: 800-672-7667, F: 804-726-6027, www.rbrtactical.com
Custom Manufacturing; Law Enforcement

RCBS/ATK Commercial Products, 605 Oro Dam Blvd., Oroville, CA 95965, P: 800-533-5000, F: 530-533-1647, www.rcbs.com
Reloading

Real Geese/Webfoot-LSP, 130 Cherry St., P.O. Box 675, Bradner, OH 43406, P: 419-800-8104, F: 888-642-6369, www.realgeese.com
Bags & Equipment Cases; Custom Manufacturing; Decoys; Emblems & Decals; Home Furnishings; Hunting Accessories; Printing Services; Retail Packaging

Realtree® Camouflage, P.O. Box 9638, Columbus, GA 31908, P: 800-992-9968, F: 706-569-9346, www.realtree.com
Camouflage; Videos

Recknagel, Landwehr 4, Bergrheinfeld, 97493, GERMANY, P: 011 49972184366, F: 011 49972182969, www.recknagel.de
Gun Parts/Gunsmithing; Scopes, Sights & Accessories

Recognition Services, 8577 Zionsville Rd., Indianapolis, IN 46268, P: 877-808-9400, F: 877-808-3565, www.we-belong.com
Custom Manufacturing; Emblems & Decals; Law Enforcement; Outfitter

ReconRobotics, Inc., 770 W. 78th St., Edina, MN 55439, P: 952-935-5515, F: 952-935-5508, www.reconrobotics.com
Law Enforcement

Redding Reloading Equipment, 1089 Starr Rd., Cortland, NY 13045, P: 607-753-3331, F: 607-756-8445, www.redding-reloading.com
Lubricants; Reloading

Redman Training Gear, 10045 102nd Terrace, Sebastian, FL 32958, P: 800-865-7840, F: 800-459-2598, www.redmangear.com
Law Enforcement; Training & Safety Equipment

Redwolf Airsoft Specialist, 7A-C, V GA Building, 532 Castle Peak Rd., Cheung Sha Wan, HONG KONG, P: 011 85228577665, F: 011 85229758305, www.redwolfairsoft.com
Airsoft

Reel Wings Decoy Co., Inc., 1122 Main Ave., Fargo, ND 58103, P: 866-55DECOY, F: 701-293-8234, www.reelwings.com
Camouflage; Decoys; Wholesaler/Distributor

Reflective Art, Inc., 403 Eastern Ave. SE, Grand Rapids, MI 49508, P: 800-332-1075, F: 616-452-2112, www.reflectiveartinc.com
Home Furnishings

Reliable of Milwaukee, P.O. Box 563, Milwaukee, WI 53201, P: 800-336-6876, F: 414-272-6443, www.reliableofmilwaukee.com
Archery; Bags & Equipment Cases; Camouflage; Footwear; Gloves, Mitts, Hats; Hunting Accessories; Men & Women's Clothing

Reminton Apparel/The Brinkmann Corp., 4215 McEwen Rd., Dallas, TX 75244, P: 877-525-9070, F: 800-780-0109, www.brinkmann.net
Camouflage; Gloves, Mitts, Hats; Hunting Accessories; Men's Clothing

Remington Arms Co., Inc., 870 Remington Dr., P.O. Box 700, Madison, NC 27025, P: 800-243-9700
Ammunition; Cutlery; Firearms; Footwear; Gun Parts/Gunsmithing; Hunting Accessories

Repel Products, P.O. Box 348, Marion, IA 52302, P: 866-921-1810, F: 319-447-0967, www.repelproducts.com
Archery; Hunting Accessories; Sports Accessories; Wildlife Management

Rescomp Handgun Technologies/CR Speed, P.O. Box 11786, Queenswood, 0186, SOUTH AFRICA, P: 011 27123334768, F: 011 27123332112, www.crspeed.co.za
Bags & Equipment Cases; Custom Manufacturing; Holsters; Law Enforcement; Scopes, Sights & Accessories; Sports Accessories; Wholesaler/Distributor

Revision Eyewear, Ltd., 7 Corporate Dr., Essex Junction, VT 05452, CANADA, P: 802-879-7002, F: 802-879-7224, www.revisionready.com
Eyewear; Hunting Accessories; Law Enforcement; Paintball Accessories; Shooting Range Equipment; Sports Accessories; Training & Safety Equipment

Rich-Mar Sports, North 7125 1280 St., River Falls, WI 54022, P: 952-881-6796, F: 952-884-4878, www.richmarsports.com
Cooking Equipment/Accessories; Hunting Accessories; Law Enforcement; Sports Accessories; Training & Safety Equipment

Ridge Outdoors U.S.A., Inc./Ridge Footwear, P.O. Box 389, Eustis, FL 32727-0389, P: 800-508-2668, F: 866-584-2042, www.ridgeoutdoors.com
Footwear; Law Enforcement; Men & Women's Clothing; Sports Accessories

Ring's Manufacturing, 99 East Dr., Melbourne, FL 32904, P: 800-537-7464, F: 321-951-0017, www.blueguns.com
Custom Manufacturing; Law Enforcement; Training & Safety Equipment

Rio Ammunition, Fountainview, Suite 207, Houston, TX 77057, P: 713-266-3091, F: 713-266-3092, www.rioammo.com, www.ueec.es
Ammunition; Black Powder/Smokeless Powder; Law Enforcement

Rio Bonito Ranch, 5309 Rio Bonito Ranch Rd., Junction, TX 76849, P: 800-864-4303, F: 325-446-3859, www.riobonito.com
Outfitter

Rite In The Rain, 2614 Pacific Hwy. E, Tacoma, WA 98424, P: 253-922-5000, F: 253-922-5300, www.riteintherain.com
Archery; Backpacking; Camping; Custom Manufacturing; Law Enforcement; Printing Services; Sports Accessories; Targets

River Oak Outdoors, Inc., 705 E. Market, Warrensburg, MO 64093, P: 660-580-0256, F: 816-222-0427, www.riveroakoutdoors.com
Custom Manufacturing; Game Calls; Gun Cabinets/Racks/Safes; Home Furnishings; Hunting Accessories; Sports Accessories

River Rock Designs, Inc., 900 RR 620 S, Suite C101-223, Austin, TX 78734, P: 512-263-6985, F: 512-263-1277, www.riverrockledlights.com
Backpacking; Camping; Hunting Accessories; Law Enforcement; Lighting Products; Sports Accessories; Training & Safety Equipment

River's Edge Treestands, Inc./Ardisam, Inc./Yukon Tracks, 1690 Elm St., Cumberland, WI 54829, P: 800-450-3343, F: 715-822-2124, www.huntriversedge.com, www.ardisam.com
Archery; Blinds; Camouflage; Gloves, Mitts, Hats; Hunting Accessories; Treestands

Rivers Edge Products, One Rivers Edge Ct., St. Clair, MO 63077, P: 888-326-6200, F: 636-629-7557, www.riversedgeproducts.com
Camouflage; Camping; Home Furnishings; Knives/Knife Cases; Leathergoods; Lighting Products; Pet Supplies; Wholesaler/Distributor

Rivers West/H2P Waterproof System, 2900 4th Ave. S, Seattle, WA 98134, P: 800-683-0887, F: 206-682-8691, www.riverswest.com
Camouflage; Law Enforcement; Men & Women's Clothing

RM Equipment, 6975 NW 43rd St., Miami, FL 33166, P: 305-477-9312, F: 305-477-9620, www.40mm.com
Firearms; Gun Grips & Stocks; Law Enforcement

RNT Calls, Inc./Buckwild Hunting Products and Quackhead Calls, 2315 Hwy. 63 N, P.O. Box 1026, Stuttgart, AR 72160, P: 877-993-4868, F: 601-829-4072, www.rntcalls.com
Custom Manufacturing; Emblems & Decals; Game Calls; Gloves, Mitts, Hats; Hunting Accessories; Scents & Lures; Videos

Robert Louis Company, Inc., 31 Shepard Hill Rd., Newtown, CT 06470, P: 800-979-9156, F: 203-270-3881, www.shotguncombogauge.com
Gun Parts/Gunsmithing; Shooting Range Equipment; Training & Safety Equipment

Rock Creek Barrels, Inc., 101 Ogden Ave., Albany, WI 53502, P: 608-862-2357, F: 608-862-2356, www.rockcreekbarrels.com
Gun Barrels

Rock River Arms, Inc., 1042 Cleveland Rd., Colona, IL 61241, P: 866-980-7625, F: 309-792-5781, www.rockriverarms.com
Custom Manufacturing; Firearms; Gun Barrels; Gun Grips & Stocks; Gun Parts/Gunsmithing; Law Enforcement; Magazines, Cartridge; Scopes, Sights & Accessories

Rockpoint Apparel, 9925 Aldine Westfield Rd., Houston, TX 77093, P: 713-699-9896, F: 713-699-9856, www.rockpoint-apparel.com
Camouflage; Custom Manufacturing; Export/Import Specialists; Gloves, Mitts, Hats; Men & Women's Clothing

Rocky Brands, 39 E. Canal St., Nelsonville, OH 45764, P: 740-753-9100, F: 740-753-7240, www.rockybrands.com
Footwear

Rocky Mountain Elk Foundation, 5705 Grant Creek Rd., P.O. Box 8249, Missoula, MT 59808, P: 800-CALL-ELK, F: 406-523-4550, www.elkfoundation.org
Books/Industry Publications; Wildlife Management

Rohrbaugh Firearms Corp., P.o. Box 785, Bayport, NY 11705, P: 800-803-2233, F: 631-242-3183, www.rohrbaughfirearms.com
Firearms

ROKON, 50 Railroad Ave., Rochester, NH 03839, P: 800-593-2369, F: 603-335-4400, www.rokon.com
Export/Import Specialists; Hunting Accessories; Sports Accessories; Vehicles, Utility & Rec

ROK Straps, 162 Locust Hill Dr., Rochester, NY 14618, P: 585-244-6451, F: 570-694-0773, www.rokstraps.com
Backpacking; Camouflage; Camping; Hunting Accessories; Pet Supplies; Sports Accessories

MANUFACTURER'S AND PRODUCT DIRECTORY

Rose Garden, The, 1855 Griffin Rd., Suite C370, Dania Beach, FL 33004, P: 954-927-9590, F: 954-927-9591, www.therosegardendb.com
Export/Import Specialists; Home Furnishings; Outdoor Art, Jewelry, Sculpture; Wholesaler/Distributor

Rose Plastic USA, LP, 525 Technology Dr., P.O. Box 698, California, PA 15419, P: 724-938-8530, F: 724-938-8532, www.rose-plastic.us
Bags & Equipment Cases; Custom Manufacturing; Gun Cases; Retail Packaging

Rossi/BrazTech, 16175 NW 49th Ave., Miami, FL 33014, P: 800-948-8029, F: 305-623-7506, www.rossiusa.com
Black Powder Accessories; Firearms

Rothco, 3015 Veterans Memorial Hwy., P.O. Box 1220, Ronkonkoma, NY 11779, P: 800-645-5195, F: 631-585-9447, www.rothco.com
Bags & Equipment Cases; Camouflage; Hunting Accessories; Knives/Knife Cases; Law Enforcement; Men & Women's Clothing; Survival Kits/First Aid; Wholesaler/Distributor

RPM, Inc./Drymate, 6665 W. Hwy. 13, Savage, MN 55378, P: 800-872-8201, F: 952-808-2277, www.drymate.com
Blinds; Camping; Custom Manufacturing; Firearms Maintenance Equipment; Home Furnishings; Hunting Accessories; Pet Supplies; Sports Accessories; Vehicles, Utility & Rec

RSR Group, Inc., 4405 Metric Dr., Winter Park, FL 32792, P: 800-541-4867, F: 407-677-4489, www.rsrgroup.com
Airguns; Ammunition; Cutlery; Firearms; Gun Cases; Holsters; Scopes, Sights & Accessories; Wholesaler/Distributor

RS International Industry/Hong Kong Co., Ltd., Room 1109, 11F, WingHing Industrial Bldg., Chai Wan Kok St., Tsuen Wan N.T., HONG KONG, P: 011 85224021381, F: 011 85224021385, www.realsword.com.hk
Airsoft

RTZ Distribution/HallMark Cutlery, 4436B Middlebrook Pike, Knoxville, TN 37921, P: 866-583-3912, F: 865-588-0425, www.hallmarkcutlery.com
Cutlery; Knifes/Knife Cases; Law Enforcement; Sharpeners

RUAG Ammotec, Uttigenstrasse 67, Thun, 3602, SWITZERLAND, P: 011 41332282879, F: 011 41332282644, www.ruag.com
Ammunition; Law Enforcement

Ruffed Grouse Society, Inc., 451 McCormick Rd., Coraopolis, PA 15108, P: 888-564-6747, F: 412-262-9207, www.ruffedgrousesociety.org
Wildlife Management

Ruger Firearms, 1 Lacey Pl., Southport, CT 06890, P: 203-259-7843, F: 203-256-3367, www.ruger.com
Firearms

Ruko, LLC, P.O. Box 38, Buffalo, NY 14207, P: 716-874-2707, F: 905-826-1353, www.rukoproducts.com
Camping; Compasses; Custom Manufacturing; Cutlery; Export/Import Specialists; Hunting Accessories; Knives/Knife Cases; Sharpeners

Russ Fields Safaris, Gameston, Alicedale Rd., P.O. Box 100, Grahamstown, East Cape, 6140, SOUTH AFRICA, P: 011 27834449753, F: 011 27466225837, www.southafricanhunting.com
Outfitter

Russian American Armory Co., 677 S. Cardinal Ln., Suite A, Scottsburg, IN 47170, P: 877-752-2894, F: 812-752-7683, www.raacfirearms.com
Firearms; Knives/Knife Cases; Magazines, Cartridge

RVJ International/Happy Feet, 6130 W. Flamingo Rd., PMB 460, Las Vegas, NV 89103, P: 702-871-6377, F: 702-222-1212, www.happyfeet.com
Books/Industry Publications; Footwear; Hunting Accessories; Men & Women's Clothing; Sports Accessories

S

S&K Industries, Inc., S. Hwy. 13, Lexington, MO 64067, P: 660-259-4691, F: 660-259-2081, www.sandkgunstocks.com
Custom Manufacturing; Gun Grips & Stocks

Saab Barracuda, LLC, 608 McNeill St., Lillington, NC 27546, P: 910-893-2094, F: 910-893-8807, www.saabgroup.com
Camouflage; Law Enforcement

Sabre Defence Industries, LLC, 450 Allied Dr., Nashville, TN 37211, P: 615-333-0077, F: 615-333-6229, www.sabredefence.com
Firearms; Gun Barrels

Sack-Ups, 1611 Jamestown Rd., Morganton, NC 28655, P: 877-213-6333, F: 828-584-6326, www.sackups.com
Archery; Black Powder Accessories; Firearms Maintenance Equipment; Gun Cases; Hunting Accessories; Knives/Knife Cases; Sports Accessories

Safari Club International, 4800 W. Gates Pass Rd., Tucson, AZ 85745, P: 520-620-1220, F: 520-618-3528, www.safariclub.org
Books/Industry Publications

Safari Nordik, 639 Labelle Blvd., Blainville, Quebec J7C 1V8, CANADA, P: 800-361-3748, F: 450-971-1771, www.safarinordik.com
Outfitter; Tours/Travel

Safari Press, 15621 Chemical Ln., Huntington Beach, CA 92649, P: 714-894-9080, F: 714-894-4949, www.safaripress.com
Books/Industry Publications

Safari Sunsets, 9735 Slater Ln., Overland Park, KS 66212, P: 877-894-1671, F: 913-894-1686, www.safarisunsets.com
Men's Clothing

Safe Guy/Gun Storage Solutions, 18317 N. 2600 East Rd., Cooksville, IL 61730, P: 309-275-1220, www.storemoreguns.com
Gun Cabinets/Racks/Safes

Safety Bullet, Inc., P.O. Box 007, Panama City, FL 32444, P: 850-866-0190, www.safetybullet.com
Gun Locks

Safety Harbor Firearms, Inc., 915 Harbor Lake Dr., Suite D, Safety Harbor, FL 34695, P: 727-725-4700, F: 727-724-1872, www.safetyharborfirearms.com
Firearms

Sage Control Ordnance, Inc./Sage International, Ltd., 3391 E. Eberhardt St., Oscoda, MI 48750, P: 989-739-7000, F: 989-739-7098, www.sageinternationalltd.com
Ammunition; Firearms; Gun Grips & Stocks; Gun Locks; Law Enforcement; Reloading

Salt River Tactical, LLC/Ost-Kraft, LLC, P.O. Box 20397, Mesa, AZ 85277, P: 480-656-2683, www.saltrivertactical.com

Bags & Equipment Cases; Firearms Maintenance Equipment; Hunting Accessories; Law Enforcement; Scopes, Sights & Accessories; Shooting Range Equipment; Wholesaler/Distributor

SAM Medical Products, P.O. Box 3270, Tualatin, OR 97062, P: 800-818-4726, F: 503-639-5425, www.sammedical.com
Backpacking; Camping; Law Enforcement; Outfitter; Shooting Range Equipment; Survival Kits/First Aid; Training & Safety Equipment

Samco Global Arms, Inc., 6995 NW 43rd St., Miami, FL 33166, P: 800-554-1618, F: 305-593-1014, www.samcoglobal.com
Ammunition; Firearms; Sports Accessories

Samson Mfg. Corp., 110 Christian Ln., Whately, MA 01373, P: 888-665-4370, F: 413-665-1163, www.samson-mfg.com
Firearms; Gun Parts/Gunsmithing; Law Enforcement; Scopes, Sights & Accessories

San Angelo/Rio Brands, 10981 Decatur Rd., Philadelphia, PA 19154, P: 800-531-7230, F: 830-393-7621, www.riobrands.com
Backpacking; Blinds; Camping; Cooking Equipment/Accessories; Gun Cabinets/Racks/Safes; Hunting Accessories; Taxidermy

Sandhurst Safaris, P.O. Box 57, Tosca, 8618, SOUTH AFRICA, P: 011 27824535683, F: 011 27539331002, www.sandhurstsafaris.com
Tours/Travel

Sandpiper of California, 687 Anita St., Suite A, Chula Vista, CA 91911, P: 866-424-6622, F: 619-423-9599, www.pipergear.com
Backpacking; Bags & Equipment Cases; Camouflage; Custom Manufacturing; Law Enforcement

Sandviper, 1611 Jamestown Rd., Morganton, NC 28655, P: 800-873-7225, F: 828-584-6326
Law Enforcement

Sante Fe Stone Works, Inc., 3790 Cerillos Rd., Sante Fe, NM 87507, P: 800-257-7625, F: 505-471-0036, www.santefestoneworks.com
Cutlery

Sargent & Greenleaf, Inc., One Security Dr., Nicholasville, KY 40356, P: 800-826-7652, F: 859-887-2057, www.sargentandgreenleaf.com
Gun Cabinets/Racks/Safes

Sarsilmaz Silah San. A.S, Nargileci Sokak, No. 4, Sarsilmaz ls Merkezi, Mercan, Eminonu, Istanbul, 34116, TURKEY, P: 011 902125133507, F: 011 902125111999, www.sarsilmaz.com
Firearms

Savage Arms, Inc., 118 Mountain Rd., Suffield, CT 06078, P: 866-233-4776, F: 860-668-2168, www.savagearms.com
Black Powder/Smokeless Powder; Firearms; Knives/Knife Cases; Law Enforcement; Shooting Range Equipment

Savannah Luggage Works, 3428 Hwy. 297 N, Vidalia, GA 30474, P: 800-673-6341, F: 912-537-4492, www.savannahluggage.com
Backpacking; Bags & Equipment Cases; Custom Manufacturing; Holsters; Law Enforcement; Training & Safety Equipment

SBR Ammunition, 1118 Glynn Park Rd., Suite E, Brunswick, GA 31525, P: 912-264-5822, F: 912-264-5888, www.sbrammunition.com
Ammunition; Firearms; Law Enforcement

Sceery Outdoors, LLC, P.O. Box 6520, Sante Fe, NM 87502; P: 800-327-4322 or

MANUFACTURER'S AND PRODUCT DIRECTORY

505-471-9110; F: 505-471-3476; www.
sceeryoutdoors.net
Decoys; Game Calls; Hunting Accessories

Scent-Lok Technologies, 1731 Wierengo Dr.,
Muskegon, MI 49442, P: 800-315-5799, F:
231-767-2824, www.scentlok.com
*Bags & Equipment Cases; Camouflage;
Gloves, Mitts, Hats; Men & Women's Clothing;
Videos*

SCENTite Blinds, P.O. Box 36635, Birmingham,
AL 35236, P: 800-828-1554, F: 205-424-
4799, www.fargasonoutdoors.com
*Archery; Backpacking; Blinds; Crossbows
& Accessories; Hunting Accessories;
Photographic Equipment; Scents & Lures;
Treestands*

Scentote, 1221 Keating, Grand Rapids, MI
49503, P: 616-742-0946, F: 616-742-0978,
www.scentote.com
*Archery; Hunting Accessories; Men's Clothing;
Scents & Lures*

Scharch Mfg., Inc/Top Brass, 10325 Cty. Rd.
120, Salida, CO 81201, P: 800-836-4683, F:
719-539-3021, www.scharch.com
*Ammunition; Magazines, Cartridge; Reloading;
Retail Packaging; Shooting Range Equipment*

Scherer Supplies, Inc., 205 Four Mile Creek
Rd., Tazewell, TN 37879, P: 423-733-2615,
F: 423-733-2073
*Custom Manufacturing; Magazines, Cartridge;
Wholesaler/Distributor*

Schmidt & Bender GmbH, Am Grossacker 42,
Biebertal, Hessen 35444, GERMANY, P:
011 496409811570, US: 800-468-3450, F:
++49-6409811511, www.schmidt-bender.de,
www.schmidtbender.com
*Hunting Accessories; Law Enforcement;
Scopes, Sights & Accessories; Sports
Accessories; Telescopes*

Schott Performance Fabrics, Inc., 2850
Gilchrist Rd., Akron, OH 44305, P: 800-321-
2178, F: 330-734-0665, www.schottfabrics.
com
*Camouflage; Export/Import Specialists;
Hunting Accessories; Men's Clothing*

Scopecoat by Devtron Diversified, 3001 E.
Cholla St., Phoenix, AZ 85028, P: 877-726-
7328, F: 602-224-9351, www.scopecoat.
com
Scopes, Sights & Accessories

SDG Seber Design Group, Inc. 2438 Cades
Way, Vista, CA 92081, P: 760-727-5555, F:
760-727-5551, www.severdesigngroup.com
*Camping; Cutlery; Knives/Knife Cases; Law
Enforcement*

Seasonal Marketing, Inc., P.O. Box 1410, La
Pine, OR 97739, P: 972-540-1656, www.
caddiswadingsysstems.net
Footwear; Hunting Accessories

Second Amendment Foundation, 12500 NE
Tenth Pl., Bellevue, WA 98005, P: 425-454-
7012, F: 425-451-3959, www.saf.org
Books/Industry Publications

SecuRam Systems, Inc., 350 N. Lantana St.,
Suite 211, Camarillo, CA 93010, P: 805-388-
2058, F: 805-383-1728, www.securamsys.
com
Gun Cabinets/Racks/Safes

Secure Firearm Products, 213 S. Main, P.O.
Box 177, Carl Junction, MO 64834, P:
800-257-8744, F: 417-649-7278, www.
securefirearmproducts.com
*Bags & Equipment Cases; Custom
Manufacturing; Gun Cases; Shooting Range
Equipment; Targets*

Secure Vault/Boyt Harness Co., One Boyt Dr.,
Osceola, IA 50213, P: 800-550-2698, F: 641-
342-2703
Gun Cabinets/Racks/Safes

Security Equipment Corp., 747 Sun Park Dr.,
Fenton, MO 63026, P: 800-325-9568, F:
636-343-1318, www.sabrered.com
*Backpacking; Camping; Custom
Manufacturing; Law Enforcement; Training &
Safety Equipment*

Seldon Technologies, Inc., P.O. Box 710,
Windsor, VT 05089, P: 802-674-2444, F:
802-674-2544, www.seldontech.com
Backpacking; Camping; Hunting Accessories

Self Defense Supply, Inc., 1819 Firman Dr.,
Suite 101, Richardson, TX 75081, P:
800-211-4186, F: 942-644-6980, www.
selfdefensesupply.com
*Airguns; Airsoft; Binoculars; Camping;
Crossbows & Accessories; Cutlery; Lighting
Products; Wholesaler/Distributor*

Sellier & Bellot, USA, Inc., P.O. Box 7307,
Shawnee Mission, KS 66207, P: 913-664-
5933, F: 913-664-5938, www.sb-usa.com
Ammunition; Law Enforcement

Sentry Group, 900 Linden Ave., Rochester, NY
14625, P: 800-828-1438, F: 585-381-8559,
www.sentrysafe.com
*Gun Cabinets/Racks/Safes; Home Furnishings;
Hunting Accessories; Law Enforcement*

Sentry Solutions, Ltd., 5 Souhegan St.,
P.O. Box 214, Wilton, NH 03086, P:
800-546-8049, F: 603-654-3003, www.
sentrysolutions.com
*Firearms Maintenance Equipment; Gun Parts/
Gunsmithing; Hunting Accessories; Lubricants;
Sharpeners; Sports Accessories*

Serbu Firearms, Inc., 6001 Johns Rd., Suite
144, Tampa, FL 33634, P: 813-243-8899, F:
813-243-8899, www.serbu.com
Firearms; Law Enforcement

Sharp Shoot R Precision, Inc., P.O. Box 171,
Paola, KS 66071, P: 785-883-4444, F: 785-
883-2525, www.sharpshootr.com
*Black Powder Accessories; Custom
Manufacturing; Firearms Maintenance
Equipment; Lubricants; Reloading; Sports
Accessories*

Shasta Wear, 4320 Mountain Lakes Blvd.,
Redding, CAR 96003, P: 800-553-2466, F:
530-243-3274, www.shastawear.com
*Emblems & Decals; Export/Import Specialists;
Gloves, Mitts, Hats; Men & Women's Clothing;
Outdoor Art, Jewelry, Sculpture; Retailer
Services; Wholesaler/Distributor*

SHE Safari, LLC, 15535 W. Hardy, Suite 102,
Houston, TX 77060, P: 281-448-4860, F:
281-448-4118, www.shesafari.com
Camouflage; Women's Clothing

Sheffield Equipment, 4569 Mission Gorge Pl.,
San Diego, CA 92120, P: 619-280-0278, F:
619-280-0011, www.sheffieldcuttingequip.
com
*Bags & Equipment Cases; Camouflage;
Custom Manufacturing; Holsters;
Leathergoods; Men & Women's Clothing*

Sheffield Tools/GreatLITE Flashlights, 165 E.
2nd St., P.O. Box 3, Mineola, NY 11501,
P: 800-457-0600, F: 516-746-5366, www.
sheffield-tools.com
*Backpacking; Camping; Cutlery; Hunting
Accessories; Knives/Knife Cases; Lighting
Products*

Shelterlogic, 150 Callender Rd., Watertown, CT
06795, P: 800-932-9344, F: 860-274-9306,
www.shelterlogic.com
*Camouflage; Camping; Custom Manufacturing;
Hunting Accessories; Law Enforcement; Pet
Supplies; Sports Accessories*

Shenzhen Champion Industry Co., Ltd.,
Longqin Rd. No. 13, Shahu, Pingshan,
Longgang Shenzhen City, GNGD 518118,
CHINA, P: 011 8675589785877, F: 011
8675589785875, www.championcase.com
*Bags & Equipment Cases; Cutlery; Gun
Cabinets/Racks/Safes; Gun Cases; Gun Locks;
Gun Parts/Gunsmithing; Home Furnishings;
Knives/Knife Cases*

Shepherd Enterprises, Inc., P.O. Box 189,
Waterloo, NE 68069, P: 402-779-2424, F:
402-779-4010, www.shepherdscopes.com
Scopes, Sights & Accessories

Sherluk Marketing, Law Enforcement & Military,
P.O. Box 156, Delta, OH 43615, P: 419-923-
8011, F: 419-923-8120, www.sherluk.com
*Firearms; Firearms Maintenance Equipment;
Gun Grips & Stocks; Gun Parts/Gunsmithing;
Law Enforcement; Wholesaler/Distributor*

Shiloh Rifle Manufacturing, 201 Centennial Dr.,
P.O. Box 279, Big Timber, MT 59011, P: 406-
932-4454, F: 406-932-5627, www.shilohrifle.
com
Black Powder Accessories; Firearms

Shirstone Optics/Shinei Group, Inc.,
Komagome-Spancrete Bldg. 8F,
Honkomagome 5-4-7, Bunkyo-Ku, Toyko,
113-0021, JAPAN, P: 011 81339439550, F:
011 81339430695, www.shirstone.com
*Binoculars; Firearms; Scopes, Sights &
Accessories*

Shocknife, Inc., 20 Railway St., Winnipeg,
Manitoba R2X 2P9, CANADA, P: 866-353-
5055, F: 204-586-2049, www.shocknife.com
*Knives/Knife Cases; Law Enforcement; Training
& Safety Equipment*

Shooter's Choice Gun Care/Ventco, Inc., 15050
Berkshire Industrial Pkwy., Middlefield, OH
44062, P: 440-834-8888, F: 440-834-3388,
www.shooters-choice.com
*Firearms Maintenance Equipment; Gun Parts/
Gunsmithing; Law Enforcement; Lubricants*

Shooters Depot, 5526 Leopard St., Corpus
Christi, TX 78408, P: 361-299-1299, F: 361-
289-9906, www.shootersdepot.com
Firearms; Gun Barrels

Shooters Ridge/ATK Commercial Products,
N5549 Cty. Tk. Z, Onalaska, WI 54650, P:
800-635-7656, F: 763-323-3890, www.
shootersridge.com
*Bags & Equipment Cases; Gun Cabinets/
Racks/Safes; Hunting Accessories; Magazines,
Cartridge; Sports Accessories*

Shooting Chrony, Inc., 2446 Cawthra Rd., Bldg.
1, Suite 10, Mississauga, Ontario L5A 3K6,
CANADA, P: 800-385-3161, F: 905-276-
6295, www.shootingchrony.com
*Archery; Black Powder Accessories; Computer
Software; Hunting Accessories; Lighting
Products; Reloading; Shooting Range
Equipment; Sports Accessories*

Shooting Ranges International, Inc./Advanced
Interactive Systems, 3885 Rockbottom
St., North Las Vegas, NV 89030, P:
702-362-3623, F: 702-310-6978, www.
shootingrangeintl.com
*Firearms; Law Enforcement; Shooting Range
Equipment*

MANUFACTURER'S AND PRODUCT DIRECTORY

Shooting Sports Retailer, 255 W. 36th St., Suite 1202, New York, NY 10018, P: 212-840-0660, F: 212-944-1884, www.shootingsportsretailer.com
Books/Industry Publications

Sierra Bullets, 1400 W. Henry St., Sedalia, MO 65301, P: 888-223-3006, F: 660-827-4999, www.sierrabullets.com
Books/Industry Publications; Computer Software; Reloading; Videos

SIG SAUER, 18 Industrial Dr., Exeter, NH 03833, P: 603-772-2302, F: 603-772-9082, www.sigsauer.com
Bags & Equipment Cases; Firearms; Holsters; Knives/Knife Cases; Law Enforcement; Training & Safety Equipment

Sightron, Inc., 100 Jeffrey Way, Suite A, Youngville, NC 27596, P: 800-867-7512, F: 919-556-0157, www.sightron.com
Binoculars; Scopes, Sights & Accessories

Silencio/Jackson Safety, 1859 Bowles Ave., Suite 200, Fenton, MO 63026, P: 800-237-4192, F: 636-717-6820, www.jacksonsafety.com
Eyewear; Hearing Protection; Law Enforcement

Silma SRL, Via I Maggio, 74, Zanano Di Sarezzo, Brescia 25068, ITALY, P: 011 390308900505, F: 011 390308900712, www.silma.net
Firearms

Silver Stag, 328 Martin St., Blaine, WA 98230, P: 888-233-7824, F: 360-332-4390, www.silverstag.com
Black Powder Accessories; Camping; Crossbows & Accessories; Custom Manufacturing; Cutlery; Hunting Accessories; Knives/Knife Cases; Outdoor Art, Jewelry, Sculpture

Silver State Armory, LLC, P.O. Box 2902, Pahrump, NV 89041, P: 775-537-1118, F: 775-537-1119
Ammunition; Firearms

Simmons, 9200 Cody St., Overland Park, KS 66214, P: 913-782-3131, F: 913-782-4189
Binoculars; Hunting Accessories; Law Enforcement; Scopes, Sights & Accessories

Simunition Operations, General Dynamics Ordnance & Tactical Systems, 5 Montée des Arsenaux, Le Gardeur, Quebec J5Z 2P4, CANADA, P: 800-465-8255, F: 450-581-0231, www.simunition.com
Ammunition; Gun Barrels; Law Enforcement; Magazines, Cartridge, Training & Safety Equipment

Sinclair International, 2330 Wayne Haven St., Fort Wayne, IN 46803, P: 800-717-8211, F: 260-493-2530, www.sinclairintl.com
Ammunition; Bags & Equipment Cases; Books; Cleaning Products; Reloading; Scopes, Sights & Accessories; Software; Targets, Videos

SISCO, 2835 Ana St., Rancho Dominguez, CA 90221, P: 800-832-5834, F: 310-638-6489, www.honeywellsafes.com
Gun Cabinets/Racks/Safes; Hunting Accessories

Sitka, Inc., 870 Napa Valley Corporate Way, Suite N, Napa, CA 94558, P: 877-SITKA MG, F: 707-253-1121, www.sitkagear.com
Men's Clothing

SKB Corp., 1607 N. O'Donnell Way, Orange, CA 92867, P: 800-654-5992, F: 714-283-0425, www.skbcases.com
Archery; Bags & Equipment Cases; Gun Cases; Hunting Accessories; Knives/Knife Cases; Law Enforcement; Sports Accessories

SKB Shotguns, 4441 S. 134th St., Omaha, NE 68137, P: 800-752-2767, P: 402-330-8040, www.skbshotguns.com
Firearms

Smith & Warren, 127 Oakley Ave., White Plains, NY 10601, P: 800-53-BADGE, F: 914-948-1627, www.smithwarren.com
Custom Manufacturing; Law Enforcement

Smith & Wesson, 2100 Roosevelt Ave., Springfield, MA 01104, P: 800-331-0852, F: 413-747-3317, www.smith-wesson.com
Firearms; Law Enforcement

Smith Optics Elite Division, 280 Northwood Way, P.O. Box 2999, Ketchum, ID 83340, P: 208-726-4477, F: 208-727-6598, www.elite.smithoptics.com
Eyewear; Law Enforcement; Shooting Range Equipment; Training & Safety Equipment

Smith's, 1700 Sleepy Valley Rd., Hot Springs, AR 71901, P: 800-221-4156, F: 501-321-9232, www.smithsedge.com
Backpacking; Camping; Cutlery; Hunting Accessories; Sharpeners

Smith Security Safes, Inc., P.O. Box 185, Tontogany, OH 43565, P: 800-521-0335, F: 419-823-1505, www.smithsecuritysafes.com
Gun Cabinets/Racks/Safes

Sniper's Hide.com/Snipers Hide, LLC, 3205 Fenton St., Wheat Ridge, CO 80212, P: 203-530-3301, F: 203-622-7331, www.snipershide.com
Books/Industry Publications; Firearms; Law Enforcement; Online Services; Training & Safety Equipment

Snow Peak USA, Inc., P.O. Box 2002, Clackamas, OR 97015, P: 503-697-3330, F: 503-699-1396, www.snowpeak.com
Backpacking; Camping; Cooking Equipment/Accessories; Cutlery

Soft Air USA Inc./Cybergun, 1452 Hughes Rd., Suite 100, Grapevine, TX 76051, P: 480-330-3358, F: 925-906-1360, www.softairusa.com
Airguns; Airsoft; Paintball Guns & Accessories

Sog Armory, Inc., 11707 S. Sam Houston Pkwy. W, Suite R, Houston, TX 77031, P: 281-568-5685, F: 285-568-9191, www.sogarmory.com
Firearms; Firearms Maintenance Equipment; Gun Barrels; Gun Grips & Stocks; Law Enforcement; Scopes, Sights & Accessories; Wholesaler/Distributor

SOG Specialty Knives, 6521 212th St. SW, Lynnwood, WA 98036, P: 888-405-6433, F: 425-771-7689, www.sogknives.com
Cutlery; Hunting Accessories; Knives/Knife Cases; Law Enforcement

Sohn Mfg., Inc., 544 Sohn Dr., Elkhart Lake, WI 53020, P: 920-876-3361, F: 920-876-2952, www.sohnmanufacturing.com
Emblems & Decals; Printing Services

Solkoa, Inc., 3107 W. Colorado Ave., Suite 256, Colorado Springs, CO 80904, P: 719-685-1072, F: 719-623-0067, www.solkoa.com
Bags & Equipment Cases; Compasses; Hunting Accessories; Law Enforcement; Survival Kits/First Aid; Training & Safety Equipment; Wholesaler/Distributor

Sona Enterprises, 7825 Somerset Blvd., Suite D, Paramount, CA 90723, P: 562-633-3002, F: 562-633-3583
Binoculars; Camouflage; Camping; Compasses; Lighting Products; Survival Kits/First Aid; Wholesaler/Distributor

SOTech/Special Operations Technologies, 206 Star of India Ln., Carson, CA 90746, P: 800-615-9007, F: 310-202-0880, www.specopstech.com
Backpacking; Bags & Equipment Cases; Custom Manufacturing; Gun Cases; Holsters; Law Enforcement; Shooting Range Equipment; Survival Kits/First Aid

Source One Distributors, 3125 Fortune Way, Suite 1, Wellington, FL 33414, P: 866-768-4327, F: 561-514-1021, www.buysourceone.com
Bags & Equipment Cases; Binoculars; Eyewear; Firearms; Knives/Knife Cases; Men's Clothing; Scopes, Sights & Accessories; Wholesaler/Distributor

Southern Belle Brass, P.O. Box 36, Memphis, TN 38101, P: 800-478-3016, F: 901-947-1924, www.southernbellebrass.com
Firearms Maintenance Equipment; Holsters; Law Enforcement; Men's Clothing; Paintball Guns; Targets; Training & Safety Equipment; Wholesaler/Distributor

Southern Bloomer Mfg. Co. & Muzzleloader Originals, 1215 Fifth St., P.O. Box 1621, Bristol, TN 37621, P: 800-655-0342, F: 423-878-8761, www.southernbloomer.com
Ammunition; Black Powder Accessories; Firearms Maintenance Equipment; Gun Parts/Gunsmithing; Hunting Accessories; Law Enforcement; Reloading; Shooting Range Equipment

SPA Defense, 3409 NW 9th Ave., Suite 1104, Ft. Lauderdale, FL 33309, P: 954-568-7690, F: 954-630-4159, www.spa-defense.com
Firearms; Law Enforcement; Scopes, Sights & Accessories; Tactical Equipment

Spartan Imports, 213 Lawrence Ave., San Francisco, CA 94080, P: 650-589-5501, F: 650-589-5552, www.spartanimports.com
Airguns; Firearms; Law Enforcement; Paintball Guns; Scopes, Sights & Accessories; Training & Safety Equipment; Wholesaler/Distributor

Spec.-Ops. Brands, 1601 W. 15th St., Monahans, TX 79756, P: 866-773-2677, F: 432-943-5565, www.specopsbrand.com
Bags & Equipment Cases; Custom Manufacturing; Holsters; Knives/Knife Cases; Law Enforcement; Shooting Range Equipment; Sports Accessories; Training & Safety Equipment

Specialty Bar Products Co., 4 N. Shore Center, Suite 110, 106 Isabella St., Pittsburgh, PA 15212, P: 412-322-2747, F: 412-322-1912, www.specialty-bar.com
Firearms; Gun Barrels; Gun Parts/Gunsmithing

Specter Gear, Inc., 1107 E. Douglas Ave., Visalia, CA 93292, P: 800-987-3605, F: 559-553-8835, www.spectergear.com
Bags & Equipment Cases; Gun Cases; Holsters; Law Enforcement

Speer Ammunition/ATK Commercial Products, 2299 Snake River Ave., Lewiston, ID 83501, P: 800-256-8685, F: 208-746-3904, www.speer-bullets.com
Ammunition; Reloading

Spiewak/Timberland Pro Valor, 463 Seventh Ave., 11th Floor, New York, NY 10018, P: 800-223-6850, F: 212-629-4803, www.spiewak.com
Footwear; Law Enforcement

MANUFACTURER'S AND PRODUCT DIRECTORY

Spitfire, Ltd., 8868 Research Blvd., Suite 203, Austin, TX 78758, P: 800-774-8347, F: 512-453-7504, www.spitfire.us
Backpacking; Camping; Sporting Range Equipment; Sports Accessories; Training & Safety Equipment

SportDOG Brand, 10427 Electric Ave., Knoxville, TN 37932, P: 800-732-0144, F: 865-777-4815, www.sportdog.com
Hunting Accessories; Pet Supplies; Training & Safety Equipment; Videos

SportEAR/HarrisQuest Outdoor Products, 528 E. 800 N, Orem, UT 84097, P: 800-530-0090, F: 801-224-5660, www.harrisquest.com
Clay Targets; Hearing Protection; Hunting Accessories; Law Enforcement; Scopes, Sights & Accessories; Shooting Range Equipment; Sports Accessories; Training & Safety Equipment

SportHill, 725 McKinley St., Eugene, OR 97402, P: 541-345-9623, F: 541-343-7261, www.sporthillhunting.com
Archery; Camouflage; Gloves, Mitts, Hats; Men & Women's Clothing; Sports Accessories

Sporting Clays Magazine, 317 S. Washington Ave., Suite 201, Titusville, FL 32796, P: 321-268-5010, F: 321-267-7216, www.sportingclays.net
Books/Industry Publications

Sporting Supplies International, Inc.®, P.O. Box 757, Placentia, CA 92871, P: 888-757-WOLF (9653), F: 714-632-9232, www.wolfammo.com
Ammunition

Sports Afield Magazine, 15621 Chemical Ln., Huntington Beach, CA 92649, P: 714-894-9080, F: 714-894-4949, www.sportsafield.com
Books/Industry Publications

Sports South, LLC, 1039 Kay Ln., P.O. Box 51367, Shreveport, LA 71115, 800-388-3845, www.Internetguncatalog.com
Ammunition; Binoculars; Black Powder Accessories; Firearms; Hunting Accessories; Reloading; Scopes, Sights & Accessories; Wholesaler/Distributor

Spot, Inc., 461 S. Milpitas Blvd., Milpitas, CA 95035, F: 408-933-4543, F: 408-933-4954, www.findmespot.com
Backpacking; Camping; Outfitter; Sports Accessories; Survival Kits/First Aid; Training & Safety Equipment

Springboard Engineering, 6520 Platt Ave., Suite 818, West Hills, CA 91307, P: 818-346-4647, F: 818-346-4647
Backpacking; Law Enforcement; Lighting Products; Sports Accessories; Survival Kits/First Aid; Training & Safety Equipment; Wholesaler/Distributor

Springfield Armory, 420 W. Main St., Geneseo, IL 61254, P: 800-680-6866, F: 309-944-3676, www.springfield-armory.com
Firearms

Spyder Paintball/Kingman Group, 14010 Live Oak Ave., Baldwin Park, CA 91706, P: 888-KINGMAN, F: 626-851-8530, www.spyder.tv
Bags & Equipment Cases; Eyewear; Gun Cases; Men's Clothing; Paintball Guns & Accessories

Spyderco, Inc., 820 Spyderco Way, Golden, CO 80403, P: 800-525-7770, F: 303-278-2229, www.spyderco.com
Knives/Knife Cases

SRT Supply, 4450 60th Ave. N, St. Petersburg, FL 33714, P: 727-526-5451, F: 727-527-6893, www.srtsupply.com
Ammunition; Export/Import Specialists; Firearms; Law Enforcement; Wholesaler/Distributor

Stack-On Products Co., 1360 N. Old Rand Rd., P.O. Box 489, Wauconda, IL 60084, P: 800-323-9601, F: 847-526-6599, www.stack-on.com
Bags & Equipment Cases; Gun Cabinets/Racks/Safes; Gun Cases; Hunting Accessories; Shooting Range Equipment; Sports Accessories; Training & Safety Equipment

Stackpole Books, Inc., 5067 Ritter Rd., Mechanicsburg, PA 17055, P: 800-732-3669, F: 717-796-0412, www.stackpolebooks.com
Books/Industry Publications

Stag Arms, 515 John Downey Dr., New Britain, CT 06051, P: 860-229-9994, F: 860-229-3738, www.stagarms.com
Firearms; Law Enforcement

Stallion Leather/Helios Systems, 1104 Carroll Ave., South Milwaukee, WI 53172, P: 414-764-7126, F: 414-764-2878, www.helios-sys.com
Bags & Equipment Cases; Holsters; Knives/Knife Cases; Law Enforcement; Leathergoods; Sports Accessories

Stansport, 2801 E. 12th St., Los Angeles, CA 90023, P: 800-421-6131, F: 323-269-2761, www.stansport.com
Backpacking; Bags & Equipment Cases; Camping; Compasses; Cooking Equipment/Accessories; Hunting Accessories; Lighting Products; Survival Kits/First Aid

Stark Equipment Corp., 55 S. Commercial St., 4th Floor, Manchester, NH 03101, P: 603-556-7772, F: 603-556-7344, www.starkequipment.com
Gun Grips & Stocks; Hunting Accessories; Law Enforcement

Starlight Cases™, 2180 Hwy. 70-A E, Pine Level, NC 27568, P: 877-782-7544, F: 919-965-9177, www.starlightcases.com
Bags & Equipment Cases; Custom Manufacturing; Gun Cabinets/Racks/Safes; Gun Cases; Hunting Accessories; Law Enforcement; Scopes, Sights & Accessories; Shooting Range Equipment

Steiner Binoculars, 97 Foster Rd., Suite 5, Moorestown, NJ 08057, P: 800-257-7742, F: 856-866-8615, www.steiner-binoculars.com
Binoculars

SteriPEN/Hydro-Photon, Inc., 262 Ellsworth Rd., Blue Hill, ME 04614, P: 888-783-7473, F: 207-374-5100, www.steripen.com
Backpacking; Camping; Cooking Equipment/Accessories; Law Enforcement; Sports Accessories; Survival Kits/First Aid; Training & Safety Equipment

Sterling Sharpener, P.O. Box 620547, Woodside, CA 94062, P: 800-297-4277, F: 650-851-1434, www.sterlingsharpener.com
Backpacking; Camping; Cooking Equipment/Accessories; Hunting Accessories; Knives/Knife Cases; Law Enforcement; Sharpeners; Survival Kits/First Aid

Stewart EFI, LLC, 45 Old Waterbury Rd., Thomaston, CT 06787, P: 800-228-2509, F: 860-283-3174, www.stewartefi.com
Ammunition; Backpacking; Custom Manufacturing; Firearms Hearing Protection; Law Enforcement; Lighting Products; Magazines, Cartridge

Steyr Arms, Inc., P.O. Box 840, Trussville, GA 35173, P: 205-467-6544, F: 205-467-3015, www.steyrarms.com
Firearms; Law Enforcement

STI International, 114 Halmar Cove, Georgetown, TX 78628, P: 512-819-0656, F: 512-819-0465, www.stiguns.com
Firearms; Gun Barrels; Gun Parts/Gunsmithing

Stil Crin SNC, Via Per Gottolengo, 12A, Pavone Mella, Brescia 25020, ITALY, P: 011-390309599496, F: 011-390309959544, www.stilcrin.it
Firearms Maintenance Equipment; Gun Cases; Gun Locks; Lubricants

Stoeger Industries, 17603 Indian Head Hwy., Accokeek, MD 20607, P: 800-264-4962, F: 301-283-6988, www.stoegerindustries.com
Airguns; Firearms

Stoney-Wolf Productions, 130 Columbia Court W, Chaska, MN 55318, P: 800-237-7583, F: 952-361-4217, www.stoneywolf.com
Books/Industry Publications; Computer Software; Food; Videos

Stoney Point Products, Inc., 9200 Cody, Overland Park, KS 66214, P: 800-221-9035, F: 800-548-0446, www.stoneypoint.com
Backpacking; Hearing Protection; Hunting Accessories; Shooting Range Equipment; Sports Accessories

Stormy Kromer Mercantile, 1238 Wall St., Ironwood, MI 49938, P: 888-455-2253, F: 906-932-1579, www.stormykromer.com
Camouflage; Gloves, Mitts, Hats; Men's Clothing

Strangler Chokes, Inc., 7958 US Hwy. 167 S, Winnfield, LA 71483, P: 318-201-3474, F: 318-473-0982
Custom Manufacturing; Firearms; Gun Barrels; Gun Parts/Gunsmithing; Hunting Accessories; Scopes, Sights & Accessories

Streamlight, Inc., 30 Eagleville Rd., Eagleville, PA 19403, P: 800-523-7488, F: 800-220-7007, www.streamlight.com
Hunting Accessories; Law Enforcement; Lighting Products; Training & Safety Equipment

Streamworks, Inc., 3233 Lance Dr., Suite B, Stockton, CA 92505, P: 209-337-3307, F: 209-337-3342, www.hattail.com
Hearing Protection

Streetwise Security Products/Cutting Edge Products, Inc., 235-F Forlines Rd., Winterville, NC 28590, P: 800-497-0539, F: 252-830-5542, www.streetwisesecurity.net
Law Enforcement

Strider Knives, Inc., 120 N. Pacific St., Suite L7, San Marcos, CA 92069, P: 760-471-8275, F: 503-218-7069, www.striderknives.com
Backpacking; Custom Manufacturing; Cutlery; Hunting Accessories; Knives/Knife Cases; Law Enforcement; Training & Safety Equipment

Strike-Hold/MPH System Specialties, Inc., P.O. Box 1923, Dawsonville, GA 30534, P: 866-331-0572, F: 325-204-2550, www.strikehold.com
Black Powder Accessories; Export/Import Specialists; Firearms Maintenance Equipment; Hunting Accessories; Law Enforcement; Lubricants; Paintball Accessories; Wholesaler/Distributor

Strong Leather Co., 39 Grove St., P.O. Box 1195, Gloucester, MA 01930, P: 800-225-0724, F: 866-316-3666, www.strongbadgecase.com

MANUFACTURER'S AND PRODUCT DIRECTORY

Bags & Equipment Cases; Holsters; Law Enforcement; Leathergoods

Sturm, 430 S. Erwin St., Cartersville, GA 30120, P: 800-441-7367, F: 770-386-6654, www.sturm-miltec.com
Camouflage; Camping; Firearms; Gun Grips & Stocks; Magazines, Cartridge; Men's Clothing; Scopes, Sights & Accessories

Sun Optics USA, 1312 S. Briar Oaks Rd., Cleburne, TX 76031, P: 817-447-9047, F: 817-717-8461
Binoculars; Custom Manufacturer; Gun Parts/Gunsmithing; Hunting Accessories; Scopes, Sights & Accessories

Sunbuster/Gustbuster, 1966-B Broadhollow Rd., Farmingdale, NY 11735, P: 888-487-8287, F: 631-777-4320, www.sunbuster.info
Clay Targets; Custom Manufacturing; Eyewear; Hunting Accessories; Law Enforcement; Shooting Range Equipment; Sports Accessories; Wholesaler/Distributor

Sunlite Science & Technology, Inc., 345 N. Iowa St., Lawrence, KS 66044, P: 785-832-8818, F: 913-273-1888, www.powerledlighting.com
Camping; Hunting Accessories; Law Enforcement; Lighting Products; Sports Accessories; Survival Kits/First Aid; Tours/Travel; Training & Safety Equipment

Sunny Hill Enterprises, Inc., W. 1015 Cty. HHH, Chilton, WI 53014, P: 920-898-4707, F: 920-898-4749, www.sunny-hill.com
Custom Manufacturing; Firearms; Gun Barrels; Gun Parts/Gunsmithing; Law Enforcement; Magazines, Cartridge

Super Seer Corp., P.O. Box 700, Evergreen, CO 80437, P: 800-645-1285, F: 303-674-8540, www.superseer.com
Law Enforcement

Super Six Classic, LLC, 635 Hilltop Trail W, Fort Atkinson, WI 53538, P: 920-568-8299, F: 920-568-8259
Firearms

Superior Arms. 836 Weaver Blvd., Wapello, IA 52653, P: 319-523-2016, F: 319-527-0188, www.superiorarms.com
Firearms

Superior Concepts, Inc., 10791 Oak St., P.O. Box 465, Donald, OR 97020, P: 503-922-0488, F: 503-922-2236, www.laserstock.com
Gun Grips & Stocks; Gun Parts/Gunsmithing; Hunting Accessories; Magazines, Cartridge; Scopes, Sights & Accessories

Sure Site, Inc., 351 Dion St., P.O. Box 335, Emmett, ID 83617, P: 800-627-1576, F: 208-365-6944, www.suresiteinc.com
Shooting Range Equipment; Targets

SureFire, LLC, 18300 Mount Baldy Circle, Fountain Valley, CA 92708, P: 800-828-8809, F: 714-545-9537, www.surefire.com
Knives/Knife Cases; Lighting Products; Scopes, Sights & Accessories

Surgeon Rifles, 48955 Moccasin Trail Rd., Prague, OK 74864, P: 405-567-0183, F: 405-567-0250, www.surgeonrifles.com
Firearms; Gun Parts/Gunsmithing; Law Enforcement

Survival Armor, Inc., 13881 Plantation Rd., International Center I, Suite 8, Ft. Myers, FL 33912, P: 866-868-5001, F: 239-210-0898, www.survivalarmor.com
Law Enforcement; Training & Safety Equipment

Survival Corps, Ltd., Ostashkovskoe Shosse, house 48a, Borodino, Moscow Obl,

Mitishinski Region, 141031, RUSSIAN FEDERATION, P: 011 74952257985, F: 011 74952257986, www.survivalcorps.ru
Bags & Equipment Cases; Camouflage; Holsters; Law Enforcement; Outfitter

Swany America Corp., 115 Corporate Dr., Johnstown, NY 12095, P: 518-725-3333, F: 518-725-2026, www.swanyhunting.com
Gloves, Mitts, Hats

Swarovski Optik North America, 2 Slater Rd., Cranston, RI 02920, P: 800-426-3089, F: 401-734-5888, www.swarovskioptik.com
Bags & Equipment Cases; Binoculars; Knives/Knife Cases; Scopes, Sights & Accessories; Telescopes; Wholesaler/Distributor

SWAT Magazine, 5011 N. Ocean Blvd., Suite 5, Ocean Ridge, FL 33435, P: 800-665-7928, F: 561-276-0895, www.swatmag.com
Books/Industry Publications; Law Enforcement; Online Services; Retailer Services; Training & Safety Equipment

Swift Bullet Co., 201 Main St., P.O. Box 27, Quinter, KS 67752, P: 785-754-3959, F: 785-754-2359, www.swiftbullets.com
Ammunition

Switch Pack, LLC, 302 NW 4th St., Grants Pass, OR 97526, P: 541-479-3919, F: 541-474-4573
Backpacking; Blinds; Hunting Accessories; Retailer Services; Sports Accessories; Wholesaler/Distributor

SWR Manufacturing, LLC, P.O. Box 841, Pickens, SC 29671, P: 864-850-3579, F: 864-751-2823, www.swrmfg.com
Firearms; Hearing Protection; Law Enforcement; Recoil Protection Devices & Services; Training & Safety Equipment

Sylvansport, 10771 Greenville Hwy., Cedar Mountain, NC 28718, P: 828-883-4292, F: 828-883-4817, www.sylvansport.com
Backpacking; Camping; Hunting Accessories; Sports Accessories; Tours/Travel; Vehicles, Utility & Rec

Systema Co., 5542 S. Integrity Ln., Fort Mohave, AZ 86426, P: 877-884-0909, F: 267-222-4787, www.systema-engineering.com
Airguns; Airsoft; Law Enforcement; Training & Safety Equipment

Szco Supplies, Inc., 2713 Merchant Dr., P.O. Box 6353, Baltimore, MD 21230, P: 800-232-6998, F: 410-368-9366, www.szco.com
Camping; Custom Manufacturing; Cutlery; Hunting Accessories; Knives/Knife Cases; Pet Supplies; Sharpeners; Wholesaler/Distributor

T

T.Z. Case, 1786 Curtiss Ct., La Verne, CA 91750, P: 888-892-2737, F: 909-392-8406, www.tzcase.com
Airguns; Archery; Custom Manufacturing; Firearms; Gun Cases; Hunting Accessories

Tac Force, 8653 Garvey Ave., Suite 202, Rosemead, CA 91733, P: 626-453-8377, F: 626-453-8378, www.tac-force.com
Backpacking; Bags & Equipment Cases; Gloves, Mitts, Hats; Gun Cases; Holsters; Law Enforcement; Paintball Accessories

Tac Wear, Inc., 700 Progress Ave., Suite 7, Toronto, Ontario M1H 2Z7, CANADA, P: 866-TAC-WEAR, F: 416-289-1522, www.tacwear.com
Gloves, Mitts, Hats; Hunting Accessories; Law Enforcement; Men & Women's Clothing;

Sports Accessories; Training & Safety Equipment

Tactical & Survival Specialties, Inc. (TSSI), 3900 Early Rd., P.O. Box 1890, Harrisonburg, VA 22801, P: 877-535-8774, F: 540-434-7796, www.tacsurv.com
Bags & Equipment Cases; Custom Manufacturing; Knives/Knife Cases; Law Enforcement; Men & Women's Clothing; Survival Kits/First Aid; Training & Safety Equipment; Wholesaler/Distributor

Tactical Assault Gear (TAG), 1330 30th St., Suite A, San Diego, CA 92154, P: 888-899-1199, F: 619-628-0126, www.tacticalassaultgear.com
Bags & Equipment Cases; Holsters; Men's Clothing

Tactical Command Industries, Inc., 2101 W. Tenth St., Suite G, Antioch, CA 94509, P: 888-990-1600, F: 925-756-7977, www.tacticalcommand.com
Custom Manufacturing; Hearing Protection; Law Enforcement; Training & Safety Equipment; Two-Way Radios

Tactical Electronics/SPA Defense, P.O. Box 152, Broken Arrow, OK 74013, P: 866-541-7996, F: 918-249-8328, www.tacticalelectronics.com
Photographic Equipment

Tactical Innovations, Inc., 345 Sunrise Rd., Bonners Ferry, ID 83805, P: 208-267-1585, F: 208-267-1597, www.tacticalinc.com
Firearms; Gun Barrels; Gun Grips & Stocks; Holsters; Law Enforcement; Magazines, Cartridge; Wholesaler/Distributor

Tactical Medical Solutions, Inc., 614 Pinehollow Dr., Anderson, SC 29621, P: 888-TACMED1, F: 864-224-0064
Law Enforcement; Survival Kits/First Aid; Training & Safety Equipment

Tactical Operations Products, 20972 SW Meadow Way, Tualatin, OR 97062, P: 503-638-9873, F: 503-638-0524, www.tacoproducts.com
Airsoft; Backpacking; Bags & Equipment Cases; Camping; Law Enforcement; Lighting Products; Paintball Accessories

Tactical Products Group, Inc., 755 NW 17th Ave., Suite 108, Delray Beach, FL 33445, P: 866-9-TACPRO, F: 561-265-4061, www.tacprogroup.com
Export/Import Specialists; Footwear; Gun Cases; Holsters; Knives/Knife Cases; Law Enforcement; Men's Clothing; Wholesaler/Distributor

Tactical Rifles, 19250 Hwy. 301, Dade City, FL 33523, P: 352-999-0599, F: 352-567-9825, www.tacticalrifles.net
Firearms

Tactical Solutions, 2181 Commerce Ave., Boise, ID 83705, P: 866-333-9901, F: 208-333-9909, www.tacticalsol.com
Firearms; Gun Barrels; Gun Grips & Stocks; Gun Parts/Gunsmithing; Scopes, Sights & Accessories; Wholesaler/Distributor

TacticalTECH1, 251 Beulah Church Rd., Carrollton, GA 30117, P: 800-334-3368, F: 770-832-1676
Bags & Equipment Cases; Eyewear; Law Enforcement; Lighting Products; Training & Safety Equipment

TAG Safari Clothes, 1022 Wirt Rd., Suite 302, Houston, TX 77055, P: 800-TAG-2703, F: 713-688-6806, www.tagsafari.com

MANUFACTURER'S AND PRODUCT DIRECTORY

Camping; Footwear; Gun Cases; Leathergoods; Men & Women's Clothing; Online Services; Wholesaler/Distributor

Tagua Gun Leather, 3750 NW 28th St., Miami, FL 33142, P: 866-678-2482, F: 866-678-2482, www.taguagunleather.com
Firearms; Holsters; Hunting Accessories; Law Enforcement; Leathergoods; Wholesaler/ Distributor

Talley Manufacturing, Inc., 9183 Old Number Six Hwy., P.O. Box 369, Santee, SC 29142, P: 803-854-5700, F: 803-854-9315, www.talleyrings.com
Black Powder Accessories; Custom Manufacturing; Gun Parts/Gunsmithing; Hunting Accessories; Scopes, Sights & Accessories; Sports Accessories

Tandy Brands Outdoors, 107 W. Gonzales St., Yoakum, TX 77995, P: 800-331-9092, F: 361-293-9127, www.tandybrands.com
Bags & Equipment Cases; Custom Manufacturing; Hunting Accessories; Knives/ Knife Cases; Leathergoods; Shooting Range Equipment; Sports Accessories

TangoDown, Inc., 1588 Arrow Hwy., Unit F, La Verne, CA 91750-5334, P: 909-392-4757, F: 909-392-4802, www.tangodown.com
Gun Grips & Stocks; Law Enforcement; Lighting Products; Magazines, Cartridge; Scopes, Sights & Accessories; Targets

TAPCO, Inc., 3615 Kennesaw N. Industrial Pkwy., P.O. Box 2408, Kennesaw, GA 30156-9138, P: 800-554-1445, F: 800-226-1662, www.tapco.com
Custom Manufacturing; Firearms Maintenance Equipment; Gun Grips & Stocks; Gun Parts/ Gunsmithing; Law Enforcement; Magazines, Cartridge; Recoil Protection Devices & Services; Wholesaler/Distributor

Target Shooting, Inc., 1110 First Ave. SE, Watertown, SD 57201, P: 800-611-2164, F: 605-882-8840, www.targetshooting.com
Scopes, Sights & Accessories; Shooting Range Equipment

Tasco/Bushnell Outdoor Products, 9400 Cody, Overland Park, KS 66214, P: 800-221-9035, F: 800-548-0446, www.tasco.com
Binoculars; Scopes, Sights & Accessories; Telescopes

Taser International, 1700 N. 85th St., Scottsdale, AZ 85255, P: 800-978-2737, F: 480-991-0791, www.taser.com
Law Enforcement

Task Holsters, 2520 SW 22nd St., Suite 2-186, Miami, FL 33145, P: 305-335-8647, F: 305-858-9618, www.taskholsters.com
Bags & Equipment Cases; Export/Import Specialists; Gun Cases; Holsters; Hunting Accessories; Law Enforcement; Leathergoods; Wholesaler/Distributor

Taurus International Manufacturing, Inc., 16175 NW 49th Ave., Miami, FL 33014, P: 800-327-3776, F: 305-623-7506, www.taurususa.com
Firearms

Taylor Brands, LLC/Imperial Schrade & Smith & Wesson Cutting Tools, 1043 Fordtown Rd., Kingsport, TN 37663, P: 800-251-0254, F: 423-247-5371, www.taylorbrandsllc.com
Backpacking; Camping; Cutlery; Hunting Accessories; Knives/Knife Cases; Law Enforcement

Taylor's & Co., Inc., 304 Lenoir Dr., Winchester, VA 22603, P: 800-655-5814, F: 540-722-2018, www.taylorsfirearms.com

Black Powder Accessories; Firearms; Firearms Maintenance Equipment; Gun Parts/ Gunsmithing; Wholesaler/Distributor

Team Realtree®, P.O. Box 9638, Columbus, GA 31908, P: 800-992-9968, F: 706-569-9346, www.realtree.com
Camouflage; Men & Women's Clothing

Team SD/TSD Sports, 901 S. Fremont Ave., Suite 218, Alhambra, CA 91803, P: 626-281-0979, F: 626-281-0323, www.airsoftsd.com
Airguns; Airsoft; Paintball Guns & Accessories; Scopes, Sights & Accessories; Sports Accessories; Training & Safety Equipment; Wholesaler/Distributor

Team Wendy, 17000 St. Clair Ave., Bldg. 1, Cleveland, OH 44110, P: 877-700-5544, F: 216-738-2510, www.teamwendy.com
Custom Manufacturing; Hunting Accessories; Law Enforcement; Sports Accessories; Training & Safety Equipment

TEARepair, Inc., 2200 Knight Rd., Bldg. 2, P.O. Box 1879, Land O'Lakes, FL 34639, P: 800-937-3716, F: 813-996-4523, www.tear-aid.com
Camping; Hunting Accessories; Retail Packaging; Sports Accessories; Survival Kits/ First Aid; Wholesaler/Distributor

Tech Mix, Inc., 740 Bowman St., Stewart, MN 55385, P: 877-466-6455, F: 320-562-2125, www.techmixinc.com
Pet Supplies

Technoframes, Via Aldo Moro 6, Scanzorosciate Bergamo, 24020, ITALY, P: 866-246-1095, F: 011 39035668328, www.technoframes.com
Ammunition; Bags & Equipment Cases; Gun Cases; Hunting Accessories; Magazines, Cartridge; Reloading; Shooting Range Equipment

Tecomate Seed, 33477 Hwy. 99E, Tangent, OR 97389, P: 800-547-4101, F: 541-926-9435, www.tecomateseed.com
Wildlife Management

Teijin Aramid USA, Inc., 801-F Blacklawn Rd., Conyers, GA 30012, P: 800-451-6586, F: 770-929-8138, www.teijinaramid.com
Law Enforcement

Television Equipment Associates, Inc., 16 Mount Ebo Rd. S, P.O. Box 404, Brewster, NY 10509, P: 310-457-7401, F: 310-457-0023, www.swatheadsets.com
Law Enforcement

Temco Communications, Inc., 13 Chipping Campden Dr., South Barrington, IL 60010, P: 847-359-3277, F: 847-359-3743, www.temcom.net
Hearing Protection; Law Enforcement; Two-Way Radios

Ten-X Ammunition, Inc., 5650 Arrow Hwy., Montclair, CA 91763, P: 909-605-1617, F: 909-605-2844, www.tenxammo.com
Ammunition; Custom Manufacturing; Law Enforcement; Reloading; Training & Safety Equipment; Wholesaler/Distributor

TenPoint Crossbow Technologies, 1325 Waterloo Rd., Suffield, OH 44260, P: 800-548-6837, F: 330-628-0999, www.tenpointcrossbows.com
Archery; Crossbows & Accessories

Teton Grill Co., 865 Xenium Lane N, Plymouth, MN 55441, P: 877-838-6643, F: 763-249-6385, www.tetongrills.com
Cooking Equipment/Accessories; Custom Manufacturing; Cutlery; Knives/Knife Cases

Tetra® Gun Care, 8 Vreeland Rd., Florham Park, NJ 07932, P: 973-443-0004, F: 973-443-0263, www.tetraguncare.com
Firearms Maintenance Equipment; Gun Parts/ Gunsmithing; Lubricants

Texas Hunt Co., P.O. Box 10, Monahans, TX 79756, P: 888-894-8682, F: 432-943-5565, www.texashuntco.com
Bags & Equipment Cases; Hunting Accessories; Knives/Knife Cases; Vehicles, Utility & Rec; Wholesaler/Distributor

Texsport, P.O. Box 55326, Houston, TX 77255, P: 800-231-1402, F: 713-468-1535, www.texsport.com
Backpacking; Bags & Equipment Cases; Camouflage; Camping; Compasses; Cooking Equipment/Accessories; Lighting Products; Wholesaler/Distributor

Thermacell/The Schawbel Corp., 100 Crosby Dr., Suite 102, Bedford, MA 01730, P: 866-753-3837, F: 781-541-6007, www.thermacell.com
Archery; Backpacking; Camouflage; Camping; Crossbows & Accessories; Holsters; Hunting Accessories; Scents & Lures

Thermore, 6124 Shady Lane SE, Olympia, WA 98503, P: 800-871-6563, www.thermore.com
Gloves, Mitts, Hats; Men & Women's Clothing; Pet Supplies

Thompson/Center Arms, A Smith & Wesson Co., P.O. Box 5002, Rochester, NH 01104, P: 603-332-2333, F: 603-332-5133, www.tcarms.com
Black Powder Accessories; Black Powder/ Smokeless Powder; Firearms; Gun Barrels; Hunting Accessories

Thorogood Shoes, 108 S. Polk St., Merrill, WI 54452, P: 800-826-0002, F: 800-569-6817, www.weinbrennerusa.com
Footwear; Law Enforcement; Leathergoods; Men & Women's Clothing

Thunderbolt Customs, Inc., 7296 S. Section Line Rd., Delaware, OH 43015, P: 740-917-9135, www.thunderboltcustoms.com
Backpacking; Black Powder Accessories; Camping; Firearms; Hunting Accessories; Pet Supplies; Scopes, Sights & Accessories; Shooting Range Accessories

Tiberius Arms, 2717 W. Ferguson Rd., Fort Wayne, IN 46809, P: 888-982-2842, F: 260-572-2210, www.tiberiusarms.com
Airguns; Law Enforcement; Paintball Guns & Accessories; Training & Safety Equipment

Tiger-Vac, Inc., 73 SW 12 Ave., Bldg. 1, Suite 7, Dania, FL 33004, P: 800-668-4437, F: 954-925-3626, www.tiger-vac.com
Shooting Range Equipment; Training & Safety Equipment

Timney Manufacturing, Inc., 3940 W. Clarendon Ave., Phoenix, AZ 85019, P: 866-4TIMNEY, F: 602-241-0361, www.timneytriggers.com
Firearms Maintenance Equipment; Gun Locks; Gun Parts/Gunsmithing

Tinks, 10157 Industrial Dr., Covington, GA 30014, P: 800-624-5988, F: 678-342-9973, www.tinks69.com
Archery; Hunting Accessories; Scents & Lures; Videos

Tisas-Trabzon Gun Industry Corp., Degol Cad. No: 13-1 Tandogan Ankara, 06580, TURKEY, P: 011 903122137509, F: 011 903122138570, www.trabzonsilah.com
Firearms; Gun Barrels

MANUFACTURER'S AND PRODUCT DIRECTORY

TMB Designs, Unit 11, Highgrove Farm Ind Est Pinvin, Pershore, Worchestershire WR10 2LF, UNITED KINGDOM, P: 011 441905840022, F: 011 441905850022, www.cartridgedisplays.com
Ammunition; Custom Manufacturing; Emblems & Decals; Hunting Accessories; Outdoor Art, Jewelry, Sculpture; Sports Accessories

Toadbak, Inc., P.O. Box 18097, Knoxville, TN 37928-8097, P: 865-548-1283
Camouflage; Men's Clothing

Tony's Custom Uppers & Parts, P.O. Box 252, Delta, OH 43515, P: 419-822-9578, F: 419-822-9578
Custom Manufacturing; Gun Barrels; Gun Parts/Gunsmithing; Wholesaler/Distributor

Tool Logic, Inc., 2290 Eastman Ave., Suite 109, Ventura, CA 93003, P: 800-483-8422, F: 805-339-9712, www.toollogic.com
Backpacking; Compasses; Cutlery; Knives/ Knife Cases; Lighting Products; Sports Accessories; Survival Kits/First Aid

Top Brass Tackle/dba Cypress Knees Publishing, P.O. Box 209, Starkville, MS 39760, P: 662-323-1559, F: 662-323-7466, www.outdooryouthadventures.com
Books/Industry Publications

TOPS Knives, P.O. Box 2544, Idaho Falls, ID 82403, P: 208-542-0113, F: 208-552-2945, www.topsknives.com
Backpacking; Custom Manufacturing; Hunting Accessories; Knives/Knife Cases; Law Enforcement; Leathergoods; Men's Clothing; Survival Kits/First Aid

Torel, 107 W. Gonzales St., Yoakum, TX 77995, P: 800-331-9092, F: 361-293-9127, www.tandybrands.com
Bags & Equipment Cases; Custom Manufacturing; Hunting Accessories; Knives/ Knife Cases; Leathergoods; Shooting Range Equipment; Sports Accessories

Torrey Pines Logic, Inc., 12651 High Bluff Dr., Suite 100, San Diego, CA 92130, P: 858-755-4549, F: 858-350-0007, www.tplogic.com
Binoculars; Law Enforcement; Scopes, Sights & Accessories; Telescopes

Traditions Performance Firearms, 1375 Boston Post Rd., P.O. Box 776, Old Saybrook, CT 06475-0776, P: 800-526-9556, F: 860-388-4657, www.traditionsfirearms.com
Black Powder Accessories; Firearms; Hunting Accessories; Scopes, Sights & Accessories

Transarms Handels GmbH & Co. KG, 6 Im Winkel, Worms, Rheinland Pfalz 67547, GERMANY, P: 011 490624197770, F: 011 4906241977777
Ammunition; Export/Import Specialists; Firearms; Firearms Maintenance Equipment; Gun Barrels; Gun Parts/Gunsmithing; Law Enforcement; Magazines, Cartridge

Traser H3 Watches, 2930 Domingo Ave., Suite 159, Berkeley, CA 94705, P: 510-479-7523, F: 510-479-7532, www.traserusa.com
Custom Manufacturing; Export/Import Specialists; Law Enforcement; Lighting Products; Men's Clothing; Training & Safety Equipment; Wholesaler/Distributor

Tree Talon, 148 Main St., P.O. Box 1370, Bucksport, ME 04416, P: 207-469-1900, F: 207-469-6121, www.treetalon.com
Hunting Accessories

Tri-Tronics, Inc., 1705 S. Research Loop, Tucson, AZ 85710, P: 800-765-2275, F: 800-320-3538, www.tritronics.com
Hunting Accessories; Pet Supplies; Sports Accessories

Trijicon, Inc., 49385 Shafer Ave., P.O. Box 930059, Wixom, MI 48393, P: 800-338-0563, F: 248-960-7725, www.trijicon.com
Scopes, Sights & Accessories

Triple K Manufacturing Co., Inc., 2222 Commercial St., San Diego, CA 92113, P: 800-521-5062, F: 877-486-6247, www.triplek.com
Black Powder Accessories; Gun Parts/ Gunsmithing; Holsters; Hunting Accessories; Law Enforcement; Leathergoods; Magazines, Cartridge; Pet Supplies

Tristar Sporting Arms, Ltd., 1816 Linn St., North Kansas City, MO 64116, P: 816-421-1400, F: 816-421-4182, www.tristarsporting.com
Export/Import Specialists; Firearms

Trophy Animal Health Care, 1217 W. 12th St., Kansas City, MO 64101, P: 800-821-7925, F: 816-474-0462, www.trophyanimalcare.com
Pet Supplies

Troy Industries, Inc., 128 Myron St., West Springfield, MA 01089, P: 866-788-6412, F: 413-383-0339, www.troyind.com
Firearms; Gun Grips & Stocks; Gun Parts/ Gunsmithing; Law Enforcement; Scopes, Sights & Accessories

Tru Hone Corp., 1721 NE 19th Ave., Ocala, FL 34470, P: 800-237-4663, F: 352-622-9180, www.truhone.com
Sharpeners

TruckVault, Inc., 211 Township St., P.O. Box 734, Sedro Woolley, WA 98284, P: 800-967-8107, F: 800-621-4287, www.truckvault.com
Custom Manufacturing; Gun Cabinets/Racks/ Safes; Hunting Accessories; Law Enforcement; Pet Supplies; Sports Accessories; Training & Safety Equipment

True North Tactical, 500 N. Birdneck Rd., Suite 200, Virginia Beach, VA 23451, P: 800-TNT-1478, F: 757-491-9652, www.truenorthtactical.com
Backpacking; Bags & Equipment Cases; Gun Cases; Holsters; Law Enforcement; Wholesaler/Distributor

TrueTimber Outdoors, 150 Accurate Way, Inman, SC 29349, P: 864-472-1720, F: 864-472-1834, www.truetimber.com
Bags & Equipment Cases; Blinds; Camouflage; Footwear; Gloves, Mitts, Hats; Hunting Accessories; Men & Women's Clothing

Truglo, Inc., 710 Presidential Dr., Richardson, TX 75081, P: 888-8-TRUGLO, F: 972-774-0323, www.truglo.com
Archery; Binoculars; Black Powder Accessories; Crossbows & Accessories; Hunting Accessories; Law Enforcement; Scopes, Sights & Accessories; Watches

Trulock Tool, 113 Drayton St. NW, P.O. Box 530, Whigham, GA 39897, P: 800-293-9402, F: 229-762-4050, www.trulockchokes.com
Ammunition; Custom Manufacturing; Firearms Maintenance Equipment; Gun Parts/Gunsmithing; Hunting Accessories; Recoil Protection Devices & Services; Sports Accessories; Wholesaler/Distributor

Trumark Mfg. Co., Inc., 1835 38th St., Boulder, CO 80301, P: 800-878-6272, F: 303-442-1380, www.slingshots.com
Archery; Backpacking; Crossbows & Accessories; Hunting Accessories; Sports Accessories

Tuff-N-Lite, 325 Spencer Rd., Conover, NC 28613, P: 877-883-3654, F: 828-322-7881, www.tuffnlite.com
Gloves, Mitts, Hats; Men & Women's Clothing

TuffForce, 1734 Ranier Blvd., Canton, MI 48187, P: 800-382-7989, F: 888-686-0373, www.tufforce.com
Bags & Equipment Cases; Gun Cases; Gun Grips & Stocks; Holsters; Hunting Accessories; Law Enforcement; Scopes, Sights & Accessories; Wholesaler/Distributor

Tunilik Adventure, 11600 Philippe Panneton, Montreal, Quebec H1E 4G4, CANADA, P: 866-648-1595, F: 514-648-1431, www.adventuretunilik.com
Outfitter

TurtleSkin Protective Products, 301 Turnpike Rd., New Ipswich, NH 03071, P: 888-477-4675, F: 603-291-1119, www.turtleskin.com
Gloves, Mitts, Hats; Hunting Accessories; Law Enforcement; Men & Women's Clothing; Sports Accessories

U

U.S. Armament Corp., 121 Valley View Dr., Ephrata, PA 17522, P: 717-721-4570, F: 717-738-4890, www.usarmamentcorp.com
Firearms

U.S. Armor Corp., 16433 Valley View Ave., Cerritos, CA 90703, P: 800-443-9798, F: 562-207-4238, www.usarmor.com
Law Enforcement; Training & Safety Equipment

U.S. Explosive Storage, LLC, 355 Industrial Park Dr., Boone, NC 28607, P: 877-233-1481, F: 800-295-1653, www.usexplosive.com
Custom Manufacturing; Firearms Maintenance Equipment; Gun Cabinets/Racks/Safes; Law Enforcement; Magazines, Cartridge; Training & Safety Equipment

U.S. Fire-Arms Mfg. Co., Inc., P.O. Box 1901, Hartford, CT 06144-1901, P: 860-296-7441, F: 860-296-7688, www.usfirearms.com
Firearms; Gun Parts/Gunsmithing

U.S. Optics, Inc., 150 Arovista Circle, Brea, CA 92821, P: 714-582-1956, F: 714-582-1959, www.usoptics.com
Custom Manufacturing; Law Enforcement; Scopes, Sights & Accessories

U.S. Tactical Supply, Inc., 939 Pacific Blvd. SE, Albany, OR 97321, P: 877-928-8645, F: 541-791-2965, www.ustacticalsupply.com
Bags & Equipment Cases; Gun Parts/ Gunsmithing; Holsters; Hunting Accessories; Knives/Knife Cases; Law Enforcement; Scopes, Sights & Accessories; Wholesaler/ Distributor

Uberti, A., 17603 Indian Head Hwy., Accokeek, MD 20607-2501, P: 800-264-4962, F: 301-283-6988, www.uberti.com
Firearms

Ultimate Hunter, Inc., 610 Prather, P.O. Box 542, Maryville, MO 64468, P: 660-562-3838, F: 660-582-4377, www.ambushlures.com
Decoys

Ultimate Survival Technologies, LLC, 14428 167th Ave. SE, Monroe, WA 98272, P: 866-479-7994, F: 206-965-9659, www.ultimatesurvival.com
Backpacking; Bags & Equipment Cases; Camping; Hunting Accessories; Law Enforcement; Men's Clothing; Sports Accessories; Survival Kits/First Aid

Ultra Dot Distribution, 6304 Riverside Dr., P.O. Box 362, Yankeetown, FL, 34498, P: 352-447-2255, F: 352-447-2266, www.ultradotusa.com
Scopes, Sights & Accessories

MANUFACTURER'S AND PRODUCT DIRECTORY

Ultra Lift Corp., 475 Stockton Ave., Unit E, San Jose, CA 95126, P: 800-346-3057, F: 408-297-1199, www.ultralift.com/safes.html
Custom Manufacturing; Gun Cabinets/Racks/Safes; Gun Cases; Retailer Services; Sports Accessories; Training & Safety Equipment

Ultra Paws, 12324 Little Pine Rd. SW, Brainerd, MN 56401, P: 800-355-5575, F: 218-855-6977, www.ultrapaws.com
Backpacking; Hunting Accessories; Law Enforcement; Outfitter; Pet Supplies; Survival Kits/First Aid; Training & Safety Equipment; Wholesaler/Distributor

Ultramax Ammunition/Wideview Scope Mount, 2112 Elk Vale Rd., Rapid City, SD 57701, P: 800-345-5852, F: 605-342-8727, www.ultramaxammunition.com
Ammunition

Ultrec Engineered Products, LLC, 860 Maple Ridge Ln., Brookfield, WI 53045, P: 262-821-2023, F: 262-821-1156, www.ultrec.com
Backpacking; Binoculars; Firearms; Hunting Accessories; Law Enforcement; Photographic Equipment; Shooting Range Equipment; Training & Safety Equipment

Umarex/Umarex, USA/RAM–Real Action Marker, 6007 S. 29th St., Fort Smith, AR 72908, P: 479-646-4210, F: 479-646-4206, www.umarexusa.com, www.trainingumarexusa.com
Airguns; Airsoft; Ammunition; Firearms; Law Enforcement; Paintball Guns; Scopes, Sights & Accessories; Training & Safety Equipment

Uncle Mike's/Bushnell Outdoor Accessories, 9200 Cody St., Overland Park, KS 66214, P: 800-423-3537, F: 800-548-0446, www.unclemikes.com
Bags & Equipment Cases; Gloves, Mitts, Hats; Gun Cases; Holsters; Hunting Accessories

Under Armour Performance, 1020 Hull St., Third Floor, Baltimore, MD 21230, P: 888-427-6687, F: 410-234-1027, www.underarmour.com
Bags & Equipment Cases; Camouflage; Gloves, Mitts, Hats; Law Enforcement; Men & Women's Clothing; Outfitter; Sports Accessories

United Cutlery Corp., 201 Plantation Oak Dr., Thomasville, GA 31792, P: 800-548-0835, F: 229-551-0182, www.unitedcutlery.com
Camping; Compasses; Custom Manufacturing; Cutlery; Knives/Knife Cases; Law Enforcement; Sharpeners; Wholesaler/Distributor

United Shield International, 1606 Barlow St., Suite 1, Traverse City, MI 49686, P: 800-705-9153, F: 231-933-5368, www.unitedshield.net
Law Enforcement

United Weavers of America, Inc., 3562 Dug Gap Rd. SW, Dalton, GA 30721, P: 800-241-5754, F: 706-226-8844, www.unitedweavers.net
Home Furnishings

Universal Power Group, 1720 Hayden, Carrollton, TX 75006, P: 866-892-1122, F: 469-892-1123, www.upgi.com, www.deerfeeder.com
Blinds; Camping; Decoys; Export/Import Specialists; Feeder Equipment; Hunting Accessories; Lighting Products; Wholesaler/Distributor

Urban–E.R.T. Slings, LLC, P.O. Box 429, Clayton, IN 46118, P: 317-223-6509, F: 317-539-2710, www.urbanertslings.com
Firearms; Hunting Accessories; Law Enforcement; Paintball Accessories

US Night Vision Corp., 3845 Atherton Rd., Suite 9, Rocklin, CA 95765, P: 800-500-4020, F: 916-663-5986, www.usnightvision.com
Binoculars; Hunting Accessories; Law Enforcement; Paintball Accessories; Scopes, Sights & Accessories; Sports Accessories; Training & Safety Equipment; Wholesaler/Distributor

US Peacekeeper Products, Inc., W245, N5570 Corporate Circle, Sussex, WI 53089, P: 800-428-0800, F: 262-246-4845, uspeacekeeper.com
Bags & Equipment Cases; Gloves, Mitts, Hats; Hunting Accessories; Men & Women's Clothing

Uselton Arms, 390 Southwinds Dr., Franklin, TN 37064, P: 615-595-2255, F: 615-595-2254, www.useltonarms.com
Custom Manufacturing; Firearms; Gun Barrels; Gun Grips & Stocks; Gun Parts/Gunsmithing; Law Enforcement

V

V.H. Blackinton & Co., Inc., 221 John Dietsch Blvd., P.O. Box 1300, Attleboro Falls, MA 02763, P: 800-699-4436, F: 508-695-5349, www.blackinton.com
Custom Manfucturing; Emblems & Decals; Law Enforcement

V-Line Industries, 370 Easy St., Simi Valley, CA 93065, P: 805-520-4987, F: 805-520-6470, www.vlineind.com
Gun Cabinets; Racks/Safes; Gun Cases

Valdada Optics, P.O. Box 270095, Littleton, CO 80127, P: 303-979-4578, F: 303-979-0256, www.valdada.com
Binoculars; Compasses; Custom Manufacturing; Law Enforcement; Photographic Equipment; Scopes, Sights & Accessories; Telescopes; Wholesaler/Distributor

Valiant Armoury, 3000 Grapevine Mills Pkwy., Suite 101, Grapevine, TX 76051, P: 877-796-7374, F: 972-539-9351, www.valliantarmouryswords.com
Wholesaler/Distributor

Valley Operational Wear, LLC/OP Wear Armor, P.O. Box 9415, Knoxville, TN 37940, P: 865-259-6248, F: 865-259-6255
Law Enforcement

Valley Outdoors, P.O. Box 108, Fort Valley, GA 31030, P: 478-397-0531, F: 478-825-3398, www.valleyoutdoors.us
Outfitter

Valor Corp., 1001 Sawgrass Corporate Pkwy., Sunrise, FL 33323, P: 800-899-VALOR, F: 866-248-9594, www.valorcorp.com
Airguns; Ammunition; Cutlery; Firearms; Knives/Knife Cases; Law Enforcement; Magazines, Cartridge; Wholesaler/Distributor

Vang Comp Systems, 400 W. Butterfield Rd., Chino Valley, AZ 86323, P: 928-636-8455, F: 928-636-1538, www.vangcomp.com
Firearms; Gun Barrels; Gun Parts/Gunsmithing

Vanguard USA, Inc., 9157 E. M-36, Whitmore Lake, MI 48189, P: 800-875-3322, F: 888-426-7008, www.vanguardworld.com
Archery; Bags & Equipment Cases; Binoculars; Gun Cases; Hunting Accessories; Photographic Equipment; Scopes, Sights & Accessories; Shooting Range Equipment

Vector Optics, 3964 Callan Blvd., South San Francisco, CA 94080, P: 415-632-7089,

CHINA, P: 011 862154040649, www.vectoroptics.com
Scopes, Sights & Accessories; Sports Accessories; Wholesaler/Distributor

Vega Holster srl, Via Di Mezzo 31 Z.I., Calcinaia (PI), 56031, ITALY, P: 011 390587489190, F: 011 390587489901, www.vegaholster.com
Bags & Equipment Cases; Gun Cases; Holsters; Hunting Accessories; Law Enforcement; Leathergoods; Shooting Range Equipment

Vega Silah Sanayi, Ltd., Tigcilar Sokak No. 1 Mercan, Eminonu, Istanbul, 34450, TURKEY, P: 011 902125200103, F: 011 902125120879
Firearms

Verney-Carron SA, 54 Blvd. Thiers, Boite Postale 72, St. Etienne Cedex 1, 42002, FRANCE, P: 011 33477791500, F: 011 33477790702, www.verney-carron.com
Custom Manufacturing; Firearms; Gun Barrels; Law Enforcement; Wholesaler/Distibutor

Versatile Rack Co., 5232 Alcoa Ave., Vernon, CA 90058, P: 323-588-0137, F: 323-588-5067, www.versatilegunrack.com
Firearms Maintenance Equipment; Gun Cabinets/Racks/Safes; Gun Cases; Gun Locks; Hunting Accessories; Reloading; Shooting Range Equipment; Sports Accessories

VibraShine, Inc./Leaf River Outdoor Products, 113 Fellowship Rd., P.O. Box 557, Taylorsville, MS 39168, P: 601-785-9854, F: 601-785-9874, www.myleafriver.com
Firearms Maintenance Equipment; Hunting Accessories; Photographic Equipment; Reloading

Victorinox Swiss Army, 7 Victoria Dr., Monroe, CT 06468, P: 800-243-4032, F: 800-243-4006, www.swissarmy.com
Camping; Cutlery; Hunting Accessories; Knives/Knife Cases; Lighting Products; Sports Accessories

Vintage Editions, Inc., 88 Buff Ln., Taylorsville, NC 28681, P: 800-662-8965, F: 828-632-4187, www.vintageeditions.com
Custom Manufacturing; Home Furnishings; Hunting Accessories; Pet Supplies; Sports Accessories

Virginia Blade, 5177 Boonsboro Rd., Lynchburg, VA 24503, P: 434-384-1282, F: 434-384-4541

Viridian Green Laser Sights/Laser Aiming Systems Corp., 12637 Sable Dr., Burnsville, MN 55337, P: 800-990-9390, F: 952-882-6227, www.viridiangreenlaser.com
Holsters; Law Enforcement; Lighting Products; Scopes, Sights & Accessories

Vixen Optics, 1010 Calle Cordillera, Suite 106, San Clemente, CA 92673, P: 949-429-6363, F: 949-429-6826, www.vixenoptics.com
Binoculars; Scopes, Sights & Accessories; Telescopes; Wholesaler/Distributor

Vltor Weapon Systems, 3735 N. Romero Rd., Tucson, AZ 85705, P: 866-468-5867, F: 520-293-8807, www.vltor.com
Firearms; Gun Grips & Stocks; Gun Parts/Gunsmithing; Law Enforcement; Recoil Protection Devices & Services

Volquartsen Custom, 24276 240th St., P.O. Box 397, Carroll, IA 51401, P: 712-792-4238, F: 712-792-2542, www.volquartsen.com
Custom Manufacturing; Firearms; Gun Barrels; Gun Grips/Stocks; Gun Parts/Gunsmithing

MANUFACTURER'S
AND PRODUCT DIRECTORY

Vortex Optics, 2120 W. Greenview Dr., Middleton, WI 53562, P: 800-426-0048, F: 608-662-7454
Binoculars; Scopes, Sights & Accessories

Vyse-Gelatin Innovations, 5024 N. Rose St., Schiller Park, IL 60176, P: 800-533-2152, F: 800-533-2152, www.vyse.com
Airguns; Ammunition; Firearms; Law Enforcement; Magazines, Cartridge; Paintball Guns & Accessories; Shooting Range Equipment

Vytek, 195 Industrial Rd., Fitchburg, MA 01420, P: 978-342-9800, F: 978-342-0606, www.vy-tek.com
Custom Manufacturing; Emblems & Decals; Retailer Services; Sports Accessories

W

W.R. Case & Sons Cutlery Co., Owens Way, Bradford, PA 16701, P: 800-523-6350, F: 814-368-1736, www.wrcase.com
Cutlery; Knives/Knife Cases; Sharpeners

Walls Industries, Inc., 1905 N. Main, Cleburne, TX 76033, P: 800-433-1765, F: 817-645-8544, www.wallsoutdoors.com
Camouflage; Gloves, Mitts, Hats; Men's Clothing

Walther USA, 2100 Roosevelt Ave., Springfield, MA 01104, P: 800-372-6454, F: 413-747-3317, www.waltheramerica.com
Bags & Equipment Cases; Firearms; Knives/Knife Cases; Law Enforcement; Lighting Products

Warson Group, Inc., 121 Hunter Ave., Suite 204, St. Louis, MO 63124, P: 877-753-2426, F: 314-721-0569, www.warson-group.com
Footwear

Watershed Drybags, 2000 Riverside Dr., Asheville, NC 28804, P: 828-252-7111, F: 828-252-7107, www.drybags.com
Backpacking; Bags & Equipment Cases; Camping; Gun Cases; Hunting Accessories; Law Enforcement; Survival Kits/First Aid; Training & Safety Equipment

WD-40 Co., 1061 Cudahy Pl., San Diego, CA 92110, P: 800-448-9340, F: 619-275-5823, www.wd40.com
Lubricants

Weatherby, Inc., 1605 Commerce Way, Paso Robles, CA 93446, P: 800-227-2016, F: 805-237-0427, www.weatherby.com
Ammunition; Custom Manufacturing; Firearms

Weaver Optics/ATK Commercial Products, N5549 Cty. Tk. Z, Onalaska, WI 54650, P: 800-635-7656, F: 763-323-3890, www.weaveroptics.com
Binoculars; Scopes, Sights & Accessories

Weber's Camo Leather Goods/Wilderness Dreams Lingerie & Swimwear, 615 Nokomis St., Suite 400, Alexandria, MN 56308, P: 320-762-2816, F: 320-763-9762, www.webersleather.com
Bags & Equipment Cases; Camouflage; Footwear; Home Furnishings; Hunting Accessories; Leathergoods; Men & Women's Clothing

Wellco Enterprises, 150 Westwood Circle, P.O. Box 188, Waynesville, NC 28786, P: 800-840-3155, F: 828-456-3547, www.wellco.com
Footwear; Law Enforcement

Wells Creek Outfitters, 803-12 SW 12th St., Bentonville, AR, 72712, P: 479-273-1174, F: 479-273-0137

Camouflage; Hunting Accessories; Men's Clothing

Wenger N.A./Wenger, Maker of the Genuine Swiss Army Knife, 15 Corporate Dr., Orangeburg, NY 10962, P: 800-431-2996, F: 845-425-4700, www.wengerna.com
Backpacking; Camping; Cutlery; Footwear; Hunting Accessories; Knives/Knife Cases; Watches

Western Powders, Inc., P.O. Box 158, Miles City, MT 59301, P: 800-497-1007, F: 406-234-0430, www.blackhorn209.com
Black Powder/Smokeless Powder; Firearms Maintenance Equipment; Lubricants; Reloading; Wholesaler/Distributor

Western Rivers, Inc., 1582 N. Broad St., Lexington, TN 38351, P: 800-967-0998, F: 731-967-1243, www.western-rivers.com
Decoys; Game Calls; Hunting Accessories; Lighting Products; Pet Supplies; Scents & Lures; Scopes, Sights & Accessories

Westfield Outdoor, Inc., 1593 Esprit Dr., Westfield, IN 46074, P: 317-569-0679, F: 317-580-1834, www.westfieldoutdoor.com
Backpacking; Camping

White Flyer Targets/Div. Reagent Chemical & Research, Inc., 115 Route 202/31 S, Ringoes, NJ 08851, P: 800-322-7855, F: 908-284-2113, www.whiteflyer.com
Clay Targets; Firearms; Shooting Range Equipment; Targets

Whites Boots, E. 4002 Ferry Ave., Spokane, WA 99202, P: 509-535-2422, F: 509-535-2423, www.whitesboots.com
Footwear

Whitetails Unlimited, 2100 Michigan St., Sturgeon Bay, WI 54235, P: 920-743-6777, F: 920-743-4658, www.whitetailsunlimited.com
Online Services; Outdoor Art, Jewelry, Sculpture; Videos; Wildlife Management

Wilcox Industries Corp., 25 Piscataque Dr., Newington, NH 03801, P: 603-431-1331, F: 603-431-1221, www.wilcoxind.com
Law Enforcement; Scopes, Sights & Accessories

Wild West Guns, LLC, 7100 Homer Dr., Anchorage, AK 99518-3229, P: 800-992-4570, F: 907-344-4005, www.wildwestguns.com
Custom Manufacturing; Firearms; Gun Parts/Gunsmithing; Outfitter; Recoil Protection Devices & Services; Scopes, Sights & Accessories; Wholesaler/Distributor

Wild Wings, LLC, 2101 S. Hwy. 61, P.O. Box 451, Lake City, MN 55041, P: 800-445-6413, F: 651-345-2981, www.wildwings.com
Decoys; Home Furnishings; Outdoor Art, Jewelry, Sculpture; Wholesaler/Distributor

Wilderness Calls, 12118 Capur St., Orlando, FL 38837, P: 407-620-8833, F: 407-620-8853

Wilderness Mint, P.O. Box 1866, Orting, WA 98360, P: 800-294-9600, F: 360-893-4400, www.wildernessmint.com
Emblems & Decals; Hunting Accessories; Outdoor Art, Jewelry, Sculpture; Watches

Wildfowler Outfitter/Tundra Quest, LLC, 5047 Walnut Grove, San Gabriel, CA 91776, P: 877-436-7177, F: 626-286-9918
Archery; Blinds, Custom Manufacturing; Export/Import Specialists; Feeder Equipment; Men's Clothing; Outfitter; Treestands

Wildlife Research Center, Inc., 14485 Azurite St. NW, Ramsey, MN 55303, P: 800-873-5873, F: 763-427-8354, www.wildlife.com

Scents & Lures

Wildsteer, 9 Avenue Eugene Brisson, Bourges, F-18000, FRANCE, P: 011 33248211380, F: 011 33248211380, www.wildsteer.com
Archery; Knives/Knife Cases; Leathergoods

Wiley X., Inc., 7491 Longard Rd., Livermore, CA 94551, P: 800-776-7842, F: 925-455-8860, www.wileyx.com
Eye Protection

William Henry Studio, 3200 NE Rivergate St., McMinnville, OR 97128, P: 888-563-4500, F: 503-434-9704, www.williamhenrystudio.com
Cutlery; Knives/Knife Cases

Williams Gun Sight Co., 7389 Lapeer Rd., Davison, MI 48423, P: 800-530-9028, F: 810-658-2140, www.williamsgunsight.com
Black Powder Accessories; Books/Industry Publications; Compasses; Gun Parts/Gunsmithing; Hunting Accessories; Scopes, Sights & Accessories

Wilson Arms Co., 97 Leetes Island Rd., Branford, CT 06405, P: 203-488-7297, F: 203-488-0135, www.wilsonarms.com
Custom Manufacturing; Firearms; Gun Barrels

Winchester Ammunition/Div. Olin Corp., 427 N. Shamrock St., East Alton, IL 62024, P: 618-258-2365, F: 618-258-3609, www.winchester.com
Ammunition

Winchester Repeating Arms, 275 Winchester Ave., Morgan, UT 84050, P: 801-876-3440, F: 801-876-3737, www.winchesterguns.com
Firearms

Winchester Safes/Granite Security Products, Inc., 4801 Esco Dr., Fort Worth, TX 76140, P: 817-561-9095, F: 817-478-3056, www.winchestersafes.com
Gun Cabinets/Racks/Safes

Winchester Smokeless Propellant, 6231 Robinson, Shawnee Mission, KS 66202, P: 913-362-9455, F: 913-362-1307
Black Powder/Smokeless Powder; Reloading

Winfield Galleries, LLC, 2 Ladue Acres, Ladue, MO 63124, P: 314-645-7636, F: 314-781-0224, www.winfieldgalleries.com
Computer Software; Outdoor Art, Jewelry, Sculpture

Wing-Sun Trading, Inc., 15501 Heron Ave., La Mirada, CA 90638, P: 866-944-1068, F: 714-522-6417
Backpacking; Binoculars; Camping; Compasses; Lighting Products; Photographic Equipment; Scopes, Sights & Accessories; Wholesaler/Distributor

Witz Sport Cases, 11282 Pyrites Way, Gold River, CA 95670, P: 800-499-1568, F: 916-638-1250, www.witzprod.com
Bags & Equipment Cases

Wolf Peak International, 1221 Marshall Way, Layton, UT 84041, P: 866-953-7325, F: 801-444-9353, www.wolfpeak.net
Airguns; Airsoft; Backpacking; Camouflage; Eyewear; Hunting Accessories; Law Enforcement; Shooting Range Equipment

Wolfe Publishing Co., 2625 Stearman Rd., Suite A, Prescott, AZ 86301, P: 800-899-7810, F: 928-778-5124, www.riflemagazine.com
Books/Industry Publications; Footwear; Gun Cabinets/Racks/Safes; Online Services; Outdoor Art, Jewelry, Sculpture

Wolverine, 9341 Courtland Dr., Rockford, MI 49351, P: 800-253-2184, F: 616-866-5666, www.wolverine.com
Footwear; Gloves, Mitts, Hats; Men's Clothing

MANUFACTURER'S AND PRODUCT DIRECTORY

Woods Outfitting, P.O. Box 3037, Palmer, AK 99645, P: 907-746-2534, F: 907-745-6283, www.woods-outfitting.com
Outfitter

Woods Wise Products, P.O. Box 681552, Franklin, TN 37068, P: 800-735-8182, F: 931-364-7925, www.woodswise.com
Blinds; Custom Manufacturing; Decoys; Game Calls; Hunting Accessories; Scents & Lures; Videos

Woolrich, Inc./Elite Series Tactical, 1 Mill St., Woolrich, PA 17779, P: 800-996-2299, F: 570-769-7662, www.woolrich.com, www.woolricheliteseriestactical.com
Footwear; Gloves, Mitts, Hats; Home Furnishings; Law Enforcement; Men & Women's Clothing; Wholesaler/Distributor

World Famous Sports, 3625 Dalbergia St., Suite A, San Diego, CA 92113, P: 800-848-9848, F: 619-231-1717, www.worldfamoussports.com
Bags & Equipment Cases; Camouflage; Camping; Gloves, Mitts, Hats; Hunting Accessories; Men & Women's Clothing

Wrangler Rugged Wear/Wrangler ProGear, 400 N. Elm St., Greensboro, NC 27401, P: 336-332-3977, F: 336-332-3518, www.wrangler.com
Men's Clothing

Wycon Safari Inc. (WY)/Wynn Condict, P.O. Box 1126, Saratoga, MY 82331, P: 307-327-5502, F: 307-327-5332, www.wyconsafariinc.com
Outfitter

X

X-Caliber Accuracy Systems, 1837 First St., Bay City, MI 48708, P: 989-893-3961, F: 989-893-0241, www.xcaliberaccuracy.com
Hunting Accessories

X-Caliber Tactical, 1111 Winding Creek Pl., Round Rock, TX 78664, P: 512-524-2621, www.xcalibertactical.com
Airguns; Airsoft; Custom Manufacturing; Export/Import Specialists; Law Enforcement; Wholesaler/Distributor

Xenonics Holdings, Inc., 2236 Rutherford Rd., Suite 123, Carlsbad, CA 92008, P: 760-448-9700, FL 760-929-7571, www.xenonics.com
Law Enforcement; Lighting Products

XGO/Polarmax, 5417 N.C. 211, P.O. Box 968, West End, NC 27376, P: 800-552-8585, F: 910-673-3875, www.xgotech.com
Men & Women's Clothing

Xisico USA, Inc./Rex Optics USA, Inc., 16802 Barker Springs, Suite 550, Houston, TX 77084, P: 281-647-9130, F: 208-979-2848, www.xisicousa.com
Airguns; Ammunition; Binoculars; Scopes, Sights & Accessories

XS Sight Systems, 2401 Ludella St., Fort Worth, TX 76105, P: 888-744-4880, F: 800-734-7939, www.xssights.com
Gun Parts/Gunsmithing; Law Enforcement; Scopes, Sights & Accessories

Y

Yaktrax, 9221 Globe Center Dr., Morrisville, NC 27560, P: 800-446-7587, F: 919-544-0975, www.yaktrax.com
Backpacking; Camping; Footwear; Sports Accessories

Yamaha Motor Corp., U.S.A., 6555 Katella Ave., Cypress, CA 90630, P: 714-761-7300, F: 714-503-7184
Vehicles, Utility & Rec

Yankee Hill Machine Co., Inc., 20 Ladd Ave., Suite 1, Florence, MA 01062, P: 877-892-6533, F: 413-586-1326, www.yhm.net
Firearms; Gun Barrels; Gun Cases; Gun Parts/Gunsmithing; Law Enforcement; Scopes, Sights & Accessories

Yukon Advanced Optics, 201 Regency Pkwy., Mansfield, TX 76063, P: 817-453-9966, F: 817-453-8770
Archery; Backpacking; Binoculars; Camping; Custom Manufacturing; Hunting Accessories; Scopes, Sights & Accessories; Wholesaler/Distributor

Z

Z-Blade, Inc., 28280 Alta Vista Ave., Valencia, CA 91355, P: 800-734-5424, F: 661-295-2615, www.pfimold.com
Custom Manufacturing; Hunting Accessories; Knives/Knife Cases

Zak Tool, 319 San Luis Rey Rd., Arcadia, CA 91007, P: 615-504-4456, F: 931-381-2568, www.zaktool.com
Law Enforcement; Training & Safety Equipment

Zanotti USA, 7907 High Knoll Ln., Houston, TX 77095, P: 281-414-2184, www.zanottiusa.com
Custom Manufacturing; Firearms

Zarc International, Inc., P.O. Box 108, Minonk, IL 61760, P: 800-882-7011, F: 309-432-3490, www.zarc.com
Law Enforcement; Retail Packaging

Zephyr Graf-x, 5443 Earhart Rd., Loveland, CO 80538, P: 970-663-3242, F: 970-663-7695, www.zhats.com
Camouflage; Custom Manufacturing; Gloves, Mitts, Hats; Men & Women's Clothing; Retailer Services

Zero Tolerance Knives, 18600 SW Tetaon Ave., Tualatin, OR 97062, P: 800-325-2891, F: 503-682-7168, www.ztknives.com
Knives/Knife Cases; Law Enforcement

Ziegel Engineering Working Designs, Jackass Field Carts, 2108 Lomina Ave., Long Beach, CA 90815, P: 562-596-9481, F: 562-598-4734, www.ziegeleng.com
Archery; Bags & Equipment Cases; Black Powder Accessories; Custom Manufacturing; Gun Cabinets/Racks/Safes; Gun Cases; Law Enforcement; Shooting Range Equipment

Zippo Manufacturing Co., 33 Barbour St., Bradford, PA 16701, P: 814-368-2700, F: 814-362-1350, www.zippo.com
Camping; Knives/Knife Cases; Lighting Products; Sports Accessories

Zistos Corp., 1736 Church St., Holbrook, NY 11741, P: 631-434-1370, F: 631-434-9104, www.zistos.com
Law Enforcement

Zodi Outback Gear, P.O. Box 4687, Park City, UT 84060, P: 800-589-2849, F: 800-861-8228
Archery; Backpacking; Camping; Cooking Equipment/Accessories; Hunting Accessories; Pet Supplies; Sports Accessories; Training & Safety Equipment

ZOLL Medical Corp., 269 Mill Rd., Chelmsford, MA 01824, P: 800-348-9011, F: 978-421-0025, www.zoll.com
Law Enforcement; Survival Kits/First Aid; Training & Safety Equipment

NUMBERS

10 Minute Deer Skinner, P.O. Box 158, Stillwater, OK 74076; P: 405-377-2222, F: 405-624-6060, www.tenminutedeerskinner.com
Cooking Equipment/Accessories; Hunting Accessories; Outfitter, Videos

32north Corp - STABILicers, 6 Arctic Circle, Buddeford, ME 04005, P: 800-782-2423, F: 207-284-5015, www.32north.com
Backpacking; Footwear; Hunting Accessories; Law Enforcement; Sports Accessories

3M Thinsulate™ Insulation / 3M Scotchgard™ Protector, 3M Center Building 235-2F-06, St. Paul, MN 55144-1000, P: 800-364-3577, F: 651-737-7659, www.thinsulate.com
Men & Women's Clothing; Footwear; Gloves, Mitts, Hats

3Point5.com, 224 South 200 West, Suite 230, Salt Lake City, UT 84101, P: 801-456-6900/2007, F: 801-485-5039, www.3point5.com

5.11 Tactical Series, 4300 Spyres Way, Modesto, CA 95356, P: 866-451-1726/348, F: 209-548-5348, www.511tactical.com
Bags & Equipment Cases; Men & Women's Clothing; Eyewear; Footwear; Gloves, Mitts, Hats; Law Enforcement; Watches

5-Hour Energy, 46570 Humboldt Drive, Novi, MI 48377, P: 248-960-1700/209, F: 248-960-1980, www.fivehour.com
Food; Hunting Accessories; Law Enforcement; Outfitter; Sports Accessories; Wholesaler/Distributor

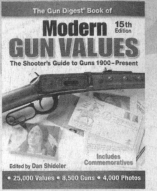

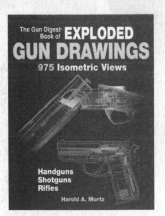

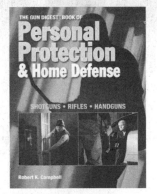